DIRECTORY OF FOREIGN FIRMS OPERATING IN THE UNITED STATES

11th Edition

Edited & Published by Uniworld Business Publications, Inc.

Uniworld Business Publications, Inc.
257 Central Park West
New York, NY 10024-4110
Tel: (212)496-2448 Fax: (212)769-0413
uniworldbp@aol.com
www.uniworldbp.com

First Edition	1969
Second Edition	1972
Third Edition	1975
Fourth Edition	1978
Fifth Edition	1986
Sixth Edition	1989
Seventh Edition	1992
Eighth Edition	1995
Ninth Edition	1998
Tenth Edition	2000
Eleventh Edition	2002

Published by
Uniworld Business Publications, Inc.
257 Central Park West
New York, N.Y. 10024-4110

ISBN: 0-8360-0046-3

Library of Congress Catalog Card Number: 85-051906

Printed in the United States of America

Table Of Contents

PART ONE
FOREIGN FIRMS OPERATING IN THE UNITED STATES   1
(Grouped by Country)

PART TWO
ALPHABETICAL LISTING OF FOREIGN FIRMS

PART THREE
ALPHABETICAL LISTING OF AMERICAN AFFILIATES

PART FOUR
PUBLISHER'S NOTES – Related Publications

Introduction

This is the 11th Edition of **DIRECTORY OF FOREIGN FIRMS OPERATING IN THE UNITED STATES.** First published in 1969, it has been an authoritative and valuable source of information for corporations, agencies, organizations, institutions, and individuals involved in many forms of international commerce or investment. The current edition contains 2,800 foreign firms in 79 countries and over 7,200 businesses in the US that they own, wholly, or in part. Only the American headquarters and selected locations of each branch, subsidiary or affiliate are listed.

Foreign Direct Investment in the United States
(Historical-cost Basis in US $ Billions, by Country of Ultimate Beneficial Owner)
U.S. Bureau of Economic Analysis, *Revised 2000

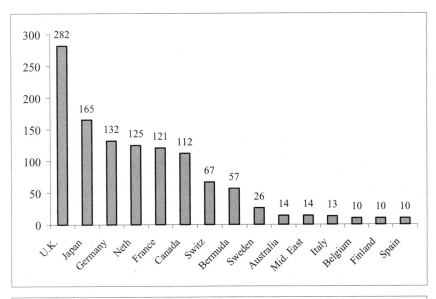

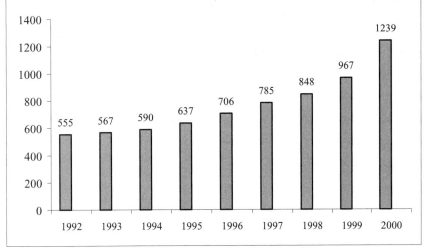

SOURCE AND ACCURACY OF LISTINGS

Firms in the 10th Edition were actively researched by our staff over a six-month period. The primary sources of information for all entries were inquiries sent to the corporations and/or annual reports provided by them. Direct telephone, fax and e-mail contact were used extensively for verification and clarification, as well as print and electronic media. Overseas companies in the 10th Edition, which no longer have a US subsidiary, were deleted, as were US firms whose ownership by foreign firms had ceased. Nearly 800 new firms were identified as the beneficial owner of companies operating in the US.

The aim of this Directory is to provide accurate, up-to-date listings, but the Editor and Publisher cannot guarantee that the information received from a company or other source is correct. Also, as extensive as this Directory may be, it does not claim to be all-inclusive. It contains only what has been disclosed to us. In addition, the designations and listings are not to be considered definitive as to legal status or the relationship between the foreign and American firms. Some US companies included here are technically owned by other US companies that, in turn, are owned by non-US firms. "Foreign-owned," therefore, refers to the ultimate owner. Also, no assumptions should be made if the percentage of ownership is not specified. Neither the direct nor indirect nature of ownership, nor the degree of participation, is of primary importance to the purpose of this directory.

In a compilation of this scope inaccuracies are inevitable. It would be appreciated if the reader would inform the Publisher of inaccuracies so corrections can be made in all future publications.

ACKNOWLEDGMENTS

We thank, most sincerely, the many company representatives who cooperated generously in providing information for this directory, and those who assisted in its preparation; Associate Editor Lynn Sherwood, Associate Publisher Debra Lipian, and Publishing Consultant David Bornstein.

Barbara D. Fiorito, Editor
Uniworld Business Publications, Inc.

Key to Abbreviations

The following abbreviations have been used in the Directory

A/C	Air Conditioning	Equip	Equipment
Access	Accessories	Exch	Exchange
Adv	Advertising	Exec	Executive
Affil	Affiliate(d)	Exp	Export(er)
Agcy	Agent/Agency	EVP	Executive Vice President
Agric	Agriculture	Fax	Facsimile
Arch	Architect(ural)	Fin	Financial/Finance
Assur	Assurance	Fl	Floor
Auto	Automotive	For	Foreign
Aux	Auxiliary	Furn	Furniture
Bldg	Building	Fwdg	Forwarding
Bus	Business	Gds	Goods
CEO	Chief Executive Officer	Gen	General
COO	Chief Operating Officer	Gov	Governor
Chem	Chemical	Hdwe	Hardware
Chrm	Chairman	Hos	Hospital
Cir	Circulation	Hydr	Hydraulic(s)
Corn	Components	Imp	Import(er)
Coml	Commercial	Ind	Industrial/Industry
Commun	Communications	Inf	Information
Conslt	Consultant/Consulting	Ins	Insurance
Constr	Construction	Inspec	Inspect(ion)
Cont	Controller	Instru	Instrument
Corp	Corporate	Intl	International
Cust	Customer	Invest	Investment
Dept	Department	JV	Joint Venture
Devel	Development	Lab	Laboratory
Diag	Diagnostic	Liq	Liquid
Dir	Director	Mach	Machine(ry)
Dist	District	Maint	Maintenance
Distr	Distributor/Distribution	Mat	Material
Divers	Diversified	Mdse	Merchandise
Dom	Domestic	Mdsng	Merchandising
Econ	Economist	Meas	Measurement
Educ	Education(al)	Med	Medical
Elec	Electrical	Mfg	Manufacturing
Electr	Electronic	Mfr.	Manufacture(r)
Emp	Employee(s)	Mgmt	Management
Engr	Engineer(ing)	Mng	Managing
Envi	Environmental	Mgr	Manager

(continued)

Mkt	Market	Rel	Relations
Mktg	Marketing	Rep	Representative
Mil	Million	Ret	Retail(er)
Oper	Operation	Rev	Revenue
Ops	Operations	Rfg	Refining
Orgn	Organization(al)	Ry	Railway
Pass	Passenger	Sci	Scientific
Petrol	Petroleum	Spec	Special(ty)/Specialized
Pharm	Pharmaceutical	Sta	Station
Plt	Plant	Subs	Subsidiary
Prdt(s)	Product(s)	Super	Supervision
Pres	President	SVP	Senior Vice President
Prin	Principal	Sys	System
Print	Printing	TV	Television
Prod	Process(ing)	Tech	Technical/Technology
Prod	Production	Tel	Telephone
Prog	Programming	Telecom	Telecommunications
Ptnr	Partner	Temp	Temperature
Pub	Publishing	Trans	Transmission
Publ	Publisher	Transp	Transport(ation)
R&D	Research & Development	VP	Vice President
Recre	Recreation(al)	Whl	Wholesale(r)
Refrig	Refrigeration	Whse	Warehouse
Reins	Reinsurance		

Company Designations

Abbreviation	Term	Country
AB	Aktiebolag	Sweden
AG	Aktiengesellschaft	Austria, Germany, Switzerland
AS	Anonim Sirketi	Turkey
A/S	Aktieselskab	Denmark
	Aksjeselskap	Norway
BV	Beslotene Vennootschap	Netherlands
CA	Compania Anonima	Venezuela
CIE	Compagnie	Belgium, France
CO	Company	Canada, England, U.S.
CORP	Corporation	England, U.S.
GMBH	Gesellschaft mit beschrankter Haftung	Austria, Germany
INC	Incorporated	Canada, England, U.S.
KG	Kommanditgesellschaft	Germany
KK	Kabushiki Kaisha	Japan
LTD	Limited	Canada, England, U.S.
Mli	Maatschappij	Netherlands
NV	Naamioze Vennoostchap	Belgium, Netherlands
OYJ	Osakeyhtio	Finland
P/L	Proprietary Limited	Australia
PLC	Public Limited Company	England, Scotland
PT	Perusahaan Terbatas	Indonesia
SA	Sociedad Anonima	Argentina, Brazil, Colombia Spain, Venezuela
	Societe Anonyme	Belgium, France, Switzerland
SpA	Societa per Azioni	Italy
SPRL	Societe de Personnes a Responsabilite Limitee	Belgium
SRL, srl	Societa a Responsabilita Limitata	Italy

Notes on Alphabetizing

Alphabetizing in this directory is by computer sort, which places numerals before letters; and among names, places blanks, hyphens and ampersands before letters. Thus, 3D Co. precedes A Z Co., which precedes A-Z Co., which precedes A&Z Co., which precedes Abiz Co.

Names such as The Jones Corp., Charles Jones Inc., and L. M. Jones & Co. are alphabetized conventionally: all will be found under J.

Names, which consist of initials, only (e.g., LFM Co.) are in strict alphabetical order: Lewis Corp., LFM Co., and Lintz Inc.

While the custom in most countries is to place company designations (Co., Inc., etc.) at the end of the firm's name, that is not always the case. For example, Finland's "Oyj" and Sweden's "AB" sometimes appear at the end and sometimes at the beginning of the company's name. In this directory they have been disregarded in alphabetizing. The reader is advised to check more than one location when looking for a firm whose listing might be affected by the company designation.

Special Notes

An asterisk (*) has been placed prior to the address of all firms that had offices in the New York City World Trade Center complex. Some of these businesses have moved to permanent locations, others have temporary facilities and still others were not reachable, and therefore show the last known contact information.

All revenue (Rev) figures have been converted to US $ and are quoted in millions.

FOREIGN FIRMS OPERATING IN THE UNITED STATES
(Grouped by country)

Part One groups foreign firms by country. Within each country, the foreign firms are listed alphabetically noted by a bullet. The American firm(s) owned by or affiliated with the foreign firm is indented.

Argentina

- **AEROLINEAS ARGENTINAS**
Torre Bouchard 547, 1106 Buenos Aires, Argentina
CEO: Diego Cousino, Pres. & CEO   Tel: 54-11-4310-3000
Bus: *Commercial air transport services.*   Fax: 54-11-4310-3585
    www.aerolinas.com.ar

    AEROLINEAS ARGENTINAS
    630 Fifth Avenue, Ste. 1661, New York, NY   10111
    CEO: Marcelo Moscheni, VP   Tel: (212) 698-2077   %FO: 100
    Bus: *International commercial air*   Fax: (212) 698-2067   Emp: 15
    transport services.

    AEROLINEAS ARGENTINAS
    6100 Blue Lagoon Drive, Ste. 210, Miami, FL   33126
    CEO: Lillana Bechara, Dir.   Tel: (305) 261-0100   %FO: 100
    Bus: *International commercial air*   Fax: (305) 264-9116   Emp: 35
    transport services.

- **ALLENDE & BREA**
Maipú 1300, 10th Fl., 1006 Buenos Aires, Argentina
CEO: Enrique Garrido, Mng. Prtn.   Tel: 54-11-4318-9900
Bus: *International law firm.*   Fax: 54-11-4313-9999   Emp: 100
    www.allendebrea.com

    ALLENDE & BREA
    10 Rockefeller Plaza, Ste. 1001, New York, NY   10020
    CEO: Osvaldo J. Marzorati, Mng. Ptnr.   Tel: (212) 698-2230   %FO: 100
    Bus: *International law firm.*   Fax: (212) 489-7317

- **AMARIN TECHNOLOGIES SA**
San Juan Av. 2266, C1232AAR Buenos Aires, Argentina
CEO: Sergio Lucero, Mng. Dir.   Tel: 54-11-4942-3319   Rev: $2,600
Bus: *Engaged in development of innovative*   Fax: 54-11-4943-3561   Emp: 100
pharmaceutical products using its   www.amarincorp.com
proprietary topical and transdermal
drug delivery technologies and know-
how to offer improved formulations of
established drugs.

AMARIN PHARMACEUTICALS
25 Independence Boulevard, Warren, NJ   07059
CEO: Richard Stewart, CEO   Tel: (908) 580-5535   %FO: 100
Bus: *Research and development and*   Fax: (908) 580-9390
sale and marketing of pain
management pharmaceuticals.

● **BANCO DE GALICIA Y BUENOS AIRES**
General Juan D. Peron 407, 2 Piso, 1038 Buenos Aires, Argentina
CEO: Eduardo J. Escasany, Chmn. & CEO   Tel: 54-11-329-6000   Rev: $1,792
Bus: *General banking services.*   Fax: 54-11-329-6100   Emp: 8,865
                                          www.bancogalicia.com.ar

BANCO DE GALICIA Y BUENOS AIRES
300 Park Avenue, 20th Fl., New York, NY   10022
CEO: Hector E. Arzeno, EVP   Tel: (212) 906-3700   %FO: 100
Bus: *General banking services.*   Fax: (212) 906-3777

● **BANCO DE LA NACION ARGENTINA**
Bartolmoe Mitre 326, 1036 Buenos Aires, Argentina
CEO: Eduardo J. Escasany   Tel: 54-11-347-6000   Rev: $1,792
Bus: *Commercial banking services.*   Fax: 54-11-347-8097   Emp: 8,865
                                          www.bna.com.ar

BANCO DE LA NACION ARGENTINA
299 Park Avenue, 2nd Fl., New York, NY   10171
CEO: Jorge del Rio, SVP   Tel: (212) 303-0600   %FO: 100
Bus: *Commercial banking services.*   Fax: (212)303-0805

BANCO DE LA NACION ARGENTINA
777 Brickell Avenue, Miami, FL   33131
CEO: Arturo Almada, Mgr.   Tel: (305) 371-7500   %FO: 100
Bus: *Commercial banking services.*   Fax: (305) 374-7805

● **BANCO DE LA PROVINCIA DE BUENOS AIRES**
San Martin 137, Buenos Aires, Argentina
CEO: Dr. Carlos E. Sanchez, Chmn.   Tel: 54-11-331-4011
Bus: *General banking services.*   Fax: 54-11-331-8375   Emp: 13,730
                                          www.bpba.com

BANCO DE LA PROVINCIA DE BUENOS AIRES
609 Fifth Avenue, 3rd Fl., New York, NY   10017
CEO: Ricardo Sturla, Mgr.   Tel: (212) 292-5400   %FO: 100
Bus: *Commercial & investment*   Fax: (212) 688-6827   Emp: 37
banking, trade finance.

● **INDUSTRIAS METALURGICAS PESCARMONA SAIC**
Carril Rodriguez Pena 2451, 5503 Godoy Cruz, Mendoza, Argentina
CEO: Enrique M. Pescarmona, Pres.   Tel: 54-61-498300
Bus: *Mfr. of hydromechanical equipment,*   Fax: 54-61-316124   Emp: 1,100
       turnkey hydroelectric plants, and
       container handling equipment.

IMPSA INTERNATIONAL INC.
1910 Cochran Road, Ste. 536, Pittsburgh, PA   15220
CEO: Gerald L. Katz, Pres.   Tel: (412) 344-7003   %FO: 100
Bus: *Sales/purchasing/service turbines,*   Fax: (412) 344-7009   Emp: 10
       generators, gates & valves,
       cranes, pressure vessels.

Australia

- **AMCOR LTD.**
679 Victoria Street, Abbottford VIC 3067, Australia
CEO: Russell Jones, CEO   Tel: 61-3-9226-9000   Rev: $3,430
Bus: *Mfr./sales paper and wood products and*   Fax: 61-3-9226-9050   Emp: 17,500
packaging.   www.amcor.co.au

   AMCOR PACKAGING USA INC.
6600 Valley View Street, Buenos Park, CA 90620
CEO: Mark Condron, VP   Tel: (714) 562-2001   %FO: 100
Bus: *Holding company for sales of*   Fax: (714) 562-2030
paper and wood products.

   AMCOR SUNCLIPSE INC.
6600 Valley View Street, Buena Park, CA 90620
CEO: Philip E. Shelton, Chmn.   Tel: (714) 562-6000   %FO: 100
Bus: *Sales/distribution of corrugated*   Fax: (714) 562-6059
box and packaging.

   KIMBERLY-CLARK CORPORATION, TECHNICAL PAPER DIV.
1400 Holcolm Bridge Road, Roswell, GA 30076
CEO: Mark Streich, Pres.   Tel: (770) 587-8909   %FO: JV
Bus: *Mfr./sales paper products.*   Fax: (770) 587-8840

- **ANSELL INTERNATIONAL, DIV. PACIFIC DUNLOP**
530 Springvale Road, PO Box 4584, Glen Waverley VIC 3150, Australia
CEO: Harry Boon, Chmn.   Tel: 61-3-9264-0888   Rev: $3,287
Bus: *Mfr. latex and rubber products and*   Fax: 61-3-9264-0886   Emp: 12,000
needles.   www.ansell.com

   ANSELL HEALTHCARE INC.
200 Schulz Drive, Red Bank, NJ 07701
CEO: Harry Boon, CEO   Tel: (732) 345-5400
Bus: *Sales/distribution of industrial and*   Fax: (732) 345-9695
medical gloves.

- **ARISTOCRAT LEISURE LIMITED**
71 Longueville Road Lane, Cove NSW 2066, Australia
CEO: D. H. Randall, CEO   Tel: 61-2-9413-6300   Rev: $298
Bus: *Mfr. video gaming machines.*   Fax: 61-2-9420-1354   Emp: 1,886
   www.aristocrat.com.au

ARISTOCRAT TECHNOLOGIES INC.
7160 Bermuda Road, Ste. 240, Las Vegas, NV   89119
CEO: Jennifer Martinez, HR	Tel: (702) 952-4800	%FO: 100
Bus: *Mfr. video gaming machines.*	Fax: (702) 952-5243	Emp: 120

CASINO DATA SYSTEMS, INC.
3300 Birtcher Drive, Las Vegas, NV   89118
CEO: Steve Weiss, CEO   Tel: (702) 269-5000   %FO: 100
Bus: *Mfr. video slot machines and*   Fax: (702) 269-5171
     technology driven products for the
     gaming industry.

• **ASI ENTERTAINMENT INC.**
1601 Main Road, Ste. 3, Research VIC 3095, Australia
CEO: Ronald J. Chapman, CEO   Tel: 61-3-9-437-1233
Bus: *Supplies in-flight video entertainment*   Fax: 61-3-9-437-1234
     systems to airlines and ground   www.asientertainment.com
     communications.

ASI ENTERTAINMENT
101 North Brand Blvd., Ste. 1700, Glendale, CA   91203
CEO: David Castler, Pres. & CEO   Tel: (818) 637-5611
Bus: *Specializes in research for*   Fax: (818) 637-6402
     television programming.

AUDIENCE RESEARCH & DEVELOPMENT
8828 Stemmons, Ste. 600, Dallas, TX   75247
CEO: William Taylor, Sales   Tel: (214) 630-5097
Bus: *Advises local broadcast stations,*   Fax: (214) 630-5097
     television programming producers
     and newspapers.

MEDIA ADVISORS INTERNATIONAL
8828 Stemmons Street, Ste. 600, Dallas, TX   75247
CEO: William Duff   Tel: (214) 630-5691   %FO: 100
Bus: *Provides audience information to*   Fax: (214) 630-4951
     media.

• **AUSTRALIA & NEW ZEALAND BANKING GROUP LTD.**
Level 2, 100 Queen Street, Melbourne, VIC 3000, Australia
CEO: Charles Goode, Chmn.   Tel: 61-3-9273-6141   Rev: $6,962
Bus: *International banking services.*   Fax: 61-3-9273-6142   Emp: 23,134
                        www.anz.com.au

AUSTRALIA & NEW ZEALAND BANKING GROUP LTD.
1177 Avenue of the Americas, 6th Fl., New York, NY   10036
CEO: Roy Marsden, EVP   Tel: (212) 801-9800   %FO: 100
Bus: *International banking services.*   Fax: (212) 801-9859

• AUSTRALIAN BROADCASTING CORP.
700 Harris Street, Ultimo 2007, GPO Box 9994, Sydney NSW 2001, Australia
CEO: Jonathan Shier   Tel: 61-2-9339-1500
Bus: *Engaged in television and radio*   Fax: 61-2-9333-5305   Emp: 4,000
broadcasting.   www.abc.net.au

AUSTRALIAN BROADCASTING CORPORATION
630 Fifth Avenue, Ste. 2260, New York, NY   10111
CEO: Maggie M. Jones, Mgr.   Tel: (212) 332-2540   %FO: 100
Bus: *TV & radio broadcasting.*   Fax: (212) 332-2546

• BARBEQUES GALORE LIMITED
327 Chisholm Road, Auburn NSW 2144, Australia
CEO: Sam Linz, Chmn.   Tel: 61-2-9704-4177   Rev: $167
Bus: *Mfr. grills, smokers, sauces, cookbooks,*   Fax: 61-2-9704-4201   Emp: 1,350
and barbecue accessories.   www.bbqgalore.com

BARBEQUES GALORE LIMITED
15041 Bake Parkway, Ste. A, Irvine, CA   92618
CEO: Sydney Selati, Pres.   Tel: (949) 597-2400   %FO: 100
Bus: *Mfr. grills, smokers, sauces,*   Fax: (949) 597-2452
cookbooks, and barbecue
accessories.

• BHP BILLITON LIMITED
BHP Tower, 600 Bourke Street, 40th Fl., Melbourne, VIC 3000, Australia
CEO: Paul M. Anderson, CEO   Tel: 61-3-9609-3333   Rev: $12,840
Bus: *Engaged in exploration of petroleum,*   Fax: 61-3-9609-3015   Emp: 35,000
copper, steel and minerals. (JV of BHP   www.bhpbilliton.com
BILLITON PLC. UK)

BHP BUILDING PRODUCTS, INC.
2110 Enterprise Blvd., Sacramento, CA   95691
CEO: Joe Coubal, Pres.   Tel: (916) 372-0933   %FO: 100
Bus: *Distribution/sales steel products.*   Fax: (916) 372-5442

BHP BUILDING PRODUCTS, INC.
2141 Milwaukee Way, Tacoma, WA   98401
CEO: Steve Staulding, Mgr.   Tel: (253) 383-4955   %FO: 100
Bus: *Plant; steel products.*   Fax: (206) 272-0791

BHP COPPER
550 California Street, San Francisco, CA 94104
CEO: Harry Smith, SVP Tel: (415) 981-1515 %FO: 100
Bus: *Copper mining & processing.* Fax: (415) 774-2026

BHP PETROLEUM (AMERICA) INC.
1360 Post Oak Blvd., Ste. 500, Houston, TX 77056-3020
CEO: Bernie Wirth, Pres. Tel: (713) 961-8500 %FO: 100
Bus: *Engaged in exploration and* Fax: (713) 961-8400
production of oil and gas.

● BILLABONG INTERNATIONAL LTD.
1 Billabong Place, Burleigh Heads QLD 4220, Australia
CEO: Matthew Perrin, CEO Tel: 61-75-589-9899 Rev: $74
Bus: *Mfr. sporting products, including* Fax: 61-75-589-9800 Emp: 500
surfboards, snowboards, skateboards www.billabong.com
and sports apparel.

BILLABONG USA, INC.
1946 Placentia Avenue, Costa Mesa, CA 92627
CEO: Mark Machado, Mgr. Tel: (714) 548-9375 %FO: 100
Bus: *Mfr. sporting products, including* Fax: (714) 548-9521
surfboards, snowboards,
skateboards and sports apparel.

● BORAL LIMITED
Level 39, 50 Bridge Street, GPO Box 910, Sydney NSW 2001, Australia
CEO: Dr. Ken Moss, Chmn. Tel: 61-2-9232-6300 Rev: $3,200
Bus: *Mfr./distributor building and* Fax: 61-2-9233-6605 Emp: 18,600
construction materials (bricks, timber, www.boral.com.au
tiles); and energy marketing/exploration.

BORAL INDUSTRIES, INC.
200 Mansell Court East, Ste. 310, Roswell, GA 30076
CEO: Dennis Brown, CEO Tel: (770) 645-4500 %FO: 100
Bus: *Mfr./distributor building &* Fax: (770) 801-9922
construction materials.

BORAL MATERIAL TECHNOLOGIES INC.
2930 Inland Empire Blvd., Ste. 102, Ontario, CA 91764
CEO: Ed Reed Tel: (909) 466-5271
Bus: *Mfr./distributor building &* Fax: (800) 864-4521
construction materials.

BORAL MATERIAL TECHNOLOGIES INC.
227 Pearl Street, Auburndale, FL   33823
CEO: Mitchell Smith, Mgr.   Tel: (863) 967-6626
Bus: *Mfr./distributor building &*   Fax: (863) 967-6626
construction materials.

BORAL MATERIAL TECHNOLOGIES INC.
45 NE Loop 410, Ste. 700, San Antonio, TX   78216
CEO: Gerry Gordon, Pres.   Tel: (210) 349-4069   %FO: 100
Bus: *Mfr./distributor building &*   Fax: (210) 349-8512
construction materials.

BORAL MATERIAL TECHNOLOGIES INC.
7500 N. Dreamy, Draw No. 234, Phoenix, AZ   85011
CEO: Bob Kepford, Mgr.   Tel: (602) 861-5100   %FO: 100
Bus: *Mfr./distributor building &*   Fax: (602) 861-0885
construction materials.

● **BRAMBLES INDUSTRIES LIMITED**
Level 40 Gateway, 1 Macquarie Place, Sydney NSW 2000, Australia
CEO: John E. Fletcher, CEO   Tel: 61-2-9256-5222   Rev: $2,939
Bus: *Engaged in materials handling,* Fax: 61-2-9256-5299   Emp: 14,550
industrial services and equipment www.bil.com.au
operations.

BRAMBLES INC.
400 North Michigan Avenue, Ste. 610, Chicago, IL   60611
CEO: Gerard Legtmann, Pres.   Tel: (312) 836-0200   %FO: 100
Bus: *Provides equipment supply*   Fax: (312) 836-1045
services and security services.

● **COMMONWEALTH BANK OF AUSTRALIA**
Level 1, 48 Martin Place, Sydney, NSW 1155, Australia
CEO: John T. Ralph, Chmn.   Tel: 61-2-9378-2000   Rev: $6,778
Bus: *General banking, investment and life* Fax: 61-2-9378-3317 Emp: 37,130
insurance services.   www.commbank.com.au

COMMONWEALTH BANK OF AUSTRALIA
599 Lexington Avenue, 17th Fl., New York, NY   10022
CEO: Ian M. Phillips, EVP   Tel: (212) 848-9200   %FO: 100
Bus: *International banking services.* Fax: (212) 336-7725

● **CSR LIMITED**

9 Help St., Level 1, Chatswood, NSW 2067, Australia

CEO: Peter M. Kirby, CEO

Bus: *Mfr./distribution building and construction materials; real estate and sugar industry investments.*

Tel: 61-2-9235-8000
Fax: 61-2-9235-8044
www.csr.com.au

Rev: $4,480
Emp: 17,100

CSR AMERICA INC.

1501 Belvedere Road, West Palm Beach, FL 33406

CEO: David Clarke, Pres.

Bus: *Building and construction materials.*

Tel: (561) 833-5555
Fax: (561) 655-6876

%FO: 100

CSR ASSOCIATES

6300 Glenwood Avenue, Everett, WA 98203

CEO: Neill Evans, Pres.

Bus: *Mfr. concrete pipe, box culvert, precast structures, and building components.*

Tel: (425) 355-2111
Fax: (425) 348-6378

%FO: 100

CSR HYDRO CONDUIT

8600 North Welby Road, Denver, CO 80229-5103

CEO: Ed Anderson, Mgr.

Bus: *Mfr. concrete pipe, box culvert, precast structures, and building components.*

Tel: (303) 288-6677
Fax: (303) 288-4238

%FO: 100

CSR HYDRO CONDUIT CORPORATION

16701 Greenpoint Park Drive, Suite 350, Houston, TX 77060

CEO: Adrian Driver, Pres.

Bus: *Mfr. concrete pipe, box culvert, precast structures, and building components.*

Tel: (281) 872-3500
Fax: (281) 872-5709

%FO: 100

CSR INC,

7150 Pollock Drive, Las Vegas, NV 89119

CEO: Robert Albano, VP

Bus: *Mfr./distribution of building materials.*

Tel: (702) 260-9900
Fax: (702) 260-9903

%FO: 100

CSR INC,

4242 West Buckeye Road, Phoenix, AZ 85009

CEO: David Clarke, Pres.

Bus: *Mfr./distribution of building materials.*

Tel: (602) 278-3526
Fax: (602) 484-0705

%FO: 100

CSR INC,
69 Neck Road, Westfield, MA   01085
CEO: David Clarke, Pres.   Tel: (800) 331-4605   %FO: 100
Bus: *Mfr./distribution of building*   Fax: (413) 562-7010
    materials.

CSR WILSON
802 Allied Road, La Platte, NE   68123
CEO: Jim Sautter, Pres.   Tel: (402) 293-1100   %FO: 100
Bus: *Mfr. concrete pipe and ready-mix*   Fax: (402) 293-1298
    concrete.

● **DAVNET LIMITED**
Level 7, 209 Castlereagh Street, Sydney NSW 2000, Australia
CEO: Stephen L. Moignard, CEO   Tel: 61-2-9272-9600   Rev: $85
Bus: *Engaged in telecommunications.* Fax: 61-2-9272-9605   Emp: 30
    www.davnet.com.au

    DAVNET LIMITED
    233 South Wacker Drive, Ste. 4620, Chicago, IL   60606
    CEO: Yung Hahn, CEO   Tel: (312) 377-4620   %FO: 100
    Bus: *Engaged in telecommunications.*   Fax: (312) 377-4630

● **JOHN FAIRFAX LTD.**
Level 19, Darling Park 201 Sussex Street, Box 506 GPO, Sydney NSW 2000, Australia
CEO: Brian Powers, Chmn.   Tel: 61-2-9282-2822   Rev: $803
Bus: *Magazine and newspaper publishing.*   Fax: 61-2-9282-1640   Emp: 4,500
    www.fairfax.com.au

    JOHN FAIRFAX (US) LTD
    317 Madison Avenue, Ste.1720, New York, NY   10017
    CEO: Jeanne Shelley, Pres.   Tel: (212) 972-4200   %FO: 100
    Bus: *Magazine and newspaper*   Fax: (212) 972-3331   Emp: 5
    publishing.

● **F. H. FAULDING & COMPANY LIMITED**
115 Sherriff Street, Underdale, South Australia 5032, Australia
CEO: Edward D. Tweddell, CEO   Tel: 61-8-8205-6500   Rev: $2,406
Bus: *Mfr. generic pharmaceuticals and*   Fax: 61-8-8234-5648   Emp: 4,300
    healthcare products.   www.faulding.com

    FAULDING HEALTHCARE INC.
    100 West Cypress Creek Rd., Ste. 885, Ft. Lauderdale, FL   33309
    CEO: David Murphy, CEO   Tel: (954) 776-8240   %FO: 100
    Bus: *Mfr. generic pharmaceuticals and*   Fax: (954) 776-8245
    healthcare products.

FAULDING LABORATORIES

5511 Capital Centre Drive, Ste. P116, Raleigh, NC   27606

CEO: Alan Mock, VP Mktg.   Tel: (919) 233-5788   %FO: 100

Bus: *Mfr. generic pharmaceuticals and*   Fax: (919) 233-3871
    healthcare products.

FAULDING ORAL PHARMACEUTICALS, INC.

200 Elmore Avenue, Elizabeth, NJ   07207

CEO: Frank Condella, Jr.   Tel: (908) 527-9100   %FO: 100

Bus: *Mfr. generic pharmaceuticals and*   Fax: (908) 527-0649
    healthcare products.

FAULDING PHARMACEUTICALS, INC.

4971 Southridge Boulevard, Memphis, TN   38141

CEO: Frank Condella, Jr.   Tel: (901) 542-3410   %FO: 100

Bus: *Distribution center.*   Fax: (901) 542-3470

FAULDING PHARMACEUTICALS, INC.

650 From Road, 5th Fl., Paramus, NJ   07652

CEO: Frank Condella, Jr.   Tel: (201) 225-5500   %FO: 100

Bus: *Mfr. generic pharmaceuticals and*   Fax: (201) 225-5520
    healthcare products.

PUREPAC PHAMACEUTICAL CO., DIV. FAULDING

200 Elmora Avenue, Elizabeth, NJ   07207

CEO: Michael Nestor, COO   Tel: (908) 527-9100   %FO: 100

Bus: *Mfr. generic pharmaceuticals and*   Fax: (908) 527-9100
    healthcare products.

● FOSTER'S BREWING GROUP LTD.

77 Southbank Boulevard, Southbank VIC 3006, Australia

CEO: Ted Kunkel, Pres. & CEO   Tel: 61-3-9633-2000   Rev: $3,100

Bus: *Engaged in brewing and sales of beer.*   Fax: 61-3-9633-2002   Emp: 8,200
                            www.foster.com.au

FOSTER'S USA LLC

3939 West Highland Blvd., Milwaukee, WI   53208-2866

CEO: Richard Scully   Tel: (414) 931-2000   %FO:

Bus: *Sales/distribution of Molson beer.*   Fax: (414) 931-3735

● JAMES HARDIE INDUSTRIES LTD.

Level 9, 65 York Street, Sydney NSW 2000, Australia

CEO: P. D. Macdonald, CEO   Tel: 61-2-9290-5333   Rev: $1,070

Bus: *Mfr. cement and building materials.*   Fax: 61-2-9262-4394   Emp: 3,700
                            www.jameshardie.com

HARDIE PIPE, DIV. JAMES HARDIE
PO Box 23272, Tampa, FL   33622-3272
CEO: Kerry Ngo   Tel: (813) 207-7000   %FO: 100
Bus: *Mfr./sales pipe.*   Fax: (813) 207-7098

JAMES HARDIE EXPORT
5931 East Marginal Way South, Seattle, WA   98134
CEO: George Petras   Tel: (206) 768-3773   %FO: 100
Bus: *Sales building products, including*   Fax: (206) 768-3794
    fiber cement and gypsum.

JAMES HARDIE INC.
26300 LaAlameda, Ste. 250, Mission Viejo, CA   92691
CEO: Randal Cecala, VP   Tel: (949) 348-1800   %FO: 100
Bus: *Mfr./sales building products,*   Fax: (949) 367-1294
    including fiber cement and gypsum.

● **HOYTS CINEMAS LIMITED**
Level 6, Hoyts Center, 505-523 George Street, Sydney NSW 2000, Australia
CEO: Ashok Jacob, Chmn.   Tel: 61-2-9273-7373   Rev: $312
Bus: *Owns and operates theater chains.* Fax: 61-2-9273-7356   Emp: 6,500
                                        www.hoyts.com.au

HOYTS CINEMAS CORPORATION
One Exeter Plaza, Boston, MA   02116
CEO: Paul Johnson, Dir.   Tel: (617) 267-2700   %FO: 100
Bus: *Owns and operates theater chains.* Fax: (617) 262-0707

● **ILUKA RESOURCES LTD. (FORMERLY RENISON GOLDFIELDS CONSOLIDATED LTD.)**
5th Fl., 553 Hay Street, Perth, WA 6000, Australia
CEO: Dr. Richard Aldous, CEO   Tel: 61-89-221-7611
Bus: *Titanium minerals, tin, coal and*   Fax: 61-89-221-7744
    quicklime.   www.iluka.com

ILUKA RESOURCES, INC.
12472 St. John Church Road, Stony Creek, VA   23882-0129
CEO: Alan Sale, Mgr.   Tel: (804) 246-8016   %FO: 100
Bus: *Non-metallic mineral services.*   Fax: (804) 246-3039

ILUKA RESOURCES, INC.
1223 Warner Road, Green Cove Springs, FL   32043
CEO: Graeme Sloan, Gen. Mgr.   Tel: (904) 284-9832   %FO: 100
Bus: *Non-metallic mineral services.*   Fax: (904) 284-4006

● **KIMBERLY-CLARK AUSTRALIA PTY LTD. (DIV. AMCOR)**
52 Alfred Street, Milsons Point NSW2061, Australia
CEO: Russell Jones, Dir.   Tel: 61-2-9963-8888
Bus: *Mfr./markets tissue and personal care*   Fax: 61-2-9957-5687
products. (JV with Kimberly-Clark   www.kca.com.au
Corp., U.S.).

    KIMBERLY-CLARK CORPORATION, TECHNICAL PAPER DIV.
    1400 Holcolm Bridge Road, Roswell, GA 30076
    CEO: Mark Streich, Pres.   Tel: (770) 587-8909   %FO: JV
    Bus: *Mfr./sales paper products.*   Fax: (770) 587-8840

● **LEND LEASE CORPORATION LIMITED**
Level 46, Tower Bldg., Australia Square, Sydney NSW 2000, Australia
CEO: Stuart Hornery, Chmn.   Tel: 61-2-9236-6065   Rev: $2,140
Bus: *Engaged in the management of property*   Fax: 61-2-9252-2192   Emp: 7,100
funds.   www.lendlease.com.au

    LEND LEASE AGRI-BUSINESS
    12747 Olive Street Road, Ste. 350, St. Louis, MO 63141
    CEO: Richard Henderson, CEO   Tel: (314) 434-7159
    Bus: *Engaged in the management of*   Fax: (314) 434-1091
    property funds.

    LEND LEASE CORPORATION
    3424 Peachtree Road NE, Ste. 800, Atlanta, GA 30326
    CEO: Sheryl K. Pressier, CEO   Tel: (404) 848-8600   %FO: 100
    Bus: *Engaged in the management of*   Fax: (404) 848-8910
    property funds.

    LEND LEASE CORPORATION
    787 Seventh Avenue, 46th Fl., New York, NY 10019
    CEO: Matthew Banks, CEO   Tel: (212) 554-1600   %FO: 100
    Bus: *Engaged in the management of*   Fax: Emp: 800
    property funds.

    LEND LEASE ROSEN REAL ESTATE SECURITIES LLC
    1995 University Avenue, Ste. 500, Berkeley, CA 94704
    CEO: Kenneth R. Rosen, Chmn.   Tel: (510) 849-8360   %FO: 100
    Bus: *Engaged in real estate securities.*   Fax:

● **MACQUARIE BANK LIMITED**
No. 1 Martin Place, Sydney NSW 2000, Australia
CEO: Allan Moss, CEO   Tel: 61-2-9237-3333   Rev: $104
Bus: *Engaged in investment banking.*   Fax: 61-2-9237-3350   Emp: 4,000
                                             www.macquarie.com.au

MACQUARIE BANK
600 Fifth Avenue, Level 21, New York, NY   10020
CEO: Jerome Silvey, EVP   Tel: (212) 548-6500   %FO: 100
Bus: *Investment banking.*   Fax: (212) 399-8928

MACQUARIE BANK
440 South LaSalle Street, Ste. 2940, Chicago, IL   60605
CEO: Jerome Silvey, EVP   Tel: (312) 521-6888   %FO: 100
Bus: *Investment banking.*   Fax: (312) 521-6877

MACQUARIE BANK
101 California Street, Ste. 2095, San Francisco, CA   94111
CEO: Jerome Silvey, EVP   Tel: (415) 645-8090   %FO: 100
Bus: *Investment banking.*   Fax: (415) 989-2145

● **MEAT & LIVESTOCK AUSTRALIA LTD.**
Locked Bag 991, North Sydney NSW 2059, Australia
CEO: Richard Brooks, Mng. Dir.   Tel: 61-2-9463-9180
Bus: *Promotion and marketing of Australian*   Fax: 61-2-9463-9123
meat and livestock.   www.australian-lamb.com

MEAT AND LIVESTOCK AUSTRALIA LTD.
750 Lexington Ave., 17th Fl., New York, NY   10022
CEO: Frances Cassidy, CEO   Tel: (212) 486-2405   %FO: 100
Bus: *Promotion and marketing of*   Fax: (212) 355-1471
Australian meat and livestock.

● **MINCOM LIMITED**
61 Wyandra Street, Teneriffe QLD 4005, Australia
CEO: Frank Berger, Mng. Dir.   Tel: 61-7-3303-3333
Bus: *Mfr. computer software.*   Fax: 61-7-3303-3232
                                       www.mincom.com

MINCOM, INC.
1675 Broadway, Ste. 900, Denver, CO   80202
CEO: Brett Roveda, Pres.   Tel: (303) 446-9000   %FO: 100
Bus: *Mfr./sales computer software.*   Fax: (303) 446-8664

● **NATIONAL AUSTRALIA BANK LIMITED**
500 Bourke Street, GPO Box 84A, Melbourne VIC 3001 Australia
CEO: Francis J. Cicutto, CEO   Tel: 61-3-9641-3500   Rev: $13,051
Bus: *International banking, investment and*   Fax: 61-3-9641-4916   Emp: 51,550
insurance services.   www.national.com.au

HOMESIDE INC.
7301 Baymeadows Way, Jacksonville, FL   32256
CEO: Joseph K. Pickett, CEO   Tel: (904) 281-3000   %FO: 100
Bus: *Financial and lending services.*   Fax: (904) 281-3745

MICHIGAN NATIONAL BANK
PO Box 9065, Farmington Hills, MI   48333-9065
CEO: James A. Williams, Chmn.   Tel: (248) 473-3000   %FO: 100
Bus: *Engaged in commercial banking.*   Fax: (248) 442-5713

MICHIGAN NATIONAL CORPORATION
27777 Inkster Road, Farmington Hills, MI   48333-9065
CEO: Douglas E. Ebert, CEO   Tel: (248) 473-3000   %FO: 100
Bus: *Financial services holding*   Fax: (248) 473-3086
    company.

NATIONAL AUSTRALIA BANK LTD.
200 Park Avenue, 34th Fl., New York, NY   10166
CEO: Thomas W. Hunersen, EVP   Tel: (212) 916-9500   %FO: 100
Bus: *International banking, investment*   Fax: (212) 983-1969
    and insurance services.

● **THE NEWS CORPORATION LTD.**
2 Holt Street, Surrey Hills, Sydney, NSW 2010, Australia
CEO: K. Rupert Murdoch, Chmn. & CEO   Tel: 61-2-288-3000   Rev: $13,800
Bus: *Publishing, broadcasting, filmed*   Fax: 61-2-228-3292   Emp: 30,000
    entertainment.   www.newscorp.com

FOX BROADCASTING COMPANY
10201 West Pico Boulevard, Los Angeles, CA   90035
CEO: David Nevins, EVP   Tel: (323) 277-2211   %FO: 100
Bus: *Program services.*   Fax: (323) 203-2735

FOX ENTERTAINMENT GROUP, INC.
1211 Avenue of the Americas, 2nd Fl., New York, NY   10036
CEO: Peter Chernin, Pres. & COO   Tel: (212) 556-2400   %FO: 100
Bus: *Develops and produces*   Fax: (212) 852-7145
    programming.

FOX KIDS WORLDWIDE
10960 Wilshire Boulevard, Los Angeles, CA   90024
CEO: Halm Saban, Chmn. & CEO   Tel: (310) 235-5100   %FO: 100
Bus: *Distributes animated and live-*   Fax:
    action children's television
    programming.

FOX NEWS
1211 Avenue of the Americas, 2nd Fl., New York, NY   10036
CEO: Roger Alles, Chmn. & CEO   Tel: (212) 556-2500   %FO: 100
Bus: *General news service.*   Fax: (212) 301-8599

HARPER COLLINS PUBLISHERS INC.
10 East 53rd Street, New York, NY   10022
CEO: Jane Friedman, Pres. & CEO   Tel: (212) 207-7000   %FO: 100
Bus: *Book publishing.*   Fax: (212) 207-7145   Emp: 3,000

LOS ANGELES DODGERS INC.
1000 Elysian Park Avenue, Los Angeles, CA   90012
CEO: Robert A. Daly, CEO   Tel: (323) 224-1500   %FO: 100
Bus: *Major league baseball team.*   Fax: (323) 224-1269

NEW YORK POST
1211 Avenue of the Americas, New York, NY   10036-8790
CEO: Martin Singerman, Pres. & Pub. Tel: (212) 930-8000   %FO: 100
Bus: *Daily metropolitan newspaper.* Fax: (212) 930-8540

NEWS AMERICA MARKETING
1211 Avenue of the Americas, 5th Fl., New York, NY   10036
CEO: Paul Carlucci, Chmn.   Tel: (212) 782-8000   %FO: 100
Bus: *Engaged in single-source*   Fax: (212) 575-5845
   marketing services.

NEWS AMERICA PUBLISHING GROUP
1211 Avenue of the Americas, New York, NY   10036
CEO: Anthea Disney, CEO   Tel: (212) 852-7000   %FO: 100
Bus: *Telephone and marketing service.* Fax: (212) 852-7147   Emp: 4,700

NEWS CORP ONE
1211 Avenue of the Americas, New York, NY   10036
CEO: Kayne Lanahan, SVP   Tel: (212) 556-8116   %FO: 100
Bus: *Creates customized, integrated* Fax: (212) 556-8119
   media and marketing solutions.

NEWS CORPORATION
1211 Avenue of the Americas, 3rd Fl., New York, NY   10036
CEO: Peter Chernin, Pres. & COO   Tel: (212) 852-7000   %FO: 100
Bus: *Newspaper & magazine*   Fax: (212) 852-7145   Emp: 30,000
   publishing. (The New York Post,
   Soap Opera News & TV Guide.)

RAWKUS ENTERTAINMENT LC

676 Broadway, 4th Fl., New York, NY 10012

CEO: K. Rupert Murdoch, Pres. Tel: (212) 358-7890 %FO: 100

Bus: *Record company specializing in* Fax: (212) 358-7962
alternative and hip-hop music.

TV GUIDE

1211 Avenue of the Americas, 4th Fl., New York, NY 10036

CEO: Henry C. Yuen, CEO Tel: (212) 852-7500 %FO: 100

Bus: *Weekly television magazine.* Fax: (212) 852-7500 Emp: 1,700

THE WEEKLY STANDARD

1150 17th Street NW, Ste. 505, Washington, DC 20036

CEO: Fred Barnes, Editor Tel: (202) 293-4900 %FO: 100

Bus: *Weekly political magazine.* Fax: (202) 293-4901

• NOVOGEN LIMITED

140 Wicks Road, North Ryde NSW 2113, Australia

CEO: Chris Naughton, CEO Tel: 61-298-780-088 Rev: $16

Bus: *Mfr. non-prescription pharmaceuticals.* Fax: 61-298-780-005 Emp: 75

www.novogen.com

NOVOGEN INC.

One Landmark Square, Ste. 240, Stamford, CT 06901

CEO: Warren Lancaster, VP Tel: (203) 327-1188 %FO: 100

Bus: *Mfr. non-prescription* Fax: (203) 327-0011
pharmaceuticals.

• ORBITAL ENGINE CORPORATION LIMITED

One Whipple Street, Balcatta WA 6021, Australia

CEO: Kim Christopher Schlunke, CEO Tel: 61-8-9441-2311 Rev: $28

Bus: *Engaged in direct fuel injection* Fax: 61-8 9441-2133 Emp: 260
technology to reduce fuel use and www.orbeng.com.au
emissions in engines.

ORBITAL ENGINE COMPANY INC.

PO Box 338, Tecumseh, MI 49286

CEO: Kim C. Schlunke, CEO Tel: (517) 423-6623 %FO: 100

Bus: *Engaged in direct fuel injection* Fax: (517) 423-6079
technology to reduce fuel use and
emissions in engines.

SYNERJECT
201 Enterprise Drive, Newport News, VA   23603
CEO: Marianne Tully, VP   Tel: (757) 890-4900   %FO: 100
Bus: *Engaged in direct fuel injection*   Fax: (757) 890-4933
technology to reduce fuel use and
emissions in engines.

● **ORICA LIMITED**
One Nicholson Street, Melbourne VIC 3000, Australia
CEO: Malcolm Broomhead, CEO   Tel: 61-3-9665-7111   Rev: $2,163
Bus: *Mfr. chemicals and explosives.*   Fax: 61-3-9665-7937   Emp: 9,000
                                          www.orica.com.au

   ORICA USA INC.
   9781 South Meridian Blvd., Englewood, CO   80112-5911
   CEO: David Taylor, Pres.   Tel: (303) 268-5000   %FO: 100
   Bus: *Mfr. chemicals.*   Fax: (303) 268-5250

● **PACIFIC DUNLOP LIMITED**
Level 41, 101 Collins Street, Melbourne VIC 3000, Australia
CEO: Rodney L. Chawick, CEO   Tel: 61-3-9270-7270   Rev: $3,425
Bus: *Consumer, automotive, healthcare,* Fax: 61-3-9270-7300   Emp: 37,835
industrial and electrical products.   www.pacdun.com

   ANSELL HEALTHCARE INC.
   200 Schulz Drive, Red Bank, NJ   07701
   CEO: Harry Boon, CEO   Tel: (732) 345-5400   %FO: 100
   Bus: *Mfr. latex and rubber products.* Fax: (732) 219-5114   Emp: 12,000

   PACIFIC DUNLOP HOLDINGS INC.
   6121 Lakeside Drive, Suite 200, Reno, NV   89511
   CEO: Steve Geerling   Tel: (775) 824-4600   %FO: 100
   Bus: *Diversified mfr./sales/service;* Fax: (775) 824-4626
   consumer, automotive, healthcare,
   industrial & electrical groups.

● **PASMINCO LTD. (FORMERLY SAVAGE RESOURCES, LTD.)**
Level 15, 380 St. Kilda Road, GPO Box 1291K, Melbourne VIC 3004, Australia
CEO: Greig Gailey, CEO   Tel: 61-3-9288-0333
Bus: *Produces zinc, lead and silver.*   Fax: 61-3-9288-0406   Emp: 3,800
                                          www.pasminco.com.au

   PASMINCO ZINC US INC.
   1800 Zinc Plant Road, PO Box 1104, Clarksville, TN   37041-1104
   CEO: Gerog Gailey, CEO   Tel: (931) 552-4200   %FO: 100
   Bus: *Zinc mining and refining.*   Fax: (931) 552-0471   Emp: 260

● **PETSEC ENERGY LTD.**
Level 13, Gold Fields House, One Alfred Street, Sydney NSW 2000, Australia
CEO: Terrence N. Fern, Chmn. & CEO   Tel: 61-2-9247-4605   Rev: $110
Bus: *Engaged in exploration and production*   Fax: 61-2-9251-2410   Emp: 33
   of oil and gas.   www.petsec.com

   PETSEC ENERGY INC.
   143 Ridgeway Drive, Lafayette, LA   70503
   CEO: Ross Keogh, VP   Tel: (337) 989-1942   %FO: 100
   Bus: *Engaged in exploration and*   Fax: (337) 981-8784
      production of oil and gas.

● **QANTAS AIRWAYS LTD.**
Qantas Centre, Level 9, Bldg. A, 203 Coward Street, Mascot, NSW 2000, Australia
CEO: Geoff Dixon, CEO   Tel: 61-2-9691-3636   Rev: $5,437
Bus: *Commercial airline and hotel operators.*   Fax: 61-2-9691-3339   Emp: 29,215
      www.qantas.com.au

   QANTAS AIRWAYS LTD.
   841 Apollo Street, Ste. 400, El Segundo, CA   90245
   CEO: Ken Groves, VP   Tel: (310) 726-1400   %FO: 100
   Bus: *Air transport services.*   Fax: (310) 726-1401

● **QBE INSURANCE GROUP LIMITED**
Level 2, 82 Pitt Street, Sydney 2000, Australia
CEO: Frank O'Halloran, CEO   Tel: 61-2-9375-444   Rev: $2,726
Bus: *Engaged in general insurance.*   Fax: 61-2-9235-3166   Emp: 2,500
      www.gbe.com.au

   QBE INSURANCE CORPORATION
   88 Pine Street, 16th Fl., New York, NY   10005
   CEO: Abe Altman, CEO   Tel: (212) 422-1212   %FO: 100
   Bus: *Engaged in general insurance.*   Fax: (212) 422-1212

● **SANTOS LTD.**
Level 29, Santos House, 91 King William Street, Adelaide 5000, Australia
CEO: John Ellice-Flint, CEO   Tel: 61-8-8218-5111   Rev: $834
Bus: *Engaged in oil and gas production.*   Fax: 61-8-8218-5476   Emp: 1,630
      www.santos.com.au

   SANTOS USA CORPORATION
   2500 Tanglewilde, Ste. 160, Houston, TX   77063
   CEO: Kathleen Hogenson, Pres.   Tel: (713) 975-3700   %FO: 100
   Bus: *Engaged in oil and gas production.*   Fax: (713) 975-3711

- **SOLUTION 6 HOLDINGS LIMITED**
Level 21,Town Hall House, 456 Kent Street, Sydney NSW 2000, Australia
CEO: Neil Gamble, CEO   Tel: 61-2-9278-0666
Bus: *Mfr. computer software.*   Fax: 61-2-9278-0555
                                        www.solution6.com

    SOLUTION 6 NORTH AMERICA
    101 North Monroe Street, Ste. 800, Tallahassee, FL   32301
    CEO: Anita Prater   Tel: (850) 224-2200   %FO: 100
    Bus: *Mfr./sales computer software.*   Fax: (850) 224-7260

- **TELSTRA CORPORATION LIMITED**
Level 41, 242 Exhibition Street, Melbourne, VIC 3000, Australia
CEO: Dr. Zygmunt E. Switkowski, CEO   Tel: 61-3-9634-6400   Rev: $11,845
Bus: *Telecommunications services.*   Fax: 61-3-9632-3215   Emp: 50,760
                                        www.telstra.com.au

    TELSTRA INC.
    50 Francisco Street, Ste. 105, San Francisco, CA   94133
    CEO: David Mitsak, Mgr.   Tel: (415) 788-5951   %FO: 100
    Bus: *Telecommunications services.*   Fax: (415) 788-5902   Emp: 14

    TELSTRA INC.
    871 Belle Avenue, Teaneck, NJ   07666
    CEO: William Costa, VP   Tel: (201) 836-9494   %FO: 100
    Bus: *Telecommunications services.*   Fax: (201) 836-9494

- **J.B. WERE & SON INC.**
101 Collins Street, 16th Floor, Melbourne VIC 3000, Australia
CEO: Terry Campbell, Pres.   Tel: 61-3-9679-1111
Bus: *Financial services: securities.*   Fax: 61-3-9679-1493
                                        www.jbwere.com.au

    J.B. WERE & SON INC.
    101 East 52nd Street, 34th Fl., New York, NY   10022
    CEO: Matthew Goodson, Pres.   Tel: (212) 824-4500   %FO: 100
    Bus: *Financial services; securities.*   Fax: (212) 824-4501

- **WESTFIELD HOLDINGS LIMITED**
24th Fl., Westfield Tower Three, 200 William Street, Sydney NSW 2011, Australia
CEO: Frank Lowy, Chmn.   Tel: 61-2-9358-7000
Bus: *Engaged in design, building and   Fax: 61-2-9358-7077
managing shopping centers.*   www.westfield.com.au

WESTFIELD AMERICA, INC.
11601 Wilshire Boulevard, 12th Fl., Los Angeles, CA   90025
CEO: Peter S. Lowy, CEO

Tel: (310) 478-4456

%FO: 100

Bus: *Engaged in leasing, operating and*   Fax: (310) 478-1267
developing shopping centers.

● **WESTPAC BANKING CORP**
60 Martin Place, Sydney, NSW 2000, Australia
CEO: John Uhrig, Chmn.

Tel: 61-2-9226-3311

Rev: $6,540

Bus: *International banking and insurance*   Fax: 61-2-9226-4128
services.   www.westpac.com.au

Emp: 31,000

WESTPAC BANKING CORP
575 Fifth Avenue, 39th Fl., New York, NY   10017-2422
CEO: Manuela Adl, Mng. Prtn.

Tel: (212) 551-1800

%FO: 100

Bus: *General international banking*   Fax: (212) 818-2800
services.

Emp: 445

● **WMC LIMITED**
Level 16, IBM Centre, 60 City Road, Southbank VIC, Australia
CEO: Hugh M. Morgan, CEO

Tel: 61-3-9685-6000

Rev: $1,540

Bus: *Engaged in mining of alumina, copper,*   Fax: 61-3-9686-3569
gold nickel and phosphate.   www.wmc.com.au

Emp: 5,540

WMC CORPORATE SERVICES INC.
8008 East Araphoc Court, Ste. 110, Englewood, CO   80112
CEO: Christopher B. Leptos, Mgr.

Tel: (303) 268-8300

%FO: 100

Bus: *Engaged in mining exploration.*   Fax: (303) 268-8370

Austria

● **AUSTRIAN AIRLINES AG**
Fontanastrassa 1, A-1107 Vienna, Austria
CEO: Dr. Rudolf Streicher, Chmn.   Tel: 43-1-683511
Bus: *Commercial air transport services.*   Fax: 43-1-685505   Emp: 3,200
www.austrianair.com

AUSTRIAN AIRLINES
17-20 Whitestone Expressway, Whitestone, NY   11357
CEO: Guenter Hude, Mgr.   Tel: (718) 670-8600   %FO: 100
Bus: *Air transport services.*   Fax: (718) 670-8619   Emp: 70

● **BANK AUSTRIA CREDITANSTALT, DIV. HVB GROUP**
Vordere Zollamtsstrasse 13, A-1030 Vienna, Austria
CEO: Guido Schmidt-Chiari, Chmn.   Tel: 43-1-711-91-0
Bus: *Engaged in electronic banking services.*   Fax: 43-1-711-91-56155   Emp: 20,000
www.bacai.com

BANK AUSTRIA CREDITANSTALT
2 Greenwich Plaza, 4th Fl., Greenwich, CT   06830-6353
CEO: Gary P. Kearns, COO   Tel: (203) 861-6464   %FO: 100
Bus: *International banking services.*   Fax: (203) 861-1414

BANK AUSTRIA CREDITANSTALT
50 California Street, Ste. 3005, San Francisco, CA   94111
CEO: Jack Bertges, SVP   Tel: (415) 788-1371   %FO: 100
Bus: *International banking services.*   Fax: (415) 781-0622

BANK AUSTRIA CREDITANSTALT
245 Park Avenue, 32nd Fl., New York, NY   10167
CEO: Wolfgang Schoellkopf, CEO   Tel: (212) 856-1000   %FO: 100
Bus: *Investment advisory services.*   Fax: (212) 856-1661

BANK AUSTRIA CREDITANSTALT
2 Arvinia Drive, Ste. 1680, Atlanta, GA   30346
CEO: Robert Biringer, Mgr.   Tel: (770) 390-1850   %FO: 100
Bus: *International banking services.*   Fax: (770) 390-1851

CA IB SECURITIES INC.
245 Park Avenue, 32nd Fl., New York, NY   10167
CEO: Gyula Schuch   Tel: (212) 856-1000   %FO: 100
Bus: *Investment advisory services.*   Fax: (212) 856-1661

● **BERNDORF BAND GMBH**

Leobersdprfer Str. 26, A-2560 Berndorf, Austria

CEO: Mr. Helmut Baresch Tel: 43-2672-800-350
Bus: *Production of stainless and carbon* Fax: 43-2672-84176 Emp: 300
conveyor belting. www.berndorf-band.at

   BERNDORF BELT SYSTEMS, INC.

   850 Commerce Parkway, Carpentersville, IL   60110

   CEO: Maurice Farissier Tel: (847) 649-0200 %FO: 100
   Bus: *Mfr./distributor of conveyor* Fax: (847) 649-0223 Emp: 32
   systems and related equipment.

   BERNDORF ICB

   7703 Park Place Road, York, SC   29745

   CEO: Dietmar Müller Tel: (803) 684-1112 %FO: 100
   Bus: *Mfr./distributor of conveyor* Fax: (803) 684-7750
   systems and related equipment.

● **BOEHLER-UDDEHOLM AG**

Modecenterstraße 14/A/3, A-1030 Vienna, Austria

CEO: Claus J. Raidl, Chmn. & CEO Tel: 43-1-798-69010 Rev: $1,274
Bus: *Mfr. and production of high-* Fax: 43-1-798-6901-713 Emp: 9,050
performance steels for drills and mining www.buag.co.at
tools.

   BOHLER-UDDEHOLM AMERICA INC.

   4902 Tollview Drive, Rolling Meadows, IL   60008-3729

   CEO: Erik Spencer, Pres. Tel: (847) 577-2220 %FO: 100
   Bus: *Sales/distribution of high-* Fax: (847) 577-8028
   performance steels.

● **CASINOS AUSTRIA INTERNATIONAL LTD. (CAI)**

Dr. Karl Lueger Ring 14, A-1015 Vienna, Austria

CEO: Hermann Pamminger Tel: 43-1-534-40-504 Rev: $60
Bus: *Casino operations.* Fax: 43-1-532-92-07 Emp: 1,250
   www.caicasinos.com

   CASINOS AUSTRIA MARITIME

   4651 Sheridan Street, Suite 303, Hollywood, FL   33021

   CEO: Hermann Pamminger Tel: (954) 964-4131 %FO: 100
   Bus: *Casino operations.* Fax: (954) 964-4246 Emp: 60

• ELIN EBG ELEKTROTECHNIK GMBH
Penzingerstraße 76, A-1141 Vienna, Austria
CEO: Klaus Sernetz — Tel: 43-1-899-90-0
Bus: *Engaged in electrical plant engineering* — Fax: 43-1-894-6468 — Emp: 5,000
and infrastructure engineering. — www.elinebg.at

AMERICAN ELIN CORPORATION
405 Lexington Avenue, 42nd Fl., New York, NY 10174
CEO: Walter Paminger, Pres. — Tel: (212) 808-4470 — %FO: 100
Bus: *Metallurgical, energy and* — Fax: (212) 808-4473 — Emp: 10
environmental engineering
services.

• EMCO MAIER GMBH
Salvachtal Bundesstraße Nord 58, PO Box 131, A-5400 Hallein, Austria
CEO: Herbert Maier, Pres. — Tel: 43-6245-891-0
Bus: *Mfr. industrial machinery.* — Fax: 43-6245-869-65
www.emcomaier.com

EMCO MAIER CORPORATION
2757 Scioto Parkway, Columbus, OH 43026
CEO: Michael Wicken, Pres. — Tel: (614) 771-5991 — %FO: 100
Bus: *Mfr./ distribution industrial* — Fax: (614) 771-5990
machinery.

• ERSTE BANK AG
Graben 21, A-1010 Vienna, Austria
CEO: Herbert Schimetschek, Pres. — Tel: 43-1-711-94-0 — Rev: $3,346
Bus: *Commercial banking, real estate* — Fax: 43-1-711-94 — Emp: 8,415
financing and asset management. — www.erstebank.at

ERSTE BANK
280 Park Avenue, W. Bldg, 32nd Fl., New York, NY 10017
CEO: Hans Krikava, Mgr. — Tel: (212) 984-5600 — %FO: 100
Bus: *Commercial banking, real estate* — Fax: (212) 986-1423
financing and asset management.

• GLOCK GMBH
PO Box 9, A-2232 Deutsch-Wagram, Austria
CEO: Gaston Glock, Pres. — Tel: 43-2247-90300-0
Bus: *Supplies pistols to armies and civilians.* — Fax: 43-2247-90300-312
www.glock.com

GLOCK INC.
6000 Highlands Parkway, Smyrna, GA 30082
CEO: Paul Jannuzzo, VP   Tel: (770) 432-1202   %FO: 100
Bus: *Sales of pistols.*   Fax: (770) 433-8719

● **GRASS HOLDING AG**
Grass Platz 1, A-6973 Hoechst, Austria
CEO: H. Grass, Chmn. & CEO   Tel: 43-5578-7010   Rev: $115
Bus: *Mfr. hinges, brackets and other steel*   Fax: 43-5578-70159   Emp: 1,062
fittings for use in office and household   www.grass.at
furniture.

   GRASS AMERICA INC.
   PO Box 1019, Kernersville, NC 27284
   CEO: Kerry Kerr   Tel: (336) 996-4041   %FO: 100
   Bus: *Distribution/sales hinges, brackets*   Fax: (336) 996-5149   Emp: 200
   and other steel fittings for use in
   office and household furniture.

● **HOERBIGER INTERNATIONAL AB**
Prinz-Eugen Straße 70, A-1040 Vienna, Austria
CEO: Dr. Gerd Unterburg, CEO   Tel: 43-1-505-14160
Bus: *Mfr. electrical linear actuators, band*   Fax: 43-1-505-1416-20
cylinders, pneumatic valves & cylinders.   www.hoerbiger-origa.com

   HOERBIGER-ORIGA CORPORATION
   100 West Lake Drive, Glendale Heights, IL 60139
   CEO: Joseph M. Hughes, Pres. & CEO   Tel: (630) 871-8300   %FO: 100
   Bus: *Mfr./sale/service electrical linear*   Fax: (630) 871-1515
   actuators, band cylinders,
   pneumatic valves & cylinders.

● **PLAUT GMBH**
Modecenterstraße 14, A-1030 Vienna, Austria
CEO: Erich Lebeiner, CEO   Tel: 43-1-79570-0   Rev: $291
Bus: *Engaged in management consulting,*   Fax: 43-1-7986968   Emp: 5,000
strategy consulting and IT-outsourcing.   www.plaut.de

   EDGEWING, DIV. PLAUT
   1050 Winter Street, Waltham, MA 02451
   CEO: Paul Shaughnessy, Pres.   Tel: (781) 768-0600   %FO: 100
   Bus: *Provides e-business solutions.*   Fax: (781) 768-0508

PLAUT CONSULTING, INC.
1050 Winter Street, Waltham, MA   02451
CEO: Klaus Schottenhamel, Pres. Tel: (781) 768-0500 %FO: 100
Bus: *Engaged in management* Fax: (781) 768-0508
  consulting services.

● RED BULL GMBH
Brunn 115, A-5330 Fuschi am See, Austria
CEO: Dietrich Mateschitz, CEO Tel: 43-662-6582-0 Rev: $1,200
Bus: *Mfr. non-alcoholic, energy drink.* Fax: 43-662-6582-31 Emp: 550
  www.redbull.at

RED BULL NORTH AMERICA, INC.
70 Hudson Street, 6th Fl., Hoboken, NJ   07030
CEO: Dietrich Mateschitz, Pres. Tel: (201) 239-7171 %FO: 100
Bus: *Sales of non-alcoholic, energy* Fax: (201) 239-7666
  drink.

RED BULL NORTH AMERICA, INC.
2525 Colorado Boulevard, Ste. 320, Santa Monica, CA   90404
CEO: Kimberly Torres, HR Tel: (310) 393-4647 %FO: 100
Bus: *Sales of non-alcoholic, energy* Fax: (310) 230-2361
  drink.

● RHI AG
Mommsengaße 35, A-1040 Vienna, Austria
CEO: Rudolf Kanzi Tel: 43-1-50213-0 Rev: $1,580
Bus: *Mfr. refractory, insulating and* Fax: 43-1-50213-368 Emp: 14,500
  waterproofing products. www.rhi.at

RHI REFRACTORIES AMERICA
600 Grant Street, 51st Fl., Pittsburgh, PA   15219
CEO: Jess Hutchinson, CEO Tel: (412) 562-6200 %FO: 100
Bus: *Mfr., distribution and sales of* Fax: (412) 562-6421
  refractory products for heat
  processing applications.

● ROSENBAUER INTERNATIONAL AG
Paschinger Straße 90, A-4060 Leonding Österreich, Austria
CEO: Julian Wagner, Pres. & CEO Tel: 43-732-6794-0
Bus: *Engaged in fire-fighting technology;* Fax: 43-732-6794-83
  vehicles, components and equipment. www.rosenbauer.co.at

ROSENBAUER AMERICA
25900 Fallbrook Avenue, Wyoming, MN   55092
CEO: John Heffren, Pres.   Tel: (651) 462-1000   %FO: 100
Bus: *Engaged in fire-fighting*   Fax: (651) 462-1700
technology; vehicles, components
and equipment.

• SEZ AG
Draubodenweg 29, A-9500 Villach, Austria
CEO: Egon Putzi, Pres. & CEO   Tel: 43-42-42-204   Rev: $50
Bus: *Chemical spin etch systems for* Fax: 43-42-42-20421   Emp: 620
semiconductor wafers.   www.sez.com

SEZ AMERICA, INC.
4824 South 40th Street, Phoenix, AZ   85040
CEO: Donald P. Baumann, EVP & GM   Tel: (602) 437-5050   %FO: 100
Bus: *Chemical spin etch systems for* Fax: (602) 437-4949   Emp: 50
semiconductor wafers.

SEZ AMERICA, INC.
18484 Preston Road, Ste. 102-121, Dallas, TX   75252
CEO: Donald P. Baumann, EVP & GM   Tel: (972) 596-6644   %FO: 100
Bus: *Chemical spin etch systems for* Fax: (972) 596-6688
semiconductor wafers.

SEZ AMERICA, INC.
15 Green Meadow Road, Florida, NY   10921
CEO: Debbie Bagget   Tel: (845) 651-3255   %FO: 100
Bus: *Chemical spin etch systems for* Fax: (845) 651-3256
semiconductor wafers.

SEZ AMERICA, INC.
1405 Preston Avenue, Austin, TX   78703
CEO: Debbie Bagget   Tel: (512) 481-0403   %FO: 100
Bus: *Chemical spin etch systems for* Fax: (512) 481-0407
semiconductor wafers.

• TOPCALL INTERNATIONAL AG
Talpagaße 1, A-1230 Vienna, Austria
CEO: Herbert Blieberger, CEO   Tel: 43-1-86353-0
Bus: *Engaged in management and*   Fax: 43-1-86353-21
communication business solutions.   www.topcall.com

TOPCALL CORPORATION
200 Chester Field Parkway, Malvern, PA 19355

CEO: Denis O'Neil, Pres.	Tel: (610) 240-4304	%FO: 100
Bus: *Engaged in management and communication business solutions.*	Fax: (610) 240-4340	

• UNITEK MASCHINEN GMBH
Dresdner Straße 38-40, A-1200 Vienna, Austria

CEO: K. Streitenberger, Mng. Dir.	Tel: 43-1-332-5510	
Bus: *Fixed center crossheads and color change systems for wire extrusion.*	Fax: 43-1-332-5515 www.unitek.at	Emp: 35

UNITEK NORTH AMERICA, INC.
One Evergreen Avenue, Hampton, CT 06518

CEO: Thomas J. Siedlarz, Pres.	Tel: (203) 230-5947	%FO: 80
Bus: *Fixed center crossheads and color change systems for wire extrusion.*	Fax: (203) 230-9864	Emp: 5

• VA TECHNOLOGIE AG
Lunzerstraße 64, A-4031 Linz Österreich, Austria

CEO: Erich Becker, CEO	Tel: 43-732-6986-9222	Rev: $3,658
Bus: *Metallurgical, energy and environmental engineering services; steel milling technology, hydroelectric turbines and industrial gas cleaning systems.*	Fax: 43-732-6980-3416 www.vatech.co.at	Emp: 22,150

VA TECH ELIN USA CORPORATION
48 Miller Avenue, Jackson, TN 38305

CEO: Bob Kelley, Mgr.	Tel: (901) 664-7644	%FO: 100
Bus: *Mfr./service transformers.*	Fax: (901) 664-5372	

VAI AUTOMATION, INC.
2390 Pipestone Road, Benton Harbor, MI 49023-1408

CEO: Mahesh K. Seth, Mgr.	Tel: (616) 926-2148	%FO: 100
Bus: *Metallurgical, energy and environmental engineering services.*	Fax: (616) 926-6854	

VOEST-ALPINE INDUSTRIES, INC.
541 Tech Drive, Canonsburg, PA 15317

CEO: John Kelman, Pres.	Tel: (724) 514-8400	%FO: 100
Bus: *Metallurgical, energy and environmental engineering services; steel milling technology, hydroelectric turbines and industrial gas cleaning systems.*	Fax: (724) 514-8354	

VOEST-ALPINE INTERNATIONAL

60 East 42nd Street, Ste. 4510, New York, NY 10165

CEO: Gerhard Nussbaumer, CFO Tel: (212) 922-2000 %FO: 100

Bus: *Metallurgical, energy and environmental engineering services; steel milling technology, hydroelectric turbines and industrial gas cleaning systems.* Fax: (212) 922-3810

VOEST-ALPINE TUBULAR CORPORATION

10260 Westheimer, Ste. 630, Houston, TX 77042

CEO: Robert A. Scott, Mgr. Tel: (713) 784-9990 %FO: 100

Bus: *Metallurgical, energy and environmental engineering services; steel milling technology, hydroelectric turbines and industrial gas cleaning systems.* Fax: (713) 784-9980

● VOEST-ALPINE AG

Straße 1, A-4020 Linz, Austria

CEO: Horst Paschinger, Mng. Dir. Tel: 43-732-6585-8015 Rev: $3,037

Bus: *Mfr. mechanical cutting equipment for mining of coal and rocks. (JV with Sandvik Tamrock, Sweden)* Fax: 43-732-6980-8021
www.voest.co.at

VOEST-ALPINE STEEL CORP.

500 Mamaroneck Ave, Suite 310, Harrison, NY 10528

CEO: Wolfgang Neubauer, Pres. Tel: (914) 899-3700 %FO: JV

Bus: *Sales/distribution of high-quality steel flat and long products.* Fax: (914) 381-0509

● WIENERBERGER BAUSTOFFINDUSTRIE AG

Wienerbergerstraße 7, A-1102 Vienna, Austria

CEO: Wolfgang Reithofer, CEO Tel: 43-1-601-92-0 Rev: $1,458

Bus: *Engaged in manufacture of building materials and real estate development.* Fax: 43-1-601-92-473 Emp: 10,378
www.wienerberger.com

GENERAL SHALE PRODUCTS CORPORATION

PO Box 813250, Smyrna, GA 30081

CEO: Erhard Schaschl, CEO Tel: (404) 799-8541

Bus: *Mfr. facing bricks, concrete block, lightweight aggregates and sand.* Fax: (404) 799-8892

GENERAL SHALE PRODUCTS CORPORATION
3211 North Roan Street, Johnson City, TN   37602

CEO: Erhard Schaschl, CEO   Tel: (423) 282-4661

Bus: *U.S. headquarters. Mfr. facing*   Fax: (423) 952-4104   Emp: 1,450
     bricks, concrete block, lightweight
     aggregates and sand.

• WINTERSTEIGER
Dimmelstrave 9, A-4910 Ried, Austria

CEO: Diderik Schnitler, Chmn.   Tel: 43-7752-919-0   Rev: $35

Bus: *Ski tuning machines, agricultural*   Fax: 43-7752-919-57   Emp: 300
    machines, woodworking machines.   www.wintersteiger.com

WINTERSTEIGER
217 Wright Brothers Drive, Salt Lake City, UT   84116

CEO: Fritz Hoeckner, CEO   Tel: (801) 355-6550   %FO: 100

Bus: *Ski tuning machines, agricultural*   Fax: (801) 355-6541   Emp: 25
    machines, woodworking machines.

• WITTMANN ROBOT GMBH
Lichtblaustraße 10, A-1220 Vienna, Austria

CEO: Dr. Werner Wittmann, Pres.   Tel: 43-1-250-390

Bus: *Mfr. of water flow regulators,*   Fax: 43-1-259-7170   Emp: 260
   temperature controllers and automation   www.wittmann-robot.at
   systems for plastic industry.

WITTMANN ROBOT & AUTOMATION SYSTEMS
One Technology Park Drive, Torrington, CT   06790

CEO: Duane D. Royce   Tel: (860) 496-9603   %FO: 100

Bus: *Mfr. of water flow regulators,*   Fax: (860) 482-2069
   temperature controllers and
   automation systems for plastic
   industry.

• WOLFORD AG
Wolfordstraße 1, A-6901 Bregenz, Austria

CEO: Firtz Humer, Chmn.   Tel: 43-5574-690-1454   Rev: $135

Bus: *Mfr. hosiery, lingerie, bodysuits and*   Fax: 43-5574-690-1545   Emp: 1,820
   swimwear.   www.wolford.com

WOLFORD AMERICA
540 Madison Avenue, New York, NY   10022

CEO: Karen Schneider, Pres.   Tel: (212) 453-5556   %FO: 100

Bus: *Sales/distribution of hosiery and*   Fax: (212) 453-5563
   lingerie.

WOLFORD BOUTIQUES
54 East Oak Street, Chicago, IL   60611
CEO: Karen Schneider, Pres.   Tel: (312) 642-8787
Bus: *Sales/distribution of hosiery and*   Fax: (312) 642-8787
lingerie.

WOLFORD BOUTIQUES
3333 Bristol Street, St. 2419, Costa Mesa, CA   92626
CEO: Karen Schneider, Pres.   Tel: (714) 556-7900
Bus: *Sales/distribution of hosiery and*   Fax: (714) 556-7927
lingerie.

• ZUMTOBEL STAFF GMBH
Schweizer Straße 30, Postfach 72, A-6851 Dornbirn, Austria
CEO: Jürg Zumtobel, Chmn.   Tel: 43-5572-390-0
Bus: *Mfr. lighting fixtures.*   Fax: 43-5572-22826   Emp: 2,860
www.zumtobelstaff.com

ZUMTOBEL STAFF LIGHTING, INC.
141 Lanza Avenue, Garfield, NJ   07026
CEO: Wolfgang Egger, Pres.   Tel: (973) 340-8900   %FO: 100
Bus: *Mfr. lighting fixtures.*   Fax: (973) 340-9898   Emp: 100

ZUMTOBEL STAFF LIGHTING, INC.
300 Route 9W North, PO Box 1020, Highland, NY   12528
CEO: Wolfgang Egger, Pres.   Tel: (845) 691-6262   %FO: 100
Bus: *Mfr. lighting fixtures.*   Fax: (914) 691-6289   Emp: 100

Bahamas

- **STEINER LEISURE LIMITED**
Saffrey Square, Ste. 104A, Nassau, Bahamas
CEO: Leonard I. Fluxman, CEO   Tel: 242-356-0006   Rev: $162
Bus: *Operates spas on cruise ship lines.*   Fax: 242-356-6260   Emp: 1,585
www.steinerleisure.com

    STEINER USA INC.
    770 South Dixie Hwy., Ste. 200, Coral Gables, FL   33146
    CEO: Jan Green, Mgr.   Tel: (305) 358-9002   %FO: 100
    Bus: *Manages spas on cruise ship lines.*   Fax: (305) 372-9310

- **SUN INTERNATIONAL HOTELS LIMITED**
Coral Towers, Paradise Island, Bahamas
CEO: Solomon Kerzner, CEO   Tel: 242-363-6000   Rev: $885
Bus: *Owns and manages resort facilities and*   Fax: 242-363-5401   Emp: 9,600
casinos.   www.sunint.com

    MOHEGAN SUN CASINO/TRIBAL GAMING AUTHORITY
    One Mohegan Sun Boulevard, Uncasville, CT   06382
    CEO: William Velardo, VP   Tel: (860) 204-8000
    Bus: *Casino, hotel and restaurant*   Fax: (860) 204-7167
    facility owned by the Mohegan
    Tribe of Indians.

Bahrain

● **ARAB BANKING CORPORATION**
PO Box 5698, ABC Tower, Diplomatic Area, Manama, Bahrain
CEO: A. Yousef Al-Hunalf, Chmn.   Tel: 973-532-235
Bus: *International banking services.*   Fax: 973-533-062
                                            www.arabbanking.com

> **ARAB BANKING CORPORATION**
> 600 Travis Street, Ste. 1900, Houston, TX   77002
> CEO: Harold Dietler, Rep.   Tel: (713) 227-8444   %FO: 100
> Bus: *International banking services.*   Fax: (713) 227-6507

> **ARAB BANKING CORPORATION**
> 555 South Flower Street, 46th Fl., Los Angeles, CA   90017
> CEO: Richard B. Whelan, Mgr.   Tel: (213) 689-0121   %FO: 100
> Bus: *International banking services.*   Fax: (213) 689-1048

> **ARAB BANKING CORPORATION**
> 277 Park Avenue, 32nd Fl., New York, NY   10173-3299
> CEO: Geoffrey Milton, VP   Tel: (212) 583-4720   %FO: 100
> Bus: *International banking services.*   Fax: (212) 583-0921

● **GULF AIR COMPANY GSC**
Gulf Air Headquarters, Manama, Bahrain
CEO: H.E. Ibrahim Adbulla AlHamer, Pres.   Tel: 973-322200   Rev: $75
Bus: *Commercial air transport services.*   Fax: 973-338980   Emp: 4,402
                                            www.gulfairco.com

> **GULF AIR COMPANY GSC**
> 104 South Central Avenue, Valley Stream, NY   11580
> CEO: H.E. Ibrahim Abdulla AlHamer   Tel: (516) 568-0860   %FO: 100
> Bus: *Commercial air transport services.*   Fax: (516) 553-2824   Emp: 8

● **GULF INTERNATIONAL BANK (GIB)**
PO Box 1017 Al-Dowali Building, 3 Palace Avenue, Manama, Bahrain
CEO: Dr. Khaled Al-Fayez   Tel: 973-534000
Bus: *Engaged in corporate and institutional*   Fax: 973-522633
banking, investment banking, asset   www.gibon.com
management, treasury and financial
markets.

GULF INVESTMENT CORPORATION
335 Madison Avenue, 21st Fl., New York, NY   10017
CEO: Issa N. Baconi, SVP   Tel: (212) 922-2300   %FO: 100
Bus: *International banking services.*   Fax: (212) 922-2339

• **INVESTCORP BANK E.C.**
Investcorp House, PO Box 5340, Manama, Bahrain
CEO: Abdul-Rahman S. Al-Ateeqi, Chmn.   Tel: 973-530000   Rev: $332
Bus: *Manages real estate, investments and* Fax: 973-530816   Emp: 250
mergers and acquisitions.   www.investcorp.com

INVESTCORP USA
280 Park Avenue, 37th Fl. West, New York, NY   10017
CEO: Savio W. Tuing, COO   Tel: (212) 599-4700   %FO: 100
Bus: *Manages real estate, investments*   Fax: (212) 983-7073
and acquisitions.

Barbados

- **EVEREST RE GROUP LTD.**

c/o ABG Financial Services Inc., Wildey Business Park, Wildey Road, St. Michael, Barbados

CEO: Joseph V. Taranto, CEO	Tel: 246-228-7398	Rev: $1,480
Bus: *Underwriter of property and casualty reinsurance.*	Fax: 903-604-3322 www.everestre.com	Emp: 440

EVEREST NATIONAL INC., DIV. EVEREST RE GROUP

477 Martinsville Road, PO Box 830, Liberty Corner, NJ   07938-0830

CEO: Larry A. Frakes, Pres.	Tel: (908) 604-3000	%FO: 100
Bus: *Engaged in insurance.*	Fax: (908) 604-3450	

EVEREST RE GROUP

1200 Brickell Avenue, Ste. 600, Miami, FL   33131

CEO: Thomas J. Gallagher	Tel: (305) 371-8200	%FO: 100
Bus: *Engaged in insurance.*	Fax: (305) 789-3936	

EVEREST RE GROUP

120 Broadway, Ste. 2800, New York, NY   10271

CEO: James Ruden, VP	Tel: (212) 619-0002	%FO: 100
Bus: *Engaged in insurance.*	Fax: (212) 267-1917	

EVEREST RE GROUP

311 South Wacker Drive, Ste. 2375, Chicago, IL   60606

CEO: Thomas J. Gallagher	Tel: (312) 939-2900	%FO: 100
Bus: *Engaged in insurance.*	Fax: (312) 939-6911	

Belgium

● **AGFA-GEVAERT GROUP**
Septestraat 27, B-2640 Mortsel, Belgium
CEO: Klaus Seeger, Chmn. & CEO   Tel: 32-3-444-2111   Rev: $1,814
Bus: *Mfr. photographic and electronic*   Fax: 32-3-444-7094   Emp: 21,900
imaging equipment.   www.agfa.com

   AGFA-GEVAERT GROUP
   100 Challenger Road, Ridgefield Park, NJ   07660-2199
   CEO: Erhard Rettinghaus, Pres.   Tel: (201) 641-9566   %FO: 100
   Bus: *Photographic, imaging*   Fax: (201) 440-1512
   technologies.

● **BANQUE BRUXELLES LAMBERT**
24 Avenue Marnix, B-1050 Brussels, Belgium
CEO: Luc Vandewalle, CEO   Tel: 32-2-517-2111
Bus: *General banking services.*   Fax: 32-2-517-3663
   www.bbl.be

   BANK BRUSSELS LAMBERT
   630 Fifth Avenue, 6th Floor, New York, NY   10111-0020
   CEO: Ludwig Hoogstoel, Mgr.   Tel: (212) 218-5200   %FO: 100
   Bus: *International banking services.*   Fax: (212) 333-5786   Emp: 100

● **BARCO N.V.**
President Kennedy Park 35, B-8500 Kortrijk, Belgium
CEO: Hugo Vandamme, Pres. & CEO   Tel: 32-56-262-611   Rev: $886
Bus: *Integrated systems for textile industry,*   Fax: 32-56-262-690   Emp: 4,765
graphic displays, broadcast monitors.   www.barco.com

   BARCO DISPLAY SYSTEMS, INC.
   3059 Premier Pkwy., Duluth, GA   30097
   CEO: Dave Scott, VP   Tel: (678) 475-8000
   Bus: *Mfr. vision systems.*   Fax: (678) 475-8100

   BARCO ELECTRONIC TOOLING SYSTEMS, INC.
   30 South Satellite Road, South Windsor, CT   06074
   CEO: Stan Huber, Mgr.   Tel: (860) 291-7000   %FO: 100
   Bus: *Mfr. electronic tooling systems.*   Fax: (860) 291-7001   Emp: 180

BARCO GRAPHICS INC.
163 Technology Drive, Ste. 100, Irvine, CA   92618
CEO: Steve Klein, VP   Tel: (949) 788-7300
Bus: *Mfr. graphics systems.*   Fax: (949) 788-7330

BARCO VISION, INC.
4420 Taggert Creek Road, Ste. 101, Charlotte, NC   28208
CEO: Steve Altman, VP   Tel: (704) 392-9371   %FO: 100
Bus: *Automation division.*   Fax: (704) 399-5588   Emp: 30

• BARCONET NV
Luipaardstraat 12, B-8500 Kortrijk, Belgium
CEO: Jos Vancoppernolle, COO   Tel: 32-56-445-139
Bus: *Provider of multimedia distribution*   Fax: 32-56-445-010   Emp: 700
    solutions for broadband and broadcast   www.barconet.com
    applications.

BARCONET, INC.
3240 Town Point Drive, Kennesaw, GA   30144
CEO: Robert Cunningham, Mgr.   Tel: (770) 590-3629   %FO: 100
Bus: *Provider of multimedia*   Fax: (770) 590-3610
    distribution solutions for
    broadband and broadcast
    applications, including projection
    systems.

• NV BEKAERT SA
President Kennedy Park 18, B-8500 Kortrijk, Belgium
CEO: Raf Decaluwé, CEO   Tel: 32-56-230-511   Rev: $2,500
Bus: *Mfr. producer of high-grade steel cord,*   Fax: 32-56-230543   Emp: 17,000
    steel wire and fences.   www.bekaert.com

BEKAERT CORP.
2000 Isaac Shelby Drive, Shelbyville, KY   40065
CEO: David R. Best, Pres.   Tel: (502) 633-6722   %FO: 100
Bus: *Mfr. wire and wire products.* Fax: (502) 633-1561

BEKAERT CORPORATION
3200 West Market Street, Ste. 300, Akron, OH   44333
CEO: David R. Best, Pres. & CEO   Tel: (330) 867-3325   %FO: 100
Bus: *U.S. headquarters for production*   Fax: (330) 873-3424
    of high-grade steel cord, steel wire
    and fences.

BEKAERT CORPORATION
1395 South Marietta Parkway, Bldg. 500, Marietta, GA   30067
CEO: Henri-Jean Velge, Pres.   Tel: (770) 421-8520   %FO: 100
Bus: *Mfr. steel wire & wire products.*   Fax: (770) 421-8521

BEKAERT CORP.
8401 N.W. 53rd Terrace, Ste. 109, Miami, FL   33166
CEO: David R. Best, Pres.   Tel: (305) 463-8979   %FO: 100
Bus: *Mfr. steel cord and wire.*   Fax: (305) 463-8959

BEKAERT CORP.
PO Box 1205, Rome, GA   30161
CEO: David R. Best, Pres.   Tel: (706) 235-4481   %FO: 100
Bus: *Mfr. steel cord.*   Fax: (706) 235-2160

BEKAERT CORP.
One Bekaert Road, Dyersburg, TN   38024
CEO: David R. Best, Pres.   Tel: (901) 285-0897   %FO: 100
Bus: *Mfr. steel cord.*   Fax: (901) 285-1584

BEKAERT CORP.
One Bekaert Road, Rogers, AZ   72756-1948
CEO: David R. Best, Pres.   Tel: (501) 631-7661   %FO: 100
Bus: *Mfr. steel cord.*   Fax: (501) 631-8174

BEKAERT CORP.
2121 Latimer Drive, Muskegon, MI   49442
CEO: David R. Best, Pres.   Tel: (231) 777-2575   %FO: 100
Bus: *Mfr. wire and wire products.*   Fax: (231) 773-4863

BEKAERT CORP.
7510 N. Caldwell Avenue, Niles, IL   60714
CEO: David R. Best, Pres.   Tel: (847) 588-1864   %FO: 100
Bus: *Service for Bakaert products.*   Fax: (847) 588-1872

BEKAERT CORP.
PO Box 13159, Research Triangle Park, NC   27709-3159
CEO: David R. Best, Pres.   Tel: (919) 485-8995   %FO: 100
Bus: *Mfr. advanced materials.*   Fax: (919) 485-8993

BEKAERT CORP.
1881 Bekaert Drive, Van Buren, AR   72956-6801
CEO: David R. Best, Pres.   Tel: (501) 474-5211   %FO: 100
Bus: *Mfr. wire products.*   Fax: (501) 474-9075

CONTOURS, LTD.
East Pine & Lake Streets, Orrville, OH   44667-0608
CEO: Jim Balzarini, Mgr.   Tel: (330) 683-5060   %FO: 100
Bus: *Mfr./sales of flat and shaped wire.*   Fax: (330) 683-0446

SOLIDLOCK INC.
7040 International Drive, Louisville, KY   40258
CEO: Willy Snaet   Tel: (502) 933-4404   %FO: 100
Bus: *Mfr. wire and wire products.*   Fax: (502) 933-4404

● BELGACOM SA
Blvd. du Roi Albert II 27, B-1030 Brussels, Belgium
CEO: John J. Goossens, Pres. & CEO   Tel: 32-2-202-4111   Rev: $4,841
Bus: *Telecommunications services.*   Fax: 32-2-203-55-35   Emp: 23,475
                                       www.belgacom.be

BELGACOM NORTH AMERICA
320 Post Road West, Suite 250, Westport, CT   06880-4748
CEO: Susan Mirbach, Pres.   Tel: (203) 221-5250   %FO: 100
Bus: *Telecommunications services,*   Fax: (203) 222-8401   Emp: 14
     branch office.

● BROWNING SA
Parc Indust des Hauts-Sarts, 3 ème Ave. 25, B-4040 Herstal, Belgium
CEO: Philippe Tennesson, Pres.   Tel: 32-42-405-211
Bus: *Hunting, shooting and fishing products.*   Fax: 32-42-405-212
                                       www.browningint.com

BROWNING
One Browning Place, Morgan, UT   84050-9326
CEO: Charles Guevremont, Pres.   Tel: (801) 876-2711   %FO: 100
Bus: *Distributor hunting, fishing &*   Fax: (801) 876-3331
     shooting products.

● DE BANDT, VAN HECKE & LAGAE
Rue Brederode 13, B-1000 Brussels, Belgium
CEO: Alec Burnside   Tel: 32-2-501-9411
Bus: *Engaged in international law practice.*   Fax: 32-2-501-9494
                                       www.debandt.com

DE BANDT, VAN HECKE & LAGAE
1345 Avenue of the Americas, New York, NY   10105
CEO: Caird Forbes-Cockell, Mng. Prtn.   Tel: (212) 424-9000   %FO: 100
Bus: *International law firm.*   Fax: (212) 424-9100   Emp: 3

● **DELHAIZE LE LION GROUP SA**
Rue Osseghem 53, Molenbeek-St.-Jean, B-1080 Brussels, Belgium
CEO: Gui de Vaucleroy, Chmn.   Tel: 32-2-412-2111   Rev: $17,500
Bus: *General merchandise and food retailers.* Fax: 32-2-412-2194   Emp: 134,650
www.delhaize-le-lion.be

    DELHAIZE AMERICA
    950 East Paces Ferry, Suite 2160, Atlanta, GA   30326
    CEO: Pierre-Olivier Beckers, Chmn.   Tel: (404) 365-8435   %FO: 100
    Bus: *Holding company.*   Fax: (404) 365-8358

    DELHAIZE AMERICA
    PO Box 1330, Salisbury, NC   28145-1330
    CEO: R. William McCanless, CEO   Tel: (704) 633-8250   %FO: 51
    Bus: *Supermarket chain.*   Fax: (704) 636-4940   Emp: 48,360

    HANNAFORD BROTHERS CO.
    145 Pleasant Hill Road, Scarborough, ME   04074
    CEO: Hugh G. Farrington, CEO   Tel: (207) 883-2911   %FO: 100
    Bus: *Retail supermarkets.*   Fax: (207) 885-3165

    SUPER DISCOUNT MARKETS, INC
    420 Thornton Road, Suite 103, Lithia Springs, GA   30122
    CEO: Preston Slayden, Pres. & CEO   Tel: (770) 732-6800   %FO: 100
    Bus: *Supermarket chain.*   Fax: (770) 732-6818

● **DEXIA BANQUE INTERNATIONALE A LUXEMBOURG**
Blvd. Pacheco 44, B-1000 Brussels, Belgium
CEO: Marc Hoffmann   Tel: 32-2-222-1111   Rev: $14,157
Bus: *Financial institution engaged in asset* Fax: 32-2-222-4032   Emp: 10,300
management, public works loans and www.dexia.com
insurance. (JV with Dexia France)

    BCEE LUXEMBOURG SA
    712 Fifth Avenue, New York, NY   10019
    CEO: Egide Thein, Reg. Rep.   Tel: (212) 245-7100   %FO: 100
    Bus: *Banking; representative office.*   Fax: (212) 245-7373   Emp: 1

    DEXIA BANK
    445 Park Avenue, New York, NY   10022
    CEO: Jan E. Van Panhuys, Gen. Mgr.   Tel: (212) 705-0700   %FO: 100
    Bus: *General banking services.*   Fax: (212) 705-0701

● **ETEX GROUP SA**

Avenue de Tervueren 361, B-1150 Brussels, Belgium

CEO: David Trapnell, CEO
Tel: 32-2-778-1211

Bus: *Mfr. building materials and systems,*
including roofs, plastics, boards, floors
and walls.
Fax: 32-2-778-1212
www.etexgroup.com
Emp: 25,900

CANPLAS INC.

11402 East 53rd Avenue, Ste. 200, Denver, CO   80239

CEO: Jeff Bailey, Pres.
Tel: (303) 373-1918
%FO: 100

Bus: *Mfr. injection molded components*
for the construction industry.
Fax: (303) 373-1923

CEMPLANK

PO Box 99, Blandon, PA   19510

CEO: Toussaint Dolmans, Pres. & CEO
Tel: (610) 926-5533
%FO: 100

Bus: *Mfr. building materials.*
Fax: (610) 916-4916

CÉRAMICA SAN LORENZO INC.

10012 Norwalk Blvd., Ste. 110, Santa Fe Springs, CA   90670

CEO: J. Fernando
Tel: (562) 944-3957
%FO: 100

Bus: *Mfr. building materials.*
Fax: (562) 944-3198

ETERNIT, INC., DIV. ETEX

610 Corporate Drive, Reading, PA   19605

CEO: Tony Wilson
Tel: (610) 926-0100
%FO: 100

Bus: *Mfr. building materials.*
Fax: (610) 926-9232

● **FONDERIES MAGOTTEAUX SA**

Vaux Sous, B-4601 Chevremont, Belgium

CEO: Walter Mersch, CEO
Tel: 32-43-617-550

Bus: *Mfr. white iron grinding media, iron*
and steel castings.
Fax: 32-43-617-617
www.magotteaux.com

AMERICAN MAGOTTEAUX CORPORATION

2409 21st Avenue, PO Box 120915, Nashville, TN   37212

CEO: Walter Mersch, CEO
Tel: (615) 385-3055
%FO: 100

Bus: *Grinding media, iron and steel*
castings
Fax: (615) 297-6743

WOLLASTON ALLOYS INC.

205 Wood Road, Braintree, MA   02184

CEO: David Bernardi, Pres.
Tel: (781) 848-3333
%FO: 100

Bus: *Stainless steel valves and pumps,*
defense castings.
Fax: (781) 848-3993

● **FORTIS (B)**

Rue Royale 20, B-1000 Brussels, Belgium

CEO: Maurice Lippens, Chmn.	Tel: 32-2-510-5211	Rev: $44,650
Bus: *Provides specialty insurance and*	Fax: 32-2-510-5626	Emp: 1,148
investment products to businesses,	www.ag.be	
associations, financial service		
organizations and individuals. (See joint		
parent: Fortis Amev, Netherlands		

ASSURANT GROUP

260 Interstate North Circle, SE, Atlanta, GA   30339-2210

CEO: Bruce Camacho, Pres.	Tel: (770) 763-1000	%FO: 100
Bus: *Provides specialty insurance.*	Fax: (770) 859-4403	

CORE INC.

18881 Von Karman Ave., Ste. 1750, Irvine, CA   92612

CEO: George C. Carpenter IV, CEO	Tel: (949) 477-8089	%FO: 100
Bus: *Provider of employee absence*	Fax: (949) 442-2109	Emp: 600
management.		

FORTIS BENEFITS INSURANCE COMPANY

2323 Grand Boulevard, Kansas City, MO   64108

CEO: Michael Peninger, Pres. & CEO	Tel: (816) 474-2345	%FO: 100
Bus: *Specializes in non-medical*	Fax: (816) 881-8646	
employee benefits.		

FORTIS FAMILY INSURANCE

10 Glenlake Parkway, Suite 500, Atlanta, GA   30328

CEO: Alan W. Feagin, Pres.	Tel: (404) 659-3300	%FO: 100
Bus: *Provides preneed insurance*	Fax: (404) 524-4945	
products that help individuals		
arrange and fund their own		
funeral plans.		

FORTIS FINANCIAL GROUP

500 Bielenberg Drive, Woodbury, MN   55125

CEO: Dean C. Kopperud, Pres.	Tel: (612) 738-4000	%FO: 100
Bus: *Financial services; mutual funds,*	Fax: (612) 738-5534	
insurance & annuities.		

FORTIS FINANCIAL SERVICES

520 Madison Avenue, New York, NY   10022

CEO: Jacques Thys	Tel: (212) 418-6813	%FO: 100
Bus: *Engaged in financial services.*	Fax: (212) 644-5950	

FORTIS FINANCIAL SERVICES
301 Tresser Blvd., Stamford, CT   06901
CEO: John Connors, Pres.   Tel: (203) 705-5700   %FO: 100
Bus: *Engaged in financial services.*   Fax: (203) 705-5906

FORTIS HEALTH, DIV. FORTIS INC.
501 W. Michigan Avenue, Milwaukee, WI   53203
CEO: Jack Gochenaur, SVP   Tel: (414) 271-3011   %FO: 100
Bus: *Developer and provider of*   Fax: (414) 224-0472
   individual medical, small
   employer, short term and student
   health insurance products.

FORTIS INC.
One Chase Manhattan Plaza, New York, NY   10005
CEO: J. Kerry Clayton, CEO   Tel: (212) 859-7000   %FO: 100
Bus: *Financial services holding*   Fax: (212) 859-7071   Emp: 6,040
   company.

FORTIS INSURANCE
501 W. Michigan Avenue, Milwaukee, WI   53201-2989
CEO: Benjamin M. Cutler, CEO   Tel: (414) 271-3011   %FO: 100
Bus: *Financial services.*   Fax: (414) 271-0879

JOHN ALDEN FINANCIAL CORPORATION
7300 Corporate Center Drive, Miami, FL   33126
CEO: Glendon E. Johnson, Pres. & CEO Tel: (305) 715-2000
Bus: *Provides group health indemnity,*   Fax: (305) 715-3172
   managed indemnity and HMO
   products, as well as other
   insurance-related products and
   services.

NORTH STAR, DIV. JOHN ALDEN
1210 Northbrook Drive, Ste. 140, Trevose, PA   19053
CEO: Jay Sinacole, Mgr.   Tel: (215) 357-6434
Bus: *Provides small group health*   Fax: (215) 357-6656
   insurance.

● **ICOS VISION SYSTEMS CORPORATION N.V.**
Research Park Haasrode, Zone 1, Esperantolaan 9, B-3001 Heverlee, Belgium
CEO: Joseph Verjans, Pres. & CEO   Tel: 32-16-39-8220   Rev: $48
Bus: *Mfr. machine vision and inspection*   Fax: 32-16-40-0067   Emp: 175
   systems to electronic and automotive   www.icos.be
   industries.

ICOS VISION SYSTEMS INC.
2000 Wyatt Drive, Ste. 13, Santa Clara, CA   95054

CEO: Dale Christman, Pres.

Bus: *Mfr. machine vision and inspection systems to electronic and automotive industries.*

Tel: (408) 567-9511
Fax: (408) 567-9512

• INTERBREW S.A
Vaartstraat 94, B-3000 Leuven, Belgium

CEO: Hugo Powell, CEO

Bus: *Brews beers (Rolling Rock, Labatt, & Tecate); bottles soft drinks, juices and water; operates restaurants.*

Tel: 32-16-24-7111
Fax: 32-16-247-407
www.interbrew.com

Rev: $4,531
Emp: 24,350

LABATT USA
101 Merritt 7, PO Box 5075, Norwalk, CT   06856-5075

CEO: Mark Portelance, CEO

Bus: *Brews beers; bottles soft drinks, juices, & water; operates restaurants. (U.S. Brands; Rolling Rock, Labatt, & Tecate.)*

Tel: (203) 750-6600
Fax: (203) 750-6699

%FO: JV

• KBC BANK AND INSURANCE HOLDING CO.
Havenlaan 2, B-1080 Brussels, Belgium

CEO: Remi Vermeiren, Pres.

Bus: *General banking services.*

Tel: 32-78-152-154
Fax: 32-3-206-6-208
www.kbc.be

Rev: $14,580
Emp: 39,075

KBC BANK NV
125 West 55th Street, 10th Fl., New York, NY   10019

CEO: Rik Scheerlinck, SVP

Bus: *International banking services.*

Tel: (212) 541-0600
Fax: (212) 956-5580

%FO: 100
Emp: 114

KBC BANK NV
1349 Peachtree St., Ste. 1750, Atlanta, GA   30309

CEO: Michael Sawicki, Reg. Mgr.

Bus: *International banking services.*

Tel: (404) 876-2556
Fax: (404) 876-3212

%FO: 100
Emp: 6

KBC BANK NV
515 South Figueroa Street, Ste. 1920, Los Angeles, CA   90071

CEO: Thomas Jackson, Reg. Mgr.

Bus: *International banking services.*

Tel: (213) 624-0401
Fax: (213) 629-6801

%FO: 100
Emp: 6

- **LERNOUT & HAUSPIE SPEECH PRODUCTS N.V.**

Flanders Language Valley 50, Sint-Krispijnstraat 7, B-8900 Leper, Belgium

CEO: Philippe Bodson, CEO   Tel: 32-57-228-888   Rev: $2,021

Bus: *Mfr. of speech dictation, translation and* Fax: 32-57-208-489   Emp: 6,150
recognition products.   www.lhs.com

   LERNOUT & HAUSPIE DIRECT INC.

   18940 US Hwy 19N, Clearwater, FL 33764

   CEO: Peter Hauser, Pres. & CEO   Tel: (800) 843-1224

   Bus: *Mfr. personal speech recognition*   Fax: (813) 524-1818
   products.

   LERNOUT & HAUSPIE SPEECH PRODUCTS INC.

   1420 Beverly Road, Ste. 350, McLean, VA 22101

   CEO: Peter Hauser, Pres. & CEO   Tel: (703) 821-5000

   Bus: *Mfr. personal speech recognition*   Fax: (703) 734-5703
   products.

   LERNOUT & HAUSPIE SPEECH PRODUCTS INC.

   52 Third Avenue, Burlington, MA 01803

   CEO: Peter Hauser, Pres. & CEO   Tel: (781) 203-5000

   Bus: *Mfr. personal speech recognition*   Fax: (781) 238-0986
   products.

- **PICANOL NV**

Polenlaan 3/7, B-8900 Leper, Belgium

CEO: Patrick Steverlynck, Pres.   Tel: 32-57-222-111

Bus: *Mfr./sale weaving machine & parts,*   Fax: 32-57-222-001
technical service for installation &   www.picanol.be
training.

   PICANOL OF AMERICA INC

   Ketron Court, PO Box 5519, Greenville, SC 29606

   CEO: James C. Thomas   Tel: (864) 288-5475   %FO: 100

   Bus: *Sale weaving machine & parts,*   Fax: (864) 297-5081   Emp: 50
   technical service for installation &
   training.

- **SABENA GROUP SA/NV**

Avenue Mounierlaan 2, B-1200 Brussels, Belgium

CEO: Christoph Müller, CEO   Tel: 32-2-723-3111   Rev: $2,298

Bus: *International air transport services.*   Fax: 32-2-723-8399   Emp: 11,295
                  www.sabena.com

SABENA BELGIAN WORLD AIRLINES
41 Pinelawn Road, Melville, NY 11747
CEO: Reto Wilhelm, VP   Tel: (631) 844-4500   %FO: 100
Bus: *International air transport.*   Fax:

• **SAIT-STENTO BV**
Ruisbroeksesteenweg 66B, B-1180 Brussels, Belgium
CEO: V. Van Overbeek, Mng. Dir.   Tel: 32-2-370-5311
Bus: *Engaged in wireless communication.* Fax: 32-2-370-5111
                                          www.sait-stento.com

RADIO HOLLAND USA INC.
3822 18th Avenue West, Seattle, WA 98119
CEO: Gregg Ferrando, Branch Mgr.   Tel: (206) 270-8671
Bus: *Sales/service of marine/industrial* Fax: (206) 270-8754
electronics and communication
and nautical instruments.

RADIO HOLLAND USA INC.
3007 Greene Street, Hollywood, FL 33020
CEO: Tim Schadt, Branch Mgr.   Tel: (954) 920-8400
Bus: *Sales/service of marine/industrial* Fax: (954) 920-8455
electronics and communication
and nautical instruments.

RADIO HOLLAND USA INC.
309 South Cloverdale, #B 29-30, Seattle, WA 95108
CEO: Gregg Ferrando, Branch Mgr.   Tel: (206) 768-1601
Bus: *Sales/service of marine/industrial* Fax: (206) 768-1603
electronics and communication
and nautical instruments.

RADIO HOLLAND USA INC.
910 Minnehaha, Ste. 3, Vancouver, WA 98665
CEO: Bonnie M. Moore, Branch Mgr.   Tel: (360) 373-0519
Bus: *Sales/service of marine/industrial* Fax: (360) 737-0543
electronics and communication
and nautical instruments.

RADIO HOLLAND USA INC.
1965 East Spring Street, Long Beach, CA 90806
CEO: William E. Wheeler, Branch Mgr.   Tel: (562) 595-0039
Bus: *Sales/service of marine/industrial* Fax: (562) 986-0236
electronics and communication
and nautical instruments.

RADIO HOLLAND USA INC.

5233 IH-37, Ste. A-1, Corpus Christi, TX   78408

CEO: Arlin G. Shook, Branch Mgr.   Tel: (361) 883-5283

Bus: *Sales/service of marine/industrial*   Fax: (361) 883-5285
electronics and communication
and nautical instruments.

RADIO HOLLAND USA INC.

1506 Technology Drive, Chesapeake, VA   23320

CEO: William W. Bonner, Branch Mgr.   Tel: (757) 436-2360

Bus: *Sales/service of marine/industrial*   Fax: (757) 436-4609
electronics and communication
and nautical instruments.

RADIO HOLLAND USA INC.

500 South 31st Street, Kenilworth, NJ   07033-1306

CEO: Martin J. Powell, Branch Mgr.   Tel: (908) 298-9100

Bus: *Sales/service of marine/industrial*   Fax: (908) 298-9118
electronics and communication
and nautical instruments.

RADIO HOLLAND USA INC.

5515 Pepsi Street, Ste. C, Harahan, LA   70123-3221

CEO: Patrick J. Farrell, Branch Mgr.   Tel: (504) 733-4024

Bus: *Sales/service of marine/industrial*   Fax: (504) 733-4027
electronics and communication
and nautical instruments.

RADIO HOLLAND USA INC.

701 A South Conception, Mobile, AL   36603-2102

CEO: Billy P. Woolridge, Branch Mgr.   Tel: (334) 432-3109

Bus: *Sales/service of marine/industrial*   Fax: (334) 433-8223
electronics and communication
and nautical instruments.

RADIO HOLLAND USA INC.

8943 Gulf Freeway, Houston, TX   77017-7004

CEO: Jacob Plenter, Pres.   Tel: (713) 943-3325

Bus: *Sales/service of marine/industrial*   Fax: (713) 943-3802
electronics and communication
and nautical instruments.

• SOCONORD SA

287 Ave. Louise, B-1050 Brussels, Belgium

CEO: Jacques Focquet, Pres.   Tel: 32-2-640-7430

Bus: *Engaged in pipes and tubular products*   Fax: 32-2-647-7297
for the gas and oil industry.   www.soconord.com

SOCONORD CORPORATION
333 North Sam Houston Pkwy. East, Ste. 1020, Houston, TX   77060-2415

CEO: Luke Vollemaere, VP

Bus: *Sales/distribution of pipes and tubular products for the gas and oil industry.*

Tel: (281) 820-9400

Fax: (281) 820-5800

• SOLVAY SA
Rue du Prince Albert 33, B-1050 Brussels, Belgium

CEO: Alois Michielsen, Chmn.

Bus: *Chemicals, plastics, human and health products.*

Tel: 32-2-509-6111

Fax: 32-2-509-6624

www.solvay.com

Rev: $8,345

Emp: 32,300

HEDWIN CORP
1600 Roland Heights Avenue, Baltimore, MD   21211

CEO: David Rubley, Pres.

Bus: *Mfr./distributor plastic containers, automotive parts and film.*

Tel: (410) 467-8209

Fax: (410) 467-1761

%FO: 100

SOLVAY AMERICA INC.
3333 Richmond Avenue, Houston, TX   77098

CEO: M. Whitson Sadler, Pres.

Bus: *Holding company. U.S. headquarters.*

Tel: (713) 525-6000

Fax: (713) 525-7887

%FO: 100

SOLVAY AUTOMOTIVE INC.
2565 West Maple Road, Troy, MI   48084

CEO: M. Whitson Sadler, Pres.

Bus: *Mfr. gas tanks and plastic parts for auto industry; design, test, mfr. blow-molded plastic components.*

Tel: (248) 435-3300

Fax: (248) 435-3957

%FO: 100

Emp: 516

SOLVAY ENGINEERED POLYMERS
1200 Harmon Road, Auburn Hills, MI   48326

CEO: Joseph Greulich, Pres.

Bus: *Mfr. thermoplastic polyolefins for auto industry.*

Tel: (248) 391-9500

Fax: (248) 391-9501

SOLVAY FLUORIDES, INC.
1630 Des Peres Road, Ste. 210, St. Louis, MO   63131

CEO: Wayne Brasser, Pres.

Bus: *Distributor of chemicals.*

Tel: (314) 965-7100

Fax: (314) 965-7100

%FO: 100

SOLVAY INDUSTRIAL FILMS INC.

1207 East Lincoln Way, Laporte, IN   46350

CEO: Frederick W. Young, Pres.   Tel: (219) 324-6886   %FO: 100

Bus: *Mfr./distribution high-clarity*   Fax: (219) 324-8696
polypropylene film.

SOLVAY INTEROX

3333 Richmond Avenue, Houston, TX   77227

CEO: Gary Hall, Pres.   Tel: (713) 525-6500   %FO: 100

Bus: *Mfr./distribution peroxygen*   Fax: (713) 524-9032
chemicals.

SOLVAY PHARMACEUTICALS INC.

901 Sawyer Road, Marietta, GA   30062

CEO: Harold H. Shievin, CEO   Tel: (770) 578-9000   %FO: 100

Bus: *Mfr./distributor pharmaceuticals.*   Fax: (770) 578-5597

SOLVAY POLYMERS INC

3333 Richmond Avenue, Houston, TX   77098-3099

CEO: David G. Birney, Pres.   Tel: (713) 525-4000   %FO: 100

Bus: *Mfr. thermoplastic polyolefins for*   Fax: (713) 522-2435   Emp: 300
auto industry.

SOLVAY SPECIALTY CHEMICALS, INC.

30 Two Bridges Road, Fairfield, NJ   07006-1530

CEO: Thomas Johnson, Pres.   Tel: (973) 882-7900   %FO: 100

Bus: *Mfr./distribution semiconductor*   Fax: (973) 882-7967   Emp: 133
gases, safety-related products.

● SWIFT

Avenue Adele 1, B-1310 La Hulpe, Belgium

CEO: Leonard H. Schrank, CEO   Tel: 32-2-655-3111   Rev: $450

Bus: *Engaged in global communications.*   Fax: 32-2-655-3226   Emp: 1,570
www.swift.com

SWIFT TECHNOLOGY CENTER

9615 Center Street, Manassas, VA   20110-5521

CEO: Leonard H. Schrank, CEO   Tel: (703) 365-6000   %FO: 100

Bus: *Engaged in international banking.*   Fax: (703) 365-6410

SWIFT TECHNOLOGY CENTER

200 Park Avenue, 38th Fl., New York, NY   10166

CEO: Leonard H. Schrank, CEO   Tel: (212) 455-1800   %FO: 100

Bus: *Engaged in international banking.*   Fax: (212) 455-1817

- **TRACTEBEL S.A. (FORMERLY POWERFIN SA)**
  Place du Trone 1, B-1000 Brussels, Belgium
  CEO: Jean-Pierre Hansen, CEO   Tel: 32-2-510-7111   Rev: $12,970
  Bus: *Electric power production, gas and*   Fax: 32-2-510-7388   Emp: 60,500
  electric distribution, communications,   www.tractebel.com
  technical services, real estate and
  engineering.

  ### TRACTEBEL ENERGY MARKETING INC.
  1177 West Loop South, Ste. 800, Houston, TX 77027-9006
  CEO: William P. Utt, Pres.   Tel: (713) 350-1400   %FO: 100
  Bus: *Independent power production.*   Fax: (713) 548-5151   Emp: 115

  ### TRACTEBEL POWER INC.
  1177 West Loop South, Ste. 800, Houston, TX 77027-9006
  CEO: Phillippe van Marcke, EVP   Tel: (713) 552-2501   %FO: 100
  Bus: *Power generation.*   Fax: (713) 552-2416

- **UCB S.A.**
  Allee de la Recherche 60, B-1070 Brussels, Belgium
  CEO: Georges Jacobs, Chmn.   Tel: 32-2-599-9999   Rev: $1,855
  Bus: *Mfr. specialty chemicals and*   Fax: 32-2-599-9900   Emp: 9,200
  pharmaceuticals.   www.ucb-group.com

  ### UCB FILMS INC.
  1900 Lake Park Drive, Smyrna, GA 30080
  CEO: Andy Newman, Pres.   Tel: (770) 437-5732   %FO: 100
  Bus: *Mfr. flexible films for food*   Fax: (770) 333-6980
  packaging and various industrial
  applications.

  ### UCB INC.
  2000 Lake Park Drive, Smyrna, GA 30080
  CEO: Rich Kemmerer, Pres.   Tel: (770) 434-6188   %FO: 100
  Bus: *Mfr. specialty chemicals.*   Fax: (770) 437-5749

  ### UCB PHARMA INC.
  1950 Lake Park Drive, Smyrna, GA 30080
  CEO: Tony Tebbutt, Pres.   Tel: (770) 437-5500   %FO: 100
  Bus: *Mfr. prescription medicines.*   Fax: (770) 437-5506

- **U.V. UMICORE S.A.**
  Broekstraat 31 rue du Marais, B-1000 Brussels, Belgium
  CEO: Thomas Leysen, CEO   Tel: 32-2-227-7111   Rev: $3,611
  Bus: *Production zinc, copper, precious*   Fax: 32-2-227-79-00   Emp: 7,892
  metals, and advanced materials.   www.um.be

UMICORE ELECTRO-OPTIC MATERIALS

3 Foundry Street, Bldg. 1, Lowell, MA   01852

CEO: Mark Caffarey, CEO   Tel: (978) 458-8329   %FO: 100

Bus: *Production zinc, copper, precious*   Fax: (978) 458-8414
   metals, and advanced materials.

UMICORE INC.

Magnolia Building, 3120 Highlands Blvd., Suite 110, Raleigh, NC   27604

CEO: Mark Caffarey, CEO   Tel: (919) 874-7171   %FO: 100

Bus: *Production zinc, copper, precious*   Fax: (919) 874-7195
   metals, and advanced materials.

UMICORE INC.

PO Box 1329, Laurinburg, NC   28352

CEO: Peter Stenzel   Tel: (910) 844-5614   %FO: 100

Bus: *Production zinc, copper, precious*   Fax: (910) 844-9224
   metals, and advanced materials.

UMICORE SEMICONDUCTOR PROCESSING INC.

12 Channel Street, Suite 702, Boston, MA   02210

CEO: Jim Higgins, Mgr.   Tel: (617) 345-9936   %FO: 100

Bus: *Production zinc, copper, precious*   Fax: (617) 345-9271
   metals, and advanced materials.

UMICORE USA INC.

PO Box 913, 2923 NY54 East, Coulington, TN   38019-0913

CEO: Thomas Leysen   Tel: (901) 476-1813   %FO: 100

Bus: *Production zinc, copper, precious*   Fax: (502) 563-2284
   metals, and advanced materials.

● **XEIKON NV**

Vredebaan 72, B-2640 Mortsel, Belgium

CEO: Alfons Buts, CEO   Tel: 32-3-443-1311   Rev: $174

Bus: *Develops and manufactures color*   Fax: 32-3-443-1309   Emp: 1,000
   printing systems.   www.xeikon.com

   XEIKON AMERICA INC.

   1360 N. Wood Dale Road, Wood Dale, IL   60191

   CEO: Mike Bertolani, VP Sales   Tel: (630) 616-5600   %FO: 100

   Bus: *Develops/manufactures color*   Fax: (616) 616-9535
      printing systems.

● **ZEYEN BEGHIN FEIDER**

Ave. de Tervuren 268A, B-1150 Brussels, Belgium

CEO: Carlos Zeyen   Tel: 32-2-778-2211

Bus: *International law firm.*   Fax: 32-2-763-2185

ZEYEN BEGHIN FEIDER
10 East 50th St., 23 Fl., New York, NY   10022
CEO: Helen Sprenger, Mng. Prtn.   Tel: (212) 759-9000   %FO: 100
Bus: *International law firm.*   Fax: (212) 759-9018

Belize

• CARLISLE HOLDINGS LIMITED

60 Market Square, PO Box 1764 Belize City, Belize

CEO: Ian R. Pluthero, CEO   Tel: 501-2-72660   Rev: $1,241

Bus: *ü*   Fax: 501-2-75854   Emp: 62,000

www.carlisleholdings.com

CARLISLE GROUP

4800 North Federal Hwy., Ste. 200 B, Boca Raton, FL   33431

CEO: Peter Gaze, COO   Tel: (561) 368-3899

Bus: *Engaged in outsourcing services,*   Fax: (561) 368-5033
*principally to owners of
commercial real estate and the
property management industry.*

ONESOURCE, DIV. CARLISLE GROUP US

1600 Parkwood Circle, Atlanta, GA   30339

CEO: Rich Kissane, Pres.   Tel: (770) 436-9900

Bus: *Engaged in a full range of*   Fax: (770) 226-8512   Emp: 42,000
*facilities services, including
janitorial, landscaping, security
services and general repair and
maintenance.*

Bermuda

• **ACCENTURE LTD. (FORMERLY ANDERSEN CONSULTING)**
41 Cedar Avenue, Hamilton HM12, Bermuda
CEO: Joe W. Forehand, Chmn. & CEO Tel: 441-296-8262 Rev: $9,752
Bus: *Engaged in management and* Fax: 441-296-4245 Emp: 70,000
technology consulting. www.accenture.com

   ACCENTURE LTD.
   901 Main Street, Ste. 5400, Dallas, TX 75202
   CEO: Doug Boerr Tel: (214) 853-1000 %FO: 100
   Bus: *Engaged in management and* Fax: (214) 853-2000
   technology consulting.

   ACCENTURE LTD.
   41 South High Street, Ste. 2000, Columbus, OH 6142219900
   CEO: Doug Boerr Tel: (614) 228-0692 %FO: 100
   Bus: *Engaged in management and* Fax: (614) 228-0692
   technology consulting.

   ACCENTURE LTD.
   200 Public Square, Ste. 1900, Cleveland, OH 44114
   CEO: Doug Boerr Tel: (216) 535-5350 %FO: 100
   Bus: *Engaged in management and* Fax: (216) 535-5350
   technology consulting.

   ACCENTURE LTD.
   165 Madison Avenue, 16th Fl., Memphis, TN 38103
   CEO: M. Finnegan Tel: (901) 575-9500 %FO: 100
   Bus: *Engaged in management and* Fax: (901) 527-7119
   technology consulting.

   ACCENTURE LTD.
   Two Hannover Square, Ste. 1520, Raleigh, NC 27601
   CEO: Charlotte Trudel Tel: (919) 836-1200 %FO: 100
   Bus: *Engaged in management and* Fax: (919) 821-0561
   technology consulting.

   ACCENTURE LTD.
   One Biscayne Tower, Ste. 2000, Miami, FL 33131
   CEO: Doug Boerr Tel: (786) 425-7000 %FO: 100
   Bus: *Engaged in management and* Fax: (305) 358-3122
   technology consulting.

ACCENTURE LTD.

7500 College Blvd., Ste. 1400, Overland Park, KS 66210

CEO: Doug Boerr   Tel: (913) 319-1000   %FO: 100

Bus: *Engaged in management and*   Fax: (913) 319-1900
    technology consulting.

ACCENTURE LTD.

11951 Freedom Drive, Reston, VA 20190

CEO: Charlotte Trudel   Tel: (703) 947-2000   %FO: 100

Bus: *Engaged in management and*   Fax: (703) 947-2200
    technology consulting.

ACCENTURE LTD.

133 Peachtree Street NE, Ste. 2600, Atlanta, GA 30303

CEO: Doug Boerr   Tel: (404) 880-9100   %FO: 100

Bus: *Engaged in management and*   Fax: (404) 589-4200
    technology consulting.

ACCENTURE LTD.

500 Woodward Avenue, Ste. 2900, Detroit, MI 48226-3424

CEO: Doug Boerr   Tel: (313) 887-2000   %FO: 100

Bus: *Engaged in management and*   Fax: (313) 887-2050
    technology consulting.

ACCENTURE LTD.

201 East Fourth Street, Ste. 1600, Cincinnati, OH 45202

CEO: Doug Boerr   Tel: (513) 455-1001   %FO: 100

Bus: *Engaged in management and*   Fax: (513) 455-1600
    technology consulting.

ACCENTURE LTD.

100 East Wisconsin Ave., Ste. 2100, Milwaukee, WI 53202

CEO: Tom Arenberg, Mng. Prtn.   Tel: (414) 212-1000   %FO: 100

Bus: *Engaged in management and*   Fax: (414) 212-3620
    technology consulting.

ACCENTURE LTD.

111 Washington Avenue, Albany, NY 12210

CEO: Doug Boerr   Tel: (518) 462-4762   %FO: 100

Bus: *Engaged in management and*   Fax: (518) 462-4762
    technology consulting.

ACCENTURE LTD.

161 North Clark Street, Chicago, IL 60601

CEO: Michael C. Fox   Tel: (312) 693-0161   %FO: 100

Bus: *Engaged in management and*   Fax: (312) 652-2329
    technology consulting.

ACCENTURE LTD.
2101 Rosecrans Ave., Ste. 3300, El Segundo, CA   90245
CEO: Doug Boerr   Tel: (310) 726-2700   %FO: 100
Bus: *Engaged in management and*   Fax: (310) 726-2950
    technology consulting.

ACCENTURE LTD.
100 North Tryon Street, Ste. 3900, Charlotte, NC   28202-4000
CEO: Doug Boerr   Tel: (704) 332-6411   %FO: 100
Bus: *Engaged in management and*   Fax: (704) 370-5700
    technology consulting.

ACCENTURE LTD.
100 William Street, Wellesley, MA   02181-9151
CEO: Doug Boerr   Tel: (617) 454-4000   %FO: 100
Bus: *Engaged in management and*   Fax: (617) 454-4001
    technology consulting.

ACCENTURE LTD.
1501 S. McPac Expwy., Ste. 300, Austin, TX   78746
CEO: Doug Boerr   Tel: (512) 472-2323   %FO: 100
Bus: *Engaged in management and*   Fax: (512) 476-7765
    technology consulting.

ACCENTURE LTD.
1345 Avenue of the Americas, New York, NY   10105
CEO: Doug Boerr   Tel: (917) 452-4400   %FO: 100
Bus: *Engaged in management and*   Fax: (917) 527-9915
    technology consulting.

ACCENTURE LTD.
2929 Allen Pkwy., Ste. 2000, Houston, TX   77019-7107
CEO: Doug Boerr   Tel: (713) 837-1500   %FO: 100
Bus: *Engaged in management and*   Fax: (713) 837-1593
    technology consulting.

ACCENTURE LTD.
112 East Jefferson Street, Tallahassee, FL   32301
CEO: Doug Boerr   Tel: (850) 513-0620   %FO: 100
Bus: *Engaged in management and*   Fax: (850) 513-3500
    technology consulting.

ACCENTURE LTD.
One Financial Plaza, Hartford, CT   06103
CEO: Doug Boerr   Tel: (860) 756-2000   %FO: 100
Bus: *Engaged in management and*   Fax: (860) 756-2888
    technology consulting.

ACCENTURE LTD.
128 Third Street South, St. Petersburg, FL   33701
CEO: Doug Boerr   Tel: (727) 897-7000   %FO: 100
Bus: *Engaged in management and*   Fax: (727) 897-7099
     technology consulting.

ACCENTURE LTD.
1010 Market Street, St. Louis, MO   63101
CEO: Todd Charow   Tel: (314) 345-3000   %FO: 100
Bus: *Engaged in management and*   Fax: (314) 345-3505
     technology consulting.

ACCENTURE LTD.
111 Monument Circle, Ste. 4300, Indianapolis, IN   46204-5143
CEO: Doug Boerr   Tel: (317) 231-1300   %FO: 100
Bus: *Engaged in management and*   Fax: (317) 231-1500
     technology consulting.

ACCENTURE LTD.
1215 K Street, 17th Fl., Sacramento, CA   95814
CEO: Doug Boerr   Tel: (916) 503-1626   %FO: 100
Bus: *Engaged in management and*   Fax: (916) 503-3606
     technology consulting.

ACCENTURE LTD.
1255 Treat Boulevard, Walnut Creek, CA   94596
CEO: Doug Boerr   Tel: (925) 974-5200   %FO: 100
Bus: *Engaged in management and*   Fax: (925) 974-5399
     technology consulting.

ACCENTURE LTD.
One Market Street, 38th Fl., San Francisco, CA   94105
CEO: Doug Boerr   Tel: (415) 537-5000   %FO: 100
Bus: *Engaged in management and*   Fax: (415) 537-5038
     technology consulting.

ACCENTURE LTD.
One North Old State, Ste. 333, Springfield, IL   62710
CEO: Doug Boerr   Tel: (217) 522-2718   %FO: 100
Bus: *Engaged in management and*   Fax: (217) 522-2952
     technology consulting.

ACCENTURE LTD.
2527 Camino Ramon, Ste. 170, San Ramon, CA   94583
CEO: Michelle A. Snoddy   Tel: (925) 358-7000   %FO: 100
Bus: *Engaged in management and*   Fax: (925) 358-7200
     technology consulting.

ACCENTURE LTD.

605 Fifth Avenue South, Ste. 800, Seattle, WA   98104

CEO: David Andrews Tel: (206) 839-2000 %FO: 100

Bus: *Engaged in management and* Fax: (206) 839-2008
technology consulting.

● **ACE LIMITED**

30 Woodbourne Avenue, Hamilton HM 08, Bermuda

CEO: Brian Duperreaault, CEO Tel: 441-295-5200 Rev: $5,267

Bus: *Engaged in property and casual* Fax: 441-295-5221 Emp: 7,933
insurance. www.ace.bm

ACE CASUALTY SOLUTIONS

PO Box 41484, Philadelphia, PA   19101-1484

CEO: Gregory W. Springer Tel: (215) 640-1000 %FO: 100

Bus: *Engaged in casualty insurance* Fax: (215) 640-1484
services.

ACE FINANCIAL SOLUTIONS

1133 Avenue of the Americas, New York, NY   10036

CEO: Robert Omahne, Pres. Tel: (212) 642-7803 %FO: 100

Bus: *Financial underwriting solutions.* Fax: (212) 642-7889

ACE GUARANTY RE, INC.

1325 Avenue of the Americas, New York, NY   10019

CEO: Joseph W. Swain, Pres. Tel: (212) 974-0100 %FO: 100

Bus: *Reinsurance for the municipal* Fax: (212) 581-3268
bond industry.

ACE HOLDING USA

1601 Chestnut Street, PO Box 41484, Philadelphia, PA   19101-1484

CEO: Dennis B. Reding, Pres. & CEO Tel: (215) 640-1000 %FO: 100

Bus: *Engaged in property and casual* Fax: (215) 640-2489
insurance.

● **AMERICAN SAFETY INSURANCE GROUP, LTD.**

44 Church Street, Hamilton HMHX, Bermuda

CEO: Lloyd A. Fox Tel: 441-295-5688 Rev: $17

Bus: *Insurance services.* Fax: 441-292-1867 Emp: 55
www.americansafetygroup.com

AMERICAN SAFETY

1845 The Exchange, Ste. 200, Atlanta, GA   30339

CEO: Lloyd A. Fox, Pres. Tel: (770) 916-1908 %FO: 100

Bus: *Insurance services.* Fax: (770) 916-0618

- **B+H OCEAN CARRIERS LTD.**
Par LaVille Place, 14 Par-la-Ville Road, 3rd Fl., Hamilton HM JX, Bermuda

CEO: Michael S. Hudner, CEO	Tel: 441-295-6875	Rev: $45
Bus: *Engaged in dry bulk and liquid cargo transport.*	Fax: 441-295-6796 www.bhocean.com	Emp: 250

NAVINVEST MARINE SERVICES, DIV. B+H OCEAN
One Little Harbor Landing, Portsmouth, RI 02871

CEO: Susan Lockwood, HR	Tel: (401) 682-1100	%FO: 100
Bus: *Engaged in dry bulk and liquid cargo transport.*	Fax: (401) 682-1100	

- **BACARDI LIMITED**
65 Pitts Bay Road, Pembroke HM 08, Bermuda

CEO: Ruben Rodriguez, Pres. & CEO	Tel: 441-295-4345	Rev: $2,800
Bus: *Mfr. wine and spirits, including Bacardi rum, Martini vermouth, Dewar's scotch and Bombay gin.*	Fax: 441-292-0562 www.bacardi.com	Emp: 6,000

BACARDI MARTINI USA
2100 Biscayne Boulevard, Miami, FL 33137

CEO: Rudy Ruiz, Pres. & CEO	Tel: (305) 573-8511	%FO: 100
Bus: *Sales/distribution of wine and spirits, including Bacardi rum and Martini vermouth.*	Fax: (305) 576-7507	

- **THE BANK OF BERMUDA LTD.**
6 Front Street, Hamilton HM-DX, Bermuda

CEO: Henry B. Smith, CEO	Tel: 809-295-4000	
Bus: *International commercial banking and trust services.*	Fax: 809-295-7093 www.bankofbermuda.com	Emp: 1,800

BANK OF BERMUDA (NEW YORK) LTD
570 Lexington Avenue, 25th Fl., New York, NY 10022

CEO: Peter McClean, Chmn.	Tel: (212) 980-4500	%FO: 100
Bus: *International banking & trust services.*	Fax: (212) 980-5079	Emp: 42

- **BERMUDA DEPARTMENT OF TOURISM**
PO Box 465, HM 465, Hamilton HMBX, Bermuda

CEO: Gary Phillips, Dir.	Tel: 441-292-0023
Bus: *Engaged in tourism and travel.*	Fax: 441-292-7537 www.bermudatourism.com

BERMUDA DEPARTMENT OF TOURISM
205 East 42nd Street, 16th Fl., New York, NY   10017
CEO: Toby Dillas, Dir.   Tel: (212) 818-9800   %FO: 100
Bus: *Engaged in tourism and travel.*   Fax: (212) 983-5289

● GLOBAL CROSSING LTD.
Wessex House, 45 Reid Street, Hamilton HM 12, Bermuda
CEO: David A. Walsh, COO   Tel: 441-296-8600   Rev: $3,790
Bus: *Engaged in data transport*   Fax: 441-296-8607   Emp: 16,400
telecommunications.   www.globalcrossing.com

GLOBAL CROSSING INC.
Seven Giralda Farms, Madison, NJ   07940
CEO: Joseph P. Clayton, CEO   Tel: (973) 410-8300   %FO: 100
Bus: *Engaged in data transport*   Fax: (973) 410-8330
telecommunications.

GLOBAL CROSSING INC.
360 North Crescent Drive, Beverly Hills, CA   90210
CEO: Joseph P. Clayton, CEO   Tel: (310) 385-5200   %FO: 100
Bus: *Engaged in data transport*   Fax: (310) 385-3700
telecommunications.

● GLOBALSTAR TELECOMMUNICATIONS LIMITED
Cedar House, 41 Cedar Avenue, Hamilton HM 12, Bermuda
CEO: Anthony J. Navarra, Pres.   Tel: 441-295-2244   Rev: $
Bus: *Engaged in satellite based mobile phone* Fax: 441-295-2244   Emp: 450
network.   www.globalstar.com

GLOBALSTAR
3200 Zanker Road, Bldg. 260, San Jose, CA   95134
CEO: Gloria Everett, EVP   Tel: (408) 933-4000   %FO: 100
Bus: *Engaged in satellite based mobile*   Fax: (408) 933-4100
phone network.

● INTERWAVE COMMUNICATIONS INTERNATIONAL, LTD.
2 Church Street, PO Box HM 1022, Hamilton HM DX, Bermuda
CEO: Priscilla M. Lu, CEO   Tel: 44-1-395-5950   Rev: $27
Bus: *Mfr. wireless systems.*   Fax: 44-1-395-5950   Emp: 200
www.iwv.com

INTERWAVE COMMUNICATIONS
312 Constitution Drive, Menlo Park, CA   94025
CEO: Priscilla M. Lu, Pres.   Tel: (650) 838-2100   %FO: 100
Bus: *Sales wireless network solutions.*   Fax: (650) 321-6250

INTERWAVE COMMUNICATIONS
6650 Lusk Blvd., Ste. B-013, San Diego, CA   92121
CEO: Priscilla M. Lu, Pres.   Tel: (858) 597-5200   %FO: 100
Bus: *Sales wireless network solutions.*   Fax: (858) 598-5201

● MUTUAL RISK MANAGEMENT LTD.
44 Church Street, Hamilton HM 12, Bermuda
CEO: Robert A. Mulderig, CEO   Tel: 441-295-5688   Rev: $498
Bus: *Engaged in risk insurance.*   Fax: 441-292-1867   Emp: 1,373
                                       www.mutrisk.com

CAPTIVE RESOURCES, INC.
201 East Commerce Drive, Schaumburg, IL   60173-5338
CEO: Roland B. Gray, VP   Tel: (847) 781-1400   %FO: 100
Bus: *Provides insurance services.*   Fax: (847) 781-1455

THE LEGION COMPANIES
One Logan Square, Ste. 1400, Philadelphia, PA   19103
CEO: Robert A. Mulderig, Chmn.   Tel: (215) 963-1200   %FO: 100
Bus: *Engaged in insurance services.* Fax: (215) 963-1205

PROFESSIONAL RISK MANAGEMENT SERVICES, INC.
1515 Wilson Blvd., Ste. 800, Arlington, VA   22209
CEO: Martin G. Tracy, Pres. & CEO   Tel: (703) 276-6742   %FO: 100
Bus: *Engaged in insurance services.* Fax: (703) 276-9419

● ORIENT-EXPRESS HOTELS LTD.
41 Cedar Avenue, PO Box HM 1179, Hamilton HM EX, Bermuda
CEO: Simon M. C. Sherwood, CEO   Tel: 441-295-2244   Rev: $268
Bus: *Manager of luxury hotels.*   Fax: 441-292-8666   Emp: 4,600
                                       www.orient-expresshotels.com

WINDSOR COURT HOTEL
300 Gravier Street, New Orleans, LA   70130
CEO: Dean P. Andrews, VP   Tel: (504) 523-6000   %FO: 100
Bus: *Manager of luxury hotel.*   Fax: (504) 523-4513

● PARTNER RE LTD.
106 Pitts Bay Road, Pembroke HM 08, Bermuda
CEO: Patrick Thiele, Pres. & CEO   Tel: 441-292-0888   Rev: $1,526
Bus: *Engaged in reinsurance.*   Fax: 441-292-7010   Emp: 615
                                       www.partnerre.com

PARTNER REINSURANCE CO AGRICULTURAL SERVICES

10000 College Boulevard Suite 250, Overlook Park, KS   66210-1473

CEO: Alan Walter

Bus: *Agricultural reinsurance services.*

Tel: (913) 486-8745

Fax: (913) 696-1826

%FO: 100

PARTNER REINSURANCE CO OF THE US

One Greenwich Plaza, Greenwich, CT   06830-6352

CEO: Scott D. Moore, CEO

Bus: *Reinsurance services.*

Tel: (203) 485-4200

Fax: (203) 485-4300

%FO: 100

• PXRE GROUP LTD.

99 Front Street, Hamilton HM12, Bermuda

CEO: Gerald L. Radke, CEO

Bus: *Provides re-insurance.*

Tel: 441-296-5858

Fax: 441-296-6162

www.pxregroup.com

Rev: $199

Emp: 88

MARINE & AEROSPACE

399 Thornall Street, 14th Fl., Edison, NJ   08837

CEO: Charles Volker, SVP

Bus: *Engaged in catastrophe insurance services.*

Tel: (732) 906-8100

Fax: (732) 906-9283

%FO: 100

PXRE REINSURANCE COMPANY

399 Thornall Street, 14th Fl., Edison, NJ   08837

CEO: Gordon Forsyth III, EVP

Bus: *Engaged in re-insurance.*

Tel: (732) 906-8100

Fax: (732) 906-9283

%FO: 100

• RENAISSANCE RE HOLDINGS LTD.

Renaissance House, 8-12 East Broadway, Pembroke HM 19, Bermuda

CEO: James N. Stanard, CEO

Bus: *Engaged in catastrophe reinsurance.*

Tel: 441-295-4513

Fax: 441-292-9453

www.renre.com

Rev: $350

Emp: 100

DESOTO INSURANCE COMPANY

PO Box 901002, Ft. Worth, TX   76113-2002

CEO: Maria Vizcarrondo, Pres.

Bus: *Engaged in catastrophe reinsurance.*

Tel: (877) 843-4554

Fax: (877) 843-4554

%FO: 100

RENAISSANCE RE US HOLDINGS

319 West Franklin Street, Ste. 104, Richmond, VA   23220

CEO: Mark Rickey, Pres.

Bus: *Engaged in catastrophe reinsurance.*

Tel: (804) 344-3600

Fax: (804) 344-4075

%FO: 100

● **SILVERSTAR HOLDINGS, LTD.**

Clarendon House, Church Street, Hamilton HM CX, Bermuda

CEO: Clieve Kabatznik, CEO	Tel: 441-295-1422	Rev: $1
Bus: *Holding company for college football fantasy sports games.*	Fax: 441-292-4720	Emp: 2,300
	www.silverstarholdings.com	

SILVERSTAR HOLDINGS

6100 Glades Road, Ste. 305, Boca Raton, FL   33434

CEO: Cleve Kabatznik, CEO	Tel: (561) 479-0040	%FO: 100
Bus: *Holding company investing in profitable businesses.*	Fax: (561) 479-0757	

● **W. P. STEWART & CO. LTD.**

Trinity Hall, 43 Cedar Avenue, Hamilton HM LX, Bermuda

CEO: William P. Stewart, CEO	Tel: 441-295-8585	Rev: $203
Bus: *Offers asset management services.*	Fax: 441-296-6823	Emp: 80
	www.wpstewart.com	

W. P. STEWART & CO.

527 Madison Avenue, 20th Fl., New York, NY   10022

CEO: Robert C. Rohn, CEO	Tel: (212) 750-8585	%FO: 100
Bus: *Asset management.*	Fax: (212) 980-8039	

● **TYCO INTERNATIONAL, LTD.**

90 Pitts Bay Road, 2nd Fl., Pembroke HM08, Bermuda

CEO: L. Dennis Kozlowski, Chmn. & CEO	Tel: 441-292-8674	Rev: $22,000
Bus: *Engaged in security monitoring/fire protection services, disposable medical products/surgical instruments, undersea fiber optic cables, electrical connectors and industrial valves and plastic films.*	Fax: 441-295-9647	Emp: 120,000
	www.tyco.com	

ALLIED TUBE & CONDUIT

16100 South Lathrop Avenue, Harvey, IL   60426

CEO: Robert P. Mead, Pres.	Tel: (708) 339-1610	%FO: 100
Bus: *Mfr. tubular and pipe products.*	Fax: (708) 339-2399	

DULMISON, INC

1725 Purcell Road, Lawrenceville, GA   30043

CEO: Douglas Brasell, Pres.	Tel: (770) 339-3350	%FO: 100
Bus: *Sales/distribution of vibration control devices and support hardware for fiber optic cables.*	Fax: (770) 339-3770	

EARTH TECH
100 West Broadway, Ste. 8000, Long Beach, CA   90802
CEO: Diane Creel, Pres.   Tel: (562) 951-2000   %FO: 100
Bus: *Engaged in fire and safety systems.* Fax: (562) 951-2100

LUDLOW TECHNICAL PRODUCTS
2 Ludlow Park Drive, Chicopee, MA   01022
CEO: L. A. Carrier, Pres.   Tel: (413) 593-6400   %FO: 100
Bus: *Mfr. products for the office*   Fax: (413) 593-6114
     imaging industries.

MA COM
PO Box 3295, Lowell, MA   01853
CEO: Rick D. Hess, VP   Tel: (978) 442-5000   %FO: 100
Bus: *Mfr. radio frequency and*   Fax: (978) 442-5350
     microwave components.

RAYCHEM INC.
300 Constitution Drive, Menlo Park, CA   94025
CEO: Richard A. Kashnow, Pres.   Tel: (650) 361-3333   %FO: 100
Bus: *Provides passive electronic*   Fax: (650) 361-7173
     components.

SIMPLEX TECHNOGIES INC.
PO Box 479, Portsmouth, NH   03801
CEO: William Jackson, Pres.   Tel: (603) 436-6100   %FO: 100
Bus: *Designs cables for commercial*   Fax: (603) 427-0701
     communications.

TYCO ELECTRONICS
441 Friendship Road, Harrisburg, PA   17111
CEO: Juergen W. Gromer, Pres.   Tel: (717) 564-0100   %FO: 100
Bus: *Mfr. electrical and electronic*   Fax: (717) 986-7575
     connectors and connector
     assemblies.

TYCO FIRE AND SECURITY SERVICES
One Town Center Road, Boca Raton, FL   33486
CEO: Jerry Boggess, Pres.   Tel: (561) 988-3600   %FO: 100
Bus: *Provides fire protection.*   Fax:

TYCO HEALTHCARE GROUP
15 Hampshire Street, Mansfield, MA   02048
CEO: R. J. Meelia, Pres.   Tel: (508) 261-8000   %FO: 100
Bus: *Mfr. health care products.*   Fax: (508) 261-8145

TYCO INTERNATIONAL LTD.
One Tyco Park, Exeter, NH   03833
CEO: J. Brad McGee, EVP   Tel: (603) 778-9700   %FO: 100
Bus: *Home and office security systems.*   Fax: (603) 778-7330

TYCO PLASTICS AND ADHESIVES
8 Amelia Drive, Nantucket, MA   02554
CEO: Steve McDonough, Pres.   Tel: (508) 325-0004   %FO: 100
Bus: *Produces industrial and consumer*   Fax:
   products.

UNISTRUT CORP.
1140 West Thorndale Avenue, Itasca, IL   60143
CEO: Ron Jones, Pres.   Tel: (800) 468-9510   %FO: 100
Bus: *Mfr. steel framing structures.*   Fax: (630) 773-4214

UNITED STATES SURGICAL CORP.
150 Glover Avenue, Norwalk, CT   06856
CEO: Kevin Gould, CEO   Tel: (203) 845-1000   %FO: 100
Bus: *Mfr. surgical staplers.*   Fax: (203) 845-4478

● **WHITE MOUNTAINS INSURANCE GROUP, LTD.**
12 Church Street, Ste. 322, Hamilton HM 11, Bermuda
CEO: John J. Bryne, CEO   Tel: 441-296-6011   Rev: $850
Bus: *Engaged in insurance services.*   Fax: 44-296-9904   Emp: 255
                   www.whitemountains.com

FOLKSAMERICA REINSURANCE COMPANY
900 South Avenue, Staten Island, NY   10314-3403
CEO: John J. Bryne, CEO   Tel: (718) 568-2264   %FO: 100
Bus: *Engaged in insurance services.*   Fax: (718) 568-2265

FOLKSAMERICA REINSURANCE COMPANY
One Liberty Plaza, New York, NY   10006
CEO: Steven E. Fass, CEO   Tel: (212) 312-2500   %FO: 100
Bus: *Engaged in insurance services.*   Fax: (212) 385-2279

FOLKSAMERICA REINSURANCE COMPANY
599 West Putnam Avenue, Greenwich, CT   06831
CEO: Brian Gulbransen, SVP   Tel: (203) 618-3200   %FO: 100
Bus: *Engaged in insurance services.*   Fax: (203) 618-3250

FOLKSAMERICA REINSURANCE COMPANY
806 Douglas Road, Coral Gables, FL   33134
CEO: Rafael A. Saer   Tel: (305) 444-6660   %FO: 100
Bus: *Engaged in insurance services.*   Fax: (305) 444-7727

WHITE MOUNTAINS INSURANCE GROUP
80 South Main Street, Hanover, NH   03755-2053

CEO:John J. Bryne, CEO	Tel: (603) 643-1567	%FO: 100
Bus: *Engaged in insurance services.*	Fax: (603) 643-4562	

Brazil

● **AGC OPTOSYSTEMS INDÚSTRIA E COMÉRCIO LTDA.**
Rua Panaçu, 54, 04264-080 São Paulo SP, Brazil

CEO: Jonah Trunk, Pres.	Tel: 55-11-272-1544	Rev: $11
Bus: *Mfr. optical instruments, lenses and communications equipment.*	Fax: 55-11-274-3977 www.agc.com.br	Emp: 45

AGC LIGHTWAVE, INC.
1025 South Semoran Boulevard, Ste. 1093, Winter Park, FL   32792-5511

CEO: Jonah Trunk, Pres.	Tel: (407) 679-7780	%FO: 100
Bus: *Optical instruments, lenses; communications equipment.*	Fax: (407) 677-1472	

● **ALTUS SISTEMAS DE INFORMÁTICA SA**
Av. São Paulo, 555, 90230-161Porto Alegre RS, Brazil

CEO: Ricardo Felizzola, Chmn.	Tel: 55-51-337-3633	Rev: $12
Bus: *Mfr. industrial automation systems.*	Fax: 55-51-337-3632 www.altus-usa.com	Emp: 150

ALTUS AUTOMATION SYSTEMS CORP., INC.
9050 Pines Blvd., Suite 210, Pembroke Pines, FL   33024

CEO: Joni Girardi, Sales	Tel: (954) 450-0480	%FO: 100
Bus: *Electronics, computers, relays & Industrial controls.*	Fax: (954) 438-1995	

● **ARACRUZ CELULOSE SA**
Rua Lauro Muller, 116, 21o./22o. Andares, 22299-900 Rio de Janeiro, RJ Brazil

CEO: Luiz Kaufmann, Pres.	Tel: 55-21-545-8111	Rev: $460
Bus: *Pulp mills, forestry services.*	Fax: 55-21-295-7943 www.aracruz.com.br	Emp: 2,000

ARACRUZ CORPORATION
140 Winchime Court, Raleigh, NC   27615

CEO: Kimberly Bullard	Tel: (919) 847-9437	%FO: 100
Bus: *Paper & pulp mills; forestry services.*	Fax: (919) 847-9265	Emp: 5

● **ARBI PARTICIPAÇÕES, S.A..**
Av. Almirante Borroso, 52, 11o. andar, RJ 20031-000 Rio de Janeiro, Brazil

CEO: Daniel B. Birmann, Pres.	Tel: 55-21-212-8282	Rev: $996
Bus: *Investment advisor services.*	Fax: 55-21-220-5232 www.arbisf.com	Emp: 1,200

ARBI TRANSNATIONAL, INC.
601 California Street, Suite 615, San Francisco, CA   94108
CEO: Terry Vogt, Pres.   Tel: (415) 989-2884   %FO: 100
Bus: *Investment advisory.*   Fax: (415) 989-2904   Emp: 6

• BANCO BANDEIRANTES S.A.
Rua Boavista, 162, 7o.andar, SP 01014-902 São Paulo, Brazil
CEO: Antonio Tomas Correla, Chmn.   Tel: 55-11-233-7155
Bus: *Commercial banking services.*   Fax: 55-11-233-7329   Emp: 4,900
                                      www.bandeirantes.com.br

BANCO BANDEIRANTES S.A.
280 Park Avenue, 38th Fl., New York, NY   10017
CEO: Roberto L. Paladini, Dir.   Tel: (212) 972-7455   %FO: 100
Bus: *Commercial banking services.* Fax: (212) 949-9158   Emp: 6

• BANCO BOZANO, SIMONSEN S.A.
Av. Rio Branco, 138, 16o. andar, RJ 20057-900 Rio de Janeiro, Brazil
CEO: Paulo V. Ferraz, Pres.   Tel: 55-21-508-4000
Bus: *Banking services.*   Fax: 55-21-508-4053   Emp: 350
                                     www.bozano.com.

BOZANO SIMONSEN SECURITIES S.A.
590 Fifth Avenue, 2nd Fl., New York, NY   10036-4702
CEO: Jose Lavaquial, Rep.   Tel: (212) 869-3690   %FO: 100
Bus: *Representative office.*   Fax: (212) 869-3654   Emp: 3

BOZANO SIMONSEN SECURITIES S.A.
1200 Brickell Avenue, Ste. 1480, Miami, FL   33131
CEO: Jose Lavaquial, Rep.   Tel: (305) 530-0078
Bus: *Miami branch office.*   Fax: (305) 530-9004

• BANCO BRADESCO SA
Av. Ipiranga 282, 10 andar, CX Postal 1250, CEP 01046-920 São Paulo SP, Brazil
CEO: Lázaro de Mello Brandão, Chmn. Tel: 55-11-235-9566   Rev: $10,754
Bus: *Commercial banking services.* Fax: 55-11-256-8442   Emp: 65,800
                                     www.bradesco.com.br

BANCO BRADESCO SA
450 Park Avenue, 32nd & 33 Fls., New York, NY   10022
CEO: Joao Albino Winkelmann, Mgr.   Tel: (212) 688-9855   %FO: 100
Bus: *International commercial banking* Fax: (212) 754-4032   Emp: 30
     services.

- **BANCO DO BRASIL**

Ed. Sede III, Bloco C, 24 andar SBS, Quadro 4 Lote 32, 70089-900 Brasilia, DF Brazil
CEO: Paulo Enrico Maria Zaghen, CEO   Tel: 55-61-310-3400   Rev: $18,654
Bus: *Commercial banking services.*   Fax: 55-61-310-2563   Emp: 69,435
www.bancobrasil.com.br

BANCO DO BRASIL S.A.
2 South Biscayne Blvd., Ste. 3870, Miami, FL   33131
CEO: Roberto Barroso, Gen. Mgr.   Tel: (305) 358-3586   %FO: 100
Bus: *International commercial banking*   Fax: (305) 577-0541
services.

BANCO DO BRASIL S.A.
2 North LaSalle Street, Ste. 2005, Chicago, IL   60602
CEO: Julio Cesar Picolli, Rep.   Tel: (312) 236-9766   %FO: 100
Bus: *International commercial banking*   Fax: (312) 236-1591
services.

BANCO DO BRASIL S.A.
811 Wilshire Boulevard, Los Angeles, CA   90017-2624
CEO: Paulo Guimaraes   Tel: (213) 688-2996   %FO: 100
Bus: *International commercial banking*   Fax: (213) 688-2994   Emp: 21
services.

BANCO DO BRASIL S.A.
550 Fifth Avenue, New York, NY   10036
CEO: Rubens Amanal, Mgr.   Tel: (212) 626-7000   %FO: 100
Bus: *Savings institution.*   Fax: (212) 626-7045   Emp: 210

BANCO DO BRASIL S.A.
2020 K Street NW, Suite 450, Washington, DC   20006
CEO: Akira Ensiki, Mgr.   Tel: (202) 857-0320   %FO: 100
Bus: *International commercial banking*   Fax: (202) 872-8649   Emp: 100
services.

- **BANCO DO ESTADO DE SÃO PAULO SA**

Praça de Republic 295, 10 andar, CEP 01045-001 São Paulo, SP, Brazil
CEO: Arthur Campos Tavares, Dir.   Tel: 55-11-223-5045
Bus: *State commercial bank. (JV of Banco*   Fax: 55-11-223-5783   Emp: 23,400
Santander, Spain)   www.banespa.com.br

BANCO DO ESTADO DE SÃO PAULO SA
399 Park Avenue, 39th Fl., New York, NY   10022
CEO: Luis Escovar, Mgr.   Tel: (212) 715-2800   %FO: 100
Bus: *International commercial banking*   Fax: (212) 371-1034   Emp: 52
services.

● **BANCO DO ESTADO DO PARANÁ SA**
Praça Antonio Prado 6, 6 Andar, São Paulo, Brazil
CEO: Eduardo Guimaraes, Chmn.   Tel: 55-11-249-9090   Rev: $3,294
Bus: *General banking services.*   Fax: 55-11-239-2414   Emp: 12,000
                                           www.banespa.com.br

   BANCO DO ESTADO DO PARANA SA
   399 Park Avenue, 39th Fl., New York, NY   10022
   CEO: Luis Escovar, Mgr.   Tel: (212) 715-2800   %FO: 100
   Bus: *International commercial banking*   Fax: (212) 371-1034   Emp: 10
   services.

● **BANCO DO ESTADO DO RIO GRANDE DO SUL SA**
Rua Capitão Montanha, 177 Porto Alegre, 90018-900 RS, Brazil
CEO: Jose Verle, Pres.   Tel: 55-51-215-2887
Bus: *General banking services.*   Fax: 55-51-228-6473   Emp: 10,000
                                           www.banrisul.com.br

   BANRISUL
   500 Fifth Ave., Ste. 2310, New York, NY   10110
   CEO: Carlos R. Becker, Gen.Mgr.   Tel: (212) 827-0390   %FO: 100
   Bus: *Banking services.*   Fax: (212) 869-0844   Emp: 4

● **BANCO FIBRA SA**
Av. Brigadeiro Faria Lima, 3064-7° Andar, 01451-000 São Paulo SP, Brazil
CEO: Benjamin Steinbruch, Pres.   Tel: 55-11-3811-4700
Bus: *Security brokers, dealers and flotation*   Fax: 55-11-3847-6744   Emp: 450
services.   www.bancofibra.com

   FIBRA SECURITIES INC.
   300 Park Avenue, 17th Fl., New York, NY   10022
   CEO: Yukio Aoki, Mng. Dir.   Tel: (212) 572-6390   %FO: 100
   Bus: *Security brokers, dealers, &*   Fax: (212) 572-6458   Emp: 8
   flotation services.

● **BANCO INDUSVAL S.A**
Rua Boavista 356, 7o.andar, SP 01014 São Paulo, Brazil
CEO: Luiz Masagão Ribeiro, Pres.   Tel: 55-11-225-6888
Bus: *Security brokers, dealers and flotation*   Fax: 55-11-225-0815   Emp: 178
services.   www.indusval.com.br

   INDUSVAL USA CORPORATION
   140 Broadway, 45th Fl., New York, NY   10005
   CEO: George Lee Rexing, EVP   Tel: (212) 858-7528   %FO: 100
   Bus: *Broker, dealer & investment*   Fax: (212) 858-7741   Emp: 4
   advisory.

● **BANCO ITAÚ S.A.**
Rua Boavista, 176, SP 01092-900 São Paulo, Brazil
CEO: Roberto Egydio Setubal, Pres.   Tel: 55-11-237-3000   Rev: $5,399
Bus: *Investment and commercial banking.*   Fax: 55-11-277-1044   Emp: 39,000
www.itau.com.br

    BANCO ITAÚ S.A.
    540 Madison Avenue, 24th Fl., New York, NY   10022
    CEO: Marcelo Sanchez, Gen. Mgr.   Tel: (212) 486-1380   %FO: 100
    Bus: *International banking services.*   Fax: (212) 888-9342   Emp: 24

● **BANCO MERCANTIL DE SÃO PAULO S.A**
Av. Paulista, 1450, SP 01310-100 São Paulo, Brazil
CEO: Gastão Eduardo de Bueno Vidigal, Pres. Tel: 55-11-252-2121
Bus: *Commercial banking services.*   Fax: 55-11-284-3312   Emp: 6,700
www.finasa.com.br

    BANCO MERCANTIL DE SÃO PAULO S.A
    450 Park Avenue, 14th Fl., New York, NY   10022-2636
    CEO: Irones Oliveira Paula, Gen. Mgr.   Tel: (212) 888-0030   %FO: 100
    Bus: *International banking services.*   Fax: (212) 888-4631   Emp: 7

● **BANCO PACTUAL S.A.**
Av. Rebulica do Chile, 230, 29o.andar, RJ 20031-170 Rio de Janeiro, Brazil
CEO: Luiz Cesar Fernandes, Pres.   Tel: 55-21-514-9600
Bus: *Investment banking and investment* Fax: 55-21-514-8600   Emp: 300
advisory services.   www.pactual.com.br

    PACTUAL CAPITAL CORPORATION
    527 Madison Avenue, 11th Fl., New York, NY   10022
    CEO: Thomas W. Keesee III, Mng. Dir.   Tel: (212) 702-4100   %FO: 100
    Bus: *Investment banking.*   Fax: (212) 702-4110   Emp: 7

● **BANCO REAL SA**
Av. Paulista 1374, 01310-916 São Paulo, Brazil
CEO: Fabio Colletti Barbosa, Pres.   Tel: 55-11-3174-9045   Rev: $4,029
Bus: *National commercial bank.*   Fax: 55-11-3174-9222   Emp: 15,000
www.realcom.br

    BANCO REAL INTL INC
    200 West Adams St., Ste. 1610, Chicago, IL   60606
    CEO: Thomas P. Campbell, Gen. Mgr.   Tel: (312) 853-3421   %FO: 100
    Bus: *International banking services.*   Fax: (312) 853-3424   Emp: 5

BANCO REAL SA

680 Fifth Ave., 6th Fl., New York, NY   10019

CEO: Humberto Mourao de Carvalho,   Tel: (212) 469-5100   %FO: 100
      Reg. Dir.

Bus: *International banking services.*   Fax: (212) 307-5627   Emp: 50

BANCO REAL SA

1800 K Street, NW, Suite 301, Washington, DC   20006

CEO: Henrique Campos, Gen. Mgr.   Tel: (202) 452-6870   %FO: 100

Bus: *International banking services.*   Fax: (202) 452-6873   Emp: 6

BANCO REAL SA

South Biscayne Blvd., Suite 1870, Miami, FL   33131

CEO: Fernando Biuno Pinto, Gen. Mgr.   Tel: (305) 358-2433   %FO: 100

Bus: *International banking services.*   Fax: (305) 375-8214   Emp: 25

● **BANQUE SUDAMERIS**

Av. Paulista, 1000. 7o. andar, SP 01310-912 São Paulo, Brazil

CEO: Giovanni Urizio, Dir.   Tel: 55-11-283-9633

Bus: *Investment banking services.*   Fax: 55-11-289-1239   Emp: 3,800
                                         www.sudameris.com.br

BANK SUDAMERIS-MIAMI

1200 Brickell Avenue, 7th Fl., Miami, FL   33131

CEO: Robert Marcuse, Gen. Mgr.   Tel: (305) 372-2200   %FO: 100

Bus: *Investment banking.*   Fax: (305) 374-1137   Emp: 58

● **BM & F - BOLSA DE MERCADORIAS E FUTUROS**

Praça Antonio Prado, 48, SP 01010-901 São Paulo, Brazil

CEO: Edemir Pinto, CEO   Tel: 55-11-232-7563

Bus: *Commodities, futures, and options*   Fax: 55-11-232-7565   Emp: 288
      exchanges.   www.bmf.com.br

BM & F USA

450 Park Avenue, Ste. 2704, New York, NY   10022-2605

CEO: Luiz F. Forbes, Pres.   Tel: (212) 750-4197   %FO: 100

Bus: *International financial advisory*   Fax: (212) 750-4198   Emp: 3
      firm.

● **BRAZMEDIA INTERNACIONAL PUBLICIDADE E EDIÇÕES LTDA.**

Alameda Gabriel Monteiro da Silva, 366, SP 01442-900 São Paulo, Brazil

CEO: Les Bilyk, Pres.   Tel: 55-11-853-4133

Bus: *Media and advertising placement in*   Fax: 55-11-852-6485   Emp: 17
      Brazilian publications.   www.brazmedia.com

THE N. DEFILIPPES CORPORATION
130 West 42nd Street, Ste. 714, New York, NY   10036-7800

CEO: Veronica Shay, VP	Tel: (212) 391-0002	%FO: 100
Bus: *Advertising agency.*	Fax: (212) 391-7666	Emp: 10

● COMPANHIA CACIQUE DE CAFÊ SOLÚVEL
Av. das Nações Unidas, 10989, 10o ao 11o. andares, SP 04578-000 São Paulo, Brazil

CEO: Sérgio Coimbra, Pres.   Tel: 55-11-3054-8200

Bus: *Mfr. roasted coffee.*   Fax: 55-11-3849-7278   Emp: 2,000

www.cafepele.com.br

BRASTRADE (BRAZILIAN TRADING COMPANY, INC.)
120 Wall Street, Suite 1801, New York, NY   10005

CEO: Sérgio C. Pereria, Pres.	Tel: (212) 363-2575	%FO: 100
Bus: *Coffee brokers & dealers.*	Fax: (212) 514-6119	Emp: 11

● COMPANHIA VALE DO RIO DOCE
Av. Graca Aranha 26, 20005-900 Rio de Janeiro, Brazil

CEO: Jorio Dauster, Pres.   Tel: 55-21-3814-4477

Bus: *Provides mining and exposition of iron*   Fax: 55-21-3814-4040   Emp: 11,500
ore.   www.curd.com.br

RIO DOCE AMERICA INC.
546 Fifth Avenue, 12th Fl., New York, NY   10036

CEO: Armando Santos, Pres.	Tel: (212) 589-9800	%FO: 100
Bus: *Import/export.*	Fax: (212) 391-1000	

● DEMAREST E ALMEIDA
Alameda Campinas 1070, SP 01404-002 São Paulo, Brazil

CEO: Altamiro Boscoli, Ptnr.   Tel: 55-11-888-1800

Bus: *International law firm.*   Fax: 55-11-888-1700

www.demarest.com.br

DEMAREST E. ALMEIDA
509 Madison Avenue, Ste. 506, New York, NY   10169

CEO: Isabel C. Franco, Ptnr.	Tel: (212) 371-9191	%FO: 100
Bus: *International law firm.*	Fax: (212) 371-5551	

● DURATEX SA
Av. Paulista 1938, CEP 01310-200 São Paulo, Brazil

CEO: Paulo Setubal, Pres.   Tel: 55-11-3179-7733

Bus: *Mfr./sale hardboard and particle board.*   Fax: 55-11-3179-7707

www.duratex.com.br

DURATEX NORTH AMERICA, INC.
1208 Eastchester Drive, Suite 202, High Point, NC   27265
CEO: Gary Wikstrom, Mgr.   Tel: (336) 885-1500   %FO: 100
Bus: *Mfr./sale hardboard &*   Fax: (336) 885-1501
particleboard.

● EMBRAER, EMPRESA BRASILEIRA DE AERONAUTICA S.A.
Caixa Postal 343, SP 12227-901, São José dos Campos, Brazil
CEO: Mauricio Botelho, Pres.   Tel: 55-123-25-1000   Rev: $1,300
Bus: *Mfr. aircraft, engines and parts.*   Fax: 55-123-25-1090   Emp: 7,000
www.embraer.com.br

EMBRAER AIRCRAFT CORPORATION
276 SW 34th Street, Ft. Lauderdale, FL   33315
CEO: Mark Hale, VP   Tel: (954) 359-3700   %FO: 100
Bus: *Aircraft engines and parts.* Fax: (954) 359-8170   Emp: 76

● GAFISA PARTICIPAÇÕES S.A.
Av. Brigadeiro Faria Lima, 1355- 22 andar. Pinheiros, SP 01452-002 São Paulo, Brazil
CEO: Carlos Moasyr Gomes de Alemeida,   Tel: 55-11-817-9000
Chrm.
Bus: *Real estate services.*   Fax: 55-11-814-0881   Emp: 2,853
www.gafisa.com.br

GAFISA (USA) INC.
16 East 52nd Street, 9th Fl., New York, NY   10022
CEO: Raul Leite Luna, Pres.   Tel: (212) 888-5155   %FO: 100
Bus: *Real estate agents & managers.*   Fax: (212) 888-5470   Emp: 15

● GAZETA MERCANTIL S.A.
Rua Engenheiro Francisco Pitta de Brito, 125, SP 04753-080 São Paulo, Brazil
CEO: Antonio Costa Filho, Dir.   Tel: 55-11-547-3090
Bus: *Books, periodicals and newspapers.*   Fax: 55-11-547-3011   Emp: 500
www.gazetamercantil.com

GAZETA MERCANTIL
1101 Brickell Avenue, Ste. 401, Miami, FL   33131
CEO: Marcos Maranhão. VP   Tel: (305) 371-7090   %FO: 100
Bus: *Books, periodicals & newspapers.*   Fax: (305) 371-5419

GAZETA MERCANTIL
441 Lexington Avenue, New York, NY   10017
CEO: William Duke   Tel: (212) 949-0464   %FO: 100
Bus: *Books, periodicals & newspapers.*   Fax: (212) 949-0487   Emp: 2

● **GERDAU SA**
Avenida Farrapos 1811, 90220-005 Porto Alegre, Rio Grande do Sul, Brazil

CEO: Jorge Gerdau Johannpeter, CEO	Tel: 55-51-323-2000	Rev: $2,675
Bus: *Mfr. long-rolled steel.*	Fax: 55-51-323-2080	Emp: 12,350
	www.gerdau.com.br	

   AMERISTEEL CORPORATION
   5100 West Lemon Street, Ste. 312, Tampa, FL   33609

CEO: Thomas J. Landa, VP	Tel: (813) 826-8383	%FO: 100
Bus: *Mfr. long-rolled steel.*	Fax: (813) 826-8383	

   AMERISTEEL STEEL MILL
   1919 Tennessee Avenue, Knoxville, TN   37921

CEO: Jim Oliver, VP	Tel: (423) 546-0102	%FO: 100
Bus: *Mfr. long-rolled steel.*	Fax: (423) 546-0102	

   AMERISTEEL STEEL MILL
   801 AmeriSteel Road, Jackson, TN   38305

CEO: Jimmy Sloop, Plant Mgr.	Tel: (901) 424-5600	%FO: 100
Bus: *Mfr. long-rolled steel.*	Fax: (901) 424-5600	

   AMERISTEEL STEEL MILL
   Hwy. 217 Yellow Water Road, Baldwin, FL   32234

CEO: Richard Phillips	Tel: (904) 266-4261	%FO: 100
Bus: *Mfr. long-rolled steel.*	Fax: (904) 266-4261	

● **GLOBO CABO SA**
Rua Verbo Divino, 1356 04719-002 São Paulo, SP, Brazil

CEO: Roberto Irineu Marinho, VP	Tel: 55-11-5186-2606	Rev: $556
Bus: *Engaged in cable television broadcasting.*	Fax: 55-11-5186-2606	Emp: 6,300
	www.globocabo.com	

   GLOBO INTERNATIONAL TV NETWORK
   909 Third Avenue, 21st Fl., New York, NY   10022

CEO: Roberto Irineu Marinho, VP	Tel: (212) 446-3000
Bus: *Engaged in television broadcasting.*	Fax: (212) 446-3000

● **IOCHPE-MAXION S.A.**
Av. Eng. Luiz Carlos Berrini No. 1253-14° Andar, SP 04571-01, Brooklin Novo São Paulo, Brazil

CEO: Dan Ioschpe, CEO	Tel: 55-11-5508-3800	Rev: $433
Bus: *Motor vehicles, car bodies, parts and accessories.*	Fax: 55-11-5508-3821	Emp: 9,500
	www.maxion-motores.com.br	

IOCHPE-MAXION USA INC.
9100 S. Dadeland Blvd., Ste 1101, Miami, FL   33156

CEO: Salamon Iochpe, Pres.

Bus: *Motor vehicles: car bodies, parts and accessories.*

Tel: (305) 670-8030

Fax: (305) 670-9966

%FO: 100

Emp: 14

• MANGELS INDUSTRIAL S.A.
Rua Verbo Divino, 1488 3° andar Bloco A, 04719-904 São Paulo SP, Brazil

CEO: Roberto Mangels, Chmn.

Bus: *Motor vehicle wheels, parts and accessories.*

Tel: 55-11-5188-8800

Fax: 55-11-5181-0155

www.mangels.com.br

Emp: 1,700

MANGELS USA INC.
710 Rimpau Ave. Ste. 202, Corona, CA   92879

CEO: Mark R. Mangels, Mgr.

Bus: *Mfr. wheels, parts and accessories.*

Tel: (909) 737-2117

Fax: (909) 737-0292

%FO: 100

Emp: 16

• ODEBRECHT S.A.
Avenida Tancredo Neves, 450-29 andar, 41827-900 Salvador Bahia, Brazil

CEO: Emilio Odebrecht, Chmn.

Bus: *Holding company engaged in engineering, construction and offshore drilling.*

Tel: 55-71-340-1111

Fax: 55-71-341-9129

www.odebrecht.com.br

Rev: $3,138

ODEBRECH CONSTRUCTION, INC.
201 Alhambra Circle, Ste. 1400, Coral Cables, FL   33134

CEO: Luiz Augusto Rocha, Pres. & CEO

Bus: *Engaged in heavy construction.*

Tel: (305) 445-1165

Fax: (305) 445-9392

%FO: 100

• PETROBRÁS (PETRÓLEO BRASILEIRO S.A.)
Av. República do Chile, 65, RJ 20132-900 Rio de Janeiro, Brazil

CEO: Joel Mendes Rennó, Pres.

Bus: *Engaged in petroleum exploration, drilling, production and pipeline transportation.*

Tel: 55-21-534-4477

Fax: 55-21-534-3247

www.petrobras.com.br

Rev: $25,518

Emp: 35,890

PETROBRÁS (NY) - PETRÓLEO BRASILEIRO S.A.
1330 Avenue of the Americas, 16th Fl., New York, NY   10019

CEO: Ted Helm, Gen. Mgr.

Bus: *Petroleum, oil & gas production - drilling & refining services; natural health products.*

Tel: (212) 974-0777

Fax: (212) 974-1169

%FO: 100

Emp: 15

● **SÃO PAULO ALPARGATAS S.A.**
Rua Urussuí, 300, SP 04542-903 São Paulo, Brazil
CEO: Fernando Tigre, Mgr. Tel: 55-11-827-7322 Rev: $512
Bus: *Mfr. textiles.* Fax: 55-11-820-8866 Emp: 17,175
 www.alpargatas.com.br

 EXPASA FLORIDA, INC.
 8284 14th Street, NW, Miami, FL 33126
 CEO: Nelson Ortega, Pres. Tel: (305) 279-7810 %FO: 100
 Bus: *Export/import textiles.* Fax: (305) 274-8207 Emp: 12

● **SMAR EQUIPAMENTOS INDUSTRIAS LTDA.**
Rua Dr. Antonio Furlan Jr., 1028, SP 14170-480 Sertãozinho, Brazil
CEO: Edmundo Corini, Pres. Tel: 55-16-645-6455 Rev: $30
Bus: *Ind. measurement instruments, display* Fax: 55-16-645-6450 Emp: 730
 & control, and machinery. www.smar.com

 SMAR INTERNATIONAL CORPORATION
 6001 Stonington Street, Ste. 100, Houston, TX 77041
 CEO: Paulo Garrone, Gen. Mgr. Tel: (713) 849-2021 %FO: 100
 Bus: *Ind. measurement instruments,* Fax: (713) 849-2022 Emp: 25
 display and control machinery

● **TRANSBRASIL LINHAS AEREAS**
Rua Galeao Pantaleao Telles 40, Jardim Aeroporto, 04355-040 São Paulo SP, Brazil
CEO: Antonio Celso Cipriani, CEO Tel: 55-11-533-7111 Rev: $700
Bus: *International air transport services.* Fax: 55-11-543-9083 Emp: 4,200
 www.transbrasil.com.br

 TRANSBRASIL AIRLINES INC.
 5757 Blue Lagoon Drive, Suite 400, Miami, FL 33126
 CEO: Flavio Carvalho, VP Tel: (305) 591-8322 %FO: 100
 Bus: *International air transport* Fax: (305) 477-9509 Emp: 151
 services.

 TRANSBRASIL AIRLINES INC.
 500 Fifth Avenue, Suite 1710, New York, NY 10110
 CEO: Lincoln Delborne, Mgr. Tel: (212) 944-7374 %FO: 100
 Bus: *International air transport* Fax: (212) 944-7458 Emp: 20
 services.

● **UNIBANCO (UNIÃN DE BANCOS BRASILERIOS S.A.)**
Av. Eusãébio Matoso 891, 4o. andar, SP 05423-180 São Paulo, Brazil
CEO: Fernando Barreira Sotelino, Pres. Tel: 55-3789-8000 Rev: $5,412
Bus: *Commercial banking services.* Fax: 55-3097-4763 Emp: 19,450
 www.unibanco.com.br

UNIBANCO NEW YORK (UNIÃN DE BANCOS BRASILERIOS S.A.)
65 East 55th Street, 29th Fl., New York, NY   10022
CEO: George Lieblein, Gen. Mgr.   Tel: (212) 832-1700   %FO: 100
Bus: *Commercial banking.*   Fax: (212) 752-2076   Emp: 27

UNIBANCO NEW YORK (UNIÃN DE BANCOS BRASILERIOS S.A.)
701 Brickell Avenue, Suite 2030, Miami, FL   33131
CEO: Marcos Rodrigues Pereira, Mgr.   Tel: (305) 372-0100   %FO: 100
Bus: *Commercial banking.*   Fax: (305) 374-5652   Emp: 15

● **VARIG BRAZILIAN AIRLINES SA**
Av. Almiranti Silvio de Noronha 365, 20021-010 Rio de Janeiro RJ, Brazil
CEO: Dr. Ozires Silva, Pres.   Tel: 55-21-272-5310   Rev: $3,500
Bus: *International commercial air transport*   Fax: 55-21-272-5720   Emp: 17,700
      services.   www.varig.com.br

VARIG BRAZILIAN AIRLINES
380 Madison Avenue, New York, NY   10017
CEO: Carlos O. Muzzio, Dir.   Tel: (212) 850-8200   %FO: 100
Bus: *Commercial air transport services.*   Fax: (212) 850-8201   Emp: 360

● **VOTORANTIM**
1357 - 6 andar, Cerqueira Cesar, SP 01470-908 São Paulo, Brazil
CEO: José Ermírio de Moraes Filho, Chmn.   Tel: 55-11-269-4000   Rev: $578
Bus: *Mfr. paper, chemicals and allied*   Fax: 55-11-820-0330   Emp: 3,980
      products.   www.vcp.com.br

VOTORANTIM INTERNATIONAL NORTH AMERICA, INC.
111 Continental Dr., Ste. 111, Newark, DE   19713
CEO: Eduardo Scabbia, Mng. Dir.   Tel: (302) 454-8300   %FO: 100
Bus: *Import/export commodity sales*   Fax: (302) 454-8309   Emp: 6
      office.

● **WEG INDUSTRIAS SA**
Av. Prefeito Waldemar Grubba 3300, SC 89256-900 Jaraguá do Sul, Brazil
CEO: Eggon João da Silva, CEO   Tel: 55-47-372-4000   Rev: $332
Bus: *Mfr./sales electric motors.*   Fax: 55-47-372-4010   Emp: 7,000
                                          www.weg.com.br

WEG ELECTRIC MOTORS CORPORATION
11705 W. 83rd Terrace, Ste. 100, Lenexa, KS   66215
CEO: Don Lennard, Mgr.   Tel: (913) 492-7000   %FO: 100
Bus: *Mfr./sales electric motors.*   Fax: (913) 492-6999

WEG ELECTRIC MOTORS CORPORATION
5150 NW 109th Avenue, Ste. 2, Sunrise, FL   33351
CEO: Adolfo Steingraber, Mgr.   Tel: (954) 749-7987   %FO: 100
Bus: *Mfr./sales electric motors.*   Fax: (954) 749-3490

WEG ELECTRIC MOTORS CORPORATION
1327 Northbrook Parkway, Suwanee, GA   30024
CEO: Mark Howze, Mgr.   Tel: (770) 338-5656   %FO: 100
Bus: *Mfr./sales electric motors.*   Fax: (770) 338-1632

WEG ELECTRIC MOTORS CORPORATION
252 Ginbert Drive, Virginia Beach, VA   23452
CEO: Marco Marino, Sales   Tel: (757) 340-4142   %FO: 100
Bus: *Mfr./sales electric motors.*   Fax: (757) 340-3530

British Virgin Islands

● **UTI WORLDWIDE INC.**
8 Columbus Centre, Pelican Drive, Road Town, Tortola, BWI
CEO: Roger I. MacFarlane, CEO   Tel: 284-494-4561   Rev: $302
Bus: *Provides freight forwarding, customs*   Fax: 284-494-4568   Emp: 5,600
brokerage and warehousing services.   www.go2uti.com

UNION-TRANSPORT CORPORATION
120 Eastern Avenue, Chelsea, MA   02150
CEO: Greg Mongomery, Pres.   Tel: (617) 889-5588   %FO: 100
Bus: *Provides freight forwarding and*   Fax: (617) 889-6580
customs brokerage services.

UNION-TRANSPORT CORPORATION
1660 Walt Whitman Road, Melville, NY   11747
CEO: Greg Mongomery, Pres.   Tel: (631) 755-3500   %FO: 100
Bus: *Provides freight forwarding and*   Fax: (631) 755-3550
customs brokerage services.

UNION-TRANSPORT CORPORATION
745 N. Dillon Drive, Wood Dale, IL   06191
CEO: Greg Mongomery, Pres.   Tel: (630) 694-0680   %FO: 100
Bus: *Provides freight forwarding and*   Fax: (630) 694-0684
customs brokerage services.

UNION-TRANSPORT CORPORATION
38 Romney, Charleston, SC   29403
CEO: Greg Mongomery, Pres.   Tel: (843) 722-4163   %FO: 100
Bus: *Provides freight forwarding and*   Fax: (843) 577-6230
customs brokerage services.

UNION-TRANSPORT CORPORATION
228 North Avenue East, Elizabeth, NJ   07201
CEO: Greg Mongomery, Pres.   Tel: (908) 820-9700   %FO: 100
Bus: *Provides freight forwarding and*   Fax: (908) 820-8774
customs brokerage services.

UNION-TRANSPORT CORPORATION
2700 Broening Hwy., Ste. 211, Baltimore, MD   21222
CEO: Greg Mongomery, Pres.   Tel: (410) 631-7225   %FO: 100
Bus: *Provides freight forwarding and*   Fax: (410) 631-7140
customs brokerage services.

UNION-TRANSPORT CORPORATION
1900-G Center Park Drive, Charlotte, NC   28217

CEO: Greg Mongomery, Pres.   Tel: (704) 357-9722   %FO: 100

Bus: *Provides freight forwarding and*   Fax: (704) 357-9717
     customs brokerage services.

UNION-TRANSPORT CORPORATION
475 Plaza Drive, College Park, GA   30349

CEO: Greg Mongomery, Pres.   Tel: (404) 762-1887   %FO: 100

Bus: *Provides freight forwarding and*   Fax: (404) 762-9076
     customs brokerage services.

UNION-TRANSPORT CORPORATION
755 Port American Place, Ste. 300, Grapevine, TX   76051

CEO: Greg Mongomery, Pres.   Tel: (817) 424-0037   %FO: 100

Bus: *Provides freight forwarding and*   Fax: (817) 424-3072
     customs brokerage services.

Burkina Faso

- **AIR AFRIQUE**
  1 Avenue de Bassa Warga, 01 BP 141 Ouagadougou, Burkina Faso
  CEO: Yves Roland Billecart, Pres.   Tel: 226-30-60-20   Rev: $286
  Bus: *Commercial air transport services.*   Fax: 226-31-15-28   Emp: 4,209
                                             www.airafrique.com

  AIR AFRIQUE
  1350 Avenue of the Americas, 6th Floor, New York, NY   10019
  CEO: Yves Roland Billecart, Pres.   Tel: (212) 586-5908   %FO: 100
  Bus: *International commercial air*   Fax: (212) 541-7539   Emp: 50
       transport services.

Canada

- **360 NETWORKS INC.**
  1066 West Hastings Street, Ste. 1500, Vancouver BC, V6E 3X1, Canada
  CEO: Gregory B. Maffei, CEO   Tel: (604) 681-1994   Rev: $511
  Bus: *Provides broadband network and*   Fax: (604) 681-6822   Emp: 1,900
  telecommunications services.   www.360.net

  ### 360 NETWORKS INC.
  350 Park Avenue, 21st Fl., New York, NY   10022
  CEO: Jerry Tharp, Pres.   Tel: (212) 940-7200   %FO: 100
  Bus: *Provides broadband network and*   Fax: (212) 940-7234
  telecommunications services.

  ### 360 NETWORKS INC.
  16000 North Dallas Pkwy., Ste. 225, Dallas, TX   75248
  CEO: Jerry Tharp, Pres.   Tel: (469) 374-4300   %FO: 100
  Bus: *Provides broadband network and*   Fax: (469) 374-4379
  telecommunications services.

- **724 SOLUTIONS INC.**
  4101 Yonge Street, Ste. 702, Toronto ON, M2P 1N6, Canada
  CEO: John Sims, CEO   Tel: (416) 226-2900   Rev: $21
  Bus: *Provides online banking and financial*   Fax: (416) 226-4456   Emp: 710
  services over wireless devices.   www.724.com

  ### 724 SOLUTIONS INC.
  108 Wild Basin Road, Ste. 110, Austin, TX   78746
  CEO: Jim Sink, VP   Tel: (512) 306-4200   %FO: 100
  Bus: *Provides online banking and*   Fax: (512) 329-0167
  financial services over wireless
  devices.

- **ABITIBI-CONSOLIDATED INC.**
  1155 rue Metcalfe, Ste. 800, Montréal PQ, H3B 542, Canada
  CEO: John W. Weaver, Pres. & CEO   Tel: (514) 875-2160   Rev: $3,785
  Bus: *Mfr. newsprint, groundwood paper,*   Fax: (514) 394-2272   Emp: 18,000
  pulp, and lumber.   www.abicon.com

  ### ABITIBI CONSOLIDATED
  Four Gannett Drive, White Plains, NY   10604
  CEO: Andre M. J. Van Hattum, Pres.   Tel: (914) 640-8600   %FO: 100
  Bus: *U.S. headquarters.*   Fax: (914) 640-8900

ABITIBI RECYCLING, INC.
2350 North Belt East, Ste. 600, Houston, TX 77032
CEO: Vincent A. Benvenuti, Pres.　　Tel: (281) 539-7000
Bus: *Engaged in paper recycling.*　　Fax: (281) 539-7906

ABITIBI-CONSOLIDATED SAKES
222 South Riverside Plaza, Chicago, IL 60606
CEO: Michael D. Dudgeon, Pres.　　Tel: (312) 575-8888　　%FO: 100
Bus: *Sales.*　　Fax: (312) 575-8855

ALABAMA RIVER NEWSPRINT COMPANY
PO Box 10, Perdue Hill, AL 36470
CEO: T. Thorsteinson, Mgr.　　Tel: (334) 575-2800　　%FO: JV
Bus: *Production of newsprint.*　　Fax: (334) 743-6427

AUGUSTA NEWSPRINT COMPANY
PO Box 1647, Augusta, GA 30913
CEO: Bob Collez, Mgr.　　Tel: (706) 798-3440　　%FO: JV
Bus: *Production of newsprint.*　　Fax: (706) 793-4149

● **ABLEAUCTIONS.COM, INC.**
1963 Lougheed Highway, Coquitlam B,C V3K 3T8, Canada
CEO: Abdul Ladha, CEO　　Tel: (604) 521-2253　　Rev: $11
Bus: *On-line auctioneer for charities.*　　Fax: (604) 521-5093　　Emp: 100
　　www.ableauctions.com

ABLEAUCTIONS.COM, INC.
7303 East Earll Drive, Scottsdale, AZ 85251
CEO: Dan Bouchard, VP　　Tel: (602) 979-9600　　%FO: 100
Bus: *On-line auction house.*　　Fax: (602) 979-9600

● **ACRES INTERNATIONAL LTD.**
480 University Ave, Toronto ON, M5G 1V2, Canada
CEO: Oskar T. Sigvaldason, Pres.　　Tel: 416-595-2000
Bus: *Engaged in engineering services.*　　Fax: 416-595-2004　　Emp: 700
　　www.acres.com

ACRES INTERNATIONAL CORPORATION
3100 Richmond Avenue, Ste. 550, Houston, TX 77098
CEO: Jacob A. Argauer Jr., Pres.　　Tel: (713) 527-8481　　%FO: 100
Bus: *Engineering services.*　　Fax: (713) 526-8766

ACRES INTERNATIONAL CORPORATION
1750 Pennsylvania Avenue NW, Washington, DC 20006
CEO: Jacob A. Argauer Jr., Pres.　　Tel: (202) 393-2027　　%FO: 100
Bus: *Engineering services.*　　Fax: (202) 393-5721

ACRES INTERNATIONAL CORPORATION
125 Wolf Road, Albany, NY   12205
CEO: Jacob A. Argauer Jr., Pres.   Tel: (518) 453-6353   %FO: 100
Bus: *Engineering services.*   Fax: (518) 438-7285

ACRES INTERNATIONAL CORPORATION
140 John James Audubon Pkwy, Amherst, NY   14228
CEO: Terry A. Hernaha, VP   Tel: (716) 689-3737   %FO: 100
Bus: *Engineering services.*   Fax: (716) 689-3749

ACRES INTERNATIONAL CORPORATION
150 Nickerson Street, Ste. 310, Seattle, WA   98109
CEO: Jacob A. Argauer Jr., Pres.   Tel: (206) 352-5730   %FO: 100
Bus: *Engineering services.*   Fax: (206) 352-5734

ACRES INTERNATIONAL CORPORATION
311 4th Street South, Ste. 116, Grand Forks, ND   58201
CEO: Jacob A. Argauer Jr., Pres.   Tel: (701) 746-8655   %FO: 100
Bus: *Engineering services.*   Fax: (701) 775-2295

● **AGRIUM INC.**
13131 Lake Fraser Drive SE, Calgary AB, T2J 7E8, Canada
CEO: John M. Van Brunt, Pres. & CEO   Tel: (403) 225-7000   Rev: $1,873
Bus: *Mfr. fertilizers and wholesale and retail* Fax: (403) 225-7609   Emp: 4,535
    plant growth nutrients.   www.agrium.com

AGRIUM INC.
1551 Farm Road, PO Box 5067, Borger, TX   79008-5067
CEO: Larry Wood, Plant Mgr.   Tel: (806) 274-5204   %FO: 100
Bus: *Mfr. fertilizers.*   Fax: (806) 274-2021

AGRIUM INC.
22292 SW 89th Road, Beatrice, NE   68310-6872
CEO: Don McCarthy, Mgr.   Tel: (402) 223-5271   %FO: 100
Bus: *Mfr. fertilizers.*   Fax: (402) 228-3862

AGRIUM INC.
4582 South Ulster Street, Ste. 1400, Denver, CO   80237
CEO: John M. Van Brunt, Pres.   Tel: (803) 804-4400   %FO: 100
Bus: *Mfr. fertilizers.*   Fax: (803) 804-4476

● **AIMTRONICS CORPORATION INC.**
1245 California Avenue, Brockville ON, K6V 5Y6, Canada
CEO: Michael Marti, Pres.   Tel: (613) 342-5041
Bus: *Mfr. surface mounts and circuit boards.* Fax: (613)342-1774   Emp: 500
                                        www.aimtronics.com

AIMTRONICS
100 Chimney Point Drive, Ogdensburg, NY   13669

CEO: Rod Bush, Dir.   Tel: (315) 393-3573   %FO: 100

Bus: *Produces electronic equipment*   Fax: (315) 393-3573
      and components.

● AIR CANADA
Air Canada Centre, PO Box 14000, St-Laurent PQ, H4Y 1H4, Canada

CEO: Robert A. Milton, CEO   Tel: (514) 422-5000   Rev: $3,800

Bus: *Commercial air transport services.*   Fax: (514) 422-5799   Emp: 22,837

      www.aircanada.ca

AIR CANADA
1133 Ave. of the Americas, 16th Fl., New York, NY   10036

CEO: Robert A. Milton, CEO   Tel: (212) 869-8840

Bus: *Commercial air transport services.*   Fax: (212) 930-8355

● ALCAN ALUMINUM LTD.
1188 Sherbrooke Street West, Montréal PQ, H3A 3G2, Canada

CEO: Jacques Bougie, Pres. & CEO   Tel: (514) 848-8000   Rev: $7,800

Bus: *Mfr./sale aluminum products.*   Fax: (514) 848-8115   Emp: 36,000

      www.alcan.com

ALCAN ALUMINUM CORPORATION
6060 Parkland Blvd., Cleveland, OH   44124-4185

CEO: Brian Strugell, Pres.   Tel: (440) 423-6600   %FO: 100

Bus: *Aluminum plate, foil products,*   Fax: (440) 423-6667
      electronic equipment, agricultural
      products.

● ALIANT INC.
PO Box 800, Central RPO, Halifax NS, B3J 2W3, Canada

CEO: Stephen G. Wetmore, CEO   Tel: (877) 225-4268   Rev: $1,517

Bus: *Engaged in telecommunications and*   Fax: (877) 355-9988   Emp: 9,350
      internet solution services.   www.aliant.ca

PREXAR, INC.
40 Summer Street, Bangor, ME   04401

CEO: Daniel J. Doiron, Pres.   Tel: (207) 974-4300   %FO: 100

Bus: *Engaged in telecommunications*   Fax: (207) 974-4378
      and internet services.

ROCKET SCIENCE INTERNET SOLUTIONS, INC.
282 Corporate Drive, Portsmouth, NH   03801

CEO: Daniel J. Doiron, Pres.   Tel: (603) 334-6444   %FO: 100

Bus: *Internet solutions.*   Fax: (603) 334-6457

• **ALLIANCE ATLANTIS COMMUNICATIONS INC.**

121 Bloor Street East, Ste. 1500, Toronto ON, M4W 3M5, Canada

CEO: Michael MacMillan, Chmn.	Tel: (416) 934-7144	Rev: $420
Bus: *Broadcaster and international distributor of filmed entertainment for TV and cinema.*	Fax: (416) 967-5884 www.allianceatlantis.com	Emp: 350

ALLIANCE ATLANTIS COMMUNICATIONS INC.

808 Wilshire Boulevard, Ste. 400, Santa Monica, CA 90401

CEO: Michael MacMillan, CEO	Tel: (310) 899-8000
Bus: *Engaged in production and distribution of films and TV shows.*	Fax: (310) 899-8100

• **ALLIANCE FOREST PRODUCTS INC.**

1000 de la Gauchtière West, Ste. 2820, Montréal PQ, H3B 4W5, Canada

CEO: Pierre Monahan, Pres. & CEO	Tel: (514) 954-2100	Rev: $725
Bus: *Mfr. paper, pulp, lumber and newsprint.*	Fax: (514) 954-2167 www.alliance-forest.com	Emp: 3,500

ALLIANCE FOREST PRODUCTS INC.

1700 5089 Plant Road, Coosa Pines, AL 35044-0559

CEO: Kevin B. Wassil	Tel: (256) 378-5541	%FO: 100
Bus: *Mfr. paper, pulp, lumber and newsprint.*	Fax: (256) 378-2169	

• **ANACHEMIA CANADA LTD.**

255 rue Norman, Ville St. Pierre PQ, H8R 1A3, Canada

CEO: Ivoj K. Kudrnac, Pres.	Tel: (514) 489-5711
Bus: *Engaged in manufacture of chemicals and distribution of lab equipment.*	Fax: (514) 363-5281 www.anachemia.com

ANACHEMIA CHEMICALS

3 Lincoln Boulevard, Rouses Point, NY 12979

CEO: Russell Lavigne, Mgr.	Tel: (518) 297-4444	%FO: 100
Bus: *Mfr. chemicals, lab chemicals/solvents, etc.*	Fax: (518) 297-2960	

ANACHEMIA SCIENCE

738 Spice Island Drive, Sparks, NV 89431

CEO: Peter Cavender, Mgr.	Tel: (775) 331-2300	%FO: 100
Bus: *Engaged in marketing and distribution of chemicals.*	Fax: (775) 331-2646	

● **ARMBRO CORPORATION**
3660 Midland Avenue, Toronto ON, M1V 4V3, Canada
CEO: John M. Beck, Pres. & CEO   Tel: (416) 754-8735   Rev: $412
Bus: *Provides services in construction and*   Fax: (416) 754-8736   Emp: 4,244
engineering. (JV Hochtief AG)   www.armbro.ca

    BFC FRONTIER, INC.
    19217 36th Avenue West, Lynnwood, WA 98036
    CEO: George Kramer, VP   Tel: (425) 774-2945   %FO: 100
    Bus: *Commercial construction services.*   Fax: (425) 771-8094

● **ARMSTRONG, S.A. LTD.**
23 Bertrand Avenue, Scarborough ON, M1L 2P3, Canada
CEO: Charles A. Armstrong, Pres.   Tel: (416) 755-2291
Bus: *Mfr. pumps and pumping equipment.*   Fax: (416) 759-9101   Emp: 200
    www.armstrongpumps.com

    ARMSTRONG PUMPS INC.
    93 East Avenue, North Tonawanda, NY 14120
    CEO: Antoine Meo, VP   Tel: (716) 693-8813   %FO: 100
    Bus: *Mfr. pumps, pumping equipment.*   Fax: (716) 693-8970   Emp: 100

● **AT PLASTICS INC.**
134 Kennedy Road South, Brampton ON, L6W 3G5, Canada
CEO: Gary Connaughty, Pres. & CEO   Tel: (905) 451-1630   Rev: $195
Bus: *Mfr. specialty plastics.*   Fax: (905) 451-7650   Emp: 675
    www.atplas.com

    AT PLASTICS CORPORATION
    111 Hilltown Village Center, Chesterfield, MO 63017
    CEO: Arnold L. Cader   Tel: (636) 230-8390   %FO: 100
    Bus: *Mfr. specialty plastics.*   Fax: (636) 532-7556

    AT PLASTICS CORPORATION
    101 Sierra Drive, Peachtree City, GA 30269
    CEO: Peter Connelly, Mgr.   Tel: (770) 376-1912   %FO: 100
    Bus: *Mfr. specialty plastics.*   Fax: (770) 376-1919

● **ATI TECHNOLOGIES INC.**
33 Commerce Valley Drive East, Thornhill ON, L3T 7N6, Canada
CEO: David Orton, CEO   Tel: (905) 852-2600   Rev: $1,372
Bus: *Mfr. graphics accelerator chips.*   Fax: (905) 882-2620   Emp: 1,850
    www.atitech.ca

ATI TECHNOLOGIES SYSTEMS CORP.

1100 Northwest Compton Drive, Beaverton, OR   97006

CEO: Henry Quan, VP   Tel: (503) 531-2090   %FO: 100

Bus: *Mfr. graphics accelerator chips.*   Fax:

● **ATS AUTOMATION TOOLING SYSTEMS INC.**

250 Royal Oak Road, PO Box 32100, Preston Centre, Cambridge ON, N3H 5M2, Canada

CEO: Lawrence G. Tapp, Chmn.   Tel: (519) 653-6500   Rev: $340

Bus: *Mfr. automated production and test*   Fax: (519) 653-6533   Emp: 3,400
     systems.   www.atsautomation.com

ACCU-FAB SYSTEMS INC.

2121 NE Jack London Street, Corvallis, OR   97333

CEO: Bill Robinson   Tel: (541) 758-3329

Bus: *Mfr. automated production and*   Fax: (541) 758-3072
     test systems.

ATS CAROLINA

PO Box 12650, Rock Hill, SC   29731

CEO: Klaus D. Woerner, CEO   Tel: (803) 324-9300   %FO: 100

Bus: *Mfr. automated production and*   Fax: (803) 324-9360
     test systems.

ATS MICHIGAN SALES & SERVICE INC.

7060 Kensington Road, Brighton, MI   48116

CEO: Klaus D. Woerner, CEO   Tel: (248) 446-5006

Bus: *Mfr. automated production and*   Fax: (248) 446-5007
     test systems.

ATS OHIO INC.

425 Enterprise Drive, Westerville, OH   43081

CEO: Klaus D. Woerner, CEO   Tel: (514) 888-2344

Bus: *Mfr. automated production and*   Fax: (614) 888-3875
     test systems.

ATS SYSTEMS CALIFORNIA, INC.

4763 Bennett Drive, Livermore, CA   94550

CEO: Klaus D. Woerner, CEO   Tel: (925) 606-2000

Bus: *Mfr. automated production and*   Fax: (925) 371-0798
     test systems.

ECO SNOW SYSTEMS, INC.

4935A Southfront Road, Livermore, CA   94550

CEO: Klaus D. Woerner, CEO   Tel: (925) 606-2000   %FO: 100

Bus: *Mfr. automated production and*   Fax: (925) 371-0798
     test systems.

● **BALLARD POWER SYSTEMS INC.**
9000 Glenlyon Parkway, Burnaby BC, V5J 5J9, Canada

CEO: Layle K. Smith, CEO	Tel: (604) 454-0900	Rev: $16
Bus: *Develops fuel cell power systems.*	Fax: (604) 454-4700	Emp: 500
	www.ballard.com	

   BALLARD POWER SYSTEMS CORPORATION
   12190 Tech Center Drive, Poway, CA   92064

CEO: Neil Otto, VP	Tel: (619) 679-3270	%FO: 100
Bus: *Provides fuel cell power systems.*	Fax: (619) 679-4901	

● **BANK OF MONTREAL**
119 St. Jacques, Montréal PQ, H2Y 1L6, Canada

CEO: Matthew W. Barrett, Chmn.	Tel: (514) 877-7373	Rev: $12,231
Bus: *Commercial banking services.*	Fax: (514) 877-7399	Emp: 33,200
	www.bom.com	

   BANK OF MONTREAL
   3 Times Square, New York, NY   10036

CEO: Sanjiv Tandon, SVP	Tel: (212) 758-6300	%FO: 100
Bus: *Commercial banking services.*	Fax: (212) 702-1193	

   HARRIS BANKCORP INC.
   111 West Monroe Street, Chicago, IL   60603

CEO: Alan G. McNally, Chmn.	Tel: (312) 461-2121	%FO: 100
Bus: *Commercial banking services.*	Fax: (312) 461-7385	

   HARRIS INVESTMENT MANAGEMENT CORP
   190 South LaSalle Street, Chicago, IL   60690-0755

CEO: Donald G. M. Coxe, Chmn.	Tel: (312) 461-5365	%FO: 100
Bus: *Investment management services.*	Fax: (312) 765-8160	

   HARRIS INVESTORS DIRECT, INC.
   111 West Monroe Avenue, Chicago, IL   60603

CEO: Rod Trautvetter, Pres.	Tel: (312) 461-6000	%FO: 100
Bus: *Investment services.*	Fax: (312) 461-5755	

● **BARRICK GOLD CORP.**
Royal Bank Plaza, 200 Bay Street, PO Box 119, Toronto ON, M5J 2J3, Canada

CEO: Randall Oliphant, Pres. & CEO	Tel: (416) 861-9911	Rev: $1,330
Bus: *Engaged in gold mining.*	Fax: (416) 861-2492	Emp: 4,300
	www.barrick.com	

BARRICK GOLDSTRIKE MINES, INC.
801 Pennsylvania Avenue NW, Ste. 730, Washington, DC   20004
CEO: Michael J. Brown, VP   Tel: (202) 638-0026   %FO: 100
Bus: *U.S. representative office.*   Fax: (202) 638-7787

HOMESTAKE MINING COMPANY
1600 Riviera Avenue, Walnut Creek, CA   94546-3568
CEO: Jack E. Thompson, CEO   Tel: (925) 817-1300   %FO: 100
Bus: *Engaged in mining of precious*   Fax: (925) 746-0563
metals.

● BATA LIMITED
59 Wynford Drive, North York, Don Mills ON, M3C 1K3, Canada
CEO: Rino Rizzo, Pres.   Tel: (416) 446-2020
Bus: *Mfr./sale/distribution of children's*   Fax: (416) 443-8861
shoes, athletic and seasonal footwear,   www.toronto.bata.com
industrial boots and casual and dress
shoes.

BATA SHOE COMPANY INC.
4501 Pulaski Highway, Belcamp, MD   21017
CEO: David Talbot, Pres.   Tel: (410) 272-2000   %FO: 100
Bus: *Rubber, canvas and plastic*   Fax: (410) 272-3346
footwear.

● BCE INC.
1000 rue de la Gauchtière Quest, Bureau 3700 Montréal PQ, H3B 4Y7, Canada
CEO: Jean C. Monty, Pres. & CEO   Tel: (514) 870-8777   Rev: $18,094
Bus: *Provides communications and*   Fax: (514) 870-5424   Emp: 55,000
telecommunications services.   www.bce.com

CGI USA
600 Federal Street, Andover, MA   01810
CEO: Luc Pinard, VP   Tel: (978) 682-5500   %FO: 100
Bus: *Information technology services.*   Fax: (978) 686-0130

● BENTALL CORPORATION
1055 Dunsmuir Street, Ste. 1800, PO Box 49001, Vancouver BC, V7X 1B1, Canada
CEO: Mark Shuparski, Pres.   Tel: (604) 661-5000
Bus: *Real estate development services.*   Fax: (604) 661-5055   Emp: 150
www.bentall.com

BENTALL US PARTNERS
320 108th Avenue NE, Ste. 200, Bellevue, WA   98004
CEO: Gary Carpenter, CEO   Tel: (425) 643-4300   %FO: 100
Bus: *Real estate development services.*   Fax: (425) 643-7215

• BERNARD CALLEBAUT CHOCOLATERIE
1313 First Street SE, Calgary AB, T2G 5L1, Canada
CEO: Bernard Callebaut, Chmn. & Pres.   Tel: (403) 265-5777
Bus: *High quality confectioner and artisan*   Fax: (403) 265-7738
chocolatier.   www.bernardcallebaut.com

BERNARD C. CHOCOLATERIE
73-655 El Paseo, Ste. J, Palm Desert, CA   92260
CEO: JoAnn Van Valkenburg, Mgr.   Tel: (760) 341-8558   %FO: 100
Bus: *High quality, decorative*   Fax: (760) 773-0388
chocolates.

BERNARD C. CHOCOLATERIE
2820 S. Alma School Road, Bashas' Plaza, Chandler, AZ   85248
CEO: Murray Kuzek   Tel: (602) 855-1000   %FO: 100
Bus: *High quality, decorative*   Fax: (602) 855-1001
chocolates.

BERNARD C. CHOCOLATERIE
Sunset Corners, 825 South Waukegan Road, Lake Forest, IL   60045
CEO: Helen Shum, Mgr.   Tel: (847) 283-9927   %FO: 100
Bus: *High quality, decorative*   Fax: (847) 283-9928
chocolates.

BERNARD C. CHOCOLATERIE
440 - 5th Street, Lake Oswego, OR   97034
CEO: Ron Cameron   Tel: (503) 675-7500   %FO: 100
Bus: *High quality, decorative*   Fax: (503) 675-0500
chocolates.

• BID.COM INTERNATIONAL INC.
6725 Airport Road, Ste. 201, Mississauga ON, L4V 1V2, Canada
CEO: Jeffrey Lymburner, Pres. & CEO   Tel: (905) 6727467   Rev: $8
Bus: *Markets site-hosting services and*   Fax: (905) 672-5705   Emp: 62
auction systems to corporations.   www.bid.com

BID.COM INTERNATIONAL INC.
980 Ninth Street, 16th Fl., Sacramento, CA   95814-2736
CEO: J. Austin Ice, Mgr.   Tel: (916) 449-9531   %FO: 100
Bus: *Markets site-hosting services and*   Fax: (916) 449-9531
auction systems to corporations.

BID.COM INTERNATIONAL INC.
11 Penn Plaza, Ste. 5029, New York, NY   10001
CEO: Scott Lewis, Dir.   Tel: (212) 946-2895   %FO: 100
Bus: *Markets site-hosting services and*   Fax: (212) 946-2895
auction systems to corporations.

• BOMBARDIER INC.

800 René-Lévesque Blvd., Montréal PQ, H3N 1Y8, Canada

CEO: Robert E. Brown, Pres.	Tel: (514) 861-9481	Rev: $9,420
Bus: *Civil aerospace; mfr. diesel electric locomotives, engines; water, snow craft; defense systems and lease financing.*	Fax: (514) 861-7053 www.bombardier.com	Emp: 56,000

BOMBARDIER AEROSPACE

2400 Aviation Way, Bridgeport, WV   26330

CEO: Troy Jonas, VP	Tel: (304) 842-6300	%FO: 100
Bus: *Refurbishing center for civil and military aircraft.*	Fax: (304) 842-3632	

BOMBARDIER CAPITAL

261 Mountain View Drive, Colchester, VT   05446

CEO: William Crowe, VP	Tel: (802) 654-8100	%FO: 100
Bus: *Financing and leasing services.*	Fax: (802) 654-8421	

BOMBARDIER MOTOR CORPORATION OF AMERICA

6545 US Highway 1, Grant, FL   32949

CEO: Henri Lonski, Pres.	Tel: (321) 722-4000	%FO: 100
Bus: *Sales/distribution of diesel electric locomotives and engines.*	Fax: (321) 722-4039	

BOMBARDIER TRANSIT CORPORATION

101 Park Avenue, Ste. 2609, New York, NY   10178

CEO: Peter Stangl, Pres.	Tel: (212) 682-5860	%FO: 100
Bus: *Defense systems and lease financing.*	Fax: (212) 682-5767	

LEARJET INC.

One Learjet Way, Wichita, KS   67277

CEO: James Ziegler, VP	Tel: (316) 946-2000	%FO: 100
Bus: *Mfr. executive aircraft.*	Fax: (316) 946-5767	

• BROOKFIELD COMMERCIAL PROPERTIES, LTD.

181 Bay Street, Ste. 4300, PO Box 739, Toronto ON, M5J 2T3, Canada

CEO: J. Bruce Flatt, Pres. & CEO	Tel: (416) 369-8200	Rev: $1,825
Bus: *Develops commercial and retail real estate.*	Fax: (416) 369-0973 www.brookfield.ca	Emp: 2,500

BROOKFIELD HOMES

5960 Inglewood Drive, Ste. 200, Pleasanton, CA   94588

CEO: John Ryan, Pres.	Tel: (925) 463-2600	
Bus: *Develop commercial and retail real estate.*	Fax: (925) 227-8740	

BROOKFIELD HOMES

12865 Point Del Mar Way, Ste. 200, Del Mar, CA   92014

CEO: Steve Doyle, Pres.   Tel: (858) 481-8500   %FO: 100

Bus: *Develop commercial and retail*   Fax: (858) 481-9375
  real estate.

COSCAN WASHINGTON INC.

8521 Leesburg Pike, Vienna, VA   22182

CEO: Robert C. Hubbell, Pres.   Tel: (703) 356-9090   %FO: 100

Bus: *Develop commercial and retail*   Fax: (703) 442-4828
  real estate.

COSCAN WATERWAYS, INC.

20803 Biscayne Blvd., Ste. 103, Aventura, FL   33180

CEO: Al Piazza, Pres.   Tel: (305) 935-0255

Bus: *Develop commercial and retail*   Fax: (305) 932-9870
  real estate.

● **BURNTSAND INC.**

1075 West Georgia Street, Ste. 1500, Vancouver BC, V6E 3C9, Canada

CEO: Paul Berten, CEO   Tel: (604) 608-6400   Rev: $48

Bus: *Engaged in e-commerce and consulting.*   Fax: (604) 608-6412   Emp: 400
                                   www.burntsand.com

BURNTSAND INC.

333 West San Carlos Street, Ste. 1250, San Jose, CA   95110

CEO: Joseph Garappolo, VP   Tel: (408) 271-0200   %FO: 100

Bus: *Engaged in e-commerce and*   Fax: (408) 271-0230
  consulting.

BURNTSAND INC.

1010 Lamar Street, Ste. 400, Houston, TX   77002

CEO: Marc Karstaedt, VP   Tel: (713) 890-8000   %FO: 100

Bus: *Engaged in e-commerce and*   Fax: (713) 890-8001
  consulting.

BURNTSAND INC.

S17 Route One South, Ste. 5600, Iselin, NJ   08830

CEO: Markus Luft, VP   Tel: (732) 404-9400   %FO: 100

Bus: *Engaged in e-commerce and*   Fax: (732) 404-1400
  consulting.

● **CAE INC.**

Royal Bank Plaza, Ste. 3060, PO Box 30, Toronto ON, M5J 2J1, Canada

CEO: Derek H. Burney, Pres. & CEO   Tel: (416) 865-0070   Rev: $803

Bus: *Mfr. flight simulators, training services,*   Fax: (416) 865-0337   Emp: 6,100
  forest product machinery and equipment. www.cae.ca

CAE RANSOHOFF INC.
4933 Provident Drive, Cincinnati, OH   45246
CEO: John E. Caldwell, Pres.   Tel: (513) 870-0100
Bus: *Mfr. flight simulators, training*   Fax: (513) 870-1781
    services, rail equipment service,
    forest product machinery &
    equipment.

CAE USA, INC.
4908 Tampa West Blvd., Tampa, FL   33634
CEO: John Lenyo, CEO   Tel: (813) 885-7481   %FO: 100
Bus: *Mfr. flight simulators.*   Fax: (813) 887-1419

● **CAISSE DE DÉPÔT ET PLACEMENT DU QUÉBEC**
1981 Avenue McGill College, Montréal PQ, H3A 3C7, Canada
CEO: Jean-Claude Scraire, CEO   Tel: (514) 842-3261
Bus: *Engaged in private investment and real*   Fax: (514) 8472498
    estate management.   www.lacaisse.com

    BENTALL US, INC.
    320 108th Avenue NE, Ste. 200, Bellevue, WA   98004
    CEO: Gary J. Carpenter, COO   Tel: (425) 643-4300   %FO: 100
    Bus: *Engaged in property management*   Fax: (425) 643-7215
        and leasing.

    BENTALL US, INC.
    7755 Centre Avenue, Ste. 845, Huntington Beach, CA   92647
    CEO: Kit Royer   Tel: (714) 894-5569   %FO: 100
    Bus: *Engaged in property management*   Fax: (714) 373-5348
        and leasing.

● **CAMBIOR, INC.**
1111 St. Charles St. West, Ste. 750, Longueuil PQ, J4K 5G4, Canada
CEO: Louis P. Gignac, Pres. & CEO   Tel: (405) 677-0040   Rev: $209
Bus: *Engaged in gold exploration.*   Fax: (405) 677-3382   Emp: 1,600
                                       www.cambior.com

    CAMBIOR USA INC.
    1315 Greg Street, Ste. 110, Sparks, NV   89431
    CEO: Louis P. Gignac, Pres. & CEO Tel: (775) 351-1116
    Bus: *Gold exploration.*   Fax: (775) 351-1119

    CAMBIOR USA INC.
    8101 East Prentice Avenue, Ste. 800, Englewood, CO   80111
    CEO: Gary Parkison   Tel: (303) 694-4936
    Bus: *US headquarters location.*   Fax: (303) 773-0733

● **THE CANADA LIFE ASSURANCE COMPANY**
330 University Avenue, Toronto ON, M5G IR8, Canada
CEO: David A. Nield, Pres. & CEO   Tel: (416) 597-1456   Rev: $3,655
Bus: *Provides insurance services.*   Fax: (416) 597-3892
                                              www.canadalife.com

    THE CANADA LIFE ASSURANCE COMPANY OF AMERICA
    6201 Power Ferry Road, PO Box 105087, Atlanta, GA   30348
    CEO: Ron Beetam, VP   Tel: (770) 953-1959   %FO: 100
    Bus: *Provides insurance services.*   Fax: (770) 953-1959

● **CANADIAN IMPERIAL BANK OF COMMERCE (CIBC)**
Commerce Court, 25 King Street, Toronto ON, M5L 1A2, Canada
CEO: John S. Hunkin, Chmn. & CEO   Tel: (416) 980-2210   Rev: $15,184
Bus: *General banking services.*   Fax: (416) 980-5026   Emp: 44,215
                                              www.cibc.com

    CANADIAN IMPERIAL BANK OF COMMERCE.
    *425 Lexington Avenue, New York, NY   10017
    CEO: Paul D. Rogers, CEO   Tel: (212) 667-7000   %FO: 100
    Bus: *Commercial & investment*   Fax: (212) 885-4936   Emp: 300
    banking, securities brokerage &
    asset management services.

● **CANADIAN MEDICAL LABORATORIES LIMITED**
1644 Almco Blvd., Mississauga ON, L4W 2V2, Canada
CEO: Dr. John D. Mull, CEO   Tel: (905) 565-0043   Rev: $124
Bus: *Engaged in diagnostic laboratory*   Fax: (905) 565-1776   Emp: 1,300
services, trials and studies.   www.canmedlab.com

    SUMMIT RESEARCH NETWORK, C/O
    PACIFIC NORTHWEST CLINICAL RESEARCH CTR.
    1849 NW Kearney, Ste. 201, Portland, OR   97209
    CEO: Ward T. Smith, MD   Tel: (503) 228-2273   %FO: 100
    Bus: *Engaged in diagnostic and clinical*   Fax: (503) 228-2273
    research studies.

● **CANADIAN NATIONAL RAILWAY COMPANY**
935 de la Gauchetiére Street West, Montréal PQ, H3B 2M9, Canada
CEO: Paul M. Tellier, Pres. & CEO   Tel: (514) 399-5430   Rev: $3,620
Bus: *Railway & intermodal transportation,*   Fax: (514) 399-5586   Emp: 17,200
telecommunications.   www.cn.ca

CANADIAN NATIONAL ILLINOIS CENTRAL
720 North President, Ste. 200, Jackson, MS 39202
CEO: Terry McManaman, VP   Tel: (601) 592-1866   %FO: 100
Bus: *Operates freight railroad.*   Fax: (601) 592-1966

CANADIAN NATIONAL ILLINOIS CENTRAL
455 North Cityfront Plaza Drive, Chicago, IL 60611-5504
CEO: Ed Harris, VP   Tel: (312) 755-7500   %FO: 100
Bus: *Operates freight railroad.*   Fax: (312) 755-7839

CANADIAN NATIONAL RAILWAY COMPANY
2800 Livernois Avenue, Ste. 300, Troy, MI 48083-1222
CEO: John Fenton, Mgr.   Tel: (248) 740-6000   %FO: 100
Bus: *Holding company.*   Fax: (248) 740-6276

● **CANADIAN PACIFIC LTD.**
1800 Bankers Hall East, 855 Second Street SW, Calgary AL, T2P 4Z5, Canada
CEO: David P. O'Brien, Chmn.   Tel: (403) 218-8000   Rev: $10,737
Bus: *Transportation, waste services, energy,*   Fax: (403) 218-8005   Emp: 43,152
real estate, hotels, telecommunications.   www.cp.com

    CANADIAN PACIFIC RAILWAY
    105 South Fifth Street, Minneapolis, MN 55402
    CEO: Robert J. Ritchie, Pres.   Tel: (612) 347-8000   %FO: 100
    Bus: *Transportation & real estate*   Fax: (612) 347-8000   Emp: 4,500
    services.

● **CANADIAN TECHNICAL TAPE LTD.**
455 Cote Vertu, Montréal PQ, H4N 1E8, Canada
CEO: Leonard Cohen, Pres.   Tel: (514) 334-1510
Bus: *Mfr. pressure sensitive tape.*   Fax: (514) 745-0764   Emp: 600
    www.cantechtape.com

    CANTECH INDUSTRIES INC.
    2222 Eddie Williams Drive, Johnson City, TN 37601
    CEO: George Schneider, Mgr.   Tel: (423) 928-8331   %FO: 100
    Bus: *Mfr. pressure sensitive tapes.*   Fax: (423) 928-0311   Emp: 60

● **CANFOR CORPORATION**
2900-1055 Dunsmuir Street, Bentall Postal Sta., Vancouver BC, V7X 1B5, Canada
CEO: David L. Emerson, CEO   Tel: (604) 661-5241   Rev: $1,512
Bus: *Producer of softwood lumber and*   Fax: (604) 661-5235   Emp: 6,575
market pulp.   www.canfor.com

CANFOR (USA) CORPORATION
4395 Curtis Road, Bellingham, WA   98225
CEO: George Layton, Mng. Dir.   Tel: (360) 647-2434   %FO: 100
Bus: *Mfr. pulp, paper, wood products.*   Fax: (360) 647-2437

● CANWEST GLOBAL COMMUNICATIONS CORP.
3100 TD Centre, 201 Portage Avenue, Winnipeg MN, R3B 3L7, Canada
CEO: Leonard J. Asper, CEO   Tel: (204) 956-2025   Rev: $497
Bus: *Engaged in media and*   Fax: (204) 947-9841   Emp: 720
telecommunications; internet, TV and   www.canwestglobal.com
newspapers.

FIREWORKS TELEVISION
421 South Beverly Drive, 7th Fl., Beverly Hills, CA   90212
CEO: Robb Dalton   Tel: (310) 789-4700   %FO: 100
Bus: *Engaged in television production.*   Fax: (310) 789-4799

LIFESERV CORPORATION
1440 N. Dayton Street, Ste. 100, Chicago, IL   60622
CEO: Rob Reynolds, Pres.   Tel: (312) 573-0343   %FO: JV
Bus: *Engaged in web powered services.*   Fax: (312) 573-0468

● CASCADES INC.
404 Marie-Victorin Blvd., PO Box 30, Kingsey Falls PQ, J0A 1B0, Canada
CEO: Laurent Lemaire, Pres. & CEO   Tel: (819) 363-5100   Rev: $1,808
Bus: *Mfr. paper and packaging products and*   Fax: (819) 363-5155   Emp: 12,000
boxboard sheeting.   www.cascades.com

CASCADES INC.
2255 Global Way, Hebron, KY   41048
CEO: Alain Lemaire, EVP   Tel: (606) 586-1100   %FO: 100
Bus: *Mfr. paper and packaging*   Fax: (606) 334-6941
products.

CASCADES PAPERBOARD DIV.
8700 Larkin Road, Savage, MD   29763
CEO: Alain Lemaire, EVP   Tel: (410) 724-5130   %FO: 100
Bus: *Mfr. and distribution of boxboard*   Fax: (410) 888-9048
sheeting.

● CCL INDUSTRIES INC.
105 Gordon Baker Rd, Willowdale ON, M2H 3P8, Canada
CEO: Donald G. Lang, Pres. & CEO   Tel: (416) 756-8500   Rev: $1,060
Bus: *Mfr. cleaning and sanitation products,*   Fax: (416) 391-5558   Emp: 7,300
paints, toilet preparations.   www.cclind.com

CCL CONTAINER, INC.
One Llodio Drive, Hermitage, PA   16148
CEO: Samuel Ragusa, VP
Bus: *Mfr. aluminum and aerosol containers.*

Tel: (724) 981-4420
Fax: (724) 342-1116

CCL LABEL, INC.
6133 North River Road, Ste. 500, Rosemont, IL   60018
CEO: Christine A. Schaefer, Dir.
Bus: *Mfr. labels.*

Tel: (847) 773-8888
Fax: (847) 773-8004

%FO: 100

● **CELESTICA INC.**
12 Concorde Place, 7th Fl. Toronto ON, M3C 3R8, Canada
CEO: Eugene V. Polistuk, Pres. & CEO
Bus: *Engaged in providing services to electronics computer manufacturers.*

Tel: (416) 448-2200
Fax: (416) 448-5527
www.celestica.com

Rev: $3,250
Emp: 14,000

CELESTICA INC.
20 Alpha Road, Chelmsford, MA   01824
CEO: J. Marvin MaGee, Pres.
Bus: *Engaged in providing services to electronics computer manufacturers.*

Tel: (978) 250-3100
Fax: (978) 250-3180

%FO: JV

CELESTICA INC.
4701 Technology Parkway, Ft. Collins, CO   80525
CEO: J. Marvin MaGee, Pres.
Bus: *Engaged in providing services to electronics computer manufacturers.*

Tel: (970) 207-5000
Fax:

%FO: JV

CELESTICA INC.
72 Pease Boulevard, Newington, NH   03801
CEO: J. Marvin MaGee, Pres.
Bus: *Engaged in providing services to electronics computer manufacturers.*

Tel: (603) 334-4000
Fax: (603) 334-4300

%FO: JV

● **CGI GROUP INC.**
1130 Sherbrooke Street West, 5th Fl., Montréal PQ, H3A 2M8, Canada
CEO: Serge Godin, CEO
Bus: *Engaged in information technology services.*

Tel: (514) 841-3200
Fax: (514) 841-3299
www.cgi.ca

Rev: $956
Emp: 10,000

CGI GROUP INC.
One Penn Plaza, Ste. 3415, New York, NY   10119
CEO: Pierre Turcotte, SVP Tel: (212) 268-2727 %FO: 100
Bus: *Engaged in information* Fax: (212) 971-0746
technology services.

CGI GROUP INC.
One Jenner, Ste. 200, Irvine, CA   92618
CEO: Ken Dickinson, SVP Tel: (949) 341-0444 %FO: 100
Bus: *Engaged in information* Fax: (949) 341-0480
technology services.

CGI GROUP INC.
1225 North Loop West, Ste. 825, Houston, TX   77008
CEO: Ken Dickinson, SVP Tel: (713) 868-5537 %FO: 100
Bus: *Engaged in information* Fax: (713) 868-4014
technology services.

● **CHANGEPOINT CORPORATION**
1595 16th Avenue, Ste. 700, Richmond Hill ON, L4B 3N9, Canada
CEO: Gerald W. Smith, CEO Tel: (905) 886-7000 Rev: $6
Bus: *Mfr. software for information* Fax: (905) 886-7023 Emp: 150
technology solutions. www.changepoint.com

CHANGEPOINT CORPORATION
9700 Higgins Road, Ste. 500, Rosemont, IL   60018
CEO: Gerald W. Smith, Pres. Tel: (847) 993-1400 %FO: 100
Bus: *Mfr. software for information* Fax:
technology solutions.

● **CIRQUE DU SOLEIL INC.**
8400 Second Avenue, Montréal PQ, H1Z 4M6, Canada
CEO: Guy Laliberté, CEO Tel: (514) 722-2324 Rev: $327
Bus: *Cirque Du Soleil (Circus of the Sun) is* Fax: (514) 722-3692 Emp: 2,100
a circus art performance troupe. www.cirquedusoleil.com

CIRQUE DU SOLEIL INC.
3600 Las Vegas Boulevard South, Las Vegas, NV   89109
CEO: Guy Laliberte, Pres. Tel: (702) 693-7790 %FO: 100
Bus: *Cirque Du Soleil (Circus of the* Fax: (702) 693-7768
Sun) is a circus art performance
troupe.

● **CLARICA LIFE INSURANCE COMPANY**
227 King Street South, Waterloo ON, N2J 4C5, Canada

CEO: Robert M. Astley, Pres. & CEO   Tel: (519) 888-2290   Rev: $3,804

Bus: *Provides individual and group*   Fax: (519) 888-2171   Emp: 7,500
insurance, investment solutions and   www.clarica.com
retirement plans.

     CLARICA LIFE INSURANCE COMPANY
     13890 Bishop's Drive, Ste. 300, Brookfield, WI   53005

     CEO: Ronald Butkiewicz, Pres. & CEO   Tel: (262) 797-3900   %FO: 100

     Bus: *Provides life insurance products*   Fax: (262) 797-3919
     and services.

● **CLEARLY CANADIAN BEVERAGE CORPORATION**
1820-999 W. Hastings Street Vancouver BC, V6C 2W2, Canada

CEO: Douglas L. Mason, CEO   Tel: (604) 683-0312   Rev: $29

Bus: *Mfr. beverages.*   Fax: (604) 683-2256   Emp: 120
     www.clearly.ca

     CC BEVERAGE CORPORATION
     PO Box 326, Burlington, WA   98233

     CEO: James J. Duffy, Pres.   Tel: (360) 757-4441   %FO: 100

     Bus: *Mfr. beverages.*   Fax: (360) 757-4441

● **COGNICASE INC.**
111 Duke Street, 9th Fl., Montréal PQ, H3C 2M1, Canada

CEO: Ronald Brisebois, CEO   Tel: (514) 228-8888   Rev: $192

Bus: *Engaged in information technology;*   Fax: (514) 228-8959   Emp: 3,800
consulting and systems integration   www.cognicase.ca
services.

     COGNICASE INC.
     25 Independence Boulevard, Warren, NJ   07059

     CEO: Ron Sedwin, Sales   Tel: (908) 542-1000   %FO: 100

     Bus: *Engaged in information*   Fax: (908) 542-0100
     technology; consulting and
     systems integration services.

● **COGNOS INCORPORATED**
3755 Riverside Drive, PO Box 9707, Ottawa ON, K1G 4K9, Canada

CEO: Renato Zambonini, CEO   Tel: (613) 738-1440   Rev: $386

Bus: *Development/marketing computer*   Fax: (613) 738-0002   Emp: 2,150
software.   www.cognos.com

COGNOS CORPORATION
Two Meridian Crossing, Ste. 330, Richfield, MN   55423

CEO: Bill Steele	Tel: (612) 367-2800	%FO: 100
Bus: *Marketing/sales computer software.*	Fax: (612) 866-4822	

COGNOS CORPORATION
67 South Bedford Street, Ste. 1005, Burlington, MA   01803-5164

CEO: Nancy DeFilippis	Tel: (781) 229-6600	%FO: 100
Bus: *Marketing/sales computer software.*	Fax: (781) 229-9844	Emp: 205

COGNOS CORPORATION
4675 McArthur Court, Ste. 300, Newport Beach, CA   92660

CEO: Brenna Ryan	Tel: (949) 471-6100	%FO: 100
Bus: *Marketing/sales computer software.*	Fax: (949) 471-6199	

COGNOS CORPORATION
908 Blue Heron Drive, Highland, MI   48357

CEO: Dean Dolley	Tel: (248) 889-8020	%FO: 100
Bus: *Marketing/sales computer software.*	Fax: (248) 889-8021	

COGNOS CORPORATION
One Penn Plaza, Ste. 2115, New York, NY   10119

CEO: Julie Cortes	Tel: (212) 548-8300	%FO: 100
Bus: *Marketing/sales computer software.*	Fax: (212) 548-8399	

COGNOS CORPORATION
6155 South Jericho Court, Aurora, CO   80016

CEO: Michael Tagtow	Tel: (303) 627-9432	%FO: 100
Bus: *Marketing/sales computer software.*	Fax: (303) 627-4883	

COGNOS CORPORATION
425 North Martindale, Ste. 930, Schaumburg, IL   60173

CEO: Dave King	Tel: (847) 240-5222	%FO: 100
Bus: *Marketing/sales computer software.*	Fax: (847) 240-0252	

COGNOS CORPORATION
405 Sherrin Avenue, Louisville, KY   40207

CEO: Kim Smith	Tel: (502) 896-2673	%FO: 100
Bus: *Marketing/sales computer software.*	Fax: (502) 896-2673	

COGNOS CORPORATION

5181 Natorp Boulevard, Ste. 210, Mason, OH   45040

CEO: Carrie Leonardo	Tel: (513) 229-2700	%FO: 100
Bus: *Marketing/sales computer software.*	Fax: (513) 229-0300	

COGNOS CORPORATION

668 North 44th Street, Ste. 300, Phoenix, AZ   85008

CEO: Tom Mokry	Tel: (602) 685-1115	%FO: 100
Bus: *Marketing/sales computer software.*	Fax: (602) 685-1116	

COGNOS CORPORATION

400 Interstate N. Parkway, Ste. 770, Atlanta, GA   30339-5017

CEO: Mairin Friday	Tel: (770) 951-0294	%FO: 100
Bus: *Marketing/sales computer software.*	Fax: (770) 956-1698	

COGNOS CORPORATION

10900 NE 4th Street, Ste. 1030, Bellevue, WA   98004

CEO: Brenna Ryan	Tel: (425) 698-6400	%FO: 100
Bus: *Marketing/sales computer software.*	Fax: (425) 451-2963	

COGNOS CORPORATION

2020 Main Street, Ste. 750, Irving, TX   92614

CEO: Brenna Ryan	Tel: (972) 556-1122	%FO: 100
Bus: *Marketing/sales computer software.*	Fax: (972) 556-1004	

● **COMINCO LTD.**

500-200 Burrard Street, Vancouver BC, V6C 3L7, Canada

CEO: David A. Thompson, CEO	Tel: (604) 682-0611	Rev: $1,251
Bus: *Mining, smelting, refining mineral exploration .*	Fax: (604) 685-3019	Emp: 5,125
	www.cominco.com	

COMINCO AMERICAN INC.

15918 East Euclid Avenue, Spokane, WA   99220-3087

CEO: Jeffrey Clark	Tel: (509) 747-6111	%FO: 100
Bus: *Base metal mining.*	Fax: (509) 459-4400	

● **COMPUTALOG LTD., DIV. PRECISION DRILLING**

150-6th Avenue SW, Ste. 4500, Calgary AB, T2P 3Y7, Canada

CEO: Hank B. Swartout, CEO	Tel: (403) 265-6060	Rev: $60
Bus: *Engaged in oil and gas exploration.*	Fax: (403) 218-2424	Emp: 1,050
	www.computalog.com	

COMPUTALOG INC.
500 Winscott Road, Ft. Worth, TX   76126
CEO: Marlene McPeek, Sales   Tel: (817) 249-7200   %FO: 100
Bus: *Engaged in oil and gas*   Fax: (817) 249-7284
      exploration.

• CONSUMERS PACKAGING INC.
777 Kipling Avenue, Toronto ON, M8Z 5Z4, Canada
CEO: Brent Ballantyne, CEO   Tel: (416) 232-3000   Rev: $1,029
Bus: *Mfr. bottles and jars for food and*   Fax: (416) 232-3378   Emp: 2,400
beverage production.   www.consumersglass.com

ANCHOR GLASS INC.
4343 Anchor Plaza Parkway, Tampa, FL   33634
CEO: Rick Deneau, Pres.   Tel: (813) 884-0000   %FO: 100
Bus: *Mfr. bottles and jars for food and*   Fax: (813) 886-3456
beverage production.

• COOLBRANDS INTERNATIONAL INC. (FORMERLY YOGEN FRUZ WORLD-WIDE INC.)
8300 Woodbine Avenue, 5th Fl., Markham ON, L3R 9Y7, Canada
CEO: David J. Stein, Pres. & CEO   Tel: (905) 479-8762   Rev: $66
Bus: *Mfr. frozen yogurt deserts.*   Fax: (905) 479-5235   Emp: 420
    www.yogenfruz.com

COOLBRANDS INTERNATIONAL INC.
4175 Veteran's Hwy., 3rd Fl., Ronkonkoma, NY   11779
CEO: John Kaczynski, SVP   Tel: (631) 737-9700   %FO: 100
Bus: *Mfr. frozen ice cream deserts.*   Fax: (631) 737-9792

ESKIMO PIE CORPORATION
901 Moorefield Park Drive, Richmond, VA   23236
CEO: David B. Kewer, CEO   Tel: (804) 560-8400   %FO: 100
Bus: *Mfr. frozen ice cream deserts.*   Fax: (804) 330-3537

• CO-STEEL INC.
300 Consilium Place, Ste. 800, Toronto ON, M1H 3G2, Canada
CEO: Terry G. Newman, CEO   Tel: (416) 297-3700   Rev: $985
Bus: *Mfr. steel rod, bar and structural shapes.*   Fax: (416) 297-3740   Emp: 2,200
    www.costeel.com

CO-STEEL
PO Box 5341, Bethlehem, PA   18015
CEO: Gary Wright   Tel: (610) 954-7705
Bus: *Mfr. wire rod coils and steel rod,*   Fax: (610) 954-7750
bar & structural shapes.

CO-STEEL RARITAN INC.
225 Elm Street, PO Box 309, Perth Amboy, NJ   08862
CEO: Steve Gresham   Tel: (732) 442-1600   %FO: 100
Bus: *Mfr. wire rod coils and steel rod,*   Fax: (732) 442-3957   Emp: 485
 bar & structural shapes.

CO-STEEL SAYREVILLE
North Crossman Road, Sayreville, NJ   08871-0249
CEO: Bill Skeens, Mgr.   Tel: (732) 721-6600
Bus: *Mfr. wire rod coils and steel rod,*   Fax: (732) 721-8784
 bar & structural shapes.

GALLATIN STEEL
RR #1, Box 320, Ghent, KY   41045-9704
CEO: Don B. Daily, VP   Tel: (859) 567-3100
Bus: *Mfr. wire rod coils and steel rod,*   Fax: (859) 567-3169
 bar & structural shapes.

● COTT CORPORATION
207 Queen's Quay West, Ste. 800, Toronto ON, M5J 1A7, Canada
CEO: Frank E. Weise III, CEO   Tel: (416) 203-3898   Rev: $1,020
Bus: *Mfr. bottled and canned soft*   Fax: (416) 203-8268   Emp: 2,000
 drinks/carbonated waters.   www.cott.com

COTT BEVERAGES
5405 Cypress Center Drive, Ste. 100, Tampa, FL   33609
CEO: David G. Bluestein, Pres.   Tel: (813) 342-2500   %FO: 100
Bus: *US headquarters for soft drinks.*   Fax:

● COUNSEL CORPORATION
PO Box 435, 130 King Street West, Toronto ON, M5X 1E3, Canada
CEO: Allan Silber, CEO   Tel: (416) 866-3000   Rev: $35
Bus: *Engaged in e-commerce and*   Fax: (416) 866-3061   Emp: 1,200
 pharmaceuticals.   www.counselcorp.com

IBT TECHNOLOGIES, INC.
8601 FM 2222, Ste. 100, Austin, TX   78730-2326
CEO: Dr. William Cunningham, CEO   Tel: (512) 327-4899   %FO:
Bus: *Engaged in internet based and e-*   Fax: (512) 327-2643
 learning.

PROSCAPE TECHNOLOGIES, INC.
501 Office Center Drive, Fort Washington, PA   19034
CEO: Keith DeVault, VP Mktg.   Tel: (215) 540-8100   %FO:
Bus: *Develops, markets, and supports*   Fax: (215) 540-8117
 marketing and sales systems.

● **CSA INTERNATIONAL (CANADIAN STANDARDS ASSOCIATION)**

90 Burnhamthorpe Road West, Ste. 300, Mississauga ON, L5B 3C3, Canada

CEO: Rob M. Griffin, Pres. & CEO

Bus: *Engaged in national and international management system registration and certification.*

Tel: (905) 272-3920
Fax: (905) 272-3942
www.qmi.com

QMI, DIV. CSA INTL.

8501 East Pleasant Valley Road, Cleveland, OH 44131-5575

CEO: Jeanette Preston, Mgr.

Bus: *Engaged in national and international management system registration and certification.*

Tel: (216) 901-1911
Fax: (216) 520-8967

QMI, DIV. CSA INTL.

2805 Barranca Parkway, Irvine, CA 92606

CEO: Anna Hun, Mgr.

Bus: *Engaged in national and international management system registration and certification.*

Tel: (949) 733-4333
Fax: (949) 733-4316

QMI, DIV. CSA INTL.

900 West Sproul Road, Ste. 103, Springfield, PA 19064

CEO: Bud Cuthberg, Dir.

Bus: *Engaged in national and international management system registration and certification.*

Tel: (610) 544-7880
Fax: (610) 544-9682

● **CYBERPLEX INC.**

267 Richmond Street West, Toronto ON, M5V 3M6, Canada

CEO: William D. Hopkins, CEO

Bus: *Provides web site design and marketing and e-commerce solutions and services.*

Tel: (416) 597-8889
Fax: (416) 597-2345
www.cyberplex.com

Rev: $31
Emp: 315

CYBERPLEX INC.

15 Dartmouth Place, Boston, MA 02116

CEO: Christopher DeGrace

Bus: *Provides web site design and marketing and e-commerce solutions and services.*

Tel: (617) 859-9361
Fax: (617) 859-9363

%FO: 100

CYBERPLEX INC.

205 Liberty Square, Norwalk, CT 06855

CEO: Kim Konte

Bus: *Provides web site design and marketing and e-commerce solutions and services.*

Tel: (203) 299-0777
Fax: (203) 299-0898

%FO: 100

CYBERPLEX INC.
100 Shoreline Hwy., Ste. 100, Mill Valley, CA 94941
CEO: Bruce Randall   Tel: (415) 339-1830   %FO: 100
Bus: *Provides web site design and*   Fax: (415) 339-1979
  marketing and e-commerce
  solutions and services.

CYBERPLEX INC.
310 Washington Boulevard, Ste. 212, Marina Del Rey, CA 90292
CEO: Chris Vulovic   Tel: (310) 577-9119   %FO: 100
Bus: *Provides web site design and*   Fax: (310) 577-9109
  marketing and e-commerce
  solutions and services.

CYBERPLEX INC.
7000 North Mopac, Ste. 150, Austin, TX 78731
CEO: Paul Saper   Tel: (512) 795-3095   %FO: 100
Bus: *Provides web site design and*   Fax: (512) 343-6175
  marketing and e-commerce
  solutions and services.

• **DATAMIRROR CORPORATION**
3100 Steeles Avenue East, Ste. 700, Markham ON, L3R 8T3, Canada
CEO: Nigel Stokes, CEO   Tel: (905) 425-0310   Rev: $29
Bus: *Mfr. database software.*   Fax: (905) 415-0340   Emp: 270
                                         www.datamirror.com

   DATAMIRROR CORPORATION
  One Tower Lane, Ste. 1700, Oakbrook Terrace, IL 60181
  CEO: Dan Cipriano, Mgr.   Tel: (630) 573-2927   %FO: 100
  Bus: *Mfr. database software.*   Fax: (630) 954-0650

   DATAMIRROR CORPORATION
  90 Park Avenue, 16th Fl., New York, NY 10021
  CEO: Sam Webster, Mgr.   Tel: (212) 984-0608   %FO: 100
  Bus: *Mfr. database software.*   Fax: (212) 351-5098

• **DATAWAVE SYSTEMS, INC.**
101 West Fifth Avenue, Vancouver BC, V5Y 4A5, Canada
CEO: Josh Emanual, CEO   Tel: (604) 874-1302   Rev: $10
Bus: *Engaged in merchandising of prepaid* Fax: (604) 874-1503   Emp: 60
  phone cards.   www.datawave.ca

DATAWAVE SYSTEMS, INC.
231 West Parkway, Pompton Plains, NJ 07444
CEO: Ron Bozek, VP   Tel: (973) 839-9100   %FO: 100
Bus: *Engaged in merchandising of*   Fax: (973) 616-0022
prepaid phone cards.

• DAVIES, WARD, PHILLIPS & VINEBERG LLP
1 First Canadian Place, Toronto ON, M5X 1B1, Canada
CEO: William O'Reilly, CEO   Tel: (416) 863-0900
Bus: *International law firm.*   Fax: (416) 863-5573   Emp: 200

DAVIES, WARD, PHILLIPS & VINEBERG LLP
430 Park Avenue, 10th Fl., New York, NY 10022
CEO: Steven Levin, Ptnr.   Tel: (212) 308-8866   %FO: 100
Bus: *International law firm.*   Fax: (212) 308-0132

• DAYTON MINING CORPORATION
595 Burrard Street, Ste. 2393, Vancouver BC, V7X 1K8, Canada
CEO: William H. Myckatyn, CEO   Tel: (604) 662-8383   Rev: $36
Bus: *Engaged in mining.*   Fax: (604) 684-1329   Emp: 75
www.dayton-mining.com

DENTON RAWHIDE MINE, C/O KENNECOTT RAWHIDE MINING
PO Box 2070, Fallon, NV 89407
CEO: Kevin T. Hegerle, Gen. Mgr.   Tel: (775) 945-1015   %FO: 100
Bus: *Produces minerals and metals.*   Fax: (775) 945-1213   Emp: 185

• DECOMA INTERNATIONAL INC.
50 Casmir Court, Concord ON, L4K 4J5, Canada
CEO: Alan J. Power, CEO   Tel: (905) 669-2888   Rev: $353
Bus: *Mfr. exterior auto components.*   Fax: (905) 669-5075   Emp: 13,500
www.decoma.com

DECOMA CORPORATION
PO Box 1625, Troy, MI 48084-1625
CEO: Alan J. Power, Pres.   Tel: (248) 729-2600   %FO: 100
Bus: *Engaged in exterior systems*   Fax: (248) 729-2500
engineering.

• DELANO TECHNOLOGY CORPORATION
302 Town Centre Boulevard, Markham ON, L3R OE8, Canada
CEO: John Foresi, CEO   Tel: (905) 947-2222   Rev: $31
Bus: *Engaged in e-commerce.*   Fax: (905) 947-2120   Emp: 500
www.delanotech.com

DELANO TECHNOLOGY CORPORATION
550 W. Washington Blvd., Ste. 300, Chicago, IL   80237
CEO: James Wentzell, VP   Tel: (312) 985-5500   %FO: 100
Bus: *Engaged in e-commerce solutions.*   Fax: (312) 985-5550

DELANO TECHNOLOGY CORPORATION
4600 S. Syracuse St., 9th Fl., Denver, CO   80237
CEO: James Wentzell, VP   Tel: (303) 256-6230   %FO: 100
Bus: *Engaged in e-commerce solutions.*   Fax: (303) 256-6230

DELANO TECHNOLOGY CORPORATION
425 Market Street, San Francisco, CA   94105
CEO: James Wentzell, VP   Tel: (415) 955-2619   %FO: 100
Bus: *Engaged in e-commerce solutions.*   Fax: (415) 955-2619

DELANO TECHNOLOGY CORPORATION
250 West 34th Street, Ste. 3600, New York, NY   10119
CEO: James Wentzell, VP   Tel: (646) 756-2635   %FO: 100
Bus: *Engaged in e-commerce solutions.*   Fax: (646) 756-2633

DELANO TECHNOLOGY CORPORATION
7701 France Avenue S., Ste. 200, Edina, MN   55435
CEO: James Wentzell, VP   Tel: (763) 416-9015   %FO: 100
Bus: *Engaged in e-commerce solutions.*   Fax: (763) 416-9022

DELANO TECHNOLOGY CORPORATION
14785 Preston Road, Ste. 550, Dallas, TX   75240
CEO: James Wentzell, VP   Tel: (972) 789-5197   %FO: 100
Bus: *Engaged in e-commerce solutions.*   Fax: (972) 789-5168

DELANO TECHNOLOGY CORPORATION
116 Village Blvd., 2nd Fl., Princeton, NJ   08540
CEO: James Wentzell, VP   Tel: (609) 734-4307   %FO: 100
Bus: *Engaged in e-commerce solutions.*   Fax: (609) 734-4342

DELANO TECHNOLOGY, ANALYTICS DIV.
15721 College Boulevard, Lenexa, KS   66219
CEO: James Wentzell, VP   Tel: (913) 438-9444   %FO: 100
Bus: *Engaged in e-commerce solutions.*   Fax: (913) 438-9449

● **DENTECH PRODUCTS LTD.**
3168-262 Street, Langley BC, V4W 2Z6, Canada
CEO: Steve White, Pres.   Tel: (604) 856-0410
Bus: *Mfr. dental equipment.*   Fax: (604) 856-0424   Emp: 52
                                   www.dentechcorp.com

DENTECH CORPORATION
1835 Liberty Street, Lyden, WA   98264
CEO: Kelvin Lambright   Tel: (360) 354-3978   %FO: JV
Bus: *Assembly/sale dental equipment.*   Fax: (360) 318-1630   Emp: 45

• DERLAN INDUSTRIES LTD.
145 King Street East, Suite 500, Toronto ON, M5C 2Y7, Canada
CEO: Dermot G. Coughlin, Pres. & CEO   Tel: (416) 364-5852   Rev: $117
Bus: *Holding company.*   Fax: (416) 362-5334   Emp: 3,800
www.derlan.com

K&M ELECTRONICS INC.
11 Interstate Drive, West Springfield, MA   01089
CEO: John Marriott, Pres.   Tel: (413) 781-1350   %FO: 100
Bus: *Mfr. power supplies, lighting fixtures.*   Fax: (413) 737-0608   Emp: 500

• THE DESCARTES SYSTEMS GROUP INC.
120 Randall Drive, Waterloo ON, N2V 1C6, Canada
CEO: Peter J. Schwartz, CEO   Tel: (519) 746-8110   Rev: $67
Bus: *Mfr. supply chain management software.*   Fax: (519) 747-0082   Emp: 500
www.descartes.com

DESCARTES SYSTEMS GROUP
5959 West Century Blvd., Ste. 914, Los Angeles, CA   90045
CEO: Willen Galle, Pres.   Tel: (310) 337-0447   %FO: 100
Bus: *Mfr. supply chain management software.*   Fax: (310) 337-0575

DESCARTES SYSTEMS GROUP
2633 North Innsbruck Drive, Ste. D, St. Paul, MN   55112
CEO: Jae Young Choi, Pres.   Tel: (651) 633-4251   %FO: 100
Bus: *Mfr. supply chain management software.*   Fax: (651) 631-9029

DESCARTES SYSTEMS GROUP
6800 Jericho Turnpike, Ste. 120W, Syosset, NY   11791
CEO: Willen Galle, Pres.   Tel: (516) 393-5900   %FO: 100
Bus: *Mfr. supply chain management software.*   Fax: (516) 393-5900

DESCARTES SYSTEMS GROUP
200 Hightower Blvd., Pittsburgh, PA   15205-1123
CEO: Todd Handcock, Mgr.   Tel: (412) 788-2466   %FO: 100
Bus: *Mfr. supply chain management software.*   Fax: (412) 788-4821

DESCARTES SYSTEMS GROUP
1410 Spring Hill Road, Ste. 200, McLean, VA   22102-3008
CEO: Mel Steinke   Tel: (703) 790-8300   %FO: 100
Bus: *Mfr. supply chain management*   Fax: (703) 790-8333
     software.

TRANSETTLEMENT, DIV. DESCARTES
1745 Phoenix Boulevard, Ste. 470, Atlanta, GA   30349-5534
CEO: Joe Tenney, CEO   Tel: (770) 996-8109   %FO: 100
Bus: *Mfr. supply chain management*   Fax: (770) 996-8109
     software.

● **DOFASCO, INC.**
PO Box 2460, Hamilton ON, L8N 3J5, Canada
CEO: John Mayberry, Pres. & CEO   Tel: (905) 544-3761   Rev: $2,172
Bus: *Mfr. steel and steel products.*   Fax: (905) 545-3236   Emp: 7,360
                                   www.dofasco.ca

DOFASCO, U.S.A., INC.
26877 Northwest Hwy, Ste.104, Southfield, MI   48034-8431
CEO: David Black, Gen. Mgr.   Tel: (248) 357-3090   %FO: 100
Bus: *Mfr./sale steel and steel products.*   Fax: (248) 357-9888

GALLATIN STEEL COMPANY
Route One, Box 320, Ghent, KY   41045
CEO: Don B. Daily, VP & Gen. Mgr. Tel: (859) 567-3100   %FO: JV
Bus: *Mfr./sale steel and steel products.*   Fax: (859) 567-3169

● **DOREL INDUSTRIES INC.**
4750 Des Grandes Prairies, Montréal PQ, H1R 1A3, Canada
CEO: Martin Schwartz, Chmn.   Tel: (514) 523-5701   Rev: $800
Bus: *Mfr. general household furniture,*   Fax: (514) 523-5701   Emp: 3,800
     including juvenile furnishings.   www.dorel.com

AMERIWOOD INDUSTRIES
305 East South First Street, Wright City, MO   40283
CEO: Bob Klassen, Pres.   Tel: (636) 745-3351   %FO: 100
Bus: *Mfr. household furnishings,*   Fax: (636) 745-1007
     including juvenile furniture.

COSCO INC.
2525 State Street, Columbus, IN   47201
CEO: Nick Costides, Pres.   Tel: (812) 372-0141   %FO: 100
Bus: *Mfr. juvenile furniture & vehicles,*   Fax: (812) 372-0911   Emp: 1,100
     padded seats.

INFANTINO
9404 Cabot Drive, San Diego, CA   92126
CEO: Michael Silberstein, Pres.   Tel: (858) 689-1221   %FO: 100
Bus: *Mfr. juvenile soft goods and*   Fax: (858) 689-1099
      accessories.

SAFETY FIRST
45 Dan Road, Canton, MA   02021
CEO: Jeff Hale, VP   Tel: (781) 364-3100
Bus: *Mfr. juvenile car seats.*   Fax: (800) 723-3065

● **DYNACARE INC.**
20 Eglinton Avenue West, Toronto ON, M4R 2H1, Canada
CEO: Harvey A. Shapiro, CEO   Tel: (416) 487-1100   Rev: $353
Bus: *Engaged in clinical laboratory testing*   Fax: (416) 487-8769   Emp: 5,500
      services.   www.dynacare.com

   DYNACARE INC.
   1310 East Division Street, Mount Vernon, WA   98273
   CEO: Valary Woll, Sales   Tel: (360) 424-6137   %FO: 100
   Bus: *Engaged in clinical laboratory* Fax: (360) 416-2222
         testing services.

   DYNACARE INC.
   819 Boylston Avenue, 2nd Fl., Seattle, WA   98104
   CEO: David Anderson   Tel: (206) 386-2672   %FO: 100
   Bus: *Engaged in clinical laboratory* Fax: (206) 386-6009
         testing services.

   DYNACARE INC.
   3221 Third Avenue, South Birmingham, AL   35222
   CEO: Barbara Burkhart, Sales   Tel: (205) 251-4191   %FO: 100
   Bus: *Engaged in clinical laboratory* Fax: (205) 251-4250
         testing services.

   DYNACARE INC.
   1-31 North Flowood Drive, Jackson, MS   39208
   CEO: Martha Barrett, Sales   Tel: (601) 932-1333   %FO: 100
   Bus: *Engaged in clinical laboratory* Fax: (601) 932-1293
         testing services.

   DYNACARE INC.
   14900 Landmark Blvd., Ste. 200, Dallas, TX   75240
   CEO: Steve Ho, SVP   Tel: (972) 387-3200   %FO: 100
   Bus: *Engaged in clinical laboratory* Fax: (972) 387-3212
         testing services.

DYNACARE INC.
1101 Nott Street, Schenectady, NY   12303

CEO: Wendy Rosher, Sales

Bus: *Engaged in clinical laboratory testing services.*

Tel: (518) 243-4047
Fax: (518) 243-1443

%FO: 100

● DYNEGY CANADA INC.
350 Seventh Avenue SW, Ste. 2200, Calgary AB, T2P 3N9, Canada

CEO: Stephen W. Bergstrom, CEO

Bus: *Produces natural gas and services natural gas gathering & processing services, crude oil and electric power and related management services.*

Tel: (403) 213-6000
Fax: (403) 213-6005
www.dynegy.com

DYNEGY INC.
1000 Louisiana Street, Ste. 5800, Houston, TX   77002

CEO: Chuck Watson, Pres. & CEO

Bus: *Provides natural gas services.*

Tel: (713) 507-6400
Fax: (713) 507-6405

%FO: 100

● EMCO LTD.
620 Richmond Street, PO Box 5252, London ON, N6A 4L6, Canada

CEO: Douglas E. Speers, Pres. & CEO

Bus: *Mfr. fluid handling systems and equipment.*

Tel: (519) 645-3900
Fax: (519) 645-2465
www.emcoltd.com

Rev: $830
Emp: 3,000

METCRAFT INC
13910 Kessler Drive, Grandview, MO   64030

CEO: Steve McIlwaine, Pres.

Bus: *Stainless steel fabrication for institutional, commercial markets.*

Tel: (816) 761-3250
Fax: (816) 761-0544

%FO: 100
Emp: 60

● EMERA INC.
1894 Barrington Street, PO Box 910, Halifax NS, B3J 2W5, Canada

CEO: David Mann, CEO

Bus: *Engaged in energy services, oil, diesel fuel, gas and lubricants.*

Tel: (902) 428-6250
Fax: (902) 428-6181
www.emera.com

Rev: $598
Emp: 1,785

BANGOR HYDRO ELECTRIC COMPANY
PO Box 932, 33 State Street, Bangor, ME   04401

CEO: Bob Briggs, Pres.

Bus: *Provides electrical services.*

Tel: (207) 945-5621
Fax: (207) 947-2414

%FO: 100

● **ENBRIDGE PIPELINES, INC.**
3000 Fifth Ave. Place, 425 - 1st St. Southwest, Calgary AB, T2P 3L8, Canada
CEO: Patrick D. Daniel, CEO | Tel: (403) 231-3900 | Rev: $1,963
Bus: *Crude petroleum pipelines and natural* | Fax: (403) 231-3920 | Emp: 5,500
gas distribution and utility. | www.enbridge.com

    LAKEHEAD PIPELINE COMPANY
    21 West Superior Street, Duluth, MN 55802
    CEO: Denise Hamsher, Mgr. | Tel: (218) 725-0100 | %FO: 100
    Bus: *Crude petrol pipelines.* | Fax: (218) 725-0109 | Emp: 360

● **ENVOY COMMUNICATIONS GROUP, INC.**
26 Duncan Street, Toronto ON, M5V 2B9, Canada
CEO: Geoffrey B. Genovese, CEO | Tel: (416) 593-1212 | Rev: $39
Bus: *Provides full-services marketing and* | Fax: (416) 593-4434 | Emp: 300
advertising services. | www.envoygrp.com

    HAMPEL STEFANIDES, INC.
    111 Fifth Avenue, New York, NY 10003
    CEO: Brian Goodall, Pres. | Tel: (212) 677-5200 | %FO: 100
    Bus: *Provides advertising and* | Fax: (212) 677-5200
    marketing services.

● **EXCO TECHNOLOGIES LIMITED (ABSORBED TECSYN INTL INC.)**
130 Spy Court Markham ON, L3R 5H6, Canada
CEO: Brian A. Robbins, Pres. & CEO | Tel: (905) 477-3065 | Rev: $118
Bus: *Engaged in casting and extrusion* | Fax: (905) 477-2449 | Emp: 1,000
technology for automobile industry. | www.excocorp.com

    EDCO TOOL AND SUPPLY, INC.
    PO Box 4127, Toledo, OH 43609
    CEO: Sam Edelman | Tel: (419) 276-8181 | %FO: 100
    Bus: *Mfr. tools.* | Fax: (419) 276-8285

    TECSYN INC., DIV. EXCO
    PO Box 160430 Freeport Center Bldg. A-16-A, Clearfield, UT 84016-0430
    CEO: G. Wayne Corbett, Pres. | Tel: (801) 773-8756 | %FO: 100
    Bus: *Mfr. baler, tomato and industrial* | Fax: (801) 773-8664 | Emp: 100
    twines.

    TECSYN INC., DIV. EXCO
    4950 Gilmer Drive, Huntsville, AL 35805
    CEO: G. Wayne Corbett, Pres. | Tel: (256) 722-9092 | %FO: 100
    Bus: *Mfr. pressed powdered metal* | Fax: (256) 722-7939 | Emp: 12
    products.

● **EXTENDICARE INC.**

3000 Steeles Avenue, East Markham ON, L3R 9W2, Canada

CEO: Mel A. Rhinelander, CEO   Tel: (905) 470-4000   Rev: $1,200

Bus: *Operators of long-term care, medical*   Fax: (905) 470-5588   Emp: 38,800
specialty services, including subacute   www.extendicare.com
care and rehabilitative therapy services,
medical supplies and services.

EXTENDICARE HEALTH SERVICES, INC.

111 West Michigan Street, Milwaukee, WI   53203-2903

CEO: John G. McLaughlin, Pres.   Tel: (414) 908-8000   %FO: 100

Bus: *Operates nursing care centers,*   Fax: (414) 908-8059
retirement centers and
pharmaceutical services.

● **FAHNESTOCK VINER HOLDINGS INC.**

20 Eglinton Avenue West, Ste. 1110, PO Box 2015, Toronto ON, M4R 1K8, Canada

CEO: Albert G. Lowenthal, Chmn. & CEO   Tel: (416) 322-1515   Rev: $316

Bus: *Engaged in securities and trading.*   Fax: (416) 322-7007   Emp: 1,285
www.fahnestock.com

FAHNESTOCK & COMPANY INC.

7373 North Scottsdale Rd., Ste. B274, Scottsdale, AZ   85253

CEO: Albert G. Lowenthal, CEO   Tel: (480) 596-1211   %FO: 100

Bus: *Engaged in retail and discount*   Fax: (800) 253-6825
brokerage.

FAHNESTOCK & COMPANY INC.

601 Montgomery Street, Ste. 845, San Francisco, CA   94111

CEO: James D. Gerson, SVP   Tel: (415) 693-9301   %FO: 100

Bus: *Engaged in retail and discount*   Fax: (415) 693-9333
brokerage.

FAHNESTOCK & COMPANY INC.

125 Broad Street, New York, NY   10004

CEO: Albert G. Lowenthal, CEO   Tel: (212) 668-8000   %FO: 100

Bus: *Engaged in retail and discount*   Fax: (212) 943-8728
brokerage.

FAHNESTOCK & COMPANY INC.

501 St. Vrain Lane, Ste. 202, Estes Park, CO   80517

CEO: Albert G. Lowenthal, CEO   Tel: (970) 586-1895   %FO: 100

Bus: *Engaged in retail and discount*   Fax: (800) 800-9138
brokerage.

FAHNESTOCK ASSET MANAGEMENT

150 East 52nd Street, 29th Fl., New York, NY   10022

CEO: Craig Hutchison, Mng. Dir.   Tel: (212) 644-3200

Bus: *Asset management and investment*   Fax: (212) 486-1007
banking services.

FIRST OF MICHIGAN CORPORATION

300 River Place, Ste. 4000, Detroit, MI   48207

CEO: Lenore P. Denys, SVP   Tel: (313) 259-2600   %FO: 100

Bus: *Engaged in retail and discount*   Fax: (313) 259-7853
brokerage.

FREEDOM INVESTMENTS, INC.

11442 Miracle Hills Drive, Ste. 501, Omaha, NE   68154

CEO: Brewster Ellis, Pres.   Tel: (402) 431-8500

Bus: *Investment banking services.*   Fax: (402) 431-8563

● FAIRFAX FINANCIAL HOLDINGS LIMITED

95 Wellington Street West, Ste. 800, Toronto ON, M5J 2N7, Canada

CEO: V. Prem Watsa, Chmn. & CEO   Tel: (416) 367-4941   Rev: $5,788

Bus: *Engaged in life, property and casualty*   Fax: (416) 367-4946   Emp: 9,442
insurance and investment management.   www.fairfax.ca

CRUM & FORSTER HOLDINGS, INC.

305 Madison Avenue, Morristown, NJ   07960

CEO: Bruce A. Esselborn, CEO   Tel: (973) 490-6600   %FO: 100

Bus: *Engaged in insurance.*   Fax: (973) 490-6600

ODYSSEY AMERICA REINSURANCE CORP.

300 First Stamford Place, Stamford, CT   06902

CEO: Michael Wacek, CEO   Tel: (203) 977-8000   %FO: 100

Bus: *Engaged in reinsurance.*   Fax: (203) 940-8183

RANGER INSURANCE

PO Box 2807, Houston, TX   77252

CEO: Philip J. Broughton, Pres.   Tel: (713) 954-8100

Bus: *Engaged in property and casualty*   Fax: (713) 954-8335
insurance.

TIG INSURANCE COMPANY

5205 North O'Connor Blvd., Irving, TX   75039

CEO: Courtney C. Smith, CEO   Tel: (972) 831-5000   %FO: 100

Bus: *Engaged in property and casualty*   Fax: (972) 831-6550
insurance.

● **FAIRMONT HOTELS & RESORTS INC.**
100 Wellington Street West, Ste. 1600, Toronto ON, M5K 1B7, Canada
CEO: William R. Fatt, CEO   Tel: (416) 874-2600   Rev: $350
Bus: *Management of luxury hotels.*   Fax: (416) 874-2601   Emp: 4,200
     www.fairmont.com

     THE FAIRMONT CHICAGO
     200 North Columbus Drive, Chicago, IL   60602
     CEO: Kevin Frid, Mgr.   Tel: (312) 565-8000   %FO: 100
     Bus: *Engaged in hotel management.*   Fax: (312) 861-3656

     THE FAIRMONT COPLEY PLAZA
     136 St. James Avenue, Boston, MA   02116
     CEO: Jon Crellin, Mgr.   Tel: (617) 267-5300   %FO: 100
     Bus: *Engaged in hotel management.*   Fax: (617) 247-6681

     THE FAIRMONT DALLAS
     1717 North Akard Street, Dallas, TX   75201
     CEO: Cyril Isnard, Mgr.   Tel: (214) 720-2020   %FO: 100
     Bus: *Engaged in hotel management.*   Fax: (214) 720-7403

     FAIRMONT HOTELS & RESORTS INC.
     950 Mason Street, San Francisco, CA   94108
     CEO: Lewis Wolff   Tel: (415) 772-5000   %FO: 100
     Bus: *Engaged in hotel management.*   Fax: (415) 772-5013

     THE FAIRMONT KANSAS CITY AT THE PLAZA
     401 Ward Parkway, Kansas City, MO   64112
     CEO: Mike Casola, Mgr.   Tel: (816) 756-1500   %FO: 100
     Bus: *Engaged in hotel management.*   Fax: (816) 303-0734

     THE FAIRMONT KEA LANI MAUI
     4100 Wailea Alanui Drive, Maui, HI   96753
     CEO: Christof Luedi, Mgr.   Tel: (808) 875-4100   %FO: 100
     Bus: *Engaged in hotel management.*   Fax: (808) 875-1200

     THE FAIRMONT MIRAMAR HOTEL
     101 Wilshire Blvd., Santa Monica, CA   90401
     CEO: Karl Buchta, Mgr.   Tel: (310) 576-7777   %FO: 100
     Bus: *Engaged in hotel management.*   Fax: (310) 458-7912

     THE FAIRMONT NEW ORLEANS
     123 Baronne Street, New Orleans, LA   70112
     CEO: Ray Tackaberry, Mgr.   Tel: (504) 529-7111   %FO: 100
     Bus: *Engaged in hotel management.*   Fax: (504) 529-4764

THE FAIRMONT SAN JOSE
170 South Market Street, San Jose, CA   95113
CEO: Fred Hansen, Mgr.   Tel: (408) 998-1900   %FO: 100
Bus: *Engaged in hotel management.*   Fax: (408) 287-1648

THE FAIRMONT SCOTTSDALE PRINCESS
7575 East Princess Drive, Scottsdale, AZ   85255
CEO: John Williams, Mgr.   Tel: (480) 585-4848   %FO: 100
Bus: *Engaged in hotel management.*   Fax: (480) 585-0086

THE PLAZA
Fifth Avenue at Central Park South, New York, NY   10019
CEO: Gary Schweikert, Mgr.   Tel: (212) 759-3000   %FO: 100
Bus: *Engaged in hotel management.*   Fax: (212) 546-5324

● **FAKESPACE SYSTEMS INC.**
809 Wellington Street North, Kitchener ON, N2G 4J6, Canada
CEO: Daniel P. Wright, Chmn. & CEO   Tel: (519) 749-3111
Bus: *Mfr. visualization and interaction*   Fax: (519) 749-3151   Emp: 800
products and workspace solutions.   www.fakespacesystems.com

FAKESPACE SYSTEMS, INC.
1395 Piccard Drive, Rockville, MD   20850
CEO: William Lackner   Tel: (240) 632-0011   %FO: 100
Bus: *Mfr. visualization and interaction*   Fax: (240) 632-0044
products and workspace solutions.

FAKESPACE SYSTEMS, INC.
39650 Orchard Hill Place, Novi, MI   48375
CEO: Ken Holsgrove   Tel: (248) 735-4300   %FO: 100
Bus: *Mfr. visualization and interaction*   Fax: (248) 735-4310
products and workspace solutions.

FAKESPACE SYSTEMS, INC.
17663 Trenton Drive, Castro Valley, CA   94546
CEO: Frank Hepburn   Tel: (510) 581-4238   %FO: 100
Bus: *Mfr. visualization and interaction*   Fax: (510) 581-4238
products and workspace solutions.

● **FALCONBRIDGE LTD.**
95 Wellington Street West, Ste. 1200, Toronto ON, M5J 2V4, Canada
CEO: Øyvind Hushovd, CEO   Tel: (416) 956-5700   Rev: $1,100
Bus: *Nickel mining company.*   Fax: (416) 956-5757   Emp: 6,650
www.falconbridge.com

FALCONBRIDGE US, INC.
4955 Steubenville Pike, Ste. 245, Pittsburgh, PA   15205
CEO: James H. Moore, Pres.   Tel: (412) 787-0220   %FO: 100
Bus: *Nickel mining.*   Fax: (412) 787-0287

● FIRSTSERVICE CORPORATION
1140 Bay Street, Ste. 4000, Toronto ON, M5S 2B4, Canada
CEO: Jay S. Hennick, CEO   Tel: (416) 960-9500   Rev: $425
Bus: *Engaged in property management and*   Fax: (416) 960-5333   Emp: 9,700
    business services through franchise   www.firstservice.com
    units.

CALIFORNIA CLOSETS COMPANY, INC.
1000 Fourth Street, Ste. 800, San Rafael, CA   94901
CEO: D. Scott Patterson, SVP   Tel: (415) 256-8500   %FO: 100
Bus: *Mfr. closet shelving systems and*   Fax: (415) 256-8501
    organizing systems.

CERTA PROPAINTERS LTD.
150 Green Treet Road, Ste. 1003, Oaks, PA   19456
CEO: Jay S. Hennick, Pres.   Tel: (610) 650-9999   %FO: 100
Bus: *Engaged in painting services.*   Fax: (620) 650-9997

COLLEGE PRO PAINTERS LTD.
313 Pleasant Street, Watertown, MA   02472
CEO: Jay S. Hennick, Pres.   Tel: (617) 924-1300   %FO: 100
Bus: *Engaged in painting services.*   Fax: (617) 924-8122

INTERCON SECURITY
2311 West 22nd Street, Ste. 201, Oak Brook, IL   60523
CEO: D. Scott Patterson, SVP   Tel: (630) 645-0200   %FO: 100
Bus: *Engaged in security.*   Fax: (630) 645-0106

STAINED GLASS OVERLAY, INC.
1827 North Case Street, Orange, CA   92865
CEO: Jay S. Hennick, Pres.   Tel: (714) 974-6124   %FO: 100
Bus: *Mfr. stained glass.*   Fax: (714) 974-6529

THE WENTWORTH GROUP
901 South Tropper Road, PO Box 80690, Valley Forge, PA   19484
CEO: Jay S. Hennick, Pres.   Tel: (610) 650-0600   %FO: 100
Bus: *Engaged in real estate*   Fax: (610) 650-0700
    management, marketing, financial
    and consulting services.

● **FISHERY PRODUCTS INTERNATIONAL LTD.**
PO Box 550, St. Johns NF, A1C 5L1, Canada
CEO: Victor L .Young, CEO   Tel: (709) 570-0000
Bus: *Supplies frozen seafood products.*   Fax: (709) 570-0479
                                         www.fpil.com

    FISHERY PRODUCTS INTERNATIONAL CLOUSTIN, INC.
    18 Electronics Avenue, Danvers, MA   01923
    CEO: John D. Cummings, Pres.   Tel: (978) 777-2660   %FO: 100
    Bus: *Supplies frozen seafood products.*   Fax: (978) 777-7458

● **FLONETWORK INC.**
280 King Street East, Toronto ON, M5A 1K3, Canada
CEO: Eric Goodwin, CEO   Tel: (416) 369-1100   Rev: $1
Bus: *Provides direct marketing services.*   Fax: (416) 369-9037   Emp: 9
                                     www.flonetwork.com

    FLONETWORK INC.
    391 East Putnam Avenue, Ste. 2902, Cos Cob, CT   06807
    CEO: Regina A. Brady, VP   Tel: (203) 552-6841   %FO: 100
    Bus: *Direct marketing services.*   Fax: (203) 552-6846

    FLONETWORK INC.
    10 East 40th Street, New York, NY   10016
    CEO: Eric Goodwin, CEO   Tel: (646) 485-3271   %FO: 100
    Bus: *Direct marketing services.*   Fax: (646) 485-3274

● **FOUR SEASONS HOTELS**
1165 Leslie Street, Toronto ON, M3C 2K8, Canada
CEO: Wolf H. Hengst, Pres. & CEO   Tel: (416) 449-1750   Rev: $237
Bus: *First class hotel and resort chain.*   Fax: (416) 441-4374   Emp: 26,750
                                     www.fourseasons.com

    FOUR SEASONS & REGENT HOTELS
    505 Park Avenue, 6th Fl., New York, NY   10022
    CEO: Kathleen Dickson, Reg. Dir. of   Tel: (212) 980-0101
        Sales
    Bus: *Worldwide sales office.*   Fax: (212) 980-8270

    FOUR SEASONS & REGENT HOTELS
    350 South Beverly Drive, Ste. 220, Beverly Hills, CA   90212-4814
    CEO: Michael Erickson, Reg. Dir. of   Tel: (310) 286-7545
        Sales
    Bus: *Worldwide sales office.*   Fax: (310) 274-2620

FOUR SEASONS & REGENT HOTELS
2777 Stemmons Freeway, Ste. 1632, Dallas, TX   75207
CEO: Wendy Lash, Reg. Dir. of Sales   Tel: (214) 634-7200
Bus: *Worldwide sales office.*   Fax: (214) 634-7208

FOUR SEASONS HOTELS
1025 Thomas Jefferson Street N.W., Ste. 306-E, Washington, DC   20007
CEO: Kathy Austgen, Reg. Dir. of Sales   Tel: (202) 333-7141
Bus: *Worldwide sales office.*   Fax: (202) 337-8035

FOUR SEASONS REGENT HOTELS & RESORTS
75 Fourteenth Street, Atlanta, GA   30309
CEO: Tom Stafford, Reg. Dir. of Sales   Tel: (404) 249-1580
Bus: *Worldwide sales office.*   Fax: (404) 249-7226

FOUR SEASONS RESORTS & HOTELS
900 North Michigan Avenue, Ste, 804, Chicago, IL   60611
CEO: Rhonda Chesney, Reg. Dir. of   Tel: (312) 944-4949
    Sales
Bus: *Worldwide sales office.*   Fax: (312) 944-6798

● **FRISCO BAY INDUSTRIES LTD.**
160 Graveline Street, St. Laurent PQ, H4T 1R7, Canada
CEO: Barry E. Katsof, CEO   Tel: (514) 738-7300   Rev: $24
Bus: *Mfr. integrated security systems and*   Fax: (514) 735-7039   Emp: 170
    self-service banking systems.   www.friscobay.com

FRISCO BAY INDUSTRIES INC.
1055 Parsippany Boulevard, Parsippany, NJ   07054
CEO: Robert Gagnon   Tel: (973) 257-5506   %FO: 100
Bus: *Mfr. integrated security systems*   Fax: (973) 257-5510
    and self-service banking systems.

● **G.T.C. TRANSCONTINENTAL GROUP LTD.**
1, Place Ville Marie, Bureau 3315, Montréal PQ, H3B 3N2, Canada
CEO: Remi Marcoux, Chmn.   Tel: (514) 954-4000   Rev: $865
Bus: *Engaged in commercial printing.*   Fax: (514) 954-4016   Emp: 8,950
    www.transcontinental-gtc.com

MIAMI VALLEY PUBLISHING CO., INC.
678 Yellow Springs Fairfield Road, Fairborn, OH   45324
CEO: Ralph Pontillo, Mgr.   Tel: (937) 879-5678   %FO: 100
Bus: *Engaged in commercial printing.*   Fax: (937) 878-5283

NEWTOWN CPC

169 Friends Lane, Newtown, PA   18940

CEO: James Corr, Mgr.   Tel: (215) 968-5001   %FO: 100

Bus: *Printing plant engaged in direct*   Fax: (215) 968-5852
      marketing.

SPECTRA GRAPHICS

One Forms Lane, Willow Grove, PA   19090

CEO: Richard Weissman, Pres.   Tel: (215) 659-4000   %FO: 100

Bus: *Printing plant engaged in direct*   Fax: (215) 659-3122
      marketing.

TRANSCON PRINTING INC.

678 Yellow Springs Fairfield Road, Fairborn, OH   45324

CEO: Ralph Pontillo, Mgr.   Tel: (937) 879-5678   %FO: 100

Bus: *Engaged in commercial printing.*   Fax: (937) 878-5283

● **GEAC COMPUTER CORP. LTD.**

4100 Yonge St., 6th Fl., Toronto ON, M2P 2B5, Canada

CEO: John E. Caldwell, CEO   Tel: (416) 642-1960   Rev: $669

Bus: *Mfr. automation systems for diverse*   Fax: (416) 642-1961   Emp: 5,026
      industries and services.   www.geac.com

AMSI

1831 NW Freeway, Ste. 500, Houston, TX   77040

CEO: Mike Mullin, Mgr.   Tel: (713) 690-2674   %FO: 100

Bus: *Mfr. software.*   Fax: (713) 690-0330

GEAC COMPUTERS, LIBRARY SYSTEMS DIV.

9 Technology Drive, Westborough, MA   01581

CEO: John Brooks, Mgr.   Tel: (508) 871-6800   %FO: 100

Bus: *Mfr. library automation software.*   Fax: (508) 871-6850

GEAC ENTERPRISE SOLUTIONS

161 Gaither Drive, Ste. 200, Mt. Laurel, NJ   08054

CEO: Donna Smith   Tel: (856) 231-9400   %FO: 100

Bus: *Mfr. software.*   Fax: (856) 231-9874

GEAC ENTERPRISE SOLUTIONS

72 Eagle Rock Avenue, 2nd Fl., East Hanover, NJ   07936-3151

CEO: John E. Caldwell, CEO   Tel: (973) 599-7500   %FO: 100

Bus: *Mfr. software.*   Fax: (973) 599-7500

GEAC INTERREALTY, INC.

1951 Kidwell Drive, Vienna, VA   22182

CEO: Larry Dressel, Mgr.   Tel: (703) 610-5000   %FO: 100

Bus: *Mfr. realty automation software.*   Fax: (703) 610-5000

GEAC PUBLISHING SOFTWARE INC.
3707 West Cherry Street, Tampa, FL   33607

CEO: Bernard Grinberg, Pres.   Tel: (813) 872-9990   %FO: 100

Bus: *Mfr. newspaper and magazine*   Fax: (813) 872-2751
publishing software.

GEAC SMART ENTERPRISE SOLUTIONS
66 Perimeter Center East, Atlanta, GA   30346

CEO: Steve Shine, Mgr.   Tel: (404) 239-2000   %FO: 100

Bus: *Sale/service retail banking*   Fax: (404) 239-2220
software.

• GENESIS MICROCHIP INCORPORATED
165 Commerce Valley Drive West, Thornill ON, L3T 7V8, Canada

CEO: Paul M. Russo, Chmn.   Tel: (905) 889-5400   Rev: $64

Bus: *Engaged in design of integrated circuits.*   Fax: (905) 889-0035   Emp: 170

www.genesis-microchip.com

GENESIS MICROCHIP CORP.
2150 Gold Street, Alviso, CA   95002

CEO: Amnon Fisher, Pres.   Tel: (408) 262-6599   %FO: 100

Bus: *Engaged in design of integrated*   Fax: (408) 262-7989
circuits.

• GLOBAL LIGHT TELECOMMUNICATIONS INC.
999 West Hastings Street, Ste. 530, Vancouver BC, V6C 2W2, Canada

CEO: W. Gordon Blankstein, CEO   Tel: (604) 688-0553   Rev: $68

Bus: *Engaged in telecommunications.*   Fax: (604) 688-7330   Emp: 15

www.ggbtelecom.com

NEW WORLD NETWORK USA INC.
265 Davidson Avenue, Ste. 127, Somerset, NJ   08873

CEO: David W. Warnes, Pres.   Tel: (732) 868-8400   %FO: 100

Bus: *Engaged in telecommunications.*   Fax: (732) 868-8340

NEW WORLD NETWORK USA INC.
2977 McFarlane Road, Ste. 300, Coconut Grove, FL   33133

CEO: David W. Warnes, Pres.   Tel: (305) 529-8700   %FO: 100

Bus: *Engaged in telecommunications.*   Fax: (305) 529-8701

• GORAN CAPITAL INC.
2 Eva Road, Suite 200, Toronto ON, M9C 2A8, Canada

CEO: Alan G. Symons, Pres. & CEO   Tel: (416) 622-0600   Rev: $473

Bus: *Engaged in property and casualty*   Fax: (416) 622-8809   Emp: 1,200
insurance and auto and crop insurance.   www.goralcapital.com

IGF INSURANCE
6000 Grand Avenue, Des Moines, IA   50321
CEO: Dennis Daggett, Pres.   Tel: (515) 633-1000   %FO: 100
Bus: *Engaged in crop insurance.*   Fax: (515) 633-1012

SUPERIOR INSURANCE GROUP
4720 Kingsway Drive, Indianapolis, IN   46205
CEO: Gene Yerent, CEO   Tel: (317) 259-6300   %FO: 100
Bus: *Engaged in non-standard auto*   Fax: (317) 259-6395
insurance.

SYMONS INTERNATIONAL GROUP
4720 Kingsway Drive, Indianapolis, IN   46205
CEO: Douglas H. Symons, CEO   Tel: (317) 259-6300   %FO: 100
Bus: *Engaged in crop and non-standard* Fax: (317) 259-6395
auto insurance.

● GREAT PACIFIC ENTERPRISES
Ste. 1600, 1055 West Hastings Street, Vancouver BC, V6E 2H2, Canada
CEO: Jimmy Pattison, Pres.   Tel: (604) 688-6764
Bus: *Mfr. plastics and industrial machinery.* Fax: (604) 687-2601
                                         www.pacific-nutrition.com

CONTINENTAL SUPERBAG COMPANY
11 Cliffside Drive, Cedar Grove, NJ   07009
CEO: Ronald Basso, VP   Tel: (973) 239-4030   %FO: 100
Bus: *Mfr. plastic shopping bags.*   Fax: (973) 239-9289

● THE GREAT-WEST LIFE ASSURANCE COMPANY
100 Osborne Street North, PO Box 6000, Winnipeg MN, R3C 3A5, Canada
CEO: Raymond L. McFeetors, CEO   Tel: (204) 946-1190   Rev: $10,185
Bus: *Provides group executive benefit* Fax: (204) 946-8818   Emp: 6,880
planning and health and life insurance www.gwl.ca
services.

GREAT-WEST LIFE & ANNUITY INSURANCE COMPANY
8515 East Orchard Road, Greenwood Village, CO   80111
CEO: William T. McCallum, Pres. &   Tel: (303) 689-3000   %FO: 100
CEO
Bus: *Provides executive benefit*   Fax: (303) 689-3198
planning and health and life
insurance services.

- **GROUPE TRANSCONTINENTAL GTC LTEE**

One Place Ville Maire, Rm. 3315, Montréal PQ, H3B 3N2 Canada

CEO: Remi Marcoux, Chmn.   Tel: (514) 954-4000

Bus: *Commercial printing, graphic design &*   Fax: (514) 954-4016   Emp: 3,300
periodicals.   www.transcontinental-gtc.com

TRANSCONTINENTAL PRINTING, INC.

678 Yellow Spring-Fairfield, Fairborn, OH   45324

CEO: Ralph Pontillo, Pres.   Tel: (937) 879-5678   %FO: 100

Bus: *Commercial offset printing*   Fax: (937) 878-5283   Emp: 240
products & services.

- **GSI LUMONICS INC.**

105 Schneider Road, Kanata ON, K2K 1Y3, Canada

CEO: Charles D. Winston, CEO   Tel: (613) 592-1460   Rev: $374

Bus: *Develop/mfr. lasers and laser systems.*   Fax: (613) 592-5706   Emp: 1,150
     www.gsilumonics.com

GSI LUMONICS CORPORATION

60 Fordham Road, Wilmington, MA   01887

CEO: Rob Maclean   Tel: (978) 661-4300   %FO: 100

Bus: *Mfr. lasers and laser-based*   Fax: (978) 988-8798
advanced manufacturing systems.

GSI LUMONICS CORPORATION

22300 Haggerty Road, Northville, MI   48167

CEO: John George, Dir.   Tel: (248) 449-8989   %FO: 100

Bus: *Mfr. lasers and laser-based*   Fax: (248) 735-2460
advanced manufacturing systems.

GSI LUMONICS CORPORATION

8401 Jefferson Highway, Maple Grove, MN   55369

CEO: Cathy Olson, Mgr.   Tel: (763) 315-1780   %FO: 100

Bus: *Mfr. lasers and laser-based*   Fax: (736) 315-1770   Emp: 75
advanced manufacturing systems.

GSI LUMONICS CORPORATION

130 Lombard Street, Oxnard, CA   93031-9010

CEO: Charles D. Winston, CEO   Tel: (805) 485-5559   %FO: 100

Bus: *Mfr. lasers and laser-based*   Fax: (805) 485-3310   Emp: 150
advanced manufacturing systems.

GSI LUMONICS CORPORATION

5390 Kazuko Court, Moorpark, CA   93021

CEO: Charles Winston, CEO   Tel: (805) 529-3324   %FO: 100

Bus: *Mfr. lasers and laser-based*   Fax: (805) 529-4298
advanced manufacturing systems.

● **HARLEQUIN ENTERPRISES LTD.**
225 Duncan Mill Rd, Don Mills ON, M3B 3K9, Canada
CEO: Brian Hickey, Pres.   Tel: (416) 445-5860
Bus: *Publishing.*   Fax: (416) 445-8655   Emp: 1,200
                                  www.romance.net

    HARLEQUIN BOOKS
    300 East 42nd Street, 6th Fl., New York, NY 10017
    CEO: Debra Matteucci   Tel: (212) 682-6080   %FO: 100
    Bus: *Publishing.*   Fax: (212) 682-4539

    HARLEQUIN BOOKS DISTRIBUTION CENTRE
    3010 Walden Avenue, Depew, NY 14043
    CEO: Jim Robinson, VP   Tel: (716) 684-1800   %FO: 100
    Bus: *Book distribution.*   Fax: (716) 684-5066

● **HEMOSOL INC.**
2 Meridian Road, Toronto ON, M9W 4Z7, Canada
CEO: John W. Kennedy, Pres. & CEO   Tel: (416) 798-0700   Rev: $
Bus: *Mfr. blood substitute.*   Fax: (416) 798-0152   Emp: 150
                                      www.hemosol.com

    HEMOSOL USA INC.
    8 Wood Hollow Road, Ste. 301, Parsippany, NJ 07054
    CEO: Dirk Alkema, VP   Tel: (973) 781-0200   %FO: 100
    Bus: *Mfr. blood substitute.* Fax: (973) 781-9840

● **HOLLINGER, INC.**
10 Toronto Street, Toronto ON, M5C 2B7 Canada
CEO: Conrad M. Black, Chmn.   Tel: (416) 363-8721   Rev: $2,140
Bus: *International newspaper publishing.* Fax: (416) 364-2088   Emp: 16,500
                                      www.hollinger.com

    AMERICAN PUBLISHING MANAGEMENT SERVICES, INC.
    401 N. Wabash Avenue, Ste. 740, Chicago, IL 60611
    CEO: Jerry J. Strader, Pres. Tel: (312) 321-2299   %FO: 100
    Bus: *Newspaper publishing.* Fax: (312) 321-0629

    CHICAGO SUN-TIMES
    401 N. Wabash Avenue, Ste. 740, Chicago, IL 60611
    CEO: F. David Radler, Pub.   Tel: (312) 321-3000   %FO: 100
    Bus: *Daily newspaper.*   Fax: (312) 321-0629

HOLLINGER INC.
401 N. Wabash Avenue, Ste. 740, Chicago, IL   60611
CEO: Jerry J. Strader, Pres.   Tel: (312) 321-2299   %FO: 100
Bus: *Newspaper publishing.*   Fax: (312) 321-0629   Emp: 3,100

● **HUMMINGBIRD LTD.**
1 Sparks Avenue, North York ON, M2H 2W1, Canada
CEO: Alan Barry Litwin, Pres.   Tel: (416) 496-2200   Rev: $238
Bus: *Mfr. software.*   Fax: (416) 496-2207   Emp: 1,400
                                      www.hummingbird.com

  HUMMINGBIRD USA INC.
  100 Mill Plain Road, 3rd Fl., Danbury, CT   06811
  CEO: Peter Auditore, VP   Tel: (877) 359-4866   %FO: 100
  Bus: *Mfr. software.*   Fax: (877) 359-4866

  HUMMINGBIRD USA INC.
  25 Burlington Mall Road, Burlington, MA   01803
  CEO: Peter Auditore, VP   Tel: (877) 359-4866   %FO: 100
  Bus: *Mfr. software.*   Fax: (877) 359-4866

● **HUSKY INJECTION MOLDING SYSTEMS LTD.**
500 Queen Street South, Bolton ON, L7E 5S5, Canada
CEO: Robert Schad, Chmn. & CEO   Tel: (905) 951-5000   Rev: $700
Bus: *Mfr. injection molding equipment for*   Fax: (905) 951-5324   Emp: 3,000
manufacture of plastic products.   www.husky.on.ca

  HUSKY INJECTION MOLDING SYSTEMS LTD.
  101 Carnegie Center, Ste. 305, Princeton, NJ   08540
  CEO: Robert Schad   Tel: (609) 514-0200   %FO: 100
  Bus: *Mfr. injection molding equipment*   Fax: (609) 514-1080
       for manufacture of plastic
       products.

  HUSKY INJECTION MOLDING SYSTEMS LTD.
  364 Littleton Road, Ste. 3, Westford, MA   01886
  CEO: Bruce Coxhead   Tel: (978) 692-0077   %FO: 100
  Bus: *Mfr. injection molding equipment*   Fax: (978) 692-0077
       for manufacture of plastic
       products.

  HUSKY INJECTION MOLDING SYSTEMS LTD.
  7341 5215 North O'Connor Blvd., Ste. 1030, Irving, TX   75035
  CEO: Wayne Harper, Mgr.   Tel: (972) 831-7340   %FO: 100
  Bus: *Mfr. injection molding equipment*   Fax: (972) 831-7341
       for manufacture of plastic
       products.

HUSKY INJECTION MOLDING SYSTEMS LTD.
105 Terry Drive Suite 119, Newtown, PA   18940
CEO: Michael Kirschnick   Tel: (215) 497-9700   %FO: 100
Bus: *Mfr. injection molding equipment*   Fax: (215) 497-9700
    for manufacture of plastic
    products.

• **ID BIOMEDICAL CORPORATION**
1510 800 West Pender, Vancouver BC, V6C 2V6, Canada
CEO: Anthony F. Holler, CEO   Tel: (604) 431-9314   Rev: $9
Bus: *Engaged in gene therapy.*   Fax: (604) 431-9378   Emp: 30
                                      www.idbiomed.com

    ID BIOMEDICAL CORPORATION
    UMBC Technology Center, Rolling Road, Baltimore, MD   21227
    CEO: George Lowell, MD   Tel: (410) 455-5614
    Bus: *Engaged in gene therapy.*   Fax: (410) 455-5606

    ID BIOMEDICAL CORPORATION
    19204 North Creek Parkway, Ste. 100, Bothell, WA   98011
    CEO: George Lowell, MD   Tel: (425) 482-2601   %FO: 100
    Bus: *Engaged in gene therapy.*   Fax: (425) 482-2502

• **IMAX CORPORATION**
2525 Speakman Drive, Mississauga ON, L5K 1B1, Canada
CEO: Bradley J. Wechsler, Co-Chair   Tel: (905) 403-6500   Rev: $201
Bus: *Mfr. and leasing of projection and*   Fax: (905) 403-6450   Emp: 701
    sound systems for IMAX giant screen   www.imax.com
    theaters.

    DAVID KEIGHLEY PRODUCTIONS 70 MM INC.
    2111 Park Office Circle, Birmingham, AL   35244
    CEO: David B. Keighley, Pres.   Tel: (205) 982-8100   %FO: 100
    Bus: *Engaged in laboratory post*   Fax:
        production and image quality
        assurance.

    SONICS ASSOCIATES, INC.
    959 Seward Street, Los Angeles, CA   90038
    CEO: Richard L. Gelfond, Pres.   Tel: (323) 957-2442   %FO: 100
    Bus: *Designs, installs, and maintains*   Fax:
        sound systems and components for
        IMAX theaters, theme parks, and
        various large capacity facilities.

● **INCO LIMITED**

145 King Street West, Suite 1500, Toronto ON, M5H 4B7, Canada

CEO: Scott M. Hand, Pres. & CEO   Tel: (416) 361-7511   Rev: $2,917

Bus: *Mines/processes nickel, copper,*   Fax: (416) 361-7782   Emp: 11,000
      precious metals, cobalt.   www.incoltd.com

    INCO UNITED STATES INC.

    PO Box 720, Ellwood City, PA   16117

    CEO: Kenneth L. Money, EVP   Tel: (724) 758-5515   %FO: 100

    Bus: *Mfr. nickel, copper and precious*   Fax: (724) 758-9311
        metals.

    NOVAMET SPECIALTY PRODUCTS CORP

    681 Lawlins Road, Wyckoff, NJ   07481

    CEO: Lou Koehler, CEO   Tel: (201) 891-7976   %FO: 100

    Bus: *Mfr. conductive additives.*   Fax: (201) 891-9467

● **INDUSTRIAL-ALLIANCE LIFE INSURANCE CO.**

1080 St Louis Road, Sillery PQ, G1K 7M3, Canada

CEO: Jacques Carrière, VP   Tel: (418) 684-5000   Rev: $1,580

Bus: *Life insurance services.*   Fax: (418) 684-5294   Emp: 10,600
        www.inalco.com

    NORTH WEST LIFE OF AMERICA

    PO Box 8118, Blaine, WA   98231

    CEO: John B. Gill, Pres.   Tel: (360) 715-8935   %FO: 99

    Bus: *Insurance services.*   Fax: (360) 715-8953   Emp: 20

● **INFOWAVE SOFTWARE INC.**

4664 Lougheed Hwy., Ste. 188, Burnby BC, V5C 5T5, Canada

CEO: Thomas U. Koll, CEO   Tel: (604) 473-3600   Rev: $8

Bus: *Develops software for wireless*   Fax: (604) 473-3699   Emp: 115
      communications.   www.infowave.com

    INFOWAVE SOFTWARE INC.

    3535 Factoria Blvd. SE, Ste. 500, Bellevue, WA   98006

    CEO: Jeff Feinstein, SVP   Tel: (425) 806-3100   %FO: 100

    Bus: *Develops software for wireless*   Fax: (425) 806-3100
        communications.

● **INMET MINING CORPORATION**

330 Bay Street, Ste. 1000, Toronto ON, M5H 2S8, Canada

CEO: Richard Ross, Pres.   Tel: (416) 361-6400   Rev: $47

Bus: *Engaged in mining.*   Fax: (416) 368-4692   Emp: 740
        www.inmet-mining.com

INMET MINING CORPORATION
1315 Greg Street, Ste. 110, Sparks, NV   89431
CEO: Samuel Nunnemaker, Dist.   Tel: (775) 826-4040   %FO: 100
    Geologist
Bus: *Engaged in mining exploration.*   Fax: (775) 826-4007

• **INTERNATIONAL ABSORBENTS INC.**
1569 Dempsey Road, North Vancouver BC, V7K 1S8, Canada
CEO: Gordon L. Ellis, CEO   Tel: (604) 681-6181   Rev: $10
Bus: *Mfr. biodegradable absorption products.* Fax: (604) 904-4105   Emp: 42
    www.absorbent.com

    INTERNATIONAL ABSORBENTS INC.
    1051 Hilton Avenue, Bellingham, WA   98225
    CEO: Shawn Dooley, VP   Tel: (604) 681-6181   %FO: 100
    Bus: *Mfr. and sales of biodegradable*   Fax: (604) 514-6559
       absorption products.

• **INTERTAPE POLYMER GROUP**
110 E. Montee de Liesse, Montréal PQ, H4T 1N4, Canada
CEO: Melbourne F. Yull, CEO   Tel: (514) 731-7591   Rev: $375
Bus: *Mfr. packaging/masking tape.*   Fax: (514) 731-5039   Emp: 2,440
    www.intertapepolymer.com

    INTERTAPE POLYMER GROUP
    3647 Cortez Road West, Bradenton, FL   34210
    CEO: Cullen Jones   Tel: (941) 727-5788   %FO: 100
    Bus: *Sales/distribution of*   Fax: (941) 727-1568
       packing/masking tape.

    INTERTAPE POLYMER GROUP
    317 Kendall Avenue, Marysville, MI   48040
    CEO: Dan Croteau   Tel: (810) 364-9000   %FO: 100
    Bus: *Sales/distribution of*   Fax: (810) 364-9000
       packing/masking tape.

• **INTRAWEST CORPORATION**
200 Burrard Street, Ste. 800, Vancouver BC, B6C 3L6, Canada
CEO: Joe. S. Houssian, Pres. & CEO   Tel: (604) 669-9777   Rev: $407
Bus: *Owns and operates ski resorts and* Fax: (604) 669-0605   Emp: 12,300
    affiliated hotels and restaurants.   www.intrawest.com

    MOUNTAIN CREEK SKI RESORT
    Route 94, Vernon, NJ   07044
    CEO: James J. Gibbons, Pres.   Tel: (973) 827-2000
    Bus: *Ski resort and water park.*   Fax:

- **IPSCO, INC.**
  Armour Road, PO Box 1670, Regina SK, S4P 3C7, Canada
  CEO: Roger Phillips, Pres. & CEO   Tel: (306) 924-7700   Rev: $950
  Bus: *Mfr. steel and pipe.*   Fax: (306) 924-7500   Emp: 1,900
     www.ipsco.com

  ### IPSCO STEEL, INC.
  1770 Bill Sharp Boulevard, Muscatine, IA 52761
  CEO: Charles Sanida, Pres.   Tel: (319) 381-5300   %FO: 100
  Bus: *Steel mill operators.*   Fax: (319) 381-5329

  ### IPSCO TUBULARS INC.
  2011 Seventh Avenue, PO Box 18, Camanche, IA 52730-0180
  CEO: Dave Britten, Pres.   Tel: (319) 242-0000   %FO: 100
  Bus: *Steel pipe mill operator.*   Fax: (319) 242-9408

  ### PAPER CAL STEEL COMPANY
  2500 West County Road D, Ste. 1, Roseville, MN 55113
  CEO: Dayton Barkley, VP   Tel: (612) 631-9031   %FO: 100
  Bus: *Steel service center.*   Fax: (612) 631-9670   Emp: 40

- **IVACO INC.**
  Place Mercantile, 770 rue Sherbrooke, Montréal PQ, H3A 1G1, Canada
  CEO: Paul Ivanier, Pres. & CEO   Tel: (514) 288-4545
  Bus: *Mfr./fabrication of steel and other*   Fax: (514) 284-9414   Emp: 5,000
      diversified products.   www.ivaco.com

  ### IFC USA CORP.
  PO Box 216, Swanton, VT 05488
  CEO: Peter Kasper, Mgr.   Tel: (450) 658-8741   %FO: 100
  Bus: *Mfr. fastener products.*   Fax: (450) 447-0114

  ### IVACO STEEL MILLS LTD.
  920 Providence Road, Ste. 305, Towson, MD 21286
  CEO: Donald Habersack, Mgr.   Tel: (410) 823-7696   %FO: 100
  Bus: *Mfr. wire rods & wire products*   Fax: (410) 823-3081   Emp: 10

  ### IVACO STEEL PROCESSING, INC.
  3937 River Road, Tonawanda, NY 14151-0646
  CEO: Renee Klawon, Mgr.   Tel: (716) 874-5681   %FO: 100
  Bus: *Mfr. wire products and wire rod*   Fax: (716) 874-4440
      processing.

  ### SIVACO WIRE GROUP
  24 Herring Road, Newnan, GA 30265-1006
  CEO: Barry Retter, VP   Tel: (770) 253-6333   %FO: 100
  Bus: *Mfr. wire and wire products.*   Fax: (770) 253-3550   Emp: 600

● **IVANHOE ENERGY INC.**
200 Burrard Street, 9th Fl., Vancouver BC, V6C 3L6, Canada
CEO: E. Leon Daniel, CEO   Tel: (604) 688-8323   Rev: $1
Bus: *Engaged in energy.*   Fax: (604) 662-2060   Emp: 70
                                   www.ivanhoe-energy.com

    IVANHOE ENERGY USA INC.
    1200 Discovery Way, 3rd Fl., Bakersfield, CA   93389-9279
    CEO: Leon Daniel   Tel: (661) 325-4026   %FO: 100
    Bus: *Engaged in energy.*   Fax: (661) 325-4440

● **THE JEAN COUTU GROUP (PJC) INC.**
530 Beriault, Longueuil PQ, J4G 1SI, Canada
CEO: Jean Coutu, Chmn.   Tel: (450) 646-9611   Rev: $1,722
Bus: *Owns and operates chain drugstores,*   Fax: (450) 646-5649   Emp: 6,275
   including Jean Coutu, Maxi Drug and   www.jeancoutu.com
   Brooks Pharmacy.

    MAXI/BROOKS PHARMACY INC.
    50 Service Road, Warwick, RI   02886
    CEO: Michelle Coutu, Pres. & CEO   Tel: (401) 825-3900   %FO: 100
    Bus: *Owns and operates chain*   Fax: (401) 825-3996
       drugstores.

● **KINGSWAY FINANCIAL SERVICES INC.**
5310 Explorer Drive, Ste. 200, Mississauga ON, l4W 5H8, Canada
CEO: William G. Star, CEO   Tel: (905) 629-7888   Rev: $430
Bus: *Provides casualty and property*   Fax: (905) 629-5008   Emp: 1,000
   insurance services.   www.kingsway-financial.com

    AVALON RISK MANAGEMENT, INC.
    84 Wharf Street, Salem, MA   01970
    CEO: Anna Alajajian   Tel: (978) 740-5677   %FO: 100
    Bus: *Provides casualty and property*   Fax: (978) 740-6627
       insurance services.

    AVALON RISK MANAGEMENT, INC.
    3315 East Algonquin Road, Ste. 340, Rolling Meadows, IL   60008
    CEO: Gary C. Bhojwani, Pres.   Tel: (847) 670-8970   %FO: 100
    Bus: *Provides casualty and property*   Fax: (847) 670-9260
       insurance services.

    AVALON RISK MANAGEMENT, INC.
    4801 Woodway Drive, Ste. 300 E, Houston, TX   7056
    CEO: Charlotte McCanless   Tel: (713) 964-2685   %FO: 100
    Bus: *Provides casualty and property*   Fax: (713) 964-2686
       insurance services.

HAMILTON RISK
8686 NW 68th Street, Miami, FL   33166
CEO: Juvenal Llanes, Mgr.   Tel: (305) 477-2207   %FO: 100
Bus: *Provides casualty and property*   Fax: (305) 477-7072
insurance services.

● **KIPP & ZONEN INC.**
1503 Fletcher Road, Saskatoon SK, S7M 5S5, Canada
CEO: James Yule, Pres.   Tel: (306) 934-0101
Bus: *Mfr. instruments for scientific research.*   Fax: (306) 978-2339
www.kippzonen.com

KIPP & ZONEN INC.
125 Wilbur Place, Bohemia, NY   11716
CEO: Reinhold Rosemann, VP   Tel: (516) 589-2065   %FO: 100
Bus: *Mfr. instruments for scientific*   Fax: (516) 589-2068
research.

● **LAIDLAW INC.**
3221 North Service Road, Burlington ON, L7N 3G2, Canada
CEO: John R. Grainger, CEO   Tel: (905) 3361800   Rev: $3,690
Bus: *Holding company: ambulances,*   Fax: (905) 336-3976   Emp: 80,000
passengers services and food services.   www.laidlaw.com

GREYHOUND LINES, INC.
15110 North Dallas Parkway, Ste. 600, Dallas, TX   75248
CEO: Craig Lentzsch, CEO   Tel: (972) 789-7000
Bus: *Inter-city bus transportation.*   Fax: (972) 387-1874

LAIDLAW TRANSIT CORPORATION
35 Troy Lane, Lincoln Park, NJ   07035
CEO: Laura Stoddart, Mgr.   Tel: (973) 696-1441   %FO: JV
Bus: *School bus operators.*   Fax: (973) 696-8883

SAFETY-KLEEN CORPORATION
1301 Gervais Street, Ste. 300, Columbia, SC   29201
CEO: David E. Thomas Jr.   Tel: (803) 933-4200
Bus: *Provides hazardous waste removal.*   Fax: (803) 933-4345

SC FOOD SERVICE (USA), INC.
816 South Military Trail, Deerfield Beach, FL   33442
CEO: Brian Worts, Pres.   Tel: (954) 481-9555   %FO: 100
Bus: *Food industry; operates Manchu-*   Fax: (954) 481-9670
Wok restaurants in food courts.

• LEITCH TECHNOLOGY CORPORATION

25 Dyas Road, North York ON, M3B 1V7, Canada

CEO: John A. MacDonald, Pres. & CEO   Tel: (416) 445-9640   Rev: $143

Bus: *Mfr. products for processing audio and*   Fax: (416) 445-4308   Emp: 700
video signals.   www.leitch.com

LEITCH INC.

6108 River Landings Drive, Raleigh, NC 27604

CEO: Jill Walters   Tel: (919) 876-9765   %FO: 100

Bus: *Mfr./sales of products for*   Fax: (919) 876-9766
processing audio and video
signals.

LEITCH INC.

780 Main Street, Royersford, PA 19468

CEO: Jim Lien   Tel: (610) 792-5230   %FO: 100

Bus: *Mfr./sales of products for*   Fax: (610) 792-5231
processing audio and video
signals.

LEITCH INC.

57 Gould Street, Stoneham, MA 02180

CEO: John Margardo   Tel: (781) 438-5240   %FO: 100

Bus: *Mfr./sales of products for*   Fax: (781) 438-5231
processing audio and video
signals.

LEITCH INC.

73 Evans Avenue, Oceanside, NY 11572

CEO: Keith Andoos   Tel: (516) 594-3372   %FO: 100

Bus: *Mfr./sales of products for*   Fax: (516) 594-3373
processing audio and video
signals.

LEITCH INC.

920 Corporate Lane, Chesapeake, VA 23320-3641

CEO: Warren East, COO   Tel: (757) 548-2300   %FO: 100

Bus: *Mfr./sales of products for*   Fax: (757) 548-4088
processing audio and video
signals.

LEITCH INC.

943 South Mallard Drive, Palatine, IL 60067-7032

CEO: Gary A. Schutte   Tel: (847) 358-7545   %FO: 100

Bus: *Mfr./sales of products for*   Fax: (847) 358-8909
processing audio and video
signals.

LEITCH INC.
4515 Florida National Drive, Ste. 208, Lakeland, FL   33813
CEO: Todd Riggs   Tel: (863) 701-9000   %FO: 100
Bus: *Mfr./sales of products for*   Fax: (863) 701-9400
  processing audio and video
  signals.

LEITCH INC.
1860 Aurora Court, Brentwood, CA   94513
CEO: Richard Sutherland   Tel: (925) 513-2773   %FO: 100
Bus: *Mfr./sales of products for*   Fax: (925) 513-2793
  processing audio and video
  signals.

LEITCH INC.
1103 Crockett Court, Southlake, TX   76092
CEO: John Nielsen   Tel: (817) 251-0165   %FO: 100
Bus: *Mfr./sales of products for*   Fax: (817) 251-0242
  processing audio and video
  signals.

LEITCH INC.
1912 Des Plaines Avenue, Park Ridge, IL   60068
CEO: Alan Cherne   Tel: (847) 692-6704   %FO: 100
Bus: *Mfr./sales of products for*   Fax: (847) 692-6705
  processing audio and video
  signals.

LEITCH INC.
204 West Hills Way, Woodstock, GA   30189
CEO: Greg Weot   Tel: (678) 445-5650   %FO: 100
Bus: *Mfr./sales of products for*   Fax: (678) 445-5651
  processing audio and video
  signals.

LEITCH LATIN AMERICA
14750 NW 77th Court, Ste. 105, Miami Lakes, FL   33016
CEO: Edel Garcia   Tel: (305) 512-0045   %FO: 100
Bus: *Mfr./sales of products for*   Fax: (305) 362-0034
  processing audio and video
  signals.

● **LINAMAR CORPORATION**
301 Massey Road, Guelph ON, N1K 1B2, Canada
CEO: Frank J. Hasenfratz, Chmn. & CEO   Tel: (519) 836-7550   Rev: $650
Bus: *Mfr. precision machine components.*   Fax: (519) 824-8479   Emp: 8,600
  www.linamar.ca

EAGLE MANUFACTURING LLC
7100 Industrial Road, Florence, KY   41042
CEO: Linda Hasenfratz, COO   Tel: (606) 282-5900   %FO: 100
Bus: *Mfr. precision machine*   Fax: (606) 282-5925
components.

LINAMAR USA INC.
9401 Harrison Road, Romulus, MI   48174
CEO: Linda Hasenfratz, COO   Tel: (734) 946-0610   %FO: 100
Bus: *Mfr. precision machine*   Fax: (734) 946-0610
components.

PROMET, INC.
950 Bridgeview North, Saginaw, MI   48604
CEO: Linda Hasenfratz, COO   Tel: (517) 755-1900   %FO: 100
Bus: *Mfr. precision machine*   Fax: (517) 755-1981
components.

● **LMI (LASER MEASUREMENT INTERNATIONAL INC.)**
7088 Venture Street, Ste. 205, Delta BC, V4G IH5, Canada
CEO: Leonard Metcalfe, CEO   Tel: (604) 940-0141
Bus: *Mfr. optoelectronic monitoring and*   Fax: (604) 940-0793
measuring equipment.   www.lmint.com

LMI TECHNOLOGIES, INC.
21654 Melrose Avenue, Southfield, MI   48075-7905
CEO: Sven Johansson, VP & Gen.Mgr.   Tel: (248) 355-5900   %FO: 100
Bus: *Optoelectronic*   Fax: (248) 355-3283   Emp: 10
monitoring/measuring equipment.

● **LML PAYMENT SYSTEMS INC.**
1140 West Pender Street, Ste. 1680, Vancouver BC, Canada
CEO: Patrick H. Gaines, CEO   Tel: (604) 689-4440   Rev: $10
Bus: *Provides check verification and*   Fax: (604) 689-4413   Emp: 150
electronic payment system software.   www.lmlpayment.com

LML PAYMENT SYSTEMS CORP.
1330 Riverbend Drive, Ste. 600, Dallas, TX   75247
CEO: H. Gaines, Pres.   Tel: (214) 678-2000   %FO: 100
Bus: *Provides check verification and*   Fax: (214) 678-2001
electronic payment system
software.

● **LOBLAW COMPANIES LIMITED, DIV. GEORGE WESTON LIMITED**

22 St. Clair Avenue East, Toronto ON, M4T 2S8, Canada

CEO: John A. Lederer, Pres. & CEO   Tel: (416) 922-8500   Rev: $13,425

Bus: *Food retailer and wholesale distributor.*   Fax: (416) 922-7791   Emp: 114,000

www.loblaw.com

    LOBLAW COMPANIES LIMITED

    8725 West Higgins Road, Chicago, IL   60603

    CEO: Richard J. Currie, Pres.   Tel: (773) 693-4520   %FO: 100

    Bus: *Food retailer and wholesale*   Fax: (773) 693-4533
      distributor.

● **LOEWEN GROUP, INC.**

2225 Sheppard Avenue East, 11th Floor, Atria III, Toronto ON, M2J 5C2, Canada

CEO: Paul A. Houston, CEO   Tel: (604) 299-9321   Rev: $900

Bus: *Operates funeral homes and cemeteries.*   Fax: (604) 473-7330   Emp: 10,800

www.loewengroup.com

    LOEWEN GROUP

    3190 Tremont Avenue, Trevose, PA   19053

    CEO: Robert B. Lundgren, Pres. & CEO   Tel: (215) 364-7770   %FO: 100

    Bus: *Operates funeral homes and*   Fax: (215) 364-7770
      cemeteries.

● **MAAX INC.**

640 Cameron Road, Sainte-Marie PQ, G6E 1B2, Canada

CEO: Placide Poulin, CEO   Tel: (418) 387-4155   Rev: $298

Bus: *Designs and manufactures acrylic and*   Fax: (418) 386-4520   Emp: 2,755
fiberglass showers and bathtubs.   www.maax.com

    MAAX INC.

    2150 Division Street, Bellingham, WA   98226-9129

    CEO: Andre Heroux, Pres.   Tel: (360) 734-0616   %FO: 100

    Bus: *Mfr. showers and bathtubs.*   Fax: (360) 733-6985

    PEARL BATHS, INC.

    9224 73rd Avenue, Minneapolis, MN   55428

    CEO: Rob Larson   Tel: (800) 328-2531   %FO: 100

    Bus: *Mfr. acrylic and fiberglass*   Fax: (763) 424-9808
      showers and bathtubs.

● **MACLEAN HUNTER PUBLISHING LTD. (SUB. ROGERS COMMUNICATIONS))**
777 Bay Street, Toronto ON, M5W 1A7, Canada
CEO: George Condon, CEO   Tel: (416) 596-5000
Bus: *Publisher of consumer magazine and*   Fax: (416) 593-3175   Emp: 12,000
business publications, newspapers,   www.rogers.com
cable TV, radio and television, printing,
book distribution, radio paging, trade
shows.

   ROGERS M&N COMPANY
   450 Seventh Avenue, New York, NY   10123
   CEO: Robert Webster, Pres.   Tel: (212) 629-8229   %FO: 100
   Bus: *Medical education publication.*   Fax: (212) 629-8559

● **MAGELLAN AEROSPACE CORPORATION**
55 York Street, Ste. 1450, Toronto ON, M5J 1R7, Canada
CEO: Richard A. Neill, Pres.   Tel: (416) 365-0565   Rev: $388
Bus: *Mfr. aircraft components,*   Fax: (416) 365-2131   Emp: 3,280
communications hardware.   www.malaero.com

   AERONCA INC.
   1712 Germantown Road, Middletown, OH   45042
   CEO: James Stine, EVP   Tel: (513) 422-2751   %FO: 100
   Bus: *Aircraft/aerospace parts and*   Fax: (513) 422-0812   Emp: 330
   assemblies.

● **MAGNA INTERNATIONAL INC.**
337 Magna Drive, Aurora ON, L4G 7K1, Canada
CEO: James Nicol, Pres.   Tel: (905) 726-2462   Rev: $10,513
Bus: *Holding company.*   Fax: (905) 726-7164   Emp: 59,000
                                                  www.magnaint.com

   EAGLE BEND MANUFACTURING INC.
   1000 JD Yarnell Industrial Pkwy., Clinton, TN   37716
   CEO: Walter Himsl, Pres.   Tel: (865) 457-3800   %FO: 100
   Bus: *Mfr. motor vehicle parts and*   Fax: (865) 457-0140
   accessories.

   MAGNA INTERIOR SYSTEMS
   27300 Haggerty Road, Ste. F-10, Farmington Hills, MI   48331
   CEO: Walter Himsl, Pres.   Tel: (248) 553-9500   %FO: 100
   Bus: *Mfr. interior systems.*   Fax: (248) 957-2370

MAGNA INTERNATIONAL OF AMERICA
600 Wilshire Drive, Troy, MI   48084
CEO: Walter Himsl, Pres.   Tel: (248) 729-2400   %FO: 100
Bus: *Mfr. exterior systems.*   Fax: (248) 729-2520

MAGNA MIRROR SYSTEMS
17177 North Laurel Park, Ste. 307, Livonia, MI   48152
CEO: Patrick Graham, Mgr.   Tel: (734) 953-5555   %FO: 100
Bus: *Mfr. auto mirrors.*   Fax: (734) 953-5758

MAGNA SEATING SYSTEMS
19700 Haggerty Road, South Bldg., Livonia, MI   48152
CEO: Patrick Graham, Mgr.   Tel: (734) 432-4514   %FO: 100
Bus: *Mfr. seating systems.*   Fax: (734) 591-1146

● **MANULIFE FINANCIAL CORPORATION**
200 Bloor Street East, Toronto ON, M4W 1E5, Canada
CEO: Dominic D'Alessandro, CEO   Tel: (416) 926-0100   Rev: $9,437
Bus: *Life insurance and financial services.*   Fax: (416) 926-5410   Emp: 28,000
                                  www.manulife.com

THE MANUFACTURERS LIFE INSURANCE COMPANY
73 Tremont Street, Boston, MA   02107
CEO: John D. DesPrez III, Chmn.   Tel: (617) 854-4300   %FO: 100
Bus: *Mutual funds, annuities*   Fax: (617) 854-8600   Emp: 138

● **MAPLE LEAF FOODS INC.**
30 St. Clair Avenue West, Ste. 1500, Toronto ON, M4V 3A2, Canada
CEO: G. Wallace F. McCain, Chmn. Tel: (416) 926-2000   Rev: $2,631
Bus: *Mfr./distributes fresh, processed and*   Fax: (416) 926-2018   Emp: 12,000
canned foods and animal feeds. www.mapleleaf.ca

MAPLE LEAF BAKERY, INC.
1011 East Touhy Avenue, Ste. 500, Des Plaines, IL   60018
CEO: Richard Lan, Pres.   Tel: (847) 655-8100   %FO: 100
Bus: *Mfr./distributes fresh, processed*   Fax: (847) 655-8110
*and canned foods and animal
feeds.*

MAPLE LEAF FOODS INC.
220 South Orange Avenue, Livingston, NJ   07039
CEO: Richard Lan, Pres.   Tel: (973) 597-1991   %FO: 100
Bus: *Mfr./distributes fresh, processed*   Fax: (973) 597-1183
*and canned foods and animal
feeds.*

● **McCAIN FOODS, LTD.**
107 Main Street, Florenceville NB, E0J 1K0, Canada
CEO: Harrison McCain, Chmn.   Tel: (506) 392-5541   Rev: $3,500
Bus: *Food processing, storage and transport.* Fax: (506) 392-8156   Emp: 16,000
                                      www.mccain.com

   MC CAIN FOODS USA, INC.
   2905 Butterfield Road, Oak Brook, IL   60523-1102
   CEO: Gilles Lessard, Chmn. & CEO   Tel: (630) 472-0420   %FO: 100
   Bus: *Mfr. potato & vegetable*   Fax: (630) 472-0451   Emp: 1,885
        specialties, pizza products.

● **MDC CORPORATION INC.**
45 Hazelton Avenue, Toronto ON, M5R 2E3, Canada
CEO: Miles S. Nadal, Pres. & CEO   Tel: (416) 960-9000   Rev: $778
Bus: *Engaged in printing of checks, stamps,* Fax: (416) 960-9555   Emp: 4,850
     travel and event tickets.   www.mdccorp.com

   CYBERSIGHT, LLC
   220 NW Second Avenue, Ste. 1100, Portland, OR   97209
   CEO: Andrew Shakman, Pres. & CEO   Tel: (503) 228-4008
   Bus: *Engaged in advertising and*   Fax: (503) 228-3629
        internet-based marketing.

   PRO-IMAGE CORPORATION
   1805 Loucks Road, York, PA   17404
   CEO: Joe E. Bugelli, Pres. & CEO   Tel: (717) 764-5880
   Bus: *Pre-press composition of scholarly* Fax: (717) 764-6140
        and technical books and journals
        with emphasis on mathematics,
        chemistry and medical titles.

● **MDS INC.**
100 International Boulevard, Toronto ON, M9W 6J6, Canada
CEO: John A. Rogers, CEO   Tel: (416) 675-4530   Rev: $931
Bus: *Distributes medical supplies and home* Fax: (416) 675-0688   Emp: 10,350
     health care products and provides   www.mdsintl.com
     management of automated lab systems.

   MDS PANLABS
   11804 North Creek Parkway South, Bothell, WA   98011
   CEO: Pamela Dean, Sales Mgr.   Tel: (425) 487-8200   %FO: 100
   Bus: *Distributes medical supplies and*   Fax: (425) 487-3787
        home health care products and
        provides management of
        automated lab systems.

MDS PANLABS

4 Crystal Court, Sicklerville, NJ   08081

CEO: Ben Palombo, R.N., Mgr.   Tel: (609) 262-7839

Bus: *Distributes medical supplies and*   Fax: (609) 262-8994
home health care products and
provides management of
automated lab systems.

MDS PANLABS

HC-89, Box 450, Pocono Pines, PA   18350

CEO: Robert Krell, Ph.D., Mgr.   Tel: (570) 643-1022

Bus: *Distributes medical supplies and*   Fax: (570) 643-7705
home health care products and
provides management of
automated lab systems.

MDS PANLABS

2 Pimlico Court, Bedford, NH   03110

CEO: Livia Gorini, M.S., Mgr.   Tel: (603) 629-9173

Bus: *Distributes medical supplies and*   Fax: (603) 644-0749
home health care products and
provides management of
automated lab systems.

MDS PANLABS

147 Ancient Oak Road, Bethlehem, CT   06751

CEO: Mark Crane, Mgr.   Tel: (203) 266-7972

Bus: *Distributes medical supplies and*   Fax: (203) 266-7842
home health care products and
provides management of
automated lab systems.

MDS PANLABS

623 El Mirador Drive, Fullerton, CA   92835

CEO: Dave McMillen, Mgr.   Tel: (714) 449-9080   %FO: 100

Bus: *Distributes medical supplies and*   Fax: (714) 449-1969
home health care products and
provides management of
automated lab systems.

MDS PANLABS

PO Box 447, 1083 Taylorsville Road, Washington Crossing, PA   18977

CEO: Corey Jacklin, Mgr.   Tel: (215) 369-0965   %FO: 100

Bus: *Distributes medical supplies and*   Fax: (215) 369-0967
home health care products and
provides management of
automated lab systems.

MDS PANLABS
221 West Street Road, Ste. 7, Feasterville, PA 19053
CEO: Benjamin Blank, Ph.D., Mgr.   Tel: (215) 364-6650   %FO: 100
Bus: *Distributes medical supplies and*   Fax: (215) 364-6652
home health care products and
provides management of
automated lab systems.

● **METHANEX CORPORATION**
1800 Waterfront Center, 200 Burrard Street, Vancouver BC, V8C 3M1, Canada
CEO: Pierre Choquette, CEO   Tel: (604) 661-2600   Rev: $1,061
Bus: *Mfr. methanol.*   Fax: (604) 661-2676   Emp: 850
www.methanex.com

    METHANEX CORPORATION
    12377 Merit Drive, Ste. 490, Dallas, TX   75251
    CEO: Pierre Choquette, Pres.   Tel: (972) 702-0909   %FO: 100
    Bus: *Mfr. methanol.*   Fax: (972) 233-1266

● **MITEL CORPORATION**
350 Legett Drive, Kanata ON, K2K 2W7, Canada
CEO: Kirt K. Mandy, Pres. & CEO   Tel: (613) 592-2122   Rev: $963
Bus: *Design/mfr. semiconductor devices,*   Fax: (613) 592-4784   Emp: 5,775
components & integrated circuits,   www.mitel.com
telephone systems and call centers. (JV
with General Electric Co Plc, UK)

    MITEL, INC.
    3200 Bristol Street, Ste. 200, Costa Mesa, CA   92626
    CEO: Dave Schuler, Mgr.   Tel: (724) 435-4006   %FO: JV
    Bus: *Mfr./sales semiconductor devices,*   Fax: (724) 431-3073
    components & integrated circuits,
    telephone and call centers..

    MITEL, INC.
    800 Corporate Drive, Ste. 221, St. Lauderdale, FL   33334
    CEO: Paul Alfano, Mgr.   Tel: (954) 928-0604   %FO: JV
    Bus: *Mfr./sales semiconductor devices,*   Fax: (954) 928-0688
    components & integrated circuits,
    telephone and call centers..

    MITEL, INC.
    3030 LBJ Freeway, Ste. 1700, Dallas, TX   75234
    CEO: Mark Koster, Mgr.   Tel: (214) 353-5200   %FO: JV
    Bus: *Mfr./sales semiconductor devices,*   Fax: (214) 353-5250
    components & integrated circuits,
    telephone and call centers..

MITEL, INC.

205 Van Buren Street, Ste. 400, Herndon, VA   22170-7020

CEO: Carl Currurthers, Pres.

Tel: (703) 318-7020

%FO: JV

Bus: *Mfr./sales semiconductor devices, components & integrated circuits, telephone and call centers..*

Fax: (703) 318-0591

● **THE MOLSON COMPANIES LTD.**

1555 Notre Dame St. East, Montréal PQ, H2L 2R5, Canada

CEO: Daniel J. O'Neill, CEO

Tel: (514) 521-1786

Rev: $1,180

Bus: *Engaged in beer brewing, retail merchandising and sports and entertainment field.*

Fax: (514) 598-6969

www.molson.com

Emp: 3,000

MOLSON USA, DIV. MILLER BREWING COMPANY

3939 West Highland Boulevard, Milwaukee, WI   53208-2866

CEO: John Rooney, VP

Tel: (414) 931-2000

%FO: JV

Bus: *Sales/distribution of beer (Molson & Foster) in the U.S. (JV with Miller Brewing).*

Fax: (414) 931-3735

● **MONARCH INDUSTRIES LTD.**

PO Box 429, 889 Erin Street, Winnipeg MB, R3C 3E4, Canada

CEO: Gene D. Dunn, Pres. & CEO

Tel: (204) 786-7921

Bus: *Mfr. centrifugal pumps, concrete mixers, hydraulic cylinders, water systems, self priming pumps.*

Fax: (204) 889-9120

www.monarchinc.com

Emp: 375

MONARCH INDUSTRIES INC.

PO Box 20476, Minneapolis, MN   55420

CEO: Gene D. Dunn, Pres. & CEO

Tel: (612) 884-0226

%FO: 100

Bus: *Distribute centrifugal pumps, concrete mixers, hydraulic cylinders, water systems, self priming pumps.*

Fax: (612) 889-9120

● **MOORE CORP. LTD.**

One First Canadian Plaza, Toronto ON, M5X 1G5 Canada

CEO: Thomas E. Kierans, Chmn.

Tel: (416) 364-2600

Rev: $2,258

Bus: *Mfr. business forms and systems, information management services.*

Fax: (416) 364-1667

www.moore.com

Emp: 16,200

MOORE NORTH AMERICA, INC.
1200 Lakeside Drive, Bannockburn, IL   60015

CEO: Gary Ampulski, Pres.   Tel: (847) 607-6000   %FO: 100

Bus: *Mfr. business forms and systems*   Fax: (847) 607-7250
and information management
services.

MOORE PROCESS AUTOMATION SOLUTIONS
1201 Sumney Town Pike, Spring House, PA   19477-0900

CEO: Donald Bogle, Pres.   Tel: (215) 646-7400   %FO: 100

Bus: *Mfr. business forms and systems*   Fax: (215) 283-6358
and information management
services.

• MOSAID TECHNOLOGIES INCORPORATED
11 Hines Road, Kanata ON, K2K 2X1, Canada

CEO: George J. J. Cwynar, CEO   Tel: (613) 599-9539   Rev: $33

Bus: *Semiconductors.*   Fax: (613) 591-8148   Emp: 200

                                    www.mosaid.com

MOSAID SYSTEMS INC.
3375 Scott Blvd., Ste. 206, Santa Clara, CA   95054

CEO: James D. Skippen   Tel: (408) 727-7199   %FO: 100

Bus: *Semiconductors.*   Fax: (408) 727-0479

MOSAID SYSTEMS INC.
11921 North Mopac Expwy., Ste. 310, Austin, TX   78759-3513

CEO: G. Glenn Evans   Tel: (512) 231-0331   %FO: 100

Bus: *Semiconductors.*   Fax: (512) 997-7665

• MOUNTAIN PROVINCE DIAMONDS INC.
1205-789 West Pender Street, Vancouver BC, V6C 1H2, Canada

CEO: Jan W. Vandersande, CEO   Tel: (604) 687-0122   Rev: $1

Bus: *Diamond exploration. (JV of DeBeers).*   Fax: (604) 684-7208   Emp: 20

                                    www.mountainprovince.com

MOUNTAIN PROVINCE DIAMONDS INC.
3633 East Inland Empire Blvd., Ste. 265, Ontario, CA   91764

CEO: Alan K. Decker   Tel: (800) 220-1943   %FO: 100

Bus: *Diamond exploration.*   Fax: (800) 220-1943

• NATIONAL BANK OF CANADA
600 rue de la Gauchetiére W., Montréal PQ, H3B 4L2 Canada

CEO: Andre Berard, CEO   Tel: (514) 394-5000   Rev: $2,930

Bus: *General banking services.*   Fax: (514) 394-8434   Emp: 17,100

                                    www.nbc.ca

NATBANK

4031 Oakwood Blvd., Hollywood, FL 33020

CEO: Raymond Gelinas, CEO   Tel: (954) 923-4933   %FO: 100

Bus: *General banking services.*   Fax: (954) 923-3347

NATIONAL BANK OF CANADA - Chicago Branch

225 West Washington Street, Ste. 1100, Chicago, IL 60606

CEO: Leroy Irvin, Mgr.   Tel: (312) 263-1616   %FO: 100

Bus: *Commercial banking services.*   Fax: (312) 558-8888

NATIONAL BANK OF CANADA

125 West 55th Street, 23rd Fl., New York, NY 10019

CEO: Frank Devries, SVP   Tel: (212) 632-8500   %FO: 100

Bus: *Commercial banking.*   Fax: (212) 632-8545

NATIONAL BANK OF CANADA - Agency

725 South Figueroa Street, Los Angeles, CA 90017

CEO: David Shaw, Mgr.   Tel: (213) 629-3300   %FO: 100

Bus: *Commercial banking services.*   Fax: (213) 629-3810

● **NBS TECHNOLOGIES INC.**

5935 Airport Road, Ste. 600, Mississauga ON, L4V 1W5, Canada

CEO: Ken Kivenko, Pres. & CEO   Tel: (905) 671-3334

Bus: *Engaged in electronic business*   Fax: (905) 671-0690
     equipment.   www.nbstech.com

CARD TECHNOLOGY CORPORATION

70 Eisenhower Drive, Paramus, NJ 07652

CEO: Nayri Artun, Pres.   Tel: (201) 845-7373   %FO: 100

Bus: *Engaged in card technology.*   Fax: (201) 845-3337

● **NEXFOR (FORMERLY NORANDA FOREST)**

Suite 500, 1 Toronto Street, Toronto ON, M5C 2W4, Canada

CEO: Ian Young, SVP   Tel: (416) 643-8820   Rev: $1,580

Bus: *Pulp, paper and lumber products.*   Fax: (416) 643-8827   Emp: 9,000
                                    www.nexfor.com

FRASER PAPER, LTD.

PO Box 10055, Stamford, CT 06902

CEO: Richard J. Chapel, Dir.   Tel: (203) 705-2800   %FO: 100

Bus: *Mfr./sales paper products.*   Fax: (203) 705-2801   Emp: 10

FRASER PAPER, LTD.

PO Box 340, Park Falls, WI 54552

CEO: C. S. Souther, HR   Tel: (715) 762-3231   %FO: 100

Bus: *Mfr./sales paper products.*   Fax: (715) 762-3231

J. P. LEVESQUE & SONS LTD.
PO Box 429, Ashland, ME   04732
CEO: Charles Gordon, VP   Tel: (207) 435-6401   %FO: 100
Bus: *Mfr./sales paper products.*   Fax: (207) 425-6117

● **NORANDA INC.**
181 Bay Street, Ste. 4100, PO Box 755, BCE Place, Toronto ON, M5J 2T3, Canada
CEO: David W. Kerr, Pres. & CEO   Tel: (416) 982-7111   Rev: $3,910
Bus: *Processes natural resources, including*   Fax: (416) 982-7423   Emp: 18,000
    mining and metals.   www.noranda.com

    AMERICAN RACING EQUIPMENT, INC.
    19067 South Reyes Drive, Rancho Dominguez, CA   90221
    CEO: Robert Hange, Pres.   Tel: (310) 761-4054   %FO: 100
    Bus: *Sales natural resources and*   Fax: (310) 537-6762
        products.

    MICRO METALLICS CORPORATION
    1695 Monterey Hwy., San Jose, CA   95112
    CEO: Steve Skurnac, Pres.   Tel: (408) 998-4930   %FO: 100
    Bus: *Processes precious metal-bearing*   Fax: (408) 998-5033
        electronic materials.

    NORANDA ALUMINUM, INC.
    1000 Corporate Center Drive, Ste. 300, Franklin, TN   37067
    CEO: William Brooks, Pres.   Tel: (615) 771-5700   %FO: 100
    Bus: *Primary aluminum, aluminum*   Fax: (615) 771-5703   Emp: 1,200
        sheet and foil.

    NORANDA SAMPLING INC.
    80 Commercial Way, East Providence, RI   02914
    CEO: Robert Stanley, Mgr.   Tel: (401) 438-9220   %FO: 100
    Bus: *Sales natural resources and*   Fax: (401) 438-1237
        products.

    NORANDA USA
    750 Old Hickory Blvd., Ste. 102, Brentwood, TN   37027
    CEO: Steve Sutherland, Pres.   Tel: (615) 771-5700   %FO: 100
    Bus: *Sales natural resources and*   Fax: (615) 371-1251
        products.

● **NORTEL NETWORKS CORPORATION**
8200 Dixie Road, Ste. 100, Brampton ON, L6T 5P6, Canada

CEO: John A. Roth, CEO	Tel: (905) 863-0000	Rev: $30,275
Bus: *Global supplier of communications networks and services for data and telephony, engaged in remote information processing systems.*	Fax: (905) 863-8408 www.nortelnetworks.com	Emp: 94,500

NORTEL NETWORKS
4001 Chapel Hill Nelson Highway, Research Triangle Park, NC 27709

CEO: J. A. Craig, EVP	Tel: (919) 992-5000	%FO: 100
Bus: *Engaged in remote information processing systems.*	Fax: (919) 992-5000	

NORTEL NETWORKS
2376 B. Glenville Drive, Richardson, TX 75082-4399

CEO: James Long, Pres.	Tel: (972) 684-1000	%FO: 100
Bus: *Engaged in remote information processing systems.*	Fax: (972) 684-1000	

PERIPHONICS, DIV. NORTEL
4000 Veterans Memorial Highway, Bohemia, NY 11716-1024

CEO: Peter Cohen, Pres.	Tel: (631) 468-9000	%FO: 100
Bus: *Engaged in remote information processing systems.*	Fax: (631) 981-2689	

● **NOVA CHEMICALS CORPORATION**
645 Seventh Avenue, SW, PO Box 2518 Station M, Calgary AB, T2P 5C6, Canada

CEO: Jeffrey M. Lipton, CEO	Tel: (403) 750-3600	Rev: $3,916
Bus: *Mfr. chemicals, including polyethylene and polystyrene.*	Fax: (403) 269-7410 www.novachem.com	Emp: 4,750

NOVA CHEMICALS CORPORATION
3 Kingwood Place, 800 Rockmead Drive, Kingwood, TX 77339

CEO: Rick Seguin, Mgr.	Tel: (281) 359-6283	%FO: 100
Bus: *Mfr. chemicals, including polyethylene and polystyrene.*	Fax: (281) 359-7288	

NOVA CHEMICALS CORPORATION
950 Worcester Street, Indian Orchard, MA 01151

CEO: Richard MacKay, Mgr.	Tel: (413) 747-4091	%FO: 100
Bus: *Mfr. chemicals, including polyethylene and polystyrene.*	Fax:	

NOVA CHEMICALS CORPORATION
2655 LeJeune Road, Ste. 531, Coral Gables, FL   33134
CEO: Jeffrey M. Lipton, Pres. & CEO   Tel: (305) 461-5999   %FO: 100
Bus: *Mfr. chemicals, including*   Fax: (305) 461-5030
     polyethylene and polystyrene.

NOVA CHEMICALS CORPORATION
29201 Telegraph Road, Ste. 500, Southfield, MI   48034
CEO: Ronald R. Hornack, VP   Tel: (248) 353-6730   %FO: 100
Bus: *Mfr. chemicals, including*   Fax: (248) 353-6195
     polyethylene and polystyrene.

NOVA CHEMICALS CORPORATION
400 Frankfort Road, Monaca, PA   15061
CEO: Wes Lucas, Mgr.   Tel: (724) 770-5510   %FO: 100
Bus: *Mfr. chemicals, including*   Fax: (724) 770-5625
     polyethylene and polystyrene.

NOVA CHEMICALS CORPORATION
5100 Bainbridge Blvd., Chesapeake, VA   23320
CEO: Pete Graham, Mgr.   Tel: (757) 494-2511   %FO: 100
Bus: *Mfr. chemicals, including*   Fax: (757) 494-2511
     polyethylene and polystyrene.

NOVA CHEMICALS CORPORATION
PO Box 600, Township Road 97, Belpre, OH   45714
CEO: Cliff Hardaway, Mgr.   Tel: (740) 423-6228   %FO: 100
Bus: *Mfr. chemicals, including*   Fax: (740) 423-6228
     polyethylene and polystyrene.

NOVA CHEMICALS CORPORATION
Park West 2, Ste. 200, 2000 Cliff Mine Road, Pittsburgh, PA   15275
CEO: Grant C. Thomson, VP Sales   Tel: (412) 490-4000   %FO: 100
Bus: *Mfr. chemicals, including*   Fax: (412) 494-4861
     polyethylene and polystyrene.

NOVA CHEMICALS CORPORATION
786 Hardy Road, Painesville, OH   44077
CEO: John Feraco, Mgr.   Tel: (403) 750-4380   %FO: 100
Bus: *Mfr. chemicals, including*   Fax: (403) 750-4380
     polyethylene and polystyrene.

STYRENICS TECHNOLOGY
1550 Coraopolis Heights Road, Moon Township, PA   15108
CEO: Lynne Manuel, VP   Tel: (412) 490-4073   %FO: 100
Bus: *Engaged in research.*   Fax: (412) 490-4073

● **NOVAMERICAN STEEL INC.**
2175 Hymus Boulevard, Dorval PQ, H9P 1JB, Canada
CEO: D. Bryan Jones, Chmn.   Tel: (514) 335-6682   Rev: $480
Bus: *Mfr./distributes steel products.*   Fax: (514) 683-5285   Emp: 950
                                        www.novamerican.com

> **AMERICAN STEEL AND ALUMINUM CORPORATION**
> 425 Homestead Avenue, Hartford, CT   06112
> CEO: Joseph Pfeffer   Tel: (860) 527-2681   %FO: 100
> Bus: *Mfr./distribute steel products.*   Fax: (860) 244-9563

> **AMERICAN STEEL AND ALUMINUM CORPORATION**
> 11111 Leadbetter Road, Ashland, VA   23005
> CEO: Neil Snellings   Tel: (804) 798-6031   %FO: 100
> Bus: *Mfr./distribute steel products.*   Fax: (804) 798-4010

> **AMERICAN STEEL AND ALUMINUM CORPORATION**
> 4601 Crown Road, Liverpool, NY   13088
> CEO: Jack Chaney   Tel: (315) 451-6990   %FO: 100
> Bus: *Mfr./distribute steel products.*   Fax: (315) 451-8946

> **AMERICAN STEEL AND ALUMINUM CORPORATION**
> 197 Dexter Street, Cumberland, RI   02864
> CEO: Mike Ryan   Tel: (401) 728-8000   %FO: 100
> Bus: *Mfr./distribute steel products.*   Fax: (401) 726-6980

> **AMERICAN STEEL AND ALUMINUM CORPORATION**
> 2751 Spring Garden Drive, Middletown, PA   17057
> CEO: Frank Peredna   Tel: (717) 939-7861   %FO: 100
> Bus: *Mfr./distribute steel products.*   Fax: (717) 939-3264

> **AMERICAN STEEL AND ALUMINUM CORPORATION**
> 27 Elm Street, Auburn, MA   01501
> CEO: Bob Pierson   Tel: (508) 832-9681   %FO: 100
> Bus: *Mfr./distribute steel products.*   Fax: (508) 832-3719

> **AMERICAN STEEL AND ALUMINUM CORPORATION**
> 1080 University Avenue, Norwood, MA   02062
> CEO: Mark Willwerth   Tel: (781) 762-8014   %FO: 100
> Bus: *Mfr./distribute steel products.*   Fax: (781) 762-8804

> **AMERICAN STEEL AND ALUMINUM CORPORATION**
> One West Albany Drive, Albany, NY   12205
> CEO: Bob Boyea   Tel: (518) 489-3281   %FO: 100
> Bus: *Mfr./distribute steel products.*   Fax: (518) 489-0007

AMERICAN STEEL AND ALUMINUM CORPORATION

115 Wallace Avenue, South Portland, ME   04106

CEO: Peter Brissette	Tel: (207) 772-4641	%FO: 100
Bus: *Mfr./distribute steel products.*	Fax: (207) 772-0359	

BETHNOVA TUBE, LLC

PO Box 1179, Jeffersonville, IN   47130

CEO: Chuck Yingst	Tel: (812) 285-9796	%FO: 100
Bus: *Mfr./distribute steel products.*	Fax: (812) 285-8832	

NOVA TUBE AND STEEL

600 Dean Sievers Place, Morrisville, PA   19067

CEO: Bill Ward	Tel: (215) 295-8813	%FO: 100
Bus: *Mfr. structural tubing.*	Fax: (215) 295-8798	

● NURUN INC.

1260 Lebourgneuf Boulevard, Ste. 250, Quebec City PQ, G2K 2G2, Canada

CEO: Jacques-Herve Roubert, CEO	Tel: (418) 627-2001	Rev: $85
Bus: *Engaged in e-commerce.*	Fax: (418) 627-2023	Emp: 1,277
	www.nurun.com	

NURUN INC.

980 Washington Street, Ste. 222, Dedham, MA   02026

CEO: Ron Cheung, VP	Tel: (781) 410-2000	%FO: 100
Bus: *Engaged in e-commerce.*	Fax: (781) 410-2163	

NURUN INC.

273-C West 83rd Street, Ste. C, Burr Ridge, IL   60521

CEO: Diane Cloutier, VP	Tel: (630) 455-2660	%FO: 100
Bus: *Engaged in e-commerce.*	Fax: (630) 455-6480	

NURUN INC.

90 Broad Street, 7th Fl., New York, NY   10004

CEO: Taneshea Nash Laird, Pres.	Tel: (212) 825-5290	%FO: 100
Bus: *Engaged in e-commerce.*	Fax: (212) 826-5628	

NURUN INC.

645 Griswold, Ste. 1300, Detroit, MI   48226

CEO: Diane Cloutier, VP	Tel: (313) 237-6880	%FO: 100
Bus: *Engaged in e-commerce.*	Fax: (313) 237-6888	

● NYMOX PHARMACEUTICAL CORPORATION

9900 Cavendish Boulevard, St. Laurent PQ, H4 2V2, Canada

CEO: Paul Averback, CEO	Tel: (514) 332-3222	Rev: $2
Bus: *Engaged in biotechnology.*	Fax: (514) 332-9669	Emp: 30
	www.nymox.com	

NYMOX CORPORATION
230 West Passaic Street, Maywood, NJ 07607
CEO: Michael Munzar, MD   Tel: (800) 936-9669   %FO: 100
Bus: *Engaged in biotechnology.*   Fax: (514) 332-2227

● **ONEX CORPORATION**
161 Bay Street, PO Box 700, Toronto ON, M5J 2S1, Canada
CEO: Gerald W. Schwartz, Chmn. & CEO   Tel: (416) 362-7711   Rev: $83,000
Bus: *Holding company engaged in airline*   Fax: (416) 362-6803   Emp: 53,000
catering, electronics manufacturing,   www.onexcorp.com
auto and building products and
telecommunications.

    CLIENTLOGIC CORPORATION
    3102 West End Avenue, Ste. 1000, Nashville, TN 37203
    CEO: Mark Briggs, CEO   Tel: (615) 301-7100   %FO: 100
    Bus: *Provides outsourced customer*   Fax: (615) 301-7150
    service.

    HIDDEN CREEK INDUSTRIES
    4508 Ids Center, Minneapolis, MN 55402
    CEO: Tony Johnson, Pres.   Tel: (612) 332-2335   %FO: 100
    Bus: *Engaged in industrial management.*   Fax: (612) 332-2335

    J. L. FRENCH AUTOMOTIVE CASTINGS
    3101 South Taylor Drive, Sheboygan, WI 53081
    CEO: Charles M. Waldon, CEO   Tel: (920) 458-7724   %FO: 100
    Bus: *Mfr. aluminum die-cast*   Fax: (920) 458-7724
    components.

    MAGNATRAX CORPORATION
    1150 State Docks Road, Eufaula, AL 36027
    CEO: Robert Ammerman, CEO   Tel: (334) 687-5490   %FO: 100
    Bus: *Mfr. engineered metal building*   Fax: (334) 687-9297
    systems.

    ONEX FOOD SERVICES, INC.
    524 East Lamar Blvd., Arlington, TX 76011
    CEO: Daniel J. Altobello, Chmn.   Tel: (817) 792-2300   %FO: 100
    Bus: *Engaged in catering services.*   Fax: (817) 792-2300

    ONEX INVESTMENT CORP.
    712 Fifth Avenue, New York, NY 10019
    CEO: Robert M. LeBlanc, Dir.   Tel: (212) 582-2211   %FO: 100
    Bus: *Engaged in finance.*   Fax: (212) 582-2211

SKY CHEFS, INC.
524 East Lamar Blvd., Arlington, TX   76011
CEO: Michael Z. Kay, Pres. & CEO   Tel: (817) 792-2300   %FO: 100
Bus: *Engaged in airline catering*   Fax: (817) 792-2123
   services.

• **ONTARIO DIE COMPANY INTERNATIONAL**
235 Gage Avenue, PO Box 33, Kitchener ON, N2M 2C9, Canada
CEO: Gary Levene, Pres.   Tel: (519) 745-1002
Bus: *Mfr. die cuts and machinery leasing.*   Fax: (519) 745-0051
                                         www.ontariodie.com

   ONTARIO DIE COMPANY OF AMERICA
   PO Box 610397, Port Huron, MI   48601
   CEO: Mike Geffros, EVP   Tel: (810) 987-5060   %FO: 100
   Bus: *Mfr./sales die cuts and machinery*   Fax: (810) 987-3688
      leasing.

   ONTARIO DIE OF TENNESSEE
   1425 Toshiba Drive, Lebanon, TN   37087
   CEO: Dieter Kroger, Mgr.   Tel: (615) 443-0808   %FO: 100
   Bus: *Machinery plant.*   Fax: (615) 443-4716

   ONTARIO DIE OF TEXAS
   9641 Plaza Circle, El Paso, TX   79907
   CEO: Jim Thompson, Mgr.   Tel: (915) 858-1900   %FO: 100
   Bus: *Machinery plant.*   Fax: (915) 858-6964

• **OPEN TEXT CORPORATION**
185 Columbia Street West, Waterloo ON, N2L 5Z5, Canada
CEO: P. Thomas Jenkins, CEO   Tel: (519) 888-7111   Rev: $147
Bus: *Mfr. software products.*   Fax: (519) 888-0677   Emp: 400
                                        www.opentext.com

   OPEN TEXT
   15444 NE 95th Street, Ste. 244, Redmond, WA   98052
   CEO: P. Thomas Jenkins, CEO   Tel: (425) 897-2300   %FO: 100
   Bus: *Mfr. software products.*   Fax: (425) 897-2349

   OPEN TEXT
   3877 West Six Mile Road, Ste. 101, Livonia, MI   48152
   CEO: P. Thomas Jenkins, CEO   Tel: (734) 542-5955   %FO: 100
   Bus: *Mfr. software products.*   Fax: (734) 542-1805

OPEN TEXT

1320 Old Chain Bridge Road, Ste. 450, McLean, VA   22101

CEO: P. Thomas Jenkins, CEO   Tel: (703) 827-5510   %FO: 100

Bus: *Mfr. software products.*   Fax: (703) 827-5510

OPEN TEXT

5080 Tuttle Crossing Blvd., M/S 7-8, Dublin, OH   43016

CEO: P. Thomas Jenkins, CEO   Tel: (614) 761-7290   %FO: 100

Bus: *Mfr. software products.*   Fax: (614) 761-7290

OPEN TEXT

2201 South Waukegan Road, Bannockburn, IL   60015

CEO: P. Thomas Jenkins, CEO   Tel: (847) 267-9330   %FO: 100

Bus: *Mfr. software products.*   Fax: (847) 267-9332

● **OSLER, HOSKIN & HARCOURT LLP**

1 First Canadian Place, PO Box 50, Toronto ON, M5X 1B8, Canada

CEO: Terrence Burgoyne   Tel: (416) 362-2111

Bus: *Canadian law firm, barristers and*   Fax: (416) 862-6666
 solicitors; patent and trade-mark agents. www.osler.com

OSLER, HOSKIN & HARCOURT

280 Park Avenue, Suite 30W, New York, NY   10017

CEO: Stephen Sigurdson, Mng. Prtn.   Tel: (212) 867-5800   %FO: 100

Bus: *NY office of Canadian law firm.*   Fax: (212) 867-5802

● **PANCANADIAN PETROLEUM LIMITED**

150 9th Avenue SW, PO Box 2850, Calgary AB, T2P 2S5, Canada

CEO: David A. Tuer, Pres. & CEO   Tel: (403) 290-2000   Rev: $4,815

Bus: *Engaged in oil exploration and*   Fax: (403) 290-2950   Emp: 2,000
 production.   www.pcp.ca

NARCO

16 East Granite Street, Butte, MT   59701

CEO: Jim Benner, VP   Tel: (406) 782-4233   %FO: 100

Bus: *Engaged in oil exploration and*   Fax: (406) 496-5300
 production.

NARCO

1700 Broadway, Ste. 2000, Denver, CO   80290

CEO: Jim Benner, VP   Tel: (303) 861-9183   %FO: 100

Bus: *Engaged in oil exploration and*   Fax: (303) 839-3050
 production.

PANCANADIAN ENERGY SERVICES INC.

1200 Smith, Ste. 900, Houston, TX 77002

CEO: Larry LeBlanc, VP

Bus: *Specialty chemicals and natural gas liquids, magnesium; operates gas pipelines; property development.*

Tel: (713) 331-5000

Fax: (713) 331-5333

%FO: 100

• JIM PATTISON GROUP

1055 West Hastings Street, Ste. 1600, Vancouver BC, V6E 2H2, Canada

CEO: James Pattison, CEO

Bus: *Engaged in manufacturing of specialty packaging, grocery stores, magazine distribution, Ripley's Believe It or Not museums.*

Tel: (604) 688-6764

Fax: (604) 687-2601

www.jimpattison.com

Rev: $5,000

Emp: 24,000

CONTINENTAL SUPERBAG COMPANY

11 Cliffside Drive, Cedar Grove, NJ 07009

CEO: Warren Basso, Pres.

Bus: *Mfr. upscale, plastic shopping bags.*

Tel: (973) 239-4030

Fax: (973) 239-9289

%FO: 100

GENPAK CORPORATION

68 Warren Street, Glens Fall, NY 12801

CEO: James Reilly, Pres.

Bus: *Mfr. foam, take-out containers.*

Tel: (518) 798-9511

Fax: (518) 798-3302

THE NEWS GROUP

9081 Northfield Drive, Fort Mill, SC 29715

CEO: Mike Cooke, Pres.

Bus: *Publication wholesaler.*

Tel: (803) 548-2297

Fax: (803) 802-6701

%FO: 100

RIPLEY'S ENTERTAINMENT, INC., DIV. PATTISON GROUP

5728 Major Boulevard, Orlando, FL 32189

CEO: Robert Masterson, Pres.

Bus: *Museums, aquariums, moving theater simulators and Guinness World of Records Attractions.*

Tel: (407) 345-8010

Fax: (407) 345-8010

%FO: 100

STROUT PLASTICS, DIV. JIM PATTISON GROUP

9611 James Avenue, Bloomington, MN 55431

CEO: Thomas S. Everett, VP

Bus: *Mfr. flexible packaging.*

Tel: (612) 881-8673

Fax: (612) 881-9697

%FO: 100

Emp: 180

• PCL CONSTRUCTION GROUP INC.

5410 99th Street, Bldg. 2, Edmonton AB, T6E 3P4, Canada

CEO: Ross Grieve, Pres. & CEO	Tel: (780) 435-9711	Rev: $2,800
Bus: *Engaged in industrial, civil and commercial construction.*	Fax: (780) 436-2247 www.pcl.ca	Emp: 5,500

A. T. CURD STRUCTURES, INC.

2239 W. Stonehurst Drive, Rialto, CA   92377

CEO: Jeff McDonald, Plant Mgr.	Tel: (909) 357-0197	%FO: 100
Bus: *Engaged in industrial, civil and commercial construction.*	Fax: (919) 357-9860	

PCL CIVIL CONSTRUCTORS, INC.

2000 South Colorado Blvd., Tower Two, Ste. 2500, Denver, CO   80222

CEO: Peter Beaupre, Pres.	Tel: (303) 365-6400	%FO: 100
Bus: *U.S. headquarters location for industrial, civil and commercial construction.*	Fax: (303) 365-6490	

PCL CIVIL CONSTRUCTORS, INC.

195 East Reno, Ste. C, Las Vegas, NV   89119

CEO: Charles Houston, VP	Tel: (702) 895-7575	%FO: 100
Bus: *Engaged in industrial, civil and commercial construction.*	Fax: (702) 895-9191	

PCL CIVIL CONSTRUCTORS, INC.

9900 West Sample Road, Ste. 203, Coral Springs, FL   33065

CEO: Jerry Harder, VP	Tel: (954) 345-1725	%FO: 100
Bus: *Engaged in industrial, civil and commercial construction.*	Fax: (954) 341-4576	

PCL CONSTRUCTION SERVICES, INC.

6649 Westwood Blvd., Ste. 220, Orlando, FL   32821

CEO: Shaun Yancey, VP	Tel: (407) 363-0059	%FO: 100
Bus: *Engaged in industrial, civil and commercial construction.*	Fax: (407) 363-0171	

PCL CONSTRUCTION SERVICES, INC.

1729 West Greentree Dr., Ste. 105, Tempe, AZ   85254

CEO: Luis Ventoza, VP	Tel: (480) 829-6333	%FO: 100
Bus: *Engaged in industrial, civil and commercial construction.*	Fax: (480) 829-8252	

PCL CONSTRUCTION SERVICES, INC.
5875 El Cajon Blvd., Ste. 204, San Diego, CA   92115

CEO: Mike McKinney, VP	Tel: (619) 229-9540	%FO: 100
Bus: *Engaged in industrial, civil and commercial construction.*	Fax: (619) 229-9520	

PCL CONSTRUCTION SERVICES, INC.
15405 Southeast 37th Street, Bellevue, WA   98006

CEO: Ted Cook, VP	Tel: (424) 454-8020	%FO: 100
Bus: *Engaged in industrial, civil and commercial construction.*	Fax: (425) 454-5924	

PCL CONSTRUCTION SERVICES, INC.
12200 Nicollet Avenue South, Burnsville, MN   55337

CEO: Fred Auch, VP	Tel: (952) 882-9600	%FO: 100
Bus: *Engaged in industrial, civil and commercial construction.*	Fax: (952) 882-9900	

PCL CONSTRUCTION SERVICES, INC.
200 Burchett Street, Glendale, CA   91203

CEO: Andy Curd, VP	Tel: (818) 246-3481	%FO: 100
Bus: *Engaged in industrial, civil and commercial construction.*	Fax: (818) 247-5775	

PCL CONSTRUCTION SERVICES, INC.
2131 Kingston Court SE, Ste. 106, Marietta, GA   30067

CEO: Patrick Malone	Tel: (770) 541-7701	%FO: 100
Bus: *Engaged in industrial, civil and commercial construction.*	Fax: (770) 541-7703	

● PERMA FLEX INC.
6015 Kestrel Road, Mississauga ON, L5T 1S8, Canada

CEO: Glen Colhurst, Mgr.	Tel: (905) 670-0670
Bus: *Mfr. rollers and roller coverings.*	Fax: (905) 670-3299
	www.perma-flex.com

PERMA FLEX ENGINEERING INC.
PO Box 422, Orange, MA   01364

CEO: Mike Hebert, Mgr.	Tel: (978) 544-7803	%FO: 100
Bus: *Mfr. rollers and roller coverings.*	Fax: (978) 544-6748	

PERMA FLEX NORTH AMERICA INC.
375 Bellevue Road, Newark, DE   19713

CEO: Michael Berwick, EVP	Tel: (302) 731-7880	%FO: 100
Bus: *Mfr. rollers and roller coverings.*	Fax: (302) 731-7523	

PERMA FLEX SOUTHERN INC.
PO Box 2389, Salisbury, NC 28114-2389
CEO: Doug Angel, Mgr.   Tel: (704) 633-1201   %FO: 100
Bus: *Mfr. rollers and roller coverings.* Fax: (704) 633-1219

● **PHARMASCIENCE INC.**
6111 Avenue Royalmount, Suite 100, Montréal PQ, H4P 2T4, Canada
CEO: Morris Goodman, Chrm. Tel: (514) 340-9800
Bus: *Pharmaceuticals, surgical supplies.* Fax: (514) 342-7764 Emp: 100
            www.pharmascience.com

  AMD-RITMED INC.
  175 Rano Street, Buffalo, NY 14207
  CEO: Tammy Chase, Gen. Mgr. Tel: (716) 871-9164   %FO: 100
  Bus: *Mfr. disposable O/R supplies.* Fax: (716) 871-3415   Emp: 28

● **PLACER DOME INC.**
PO Box 49330, Bentail Postal Station, Vancouver BC, V7X 1P1, Canada
CEO: Jay K. Taylor, Pres.   Tel: (604) 682-7082   Rev: $1,413
Bus: *Mineral exploration, development and* Fax: (604) 682-7092   Emp: 12,000
  production.   www.placerdome.com

  PLACER DOME INC.
  1125 17th Street, Ste. 2310, Denver, CO 80202
  CEO: William Hayes, CEO   Tel: (303) 675-0055   %FO: 100
  Bus: *Mineral exploration, development* Fax: (303) 675-0707   Emp: 950
  and production.

● **PMC-SIERRA, INC.**
105-8555 Baxter Place, Burnaby BC, V5A 4V7, Canada
CEO: Robert L. Bailey, CEO   Tel: (604) 415-6000   Rev: $695
Bus: *Mfr. broadband chips for network* Fax: (604) 415-6209   Emp: 1,700
  infrastructure applications. www.pmc-sierra.com

  PMC-SIERRA, INC.
  One Apple Hill Drive, Ste. 224, Natick, MA 01760-2083
  CEO: Gregory D. Aasen, COO Tel: (508) 560-3431   %FO: 100
  Bus: *Mfr. broadband chips for network* Fax: (508) 650-3434
  infrastructure applications.

  PMC-SIERRA, INC.
  Two Mid America Plaza, Ste. 800, Oakbrook Terrace, IL 60181
  CEO: Gregory D. Aasen, COO Tel: (630) 954-2324   %FO: 100
  Bus: *Mfr. broadband chips for network* Fax: (630) 954-2259
  infrastructure applications.

PMC-SIERRA, INC.
4825 Creekstone Drive, Ste. 200, Durham, NC   27703
CEO: Gregory D. Aasen, COO   Tel: (919) 474-5125   %FO: 100
Bus: *Mfr. broadband chips for network*   Fax: (919) 474-5050
     infrastructure applications.

PMC-SIERRA, INC.
3975 Freedom Circle, Santa Clara, CA   95054
CEO: Gregory D. Aasen, COO   Tel: (405) 239-8000   %FO: 100
Bus: *Mfr. broadband chips for network*   Fax: (408) 492-1157
     infrastructure applications.

PMC-SIERRA, INC.
850 Central Parkway East, Ste. 140, Plano, TX   75074
CEO: Gregory D. Aasen, COO   Tel: (972) 423-4135   %FO: 100
Bus: *Mfr. broadband chips for network*   Fax: (972) 424-0141
     infrastructure applications.

● **POLYAIR INTER PACK INC.**
258 Attwell Drive, Toronto ON, M9VV 5B2, Canada
CEO: Henry Schnurbach, CEO   Tel: (416) 740-2687   Rev: $105
Bus: *Mfr. protective foam packaging*   Fax: (416) 740-2692   Emp: 750
     materials.   www.polyair.com

POLYAIR INTER PACK INC.
808 East 113th Street, Chicago, IL   60628
CEO: Chris French   Tel: (773) 995-1818   %FO: 100
Bus: *Mfr. protective foam packaging*   Fax: (773) 995-7725
     materials.

POLYAIR INTER PACK INC.
6035-B LeGrange Blvd., Atlanta, GA   30336
CEO: Chris French   Tel: (404) 344-4413   %FO: 100
Bus: *Mfr. protective foam packaging*   Fax: (404) 629-6148
     materials.

POLYAIR INTER PACK INC.
1692 Jenks Drive, Ste. 102, Corona, CA   92880
CEO: Chris French   Tel: (909) 737-7125   %FO: 100
Bus: *Mfr. protective foam packaging*   Fax: (909) 737-8021
     materials.

POLYAIR INTER PACK INC.
1100 Performance Place, Youngstown, OH   44502
CEO: Chris French   Tel: (330) 744-8812   %FO: 100
Bus: *Mfr. protective foam packaging*   Fax: (330) 744-1228
     materials.

POLYAIR INTER PACK INC.

300 Spencer Mattingly Lane, Bardstown, KY 40004

CEO: Chris French   Tel: (502) 348-7020   %FO: 100

Bus: *Mfr. protective foam packaging*   Fax: (502) 348-5511
materials.

● **POLYDEX PHARMACEUTICALS LIMITED**

421 Comstock Road, Toronto ON, M1L 2H5, Canada

CEO: George G. Usher, CEO   Tel: (416) 755-2231   Rev: $14

Bus: *Mfr. veterinary drugs.*   Fax: (416) 755-0334   Emp: 100
                                    www.polydex.com

SPARHAWK VETERINARY LABORATORIES, INC.

12340 Santa Fe Drive, Lenexa, KS 66215

CEO: Bert Hughes   Tel: (913) 888-7500   %FO: 100

Bus: *Mfr./sales veterinary drugs.*   Fax: (913) 888-7500

● **POTASH CORPORATION OF SASKATCHEWAN INC. (PCS)**

122 First Avenue South, Ste. 500, Saskatoon SK, S7K 7G3, Canada

CEO: William J. Doyle, CEO   Tel: (306) 933-8500   Rev: $2,232

Bus: *Engaged in producing fertilizers.*   Fax: (306) 933-8844   Emp: 5,340
                                          www.potashcorp.com

PCS FEED GROUP

PO Box 500, 1637 Westfront Street, Buffalo, IA 52728

CEO: William J. Doyle, Pres. & CEO   Tel: (319) 381-1130   %FO: 100

Bus: *Engaged in minimizing emissions*   Fax: (319) 381-1130
through the use of advanced
control technology.

PCS NITROGEN

3175 Lenox Park Boulevard, Ste 400, Memphis, TN 38115

CEO: Jim Dietz, Mgr.   Tel: (901) 758-5200   %FO: 100

Bus: *Produces nitrogen.*   Fax: (901) 758-5379

PCS PHOSPHATE INC.

3101 Glenwood Avenue, Raleigh, NC 27612

CEO: William J. Doyle, Pres. & CEO   Tel: (919) 881-2700   %FO: 100

Bus: *Engaged in minimizing emissions*   Fax: (919) 881-2847
through the use of advanced
control technology.

PCS PHOSPHATE INC.
PO Box 300, County Road 137, White Springs, FL   32096
CEO: William J. Doyle, Pres. & CEO   Tel: (904) 397-8101   %FO: 100
Bus: *Engaged in minimizing emissions*   Fax: (904) 397-8371
through the use of advanced
control technology.

● **POWER FINANCIAL LTD.**
751 Victoria Square, Montréal PQ, Canada H2Y 2K4
CEO: Paul Desmarais, Jr., CEO   Tel: (514) 286-7400   Rev: $9,800
Bus: *Holding company.*   Fax: (514) 286-7424   Emp: 23,000
www.powercorp.ca

THE GREAT-WEST LIFE ASSURANCE COMPANY
8505-8515 East Orchard Road, Englewood, CO   80111
CEO: William T. McCallum, CEO   Tel: (303) 889-3000   %FO: 99
Bus: *Life & health insurance and*   Fax: (303) 689-5220
annuities.

● **PRECISION DRILLING CORPORATION**
4200 Petro Canada Centre, 150 6th Avenue SW, Calgary AB, T2P 3Y7, Canada
CEO: Hank B. Swartout, CEO   Tel: (403) 716-4500   Rev: $904
Bus: *Oil well drilling contractor.*   Fax: (403) 264-0251   Emp: 10,575
www.precisiondrilling.com

COMPUTALOG USA INC.
500 Winscott Road, Ft. Worth, TX   76126
CEO: Steve Upperman   Tel: (817) 249-7200   %FO: 100
Bus: *Oil well drilling contractor.*   Fax: (817) 249-7222

NORTHLAND-NORWARD ENERGY SERVICES.
PO Box 1195, Evanston, WY   82930
CEO: Dave Garnier, Mgr.   Tel: (307) 789-5590   %FO: 100
Bus: *Oil well drilling contractor.*   Fax: (307) 789-5593

NORTHLAND-NORWARD ENERGY SERVICES.
7090 Barton Drive, Casper, WY   82604
CEO: Bruce Fields, Mgr.   Tel: (307) 577-8875   %FO: 100
Bus: *Oil well drilling contractor.*   Fax: (307) 577-9182

NORTHLAND-NORWARD ENERGY SERVICES.
363 North Sam Houston Pkwy. East, Ste. 1700, Houston, TX   77060
CEO: Bob Pilko, Mgr.   Tel: (281) 260-5600   %FO: 100
Bus: *Oil well drilling contractor.*   Fax: (281) 260-5670

● **PREMDOR INC.**
1600 Britannia Road East, Mississauga ON, L4W 1J2, Canada

CEO: Philip S. Orsino, Pres. & CEO	Tel: (905) 670-6500	Rev: $1,292
Bus: *Mfr. interior and exterior doors.*	Fax: (905) 670-6520	Emp: 1,200
	www.premdor.com	

    PREMDOR CORPORATION
    210 Haleyville Industrial Road, Haleyville, AL   35565

CEO: Lawrence P. Repar, VP Sales	Tel: (205) 486-9216	%FO: 100
Bus: *Mfr./sales interior and exterior doors.*	Fax: (205) 486-4324	

    PREMDOR CORPORATION
    PO Box 285, Corning, CA   96021

CEO: Lawrence P. Repar, VP Sales	Tel: (530) 824-2121	%FO: 100
Bus: *Mfr./sales interior and exterior doors.*	Fax: (530) 824-4374	

    PREMDOR CORPORATION
    PO Box 218, North Platte, NE   69101

CEO: Lawrence P. Repar, VP Sales	Tel: (308) 534-1102	%FO: 100
Bus: *Mfr./sales interior and exterior doors.*	Fax: (308) 534-4482	

    PREMDOR CORPORATION
    PO Box 1, Walkerton, IN   46574

CEO: Lawrence P. Repar, VP Sales	Tel: (219) 586-3192	%FO: 100
Bus: *Mfr./sales interior and exterior doors.*	Fax: (219) 586-7282	

    PREMDOR US HOLDINGS INC.
    One North Dale Mabry Hwy., Ste. 950, Tampa, FL   33609

CEO: Lawrence P. Repar, VP Sales	Tel: (813) 877-2726	%FO: 100
Bus: *Mfr./sales interior and exterior doors.*	Fax: (813) 739-0115	

● **PREVOST CAR INC.**
35 Blvd. Gagnon, Ste Claire PQ, G0R 2V0, Canada

CEO: Georges Bourelle, Pres. & CEO	Tel: (418) 883-3391	
Bus: *Mfr. intercity coaches and special purpose vehicles. (JV Volvo Bus and Henly's Group Plc)*	Fax: (418) 883-4157	Emp: 1,500
	www.prevostcar.com	

PREVOST CAR INC.
862 Valley Brook Avenue, Lyndhurst, NJ   07071

CEO: Dan Marrazzo, Mgr.	Tel: (201) 933-3900	%FO: 100
Bus: *Sales/service intercity coaches &* *special purpose vehicles*	Fax: (201) 933-2785	Emp: 33

● **QUEBECOR INC.**
612 St. Jacques Street, Montréal PQ, H3C 4M8, Canada

CEO: Eric Peladeau, Pres. & CEO	Tel: (514) 877-9777	Rev: $7,490
Bus: *Commercial printing services and* *distributors of French language books* *and CD-ROMS.*	Fax: (514) 877-9757 www.quebecor.com	Emp: 60,000

QUEBECOR WORLD (USA) CORP.
340 Pemberwick Road, Greenwich, CT   06831

CEO: Marc L. Reisch, CEO	Tel: (203) 532-4200	%FO: 100
Bus: *Distributes print and digital* *information.*	Fax: (203) 532-4372	Emp: 16,000

● **RAND A TECHNOLOGY CORPORATION**
5785 Solar Drive, Mississauga ON, L4W 5B8, Canada

CEO: Brian Semkiw, CEO	Tel: (905) 625-2000	Rev: $280
Bus: *Resale of software and hardware.*	Fax: (905) 625-2035 www.rand.com	Emp: 1,300

RAND WORLDWIDE
675 Mansell Road, Ste. 115, Roswell, GA   30076

CEO: Phil Stephenson, Pres.	Tel: (770) 518-9691	%FO: 100
Bus: *Resale of software and hardware.*	Fax: (770) 581-1869	

RAND WORLDWIDE
4 Greentree Center, Ste. 303, Marlton, NJ   08053

CEO: Phil Stephenson, Pres.	Tel: (856) 797-7060	%FO: 100
Bus: *Resale of software and hardware.*	Fax: (856) 797-7066	

RAND WORLDWIDE
2030 E. Algonquin Road, Ste. 402, Schaumburg, IL   60173

CEO: Phil Stephenson, Pres.	Tel: (847) 303-6460	%FO: 100
Bus: *Resale of software and hardware.*	Fax: (847) 303-6471	

RAND WORLDWIDE
23550 Commerce Park, Beachwood, OH   44122

CEO: Phil Stephenson, Pres.	Tel: (216) 292-3457	%FO: 100
Bus: *Resale of software and hardware.*	Fax: (216) 765-0027	

RAND WORLDWIDE
10355 Westmoor Drive, Ste. 200, Westminster, CO   80021
CEO: Phil Stephenson, Pres.   Tel: (303) 410-0060   %FO: 100
Bus: *Resale of software and hardware.*   Fax: (303) 410-0070

RAND WORLDWIDE
100 Great Meadow Road, Ste. 500, Wethersfield, CT   06109-2375
CEO: Phil Stephenson, Pres.   Tel: (860) 571-7242   %FO: 100
Bus: *Resale of software and hardware.*   Fax: (860) 571-7250

RAND WORLDWIDE
815 Shore Drive, Boynton Beach, FL   33435
CEO: Phil Stephenson, Pres.   Tel: (561) 735-9971   %FO: 100
Bus: *Resale of software and hardware.*   Fax: (760) 281-8876

RAND WORLDWIDE
4835 LBJ Freeway, Ste. 100, Dallas, TX   75244
CEO: Phil Stephenson, Pres.   Tel: (972) 991-1404   %FO: 100
Bus: *Resale of software and hardware.*   Fax: (972) 991-1447

RAND WORLDWIDE
6039 Schumacher Park Drive, Cincinnati, OH   45069
CEO: Phil Stephenson, Pres.   Tel: (513) 777-6775   %FO: 100
Bus: *Resale of software and hardware.*   Fax: (513) 777-1276

RAND WORLDWIDE
1819 Sardis Road North, Ste. 300, Charlotte, NC   28270
CEO: Phil Stephenson, Pres.   Tel: (704) 849-7995   %FO: 100
Bus: *Resale of software and hardware.*   Fax: (704) 849-0096

RAND WORLDWIDE
321 Commonwealth Road, Ste. 100, Wayland, MA   01778
CEO: Phil Stephenson, Pres.   Tel: (508) 655-0885   %FO: 100
Bus: *Resale of software and hardware.*   Fax: (508) 655-4196

● **RAYCO ELECTRONICS SYSTEMS, DIV. RAYCO TECHNOLOGY**
2440 Ave. Dalton, Ste-Foy PQ, G1P 3X1, Canada
CEO: Norman Hinse, CEO   Tel: (418) 654-0404
Bus: *Engaged in supply crane and heavy*   Fax: (418) 654-3674   Emp: 100
equipment monitoring and safety   www.raycotech.com
systems.

WYLIE SYSTEMS INC.
420 North Walnut Avenue, Broken Arrow, OK   74012
CEO: Normand Hinse, Pres. & CEO   Tel: (918) 252-1957   %FO: 100
Bus: *Distribution/service crane safety*   Fax: (918) 252-2048   Emp: 5
systems.

● **RBC DOMINION SECURITIES, DIV. ROYAL BANK OF CANADA**
PO Box 50, Royal Bank Plaza, Toronto ON, M5J 2WJ, Canada
CEO: Gordon Nixon, CEO   Tel: (416) 842-2000
Bus: *Investment broker.*   Fax: (416) 842-2100   Emp: 2,000
                                       www.rbcds.com

    RBC DOMINION SECURITIES, INC.
    165 Broadway, New York, NY   10006-1404
    CEO: Bruce MacDonald, CEO   Tel: (212) 858-7000   %FO: 100
    Bus: *Investment broker.*   Fax: (212) 858-7180

● **RBC FINANCIAL GROUP (FORMERLY ROYAL BANK OF CANADA)**
200 Bay Street, Toronto ON, M5J 2JS, Canada
CEO: Gordon J. Feeney   Tel: (416) 974-5151   Rev: $14,963
Bus: *General banking services.*   Fax: (416) 955-7800   Emp: 49,230
                                       www.royalbank.com

    BULL & BEAR SECURITIES, INC.
    *One Liberty Plaza, New York, NY   10006-1404
    CEO: Brian Kape, CEO   Tel: (212) 428-6200   %FO: 100
    Bus: *Commercial banking services.*   Fax: (212) 428-6961

    DAIN RAUSCHER CORPORATION
    60 South Sixth Street, Minneapolis, MN   55402-4422
    CEO: Irving Weiser, CEO   Tel: (612) 313-1234   %FO: 100
    Bus: *Engaged in corporate,*   Fax: (612) 371-7619   Emp: 3,700
       institutional and individual
       investment services.

    DAIN RAUSCHER CORPORATION
    65 East 55th Street, New York, NY   10022
    CEO: Irving Weiser, CEO   Tel: (212) 593-2110   %FO: 100
    Bus: *Engaged in corporate,*   Fax: (212) 593-2120
       institutional and individual
       investment services.

    RBC FINANCIAL GROUP
    One Liberty Plaza, New York, NY   10006-1404
    CEO: Bruce Rothney   Tel: (212) 428-6200   %FO: 100
    Bus: *Commercial banking services.*   Fax: (212) 428-3011   Emp: 500

    SECURITY FIRST NETWORK BANK
    3475 Piedmont Road, Ste. 300, Atlanta, GA   30305
    CEO: Ashif N. Ratanshi, CEO   Tel: (404) 495-6000   %FO: 100
    Bus: *Commercial banking services.*   Fax: (404) 495-6000

● **RECOCHEM INC.**
850 Montee de Liesse, Montréal PQ, H4T 1P4, Canada
CEO: Eva Kuchar, VP   Tel: (514) 341-3550
Bus: *Mfr. chemicals.*   Fax: (514) 341-6553   Emp: 450
                                        www.recochem.com

   RECOCHEM (USA)
   182 West Central Street, Natick, MA   01760
   CEO: Bert White, VP   Tel: (508) 650-5800   %FO: 100
   Bus: *Mfr./sales chemicals.*   Fax: (508) 651-0294

● **RIO ALGOM LTD.**
120 Adelaide Street West, Toronto ON, M5H 1W5, Canada
CEO: Patrick M. James, Pres. & CEO   Tel: (416) 367-4000   Rev: $1,375
Bus: *Mining and metals distributor.*   Fax: (416) 365-6870   Emp: 2,774
                                        www.rioalgom.com

   RIO ALGOM MINING CORPORATION
   6305 Waterford Blvd., Ste. 325, Oklahoma City, OK   73118
   CEO: Robert P. Luke, Pres.   Tel: (405) 848-1190   %FO: 100
   Bus: *Uranium mining.*   Fax: (405) 848-1208   Emp: 100

● **RITCHIE BROS. AUCTIONEERS INCORPORATED**
9200 Bridgeport Road, Richmond BC, V6X 1S1, Canada
CEO: David E. Ritchie, CEO   Tel: (604) 273-7564   Rev: $106
Bus: *Auctioneer.*   Fax: (604) 273-6873   Emp: 1,515
                                        www.rbauction.com

   RITCHIE BROS. AUCTIONEERS
   3901 Faulkner Drive, PO Box 6429, Lincoln, NE   68506-0429
   CEO: Michael G. Ritchie, VP   Tel: (402) 421-3631   %FO: 100
   Bus: *Auctioneer.*   Fax: (402) 421-1738

● **RUSSEL METALS INC.**
1900 Minnesota Court, Ste. 210, Mississauga ON, l5N 3C9, Canada
CEO: Edward M. Siegel Jr., CEO   Tel: (905) 819-7777   Rev: $1,022
Bus: *Engaged in steel distribution.*   Fax: (905) 819-7409   Emp: 1,900
                                        www.russelmetals.com

   SUNBELT GROUP INC.
   1990 Post Oak Boulevard, Ste. 1550, Houston, TX   77056-3813
   CEO: Gerhard Adenacker, Pres.   Tel: (713) 840-0550   %FO: 100
   Bus: *Engaged in steel distribution.*   Fax: (713) 840-8727

● **SAND TECHNOLOGY INC.**
215 Redfern, Ste. 415, Westmount PQ, H3Z 3I5, Canada
CEO: Arthur G. Ritchie, CEO   Tel: (514) 939-3477   Rev: $5
Bus: *Mfr. analytical processing software.*   Fax: (514) 939-2042   Emp: 65
www.sandtechnology.com

   SAND TECHNOLOGY CORPORATION
   555 Woodbridge Towers, Route 1, South Iselin, NJ   08830
   CEO: Jerome Shattner, Pres.   Tel: (732) 750-4848   %FO: 100
   Bus: *Mfr./sales analytical processing   Fax: (732) 750-4848
      software.*

● **SANDWELL ENGINEERING, INC.**
Park Place, 666 Burrard Street, Vancouver BC, V6C 2X8, Canada
CEO: Alan Pyatt, Pres. & CEO   Tel: (604) 684-0055
Bus: *Engineering, plan, design, project and   Fax: (604) 684-7533   Emp: 1,700
   construction management.*   www.sandwell.com

   SANDWELL INC.
   2690 Cumberland Pkwy., Atlanta, GA   30339
   CEO: Jon Ferguson, VP   Tel: (770) 433-9336   %FO: 100
   Bus: *Engineering, planning, design,   Fax: (770) 433-9518   Emp: 350
      project & construction
      management*

● **SAPUTO GROUP INC.**
6869 Metropolitan East, Montréal PQ, H1P 1X8, Canada
CEO: Emanuele Saputo, CEO   Tel: (514) 328-6662   Rev: $1,371
Bus: *Mfr. mozzarella and specialty cheeses,   Fax: (514) 328-3356   Emp: 8,450
   butter and whey protein.*   www.saputo.com

   SAPUTO CHEESE INC.
   5611 East Imperial, South Gate, CA   90280
   CEO: Tim Yoshonis, Sales Mgr.   Tel: (562) 862-7686   %FO: 100
   Bus: *Mfr. cheeses.*   Fax: (562) 862-7756

   SAPUTO CHEESE INC.
   25 Tri State Industrial Office Park, Lincolnshire, IL   60069
   CEO: Rick Gillespie   Tel: (847) 267-1100   %FO: 100
   Bus: *Mfr. cheeses.*   Fax: (847) 267-0618

• **SCOTIABANK (THE BANK OF NOVA SCOTIA)**

44 King Street, Toronto ON, M5H 1H1, Canada

CEO: Peter C. Godsoe, CEO   Tel: (416) 866-6161   Rev: $12,405

Bus: *Provides commercial, corporate,*   Fax: (416) 866-6430   Emp: 54,000
investment and international banking   www.scotiabank.ca
services.

  SCOTIABANK

  28 State Street, 17th Fl., Boston, MA   02109

  CEO: Terrance Pitcher, Mng. Dir.   Tel: (617) 624-7609   %FO: 100

  Bus: *Provides corporate, investment*   Fax: (617) 624-7607
     banking and capital market
     services.

  SCOTIABANK

  888 SW Fifth Avenue, Portland, OR   97204

  CEO: Michael Brown, VP   Tel: (503) 222-5233   %FO: 100

  Bus: *Provides corporate, investment*   Fax: (503) 222-5502
     banking and capital market
     services.

  SCOTIABANK

  580 California Street, Ste. 2100, San Francisco, CA   94104

  CEO: James York, VP   Tel: (415) 986-1100   %FO: 100

  Bus: *Provides corporate, investment*   Fax: (415) 397-0791
     banking and capital market
     services.

  SCOTIABANK

  181 West Madison Street, Chicago, IL   60602

  CEO: Chris Allen, Mng. Dir.   Tel: (312) 201-4100   %FO: 100

  Bus: *Provides corporate, investment*   Fax: (312) 201-4108
     banking and capital market
     services.

  SCOTIABANK

  *One Liberty Plaza, 26th Fl., New York, NY   10006

  CEO: Kevin Ray, EVP   Tel: (212) 225-5233   %FO: 100

  Bus: *Provides corporate, investment*   Fax: (212) 225-6464
     banking and capital market
     services.

SCOTIABANK

1100 Louisiana Street, Ste. 300, Houston, TX   77002

CEO: Larry Lloyd, Mng. Dir.   Tel: (713) 752-0900   %FO: 100

Bus: *Provides corporate, investment*   Fax: (713) 752-2425
   banking and capital market
   services.

SCOTIABANK

600 Peachtree Street NE, Ste. 2700, Atlanta, GA   30308

CEO: William Brown, VP   Tel: (404) 877-1500   %FO: 100

Bus: *Provides corporate, investment*   Fax: (404) 888-8998
   banking and capital market
   services.

● **THE SEAGRAM COMPANY LTD.**

1430 Peel Street, Montréal PQ, H3A 1S9, Canada

CEO: Edgar M. Bronfman Jr., Pres. & CEO   Tel: (514) 849-5271   Rev: $12,312

Bus: *Mfr. and distributes distilled spirits,*   Fax: (514) 987-5224   Emp: 24,200
   wines and beverages; entertainment   www.seagram.com
   products and operates theme parks.

MCA NASHVILLE

60 Music Square East, Nashville, TN   37203

CEO: Tony Brown, Pres.   Tel: (615) 244-8944   %FO: 100

Bus: *Mfr. and distributes recorded*   Fax:
   music.

MCA RECORDS

2220 Colorado Avenue, Santa Monica, CA   90404

CEO: Jay Boberg, Pres.   Tel: (310) 865-4000

Bus: *Music recording and publishing.*   Fax:

JOSEPH E. SEAGRAM & SONS INC.

375 Park Avenue, New York, NY   10152-0192

CEO: Edgar M. Bronfman Jr., Pres.   Tel: (212) 572-7000   %FO: 100

Bus: *Distilled spirits & wines.*   Fax: (212) 838-5052

SEAGRAM AMERICAS

800 Third Avenue, New York, NY   10152-0192

CEO: Stephen N. Fisher, Pres.   Tel: (212) 572-7000   %FO: 100

Bus: *Distribution distilled spirits, wines*   Fax: (212) 572-7058
   and beverages.

SEAGRAM CHATEAU & ESTATE WINES COMPANY

2600 Campus Drive, Ste.160, San Mateo, CA   94403

CEO: Samuel Bronfman II, Pres.   Tel: (650) 378-3800   %FO: 100

Bus: *Mfr. & distribution wines and*   Fax: (650) 378-3820
    spirits.

THE SEAGRAM SPIRITS & WINE GROUP

375 Park Avenue, 5th Fl., New York, NY   10152

CEO: Steven J. Kalagher, Pres. & CEO   Tel: (212) 572-7000   %FO: 100

Bus: *U.S. Headquarters; distilled spirits* Fax: (212) 572-1022
    and wines.

SPENCER GIFTS

6826 Black Horse Pike, Egg Harbor Township, NJ   08234

CEO: John Hacala, CEO   Tel: (609) 645-3300

Bus: *Retail store gift chain.*   Fax:

UNIVERSAL CONSUMER PRODUCTS GROUP

100 Universal City Plaza, Bldg. 509, 15th Fl., Universal City, CA   91608

CEO: Cynthia C. Cleveland, Pres.   Tel: (818) 777-5391

Bus: *Retail stores operations.*   Fax:

UNIVERSAL MUSIC & VIDEO DISTRIBUTION

Ten Universal City Plaza, Ste. 400, Universal City, CA   91608

CEO: Jim Urie, Pres.   Tel: (818) 777-4400   %FO: 100

Bus: *Handles sales and marketing for*   Fax:
    Universal Music Group.

UNIERSAL MUSIC GROUP

1755 Broadway, New York, NY   10019

CEO: Doug Morris, CEO   Tel: (212) 373-0600   %FO: 100

Bus: *Mfr. and distributes recorded*   Fax:
    music.

UNIVERSAL MUSIC GROUP

2220 Colorado Avenue, Santa Monica, CA   90404

CEO: Zach Horowitz, Pres.   Tel: (310) 865-5000   %FO: 100

Bus: *Music publishing and live event*   Fax:
    concerts.

UNIVERSAL PICTURES

100 Universal City Plaza, Universal City, CA   91608

CEO: Rick Finkelstein, Pres.   Tel: (818) 777-1000   %FO: 100

Bus: *Creates and distributes theatrical* Fax:
    and non-theatrical filmed
    entertainment.

UNIVERSAL STUDIOS, INC.
100 Universal City Plaza, Universal City, CA 91608
CEO: Ron Meyer, Pres. & COO   Tel: (818) 777-1000   %FO: 100
Bus: *Motion picture, TV production and*   Fax: (818) 866-1440   Emp: 14,000
distribution, music recording and
publishing, communications, real
estate.

UNIVERSAL TELEVISION AND NETWORKS GROUP
100 Universal City Plaza, Universal City, CA 91608
CEO: Blair Westlake, Chmn.   Tel: (818) 777-1000   %FO: 100
Bus: *Engaged in production,*   Fax:
distribution and networks
operations.

VERVE MUSIC GROUP
1755 Broadway, New York, NY 10019
CEO: Tommy LiPuma, Pres.   Tel: (212) 373-0600   %FO: 100
Bus: *Music recording and publishing.*   Fax: (212) 373-0600

● **SEMANTIX, INC.**
55 rue Prince, Montréal PQ, H3C 2M7, Canada
CEO: Andy Ras-Work, CEO   Tel: (514) 848-9621
Bus: *Mfr. software.*   Fax: (514) 848-9741
   www.semantix.com

SEMANTIX, INC.
13530 Dulles Technology Drive, Ste. 150, Herndon, VA 20171
CEO: Rob Johnston   Tel: (703) 234-0341   %FO: 100
Bus: *Mfr./sales software.*   Fax: (703) 234-0341

● **SENSE TECHNOLOGIES INC.**
305-595 Howe Street, Vancouver BC, V6C 2T5, Canada
CEO: Gerald McIlhargey, CEO   Tel: (604) 682-7878
Bus: *Mfr. microwave radar technology*   Fax: (604) 688-9727   Emp: 5
systems for truck backups.   www.sensetech.com

SENSE TECHNOLOGIES INC.
14441 Dupont Court, Ste. 103, Omaha, NE 68144
CEO: G. R. McIlhargey, Pres.   Tel: (604) 682-0074
Bus: *Mfr./sales microwave radar*   Fax: (604) 688-9727
technology systems for truck
backups.

• SHAWCOR LTD.

25 Bethridge Road, Toronto ON, M9W 1M7, Canada

CEO: Leslie E. Shaw	Tel: (416) 743-7111	Rev: $312
Bus: *Mfr. pipeline coatings.*	Fax: (416) 743-7199	Emp: 2,200
	www.shawcor.com	

BREDERO-SHAW

2350 N. Sam Houston Pkwy. East, Houston, TX   77032

CEO:L. Evans	Tel: (281) 886-2350
Bus: *Mfr. pipe coatings.*	Fax: (281) 886-2351

DSG-CANUSA

173 Commerce Blvd., Loveland, OH   45140

CEO: Scott James	Tel: (513) 683-7800	%FO: 100
Bus: *Mfr. pipe coatings.*	Fax: (513) 683-7809	

OMSCO

PO Box 230589, Houston, TX   77223-0589

CEO: W. Steve Fowler, VO	Tel: (713) 844-3700	%FO: 100
Bus: *Mfr. valves and pipes.*	Fax: (713) 926-7103	

• SHIRE-BIOCHEM PHARMA INC., DIV. SHIRE PHARMACEUTICALS

275 Armand-Frappier Boulevard, Laval PQ, H7V 4A7, Canada

CEO: Dr. Francesco Bellini, CEO	Tel: (450) 681-1744	Rev: $217
Bus: *Engaged in the development of HIV drugs.*	Fax: (450) 978-7755	Emp: 500
	www.biochem-pharma.com	

BIOGLAN PHARMA INC.

7 Great Valley Parkway, Ste. 301, Malvern, PA   19355

CEO: Frederick J. Andrew	Tel: (610) 232-2000	%FO: 100
Bus: *Engaged in the development of HIV drugs.*	Fax: (610) 232-2020	

• SICO INC.

2505 de la Metropole Street, Longueuil PQ, Canada J4G 1E5

CEO: Pierre Brodeur, CEO	Tel: (514) 527-5111	
Bus: *Paint, coatings, sealants, concrete admixtures.*	Fax: (514) 646-7699	Emp: 1,000
	www.sico.com	

HANCOCK PAINTS INC.

24 Plain Street, Braintree, MA   02184

CEO: Sal Giglio	Tel: (781) 794-9800	%FO: 100
Bus: *Mfr. paint, industry coatings.*	Fax: (781) 794-9809	

● **SIERRA WIRELESS, INC.**
13811 Wireless Way, Richmond BC, V6V 3A4, Canada
CEO: David B. Stucliffe, CEO   Tel: (604) 231-1100   Rev: $54
Bus: *Mfr. modems and software for wireless*   Fax: (604) 231-1109   Emp: 250
communication.   www.sierrawireless.com

    SOLECTRON CORPORATION
    847 Gibraltar Drive, Milpitas, CA 95035
    CEO: Koichi Nishimura, CEO   Tel: (408) 957-8500   %FO: 100
    Bus: *Engaged in electronics*   Fax: (408) 957-2855
    manufacturing and supply-chain
    management services.

● **SILENT WITNESS ENTERPRISES LTD.**
6554 175th Street, Surrey BC, V3S 4G5, Canada
CEO: Rob Bakshi, CEO   Tel: (604) 574-1526   Rev: $27
Bus: *Mfr. video surveillance systems.*   Fax: (604) 574-7736   Emp: 110
    www.silent-witness.com

    SILENT WITNESS ENTERPRISES
    PO Box 1950, Blaine, WA 98231
    CEO: John Jennings   Tel: (604) 574-1526   %FO: 100
    Bus: *Sales/distribution of video*   Fax: (604) 574-1527   Emp: 125
    surveillance systems.

● **SIMEX INC.**
511 King Street West, Ste. 130, Toronto ON, M5V 2Z4, Canada
CEO: Michael Needham, CEO   Tel: (416) 597-1585   Rev: $19
Bus: *Designs motion simulation machines.*   Fax: (416) 597-0530   Emp: 80
    www.simex.ca

    SIMEX DIGITAL STUDIOS
    3250 Ocean Park Blvd, Ste. 100, Santa Monica, CA 90405
    CEO: Michael Needham, Pres.   Tel: (310) 664-9500   %FO: 100
    Bus: *Designs motion simulation*   Fax: (310) 664-9977
    machines.

● **A.G. SIMPSON AUTOMOTIVE SYSTEMS**
675 Progress Avenue, Scarborough ON, M1H 2W9, Canada
CEO: Robert A. Simpson, Chmn.   Tel: (416) 438-6650   Rev: $409
Bus: *Mfr. bumper systems, metal brackets,*   Fax: (416) 431-8756   Emp: 3,000
fuel tank straps and tailgates.   www.agsimpson.com

A. G. SIMPSON AUTOMOTIVE

6640 Sterling Drive South, Ste. 11, Sterling Heights, MI 48312

CEO: Robert A. Simpson, Pres. Tel: (810) 558-5400 %FO: 100

Bus: *Mfr. bumper systems, metal brackets, fuel tank straps and tailgates.* Fax: (810) 939-7744

A. G. SIMPSON AUTOMOTIVE

1304 East Maple Road, Troy, MI 48034

CEO: Robert A. Simpson, Pres. Tel: (248) 925-5600 %FO: 100

Bus: *Mfr. bumper systems, metal brackets, fuel tank straps and tailgates.* Fax: (248) 616-0865

A. G. SIMPSON AUTOMOTIVE

One Simpson Boulevard, Dickson, TN 37055

CEO: Robert A. Simpson, Pres. Tel: (615) 446-7725 %FO: 100

Bus: *Mfr. bumper systems, metal brackets, fuel tank straps and tailgates.* Fax: (615) 446-8118

• SINCLAIR TECHNOLOGIES LTD.

85 Mary Street, Aurora ON, L4G 3G9, Canada

CEO: Douglas Jones, Pres. Tel: (905) 727-0165

Bus: *Mfr. antennas & filters for radio communication systems.* Fax: (905) 727-0861 Emp: 170
www.sinctech.com

SINCLAIR TECHNOLOGIES INC.

55 Oriskany Drive, Tonawanda, NY 14150

CEO: Gord Tupling Tel: (716) 874-3682 %FO: 100

Bus: *Mfr. antennas and filters for radio communication systems.* Fax: (716) 874-4007 Emp: 65

• SKYJACK, INC.

55 Campbell Road, Guelph ON, N1H 1B9, Canada

CEO: J. J. Wintermans, CEO Tel: (519) 837-0888 Rev: $182

Bus: *Mfr. scissor lift work platforms.* Fax: (519) 837-3102 Emp: 1,400
www.skyjack.on.ca

SKYJACK, INC.

PO Box 249 Highway 4, South Emmetsburg, IA 50536

CEO: David J. Stewart, VP Tel: (712) 852-2724 %FO: 100

Bus: *Mfr. scissor lift work platforms.* Fax: (712) 852-2952

SKYJACK, INC.
3451 Swenson Avenue, St. Charles, IL   60174
CEO: David J. Stewart, VP   Tel: (630) 262-0005   %FO: 100
Bus: *Mfr. scissor lift work platforms.*   Fax: (630) 262-0006

SKYJACK, INC.
PO Box 399 990 Vernon Road, Wathena, KS   66090
CEO: David J. Stewart, VP   Tel: (785) 989-4646   %FO: 100
Bus: *Mfr. scissor lift work platforms.*   Fax: (785) 989-4594

• SLATER STEEL INC.
6711 Mississauga Rd., Ste. 202, Mississauga ON, L5N 2W3, Canada
CEO: Paul A. Kelly, Pres. & CEO   Tel: (905) 567-1822   Rev: $480
Bus: *Steel products and special steel,*   Fax: (905) 567-0946   Emp: 1,466
     hardware for electric transmission.   www.canadiansteel.ca

SLATER STEEL INC.
2400 Taylor Street West, PO Box 630, Fort Wayne, IN   46801
CEO: Pete Anderson, Pres.   Tel: (219) 434-2800   %FO: 100
Bus: *Mfr. stainless & special alloy steel.*   Fax: (219) 434-2801   Emp: 720

• SMTC CORPORATION
635 Hood Road, Markham ON, L3R 4N6, Canada
CEO: Paul Walker, CEO   Tel: (905) 479-1810   Rev: $782
Bus: *Mfr. electronics.*   Fax: (905) 479-1877   Emp: 5,000
      www.smtc.com

SMTC PENSAR DESIGN
109 Constitution Blvd., Unite 160, Franklin, MA   01038
CEO: Paul Walker, CEO   Tel: (508) 520-5800   %FO: 100
Bus: *Mfr. electronics.*   Fax: (508) 553-9351

SMTC PENSAR DESIGN
15700 Long Vista Drive, Austin, TX   78728
CEO: Paul Walker, CEO   Tel: (512) 310-4300   %FO: 100
Bus: *Mfr. electronics.*   Fax: (512) 310-4301

SMTC PENSAR DESIGN
2222 East Pensar Drive, Appleton, WI   54911
CEO: Paul Walker, CEO   Tel: (920) 739-4355   %FO: 100
Bus: *Mfr. electronics.*   Fax: (920) 739-9615

SMTC PENSAR DESIGN
2302 Trade Zone Boulevard, San Jose, CA   95131
CEO: Paul Walker, CEO   Tel: (408) 934-7100   %FO: 100
Bus: *Mfr. electronics.*   Fax: (408) 934-7101

SMTC PENSAR DESIGN
5601 Wilkinson Boulevard, Charlotte, NC 28208
CEO: Paul Walker, CEO   Tel: (704) 394-6341   %FO: 100
Bus: *Mfr. electronics.*   Fax: (704) 394-1722

● **SNC LAVALIN GROUP INC.**
455 Rene-Levesque Boulevard, West Montréal PQ, H2Z 1Z3, Canada
CEO: Jacques Lamarre, Pres. & CEO   Tel: (514) 393-1000   Rev: $1,130
Bus: *Engaged in pulp, paper,*   Fax: (514) 393-0156   Emp: 8,200
pharmaceuticals, biotechnology,   www.snc-lavalin.com
chemicals, petroleum, agriculture and
engineering.

SNC LAVALIN INTERNATIONAL, INC.
1775 I Street, N.W., Suite 600, Washington, DC 20006
CEO: David W. Brown, Pres.   Tel: (202) 293-7601   %FO: 100
Bus: *Engaged in pulp, paper,*   Fax: (202) 887-7018
pharmaceuticals, biotechnology,
chemicals, petroleum, agriculture
and engineering.

● **SOBEYS CANADA INC.**
115 King Street, Stellarton NS, B0K 1S0, Canada
CEO: Douglas B. Stewart, CEO   Tel: (902) 752-8371
Bus: *Retail groceries.*   Fax: (902) 752-2960
www.sobeysweb.com

OSHAWA GROUP PRODUCE, INC.
1903 S. Congress Avenue, Ste. 300, Boynton Beach, FL 33426
CEO: Maria Buffone, Mgr.   Tel: (561) 731-2722   %FO: 26
Bus: *Wholesale food distribution,*   Fax: (561) 731-1463
supermarkets and drug stores.

● **SOLIDUM SYSTEMS CORPORATION**
940 Belfast Road, Ste. 217, Ottawa ON, K1G 4A2, Canada
CEO: Leo Lax, CEO   Tel: (613) 244-4804
Bus: *Provides hardware and software*   Fax: (613) 244-4803
solutions.   www.solidum.com

SOLIDUM SYSTEMS
269 Mount Hermon Road, Ste. 102, Scotts Valley, CA 95066
CEO: Charlie Jenkins   Tel: (831) 461-0940   %FO: 100
Bus: *Provides hardware and software*   Fax: (831) 461-0960
solutions.

● **SPECTRAL DIAGNOSTICS INC.**

135-2 The West Mall, Toronto ON, M9C 1C2, Canada

CEO: Douglas C. Ball, CEO	Tel: (416) 626-3233	Rev: $7
Bus: *Mfr. blood test kits for health care professionals.*	Fax: (416) 626-7383 www.spectraldiagnostics.com	Emp: 100

   SPECTRAL DIAGNOSTICS INC.

   85 First Street, Whitestone, VA   22578

CEO: Grant Frazier, VP	Tel: (804) 435-9850	%FO: 100
Bus: *Mfr./sales blood test kits for health care professionals.*	Fax: (804) 435-9851	

● **SPECTRUM SIGNAL PROCESSING INC.**

2700 Production Way, Ste. 200, Burnaby BC, V5A 4X1, Canada

CEO: Pascal Spotheifer, CEO	Tel: (604) 421-5422	Rev: $26
Bus: *Engaged in software and wireless systems.*	Fax: (604) 421-1764 www.spectrumsignal.com	Emp: 175

   SPECTRUM SIGNAL PROCESSING INC.

   1140 Corporate Drive, Landover, MD   20785

CEO: Mike Farley	Tel: (301) 459-8888	%FO: 100
Bus: *Engaged in software and wireless systems.*	Fax: (301) 459-8887	

   SPECTRUM SIGNAL PROCESSING INC.

   17451 Bastanchury Road, Ste. 204, Yorba Linda, CA   92886

CEO: Tom Spurlock	Tel: (714) 577-6950	%FO: 100
Bus: *Engaged in software and wireless systems.*	Fax: (714) 577-6910	

   SPECTRUM SIGNAL PROCESSING INC.

   99 Trophy Club Drive, Trophy Club, TX   76262

CEO: Mark Whaylen	Tel: (817) 430-5840	%FO: 100
Bus: *Engaged in software and wireless systems.*	Fax: (817) 430-5839	

● **ST. LAWRENCE CEMENT, INC.**

1945 Graham Boulevard, Mount-Royal PQ, H3R 1H1, Canada

CEO: Patrick Dolberg, CEO	Tel: (514) 340-1881	Rev: $703
Bus: *Cement, concrete, aggregates, construction services.*	Fax: (514) 342-8154 www.stlawrencecement.com	Emp: 2,500

   INDEPENDENT CEMENT CORPORATION

   3 Columbia Circle, Albany, NY   12203

CEO: Dennis W. Skidmore, Pres.	Tel: (518) 452-3001	%FO: 100
Bus: *Mfr./distribution cement.*	Fax: (518) 452-3045	Emp: 23

- **STAKE TECHNOLOGY LTD.**

  2838 Highway 7, Norval ON, L0P 1KO, Canada

  CEO: Jeremy N. Kendall, CEO   Tel: (905) 445-1990 Rev: $68

  Bus: *Sales of organic corn and soy products.* Fax: (905) 455-2529 Emp: 275

  www.staketech.com

  ### BEI PECAL

  2 Elaine Street, New Orleans, LA   70126

  CEO: Allan Jones, Mgr.   Tel: (504) 243-2205 %FO: 100

  Bus: *Abrasives market.*   Fax: (504) 243-2204

  ### SUNRICH INC.

  3824 SW 93rd Street, Hope, MN   56046

  CEO: Allan Routh, CEO   Tel: (507) 451-4724 %FO: 100

  Bus: *Engaged in agritech.*   Fax: (507) 451-4724

- **STELCO, INC.**

  Stelco Tower, 100 King West, PO Box 2030, Hamilton ON, L8N 3T1, Canada

  CEO: James C. Alfano, Pres. & CEO Tel: (905) 528-2511 Rev: $2,143

  Bus: *Blast furnaces and steel mills.* Fax: (905) 577-4412 Emp: 11,143

  www.stelco.ca

  ### CHIMHOLD COAL COMPANY, INC.

  32601 Highway 194 East, Phelps, KY   41553

  CEO: Brian Warry, Pres.   Tel: (606) 456-3432 %FO: 100

  Bus: *Coal production.*   Fax: (606) 456-8565 Emp: 260

  ### STELCO INC.

  2855 Coolridge Street, Ste. 203, Troy, mi   48084

  CEO: Link Simpson, VP   Tel: (248) 649-3460 %FO: 100

  Bus: *Mfr. hot and cold rolled steel* Fax: (248) 649-1104
     sheets.

- **STS SYSTEMS, INC.**

  2800 Trans-Canada Highway, Pointe-Claire PQ, H9R 1B1, Canada

  CEO: Howard Stotland, Pres.   Tel: (514) 426-0822

  Bus: *Mfr. computer software services.* Fax: (514) 426-0524 Emp: 1,300

  www.stssystems.com

  ### STS SYSTEMS, INC.

  575 Lexington Avenue, Ste. 410, New York, NY   10022

  CEO: Stanley E. Zack, SVP   Tel: (212) 572-9637 %FO: 100

  Bus: *Mfr. computer software services.* Fax: (212) 572-9638

STS SYSTEMS, INC.
3111 Camino del Rio North, Ste. 1201, San Diego, CA   92108
CEO: Stanley E. Zack, SVP Tel: (619) 282-2163 %FO: 100
Bus: *Mfr. computer software services.* Fax: (619) 282-3368

STS SYSTEMS, INC.
110 South Jefferson Road, Whippany, NJ   07981
CEO: Stanley E. Zack, SVP Tel: (973) 781-9400 %FO: 100
Bus: *Mfr. computer software services.* Fax: (973) 781-9686

• SUN LIFE FINANCIAL SERVICES OF CANADA
150 King Street West, Toronto ON, M5H 1J9, Canada
CEO: C. James Prieur, Pres. & CEO Tel: (416) 979-9966 Rev: $10,591
Bus: *Insurance, pensions and mutual funds.* Fax: (416) 585-9546 Emp: 11,222
           www.sunlife.com

CLARENDON INSURANCE AGENCY, INC.
One Sun Life Executive Park, Wellesley Hills, MA   02481
CEO: Ronald Fernandes, Pres. Tel: (781) 237-6030 %FO: 100
Bus: *Insurance services.* Fax: (781) 237-6030

MFS INVESTMENT MANAGEMENT
500 Boylston Street, Boston, MA   02116
CEO: James L. Shames, CEO Tel: (617) 954-5000 %FO: 100
Bus: *Investment management services.* Fax: (617) 556-4888

SUN LIFE FINANCIAL SERVICES OF CANADA
One Sun Life Executive Park, Wellesley Hills, MA   02181
CEO: Donald A. Stewart, CEO Tel: (781) 237-6030 %FO: 100
Bus: *Insurance, pensions and mutual funds.* Fax: (781) 237-6309

SUN LIFE INSURANCE AND ANNUITY CO. OF NEW YORK
122 East 42nd Street, New York, NY   10017
CEO: Donald A. Stewart, Chmn. Tel: (212) 983-6352 %FO: 100
Bus: *Individual, variable and fixed annuity contracts and group life contracts.* Fax: (212) 983-6352

• TARO PHARMACEUTICAL INDUSTRIES LTD.
130 East Drive, Brampton ON, L6T 1C1, Canada
CEO: Aaron Levitt, CEO Tel: (905) 791-8276 Rev: $103
Bus: *Research/mfr./sale pharmaceuticals.* Fax: (905) 791-4473 Emp: 600
           www.taro.ca

TARO PHARMACEUTICALS USA INC.
5 Skyline Drive, Hawthorne, NY   10532

CEO: Richard J. Anderson, VP	Tel: (914) 345-9001	%FO: 100
Bus: *Research/mfr./sale pharmaceuticals.*	Fax: (914) 345-8728	Emp: 25

● **TD CANADA TRUST INC.**
161 Bay Street, Toronto ON, M5J 2T2, Canada

CEO: W. Edmund Clark, Pres. & CEO	Tel: (416) 361-8000	Rev: $2,500
Bus: *Engaged in banking and investment management services.*	Fax: (416) 361-4633 www.canadatrust.com	Emp: 14,150

TD WATERHOUSE SECURITIES
100 Wall Street, New York, NY   10005

CEO: Bill Handy	Tel: (212) 806-3500
Bus: *Investment banking services.*	Fax: (212) 809-1689

● **TECK CORPORATION**
200 Burrand Street, Ste. 600, Vancouver BC, V6C 3L9, Canada

CEO: Norman B. Keevil, CEO	Tel: (604) 687-1117	Rev: $804
Bus: *Mining of gold, coal and copper.*	Fax: (604) 687-6100 www.teckcorp.ca	Emp: 7,200

TECK COMINCO INC.
15918 East Euclid Avenue, Spokane, WA   99216-1815

CEO: Steven G. Dean, Pres.	Tel: (509) 922-8787	%FO: 100
Bus: *Mining of gold, coal and copper.*	Fax: (509) 922-8767	

● **TEKNION CORPORATION**
1150 Flint Road, Toronto ON, M3J 2J5, Canada

CEO: David Feldberg, CEO	Tel: (416) 661-3370	Rev: $595
Bus: *Mfr. portable sheetrock walls.*	Fax: (416) 661-7970 www.teknion.com	Emp: 5,000

TEKNION CORPORATION
250 Sutter Street, Ste 300, San Francisco, CA   94108

CEO: Walsh Kaiser, VP	Tel: (415) 397-1380	%FO: 100
Bus: *Mfr./sales portable sheetrock walls.*	Fax: (415) 397-1381	

TEKNION CORPORATION
5201 Great American Parkway, Ste. 446, Santa Clara, CA   95054

CEO: Walsh Kaiser, VP	Tel: (408) 970-0891	%FO: 100
Bus: *Mfr./sales portable sheetrock walls.*	Fax: (408) 970-0894	

TEKNION CORPORATION
631 Wilshire Blvd., Ste., Santa Monica, CA   90401

CEO: Walsh Kaiser, VP   Tel: (310) 300-3800   %FO: 100

Bus: *Mfr./sales portable sheetrock walls.*   Fax: (310) 300-3224

TEKNION CORPORATION
1048 Merchandise Mart, Chicago, IL   60654

CEO: Monty Brown, Pres.   Tel: (312) 321-1286   %FO: 100

Bus: *Mfr./sales portable sheetrock walls.*   Fax: (312) 321-1388

● TELEGLOBE INC.
1000 de la Gauchtière Street West, 24th Fl., Montréal PQ, H3B 4X5, Canada

CEO: Terry Jarman, Pres. & CEO   Tel: (514) 868-8124   Rev: $2,873

Bus: *International telecommunications services and products.*   Fax: (514) 868-7234   Emp: 5,295

www.teleglobe.com

EXCEL COMMUNICATIONS, INC.
8750 North Central Expressway, Dallas, TX   75231

CEO: Selby Shaver, Pres. & CEO   Tel: (214) 863-8000   %FO: 100

Bus: *Provides telecommunications services.*   Fax: (214) 863-8841

TELEGLOBE COMMUNICATIONS CORP.
11480 Commerce Park Drive, Reston, VA   20191

CEO: Terence J. Jarman, CEO   Tel: (703) 755-2000   %FO: 100

Bus: *Provides telecommunications services.*   Fax: (703) 260-0000

● TESCO CORPORATION
6204, 6A Street SE, Calgary AB, T2H 2B7, Canada

CEO: Robert M. Tessari, CEO   Tel: (403) 233-0757   Rev: $103

Bus: *Mfr. drilling equipment for oil and gas industry.*   Fax: (403) 252-3362   Emp: 750

www.tescocorp.com

TESCO CORPORATION
11330 Brittmoore Park Drive, Houston, TX   77041

CEO: Barry Knichel, Dir.   Tel: (713) 849-5900   %FO: 100

Bus: *Mfr./sales drilling equipment for oil and gas industry.*   Fax: (713) 849-0075

● **THINKPATH.COM INC.**

55 University Avenue, Ste. 505, Toronto ON, M5J 2H7, Canada

CEO: Declan French, CEO   Tel: (416) 364-8800   Rev: $44

Bus: *Provides information technology,*   Fax: (416) 364-2424   Emp: 180
      engineering services and recruitment.   www.thinkpath.com

    CAD CAM INC.

    6160 Peachtree-Dunwoody Rd., Ste. B100, Atlanta, GA   30328

    CEO: Tim Long, Mgr.   Tel: (770) 350-9323   %FO: 100

    Bus: *Provides information technology.*   Fax: (770) 350-0039

    THINKPATH.COM INC.

    2505 Taylor Road, Columbus, IN   47203

    CEO: Jeff Anderson, Mgr.   Tel: (812) 376-8519   %FO: 100

    Bus: *Engaged in engineering services*   Fax: (812) 376-7530
      and recruitment.

    THINKPATH.COM INC.

    1211 N. Westshore Blvd., Ste. 410, Tampa, FL   33607

    CEO: Ed Godwin, Mgr.   Tel: (813) 636-8227   %FO: 100

    Bus: *Engaged in engineering services*   Fax: (813) 636-9059
      and recruitment.

    THINKPATH.COM INC.

    375 Totten Pond Road, Ste. 200, Waltham, MA   02451

    CEO: Denise Dunne, Mgr.   Tel: (781) 890-6444   %FO: 100

    Bus: *IT documentation recruitment.*   Fax: (781) 890-3355

    THINKPATH.COM INC.

    1941 Savage Road, Ste. 400C, Charleston, SC   29407

    CEO: Jeff Sheidow, Mgr.   Tel: (843) 556-2511   %FO: 100

    Bus: *Engaged in engineering services*   Fax: (843) 556-1920
      and recruitment.

    THINKPATH.COM INC.

    110 Boggs Lane, Ste. 365, Cincinnati, OH   45246

    CEO: Dave Hoffman, Mgr.   Tel: (513) 326-4760   %FO: 100

    Bus: *Engaged in engineering services*   Fax: (513) 326-4765
      and recruitment.

    THINKPATH.COM INC.

    2800 East River Road, 4th Fl., Dayton, OH   45439

    CEO: Bob Liput, Mgr.   Tel: (937) 643-4100   %FO: 100

    Bus: *Engaged in engineering services*   Fax: (937) 643-4110
      and recruitment.

THINKPATH.COM INC.
25840 Sherwood, Warren, MI 48091
CEO: Rick Simon, Mgr.   Tel: (810) 754-2700   %FO: 100
Bus: *Engaged in engineering services*   Fax: (810) 754-3700
and recruitment.

THINKPATH.COM INC.
8455 Keystone Crossing, Ste. 201, Indianapolis, IN 46240
CEO: Mike Tribul, Mgr.   Tel: (317) 253-2204   %FO: 100
Bus: *Engaged in engineering services*   Fax: (317) 253-2294
and recruitment.

THINKPATH.COM INC.
195 Broadway, Ste. 1801, New York, NY 10007
CEO: Michelle French, Mgr.   Tel: (212) 566-4223   %FO: 100
Bus: *Engaged in training.*   Fax: (212) 566-4214

THINKPATH.COM INC.
PO Box 1063, Toms River, NJ 08754-1063
CEO: Grace Piscopo, Mgr.   Tel: (732) 267-4849   %FO: 100
Bus: *Engaged in recruitment.*   Fax: (732) 286-9991

● **THE THOMSON CORP.**
PO Box 24, Toronto-Dominion Tower, Ste. 2706, Toronto ON, M5K 1A1, Canada
CEO: Richard J. Harrington, CEO   Tel: (416) 360-8700   Rev: $5,752
Bus: *Publishing, newspapers, information*   Fax: (416) 360-8812   Emp: 32,500
services, leisure travel.   www.thomcorp.com

FAUKNER & GRAY
11 Penn Plaza, New York, NY 10001
CEO: John Love, Pres.   Tel: (212) 967-7000   %FO: 100
Bus: *Book publishing.*   Fax: (212) 967-7155   Emp: 100

THOMSON & THOMSON
500 Victory Blvd., North Quincy, MA 02171
CEO: Kim Graven Neilsen, CEO   Tel: (617) 479-1600   %FO: 100
Bus: *Engaged in research.*   Fax: (617) 786-8273

THOMSON FINANCIAL
22 Thomson Place, Boston, MA 02210
CEO: Patrick Tierney, CEO   Tel: (617) 345-2000   %FO: 100
Bus: *Regulatory and financial*   Fax: (617) 772-5007
information services.

THOMSON LEARNING, INC.
Metro Center, One Station Place, 8th Fl., Stamford, CT   06902
CEO: Robert S. Christie, Pres.   Tel: (203) 969-8700   %FO: 100
Bus: *U.S. headquarters. Holding*   Fax: (203) 977-8354
   company.

THOMSON TAX & ACCOUNTING INC.
395 Hudson Street, 4th Fl., New York, NY   10014
CEO: George Taylor, Pres.   Tel: (212) 367-6300   %FO: 100
Bus: *Book publishing.*   Fax: (212) 367-6305   Emp: 100

WEST GROUP
610 Opperman Drive, Eagan, MN   55123
CEO: Brian H. Hall, CEO   Tel: (651) 687-7000   %FO: 100
Bus: *Provides legal information.*   Fax: (651) 687-5827

● **TIMMINCO LIMITED**
Water Park Place, 9th Fl., 10 Bay Street, Toronto ON, M5J 2R8, Canada
CEO: J. Thomas Timmins, Pres.   Tel: (416) 364-5171
Bus: *Engaged in the production of non-* Fax: (416) 364-3451
   ferrous metals.

TIMMINCO TECHNOLOGY CORPORATION
750 Lake Cook Road, Ste. 405, Buffalo Grove, IL   60089
CEO: Anthony S. Meketa, VP   Tel: (847) 215-6770   %FO: 100
Bus: *Sales/distribution of non-ferrous* Fax: (847) 215-6774
   metals.

● **TLC LASER EYE CENTERS INC.**
5280 Solar Drive, Ste. 300, Mississauga ON, L4W 5M8, Canada
CEO: Elias Vamvakas, CEO   Tel: (905) 602-2020   Rev: $175
Bus: *Operates laser eye clinics.*   Fax: (905) 602-2025   Emp: 760
                                         www.tlcvision.com

TLC LASER EYE CENTERS
115 East 57th Street, 16th Fl., New York, NY   10022
CEO: John J. Klobnak, CEO   Tel: (212) 588-0100   %FO: 100
Bus: *Laser eye clinic.*   Fax: (212) 588-0406

TLC LASER EYE CENTERS
75 Kings Highway, Fairfield, CT   06430
CEO: James C. Wachtman, Pres.   Tel: (203) 334-2020   %FO: 100
Bus: *Laser eye clinic.*   Fax: (203) 334-2401

TLC LASER EYE CENTERS
555 Fairmont Avenue, Ste. 201, Towson, MD 21286

CEO: James C. Wachtman, Pres.
Bus: *Laser eye clinic.*

Tel: (410) 832-1852
Fax: (410) 832-5480

%FO: 100

● TOROMONT INDUSTRIES LTD.
PO Box 20011, Concord ON, L4K 4T1, Canada

CEO: Hugo T. Sorensen, Pres. & CEO
Bus: *Mfr. refrigeration and heating equipment and distributes construction equipment.*

Tel: (416) 667-5511
Fax: (416) 667-5566
www.toromont.com

Rev: $534
Emp: 2,300

AERO TECH MANUFACTURING INC.
395 West 1100 North, North Salt Lake, UT 84054

CEO: Jerry Quest, Pres.
Bus: *Refrigeration equipment.*

Tel: (801) 292-0493
Fax: (801) 292-9908

%FO: 100
Emp: 100

● TORONTO-DOMINION BANK
55 King St. West, Box 1, Toronto ON, M5K 1A2, Canada

CEO: A. Charles Baillie, Chmn.
Bus: *Engaged in banking and financial services.*

Tel: (416) 982-8222
Fax: (416) 944-5718
www.tdbank.ca

Rev: $13,181
Emp: 44,798

TD SECURITIES INC.
31 West 52nd Street, New York, NY 10019-6101

CEO: Peter A. E. Bethlenfalvy, CEO
Bus: *Investment banking services.*

Tel: (212) 827-7000
Fax: (212) 262-1922

%FO: 100

TD WATERHOUSE INVESTOR SERVICES, INC.
100 Wall Street, 28th Fl., New York, NY 10005

CEO: Frank Petrilli, Pres. & CEO
Bus: *Securities brokerage and investment services.*

Tel: (212) 344-7500
Fax: (212) 509-8122

%FO: 100

TORONTO-DOMINION HOLDINGS (USA) INC.
909 Fannin Street, Houston, TX 77010

CEO: Carole Clause, Assoc. VP
Bus: *Bank holding company.*

Tel: (713) 653-8200
Fax: (713) 951-9921

%FO: 100

● TORSTAR CORPORATION
One Yonge Street, Toronto ON, M5E 1P9, Canada

CEO: David A. Galloway, CEO
Bus: *Publishes romance novels.*

Tel: (416) 869-4010
Fax: (416) 869-4183
www.torstar.com

Rev: $965
Emp: 800

HARLEQUIN
PO Box 5190, Buffalo, NY   14240-5190
CEO: Katherine Orr, VP   Tel: (416) 445-5860   %FO: 100
Bus: *Publishes romance novels.*   Fax: (416) 448-7140

● **TRACTEL LTD. SWINGSTAGE GROUP**
1615 Warden Avenue, Scarborough ON, MIR2T3, Canada
CEO: Dennis Pradon, Chmn.   Tel: (416) 298-8822
Bus: *Engineering lifting and materials   Fax: (416) 298-1053
handling, electronic load measuring   www.tractel.com
and fall arrest equipment.*

   TRACTEL LTD., SWINGSTAGE DIV.
   315 Cloverleaf Drive, Ste. E, Baldwin Park, CA   91706
   CEO: Jean Louis Weicker, Pres.   Tel: (626) 937-6727
   Bus: *Engineering lifting and materials   Fax: (626) 937-6727
   handling, electronic load
   measuring and fall arrest
   equipment.*

   TRACTEL LTD., SWINGSTAGE DIV.
   12 Prince Street, New York, NY   10012
   CEO: Brian Timmins, Mgr.   Tel: (212) 431-3441
   Bus: *Engineering lifting and materials   Fax: (212) 431-3767
   handling, electronic load
   measuring and fall arrest
   equipment.*

   TRACTEL LTD., SWINGSTAGE DIV.
   PO Box 68, Westwood, MA   02097
   CEO: Jean Louis Weicker, Pres.   Tel: (781) 329-5650
   Bus: *Engineering lifting and materials   Fax: (781) 329-6530
   handling, electronic load
   measuring and fall arrest
   equipment.*

● **TRANS ALTA CORPORATION**
Box 19 Station M, 110-12 Avenue SW, Calgary AB, T2P 2MI, Canada
CEO: Stephen G. Snyder, Pres. & CEO   Tel: (403) 267-7110   Rev: $1,059
Bus: *Engaged in energy management;   Fax: (403) 267-2559   Emp: 2,365
electric and gas.*   www.transalta.com

   MEGA INTERNATIONAL, INC.
   404 Wyman Street, Waltham, MA   02451-1264
   CEO: Bob Decker   Tel: (781) 890-3442   %FO: 100
   Bus: *Provides visual analysis and   Fax: (781) 890-3103
   design solutions for e-business.*

TRANS ALTA CORPORATION
1126 South Gold Street, Centralia, WA 98531
CEO: Stephen G. Snyder, Pres.   Tel: (360) 330-0275   %FO: 100
Bus: *Engaged in energy management;*   Fax: (360) 330-0276
electric and gas.

TRANS ALTA ENERGY MARKETING
4004 Kruse Way Place, Ste. 150, Lake Oswego, OR 97035
CEO: Steve Lincoln   Tel: (503) 675-3800   %FO: 100
Bus: *Engaged in energy management;*   Fax: (503) 675-3808
electric and gas.

● **TRANSCANADA PIPELINES LTD.**
111 5th Ave. SW, Calgary AB, T2P 3Y6, Canada
CEO: Harold N. Kvisle, Pres. & CEO   Tel: (403) 267-6100   Rev: $14,107
Bus: *Natural gas marketing and transmission* Fax: (403) 267-8993   Emp: 4,900
and electric power generation.   www.transcanada.com

GREAT LAKES GAS TRANSMISSION COMPANY
5250 Corporate Drive, Troy, MI 48098
CEO: Greg A. Lohnef, Pres.   Tel: (248) 205-7400   %FO: 100
Bus: *Natural gas transmission.*   Fax: (248) 205-7612

IROQUOIS GAS TRANSMISSION SYSTEM
One Corporate Drive, Suite 600, Shelton, CT 06484-6211
CEO: Craig R. Frew, Pres.   Tel: (203) 926-7200   %FO: 50
Bus: *Natural gas transmission.*   Fax: (203) 929-9501   Emp: 282

● **TRIVERSITY INC.**
3550 Victoria Park Avenue, Suite 400, Toronto ON, M2H 2N5, Canada
CEO: David Thomas, Pres. & CEO   Tel: (416) 791-7100
Bus: *Computer software & services.*   Fax: (416) 791-7107
www.triversity.com

TRIVERSITY CORPORATION
311 Sinclair Street, Bristol, PA 19007
CEO: David Thompson, Pres. & CEO   Tel: (215) 785-4321   %FO: 100
Bus: *Computer software & services.*   Fax: (215) 785-5329

● **TRIZEC HAHN CORP.**
181 Bay Street, Toronto ON, M5J 2T3, Canada
CEO: Christopher Mackenzie, Pres.   Tel: (416) 361-7200   Rev: $1,176
Bus: *Develop, own and manage commercial* Fax: (416) 364-1503   Emp: 2,520
income property.   www.trizechahn.com

TRIZEC HAHN INC.

4350 La Jolla Village Drive, San Diego, CA   92122-1233

CEO: Lee H. Wagman, Pres.	Tel: (858) 546-1001	%FO: 100
Bus: *Real estate development and management.*	Fax: (858) 546-3413	Emp: 1,900

TRIZEC HAHN INC.

233 South Wacker Drive, Ste. 4600, Chicago, IL   60606

CEO: Casey R. Wold, Pres.	Tel: (312) 466-3000	%FO: 100
Bus: *Real estate development and management.*	Fax: (312) 466-1710	Emp: N/S

● **TROJAN TECHNOLOGIES INC.**

3020 Gore Road, London ON, N5V 4T7, Canada

CEO: Henry J. Vander Laan, Pres. & CEO	Tel: (519) 457-3400	Rev: $46
Bus: *Mfg. pollution & treatment controls & filtration products.*	Fax: (519) 457-3030 www.trojanuv.com	Emp: 300

TROJAN TECHNOLOGIES INC.

2050 Peabody Road, Suite 200, Vacaville, CA   95687

CEO: Neil Brown	Tel: (707) 469-2680	%FO: 100
Bus: *Mfg. pollution & treatment controls & filtration products.*	Fax: (707) 469-2688	

● **TUCOWS INC.**

96 Mowat Avenue, Toronto ON, M6K 3M1, Canada

CEO: Elliot Noss, Pres. & CEO	Tel: (416) 535-0123	Rev: $11
Bus: *Computer software & services.*	Fax: (416) 531-5584 www.tucows.com	Emp: 46

TUCOWS INC.

590 North Gulph Road, King of Prussia, PA   19403-2800

CEO: Scott Swedorski, Pres.	Tel: (800) 860-9227	%FO: 100
Bus: *Computer software & services.*	Fax: (610) 971-8859	

TUCOWS INC.

4100 Pier North Drive, Suite A, Flint, MI   48504

CEO: Scott Swedorski, Pres.	Tel: (810) 720-1155	%FO: 100
Bus: *Computer software & services.*	Fax: (810) 720-0520	

● **TUNDRA SEMICONDUCTOR CORPORATION**

603 March, Kanata ON, K2K 2M5, Canada

CEO: Adam Chowaniec, Pres. & CEO	Tel: (613) 592-0714
Bus: *Mfg. electronics and semiconductor products.*	Fax: (613) 599-2310 www.tundra.com

QUADIC SYSTEMS, DIV. TUNDRA
39 Darling Avenue, South Portland, ME   04106
CEO: Mark Cohen   Tel: (207) 773-2662   %FO: 100
Bus: *Mfg. electronics & semiconductor* Fax: (207) 773-1550
    products.

TUNDRA SEMICONDUCTOR CORPORATION
101-1265 Montecito Avenue, Mountain View, CA   94043
CEO: Thomas Wilson, Mgr.   Tel: (650) 960-0282   %FO: 100
Bus: *Mfg. electronics & semiconductor* Fax: (650) 960-0321
    products.

TUNDRA SEMICONDUCTOR CORPORATION
4100 Spring Valley Road, Ste. 50, Dallas, TX   75244
CEO: Kurt Weber   Tel: (214) 420-9315   %FO: 100
Bus: *Mfg. electronics & semiconductor* Fax: (214) 420-9316
    products.

• VELAN INC.
2125 Ward Ave., Montréal PQ, H4M 1T6, Canada
CEO: A. K. Velan, Pres.   Tel: (514) 748-7743
Bus: *Mfr. forged and cast pressure valves.*   Fax: (514) 748-8635
                                         www.velan.com

VELAN-VALVE CORPORATION
94 Avenue C, Williston, VT   05495-9732
CEO: Michael A. Parsons, Mgr.   Tel: (802) 863-2561   %FO: 100
Bus: *Mfr. steel gates and cast valves.* Fax: (802) 862-4014

• VISIBLE GENETICS INC.
700 Bay Street, Ste. 1000, Toronto ON, M5G 1Z6, Canada
CEO: Richard T. Daly, CEO   Tel: (416) 813-3240   Rev: $13
Bus: *Engaged in pharmaceutical*   Fax: (416) 813-3250   Emp: 35
    development.   www.visgen.com

VISIBLE GENETICS CORPORATION
25 Crestridge Drive, Ste. 200, Suwanee, GA   30024
CEO: Donna J.DeLong, Dir.   Tel: (678) 318-2621   %FO: 100
Bus: *Engaged in pharmaceutical*   Fax: (678) 398-2911
    development.

• VITRAN CORPORATION INC.
70 University Avenue, Ste. 350, Toronto ON, M5J 2M4 Canada
CEO: Richard D. McGraw, CEO   Tel: (416) 596-7664   Rev: $340
Bus: *Freight shipping and logistics services.*   Fax: (416) 596-8039 Emp: 3,000
                                         www.vitranexpress.com

VITRAN EXPRESS INC.
PO Box 7004, Indianapolis, IN   46219
CEO: Richard D. McGraw, Pres. & CEO   Tel: (317) 803-6400
Bus: *Freight shipping and logistics*   Fax: (317) 543-1228
services.

● **WATERSAVE LOGIC CORP.**
1103-1166 Alberni Street, Vancouver BC, V6E323, Canada
CEO: David Nelson, Pres.   Tel: (604) 688-2464
Bus: *Mfr. ceramic sanitary ware, vitreous*   Fax: (604) 688-0097   Emp: 4
china.   www.watersavelogic.com

  WP INDUSTRIES INC.
  14405 Best Avenue, Norwalk, CA   90650
  CEO: Hans O. Andersson, CEO   Tel: (562) 229-0910   %FO: 100
  Bus: *Mfr. ceramic sanitary ware.*   Fax: (562) 229-0930   Emp: 88

● **WAWANESA MUTUAL INSURANCE COMPANY**
191 Broadway, Winnipeg MN, R3C 3P1, Canada
CEO: Gregg Hanson, Pres. & CEO   Tel: (204) 985-3511   Rev: $700
Bus: *Engaged in property and casualty*   Fax: (204) 942-7724   Emp: 1,300
insurance.   www.wawanesa.com

  WAWANESA MUTUAL INSURANCE COMPANY
  9050 Friars Road, San Diego, CA   92108
  CEO: Grey Hanson, Pres.   Tel: (619) 285-6010   %FO: 100
  Bus: *Engaged in property and casualty*   Fax: (619) 285-6020
  insurance.

● **GEORGE WESTON LTD.**
22 St. Clair Avenue East, Ste. 101, Toronto ON, M4T 2S7, Canada
CEO: Richard Currie, CEO   Tel: (416) 922-2500   Rev: $9,575
Bus: *Bakery and confectionery products,*   Fax: (416) 922-4395   Emp: 124,000
groceries, fisheries.   www.weston.ca

  INTERBAKE FOODS INC.
  2821 Emerywood Parkway, Ste. 210, Richmond, VA   23294
  CEO: Ray Baxter, Pres.   Tel: (804) 755-7107   %FO: 100
  Bus: *Mfr./distribution crackers &*   Fax: (804) 755-7173
  cookies.

● **WP INDUSTRIES INC.**
1103-1166 Alberni Street, Vancouver BC, V6E 3ZD3, Canada
CEO: David Nelson   Tel: (604) 688-2464
Bus: *Mfr. china.*   Fax: (604) 688-0097

WP INDUSTRIES INC.
11821 Industrial Avenue, South Gate, CA   90280
CEO: Darryl Wint, Sales Mgr.   Tel: (562) 529-6560
Bus: *Sales/distribution of china.*   Fax: (562) 630-5040

● **ZEMEX CORPORATION**
BCE Place, 161 Bay Street, Ste. 3750, Toronto ON, M5J 2S1, Canada
CEO: Richard L. Lister, CEO   Tel: (416) 365-8080   Rev: $77
Bus: *Production of industrial minerals.* Fax: (416) 365-8094   Emp: 450
                                        www.zemex.com

   ETS SCHAEFER CORPORATION
   8050 Highland Pointe Parkway, Macedonia, OH   44056
   CEO: Allen J. Palmiere   Tel: (330) 468-6600   %FO: 100
   Bus: *Aluminum recycling.*   Fax: (330) 468-6610

   ZEMEX MICA INC.
   112 Greenwood Road, Spruce Pine, NC   28777
   CEO: Richard L. Lister, Pres.   Tel: (828) 765-8022   %FO: 100
   Bus: *Mfr. mica for use in ceramic tiles,* Fax: (828) 765-8988
        glassware and plumbing fixtures.

● **ZI CORPORATION**
500 Fourth Avenue SW, Ste. 300, Calgary AB, T2P 26V, Canada
CEO: Michael E. Lobsinger, CEO   Tel: (403) 233-8875   Rev: $4
Bus: *Mfr. software for wireless headsets.* Fax: (403) 233-8878   Emp: 230
                                        www.zicorp.com

   ZI CORPORATION
   685 Market Street, Ste. 460, San Francisco, CA   94105
   CEO: Dan McKillen, Pres.   Tel: (415) 536-2740   %FO: 100
   Bus: *Mfr./sales software.*   Fax: (415) 536-2748

Cayman Islands

● **FRUIT OF THE LOOM, LTD.**

PO Box 31311 SMB, Grand Cayman, Cayman Islands

CEO: Brian Wolfson   Tel: 345-945-8210   Rev: $1,835

Bus: *Mfr. basic family apparel, including*   Fax: 345-949-6690   Emp: 31,000
     underwear and outerwear.   www.fruit.com

     FRUIT OF THE LOOM, INC.

     One Fruit of the Loom Drive, Bowling Green, KY   42102

     CEO: Dennis Bookshester, CEO   Tel: (270) 781-6400   %FO: 100

     Bus: *Mfr. family apparel and*   Fax: (270) 781-5288
       underwear.

● **GARMIN LTD.**

Queensgate House, PO Box 3046 4SMB, 113 S. Church St., George Town, Cayman Islands

CEO: Min H. Kao, CEO   Tel: 345-946-5203   Rev: $346

Bus: *Mfr. digital navigation products.*   Fax: 345-945-2197   Emp: 1,290
     www.garmin.com

     GARMIN INTERNATIONAL INC.

     1200 East 151st Street, Olathe, KS   66062

     CEO: Gary L. Burrell, Pres.   Tel: (913) 397-8200   %FO: 100

     Bus: *Mfr. digital navigation products.*   Fax: (913) 397-8282

● **O2MICRO INTERNATIONAL LIMITED**

The Grand Pavillion, West Bay Road, George Town, Grand Cayman, Cayman Islands

CEO: Sterling Du   Tel: 345-945-1110   Rev: $40

Bus: *Mfr. integrated circuits.*   Fax: 345-945-1110   Emp: 120
     www.o2micro.com

     L-SQUARED INC.

     15247 NW Greenbrier Parkway, Beaverton, OR   97006

     CEO: Marcel Hendrickx, VP   Tel: (503) 629-8555   %FO: 100

     Bus: *Mfr./sales integrated circuits.*   Fax: (503) 629-8555

     O2MICRO USA INC.

     3118 Patrick Henry Drive, Santa Clara, CA   95054

     CEO: Max Huang, VP   Tel: (408) 987-5920   %FO: 100

     Bus: *Mfr./sales integrated circuits.*   Fax: (408) 987-5920

Channel Islands, U.K.

- **LONDON PACIFIC GROUP LIMITED**
Minden House, 6 Minden Place, Saint Helier, Jersey JE2 4Q, Channel Islands
CEO: Arthur I. Trueger, Chmn. & CEO   Tel: 44-1534-6077000   Rev: $156
Bus: *Provides financial services including*   Fax: 44-1534-607-899   Emp: 300
venture capital investments, life   www.londonpacific.com
insurance, trust and fund management.

BERKELEY INTERNATIONAL CAPITAL
650 California Street, San Francisco, CA   94104
CEO: Bernard R. Geiger   Tel: (415) 249-0450   %FO: 100
Bus: *Development stage investment in*   Fax: (415) 249-0450
technology.

LONDON PACIFIC GROUP LTD.
1755 Creekside Oaks Drive, Sacramento, CA   95833
CEO: Ian Whitehead, Pres.   Tel: (916) 641-4200   %FO: 100
Bus: *Provides financial services*   Fax: (916) 641-4298

Chile

- **BANCO DE CHILE**
Ahumada 251, 3rd Fl., Santiago, Chile
CEO: René Lehuedé Fuenzalida, Pres.   Tel: 56-2-637-2111
Bus: *Commercial banking services.*   Fax: 56-2-637-2103   Emp: 4,000
www.bancochile.cl

    BANCO DE CHILE - New York Branch
    535 Madison Avenue, 9th Fl., New York, NY   10022
    CEO: Hernan L. Donoso, Gen.Mgr.   Tel: (212) 758-0909   %FO: 100
    Bus: *General banking services.*   Fax: (212) 593-9770   Emp: 33

    BANCO DE CHILE - Miami Agency
    200 South Biscayne Boulevard, Miami, FL   33131-5307
    CEO: Matias Herrera, Gen. Mgr.   Tel: (305) 373-0041   %FO: 100
    Bus: *International banking services.*   Fax: (305) 373-6465   Emp: 10

- **BANCO SANTIAGO**
Bandera 201, Santiago, Chile
CEO: Andronico Luksic, Chmn.   Tel: 56-2-692-4000   Rev: $1,204
Bus: *Commercial banking services.*   Fax: 56-2-672-6569   Emp: 4,715
www.bsantiag.cl

    BANCO SANTIAGO
    375 Park Avenue, Ste. 2601, New York, NY   10152
    CEO: Carlos F. Singer, Rep.   Tel: (212) 826-0550   %FO: 100
    Bus: *Commercial banking services.*   Fax: (212) 826-1218   Emp: 2

- **CHILE FAST**
Manquelhue Norte 444, Apoquindo 5856, Las Condes Santiago, Chile
CEO: Ana Maria Carey, Mgr.   Tel: 56-2-201-3611
Bus: *Engaged in tourism and cargo transport.*   Fax: 56-2-240-0450
www.fastair.cl

    INTER-HEMISPHERE TOURS
    82 Wall Street, Ste. 1009, New York, NY   10005
    CEO: Cecilia Carey, Pres.   Tel: (212) 344-4690   %FO: JV
    Bus: *Engaged in tourism and cargo transport.*   Fax: (212) 344-0004   Emp: 2

● **CORPORACION NACIONAL DE COBRE DE CHILE (CODELCO)**

Huerfanos 1270, Casilla 150-D, Santiago, Chile

CEO: Marcos Lima Aravena, Pres.	Tel: 56-2-690-3000	Rev: $2,500
Bus: *Operates mines and generates and distributes electric power.*	Fax: 56-2-672-1473 www.codelcochile.com	Emp: 18,200

CODELCO USA INC.

177 Broad Street, 14th Fl., Stamford, CT 06901

CEO: Joan Dennen, Mgr.	Tel: (203) 425-4321	%FO: 100
Bus: *U.S. headquarters operation.*	Fax: (203) 425-4322	

● **CSAV (COMPAÑIA SUD AMERICANA DE VAPORES)**

Plaza Sotomayor 50, PO Box 49-V, 236171 Valparaiso, Chile

CEO: Francisco Silva Donoso, CEO	Tel: 56-32-203000
Bus: *Cargo and freight handling services.*	Fax: 56-32-203333 www.csav.cl

CSAV/CHILEAN LINE INC.

99 Wood Avenue, Ste. 9, Iselin, NJ 08830

CEO: Alberto Camacho, Pres.	Tel: (732) 635-2600	%FO: 100
Bus: *Cargo and freight handling services.*	Fax: (732) 635-2601	

CSAV/CHILEAN LINE INC.

249 East Ocean Blvd., Ste. 1000, Los Angeles, CA 90802

CEO: Eric Chang, Pres.	Tel: (562) 983-7699	%FO: 100
Bus: *Cargo and freight handling services.*	Fax: (562) 983-7668	

CSAV/CHILEAN LINE INC.

1071 Morrison Drive, Ste. 2C, Charleston, SC 29404

CEO: Richard Soubeyroux, Pres.	Tel: (843) 853-1150	%FO: 100
Bus: *Cargo and freight handling services.*	Fax: (843) 853-7226	

TRANSCO AGENCIES INC.

2310 Burning Highway, Baltimore, MD 21224

CEO: Vince Signorello, Mgr.	Tel: (410) 489-2633
Bus: *Agents for cargo and freight handling services.*	Fax: (410) 633-2630

● **LAN CHILE AIRLINES**

Edificio Corp., Lan Chile Americo, Vespucio, 839 Rench, Estado 10, Santiago, Chile

CEO: Enrique Cueto, Pres.	Tel: 56-2-565-5225	Rev: $1,000
Bus: *International commercial air transport.*	Fax: 56-2-565-2584 www.lanchile.cl	Emp: 8,000

LAN CHILE AIRLINES
630 Fifth Avenue, Suite 809, New York, NY   10111
CEO: Rolando Damas, Reg. Sales Mgr.   Tel: (212) 582-3250   %FO: 100
Bus: *International commercial air*   Fax: (212) 582-6863
transport services.

LAN CHILE AIRLINES
9700 South Dixie Hwy, PH 11th Fl., Miami, FL   33156-9655
CEO: Alexandre De Gunten, VP   Tel: (305) 670-1961   %FO: 100
Bus: *International commercial air*   Fax: (305) 670-9553
transport services.

LAN CHILE AIRLINES
1960 East Grand Avenue, Ste. 522, El Segundo, CA   90245
CEO: Buddy Lander, Reg. Sales Mgr.   Tel: (310) 416-9061   %FO: 100
Bus: *International commercial air*   Fax: (310) 416-9864
transport services.

● MASISA S.A.
Los Conquistadores 1700, 12th Fl.. PO Box 663, Correo Central Santiago, Chile
CEO: Juan Obach González   Tel: 56-2-707-8800   Rev: $190
Bus: *Mfr. particleboard, fiberboard and*   Fax: 56-2-234-2666   Emp: 1,000
related products.   www.masisa.com

GEORGIA-PACIFIC GROUP
133 Peachtree Street NE, 41st St., Atlanta, GA   30303
CEO: Alston D. Correll, Chmn.   Tel: (404) 652-4000   %FO: 50
Bus: *Mfr. particleboard, fiberboard and*   Fax: (404) 230-5774
related products.

● SOCIEDAD QUIMICA Y MINERA DE CHILE S.A.
Miraflores 222, Piso 11, Santiago, Chile
CEO: Patricio Contesse Gonzalez, CEO   Tel: 56-2-632-6888   Rev: $502
Bus: *Production and distribution of specialty*   Fax: 56-2-633-4223   Emp: 3,850
fertilizers and industrial chemicals.   www.sqm.com

SQM NORTH AMERICA INC.
3101 Tower Creek Pkwy., Ste. 450, Atlanta, GA   30339
CEO: Guillermo Farias, Pres.   Tel: (770) 916-9400   %FO: 100
Bus: *Mfr. specialty fertilizers.*   Fax: (770) 916-9401

China (PRC)

- **AIR CHINA**

Beijing Capital International Airport, Beijing 100621, China PRC
CEO: Wang Li An, Pres.   Tel: 86-10-6456-3201   Rev: $996
Bus: *Commercial air transport services.*   Fax: 86-10-6456-3831   Emp: 14,000
                                    www.airchina.com

    AIR CHINA INTERNATIONAL INC.

    222 North Sepulveda Blvd., Ste. 1500, Los Angeles, CA 90049
    CEO: Ms. Shao, Sales Mgr.   Tel: (310) 322-6686   %FO: 100
    Bus: *Commercial air transport services.*   Fax: (310) 322-1133

    AIR CHINA INTERNATIONAL INC.

    540 California Street, San Francisco, CA 94104
    CEO: Mr. Chen, Gen. Mgr.   Tel: (415) 981-1688   %FO: 100
    Bus: *Commercial air transport services.*   Fax: (415) 392-6214

    AIR CHINA INTERNATIONAL INC.

    45 East 49th Street, New York, NY 10017
    CEO: Mr. Jia, Mgr.   Tel: (212) 935-0110   %FO: 100
    Bus: *Commercial air transport services.*   Fax: (212) 935-7951

- **BANK OF CHINA**

410 Fuchengmen Nei Dajie, Beijing 100818, China PRC
CEO: Liu Mingkang, Pres. & CEO   Tel: 86-10-6601-6688   Rev: $19,495
Bus: *Commercial banking services.*   Fax: 86-10-6601-6869   Emp: 192,275
                                      www.bankofchina.com

    BANK OF CHINA

    410 Madison Avenue, New York, NY 10017
    CEO: Chuanjie Li, Mgr.   Tel: (212) 935-3101   %FO: 100
    Bus: *International banking services.*   Fax: (212) 593-1831   Emp: 280

    BANK OF CHINA

    444 South Flower Street, 39th Fl., Los Angeles, CA 90071
    CEO: Xiaoming Luo, Mgr.   Tel: (213) 688-8700   %FO: 100
    Bus: *International banking services.*   Fax: (213) 688-0198   Emp: 100

    BANK OF CHINA

    42-44 East Broadway, New York, NY 10002
    CEO: Haiping Liu, Mgr.   Tel: (212) 925-2355   %FO: 100
    Bus: *International banking services.*   Fax: (212) 431-6157

- **BANK OF COMMUNICATIONS**

18 Xian Zia Road, Shanghai 200335, China PRC

CEO: Jie Yan Yin, Chmn.   Tel: 86-21-6275-1234

Bus: *Commercial banking services.*   Fax: 86-21-6275-6784

    BANK OF COMMUNICATIONS

    55 Broadway, 31/32 Fls., New York, NY   10006-3008

    CEO: De Cai Li, Mgr.   Tel: (212) 376-8030   %FO: 100

    Bus: *Commercial banking services.*   Fax: (212) 376-8089

- **CHINA EASTERN AIRLINES CORPORATION LIMITED**

2550 Hongqiao Road, Hongqiao International Airport, Shanghai 200335, China PRC

CEO: Liu Shaoyong, Pres.   Tel: 86-21-6268-6268   Rev: $1,356

Bus: *Passenger and cargo airline services.*   Fax: 86-21-6268-8668   Emp: 8,500

    www.cea.com.cn

    CHINA EASTERN AIRLINES

    1215 4th Avenue, Ste. 310, Seattle, WA   98161

    CEO: Kaihong Duan, Gen. Mgr.   Tel: (206) 343-5583   %FO: 100

    Bus: *Passenger airline services.*   Fax: (206) 343-5244

    CHINA EASTERN AIRLINES

    380 World Way, Tom Bradley Intl Terminal, Los Angeles, CA   90045

    CEO: Kaihong Duan, Gen. Mgr.   Tel: (310) 646-1849   %FO: 100

    Bus: *Passenger airline services.*   Fax: (310) 645-1758

    CHINA EASTERN AIRLINES

    55 South Lake Avenue, Ste. 120, Pasadena, CA   91101

    CEO: Steven Bak, Operations Mgr.   Tel: (818) 583-1500   %FO: 100

    Bus: *Passenger and cargo airline*   Fax: (818) 583-1515
       services.

    CHINA EASTERN AIRLINES

    Main Terminal Rm. 5625 T, Sea-Tac International Airport, Seattle, WA   98158

    CEO: Steven Bak, Operations Mgr.   Tel: (206) 431-9155   %FO: 100

    Bus: *Cargo airline services.*   Fax: (206) 431-9171

    CHINA EASTERN AIRLINES

    625 N. Michigan Avenue, Ste. 1206, Chicago, IL   60611

    CEO: X. Huang, Mgr.   Tel: (312) 337-8008   %FO: 100

    Bus: *Passenger airline services.*   Fax: (312) 337-8120

    CHINA EASTERN AIRLINES

    PO Box 6608, O'Hare International Airport, Chicago, IL   60601

    CEO: Shirley Cao, Mgr.   Tel: (773) 686-0107   %FO: 100

    Bus: *Cargo airline services.*   Fax: (773) 686-0125

- **CHINA INTERNATIONAL TRUST & INVESTMENT CORPORATION (CITIC)**
Capital Mansion 6, Xinuan Nanlu, Beijing 10004, China PRC
CEO: Kong Dan, CEO   Tel: 86-10-6466-8866   Rev: $3,923
Bus: *Engaged in overseeing the government's* Fax: 86-10-6466-1186   Emp: 23,400
    international investments.   www.citic.com

    CITIFOR INC.
    7272 Columbia Center, 701 Fifth Avenue, Seattle, WA   98104-7090
    CEO: Qin Xiao, Pres.   Tel: (206) 622-3770   %FO: 100
    Bus: *Engaged in international*   Fax: (206) 622-6714
        investments.

- **CHINA NATIONAL CHEMICALS IMPORT & EXPORT CORPORATION**
Sinochem Tower A2, Fixingmenwai Dajie, Beijing 100045, China PRC
CEO: Lin Deshu, CEO   Tel: 86-10-6856-8888   Rev: $18,000
Bus: *Mfr./import/export chemicals and* Fax: 86-10-6856-8890   Emp: 6,450
    specialty chemical products.   www.sinochem.com

    SINO-CHEM AMERICA HOLDINGS, INC
    *Two World Trade Center, Ste. 2222, New York, NY   10048
    CEO: Keziang Wang, Pres.   Tel: (212) 488-8060   %FO: 100
    Bus: *U.S. headquarters.*   Fax: (212) 488-1140   Emp: 6
        Mfr./import/export chemicals and
        specialty chemical products.

    SINO-CHEM POLYMERS INC.
    *Two World Trade Center, Ste. 2222, New York, NY   10048
    CEO: Linmin Gu, Pres.   Tel: (212) 432-2100   %FO: 100
    Bus: *Mfr./import/export chemicals and* Fax: (212) 432-9179   Emp: 10
        specialty chemical products.

    SINOCHEM U.S.A. INC.
    *Two World Trade Center Suite 2222, New York, NY   10048
    CEO: Tel: (212) 432-2100   %FO: 100
    Bus: *Sales of chemicals and specialty* Fax: (212) 432-9179
        chemical products

    US AGROCHEMICAL CORPORATION, DIV. SINO-CHEM
    3225 State Road, 630 West, Fort Meade, FL   33841
    CEO: Xiangyuan Shen, VC   Tel: (863) 285-8121   %FO: 100
    Bus: *Mfr./import/export chemicals and* Fax: (863) 285-7984
        specialty chemical products.

• CHINA NATIONAL FOREIGN TRADE TRANSPORTATION CORP.

Jiuling Bldg. No. 21, Xisanhuan Beilu, Beijing, China PRC

CEO: N/A   Tel: 86-10-6840-5005

Bus: *Freight forwarding services.*   Fax: 86-10-6840-5009

                                           www.china-interocean.com

CHINA INTEROCEAN TRANSPORT INC.

501 Grandview Drive, Suite 101, South San Francisco, CA   94080-4902

CEO: Si Yuen Chen, Mgr.   Tel: (650) 588-7685   %FO: 100

Bus: *Freight forwarding services.*   Fax: (650) 588-3157

CHINA INTEROCEAN TRANSPORT INC.

2300 E. Higgins Road, Ste. 213A, Chicago, IL   60007

CEO: M. Xijin, Mgr.   Tel: (847) 437-5900   %FO: 100

Bus: *Freight forwarding services.*   Fax: (847) 437-5902

CHINA INTEROCEAN TRANSPORT INC.

2099 South Atlantic Blvd. Unit I, Monterey Park, CA   91745

CEO: M. Jiang, Mgr.   Tel: (323) 262-7718   %FO: 100

Bus: *Freight forwarding services.*   Fax: (323) 262-7719

CHINA INTEROCEAN TRANSPORT INC.

JFK Airport Bldg. #75, North Hangar Road, Ste. 203, Jamaica, NY   11430

CEO: Wayne, Mgr.   Tel: (718) 656-3098   %FO: 100

Bus: *Freight forwarding services.*   Fax: (718) 656-3098

SINO-AM MARINE COMPANY

601 E. Linden Avenue, Linden, NJ   07036

CEO: M. Liumin, Mgr.   Tel: (908) 862-0800   %FO: 100

Bus: *Freight forwarding services.*   Fax: (908) 862-0876

• CHINA SOUTHERN AIRLINES COMPANY LTD.

Baiyun International Airport, Guangzhou, China PRC

CEO: Xu Jie Bo, CEO   Tel: 86-20-8612-4738   Rev: $1,835

Bus: *International passenger and cargo*   Fax: 86-20-8665-9040   Emp: 15,850
     carrier, engaged in operation of hotels,   www.cs-air.com
     restaurants and duty-free shops.

CHINA SOUTHERN AIRLINES COMPANY LTD.

6300 Wilshire Boulevard, Los Angeles, CA   90048

CEO: Liao Weijia, Mgr.   Tel: (323) 653-8088   %FO: 100

Bus: *International passenger and cargo*   Fax: (323) 653-8066
     carrier, engaged in operation of
     hotels, restaurants and duty-free
     shops.

● **CHINA STATE CONSTRUCTION ENGINEERIG CORP. (CSCEC)**
9 Sanlihe Road, Xiheng District, Beijing 100835, China PRC
CEO: Ma Tinggui, Pres.   Tel: 86-10-6839-3368   Rev: $5,000
Bus: *Engaged in civil engineering and*   Fax: 86-10-6831-4326   Emp: 1,480
      construction.   www.cscec.com

    CSCEC INC
    *One World Trade Center, Ste. 3861, New York, NY   10048
    CEO: Qingyu Meng, CEO   Tel: (212) 488-8964   %FO: 100
    Bus: *Engaged in civil engineering and* Fax: (212) 488-8296
          construction.

● **COFCO**
Jian Guo Men Nei Street, Beijing 10005, China PRC
CEO: Zhou Ming Chen, Pres.   Tel: 86-10-6526-8888   Rev: $12,100
Bus: *Import and exports of grains and*   Fax: 86-10-6527-8619   Emp: 28,000
      foodstuffs.   www.cofco.com.cn

    CEROIL FOOD INC.
    910 Sylvan Avenue, Englewood Cliffs, NJ   07632
    CEO: Yue Guo, Pres.   Tel: (201) 568-6788   %FO: 100
    Bus: *Engaged in commodity trading.*   Fax: (201) 569-2008

    FOREC TRADING INC.
    201 South Lake Avenue, Ste. 801, Pasadena, CA   91101
    CEO: Yeming Liu, VP   Tel: (626) 583-8989   %FO: 100
    Bus: *Imports/exports food products and* Fax: (626) 583-1583
          textiles.

● **COSCO (CHINA OCEAN SHIPPING CO.)**
412 Huanshi Road East, Guangzhou, China PRC
CEO: Captain Wei Jiafu, Pres. & CEO   Tel: 86-20-8776-5567
Bus: *Engaged in international shipping,*   Fax: 86-20-8776-5636   Emp: 700
      warehousing, insurance and real estate. www.cosco.com

    COSCO
    Westbrook Corp. Tower 4, Ste. 200, Westchester, IL   60154
    CEO: Carole Cirino, EVP   Tel: (708) 531-8001   %FO: 100
    Bus: *Engaged in international shipping* Fax: (708) 531-8081
          and warehousing.

    COSCO
    1201 Roberts Blvd., Ste. 203, Kennesaw, GA   30328
    CEO: Jeff Hall, Mgr.   Tel: (770) 419-1123   %FO: 100
    Bus: *Engaged in international shipping* Fax: (770) 419-7772
          and warehousing.

COSCO
Parkshore Centre, One Posten Rd., Charleston, SC   29407
CEO: Carl Bollettino, Mgr.   Tel: (843) 769-5443   %FO: 100
Bus: *Engaged in international shipping*   Fax: (843) 769-9808
    and warehousing.

COSCO
9 Koger Center, Ste. 101, Norfolk, VA   23502
CEO: Mike Abbott, Mgr.   Tel: (757) 461-6444   %FO: 100
Bus: *Engaged in international shipping*   Fax: (757) 461-6474
    and warehousing.

COSCO
606 South Olive Street, Ste. 1100, Los Angeles, CA   90014
CEO: Zhou Hu, Pres.   Tel: (213) 689-6700   %FO: 100
Bus: *Engaged in international shipping*   Fax: (213) 627-2804
    and warehousing.

COSCO
100 Lighting Way, Secaucus, NJ   07094
CEO: Frank Grossi, EVP   Tel: (201) 422-0500   %FO: 100
Bus: *Engaged in international shipping*   Fax: (201) 422-8956
    and warehousing.

COSCO
100 Spear Street, Ste. 1711, San Francisco, CA   94109
CEO: Walter Schreiber, EVP   Tel: (415) 778-7888   %FO: 100
Bus: *Engaged in international shipping*   Fax: (415) 882-9286
    and warehousing.

COSCO
20525 Center Ridge Road, Rocky River, OH   44116
CEO: John Robinson, Mgr.   Tel: (440) 356-4640   %FO: 100
Bus: *Engaged in international shipping*   Fax: (440) 356-4641
    and warehousing.

COSCO
401 East Pratt Street, Ste. 655, Baltimore, MD   21202
CEO: Gene Johnson, Mgr.   Tel: (410) 468-1300   %FO: 100
Bus: *Engaged in international shipping*   Fax: (410) 468-1323
    and warehousing.

COSCO
15333 JFK Blvd., Ste. 550, Houston, TX   77032
CEO: Dugan Graddy, VP   Tel: (281) 765-6800   %FO: 100
Bus: *Engaged in international shipping*   Fax: (281) 765-6801
    and warehousing.

COSCO
1601 - 5th Avenue, Ste. 850, Seattle, WA 98101
CEO: Tim Banks, EVP   Tel: (206) 654-4500   %FO: 100
Bus: *Engaged in international shipping* Fax: (206) 654-4599
  and warehousing.

● **INDUSTRIAL AND COMMERCIAL BANK OF CHINA**
No. 55 Fuxingmennei Dajie, Beijing 100031, China PRC
CEO: Jiang Jianquing, CEO   Tel: 86-10-6610-7116
Bus: *State-owned commercial bank.* Fax: 86-10-6610-8213
                                     www.icbc.com.cn

INDUSTRIAL AND COMMERCIAL BANK OF CHINA
375 Park Avenue, Ste. 3508, New York, NY 10152
CEO: Y. Wang, Rep.   Tel: (212) 838-7799   %FO: 100
Bus: *Bank services.*   Fax: (212) 838-5770

● **JUN HE LAW OFFICE**
China Resources Bldg., 20th Fl., 8 Jianguomenbei Avenue, Beijing 100005, China PRC
CEO: Xiaolin Zhou, Prtn.   Tel: 86-10-8519-1300
Bus: *International law firm.*   Fax: 86-10-8519-1350   Emp: 85
                                     www.junhe.com

JUN HE LAW OFFICE
One World Trade Center, Ste. 7717, New York, NY 10048
CEO: Wei Zhang, Ptnr.   Tel: (212) 775-8610   %FO: 100
Bus: *International law firm.*   Fax: (212) 775-8533

● **SINOPEC SHANGHAI PETROCHEMICAL COMPANY LIMITED**
2 Wei Er Road, Jinshanwei, Shanghai 200540, China PRC
CEO: Lu Yiping, Pres.   Tel: 86-21-5794-3143   Rev: $1,295
Bus: *Mfr. ethylene and petroleum-based fuels* Fax: 86-21-5794-0050   Emp: 38,000
  and oils, including benzene. (JV with www.spc.com.cn
  Union Carbide Corp., US)

UNION CARBIDE CORPORATION
39 Old Ridgebury Road, Danbury, CT 06817
CEO: William H. Joyce, Chmn.   Tel: (203) 794-2000   %FO: JV
Bus: *Mfr. industrial chemicals, plastics* Fax: (203) 794-6269
  and resins.

Colombia

● **BANCAFE (BANCO CAFETERO)**
Calle 28 #13A-15, Apartado Aereo 240332, Bogotá, Colombia
CEO: Gilberto Gomez, Pres.   Tel: 57-1-284-6800
Bus: *International banking services.*   Fax: 57-1-286-8893   Emp: 6,900
                              www.bancafe.com

     BANCAFE INTERNATIONAL MIAMI
     801 Brickell Avenue, PH-1, Miami, FL 33131
     CEO: Alfredo Quintero, Pres.   Tel: (305) 372-9909   %FO: 100
     Bus: *International banking services.* Fax: (305) 372-1797   Emp: 35

● **BANCO COLPATRIA SA**
Carretera 13, 93B-11 Floor 1, Bogotá, Colombia
CEO: Santiago Perdomo, Pres.   Tel: 57-1-661-1104
Bus: *International banking services.*   Fax: 57-1-616-1184   Emp: 480
                              www.colpatria.com.co

     BANCO COLPATRIA S.A.
     801 Brickell Avenue, Ste. 2360, Miami, FL 33131
     CEO: Carlos R. Pancheco, Mgr.   Tel: (305) 374-4026   %FO: 100
     Bus: *International banking services.* Fax: (305) 372-0605   Emp: 5

● **BANCO DE BOGOTA**
Calle 36 #7-47, Bogotá, Colombia
CEO: Alejandro Figueroa, Gen. Mgr. Tel: 57-1-288-1188
Bus: *International banking services.*   Fax:
                              www.bancodebogota.com.co

     BANCO DE BOGOTA
     375 Park Avenue, Ste. 307, New York, NY 10152
     CEO: John J. Kennedy, Mgr.   Tel: (212) 230-1857   %FO: 100
     Bus: *International banking services.* Fax: (212) 319-6976   Emp: 50

     BANCO DE BOGOTA INTERNATIONAL CORPORATION
     200 South Biscayne Boulevard, Miami, FL 33131
     CEO: Matias Herrera, Mgr.   Tel: (305) 373-0041   %FO: 100
     Bus: *International banking services.* Fax: (305) 373-6465   Emp: 10
       Sub of Banco de Bogota.

- **BBV BANCO GANADERO, S.A.**
Carrera 9a, No. 71-52, 53851 Bogotá, Colombia
CEO: Jose M. Ayala Vargas, CEO   Tel: 57-1-312-4666   Rev: $822
Bus: *International banking services.*   Fax: 57-1-235-9829   Emp: 5,800
     www.bbv.es

     BANCO GANADERO, S.A.
     1150 South Miami Avenue, Miami, FL   33130
     CEO: J. Zavier, Mgr.   Tel: (305) 374-3955   %FO: 100
     Bus: *International banking services.*   Fax: (305) 374-7710

Costa Rica

● **BANCO INTERNACIONAL DE COSTA RICA, S.A.**

Barrio Tournon, San Jose, Costa Rica

CEO: Alfonso Guardia Mora, Chmn.

Bus: *International banking services.*

Tel: 506-243-1000

Fax: 506-243-8866

www.bicsa.com

BANCO INTERNACIONAL DE COSTA RICA, S.A.

201 South Biscayne Blvd., Ste. 2700, Miami, FL   33131

CEO: Percy A. Elbrecht, SVP

Bus: *Banking services.*

Tel: (305) 374-0855

Fax: (305) 381-6971

%FO: 100

● **CREDOMATIC INTERNATIONAL CORPORATION**

Calle O, Avenidas 3 y 5, 5to Piso, San Jose, Costa Rica

CEO: Ernesto Castegnaro, CEO

Bus: *Largest credit card operation in Central America; issues both local and international (MasterCard and VISA) cards.*

Tel: 506-257-6512

Fax:

www.credomatic.fi.cr

Rev: $1,000

BAC FLORIDA BANK

848 Brickell Avenue, Ste. 300, Miami, FL   33131

CEO: Walter Carvalho, Mgr.

Bus: *Issues local and international credit cards.*

Tel: (305) 789-7000

Fax: (305) 374-1402

%FO: 100

Cyprus

- **CYPRUS AIRWAYS LTD.**
  21 Alkeou Street, Nicosia, Cyprus
  CEO: Vasillis G. Rologis, Chmn.
  Bus: *Commercial air transport services.*

  Tel: 35-72-443054
  Fax: 35-72-443167
  www.cyprusair.com.cy

  Rev: $302
  Emp: 2,000

  CYPRUS AIRWAYS LTD.
  311 West 54th Street, New York, NY   10019
  CEO: Vasillis G. Rologis, Chmn.
  Bus: *Commercial air transport services.*

  Tel: (212) 714-2190
  Fax: (212) 714-2543

  %FO: 100

Czech Republic

● **CENTROTEX COMPANY LTD.**
nam. Hrdinu, 3/2634, 190 61 Prague 4, Czech Republic
CEO: Jitka Susová
Bus: *Trading company.*

Tel: 420-2-6115-1111
Fax: 420-2-6121-1464
www.centrotex.cz

CENTROTEX USA, INC.
990 Avenue of the Americas, New York, NY 10018
CEO: Miroslav Tvaruzek, Pres.
Bus: *Trading company; import/export of textiles.*

Tel: (212) 947-8094
Fax: (212) 947-8228

%FO: 100
Emp: 2

● **CZECH AIRLINES LTD.**
Letiste Ruzyne, Prague, Czech Republic
CEO: Antonin Jakubse, Pres.
Bus: *Commercial air transport services.*

Tel: 420-23-341540
Fax: 420-23-162774
www.csa.cz

Rev: $244
Emp: 4,300

CZECH AIRLINES LTD.
35 East Wacker Drive, Ste. 1078, Chicago, IL 60601
CEO: Jaroslav Simecek, Dir.
Bus: *Commercial air transport services.*

Tel: (312) 201-1781
Fax: (312) 201-1783

%FO: 100

CZECH AIRLINES LTD.
1350 Avenue of the Americas, Ste. 601, New York, NY 10036
CEO: Miroslav Belovsky, Gen. Mgr.
Bus: *Commercial air transport services.*

Tel: (212) 765-6022
Fax: (212) 765-6588

%FO: 100

● **PRECIOSA AS**
Opietalova 17, 466 67 Jablonec nad Nisou, Czech Republic
CEO: Ing. Ivo Schötta, Dir.
Bus: *Engaged in design and manufacture of glass cutting and polishing machines, machine-cut glass stones, light fittings and cut crystal figurines.*

Tel: 420-428-415111
Fax: 420-428-311761
www.preciosa.com

PRECIOSA INTERNATIONAL, INC.
41 Madison Avenue, 16th Fl., New York, NY   10010
CEO: Jaroslav Hanys, Pres.   Tel: (212) 889-3741   %FO: 100
Bus: *Sales/distribution of machine-cut*   Fax: (212) 684-1874
     glass stones, including beads,
     fancy stones and chandelier
     trimmings.

SENOV LIMITED
41 Madison Avenue, 16th Fl., New York, NY   10010
CEO: Michael Kamir, Mgr.   Tel: (212) 889-3741   %FO: 100
Bus: *Sales/distribution of hand made*   Fax: (212) 684-1874
     chandeliers.

● **UNIPLET A.S.**
Prumyslova Ctvrt, 674 01 Trebic, Czech Republic
CEO: Otakar Curda, VP   Tel: 420-618-776
Bus: *Mfr. small diameter hosiery knitting*   Fax: 420-618-840-641
     machines.   www.uniplet.cz

UNIPLET COMPANY LTD.
6012-A Old Pineville Road, Charlotte, NC   28217
CEO: Otakar Curda, VP   Tel: (704) 521-9303   %FO: 100
Bus: *Sales, service and support for*   Fax: (704) 521-8379
     hosiery knitting machines.

Denmark

- **AALBORG PORTLAND HOLDING A/S, DIV. FLS INDUSTRIES**
PO Box 165, DK-9100 Aalborg, Denmark
CEO: Bjarne Moltke Hansen, CEO — Tel: 45-98-16-7777 — Rev: $1,528
Bus: *Mfr. building products, including white* — Fax: 45-98-10-1186 — Emp: 3,500
cement and concrete. — www.aph.dk

> **AALBORG ENERGY CONSULTANTS INC.**
> 300 Knickerbocker Road, Cresskill, NJ 07626
> CEO: Greta Ostbirk, Pres. — Tel: (201) 871-4777 — %FO: 100
> Bus: *Energy consultants.* — Fax: (201) 569-1961

- **AARHUS OLIEFABRIK A/S**
MP Bruuns Gade 27, PO Box 50, DK-8100 Aarhus C, Denmark
CEO: Erik Højsholt, CEO — Tel: 45-87-30-6000 — Rev: $666
Bus: *Produces specialty fats and oils.* — Fax: 45-87-30-6012 — Emp: 3,928
www.aarhus.com

> **AARHUS INC.**
> 131 Marsh Street, Port Newark, NJ 07114
> CEO: Carl Heckel, Mgr. — Tel: (973) 344-1300 — %FO: 100
> Bus: *Produces specialty fats and oils.* — Fax: (973) 344-9049

- **ALK-ABELLÓ LABORATORIES AS, DIV. CHR. HANSEN GROUP**
Boge Allé 10-12, PO Box 408, DK-2970 Horsholm, Denmark
CEO: Jens Bager, Pres. — Tel: 45-45-76-7777
Bus: *Develops allergy products for the* — Fax: 45-45-76-5152
diagnosis, prevention and cure of — www.alk-abello.com
allergies.

> **ALK-ABELLÓ LABORATORIES INC.**
> 27 Village Lane, Wallingford, CT 06492
> CEO: Brian J. DeBari, Pres. — Tel: (203) 949-2727 — %FO: 100
> Bus: *Research for allergy treatment* — Fax: (203) 949-2718
> *products.*

> **ALK-ABELLÓ LABORATORIES INC.**
> 1700 Royston Lane, Round Rock, TX 78664
> CEO: Brian J. DeBari, Pres. — Tel: (512) 251-0037 — %FO: 100
> Bus: *Develops allergy products for the* — Fax: (512) 251-8450
> *diagnosis, prevention and cure of*
> *allergies and the relief of*
> *symptoms.*

● **ARLA FOODS AMBA**
Skanderborgvej 277, PO Box 2400, DK-8260 Viby, Denmark
CEO: Lars Lamberg, Chmn.   Tel: 45-89-38-1000
Bus: *Engaged in production of fresh milk*   Fax: 45-86-28-1691
products, cheeses, yogurts and specialty   www.arlafoods.com
products.

    MEDIPHARM INC.
    10215 Dennis Drive, Des Moines, IA   50322
    CEO: Mark Richards, Dir.   Tel: (515) 254-1280   %FO: 100
    Bus: *Engaged in concentrates and*   Fax: (515) 254-1356
    cultures for the food industry.

● **BANG & OLUFSEN HOLDING A/S**
Peter Bangs Vej 15, DK-7600 Struer, Denmark
CEO: Torben B. Sorensen, Pres. & CEO   Tel: 45-96-84-1122   Rev: $468
Bus: *Mfr. electronics.*   Fax: 45-97-85-1888   Emp: 2,790
                                    www.bang-olufsen.com

    BANG & OLUFSEN
    927 Broadway, New York, NY   10010
    CEO: Anders Knutsen, CEO   Tel: (212) 388-9792   %FO: 100
    Bus: *Sales of electronic equipment.*   Fax: (212) 388-0657

    BANG & OLUFSEN
    86 Greenwich Avenue, Greenwich, CT   06830
    CEO: Anders Knutsen, CEO   Tel: (203) 625-3388   %FO: 100
    Bus: *Sales of electronic equipment.*   Fax: (203) 625-8666

    BANG & OLUFSEN
    952 Madison Avenue, New York, NY   10021
    CEO: Anders Knutsen, CEO   Tel: (212) 879-6161   %FO: 100
    Bus: *Sales of electronic equipment.*   Fax: (212) 794-4998

    BANG & OLUFSEN
    Roosevelt Field Mall, Ste. 2082, Garden City, NY   11530
    CEO: Anders Knutsen, CEO   Tel: (516) 248-4198   %FO: 100
    Bus: *Sales of electronic equipment.*   Fax: (516) 248-4430

    BANG & OLUFSEN
    1200 Morris Tpke., Ste. 206, Short Hills, NJ   07078
    CEO: Anders Knutsen, CEO   Tel: (973) 258-0808   %FO: 100
    Bus: *Sales of electronic equipment.*   Fax: (973) 258-9121

- **BELLE SYSTEMS A/S**
Universitetsparken 7, DK-4000 Roskilde, Denmark
CEO: Erik Froberg, CEO   Tel: 45-70-12-2500
Bus: *Mfr. computer software and services.*   Fax: 45-70-12-2501
                                         www.bellesystems.com

> **BELL SYSTEMS, DIV. DIGIQUANT**
> 1000 Abernathy Road, Ste. 1800, Atlanta, GA 30328
> CEO: Michael O'Laughlin, VP   Tel: (770) 206-4600   %FO: 100
> Bus: *Mfr. computer software.*   Fax: (770) 206-4690

- **CRISPLANT INDUSTRIES A/S**
Pedersens Vej 10, DK-8200 Årthus, Denmark
CEO: Ebbe Funk, Dir.   Tel: 45-87-41-4141   Rev: $1,192
Bus: *Manufactures automated high-speed* Fax: 45-87-41-4120   Emp: 800
sortation systems.   www.crisplantinc.com

> **CRISPLANT, INC.**
> 7495 New Technology Way, Frederick, MD 21703
> CEO: Jan Reynolds, HR   Tel: (301) 663-8710   %FO: 100
> Bus: *Sales/distribution/service*   Fax: (301) 662-0449   Emp: 90
> *automated high-speed sortation*
> *systems.*

- **L DAEHNFELDT A/S**
PO Box 185, DK-5100 Odense C, Denmark
CEO: P. B. Jorgensen, Dir.   Tel: 45-66-17-5506
Bus: *Engaged in seed production and sales.* Fax: 45-66-17-5505
                                         www.daehnfeldt.com

> **DAEHNFELDT INC.**
> PO Box 38, North Manchester, IN 46962-0038
> CEO: Joe R. Messer, Pres.   Tel: (219) 982-7969   %FO: 100
> Bus: *Seed production and sales.*   Fax: (219) 982-7970   Emp: 18

- **DANFOSS A/S**
DK-6430 Nordborg, Denmark
CEO: Jørge M. Clausen, Pres.   Tel: 45-74-882222   Rev: $1,700
Bus: *Refrigeration controls, heating and* Fax: 45-74-880949   Emp: 17,000
water controls and motion controls.   www.danfoss.com

> **DANFOSS BAUER**
> 31 Schoolhouse Road, Somerset, NJ 08873
> CEO: Steffen Habermann   Tel: (732) 469-8770   %FO: 100
> Bus: *Mfr. of DC electronic frequency* Fax: (732) 469-8773
> *converters.*

DANFOSS BUILDING AND COMFORT CONTROLS
3435 Box Hill Corporate Center Drive, Ste. C, Abingdon, MD   21009

CEO: Roger Maves   Tel: (443) 512-0266   %FO: 100
Bus: *Mfr. controls.*   Fax: (443) 512-0270

DANFOSS DRIVES
2995 Eastrock Drive, Rockford, IL   61109

CEO: Ross Waite, Pres.   Tel: (815) 398-2770   %FO: 100
Bus: *Mfr. AC electronic frequency*   Fax: (815) 398-2869   Emp: 135
converters.

DANFOSS FLUID POWER
1201 Pelzer Highway, Easley, SC   29642

CEO: Roy Taylor, Dir.   Tel: (864) 855-2884   %FO: 100
Bus: *Mfr. Hydraulic components.*   Fax: (864) 855-5885

DANFOSS FLUID POWER
8635 Washington Avenue, Racine, WI   53406-3773

CEO: Preben Pedersen, Pres.   Tel: (414) 884-7400   %FO: 100
Bus: *Mfr. hydraulic integrated circuits,*   Fax: (414) 884-7470   Emp: 600
motors, pumps, power units, and
manual & electrically operated
valves.

DANFOSS GRAHAM
PO Box 245041, Milwaukee, WI   53224

CEO: Charles Manz, EVP   Tel: (414) 355-8800   %FO: 100
Bus: *Mfr. of DC electronic frequency*   Fax: (414) 355-6117   Emp: 130
converters.

DANFOSS MANEUROP, LTD.
1775-G MacLeod Drive, Lawrenceville, GA   30243

CEO: Joe Orosz, VP   Tel: (678) 377-5100   %FO: 100
Bus: *Mfr. refrigerant compressors and*   Fax: (678) 377-5101   Emp: 60
condensing units.

DANFOSS VIDEK USA
2200 Brighton Henriette Town Line Road, Rochester, NY   14623-2706

CEO: Wes M. Perdue, Pres.   Tel: (716) 292-6210   %FO: 100
Bus: *Vision product for the optimizing*   Fax: (716) 292-5884   Emp: 21
of production processes.

DANFOSS, INC.
7941 Corporate Drive, Baltimore, MD   21236
CEO: Robert W. Wilkins, Pres.   Tel: (410) 931-8250   %FO: 100
Bus: *Refrigerant flow controls,*   Fax: (410) 931-8256   Emp: 142
    industrial controls & compressors,
    refrigeration compressors,
    condensing units, electronic
    products.

FLOMATIC CORPORATION
145 Murray Street, Glens Falls, NY   12801-4424
CEO: Bo Andersson, Pres.   Tel: (518) 761-9797   %FO: JV
Bus: *Mfr./sale check valves, foot valves,* Fax: (518) 761-9798   Emp: 50
    back flow preventers, control
    valves.

INSTRUMARK INTERNATIONAL
1124 Wrigley Way, Milpitas, CA   95035
CEO: Bo Andersson, Pres.   Tel: (408) 262-0717   %FO: 100
Bus: *Mfr. flow products.*   Fax: (408) 262-3610

● **DANISCO A/S**
Langebrogade 1, PO Box 17, DK-1001 Copenhagen K, Denmark
CEO: Alf Duch-Pedersen, CEO   Tel: 45-32-66-2000   Rev: $3,397
Bus: *Food and beverages, sweeteners, food* Fax: 45-32-66-2175   Emp: 17,712
    ingredients and packaging.   www.danisco.com

DANISCO CULTOR INC.
201 New Century Parkway, New Century, KS   66031
CEO: Germain Despres, Pres.   Tel: (913) 764-8100   %FO: 100
Bus: *Mfr./sale food ingredients.*   Fax: (913) 764-5407   Emp: 240

DANISCO INGREDIENTS USA, INC.
4509 South 50th Street, St. Joseph, MO   64507
CEO: Gary King, Mgr.   Tel: (816) 232-8423   %FO: 100
Bus: *Mfr./sale food ingredients.*   Fax: (816) 232-2045

FINNSUGAR BIOPRODUCTS, INC.
1895C Rohlwing Road, Rolling Meadows, IL   60008-8550
CEO: M. Monten, Pres.   Tel: (847) 670-7400
Bus: *Mfr. ingredients for animal feed.*   Fax: (847) 670-7444

GENENCOR INTERNATIONAL INC.
200 Meridian Centre Blvd., Rochester, NY   14618-3916
CEO: Karl Sanford, VP   Tel: (716) 256-5200
Bus: *Mfr. enzymes.*   Fax: (716) 256-5952

GENENCOR INTERNATIONAL INC.
925 Page Mill Road, Palo Alto, CA 94304
CEO: W. Thomas Mitchell, CEO   Tel: (650) 846-7500
Bus: *Mfr. enzymes.*   Fax: (650) 846-7500

● DANSKE BANK A/S (FORMERLY DEN DANSKE BANK)
2-12 Holmens Kanal, DK-1092 Copenhagen, Denmark
CEO: Paul J. Svanholm, Chmn.   Tel: 45-33-44-0000   Rev: $6,661
Bus: *General commercial banking services.*   Fax: 45-33-18-5873   Emp: 18,930
www.danskebank.de

DANSKE BANK
280 Park Avenue, 4th Fl. East Bldg., New York, NY 10017-1216
CEO: James M. Stewart, Gen. Mgr.   Tel: (212) 984-8400   %FO: 100
Bus: *International commercial banking*   Fax: (212) 370-9239   Emp: 65
services.

● DFDS A/S
Sankt Annae Plads 30, DK-1295 Copenhagen, Denmark
CEO: Thorleif Blok, CEO   Tel: 45-33-42-3342
Bus: *Shipping line, engaged in travel and*   Fax: 45-33-42-3341   Emp: 5,000
transport services.   www.dfds.dk

DFDS DAN TRANSPORT CORPORATION
1210 Corbin Street, Elizabeth, NJ 07201
CEO: Jorgen Moller, Pres.   Tel: (908) 353-0800   %FO: 100
Bus: *Engaged in international freight*   Fax: (908) 353-8717
forwarding.

DFDS SEAWAYS (USA) INC.
6555 NW 9th Ave., Ste. 207, Ft. Lauderdale, FL 33309
CEO: Josie Julian, Dir.   Tel: (954) 491-7909   %FO: 100
Bus: *Marketing/reservations travel &*   Fax: (954) 491-7958   Emp: 5
transport.

● ENKOTEC A/S
Sverigesvej 26, DK-8660 Skanderborg, Denmark
CEO: Svend-Helge Sorensen, Pres.   Tel: 45-86-52-4444
Bus: *Mfr. rotary forming nail machines and*   Fax: 45-86-52-4813   Emp: 60
cold forgers.   www.encotech.com

ENKOTEC CO INC
31200 Solon Road, Ste. 16, Cleveland, OH 44139-3523
CEO: Jan Sørige, Pres.   Tel: (440) 349-2800   %FO: 100
Bus: *Sale/service rotary forming nail*   Fax: (440) 349-3575   Emp: 7
machines, and cold formers.

- **EPOKE A/S**

Vejenvej 50, Askov Postbox 230, DK-6600 Vejen, Denmark

CEO: Thyge Hvass Rasmussen, Pres.   Tel: 45-76-96-2200

Bus: *Sales/distribution of snow removal*   Fax: 45-76-36-3867   Emp: 400
equipment, spreaders, de-icing and anti- www.epoke.com
icing equipment.

    EPOKE INC.

    2557 Glenn Drive, Canyon Lake, TX   78133

    CEO: Bill Vandemark, VP   Tel: (705) 653-0317   %FO: 100

    Bus: *Spreaders, de-icing & anti-icing*   Fax: (705) 653-4732
       equipment.

- **FLS INDUSTRIES A/S**

Vigersleve Alle 77, DK-2500 Valby, Copenhagen, Denmark

CEO: Peter Assam, Pres. & CEO   Tel: 45-36-18-1800   Rev: $2,271

Bus: *Engineering, building materials, real*   Fax: 45-36-30-4441   Emp: 14,640
estate, aerospace services.   www.flsindustries.dk

    F. L. SMIDTH INC.

    2040 Avenue C, Bethlehem, PA   18017

    CEO: Frank Gad, Pres.   Tel: (610) 264-6011   %FO: 100

    Bus: *Supplier of custom equipment,*   Fax: (610) 264-6170   Emp: 1,163
       systems, products & processes for
       cement, pulp, paper, mining, and
       chemical industry.

    FLS MILJO

    100 Glenborough Drive, Houston, TX   77067-3611

    CEO: Preben Laursen, Pres.   Tel: (281) 539-3400   %FO: 100

    Bus: *Supplier electro static,*   Fax: (281) 539-3411
       precipitators.

    FULLER BULK HANDLING CORPORATION

    3225 Schoenersville Road, Bethlehem, PA   18016

    CEO: Jack Hilbert   Tel: (610) 264-6055   %FO: 100

    Bus: *Distribute cement.*   Fax: (610) 264-6735

    FULLER COMPANY

    2040 Avenue C, Bethlehem, PA   18017

    CEO: Jack Hilbert, Pres.   Tel: (610) 264-6011   %FO: 100

    Bus: *Mfr. fabric filter dust collectors*   Fax: (610) 264-6701
       and pneumatic conveying
       equipment.

● **FOSS ELECTRIC A/S**

Slangerupgade 69, DK-3400 Hillerod, Denmark

CEO: Peter Foss, CEO   Tel: 45-42-26-3366

Bus: *Electronic equipment, measure control*   Fax: 45-42-26-9322   Emp: 700
devices.   www.foss.dk

    FOSS NIRSYSTEMS

    12101 Tech Road, Silver Spring, MD   20904

    CEO: Donald R. Webster, Pres.   Tel: (301) 680-9600

    Bus: *Mfr. of near-infrared spectroscopy*   Fax: (301) 326-0134
    equipment and chemical analyzers.

    FOSS NORTH AMERICA

    7682 Executive Drive, Eden Prairie, MN   55344

    CEO: Brendan P. Martin, Pres.   Tel: (952) 974-9892   %FO: 100

    Bus: *Sale/service analytical instruments*   Fax: (952) 974-9823   Emp: 45
    for dairy, food & feed industry.

● **GN RESOUND AS, SUB. GN GREAT NORDIC A/S**

Mårkærvej 2A, PO Box 224, DK-2630 Taastrup, Denmark

CEO: Jesper Mailind, CEO   Tel: 45-72-11-1111

Bus: *Mfr. and sales of audiological*   Fax: 45-72-11-1111
diagnostic systems and measurement   www.gnresound-group.com
equipment.

    GN RESOUND NORTH AMERICA

    8001 Bloomington Freeway, Bloomington, MN   55420

    CEO: Jay Grooters, VP   Tel: (800) 248-4327   %FO: 100

    Bus: *Sales of audiological diagnostic*   Fax: (952) 769-8001
    systems and measurement
    equipment.

● **GREAT NORDIC A/S**

Mårkaervej 2A, Postbox 224, DK-2630 Taastrup, Denmark

CEO: Jørn Kildegaard, Pres. & CEO   Tel: 45-43-71-4100   Rev: $15,000

Bus: *Mfr. hearing healthcare products and*   Fax: 45-43-71-4104   Emp: 2,500
services.   www.gn.dk

    GN RESOUND, INC.

    8001 Bloomington Freeway, Bloomington, MN   55420

    CEO: Carsten Trads, Pres.   Tel: (800) 248-4327   %FO: 100

    Bus: *Sales/distribution of hearing*   Fax: (800) 248-4327   Emp: 140
    instruments.

SONUS USA INC.
111 SW Fifth Avenue, Ste. 1620, Portland, OR   97204
CEO: Paul C. Campbell, SVP   Tel: (503) 225-9152   %FO: 100
Bus: *Sales/distribution of hearing*   Fax: (503) 225-9309
     instruments.

• GROUP 4 FALCK A/S
Polititorvet, DK-1780 Copenhagen 5, Denmark
CEO: Lars Norby Johansen, CEO   Tel: 45-70-13-4343   Rev: $2,315
Bus: *Engaged in security systems.*   Fax: 45-33-91-0026   Emp: 111,325
     www.group4falck.com

GROUP 4 INC.
1420 Spring Hill Road, Ste. 600, McLean, VA   22102-3006
CEO: Hans Bennetzen, COO   Tel: (703) 749-1286   %FO: 100
Bus: *Engaged in security systems.*   Fax: (703) 790-6082

GROUP 4 SECURITIES TECHNOLOGY CORP.
20710 Manhattan Place, Torrance, CA   90501-1829
CEO: Hans Bennetzen, COO   Tel: (301) 518-2380   %FO: 100
Bus: *Engaged in security systems.*   Fax: (310) 834-0685

• HALDOR TOPSOE A/S
PO Box 213, Nymollevej 55, DK-2800 Lyngby, Denmark
CEO: Haldor Topsoe, Chmn.   Tel: 45-45-27-2000
Bus: *Engineering/licensing, chemical process*   Fax: 45-45-27-2999   Emp: 1,000
     development, mfr./research/sale catalyst.   www.haldortopsoe.com

HALDOR TOPSOE INC.
17629 El Camino Real, Ste. 300, Houston, TX   77058
CEO: Alex Barlowen, EVP   Tel: (281) 228-5000   %FO: 100
Bus: *Engineering/licensing, chemical*   Fax: (281) 228-5019   Emp: 150
     process development,
     mfr./research/sale catalyst.

HALDOR TOPSOE INC.
770 The City Drive, Ste. 8400, Orange, CA   92668
CEO: Emiliano de la Fuente, EVP   Tel: (714) 621-3800   %FO: 100
Bus: *Engineering/licensing, chemical*   Fax: (714) 748-4188
     process development,
     mfr./research/sale catalyst.

● **CHRISTIAN HANSEN HOLDING A/S**

10-12 Bøge Allé, PO Box 407, DK-2970 Hørsholm, Denmark

CEO: Erik Sørensen, Pres. & CEO Tel: 45-45-747474 Rev: $515

Bus: *Supplies ingredients; food industry,* Fax: 45-45-765576 Emp: 3,525
pharmaceuticals and diagnostics for www.chr-hansen.com
specific allergy disease treatment.

CHRISTIAN HANSEN INC. BIOSYSTEMS

9015 West Maple Street, Milwaukee, WI 53214-4298

CEO: Donald H. Combs, Pres. Tel: (414) 476-3630 %FO: 100

Bus: *Mfr. supplies for dairy and* Fax: (414) 259-9399
agricultural industry.

VESPA LABORATORIES INC., SUB. ALK-ABELLÓ

1095 Upper Georges Valley Road, Spring Mills, PA 16875

CEO: Miles W. Guralnick, Pres. Tel: (814) 422-8165 %FO: 100

Bus: *Research/mfr./mktg. insect venom* Fax: (814) 422-8424
therapies.

● **HARDI INTERNATIONAL A/S**

Helgeshoj Alle 38, DK-2630 Taastrup, Denmark

CEO: Mogens Nehen-Hansen, Dir. Tel: 45-43-71-1900

Bus: *Mfr. agricultural sprayers.* Fax: 45-43-71-3355 Emp: 750
www.hardi.dk

HARDI, INC.

1500 West 76th Street, Davenport, IA 52806-1356

CEO: Tom Kinzenbaw, Pres. Tel: (319) 386-1730 %FO: 100

Bus: *Mfr./distribution agricultural* Fax: (319) 386-1710 Emp: 40
sprayers.

● **IKEA INTERNATIONAL A/S**

Ny Strandvej 21, DK-3053 Humlebaeck, Denmark

CEO: Anders Dahlvig, Pres. Tel: 45-49-15-5000 Rev: $8,500

Bus: *Retail and mail-order furniture and* Fax: 45-49-15-5001 Emp: 58,000
household items. www.ikea.com

IKEA NORTH AMERICA

2982 El Camino Real Blvd., Tustin, CA 92680

CEO: Jan Kjellman, Pres. Tel: (714) 838-4000 %FO: 100

Bus: *Retail and mail-order furniture &* Fax:
household items.

IKEA NORTH AMERICA

20700 S. Avalon Blvd., Carson, CA   90746

CEO: Jan Kjellman, Pres. Tel: (310) 527-4532 %FO: 100

Bus: *Retail and mail-order furniture &* Fax:
household items.

IKEA NORTH AMERICA

Media City Center, 600 N. San Fernando Blvd., Burbank, CA   91502

CEO: Jan Kjellman, Pres. Tel: (818) 842-4532 %FO: 100

Bus: *Retail and mail-order furniture &* Fax:
household items.

IKEA NORTH AMERICA

7810 Katy Freeway, Houston, TX   77024

CEO: Jan Kjellman, Pres. Tel: (713) 688-7867 %FO: 100

Bus: *Retail and mail-order furniture &* Fax:
household items.

IKEA NORTH AMERICA

1800 E. McConnor Pkwy., Schaumburg, IL   60173

CEO: Jan Kjellman, Pres. Tel: (847) 969-9700 %FO: 100

Bus: *Retail and mail-order furniture &* Fax: (847) 969-9244
household items.

IKEA NORTH AMERICA

8352 Honeygo Blvd., Baltimore, MD   21236

CEO: Jan Kjellman, Pres. Tel: (410) 931-5400 %FO: 100

Bus: *Retail and mail-order furniture &* Fax:
household items.

IKEA NORTH AMERICA

600 SW 43rd Street, Renton, WA   98055

CEO: Bjorn Bayley, Pres. Tel: (425) 656-2980 %FO: 100

Bus: *Retail and mail-order furniture &* Fax: (425) 656-8104
household items.

IKEA NORTH AMERICA

Town Centre, 2001 Park Manor Blvd., Pittsburgh, PA   15205

CEO: Jim Anastos, Mgr. Tel: (412) 747-0747 %FO: 100

Bus: *Retail and mail-order furniture &* Fax:
household items.

IKEA NORTH AMERICA

1100 Broadway Mall, Hicksville, NY   11801

CEO: Jan Kjellman, Pres. Tel: (516) 681-4532 %FO: 100

Bus: *Retail and mail-order furniture &* Fax:
household items.

IKEA NORTH AMERICA
2149 Fenton Parkway, San Diego, CA   92108
CEO: Renee Hausler, Mgr.   Tel: (619) 563-4532   %FO: 100
Bus: *Retail and mail-order furniture*   Fax:
and household items.

IKEA NORTH AMERICA
1000 Center Drive, Elizabeth, NJ   07202
CEO: Jan Kjellman, Pres.   Tel: (908) 289-4488   %FO: 100
Bus: *Retail and mail-order furniture &*   Fax:
household items.

IKEA NORTH AMERICA HDQRTS.
496 West Germantown Pike, Plymouth Meeting, PA   19462
CEO: Jan Kjellman, Pres.   Tel: (610) 834-0150   %FO: 100
Bus: *Retail and mail-order furniture &*   Fax: (610) 834-0872
household items.

IKEA NORTH AMERICA
17621 E. Gale Ave., City of Industry, CA   91748
CEO: Jan Kjellman, Pres.   Tel: (626) 912-4532   %FO: 100
Bus: *Retail and mail-order furniture &*   Fax:
household items.

IKEA NORTH AMERICA
2700 Potomac Circle, Ste. 888, Woodbridge, VA   22192
CEO: Tomas Franzen, Mgr.   Tel: (703) 494-4532   %FO: 100
Bus: *Retail and mail-order furniture &*   Fax:
household items.

● **INCENTIVE GROUP A/S (FORMERLY KEW INDUSTRI A/S)**
Kongens Nytorv 28, PO Box 2764, DK-1013 Copenhagen, Denmark
CEO: Jørgen Frost, CEO   Tel: 45-72-18-1000   Rev: $314
Bus: *Mfr. high pressure cleaners and related*   Fax: 45-72-18-1000   Emp: 2,985
cleaning equipment.   www.incentive-dk.com

ALTO US INC.
16253 Swingley Ridge Rd., Ste. 200, Chesterfield, MO   63017
CEO: Althea Hensley, HR   Tel: (636) 530-0871   %FO: 100
Bus: *U. S. headquarters. Mfr. of rider,*   Fax: (636) 530-0872
sweeper, scrubber equipment.

ALTO US INC.
2100 Hwy 265, Springdale, AR 72764

CEO: Bob Jones, VP

Tel: (501) 750-1000

Bus: *Mfr. of sanders, vacuums, polishers, carpet cleaning equipment.*

Fax: (501) 756-0719

• LABOTEK A/S
PO Box 100, DK-3600 Frederikssund, Denmark

CEO: Peter Jurgensen, CEO

Tel: 45-48-21-8411

Bus: *Auxiliary plastic processing equipment.*

Fax: 45-48-21-8000

www.labotek.com

Emp: 100

LABOTEK INC.
1170-F University Avenue, Rochester, NY 14607

CEO: Thomas A. Elias, Pres.

Tel: (716) 244-4840

%FO: 100

Bus: *Sale of plastic processing equipment.*

Fax: (716) 244-1690

Emp: 3

• J. LAURITZEN A/S
28 Sankt Annae Plads, PO Box 2147, DK-1291 Copenhagen, Denmark

CEO: Michael Christiansen, Chmn.

Tel: 45-33-96-8000

Rev: $420

Bus: *Ship owner and operator.*

Fax: 45-33-96-8001

Emp: 1,075

www.j-lauritzen.dk

J. LAURITZEN (USA) INC.
4 Landmark Square, Ste. 150, Stamford, CT 06901

CEO: Jorgen Kragh, Mgr.

Tel: (203) 961-8661

%FO: 100

Bus: *Ship owner & operator.*

Fax: (203) 964-0350

Emp: 20

LAURITZEN COOL
PO Box 639, Port Hueneme, CA 93044

CEO: Gerald A. Fountain, Pres.

Tel: (805) 488-1222

%FO: 100

Bus: *Steamship agent for water transportation.*

Fax: (805) 986-8320

Emp: 10

LAURITZEN KOSAN TANKERS
2600 SW 30th Avenue, Ft. Lauderdale, FL 33312

CEO: David Bayer

Tel: (954) 584-0524

%FO: 100

Bus: *Shipping and tanker services.*

Fax: (954) 584-0037

LAURITZEN REEFERS
PO Box 32088, Long Beach, CA 90832

CEO: Jens Hedelund

Tel: (310) 833-0350

%FO: 100

Bus: *Shipping services.*

Fax: (310) 833-2503

• **LEGO GROUP A/S**
Lego Center, DK-7190 Billund,Vejen, Denmark

CEO: Kjeld Kirk Kristiansen, Pres. & CEO	Tel: 45-79-50-6070	Rev: $1,194
Bus: *Educational toys; plastic bricks.*	Fax: 45-75-35-3360	Emp: 7,670
	www.lego.com	

LEGO SYSTEMS, INC.
555 Taylor Road, Enfield, CT   06083-1600

CEO: Peter Eio, Pres.	Tel: (860) 749-2291	%FO: 100
Bus: *Educational toys; plastic bricks.*	Fax: (860) 763-7743	

• **A. P. MOLLER A/S**
50, Esplanaden, DK-1098 Copenhagen K, Denmark

CEO: Jess Søderberg, CEO	Tel: 45-33-63-3363	Rev: $10,630
Bus: *Engaged in shipping, exploration for and production of oil and gas, shipbuilding, aviation, industry, supermarkets and EDP services.*	Fax: 45-33-63-4784 www.apmoller.com	

MAERSK DATA INC.
465 South Street, Ste. 200, PO Box 1992, Morristown, NJ   07962-1992

CEO: Tom Thomsen	Tel: (973) 490-3400	%FO: 100
Bus: *Engaged in shipping.*	Fax: (973) 734-3600	

MAERSK INC.
8686 New Trails Drive, Houston, TX   77301

CEO: Greg Moore	Tel: (281) 297-7200	%FO: 100
Bus: *Engaged in shipping.*	Fax: (281) 297-7319	

MAERSK INC.
401 East Pratt Street, Ste. 1634, Baltimore, MD   21202

CEO: Tom Thomsen	Tel: (410) 332-0500	%FO: 100
Bus: *Engaged in shipping.*	Fax: (410) 332-0927	

MAERSK INC.
115 Perimeter Center Place NE, Atlanta, GA   30346-1274

CEO: Edward Wilkes, Mgr.	Tel: (770) 399-1909	%FO: 100
Bus: *Engaged in shipping.*	Fax: (770) 399-4100	

MAERSK INC.
PO Box 880, Madison, NJ   07940-0880

CEO: Thomas Thomsen, Pres.	Tel: (973) 514-5000	%FO: 100
Bus: *Engaged in shipping.*	Fax: (973) 514-5410	

MAERSK INC.
1101 17th Street, NW, Ste. 610, Washington, DC   20036
CEO: Mark Johnson, Dir.   Tel: (202) 887-6770   %FO: 100
Bus: *Engaged in shipping.*   Fax: (202) 887-5014

MAERSK INC.
546 Long Point Road, Ste. 200, Mt. Pleasant, SC   29465
CEO: Diana Lucas, Mgr.   Tel: (843) 881-2700   %FO: 100
Bus: *Engaged in shipping.*   Fax: (843) 849-2674

MAERSK SEALAND INC.
790 NW 107th Avenue, Miami, FL   33172
CEO: Tony Scioscia, Pres.   Tel: (305) 220-6660   %FO: 100
Bus: *Engaged in shipping.*   Fax: (305) 220-7065

● **NAVISION SOFTWARE A/S**
Frydenlunds Alle 6, DK-2950 Vedbaek, Denmark
CEO: Jesper Balser, Pres. & CEO   Tel: 45-45-65-5000
Bus: *Mfr. computer software.*   Fax: 45-45-65-5001
                                       www.navision.com

   NAVISION US, INC.
   3505 Koger Blvd., Ste. 400, Duluth, GA   30096
   CEO: John Frederiksen, Pres.   Tel: (678) 226-8300   %FO: 100
   Bus: *Mfr./sales computer software.*   Fax: (678) 226-8305

● **NILFISK-ADVANCE GROUP, DIV. NKT HOLDING**
Sognevej 25. DK-2605 Broendby, Denmark
CEO: Johan Molin, Pres. & CEO   Tel: 45-43-23-8100
Bus: *Mfr. equipment for professional* Fax: 45-43-43-7700   Emp: 2,600
   cleaning.   www.nilfisk-advance.dk

   EUROCLEAN USA INC.
   1151 Bryn Mawr Avenue, Itasca, IL   60143
   CEO: Eric J. Titus   Tel: (630) 773-2111   %FO: 100
   Bus: *Mfr. commercial and industrial* Fax: (630) 773-2859
      floorcare equipment.

   NILFISK-ADVANCE AMERICA INC.
   300 Technology Drive, Malvern, PA   19355
   CEO: Bob Magdelain, Pres.   Tel: (610) 647-6420   %FO: 100
   Bus: *Mfr. specialty vacuum cleaners.* Fax: (610) 647-6427

NILFISK-ADVANCE INC.

14600 21st Avenue North, Plymouth, MN   55447

CEO: R. Moody

Bus: *Mfr. equipment for professional cleaning; commercial and industrial floor care.*

Tel: (763) 745-3500

Fax: (763) 745-3718

%FO: 100

• NIRO A/S, DIV. METALLGESELLSCHAFT AG

305 Gladsaxevej, DK-2860 Soeborg, Denmark

CEO: Niels Graugaard, Pres.

Bus: *Mfr. industrial spray dryers, fluid bed dryers, homogenizers, membrane filtration, extraction and heating and cooling plants for processing liquid and solid materials.*

Tel: 45-39-545454

Fax: 45-39-545800

www.niro.com

Emp: 300

NIRO INC.

1600 O'Keefe Road, PO Box 268, Hudson, WI   54016

CEO: Ron Matzek, VP

Bus: *Mfr./sale industrial drying agglomeration equipment, consulting, industrial testing facilities. Food and dairy division.*

Tel: (715) 386-9371

Fax: (715) 386-9376

%FO: 100

NIRO INC.

9165 Rumsey Road, Columbia, MD   21045

CEO: Steven Kaplan, Pres.

Bus: *Mfr./sale industrial drying agglomeration equipment, consulting, industrial testing facilities. Spare parts, repairs and marketing.*

Tel: (410) 997-8700

Fax: (410) 997-5021

%FO: 100

Emp: 170

• NORDFAB A/S

Industrigade 13, DK-9550 Mariager, Denmark

CEO: Stig Hoffmeyer, Dir.

Bus: *Mfr. air pollution control systems.*

Tel: 45-98-583422

Fax: 45-98-624071

www.nordfab.com

Emp: 150

DISA SYSTEMS INC.

102 Transit Avenue, PO Box 429, Thomasville, NC   27360

CEO: Niels Pedersen, Pres.

Bus: *Mfr./distribution/service air pollution control systems.*

Tel: (336) 889-5599

Fax: (336) 884-7873

%FO: 100

Emp: 100

• NOVO NORDISK A/S

Novo Allé, DK-2880 Bagsvaerd, Denmark

CEO: Mads Øvlisen, Pres. & CEO Tel: 45-44-448888 Rev: $2,595

Bus: *Pharmaceuticals company: leader in* Fax: 45-44-490555 Emp: 15,185
diabetes care, mfr./markets www.novo.dk
pharmaceutical products.

NOVO NORDISK BIOCHEM NORTH AMERICA, INC.

77 Perrys Chapel Church Road, PO Box 576, Franklinton, NC 27525-0576

CEO: Lee Yarbrough, Pres. Tel: (919) 494-2014 %FO: 100

Bus: *Biotechnology R&D.* Fax: (919) 494-3461

NOVO NORDISK BIOTECH, INC.

1497 Drew Avenue, Davis, CA 95616

CEO: Glenn E. Nedwin, Pres. Tel: (530) 757-8100 %FO: 100

Bus: *Biopesticide R&D.* Fax: (530) 758-0317 Emp: 35

NOVO NORDISK OF NORTH AMERICA, INC.

405 Lexington Avenue, Ste. 6400, New York, NY 10174-6401

CEO: Henrik Aagaard, Pres. Tel: (212) 867-0123 %FO: 100

Bus: *North American operations* Fax: (212) 867-0298 Emp: 12
headquarters.

NOVO NORDISK PHARMACEUTICAL IND., INC.

3612 Powhatan Road, Clayton, NC 27520

CEO: John R. Pratt, Gen. Mgr. Tel: (919) 550-2200 %FO: 100

Bus: *Mfr./sales pharmaceuticals.* Fax: (919) 553-4057

NOVO NORDISK PHARMACEUTICALS, INC. , LARON DIV

1776 North Pine Island Road, Ste. 108, Plantation, FL 33322

CEO: Guillermo J. Rodriguez, Pres. Tel: (954) 424-0006 %FO: 100

Bus: *Mfr./sales pharmaceuticals.* Fax: (954) 424-0074

NOVO NORDISK PHARMACEUTICALS, INC.

100 Overlook Center, Ste. 200, Princeton, NJ 08540-7810

CEO: Martin Soeters, Pres. Tel: (609) 987-5800 %FO: 100

Bus: *Pharmaceutical sales.* Fax: (609) 921-8082

ZYMOGENETICS INC.

1201 East Lake Avenue East, Seattle, WA 98105-3702

CEO: Bruce Carter, Pres. Tel: (206) 442-6600 %FO: 100

Bus: *Biotechnology research and* Fax: (206) 442-6608 Emp: 100
development.

● **OLICOM A/S**
Nybrovej 110, DK-2800 Lyngby, Denmark
CEO: Boji Rinhart, Pres. & CEO   Tel: 45-45-27-0000   Rev: $207
Bus: *Complete networking services.*   Fax: 45-45-27-0101   Emp: 750
                                         www.olicom.dk

    OLICOM USA INC.
    800 E. Campbell Road, Ste. 199, Richardson, TX   75081
    CEO: Pat Bruno Larsen, Pres.   Tel: (972) 301-4688   %FO: 100
    Bus: *Complete networking solutions.* Fax: (972) 302-4689   Emp: 80

● **ORTOFON DK**
Telegafvej 5, DK-2750 Ballerup, Denmark
CEO: Anna Rohmann, Pres.   Tel: 45-44-68-1033
Bus: *Mfr. phonograph cartridges.*   Fax: 45-44-68-0920   Emp: 100
                                         www.ortofon.dk

    ORTOFON INC.
    1363-42 Veterans Highway, Hauppauge, NY   11788
    CEO: Frank Konopasek, VP   Tel: (631) 979-5828   %FO: 100
    Bus: *Phonograph cartridges.*   Fax: (631) 979-5920

● **PHASE ONE DENMARK A/S**
Roskildevej 39, DK-2000 Frederiksberg, Denmark
CEO: Anders S. Anderson   Tel: 45-36-46-0111
Bus: *Mfr. direct digital imaging camera* Fax: 45-36-46-0222
    equipment.   www.phaseone.com

    PHASE ONE - USA
    24 Woodbine Avenue, Suite 15, Northport, NY   11768
    CEO: Carston Steenberg, Pres.   Tel: (516) 757-0400   %FO: 100
    Bus: *Sales and service direct digital* Fax: (516) 757-2217   Emp: 18
    imaging camera equipment.

● **PURUP-ESKOFOT A/S (FORMERLY SCANVIEW)**
Industriparken 35-37, DK-2750 Ballerup, Denmark
CEO: William Schulin-Zeuthen, Pres. & CEO Tel: 45-44-73-6666
Bus: *Mfr. pre-press, scanning equipment.* Fax: 45-44-73-6868   Emp: 200
                                         www.purup-eskofot.com

    PURUP-ESKOFOT INC.
    500 Town Park Lane, Ste. 250, Kennesaw, GA   30144
    CEO: Knud Eric Rodbro   Tel: (770) 427-5700   %FO: 100
    Bus: *Pre-press working process and*   Fax: (770) 427-7844
    press ready printing plates.

● **RADIOMETER A/S**
Akandevej 21, Bronshoj, DK-2700 Copenhagen, Denmark
CEO: Johan Schrøder, Pres.   Tel: 45-38-273827   Rev: $181
Bus: *Electronic instruments for science,*   Fax: 45-38-272727   Emp: 1,680
medicine and industry.   www.radiometer.com

    ACCUMETRICS, INC.
    3985 Sorrento Valley Boulevard, San Diego, CA   92121
    CEO: Jurgen Frings, Pres.   Tel: (858) 643-1600   %FO: 100
    Bus: *Develop and manufacture*   Fax: (858) 643-1600
    cardiovascular diagnostic
    products.

    RADIOMETER AMERICA INC.
    810 Sharon Drive, Westlake, OH   44145
    CEO: Jurgen Frings, Pres.   Tel: (440) 871-8900   %FO: 100
    Bus: *Mfr./sale electronic instruments*   Fax: (440) 871-8117
    for science, medicine & industry.

● **SOPHUS BERENDSEN A/S**
1 Klausdalsbrovej, DK-2860 Soborg, Denmark
CEO: Henrik Brandt, CEO   Tel: 45-39-53-8500
Bus: *Provides healthcare, pest control,*   Fax: 45-39-53-8585
laundry & textile services; distribution,   www.berendsen.com
industrial parts; hydraulics/electronics.

    BERENDSEN FLUID POWER INC.
    1200 Mid-Continent Tower, 401 S. Boston, Tulsa, OK   74103-4005
    CEO: Ian Hill, Pres.   Tel: (918) 592-3781   %FO: 100
    Bus: *Distribution, industrial parts;*   Fax: (918) 592-7051
    hydraulics/electronics.

● **STRUERS A/S**
Valhøjs Alle 176, DK-2610 Rødovre Copenhagen, Denmark
CEO: John Hestehave, CEO   Tel: 45-36-70-3500
Bus: *Mfr. equipment and consumables for*   Fax: 45-38-27-2701
materialographic surface preparation of   www.struers.com
solid materials.

    STRUERS INC.
    215 Monaco Circle, Clemson, SC   29631-1259
    CEO: Garry Poirier, Mgr.   Tel: (864) 653-6858   %FO: 100
    Bus: *Sales/distribution of*   Fax: (864) 653-6858
    metallographic laboratory
    equipment and supplies.

STRUERS INC.
810 Sharon Drive, Westlake, OH   44145

CEO: Mary E. Doyle, Pres.   Tel: (440) 871-0071   %FO: 100
Bus: *Sales/distribution of*   Fax: (440) 871-8188
metallographic laboratory
equipment and supplies.

• SUPERFOS A/S
Stubbeled 2, PO Box 39, DK-2950 Vedbæk, Denmark

CEO: Per Møller, Pres.   Tel: 45-45-67-0000   Rev: $1,000
Bus: *Mfr. injection-moulded pots and pails,*   Fax: 45-45-66-0405   Emp: 6,690
table packs, plastic bottles and pharma   www.superfos.dk
packaging of plastic.

SUPERFOS PACKAGING, INC.
11301 Superfos Drive, Cumberland, MD   21502

CEO: James Mason, Pres.   Tel: (301) 759-3145   %FO: 100
Bus: *Provides packaging products &*   Fax: (301) 459-4905
services.

• TDC A/S (FORMERLY TELE DANMARK A/S)
Norregade 21, DK-0900 Copenhagen C, Denmark

CEO: Henning Dyremose, Pres. & CEO   Tel: 45-33-43-7777   Rev: $5,556
Bus: *Engaged in telecommunications*   Fax: 45-33-43-7619   Emp: 17,465
services.   www.teledanmark.dk

TELE DENMARK USA INC.
50 Main Street, Ste. 1275, White Plains, NY   10606-1920

CEO: Palle Tolstrup Nielsen, Pres.   Tel: (914) 289-0100   %FO: 100
Bus: *Telecommunications and data*   Fax: (914) 289-0105
communications services.

• THOLSTRUP CHEESE A/S
20B Lille Strandstrade, DK-1254 Copenhagen K, Denmark

CEO: T. Tholstrup   Tel: 45-33-12-6077
Bus: *Mfr. cheese and dairy products.*   Fax: 45-33-12-6077
                                       www.sagacheese.com

THOLSTRUP CHEESE INC.
One Mountain Blvd., PO Box 4194, Warren, NJ   07059-6320

CEO: Vincent Staiger, Mgr.   Tel: (908) 756-6320
Bus: *Sales/distribution of cheese and*   Fax: (908) 756-4943
dairy products.

● **TYTEX A/S**

Industrivej 21, DK-7430 Ikast, Denmark

CEO: Carsten Madsen — Tel: 45-96-60-4200

Bus: *Mfr. medical textile products.* — Fax: 45-96-60-4201 — Emp: 300

www.tytex.dk

TYTEX, INC.

601 Park East Drive, Woonsocket, RI 02895

CEO: Peter Aggersbjerg, Pres. — Tel: (401) 762-4100 — %FO: 100

Bus: *Mfr./sale textiles.* — Fax: (401) 762-4262 — Emp: 55

● **UNIBANK A/S**

Torvegade 2, DK-1256 Copenhagen, Denmark

CEO: Thorleif Krarup, Chmn. — Tel: 45-33-33-3333

Bus: *Commercial banking services.* — Fax: 45-33-33-6262

www.unibank.dk

UNIBANK A/S - NEW YORK BRANCH

13-15 West 54th Street, New York, NY 10019-5404

CEO: Peter Caroe, EVP — Tel: (212) 603-6900 — %FO: 100

Bus: *International banking services.* — Fax: (212) 603-1685 — Emp: 60

● **UNICON GROUP**

Køgevej 172, PO Box 160, DK-4000 Roskilde, Denmark

CEO: Kent Arentoft, Pres. & CEO — Tel: 45-46-3-6000

Bus: *Mfr. ready mixed concrete and concrete* — Fax: 45-46-34-6023
 blocks. — www.unicon.dk

UNICON CONCRETE INC.

100 Meredith Drive, Ste. 200A, Durham, NC 27713

CEO: Chet Miller, Pres. — Tel: (919) 544-4350

Bus: *Mfr./sales ready mixed concrete* — Fax: (919) 544-3634
 and concrete blocks.

UNICON CONCRETE INC.

1400 Key Road, PO Box 5636, Columbia, SC 29250

CEO: Andrew Stevenson, Mgr. — Tel: (803) 254-5656

Bus: *Mfr./sales ready mixed concrete* — Fax: (803) 256-2599
 and concrete blocks.

UNICON CONCRETE INC.

2511 Big Block Road, Myrtle Beach, SC 29575

CEO: Robert Steele, Mgr. — Tel: (843) 650-2900

Bus: *Mfr./sales ready mixed concrete* — Fax: (843) 650-8108
 and concrete blocks.

● **VESTAS WIND SYSTEMS A/S**

Smed Hansens Vej 27, DK-6940 Lem, Denmark

CEO: Johannes Poulsen, Mng. Dir.

Bus: *Mfr., install, maintain wind turbines and wind turbine projects.*

Tel: 45-44-44-3335

Fax: 45-44-34-1484

www.vestas.dk

Rev: $447

Emp: 625

> **VESTAS-AMERICAN WIND TECHNOLOGY, INC.**
>
> PO Box 580278, North Palm Springs, CA   92258-0100
>
> CEO: Henrik Norremark, Pres.
>
> Bus: *Sale/install/maintenance wind turbines & wind turbine projects.*
>
> Tel: (760) 329-5400
>
> Fax: (760) 329-5558
>
> %FO: 100
>
> Emp: 12

● **VIKING LIFE-SAVING EQUIPMENT A/S**

Saedding Ringvej, DK-6710 Esbjerg V, Denmark

CEO: Kjeld Amann, Mng. Dir.

Bus: *Life rafts, escape systems, survival and protection suits, mob rescue boats.*

Tel: 45-76-11-8100

Fax: 45-79-11-8101

www.viking-life.com

Emp: 500

> **VIKING LIFE-SAVING EQUIPMENT (AMERICA) INC.**
>
> 1625 North Miami Avenue, Miami, FL   33136
>
> CEO: Poul V. Jensen, Mng. Dir.
>
> Bus: *Liferafts, marine escape systems, survival a protection suits, water-activated lights, thermal protective aides.*
>
> Tel: (305) 374-5115
>
> Fax: (305) 374-1535
>
> %FO: 100
>
> Emp: 21

● **WOLFKING A/S**

Industrivej 6, DK-4200 Slagelse, Denmark

CEO: Ole Most, Mng. Dir.

Bus: *Mfr. industrial meat processing equipment.*

Tel: 45-58-50-2525

Fax: 45-58-50-1031

www.wolfking.com

Emp: 240

> **WOLFKING INC.**
>
> 825 Taylor Road, Columbus, OH   43230
>
> CEO: Jan Erik Kuhlmann, Pres.
>
> Bus: *Mfr. industrial meat processing equipment.*
>
> Tel: (614) 863-3144
>
> Fax: (614) 863-3296
>
> %FO: 100
>
> Emp: 30

Dominican Republic

- **BANCO BHD, SA**
  Winston Churchill Esq., 27 de Febrero, Santo Domingo, Dominican Republic
  CEO: Luis Molina, Chmn.
  Bus: *General banking services.*
  Tel: 809-243-3232
  Fax: 809-542-7767
  www.bhd.com.do

  ### BHD CORP.
  561 West 181st Street, New York, NY 10033
  CEO: Wilson Ramos, Mgr.
  Bus: *General banking services.*
  Tel: (212) 927-6700
  Fax: (212) 927-7768
  %FO: 100

- **TRICOM, S.A.**
  Avenida Lope de Vega 95, Ensanche Naco, Santo Domingo, Dominican Republic
  CEO: Arturo Pellerano, Pres.
  Bus: *Engaged in basic and long-distance telephone, cellular and paging services and telecommunications systems and equipment.*
  Tel: 809-476-4997
  Fax: 809-476-4412
  www.tricom.net
  Rev: $126
  Emp: 1,340

  ### ACD TRIDON NORTH AMERICA, INC.
  8100 Tridon Drive, Smyrna, TN 37167
  CEO: Michael Hottinger, Pres.
  Bus: *Mfr. of fully integrated windshield wiper systems and hose clamps and production of electronic turn signal flashers.*
  Tel: (615) 459-5800
  Fax: (615) 355-1104
  %FO: 100

  ### TRICOM U.S.A.
  One Exchange Place, Ste. 400, Jersey City, NJ 07302
  CEO: Pablo Barry, Pres.
  Bus: *Sales of long-distance telephone, cellular and paging services and telecommunications systems and equipment.*
  Tel: (201) 324-0078
  Fax: (201) 324-0688
  %FO: 100

Egypt

- **EGYPTAIR**
  Cairo International Airport, Cairo, Egypt
  CEO: Mohamed Fahim Rayan, Chmn.   Tel: 20-2-245-4400
  Bus: *Commercial air transport services.*   Fax: 20-2-245-9316   Emp: 3,000
  www.egyptair.com.eg

  EGYPTAIR
  720 Fifth Avenue, New York, NY   10022
  CEO: Samir El Shanawany, VP   Tel: (212) 581-5600   %FO: 100
  Bus: *Commercial air transport services.*   Fax: (212) 586-6599

El Salvador

● **GRUPO TACA**

Caribe Building, First Floor, San Salvador, El Salvador
San Salvador, El Salvador

CEO: Federico Bloch, Pres. & CEO	Tel: 503-298-1560	Rev: $700
Bus: *Provides airline passenger and cargo services.*	Fax: 503-298-3064 www.taca.com	Emp: 6,500

GRUPO TACA

6824 Veterans Boulevard, Metairie, LA   70003

CEO: Alfredo Schildknecht, COO	Tel: (504) 887-7411	%FO: 100
Bus: *Provides airline passenger and cargo services.*	Fax: (504) 887-7411	

GRUPO TACA

1751 NW 68th Avenue, Bldg. 706, Miami, FL   33126

CEO: Evelyn Dela Vega, Mgr.	Tel: (305) 871-1587	%FO: 100
Bus: *Provides airline passenger and cargo services.*	Fax: (305) 871-5066	

GRUPO TACA

1776 G. Street NW, Washington, DC   20006

CEO: Alfredo Schildknecht, COO	Tel: (202) 589-0810	%FO: 100
Bus: *Provides airline passenger and cargo services.*	Fax: (202) 589-0811	

England, U.K.

- **3i GROUP PLC**
91 Waterloo Road, London SE1 8XP, UK
CEO: Brian P. Larcombe, CEO
Bus: *Engaged in venture capital investments and buyouts.*

Tel: 44-207-928-3131
Fax: 44-207-928-0058
www.3igroup.com

Rev: $519
Emp: 840

3i CORPORATION
890 Winter Street, Ste. 160, Waltham, MA 02451
CEO: Peter Bollier
Bus: *Engaged in venture capital investments and buyouts.*

Tel: (781) 890-8300
Fax: (781) 890-8301

%FO: 100

3i CORPORATION
4005 Miranda Avenue, Ste. 175, Palo Alto, CA 94304
CEO: Martin Gagen
Bus: *Engaged in venture capital investments and buyouts.*

Tel: (650) 843-3131
Fax: (650) 812-0472

%FO: 100

- **THE 600 GROUP PLC**
Landmark Court, Revie Road, Leeds LS11 8JT, UK
CEO: Tony Sweeten, CEO
Bus: *Holding company; manufacturing and marketing machine tools, machine tool accessories, lasers and other engineering products.*

Tel: 44-1908-446-1545
Fax: 44-1908-446-1545
www.the600group.com

Emp: 1,260

CLAUSING INDUSTRIAL INC.
1819 North Pitcher Street, Kalamazoo, MI 49007
CEO: William Nancarrow, Pres.
Bus: *Mfr. industrial machinery, drills and equipment.*

Tel: (616) 345-7155
Fax: (616) 345-5945

%FO: 100
Emp: 100

- **ACAMBIS PLC**
Peterhouse Tech Park, 100 Fulbourn Road, Cambridge CB1 9PT, UK
CEO: John Brown, CEO
Bus: *Development of oral and nasal vaccines.*

Tel: 44-122-327-5300
Fax: 44-122-341-6300
www.acambis.com

Rev: $10
Emp: 100

ACAMBIS INC.
38 Sidney Street, Cambridge, MA   02139

CEO: Lance Gordon, VP	Tel: (617) 494-1339	%FO: 100
Bus: *Development of oral and nasal vaccines.*	Fax: (617) 494-1741	

● **ACTINIC PLC**
2 Balfour Road, Weybridge Surrey KT13 8HD, UK

CEO: Kevin S. Grumball, CEO	Tel: 44-193-287-1000	Rev: $2,892
Bus: *Mfr. e-commerce software.*	Fax: 44-193-287-1001	Emp: 39
	www.actinic.co.uk	

ACTINIC SOFTWARE LLC
63 West Prospect Street, East Brunswick, NJ   08816

CEO: Debby Stefaniak, Mgr.	Tel: (732) 238-8007	%FO: 100
Bus: *Mfr. e-commerce software.*	Fax: (732) 238-8846	

● **ADEPTRA, LTD.**
120 Wilton Road, London SW1V 1JZ, UK

CEO: Stephen Voller, CEO	Tel: 44-207-233-9733	
Bus: *Engaged in customer relationship management technology.*	Fax: 44-207-233-9744	Emp: 40
	www.adeptra.co.uk	

ADEPTRA INC.
1055 Washington Boulevard, 5th Fl., Stamford, CT   06901

CEO: Michael Callahan, SVP	Tel: (203) 355-2200	%FO: 100
Bus: *Engaged in customer relationship management technology.*	Fax: (203) 355-2300	

● **AEA TECHNOLOGY PLC**
329 Harwell, Didcot Oxfordshire OX11 ORA, UK

CEO: Peter Watson, CEO	Tel: 44-123-582-1111	Rev: $577
Bus: *Creates industrial plants and provides waste management.*	Fax: 44-123-543-2916	Emp: 4,490
	www.aeat.co.uk	

AEA TECHNOLOGY ENGINEERING SERVICES, INC.
184 B Rolling Hill Road, Mooresville, NC   28117

CEO: Robert Mullens	Tel: (704) 799-2708	%FO: 100
Bus: *Creates industrial plants and provides waste management.*	Fax: (704) 799-6426	

AEA TECHNOLOGY ENGINEERING SERVICES, INC.
241 Curry Hollow Road, Pittsburgh, PA   15236-4696

CEO: Van Walker	Tel: (412) 655-1200	%FO: 100
Bus: *Creates industrial plants and provides waste management.*	Fax: (412) 655-2928	

AEA TECHNOLOGY ENGINEERING SERVICES, INC.

1301 Moran Road, Ste. 202, Sterling, VA   20166

CEO: Laurie Judd

Bus: *Creates industrial plants and provides waste management.*

Tel: (703) 433-0720
Fax: (703) 433-9745

%FO: 100

AEA TECHNOLOGY ENGINEERING SOFTWARE, INC.

4960 Robert Mathews Pkwy., Ste. B, El Dorado Hills, CA   95762

CEO: George Bache

Bus: *Creates industrial plants and provides waste management.*

Tel: (916) 939-0246
Fax: (916) 939-0342

%FO: 100

AEA TECHNOLOGY ENGINEERING SOFTWARE, INC.

2000 Oxford Drive, Ste. 610, Bethel Park, PA   15102

CEO: Thomas Dayton

Bus: *Creates industrial plants and provides waste management.*

Tel: (412) 833-4820
Fax: (412) 833-4580

%FO: 100

● AEGIS GROUP PLC

11A West Halkin Street, London SW1X 8JL, UK

CEO: Douglas Flynn, CEO

Bus: *Engaged in media buying and planning services.*

Tel: 44-207-470-5000
Fax: 44-207-470-5099
www.aegisgroup.co.uk

Rev: $7,746
Emp: 4,175

BAI GLOBAL INC.

580 White Plains Road, Tarrytown, NY 10591

CEO: Kate Permut, VP Mktg.

Bus: *Engaged in marketing research consulting and information services.*

Tel: (914) 332-5300
Fax: (914) 631-8300

%FO: 100

CARAT INTERACTIVE

2 Wells Avenue, Newton, MA   02459

CEO: D. Brynes

Bus: *Engaged in media buying and planning services.*

Tel: (617) 303-3000
Fax: (617) 303-3063

%FO: 100

CARAT USA INC.

3390 Peachtree Road NE, Ste. 700, Atlanta, GA   30326

CEO: Arthur Kennedy, EVP

Bus: *Engaged in media buying and planning services.*

Tel: (404) 231-1232
Fax: (404) 239-9755

%FO: 100

CARAT USA INC.
5830 Mt. Moriah, Ste. 6, Memphis, TN　38115
CEO: Randy Washburn　　　　　　Tel: (901) 362-0245　　　%FO: 100
Bus: *Engaged in media buying and*　　Fax: (901) 365-4223
　　planning services.

CARAT USA INC.
401 N. Michigan Avenue, 14th Fl., Chicago, IL　60611
CEO: Susan Rowe, SVP　　　　　　Tel: (312) 384-4500　　　%FO: 100
Bus: *Engaged in media buying and*　　Fax: (312) 384-5100
　　planning services.

CARAT USA INC.
3 Park Avenue, New York, NY　10016
CEO: Charles Rutman, EVP　　　　Tel: (212) 591-9164　　　%FO: 100
Bus: *Engaged in media buying and*　　Fax: (212) 689-6005
　　planning services.

CARAT USA INC.
2450 Colorado Avenue, Ste. 300 E, Santa Monica, CA　90404
CEO: John Barnes, EVP　　　　　　Tel: (310) 255-1000　　　%FO: 100
Bus: *Engaged in media buying and*　　Fax: (310) 255-1050
　　planning services.

MARKET FACTS INC.
3390 Peachtree Road NE, Ste. 700, Atlanta, GA　30326
CEO: Irenea Seufert　　　　　　　Tel: (678) 553-2080　　　%FO: 100
Bus: *Engaged in marketing research*　　Fax: (678) 553-2081
　　consulting and information
　　services.

MARKET FACTS INC.
3040 West Salt Creek Lane, Arlington Heights, IL　60005
CEO: Tom Payne, CEO　　　　　　Tel: (847) 590-7000　　　%FO: 100
Bus: *Engaged in marketing research*　　Fax: (847) 590-7010
　　consulting and information
　　services.

MARKET FACTS, INC.
1650 Tysons Boulevard, McLean, VA　22102
CEO: Steve Weber, EVP　　　　　　Tel: (703) 790-9099　　　%FO: 100
Bus: *Engaged in marketing research*　　Fax: (703) 790-9181
　　consulting and information
　　services.

MARKET FACTS, INC.
3390 Peachtree Road NE, Ste. 700, Atlanta, GA   30326
CEO: Irenea Seufert   Tel: (678) 553-2080   %FO: 100
Bus: *Engaged in marketing research*   Fax: (678) 553-2081
consulting and information
services.

MARKET FACTS, INC.
One Apple Hill, Ste. 221, Natick, MA   01760
CEO: Bill Seymour, SVP   Tel: (508) 655-0777   %FO: 100
Bus: *Engaged in marketing research*   Fax: (508) 655-0033
consulting and information
services.

MARKET FACTS, INC.
14643 Dallas Parkway, Ste. 636, Dallas, TX   75240
CEO: Barry Davis   Tel: (972) 387-5555   %FO: 100
Bus: *Engaged in marketing research*   Fax: (972) 387-4441
consulting and information
services.

MARKET FACTS, INC.
16133 Ventura Boulevard, Ste. 1000, Encino, CA   91436
CEO: Larry Levin, SVP   Tel: (818) 380-1480   %FO: 100
Bus: *Engaged in marketing research*   Fax: (818) 380-1485
consulting and information
services.

MARKET FACTS, INC.
65 Madison Avenue, 4th Fl., Morristown, NJ   07960
CEO: Greg McMahon, SVP   Tel: (973) 605-8800   %FO: 100
Bus: *Engaged in marketing research*   Fax: (973) 605-5202
consulting and information
services.

MARKET FACTS, INC.
7900 SE 28th Street, Ste. 200, Mercer Island, WA   98040
CEO: Lindsay Holbrook, VP   Tel: (206) 236-5970   %FO: 100
Bus: *Engaged in marketing research*   Fax: (206) 236-5971
consulting and information
services.

MARKET FACTS, INC.
902 Broadway, New York, NY 10010
CEO: Gary Williams, SVP   Tel: (212) 460-8585   %FO: 100
Bus: *Engaged in marketing research*   Fax: (212) 353-1724
consulting and information
services.

MARKETING STRATEGY AND PLANNING, INC.
1775 Broadway, New York, NY 10019
CEO: Bob Slaski, EVP   Tel: (212) 373-7800   %FO: 100
Bus: *Engaged in marketing and*   Fax: (212) 307-9095
planning.

MMA/CARAT INC.
15 River Road, Ste. 101, Wilton, CT 06897
CEO: Randy Stone   Tel: (203) 834-3300   %FO: 100
Bus: *Engaged in marketing research*   Fax: (203) 834-3333
consulting and information
services.

STRATEGY RESEARCH CORPORATION
10 NW 37th Avenue, Miami, FL 33125
CEO: Richard H. Tobin, Pres.   Tel: (305) 649-5400   %FO: 100
Bus: *Engaged in marketing research*   Fax: (305) 649-6312
consulting and information
services.

TANDEM RESEARCH ASSOCIATES, INC
200 Route 17 South, Mahwah, NJ 07430
CEO: Donald E. Rupnow   Tel: (201) 529-5540   %FO: 100
Bus: *Engaged in marketing research.*   Fax: (201) 529-2659

TANDEM RESEARCH ASSOCIATES, INC
2 Executive Boulevard, Suffern, NY 10901
CEO: Daniel W. Fish   Tel: (914) 369-4900   %FO: 100
Bus: *Engaged in marketing research.*   Fax: (914) 369-1840

● AGGREGATE INDUSTRIES, PLC
Bardon Hall, Copt Oak Road, Markfield, Leicestershire LE67 9PJ, UK
CEO: Peter Tom, Pres. & CEO   Tel: 44-153-081-6600   Rev: $1,700
Bus: *Provides aggregates, paving*   Fax: 44-153-081-6666   Emp: 7,580
contracting and soil remediation   www.aggregate.com
services.

AGGREGATE INDUSTRIES, INC.
1515 First Avenue North, PO Box 499, Moorehead, MN 56560
CEO: Jeff Readder, Mgr.   Tel: (218) 236-9640   %FO: 100
Bus: *Sales/distribution of building*   Fax: (218) 236-5660   Emp: 100
   materials and fibre mesh produces.

AGGREGATE INDUSTRIES, INC.
3605 South Teller, Lakewood, CO 80235
CEO: James M. Addams, Pres.   Tel: (303) 987-2300   %FO: 100
Bus: *Sales/distribution of building*   Fax: (303) 987-9039
   materials.

AGGREGATE INDUSTRIES, INC.
2915 Water Road, Ste. 103, Eagan, MN 55121
CEO: Jonathan Wilmshurst, Pres.   Tel: (651) 686-7100   %FO: 100
Bus: *Mfr. concrete masonry units.*   Fax: (651) 686-6969   Emp: 245

● AIM GROUP PLC
16 Carlton Crescent, Southampton, Hampshire SO1 2ES, UK
CEO: Jeffrey C. Smith, Chmn. & CEO   Tel: 44-170-333-5111   Rev: $111
Bus: *Mfr. aircraft interiors.*   Fax: 44-170-322-8733   Emp: 1,200
   www.aimaviation.com

AIM AVIATION AUBURN, INC.
1530 22nd Street NW, Auburn, WA 98001
CEO: John Feutz, Gen. Mgr.   Tel: (253) 804-3355   %FO: 100
Bus: *Sales/distribution of aircraft*   Fax: (253) 804-3356
   interiors, assemblies & parts.

AIM AVIATION INC.
705 Southwest Seventh Avenue, Renton, WA 98055
CEO: Mark Potensky, Pres.   Tel: (425) 235-2750   %FO: 100
Bus: *Sales/distribution of aircraft*   Fax: (425) 228-0761   Emp: 250
   interiors, assemblies & parts.

● AIR PARTNER PLC
Platinum House, Gatwick Road, Crawley West Sussex RH 10 2RP, UK
CEO: Anthony Mack, Chmn.   Tel: 44-129-384-4800   Rev: $104
Bus: *Corporate aircraft charters.*   Fax: 44-129-353-9263   Emp: 80
   www.airpartner.com

AIR PARTNER INC.
245 Park Avenue, Ste. 62, New York, NY 10167
CEO: Alan Marler, Dir.   Tel: (212) 252-1002   %FO: 100
Bus: *Corporate aircraft charters.*   Fax: (212) 792-4191

● **AIRCLAIMS LTD.**
Cardinal Point, Newell Road Heathrow Airport, London TW 6 2AS, UK
CEO: Derek Hammond Gils, Mng. Dir.   Tel: 44-208-897-1066
Bus: *Aviation claims/loss adjustments.*   Fax: 44-208-897-0300
    www.airclaims.co.uk

    AIRCLAIMS, INC.
    7270 Northwest 12th St., Ste. 800, Miami, FL 33126
    CEO: Kenneth Forsyth, CEO   Tel: (305) 597-5666   %FO: 100
    Bus: *Aviation claims/loss adjustments.*   Fax: (305) 639-2555

● **AIRTOURS PLC**
Parkway Business Centre, 300 Princess Road, Manchester M14 7QU, UK
CEO: Tim Byrne, CEO   Tel: 44-161-232-0066   Rev: $5,777
Bus: *Travel and tour operator.*   Fax: 44-161-232-6524   Emp: 29,000
    www.airtours.com

    TRAVEL SERVICES INTERNATIONAL, INC.
    220 Congress Park Drive, Delray Beach, FL 33445-7289
    CEO: Peter McHugh, Pres. & CEO   Tel: (561) 266-0860   %FO: 100
    Bus: *Engaged in travel and tour*   Fax: (561) 266-0872   Emp: 2,142
    services.

● **ALFRED MC ALPINE PLC**
Eight Suffolk Street, London SW1Y 4HG, UK
CEO: Oliver Whitehead, CEO   Tel: 44-207-930-6255   Rev: $1,200
Bus: *Construction, building and civil*   Fax: 44-207-839-6902
engineering.   www.alfredmcalpine.co.uk

    ALFRED MC ALPINE INC.
    PO Box 33697, Charlotte, NC 28206
    CEO: W. Noel Briggs, Pres.   Tel: (704) 376-5854   %FO: 100
    Bus: *Construction, building and civil*   Fax: (704) 376-0564
    engineering.

● **ALLEN & OVERY**
One New Change, London EC4M 9QQ, UK
CEO: Guy Beringer, Sr. Prtn.   Tel: 44-207-330-3000
Bus: *International law firm.*   Fax: 44-207-330-9999   Emp: 4,000
    www.allenovery.com

    ALLEN & OVERY
    10 East 50th St., 27th Fl., New York, NY 10022
    CEO: Andrew Ballheimer   Tel: (212) 610-6300   %FO: 100
    Bus: *International law firm.*   Fax: (212) 610-6399   Emp: 19

• ALLIED DOMECQ, PLC.

24 Portland Place, London W1N 4BB, UK
CEO: Sir Christopher A. Hogg, Chmn.
Bus: *International spirits manufacturing and retailing group: wine, spirits, frozen foods & desserts, tea & coffee.*

Tel: 44-207-323-9000
Fax: 44-207-323-1742
www.allieddomecqplc.com

Rev: $7,250
Emp: 49,710

ALLIED DOMECQ SPIRITS USA

355 Riverside Avenue, Westport, CT 06880
CEO: Martin Jones, Pres. & CEO
Bus: *Sales and marketing company for distilled spirits.*

Tel: (203) 221-5400
Fax: (203) 221-5444

%FO: 100
Emp: 100

ALLIED DOMECQ WINES

375 Healdsburg Avenue, 2nd Fl., Healdsburg, CA 95448-4137
CEO: Michael Jellison, Pres.
Bus: *Sales and marketing company for wine products.*

Tel: (707) 433-8268
Fax: (707) 433-3538

%FO: 100
Emp: 150

BASKIN-ROBBINS USA, COMPANY

31 Baskin-Robbins Place, Glendale, CA 91201
CEO: Jack Shafer, CEO
Bus: *Mfr. ice cream & dessert products.*

Tel: (818) 956-0031
Fax: (818) 548-8218

%FO: 100
Emp: 200

DUNKIN' DONUTS INC.

14 Pacella Park Drive, Randolph, MA 02368
CEO: Jack Shafer, CEO
Bus: *Sales/distribution of doughnuts, baked goods and coffee.*

Tel: (781) 961-4000
Fax: (781) 963-2913

%FO: 100

MAKER'S MARK DISTILLERY, INC.

6200 Dutchman's Lane, Ste. 103, Louisville, KY 40205
CEO: T. William Samuels, Pres.
Bus: *Distillery of bourbon whiskey.*

Tel: (502) 459-7884
Fax: (502) 459-2026

%FO: 100

TOGO'S INC.

900 East Campbell Avenue, Campbell, CA 95008
CEO: Jack Shafer, CEO
Bus: *Franchised sandwich store and eatery.*

Tel: (408) 377-1754
Fax: (408) 377-1058

%FO: 100

• ALTERIAN PLC

Century Place, Newfoundland Street, Bristol BS2 9AG, UK
CEO: David Justin Eldridge, CEO
Bus: *Provides analytical software solutions.*

Tel: 44-117-970-3200
Fax: 44-117-970-3201
www.alterian.com

Rev: $2
Emp: 10

ALTERIAN, INC.
One North LaSalle, Ste. 4300, Chicago, IL 60602

CEO: Anthony Power, SVP	Tel: (312) 704-1700	%FO: 100
Bus: *Provides analytical software* *solutions.*	Fax: (312) 704-1701	

• AMEC, PLC
Sandiway House, Hartford Northwich, Cheshire CW8 2YA, UK

CEO: Peter Mason, CEO	Tel: 44-160-688-3885	Rev: $4,500
Bus: *Engaged in engineering and* *construction.*	Fax: 44-160-688-3996	Emp: 22,000
	www.amec.co.uk	

AGRA BAYMONT, INC.
14100 58th Street North, Clearwater, FL 33760-3796

CEO: Robert Brown, Pres.	Tel: (727) 539-1661	%FO: 100
Bus: *Supplies data conversion and* *related services to the geospatial* *info and tech industry.*	Fax: (727) 539-1749	

AGRA BIRWELCO, INC.
710 Route 46 East, Fairfield, NJ 07004

CEO: Alan Katz, VP	Tel: (973) 439-1140	%FO: 100
Bus: *Engaged in engineering global* *solutions.*	Fax: (973) 439-1141	

AGRA FOUNDATIONS INC.
10108 32nd Avenue West, Bldg. C3, Everett, WA 98204

CEO: Mike Hadzariga, Pres.	Tel: (425) 353-5506	%FO: 100
Bus: *Provides design and construction* *services.*	Fax: (425) 353-4151	

AGRA INFRASTRUCTURE, INC.
4435 East Holmes Avenue, Mesa, AZ 85206-3372

CEO: Jim McCluskie, Pres.	Tel: (480) 830-3700	%FO: 100
Bus: *Provides engineering and* *construction services.*	Fax: (480) 830-3903	

AMEC
6600 North Andrews Avenue, Ste. 590, Ft. Lauderdale, FL 33309

CEO: Peter Mason, CEO	Tel: (954) 771-6677	%FO: 100
Bus: *Engaged in engineering and* *construction.*	Fax: (954) 771-6694	

AMEC
1501 Lee Hwy., Ste. 204, Arlington, VA   22209
CEO: M.McGaughan   Tel: (703) 247-2700   %FO: 100
Bus: *Engaged in engineering and*   Fax: (703) 247-2701
     construction.

AMEC
148 State Street, 7th Fl., Boston, MA   02109
CEO: Peter Mason, CEO   Tel: (617) 725-2788   %FO: 100
Bus: *Engaged in engineering and*   Fax: (617) 725-4925
     construction.

AMEC
1633 Broadway, 24th Fl., New York, NY   10019
CEO: Donald H. Piser, CEO   Tel: (212) 484-0300   %FO: 100
Bus: *Engaged in engineering and*   Fax: (212) 484-0580
     construction.

AMEC
1111 Superior Avenue, Ste. 1111, Cleveland, OH   44114
CEO: Peter Mason, CEO   Tel: (216) 574-6300   %FO: 100
Bus: *Engaged in engineering and*   Fax: (216) 574-9538
     construction.

AMEC
Public Ledger Bldg., Ste. 272, Independence Square, Philadelphia, PA   19106
CEO: Peter Mason, CEO   Tel: (215) 627-4902   %FO: 100
Bus: *Engaged in engineering and*   Fax: (215) 627-5950
     construction.

AMEC
450 Sansome Street, Ste. 900, San Francisco, CA   94111
CEO: Peter Mason, CEO   Tel: (415) 399-0905   %FO: 100
Bus: *Engaged in engineering and*   Fax: (415) 399-0945
     construction.

AMEC
11920 Fairway Lakes Drive, Fort Meyers, FL   33913
CEO: Richard Kelly   Tel: (941) 561-7288   %FO: 100
Bus: *Engaged in engineering and*   Fax: (941) 561-7299
     construction.

AMEC
125 South Wacker Drive, 2nd Fl., Chicago, IL   60606
CEO: Peter Mason, CEO   Tel: (312) 541-1600   %FO: 100
Bus: *Engaged in engineering and*   Fax: (312) 541-1754
     construction.

MOORE & TABER GROUTING SERVICES

1290 North Hancock Street, Anaheim, CA   92817

CEO: John Tims, Mgr. Tel: (714) 779-0681 %FO: 100

Bus: *Engaged in engineering and* Fax: (714) 779-1459
construction.

U.S. PIPELINE, INC.

11767 Katy Freeway, Ste. 100, Houston, TX   77079

CEO: Bobby Crotts, Pres. Tel: (281) 531-6100 %FO: 100

Bus: *Engaged in engineering and* Fax: (281) 531-6700
construction.

● AMERSHAM PHARMACIA BIOTECH LTD.

Amersham Place, Little Chalfont, Buckinghamshire HP7 9NA, UK

CEO: Sir William M. Castell, CEO Tel: 44-149-454-4000 Rev: $1,917

Bus: *Mfr. equipment for biotechnology and* Fax: 44-149-454-2266 Emp: 8,750
gene sequencing research. www.apbiotech.com

AMERSHAM PHAMACIA BIOTECH, INC.

800 Centennial Avenue, PO Box 1327, Piscataway, NJ   08855-1327

CEO: Peter Coggins, Pres. Tel: (732) 457-8000 %FO: 100

Bus: *Mfr. equipment for biotechnology* Fax: (732) 457-0557
and gene sequencing research.

● AMVESCAP PLC

11 Devonshire Square, London EC2M 4YR, UK

CEO: Michael D. Benson, CEO Tel: 44-207-626-3434 Rev: $2,435

Bus: *Institutional and retail investment* Fax: 44-207-484-8962 Emp: 5,545
advisory services, mutual funds www.amvescap.coM
distribution.

AIM MANAGEMENT GROUP, INC.

11 Greenway Plaza, Ste. 100, Houston, TX   77046

CEO: Robert H. Graham, CEO Tel: (713) 626-1919 %FO: 100

Bus: *Institutional and retail investment* Fax: (713) 214-7565 Emp: 2,100
advisory services, mutual funds
distribution.

INSTITUTIONAL TRUST CO. INC.

7800 East Union Avenue, Suite 800, Denver, CO   80237

CEO: Mary Mohr, CEO Tel: (303) 930-2700 %FO: 100

Bus: *Mutual fund advisory services.* Fax: (303) 930-6307

INVESCO CAPITAL MANAGEMENT, INC.
1315 Peachtree Street, Suite 500, Atlanta, GA   30309

CEO: Terry Miller, Pres.   Tel: (404) 892-0896   %FO: 100

Bus: *Investment management holding*   Fax: (404) 724-4270
company.

INVESCO CAPITAL MANAGEMENT, INC.
One Midtown Plaza, 1360 Peach Street NE, Ste. 100, Atlanta, GA   30309

CEO: A. D. Frazier, CEO   Tel: (404) 892-0896   %FO: 100

Bus: *Institutional and retail investment*   Fax: (404) 724-4270   Emp: 2,600
advisory services.

INVESCO CAPITAL MANAGEMENT, INC.
241 Sevilla Avenue, Suite 905, Coral Gables, FL   33134

CEO: Michael Matus, SVP   Tel: (305) 443-3241   %FO: 100

Bus: *Institutional and retail investment*   Fax: (305) 443-6963
advisory services.

INVESCO MANAGEMENT & RESEARCH, INC.
1166 Avenue of the Americas, New York, NY   10036

CEO: Frank Keeler, Pres.   Tel: (212) 278-9000   %FO: 100

Bus: *Institutional and retail investment*   Fax: (212) 278-9672
advisory services.

INVESCO REALTY ADVISORS INC.
5400 LBJ Freeway, Ste. 700, Dallas, TX   75240

CEO: David Ridley, Pres.   Tel: (972) 715-7400   %FO: 100

Bus: *Realty advisors.*   Fax: (972) 715-7474

PRIMCO CAPITAL MANAGEMENT, INC.
400 West Market, Ste. 3300, Louisville, KY   40202

CEO: George Bauman, Pres.   Tel: (502) 589-2011   %FO: 100

Bus: *Institutional and retail investment*   Fax: (502) 589-2157
advisory services.

● ANGLE AMERICAN PLC
20 Carlton House Terrace, London SW1Y 5AN, UK

CEO: Anthony Trahar, CEO   Tel: 44-207-698-8888

Bus: *Engaged in gold, platinum, diamonds,*   Fax: 44-207-698-8500
base metals, coal and forest products.   www.angloamerican.co.uk

BOART LONGYEAR COMPANY
2640 West 1700 South, Salt Lake City, UT   84104

CEO: Richard Swain, Pres.   Tel: (801) 972-6430   %FO: 100

Bus: *Provides drilling products and*   Fax: (801) 977-3374
contract services to the mining
and constructions markets.

SLOPE INDICATOR COMPANY

3450 Monte Villa Parkway, Bothell, WA   98021

CEO: Peter Fordyce, Mgr.	Tel: (425) 806-2200	%FO: 100
Bus: *Mfr. geotechnical and structural monitoring instruments.*	Fax: (425) 806-2250	

● **APPLIED PRODUCT SOLUTIONS LTD. (APS)**

Unit 36, Mere View Industrial Estate ,Yaxley, Peterborough PE7 3HF, UK

CEO: Nic Berg, CEO	Tel: 44-173-324-3777	
Bus: *Mfr. refrigeration products.*	Fax: 44-173-324-3888	
	www.productsolutions.co.uk	

VIRGINIA KMP CORPORATION

4100 Platinum Way, Dallas, TX   75237

CEO: Finn Jordskogen, Pres.	Tel: (214) 330-7731	%FO: 100
Bus: *Mfr. refrigeration products.*	Fax: (214) 337-8854	Emp: 100

● **APV LTD.**

23 Gatwick Road, Crawley, West Sussex RH2 QB, UK

CEO: Donald Sorterup, Pres.	Tel: 44-129-352-7777	
Bus: *Markets specialized process plants and equipment for food and beverage industry.*	Fax: 44-129-355-2640	Emp: 12,000
	www.apv.com	

APV AMERICAS

9525 West Bryn Mawr Avenue, Rosemont, IL   60018

CEO: Craig Bergstrom, Pres.	Tel: (847) 678-4300	%FO: 100
Bus: *Mfr. food, dairy, chemical processing & automation equipment & systems.*	Fax: (847) 678-4407	Emp: 1,000

APV BAKER INC.

1200 West Ash Street, PO Box 1718, Goldsboro, NC   27530

CEO: John Hamilton, Mgr.	Tel: (919) 731-5302	%FO: 100
Bus: *Mfr. process packaging equipment for bakery/cereal industry.*	Fax: (919) 731-5455	

APV BAKER INC.

3200 Fruit Ridge Avenue, NW, Grand Rapids, MI   49504

CEO: Robert Rander, Pres.	Tel: (616) 784-3111	%FO: 100
Bus: *Mfr. process packaging equipment for bakery/cereal industry.*	Fax: (616) 784-0973	

• AREMISSOFT CORPORATION
Goldsworth House, Denton Way, Woking Surrey GU21 3LG, UK

CEO: Lycourgos K. Kyprianou, CEO	Tel: 44-148-388-5000	Rev: $123
Bus: *Develops enterprise resource planning software.*	Fax: 44-148-388-5224 www.aremissoft.co.uk	Emp: 840

AREMISSOFT CORPORATION
216 Haddon Avenue, Ste. 607, Westmont, NJ   08108

CEO: Roys Poyiadjus, Pres.	Tel: (856) 869-0770
Bus: *Develops enterprise resource planning software.*	Fax: (856) 869-0162

AREMISSOFT CORPORATION
1201 Roberts Boulevard, Ste. 207, Kennesaw, GA   30144

CEO: Charles Durling	Tel: (770) 590-4340	%FO: 100
Bus: *Develops enterprise resource planning software.*	Fax: (770) 590-4359	

• ARJO WIGGINS APPLETON PLC
45 Pall Mall, London SW1Y 5JG, UK

CEO: Kenneth J. Minton, Pres.	Tel: 44-207-941-8000	Rev: $5,208
Bus: *Mfr./distributes specialty paper products.*	Fax: 44-207-941-8008 www.paperpoint.co.uk	Emp: 19,050

APPLETON PAPERS, INC.
825 East Wisconsin Avenue, Appleton, WI   54911

CEO: Douglas P. Buth, CEO	Tel: (920) 734-9841	%FO: 100
Bus: *Distribution/sale of specialty paper products.*	Fax: (920) 749-8796	

• ARM HOLDINGS PLC
110 Fulbourn Road, Cambridge CB1 9NJ, UK

CEO: Robin Saxby, CEO	Tel: 44-122-340-0400	Rev: $151
Bus: *Develops and licenses microprocessors for fax modems, cell phones and hand-held computers.*	Fax: 44-122-340-0410 www.arm.com	Emp: 620

ARM, INC.
1981 North Broadway, Ste. 245, Walnut Creek, CA   94596

CEO: T. Garibay	Tel: (925) 944-9690	%FO: 100
Bus: *Develops and licenses microprocessors for fax modems, cell phones and hand-held computers.*	Fax: (925) 944-9612	

ARM, INC.

18300 NE Union Hill Road, Ste. 257, Redmond, WA   98052

CEO: T. Garibay   Tel: (425) 882-9781   %FO: 100

Bus: *Develops and licenses*   Fax: (425) 882-9782
microprocessors for fax modems,
cell phones and hand-held
computers.

ARM, INC.

300 West Main Street, Ste. 215, Northborough, MA   01532

CEO: Mike Spaulding   Tel: (508) 351-6525   %FO: 100

Bus: *Develops and licenses*   Fax: (508) 351-6526
microprocessors for fax modems,
cell phones and hand-held
computers.

ARM, INC.

1250 Capital of Texas Hwy., Bldg. 3, Austin, TX   78746

CEO: T. Garibay   Tel: (512) 327-9249   %FO: 100

Bus: *Develops and licenses*   Fax: (512) 314-1078
microprocessors for fax modems,
cell phones and hand-held
computers.

ARM, INC.

1902 Wright Place, Ste. 200, Carlsbad, CA   92008

CEO: Annie Murphy   Tel: (760) 918-5535   %FO: 100

Bus: *Develops and licenses*   Fax:
microprocessors for fax modems,
cell phones and hand-held
computers.

• ASHTEAD GROUP PLC

Business Park 8, Barnett Wood Lane, Leatherhead Surrey KT22 7DG, UK

CEO: George B. Burnett, CEO   Tel: 44-137-236-2300   Rev: $469

Bus: *Engaged in rental of industrial*   Fax: 44-137-237-6610   Emp: 3,729
equipment and tools, electronic survey,   www.ashtead-group.com
inspection and testing equipment.

ASHTEAD TECHNOLOGY, INC.

3311 Preston Avenue, Pasadena, TX   77505

CEO: Michael Klembus, Mgr.   Tel: (281) 991-1448   %FO: 100

Bus: *Engaged in rental of industrial*   Fax: (281) 991-1449
equipment and tools, electronic
survey, inspection and testing
equipment.

ASHTEAD TECHNOLOGY, INC.
18195 McDurmott East, Ste. A/B, Irvine, CA   92714
CEO: Steve Rozunick, VP   Tel: (949) 955-3930   %FO: 100
Bus: *Engaged in rental of industrial*   Fax: (949) 955-3932
equipment and tools, electronic
survey, inspection and testing
equipment.

ASHTEAD TECHNOLOGY, INC.
1057 East Henrietta Road, Rochester, NY   14623
CEO: Rob Phillips, Mng. Dir.   Tel: (716) 424-2140   %FO: 100
Bus: *Engaged in rental of industrial*   Fax: (716) 424-2166
equipment and tools, electronic
survey, inspection and testing
equipment.

RESPONSE RENTALS, DIV. ASHTEAD TECHNOLOGY
19407 Park Row, Ste. 170, Houston, TX   77084
CEO: Andy Holroyd, Pres.   Tel: (281) 398-9533   %FO: 100
Bus: *Engaged in international survey*   Fax: (281) 398-3052
and inspection equipment rentals.

SUNBELT RENTALS, INC.
611 Templeton Avenue, Charlotte, NC   28203
CEO: Bruce Dressel, Pres. & CEO   Tel: (704) 969-0250   %FO: 100
Bus: *Provides rental solutions.*   Fax: (704) 348-5722

• **ASPREY & GARRARD HOLDINGS LIMITED**
167 New Bond Street, London W1S 4AR, UK
CEO: Rosa Monckton, CEO   Tel: 44-207-493-6767
Bus: *Mfr. jewelry.*   Fax: 44-207-491-0384
                                         www.asprey-garrard.com

ASPREY & GARRARD HOLDINGS INC.
725 Fifth Avenue, New York, NY   10022
CEO: Philip Warner, CEO   Tel: (212) 688-1811   %FO: 100
Bus: *Mfr. jewelry.*   Fax: (212) 826-3746

• **ASSOCIATED BRITISH FOODS PLC**
Weston Centre, Bowater House, 68 Knightsbridge, London SW1X 7LQ, UK
CEO: Peter J. Jackson, CEO   Tel: 44-207-589-6363   Rev: $6,445
Bus: *Mfr. food products.*   Fax: 44-207-584-8560   Emp: 34,375
                                         www.abf.co.uk

ACH FOOD COMPANY, INC.
7171 Goodlett Farms Pkwy., Cordova, TN 38018

CEO: Daniel Antonielli, Pres.	Tel: (901) 381-3000	%FO: 100
Bus: *Sale/distribution of food products.*	Fax: (901) 381-3211	

GROSVENOR MARKETING LTD.
East 210 Route 4, Paramus, NJ 07652

CEO: Patrick M. Clode, Pres.	Tel: (201) 843-1022	%FO: 100
Bus: *Sale/distribution of food products.*	Fax: (201) 843-7869	

● ASSOCIATED BRITISH PORTS HOLDINGS PLC
150 Holborn Street, London EC1N 2LR, UK

CEO: Bo Lerenius, CEO	Tel: 44-207-430-1177	Rev: $583
Bus: *Port operator providing container handling, dredging and docking, storage and distribution.*	Fax: 44-207-430-1384 www.abports.co.uk	Emp: 3,000

AMPORS INC.
1344 World Trade Center, Baltimore, MD 21202

CEO: Jim Davis, Mgr.	Tel: (410) 625-1370	%FO: 100
Bus: *Port operator providing container handling, dredging and docking, storage and distribution.*	Fax: (410) 625-1481	

● ASSOCIATED NEWSPAPERS, LTD.
2 Derry Street, Kensington, London W85 TT, UK

CEO: Murdoch MacLennon, Mng. Dir.	Tel: 44-207-938-6000
Bus: *UK newspaper group.*	Fax: 44-207-938-6000
	www.associatednewspapers.co.uk

ASSOCIATED NEWSPAPERS N.A., INC.
477 Madison Avenue, New York, NY 10022

CEO: Ian Cobain, Bureau Chief	Tel: (212) 893-2170	%FO: 100
Bus: *Newspaper editorial bureau for UK news group.*	Fax: (212) 893-2178	Emp: 4

● ASTRA ZENECA PLC
15 Stanhope Gate, London W1K 1LN, UK

CEO: Dr. Tom McKillop, CEO	Tel: 44-207-304-5000	Rev: $9,145
Bus: *Mfr. pharmaceutical products.*	Fax: 44-207-304-5151 www.astrazeneca.com	Emp: 34,000

ASTRA ZENECA PHARMACEUTICALS
3 Werner Way, Ste. 200, Lebanon, NJ 08833

CEO: David Brennan, Pres. & CEO	Tel: (908) 236-9535
Bus: *Research, product development and marketing of pharmaceuticals.*	Fax: (908) 236-7393

ASTRA ZENECA PHARMACEUTICALS

500 N. Central Expressway, Ste. 231, Plano, TX 75074

CEO: David Brennan, Pres. & CEO   Tel: (972) 578-5454

Bus: *Research, product development*   Fax: (972) 516-1535
and marketing of pharmaceuticals.

ASTRA ZENECA PHARMACEUTICALS

2300 N. Barrington Road, Ste. 350, Hoffman Estates, IL 60195

CEO: David Brennan, Pres. & CEO   Tel: (708) 885-1160

Bus: *Research, product development*   Fax: (708) 885-6090
and marketing of pharmaceuticals.

ASTRA ZENECA PHARMACEUTICALS

587 Old Baltimore Pike, Newark, DE 19711

CEO: David Brennan, Pres. & CEO   Tel: (302) 453-3500

Bus: *Research, product development*   Fax: (302) 453-5997
and marketing of pharmaceuticals.

ASTRA ZENECA PHARMACEUTICALS

10681 Foothill Blvd., Ste. 297, Rancho Cucamonga, CA 91730

CEO: David Brennan, Pres. & CEO   Tel: (909) 941-2900

Bus: *Research, product development*   Fax: (909) 941-3090
and marketing of pharmaceuticals.

ASTRA ZENECA PHARMACEUTICALS

430 Bedford Street, Ste. 100, Lexington, MA 02173

CEO: Niklas Lidskog   Tel: (781) 861-7707

Bus: *Research, product development*   Fax: (781) 861-7787
and marketing of pharmaceuticals.

ASTRA ZENECA PHARMACEUTICALS

128 Sidney Street, Cambridge, MA 02139

CEO: Youe-Kong Shue, Mgr.   Tel: (617) 576-3900

Bus: *Research, product development*   Fax: (617) 576-3030
and marketing of pharmaceuticals.

ASTRA ZENECA PHARMACEUTICALS

One Innovation Drive, Worcester, MA 01605

CEO: Ioannis A. Papayannopoulos   Tel: (508) 421-3500

Bus: *Research, product development*   Fax: (508) 421-3581
and marketing of pharmaceuticals.

ASTRA ZENECA PHARMACEUTICALS

PO Box 4500, Westborough, MA 01581

CEO: Ivan R. Rowley, Pres. & CEO   Tel: (508) 366-1100

Bus: *Research, product development*   Fax: (508) 366-7406
and marketing of pharmaceuticals.

ASTRA ZENECA PHARMACEUTICALS

725 Chesterbrook Boulevard, Wayne, PA 19087-5677

CEO: David Brennan, Pres. & CEO   Tel: (610) 695-1000

Bus: *Research, product development*   Fax: (610) 695-1250
     and marketing of pharmaceuticals.

ASTRA ZENECA PHARMACEUTICALS

1800 Concord Pike, Wilmington, DE 19850

CEO: David Brennan, Pres. & CEO   Tel: (302) 886-3000

Bus: *Research, product development*   Fax: (302) 886-2972
     and marketing of pharmaceuticals.

ASTRA ZENECA PHARMACEUTICALS

5 Concourse Parkway, Ste. 1935, Atlanta, GA 30328-6111

CEO: David Brennan, Pres. & CEO   Tel: (770) 394-6064

Bus: *Research, product development*   Fax: (770) 394-4355
     and marketing of pharmaceuticals.

● **WS ATKINS PLC**

Woodcote Grove, Ashley Road, Epsom, Surrey KT18 5BW, UK

CEO: Robin Southwell, CEO   Tel: 44-137-272-6140   Rev: $955

Bus: *Engaged in management consulting*   Fax: 44-137-274-0055   Emp: 12,500
     services.   www.wsatkins.co.uk

     ATKINS BENHAM

     1909 East 20th Street, Ste. 2, Farmington, NM 87401

     CEO: Nicholas S. Stagg   Tel: (505) 325-4601   %FO: 100

     Bus: *Engaged in management*   Fax: (505) 325-4625
         consulting services.

     ATKINS BENHAM

     9400 N. Broadway, Oklahoma City, OK 73114

     CEO: Nicholas S. Stagg   Tel: (405) 478-5353   %FO: 100

     Bus: *Engaged in management*   Fax: (405) 478-5660
         consulting services.

     ATKINS BENHAM

     11175 Wood Elves Way, Baltimore, MD 21044

     CEO: Nicholas S. Stagg   Tel: (410) 992-6880   %FO: 100

     Bus: *Engaged in management*   Fax: (410) 922-6883
         consulting services.

● **AUTONOMY CORPORATION PLC**

St. John's Innovation Centre, Cowley Road, Cambridge CB4 OWS, UK

CEO: Michael Lynch, Mng. Dir.   Tel: 44-122-342-1220   Rev: $65

Bus: *Mfr. software for on-line media and*   Fax: 44-122-342-1583   Emp: 170
     publishing companies.   www.autonomy.com

AUTONOMY INC.
301 Howard Street, 22nd Fl., San Francisco, CA 94105
CEO: Mary Ann Moran, Pres.　　　　Tel: (415) 243-9955　　　%FO: 100
Bus: *Mfr. software for on-line media*　Fax: (415) 243-9984
　　　and publishing companies.

● **AUTOTYPE INTERNATIONAL LTD.**
Grove Road, Wantage, Oxon OX127 B2, UK
CEO: Peter Levinsohn, Pres.　　　　Tel: 44-123-577-1111　　　Rev: $394
Bus: *Mfr. of specialty films and chemicals for*　Fax: 44-123-577-1196　　Emp: 3,000
　　　the electronics industry, screen printing,　www.autotype.com
　　　digital display printing and industrial
　　　applications.

　　AUTOTYPE AMERICAS INC.
　　2050 Hammond Drive, Schaumburg, IL 60173-3810
　　CEO: Graham Cooper, Pres.　　　Tel: (847) 303-5900
　　Bus: *Mfr. films/chemicals for the screen*　Fax: (847) 303-5225
　　　　and print industry.

● **BAA PLC**
130 Wilton Road, London SW1V 1LQ, UK
CEO: Mike Hodgkinson, CEO　　　　Tel: 44-207-932-6642　　Rev: $3,160
Bus: *Airport management and operations.*　Fax: 44-207-932-6757　　Emp: 12,700
　　　　　　　　　　　　　　　　　www.baa.co.uk.

　　BAA INDIANAPOLIS INC.
　　2500 South High School Road, Indianapolis, IN 46241
　　CEO: David Roberts, Pres.　　　Tel: (317) 487-5003　　%FO: 100
　　Bus: *Airport management and*　　Fax: (317) 487-5034　　Emp: 199
　　　　operations.

　　BAA PITTSBURGH INC.
　　Pittsburgh Intl Airport, PO Box 12318, Pittsburgh, PA 15231-0318
　　CEO: Mark Knight, Pres.　　　Tel: (412) 472-5180　　%FO: 100
　　Bus: *Airport management and*　　Fax: (412) 472-5190　　Emp: 8
　　　　operations.

　　BAA USA INC.
　　45240 Business Court, Ste. 225, Sterling, VA 20166
　　CEO: David C. Suomi, VP　　　Tel: (703) 708-7998　　%FO: 100
　　Bus: *Airport management and*　　Fax: (703) 708-7991　　Emp: 7
　　　　operations.

WORLD DUTY FREE AMERICAS INC.
63 Copps Hill Road, Ridgefield, CT   06877
CEO: Steve Longdon, CEO   Tel: (203) 431-6057   %FO: 100
Bus: *Duty free shop operations in*   Fax: (203) 438-1356   Emp: 2,000
international airport terminals.

● **BAE SYSTEMS, PLC**
Warwick House, FAC, PO Box 87, Farnborough, Hampshire GU14 6YU, UK
CEO: John Weston, CEO   Tel: 44-125-237-3000   Rev: $14,435
Bus: *Mfr. aerospace products, commercial*   Fax: 44-125-237-3232   Emp: 83,400
and military aircraft, artillery, missiles,   www.bae.co.uk
defense systems.

   BAE ADVANCED SYSTEMS
   450 East Polaski Road, Greenlawn, NY   11740
   CEO: Ray Daugherty, Pres.   Tel: (631) 261-7000   %FO: 100
   Bus: *Mfr./sales of aerospace systems*   Fax: (631) 262-8019
   and equipment.

   BAE AEROSPACE SECTOR
   6500 Tracor Lane, Austin, TX   78725
   CEO: George R. Melton, Pres.   Tel: (512) 926-2800   %FO: 100
   Bus: *Mfr./sales of aerospace systems*   Fax: (512) 929-2380
   and equipment.

   BAE SYSTEMS NA
   4200 South Hulen, Ste. 600, Ft. Worth, TX   76109-4913
   CEO: Keith Fordham, VP   Tel: (817) 735-1185   %FO: 100
   Bus: *Mfr./sales of aerospace systems*   Fax: (817) 377-3345
   and equipment.

   BAE SYSTEMS NA
   15000 Conference Center Drive, Chantilly, VA   20151
   CEO: Stephen O'Sullivan, EVP   Tel: (703) 802-0361   %FO: 100
   Bus: *Mfr./sales of aerospace systems*   Fax: (703) 227-1733
   and equipment.

   BAE SYSTEMS NA
   1125 Indian Bluff, St. Louis, MO   63138
   CEO: Richard Milnes   Tel: (314) 653-6731   %FO: 100
   Bus: *Mfr. aircraft controls.*   Fax: (314) 653-6734

   BAE SYSTEMS NA
   1601 Research Boulevard, Rockville, MD   20850
   CEO: Mark H. Ronald, CEO   Tel: (301) 838-6000   %FO: 100
   Bus: *Sale & support aerospace*   Fax: (301) 838-6925   Emp: 380
   products & operations.

BAE SYSTEMS NA
1215 Jefferson Davis Hwy., Ste. 1500, Arlington, VA   22202
CEO: Cynthia Keefer   Tel: (703) 416-7777   %FO: 100
Bus: *Mfr. aircraft controls.*   Fax: (703) 416-2729

CINCINNATI ELECTRONICS CORP.
75000 Innovation Way, Mason, OH   45040
CEO: James Wimmers, Pres.   Tel: (513) 573-6100   %FO: 100
Bus: *Mfr. space electronics and*   Fax: (513) 573-6458
      infrared imaging systems.

FLIGHT SIMULATION
4908 Tampa West Blvd., Tampa, FL   33634
CEO: John Pitts, Pres.   Tel: (813) 885-7481   %FO: 100
Bus: *Mfr./sales of aerospace systems*   Fax: (813) 885-1177
      and equipment.

HECKLER & KOCH, INC.
21480 Pacific Blvd., Sterling, VA   20166
CEO: Eoin Stafford, Pres.   Tel: (703) 450-1900   %FO: 100
Bus: *Mfr./sales of aerospace systems*   Fax: (703) 450-8160
      and equipment.

HECKLER & KOCH, INC.
21480 Pacific Blvd., Sterling, VA   20166
CEO: Eoin Stafford, Pres.   Tel: (703) 450-1900   %FO: 100
Bus: *Mfr./sales of aerospace systems*   Fax: (703) 578-4508
      and equipment.

ROYAL ORDINANCE NA
4509 West Stone Drive, Kingsport, TN   37660
CEO: David Allott, Mgr.   Tel: (423) 578-6064   %FO: 100
Bus: *Mfr./sales of aerospace systems*   Fax: (423) 578-8054
      and equipment.

● **BALFOUR BEATTY PLC (FORMERLY BICC PLC)**
130 Wilton Road, London SW1V 1LQ, UK
CEO: Michael Welton, CEO   Tel: 44-207-216-6800   Rev: $3,585
Bus: *Engineering for power, construction*   Fax: 44-207-216-6950   Emp: 24,000
      and communications industries.   www.balfourbeatty.com

BALFOUR BEATTY INC.
254 South Main Street, New City, NY   10956
CEO: David Piper, Pres.   Tel: (845) 708-0885   %FO: 100
Bus: *Mfr. electric power cables and*   Fax: (845) 708-0885
      related products.

● **BALLI KLOCKNER, DIV. PRIMARY INDUSTRIES LTD.**
5 Stanhope Gate, London W1Y 5LA, UK
CEO: W. Siniscalchi, Pres.　　　　Tel: 44-207-544-8300　　　Rev: $1,400
Bus: *Engaged in trading steel and steel raw*　Fax: 44-207-630-0575
　　materials.　　　　　　　　　　www.ballisteel.com

　　PRIMARY INDUSTRIES (US) INC.
　　EAB Plaza, West Tower, 5th Fl., Uniondale, NY　11556-0155
　　CEO: W. Siniscalchi, Pres.　　　Tel: (516) 794-1122　　　%FO: 100
　　Bus: *Engaged in steel.*　　　　Fax: (516) 794-8989

　　WEBCO INTERNATIONAL, DIV. WEIRTON STEEL CORP.
　　400 Three Springs Drive, Weirton, WV　26062
　　CEO: John Walker, CEO　　　　Tel: (304) 797-2000　　　%FO: JV
　　Bus: *Engaged in steel.*　　　　Fax: (304) 797-2792

● **BALTIMORE TECHNOLOGIES PLC**
The Square Basing View, Basingstoke, Hampshire RG21 4EG, UK
CEO: Francis J. Rooney, CEO　　　Tel: 44-125-681-8800　　　Rev: $111
Bus: *Mfr. e-commerce hardware.*　　Fax: 44-125-681-2901　　　Emp: 1,185
　　　　　　　　　　　　　　www.baltimore.com

　　BALTIMORE TECHNOLOGIES INC.
　　411 Borel Avenue, Ste. 100, San Mateo, CA　94401
　　CEO: Gene Carozza　　　　　Tel: (650) 372-5270　　　%FO: 100
　　Bus: *Mfr. e-commerce hardware.*　Fax: (650) 372-5283

● **BARCLAYS BANK PLC**
54 Lombard Street, London EC3P 3AH, UK
CEO: Matthew W. Barrett, CEO　　Tel: 44-207-626-1567　　　Rev: $24,747
Bus: *International investment banking and*　Fax: 44-207-692-4252　　Emp: 74,300
　　asset management services.　　www.barclays.co.uk

　　BARCLAYS PRIVATE BANKING
　　801 Brickell Avenue, Miami, FL　33131
　　CEO: Marilyn Moll, CEO　　　Tel: (305) 374-1043　　　%FO: 100
　　Bus: *International private banking.*　Fax: (305) 579-2066　　　Emp: 500

　　BARCLAYS BANK PLC
　　801 Brickell Avenue, Miami, FL　33131
　　CEO: Gonzalo Valdes-Fauli, Mgr.　Tel: (305) 374-1043　　　%FO: 100
　　Bus: *Latin America regional office.*　Fax: (305) 579-2066
　　　Securities broker/dealer, futures
　　　commission agent and investment
　　　banking.

BARCLAYS GLOBAL INVESTORS
45 Fremont Street, San Francisco, CA   94105
CEO: Patricia C. Dunn, Chrwm.   Tel: (415) 597-2000   %FO: 100
Bus: *International investment banking*   Fax: (415) 597-2010   Emp: 3,000
    and asset management services.

BARCLAYS GROUP NORTH AMERICA
222 Broadway, New York, NY   10038
CEO: Michael Prior, Dir.   Tel: (212) 412-4000   %FO: 100
Bus: *International investment banking*   Fax: (212) 412-6995   Emp: 1,400
    and asset management services.

● **BARLOW INTERNATIONAL PLC**
16 Stratford Place, London WINN 9AF, UK
CEO: Richard M. Mansell-Jones, Chmn.   Tel: 44-207-629-6243
Bus: *Mfr./distribution of hospital, laboratory*   Fax: 44-207-409-0556
    and scientific equipment.   www.wrenn-brungart

WB GROUP LP/BRUNGART EQUIPMENT
3930 Pinson Valley Pkwy., Birmingham, AL   35217
CEO: Jim Haynes, Mgr.   Tel: (205) 520-2000   %FO: 100
Bus: *Sales/distribution of hospital,*   Fax: (205) 520-2031
    laboratory and scientific
    equipment.

WB GROUP LP/BRUNGART EQUIPMENT
3915 North Highway 301, Tampa, FL   33619
CEO: Don Tyler, Mgr.   Tel: (813) 623-6700   %FO: 100
Bus: *Sales/distribution of hospital,*   Fax: (813) 664-9763
    laboratory and scientific
    equipment.

WB GROUP LP/WRENN HANDLING LTD.
901 Westinghouse Blvd., Charlotte, NC   28273
CEO: Dan Vicini, Mgr.   Tel: (704) 588-1300   %FO: 100
Bus: *Sales/distribution of hospital,*   Fax: (704) 588-2633
    laboratory and scientific
    equipment.

WB GROUP LP/WRENN HANDLING LTD.
5191 Snapfinger Woods Drive, Decatur, GA   30036
CEO: Gene Summerford, Mgr.   Tel: (770) 987-7666   %FO: 100
Bus: *Sales/distribution of hospital,*   Fax: (770) 593-7922
    laboratory and scientific
    equipment.

WB GROUP LP/WRENN HANDLING LTD.
5511 East Shelby Drive, Memphis, TN 38141
CEO: Terry Moore, Mgr. | Tel: (901) 795-7200 | %FO: 100
Bus: *Sales/distribution of hospital, laboratory and scientific equipment.* | Fax: (901) 367-5784

WB GROUP LP/WRENN HANDLING LTD.
3149 Charleston Hwy., West Columbia, SC 29172
CEO: Jeff Smith, Mgr. | Tel: (803) 796-7300 | %FO: 100
Bus: *Sales/distribution of hospital, laboratory and scientific equipment.* | Fax: (803) 796-1667

WRENN HANDLING, INC.
PO Box 410050, Charlotte, NC 28741-0050
CEO: C. Stan Sewell, Pres. | Tel: (704) 587-1003 | %FO: 100
Bus: *Sales/distribution of hospital, laboratory and scientific equipment.* | Fax: (704) 587-0317

● **BARRATT DEVELOPMENTS PLC**
Wingrove House, Ponteland Road, Newcastle Upon Tyne NE5 3DP, UK
CEO: Frank Eaton, Chmn. | Tel: 44-191-286-6811
Bus: *Property investment, building and development.* | Fax: 44-191-271-2242
 | www.barratthomes.co.uk

   BARRATT AMERICAN INC.
   2035 Corte Del Nogal, Ste. 160, Carlsbad, CA 92009
   CEO: Michael D. Pattinson, Pres. | Tel: (760) 431-0800 | %FO: 100
   Bus: *Property investment, building and development.* | Fax: (760) 929-6424

● **BBA GROUP, PLC.**
70 Fleet Street, Fifth Fl., London EC4Y 1EU, U.K.
CEO: Roberto Quarta, CEO | Tel: 44-207-842-4900 | Rev: $2,300
Bus: *Engaged in aviation and materials technology.* | Fax: 44-207-353-5831 | Emp: 13,920
 | www.bbagroup.com

   BBA AVIATION PRODUCTS
   495 Lake Mirror Road, Atlanta, GA 30349
   CEO: M. Kennemore, Mgr. | Tel: (404) 767-5800 | %FO: 100
   Bus: *Mfr. aviation products.* | Fax: (404) 767-5900

BBA AVIATION SERVICES
8 Airport Road, Morristown, NJ   07960
CEO: David Oakes   Tel: (973) 292-1300   %FO: 100
Bus: *Mfr. nonwovens.*   Fax: (973) 292-2331

BBA FRICTION INC.
3994 Pepperell Way, Dublin, VA   24084
CEO: Peter Schmitz, Pres.   Tel: (540) 674-3550   %FO: 100
Bus: *Mfr. brake pads.*   Fax: (540) 674-1147

BBA NONWOVENS
PO Box 20, Lewisburg, PA   17837
CEO: Bette Batman   Tel: (570) 524-2281   %FO: 100
Bus: *Mfr. nonwovens.*   Fax: (570) 524-8447

BBA NONWOVENS
335 Athena Drive, Athens, GA   30601
CEO: Bruce Van Allen, CEO   Tel: (706) 549-6561   %FO: 100
Bus: *Mfr. nonwovens.*   Fax: (706) 543-1231

BBA NONWOVENS
3720 Grant Street, Washougal, WA   98671
CEO: David Ellenz, Mgr.   Tel: (360) 835-8787   %FO: 100
Bus: *Mfr. nonwovens.*   Fax: (360) 835-2546

BBA NONWOVENS
100 Elm Street, Walpole, MA   02081
CEO: Diana Magaldi   Tel: (508) 660-3300   %FO: 100
Bus: *Mfr. nonwovens.*   Fax: (508) 660-2376

BBA NONWOVENS
PO Box 579, Bethune, SC   29009
CEO: David Lackmann   Tel: (843) 334-6211   %FO: 100
Bus: *Mfr. nonwovens.*   Fax: (843) 334-6462

BBA NONWOVENS
3120 Commodity Lane, Green Bay, WI   54303
CEO: Fred Crowe, Pres. & CEO   Tel: (920) 336-0222   %FO: 100
Bus: *Mfr. nonwovens.*   Fax: (920) 336-3418

BBA NONWOVENS
PO Box 3, Colrain, MA   01340
CEO: Kerry Johnson   Tel: (413) 624-3471   %FO: 100
Bus: *Mfr. nonwovens.*   Fax: (413) 624-5590

BBA NONWOVENS INC.
840 Southeast Main Street, Simpsonville, SC   29861
CEO: Dennis Tavernetti, Pres.   Tel: (864) 967-5600   %FO: 100
Bus: *Mfr. nonwovens.*   Fax: (864) 967-5695

BBA NONWOVENS INC.
100 Elm Street, Walpole, MA   02081
CEO: David Miles, Mgr.   Tel: (508) 660-3300   %FO: 100
Bus: *Mfr. nonwovens.*   Fax: (508) 660-3300

BBA NONWOVENS INTERSPUN
12244 Nations Ford Road, Pineville, NC   28134
CEO: Frank Malaney   Tel: (704) 583-3400   %FO: 100
Bus: *Mfr. nonwovens.*   Fax: (704) 583-3410

BBA NONWOVENS-REEMAY INC.
70 Old Hickory Blvd., PO Box 511, Old Hickory, TN   37138-3651
CEO: Alec Hay, Pres.   Tel: (615) 847-7000   %FO: 100
Bus: *Mfr. nonwoven spunbonded*   Fax: (615) 847-7068
    products.

BBA US HOLDINGS, INC.
401 Edgewater Place, Ste. 670, Wakefield, MA   01880
CEO: Greg Murrer, Pres.   Tel: (781) 246-8900   %FO: 100
Bus: *U.S. holding company.*   Fax: (781) 245-3227

ITS INC.
1060 East Northwest Highway, Grapevine, TX   76051
CEO: Terry Scott   Tel: (817) 949-3250   %FO: 100
Bus: *Mfr. nonwovens.*   Fax: (817) 329-0317

● **BELRON INTERNATIONAL**
Old King's Observatory, Old Deer Park, Richmond Surrey TW9 2AE, UK
CEO: John Mason, CEO   Tel: 44-181-940-9177   Rev: $935
Bus: *Engaged in auto glass repair and* Fax: 44-181-332-0589   Emp: 12,425
    replacement.   www.belron.com

SAFELITE AUTO GLASS
1330 Main Avenue, Moorehead, MN   56560
CEO: John Barlow, Pres.   Tel: (218) 236-8849   %FO: 1
Bus: *Engaged in auto glass repair and* Fax: (218) 236-8849
    replacement.

SAFELITE AUTO GLASS
1010 Main Avenue, Fargo, ND 58103

CEO: John Barlow, Pres. Tel: (701) 237-6220 %FO: 1

Bus: *Engaged in auto glass repair and* Fax: (701) 237-6220
replacement.

SAFELITE AUTO GLASS
PO Box 2000, Columbus, OH 43216

CEO: Dee Uttermohlen, Mgr. Tel: (614) 842-3000 %FO: 1

Bus: *Engaged in auto glass repair and* Fax: (614) 842-3180
replacement.

• BENFIELD GREIG GROUP PLC
55 Bishopsgate, London EC2N 3BD, UK

CEO: Grahame Chilton, CEO Tel: 44-207-578-7000 Rev: $209

Bus: *Engaged in risk insurance and* Fax: 44-207-578-7001 Emp: 350
investment. www.benfieldgroup.com

BENFIELD BLANCH INC.
3655 North Point Pkwy., Ste. 300, Alpharetta, GA 30005

CEO: Jim Satterfield, Dir. Tel: (678) 297-0784 %FO: 100

Bus: *Engaged in risk insurance and* Fax: (678) 297-0844
investment.

BENFIELD BLANCH INC.
7701 France Avenue South, Edina, MN 55435

CEO: Paul Karon, Dir. Tel: (612) 243-2517 %FO: 100

Bus: *Engaged in risk insurance and* Fax: (612) 243-2517
investment.

BENFIELD BLANCH INC.
5000 Akara, Ste. 4500, Dallas, TX 75201

CEO: Red Fox, Dir. Tel: (214) 756-7101 %FO: 100

Bus: *Engaged in risk insurance and* Fax: (214) 756-7119
investment.

• BERMANS
Trident House, 31/33 Dale Street, Liverpool L2 2NS, UK

CEO: Keith Berman, Pres. Tel: 44-151-236-2107

Bus: *Law firm services.* Fax: 44-151-236-2107
www.bermans.co.uk

BERMANS
19 West 34th Street, New York, NY 10022

CEO: Keith Berman, Pres. Tel: (212) 956-7767 %FO: 100

Bus: *English solicitors and* Fax: (212) 956-1099
international attorneys.

- **BESPAK PLC**

Four Stanhope Gate, London W1Y 5LA, UK

CEO: R. J. Preece, CEO

Bus: *Pharmaceuticals valve delivery systems, specialty valves, pumps.*

Tel: 44-207-518-7900
Fax: 44-207-518-7905
www.bespak.co.uk

Rev: $141
Emp: 560

BESPAK INC.

2450 Laura Duncan Road, Apex, NC 27502

CEO: G. Meredith, Pres.

Bus: *Mfr./distribution pharmaceuticals valve delivery systems, specialty valves, pumps.*

Tel: (919) 387-0112
Fax: (919) 387-0116

%FO: 100
Emp: 60

- **BEVAN FUNNELL LIMITED**

Beach Road, Newhaven, East Sussex, BN9 0BZ, UK

CEO: B. B. Funnell, Chmn.

Bus: *Distributes antique reproductions and classic English furniture.*

Tel: 44-127-351-3762
Fax: 44-127-351-6735
www.bevan-funnell.co.uk

BEVAN FUNNELL, LTD.

105 Depot Place, PO Box 1109, High Point, NC 27261

CEO: Paul Braithwaite, VP

Bus: *Sales/distribution/service of antique reproductions.*

Tel: (336) 889-4800
Fax: (336) 889-7037

%FO: 100

- **BG PLC**

100 Thames Valley Park Drive, Reading, Berkshire RG6 1PT, UK

CEO: Frank Chapman, CEO

Bus: *Distributes and sells gas, implements exploration and provides technological support.*

Tel: 44-118-935-3222
Fax: 44-118-935-3233
www.bg-group.com

Rev: $3,502
Emp: 19,750

BRITISH GAS U.S. HOLDINGS, INC.

5444 Westheimer, Ste. 1775, Houston, TX 77056

CEO: Cynthia Masters, VP

Bus: *Distributes and sells gas, implements exploration and provides technological support.*

Tel: (713) 622-7101
Fax: (713) 622-7244

%FO: 100

DYNEGY, INC.

1000 Louisiana Street, Ste. 5800, Houston, TX 77002

CEO: Howard Heuston, VP

Bus: *Distributes and sells gas, implements exploration and provides technological support.*

Tel: (713) 507-6400
Fax: (713) 507-6804

%FO: 100

● **BIOTRACE LIMITED**
The Science Park, Bridgend CF31 3NA, UK
CEO: Ian R. Johnson
Bus: *Mfr. rapid tests for hygiene monitoring and microbial screening in the food, industrial and environmental markets.*
Tel: 44-165-664-1400
Fax: 44-165-676-8835
www.biotrace.com

> **BIOTRACE, INC.**
> 666 Plainsboro Road, Ste. 1050, Plainsboro, NJ 08536
> CEO: Terence Alexander Clements
> Bus: *Mfr. rapid tests for hygiene monitoring and microbial screening in the food, industrial and environmental markets.*
> Tel: (609) 897-0282
> Fax: (609) 897-0289
> %FO: 100

● **BLUE CIRCLE INDUSTRIES PLC**
84 Eccleston Square, London SW1V 1PX, U.K.
CEO: Rick Haythornthwaite, CEO
Bus: *Mfr. cement, building materials and home products. (JV LaFarge)*
Tel: 44-207-828-3456
Fax: 44-207-245-8229
www.bluecircle.co.uk
Rev: $3,900
Emp: 18,650

> **BLUE CIRCLE AGGREGAES INC.**
> 1889 F NW Beaver Ridge Circle, Norcross, GA 30017-3833
> CEO: Jim Ward, Pres.
> Bus: *Building materials and home products.*
> Tel: (770) 797-2070
> Fax: (770) 797-2097
> %FO: 100

> **BLUE CIRCLE AMERICA, INC.**
> 1800 Parkway Place, Marietta, GA 30067
> CEO: Gary Genties, Pres.
> Bus: *Building materials and home products.*
> Tel: (770) 423-4700
> Fax: (770) 423-4738
> %FO: 100

> **BLUE CIRCLE CEMENT INC.**
> 9333 Dearborn Street, Detroit, MI 48209
> CEO: George Gregory, Pres.
> Bus: *Mfr. cement and concrete products.*
> Tel: (313) 842-4600
> Fax: (313) 849-4555

> **BLUE CIRCLE MATERIALS NE**
> 475 Market Street, Elmwood Park, NJ 07470
> CEO: Susan Martinez, Sales
> Bus: *Building materials and home products.*
> Tel: (201) 797-7979
> Fax: (201) 791-9831
> %FO: 100

BLUE CIRCLE MATERIALS SE
1800 Parkway Place, Ste. 1100, Marietta, GA   30067
CEO: Ray Eastin, Pres.   Tel: (770) 423-4700   %FO: 100
Bus: *Building materials and home*   Fax: (770) 499-2807
    products.

● **BNFL**
Risley, Warrington Cheshire WA3 6AS, UK
CEO: Norman Askew, CEO   Tel: 44-925-832-000
Bus: *Mfr. nuclear fuel and operates nuclear*   Fax: 44-925-822-711
    power stations.   www.bnfl.com

   BNFL INC.
   10306 Eaton Place, Ste. 450, Fairfax, VA   22030
   CEO: Paul A. Miskimin, CEO   Tel: (703) 385-7100   %FO: 100
   Bus: *Engaged in nuclear waste*   Fax: (703) 385-7128
       management.

   BNFL INC.
   1900 M Street, Ste. 500, Washington, DC   20006
   CEO: Marily Meigs, VP   Tel: (202) 785-2635   %FO: 100
   Bus: *Engaged in nuclear waste*   Fax: (202) 785-4037
       management.

   WESTINGHOUSE ELECTRIC COMPANY
   PO Box 355, Pittsburgh, PA   15230-0355
   CEO: Charles W. Pryor Jr., CEO   Tel: (412) 374-4111   %FO: 100
   Bus: *Engaged in nuclear waste*   Fax: (412) 374-6277
       management and new plant design.

● **THE BOC GROUP PLC**
Chertsey Road, Windlesham, Surrey GU20 6HJ, UK
CEO: A. E. Isaac, CEO   Tel: 44-1276-477222   Rev: $5,000
Bus: *Industrial gas company.*   Fax: 44-127-647-1333   Emp: 42,125
                          www.boc.com

   BOC COATING TECHNOLOGY
   PO Box 2529, Fairfield, CA   94533-0252
   CEO: Rod Stradling, Pres.   Tel: (707) 425-1010   %FO: 100
   Bus: *Mfr. industrial gases.*   Fax: (707) 425-1706

   BOC EDWARDS
   301 Ballardvale Street, Wilmington, MA   01887
   CEO: Mark Rosenzweig, Pres.   Tel: (978) 658-5410
   Bus: *Mfr. high vacuum equipment and*   Fax: (978) 658-7969
       service pumps.

THE BOC GASES GROUP INC.

575 Mountain Avenue, Murray Hill, NJ   07974

CEO: Dick Grant, Pres.	Tel: (908) 665-2400	%FO: 100
Bus: *Mfr. industrial gases.*	Fax: (908) 464-9015	Emp: 9,700

● THE BODY SHOP INTERNATIONAL PLC

Watersmead, Littlehampton, West Sussex BN17 6LS, UK

CEO: Patrick Gournay, CEO	Tel: 44-190-373-1500	Rev: $486
Bus: *Mfr./retailer health and beauty products.*	Fax: 44-190-372-6250	Emp: 5,200
	www.the-body-shop.com	

THE BODY SHOP, INC.

5036 One World Way, PO Box 1409, Wake Forest, NC   27587

CEO: Peter Saunders, CEO	Tel: (919) 554-4900	%FO: 100
Bus: *Retailer health and beauty products.*	Fax: (919) 554-4361	Emp: 1,000

● BODYCOTE INTERNATIONAL PLC

Hulley Road, Macclesfield, Cheshire SK10 2SG, UK

CEO: John Chesworth, Mng. Dir.	Tel: 44-162-550-5300	Rev: $554
Bus: *Engaged in heat treatments and manufacture of metallurgical coatings.*	Fax: 44-162-550-5313	Emp: 5,800
	www.bodycote.com	

LINDBERG CORPORATION

6133 North River Road, Ste. 700, Rosemont, IL   60018

CEO: Leo G. Thompson, CEO	Tel: (847) 823-2021	%FO: 100
Bus: *Engaged in heat treatments and manufacture of metallurgical coatings.*	Fax: (847) 823-0795	Emp: 1,050

● BONEHAM & TURNER LTD.

Nottingham Road, Mansfield, Notts NG1 B4A, UK

CEO: Andrew Nicklin, Chmn.	Tel: 44-162-362-7641	
Bus: *Mfr. precision machinery and tools.*	Fax: 44-162-362-7645	Emp: 225
	www.boneham.co.uk	

BONEHAM METAL PRODUCTS, INC.

327 North 14th Street, Kenilworth, NJ   07111

CEO: Doreen Guenther, Mgr.	Tel: (908) 272-1200	%FO: 100
Bus: *Import/distribute industrial equipment.*	Fax: (908) 272-4124	Emp: 10

● **THE BOOTS COMPANY PLC. (DIV. BASF)**

One Thane Road West, Nottingham NG2 3AA, UK

CEO: Steve G. Russell, CEO   Tel: 44-115-950-6111   Rev: $8,257

Bus: *Operates ethical pharmaceuticals,*   Fax: 44-115-959-2727   Emp: 55,000
      eyewear chains, and auto parts chains.   www.boots-plc.co.uk

    KNOLL PHARMACEUTICALS INC. (DIV. BASF)

    3000 Continental Drive North, Mt. Olive, NJ 07828-1234

    CEO: Carter H. Eckert, Pres.   Tel: (973) 426-2600   %FO: 100

    Bus: *Mfr. ethical pharmaceuticals.*   Fax: (973) 426-5718   Emp: 900

● **BOVIS LEND LEASE**

Liscartan House, 127 Sloane Street, London SW1X 9BA, UK

CEO: Ross Taylor, CEO   Tel: 44-207-271-8000   Rev: $4,305

Bus: *Provides construction and project*   Fax: 44-207-853-1117   Emp: 7,000
      management.   www.bovislendlease.com

    BOVIS LEND LEASE INC.

    200 Park Avenue, New York, NY 10166

    CEO: Charles Bacon, CEO   Tel: (212) 592-6800   %FO: 100

    Bus: *Provides construction and project*   Fax: (212) 448-3922
      management.

● **BP PLC**

Britannic House, One Finsbury Circus, London EC2M 7BA, UK

CEO: Sir John P. Browne, CEO   Tel: 44-207-496-4000   Rev: $83,550

Bus: *Engaged in oil and natural resources,*   Fax: 44-207-496-4630   Emp: 80,400
      exploration, production and distribution.   www.bp.com

    AMOCO FABRICS AND FIBERS COMPANY

    900 Circle 75 Parkway, Ste. 550, Atlanta, GA 3039

    CEO: Peter Cella, Pres.   Tel: (770) 944-4601   %FO: 100

    Bus: *Mfr. fabrics and fibers.*   Fax:

    ARCO PERMIAN

    600 North Marienfield, Midland, TX 79701

    CEO: Keith I. Weiser   Tel: (915) 688-5200   %FO: 100

    Bus: *Engaged in oil and gas*   Fax: (915) 688-5271
      exploration.

    BP AMOCO CORP.

    200 East Randolph Drive, Chicago, IL 60601

    CEO: Jack Golden, EVP   Tel: (312) 856-6111   %FO: 100

    Bus: *Oil and natural resources,*   Fax: (312) 856-4883
      exploration, production and
      distribution.

BP AMOCO POLYMERS INC.
4500 McGinnis Ferry Road, Alpharetta, GA 30202
CEO: George Tacquard, Pres.   Tel: (770) 772-8200   %FO: 100
Bus: *Mfr. polymers.*   Fax: (770) 772-8213

BP EXPLORATION ALASKA INC.
900 East Benson Blvd., Anchorage, AK 99508
CEO: Richard Campbell, Pres.   Tel: (907) 564-5111   %FO: 100
Bus: *Exploration, production oil and*   Fax: (907) 564-5514   Emp: 1,295
   gas.

BP SOLAR INC.
989 Corporate Boulevard, Linthicum, MD 21090
CEO: Harry Shimp, CEO   Tel: (410) 981-0240   %FO: 100
Bus: *Mfr. photovoltaic products.*   Fax: (410) 981-0278

BP SOLAR INC.
2300 North Watney Way, Fairfield, CT 94533
CEO: Peter Beadle, Pres.   Tel: (707) 428-7800   %FO: 100
Bus: *Supplies advanced photovoltaic*   Fax: (707) 428-7878
   power systems.

BURMAH CASTROL HOLDINGS INC
1500 Valley Road, Wayne, NJ 07470
CEO: Kathleen A. Dockry   Tel: (973) 633-2200   %FO: 100
Bus: *Mfr. lubricants.*   Fax: (973) 633-1287

CASTROL CARIBBEAN AND CENTRAL AMERICA INC.
11420 North Kendall Drive, Ste. 207, Miami, FL 33176
CEO: Terence Clark, Pres. & CEO   Tel: (305) 270-9433   %FO: 100
Bus: *Mfr. lubricant products.*   Fax: (305) 270-9478

CASTROL HEAVY DUTY LUBRICANTS
9300 Pulaski Highway, Baltimore, MD 21220
CEO: Chuck Grawey, CEO   Tel: (410) 574-5000   %FO: 100
Bus: *Mfr. lubricants.*   Fax: (410) 682-9408

CASTROL NORTH AMERICA CONSUMER
1500 Valley Road, Wayne, NJ 07470
CEO: Peter Meola, CEO   Tel: (973) 633-2200   %FO: 100
Bus: *Mfr. auto and motorcycle products.* Fax: (973) 633-9867

CHEM-TREND INC.
1445 West McPherson Park Drive, Howell, MI 48843
CEO: Peter J. Hayes, Pres. & CEO Tel: (517) 546-4520   %FO: 100
Bus: *Mfr. specialized release agents for* Fax: (517) 546-6785
   plastics and rubber molding.

FOSBEL INC.
640 North Rock River Drive, Berea, OH   44017
CEO: Derek Scott, Pres.   Tel: (440) 891-0892   %FO: 100
Bus: *Mfr. glass technology products.*   Fax: (440) 891-0899

FOSECO INC.
20200 Sheldon Road, Cleveland, OH   44142
CEO: Roger Stanbridge, CEO   Tel: (440) 826-4548   %FO: 100
Bus: *Mfr. metallurgical chemicals.*   Fax: (440) 243-7658   Emp: 1,118

REMET CORPORATION
210 Commons Road, Utica, NY   13502
CEO: John Paraszczak, Pres. & CEO   Tel: (315) 797-8700   %FO: 100
Bus: *Mfr. investment casting   Fax: (315) 797-4848
    consumables.*

SERICOL INC.
1101 West Cambridge Drive, Kansas City, KS   66103
CEO: Edward J. Carhart, Pres. & CEO   Tel: (913) 342-4060   %FO: 100
Bus: *Mfr. screen printing inks for the Fax: (913) 342-4752
    graphics and textiles markets.*

VYSIS, INC.
3100 Woodcreek Drive, Downers Grove, IL   60515
CEO: John L. Bishop, Pres. & CEO   Tel: (630) 271-7000   %FO: 100
Bus: *Develops/markets genetic   Fax: (630) 271-7008   Emp: 173
    diagnostic products.*

● **BPB LTD.**
Park House, 15 Bath Road, Slough Berkshire SL1 3UF, UK
CEO: Richard Cousins, CEO   Tel: 44-175-389-8800   Rev: $2,271
Bus: *Mfr. plasterboard, insulation and Fax: 44-175-389-8888   Emp: 1,550
    flooring.*   www.bpb.com

  BPB CELOTEX
  5301 West Cypress, Ste. 300, Tampa, FL   33607
  CEO: Pam Bush, Mktg.   Tel: (813) 286-3900   %FO: 100
  Bus: *Mfr. plasterboard, insulation and Fax: (813) 286-3990
      flooring.*

● **BRAIME PRESSINGS PLC**
Hunslett Road, Leeds LS10 13Z, UK
CEO: Nicholas Braime, Pres.   Tel: 44-113-245-7491
Bus: *Mfr. seamless pressings.*   Fax: 44-113-243-5021   Emp: 300

4B ELEVATOR COMPONENTS LTD.

729 Sabrina Drive, East Peoria, IL   61611

CEO: Chris Robinson, VP

Tel: (309) 698-5611

%FO: 100

Bus: *Mfr. material handling components.*

Fax: (309) 698-5615

Emp: 5

● BRINTONS LTD.

Exchange Street, Kidderminster DY10 1AG, U.K.

CEO: Mac Brinton, Chmn.

Tel: 44-156-282-0000

Rev: $151

Bus: *Mfr. carpets.*

Fax: 44-156-251-2321

Emp: 2,000

www.brintons.co.uk

BRINTONS AXMINSTER, INC.

1856 Artistry Lane, Greenville, MS   38702

CEO: Samuel H. Silver, Pres.

Tel: (662) 332-1594

Bus: *Import/sale of carpets.*

Fax: (662) 332-1581

● BRITAX INTERNATIONAL PLC

Seton House, Warwick Tech Park, Warwick CV34 6DE, UK

CEO: Richard E. Marton, CEO

Tel: 44-192-640-0040

Rev: $1,008

Bus: *Mfr. auto components, consumer and special products, including aircraft equipment, vehicle leasing and childcare products.*

Fax: 44-192-640-6300

Emp: 6,830

www.britax.com

BRITAX AIRCRAFT INTERIOR EQUIPMENT

8011 South 187th Street, Kent, WA   98032

CEO: Kip Durrell, Pres.

Tel: (425) 656-2965

%FO: 100

Bus: *Auto components, consumer and special products, including aircraft equipment, vehicle leasing and childcare products.*

Fax: (425) 656-2975

BRITAX CHILD SAFETY, INC.

13501 South Ridge Drive, Charlotte, NC   28273

CEO: Tom Baloga, Pres.

Tel: (704) 409-1700

%FO: 100

Bus: *Mfr. childcare products.*

Fax: (704) 409-1710

BRITAX CHILD SAFETY, INC.

460 R Greenway Industrial Drive, Fort Mill, SC   29715

CEO: Tom Baloga, Pres.

Tel: (803) 802-2022

%FO: 100

Bus: *Mfr. childcare products.*

Fax: (803) 802-2023

BRITAX PUBLIC SAFETY EQUIPMENT, INC.

10986 North Warson Road, St. Louis, MO   63114-2029

CEO: Thomas O'Brien, Pres.

Tel: (314) 426-2700

%FO: 100

Bus: *Mfr. automotive components.*

Fax: (314) 426-1337

BRITAX VISION SYSTEMS INC.

1855 Busha Highway, Marysville, MI 48040

CEO: Scot Smith, Pres.	Tel: (810) 364-4141	%FO: 100
Bus: *Mfr. auto components, consumer and special products, including aircraft equipment, vehicle leasing and childcare products.*	Fax: (810) 364-6821	

• BRITISH AIRWAYS PLC

PO Box 365, Harmondsworth, West Drayton UB7 0GB, UK

CEO: Roderick Ian Eddington, CEO	Tel: 44-208-759-5511	Rev: $14,250
Bus: *International air transport services.*	Fax: 44-208-759-4314	Emp: 65,150
	www.british-airways.com	

BRITISH AIRWAYS (US), INC.

1850 K Street NW, Suite 300, Washington, DC 20006

CEO: Michael J. Trump	Tel: (202) 393-4193	%FO: 100
Bus: *Government affairs representative office.*	Fax: (202) 331-8120	

BRITISH AIRWAYS (US), INC.

75-20 Astoria Boulevard, Jackson Heights, NY 11370

CEO: Dan Brewin, EVP	Tel: (718) 397-4000	%FO: 100
Bus: *International air transport services.*	Fax: (718) 397-4364	Emp: 5,000

• BAT INDUSTRIES (BRITISH AMERICAN TOBACCO PLC)

4 Temple Place, London WC2R 2PG, UK

CEO: Martin F. Broughton, Chmn. & CEO	Tel: 44-207-845-1000	Rev: $30,375
Bus: *Mfr. tobacco products, including Kent, Benson & Hedges and Rothmans.*	Fax: 44-207-845-2118	Emp: 90,000
	www.bat.com	

BROWN & WILLIAMSON TOBACCO CORPORATION

PO Box 35090, Louisville, KY 40232

CEO: Susan Ivey, Pres. & CEO	Tel: (502) 568-7000	%FO: 100
Bus: *U.S. headquarters operation for tobacco products.*	Fax: (502) 568-7494	Emp: 6,000

BROWN & WILLIAMSON TOBACCO CORPORATION

2600 Weaver Road, Mason, GA 31217

CEO: Susan Ivey, Pres. & CEO	Tel: (912) 464-0561	%FO: 100
Bus: *Mfr. tobacco products.*	Fax: (912) 464-4048	

● **BRITISH BROADCASTING CORPORATION**

Broadcasting House, Portlands Place, London W1A 1AA, UK

CEO: Greg Dyke, Dir.	Tel: 44-207-580-4468	Rev: $4,781
Bus: *Engaged in international radio and television broadcasting.*	Fax: 44-207-765-1181 www.bbc.co.uk	Emp: 23,650

    BBC AMERICA, INC.

    7475 Wisconsin Avenue, Ste. 1100, Bethesda, MD 20814

CEO: Peter Phippen, CEO	Tel: (301) 347-2200	%FO: 100
Bus: *Engaged in international television broadcasting.*	Fax: (301) 656-8591	

● **BRITISH ENERGY PLC**

10 Lochside Place, Edinburgh EH12 9DF, UK

CEO: Oliver D. Kingsley Jr., Chmn.	Tel: 44-131-527-2000	Rev: $3,008
Bus: *Operates nuclear power plants.*	Fax: 44-131-527-2277 www.british-energy.co.uk	Emp: 5,250

    AMERGEN ENERGY

    200 Exelon Way, Kennett Square, PA 19348

CEO: Robin Jeffrey, CEO	Tel: (610) 765-5493	%FO: JV
Bus: *Operates nuclear power plants.*	Fax: (610) 765-5789	Emp: 790

● **BRITISH TELECOMMUNICATIONS PLC**

81 Newgate Street, London EC1A 7AJ, UK

CEO: Sir Peter Bonfield	Tel: 44-207-356 5000	Rev: $27,300
Bus: *Telecommunications and information systems/services.*	Fax: 44-207-356 5520 www.bt.net	Emp: 124,700

    BT NORTH AMERICA, INC.

    601 Pennsylvania Avenue NW, Ste. 725, Washington, DC 20004

CEO: James E. Graf II, Pres.	Tel: (202) 639-8222	%FO: 100
Bus: *Telecommunications services..*	Fax: (202) 434-8867	

    CONCERT COMMUNICATIONS COMPANY

    1230 Peachtree Street NE, Ste. 2000, Atlanta, GA 30309

CEO: David Dorman, CEO	Tel: (404) 879-3000	%FO: 100
Bus: *Telecommunications services.*	Fax: (404) 879-3016	

    YELLOW BOOK INC.

    40 Richards Avenue, Norwalk, CT 06854

CEO: Joseph Walsh, CEO	Tel: (203) 663-2000	%FO: 100
Bus: *Publishes community and business directories.*	Fax: (203) 663-2000	

YELLOW BOOK INC.
100 North Centre Avenue, Rockville Centre, NY   11570
CEO: Joseph Walsh, CEO   Tel: (516) 766-1900   %FO: 100
Bus: *Publishes community and business*   Fax: (516) 766-1909
    directories.

• BRITISH VITA PLC
Oldham Road, Middleton Manchester M24 2DB, UK
CEO: James Mercer, Chmn.   Tel: 44-161-643-1133   Rev: $1,409
Bus: *Mfr. foam and foam products.*   Fax: 44-161-653-5411   Emp: 15,350
    www.britishvita.com

CREST FOAM INDUSTRIES INC.
100 Carol Place, Moonachie, NJ   07074-1387
CEO: Donald E. Bellew, Pres.   Tel: (201) 807-0809   %FO: 100
Bus: *Mfr. controlled pore reticulated*   Fax: (201) 807-1113
    polyurethane foams for industrial
    applications.

IMPERIAL PACKAGING CORP.
1230 Sunset Drive, Thomasville, GA   31792
CEO: D. Williams, Mgr.   Tel: (912) 228-4554   %FO: 100
Bus: *Mfr. foam products.*   Fax: (912) 225-1726

SPARTECH CORPORATION
7733 Forsyth Boulevard, Ste. 1450, Clayton, MO   63105-1817
CEO: Bradley B. Buechler, CEO   Tel: (314) 721-4242   %FO: 100
Bus: *Mfr. extruded sheet and rollstock,*   Fax: (314) 721-1447
    specialty plastic alloys,
    compounds and color concentrates.

• BUNZL PLC
110 Park Street, London W1Y 3RB, UK
CEO: Anthony Habgood, Chmn.   Tel: 44-207-495-4950   Rev: $3,440
Bus: *Mfr. plastic products,*   Fax: 44-207-495-4953   Emp: 10,000
    marketing/distribute building materials,   www.bunzl.com
    paper & plastic disposables.

ALLIANCE PLASTICS
3123 Station Road, Erie, PA   16510
CEO: Tony Herbert, Pres.   Tel: (814) 899-7671
Bus: *Mfr. plastic protection solutions.*   Fax: (814) 898-1638

BUNZL USA INC.
701 Emerson Road, St. Louis, MO   63141
CEO: Paul Lorenzini, Pres.   Tel: (314) 997-5959   %FO: 100
Bus: *Distribution of paper & plastic*   Fax: (314) 997-1405
     products, building materials.

● **BURMAH CASTROL PLC, DIV. BP AMOCO**
Pipers Way, Swindon, Wiltshire SN3 1RE, UK
CEO: Jonathan Fry, Chmn.   Tel: 44-179-351-1521   Rev: $4,700
Bus: *Lubricants, chemicals, fuels, LNG*   Fax: 44-179-351-3506   Emp: 19,000
     transport, energy investment.   www.burmah-castrol.com

     CASTROL HOLDINGS INC.
     1500 Valley Road, Wayne, NJ   07470
     CEO: Peter Meola, Pres.   Tel: (973) 633-2200   %FO: 100
     Bus: *Mfr. industrial and auto lubricants.*   Fax: (973) 633-9867   Emp: 1,600

     CASTROL INDUSTRIAL NA INC.
     1100 West 31st Street, Downers Grove, IL   60515
     CEO: Charles Gaiser, Pres.   Tel: (630) 241-4000   %FO: 100
     Bus: *Mfr. industrial and auto lubricants.*   Fax:

● **CABLE & WIRELESS PLC**
124 Theobalds Road, London WC1X 8RX, UK
CEO: Graham Wallace, CEO   Tel: 44-207-350-4000   Rev: $12,800
Bus: *Global telecommunications services and*   Fax: 44-207-315 5000   Emp: 50,700
     products.   www.cwplc.com

     CABLE & WIRELESS COMMUNICATIONS, INC.
     777 Third Avenue, New York, NY   10017
     CEO: John Stewart, VP   Tel: (212) 407-2049   %FO: 100
     Bus: *Investor relations representatives.*   Fax: (212) 593-9069

     CABLE & WIRELESS COMMUNICATIONS, INC.
     8219 Leesburg Pike, Vienna, VA   22182-2625
     CEO: W. B. Rivers, Pres.   Tel: (703) 790-5300   %FO: 100
     Bus: *Telecommunications services &*   Fax: (703) 905-7099
     equipment.

● **CADBURY SCHWEPPES PLC**
25 Berkeley Square, London W1X 6HT, UK
CEO: John Sunderland, CEO   Tel: 44-207-409-1313   Rev: $6,950
Bus: *Mfr./franchiser confectionery products*   Fax: 44-207-830 5200   Emp: 37,425
     and soft drinks, including Snapple,   www.cadburyschweppes.com
     Mistic and Stewart's root beer.

DR. PEPPER INC.
5301 Legacy Drive, Plano, TX 75024
CEO: Jack Kilduff, Pres. & CEO   Tel: (972) 673-7000   %FO: 100
Bus: *Mfr./sales Dr. Pepper soft drinks.*   Fax: (972) 673-7980

DR. PEPPER / SEVEN-UP BOTTLING GROUP
2304 Century Center Blvd., Irving, TX 75062
CEO: Jim Turner, CEO   Tel: (972) 579-1024   %FO: 100
Bus: *Bottles/distributes soft drinks.*   Fax: (972) 721-8147

DR. PEPPER/SEVEN-UP, INC.
5301 Legacy Drive, Plano, TX 75204
CEO: Doug Tough, CEO   Tel: (972) 673-7000   %FO: 100
Bus: *Mfr. fruit drinks, franchise soft drinks.*   Fax: (972) 673-7980   Emp: 2,700

● CAPITAL SAFETY GROUP LTD.
6 Canon Harnett Court, Wolverton Mill, Milton Keynes MK1 25NF, UK
CEO: Paul T. Trinder, CEO   Tel: 44-190-831-7600
Bus: *Mfr. rescue and fall protection equipment.*   Fax: 44-190-831-7611

CAPITAL SAFETY GROUP
2915 Waters Road, Ste. 112, Eagan, MN 55121
CEO: James H. Beardsley, Pres.   Tel: (651) 686-6629
Bus: *Mfr. rescue equipment.*   Fax: (651) 686-6862

DBI/SALA
3965 Pepin Avenue, Red Wing, MN 55066
CEO: James H. Beardsley, Pres.   Tel: (651) 388-8282   %FO: 100
Bus: *Mfr. fall protection and rescue equipment.*   Fax: (651) 388-5065

PROTECTA INTERNATIONAL
8748 Clay Road, Houston, TX 77080
CEO: Paul Illick, Mgr.   Tel: (713) 460-2442
Bus: *Mfr./sales fall protection safety equipment.*   Fax: (713) 460-1990

SINCO/SALA INC.
701 Middle Street, Middletown, CT 06457
CEO: David S. Denny, Pres.   Tel: (860) 632-0500
Bus: *Mfr./sales safety nets and fall protection equipment.*   Fax: (860) 632-1509

● **CARLTON COMMUNICATIONS PLC**
25 Knightsbridge, London SWIX 7RZ, UK

CEO: Gerry Murphy, CEO	Tel: 44-207-663-6363	Rev: $3,024
Bus: *Video systems mfr., media, television &*	Fax: 44-207-663-6300	Emp: 13,400
feature film production.	www.carltonplc.co.uk	

     TECHNICOLOR FILM SERVICES
     4050 Lankershim Blvd., North Hollywood, CA   91608

CEO: Walter Schonfeld, Pres.	Tel: (818) 769-8500	%FO: 100
Bus: *Video, television and feature film*	Fax: (818) 769-1027	
production.		

● **CAZENOVE GROUP PLC**
12 Tokenhouse Yard, London EC2R 7AN, UK

CEO: David Mayhew, Chmn.	Tel: 44-207-588-2828	
Bus: *Securities broker/dealer, money*	Fax: 44-207-606-9205	Emp: 900
management, and investment banking.	www.cazenove.co.uk	

     CAZENOVE & COMPANY
     1177 Avenue of the Americas, 39th Fl., New York, NY   10036

CEO: Matthew D. Neville, Pres.	Tel: (212) 376-1225	%FO: 100
Bus: *Securities broker/dealer, money*	Fax: (212) 376-6160	Emp: 32
management, and investment		
banking.		

● **CEDAR GROUP PLC**
78 Portsmouth Road, Cobham Surrey KT11 1HY, UK

CEO: Michael G. Harrison, CEO	Tel: 44-193-258-4000	Rev: $58
Bus: *Provides business software solutions.*	Fax: 44-193-258-4001	Emp: 322
	www.cedargroup.co.uk	

     CEDAR USA INC.
     8303 Mopac, Ste. C-260, Austin, TX   78759

CEO: Tom Rump	Tel: (512) 241-2140	%FO: 75
Bus: *Provides business software*	Fax: (512) 241-0875	
solutions.		

     CEDAR USA INC.
     13402 N. Scottsdale Road, Ste. Q, Scottsdale, AZ   85254-4055

CEO: Tom Rump	Tel: (480) 607-0582	%FO: 75
Bus: *Provides business software*	Fax: (480) 607-2945	
solutions.		

CEDAR USA INC.
101 East 52nd Street, 17th Fl., New York, NY 10022
CEO: Tom Rump   Tel: (212) 308-3399   %FO: 75
Bus: *Provides business software*   Fax: (212) 308-7613
    solutions.

● **CELLTECH GROUP PLC**
216 Bath Road, Slough Berkshire SL1 4EN, UK
CEO: Dr. Peter J. Fellner, CEO   Tel: 44-175-353-4655   Rev: $60
Bus: *Mfr. pharmaceuticals.*   Fax: 44-175-353-6632   Emp: 575
                                    www.celltechgroup.com

    CELLTECH PHARMACEUTICALS
    PO Box 1701, Rochester, NY   14603
    CEO: Tom Parker, VP Sales   Tel: (716) 475-9000   %FO: 100
    Bus: *Mfr. pharmaceuticals.*   Fax: (716) 475-1016

    MEDEVA PHARMACEUTICALS
    423 LaGrange Street, West Roxbury, MA   02132-3314
    CEO: Tom Parker, VP Sales   Tel: (617) 323-7404   %FO: 100
    Bus: *Mfr. inhalation drug products.*   Fax: (617) 323-6940

● **CGNU PLC**
PO Box 420, St. Helen's 1 Undershaft, London EC3P 3DQ, UK
CEO: Richard Harvey, CEO   Tel: 44-207-283-2000   Rev: $25,921
Bus: *General insurance underwriters and*   Fax: 44-207-283-1655   Emp: 70,000
    investment advisory services.   www.cgugroup.com

    CGU CALIFORNIA INSURANCE
    801 North Brand Blvd., Ste. 800, Glendale, CA   91203
    CEO: Mark A. Koman, VP   Tel: (818) 247-5001   %FO: 100
    Bus: *Insurance services.*   Fax: (818) 637-5818

    CGU GULF INSURANCE
    504 South Service Road East, Ruston, LA   71270-3404
    CEO: M. Wayne Hanson, Pres.   Tel: (318) 255-2622   %FO: 100
    Bus: *Insurance services.*   Fax: (318) 254-4231

    CGU INSURANCE COMPANY
    One Beacon Street, Boston, MA   02108
    CEO: Robert C. Gowdy, Pres. & CEO   Tel: (617) 725-6000   %FO: 100
    Bus: *Insurance services.*   Fax: (617) 725-6702

    CGU INSURANCE COMPANY
    100 Corporate Pkwy., Ste. 200, Buffalo, NY   14226
    CEO: Alexander F. Oristian, Pres.   Tel: (716) 862-5500   %FO: 100
    Bus: *Insurance services.*   Fax: (716) 862-1289

CGU INSURANCE COMPANY
3555 Kolar Blvd., Ste. 200, Duluth, GA   30096
CEO: R. Ken Sauvage, Pres.   Tel: (678) 380-8734   %FO: 100
Bus: *Insurance services.*   Fax: (678) 380-7523

CGU INSURANCE COMPANY
One Constitution Way, Foxborough, MA   02035-2661
CEO: Michael R. Keane, Pres.   Tel: (508) 549-8747   %FO: 100
Bus: *Insurance services.*   Fax: (508) 549-8733

CGU INSURANCE COMPANY
300 North Meridian Street, Ste. 1400, Indianapolis, IN   46204-1756
CEO: William J. Mead, VP   Tel: (317) 632-1451   %FO: 100
Bus: *Insurance services.*   Fax: (317) 686-5661

CGU INSURANCE COMPANY
8405 North Fresco Street, Ste. 301, Fresno, CA   93720
CEO: Joseph Mattingly, VP   Tel: (559) 440-0105   %FO: 100
Bus: *Insurance services.*   Fax: (559) 440-0199

CGU INSURANCE COMPANY
83 Hanover Road, Florham Park, NJ   07392
CEO: William F. Dougherty, VP   Tel: (973) 593-3249   %FO: 100
Bus: *Insurance services.*   Fax: (973) 593-3279

CGU INSURANCE COMPANY
400 Locust Street, Des Moines, IA   50309
CEO: Sanford A. Miller, Pres.   Tel: (515) 471-3600   %FO: 100
Bus: *Insurance services.*   Fax: (515) 471-3600

CGU INSURANCE COMPANY
5910 North Central Expressway, Ste. 500, Dallas, TX   75206
CEO: William H. Wade II   Tel: (214) 739-3919   %FO: 100
Bus: *Insurance services.*   Fax: (214) 739-3919

INTERNATIONAL MARINE UNDERWRITERS
77 Water Street, New York, NY   10005-4488
CEO: James A. Zreblec, Chmn.   Tel: (212) 440-6500   %FO: 100
Bus: *Insurance services.*   Fax: (212) 440-6689

● **CHARTER PLC**
7 Hobart Place, London SW1W 0HH, UK
CEO: Nigel W. R. Smith, CEO   Tel: 44-207-838-7000   Rev: $1,756
Bus: *Mfr. rail tracks and welding products.*   Fax: 44-207-259-5133   Emp: 12,700
www.charterplc.com

ESAB WELDING & CUTTING GROUP
PO Box 100545, Florence, SC   29501-0545
CEO: Sam Thomas, Pres.   Tel: (843) 669-4411   %FO: 50
Bus: *Sales/distribution of welding and*   Fax: (843) 664-4459
cutting products.

● **CHLORIDE GROUP PLC**
15 Wilton Road, London SW1V 1LT, UK
CEO: Keith Hodgkinson, CEO   Tel: 44-207-834-5500
Bus: *Mfr. batteries, lighting fixtures, non-*   Fax: 44-207-630-0563   Emp: 7,800
electric transformers.   www.chloridegroup.com

CEN ELECTRONICS
One Technology Place, Caledonia, NY   14423
CEO: Verne Fleming, Mgr.   Tel: (716) 538-4421   %FO: 100
Bus: *Mfr. batteries.*   Fax: (716) 538-6017

● **CHRISTIE'S INTERNATIONAL PLC**
8 King Street, St. James, London SW1Y 6QT, UK
CEO: Christopher Balfour, Chmn.   Tel: 44-207-839-9060   Rev: $430
Bus: *Auctioneering company dealing in fine*   Fax: 44-207-839-1611   Emp: 1,850
art.   www.christies.com

CHRISTIE'S EAST
219 East 67th Street, New York, NY   10021
CEO: Edward J. Dolman, Mgr.   Tel: (212) 606-0400   %FO: 100
Bus: *Auctioning of fine art.*   Fax: (212) 737-6076

CHRISTIE'S INC.
20 Rockefeller Plaza, New York, NY   10020
CEO: Edward J. Dolman, CEO   Tel: (212) 636-2000   %FO: 100
Bus: *Auctioning of fine art.*   Fax: (212) 636-4955

CHRISTIE'S INC.
360 North Camden Drive, Beverly Hills, CA   90210
CEO: Marcia Wilson Hobbs, Chmn.   Tel: (310) 385-2600   %FO: 100
Bus: *Auctioning of fine art.*   Fax: (310) 385-9292

● **CLARKS INTERNATIONAL**
40 High Street, Somerset BA16 0YA, UK
CEO: J. D. Clothier, Mng. Dir.   Tel: 44-145-843-131
Bus: *Manufacture and sale of shoes and shoe*   Fax: 44-145-846-496
components.   www.clarks.com

THE CLARK COMPANIES
156 Oak Street, Newton Upper Falls, MA   02164
CEO: Robert Infantino, Pres.   Tel: (617) 964-1222   %FO: 100
Bus: *Shoes and shoe components.*   Fax: (617) 243-4210

● CLIFFORD CHANCE & PUNDER
200 Aldersgate Street, London EC1A 4JJ, UK
CEO: Keith Clark, Chmn.   Tel: 44-207- 600-1000   Rev: $629
Bus: *International law firm.*   Fax: 44-207-600 5555   Emp: 2,500
www.cliffordchance.com

CLIFFORD CHANCE ROGERS & WELLS
One New York Plaza, New York, NY   10004
CEO: Robert Finley, Mng. Ptnr.   Tel: (212) 709-4200   %FO: 100
Bus: *International law firm.*   Fax: (212) 709-4242   Emp: 90

● CMG PLC
Parnell House, 25 Wilton Road, London SW1 V, UK
CEO: Tom Rusting, CEO   Tel: 44-207-592-4000   Rev: $1,210
Bus: *Provides information technology*   Fax: 44-207-592-4804   Emp: 13,050
consulting.   www.cmg.com

CMG WIRELESS DATA SOLUTIONS, INC.
547 Amherst Street, 3rd Fl., Nashua, NH   03063
CEO: Ian Taylor, HR   Tel: (603) 578-4300   %FO: 100
Bus: *Provides information technology*   Fax: (603) 578-4310
consulting.

● COATS PLC
2 Fouberts' Place, London W1V 1H, UK
CEO: Martin Flower, Pres.   Tel: 44-207-302-2300   Rev: $2,383
Bus: *Mfr. textiles, yarns, fabrics and*   Fax: 44-207-302-2340   Emp: 49,450
precision engineering products.   www.coats-viyella.com

COATS & CLARK, INC.
30 Patewood Drive, Ste. 351, Greenville, SC   29615
CEO: Michael Pratt, Pres.   Tel: (864) 234-0331   %FO: 100
Bus: *Manufacturer of threads.*   Fax: (864) 234-0103   Emp: 65

COATS VIYELLA NORTH AMERICA, INC.
Two Lake Point Plaza, 4135 South Stream Drive, Charlotte, NC   28217
CEO: Thomas Smith, CEO   Tel: (704) 329-5800   %FO: 100
Bus: *U.S. holding company.*   Fax: (704) 329-5820   Emp: 180

● **COBHAM PLC**

Brook Road, Wimbourne, Dorset BH21 2BJ, UK

CEO: Gordon F. Page, CEO

Bus: *Mfr. fuel tanks and air-to-air flight refueling equipment.*

Tel: 44-120-288-2020
Fax: 44-120-284-0523
www.cobham.com

Rev: $848
Emp: 6,950

    CARLETON TECHNOLOGIES INC.

    10 Cobham Drive, Orchard Park, NY 14127

    CEO: Ms. Sherell Wozniak

    Bus: *Mfr. pneumatic systems and life support equipment.*

    Tel: (716) 662-0006
    Fax: (716) 662-0747

    %FO: 100

    CONAX FLORIDA CORPORATION

    2801 75TH Street North, St. Petersburg, FL 33710

    CEO: Glenn R. Schmidt

    Bus: *Mfr. electro-explosive actuated valves, life preserver auto inflators and gas storage systems.*

    Tel: (727) 345-8000
    Fax: (727) 345-4217

    %FO: 100

● **COMPASS GROUP PLC**

Cowley House, Guildford Street, Chertsey, Surrey KT16 9BA, UK

CEO: Michael J. Bailey, CEO

Bus: *Engaged in food service contract and catering, restaurant and food outlets.*

Tel: 44-193-257-3000
Fax: 44-193-256-9956
www.compass-group.com

Rev: $12,000
Emp: 265,000

    CANTEEN CORPORATION

    3800 South Shelby Street, Indianapolis, IN 46227

    CEO: Jeff Hart, Mgr.

    Bus: *Provides food service.*

    Tel: (317) 787-8226
    Fax: (317) 781-7739

    %FO: 100

    COMPASS GROUP FOOD SERVICE CORP.

    4808 Chesapeake Drive, Charlotte, NC 28216

    CEO: Cheryl Webster

    Bus: *Provides food service.*

    Tel: (704) 394-4177
    Fax: (704) 394-6853

    %FO: 100

    SHRM CATERING, INC.

    PO Box 80798, Lafayette, LA 70598

    CEO: John Hudelot, VP

    Bus: *Provides catering services.*

    Tel: (318) 233-9153
    Fax: (318) 264-1198

    %FO: 100

● **COOKSON GROUP PLC**

Adelphi 1-11, John Adam Street, London 6HJ WC2N, UK

CEO: Stephen L. Howard, CEO

Bus: *Mfr./process industrial materials.*

Tel: 44-207-766-4500
Fax: 44-207-747-6600
www.cooksongroup.co.uk

Rev: $3,010
Emp: 17,100

COOKSON AMERICA INC.

One Cookson Place, Providence, RI   02903

CEO: Stuart L. Daniels, Pres.

Bus: *Sales/distribution of electronics, ceramics and plastics.*

Tel: (401) 521-1000

Fax: (401) 521-5273

%FO: 100

● **CORDIANT COMMUNICATIONS GROUP**

121-141 Westbourne Terrace, London W2 6JR, UK

CEO: Charles T. Scott, Chmn.

Bus: *Engaged global marketing communications.*

Tel: 44-207-262-4343

Fax: 44-207-262-4300

www.ccgww.com

Rev: $2,600

Emp: 10,000

BATES WORLDWIDE

The Chrysler Bldg., 405 Lexington Ave., New York, NY   10174

CEO: Bill Whitehead, CEO

Bus: *Engaged in advertising and marketing.*

Tel: (212) 297-7000

Fax: (212) 986-0270

%FO: 100

Emp: 7,011

ZENITH MEDIA SERVICE, INC., DIV. BATES WORLDWIDE

299 Hudson Street, New York, NY   10014

CEO: Rich Hamilton, CEO

Bus: *Media services agency.*

Tel: (212) 859-5100

Fax: (212) 886-8803

%FO: 1

● **CORPORATE SERVICES GROUP PLC**

24 Stafford Place, London SW 1E 6NG, UK

CEO: Peter Owen, CEO

Bus: *Temporary staff services.*

Tel: 44-207-931-9900

Fax: 44-207-802-0065

www.corporateservices.co.uk

Rev: $1,857

Emp: 7,000

CORESTAFF SERVICES

1775 St. James Place, Ste. 300, Houston, TX   77056

CEO: Sally DeVite, PR

Bus: *Temporary staff services.*

Tel: (713) 438-1400

Fax: (713) 438-1763

%FO: 100

● **CORUS GROUP, PLC**

15 Great Marlborough Street, London W1F 7AS, UK

CEO: Brian S. Moffat, Chmn.

Bus: *Steel production, rollings, processing and distribution.*

Tel: 44-207-717-4444

Fax: 44-207-717-4455

www.corusgroup.com

Rev: $17,491

Emp: 64,900

AVESTAPOLARIT, INC.

3043 Crenshaw Pkwy., Richburg, SC   29729

CEO: Lou Kern, EVP

Bus: *Mfr. steel bar products.*

Tel: (803) 789-5383

Fax: (803) 789-3177

%FO:

AVESTAPOLARIT, INC.
475 North Martingale Road, Ste. 400, Schaumburg, IL 60173
CEO: Mike Rinker, Pres.   Tel: (847) 517-4050   %FO:
Bus: *Mfr. steel products.*   Fax: (847) 517-2950

AVESTAPOLARIT, INC.
1101 North Main Street, Wildwood, FL 34785
CEO: Roy Cooke, EVP   Tel: (352) 748-1313   %FO:
Bus: *Mfr. steel plate and tubular*   Fax: (352) 748-6576
     products.

AVESTAPOLARIT, INC.
3176 Abbott Road, Orchard Park, NY 14127
CEO: Paul Carpenter, VP   Tel: (716) 827-4400   %FO:
Bus: *Mfr. welding products.*   Fax: (716) 827-4404

CORUS STEEL INC.
475 North Martingale Road, Ste. 400, Schaumburg, IL 60173
CEO: Thomas E. Kinley, Pres.   Tel: (847) 619-0400   %FO: 100
Bus: *Sales/distribution of steel products.* Fax: (847) 619-0468

TUSCALOOSA STEEL CORPORATION
1700 Holt Road NE, Tuscaloosa, AL 35404
CEO: Alan Warburton, CEO   Tel: (205) 556-1310   %FO: 100
Bus: *Mfr. steel plate in coil.* Fax: (205) 556-1482

● **COUTTS & COMPANY (DIV. NATIONAL WESTMINSTER BANK PLC)**
440 Strand Street, London WC2R 0QS, UK
CEO: Lord Home, Chmn.   Tel: 44-207-753-1000
Bus: *International private banking services.* Fax: 44-207-753-1050   Emp: 3,800
                                        www.coutts.com

COUTTS (USA) INTERNATIONAL
701 Brickell Avenue, Suite 300, Miami, FL 33131
CEO: Patricia Gehle McCormack, VP   Tel: (305) 789-3700   %FO: 100
Bus: *International private banking*   Fax: (305) 789-3724   Emp: 19
     services.

● **CRODA INTL PLC**
Cowick Hall, Snaith Goole, N. Humberside, DN14 9AA, UK
CEO: Michael Humphrey, CEO   Tel: 44-140-586-0551   Rev: $601
Bus: *Chemical specialties.*   Fax: 44-140-586-0202   Emp: 2,425
                                www.croda.co.uk

CRODA INC.
7 Century Drive, Parsippany, NJ   07054-4698
CEO: Kevin F. Gallagher, Pres.   Tel: (973) 644-4900   %FO: 100
Bus: *Chemical specialties*   Fax: (973) 644-9222

● **DAILY MAIL AND GENERAL TRUST (DMGT) PLC**
Northcliffe House, 2 Derry Street, Kensington, London W8 5TT, UK
CEO: Charles J. F. Sinclair, CEO   Tel: 44-207-938-6000   Rev: $2,721
Bus: *Media holding company.*   Fax: 44-207-937-3745   Emp: 18,000
                                        www.dmgt.co.uk

DMG INFORMATION LIMITED
68 Southfield Avenue, Ste. 210, Stamford, CT   06902
CEO: Martha Notaras, EVP   Tel: (203) 973-2940   %FO: 100
Bus: *Distribution of associated*   Fax: (203) 973-2995
      newspapers.

RMS, INC.
7015 Gateway Boulevard, Newark, CA   94560
CEO: Hemant Shah, Pres.   Tel: (510) 505-2500   %FO: 100
Bus: *Provides products and services for*   Fax: (510) 505-2501
      the quantification and
      management of natural hazard
      risks.

RMS, INC.
744 Broad Street, 14th Fl., Newark, NJ   07102
CEO: Hemant Shah, Pres.   Tel: (973) 848-4900   %FO: 100
Bus: *Provides products and services for*   Fax: (973) 848-4901
      the quantification and
      management of natural hazard
      risks.

RMS, INC.
621 SW Commercial, Ste. D, Peoria, Il   61602
CEO: John Abraham   Tel: (309) 637-6350   %FO: 100
Bus: *Provides products and services for*   Fax: (309) 637-6750
      the quantification and
      management of natural hazard
      risks.

● **DANKA BUSINESS SYSTEMS PLC**
33 Cavendish Square, 18th Fl., London W1MODE, UK
CEO: David W. Kendall, Chmn.   Tel: 44-207-603-1515   Rev: $2,496
Bus: *Mfr./distributes photocopiers, fax*   Fax: 44-207-603-8448   Emp: 17,000
      machines and paper supplies.   www.danka.com

DANKA BUSINESS SYSTEMS
11201 Danka Circle North, St. Petersburg, FL   33716

CEO: Brian L. Merriman, Pres.   Tel: (727) 576-6003   %FO: 100

Bus: *Sales/distribution of photocopiers*   Fax: (727) 579-0832
      and fax machines.

• DATAMONITOR PLC
108-110 Finchley Road, London NW3 5JJ, UK

CEO: Thomas E. Gardner, CEO   Tel: 44-207-675-7000   Rev: $47

Bus: *Engaged in market analysis.*   Fax: 44-207-675-7500   Emp: 600

www.datamonitor.com

DATAMONITOR INC.
One Park Avenue, 14th Fl., New York, NY   10016-5802

CEO: Tara Rummell, PR   Tel: (212) 686-7400   %FO: 100

Bus: *Engaged in market analysis for the*   Fax: (212) 686-2626
      technology industry.

• DAWSON HOLDINGS PLC
AMP House, 9th Fl. Dingwall Road, Croydon CR0 9XA, UK

CEO: David Blundell, Mng. Dir.   Tel: 44-208-667-0770   Rev: $916

Bus: *Distributes print and media; books,*   Fax: 44-208-774-3010   Emp: 3,400
      magazines and newspapers.   www.dawson.co.uk

QUALITY BOOKS INC.
1003 W. Pines Road, Oregon, IL   61061-9680

CEO: Harold G. Sterling   Tel: (815) 732-4450   %FO: 100

Bus: *Distributor of small press books,*   Fax: (815) 732-4499
      special interest videos, audio
      tapes, CDs, CD-ROMs and DVDs.

• DCS GROUP PLC
48 George Street, London W1H 5RF, UK

CEO: Tim M. Robinson, CEO   Tel: 44-207-616-1800   Rev: $210

Bus: *Engaged in information technology*   Fax: 44-207-616-1801   Emp: 1,637
      services; computer systems for transport   www.dcsgroup.co.uk
      and logistics.

DCS TRANSPORT SOLUTIONS
426 Vista Suerte, Newport Beach, CA   92660

CEO: Linda Heath   Tel: (949) 719-9982   %FO: 100

Bus: *Engaged in information*   Fax: (949) 719-9982
      technology services.

DCS TRANSPORT SOLUTIONS
538 Broadhollow Road, Ste. 420E, Melville, NY   11747

CEO: Alice Sciara	Tel: (631) 752-7700	%FO: 100
Bus: *Engaged in information technology services.*	Fax: (631) 752-7829	

DCS TRANSPORT SOLUTIONS
1555 Mittel Boulevard, Ste. G, Wood Dale, IL   60191

CEO: Shanna Miller	Tel: (630) 595-0210	%FO: 100
Bus: *Engaged in information technology services.*	Fax: (630) 595-0212	

• DE LA RUE PLC
Jays Close, Viables, Basingstoke, Hampshire RG22 4BS, UK

CEO: Ian Much, CEO	Tel: 44-125-632-9122	Rev: $982
Bus: *Provides security print banknotes and payment systems.*	Fax: 44-125-660-5336 www.delarue.com	Emp: 7,370

DE LA RUE FARADAY
4250 Pleasant Valley Road, Chantilly, VA   22021-1213

CEO: S. L .Schulman, Pres.	Tel: (703) 263-0100	%FO: 100
Bus: *Payment card processing.*	Fax: (703) 263-0503	

DE LA RUE CARD SYSTEMS, INC.
523 James Hance Court, Exton, PA   19341

CEO: David Stonley, Pres.	Tel: (610) 524-2410	%FO: 100
Bus: *Currency handling and security systems.*	Fax:	

DE LA RUE CASH SYSTEMS INC.
2441 Warrenville Road, Ste. 100, Lisle, IL   60532

CEO: Gary Mroz, Pres.	Tel: (630) 245-0100	%FO: 100
Bus: *U.S. headquarters; currency handling and security systems.*	Fax: (888) 308-8993	

DE LA RUE SECURITY PRINT INC.
100 Powers Court, Dulles, VA   20166

CEO: Michael Little, Pres.	Tel: (703) 450-1300	%FO: 100
Bus: *Commercial printer of banknotes and security documents.*	Fax: (703) 450-1308	

DE LA RUE SYSTEMS LATIN AMERICA INC.
7270 Northwest 12th Street, Ste. 140, Miami, FL   33126

CEO: Bernardo Hernandez, Mgr.	Tel: (305) 629-8505	%FO: 100
Bus: *Currency handling and security systems.*	Fax: (305) 629-8512	

• DELCAM PLC

Small Heath Business Park, Birmingham B10 OHJ, UK

CEO: Hugh R.O. Humphreys, Mng. Dir.   Tel: 44-121-766-5544   Rev: $26

Bus: *Mfr. software for design and*   Fax: 44-121-766-5511   Emp: 230
manufacturing.   www.delcam.com

    AXSYS INCORPORATED

    29627 West Tech Drive, Wixom, MI   48393

    CEO: Mark J. Bonney, Pres. & CEO   Tel: (248) 926-8810   %FO: 100

    Bus: *Mfr. software for design and*   Fax: (248) 926-9085
    manufacturing.

    PROGRAMMING PLUS, INC.

    17685 West Lincoln Avenue, New Berlin, WI   53146

    CEO: Tom Bentley, CEO   Tel: (262) 786-3500   %FO: 100

    Bus: *Mfr. software for design and*   Fax: (262) 786-3501
    manufacturing.

    SURFWARE, INC., DIV. PROGRAMMING PLUS

    5703 Corsa Avenue, Westlake Village, CA   91362

    CEO: Alan Diehl, CEO   Tel: (818) 991-1960   %FO: 100

    Bus: *Mfr. software for design and*   Fax: (818) 991-1980
    manufacturing.

• DELTA PLC

One Kingsway, London WC2B 6XF, UK

CEO: Jon Scott-Maxwell, CEO   Tel: 44-207-836-3535   Rev: $1,475

Bus: *Mfr. engineering and electrical*   Fax: 44-207-836-4511   Emp: 11,000
equipment.   www.deltaplc.com

    ACCURATE FORGING CORPORATION

    201 Pine Street, Bristol, CT   06010

    CEO: Anna A. Petrova, Mgr.   Tel: (860) 582-3169   %FO: 100

    Bus: *Mfr. brass forgings.*   Fax: (860) 583-3495

    DELTA AMERICA, INC.

    433 South Main Street, Ste. 117, West Hartford, CT   06110

    CEO: Todd G. Atkinson, Pres.   Tel: (860) 561-2244   %FO: 100

    Bus: *Holding company.*   Fax: (860) 561-2083

    INNOVATIVE TECHNOLOGY INC.

    15470 Flight Path Drive, Brooksville, FL   34609

    CEO: Frank Casagni, Mgr.   Tel: (852) 799-0713

    Bus: *Mfr. transient voltage surge*   Fax: (852) 796-0316
    suppression products.

- **DENISON INTERNATIONAL PLC**

107 Hammersmith Road, London W14 OQH, UK

CEO: David L. Weir, CEO	Tel: 44-207-603-1515	Rev: $153
Bus: *Mfr. hydraulic products for industrial machinery.*	Fax: 44-207-603-8448 www.denisonhydraulics.com	Emp: 1,072

DENISON HYDRAULICS INC.

14249 Industrial Parkway, Marysville, OH   43040

CEO: Gary Gotting, Mgr.	Tel: (937) 644-3915	%FO: 100
Bus: *Mfr. hydraulic products for industrial machinery.*	Fax: (937) 644-3915	

- **DETA BATTERIES US LTD.**

Gryphon Works Hockley Way Alfreton Trading Estate Alfreton, Derbyshire DE55 7EG, UK

CEO: Albrecht Leuschner, Pres.	Tel: 44-177-360-4231	
Bus: *Mfr. sealed industrial and automotive batteries.*	Fax: 44-177-360-7964 www.detabatteries.co.uk	Emp: 6,000

DETA-DOUGLAS BATTERIES LLC.

500 Battery Drive, PO Box 12665, Winston-Salem, NC   27117

CEO: Thomas S. Douglas, III	Tel: (336) 650-7000	%FO: JV
Bus: *Marketing batteries.*	Fax: (336) 650-7057	Emp: 2

- **DIAGEO PLC**

8 Henrietta Place, London W1M 9AG, UK

CEO: Paul S. Walsh, CEO	Tel: 44-207-927-5200	Rev: $18,000
Bus: *Distributor of food (Pillsbury, Haagen-Dazs, Burger King), wines and spirits.*	Fax: 44-207-518-4600 www.diageo.com	Emp: 72,475

BURGER KING CORPORATION

17777 Old Cutler Road, Miami, FL   33157

CEO: Mikel Durham, Pres.	Tel: (305) 378-7011	%FO: 100
Bus: *Fast food restaurant chain.*	Fax: (305) 378-7262	Emp: 17,000

HAAGEN-DAZS SHOPPE COMPANY INC., DIV. PILLSBURY COMPANY

Pillsbury Center MS 29R1, 200 South Sixth Street, Minneapolis, MN   55402-1464

CEO: John N. Lilly, Pres.	Tel: (612) 330-4966	%FO: 100
Bus: *Mfr. of ice cream products.*	Fax: (612) 330-7080	

THE PILLSBURY COMPANY

Pillsbury Center, 200 South Sixth Street, Minneapolis, MN   55402-1464

CEO: John N. Lilly, CEO	Tel: (612) 330-4966	%FO: 100
Bus: *Sales/distribution of diversified food products.*	Fax: (612) 330-5200	Emp: 14,000

UDV NORTH AMERICA, INC.
Six Landmark Square, Stamford, CT   06901
CEO: Paul Clinton, Pres. & CEO   Tel: (203) 359-7100   %FO: 100
Bus: *Import/distribution of wines and* Fax: (203) 359-7402
     spirits.

● **DIGICA LTD., SUB DCS GROUP**
Phoenix House, Colliers Way, Nottingham NG8 6AT, UK
CEO: Richard Last, CEO   Tel: 44-115-977-1177
Bus: *Engaged in outsourcing, providing end-* Fax: 44-115-977-7000
     to-end business and technology   www.digica.com
     management solutions.

   DIGICA USA, INC.
   3434 Route 22 West, Ste. 150, Branchburg, NJ   08876
   CEO: Kevin Smith, Mgr.   Tel: (908) 526-8488   %FO: 100
   Bus: *Engaged in outsourcing, providing* Fax: (908) 526-3036
        end-to-end business and
        technology management solutions.

● **DONCASTERS PLC, SUB. ROYAL BANK PRIVATE EQUITY**
28-30 Derby Road, Melbourne, Derbyshire DE73 1FE, UK
CEO: Eric Lewis, CEO   Tel: 44-133-286-4900   Rev: $465
Bus: *Mfr. airfoils and castings.*   Fax: 44-133-286-4888   Emp: 4,075
                                        www.doncasters.com

   DONCASTERS INC.
   PO Box 1970, Springfield, MA   01101-1970
   CEO: Jim Nichols, Pres. & CEO   Tel: (413) 732-1122   %FO: 100
   Bus: *Mfr. airfoils and castings.*   Fax: (413) 732-1128

   DONCASTERS PRECISION CASTINGS INC.
   PO Box 1146, Groton, CT   06840-1146
   CEO: Jim Nichols, Pres. & CEO   Tel: (860) 449-1603   %FO: 100
   Bus: *Mfr. airfoils and castings.*   Fax: (860) 449-1615

   DONCASTERS TURBO PRODUCTS INC.
   PO Box 457, Ivoryton, CT   06442
   CEO: Jim Nichols, Pres. & CEO   Tel: (860) 767-0161   %FO: 100
   Bus: *Mfr. turbo products.*   Fax: (860) 767-3093

   PED MANUFACTURING
   PO Box 5299, Oregon City, OR   97045-8299
   CEO: Dick Brozek, Mgr.   Tel: (503) 656-9653   %FO: 100
   Bus: *Mfr. airfoils and castings.*   Fax: (503) 656-1788

SOUTHERN TOOL INC.
PO Box 2248, Anniston, AL   36202
CEO: Neil Martin
Bus: *Mfr. airfoils and castings.*
Tel: (256) 831-2811
Fax: (256) 831-0902
%FO: 100

● **DOUGHTY HANSON & CO.**
Times Place 45 Pall Mall, London SW1Y 5JG, UK
CEO: Nigel E. Doughty, Dir.
Bus: *Engaged in venture capital.*
Tel: 44-207-663-9300
Fax: 44-207-663-9350
www.doughtyhanson.com

   DOUGHTY HANSON & CO.
   150 South Wacker Drive, Ste. 750, Chicago, IL   60606
   CEO: Kevin Sherman, Pres.
   Bus: *Engaged in venture capital.*
   Tel: (312) 578-1750
   Fax: (312) 578-1812
   %FO: 100

   DOUGHTY HANSON & CO.
   152 West 57th Street, New York, NY   10019
   CEO: Kevin Luzak, CEO
   Bus: *Engaged in venture capital.*
   Tel: (212) 641-3700
   Fax: (212) 641-3750
   %FO: 100

● **DRESDNER KLEINWORT WASSERSTEIN PLC, DIV. DRESDNER BANK GROUP**
20 Fenchurch Street, London EC3P 3DB, UK
CEO: Leonard H. Fischer, CEO
Bus: *Engaged in investment banking services.*
Tel: 44-207-623-8000
Fax: 44-207-623-4069
www.drkw.com
Emp: 8,500

   DRESDNER KLEINWORT WASSERSTEIN NA INC.
   190 South LaSalle Street, Ste. 2700, Chicago, IL   60603
   CEO: Carol E. Schaefer, VP
   Bus: *Provides investment banking
       services and products.*
   Tel: (312) 444-1300
   Fax: (312) 444-1192
   %FO: 100

   DRESDNER KLEINWORT WASSERSTEIN NA INC.
   75 Wall Street, New York, NY   10005
   CEO: Ulrik Trampe, Pres.
   Bus: *Provides investment banking
       services and products.*
   Tel: (212) 429-2800
   Fax: (212) 429-2127
   %FO: 100
   Emp: 60

● **DREW SCIENTIFIC GROUP PLC**
Sowerb Woods Industrial Estate, Park Road, Barrow-In-Furness, Cumbria LA1 4QR, UK
CEO: Mike Asher, CEO
Bus: *Sales of DS30 homocysteine testing
    system, a dedicated instrument
    specifically designed for the
    measurement of homocysteine.*
Tel: 44-122-943-2089
Fax: 44-122-943-2096
www.drew-scientific.com
Rev: $5
Emp: 60

DREW SCIENTIFIC INC.
1430 East Main Road, Portsmouth, RI   02871

CEO: Grant Frazier, VP	Tel: (401) 683-4042	%FO: 100
Bus: *Sales of DS30 homocysteine testing system, a dedicated instrument specifically designed for the measurement of homocysteine.*	Fax: (401) 683-3696	

● DRUCK LTD
Fir Tree Lane, Groby, Leicester LE6 0FH, UK

CEO: John Salmon, Chrm.	Tel: 44-116-231-4314	
Bus: *Mfr. pressure measuring devices.*	Fax: 44-116-875-022 www.druck.com	Emp: 500

DRUCK INC.
4 Dunham Drive, New Fairfield, CT   06812

CEO: Robert P. Knowles, Pres.	Tel: (203) 746-0400	%FO: 100
Bus: *Mfr./distribution/service pressure measuring devices.*	Fax: (203) 746-2494	Emp: 53

● DTZ HOLDINGS PLC
1 Curzon Street, London W1A 5PZ, UK

CEO: M. D. Struckett, CEO	Tel: 44-207-408-1161	Rev: $188
Bus: *Engaged in commercial real estate services.*	Fax: 44-207-643-6000 www.dtz.com	Emp: 6,500

AEW CAPITAL MANAGEMENT, INC.
601 South Figueroa Street, Los Angeles, CA   90017

CEO: Pamela J. Herhst	Tel: (213) 689-3111	%FO: 100
Bus: *Engaged in real estate investment advisory services.*	Fax: (213) 629-9160	

AEW CAPITAL MANAGEMENT, INC.
1200 18th Street, NW, Washington, DC   20036

CEO: Pamela J. Herhst	Tel: (202) 721-1552	%FO: 100
Bus: *Engaged in real estate investment advisory.*	Fax: (212) 296-7181	

AEW CAPITAL MANAGEMENT, INC.
225 Franklin Street, Boston, MA   02110

CEO: Joseph Azrack	Tel: (617) 261-9000	%FO: 100
Bus: *Engaged in real estate investment advisory services.*	Fax: (617) 261-9555	

THE STAUBACH COMPANY

405 Lexington Avenue, 17th Fl., New York, NY   10174

CEO: Hugh Kelly   Tel: (212) 221-9700   %FO: 100

Bus: *Engaged in commercial real estate* Fax: (212) 221-8584
advisory services.

THE STAUBACH COMPANY

15601 Dallas Parkway, Suite 400, Addison, TX   75001

CEO: Roger Staubach, CEO   Tel: (972) 361-5000   %FO: 100

Bus: *Engaged in commercial real estate* Fax: (972) 361-5000
advisory services.

THE STAUBACH COMPANY

301 Howard Street, Ste. 930, San Francisco, CA   94105

CEO: Matt Alexander   Tel: (415) 908-0390   %FO: 100

Bus: *Engaged in commercial real estate* Fax: (415) 908-0391
advisory services.

THE STAUBACH COMPANY

2398 East Camelback Rd., Ste. 230, Phoenix, AZ   85016

CEO: Chris Stamets   Tel: (602) 840-9333   %FO: 100

Bus: *Engaged in commercial real estate* Fax: (602) 840-9376
advisory services.

THE STAUBACH COMPANY

2025 First Avenue, Ste. 1212, Seattle, WA   98121

CEO: Rolland Jones, VP   Tel: (206) 956-9400   %FO: 100

Bus: *Engaged in commercial real estate* Fax: (206) 956-0400
advisory services.

THE STAUBACH COMPANY

2030 Main Street, Ste. 350, Irvine, CA   92614

CEO: Brian Kjos   Tel: (949) 756-6400   %FO: 100

Bus: *Engaged in commercial real estate* Fax: (949) 756-6404
advisory services.

THE STAUBACH COMPANY

140 Glastonbury Blvd., 2nd Fl., Glastonbury, CT   06033

CEO: David Dumeer   Tel: (860) 659-9191   %FO: 100

Bus: *Engaged in commercial real estate* Fax: (860) 659-8815
advisory services.

THE STAUBACH COMPANY

225 City Line Avenue, Ste. 103, Bala Cynwyd, PA   19004

CEO: David Wirth   Tel: (610) 668-2995   %FO: 100

Bus: *Engaged in commercial real estate* Fax: (610) 668-7329
advisory services.

THE STAUBACH COMPANY
321 North Clark Street, Ste. 900, Chicago, IL 60610
CEO: Steve Swanson   Tel: (312) 245-5050   %FO: 100
Bus: *Engaged in commercial real estate*   Fax: (312) 245-5022
    advisory services.

● DUNLOP SLAZENGER INTERNATIONAL LTD.
Maxfli Court, Riverside Way, Camberley, Surrey GU15 3YL, UK
CEO: Phil Parnell, CEO   Tel: 44-127-680-3399
Bus: *Mfr. sporting and athletic goods.*   Fax: 44-127-667-9680
    www.slazenger.co.uk

DUNLOP SLAZENGER GROUP AMERICAS
Box 3070, 728 N. Pleastantburg, Greenville, SC 29602
CEO: Edward Hughes, EVP   Tel: (864) 241-2200   %FO: 100
Bus: *Sales and distribution of sporting*   Fax: (864) 241-2294
    and athletic goods.

● EASYSCREEN PLC
78 Cannon Street, London EC4N 6HH, UK
CEO: Philip H. Docker, Chmn.   Tel: 44-207-645-4600
Bus: *Mfr. software to financial institutions*   Fax: 44-207-645-4667
    for trading on electronic derivatives   www.easyscreen.com
    exchanges.

EASYSCREEN INC.
350 Fifth Avenue, New York, NY 10118
CEO: James Adam, Mng. Dir.   Tel: (212) 404-7008   %FO: 100
Bus: *Mfr. software to financial*   Fax: (212) 404-7022
    institutions for trading on
    electronic derivatives exchanges.

EASYSCREEN INC.
141 West Jackson Blvd., Ste. 2740, Chicago, IL 560604
CEO: Stanley Koenig, Mng. Dir.   Tel: (312) 939-9185   %FO: 100
Bus: *Mfr. software to financial*   Fax: (312) 939-9188
    institutions for trading on
    electronic derivatives exchanges.

● THE ECONOMIST GROUP
25 St. James's Street, London SW1A 1HG, UK
CEO: Helen Alexander, CEO   Tel: 44-207-830-7000   Rev: $372
Bus: *International business and political*   Fax: 44-207-839-2968   Emp: 1,500
    news publication. (JV with Pearson, UK) www.economistgroup.com

THE ECONOMIST EDITORIAL DIV.
1235 North Olive Drive, West Hollywood, CA 90069
CEO: Elizabeth O'Rourke, Editor   Tel: (213) 650-9249   %FO: 100
Bus: *Editorial offices.*   Fax: (213) 650-9367

THE ECONOMIST ADVERTISING DIV.
509 North June Street, Los Angeles, CA 90004
CEO: Elizabeth O'Rourke, Editor   Tel: (310) 574-5385   %FO: 100
Bus: *Advertising offices.*   Fax: (310) 574-5386

THE ECONOMIST
111 West 57th Street, New York, NY 10019
CEO: Elizabeth O'Rourke, Editor   Tel: (212) 541-5730   %FO: 100
Bus: *Publishes/distributes newspaper.*   Fax: (212) 541-9379

THE ECONOMIST
1331 Pennsylvania Avenue NW, Washington, DC 20004
CEO: Elizabeth O'Rourke, Editor   Tel: (202) 783-5753   %FO: 100
Bus: *Editorial offices.*   Fax: (202) 737-1035

THE ECONOMIST/SHENANDOAH VALLEY PRESS
Route 55 East, Strasburg, VA 22657
CEO: Elizabeth O'Rourke, Editor   Tel: (703) 465-4833   %FO: 100
Bus: *Production facilities.*   Fax: (703) 465-4835

THE ECONOMIST EDITORIAL DIV.
35 East Wacker Drive, Ste. 1960, Chicago, IL 60601
CEO: Elizabeth O'Rourke, Editor   Tel: (312) 853-3835   %FO: 100
Bus: *Editorial offices.*   Fax: (312) 704-0448

● **ED&F MAN GROUP PLC**
Sugar Quay, Lower Thames Street, London EC3R 6DU, UK
CEO: Stanley Fink, CEO   Tel: 44-207-285-3000   Rev: $517
Bus: *Engaged in agricultural commodities.*   Fax: 44-207-285-3665   Emp: 4,170
www.edfman.com

EF&F MAN ALCOHOLS INC.
1105 Parkside East, Seattle, WA 98112
CEO: A. Whitfield Huguley IV, Pres.   Tel: (206) 322-2040   %FO: 100
Bus: *Engaged in commodities.*   Fax: (206) 328-2481

EF&F MAN COCOA INC.
*Two World Financial Center, 27th Fl., New York, NY 10281-2700
CEO: Josh Connell   Tel: (212) 566-9000   %FO: 100
Bus: *Engaged in commodities trading.*   Fax: (212) 566-9412

EF&F MAN SUGAR INC.
*225 Liberty Street, 27th Fl., New York, NY   10281-6127
CEO: A. Whitfield Huguley IV, Pres.   Tel: (212) 566-9000   %FO: 100
Bus: *Engaged in sugar trading.*   Fax: (212) 566-9410

WESTWAY HOLDINGS CORP.
365 Canal Place, Ste. 2900, New Orleans, LA   70130
CEO: A. Whitfield Huguley IV, Pres.   Tel: (504) 525-9741   %FO: 100
Bus: *Engaged in financial services*   Fax: (504) 525-9741
    operations.

● **EIDOS PLC**
Wimbledon Bridge House, 1 Hartfield Road, Wimbledon, London SW19 3RU, UK
CEO: Michael P. McGarvey, CEO   Tel: 44-208-636-3000   Rev: $310
Bus: *Develops and manufactures video*   Fax: 44-208-636-3001   Emp: 580
    games.   www.eidos.com

EIDOS INTERACTIVE USA, INC
651 Brannan Street, 4th Fl., San Francisco, CA   94107
CEO: Paul Baldwin, VP Mktg.   Tel: (415) 547-1200   %FO: 100
Bus: *Sales and marketing of video*   Fax: (415) 547-1201
    games.

● **ELATERAL LIMITED**
Elateral House, Crosby Way Farnham, Surrey GU16 7XX, UK
CEO: Richard Watney, CEO   Tel: 44-125-274-0740   Rev: $500
Bus: *Provides on-line printing services.*   Fax: 44-125-274-0741   Emp: 20
    www.elateral.com

ELATERAL INC.
Jefferson Office Park, 800 Turnpike Street, Ste. 101, North Andover, MA   01845
CEO: Gail Mann   Tel: (978) 557-0789   %FO: 100
Bus: *Provides on-line printing services.*   Fax: (978) 681-0666

ELATERAL INC.
5050 El Camino Real, Ste. 202, Los Altos, CA   94024
CEO: Gail Mann   Tel: (650) 969-4666   %FO: 100
Bus: *Provides on-line printing services.*   Fax: (650) 969-4667

● **ELECTROCOMPONENTS PLC**
5000 Oxford Business Park South, International Management Centre, Oxford OX4 2BH, UK
CEO: Robert A. Lawson, CEO   Tel: 44-186-520-4000   Rev: $1,212
Bus: *Distributes electronic, electrical and*   Fax: 44-186-520-7400   Emp: 4,300
    mechanical components and tools.   www.electrocomponents.com

ALLIED ELECTRONICS INC.
7410 Pebble Drive, Ft. Worth, TX   76118
CEO: Ian Mason, CEO   Tel: (800) 433-5700   %FO: 100
Bus: *Distributes electronic, electrical*   Fax: (817) 595-6444
     and mechanical components and
     tools.

• **ELEMENTIS PLC**
One Great Tower Street, London EC3R 5AH, UK
CEO: Lyndon E. Cole, CEO   Tel: 44-207-398-1400   Rev: $865
Bus: *Produces chemicals.*   Fax: 44-207-398-1401   Emp: 3,280
                                              www.elementis.com

ELEMENTIS AMERICA INC.
300 Delaware Avenue, Ste. 1257, Wilmington, DE   19801
CEO: Mark L. Barocas, Pres.   Tel: (302) 552-3104   %FO: 100
Bus: *Holding company.*   Fax:

ELEMENTIS CHROMIUM LP
Buddy Lawrence Drive, PO Box 9912, Corpus Christi, TX   78469
CEO: Mogens Jepsen   Tel: (361) 883-6421   %FO: 100
Bus: *Produces chemicals.*   Fax: (361) 883-5145

ELEMENTIS INC.
2374 Post Road, Ste. 3, Warwick, RI   02886
CEO: Mark L. Barocas, Pres.   Tel: (401) 732-2770   %FO: 100
Bus: *Produces organoclay rheological*   Fax: (401) 732-2995
     additives, urethane and acrylic
     thickeners.

ELEMENTIS LTP
546 South Water Street, Milwaukee, WI   53204
CEO: Adel Hanna, Pres.   Tel: (414) 278-8844   %FO: 100
Bus: *Produces chemicals.*   Fax:

ELEMENTIS PIGMENTS INC.
11 Executive Drive, Fairview Heights, IL   62208
CEO: David Dutro, Pres.   Tel: (618) 628-2300   %FO: 100
Bus: *Produces chemicals.*   Fax: (618) 628-1029

HARCROS CHEMICALS INC.
5200 Speaker Road, Kansas City, KS   66016
CEO: Robert Mann, Pres.   Tel: (913) 321-3131   %FO: 100
Bus: *Produces chemicals.*   Fax: (913) 621-7718

LINATEX CORPORATION OF AMERICA
1550 Airport Road, Gallatin, TN   37066

CEO: Peter Hall, VP   Tel: (615) 230-2100   %FO: 100

Bus: *Produces chemicals.*   Fax: (615) 230-2109

RHEOX, INC.
PO Box 700, Heightstown, NJ   08920

CEO: Neil Carter, CEO   Tel: (609) 443-2000   %FO: 100

Bus: *Produces organoclay rheological*   Fax: (609) 443-2288
additives, urethane and acrylic
thickeners.

• EMI GROUP PLC
4 Tenterden Street, Hanover Square, London W1A 2AY, UK

CEO: Eric Nicoli, Chmn.   Tel: 44-207-467-2000   Rev: $3,811

Bus: *Entertainment, consumer electronics,*   Fax: 44-207-355-1308   Emp: 10,300
recorded music, music publishing and   www.emigroup.com
retail sale of recorded music and video.

CAPITOL RECORDS
1750 North Vine Street, Hollywood, CA   90028

CEO: Roy Lott, Pres.   Tel: (323) 462-6252   %FO: 100

Bus: *Full service music company.*   Fax: (323) 467-6550

EMI GROUP, INC.
2751 Centerville Road, Suite 205, Wilmington, DE   19808

CEO: Robert White, Pres.   Tel: (302) 994-4100   %FO: 100

Bus: *U.S. headquarters. Entertainment,*   Fax: (302) 994-4100
consumer electronics. Music
publisher and retailer.

EMI MUSIC PUBLISHING
1290 Avenue of the Americas, New York, NY   10104

CEO: Martin Bandier, CEO   Tel: (212) 492-1200   %FO: 100

Bus: *Recorded music, music publishing.*   Fax: (212) 245-4115

VIRGIN RECORDS AMERICA, INC.
338 N. Foothill Road, Beverly Hills, CA   90210

CEO: Nancy Berry, Chmn.   Tel: (310) 278-1181   %FO: 100

Bus: *Recorded music, music publishing.*   Fax: (310) 278-2460

• ENODIS PLC (FORMERLY BERISFORD GROUP)
40 Conduit Street, London W1R 9FB, UK

CEO: David Williams, CEO   Tel: 44-207-312-2500   Rev: $1,710

Bus: *Engaged in manufacture of commercial*   Fax: 44-207-312-2501   Emp: 7,185
food equipment and building materials.   www.berisford.co.uk

SCOTSMAN INDUSTRIES INC.
820 Forest Edge Drive, Vernon Hills, IL   60061
CEO: Randall C. Rossi, Pres.
Bus: *Mfr. coolers and freezers and beverage systems.*
Tel: (847) 215-4500
Fax: (847) 534-8823
%FO: 100

WELBILT CORPORATION
2227 Welbilt Boulevard, New Port Richey, FL   34655
CEO: Andrew Roake, CEO
Bus: *Mfr. food service equipment.*
Tel: (727) 576-8600
Fax: (727) 372-4591
%FO: 100

● ENTERPRISE OIL PLC
Grand Buildings Trafalgar Square, London WC2N 5EJ, UK
CEO: Pierre H. Jungels, CEO
Bus: *Holding company dealing in crude petroleum & natural gas & oil and gas exploration services.*
Tel: 44-207-925-4000
Fax: 44-207-925-4321
www.entoil.com
Rev: $2,753
Emp: 600

ENTERPRISE OIL SERVICES INC
111 Bagby Street, Ste. 1800, Houston, TX   77002
CEO: John R. McGoldrick, Pres.
Bus: *Deals in crude petroleum & natural gas & oil/gas exploration services.*
Tel: (713) 651-0505
Fax: (713) 970-2801
%FO: 100

● ESSELTE AB
Waterside House, Cowley Business Park, High Street, London UB8 2HE, UK
CEO: Anders Igel, Pres. & CEO
Bus: *Mfr. office equipment and stationery, packaging, printing and bookbinding, cartography, school equipment, publishing, book shops.*
Tel: 44-189-587-8700
Fax: 44-189-587-8810
www.esselte.com
Rev: $1,500
Emp: 7,000

BENSONS INTERNATIONAL SYSTEMS INC.
777 Passaic Avenue, 5th Fl., Clifton, NJ   07012
CEO: Raymond Rod, Pres.
Bus: *Mfr. bar coding systems, labeling systems labels & tags, printer supplies & consumables, imprinting services.*
Tel: (201) 939-1914
Fax: (201) 939-3224
%FO: 100

CURTIS COMPUTER PRODUCTS
441 East Bay Boulevard, Provo, UT   84606
CEO: Richard Tremmel, Pres.
Bus: *Sales/distribution of computer products and office supplies.*
Tel: (801) 373-9800
Fax: (801) 373-9847
%FO: 100

ESSELTE AMERICA CORPORATION

71 Clinton Road, Garden City, NY   11530

CEO: Louis D'Amaro, Pres.
Tel: (516) 741-3200
%FO: 100

Bus: *Mfr. bar coding systems, labeling systems, labels & tags, printer supplies & consumables, imprinting services.*
Fax: (516) 873-3320
Emp: 1,000

ESSELTE OFFICE PRODUCTS

71 Clinton Road, Garden City, NY   11530

CEO: Robert Hawes, EVP
Tel: (516) 741-3200
%FO: 100

Bus: *Sales of labeling systems labels & tags, printer supplies & consumables, imprinting services.*
Fax: (516) 747-7476

NURRE CAXTON

4615 Northwest 103rd Street, Sunrise, FL   33351

CEO: Don Fairholm, Pres.
Tel: (954) 741-0395
%FO: 100

Bus: *Mfr. bar coding systems, labeling systems labels & tags, printer supplies & consumables, imprinting services.*
Fax: (954) 749-5910

● EUROMONEY INSTITUTIONAL INVESTOR PLC

Nestor House, Playhouse Yard, London EC4V 5EX, UK

CEO: Richard Ensor, Mng. Dir.
Tel: 44-207-779-8888
Rev: $280

Bus: *Publisher of financial magazines.*
Fax: 44-207-779-8658
Emp: 1,690

www.euromoneyplc.com

INSTITUTIONAL INVESTOR INC.

488 Madison Avenue, New York, NY   10022

CEO: Jonathan Gage, CEO
Tel: (212) 224-3300
%FO: 100

Bus: *Publisher of financial, on-line and print, magazine.*
Fax: (212) 224-3300

● EXEL PLC

Ocean House, The Ring, Bracknell, Berkshire RG12 1AW, UK

CEO: John Devaney, Chmn.
Tel: 44-134-430-2000

Bus: *Supplies logistic services and home moving services.*
Fax: 44-134-430-2000

www.exel.com

EXEL DIRECT

1911 Williams Drive, Ste. 101, Oxnard, CA   93030

CEO: James Allyn, CEO
Tel: (805) 485-7979
%FO: 100

Bus: *Supplies logistic services.*
Fax: (805) 988-6387

EXEL INC.
501 West Schrock Road, Westerville, OH   43081
CEO: Bruce Edwards   Tel: (614) 890-1730   %FO: 100
Bus: *Supplies logistic services.*   Fax: (614) 898-7436

● **EXPRO INTERNATIONAL GROUP PLC**
Reading Bridge House, Reading Berkshire RG1 8PL, UK
CEO: John Dawson, CEO   Tel: 44-118-959-1341   Rev: $243
Bus: *Engaged in oil field services.* Fax: 44-118-958-9000   Emp: 1,590
                                   www.expro.co.uk

    EXPRO AMERICAS INC.
    50 Westlake Park Road, Ste. 1500, Houston, TX   77079
    CEO: Tony Kitchener, Dir.   Tel: (281) 597-9010   %FO: 100
    Bus: *Engaged in oil field services.* Fax: (281) 497-8402

    KINLEY CORPORATION
    5815 Royalton, Houston, TX   77081
    CEO: Kyle Bethel, Mgr.   Tel: (713) 664-4501   %FO: 100
    Bus: *Caliper service.*   Fax: (713) 664-1037

    SPS INC.
    580 Westlake Park Blvd., Ste. 1500, Houston, TX   77079
    CEO: David Luetchford, Pres.   Tel: (281) 597-9010   %FO: 100
    Bus: *Engaged in oil field services.* Fax: (281) 497-8402

    TRIPOINT INC.
    580 Westlake Park Blvd., Ste. 1500, Houston, TX   77079
    CEO: Stan Wall, Mgr.   Tel: (281) 597-9010   %FO: 100
    Bus: *Engaged in oil field services.* Fax: (281) 497-8402

    TRONIC INC.
    580 Westlake Park Blvd., Ste. 1500, Houston, TX   77079
    CEO: Lenny Sutherland   Tel: (281) 597-9010   %FO: 100
    Bus: *Engaged in oil field services.* Fax: (281) 497-8402

● **EYRETEL PLC**
Kings Court, Kingston Road, Leatherhead Surrey KT22 7SZ, UK
CEO: Nicholas Discombe, CEO   Tel: 44-870-600-0626   Rev: $45
Bus: *Mfr. software and hardware for* Fax: 44-870-600-0636   Emp: 280
communications and display.   www.eyretel.com

    EYRETEL INC.
    2390 East Camelback Road, Ste. 335, Phoenix, AZ   85016
    CEO: David Fitzgerald, Pres.   Tel: (602) 553-1100   %FO: 100
    Bus: *Mfr. software and hardware for* Fax: (602) 553-1001
    communications and display.

EYRETEL INC.
11720 Beltsville Drive, 3rd Fl., Calverton, MD   20705
CEO: David Fitzgerald, Pres.   Tel: (301) 586-1900   %FO: 100
Bus: *Mfr. software and hardware for*   Fax: (301) 586-1919
communications and display.

● **FCX INTERNATIONAL PLC (FORMERLY CHARLES BAYNES)**
68 Baker Street, Weybridge, Surrey KT13 8AL, UK
CEO: Bruce G. McInnes, Chmn.   Tel: 44-193-283-7700   Rev: $485
Bus: *Mfr. flow control products, industrial*   Fax: 44-193-282-0204   Emp: 1,100
tools and packaging.   www.fc-x.com

    FCX PERFORMANCE INC.
    1050 Holydell Court, Sewell, NJ   08080
    CEO: Charlie Simon, CEO   Tel: (856) 582-9500   %FO: 100
    Bus: *Distributes valves, instrumentation* Fax: (856) 582-7702
    and corrosion piping and hose
    systems for industrial and high-
    purity flow control applications.

    FCX PERFORMANCE INC.
    300 Oak Street, Unite 400, Plymouth, MA   02359
    CEO: Charlie Simon, CEO   Tel: (781) 826-4866   %FO: 100
    Bus: *Distributes valves, instrumentation* Fax: (781) 826-4698
    and corrosion piping and hose
    systems for industrial and high-
    purity flow control applications.

    FCX PERFORMANCE INC.
    1355 Sherman Road, Ste. 501, Hiawatha, IA   52233
    CEO: Charlie Simon, CEO   Tel: (319) 294-8445   %FO: 100
    Bus: *Distributes valves, instrumentation* Fax: (319) 294-8446
    and corrosion piping and hose
    systems for industrial and high-
    purity flow control applications.

    FCX PERFORMANCE INC.
    373 East Route 46 West, Fairfield, NJ   07004
    CEO: Charlie Simon, CEO   Tel: (973) 575-8350   %FO: 100
    Bus: *Distributes valves, instrumentation* Fax: (973) 575-5228
    and corrosion piping and hose
    systems for industrial and high-
    purity flow control applications.

FCX PERFORMANCE INC.
3000 East 14th Avenue, Columbus, OH   43219
CEO: Charlie Simon, CEO   Tel: (614) 253-1996   %FO: 100
Bus: *Distributes valves, instrumentation*   Fax: (614) 253-2033
and corrosion piping and hose
systems for industrial and high-
purity flow control applications.

FCX PERFORMANCE INC.
7777 Wall Street, Cleveland, OH   44125
CEO: Charlie Simon, CEO   Tel: (216) 524-9600   %FO: 100
Bus: *Distributes valves, instrumentation*   Fax: (216) 524-2676
and corrosion piping and hose
systems for industrial and high-
purity flow control applications.

FCX PERFORMANCE INC.
200 Prestige Park, Charleston, WV   25526
CEO: Charlie Simon, CEO   Tel: (304) 757-3766   %FO: 100
Bus: *Distributes valves, instrumentation*   Fax: (304) 757-3979
and corrosion piping and hose
systems for industrial and high-
purity flow control applications.

FCX PERFORMANCE INC.
2221 Kenmore Avenue, Ste. 108, Buffalo, NY   14207
CEO: Charlie Simon, CEO   Tel: (716) 873-8185   %FO: 100
Bus: *Distributes valves, instrumentation*   Fax: (716) 873-0768
and corrosion piping and hose
systems for industrial and high-
purity flow control applications.

FCX PERFORMANCE INC.
3000 East 14th Avenue, Columbus, OH   43219
CEO: Charlie Simon, CEO   Tel: (614) 253-1996   %FO: 100
Bus: *Distributes valves, instrumentation*   Fax: (614) 253-2033
and corrosion piping and hose
systems for industrial and high-
purity flow control applications.

FCX PERFORMANCE INC.
9715 Kincaid Drive, Ste. 1280, Fishers, IN   46038
CEO: Charlie Simon, CEO   Tel: (317) 577-0982   %FO: 100
Bus: *Distributes valves, instrumentation*   Fax: (317) 577-0985
and corrosion piping and hose
systems for industrial and high-
purity flow control applications.

FCX PERFORMANCE INC./SIMONE

55 North Lively Blvd., Elk Grove Village, IL   60007

CEO: Charlie Simon, CEO   Tel: (847) 806-1885   %FO: 100

Bus: *Distributes valves, instrumentation*   Fax: (847) 806-1921
and corrosion piping and hose
systems for industrial and high-
purity flow control applications.

FCX PERFORMANCE INC./SIMONE

2635 45th Street, Highland, IN   46322

CEO: Chris Hill   Tel: (219) 922-6750   %FO: 100

Bus: *Distributes valves, instrumentation*   Fax: (219) 922-6870
and corrosion piping and hose
systems for industrial and high-
purity flow control applications.

● **FENNER PLC**

Hesslewood Country Office Park, Hessle, East Yorkshire HU13 0PW, UK

CEO: Mark Abrahams, CEO   Tel: 44-148-262-6500   Rev: $470

Bus: *Mfr./distributes fluid power equipment,*   Fax: 44-148-262-6502   Emp: 3,900
industrial conveyor belting, polymer   www.fenner.com
products and power transmission.

FENNER DRIVES, INC.

311 West Stiegel Street, Manheim, PA   17545

CEO: Julian Bigden, Pres. & CEO   Tel: (717) 665-2421   %FO: 100

Bus: *Mfr./sale fluid power equipment*   Fax: (717) 665-2649   Emp: 350
and industrial belting.

FENNER FLUID POWER, INC.

5885 11th Street, Rockford, IL   61109-3699

CEO: Gary Nierhoff, Pres.   Tel: (815) 874-5556   %FO: 100

Bus: *Mfr. ac/dc hydraulic power units,*   Fax: (815) 874-7853   Emp: 200
pumps and motors.

● **FFASTFILL PLC**

10 Arthur Street, London EC4R 9AY, UK

CEO: Chris Stone, CEO   Tel: 44-207-665-8900

Bus: *Designs and markets software to*   Fax: 44-207-665-8905
traders, brokers and clearers that   www.ffastfill.com
enables trading on electronic exchanges.

FFASTFILL INC.

200 West Adams Street, Ste. 2215, Chicago, Il 60606

CEO: Jonathan Hulbert, Sales   Tel: (312) 516-2790   %FO: 100

Bus: *Designs and markets software to*   Fax: (312) 516-2799
traders, brokers and clearers that
enables trading on electronic
exchanges.

● **FILTRONIC PLC**

The Waterfront at Salts Mill Road, Saltaire Shipley, West Yorkshire BD18 3TT, UK

CEO: Messrs. Rhodes and Snowdon, Chmn.   Tel: 44-127-453-0622   Rev: $334

Bus: *Mfr. wireless electronics, including*   Fax: 44-127-453-1561   Emp: 2,900
amplifiers and related products.   www.filtronic.com

    FILTRONIC COMTEK, INC.

    300 Park Blvd., Ste. 260, Itasca, Il 60143

    CEO: Paul Blashewski   Tel: (630) 775-1000   %FO: 100

    Bus: *Mfr. wireless electronics.*   Fax: (630) 775-1050

    FILTRONIC COMTEK, INC.

    21 Continental Boulevard, Merrimack, NH 03054

    CEO: D. Jenner   Tel: (603) 424-8404   %FO: 100

    Bus: *Mfr. wireless electronics.*   Fax: (603) 424-7947

    FILTRONIC COMTEK, INC.

    3251 Olcott Street, Santa Clara, CA 95054

    CEO: Rich Lukon   Tel: (408) 988-2827   %FO: 100

    Bus: *Mfr. wireless electronics.*   Fax: (408) 970-9950

    FILTRONIC COMTEK, INC.

    31901 Comtek Lane, Salisbury, MD 21804-1788

    CEO: Biba Aidoo   Tel: (410) 341-7766   %FO: 100

    Bus: *Mfr. wireless electronics.*   Fax: (410) 548-4750

    FILTRONIC SIGTEK, INC.

    9075 Guilford Road, Ste. C-1, Columbia, MD 21046

    CEO: Jim Shea, Pres.   Tel: (410) 290-3918   %FO: 100

    Bus: *Engaged in broadband access*   Fax: (410) 290-8146

    SAGE LABORATORIES, INC., DIV. FILTRONIC

    11 Huron Drive, Natick, MA 01760-1338

    CEO: Carl A. Marguerite, CEO   Tel: (508) 653-0844   %FO: 100

    Bus: *Mfr. microwave components for*   Fax: (508) 653-5671
    telecommunications.

● **FIRST TECHNOLOGY PLC**
2 Cheapside Court, Buckhurst Road, Ascot Berkshire SL5 7RF, UK
CEO: Frederick J. Westlake, CEO   Tel: 44-134-462-2322   Rev: $181
Bus: *Mfr. vehicle safety products.*   Fax: 44-134-462-2773   Emp: 1,483
   www.firsttech.co.uk

   CONTROL DEVICES, INC.
   228 Northeast Road, Standish, ME   04084
   CEO: Frederick J. Westlake, Pres.   Tel: (207) 642-4535   %FO: 100
   Bus: *Mfr. optical sensors and crash*   Fax: (207) 642-0198
     dummies used by the automotive
     industry.

   FIRST INERTIA SWITCH LTD.
   PO Box 408, Grand Blanc, MI   48439
   CEO: Muir Perker, Pres.   Tel: (810) 695-8333   %FO: 100
   Bus: *Mfr. vehicle safety products.*   Fax: (810) 695-0589

   FIRST TECHNOLOGY INC.
   28411 Northwestern Highway, Southfield, MI   48034
   CEO: Bruce Atkinson   Tel: (248) 353-6200   %FO: 100
   Bus: *Mfr. vehicle safety products.*   Fax: (248) 353-8333

   HITEC CORPORATION
   65 Power Road, Westford, MA   01886-4199
   CEO: Michael Johns, Pres.   Tel: (978) 692-4793   %FO: 100
   Bus: *Installation of strain gages and*   Fax: (978) 692-5078
     ancillary sensors.

   HITEC CORPORATION
   12729 Universal Drive, Taylor, MI   48180
   CEO: Michael Johns, Pres.   Tel: (734) 947-2466   %FO: 100
   Bus: *Installation of strain gages and*   Fax: (734) 947-2478
     ancillary sensors.

● **FIRSTGROUP PLC**
32A Weymouth Street, London WIN 3FA, UK
CEO: Anthony Osbaldiston, CEO   Tel: 44-207-291-0500   Rev: $2,912
Bus: *Diversified transportation group.*   Fax: 44-207-636-1338   Emp: 52,000
   www.firstgroup.com

   FIRSTGROUP AMERICA, INC.
   705 Central Avenue, Ste. 500, Cincinnati, OH   45202
   CEO: John Farrell, VP   Tel: (513) 241-2200   %FO: 100
   Bus: *Engaged in diversified*   Fax: (513) 381-0149
     transportation, including school
     bus service.

● **THE ALBERT FISHER GROUP PLC**
Mark Road, Hemel Hempstead, Herts HP2 7BW, UK

CEO: Terry J. Robinson, CEO	Tel: 44-144-226-1116	Rev: $1,034
Bus: *Engaged in food processing and distribution.*	Fax: 44-144-221-2302 www.albertfisher.com	Emp: 5,871

RIVER RANCH FRESH FOODS, INC.
1156 Abbott Street, Salinas, CA   93901

CEO: James Lucas, Pres.	Tel: (831) 758-1390	%FO: 100
Bus: *Distribution, sales, source and process fresh produce.*	Fax: (831) 755-8281	

● **FKI PLC**
15-19 New Fetter Lane, London EC4A 1LY, UK

CEO: Jell Whalley, Chmn.	Tel: 44-207-832-0000	Rev: $2,121
Bus: *Diversified engineering services.*	Fax: 44-207-832-0001 www.fki.co.uk	Emp: 15,895

BELWITH INTERNATIONAL, LTD.
4300 Gerald R. Ford Freeway, Grandville, MI   49468-0127

CEO: William J. Veldboom, Pres.	Tel: (616) 531-4300	%FO: 100
Bus: *Process control systems.*	Fax: (616) 531-6055	

BRIDON AMERICAN CORPORATION
PO Box 6000, Wilkes Barre, PA   18773

CEO: John Churchfield, Pres.	Tel: (570) 822-3349	%FO: 100
Bus: *Mfr./distributes wire and rope products.*	Fax: (570) 822-9180	

BRISTOL BABCOCK INC.
1100 Buckingham Street, Watertown, CT   06795

CEO: Gregory Altman, Pres.	Tel: (860) 945-2200	%FO: 100
Bus: *Mfr./supplies flow computers, pressure gauges, process control systems and transmitters.*	Fax: (860) 945-2213	

CERTEX AMERICAS
5950 Symphony Woods Road, Columbia, MD   21044

CEO: William Adams, Pres.	Tel: (410) 884-5400	%FO: 100
Bus: *Sales/distribution of lifting and safety products and services.*	Fax: (410) 884-7330	

FAULTLESS CASTER
1421 North Garvin Street, Evansville, IN   47711-4487

CEO: Donald N. Laux, Pres.	Tel: (812) 425-1011	%FO: 100
Bus: *Process control systems.*	Fax: (812) 421-7328	

KEELER BRASS HARDWARE COMPANY
955 Godfrey Avenue, SW, Grand Rapids, MI   49503-5087
CEO: William J. Veldboom, Pres.   Tel: (616) 247-4000   %FO: 100
Bus: *Sales/distribution of brass*   Fax: (616) 247-4060
     hardware.

WEBER-KNAPP
441 Chandler Street, Jamestown, NY   14702-0518
CEO: C. H. Little, Pres.   Tel: (716) 484-9135   %FO: 100
Bus: *Process control systems.*   Fax: (716) 484-9142

● FOSECO INTERNATIONAL LTD.
PO Box 5516 Tamworth, Staffordshire B78 3XQ, UK
CEO: John G. Griffiths   Tel: 44-182-726-2021
Bus: *Produces metallurgical chemicals.*   Fax: 44-182-728-3725
     www.foseco.com

FOSECO INC.
20200 Sheldon Road, Brook Park, OH   44142
CEO: Roger Stanbridge, Pres.   Tel: (440) 826-4548   %FO: 100
Bus: *Sales/distribution of industrial*   Fax: (440) 243-7658
     chemicals.

● FRENCH CONNECTION GROUP PLC
117B Fulham Road, London SW3 6RL, UK
CEO: Stephen Marks, Pres.   Tel: 44-207-399-7000   Rev: $224
Bus: *Mfr. women's clothing; chain stores.*   Fax: 44-207-399-7001   Emp: 1,331
     www.frenchconnection.com

FRENCH CONNECTION
184-02 Jamaica Avenue, Hollis, NY   11423
CEO: Brian Sloan, EVP   Tel: (718) 465-0500   %FO: 100
Bus: *U.S. headquarters office; women's*   Fax: (718) 465-0550
     clothing chain.

FRENCH CONNECTION
512 Seventh Avenue, 25th Fl., New York, NY   10018
CEO: Michael Exelrod, Pres.   Tel: (212) 221-7504   %FO: 100
Bus: *Showroom; women's clothing.*   Fax: (212) 302-6839

● FRESHFIELDS BRUCKHAUS DERINGER LLP
65 Fleet Street, London EC4Y 1HS, UK
CEO: Anthony Salz, Mng. Prtn.   Tel: 44-207-936-4000
Bus: *International business law.*   Fax: 44-207-832-7001   Emp: 690
     www.freshfields.co.uk

FRESHFIELDS BRUCKHAUS DERINGER LLP
1300 I Street NW, 12th Fl. East, Washington, DC 20005-3314
CEO: Thomas Hechl   Tel: (202) 777-4500   %FO: 100
Bus: *International law firm.*   Fax: (202) 777-4545

FRESHFIELDS BRUCKHAUS DERINGER LLP
520 Madison Avenue, 34th Fl., New York, NY 10022
CEO: Matthew Trotter   Tel: (212) 277-4000   %FO: 100
Bus: *International law firm.*   Fax: (212) 277-4001   Emp: 8

• FRIENDS IVORY & SIME PLC
100 Wood Street, London EC2V 7AN, UK
CEO: Howard Carter, CEO   Tel: 44-207-506-1100   Rev: $111
Bus: *Engaged in investment banking and*   Fax: 44-207-506-2060   Emp: 370
venture capital.   www.friendsis.com

FRIENDS IVORY & SIME NORTH AMERICA, INC.
*PO Box 1708, Shelter Island, NY 11964
CEO: Peter Arthur   Tel: %FO: 100
Bus: *Engaged in investment banking*   Fax:
and venture capital.

• THE FUTURE NETWORK PLC
30 Monmouth Street, Bath, Avon BA1 2BW, UK
CEO: Greg Ingham, CEO   Tel: 44-122-544-2244   Rev: $380
Bus: *Magazine publisher.*   Fax: 44-122-544-6019   Emp: 1,800
www.thefuturenetwork.plc.uk

IMAGINE MEDIA, INC.
150 North Hill Drive, Brisbane, CA 94005
CEO: Chris Anderson, CEO   Tel: (415) 468-4684   %FO: 100
Bus: *Engaged in magazine publishing.*   Fax: (415) 468-4684

• GALEN HOLDINGS PLC
Seagoe Industrial Estate, Craigavon, County Armagh BT63 5UA, UK
CEO: Roger Biossonneault, CEO   Tel: 44-283-833-4974   Rev: $96
Bus: *Holding company engaged in*   Fax: 44-283-835-0206   Emp: 1,700
pharmaceuticals.   www.galenplc.com

GALEN HOLDINGS
100 Enterprise Drive, Ste. 280, Rockaway, NJ 07866
CEO: Paul Herendeen, EVP   Tel: (973) 442-3222   %FO: 100
Bus: *Engaged in pharmaceuticals.*   Fax: (973) 422-3246   Emp: 5

● **GARBAN-INTERCAPITAL PLC**

Park House, 16 Finsbury Circus, London EC2M 7UR, UK

CEO: Michael Spencer, CEO	Tel: 44-207-638-7592	Rev: $970
Bus: *Engaged in wholesale money and* *security brokerage.*	Fax: 44-207-374-6743 www.garban-intercapital.com	Emp: 2,860

    GARBAN CAPITAL MARKETS LLC

    *One World Trade Center, 25th Fl., New York, NY   10048-5597

CEO: Doug Rhoten	Tel: (212) 406-1100	%FO: 100
Bus: *Engaged in wholesale money and* *security brokerage.*	Fax: (212) 815-6587	

    GARBAN CORPORATES LLC

    *One World Trade Center, Ste. 5500, New York, NY   10048

CEO: Sal Trani	Tel: (212) 341-9299	%FO: 100
Bus: *Engaged in wholesale money and* *security brokerage.*	Fax: (212) 341-9292	

● **GEI INTERNATIONAL PLC**

Aspley Hill, Woburn Sands, Bedfordshire MK17 8NW, UK

CEO: Ian Gray, Mng. Dir.	Tel: 44-190-828-1199	
Bus: *Engineering and special products.*	Fax: 44-190-828-1233 www.gei-int.com	Emp: 1,700

    GEI MATEER BURT CO. INC.

    700 Pennsylvania Drive, Exton, PA   19341-1129

CEO: Richard Ward, Pres.	Tel: (610) 321-1100	%FO: 100
Bus: *Mfr. fillers and labelers.*	Fax: (610) 321-1199	Emp: 115

● **GEMINI GENOMICS PLC**

162 Science Park, Milton Road Cambridge, Cambridgeshire CB4 OGH, UK

CEO: Paul Kelly, Pres. & CEO	Tel: 44-122-343-5300	Rev: $
Bus: *Engaged in gene research.*	Fax: 44-122-343-5301 www.gemini-genomics.com	Emp: 80

    GEMINI GENOMICS, INC.

    189 Wells Avenue, Newton, MA   02459

CEO: Dr. Rosalind Bergemann, EVP	Tel: (617) 928-9600	%FO: 100
Bus: *Engaged in gene research.*	Fax: (617) 964-7974	

● **THE GENERICS GROUP AG**

Harston Mill, Harston, Cambridge CB2 5GG, UK

CEO: Gordon Edge, CEO	Tel: 44-122-387-5200
Bus: *Engaged in integrated technology* *consulting, development and investment.*	Fax: 44-122-387-5201 www.genericsgroup.com

THE GENERICS GROUP INC.
1601 Trapelo Road, Waltham, MA   02451
CEO: Michael Petty, Pres.   Tel: (781) 290-0500   %FO: 100
Bus: *Engaged in integrated technology*   Fax: (781) 290-0501
consulting, development and
investment.

● GENETIX GROUP PLC
Queensway, New Milton, Hampshire BH25 5NN, UK
CEO: M. A. Reid, CEO   Tel: 44-142-562-4600
Bus: *Engaged in biotechnology.*   Fax: 44-142-562-4700
      www.genetix.co.uk

GENETIX USA INC.
25 East Loop Road, Stonybrook, NY   11790-3350
CEO: Dr. Ronald Dorazio, Pres.   Tel: (631) 444-9664   %FO: 100
Bus: *Engaged in biotechnology.*   Fax: (631) 444-6626

● GENTIA SOFTWARE PLC
Tuition House, St. George's Road, Wimbledon, London SW19 4EU, UK
CEO: Steve Fluin, CEO   Tel: 44-208-971-4000   Rev: $21
Bus: *Mfr. analytical software.*   Fax: 44-208-944-1604   Emp: 220
      www.gentia.com

GENTIA SOFTWARE, INC.
4555 Mansell Road, Ste. 300, Alpharetta, GA   30022
CEO: Steve Fluin, Pres.   Tel: (770) 521-4477   %FO: 100
Bus: *Mfr. analytical software.*   Fax: (770) 521-4478

GENTIA SOFTWARE, INC.
One Northfield Plaza, Ste. 300, Northfield, IL   60093
CEO: Steve Fluin, Pres.   Tel: (847) 441-2984   %FO: 100
Bus: *Mfr. analytical software.*   Fax: (847) 441-1885

GENTIA SOFTWARE, INC.
803 Front Range Road, Littleton, CO   80120
CEO: Steve Fluin, Pres.   Tel: (303) 797-8581   %FO: 100
Bus: *Mfr. analytical software.*   Fax: (303) 797-8232

● GKN, PLC. (GUEST, KEEN, NETTLETOLDS)
PO Box 55, Ipsley Church Lane, Redditch, Worcestershire B98 OTL, UK
CEO: C.K. Chow, CEO   Tel: 44-152-751-7715   Rev: $6,150
Bus: *Mfr. automotive components.*   Fax: 44-152-751-7700   Emp: 35,520
      www.gknplc.com

AEROSPACE COMPOSITE TECHNOLOGIES INC.
2300 B West Sixth Street, Ft. Worth, TX   76107
CEO: S. G. Bowen, Mgr.   Tel: (817) 336-1900   %FO: 100
Bus: *Repairs aircraft de-icing units.*   Fax: (817) 336-5733

CHEP USA
225 East Robinson Street, Orlando, FL   32801-4393
CEO: B. L. Moore, CEO   Tel: (407) 422-4510   %FO: 100
Bus: *Operates container pooling and*   Fax: (407) 422-4614
  pallet service.

EMITEC INC.
5200 South Nelson Drive, Fountain Inn, SC   29644-8875
CEO: B. R. Hunt, VP   Tel: (864) 862-0129   %FO: 100
Bus: *Mfr./sales metal substrates for*   Fax: (864) 862-1978
  catalytic converters.

GKN AEROSPACE CHEM-TRONICS, INC.
PO Box 1604, El Cajon, CA   92022
CEO: James Legler, CEO   Tel: (619) 448-2320   %FO: 100
Bus: *Engaged in aerospace components*   Fax: (619) 258-5270
  and aviation repair.

GKN AEROSPACE INC.
1145 East 233rd Street, Carson, CA   90745
CEO: James Legler, CEO   Tel: (310) 847-1900   %FO: 100
Bus: *Produces components for the*   Fax: (310) 847-1932
  aircraft industry.

GKN ARMSTRONG WHEELS
PO Box 48, Armstrong, IA   50514-0048
CEO: R. Newlin, Pres.   Tel: (712) 864-3202   %FO: 100
Bus: *U.S. representative office.*   Fax: (712) 864-3378

GKN AUTOMOTIVE INC.
3300 University Drive, Auburn Hills, MI   48326-2362
CEO: T. R. Sloan, CEO   Tel: (248) 377-1200   %FO: 100
Bus: *Mfr./sales constant velocity*   Fax: (248) 377-1370
  products.

GKN DRIVETECH INC.
1164 Ladd Road, Walled Lake, MI   48390
CEO: W. F. Pawlick, EVP   Tel: (248) 669-3432   %FO: 100
Bus: *Operates aftermarket distribution*   Fax: (248) 669-9305
  of constant velocity joints.

GKN SINTER METALS DIV.
3300 University Drive, Auburn Hills, MI   48326-2362
CEO: Seifi Ghasemi, CEO   Tel: (248) 371-0800   %FO: 100
Bus: *Mfr. sintered metal components.*   Fax: (248) 371-0808

GKN TECHNOLOGY US
3300 University Drive, Auburn Hills, MI   48326-2362
CEO: W. Hoffmann, Mgr.   Tel: (248) 377-1200   %FO: 100
Bus: *Products development.*   Fax: (248) 377-1490

GKN WALTERSCHEID, INC.
16 West 83 Street, Burr Ridge, IL   60521-5802
CEO: E. J. Martin, Pres.   Tel: (630) 887-7022   %FO: 100
Bus: *Sales/distribution of agritechnical*   Fax: (630) 887-8386
     products.

GKN WESTLAND INC.
11921 Freedom Drive, Ste. 900, Reston, VA   20190-3409
CEO: T. W. Battaglia, CEO   Tel: (703) 318-2000   %FO: 100
Bus: *Sales/distribution of aerospace*   Fax: (703) 318-2011
     products.

HOEGANAES CORPORATION
1001 Taylors Lane, Cinnaminson, NJ   08077
CEO: Robert J. Fulton, Pres.   Tel: (609) 829-2220   %FO: 100
Bus: *Produces ferrous powered metals.*   Fax: (609) 829-7496

INTERLAKE MATERIAL HANDLING, INC.
1240 East Diehl Road, Ste. 200, Naperville, IL   60563
CEO: Daniel P. Wilson, CEO   Tel: (630) 245-8800   %FO: 100
Bus: *Mfr. and markets storage racks.*   Fax: (630) 245-8901

ITALCARDANO NA INC.
Two Rutherford Street, Greenville, SC   29602-2244
CEO: M. Vittorelli, Pres.   Tel: (864) 271-1199   %FO: 100
Bus: *Sales/distribution propeller shaft*   Fax: (864) 271-0080
     components.

MEINEKE DISCOUNT MUFFLER SHOPS, INC.
128 South Tryon Street, Ste. 900, Charlotte, NC   28202
CEO: K. D. Walker, CEO   Tel: (704) 377-8855   %FO: 100
Bus: *Muffler and brake shop franchises.*   Fax: (704) 342-4334

● **GLAXO SMITHKLINE PLC**

One New Horizon Court, Brentford, Middlesex TW8 9EP, UK

CEO: Jean-Pierre Garnier, CEO

Tel: 44-181-975-2000

Rev: $27,500

Bus: *Development/mfr./marketing human and animal health care products, over-counter medicines; clinical lab testing services; healthcare services.*

Fax: 44-181-975-2090

www.gsk.com

Emp: 100,000

BLOCK DRUG COMPANY

257 Cornelison Avenue, Jersey City, NJ 07301

CEO: Thomas R. Block, Pres.

Tel: (201) 434-3000

%FO: 100

Bus: *Mfr. healthcare products.*

Fax: (201) 434-5739

Emp: 3,185

GLAXOSMITHKLINE

5 Moore Drive, PO Box 13398, Research Triangle Park, NC 27709

CEO: Jean-Pierre Garnier, Pres.

Tel: (919) 483-2100

%FO: 100

Bus: *Mfr. pharmaceuticals.*

Fax: (919) 483-2412

GLAXOSMITHKLINE

One Franklin Plaza, Philadelphia, PA 19102

CEO: David Stout, Pres. & CEO

Tel: (215) 751-4000

%FO: 100

Bus: *Develop /mfr./marketing human & animal healthcare products, over-counter medicines; clinical lab testing services; healthcare services.*

Fax: (215) 751-3400

Emp: 22,000

● **GOLIATH INTERNATIONAL TOOLS LTD.**

Newtown Row, Aston, Birmingham, B6 4NQ, UK

CEO: Norman E. Moore, Pres.

Tel: 44-121-359-6621

Bus: *Mfr. threading tapes and ties.*

Fax: 44-121-359-7092

www.goliathinternational.com

Emp: 200

GOLIATH THREADING TOOLS INC.

9092 Telegraph Road, Redford, MI 48239

CEO: Tad C. Wrobel, Gen.Mgr.

Tel: (313) 538-2460

%FO: 100

Bus: *Distribution threading taps & dies.*

Fax: (313) 538-8099

Emp: 4

● **GRANADA PLC**

London Television Centre, Upper Ground, London SE1 9LT, UK

CEO: Steve Morrison, CEO

Tel: 44-207-620-1620

Rev: $7,968

Bus: *Owns independent television stations, pay TV and internet.*

Fax: 44-207-261-3520

www.granadamedia.com

Emp: 211,125

GRANADA ENTERTAINMENT USA
11812 San Vicente Blvd., Ste. 503, Los Angeles, CA   90049

CEO: Anthony Root, Chmn.   Tel: (310) 689-4777   %FO: 100

Bus: *Engaged in television and internet*   Fax: (310) 689-4777
services.

• THE GREAT UNIVERSAL STORES PLC
Universal House, Devonshire Street, Manchester M60 IXA, UK

CEO: John Peace, CEO   Tel: 44-207-636-4080   Rev: $8,812

Bus: *Engaged in information services,*   Fax: 44-207-631-3641   Emp: 55,575
logistics and customer care and multi-   www.gusplc.co.uk
channel retailing.

BURBERRY'S LIMITED
1350 Avenue of the Americas, New York, NY   10022

CEO: Victor J. Barnett, Chmn.   Tel: (212) 757-3700   %FO: 100

Bus: *Sales/distribution of wearing*   Fax: (212) 246-9440
apparel.

EXPERIAN INFORMATION SOLUTIONS
505 City Parkway West, Orange, CA   92868

CEO: Rick Cortese, Pres.   Tel: (714) 385-7000   %FO: 100

Bus: *Supplies Credit scoring and*   Fax: (714) 385-7349
software solutions.

EXPERIAN MARKETING SOLUTIONS
955 American lan, Schaumburg, IL   60173-4998

CEO: Scot Thomas, CEO   Tel: (847) 517-5600   %FO: 100

Bus: *Provides direct marketing services.*   Fax: (847) 517-5189

EXPERIAN NORTH AMERICA
505 City Parkway West, Orange, CA   92868

CEO: Craig Smith, CEO   Tel: (714) 385-7000   %FO: 100

Bus: *Supplies credit information, credit*   Fax: (714) 385-7349
software solutions & direct
marketing services.

• R. GRIGGS GROUP LIMITED
Cobbs Lane, Wollaston, Wellingborough, Northamptonshire NN29 7SW, UK

CEO: Max Griggs, CEO   Tel: 44-193-366-5381   Rev: $370

Bus: *Mfr. specialty footwear.*   Fax: 44-193-366-4088   Emp: 3,510
www.drmartens.com

DR. MARTENS AIRWAIR USA
PO Box 29017, Portland, OR   97296-9017

CEO: Kris J. Hamper, VP   Tel: (800) 229-1262   %FO: 100

Bus: *Mfr./sales specialty footwear.*   Fax: (503) 222-6880

● **GUINNESS LTD., DIV. DIAGEO**

Park Royal Brewery, London NW10 7RR, UK

CEO: Paul S. Walsh, CEO	Tel: 44-208-965-7700	Rev: $10,793
Bus: *Brew/marketing beers and distillers of whisky, gin and other wines and spirits.*	Fax: 44-208-965-1882 www.guinness.ie	Emp: 24,700

    GUINESS IMPORT COMPANY

    Six Landmark Square, Stamford, CT   06901

CEO: Paul Clinton, Pres. & CEO	Tel: (203) 359-7100	%FO: 100
Bus: *Import/distribution of alcoholic beverages.*	Fax: (203) 359-7402	

    GUINNESS WORLD OF RECORDS MUSEUM

    2780 Las Vegas Blvd., Las Vegas, NV   89109

CEO: Oli Lewis, Mgr.	Tel: (702) 792-3766	%FO: 100
Bus: *World record museum.*	Fax: (702) 792-0530	

● **HALMA PLC**

Misbourne Court, Rectory Way, Amersham, Buckinghamshire HP7 0DE, UK

CEO: Steven R. O'Shay, CEO	Tel: 44-149-472-1111	Rev: $371
Bus: *Supplies environmental control, fire and gas detection, safety and security products and services.*	Fax: 44-149-472-8032 www.halmaholdings.com	Emp: 2,975

    AIR PRODUCTS AND CONTROLS, INC.

    1749 East Highwood, Bldg. C, Pontiac, MI   48340

CEO: R. E. Skaggs, Pres.	Tel: (248) 332-3900	%FO: 100
Bus: *Mfr. duct detectors for smoke control systems.*	Fax: (248) 332-8807	

    AQUIONICS INC.

    21 Kenton Lands Road, Erlanger, KY   41018

CEO: D. L. McCarty, Pres.	Tel: (859) 341-0710	%FO: 100
Bus: *Mfr. ultraviolet equipment for water sterilization & disinfection.*	Fax: (859) 341-0350	

    BIO-CHEM VALVE INC.

    85 Fulton Street, Boonton, NJ   07005

CEO: Adam J. Meyers, Pres.	Tel: (973) 263-3001	%FO: 100
Bus: *Mfr. miniature valves for scientific instruments.*	Fax: (973) 263-2880	

    CASTELL INTERLOCKS INC.

    PO Box 18485, Erlanger, KY   41018

CEO: Patrick E. Kanis, Pres.	Tel: (859) 341-3075	%FO: 100
Bus: *Mfr. Interlocking safety systems.*	Fax: (859) 341-2302	

ELECTRONIC MICRO SYSTEMS INC.
125 Richfield Lane, Hauppauge, NY 11788

CEO: W. J. Seymour, Pres.   Tel: (631) 864-4742   %FO: 100

Bus: *Mfr. elevator controls and*   Fax: (631) 864-4770
communications products.

FLUID CONSERVATIN SYSTEMS INC.
2001 Ford Circle, Ste. F, Milford, OH 45150

CEO: Andrew J. Williams, Pres.   Tel: (513) 831-9335   %FO: 100

Bus: *Mfr. equipment for detecting*   Fax: (513) 831-9336
underground water leaks.

HALMA HOLDINGS, INC.
3100 East Kemper Road, Cincinnati, OH 45241

CEO: J. C. Conacher, Pres.   Tel: (513) 772-5501   %FO: 100

Bus: *U.S. headquarters holding*   Fax: (513) 772-5507
*company; firms supply
environmental control, fire & gas
detection, safety and security
products & services.*

IPC POWER RESISTORS INTL INC.
7453 Empire Drive, Unit 105, Florence, KY 41042

CEO: M. A. Horn, Pres.   Tel: (859) 282-2900   %FO: 100

Bus: *Mfr. heavy-duty electrical*   Fax: (859) 282-2909
resistors.

JANUS ELEVATOR PRODUCTS INC.
125 Ricefield Lane, Hauppauge, NY 11788

CEO: M. A. Bryne, Pres.   Tel: (631) 543-4334   %FO: 100

Bus: *Mfr. elevator controls.*   Fax: (631) 543-4372

KEELER INSTRUMENTS INC.
456 Parkway, Broomall, PA 19008

CEO: D. J. Keeler, Pres.   Tel: (610) 353-4350   %FO: 100

Bus: *Distribution of optical equipment.*   Fax: (610) 353-7814

MARATHON SENSORS INC.
3100 East Kemper Road, Cincinnati, OH 45241

CEO: Eric S. Boltz, SVP   Tel: (513) 772-7788   %FO: 100

Bus: *Mfr. control equipment for heat*   Fax: (513) 772-7853
treatment and boiler efficiency.

MOSEBACH MANUFACTURING COMPANY
1417 McLaughlin Run Road, Pittsburgh, PA   15241
CEO: G. Denny, Pres.   Tel: (412) 220-0200   %FO: 100
Bus: *Mfr. heavy-duty electrical*   Fax: (412) 220-0236
    resistors.

OKLAHOMA SAFETY EQUIPMENT CO. INC.
PO Box 1327, Broken Arrow, OK   74013
CEO: J. M. Ragosta, Pres.   Tel: (918) 258-5626   %FO: 100
Bus: *Mfr. process bursting disks.*   Fax: (918) 251-2809

PERMA PURE INC.
8 Executive Drive, Toms River, NJ   08754
CEO: D. A. Leighty, Pres.   Tel: (732) 244-0010   %FO: 100
Bus: *Provides systems for removal of*   Fax: (732) 244-8140
    moisture from gas samples.

POST GLOVER RESISTORS INC.
167 Gap Way, Erlanger, KY   41018
CEO: N. E. Gambow, Pres.   Tel: (859) 283-0778   %FO: 100
Bus: *Mfr. electrical resistors.*   Fax: (859) 283-2978

VOLK OPTICAL INC.
7893 Enterprise Drive, Mentor, OH   44060
CEO: P. L. Mastores, Pres.   Tel: (440) 942-6161   %FO: 100
Bus: *Design/manufacture optical lenses.*   Fax: (440) 942-2257

● **HANSON PLC**
1 Grosvenor Place, London SW1X 7JH, UK
CEO: Andrew J.H. Dougal, CEO   Tel: 44-207-245-1245   Rev: $3,199
Bus: *Engaged in building materials supplies*   Fax: 44-207-235-3455   Emp: 16,800
    and equipment.   www.hansonplc.com

    AGGREGATE HAULERS, INC.
    15080 Tradesmen Drive, San Antonio, TX   78249
    CEO: Randy Wyatt, Pres.   Tel: (201) 492-5501   %FO: 100
    Bus: *Supplies building materials.*   Fax: (201) 492-0031

    HANSON AGGREGATES EAST
    2300 Gateway Centre, Morrisville, NC   27560
    CEO: C. Howard Nye, Pres.   Tel: (919) 380-2500   %FO: 100
    Bus: *Produces construction aggregates*   Fax: (919) 380-2522
        and hot mix asphalt.

HANSON AGGREGATES WEST
2680 Bishop Drive, San Ramon, CA   94583
CEO: Federick A. Nelson, Pres.   Tel: (925) 328-1800   %FO: 100
Bus: *Mfr. cement and aggregates.*   Fax: (925) 328-1820

HANSON BUILDING MATERIALS AMERICA
1350 Campus Pkwy., Ste. 302, Neptune, NJ   07753
CEO: Alan J. Murray, CEO   Tel: (732) 919-9777   %FO: 100
Bus: *Supplier of aggregates, cement   Fax: (732) 919-1149*
     and road materials; construction
     services.

HANSON CONCRETE SOUTH CENTRAL
8505 Freeport Pkwy., Ste. 200, Irving, TX   75063
CEO: Tommy Abbott, Mgr.   Tel: (972) 621-0345   %FO: 100
Bus: *Mfr. cement.*   Fax: (972) 621-0280

HANSON PIPE & PRODUCTS
3500 Maple Avenue, Dallas, TX   75219-0999
CEO: James Kitzmiller, Pres.   Tel: (214) 525-5500   %FO: 100
Bus: *Mfr. concrete pipe and precast   Fax: (214) 525-5817*
     concrete products.

PIONEER INC.
8668 Sparling Lane, Dixon, CA   95620
CEO: Gary Stout   Tel: (707) 678-3281   %FO: 100
Bus: *Supplies building materials.*   Fax: (707) 678-1072

PIONEER ROOFING TILE, INC.
10605 Poplar Avenue, Fontana, CA   92337
CEO: Jeff Bobolts, Mgr.   Tel: (909) 350-4238   %FO: 100
Bus: *Mfr. roofing tiles.*   Fax: (909) 350-2298

PIONEER USA, INC.
11700 Old Katy Road, Ste. 1200, Houston, TX   77079
CEO: Michael Kane, Pres.   Tel: (281) 848-3200   %FO: 100
Bus: *Mfr. building materials.*   Fax:

● **HAYS PLC**
Guildford, Surrey GU2 5HJ, UK
CEO: John R. Cole, Mng. Dir.   Tel: 44-148-330-2203   Rev: $3,361
Bus: *Provides services for wholesale/retail   Fax: 44-148-330-0388   Emp: 27,000*
     distribution, personnel recruitment and www.hays-plc.com
     office support services.

HAYS HOME DELIVERY SERVICES
14100 B. Parke Long Court, Chantilly, VA   20151
CEO: William Jarnagin, Pres.   Tel: (703) 502-1779   %FO: 100
Bus: *Provides services for*   Fax: (703) 502-4918
     wholesale/retail distribution.

HAYS INFORMATION MANAGEMENT, INC.
2010 W. Sam Houston Parkway North, Houston, TX   77043
CEO: Grant Mackie, Pres.   Tel: (713) 468-4224   %FO: 100
Bus: *Provides information storage and*   Fax: (713) 468-7246
     management services.

● **HEATHWAY, LTD.**
Featherstone Road, Wolverton Mill, Milton Keynes MK12 6LA, UK
CEO: Adrain Wraight, Pres.   Tel: 44-190-822-2500
Bus: *Fiber optic, TV and quartz-working* Fax: 44-190-822-2564   Emp: 70
     machinery.   www.heathway.co.uk

HEATHWAY INC.
4030 C Skyron Drive, Doylestown, PA   18901
CEO: Robert Halbreiner, Pres.   Tel: (215) 348-2881   %FO: 95
Bus: *Distributor fiber optic, TV &*   Fax: (215) 348-2309   Emp: 5
     quartz-working machinery.

● **HILTON GROUP PLC**
Maple Court, Central Park, Reeds Crescent, Watford, Hertfordshire WD1 1HZ, UK
CEO: John B. H. Jackson, Chmn.   Tel: 44-192-343-4000   Rev: $5,898
Bus: *Leisure industry, gaming, real estate,* Fax: 44-192-343-4001   Emp: 53,630
     hotels, retail.   www.hiltongroup.com

HILTON INTERNATIONAL CO.
901 Ponce de Leon Blvd., Ste. 700, Coral Gables, FL   33134
CEO: Howard Friedman, Pres.   Tel: (305) 444-3444   %FO: 100
Bus: *Hotel management.*   Fax: (305) 774-3895

HILTON INTERNATIONAL COMPANY
One Wall Street, New York, NY   10005
CEO: Lisa Maggiore, Mgr.   Tel: (212) 820-1700   %FO: 100
Bus: *Hotel chain.*   Fax: (212) 809-7595

● **HOPKINSONS HOLDINGS PLC**
Birkby Grange, Birkby Hall Road, Huddersfield, West Yorkshire HD2 2UR, UK
CEO: Roger Griffin   Tel: 44-148-482-0820
Bus: *Mfr. valves and spare parts service.* Fax: 44-148-482-0484
                                          www.hopkinsons.co.uk

ATWOOD & MORRILL COMPANY, INC.
285 Canal Street, Salem, MA 01970

CEO: Robert Genier, Pres.	Tel: (978) 744-5690	%FO: 100
Bus: *Mfr. valves and spare parts service.*	Fax: (978) 744-5690	Emp: 175

● HSBC HOLDINGS PLC
10 Lower Thames Street, London EC3R 6AE, UK

CEO: John R.H. Bond, Chmn.	Tel: 44-207-260-0500	Rev: $43,400
Bus: *Banking, trade and financial services and insurance.*	Fax: 44-207-260-0501 www.hsbcgroup.com	Emp: 144,500

BSBC BUSINESS LOANS, INC.
One Marine Midland Center, 19th Fl., Buffalo, NY 14203

CEO: Wick K. Hannan, SVP	Tel: (716) 841-4450	%FO: 100
Bus: *Provides business loans.*	Fax: (716) 841-1714	

HSCB EQUATOR BANK
45 Glastonbury Blvd., Glastonbury, CT 06033

CEO: John Kearney, COO	Tel: (860) 633-9999	%FO: 100
Bus: *Commercial banking services.*	Fax: (860) 633-6799	

HSBC INC.
452 Fifth Avenue, New York, NY 10018

CEO: Youssef A. Nasr, CEO	Tel: (212) 525-5000	%FO: 100
Bus: *International banking and trade financing services.*	Fax: (212) 525-5996	

HSBC MORTGAGE CORPORATION
2929 Walden Avenue, Depew, NY 14043

CEO: David J. Hunter, Pres.	Tel: (716) 651-6611	%FO: 100
Bus: *Provides residential mortgage servicing.*	Fax: (716) 651-6949	

WELLS FARGE HSBC TRADE BANK
525 Market Street, 25th Fl., San Francisco, CA 94105

CEO: William Haddon, CEO	Tel: (415) 396-6522	%FO: JV
Bus: *International trade financing services.*	Fax: (415) 541-0299	

● HUNTINGDON LIFE SCIENCES GROUP PLC
Wooley Road, Alconbury, Huntingdon, Dambridgeshire PE28 4HS, UK

CEO: Brian Cass, CEO	Tel: 44-148-089-2000	Rev: $95
Bus: *Engaged in safety and efficacy research.*	Fax: 44-148-089-2205 www.huntingdon.com	Emp: 1,300

HUNTINGDON LIFE SCIENCES
PO Box 2360, East Millstone, NJ   08875
CEO: Fiona Fraser-Smith   Tel: (732) 873-2360   %FO: 100
Bus: *Engaged in safety and efficacy*   Fax: (732) 873-3992
   research.

● **IBSTOCK BRICK LIMITED**
Lutterworth House, Lutterworth, Leicestershire, LE17 4PS, UK
CEO: Philip R. Mengel, CEO   Tel: 44-145-555-3071
Bus: *Mfr. of high quality clay facing bricks*   Fax: 44-145-555-3182
   and paving.   www.ibstock.co.uk

   GLEN-GERY CORPORATION
   1166 Sprin Street, Wyomissing, PA   19610-6001
   CEO: Stephen G. Matsick, Pres. & CEO   Tel: (610) 374-4011   %FO: 100
   Bus: *Mfr. brick, brickwork design and*   Fax: (610) 374-1622   Emp: 1,200
      services.

● **ICL PLC, DIV. FUJITSU**
Observatory House, Windsor Road, Slough Berkshire SL1 2EY, UK
CEO: Graham Goulden   Tel: 44-175-360-4736   Rev: $4,075
Bus: *Provides information technology*   Fax: 44-175-360-4669   Emp: 19,000
   systems and services.   www.icl.co.uk

   ICL FUJITSU SOLUTIONS, INC.
   5429 LBJ Freeway, Dallas, TX   75240
   CEO: Adrian King, Pres.   Tel: (972) 716-8300   %FO: 100
   Bus: *Information technology systems*   Fax: (972) 716-8586
      and services.

● **IMI PLC**
Kynoch Works, PO Box 216, Witton, Birmingham B6 7BA, UK
CEO: Gary J. Allen, CEO   Tel: 44-121-356-4848   Rev: $2,411
Bus: *Holding company. Mfr. building*   Fax: 44-121-356-3526   Emp: 18,300
   products, liquid dispensers and designs   www.imi.plc.uk
   engineering systems.

   CANNON EQUIPMENT COMPANY
   15100 Business Parkway, Cannon Falls, MN   55068
   CEO: R. Rosa, Pres.   Tel: (651) 322-6300   %FO: 100
   Bus: *Mfr. point of sale and display*   Fax: (651) 322-1583
      equipment, mobile merchandising
      carts.

CCI, INC.
22591 Avenida Empresa, Rancho Santa Margarita, CA 92688
CEO: S. A. Carson, Pres.   Tel: (949) 858-1877   %FO: 100
Bus: *Mfr./sale/service control valves for*   Fax: (949) 858-1878
     power, oil, gas and petrochemicals
     industry.

IMI CORNELIUS INC.
One Cornelius Place, Hwy. 10 West, Anoka, MN 55303
CEO: Rick Barklay, Pres.   Tel: (612) 421-6120   %FO: 100
Bus: *Mfr. beverage dispensing systems*   Fax: (612) 427-4522
     and equipment.

IMI NORGREN COMPANY
5400 South Delaware, Littleton, CO 80120-1663
CEO: William J. Wolsky, Chmn.   Tel: (303) 794-2611   %FO: 100
Bus: *Mfr. pneumatic products.*   Fax: (303) 795-9487

● **IMPERIAL CHEMICAL INDUSTRIES PLC**
Imperial Chemical House, 9 Millbank, London SW1P 3JF, UK
CEO: Brendan R. O'Neill, CEO   Tel: 44-207-834-4444   Rev: $9,592
Bus: *Mfr. industrial and special chemicals,*   Fax: 44-207-834-2042   Emp: 53,500
     agrochemical seeds, pharmaceuticals,   www.ici.com
     films, paints, explosives, fibers, acrylics.

     ACHESON COLLOIDS COMPANY
     PO Box 120, Brookfield, OH 44403
     CEO: A.V. Parry, Mgr.   Tel: (330) 448-4541   %FO: 100
     Bus: *Mfr. electronic and engineering*   Fax: (330) 448-7922
         materials.

     ACHESON INDUSTRIES, INC.
     1600 Washington Avenue, Port Huron, MI 48060
     CEO: John D. Morell, CEO   Tel: (810) 984-5583   %FO: 100
     Bus: *Mfr. specialty lubricants,*   Fax: (810) 984-5980
         including lubricating oils and
         greases.

     NATIONAL STARCH & CHEMICAL COMPANY
     14351 Highway 221, Enoree, SC 29335
     CEO: Bill Kramer, Mgr.   Tel: (864) 969-2811   %FO: 100
     Bus: *Mfr./sales adhesives and specialty*   Fax: (864) 969-6711
         synthetic polymers.

NATIONAL STARCH & CHEMICAL COMPANY
1164 Great Southwest Parkway, Grand Prairie, TX 75050

CEO: Ann Savoca, Dir.	Tel: (972) 647-9222	%FO: 100
Bus: *Mfr. adhesives.*	Fax: (972) 660-1192	

NATIONAL STARCH & CHEMICAL COMPANY
4414 Sarellen Road, Richmond, VA 23231

CEO: Bill Powell, Dir.	Tel: (804) 222-6100	%FO: 100
Bus: *Mfr. specialty starches.*	Fax: (804) 222-3739	

NATIONAL STARCH & CHEMICAL COMPANY
4035 Senator Street, Memphis, TN 38118

CEO: Bill Irvin, Mgr.	Tel: (901) 541-9660	%FO: 100
Bus: *Mfr. adhesives.*	Fax: (901) 795-4246	

NATIONAL STARCH & CHEMICAL COMPANY
10 Finderne Avenue, Bridgewater, NJ 08807

CEO: William H. Powell, CEO	Tel: (908) 685-5000	%FO: 100
Bus: *Mfr. starches, specialty chemicals and resins.*	Fax: (908) 685-5005	Emp: 1,200

NATIONAL STARCH & CHEMICAL COMPANY
2960 Exxon Avenue, Cincinnati, OH 45241

CEO: Bill Powell, Dir.	Tel: (513) 563-0220	%FO: 100
Bus: *Mfr./sales adhesives and specialty synthetic polymers.*	Fax: (513) 733-0040	

UNIQEMA
4650 South Racine, Chicago, IL 60609

CEO: Bob Drennan, VP	Tel: (773) 376-9000	%FO: 100
Bus: *Mfr. specialty chemicals.*	Fax: (773) 376-0095	

● INCEPTA GROUP PLC
3 London Wall Buildings, London Wall, London EC2M 5SY, UK

CEO: David Wright, CEO	Tel: 44-207-282-2800	Rev: $275
Bus: *Engaged in advertising, marketing and public relations.*	Fax: 44-207-638-3444	Emp: 1,000
	www.incepta.com	

CITIGATE ALBERT FRANK
850 Third Avenue, New York, NY 10022

CEO: Chris Finn	Tel: (212) 508-3400	%FO: 100
Bus: *Engaged in advertising.*	Fax: (212) 508-3544	

CITIGATE BROADCAST
1440 Broadway, 16th Fl., New York, NY 10018

CEO: Michelle Kramer	Tel: (212) 688-6840	%FO: 100
Bus: *Engaged in public relations.*	Fax: (212) 838-3393	

CITIGATE BROADSTREET
920 Broadway, New York, NY　10010
CEO: David H. Dreyfuss　　　　　Tel: (212) 780-5700　　　%FO: 100
Bus: *Specializes in high-end corporate*　Fax: (212) 780-5710
　　videos.

CITIGATE CORPORATE BRANDING
850 Third Avenue, New York, NY　10022
CEO: Jim Quartararo　　　　　Tel: (212) 508-3436　　　%FO: 100
Bus: *Engaged in design and branding.*　Fax: (212) 508-3550

CITIGATE CORPORATE BRANDING
8360 Melrose Avenue, Los Angeles, CA　90069
CEO: Jay Toffoli　　　　　Tel: (323) 866-3400　　　%FO: 100
Bus: *Engaged in design and branding.*　Fax: (323) 866-3410

CITIGATE CORPORATE BRANDING INC.
801 Montgomery Street, 5th Fl., San Francisco, CA　94133
CEO: John McClave　　　　　Tel: (415) 274-7570　　　%FO: 100
Bus: *Engaged in design and branding.*　Fax: (415) 989-6858

CITIGATE CUNNINGHAM
101 Second Street, Ste. 2250, San Francisco, CA　94105
CEO: Dennis Maxwell　　　　　Tel: (415) 618-8727　　　%FO: 100
Bus: *Engaged in public relations.*　Fax: (415) 618-8702

CITIGATE CUNNINGHAM INC.
3801 Texas Hwy. S, Bldg., 2, Ste. 2, Austin, TX　78704
CEO: Morris Denton　　　　　Tel: (512) 652-2700　　　%FO: 100
Bus: *Engaged in public relations for*　Fax: (512) 652-2702
　　technology businesses.

CITIGATE CUNNINGHAM INC.
One Memorial Drive, Cambridge, MA　02142
CEO: Debbi Ford　　　　　Tel: (617) 494-8202　　　%FO: 100
Bus: *Engaged in public relations for*　Fax: (617) 494-8422
　　technology businesses.

CITIGATE DEWE ROGERSON
180 North Michigan Avenue, Chicago, IL　60601
CEO: Ron Kelly　　　　　Tel: (312) 372-0771　　　%FO: 100
Bus: *Engaged in public relations for*　Fax: (312) 372-1409
　　technology businesses.

CITIGATE HUDSON
62 West 45th Street, New York, NY   10036
CEO: Dave Mittereder, CEO   Tel: (212) 840-0008   %FO: 100
Bus: *Engaged in advertising.*   Fax: (212) 840-9490

COLGATE DEWE ROGERSON
1440 Broadway, New York, NY   10018
CEO: Jim Sansevero   Tel: (212) 688-6840   %FO: 100
Bus: *Engaged in public relations.*   Fax: (212) 838-3393

COLGATE DEWE ROGERSON
801 Montgomery Street, 5th Fl., San Francisco, CA   94133
CEO: Maria Stokes   Tel: (415) 274-7570   %FO: 100
Bus: *Engaged in public relations.*   Fax: (415) 989-6858

COLGATE SARD VERBINNEN
630 Third Avenue, New York, NY   10017
CEO: George Sard   Tel: (212) 687-8080   %FO: 100
Bus: *Engaged in public relations.*   Fax: (212) 687-8344

• INFORMA GROUP PLC
19 Portland Place, London W1N 3AF, UK
CEO: David S. Gilbertson, CEO   Tel: 44-207-453-2222   Rev: $443
Bus: *Engaged in electronic and print*   Fax: 44-207-436-2450   Emp: 2,633
publication information services.   www.informa.com

DRUG AND MARKET DEVELOPMENT PUBLICATIONS
PO Box 5194, Westborough, MA   01581-5194
CEO: Lorraine Wood, Mgr.   Tel: (508) 616-5566   %FO: 100
Bus: *Publishes drug and market*   Fax: (508) 616-5544
publications.

EFFRON ENTERPRISES INC.
4 Gannett Drive, White Plains, NY   10604
CEO: Lac An Vuong, Dir.   Tel: (914) 640-0200   %FO: 100
Bus: *Provides products and tools for*   Fax: (914) 694-6745
investment.

FREIBERG PUBLISHING COMPANY
2302 West First Street, Cedar Falls, IA   50613
CEO: Nicole Hintz   Tel: (319) 277-3599   %FO: 100
Bus: *Publisher of agricultural*   Fax: (319) 277-3783
magazines.

IBS USA CONFERENCES

PO Box 5195, Westborough, MA 01581-5195

CEO: Leroy Hood, Pres.   Tel: (508) 616-5500   %FO: 100

Bus: *Provides conference facilities for*   Fax: (508) 616-5522
neutral unbiased forums.

INFORMA RESEARCH SERVICES INC.

26565 Agoura Road, Ste. 300, Calabasas, CA 91302-1942

CEO: Renee Arends, HR   Tel: (818) 880-8877   %FO: 100

Bus: *Provides financial information*   Fax: (818) 880-8448
and data.

MCM, INC.

One Chase Manhattan Plaza, 37th Fl., New York, NY 10005

CEO: Sherrie Davis   Tel: (212) 509-5800   %FO: 100

Bus: *Provides high value analysis of*   Fax: (212) 908-4345
financial markets to financial
institutions.

THE TOWNSEND & SCHUPP COMPANY

100 Wells Street, Hartford, CT 06103

CEO: Fred F. Townsend Jr., Pres.   Tel: (860) 522-2214   %FO: 100

Bus: *Provides financial information*   Fax: (860) 549-6200
and statistical analysis regarding
US and Canadian insurance
markets.

WASHINGTON POLICY & ALALYSIS

1025 Thomas Jefferson Street NW, Ste. 411W, Washington, DC 20007

CEO: William Martin   Tel: (202) 965-1161   %FO: 100

Bus: *Provides government and industry*   Fax: (202) 965-1177
contacts to clients.

● INGENTA PLC

BUCS Bldg., University of Bath, The Avenue, Claverton Down, Bath BA2 7AY, UK

CEO: Mark A. Rowse, CEO   Tel: 44-122-552-6267

Bus: *Provides marketing support to*   Fax: 44-122-582-6283
publishers and website development.   www.ingenta.com

DYNAMIC DIAGRAMS INC.

12 Bassett Street, Providence, RI 02903

CEO: Paul Kahn   Tel: (401) 331-2014   %FO: 100

Bus: *Engaged in website development.*   Fax: (401) 331-2015

INGENTA INC.
44 Brattle Street, 4th Fl., Cambridge, MA   02138
CEO: Christine Lamb, VP   Tel: (617) 395-4000   %FO: 100
Bus: *Provides marketing support to*   Fax: (617) 395-4099
  publishers.

● **INMARSAT VENTURES PLC**
99 City Road, London EC1Y 1AX, UK
CEO: Michael Storey, CEO   Tel: 44-207-728-1100   Rev: $417
Bus: *Provides satellite communications*   Fax: 44-207-726-1044   Emp: 500
  services.   www.inmarsatventures.com

  AIRIA INC.
  1997 Annapolis Exchange Pkwy., Ste. 300, Annapolis, MD   21401
  CEO: Steve Cutvirth   Tel: (410) 571-8240   %FO: 100
  Bus: *Provides in-flight television*   Fax: (410) 266-2538
    services.

  SETFAIR USA INC.
  PO Box 130908, The Woodlands, TX   77383
  CEO: Ken Nelson, Reg. Mgr.   Tel: (281) 298-7420   %FO: 100
  Bus: *Engaged in maritime procurement*   Fax: (281) 298-7420
    solutions.

● **THE INNOVATION GROUP PLC**
Yarmouth House, 1300 Pkwy., Solent Business Park, Whiteley, Hampshire PO15 7AE, UK
CEO: Robert S. Terry, CEO   Tel: 44-148-956-5321   Rev: $14
Bus: *Mfr. financial software.*   Fax: 44-148-957-918   Emp: 50
                www.innovation-group.co.uk

  THE INNOVATION GROUP
  39 Old Ridgebury Road, Ste. P-4, Danbury, CT   06810
  CEO: Patricia Shea, Mktg. Dir.   Tel: (203) 743-6000   %FO: 100
  Bus: *Mfr. financial software.*   Fax: (203) 743-6003

● **INSIGNIA SOLUTIONS PLC**
Wycombe Lane, Woodburn Green High Wycombe, Buckinghamshire HP10 0HH, UK
CEO: Richard M. Noling, CEO   Tel: 44-162-853-9500   Rev: $11
Bus: *Engaged in Internet technology.*   Fax: 44-162-853-9501   Emp: 100
                www.insignia.com

  INSIGNIA SOLUTIONS INC.
  41300 Christy Street, Fremont, CA   94538-3115
  CEO: Mark McMillan, CEO   Tel: (510) 360-3700   %FO: 100
  Bus: *Engaged in Internet technology.*   Fax: (510) 360-3701

- **INTERMATRIX LTD.**
  Four Cromwell Place, London SW7 2JE, UK
  CEO: Richard van den Bergh, CEO
  Bus: *Engaged in management consulting services.*

  Tel: 44-207-591-2100
  Fax: 44-207-591-2101
  www.intermatrixgroup.com

  INTERMATRIX, INC.
  Ten Corbin Drive, Darien, CT   06820
  CEO: Dr. Jan V. Dauman, Dir.
  Bus: *Engaged in management consulting services.*

  Tel: (203) 662-1000
  Fax: (203) 655-3130

  %FO: 100

- **INTERNATIONAL GREETINGS PLC**
  Hatfield Business Park, Frobisher Way, Hatfield Hertfordshire AL10 9TQ, UK
  CEO: Anders Hedlund, Chmn.
  Bus: *Mfr. gift wrapping paper and related products.*

  Tel: 44-170-763-0630
  Fax: 44-170-763-0666
  www.internationagreetings.co.uk

  THE GIFT WRAP COMPANY
  338 Industrial Boulevard, Midway, GA   31320
  CEO: Richard Eckman, VP
  Bus: *Mfr. and sales of wrapping paper.*

  Tel: (912) 884-9727
  Fax: (912) 884-9702

  %FO: 100

- **INTERNATIONAL POWER PLC**
  Senator House, 85 Queen Victoria Street, London EC4V 4PD, UK
  CEO: Peter Giller, CEO
  Bus: *Generates and sells electricity.*

  Tel: 44-207-320-8600
  Fax: 44-207-320-8700
  www.internationalpowerplc.com

  AMERICAN NATIONAL POWER INC.
  10000 Memorial Drive, Ste. 500, Houston, TX   77024
  CEO: James Moore, CEO
  Bus: *Develops and operates generating facilities in the U.S.*

  Tel: (713) 613-4300
  Fax: (713) 613-4304

  %FO: 100

- **INTERTEK TESTING SERVICES**
  25 Saville Row, London W1S 2ES, UK
  CEO: Richard Nelson, Pres. & CEO
  Bus: *Engaged in product and commodity testing.*

  Tel: 44-207-396-3400
  Fax: 44-207-396-3480
  www.testmark.com

  Rev: $581
  Emp: 9,500

CALEB BRETT USA
505 Forge River Road, Webster, TX   77598
CEO: John Hodson, Pres.   Tel: (281) 486-8825   %FO: 100
Bus: *Assessment of crude oil, petroleum*   Fax: (281) 486-4742
     products and chemicals and
     agricultural products.

CALEB BRETT USA
134 Heinsohn Road, Ste. A, Corpus Christi, TX   78401
CEO: Rory Baker, VP   Tel: (361) 289-7474   %FO: 100
Bus: *Tests environmental chemicals,*   Fax: (361) 289-7477
     water, air and soil.

CALEB BRETT USA
333 Dalziel Road, Linden, NJ   07035
CEO: John Hodson, Pres.   Tel: (908) 862-0130   %FO: 100
Bus: *Tests environmental chemicals,*   Fax: (908) 862-4288
     water, air and soil.

ETL SEMKO
70 Codman Hill Road, Boxborough, MA   01719
CEO: Nancy Medas, Mgr.   Tel: (617) 756-6711   %FO: 100
Bus: *Tests environmental chemicals,*   Fax: (617) 758-6461
     water, air and soil.

INTERTEK TESTING SERVICES
8125 NW 53rd Street, Ste. 200, Miami, FL   33166
CEO: A. Labiosa, Mgr.   Tel: (305) 513-3000   %FO: 100
Bus: *Tests environmental chemicals,*   Fax: (305) 513-3001
     water, air and soil.

INTERTEK TESTING SERVICES
1089 East Collins Boulevard, Richardson, TX   75081
CEO: Martin Jeffus, VP   Tel: (972) 238-5591   %FO: 100
Bus: *Tests environmental chemicals,*   Fax: (972) 238-5592
     water, air and soil.

LABTEST
70 Diamond Road, Springfield, NJ   07081
CEO: Raymond Kong, VP   Tel: (973) 346-5500   %FO: 100
Bus: *Tests environmental chemicals,*   Fax: (973) 379-5232
     water, air and soil.

RAM CONSULTING, DIV. INTERTEK TESTING
1301 West 22nd Street, Ste. 888, Oak Brook, IL   60523

CEO: Gene Rider, Pres.

Bus: *Tests environmental chemicals, water, air and soil.*

Tel: (630) 623-6060

Fax: (630) 623-6074

%FO: 100

● INVENSYS PLC
Carlisle Place, London SW1P 1BX, UK

CEO: Allen M. Yurko, CEO

Bus: *Holding company for industrial manufacturing companies.*

Tel: 44-207-834-3848

Fax: 44-207-821-3879

www.invensys.com

Rev: $14,380

Emp: 121,685

EUROTHERM DRIVES
9225 Forsyth Park Drive, Charlotte, NC   28273

CEO: Dan Barnhouse, Pres.

Bus: *Mfr. speed drives and control systems.*

Tel: (704) 588-3246

Fax: (704) 588-3249

%FO: 100

FOXBORO COMPANY
33 Commercial Street, Foxboro, MA   02035

CEO: William Kettelhut, Pres.

Bus: *Provides automation systems.*

Tel: (508) 543-2700

Fax: (508) 549-2735

%FO: 100

INVENSYS
PO Box 248, Dublin, OH   43017

CEO: Bruce Henderson, Pres.

Bus: *Mfr. controls, relays, etc., for refrigeration, air conditioning and automotive industry.*

Tel: (614) 873-9200

Fax: (614) 873-9290

%FO: 100

INVENSYS AUTOMATION SYSTEMS
125 South 84 Street, Suite 100, Milwaukee, WI   53214

CEO: Robert A. Hitt, CEO

Bus: *Mfr. automation systems.*

Tel: (414) 643-3300

Fax: (414) 643-2310

%FO: 100

INVENSYS BUILDING SYSTEMS
1354 Clifford Avenue, Loves Park, IL   61111

CEO: Chris Candler, Pres.

Bus: *Mfr. temperature control products and intelligent automation systems for commercial, industrial and institutional buildings.*

Tel: (815) 637-3000

Fax: (815) 637-5300

%FO: 100

INVENSYS CLIMATE CONTROLS
8161 US Route 42 North, Plain City, OH   43064
CEO: Robert A. Hitt, Pres.   Tel: (614) 873-9200   %FO: 100
Bus: *Mfr. temperature and appliance*   Fax: (614) 873-9290
   controls.

INVENSYS CONTROL SYSTEMS
2809 Emerywood Pkwy., Richmond, VA   23261
CEO: Jim Devlin, Pres.   Tel: (804) 756-6500   %FO: 100
Bus: *Mfr. automatic controls and*   Fax: (804) 756-6565
   control systems for industry,
   commercial buildings and home
   use.

INVENSYS INC.
14409 Export Road, Laredo, TX   78045
CEO: Bruce Henderson   Tel: (956) 724-7632   %FO: 100
Bus: *Mfr. appliance controls, cooking*   Fax: (956) 724-7589
   and refrigeration systems.

INVENSYS INC.
Route 58 West, Independence, VA   24348
CEO: Jim Devlin, Pres.   Tel: (540) 773-2771   %FO: 100
Bus: *Mfr. appliance controls.*   Fax: (540) 773-3250

INVENSYS INC.
105 Washington Street, Hanover, IL   61041
CEO: Jim Devlin, Pres.   Tel: (815) 591-2151   %FO: 100
Bus: *Mfr. appliance controls, cooking*   Fax: (815) 591-2321
   and refrigeration systems.

INVENSYS INC.
703 West South Street, North Manchester, IN   46962
CEO: Jim Devlin, Pres.   Tel: (219) 982-2161   %FO: 100
Bus: *Mfr. appliance controls.*   Fax: (219) 982-3537

INVENSYS INC.
11768 James Street, Holland, MI   49424
CEO: Daniel J. Hunt   Tel: (616) 396-1467   %FO: 100
Bus: *Mfr. appliance controls, cooking*   Fax: (616) 396-0161
   and refrigeration systems.

INVENSYS INC.
210 Allen Street, West Plains, MO   65775
CEO: Jim Devlin, Pres.   Tel: (417) 256-7171   %FO: 100
Bus: *Mfr. appliance controls, cooking*   Fax: (417) 256-7855
   and refrigeration systems.

INVENSYS INC.
301 West Ohio Street, Kendalville, IN   46755
CEO: Jim Devlin, Pres.   Tel: (219) 347-1000   %FO: 100
Bus: *Mfr. appliance controls.*   Fax: (219) 349-3019

INVENSYS INC.
One Siebe Drive, New Stanton, PA   15672
CEO: M. Caliel, Pres.   Tel: (724) 925-7211   %FO: 100
Bus: *Mfr. appliance controls.*   Fax: (724) 925-4632

INVENSYS POWER SYSTEMS
8609 Six Forks Road, Raleigh, NC   27645
CEO: Tom Gutierrez, CEO   Tel: (919) 872-3020   %FO: 100
Bus: *Mfr. uninterruptible power systems.* Fax: (919) 870-3450

INVENSYS SOFTWARE SYSTEMS INC.
33 Commercial Street, Foxboro, MA   02035
CEO: Bruce Henderson, Pres.   Tel: (508) 549-3300   %FO: 100
Bus: *Mfr. temperature and appliance*   Fax: (508) 549-4500
    controls.

INVENSYS SOFTWARE SYSTEMS
2191 Fox Mill Road, Suite 500, Herndon, VA   20171
CEO: Bruce Henderson, CEO   Tel: (703) 234-6000   %FO: 100
Bus: *Mfr. software systems and*   Fax: (703) 234-6719
    solutions.

NEW ENGLAND INSTRUMENTS
245 Railroad Street, Woonsocket, RI   02895
CEO: Tony Campagna, Mgr.   Tel: (401) 769-0703   %FO: 100
Bus: *Mfr. instruments.*   Fax: (401) 769-0037   Emp: 100

POWERWARE CORPORATION
8609 Six Forks Road, Raleigh, NC   27615
CEO: Pat Steffen, CEO   Tel: (919) 872-3020   %FO: 100
Bus: *Provides power protection and*   Fax: (919) 870-3450
    management solutions.

REXNORD CORPORATION
PO Box 2022, Milwaukee, WI   53201
CEO: Peter C. Wallace, Pres.   Tel: (414) 643-3000   %FO: 100
Bus: *Mfr. power transmissions and*   Fax: (414) 643-3078
    conveying components.

VIATRAN CORPORATION
300 Industrial Drive, Grand Island, NY 14072
CEO: Dave Fleischmann, CEO   Tel: (716) 773-1700   %FO: 100
Bus: *Pressure transducers and*   Fax: (716) 773-2488   Emp: 125
transmitters; measuring systems.

• JARDINE LLOYD THOMPSON GROUP PLC
6 Crutched Friars, London EC3N 2PH, UK
CEO: Ken A. Carter, CEO   Tel: 44-207-528-4444   Rev: $461
Bus: *Insurance brokers.*   Fax: 40-207-528-4185   Emp: 3,700
www.jltgroup.com

INTERMEDIARY INSURANCE SERVICES INC.
180 Montgomery Avenue, 5th Fl., San Francisco, CA 94104
CEO: James P. Henry   Tel: (415) 398-6603   %FO: 100
Bus: *Insurance brokers.*   Fax: (415) 398-6851

JLT SERVICES CORPORATION
13 Cornell Road, Latham, NY 12110
CEO: Georgiana Carney, SVP   Tel: (518) 782-3000   %FO: 100
Bus: *Insurance brokers.*   Fax: (518) 782-3082

• JCB LTD. (JC BAMFORD EXCAVATORS LTD)
Rochester, Straffordshire ST14 5JP, UK
CEO: Sir Anthony Bamford, Chmn.   Tel: 44-188-959-0312   Rev: $1,270
Bus: *Mfr. construction and materials*   Fax: 44-188-959-0588   Emp: 3,400
handling equipment.   www.jcb.co.uk

JCB INC.
2000 Bamford Boulevard, Pooler, GA 31322
CEO: Mike Chapman, Pres.   Tel: (912) 447-2000   %FO: 100
Bus: *Mfr. construction and materials*   Fax: (912) 447-2299   Emp: 115
handling equipment.

• JOHNSON MATTHEY PLC
2-4 Cockspur Street, Trafalgar Square, London SW1Y 5BQ, UK
CEO: C. R. N. Clark, CEO   Tel: 44-207-269-8400   Rev: $6,154
Bus: *Refines & processes precious metals &*   Fax: 44-207-269-8433   Emp: 6,250
rare minerals & produces   www.matthey.com
pharmaceuticals & specialty chemicals.

JOHNSON MATTHEY INC.
460 East Swedesford Road, Wayne, PA 19087-1881
CEO: Anthony Trifiletti   Tel: (610) 971-3000   %FO: 100
Bus: *Mfr. automobile exhaust catalytic*   Fax: (610) 971-3051
systems.

● **H & R JOHNSON TILES LTD.**

Highgate Tile Works, Tunstall, Stoke-On-Trent, Staffordshire ST6 4JX, UK

CEO: David Dry, Dir. Tel: 44-178-257-5575

Bus: *Mfr. ceramic tile.* Fax: 44-178-257-7377

www.johnson-tiles.com

    H & R JOHNSON, INC.

    PO Box 234, Brielle, NJ 08730

    CEO: Paul McGinty, Mgr. Tel: (732) 528-2248 %FO: 100

    Bus: *Sales/distribution of ceramic tiles.* Fax: (732) 528-2249

● **JUST GROUP PLC**

Wye House, Granby Road, Bakewell, Derbyshire DE45 1ES, UK

CEO: Wilf Shorrocks Tel: 44-162-981-4994 Rev: $18

Bus: *Develops and markets intellectual* Fax: 44-162-981-4990 Emp: 50
property rights in children's www.justgroup.com
entertainment.

    JUST GROUP INC.

    248 Columbia Turnpike, Florham Park, NJ 07932

    CEO: Ian Miles Tel: (973) 377-8855 %FO: 100

    Bus: *Develops and markets intellectual* Fax: (973) 377-9088
    property rights in children's
    entertainment.

● **KELDA GROUP PLC**

2 The Embankment, Sovereign Street, Leeds, West Yorkshire LS1 4BG, UK

CEO: John Napier, CEO Tel: 44-113-234-3234 Rev: $965

Bus: *Provides water and wastewater services.* Fax: 44-113-234-2322 Emp: 4,300

www.keldagroup.com

    AQUARION COMPANY

    835 Main Street, Bridgeport, CT 06604-4995

    CEO: Janet M. Hansen, Pres. & CEO Tel: (203) 335-2333 %FO: 100

    Bus: *Water management.* Fax: (203) 336-5639

● **KEWILL SYSTEMS PLC**

Cedar Court, Guildford Road, Fetcham, Leatherhead, Surrey KT22 9RC, UK

CEO: Robert Malley, CEO Tel: 44-137-236-6500 Rev: $97

Bus: *Mfr. enterprise resource planning* Fax: 44-137-236-6400 Emp: 600
software. www.kewill.com

KEWILL
7701 York Avenue South, Minneapolis, MN 55435
CEO: Robert Kimball   Tel: (952) 831-7182   %FO: 100
Bus: *Mfr. enterprise resource planning*   Fax: (952) 831-2811
    software.

KEWILL
14964 NW Greenbrier Parkway, Beaverton, OR 97006
CEO: Ron Avni, Pres.   Tel: (503) 690-3036   %FO: 100
Bus: *Mfr. enterprise resource planning*   Fax: (503) 690-6866
    software.

• KINGSTON COMMUNICATIONS (HULL) PLC.
Carr Lane, Kingston-Upon-Hull HU1 3RE, UK
CEO: Steve Maine, CEO ·   Tel: 44-148-260-2100   Rev: $330
Bus: *Engaged in telecommunications.*   Fax: 44-148-232-0652   Emp: 1,900
    www.kingston-comms.com

KTL DALLAS INC.
802 North Kealy, Lewisville, TX 75057-3136
CEO: Tom Tidwell   Tel: (972) 436-9600   %FO: 100
Bus: *Telecommunications.*   Fax: (972) 436-2667

• KNOWLEDGE MANAGEMENT SOFTWARE PLC
Pencroft Way, Manchester Science Park, Manchester, Lancashire M15 6AU, UK
CEO: Stuart J. Whitstance, CEO   Tel: 44-161-227-1100
Bus: *Computer software and services.* Fax: 44-161-227-1101
    www.kmsplc.com

KNOWLEDGE MANAGEMENT SOFTWARE INC.
50 Day Street, South Norwalk, CT 06854
CEO: Dave Rosalski, COO   Tel: (203) 838-6665   %FO: 100
Bus: *Computer software and services.* Fax: (203) 838-1070

KNOWLEDGE MANAGEMENT SOFTWARE INC.
51 South Main Avenue, Ste. 320, Clearwater, FL 33765
CEO: Jeff Henning, Pres.   Tel: (727) 441-9877   %FO: 100
Bus: *Computer software and services.* Fax: (727) 441-3988

KNOWLEDGE MANAGEMENT SOFTWARE INC.
795 Folsom Street, 1st Fl., Sausalito, CA 94965
CEO: Jeff Henning, Pres.   Tel: (415) 848-2748   %FO: 100
Bus: *Computer software and services.* Fax: (415) 848-2748

KNOWLEDGE MANAGEMENT SOFTWARE INC.
50 Braintree Hill Office Park, Ste. 102, Braintree, MA   02184

CEO: Jeff Henning, Pres.   Tel: (781) 356-2717   %FO: 100

Bus: *Computer software and services.*   Fax: (781) 356-2799

● JOHN LAING PLC
133 Page Street, Mill Hill, London NW7 2ER, UK

CEO: Sir J. Martin Laing, CEO   Tel: 44-208-959-3636   Rev: $2,524

Bus: *Engaged in construction, industrial and civil engineering and property development.*   Fax: 44-208-906-5297   Emp: 8,230

www.john-laing.com

JOHN LAING HOMES INC.
8618 Westwood Center Drive, Vienna, VA   22181

CEO: Steve M. Baldwin, Pres.   Tel: (703) 827-4141   %FO: 100

Bus: *Home building company.*   Fax: (703) 827-4149   Emp: 30

JOHN LAING HOMES INC.
19600 Fairchild Road, Ste. 150, Irvine, CA   92612

CEO: Larry Webb, CEO   Tel: (949) 476-9090   %FO: 100

Bus: *Home building company.*   Fax: (949) 476-9898

● THE LAIRD GROUP PLC
3 St. James's Square, London SW1Y 4JU, UK

CEO: Ian Arnott, CEO   Tel: 44-207-468-4040   Rev: $1,637

Bus: *Mfr. security systems and electronics.*   Fax: 44-207-839-2921   Emp: 15,700

www.laird-plc.com

THE LAIRD GROUP
PO Box 650, Delaware Water Gap, PA   18327

CEO: Ron Brewer, VP   Tel: (570) 424-8510   %FO: 100

Bus: *Mfr. security systems and electronics.*   Fax: (570) 424-6213

THE LAIRD GROUP
2115 N. Fayetteville St., Asheboro, NC   27203

CEO: Ian Arnott, CEO   Tel: (336) 672-3465   %FO: 100

Bus: *Mfr. security systems and electronics.*   Fax: (336) 672-5555

THE LAIRD GROUP
505 Porter Way, Placentia, CA   92870

CEO: Ian Arnott, CEO   Tel: (714) 579-7100   %FO: 100

Bus: *Mfr. security systems and electronics.*   Fax: (714) 597-7120

THE LAIRD GROUP

3481 Rider Trail South, St. Louis, MO   63045
CEO: Lars Johnson, VP   Tel: (314) 344-9300   %FO: 100
Bus: *Mfr. security systems and* Fax: (314) 344-9333
     electronics.

• LAND INSTRUMENTS INTERNATIONAL LTD.

Stubley Lane, Dronfield S18 6DJ, U.K.
CEO: Tony Duncan, Mng. Dir.   Tel: 44-124-641-7691
Bus: *Mfr. infrared temperature measuring* Fax: 44-124-641-0585   Emp: 230
     instruments and devices.   www.landinst.com

LAND INFRARED

10 Friends Lane, Newtown, PA   18940
CEO: Ramon Biarnes, Pres.   Tel: (215) 504-8000   %FO: 100
Bus: *Sale/distribution infrared*   Fax: (215) 504-0879   Emp: 25
     temperature measuring
     instruments & devices.

• LAPORTE PLC

Nations House, 103 Wigmore Street, London W1H 9AB, UK
CEO: James Leng, CEO   Tel: 44-207-399-2400   Rev: $1,504
Bus: *Mfr./distributor chemicals.* Fax: 44-207-399-2401   Emp: 5,360
                                    www.laporteplc.com

ELECROCHEMICALS INC.

5630 Pioneer Creek Drive, Maple Plain, MN   55359
CEO: Moenes Elias, Pres.   Tel: (763) 479-2008   %FO: 100
Bus: *Mfr./distributor chemicals used in* Fax: (763) 479-3344
     printed circuit boards.

INSPEC USA

101 East Park Blvd., Ste. 201, Plano, TX   75074
CEO: Jay Janis, Mgr.   Tel: (972) 516-0702   %FO: 100
Bus: *Mfr. coatings and lubricants.* Fax: (972) 516-0624

LAPORTE COMPOUNDING

170 Pioneer Drive, Leominster, MA   01453
CEO: Robert Gingue, Dir.   Tel: (978) 537-8071   %FO: 100
Bus: *Mfr. chemical compounding*   Fax: (978) 537-8385
     products.

LAPORTE, INC.

22 Chambers Street, Princeton, NJ   08542
CEO: Michael J. Kenny, Pres.   Tel: (609) 430-1199   %FO: 100
Bus: *Mfr./distributor chemicals.* Fax: (609) 430-1524   Emp: 47

- **LAURA ASHLEY HOLDINGS PLC, SUB. UNITED INDUSTRIES**
27 Bagley's Lane, Fulham, London SW6 2AR, UK

CEO: Ng Kwan Cheong, CEO	Tel: 44-207-880-5100	Rev: $379
Bus: *Retail clothing chain.*	Fax: 44-207-880-5300	Emp: 2,765
	www.lauraashley.com	

    LAURA ASHLEY INC.
    6 St. James Avenue, Boston, MA 02116

CEO: Paul Ng, CEO	Tel: (617) 457-6000	%FO: 100
Bus: *Retail clothing chain.*	Fax: (617) 457-6060	

- **LEGAL & GENERAL GROUP, PLC.**
Temple Court, 11 Queen Victoria Street, London EC4N-4TP, UK

CEO: David Prosser, CEO	Tel: 44-207-528-6200	Rev: $47,520
Bus: *Provides life insurance.*	Fax: 44-207-528-4222	Emp: 7,900
	www.legal-and-general.co.uk	

    BANNER LIFE INSURANCE COMPANY
    1701 Research Blvd., Rockville, MD 20850

CEO: David S. Lenaburg, Pres.	Tel: (301) 279-4800	%FO: 100
Bus: *Provides life insurance.*	Fax: (301) 294-6986	

    WILLIAM PENN LIFE INSURANCE COMPANY OF NEW YORK
    100 Quentin Roosevelt Blvd., Garden City, NY 11530

CEO: Joseph Sullivan, Pres.	Tel: (516) 794-3700	
Bus: *Provides life insurance.*	Fax: (516) 229-3004	

- **LINKLATERS & ALLIANCE**
One Silk Street, London EC2Y 8HQ, UK

CEO: Terence Kyle, CEO	Tel: 44-207-456-2000	
Bus: *International non-partnership*	Fax: 44-207-456-2222	
association of European law firms.	www.linklaters-alliance.com	

    LINKLATERS & ALLIANCE
    1345 Ave. of the Americas. 19th Fl., New York, NY 10105-0302

CEO: Marianne Rosenberg	Tel: (212) 424-9000	%FO: 100
Bus: *International law firm.*	Fax: (212) 424-9100	Emp: 70

    LINKLATERS & ALLIANCE
    900 17th Street NW, Washington, DC 20006

CEO: Philippa Cottle	Tel: (202) 296-8337	%FO: 100
Bus: *International law firm.*	Fax: (202) 296-8455	Emp: 1

● **LISTER-PETTER, LTD.**
PO Box 1, Dursley, Glos G11 4HS, UK
CEO: Bonnie Dean, CEO
Tel: 44-145-354-4141
Bus: *Mfr. diesel and marine engines and generators.*
Fax: 44-145-354-6732
www.lister-petter.co.uk
Emp: 1,500

LISTER-PETTER INC.
815 East 56 Highway, Olathe, KS   66061-4914
CEO: Phil Cantrill, Pres.
Tel: (913) 764-3512
%FO: 100
Bus: *Mfr./distribution diesel, marine & natural gas engines, generators.*
Fax: (913) 764-5493
Emp: 60

● **LLOYD'S (FORMERLY LLOYD'S OF LONDON)**
One Lime Street, London EC3M 7HA, UK
CEO: Nicholas Prettjohn, CEO
Tel: 44-207-327-1000
Bus: *Insurance market services.*
Fax: 44-207-626-2389
www.lloyds.co.uk

LLOYD'S AMERICA LIMITED
1177 Avenue of the Americas, New York, NY   10036
CEO: Albert A. Skwiertz Jr, Pres.
Tel: (212) 382-4060
%FO: 100
Bus: *North America representative office.*
Fax: (212) 382-4070

● **LLOYDS TSB GROUP PLC**
71 Lombard Street, London EC3P 3BS, UK
CEO: Peter B. Ellwood, CEO
Tel: 44-207-626 1500
Rev: $23,300
Bus: *Financial services group, commercial banking services.*
Fax: 44-207-356 1369
www.lloydstsb.co.uk
Emp: 86,500

INVESTMENT ADVISERS, INC.
3700 U.S. Bank Place, Minneapolis, MN   55440
CEO: Lindsay Johnston, COO
Tel: (612) 376-2600
%FO: 100
Bus: *Provides investment management services.*
Fax: (612) 376-2616

LLOYDS BANK PLC
575 Fifth Avenue, New York, NY   10017
CEO: William Camposano, SVP
Tel: (212) 930-5000
%FO: 100
Bus: *International commercial banking services.*
Fax: (212) 930-5098

LLOYDS BANK PLC
2 South Biscayne Blvd., Ste. 3200, Miami, FL 33131
CEO: Peter J. Phillips, EVP   Tel: (305) 579-8900   %FO: 100
Bus: *International commercial banking*   Fax: (305) 371-8607
services.

● **LOGICA PLC**
Stephenson House, 75 Hampstead Road, London NW1 2PL, UK
CEO: Martin P. Read, Mng. Dir.   Tel: 44-207-637-9111   Rev: $1,285
Bus: *Systems integration, consulting and*   Fax: 44-207-468-7006   Emp: 8,100
software development.   www.logica.com

LOGICA, INC.
32 Hartwell Avenue, Lexington, MA 02173
CEO: Paul Nichols, CEO   Tel: (617) 476-8000   %FO: 100
Bus: *Systems integration, consulting*   Fax: (617) 476-8010   Emp: 400
and software development.

● **LONDON BRIDGE SOFTWARE HOLDINGS PLC**
New London Bridge House, 16th Fl., 25 London Bridge St., London SE1 9SG, UK
CEO: Jon Lee, CEO   Tel: 44-207-403-1333   Rev: $85
Bus: *Mfr. software for credit risk*   Fax: 44-207-403-8981   Emp: 520
management professionals.   www.london-bridge.com

LONDON BRIDGE GROUP
615 Crescent Executive Court, Ste. 224, Lake Mary, FL 32746
CEO: Andy Orent, VP   Tel: (407) 805-8700   %FO: 100
Bus: *Mortgage financing.*   Fax: (407) 804-0020

LONDON BRIDGE GROUP
3550 Engineering Drive, Ste. 200, Norcross, GA 30092
CEO: Dave Demster, SVP   Tel: (770) 810-8000   %FO: 100
Bus: *Mortgage financing.*   Fax: (770) 810-8015

LONDON BRIDGE PHOENIX SOFTWARE, INC.
500 International Parkway, Heathrow, FL 32746
CEO: Christopher Rowbottom, CEO   Tel: (407) 548-5100   %FO: 100
Bus: *Mfr. software for information*   Fax: (407) 548-5296
processing.

● **LORIEN PLC**
30 Brindley Road, City Park, Manchester M16 9HQ, UK
CEO: Bert Morris, Chmn.   Tel: 44-870-600-7733   Rev: $225
Bus: *Provides IT resourcing and consulting*   Fax: 44-800-731-7373
services.   www.lorien.co.uk

LORIEN, INC.
4511 Rockside Road, Ste. 250, Independence, OH   44131
CEO: Robert Brown, CEO   Tel: (216) 524-2200   %FO: 100
Bus: *Provides management and*   Fax: (216) 524-1488
   training solutions.

● **LOVELL WHITE DURRANT**
65 Holborn Viaduct, London EC1A 2DY, UK
CEO: Andrew Walker, CEO   Tel: 44-207-236-0066
Bus: *International law firm.*   Fax: 44-207-248-4212   Emp: 2,600
                                  www.lovellwhitedurrant.com

   LOVELL WHITE DURRANT
   401 9th Street NW, Ste. 1150, Washington, DC   20004
   CEO: Anne Fortney, Mng. Prtn.   Tel: (202) 783-6144   %FO: 100
   Bus: *International law firm.*   Fax: (202) 783-6250

   LOVELL WHITE DURRANT
   330 North Wabash, 19th Fl., Chicago, IL   60610
   CEO: George A. Platz   Tel: (312) 832-4400   %FO: 100
   Bus: *International law firm.*   Fax: (312) 832-4444

   LOVELL WHITE DURRANT
   900 Third Avenue, 16th Fl., New York, NY   10022
   CEO: David Alberts   Tel: (212) 909-0600   %FO: 100
   Bus: *International law firm.*   Fax: (212) 909-0666

● **LYNX GROUP PLC**
269 Banbury Road, Oxford OX2 7JF, UK
CEO: Richard Last, CEO   Tel: 44-186-531-0150   Rev: $366
Bus: *Engaged in resale of hardware and*   Fax: 44-186-531-0499   Emp: 2,142
   software.   www.lynx-group.co.uk

   LYNX FINANCIAL SYSTEMS DIVISION
   7301 N State Highway 161, Ste. 310-S, Irving, TX   75039
   CEO: Paul J. Edgeley, Mng. Dir.   Tel: (972) 830-9898
   Bus: *Engaged in resale of hardware*   Fax: (972) 830-9696
      and software.

● **M&C SAATCHI WORLDWIDE LTD.**
36 Golden Square, London W1F 9EE, UK
CEO: Moray McLennan, CEO   Tel: 44-207-543-4500   Rev: $65
Bus: *Engaged in advertising services.*   Fax: 44-207-543-4501   Emp: 425
                                  www.mcsaatch.com

M&C SAATCHI
1600 Rosecrans Avenue, Ste. 100, Manhattan Beach, CA 90266
CEO: Mindy Balgrosky   Tel: (310) 727-2881   %FO: 100
Bus: *Engaged in advertising services.*   Fax: (310) 727-2879

● **MACMILLAN LTD.**
The Macmillan Building, 4 Crinan Street, London N1 9XW, UK
CEO: Richard Charkin, CEO   Tel: 44-207-833-4000
Bus: *Publishing conglomerate.*   Fax: 44-207-843-4640   Emp: 1,900
     www.macmillan.co.uk

     GROVES DICTIONARIES, INC.
     345 Park Avenue South, New York, NY 10010-1707
     CEO: Janice Kuta, Pres.   Tel: (212) 689-9200   %FO: 100
     Bus: *Book publishing.*   Fax: (212) 689-9711

     NATURE AMERICA INC
     345 Park Avenue South, New York, NY 10010-1707
     CEO: Jan Velterop   Tel: (212) 726-9200   %FO: 100
     Bus: *Publishing.*   Fax: (212) 696-9006

     PALGRAVE, DIV. MACMILLAN GROUP
     175 Fifth Avenue, New York, NY 10010
     CEO: Philip Schwartz, COO   Tel: (212) 982-3900   %FO: 100
     Bus: *Book publishing.*   Fax: (212) 777-6359

     PICADORE, DIV. MACMILLAN GROUP
     175 Fifth Avenue, New York, NY 10010
     CEO: George Witte   Tel: (212) 674-5151   %FO: 100
     Bus: *Book publishing.*   Fax: (212) 253-9627

     ST. MARTIN'S PRESS, INC.
     175 Fifth Avenue, New York, NY 10010
     CEO: John Sargent, Pres. & CEO   Tel: (212) 726-0200   %FO: 100
     Bus: *Book publishing.*   Fax: (212) 686-9491   Emp: 500

● **MADGE NETWORKS NV**
Wexham Springs, Framewood Road, Wexham Slough SL3 6PJ, UK
CEO: Martin Maline, CEO   Tel: 44-175-366-1000   Rev: $157
Bus: *Mfr. of token ring adapters for*   Fax: 44-175-366-1011   Emp: 600
     computer networking.   www.madge.com

     MADGE NETWORKS
     One State Street Plaza, 12th Fl, New York, NY 10004
     CEO: Martin Malina, Pres.   Tel: (212) 709-1000   %FO: 100
     Bus: *Mfr./sales of token ring adapters*   Fax: (212) 709-1002
     for computer networking.

MADGE NETWORKS

860 Hillview Court, Ste. 260, Milpitas, CA 95035

CEO: Simon Gawne, VP Tel: (408) 934-8180 %FO: 100

Bus: *Mfr./sales of token ring adapters* Fax: (408) 934-8181
    for computer networking.

MADGE NETWORKS

2517 Highway 35, Bldg. B, Ste. 2030205, Manasquan, NJ 08736

CEO: Martin Maline, Pres. Tel: (732) 292-1592 %FO: 100

Bus: *Mfr./sales of token ring adapters* Fax: (732) 292-1592
    for computer networking.

● **MARCONI PLC (FORMERLY GEC)**

One Burton Street, London W1J 6AW, UK

CEO: George Simpson, CEO Tel: 44-207-493-8484 Rev: $9,111

Bus: *Mfr. diagnostic and medical machines,* Fax: 44-207-493-1974 Emp: 53,000
    medical equipment, imaging devices, www.marconi.com
    and retail systems.

MARCONI COMMUNICATIONS

1000 Fore Drive, Warrendale, PA 15086-7502

CEO: Mike Parton, CEO Tel: (724) 742-4444 %FO: 100

Bus: *Mfr. telecommunications systems,* Fax: (724) 742-7742
    products and services.

MARCONI COMMUNICATIONS

5900 Landerbrook, Ste. 300, Cleveland, OH 44124-4019

CEO: Patrick L. Welker, EVP Tel: (440) 460-3600 %FO: 100

Bus: *Mfr. telecommunications systems,* Fax: (440) 460-3690
    products and services.

MARCONI DATA SYSTEMS INC.

1500 Mittel Boulevard, Wood Dale, IL 60191-1073

CEO: Craig E. Bauer, Pres. & CEO Tel: (630) 860-7300 %FO: 100

Bus: *Mfr. telecommunications systems,* Fax: (630) 616-3657
    products and services.

MARCONI MEDICAL

2915 Courtyards Drive, Ste. C, Norcross, GA 30071

CEO: John Keating, Mgr. Tel: (770) 447-5727 %FO: 100

Bus: *Mfr./sales diagnostic and medical* Fax: (770) 416-8668
    machines.

MARCONI MEDICAL

100 Baylis Road, Ste. 140, Melville, NY 11747

CEO: Marv Siegel, Mgr.   Tel: (631) 391-6800   %FO: 100

Bus: *Mfr./sales diagnostic and medical*   Fax: (631) 391-6888
machines.

MARCONI MEDICAL

600 Beta Drive, Mayfield Village, OH 44143

CEO: Ted Nemetz, Mgr.   Tel: (440) 483-2500   %FO: 100

Bus: *Mfr./sales diagnostic and medical*   Fax: (440) 483-3933
machines.

MARCONI MEDICAL

One Marconi, Ste. F, Irvine, CA 92618

CEO: Jeffrey Powell, Mgr.   Tel: (949) 699-2300   %FO: 100

Bus: *Mfr./sales diagnostic and medical*   Fax: (949) 699-2397
machines.

MARCONI MEDICAL

2540 Metropolitan Drive, Trevose, PA 19053

CEO: Jesse Heath, Mgr.   Tel: (215) 953-7900   %FO: 100

Bus: *Mfr./sales diagnostic and medical*   Fax: (215) 953-7928
machines.

MARCONI MEDICAL

550 Bond Street, Lincolnshire, IL 60069

CEO: Rich Setzer, Mgr.   Tel: (847) 821-0200   %FO: 100

Bus: *Mfr./sales diagnostic and medical*   Fax: (847) 478-5890
machines.

MARCONI MEDICAL

860 West Airport Freeway, Ste. 509, Hurst, TX 76054

CEO: Jesse Heath, Mgr.   Tel: (817) 577-5500   %FO: 100

Bus: *Mfr./sales diagnostic and medical*   Fax: (817) 577-5512
machines.

MARCONI MEDICAL

4515 Oak Fair Blvd., Ste. 104, Tampa, FL 33610

CEO: William DeLoatche, Mgr.   Tel: (813) 626-8280   %FO: 100

Bus: *Mfr./sales diagnostic and medical*   Fax: (813) 623-1756
machines.

MARCONI MEDICAL

6601 Owens Drive, Ste. 140, Pleasanton, CA 94588

CEO: Ron Ramsey, Mgr.   Tel: (925) 467-1691   %FO: 100

Bus: *Mfr./sales diagnostic and medical*   Fax: (925) 467-1697
machines.

● **MARKS AND SPENCER PLC**

Michael House, 37-67 Baker Street, London W1A 1DN, UK

CEO: Luc Vandevelde, CEO	Tel: 44-207-935-4422	Rev: $13,046
Bus: *Retail stores, internationally markets clothing, food stuffs and household goods.*	Fax: 44-207-487-2679 www.marks-and-spencers.com	Emp: 52,150

BROOKS BROTHERS

346 Madison Avenue, New York, NY   10017

CEO: Joseph Gromek, Pres. & CEO	Tel: (212) 682-8800	%FO: 100
Bus: *Retail clothing.*	Fax: (212) 309-7372	

KING SUPERMARKETS, INC.

700 Lanidex Plaza, Parsippany, NJ   07054

CEO: Alan Levitan, Pres. & CEO	Tel: (973) 463-6300	%FO: 100
Bus: *Chain store; retail foods.*	Fax: (973) 463-6513	

MARKS AND SPENCER U.S. HOLDINGS, INC.

346 Madison Avenue, New York, NY   10017

CEO: Sir Richard Greenbury, Chmn.	Tel: (212) 697-3886	%FO: 100
Bus: *U.S. headquarters, holding company. Retails clothing, food stuffs and household goods.*	Fax: (212) 697-3857	

● **MARLEY GROUP PLC, SUB. ETEX GROUP**

Seven Oakhill Road, Seven Oaks, Kent TN13 1NQ, UK

CEO: David A. Trapnell, CEO	Tel: 44-173-245-5255
Bus: *Mfr. construction materials; roofing, plumbing and flooring.*	Fax: 44-173-274-0694 www.marleyplc.com

MARLEY FLEXCO

1401 E-6th Street, Tuscumbia, AL   35674

CEO: Larry Sims, Pres.	Tel: (256) 383-7474	%FO: 100
Bus: *Mfr./distribution of commercial flooring.*	Fax: (256) 381-0322	

MARLEY MOULDINGS

PO Box 610, Marion, VA   24354

CEO: Larry Davis, Pres.	Tel: (540) 783-8161	%FO: 100
Bus: *Mfr./distribution construction materials; moldings.*	Fax: (540) 783-3292	

● **THE MAYFLOWER CORPORATION PLC**

London Road, Loudwater, High Wycombe, Buckinghamshire HP10 9RF, UK

CEO: John W. P. Simpson, CEO	Tel: 44-149-445-0145	Rev: $891
Bus: *Provides engineering, production and assembly services for motor vehicles.*	Fax: 44-149-445-0607 www.mayflowercorp.com	Emp: 5,260

THOMAS DENNIS INC.
1408 Courtesy Road, High Point, NC   27260
CEO: Bob Price   Tel: (336) 889-4871   %FO: 100
Bus: *Provides engineering, production*   Fax: (336) 889-2589
     and assembly services for motor
     vehicles.

● **MC KECHNIE, PLC**
Leighswood Road, Aldridge, Waisall, West Midland W59 8DS, UK
CEO: Andrew John Walker, CEO   Tel: 44-192-274-3887   Rev: $1,075
Bus: *Mfr. of specialized engineering*   Fax: 44-192-251-1045   Emp: 8,400
     components and engineering plastics. www.mckechnie.co.uk

   MC KECHNIE PLASTIC COMPONENTS, N.A.
   7309 West 27th Street, Minneapolis, MN   55426
   CEO: Brian Evenson, Pres.   Tel: (612) 929-3312   %FO: 100
   Bus: *Advanced injection moulding.*   Fax: (612) 929-8404   Emp: 280

   PROPULSION TECHNOLOGY INC.
   8855 NW 35th Lane, Miami, FL   33172
   CEO: Raphael Elkayam, Pres.   Tel: (305) 594-6500   %FO: 100
   Bus: *Mfr. aerospace engine components.* Fax: (305) 594-9386

   PSM FASTENER CORPORATION
   355 Paul Avenue, St. Louis, MO   63135
   CEO: Kevin Mills, Mgr.   Tel: (314) 524-7400   %FO: 100
   Bus: *Mfr. of specialized engineering* Fax: (314) 524-7333
        components and engineering
        plastics.

   PSM FASTENER CORPORATION
   7 Industrial Road, Fairfield, NJ   07004
   CEO: Angie Smith, Mgr.   Tel: (973) 882-7887   %FO: 100
   Bus: *Mfr. of specialized engineering* Fax: (973) 227-7303
        components and engineering
        plastics.

● **MEDISYS PLC**
Dock lane Melton, Woodbridge, Suffolk IP12 1PE, UK
CEO: David Wong, CEO   Tel: 44-139-444-5914
Bus: *Health products.*   Fax: 44-139-444-5917
                                         www.medisys-group.com

   FUTURA MEDICAL CORPORATION INC.
   380 Stevens Avenue, Ste. 212, Solana Beach, CA   92075
   CEO: Harold Callicoat, Mng. Dir.   Tel: (858) 350-0130   %FO: 100
   Bus: *Health products.*   Fax: (858) 350-0124

• MEGGITT PLC

Farrs House Cowgrove, Wimborne, Dorset BH21 4EL, UK

CEO: Terry Twigger, CEO   Tel: 44-120-284-7847   Rev: $490

Bus: *Mfr. electronics, aerospace, defense and*   Fax: 44-120-284-2478   Emp: 4,200
industrial controls products.   www.meggitt.com

AVICA INC.

1175 Aviation Place, San Fernando, CA 91340

CEO: Alan Smith, Pres.   Tel: (818) 361-0900   %FO: 100

Bus: *Mfr./sales fuel connectors/metallic*   Fax: (818) 361-0518
components for aircraft.

ENDEVCO CORPORATION

30700 Rancho Viejo Road, San Juan Capistrano, CA   92675

CEO: Phil Conrad, Pres.   Tel: (949) 493-8181   %FO: 100

Bus: *Mfr. sensors and related*   Fax: (949) 661-7231
electronics.

MEGGITT AVOINICS INC.

10 Ammon Drive, Manchester, NH   03103-7406

CEO: Stephen Marshall, Pres.   Tel: (603) 669-0940   %FO: 100

Bus: *Mfr. sensors and indicators to the*   Fax: (603) 669-0931
aerospace, chemical, utility,
medical and automotive industries.

MEGGITT DEFENSE SYSTEMS

655 West Valencia Drive, Fullerton, CA   92632-2104

CEO: Quinton Miller, Pres.   Tel: (714) 525-2300   %FO: 100

Bus: *Mfr. radar electronic scoring*   Fax: (714) 525-9461
systems.

MEGGITT DEFENSE SYSTEMS

2672 Dow Avenue, Tustin, CA   92780

CEO: Dr. Roger Brum, Pres.   Tel: (714) 832-1333   %FO: 100

Bus: *Mfr. aerial towed vehicle systems.*   Fax: (714) 832-6090

MEGGITT SAFETY SYSTEMS, INC.

1915 Voyager Avenue, Simi Valley, CA   93063

CEO: John J. Stoble, Pres.   Tel: (805) 584-4100   %FO: 100

Bus: *Produces aircraft fire detection*   Fax: (805) 578-3400
and industrial fire and gas
protection systems.

MEGGITT SILICONE PRODUCTS
2010 Lafayette Avenue, McMinnville, OR   97128

CEO: Allen Hall, Pres.	Tel: (503) 472-0045	%FO: 100
Bus: *Mfr. polymer seals for aerospace markets.*	Fax: (503) 434-6454	

PIHER INTERNATIONAL CORPORATION
1640 Northwind Boulevard, Libertyville, IL   60048

CEO: George DiMartino, Pres.	Tel: (847) 918-9300	%FO: 100
Bus: *Mfr. trimmers and switches.*	Fax: (847) 918-9433	

WHITTAKER CONTROLS, INC.
12838 Saticoy Street, North Hollywood, CA   91605

CEO: John J. Stoble, Pres.	Tel: (818) 765-8160	%FO: 100
Bus: *Mfr. fluid control devices.*	Fax: (818) 759-2190	

• MERANT PLC
22-30 Old Bath Road, Newbury, Berkshire RG14 1QN, UK

CEO: J. Michael Gullard, Chmn.	Tel: 44-163-532-646	Rev: $309
Bus: *Software and services.*	Fax: 44-163-533-966	Emp: 2,000
	www.merant.com	

MERANT INC.
1500 Perimeter Park Drive, Ste. 100, Morrisville, NC   27560

CEO: Tony Hill, SVP	Tel: (919) 461-4200	%FO: 100
Bus: *Software and services.*	Fax: (919) 461-4200	

MERANT INC.
9420 Key West Avenue, Rockville, MD   20850

CEO: Michael Consoli, SVP	Tel: (301) 838-5000	%FO: 100
Bus: *Software and services.*	Fax: (301) 838-5432	

• METAL BULLETIN PLC
Park House, Park Terrace, Worcester Park, Surrey KT4 7HY, UK

CEO: Sara Davis	Tel: 44-818-279-977	Rev: $47
Bus: *Publishers of books, directories, and global news journals for the iron, steel and non-ferrous metals industries.*	Fax: 44-81-337-8943 www.2metalbulletin.com	Emp: 330

METAL BULLETIN, INC.
220 Fifth Avenue, 19th Fl., New York, NY   10001

CEO: Migdalia Perez	Tel: (212) 213-6202	%FO: 100
Bus: *Publish magazine; conference organization service.*	Fax: (212) 213-1870	Emp: 10

- **MICHAEL PAGE INTERNATIONAL PLC**
39-41 Parker Street, London WC2B 5LN, UK

CEO: Terence W. Benson, CEO	Tel: 44-207-831-2000	Rev: $638
Bus: *Engaged in recruitment.*	Fax: 44-207-269-2121	Emp: 2,300
	www.michaelpage.co.uk	

    MICHAEL PAGE INTERNATIONAL INC.
    405 Lexington Avenue, 28th Fl., New York, NY 10174

CEO: Martin C. Pike	Tel: (212) 661-4800	%FO: 100
Bus: *Engaged in recruitment.*	Fax: (212) 661-4800	

- **MICRO FOCUS GROUP LTD.**
The Lawn, 22-30 Old Bath Road, Newbury, Berkshire RG14 1QN, UK

CEO: J. Michael Gullard, Chmn.	Tel: 44-163-532-646	
Bus: *Develops and market software products.*	Fax: 44-163-532-595	Emp: 250
	www.microfocus.com	

    MICRO FOCUS INC.
    9420 Key West Avenue, Rockville, MD 20850

CEO: Charles Kelsey	Tel: (301) 838-5000	%FO: 100
Bus: *Development and marketing software products.*	Fax: (301) 838-5432	

    MICRO FOCUS INC.
    701 East Middlefield Road, Mountain View, CA 94043

CEO: Charles Kelsey	Tel: (650) 938-3700	%FO: 100
Bus: *Development and marketing software products.*	Fax: (650) 856-6134	Emp: 100

- **MINORPLANET SYSTEMS PLC**
Greenwich House, Leeds LS7 2AA, UK

CEO: Michael D. Abrahams, Chmn.	Tel: 44-113-251-1600	Rev: $25
Bus: *Mfr. satellite based tracking systems for trucking fleets.*	Fax: 44-113-274-2325	Emp: 325
	www.minorplanet.co.uk	

    MINORPLANET INC.
    1155 Kas Drive, Richardson, TX 75081

CEO: Andrew Tillmann, Dir.	Tel: (972) 301-2000	
Bus: *Mfr./sales satellite based tracking systems for trucking fleets.*	Fax: (972) 301-2403	

- **MISYS PLC**
Burleigh House, Chapel Oak, Salford Priors, Worchestershire WR11 5SH, UK

CEO: John G. Sussens, Mng. Dir.	Tel: 44-138-687-1373	Rev: $1,064
Bus: *Mfr. banking and securities software.*	Fax: 44-138-687-1045	Emp: 5,750
	www.misys.co.uk	

MEDIC COMPUTER SYSTEMS, INC.

8529 Six Forks Road, Raleigh, NC   27615

CEO: Tom Skelton, CEO   Tel: (919) 847-8102   %FO: 100

Bus: *Mfr. practice management software.*   Fax: (919) 846-1555

● MITCHELL GRIEVE LTD.

Wolsey Road, Coalville Leicester LE6 4ES, UK

CEO: Byron Head, Chmn.   Tel: 44-116-510-565

Bus: *Mfr. knitting needles and elements.*   Fax: 44-161-510-458   Emp: 600

www.martex.co.uk

MITCHELL GRIEVE (USA) INC.

9600 F Southern Pine Blvd., Charlotte, NC   28273-0694

CEO: Ian Tyson, Pres.   Tel: (704) 525-0325   %FO: 100

Bus: *Distribute needles and elements for knitting and hosiery industries, dental scalpels and blades.*   Fax: (704) 525-9471   Emp: 5

● MONSOON PLC

87 Lancaster Road, London W11 1QQ, UK

CEO: Peter M. Simon   Tel: 44-207-313-3000   Rev: $240

Bus: *Retailer of women's and children's apparel, housewares and accessories.*   Fax: 44-207-313-3020   Emp: 1,800

www.moonsoon.co.uk

MONSOON USA

1245 Worchester Street, Mall #1146, Natick, MA   01760

CEO: J. S. F. Spooner, Mng. Dir.   Tel: (508) 655-6472   %FO: 100

Bus: *Retail clothing store.*   Fax: (508) 655-6472

● MOORE STEPHENS INTERNATIONAL LIMITED

St. Paul's House, Warwick Lane, London EC4P 4BN, UK

CEO: John Harbor, Mng. Ptrn.   Tel: 44-207-334-9191

Bus: *Financial services.*   Fax: 44-207-334-7976

www.moorestephens.com

MOORE STEPHENS NORTH AMERICA, INC.

1000 Connecticut Avenue NW, Ste. 1006, Washington, DC   20036

CEO: Robert Hurd, Mgr.   Tel: (202) 463-7900   %FO: 100

Bus: *Financial services.*   Fax: (202) 296-0741

● THE MORGAN CRUCIBLE COMPANY PLC

Morgan House, Madeira Walk, Windsor, Berkshire SL4 1EP, UK

CEO: Ian P. Norris, CEO   Tel: 44-175-383-7000   Rev: $1,570

Bus: *Mfr. specialized materials and components.*   Fax: 44-175-385-0872   Emp: 15,000

www.morgancrucible.com

MORGAN ADVANCED MATERIALS
441 Hall Avenue, St. Marys, PA 15857
CEO: Ian P. Norris — Tel: (814) 781-1573
Bus: *Mfr. precision machined and* — Fax: (814) 781-9258
molded components.

NATIONAL ELECTRICAL CARBON PRODUCTS, INC.
251 Forrester Drive, Greenville, SC 29607
CEO: Michael Cox, Pres. — Tel: (864) 458-7777 — %FO: 100
Bus: *Mfr./sales of carbon components* — Fax: (864) 288-2083
for electrical applications.

● **JOHN MOWLEM & COMPANY PLC**
White Lion Court, Swan Street, Isleworth, Middlesex TW7 6RN, UK
CEO: John Gains, CEO — Tel: 44-208-568-9111 — Rev: $2,599
Bus: *Engaged in construction and* — Fax: 44-208-847-4802 — Emp: 14,000
engineering. — www.mowlem.co.uk

CHARTER BUILDERS INC.
1501 LBJ Fwy., Ste. 700, Dallas, TX 75234
CEO: Colin A. Graidage, Pres. — Tel: (972) 484-4888 — %FO: 100
Bus: *Engaged in construction and* — Fax: (972) 484-4373
engineering.

● **NATIONAL EXPRESS GROUP PLC**
75 Davies Street, London W1Y 1FA, UK
CEO: Philip White, CEO — Tel: 44-207-529-2000 — Rev: $2,990
Bus: *Engaged in train, bus and coach* — Fax: 44-207-529-2100 — Emp: 39,300
transportation. — www.nationalexpressgroup.com

BRITISH TRAVEL INTERNATIONAL
PO Box 299, Elkton, VA 22827
CEO: Philip White, Pres. — Tel: (540) 298-2232 — %FO: 100
Bus: *Engaged in travel/transportation.* — Fax: (540) 298-2232

DURHAM TRANSPORTATION
2713 River Avenue, Rosemead, CA 91770
CEO: Kathleen Hall, VP — Tel: (626) 573-0204 — %FO: 100
Bus: *Engaged in transportation.* — Fax: (626) 280-4008

NATIONAL EXPRESS CORPORATION
9011 Mountain Ridge Drive, Suite 200, Austin, TX 78759-7222
CEO: John Elliott, Pres. — Tel: (512) 343-6292 — %FO: 100
Bus: *Provides school transportation* — Fax: (512) 343-6596
services.

• THE NATIONAL GRID GROUP PLC

15 Marylebone Road, London NW1 5JD, UK
CEO: David Jefferies, Chmn.   Tel: 44-207-312-5600   Rev: $2,573
Bus: *Electric utility.*   Fax: 44-207-312-5669   Emp: 7,070
          www.ngc.co.uk

ALL ENERGY MARKETING COMPANY

95 Sawyer Road, Waltham, MA   02154
CEO: William H. Hell, Chmn.   Tel: (781) 642-9502   %FO: 100
Bus: *Electric utility.*   Fax: (781) 642-9504

GRANITE STATE ELECTRIC COMPANY

Nine Lowell Road, Salem, NH   03079
CEO: William T. Sherry, EVP   Tel: (603) 809-7000   %FO: 100
Bus: *Electric utility.*   Fax: (603) 809-7000

GRANITE STATE ENERGY, INC.

4 Park Street, Concord, NH   03301
CEO: John H. Dickson, Pres.   Tel: (781) 642-9502   %FO: 100
Bus: *Electric utility.*   Fax: (781) 642-9502

MASSACHUSETTS ELECTRIC COMPANY

55 Bearfoot Road, Northboro, MA   01532
CEO: Lawrence J. Reilly, Pres.   Tel: (508) 357-4739   %FO: 100
Bus: *Electric utility.*   Fax: (508) 357-4739

NANTUCKET ELECTRIC COMPANY

Two Fairgrounds Road, Nantucket, MA   02554
CEO: Michael F. Ryan, EVP   Tel: (508) 325-8000   %FO: 100
Bus: *Electric utility.*   Fax: (508) 325-8100

NARRAGANSETT ELECTRIC CO.

280 Melrose Street, Providence, RI   02901-1438
CEO: Michael F. Ryan, EVP   Tel: (401) 784-7000   %FO: 100
Bus: *Electric utility.*   Fax: (401) 784-7545

NATIONAL GRID USA

25 Research Drive, Westborough, MA   01582
CEO: Richard P. Sergel, CEO   Tel: (508) 389-2000   %FO: 100
Bus: *Utility holding company.*   Fax: (508) 389-3518

NEW ENGLAND ELECTRIC SYSTEM INC. (NEES)

25 Research Drive, Westborough, MA   01582
CEO: Anthony C. Pini, Pres.   Tel: (508) 389-2000   %FO: 100
Bus: *Electric utility.*   Fax: (508) 836-5487

NEW ENGLAND HYDRO FINANCE COMPANY, INC.
25 Research Drive, Westborough, MA 01582
CEO: Richard P. Sergel, Pres.   Tel: (508) 389-2000   %FO: 100
Bus: *Engaged in finance.*   Fax: (508) 389-2111

NEW ENGLAND POWER COMPANY
25 Research Drive, Westborough, MA 01582
CEO: Peter G. Flynn, Pres.   Tel: (508) 389-2000   %FO: 100
Bus: *Electric utility.*   Fax: (508) 389-2111

WAYFINDER GROUP, INC.
25 Research Drive, Westborough, MA 01582
CEO: Anthony C. Pini, Pres.   Tel: (508) 389-3200   %FO: 100
Bus: *Electric utility.*   Fax: (508) 389-3201

● NCIPHER PLC
Jupiter House, Station Road, Cambridge CB1 2JD, UK
CEO: Alexander Rupert van Someren, CEO   Tel: 44-122-372-3600   Rev: $20
Bus: *Mfr. computer hardware and software.*   Fax: 44-122-372-3601   Emp: 150
                                       www.ncipher.com

NCIPHER INC.
500 Unicorn Park Drive, Woburn, MA 01801-3371
CEO: Claire Collins, PR   Tel: (781) 994-4000   %FO: 100
Bus: *Mfr. computer hardware and*   Fax: (781) 994-4001
     software.

● NDS GROUP PLC
1 London Road, Staines, Middlesex TW18 4EX, UK
CEO: Abraham Peled, CEO   Tel: 44-208-476-8000   Rev: $243
Bus: *Mfr. broadcast software.*   Fax: 44-208-476-8100   Emp: 1,040
                                       www.nds.com

NDS AMERICAS INC.
3501 Jamboree Road, Ste. 200, Newport Beach, CA 92660
CEO: Dov Rubin   Tel: (949) 725-2500   %FO: 100
Bus: *Mfr./sales broadcast software.* Fax: (949) 725-2505

NDS AMERICAS INC.
1211 Avenue of the Americas, 18th Fl., New York, NY 10036-8795
CEO: Dov Rubin   Tel: (212) 901-4440   %FO: 100
Bus: *Mfr./sales broadcast software.* Fax: (212) 901-4472

● **NOVAR PLC**

Novar House, 24 Queens Road, Weybridge, Surrey KT13 9UX, UK

CEO: B. Jurgen Hintz, CEO

Bus: *Mfr. electrical products and aluminum extrusions for the defense and marine industries; engaged in printing for financial institutions.*

Tel: 44-193-285-0850
Fax: 44-193-282-3328
www.novar.com

Rev: $2,246
Emp: 15,360

CLARKE AMERICAN INC.

PO Box 460, San Antonio, TX 78292

CEO: Charles Korbell, Pres.

Bus: *Mfr./prints checks and financial forms for banks.*

Tel: (210) 697-8888
Fax: (210) 696-1676

%FO: 100

INDALEX ALUMINUM SOLUTIONS GROUP

2905 Old Oakwood Road, Gainesville, GA 30504

CEO: Lisa Ivey, Mgr.

Bus: *Mfr. custom and standard extrusion systems.*

Tcl: (770) 535-1349
Fax: (770) 534-0403

%FO: 100

INDALEX ALUMINUM SOLUTIONS GROUP

1500 East Murden Street, Kokomo, IN 46903

CEO: Pat Wooley, Mgr.

Bus: *Mfr. custom and standard extrusion systems.*

Tel: (708) 841-8613
Fax: (708) 841-8675

%FO: 100

INDALEX ALUMINUM SOLUTIONS GROUP

706 South State Street, Girard, OH 44420

CEO: Joseph Neiner, Pres. & CEO

Bus: *Mfr. custom and standard extrusion systems.*

Tel: (330) 545-4311
Fax: (330) 545-3119

%FO: 100

INDALEX ALUMINUM SOLUTIONS GROUP

600 North Metcalf Street, Winton, NC 27986

CEO: Penny Wicker, Mgr.

Bus: *Mfr. custom and standard extrusion systems.*

Tel: (252) 358-5811
Fax: (252) 358-1141

%FO: 100

INDALEX ALUMINUM SOLUTIONS GROUP

23841 Reedy Drive, Elkhart, IN 46514

CEO: Dan Conn, Mgr.

Bus: *Mfr. custom and standard extrusion systems.*

Tel: (219) 262-2667
Fax: (219) 264-9817

%FO: 100

INDALEX ALUMINUM SOLUTIONS GROUP
330 Elmwood Road, Mountaintop, PA   18707
CEO: Mark Turley, Mgr.   Tel: (570) 474-5935   %FO: 100
Bus: *Mfr. custom and standard*   Fax: (570) 474-6846
      extrusion systems.

INDALEX ALUMINUM SOLUTIONS GROUP
930 Sandusky Street, Fostoria, OH   44830
CEO: Amy Kuhn, Mgr.   Tel: (419) 435-8581   %FO: 100
Bus: *Mfr. custom and standard*   Fax: (419) 435-4542
      extrusion systems.

INDALEX ALUMINUM SOLUTIONS GROUP
4555 North Star Way, Modesto, CA   95356
CEO: Debbie Shatley, Mgr.   Tel: (209) 521-6400   %FO: 100
Bus: *Mfr. custom and standard*   Fax: (209) 521-7525
      extrusion systems.

INDALEX ALUMINUM SOLUTIONS GROUP
1715 West Beach Street, Watsonville, CA   95076
CEO: Carol Pacuta, Mgr.   Tel: (831) 724-2244   %FO: 100
Bus: *Mfr. custom and standard*   Fax: (831) 538-5970
      extrusion systems.

INDALEX ALUMINUM SOLUTIONS GROUP
1507 Industry Drive, Burlington, NC   27216
CEO: Connie Boswell, Mgr.   Tel: (336) 227-8826   %FO: 100
Bus: *Mfr. custom and standard*   Fax: (336) 228-9813
      extrusion systems.

INDALEX ALUMINUM SOLUTIONS GROUP
500 Four Rod Road, Berlin, CT   06037
CEO: Bob Jepson   Tel: (860) 828-4186   %FO: 100
Bus: *Mfr. custom and standard*   Fax: (860) 829-0681
      extrusion systems.

INDALEX ALUMINUM SOLUTIONS GROUP
14200 Cottage Grove Avenue, Dolton, IL   60419
CEO: Susan Szumigalski, Mgr.   Tel: (708) 841-8613   %FO: 100
Bus: *Mfr. custom and standard*   Fax: (708) 543-7529
      extrusion systems.

INDALEX ALUMINUM SOLUTIONS GROUP
3333 Copley Road, Copley, OH   44321
CEO: David Weber, CEO   Tel: (330) 670-1010   %FO: 100
Bus: *Mfr. building control systems.*   Fax: (330) 670-1029

● **NSB RETAIL SYSTEMS PLC**
1015 Arlington Business Park, Theale, Reading, Berkshire RG7 4SA, UK
CEO: Nikala S. Beckett, CEO   Tel: 44-133-228-5700   Rev: $61
Bus: *Mfr. retail software.*   Fax: 44-118-930-2855   Emp: 430
                                     www.nsb.co.uk

    NSB RETAIL USA, INC.
    400 Venure Drive, Columbus, OH   43035
    CEO: Candice DeLuca, PR   Tel: (614) 840-1448   %FO: 100
    Bus: *Mfr. retail software.*   Fax: (614) 840-1401

● **NYCOMED AMERSHAM INTL PLC**
Amersham Place, Little Chalfont, Buckinghamshire HP7 9NA, UK
CEO: William M. Castell, CEO   Tel: 44-149-454-4000   Rev: $1,917
Bus: *Radiochemicals, radiopharmaceuticals,*   Fax: 44-149-454-2266   Emp: 9,300
    devices & sources for radiography.   www.amersham.co.uk

    AMERSHAM PHARMACIA BIOTECH
    800 Centennial Avenue, Piscataway, NJ   08855-1327
    CEO: Andrew Rackear, Pres.   Tel: (732) 457-8000   %FO: 100
    Bus: *Engaged in x-ray imaging and*   Fax: (732) 457-0557
        scanning.

    NYCOMED AMERSHAM IMAGING
    101 Carnegie Center, Princeton, NJ   08540-6231
    CEO: Dan Peters, Pres.   Tel: (609) 514-6000   %FO: 100
    Bus: *Engaged in x-ray imaging and*   Fax: (609) 514-6660
        scanning.

● **OCTEL CORP.**
Global House, Bailey Lane, Manchester M90 4AA, UK
CEO: Robert E. Bew, Chmn.   Tel: 44-161-498-8889   Rev: $422
Bus: *Mfr. gas additives.*   Fax: 44-161-498-1899   Emp: 850
                                     www.octel-corp.com

    OCTEL AMERICA INC.
    200 Executive Drive, Newark, DE   19702
    CEO: Dennis Kerrison, CEO   Tel: (302) 454-8100   %FO: 100
    Bus: *Mfr. gas additives.*   Fax: (302) 451-1380

● **OLD MUTUAL PLC**
Lansdowne House, 3rd Fl., 57 Berkeley Square, London W1J 6ER, UK
CEO: Roddy Sparks, Mng. Dir.   Tel: 44-207-569-0100   Rev: $12,085
Bus: *Engaged in life and general insurance,*   Fax: 44-207-569-0200   Emp: 40,540
    retail and commercial banking services.   www.oldmutual.com

CS MCKEE

One Gateway Center, Pittsburgh, PA   15222

CEO: Eugene M. Natali, Pres.

Bus: *Engaged in equity management.*

Tel: (412) 566-1234

Fax: (412) 566-1548

%FO: 100

FIRST PACIFIC ADVISORS, INC.

11400 West Olympic Blvd., Ste. 1200, Los Angeles, CA   90064

CEO: Robert L. Rodriguez, Pres.

Bus: *Investment management.*

Tel: (310) 473-0225

Fax: (310) 996-5450

%FO: 100

FUDICIARY MANAGEMENT ASSOCIATES

55 West Monroe Street, Ste. 2550, Chicago, IL   60603

CEO: Robert F. Carr III, Pres.

Bus: *Investment management.*

Tel: (312) 930-6850

Fax: (312) 641-2511

%FO: 100

GBS

301 Commerce Street, Ste. 2001, Ft. Worth, TX   76102-4140

CEO: Frank P. Ganucheau III, Mgr.

Bus: *Investment management.*

Tel: (817) 332-9915

Fax: (817) 332-9935

%FO: 100

HEITMAN FINANCIAL LLC

180 North LaSalle Street, Ste. 3600, Chicago, IL   60601-2886

CEO: Jerome J. Claeys III, CEO

Bus: *Investment management.*

Tel: (312) 855-5700

Fax: (312) 855-5807

%FO: 100

ICM

803 Cathedral Street, Baltimore, MD   21201

CEO: Stuart M. Christhilf III, CEO

Bus: *Investment management.*

Tel: (410) 539-3858

Fax: (410) 625-9016

%FO: 100

L&B REALTY ADVISORS, INC.

8750 North Central, Ste. 800, Dallas, TX   75231-6431

CEO: Paul C. Chapman, COO

Bus: *Provides real estate advisory
    services.*

Tel: (214) 989-0800

Fax: (214) 989-0600

%FO: 100

UNITED ASSET MANAGEMENT CORPORATION

One International Place, Boston, MA   02110

CEO: James F. Orr III, CEO

Bus: *Engaged in life and general
    insurance, retail and commercial
    banking services.*

Tel: (617) 330-8900

Fax: (617) 330-1133

%FO: 100

● **OPTO INTERNATIONAL LTD.**

Tower Mill, Park Mill, Dukinfield, Cheshire SK 16 5LN, UK

CEO: John Nugent, Chmn.   Tel: 44-161-303-9136

Bus: *Mfr. clamps, tubing and display fixtures.*   Fax: 44-161-330-9136

www.optoint.co.uk

     OPTO INTERNATIONAL INC.

     220 Messner Drive. Ste. 215, Wheeling, IL   60090

     CEO: Graham Wood, Pres.   Tel: (847) 541-6786

     Bus: *Sales/distribution of clamps,*   Fax: (847) 541-8160
          tubing and display fixtures.

● **ORCHESTREAM HOLDINGS PLC**

Avon House, Kensington Village, Avonmore Road, London W14 8TS, UK

CEO: Ashley Ward, CEO   Tel: 44-207-348-1500

Bus: *Mfr. software.*   Fax: 44-207-348-1501   Emp: 100

www.orchestream.com

     ORCHESTREAM HOLDINGS

     One Penn Plaza, 43th Fl., New York, NY   10119

     CEO: Mfr. software.   Tel: (212) 629-3134   %FO: 100

     Bus: *Mfr. software.*   Fax: (212) 629-3135

     ORCHESTREAM HOLDINGS

     3435 Winchester Road, Ste. 400, Allentown, PA   18104-2209

     CEO: Mfr. software.   Tel: (610) 530-2000   %FO: 100

     Bus: *Mfr. software.*   Fax: (610) 530-2020

     ORCHESTREAM HOLDINGS

     1593 Spring Hill Road, Ste. 200, Vienna, VA   22182

     CEO: Mfr. software.   Tel: (703) 734-3706   %FO: 100

     Bus: *Mfr. software.*   Fax: (703) 734-3713

● **OSMETECH PLC**

Electra House, Electra Way, Crewe CW1 6WZ, UK

CEO: Wang Chong, CEO   Tel: 44-127-021-6444

Bus: *Health products and services.*   Fax: 44-127-021-6030

www.osmetech.plc.uk

     OSMETECH INC.

     14 Clinton Drive, Hollis, NH   03049

     CEO: Donald Hetzel, Pres.   Tel: (603) 598-2922   %FO: 100

     Bus: *Health products and services.*   Fax: (603) 595-9916

- **OXFORD INSTRUMENTS, PLC**

  Old Station Way, Bynsham Witney, Oxfordshire OX8 1TL, UK

CEO: Andrew Macintosh, CEO	Tel: 44-186-588-1437	Rev: $282
Bus: *Mfr. patient monitoring systems.*	Fax: 44-186-588-1944	Emp: 1,800
	www.oxinst.com	

  ### OXFORD INSTRUMENTS MEDICAL SYSTEMS DIV.

  12 Skyline Drive, Hawthorne, NY   10532

CEO: Michael Pattinson, Pres.	Tel: (914) 593-7100
Bus: *Distribution of neurology products and accessories.*	Fax: (914) 593-7290

- **P&O NEDLLOYD CONTAINER LINE LTD.**

  Beagle House, Braham Street, London E1 9EP, UK

CEO: haddo Meijer, CEO	Tel: 44-207-411-1000	Rev: $6,568
Bus: *Provides worldwide transport of containerized cargo.*	Fax: 44-207-441-1500	Emp: 9,000
	www.ponl.com	

  ### P&O NEDLLYOD

  One Meadowlands Plaza, East Rutherford, NJ   07073

CEO: Michael Seymour, Pres. & CEO	Tel: (201) 896-6200	%FO: 100
Bus: *Provides global container shipping.*	Fax: (201) 896-6342	

- **P&O PRINCESS CRUISES PLC**

  77 New Oxford Street, London WC1A 1PP, UK

CEO: Peter G. Ratcliffe, CEO	Tel: 44-207-805-1200	Rev: $2,423
Bus: *Cruise operator.*	Fax: 44-207-805-1240	Emp: 19,000
	www.poprincesscruises.com	

  ### PRINCESS CRUISES

  24305 Town Center Drive, Santa Clarita, CA   91355

CEO: Dean Brown	Tel: (661) 753-0000	%FO: 100
Bus: *Cruise operator.*	Fax: (661) 753-0000	

- **PA CONSULTING GROUP, LTD.**

  123 Buckingham Palace Road, London SW1W 9SR, UK

CEO: Jeremy Asher, CEO	Tel: 44-207-730-9000	Rev: $495
Bus: *Engaged in technology consulting services.*	Fax: 44-207-333-5050	Emp: 4,000
	www.pa-consulting.com	

  ### PA CONSULTING GROUP

  520 South Grand Avenue, Ste. 500, Los Angeles, CA   90070

CEO: James Cullens	Tel: (213) 689-1515	%FO: 100
Bus: *Engaged in technology consulting services.*	Fax: (213) 689-1129	

PA CONSULTING GROUP
315A Enterprise Drive, Plainsboro, NJ 08536
CEO: James Cullens   Tel: (609) 936-8300   %FO: 100
Bus: *Engaged in technology consulting* Fax: (609) 936-8811
    services.

PA CONSULTING GROUP
2711 Allen Blvd., Ste. 200, Middleton, WI 53562
CEO: James Cullens   Tel: (608) 827-7820   %FO: 100
Bus: *Engaged in technology consulting* Fax: (608) 827-7815
    services.

PA CONSULTING GROUP
Three Riverway, Ste. 30, Houston, TX 77056
CEO: James Cullens   Tel: (713) 403-5150   %FO: 100
Bus: *Engaged in technology consulting* Fax: (713) 961-4153
    services.

PA CONSULTING GROUP
One Memorial Drive, Cambridge, MA 02142
CEO: James Cullens   Tel: (617) 225-2700   %FO: 100
Bus: *Engaged in technology consulting* Fax: (617) 225-2631
    services.

PA CONSULTING GROUP
1881 Ninth Street, Ste. 302, Boulder, CO 80302
CEO: James Cullens   Tel: (303) 449-5515   %FO: 100
Bus: *Engaged in technology consulting* Fax: (303) 443-5684
    services.

PA CONSULTING GROUP
1530 Wilson Blvd., Ste. 400, Arlington, VA 22209
CEO: James Cullens   Tel: (703) 351-0300   %FO: 100
Bus: *Engaged in technology consulting* Fax: (703) 351-0342
    services.

PA CONSULTING GROUP
1776 I Street NW, Washington, DC 20006
CEO: James Cullens   Tel: (202) 223-6665   %FO: 100
Bus: *Engaged in technology consulting* Fax: (202) 296-3858
    services.

PA CONSULTING GROUP
405 Lexington Avenue, New York, NY 10174
CEO: James Cullens   Tel: (212) 973-5900   %FO: 100
Bus: *Engaged in technology consulting* Fax: (212) 973-5959
    services.

- **PACE MICRO TECHNOLOGY PLC**

Victoria Road, Saltaire, Shipley, West Yorkshire BD18 3LF, UK

CEO: Malcolm M. Miller, CEO	Tel: 44-127-453-2000	Rev: $567
Bus: *Mfr. digital satellite and cable TV receivers.*	Fax: 44-127-453-2010 www.pacemicro.com	Emp: 1,100

PACE MICRO TECHNOLOGY AMERICAS

3701 FAU Boulevard, Ste. 200, Boca Raton, FL 33431

CEO: Neil Gaydon, Pres.	Tel: (561) 995-6000	%FO: 100
Bus: *Mfr. digital satellite and cable TV receivers.*	Fax: (561) 995-6001	

- **PEARSON PLC**

Three Burlington Gardens, London W1X 1LE, UK

CEO: Marjorie M. Scardino, CEO	Tel: 44-207-411-2000	Rev: $5,792
Bus: *Newspapers and book publishing, visitor attractions, TV, investment banking.*	Fax: 44-207-828-3342 www.pearson.com	Emp: 20,000

THE FINANCIAL TIMES

1330 Avenue of the Americas, 8th Fl., New York, NY 10019

CEO: Stuart Arnold, Dir.	Tel: (212) 641-2400	%FO: 100
Bus: *Financial newspaper.*	Fax: (212) 641-2400	

HEADLAND DIGITAL MEDIA

444 Spear Street, San Francisco, CA 94105

CEO: Mark Nieker, CEO	Tel: (415) 243-4040	%FO: 100
Bus: *Publishes and distributes branded internet programming.*	Fax: (415) 243-4040	

NCS PEARSON

11000 Prairie Lakes Drive, Eden Prairie, MN 55344

CEO: David W. Smith, CEO	Tel: (952) 829-3000	%FO: 100
Bus: *Provides software and internet services for data collection.*	Fax: (952) 829-3167	Emp: 4,600

PEARSON EDUCATION

One Lake Drive, Upper Saddle River, NJ 07458

CEO: Peter Jovanovich, CEO	Tel: (201) 236-7000	%FO: 100
Bus: *Educational publisher.*	Fax: (201) 236-7000	

PEARSON, INC.
1330 Avenue of the Americas, 7th Fl., New York, NY   10019
CEO: Phillip Hoffman, Pres.   Tel: (212) 641-2400   %FO: 100
Bus: *U.S. Headquarters. Newspapers &*   Fax: (212) 641-2500
    book publishing, visitor
    attractions, TV, investment
    banking.

PENGUIN GROUP
375 Hudson Street, New York, NY   10014
CEO: David Wan, Pres.   Tel: (212) 366-2000   %FO: 100
Bus: *Book publishing.*   Fax: (212) 366-2666   Emp: 180

PENGUIN PUTNAM INC.
375 Hudson Street, New York, NY   10014
CEO: Phyllis Grann, Pres. & CEO   Tel: (212) 366-2000   %FO: 100
Bus: *Book publishing.*   Fax: (212) 366-2666

● **THE PENINSULAR & ORIENTAL STEAM NAVIGATION CO.**
79 Pall Mall, London SW1Y 5EJ, UK
CEO: Sir Bruce D. MacPhall, CEO   Tel: 44-207-930-4343   Rev: $9,800
Bus: *Real estate investment and*   Fax: 44-207-930-8572   Emp: 69,500
    development, ocean passenger/cargo   www.p-and-o.com
    shipping, construction services.

  P&O COLD LOGISTICS
  19840 Rancho Way, Dominguez Hills, CA   90221
  CEO: Bill Duffy, Pres.   Tel: (310) 632-6265
  Bus: *Provides cold storage services.*   Fax: (310) 900-7041

● **PENNA CONSULTING PLC**
1 Bow Churchyard, London EC4M 9DQ, UK
CEO: Suzie A. Mumme, CEO   Tel: 44-207-945-3505
Bus: *Engaged in staffing and outsourcing.*   Fax: 44-207-945-3506
                                     www.penna.co.uk

  MANCHESTER INC.
  One Independent Drive, Ste. 206, Jacksonville, FL   32202
  CEO: P. Smith   Tel: (610) 617-9118   %FO: 100
  Bus: *Engaged in staffing.*   Fax: (610) 617-9966

● **PENNON GROUP PLC**
Peninsula House, Rydon Lane, Exeter, Devon EX2 7HR, UK
CEO: Kenneth G. Harvey, Chmn.   Tel: 44-139-244-6677   Rev: $616
Bus: *Engaged in waste management and*   Fax: 44-139-243-4966   Emp: 3,150
    environmental services.   www.pennon-group.co.uk

HART-LATIMER ASSOCIATES, INC.
1150 East Chestnut Avenue, Santa Ana, CA 92701
CEO: Harry Hart, CEO   Tel: (714) 973-9200   %FO: 100
Bus: *Engaged in waste management.*   Fax: (714) 973-4830

● PHILLIPS, DE PURY & LUXEMBOURG
101 New Bond Street, London W1Y 0AS, UK
CEO: Christopher J. Thompson, CEO   Tel: 44-207-629-6602   Rev: $224
Bus: *Auction house.*   Fax: 44-207-629-8876   Emp: 500
www.phillips-auctions.com

PHILLIPS, DE PURY & LUXEMBOURG
7447 Forsythe Boulevard, St. Louis, MO 63105
CEO: Malcolm Ivey, Mng. Dir.   Tel: (314) 726-5515   %FO: 100
Bus: *Auction house.*   Fax: (314) 726-9908

PHILLIPS, DE PURY & LUXEMBOURG
3 West 57th Street, New York, NY 10019
CEO: Anne Suterland Fuchs, CEO   Tel: (212) 570-4830   %FO: 100
Bus: *Auction house.*   Fax: (212) 570-2207

● PHOTOBITION GROUP PLC
6 Lygon Place, Eury Street, London SW1W OJR, UK
CEO: Eddie Marchbanks, Pres. & CEO   Tel: 44-207-761-9200   Rev: $223
Bus: *Engaged in graphic design services.*   Fax: 44-207-761-9222   Emp: 1,900
www.photobition.com

PHOTOBITION GROUP
132 West 31st Street, New York, NY 10001
CEO: Eddit Marchbanks, CEO   Tel: (800) 474-5280   %FO: 100
Bus: *Engaged in graphic design services.*   Fax: (212) 594-4488

● PHOTO-ME INTERNATIONAL PLC
Church Road, Bookham, Surrey KT23 3EU, UK
CEO: Serge Crasnianski, CEO   Tel: 44-137-245-3399   Rev: $300
Bus: *Mfr. and operates coin-operated, photo booths.*   Fax: 44-137-245-9064   Emp: 2,000
www.photo-me.co.uk

PHOTO-ME USA, INC.
1123 N. Carrier Parkway, Grand Prairie, TX 75050
CEO: Matthew Carter   Tel: (972) 606-1940   %FO: 100
Bus: *Operates coin-operated, photo booths.*   Fax: (972) 606-0661

● **PIC INTERNATIONAL GROUP PLC**

Fyfield Wick, Abingdon, Oxfordshire OX13 5NA, UK

CEO: A. J. Allner, Dir.   Tel: 44-207-822-200   Rev: $5,353

Bus: *Develops and markets breeding pigs.*   Fax: 44-207-820-187   Emp: 10,500

www.pic.com

> **PIC INTERNATIONAL GROUP**
>
> 2929 Seventh Street, Ste. 103, Berkeley, CA 94710
>
> CEO: Phillip J. David, CEO   Tel: (510) 848-8266   %FO: 90
>
> Bus: *Develops and markets breeding pigs.*   Fax: (510) 848-0324   Emp: 1,500

● **PILKINGTON PLC**

Prescot Road, St. Helen's, Merseyside WA10 D3T, UK

CEO: Paolo Scaroni, CEO   Tel: 44-174-428-882   Rev: $3,398

Bus: *Mfr. glass and specialty glass products.*   Fax: 44-174-469-2660   Emp: 30,900

www.pilkington.com

> **PILKINGTON LIBBEY-OWENS-FORD COMPANY**
>
> PO Box 799, Toledo, OH 43697-0799
>
> CEO: Warren Knowlton, Chmn.   Tel: (419) 247-3731   %FO: 100
>
> Bus: *Mfr. glass and specialty glass products.*   Fax: (419) 247-3821

> **PILKINGTON NORTH AMERICA**
>
> 35717 Stanley Drive, Sterling Heights, MI 48312
>
> CEO: Scott Chaffee, VP   Tel: (810) 795-3500   %FO: 100
>
> Bus: *Mfr./sales glass for the auto industry.*   Fax: (810) 795-5190

> **PILKINGTON NORTH AMERICA**
>
> PO Box 799, Toledo, OH 43695
>
> CEO: Scott Chaffee, VP   Tel: (419) 247-3731   %FO: 100
>
> Bus: *Mfr./sales glass for the auto industry.*   Fax: (419) 247-3821

> **PILKINGTON NORTH AMERICA**
>
> 11700 Tecumseh, Clinton, MI 49236
>
> CEO: David Morris   Tel: (517) 456-7451   %FO: 100
>
> Bus: *Mfr./sales glass for the auto industry.*   Fax: (517) 456-4242

● **POWDERJECT PHARMACEUTICALS PLC**
Robert Robinson Avenue, Oxford Science Park, Oxford OX4 4GA, UK
CEO: Paul Drayson, CEO   Tel: 44-186-533-2600   Rev: $57
Bus: *Mfr. needle-free systems.*   Fax: 44-186-533-2601   Emp: 850
www.powderject.com

POWDERJECT VACCINES, INC.
585 Science Drive, Madison, WI   53711
CEO: Russ Smestad   Tel: (608) 231-3150   %FO: 100
Bus: *Mfr./sales needle-free systems.*   Fax: (608) 231-6990

● **POWERGEN PLC**
53 New Broad Street, London EC2M 1SL, UK
CEO: Nick Baldwin, CEO   Tel: 44-207-826-2826   Rev: $6,100
Bus: *Electricity generation.*   Fax: 44-207-826-2890   Emp: 8,000
www.pgen.com

LOUISVILLE GAS AND ELECTRIC
820 West Broadway, PO Box 32020, Louisville, KY   40232
CEO: Stephen R. Wood, Pres.   Tel: (502) 627-3038   %FO: 100
Bus: *Electricity generation.*   Fax: (502) 627-3699

● **PREMIER FARNELL PLC**
25/28 Old Burlington Street, London W1S 3AN, UK
CEO: John R. Hirst, CEO   Tel: 44-207-851-4100   Rev: $1,281
Bus: *Mfr. industrial and electronic*   Fax: 44-207-851-4110   Emp: 5,630
   components.   www.premierfarnell.co.uk

AKRON BRASS COMPANY
PO Box 86, Wooster, OH   44691
CEO: John Kilpatrick   Tel: (330) 264-5678   %FO: 100
Bus: *Mfr. fire fighting equipment.*   Fax: (330) 264-2944

D-A LUBRICANT COMPANY
1340 West 29th Street, Indianapolis, IN   46208
CEO: Mike Finney, Mgr.   Tel: (317) 924-1601   %FO: 100
Bus: *Mfr. auto lubricants.*   Fax: (317) 923-3884

NEWARK ELECTRONICS
217 Wilcox Avenue, Gaffney, SC   29340
CEO: William Evanson, VP   Tel: (864) 487-1900
Bus: *Warehouse facility for catalog*   Fax: (864) 487-1904
   distributor of electronic
   components, equipment and
   supplies.

NEWARK ELECTRNICS

4801 North Ravenswood, Chicago, IL 60640

CEO: William Evanson, VP   Tel: (773) 784-5100   %FO: 100

Bus: *Business-to-business catalog distributor of electronic components, equipment, and supplies.*   Fax: (773) 907-5339

NEWARK ELECTRONICS

500 North Pulaski, Chicago, IL 60624

CEO: William Evanson, VP   Tel: (773) 784-5100

Bus: *Warehouse facility for catalog distributor of electronic components, equipment and supplies.*   Fax: (773) 638-3040

PREMIER FARNELL USA

4500 Euclid Avenue, Cleveland, OH 44101

CEO: Mike Ruprich, CEO   Tel: (216) 391-8300

Bus: *Mfr. industrial and electronic components.*   Fax: (216) 587-4937

TPC WIRE & CABLE

4500 Euclid Avenue, PO Box 94884, Cleveland, OH 44101-4884

CEO: Reed Cushing, Mgr.   Tel: (216) 432-7000   %FO: 100

Bus: *Mfr. electrical and electronic cord, cable and connectors for the industrial market.*   Fax: (216) 391-1548

● PREMIER HEALTH GROUP PLC

2 Dancastle Court, Arcadia Avenue, Finchley, London N3 2JU, UK

CEO: Chris Eales, CEO   Tel: 44-181-349-2282

Bus: *Employment agencies and management services.*   Fax: 44-181-349-2218
www.premierhealth.co.uk

PREMIER HEALTH GROUP INC.

2400 Herodian Way, Ste. 110, Smyrna, GA 30305

CEO: Chris Eales, CFO   Tel: (770) 956-0500   %FO: 100

Bus: *Employment agency for healthcare services.*   Fax: (770) 956-1894

● PRESSAC PLC

100 Mansfield Road, Derby DE1 3TT, UK

CEO: George C. White, CEO   Tel: 44-1332-747-7000   Rev: $287

Bus: *Mfr. electrical and electronic components for the auto telecommunications industry.*   Fax: 44-1332-747-7200   Emp: 4,050
www.pressac.com

KAUMAGRAPH FLINT CORPORATION
4705 Industrial Drive, Millington, MI 48746
CEO: D. F. Taylor, Mng. Dir.   Tel: (518) 871-4550   %FO: 100
Bus: *Mfr./sales electrical and*   Fax: (517) 871-2291
electronic components for the auto
telecommunications industry.

PRESSAC INC.
2304 Industrial Drive SW, Cullman, AL 35055
CEO: D. Whittaker, Pres.   Tel: (256) 734-2110   %FO: 100
Bus: *Mfr./sales electrical and*   Fax: (256) 734-3123
electronic components for the auto
telecommunications industry.

● **PROFESSIONAL STAFF PLC**
Buckland House, Waterside Drive, Langley Business Park, Slough, Berkshire SL3 6EZ, UK
CEO: Ben Blackden, CEO   Tel: 44-175-358-0540   Rev: $208
Bus: *Provides staffing services to clients in*   Fax: 44-175-354-0962   Emp: 375
the technology and science fields.   www.professional-staff.com

   THE WOOLF GROUP
   5315 Highgate Centre, Highgate Drive, Durham, NC 27713
   CEO: Sharon Sawchak   Tel: (919) 425-0155   %FO: 100
   Bus: *Provides staffing services to*   Fax: (919) 425-0166
   clients in the technology and
   science fields.

● **PROFILE THERAPEUTICS PLC**
7 Town Quay, Southampton SO1 OXN, UK
CEO: M. R. Kirby, CEO   Tel: 44-124-384-0033
Bus: *Health products and services.*   Fax: 44-124-384-6146
      www.profiletherapeutics.com

   PROFILE THERAPEUTICS
   28 States Street, Ste. 1100, Boston, MA 02109
   CEO: M. R. Kirby, Pres.   Tel: (617) 573-5062   %FO: 100
   Bus: *Health products and services.*   Fax: (617) 573-5063

● **PRUDENTIAL PLC**
Laurence Pountney Hill, London EC4R 0HH, UK
CEO: Jonathan Bloomer, CEO   Tel: 44-207-220-7588   Rev: $52,115
Bus: *Insurance and financial services.*   Fax: 44-207-548-3850   Emp: 22,375
      www.prudential.co.uk

JACKSON NATIONAL LIFE INSURANCE COMPANY

5901 Executive Drive, Lansing, MI 48911

CEO: Robert P. Saltzman, Pres.	Tel: (517) 394-3400	%FO: 100
Bus: *Life insurance and annuities.*	Fax: (517) 394-7107	Emp: 1,300

● PSION PLC

12 Park Crescent, London W1B 1PH, UK

CEO: David Levin, CEO	Tel: 44-207-317-4100	Rev: $328
Bus: *Mfr. mini and hand-held computers.*	Fax: 44-207-258-7340	Emp: 1,000
	www.psion.com	

PSION TEKLOGIX INC.

1810 Airport Exchange Blvd., Ste. 500, Erlanger, KY 41018

CEO: Andrew Clegg	Tel: (859) 371-6006	%FO: 100
Bus: *Sales of mini and hand-held computers.*	Fax: (859) 371-6422	

PSION TEKLOGIX INC.

3051 Oak Grove Road, Ste. 103, Downers Grove, Il 60515

CEO: Andrew Clegg	Tel: (630) 241-2500	%FO: 100
Bus: *Sales of mini and hand-held computers.*	Fax: (630) 241-0179	

PSION TEKLOGIX INC.

7000 Peachtree Dunwoody Road, Ste. 300, Atlanta, GA 30328

CEO: Andrew Clegg	Tel: (770) 390-0555	%FO: 100
Bus: *Sales of mini and hand-held computers.*	Fax: (770) 390-0005	

PSION TEKLOGIX INC.

2255 Challenger Way, Ste. 100, Santa Rosa, CA 95407

CEO: Andrew Clegg	Tel: (707) 576-1111	%FO: 100
Bus: *Sales of mini and hand-held computers.*	Fax: (707) 576-1239	

● RACAL ELECTRONICS PLC

Western Road, Bracknell, Berkshire RG12 1RG, UK

CEO: David C. Elsbury, CEO	Tel: 44-134-448-1222	Rev: $1,229
Bus: *Diversified mfr. electronics; communications, industrial, defense, health systems and equipment.*	Fax: 44-134-445-4119	Emp: 9,000
	www.racal.com	

RACAL AVIONICS INC.

8851 Monard Drive, Silver Spring, MD 20910-1878

CEO: Steve Kemp, Gen. Mgr.	Tel: (301) 495-6695	%FO: 100
Bus: *Mfr. avionics and airborne satellite communications.*	Fax: (301) 585-7578	

RACAL COMMUNICATIONS INC.

5 Research Place, Rockville, MD 20850

CEO: Mark Lipp, Pres. & CEO   Tel: (301) 948-4420   %FO: 100

Bus: *Mfr. tactical radios.*   Fax: (301) 948-6015

THE RACAL CORPORATION

1601 North Harrison Pkwy., Sunrise, FL 33323-2899

CEO: Laurence P. Manning, Pres.   Tel: (954) 846-1601   %FO: 100

Bus: *Holding company, U.S.*   Fax: (954) 846-3030
     headquarters. diversified mfr.
     electronics; communications,
     industrial, defense, health systems
     & equipment.

RACAL INSTRUMENTS INC.

4 Goodyear Street, Irvine, CA 92718-2002

CEO: Gordon W. Taylor, Pres. & CEO   Tel: (949) 859-8999   %FO: 100

Bus: *Mfr. test/measuring instruments.*   Fax: (949) 859-7139

RACAL LANDSTAR USA

7313A Grove Road, Frederick, MD 21704

CEO: John C. Sparkman, Jr., VP   Tel: (301) 624-5505

Bus: *Survey and positioning services,*   Fax: (301) 624-5848
     tracking and telemetry.

RACAL NCS, INC.

3624 Westchase Drive, Houston, TX 77042

CEO: Anthony J. Harrison, Gen. Dir.   Tel: (713) 784-4482   %FO: 100

Bus: *Marine & survey services.*   Fax: (713) 784-8162

RACAL PELAGOS INC.

3738 Ruffin Road, San Diego, CA 92123

CEO: Randall J. Ashley, SVP   Tel: (619) 292-8922   %FO: 100

Bus: *Provides survey services.*   Fax: (619) 292-5308

RACAL RECORDERS INC.

480 Spring Park Place, Ste. 1000, Herndon, VA 20170

CEO: Chris Wooten, Mgr.   Tel: (703) 709-7114   %FO: 100

Bus: *Voice & data recorders.*   Fax: (703) 709-9529

ZAXUS, INC.

1601 N. Harrison Pkwy., Ste. 100, Sunrise, FL 33323-2899

CEO: Juan Asenio, Mgr.   Tel: (954) 846-4700

Bus: *Security solutions for card*   Fax: (954) 846-3935
     payments, e-security and network
     security.

● **THE RANK GROUP PLC**

6 Connaught Place, London W2 2EZ, UK

CEO: Mike Smith, CEO　　　　　　　Tel: 44-207-706-1111　　　Rev: $2,682

Bus: *Diversified leisure, entertainment,*　Fax: 44-207-262-9866　　Emp: 43,081
　　holiday, recreation and industrial group.　www.rank.com

　　DELUXE LABORATORIES, INC.

　　1377 North Serrano Avenue, Hollywood, CA　90027

　　CEO: Cyril Drabinsky, Pres.　　　Tel: (213) 462-6171　　　%FO: 100

　　Bus: *Research/mfr./processing film and*　Fax: (213) 466-1647
　　　　video.

　　DELUXE VIDEO SERVICES INC.

　　540 Lake Cook Road, Ste. 200, Deerfield, IL　60015

　　CEO: Peter Pacitti, CEO　　　　Tel: (847) 291-1150　　　%FO: 100

　　Bus: *Sales/service and engineering*　Fax: (847) 480-6077
　　　　customization precision instrument
　　　　to measure surface, roundness and
　　　　optical features.

　　HARD ROCK CAFÉ INTERNATIONAL, INC.

　　6100 Old Park Lane, Orlando, FL　32819

　　CEO: Peter J. Beaudrault, Pres. & CEO　Tel: (407) 445-7625　　%FO: 100

　　Bus: *Chain of theme restaurants*　　Fax: (407) 445-7937　　Emp: 3,000

　　RANK AMERICA, INC.

　　5 Concourse Pkwy., Ste. 2400, Atlanta, GA　30328

　　CEO: John H. Watson, EVP　　　Tel: (770) 392-9029　　　%FO: 100

　　Bus: *U.S. headquarters of diversified*　Fax: (770) 392-0585
　　　　leisure, entertainment, holiday,
　　　　recreation and industrial group.

　　RESORTS USA, INC.

　　Route 209, PO Box 447, Bushkill, PA　18324

　　CEO: Andy Worthington, Pres.　　Tel: (717) 588-6661　　　%FO: 100

　　Bus: *Leisure time industry.*　　　Fax: (717) 588-2787

● **RAW COMMUNICATIONS LIMITED**

28-30 Worship Street, London EC2A 2AH, UK

CEO: Ab Banerjee, CEO　　　　　　Tel: 44-207-861-0400

Bus: *Webcast and Online content providers.*　Fax: 44-207-861-0401　　Emp: 80
　　　　　　　　　　　　　　　　　www.rawcommunications.com

RAW COMMUNICATIONS INC.
17 State Street, 23rd Fl., New York, NY   10004
CEO: Nick Edwards
Bus: *Webcast and Online content providers.*

Tel: (212) 742-2222
Fax: (212) 742-8461

%FO: 100

• RECKITT BENCKISER PLC
67 Alma Road, Windsor, Berkshire SL4 3HD, UK
CEO: Alan J. Dalby, Chmn.
Bus: *Mfr. household cleaning products.*

Tel: 44-175-383-5835
Fax: 44-181-994-8920
www.reckitt.com

Rev: $4,937
Emp: 20,200

RECKITT BENCKISER
1655 Valley Road, PO Box 943, Wayne, NJ   07474
CEO: Ken Stokes, EVP
Bus: *Mfr./marketing of household cleaning products.*

Tel: (973) 633-3600
Fax: (973) 633-3633

%FO: 100

• REED INTERNATIONAL PLC
25 Victoria Street, London SW 1H OEX, UK
CEO: Crispin Davis, CEO
Bus: *Publishing holding company; leading international publisher of scientific information. (JV of Reed Int'l plc, UK and Elsevier NV, Amsterdam.*

Tel: 44-207-222-8420
Fax: 44-207-227-5799
www.reed-elsevier.com

Rev: $5,624
Emp: 35,000

BUTTERWORTH HEINEMANN INC.
225 Wildwood Avenue, Woburn, MA   01801
CEO: Norm Langlois, EVP
Bus: *Publisher of books, open learning material and electronic product for students and professionals in technology, medicine and management.*

Tel: (781) 904-2500
Fax: (781) 904-2640

%FO: 100

CAHNERS BUSINESS INFORMATION
275 Washington Street, Newton, MA   02158
CEO: Marc Teren, CEO
Bus: *Publishing.*

Tel: (617) 964-3030
Fax: (617) 558-4667

%FO: 100

CAHNERS ELECTRONIC MEDIA GROUP
One Alewife Center, 2nd Fl., Cambridge, MA   02140
CEO: Richard Bibbins, VP
Bus: *Electronic media.*

Tel: (617) 873-9300
Fax: (617) 873-9550

%FO: 100

CAHNERS TRAVEL GROUP INC.
500 Plaza Drive, Secaucus, NJ   07096
CEO: George Hundley, SVP Tel: (201) 902-2000 %FO: 100
Bus: *Travel related publishing &* Fax: (201) 319-1726
services.

CONGRESSIONAL INFORMATION SERVICE
4520 East-West Hwy, Bethesda, MD 20814
CEO: Paul Kesaris, CEO Tel: (301) 654-1550 %FO: 100
Bus: *Publishing.* Fax: (301) 654-4033

DELUXE LABORATORIES INC.
1377 North Serrano Avenue, Hollywood, CA   90027
CEO: Cyril Drabinsky, Pres. Tel: (213) 462-6171 %FO: 100
Bus: *Supplies products and services to* Fax: (213) 466-1647
film industries.

ELSEVIER SCIENCE INC.
655 Avenue of the Americas, New York, NY   10010
CEO: John Regazzi, Pres. Tel: (212) 989-5800 %FO: 100
Bus: *Publisher of science and medical* Fax: (212) 633-3990
journals.

EXCERPTA MEDICA INC.
105 Raider Boulevard, Hillsborough, NJ   08876
CEO: Mel Kosko, Mgr. Tel: (908) 874-8550 %FO: 100
Bus: *Publisher of scientific information.* Fax: (908) 874-0700

GREENWOOD PUBLISHING GROUP INC.
88 Post Road West, PO Box 5007, Westport, CT   06881
CEO: Wayne Smith, Pres. Tel: (203) 226-3571 %FO: 100
Bus: *Publishing.* Fax: (203) 222-1502

HARCOURT BRACE SCHOOL PUBLISHERS, INC., DIV. HARCOURT GENERAL
6277 Sea Harbor Drive, Orlando, FL   32887
CEO: Brian J. Knez, Pres. & CEO Tel: (407) 345-3636 %FO: 100
Bus: *Publisher of educational books.* Fax: (407) 352-1318

LEXIS-NEXIS
9393 Springboro Pike, Miamisburg, OH   45342
CEO: Lou Andreozzi, CEO Tel: (937) 865-7000 %FO: 100
Bus: *On-line information service;* Fax: (937) 865-1555
reference information & databases.

MDL INFORMATION SYSTEMS, INC.

14600 Catalina Street, San Leandro, CA   94577

CEO: Pat Rougeau, CEO

Bus: *Provides integrated solutions in the life science and chemical industries.*

Tel: (510) 895-1313
Fax: (510) 352-2870

OAG WORLDWIDE

2000 Clearwater Drive, Oak Brook, IL   60523

CEO: Nawin Gupta, SVP

Bus: *Publishes materials related to the travel industry.*

Tel: (630) 574-6000
Fax: (630) 574-6565

REED ELSEVIER, INC.

125 Park Avenue, 23rd Fl., New York, NY   10017

CEO: Paul Richardson, SVP

Bus: *U.S. headquarters for publishing holding company. JV of Reed Int'l plc, London (50%) and Elsevier NV, Amsterdam (50%).*

Tel: (212) 309-5498
Fax: (212) 309-5480

%FO: 100

REED EXHIBITION COMPANY

383 Main Avenue, Norwalk, CT   06851

CEO: Rick White, Pres.

Bus: *Exhibition/conference organization*

Tel: (203) 840-4800
Fax: (203) 840-9400

%FO: 100

● REFLEC PLC

Road One, Winsford Industrial Estate, Winsford, Cheshire CW7 3QQ, UK

CEO: Peter A White, CEO

Bus: *Develops and manufactures retro-reflective inks, tapes and ancillary products and plastic coatings for protective purposes for active wear and industrial markets.*

Tel: 44-160-659-3911
Fax: 55-160-659-3306
www.reflec.co.uk.

Rev: $3,706
Emp: 75

REFLEC USA CORP.

200 Homer Avenue, Ste. 6B, Ashland, MA   01721

CEO: Peer Richard Smith, CEO

Bus: *Develops and manufactures safety-enhancing retro-reflective fabrics for active wear, outerwear, and industrial markets.*

Tel: (508) 231-0748
Fax: (508) 231-1495

%FO: 100

● **REGUS PLC**

3000 Hillswood Drive, Chertsey, Surrey KT16 0RS, UK

CEO: Mark Dixon, CEO

Bus: *Engaged in temporary business support systems, including office facilities, meeting rooms, multi-lingual staff and complete IT infrastructure.*

Tel: 44-193-289-5500
Fax: 44-193-289-5501
www.regus.com

Rev: $629
Emp: 2,800

   REGUS BUSINESS CENTERS

   5825 Glenridge Drive, Bldg. 3, Ste. 101, Atlanta, GA　30328

   CEO: Holly Wimbish, Mgr.

   Bus: *Provides temporary business support systems.*

Tel: (404) 995-9200
Fax: (404) 843-0751

%FO: 100

   REGUS BUSINESS CENTERS

   200 South Wacker Drive, Ste. 3100, Chicago, IL　60606

   CEO: Margaret Mazzitti, Mgr.

   Bus: *Provides temporary business support systems.*

Tel: (312) 674-4500
Fax: (312) 674-4501

   REGUS BUSINESS CENTERS

   303 Twin Dolphin Drive, Ste. 600, Redwood City, CA　94065

   CEO: Lou Ann Foster, Mgr.

   Bus: *Provides temporary business support systems.*

Tel: (650) 551-9900
Fax:

   REGUS LATIN AMERICA

   5201 Blue Lagoon Drive, Penthouse, Miami, FL　33126

   CEO: Maria Zaret, Mgr.

   Bus: *Provides temporary business support systems.*

Tel: (305) 716-4040
Fax: (305) 716-4100

%FO: 100

   REGUS WORLDWIDE

   245 Park Avenue, New York, NY　10020

   CEO: Ingeborg Lariby, Mgr.

   Bus: *Provides temporary business support systems.*

Tel: (212) 792-4000
Fax: (212) 792-4001

%FO: 100

● **RENISHAW PLC**

New Mills, Wotton-under-Edge, Gloucestershire GL12 8JR, UK

CEO: David R. McMurtry, CEO

Bus: *Mfr. test probe and measurement systems.*

Tel: 44-145-352-4524
Fax: 44-145-352-4001
www.renishaw.com

Rev: $177
Emp: 1,500

RENISHAW INC.

5277 Trillium Boulevard, Hoffman Estates, IL 60192

CEO: Jeffrey Seliga	Tel: (947) 843-3666	%FO: 100
Bus: *Sales test probe and measurement equipment.*	Fax: (847) 843-1744	

● RENOLD PLC

Wythenshawe, Styal Road, Wythenshawe, Manchester M22 5WL, UK

CEO: David Cotterill, Mng. Dir.	Tel: 44-161-437-5221	Rev: $302
Bus: *Transmission chain, gears, couplings, machine tools.*	Fax: 44-161-437-7782 www.renold.com	Emp: 2,200

RENOLD, INC.

100 Bourne Street, PO Box A, Westfield, NY 14787

CEO: Tom Murrer, Pres.	Tel: (716) 326-3121	%FO: 100
Bus: *Mfr. rolling mill spindles, coupling, gears, vibrators, material handling vibratory equipment.*	Fax: (716) 326-6121	Emp: 130

● RENTOKIL INITIAL PLC

Felcourt, East Grinsteadt, West Sussex RH19 21Y, UK

CEO: Sir Clive Thompson, CEO	Tel: 44-134-283-3022	Rev: $3,932
Bus: *Transportation, electronic, leisure, industry, construction service, pest control.*	Fax: 44-134-283-5176 www.rentokil-initial.com	Emp: 120,000

INITIAL CONTRACT SERVICES

1001 Avenue of the Americas, 10th Fl., New York, NY 10018

CEO: Ed Fleury, Pres. & CEO	Tel: (212) 869-6800
Bus: *Personnel staffing.*	Fax: (212) 869-6991

INITIAL DSI TRANSPORTS INC.

15600 JFK Blvd., Ste. 600, Houston, TX 77032

CEO: William Sadler, Pres. & CEO	Tel: (281) 985-0000
Bus: *Transportation services.*	Fax: (281) 442-4616

INITIAL SECURITY SERVICES

3355 Cherry Ridge, Ste. 200, San Antonio, TX 78230

CEO: Michael Schroeder, Pres.	Tel: (210) 349-6321
Bus: *Security services.*	Fax: (210) 349-0213

RENTOKIL INC.

3750 West Deerfield Road, Ste. 1000, Riverwoods, IL 60015-0710

CEO: Randy Mestad, Mgr.	Tel: (847) 634-4250	%FO: 100
Bus: *Tropical plant services.*	Fax: (847) 634-6820	

RENTOKIL INITIAL INC.
4067 Industrial Park Drive, Bldg. 3, Norcross, GA   30071

CEO: Clive Thompson, Pres.	Tel: (770) 495-0337	%FO: 100
Bus: *Rental/staffing and resort management.*	Fax: (770) 495-8610	

RENTOKIL, INC.
3750 West Deerfield Road, Riverwoods, IL   60015

CEO: Richard Cottrill, Pres.	Tel: (847) 634-4250	%FO: 100
Bus: *Plants and pest control specialists.*	Fax: (847) 634-6820	

• RETAIL DECISIONS PLC
30 St. John's Road, Woking, Surrey GU21 1SA, UK

CEO: Caryle C. Clump, CEO	Tel: 44-148-372-8700
Bus: *Mfr. of computer software.*	Fax: 44-148-372-8400
	www.redplc.com

RETAIL DECISIONS
100 Village Court, Ste. 102, Hazlet, NJ   07730

CEO: Robert A. Gein	Tel: (732) 888-0088	%FO: 100
Bus: *Sales of computer software.*	Fax: (732) 888-4396	

• REUTERS GROUP PLC
85 Fleet Street, London EC4P 4AJ, UK

CEO: Peter J. D. Job, CEO	Tel: 44-207-250-1122	Rev: $5,371
Bus: *Produces and distributes news and financial information and photographs globally.*	Fax: 44-207-510-5896	Emp: 16,550
	www.reuters.com	

INSTINET CORPORATION
875 Third Avenue, New York, NY   10022

CEO: Douglas M. Atkin, CEO	Tel: (212) 310-9500
Bus: *Produces brokerage services via an automated financial market access and information system.*	Fax: (212) 310-9500

RADIANZ INC.
50 California Street , Ste. 1500, San Francisco, CA   94104

CEO: Doug Gilstrap, CEO	Tel: (415) 277-5402	%FO: 100
Bus: *Sales of business to business financial service network providing access to information, service, and hosting services.*	Fax: (415) 277-5402	

RADIANZ INC.
26020 Acero Street, Mission Viejo, CA   92691
CEO: Doug Gilstrap, CEO   Tel: (949) 457-0363   %FO: 100
Bus: *Sales of business to business*   Fax: (949) 457-0363
     financial service network
     providing access to information,
     service, and hosting services.

RADIANZ INC.
28 State Street, 39th Fl., Boston, MA   02109
CEO: Doug Gilstrap, CEO   Tel: (617) 557-1610   %FO: 100
Bus: *Sales of business to business*   Fax: (617) 557-1610
     financial service network
     providing access to information,
     service, and hosting services.

RADIANZ INC.
2300 North Barrington Road, Ste. 400, Hoffman Estates, IL   60195
CEO: Doug Gilstrap, CEO   Tel: (847) 490-5305   %FO: 100
Bus: *Sales of business to business*   Fax: (847) 490-1039
     financial service network
     providing access to information,
     service, and hosting services.

RADIANZ INC.
1251 Avenue of the Americas, 7th Fl., New York, NY   10020
CEO: Doug Gilstrap, CEO   Tel: (212) 899-4300   %FO: 100
Bus: *Business to Business financial*   Fax: (212) 899-4300
     service network providing access
     to information, service, and
     hosting services.

REUTERS AMERICA, INC.
3 Times Square, New York, NY   10036
CEO: Marty Filipowski   Tel: (646) 223-4000   %FO: 100
Bus: *Produces and distributes news and* Fax: (646) 436-1659
     financial information and
     photographs globally.

REUTERS AMERICA, INC.
1333 H Street NW, Washington, DC   20005
CEO: Stephen Jukes, Dir.   Tel: (202) 898-8300   %FO: 100
Bus: *Produces and distributes news and* Fax: (202) 898-8383
     financial information and
     photographs globally.

REUTERS AMERICA, INC.
1700 Broadway, New York, NY   10019
CEO: Thomas Glocer, CEO   Tel: (212) 603-3300   %FO: 100
Bus: *U.S. headquarters. Produces and*   Fax: (212) 247-0346
distributes news and financial
information and photographs
globally.

REUTERS HEALTH INFORMATION
1720 Post Road East, Ste. 221, Westport, CT   06880
CEO: Dan McKillen, CEO   Tel: (203) 319-2700   %FO: 100
Bus: *Produces and distributes premiere*   Fax: (203) 319-2711
health and medical global daily
news for professionals and
consumers on the Internet.

REUTERS HEALTH INFORMATION
45 West 36th Street, 12th Fl., New York, NY   10018
CEO: Dan McKillen, CEO   Tel: (212) 273-1700   %FO: 100
Bus: *Produces and distributes premiere*   Fax: (212) 273-1730
health and medical global daily
news for professionals and
consumers on the Internet.

TIBCO SOFTWARE INC.
6000 Fairview Road, Ste. 1200, Charlotte, NC   28210
CEO: Vivek Ranadive, CEO   Tel: (704) 552-3710   %FO: JV
Bus: *Mfr. software for enterprise*   Fax: (704) 552-3705
solutions.

TIBCO SOFTWARE INC.
Two Gateway Center, Ste. 620, Pittsburgh, PA   15222
CEO: Vivek Ranadive, CEO   Tel: (412) 553-9154   %FO: 100
Bus: *Mfr. software for enterprise*   Fax: (412) 553-9159
solutions.

TIBCO SOFTWARE INC.
200 West Franklin Street, Ste. 250, Chapel Hill, NC   27516
CEO: Vivek Ranadive, CEO   Tel: (919) 969-6500   %FO: 100
Bus: *Mfr. software for enterprise*   Fax: (919) 960-2572
solutions.

TIBCO SOFTWARE INC.
6501 Belleview Avenue, Ste. 140, Englewood, CO   80111
CEO: Vivek Ranadive, CEO   Tel: (303) 729-6000   %FO: 100
Bus: *Mfr. software for enterprise*   Fax: (720) 488-1113
solutions.

TIBCO SOFTWARE INC.
5555 Glenridge Connector, Ste. 200, Atlanta, GA   30342

CEO: Tugrul Firatli, VP   Tel: (404) 257-4123   %FO: JV

Bus: *Mfr. software for enterprise solutions.*   Fax: (404) 257-4124

TIBCO SOFTWARE INC.
15305 Dallas Parkway, Ste. 300, Addison, TX   75001

CEO: Vivek Ranadive, CEO   Tel: (972) 387-7472   %FO: 100

Bus: *Mfr. software for enterprise solutions.*   Fax: (972) 387-7473

TIBCO SOFTWARE INC.
1750 Montgomery, San Francisco, CA   94111

CEO: Vivek Ranadive, CEO   Tel: (415) 954-7131   %FO: 100

Bus: *Mfr. software for enterprise solutions.*   Fax: (415) 954-8598

TIBCO SOFTWARE INC.
8400 Normandale Lake Boulevard, Ste. 920, Minneapolis, MN   55437

CEO: Vivek Ranadive, CEO   Tel: (612) 921-8290   %FO: 100

Bus: *Mfr. software for enterprise solutions.*   Fax: (612) 921-2309

TIBCO SOFTWARE INC.
10940 Wilshire Boulevard, Los Angeles, CA   90024

CEO: Vivek Ranadive, CEO   Tel: (314) 443-4135   %FO: 100

Bus: *Mfr. software for enterprise solutions.*   Fax: (310) 443-4220

TIBCO SOFTWARE INC.
1600 Smith, Ste. 3890, Houston, TX   77002

CEO: Vivek Ranadive, CEO   Tel: (713) 344-2050   %FO: 100

Bus: *Mfr. software for enterprise solutions.*   Fax: (713) 344-2060

TIBCO SOFTWARE INC.
3165 Proter Drive, Palo Alto, CA   94304

CEO: Vivek Ranadive, CEO   Tel: (650) 846-1000   %FO: 100

Bus: *Mfr. software for enterprise solutions.*   Fax: (650) 846-1005

TIBCO SOFTWARE INC.
6905 Rockledge Drive, Ste. 600, Bethesda, MD   20817

CEO: Tugrul Firatli, VP   Tel: (301) 896-9348   %FO: JV

Bus: *Mfr. software for enterprise solutions.*   Fax: (301) 896-9711

TIBCO SOFTWARE INC.
4 Cambridge Center, 4th Fl., Cambridge, MA   02142
CEO: Vivek Ranadive, CEO   Tel: (617) 868-4700   %FO: 100
Bus: *Mfr. software for enterprise*   Fax: (617) 499-4409
    solutions.

TIBCO SOFTWARE INC.
2030 Main Street, Ste. 1300, Irvine, CA   92614
CEO: Vivek Ranadive, CEO   Tel: (949) 260-4900   %FO: 100
Bus: *Mfr. software for enterprise*   Fax: (949) 260-4799
    solutions.

TIBCO SOFTWARE INC.
5201 Blue Lagoon Drive, 8th Fl., Miami, FL   33126
CEO: Vivek Ranadive, CEO   Tel: (305) 629-3153   %FO: 100
Bus: *Mfr. software for enterprise*   Fax: (305) 629-3100
    solutions.

● REXAM PLC
114 Knightsbridge, London SW1X 7NN, UK
CEO: Rolf Borjesson, Pres. & CEO   Tel: 44-207-584-7070   Rev: $4,082
Bus: *Mfr. of coated paper, film and specialty*   Fax: 44-207-581-1149   Emp: 22,700
    substrates for imaging and electronic   www.rexam.co.uk
    technologies.

REXAM BEVERAGE CAN AMERICA
1000 Holcomb Woods Parkway, Suite 442, Roswell, GA   30076
CEO: Michael Carithers, VP   Tel: (404) 642-2267   %FO: 100
Bus: *Mfr. beverage cans.*   Fax: (404) 642-2267

REXAM CLOSURES, INC.
3245 Kansas Road, Evansville, IN   47711
CEO: Matt Steurer   Tel: (812) 867-6671   %FO: 100
Bus: *Mfr. child-resistant, dispensing*   Fax: (812) 867-7802
    and standard screw closures.

REXAM CUSTOM, INC.
700 Crestdale Street, PO Box 368, Matthews, NC   28106
CEO: Harry Barto, Pres.   Tel: (704) 847-9171   %FO: 100
Bus: *Precision coating, laminating, and*   Fax: (704) 845-4307
    finishing of flexible materials on
    contract basis.

REXAM DSI, INC.
One Canal Street, South Hadley, MA   01075
CEO: Mike Sanders, VP   Tel: (413) 533-0699   %FO: 100
Bus: *Mfr. decorative covering materials.* Fax: (413) 535-2458

REXAM GRAPHICS, INC.
28 Gaylord Street, South Hadley, MA   01075
CEO: Jerry Hill   Tel: (413) 536-7800   %FO: 100
Bus: *Mfr. precision coated imaging*   Fax: (413) 536-6226
    films and papers.

REXAM MEDICAL PACKAGING, INC.
1919 S. Butterfield Road, Mundelein, IL   60060-9735
CEO: Jim Gilstrap   Tel: (847) 918-4240   %FO: 100
Bus: *Provides packaging solutions for*   Fax: (847) 918-4600
    the healthcare market.

REXAM MEDICAL PACKAGING, INC.
PO Box 158, Mount Holly, NJ   08060-0158
CEO: Mark Eisenhand, Gen. Mgr.   Tel: (609) 267-5900   %FO: 100
Bus: *Mfr. blown extrusion film,*   Fax: (609) 267-7437   Emp: 122
    protection packaging.

REXAM MEDICAL PACKAGING, INC.
8235 220th Street West, PO Box 1089, Lakeville, MN   55044-9013
CEO: David Timmons, Gen. Mgr.   Tel: (612) 469-5461   %FO: 100
Bus: *Mfr. blown extrusion film,*   Fax: (612) 469-5337
    protection packaging.

REXAM RELEASE, INC.
5001 West 66th Street, Bedford Park, IL   60638
CEO: William R. Barker, Pres.   Tel: (708) 458-0777   %FO: 100
Bus: *Mfr. silicone-coated release films*   Fax: (708) 458-4907
    and papers.

REXAM INC
4201 Congress Street, Ste. 340, Charlotte, NC   28209
CEO: Douglas J. McGregor, Pres.   Tel: (704) 551-1500   %FO: 100
Bus: *Corporate headquarters.*   Fax: (704) 551-1570

● **RIO TINTO PLC**
6 St. James's Square, London SW1Y 4LD, UK
CEO: R. Leigh Clifford, CEO   Tel: 44-207-930-2399   Rev: $7,875
Bus: *Mining, metals and industrial minerals.*   Fax: 44-207-930-3249   Emp: 34,400
    www.riotinto.com

KENNECOTT ENERGY COMPANY
PO Box 3009, Gillette, WY   82717
CEO: Gary J. Goldberg, CEO   Tel: (307) 687-6000
Bus: *Mining, metals and industrial*   Fax: (307) 687-6015
    minerals.

KENNECOTT MINERALS
224 North 2200 West, Salt Lake City, UT   84116
CEO: William Orchow, Pres.   Tel: (801) 238-2400
Bus: *Mining, metals and industrial*   Fax: (801) 583-3129
     minerals.

KENNECOTT UTAH COPPER CORPORATION
8315 West 3595 South, Magna, UT   84044
CEO: Bruce D. Farmer, Pres. & CEO   Tel: (801) 252-3000
Bus: *Mining, metals and industrial*   Fax: (801) 252-3135
     minerals.

LUZENAC AMERICA, INC.
9000 East Nichols, Ste. 200, Englewood, CO   80112
CEO: Rich Mell, Pres.   Tel: (303) 643-0400
Bus: *Mining, metals and industrial*   Fax: (303) 643-0446
     minerals.

U.S. BORAX AND CHEMICAL CORPORATION
26877 Tourney Road, Valencia, CA   91355
CEO: Preston Chiaro, Pres.   Tel: (661) 287-5400
Bus: *Mining, metals and industrial*   Fax: (661) 287-5495
     minerals.

● **RIVERSOFT PLC**
211 Lower Richmond Road, Richmond-upon-Thames, Surrey TW9 4LN, UK
CEO: Dominic Gattuso Jr., CEO   Tel: 44-208-392-5740   Rev: $8
Bus: *Design and manufacture of software.*   Fax: 44-208-392-5741   Emp: 300
                                    www.riversoft.com

RIVERSOFT INC.
3000 Arapahoe Avenue, Boulder, CO   80303
CEO: Dominic Gattuso Jr., Pres.   Tel: (720) 544-0023   %FO: 100
Bus: *Mfr./sales software.*   Fax: (720) 406-1960

RIVERSOFT INC.
3773 Cherry Creek Drive North, Ste. 575, Denver, CO   80209
CEO: Dominic Gattuso Jr., Pres.   Tel: (303) 331-6475   %FO: 100
Bus: *Mfr./sales software.*   Fax: (303) 331-6428

RIVERSOFT INC.
650 Fifth Avenue, 21st Fl., New York, NY   10019
CEO: Dominic Gattuso Jr., Pres.   Tel: (646) 557-7000   %FO: 100
Bus: *Mfr./sales software.*   Fax: (646) 557-7100

RIVERSOFT INC.
Two Embarcadero Center, 17th Fl., San Francisco, CA   94111
CEO: Michael Werthan   Tel: (415) 875-4100   %FO: 100
Bus: *Mfr./sales software.*   Fax: (415) 875-4200

● **RMC GROUP PLC**
RMC House, Coldharbour Lane, Thorpe, Egham, Surrey TW20 8TD,UK
CEO: Stuart Walker, CEO   Tel: 44-193-256-8833   Rev: $6,925
Bus: *Produces and supplies construction*   Fax: 44-193-266-8933   Emp: 34,815
materials.   www.rmc-group.com

    RMC INDUSTRIES CORPORATION
    150 East Ponce de Leon Avenue, Ste. 450, Decatur, GA   30030
    CEO: Alan S. J. Durant, Pres.   Tel: (404) 371-1050
    Bus: *Produces and supplies*   Fax: (404) 371-1415
    construction materials.

● **ROBOTIC TECHNOLOGY SYSTEMS PLC**
Northbank Industrial Park, Irlam, Great Manchester M44 5AY, UK
CEO: Philip B. Johnson, CEO   Tel: 44-161-777-2000
Bus: *Mfr. computer software.*   Fax: 44-161-777-2002
    www.rts-group.com

    RTS WRIGHT INDUSTRIES
    1363 North Tech Blvd., Ste. 103, Gilbert, AZ   85233
    CEO: Ken Verble, EVP   Tel: (480) 545-4884   %FO: 100
    Bus: *Mfr./sales computer software.*   Fax: (480) 545-4884

    RTS WRIGHT INDUSTRIES
    707 Spence lane, Nashville, TN   37217
    CEO: Bailey Robinson, Pres. & CEO   Tel: (615) 361-6600   %FO: 100
    Bus: *Mfr./sales computer software.*   Fax: (615) 351-4549

● **ROLLS-ROYCE PLC**
65 Buckingham Gate, London SW1E 6AT, UK
CEO: John E. V. Rose, CEO   Tel: 44-207-222-9020   Rev: $8,753
Bus: *Develops/mfr. turbine engines for*   Fax: 44-207-227-9178   Emp: 73,700
aerospace, marine and industrial power   www.rolls-royce.com
uses.

    BIRD-JOHNSON, DIV. ROLLS-ROYCE
    110 Norfolk Street, Walpole, MA   02081
    CEO: Peter J. Gwyn, Pres.   Tel: (508) 668-9610   %FO: 100
    Bus: *Produces marine propulsion and*   Fax: (508) 668-5638
    control systems.

CERTIFIED ALLOY PRODUCTS, INC.
3245 Cherry Avenue, Long Beach, CA   90807
CEO: Richard N. Greenwood, Pres.   Tel: (562) 595-6621   %FO: 100
Bus: *Mfr. alloyed products.*   Fax: (562) 427-8667

ROLLS-ROYCE CORP.
2001 South Tibbs Avenue, Ste. 30, Indianapolis, IN   46241
CEO: James M. Guyette, Pres.   Tel: (317) 230-2000   %FO: 100
Bus: *Sales/distribution engines for*   Fax:
     aerospace, marine and industry.

ROLLS-ROYCE ENERGY SYSTEMS INC.
7685 South State Route 48, Maineville, OH   45039
CEO: Gale Bronneburg, Pres.   Tel: (513) 683-6100   %FO: 100
Bus: *Sales/distribution engines for*   Fax:
     aerospace, marine and industry.

ROLLS-ROYCE GEAR SYSTEMS INC.
6125 Silver Creek Drive, Park City, UT   84068
CEO: Steven Rusk, Pres.   Tel: (435) 649-1900   %FO: 100
Bus: *Sales/distribution engines for*   Fax: (435) 649-1900
     aerospace, marine and industry.

ROLLS-ROYCE, INC.
11911 Freedom Drive, Reston, VA   20190
CEO: James M. Guyette, Pres. & CEO   Tel: (703) 834-1700   %FO: 100
Bus: *U.S. headquarters. Develops/mfr.* Fax: (703) 709-6086
     turbine engines for aerospace,
     marine and industrial power uses.

SYNCROLIFT INC.
9130 South Dadeland Blvd., Ste. 102, Miami, FL   33156
CEO: Geoff Stokoe, Pres.   Tel: (305) 670-8800   %FO: 100
Bus: *Engaged in building of marine*   Fax: (305) 670-8800
     shiplift facilities.

● **N. M. ROTHSCHILD & SONS LIMITED**
New Court, St. Swithin's Lane, London EC4P 4DU, UK
CEO: David de Rothschild, CEO   Tel: 44-207-280-5000   Rev: $670
Bus: *Engaged in finances and investment* Fax: 44-207-929-1643   Emp: 725
     banking.   www.nmrothschild.com]

N. M. ROTHSCHILD & SONS INC.
370 Seventeenth Street, Denver, CO   80202
CEO: David de Rothschild, CEO   Tel: (303) 607-9890   %FO: 100
Bus: *Engaged in finances and*   Fax: (303) 607-0998
     investment banking.

ROTHSCHILD NORTH AMERICA, INC.
1251 Ave. of the Americas, 51st Fl., New York, NY   10020
CEO: Gerard Rosenfeld, CEO   Tel: (212) 403-3500   %FO: 100
Bus: *Engaged in finances and*   Fax: (212) 403-3501
    investment banking.

ROTHSCHILD NORTH AMERICA, INC.
1101 Connecticut Avenue NW, 7th Fl., Washington, DC   20036
CEO: David de Rothschild, CEO   Tel: (202) 862-1660   %FO: 100
Bus: *Engaged in finances and*   Fax: (202) 862-1699
    investment banking.

● **ROTORK PCL**
Rotork House, Brassmill Lane, Bath BA1 3QJ, UK
CEO: William H. Whiteley, CEO   Tel: 44-122-573-3200   Rev: $161
Bus: *Mfr. valve actuators.*   Fax: 44-122-573-3381   Emp: 1,000
                                      www.rotork.com

  ROTORK COMPANY
  675 Mile Crossing Boulevard, Rochester, NY   14624
  CEO: Robert H. Arnold, Pres.   Tel: (716) 328-1550   %FO: 100
  Bus: *Mfr./sales valve actuators.* Fax: (716) 328-5848

  ROTORK COMPANY
  1945 Waverly Street, Napa, CA   94558
  CEO: Tom DeGaetano   Tel: (707) 252-4679   %FO: 100
  Bus: *Mfr./sales valve actuators.* Fax: (707) 252-3574

  ROTORK COMPANY
  2682 Quevedo lane, Mission Viejo, CA   92691
  CEO: Rob Cavell   Tel: (949) 348-2913   %FO: 100
  Bus: *Sales of valve and controls.* Fax: (949) 215-7230

  ROTORK CONTROLS INC.
  PO Box 330, Plainfield, IL   60544-0330
  CEO: Mike English   Tel: (815) 436-1710   %FO: 100
  Bus: *Sales of valve and controls.* Fax: (815) 436-1789

  ROTORK CONTROLS INC.
  15 Laurel Drive, Mullica Hill, NJ   08062
  CEO: Bob Tomchak   Tel: (856) 223-1926   %FO: 100
  Bus: *Sales of valve and controls.* Fax: (856) 223-9012

  ROTORK CONTROLS INC.
  300 Round Grove Road, Ste. 1634, Lewisville, TX   75067
  CEO: Skip Kuehn   Tel: (972) 459-4957   %FO: 100
  Bus: *Sales of valve and controls.* Fax: (972) 459-4957

ROTORK CONTROLS INC.
140 Gainford Court, Duluth, GA   30097
CEO: Miguel Lopez   Tel: (770) 623-6301   %FO: 100
Bus: *Sales of valve and controls.*   Fax: (770) 623-6124

ROTORK CONTROLS INC.
419 First Street, Petaluma, CA   94952
CEO: Howard Williams   Tel: (707) 769-4880   %FO: 100
Bus: *Sales of valve and controls.*   Fax: (707) 769-4888

ROTORK CONTROLS INC.
830 Compass Drive, Erie, PA   16505
CEO: Bob Toth   Tel: (814) 835-8349   %FO: 100
Bus: *Sales of valve and controls.*   Fax: (814) 835-8909

ROTORK CONTROLS INC.
6776 Southwest Freeway, Ste. 368, Houston, TX   77074
CEO: Keith Phillips   Tel: (713) 782-5888   %FO: 100
Bus: *Sales of valve and controls.*   Fax: (713) 782-8524

ROTORK CONTROLS INC.
1717 South 341st Place, Ste. 102, Federal Way, WA   98003
CEO: Charlie Haynes   Tel: (253) 838-5500   %FO: 100
Bus: *Sales of valve and controls.*   Fax: (253) 838-5400

● **ROYAL & SUN ALLIANCE INSURANCE GROUP PLC**
30 Berkeley Square, London W1X 5HA, UK
CEO: Robert V. Mendelsohn, CEO   Tel: 44-207-636-3450   Rev: $28,900
Bus: *Insurance services.*   Fax: 44-207-636-3451   Emp: 51,730
                                           www.royal-and-sunalliance.co.uk

    ROYAL & SUN ALLIANCE FINANCIAL SERVICES
    One Chase Manhattan Plaza, 38th Fl., New York, NY   1005
    CEO: Sue Kesselman   Tel: (212) 709-3600   %FO: 100
    Bus: *Financial services.*   Fax: (212) 709-3694

    ROYAL & SUN ALLIANCE INC.
    9300 Arrowpoint Boulevard, Charlotte, NC   28273-8135
    CEO: Terry Broderick, Pres.   Tel: (704) 522-2000   %FO: 100
    Bus: *Insurance services.*   Fax: (704) 522-3200

    SAFEGUARD INSURANCE COMPANY
    9300 Arrowpoint Boulevard, Charlotte, NC   28273
    CEO: Terry Broderick, Pres.   Tel: (704) 522-2000   %FO: 100
    Bus: *Provides property and casualty   Fax: (704) 522-3200
        insurance services.*

- **ROYAL DOULTON PLC**
  Minton House, London Road, Stoke-on-Trent ST47 QD, UK
  CEO: Jack Repetto, Pres.   Tel: 44-178-229-2292   Rev: $273
  Bus: *Mfr. and distributor of ceramic*   Fax: 44-178-229-2099   Emp: 6,200
  tableware and giftware.   www.royal-doulton.co.uk

  > **ROYAL DOULTON USA INC.**
  > 700 Cottontail Lane, Somerset, NJ   08873
  > CEO: Robin Goad, VP   Tel: (732) 356-7880   %FO: 100
  > Bus: *Mfr./sales and distributor of*   Fax: (732) 764-4974
  > *ceramic tableware and giftware.*

- **ROYALBLUE GROUP PLC**
  Dukes Court, Church Street East, Woking, Surrey GU21 5BH, UK
  CEO: John R. Hamer, CEO   Tel: 44-148-374-4400   Rev: $86
  Bus: *Mfr. global financial trading software.*   Fax: 44-148-372-9131   Emp: 500
  www.royalblue.com

  > **ROYALBLUE GROUP, INC.**
  > 17 State Street, New York, NY   10004-1501
  > CEO: Chris Aspinwall   Tel: (212) 269-9000   %FO: 100
  > Bus: *Mfr./sales global financial trading*   Fax: (212) 785-4327
  > *software.*

- **RPC GROUP PLC**
  Broadfield House, Grove Street, Raunds, Northamptonshire NN9 6ED, UK
  CEO: Ron J. E. Marsh, CEO   Tel: 44-193-346-0020   Rev: $505
  Bus: *Mfr. rigid plastic packaging, including*   Fax: 44-193-346-0938   Emp: 5,430
  printing and labeling for related   www.rpc-containers.co.uk
  products.

  > **BRAMLAGE-WIKO USA, INC.**
  > 415 Eagleview Boulevard, Ste. 108, Exton, PA   19341
  > CEO: Walter Gauss, CFO   Tel: (610) 321-0300   %FO: 1
  > Bus: *Mfr. rigid plastic packaging.*   Fax: (610) 321-0394

- **RTSE NETWORKS GROUP PLC**
  80 Great Eastern Street, London EC2A 3JL, UK
  CEO: Bernard Fisher, CEO   Tel: 44-207-749-5000
  Bus: *Mfr. computer software.*   Fax: 44-207-749-5001
  www.rtse.com

  > **RTSE USA INC.**
  > 4038 148th Avenue NE, Redmond, WA   98052
  > CEO: James Iettenhofen, Pres.   Tel: (425) 605-1000   %FO: 100
  > Bus: *Mfr. computer software.*   Fax: (425) 605-1097

- **SAATCHI & SAATCHI CO. PLC, DIV. PUBLICIS**
  83/89 Whitfield Street, London W1A 4X4, UK
  CEO: Kevin Roberts, CEO   Tel: 44-207-436-4000   Rev: $7,000
  Bus: *Advertising agency.*   Fax: 44-207-436-4000   Emp: 7,000
  www.saatchi-saatchi.com

  SAATCHI & SAATCHI WORLDWIDE INC.
  375 Hudson Street, New York, NY   10014
  CEO: Kevin Roberts, CEO   Tel: (212) 463-2000   %FO: 100
  Bus: *Provides advertising and*   Fax: (212) 463-2000   Emp: 400
  marketing services.

  SIEGEL & GALE, INC.
  10 Rockefeller Plaza, New York, NY   10020
  CEO: Duncan Pollock, Pres.   Tel: (212) 707-4000
  Bus: *Interactive media group.*   Fax: (212) 707-4001

- **SAB - SOUTH AFRICAN BREWERIES LTD.**
  25 Grosvenor Street, London W1X 9FE, UK
  CEO: Jacob Meyer Kahn, Chmn.   Tel: 44-207-659-0100   Rev: $4,135
  Bus: *Distributes and brews beer and bottles*   Fax: 44-207-659-0111   Emp: 34,365
  sodas for domestic use and owns hotels.   www.sab.co.za

  PILSNER URQUELL USA INC.
  560 Sylvan Avenue, Englewood Cliffs, NJ   07632
  CEO: David Williams   Tel: (201) 569-6728   %FO: 100
  Bus: *Distributes beer.*   Fax: (201) 569-6728

- **THE SAGE GROUP PLC**
  Sage House, Benton Park Road, Newcastle-Upon-Tyne NE77LZ, UK
  CEO: Paul Walker, CEO   Tel: 44-191-255-3000   Rev: $602
  Bus: *Mfr. PC accounting software.*   Fax: 44-191-255-0306   Emp: 4,642
  www.sage.com

  BEST SOFTWARE, INC.
  11413 Isaac Newton Square, Reston, VA   20190
  CEO: Timothy A. Davenport, CEO   Tel: (703) 709-5200   %FO: 100
  Bus: *Mfr./sales PC accounting software.*   Fax: (703) 709-9359   Emp: 740

  PEACHTREE SOFTWARE, INC.
  1505 Pavilion Place, Norcross, GA   30093
  CEO: Douglas G. Meyer, Pres.   Tel: (770) 724-4000   %FO: 100
  Bus: *Mfr./sales PC accounting software.*   Fax: (770) 724-4577

SAGE SOFTWARE, INC.
56 Technology South, Irvine, CA   92618
CEO: David R. Butler, CEO   Tel: (949) 753-1222   %FO: 100
Bus: *Mfr./sales PC accounting software.*   Fax: (949) 753-1859

● **J. SAINSBURY PLC**
Stamford House, Stamford Street, London SE1 9LL, UK
CEO: Sir Peter Davis, CEO   Tel: 44-207-921-6000   Rev: $26,300
Bus: *Engaged in retail food distribution, pig*   Fax: 44-207-921-6132   Emp: 178,000
production, home improvement centers.   www.j-sainsbury.co.uk

   SHAW'S SUPERMARKETS, INC.
   140 Laurel Street, East Bridgewater, MA   02333
   CEO: Ross McLaren, Pres. & CEO   Tel: (508) 378-7211   %FO: 100
   Bus: *Owner/operator supermarket*   Fax: (508) 378-3112   Emp: 22,600
   chain; retailer.

● **SCAN SHIPPING SERVICES LIMITED**
Robert Denholm House, Bletchingley Road, Nutfield, Surrey RH1 4HW, UK
CEO: A. Simonsen, Chmn.   Tel: 44-173-782-2288
Bus: *International shipping and transport.*   Fax: 44-173-782-3188
                                      www.scan-shipping.com

   SHIPCO TRANSPORT INC.
   1235 North Loop West, Ste. 715, Houston, TX   77008
   CEO: Claus Raborg, Mgr.   Tel: (713) 861-2100   %FO: 100
   Bus: *International shipping and*   Fax: (713) 861-0055
   transport.

   SHIPCO TRANSPORT INC.
   2430 Mall Drive, Ste. 220, Charleston, SC   29418
   CEO: Hans Fenneberg, Pres.   Tel: (843) 744-8336   %FO: 100
   Bus: *International shipping and*   Fax: (843) 744-5226
   transport.

   SHIPCO TRANSPORT INC.
   80 Washington Street, PO Box 1411, Hoboken, NJ   07030
   CEO: Klaus H. Jepsen, Pres.   Tel: (201) 216-1500   %FO: 100
   Bus: *International shipping and*   Fax: (201) 216-1744   Emp: 10
   transport.

   SHIPCO TRANSPORT INC.
   8600 NW 53rd Terrace, Ste. 103, Miami, FL   33166
   CEO: Don Roberts, Mgr.   Tel: (305) 591-3900   %FO: 100
   Bus: *International shipping and*   Fax: (305) 591-3181
   transport.

SHIPCO TRANSPORT INC.
2 Crown Center, Ste. 430, Atlanta, GA 30349
CEO: Hans Fenneberg, Pres.   Tel: (770) 997-1518   %FO: 100
Bus: *International shipping and*   Fax: (770) 997-2352
  transport.

SHIPCO TRANSPORT INC.
101 East Walnut Street, Compton, CA 90248
CEO: Carsten H. Poulsen, Mgr.   Tel: (310) 637-7300   %FO: 100
Bus: *International shipping and*   Fax: (310) 637-7733
  transport.

SHIPCO TRANSPORT INC.
608-L Folcroft Street, Baltimore, MD 21224
CEO: Hans Fenneberg, Pres.   Tel: (410) 631-9922   %FO: 100
Bus: *International shipping and*   Fax: (410) 631-9153
  transport.

SHIPCO TRANSPORT INC.
610 York Road, Bensenville, IL 60106
CEO: Edie DeSoto, Mgr.   Tel: (630) 616-9100   %FO: 100
Bus: *International shipping and*   Fax: (630) 616-9105
  transport.

● **SCAPA GROUP PLC**
Oakfield House, 93 Preston New Road, Blackburn Lancashire BB1 6AY, UK
CEO: David M. Dunn, CEO   Tel: 44-125-458-0123   Rev: $470
Bus: *Mfr. specialty products for the paper*   Fax: 44-125-451-764   Emp: 3,545
  and printing industries.   www.scapa.com

SCAPA TAPES INC.
111 Great Pond Drive, Windsor, CT 06995
CEO: Stuart Ganslaw, Pres.   Tel: (860) 688-8000   %FO: 100
Bus: *Mfr. adhesive films and tapes.*   Fax: (860) 688-7000

● **SCHRODERS PLC**
31 Gresham Street, London EC2V 7QA, UK
CEO: David Salisbury, CEO   Tel: 44-207-658-6000   Rev: $1,850
Bus: *Engaged in asset management.*   Fax: 44-207-658-3870   Emp: 4,750
                                      www.schroders.com

SCHRODERS & COMPANY INC.
787 Seventh Avenue, New York, NY 10019-6016
CEO: Steven Kotler, Pres. & CEO   Tel: (212) 492-6000   %FO: 100
Bus: *Engaged in asset management.*   Fax: (212) 492-7029

- **SCIENCE SYSTEMS PLC**
  Clothier Road, Bristol BS4 5SS, UK
  CEO: Mike Love, CEO   Tel: 44-117-971-7251
  Bus: *Computer software and services.*   Fax: 44-117-972-1846
        www.sciencesystems.co.uk

  SERVICE MANAGEMENT SYSTEMS
  3135 Charlotte Pike, Ste. 100, Nashville, TN   37209
  CEO: Mike Love   Tel: (615) 399-1839   %FO: 100
  Bus: *Computer software and services.*   Fax: (615) 399-1839

- **SDL PLC**
  Butler House, Market Street, Maidenhead, Berkshire SL6 8AA, UK
  CEO: Mark Lancaster, CEO   Tel: 44-162-841-0100   Rev: $44
  Bus: *Mfr. translation software.*   Fax: 44-162-841-0505   Emp: 480
        www.sdlintl.com

  SDL USA INC.
  890 Winter Street, Waltham, MA   02451-1404
  CEO: Kathleen Bostick, VP Sales   Tel: (781) 839-7127   %FO: 100
  Bus: *Mfr./sales translation software.*   Fax: (781) 839-7011

  SDL USA INC.
  9055 Bluffview Trace, Roswell, GA   30076
  CEO: Kathleen Bostick, VP Sales   Tel: (770) 645-6742   %FO: 100
  Bus: *Mfr./sales translation software.*   Fax: (770) 645-6779

  SDL USA INC.
  651 Gateway Blvd., Ste. 450, South San Francisco, CA   94080
  CEO: Kathleen Bostick, VP Sales   Tel: (650) 635-0355   %FO: 100
  Bus: *Mfr./sales translation software.*   Fax: (650) 635-0360

  SDL USA INC.
  9 Executive Park Drive, Ste. 100, Merrimack, NH   03054-4058
  CEO: Kathleen Bostick, VP Sales   Tel: (603) 262-6500   %FO: 100
  Bus: *Mfr./sales translation software.*   Fax: (603) 262-6500

  SDL USA INC.
  701 Brazos, Ste. 500, Austin, TX   7871
  CEO: Kathleen Bostick, VP Sales   Tel: (512) 320-9170   %FO: 100
  Bus: *Mfr./sales translation software.*   Fax: (512) 320-5821

  SDL USA INC.
  144 Railroad Avenue, Ste. 100, Edmonds, WA   98020
  CEO: Kathleen Bostick, VP Sales   Tel: (425) 775-9405   %FO: 100
  Bus: *Mfr./sales translation software.*   Fax: (425) 775-4235

SDL USA INC.
5068 Plano Pkwy., Ste. 205, Plano, TX   75093
CEO: Kathleen Bostick, VP Sales   Tel: (972) 818-1170   %FO: 100
Bus: *Mfr./sales translation software.*   Fax: (972) 818-1171

SDL USA INC.
5757 Central Avenue, Ste. G, Boulder, CO   80301
CEO: Kathleen Bostick, VP Sales   Tel: (303) 440-0909   %FO: 100
Bus: *Mfr./sales translation software.*   Fax: (303) 440-6369

● **SEA CONTAINERS LTD.**
20 Upper Ground, London SE1 9PF, UK
CEO: James B. Sherwood, Pres.   Tel: 44-207-805-5000   Rev: $1,360
Bus: *Engaged in hotel and resort*   Fax: 44-207-805-5900   Emp: 8,000
management and container leasing.   www.seacontainers.com

  "21" CLUB
  21 West 52nd Street, New York, NY   10019
  CEO: Simon M. C. Sherwood, SVP   Tel: (212) 582-7200   %FO: 100
  Bus: *Private dining and banquet*   Fax: (212) 581-7138
  facilities.

  CHARLESTON PLACE
  130 Market Street, Charleston, SC   29401
  CEO: Simon M. C. Sherwood, SVP   Tel: (843) 722-4900   %FO: 100
  Bus: *Hotel specializing in southern*   Fax: (843) 722-4074
  hospitality.

  GE SEACO AMERICA LLC
  1155 Avenue of the Americas, 30th Fl., New York, NY   10036
  CEO: Robin Lynch   Tel: (212) 302-5066   %FO: 1
  Bus: *Marine container leasing*   Fax: (212) 921-4353
  companies. (JV of GE Capital)

  THE INN AT PERRY CABIN
  308 Watkins Lane, St. Michaels, MD   21663
  CEO: Simon M. C. Sherwood, SVP   Tel: (410) 745-2200   %FO: 100
  Bus: *Premier hotel and resort.*   Fax: (410) 743-3348

  WINDSOR COURT HOTEL
  300 Gravier Street, New Orleans, LA   70140
  CEO: Simon M. C. Sherwood, SVP   Tel: (504) 523-6000   %FO: 100
  Bus: *Luxury hotel.*   Fax: (504) 596-4513

• SECURICOR PLC

15 Carshalton Road, Sutton, Surrey SM1 4LD, UK

CEO: Sir Neil Macfarlane, Chmn.   Tel: 44-181-770-7000   Rev: $2,030

Bus: *Provides logistics, courier and*   Fax: 44-181-770-1145   Emp: 57,000
container delivery as well as security   www.securicor.co.uk
guard service.

SECURICOR NEW CENTURY, INC.

9609 Gayton Road, Suite 100, Richmond, VA   23233

CEO: Robert J. Shiver, CEO   Tel: (804) 754-1100   %FO: 100

Bus: *Provides logistics, courier and*   Fax: (804) 754-1100
container delivery as well as
security guard service.

SECURICOR WIRELESS INC.

90 Park Avenue, 16th Fl., New York, NY   10016

CEO: Robert J. Shiver, CEO   Tel: (212) 949-4200   %FO: 100

Bus: *Provides logistics, courier and*   Fax: (212) 984-0781
container delivery as well as
security guard service.

SECURICOR WIRELESS INC.

12833 Monarch Street, Garden Grove, CA   92841

CEO: Robert J. Shiver, CEO   Tel: (714) 893-7700   %FO: 100

Bus: *Provides logistics, courier and*   Fax: (714) 893-7550
container delivery as well as
security guard service.

SECURICOR WIRELESS INC.

340 Turnpike Street 1-3C, Canton, MA   02021

CEO: Robert J. Shiver, CEO   Tel: (781) 821-8616

Bus: *Provides logistics, courier and*   Fax: (781) 821-8636
container delivery as well as
security guard service.

SECURICOR WIRELESS INC.

1690 North Topping Avenue, Kansas City, MO   64120

CEO: Robert J. Shiver, CEO   Tel: (816) 241-8400   %FO: 100

Bus: *Provides logistics, courier and*   Fax: (816) 920-1144
container delivery as well as
security guard service.

SECURICOR WIRELESS INC.
2190 Meridian Park Blvd., Ste. 11, Concord, MA 94520

CEO: Robert J. Shiver, CEO   Tel: (905) 602-5000   %FO: 100

Bus: *Provides logistics, courier and*   Fax: (905) 602-0520
container delivery as well as
security guard service.

• SELECT APPOINTMENTS HOLDINGS LIMITED
Ziggurat, Grosvenor Road, St. Albans, Hertfordshire AL1 3HW, UK

CEO: Anthony V. Martin, Chmn.   Tel: 44-172-784-2999   Rev: $1,380

Bus: *Engaged in temporary staffing.*   Fax: 44-172-784-2841   Emp: 3,000
www.selectgroup.com

ACCOUNTPROS
50 Milk Street, 5th Fl., Boston, MA 02109

CEO: Brian Greene   Tel: (617) 482-4100   %FO: 100

Bus: *Engaged in specialty staffing;*   Fax: (617) 482-1652
accounting and banking.

AUTOMATED TEMPORARY SERVICES
1601 New Stine Road, Ste. 130, Bakersfield, CA 93309

CEO: Joseph Strong, Mgr.   Tel: (661) 832-1900

Bus: *Temporary staffing of light*   Fax: (661) 835-0188
industrial and clerical sectors.

CLINICAL ONE
7 Wheeling Avenue, Woburn, MA 01801

CEO: Greg Coir, Pres.   Tel: (781) 938-4095   %FO: 100

Bus: *Healthcare staffing.*   Fax: (877) 747-9300

DESIGN TECHNOLOGIES
10 Presidential Way, Ste. 101, Woburn, MA 01801

CEO: Nicholas J. Lento, CEO   Tel: (781) 938-1910   %FO: 100

Bus: *Engaged in specialty staffing.*   Fax: (781) 938-1410

• SENIOR PLC
59-61 High Street, Rickmansworth, Hertfordshire WD3 1RH, UK

CEO: Graham Menzies, CEO   Tel: 44-192-377-5547   Rev: $755

Bus: *Mfr. aerospace and automotive*   Fax: 44-192-389-6027   Emp: 6,400
components.   www.seniorplc.com

SENIOR AEROSPACE DIV.
16830 Ventura Boulevard, Ste. 364, Encino, CA 91436

CEO: K. Guss, CEO   Tel: (818) 379-2782   %FO: 100

Bus: *Mfr./sales aerospace and*   Fax: (818) 379-2787
automotive components.

SENIOR AEROSPACE, INC.
PO Box 12950, Wichita, KS   67277-2950
CEO: G. Frye, Mgr.   Tel: (316) 942-3208   %FO: 100
Bus: *Mfr. composites.*   Fax: (316) 942-5044

SENIOR AEROSPACE, INC.
2980 N. San Fernando Blvd., Burbank, CA   91504
CEO: L. Fleming, CEO   Tel: (818) 841-9190   %FO: 100
Bus: *Mfr./sales aerospace and*   Fax: (818) 845-4205
       automotive components.

SENIOR AEROSPACE, INC.
9106 Balboa Avenue, San Diego, CA   92123
CEO: R. Case, CEO   Tel: (858) 278-8400   %FO: 100
Bus: *Mfr./sales aerospace and*   Fax: (858) 278-8768
       automotive components.

SENIOR AEROSPACE, INC.
1075 Providence Highway, Sharon, MA   02067
CEO: P. L. Fontecchio, CEO   Tel: (781) 784-1400   %FO: 100
Bus: *Mfr./sales aerospace and*   Fax: (781) 784-1405
       automotive components.

SENIOR AEROSPACE, INC.
790 Greenfield Drive, El Cajon, CA   92021
CEO: B. Simmons, CEO   Tel: (619) 442-3451   %FO: 100
Bus: *Mfr./sales aerospace and*   Fax: (619) 588-3498
       automotive components.

SENIOR FLEXONICS INC.
815 Forestwood Drive, Romeoville, IL   60441
CEO: J. Devine, CEO   Tel: (815) 886-1140   %FO: 100
Bus: *Mfr./sales aerospace and*   Fax: (815) 886-4550
       automotive components.

SENIOR FLEXONICS INC.
2400 Longhorn Industrial Drive, New Braunfels, TX   78140
CEO: G. A. Perkins, VP   Tel: (830) 629-8080   %FO: 100
Bus: *Mfr./sales aerospace and*   Fax: (830) 629-6899
       automotive components.

SENIOR FLEXONICS, INC.
PO Box 3027, Oak Ridge, TX   37831-9960
CEO: J. Devine, VP   Tel: (865) 483-7444   %FO: 100
Bus: *Mfr./sales aerospace and*   Fax: (865) 482-5600
       automotive components.

SENIOR HOLDINGS INC.

300 East Devon Avenue, Bartlett, IL   60103

CEO: K. R. Williams, VP   Tel: (630) 837-1811   %FO: 100

Bus: *Mfr./sales aerospace and*   Fax: (630) 837-1847
automotive components.

• SERCO GROUP PLC

Dolphin House, Windmill Road, Sunbury-on-Thames, Middlesex TW16 7HT, UK

CEO: Kevin S. Beeston, CEO   Tel: 44-193-275-5900   Rev: $1,153

Bus: *Provides facilities management and*   Fax: 44-193-275-5854   Emp: 32,500
systems engineering.   www.serco.com

SERCO GROUP INC.

20 East Clementon Road, Ste. 102 South, Gibbsboro, NJ   08026

CEO: Michael Walker, Pres.   Tel: (856) 346-8800   %FO: 100

Bus: *Provides facilities management*   Fax: (856) 346-8463
and systems engineering.

• SERVICE POWER TECHNOLOGIES PLC

James House, Mere Park Marlow, Buckinghamshire SL7 1FJ, UK

CEO: Ian S. MacKinnon, CEO   Tel: 44-162-848-1616

Bus: *Mfr. computer software.*   Fax: 44-162-848-1567
www.servicepower.com

SERVICE POWER TECHNOLOGIES

711 Bestgate Road, Ste. 202, Annapolis, MD   21401

CEO: Ian S. MacKinnon, CEO   Tel: (410) 571-6333   %FO: 100

Bus: *Mfr./sales computer software.*   Fax: (410) 571-9330

• SEVEN WORLDWIDE, INC.

St. Mark's House, Shepherdess Walk, London N1 7LH, UK

CEO: Derek Ashley, CEO   Tel: 44-207-861-7777

Bus: *Engaged in graphic services.*   Fax: 44-207-871-7702
www.sevenww.co.uk

SEVEN WORLDWIDE, INC.

233 N. Michigan Avenue, Ste. 420, Chicago, IL   60601

CEO: Bob Juckniess   Tel: (312) 616-7777   %FO: 100

Bus: *Engaged in graphic services.*   Fax: (312) 616-8216

SEVEN WORLDWIDE, INC.

225 West Superior Street, Chicago, IL   60610

CEO: Tricia Frawley   Tel: (312) 943-0400   %FO: 100

Bus: *Engaged in promotional,*   Fax: (312) 943-6186
packaging, advertising and
imaging.

- **SEVERN TRENT, PLC.**

2800 Crescent, Birmingham Business Park, Birmingham B37 7YU1, UK

CEO: Robert Walker, CEO	Tel: 44-121-722-4000	Rev: $2,494
Bus: *Provides water and waste management services.*	Fax: 44-121-722-4800 www.severn-trent.com	Emp: 12,870

SEVERN TRENT ENVIRONMENTAL SERVICES

16337 Park Row, Houston, TX 77084

CEO: Len Graziano, Pres.	Tel: (281) 578-4200	%FO: 100
Bus: *Provides water and waste management services.*	Fax: (281) 398-3550	Emp: 200

SEVERN TRENT SYSTEMS, INC.

20405 Highway 249, Suite 600, Houston, TX 77070

CEO: Mike Lily, Mng. Dir.	Tel: (280) 320-7100	%FO: 100
Bus: *Provides water and waste management services.*	Fax: (280) 321-7111	Emp: 80

SEVERN TRENT US, INC.

580 Virginia Drive, Ste. 300, Fort Washington, PA 19034

CEO: Thomas Mills, VP	Tel: (215) 646-9201	%FO: 100
Bus: *Provides water and waste management services.*	Fax: (215) 283-3487	Emp: 2

- **SHERWOOD INTERNATIONAL PLC**

120 Old Broad Street, London EC2N 1AR, UK

CEO: Mike Shinya, CEO	Tel: 44-207-866-6333	Rev: $81
Bus: *Mfr. software for the insurance market.*	Fax: 44-207-904-4820 www.sherwoodinternational.com	Emp: 475

SHERWOOD INTERNATIONAL

200 Business Park Drive, Armonk, NY 10504

CEO: Craig Robinson	Tel: (914) 273-1717	%FO: 100
Bus: *Mfr./sales software for the insurance market.*	Fax: (914) 273-7790	

SHERWOOD INTERNATIONAL

200 Corporate Place, 2nd Fl., Rocky Hill, CT 06067

CEO: Craig Robinson	Tel: (860) 257-0839	%FO: 100
Bus: *Mfr./sales software for the insurance market.*	Fax: (860) 257-1470	

SHERWOOD INTERNATIONAL

200 North LaSalle, Ste. 2650, Chicago, IL 60601

CEO: Larry M. Amundsen, EVP	Tel: (312) 261-4400	%FO: 100
Bus: *Mfr./sales software for the insurance market.*	Fax: (312) 261-4445	

● **SHIRE PHARMACEUTICALS GROUP PLC**

East Anton, Andover, Hampshire SP10 5RG, UK

CEO: Rolf Stahel, CEO   Tel: 44-126-433-3455   Rev: $518

Bus: *Engaged in specialty pharmaceuticals.*   Fax: 44-126-433-3460   Emp: 1,025

www.shire.com

    SHIRE LABORATORIES INC.

    1550 East Guide Drive, Rockville, MD   10850

    CEO: Jack Khattar, Pres. & CEO   Tel: (301) 838-2500   %FO: 100

    Bus: *Engaged in drug delivery*   Fax: (301) 838-2501
    technologies.

    SHIRE PHARMACEUTICAL DEVELOPMENT INC.

    1901 Research Boulevard, Rockville, MD   20850

    CEO: Simon Tulloch, SVP   Tel: (240) 453-6400   %FO: 100

    Bus: *Sales and marketing of*   Fax: (240) 453-6404
    pharmaceuticals.

    SHIRE US INC.

    7900 Tanners Gate Drive, Florence, KY   41042

    CEO: William Nuerge, CEO   Tel: (859) 282-2100   %FO: 100

    Bus: *Sales and marketing of*   Fax: (859) 282-1794
    pharmaceuticals.

● **SIGNET GROUP PLC**

Zenith House, The Hyde, London NW9 6EW, UK

CEO: James McAdam, Chmn.   Tel: 44-207-905-9000   Rev: $2,030

Bus: *Specialty jewelry retailer.*   Fax: 44-207-408-1493   Emp: 12,520

www.signet.co.uk

    KAY JEWELERS, DIV. STERLING JEWELERS, INC.

    375 Ghent Road, Akron, OH   44333

    CEO: Terry L. Burman, CEO   Tel: (330) 668-5000   %FO: 100

    Bus: *Operates chain of Kay Jewelers*   Fax: (330) 668-5187
    and Jared.

● **SIMMONS & SIMMONS**

21 Wilson Street, London EC2M 2TX, UK

CEO: David Dickinson, Mng. Prtn.   Tel: 44-207-628-2020

Bus: *Full service, international law firm.*   Fax: 44-207-628-2070   Emp: 800

www.simmons-simmons.com

SIMMONS & SIMMONS
570 Lexington Avenue, 28th Fl., New York, NY   10022-6837
CEO: Andrew Wingfield, Mng. Ptnr.   Tel: (212) 688-6620   %FO: 100
Bus: *Full service, international law*   Fax: (212) 355-3594
firm.

• SIX CONTINENTS PLC (FORMERLY BASS PLC)
20 North Audley Street, London W1Y 1WE, UK
CEO: Tim Clarke, CEO   Tel: 44-207-409-1919   Rev: $7,600
Bus: *Brewing and soft drinks, hotels, taverns*   Fax: 44-207-409-8503   Emp: 54,000
and leisure retailing, travel services.   www.sixcontinents.com

SIX CONTINENTS HOTELS
3 Ravinia Drive, Ste. 2900, Atlanta, GA   30346-2149
CEO: John Sweetwood, Pres.   Tel: (770) 604-2000   %FO: 100
Bus: *Hotels & leisure time operations*   Fax: (770) 604-2009   Emp: 10,000
management.

• SKYEPHARMA PLC
105 Piccadilly, London W1J 7NJ, UK
CEO: Michael Ashton, CEO   Tel: 44-207-491-1777   Rev: $36
Bus: *Mfr. pharmaceuticals.*   Fax: 44-207-491-3338   Emp: 375
www.skyepharma.com

SKYEPHARMA INC.
717 Constitution Drive, Ste. 204, Exton, PA   19341
CEO: John Longenecker, Pres.   Tel: (610) 321-0400   %FO: 100
Bus: *Pharmaceuticals.*   Fax: (610) 321-0401

SKYEPHARMA INC.
10 East 63rd Street, New York, NY   10021
CEO: Lisa Carlton-Wilson   Tel: (212) 753-5780   %FO: 100
Bus: *Engaged in investor relations.*   Fax: (212) 359-3928

SKYEPHARMA INC.
10450 Science Center Drive, San Diego, CA   92121
CEO: John Longenecker, Pres.   Tel: (858) 625-2424   %FO: 100
Bus: *Pharmaceuticals.*   Fax: (858) 625-2439

• SLAUGHTER AND MAY
35 Basinghall Street, London EC2V 5DB, UK
CEO: Tim Clark   Tel: 44-207-600-1200
Bus: *International law firm.*   Fax: 44-207-600-0289
www.slaughterandmay.com

SLAUGHTER AND MAY
126 East 56th Street, New York, NY   10022-3613
CEO: Mark Cardale, CEO   Tel: (212) 888-1112   %FO: 100
Bus: *International law firm.*   Fax: (212) 888-1170

● **SLOUGH ESTATES PLC**
234 Bath Road, Slough, Berkshire SL1 4EE, UK
CEO: Derek R. Wilson, CEO   Tel: 44-175-353-7171   Rev: $420
Bus: *Owns and manages commercial and*   Fax: 44-175-382-0585   Emp: 550
retail properties.   www.sloughestates.com

SLOUGH ESTATES USA INC.
33 West Monroe Street, Ste. 2000, Chicago, IL   60603-2409
CEO: Marshall D. Lees, CEO   Tel: (312) 558-9100   %FO: 100
Bus: *Management of commercial,*   Fax: (312) 558-9041
industrial and properties.

● **SMARTLOGIK GROUP PLC**
48 Leicester Square, London WC2H 7DB, UK
CEO: Stephen J. Hill, CEO   Tel: 44-207-930-6900   Rev: $13
Bus: *Engaged in Web and e-commerce*   Fax: 44-207-925-7700   Emp: 295
products.   www.smartlogik.com

SMARTLOGIK INC.
2 Embarcadero Center, Ste. 2260, San Francisco, CA   94111
CEO: Martin Garland, EVP   Tel: (415) 362-7161   %FO: 100
Bus: *Web and e-commerce products.*   Fax: (415) 362-7113

SMARTLOGIK INC.
601 North Fairfax Street, Ste. 440, Alexandria, VA   22314
CEO: Martin Garland, EVP   Tel: (703) 549-8605   %FO: 100
Bus: *Web and e-commerce products.*   Fax: (703) 549-9634

● **SMITH & NEPHEW, INC.**
2 Temple Place, Victoria Embankment, London WC2R-3BP, UK
CEO: Chris J. O'Donnell, CEO   Tel: 44-207-836-7922   Rev: $1,750
Bus: *Develop/mfr./marketing healthcare*   Fax: 44-207-240-7088   Emp: 10,000
products; tissue repair and medical   www.smith-nephew.com
devices.

SMITH & NEPHEW INC..
N104 Q13400 Donges Bay Road, Germantown, WI   53022
CEO: James McHargue, Pres.   Tel: (414) 251-7840   %FO: 100
Bus: *Develop/mfr./marketing*   Fax: (414) 251-7758   Emp: 325
healthcare products; physical
rehabilitation products.

SMITH & NEPHEW INC..

160 Dascomb Road, Andover, MA   01810

CEO: Ronald Sparks, Pres.   Tel: (978) 749-1000   %FO: 100

Bus: *Develop/mfr./marketing*   Fax: (978) 749-1212
healthcare products; endoscopy
products.

SMITH & NEPHEW INC..

2925 Appling Road, Bartlett, TN   38134

CEO: Jerry Dowdy, Pres.   Tel: (901) 373-0200   %FO: 100

Bus: *Develop/mfr./marketing*   Fax: (901) 373-0220
healthcare products; ear, nose and
throat.

SMITH & NEPHEW INC..

2985 Scott Street, Vista, CA   92083

CEO: Les Cross, Pres.   Tel: (760) 727-1280   %FO: 100

Bus: *Develop/mfr./marketing*   Fax: (760) 734-3595
healthcare products.

SMITH & NEPHEW INC..

11775 Starkey Road, Largo, FL   33773

CEO: Rod Skaggs, Pres.   Tel: (813) 392-1261   %FO: 100

Bus: *Develop/mfr. marketing wound* Fax: (813) 299-3498
care products.

● **DAVID S. SMITH HOLDINGS PLC**

4-16 Artillery Row, London SW1P 1RZ, UK

CEO: J. Peter Williams, CEO   Tel: 44-207-932-5000   Rev: $1,890

Bus: *Mfr. corrugated packaging and paper* Fax: 44-207-932-5003   Emp: 10,440
products.   www.dssmith.uk.com

RAPAK INC.

737 Oakridge Drive, Romeoville, IL   60446

CEO: Stuart Russell   Tel: (815) 372-3600   %FO: 100

Bus: *Mfr. corrugated packaging and* Fax: (815) 372-3636
paper products.

RAPAK INC.

2801 Faber Street, Union City, CA   94587-1203

CEO: Stuart Russell   Tel: (510) 324-0170   %FO: 100

Bus: *Mfr. corrugated packaging and* Fax: (510) 324-0180
paper products.

• WH SMITH PLC

Greenbridge Road, Swindon, Wilshire SN3 3RX, UK

CEO: Richard Handover, CEO   Tel: 44-179-361-6161

Bus: *Engaged in publication of magazines*   Fax: 44-179-356-2545   Emp: 27,575
and books and distribution at airports.   www.whsmithplc.com

WH SMITH INC.

3200 Windy Hill Road, Ste. 1500 W, Atlanta, GA   30339

CEO: Stacey Crawford   Tel: (770) 952-0705   %FO: 100

Bus: *Owns and operates news and gift*   Fax: (770) 951-1352
stores and bookstores in hotels
and major airports.

• SMITHS GROUP PLC

765 Finchley Road, London NW11 8DS, UK

CEO: Keith Butler-Wheelhouse, CEO   Tel: 44-208-458-3232   Rev: $2,193

Bus: *Engaged in development, manufacture,*   Fax: 44-208-458-4380   Emp: 15,520
and sale of avionics, and single-use   www.smiths-group.com
disposable medical products for critical
care applications.

BARRINGER TECHNOLOGIES, INC.

30 Technology Drive, Warren, NJ   07059

CEO: Stanley Binder, Pres.   Tel: (908) 222-9100   %FO: 100

Bus: *Mfr. trace drug and explosive*   Fax: (908) 222-1557
detection equipment.

DURA-VENT

1177 Markley Drive, Plymouth, IN   46563

CEO: Brad Bembenick, Gen. Mgr.   Tel: (219) 936-2432   %FO: 100

Bus: *Mfr. industrial ducting.*   Fax: (219) 936-2505   Emp: 36

FLEXIBLE TECHNOLOGIES INC.

Carwellyn Road, PO Box 888, Abbeville, SC   29620

CEO: W. Ted Smith, Pres.   Tel: (864) 459-5441   %FO: 100

Bus: *Mfr. ducting & hosing.*   Fax: (864) 459-8282   Emp: 470

HYPERTRONICS CORPORATION

16 Brent Drive, Hudson, MA   01749

CEO: Fred Andreski   Tel: (978) 568-0451   %FO: 100

Bus: *Mfr. electronic connectors.*   Fax: (978) 568-0680   Emp: 145

ICORE INTL INC.

180 North Wolfe Road, Sunnyvale, CA   94086

CEO: Tess Sagnant, Pres.   Tel: (408) 732-5400   %FO: 100

Bus: *Mfr. conduit.*   Fax: (408) 720-8507   Emp: 50

JOHN CRANE NORTH AMERICA
39810 Grand River Avenue, Ste. 200, Novi, MI 48375

CEO: Don Smith
Tel: (248) 615-0700
%FO: 100

Bus: *Mfr. mechanical seals.*
Fax: (248) 615-0708

JOHN CRANE NORTH AMERICA
6400 West Oakton Street, Morton Grove, IL 60053

CEO: Robert Wasson, Pres.
Tel: (847) 967-2400
%FO: 100

Bus: *Mfr. mechanical seals.*
Fax: (847) 967-3911

POLYPHASER CORP.
PO Box 9000, Minden, NV 89423

CEO: Edward Vees, Pres.
Tel: (775) 782-2511
%FO: 100

Bus: *Mfr. lightning protection and grounding solutions.*
Fax: (775) 782-4476

SIMPS PORTEX, INC.
10 Bowman Drive, Keene, NH 03431

CEO: Jeff Spellman, Pres.
Tel: (603) 352-3812
%FO: 100

Bus: *Mfr. medical equipment.*
Fax: (603) 352-3703

SIMS BCI INC.
N7 W22025 Johnson Road, Waukesha, WI 53186-1856

CEO: Frank Katarow, Pres.
Tel: (262) 542-3100
%FO: 100

Bus: *Mfr. and markets non-invasive vital signs monitoring equipment.*
Fax: (262) 542-3315

SIMS DELTEC INC.
1265 Grey Fox Road, St. Paul, MN 55112

CEO: James Stitt, Pres.
Tel: (651) 633-2556
%FO: 100

Bus: *Mfr. volume drug delivery pumps, accessories, implantable access ports and percutaneous catheters.*
Fax: (651) 639-2530
Emp: 600

SIMS LEVEL 1
160 Weymouth Street, Rockland, MA 02370

CEO: Howard Donnelly, Pres.
Tel: (781) 878-8011
%FO: 100

Bus: *Provides systems which warm fluids or blood to body temperature for delivery into patients during surgery and trauma.*
Fax: (781) 878-8201
Emp: 222

SIMS RSP INC.
2552 McGaw Avenue, Irvine, CA 92714

CEO: Anthony Beron, Pres.
Tel: (949) 756-2250
%FO: 100

Bus: *Mfr. medical systems.*
Fax: (949) 660-8611
Emp: 136

SIMS, INC.
10 Bowman Drive, Keene, NH   03431
CEO: David S. Buyher, Pres.   Tel: (603) 352-3812   %FO: 100
Bus: *Mfr. and markets a range of single*   Fax: (603) 357-5038
     use disposable products for
     anesthesia, respiratory therapy
     and critical care.

SMITHS INDUSTRIES AEROSPACE
140000 Roosevelt Boulevard, Clearwater, FL   33762-0990
CEO: John Ferric, Pres.   Tel: (727) 536-1810   %FO: 100
Bus: *Mfr. aerospace display and*   Fax: (727) 524-0024
     control systems.

SMITHS INDUSTRIES AEROSPACE
4141 Eastern Avenue, SE, Grand Rapids, MI   49518-8727
CEO: Robert F. Ehr, Pres.   Tel: (616) 241-7000   %FO: 100
Bus: *Design, develop and*   Fax: (616) 241-7533
     manufacturing plant.

SMITHS INDUSTRIES AEROSPACE
255 Great Valley Parkway, Malvern, PA   19355
CEO: William Bova, Mgr.   Tel: (610) 296-5000   %FO: 100
Bus: *Mfr. aerospace display and*   Fax: (610) 296-3409
     control systems.

TIMES MICROWAVE SYSTEMS
358 Hall Avenue, PO Box 5039, Wallingford, CT   06492-5039
CEO: Peter Page, EVP   Tel: (203) 949-8400   %FO: 100
Bus: *Mfr. microwave cable.*   Fax: (203) 949-8423   Emp: 117

TRANSTECTOR SYSTEMS, INC.
10701 Airport Drive, Hayden Lake, ID   83835
CEO: Sean Thompson, Mng. Dir.   Tel: (208) 772-8515   %FO: 100
Bus: *Mfr. electronic surge devices.*   Fax: (208) 762-6133

TUTCO INC.
500 Gould Drive, Cookeville, TN   38501
CEO: Michael Mahoney, Pres.   Tel: (931) 432-4141   %FO: 100
Bus: *Mfr. heating elements.*   Fax: (931) 432-4140   Emp: 430

• SOPHEON PLC
Stirling House, Surrey Research Park, Guildford GU2 7RF, UK
CEO: Andy Michuda, CEO   Tel: 44-148-388-3000   Rev: $7,763
Bus: *Develops and provides knowledge*   Fax: 44-148-388-3050   Emp: 1,500
     management software, solutions and   www.sopheon.com
     services.

SOPHEON CORPORATION
6870 West 52nd Avenue, Ste. 215, Arvada, CO   80002
CEO: Andy Michuda, Pres.
Bus: *Develops and provides knowledge management software, solutions and services.*
Tel: (303) 736-4900
Fax: (303) 423-5046
%FO: 100

SOPHEON CORPORATION
2850 Metro Drive, Minneapolis, MN   55425-1566
CEO: Andy Michuda, Pres.
Bus: *Develops and provides knowledge management software, solutions and services.*
Tel: (952) 851-7500
Fax: (952) 851-7744
%FO: 100

● **SPECTRIS GROUP (FORMERLY FAIREY GROUP PLC)**
Station Road, Egham, Surrey TW20 9NP, UK
CEO: Hans D. Nilsson, CEO
Bus: *Holding company: mfr. filtration, measuring and sensing equipment, and military control systems.*
Tel: 44-107-8447-0470
Fax: 44-107-8447-0848
www.spectris.com
Rev: $693
Emp: 4,460

BETA LASERMIKE, INC.
8001 Technology Blvd, Dayton, OH   45424
CEO: Randy Eifert
Bus: *Mfr. diameter gauging and process measurement products.*
Tel: (937) 233-9935
Fax: (937) 233-7284
%FO: 100

FAIREY ARLON INC.
2920 99th Street, PO Box 807, Sturtevant, WI   53177
CEO: William S. Dawson, Pres.
Bus: *Mfr. industrial filtration equipment.*
Tel: (262) 886-0888
Fax: (262) 886-6099
%FO: 100
Emp: 30

FUSION UV SYSTEMS, INC.
910 Clopper Road, Gaithersburg, MD   20878-1357
CEO: A.D.P. Harbourne, Pres.
Bus: *Ultraviolet light processing technology for curing photosensitive inks, coating & adhesives in mfr. processes.*
Tel: (301) 527-2660
Fax: (301) 527-2661
%FO: 100

IRCON, INC.
7300 N. Natchez Avenue, Niles, IL   60714
CEO: Greg W. Pacton, Pres.
Bus: *Mfr. infrared non-contact temperature measuring instruments.*
Tel: (847) 967-5151
Fax: (847) 764-7094
%FO: 100

LUXTRON CORPORATION

2775 Northwestern Pkwy., Santa Clara, CA   95051-0941

CEO: Ed Oh, Pres.

Bus: *Mfr. semiconductor process endpoint controllers, fibreoptic thermometers & non-contact temperature measurement equipment.*

Tel: (408) 727-1600
Fax: (408) 727-1677

%FO: 100

MICROSCAN SYSTEMS, INC.

1201 Southwest 7th Street, Renton, WA   98055

CEO: Dennis Kaill, Pres.

Bus: *Mfr. high performance fixed mount bar code scanning & decoding instruments.*

Tel: (425) 226-5700
Fax: (425) 226-8340

%FO: 100

NDC INFRARED ENGINEERING LTD.

5314 Irwindale Avenue, Irwindale, CA   91706

CEO: Douglas Joy

Bus: *Design and manufacturing of on-line continuous process measuring instruments.*

Tel: (626) 960-3300
Fax: (626) 939-3870

%FO: 100

PARTICLE MEASURING SYSTEMS, INC.

5475 Airport Blvd., Boulder, CO   80301

CEO: Paul C. Kelly, Pres.

Bus: *Mfr. on-line laser based particle detection systems*

Tel: (303) 443-7100
Fax: (303) 449-6870

%FO: 100

RED LION CONTROLS INC.

20 Willow Spring Circle, RD 5, York, PA   17402

CEO: Mike Granby, Pres.

Bus: *Mfr. digital control, sensing & measuring devices.*

Tel: (717) 767-6961
Fax: (717) 764-6587

%FO: 100
Emp: 150

• SPIRAX SARCO ENGINEERING PLC

Charlton House, Cirencester Road, Cheltenham, Gloucestershire GL53 8ER, UK

CEO: Marcus J. D. Steel, CEO

Bus: *Mfr. temperature controls, steam traps, pressure reduction, pipeline auxiliary.*

Tel: 44-124-252-1361
Fax: 44-124-257-3342
www.spirax-sarco.co.uk

Rev: $415
Emp: 3,795

SPIRAX SARCO INC.

1150 Northpoint Boulevard, Blythewood, SC   29016

CEO: Tony Serivin, Pres.

Bus: *Mfr. temp control, steam traps, pressure reduction, pipeline auxiliary.*

Tel: (803) 714-9193
Fax: (803) 433-1346

%FO: 100
Emp: 300

• SPIRENT PLC (FORMERLY BOWTHORPE HOLDINGS PLC)

Crawley Business Quarter, Fleming Way, Crawley West Sussex RH10 2RZ, UK

CEO: Nicholas K. Brookes, CEO	Tel: 44-129-376-7676	Rev: $1,091
Bus: *Engaged in network technology.*	Fax: 44-129-376-7677	Emp: 9,000
	www.spirent.com	

AUTRONICS

325 East Live Oak Avenue, Arcadia, CA   91006

CEO: John Kuperhand, Pres.	Tel: (626) 445-5470	%FO: 100
Bus: *Engaged in aerospace technology, including In-Flight Entertainment Systems and manufacture of aerospace electronic products.*	Fax: (626) 446-0014	

HEKIMIAN LABORATORIES, INC.

15200 Omega Drive, Rockville, MD   20850

CEO: Jim Schleckser, Pres.	Tel: (301) 590-3600	%FO: 100
Bus: *Automated test systems for telecommunications networks.*	Fax: (301) 590-3599	

HELLERMANN TYTON

PO Box 245017, Milwaukee, WI   53224

CEO: Jim Campion, Mng. Dir.	Tel: (414) 355-1130	%FO: 100
Bus: *Mfr. communication and power network products.*	Fax: (414) 355-7341	

HELLERMANN TYTON

1250 Creekside Parkway West, Naples, FL   34180

CEO: Bob Oestreich, Mgr.	Tel: (941) 593-3773	%FO: 100
Bus: *Mfg. facility for communication and power network products.*	Fax: (941) 593-1517	

HELLERMANN TYTON

7001 Frontage Road, Hinsdale, IL   60521

CEO: Fred Plesha, Mgr.	Tel: (630) 850-8750	%FO: 100
Bus: *Distribution center for communication and power network products.*	Fax: (630) 850-7013	

PENNY & GILES DRIVES TECHNOLOGY, DIV. AUTRONICS

2532 East Cerritos Avenue, Anaheim, CA   92806

CEO: Stephen A. Nesmith, Sales	Tel: (714) 712-7911	%FO: 100
Bus: *Mfr. motor control systems for mobility, industrial and other specialist electric vehicles.*	Fax: (714) 978-9512	

SMARTBITS
26750 Agoura Road, Calabasas, CA   91302
CEO: Gil Cabral, CEO   Tel: (818) 676-2300   %FO: 100
Bus: *Engaged in analysis and*   Fax: (818) 676-2700
      measurement systems for the
      networking industry.

ZARAK SYSTEMS CORPORATION
1175 Borregas Avenue, Sunnyvale, CA   94089
CEO: Mike Horn, Mgr.   Tel: (408) 541-1010   %FO: 100
Bus: *Mfr. advanced telecom test*   Fax: (408) 541-1090
      systems and implementing
      solutions.

● **SPODE LIMITED**
Church Street, Stoke-on-Trent ST4 1BX, UK
CEO: Paul Wood, CEO   Tel: 44-178-274-4011
Bus: *Mfr. china and porcelain.*   Fax: 44-178-274-4220
                                              www.spode.co.uk

ROYAL CHINA & PORCELAIN COMPANIES
1265 Glen Avenue, Moorestown, NJ   08057-0912
CEO: M. Dilella   Tel: (856) 866-2900   %FO: 100
Bus: *Mfr./sales china and porcelain.*   Fax: (856) 866-2499

● **SPORTSWORLD MEDIA GROUP PLC**
6 Henrietta Street, London WC2E 8 PS, UK
CEO: Geoff J. Brown, CEO   Tel: 44-207-240-9626   Rev: $9
Bus: *Engaged in sports marketing, outdoor* Fax: 44-207-240-9636   Emp: 75
      advertising.   wWw.sportsworld.net

IMS FREESPORT MARKETING
27285 Las Ramblas, Ste. 120, Mission Viejo, CA   92691
CEO: Carl Thomas, EVP   Tel: (949) 494-2520   %FO: 100
Bus: *Engaged in sports marketing,*   Fax: (949) 494-2520
      outdoor advertising.

● **SSL INTERNATIONAL PLC**
Toft Hall, Tolf, Knutsford, Cheshire WA16 9PD, UK
CEO: Brian Buchan, CEO   Tel: 44-156-562-4000   Rev: $1,122
Bus: *Mfr. consumer health care products.*   Fax: 44-156-562-4001   Emp: 7,500
                                              www.ssl-international.com

SILIPOS, INC.
7049 Williams Road, Niagara Falls, NY   14303
CEO: Steve Snyder, VP   Tel: (800) 229-4404   %FO: 100
Bus: *Mfr. consumer health care*   Fax: (716) 283-0600
    products.

SSL AMERICAS INC.
3585 Engineering Drive, Ste. 200, Norcross, GA   30092-2820
CEO: Allen McMichael   Tel: (770) 582-2222   %FO: 100
Bus: *Mfr. consumer health care*   Fax: (770) 582-2233
    products.

● **ST. IVES PLC**
St. Ives House, Lavington Street, London SE1 0NX, UK
CEO: Brian Edwards, Mng. Dir.   Tel: 44-207-928-8844   Rev: $710
Bus: *Engaged in commercial printing.*   Fax: 44-207-902-6572   Emp: 5,383
                                         www.st-ives.co.uk

ST. IVES INC.
2025 McKinley Street, Hollywood, FL   33020
CEO: Wayne Angstrom, Pres. & CEO   Tel: (954) 920-7300   %FO: 100
Bus: *Engaged in multi-color web offset* Fax: (954) 929-9060
    production.

● **STAGECOACH HOLDINGS PLC**
10 Dunkeld Road, Perth, Tayside PHI 5TW, UK
CEO: Keith Cochrane, Pres. & CEO   Tel: 44-173-844-2111   Rev: $2,985
Bus: *Engaged in transportation, including* Fax: 44-173-864-3648   Emp: 43,350
    operation of ferries, buses, railway units www.stagecoachplc.com
    and airport services businesses.

COACH USA, INC.
One Riverway, Ste. 500, Houston, TX   77056-1921
CEO: Frank P. Gallagher, CEO   Tel: (713) 888-0104   %FO: 100
Bus: *Provides charter and tour buses,* Fax: (713) 888-0218
    taxi cab and airport shuttle
    services.

● **STANDARD CHARTERED, PLC**
1 Aldermanbury Square, London EC2V 7SB, UK
CEO: Patrick J. Gillam, Chmn.   Tel: 44-207-280-7500   Rev: $7,462
Bus: *International banking.*   Fax: 44-207-280-7791   Emp: 27,383
                                         www.stanchart.com

STANDARD CHARTERED, PLC.
701 Brickell Avenue, Suite 1700, Miami, FL 33131
CEO: Mark North, EVP   Tel: (305) 539-7000   %FO: 100
Bus: *International banking services.*   Fax: (305) 539-7774   Emp: 40

STANDARD CHARTERED, PLC.
One Evertrust Plaza Suite 1101, Jersey City, NJ 07302
CEO: Robert P. McDonald, Pres.   Tel: %FO: 100
Bus: *International banking services.*   Fax:
(Temporary relocation since
9/11/01 WTC bombing).

● **STOCKCUBE PLC**
23 Plaza 535, King's Road, Unit 1, London SW1D OSZ, UK
CEO: Julian Burney, CEO   Tel: 44-207-352-4001
Bus: *Provides financial services.*   Fax: 44-207-376-8966
www.stockcube.com

CHARTCRAFT INC.
PO Box 2046, New Rochelle, NY 10801
CEO: Michael Burke   Tel: (914) 632-0422   %FO: 100
Bus: *Provides financial services.*   Fax: (914) 632-0335

● **STOLT-NIELSEN SA**
Aldwych House, 71-91 Aldwych, London WC2B 4HN, UK
CEO: Niels G. Stolt-Nielsen, CEO   Tel: 44-207-611-8960   Rev: $3,233
Bus: *International transport, storage and*   Fax: 44-207-611-8965   Emp: 11,000
distribution specialty bulk liquids,   www.stoltnielsen.com
subsea contracting and aquaculture.

STOLT OFFSHORE INC.
900 Town & Country Lane, Houston, TX 77024
CEO: Quinn Hebert, Pres.   Tel: (713) 430-1100
Bus: *Provides diving and marine*   Fax: (713) 461-4731
construction services and general
contracting.

STOLTHAVEN TERMINALS (HOUSTON) INC.
15602 Jacintoport Blvd., Houston, TX 77015
CEO: Bo-Stolt-Nielsen, Pres.   Tel: (281) 457-1080   %FO: 100
Bus: *Parcel tanker operations, tank*   Fax: (281) 457-4945   Emp: 300
container sales and operations,
barge/rail sales and operations,
terminal sales and operations.

STOLT-NIELSEN TRANSPORTATION GROUP LTD.

8 Sound Shore Drive, PO Box 2300, Greenwich, CT   06836

CEO: Samuel Cooperman, Pres.	Tel: (203) 625-9400	%FO: 100
Bus: *International transport of specialty bulk liquids.*	Fax: (203) 661-7695	Emp: 500

● STRATUS HOLDINGS PLC

24C Old Burlington Street, London W1X 1RL, UK

CEO: David C. Lane, CEO	Tel: 44-207-494-6400
Bus: *Engaged in publishing.*	Fax: 44-207-494-6411
	www.houseofstratus.com

HOUSE OF STRATUS INC.

1270 Avenue of the Americas, Ste. 210, New York, NY   10020

CEO: David C. Lane, Pres.	Tel: (212) 218-7649	%FO: 100
Bus: *Engaged in publishing.*	Fax: (212) 218-7648	

● SURF CONTROL PLC

Riverside, Mountbatten Way, Congleton, Cheshire CW12 1DY, UK

CEO: Stephen Purdham, CEO	Tel: 44-126-029-6200	Rev: $14
Bus: *Mfr. Internet filtering software.*	Fax: 44-126-029-6201	Emp: 300
	www.surfcontrol.com	

SURFCONTROL USA INC.

1900 West Park Drive, Ste. 180, Westborough, MA   01581

CEO: Geoff Webb, Mgr.	Tel: (508) 870-7200	%FO: 100
Bus: *Mfr./sales Internet filtering software.*	Fax: (508) 870-7200	

SURFCONTROL USA INC.

100 Enterprise Way, Ste. 110A, Scotts Valley, CA   95066

CEO: Geoff Webb, Mgr.	Tel: (831) 431-1300	%FO: 100
Bus: *Mfr./sales Internet filtering software.*	Fax: (831) 431-1800	

● SYSTEMS UNION GROUP PLC

1 Lakeside Road, Aerospace Centre, Farnborough, Hampshire GU14 6XP, UK

CEO: Paul Coleman, CEO	Tel: 44-125-255-6000	
Bus: *Supply/service of accounting software.*	Fax: 44-125-255-6219	Emp: 445
	www.systemsunion.com	

SYSTEMS UNION LIMITED

One North Lexington Avenue, 10th Fl., White Plains, NY   10601

CEO: Mark Wolfendale, CEO	Tel: (914) 948-7770	%FO: 100
Bus: *Supply/service of accounting software.*	Fax: (914) 948-7399	Emp: 65

SYSTEMS UNION LIMITED
150 Spear Street, Ste. 1750, San Francisco, CA 94105

CEO: Mark Wolfendale, CEO	Tel: (415) 247-7989	%FO: 100
Bus: *Supply/service of accounting software.*	Fax: (415) 247-7985	Emp: 15

● TADPOLE TECHNOLOGY PLC
Science Park, Milton Road, Cambridge CB4 OTB, UK

CEO: J. Bernard Hulme, CEO	Tel: 44-122-342-8201	
Bus: *Mfr. networking computers and software.*	Fax: 44-122-342-8201 www.tadpole.com	Emp: 100

ENDEAVORS TECHNOLOGY
19700 Fairchild Avenue, Ste. 200, Irvine, CA 92612

CEO: Brian Morrow, CEO	Tel: (949) 833-2800	%FO: 100
Bus: *Mfr./sales software.*	Fax: (949) 833-2881	

TADPOLE-CARTESIA
2300 Faraday Road, Carlsbad, CA 92008

CEO: Ken Skinner, VP	Tel: (760) 929-0992	%FO: 100
Bus: *Mfr./sales software.*	Fax: (760) 931-1063	

● TATE & LYLE PLC
Sugar Quay, Lower Thames Street, London EC3R 6DQ, UK

CEO: Larry G. Pillard, CEO	Tel: 44-207-626-6525	Rev: $8,987
Bus: *Sugar refining, bulk liquid storage and agricultural consulting.*	Fax: 44-207-623-5514 www.tateandlyle.com	Emp: 21,500

CHARLESTON PACKAGING CO.
4229 Domino Avenue, North Charleston, SC 29405

CEO: Michael J. Fowler	Tel: (843) 744-1646	%FO: 100
Bus: *Mfr. paper bags.*	Fax: (843) 744-1646	

DOMINO SUGAR CORPORATION
1114 Avenue of the Americas, New York, NY 10036

CEO: Andrew Ferrier, Pres. & CEO	Tel: (212) 789-9700	%FO: 100
Bus: *Mfr. refined cane sugar.*	Fax: (212) 789-9746	

PM AG PRODUCTS, INC.
17475 Jovanna Street, Homewood, IL 60430

CEO: Michael A. Reed, Pres.	Tel: (708) 206-2030	%FO: 100
Bus: *Mfr. molasses & animal feeds.*	Fax: (708) 206-1340	

TATE & LYLE, INC.
1402 Foulk Road, #102, Wilmington, DE 19803

CEO: Larry G. Pillard, CEO	Tel: (302) 478-4773	%FO: 100
Bus: *Holding company.*	Fax: (302) 478-6915	

TATE & LYLE SUGARS INC.
2200 East Eldorado Street, Decatur, IL   62525
CEO: Clive Rutherford, CEO   Tel: (217) 423-4411   %FO: 85
Bus: *Mfr. refined sugar products.*   Fax: (217) 421-2216   Emp: 5,000

THE WESTERN SUGAR COMPANY
1700 Broadway, Ste. 1600, Denver, CO   80290
CEO: Thomas F. Chandler, Pres.   Tel: (303) 830-3939   %FO: 100
Bus: *Mfr. beet sugar.*   Fax: (303) 830-3940

● **TAYLOR & FRANCIS GROUP PLC**
11 New Fetter Lane, London EC4P 4EE, UK
CEO: Anthony R. Selvey, CEO   Tel: 44-207-583-9855   Rev: $174
Bus: *Publisher of academic books.* Fax: 44-207-842-2298   Emp: 675
                                     www.tandf.co.uk

TAYLOR & FRANCIS GROUP
29 West 35th Street, New York, NY   10001
CEO: Anthony Selvey, CEO   Tel: (212) 414-0650   %FO: 100
Bus: *Academic publications.*   Fax: (212) 414-0659

TAYLOR & FRANCIS GROUP
325 Chestnut Street, 8th Fl., Philadelphia, PA   19106
CEO: Anthony Selvey, CEO   Tel: (215) 625-8900   %FO: 100
Bus: *Academic publications.*   Fax: (215) 625-2940

● **TAYLOR NELSON SOFRES PLC**
Westgate, London W5 1UA, UK
CEO: Mike Kirkham, CEO   Tel: 44-208-967-0007   Rev: $716
Bus: *Engaged in market research.*   Fax: 44-208-967-4060   Emp: 7,125
                                     www.tnsofres.com

CMR INC.
200 West Jackson Blvd., Chicago, IL   60606-6910
CEO: Carl Dickens, VP   Tel: (312) 583-5353
Bus: *Provider of advertising*   Fax: (312) 583-5353
  expenditure data.

CMR INC.
685 Third Avenue, New York, NY   10017
CEO: David Peeler, Pres. & CEO   Tel: (212) 991-6000   %FO: 100
Bus: *Provider of advertising*   Fax: (212) 789-1400
  expenditure data.

CMR INC.
3102 Oaklawn Avenue, Ste. 510, Dallas, TX 75219
CEO: Alan Kraut　　　　　Tel: (214) 521-6421
Bus: *Provider of advertising*　　Fax: (214) 521-6421
　　expenditure data.

CMR INC.
5055 Wilshire Blvd., 7th Fl., Los Angeles, CA 90036
CEO: John J. Sarsen, Pres.　　Tel: (323) 525-2259
Bus: *Provider of advertising*　　Fax: (323) 525-2259
　　expenditure data.

TAYLOR NELSON SOFRES INTERSEARCH
410 Horsham Road, Horsham, PA 19044
CEO: Bob Michaels　　　　Tel: (215) 442-9000　　%FO: 100
Bus: *Engaged in market research.*　Fax: (215) 442-9040

● **TAYLOR WOODROW PLC**
Venture House, 42-54 London Rd., Staines, Middlesex TW18 4HF, UK
CEO: Keith R. Egerton, CEO　　Tel: 44-178-442-8650　　Rev: $2,298
Bus: *Property development, housing, general*　Fax: 44-178-442-8750　　Emp: 7,963
　　construction and trading activities.　www.taywood.co.uk

MONARCH TAYLOR WOODROW
30012 Ivy Glenn Drive, Ste. 180, Laguna Niguel, CA 92677
CEO: Gordon Craig, Pres.　　Tel: (949) 363-7010　　%FO: 100
Bus: *Property development, housing &*　Fax: (949) 363-9360
　　general construction.

TAYLOR WOODROW COMMUNITIES, INC.
623 Lakeshore Drive, Sugar Land, TX 77478
CEO: Jeffrey Anderson, Pres.　　Tel: (281) 242-4004　　%FO: 100
Bus: *Property development, housing*　Fax: (281) 242-6968
　　and general construction.

TAYLOR WOODROW FLORIDA
7129 South Beneva Road, Sarasota, FL 34238-2150
CEO: John R. Peshkin, Pres.　　Tel: (941) 927-0999　　%FO: 100
Bus: *Property development, housing*　Fax: (941) 925-4856
　　and general construction.

TAYLOR WOODROW HOMES CALIFORNIA LTD.
2441 Ridge Route Drive, Laguna Hills, CA 92653-1686
CEO: Richard E. Pope, Pres.　　Tel: (949) 581-2626　　%FO: 100
Bus: *Property development, housing*　Fax: (949) 581-2727
　　and general construction.

● **TBI PLC**
159 New Bond Street, London W1C 2UD, UK
CEO: Keith Brooks, CEO   Tel: 44-207-408-7300   Rev: $153
Bus: *Engaged in airport management.*   Fax: 44-207-408-7321   Emp: 985
www.tbiplc.co.uk

    AIRPORT GROUP INTERNATIONAL
    330 North Brand Blvd., Ste. 300, Glendale, CA   91203
    CEO: Jack Evans, CEO   Tel: (818) 409-7500   %FO: 100
    Bus: *Airport management.*   Fax: (818) 409-7979   Emp: 1,300

● **TEMPUS GROUP PLC**
1 Pemberton Row, London EC4A 3BA, UK
CEO: David Reich, CEO   Tel: 44-207-803-2803   Rev: $226
Bus: *Engaged in media communications.*   Fax: 44-207-803-2097   Emp: 2,500
www.tempusgroup.co.uk.

    VSM MEDIA INC.
    307 East 53rd Street, New York, NY   10022-4985
    CEO: Barry Allen, CEO   Tel: (212) 753-5200
    Bus: *Engaged in media communications.* Fax: (212) 753-5297

● **THALES ANTENNAS LIMITED**
First Avenue, Millbrook Trading Estate, Southampton SO15 0LJ, UK
CEO: Simon Mountfort   Tel: 44-238-070-5705   Rev: $8,600
Bus: *Develops and manufactures base station* Fax: 44-238-070-1122   Emp: 6,500
antennas.   www.racal-antennas.com

    THALES ANTENNAS INC.
    501 Tradeway, Mineral Wells, TX   76067
    CEO: Anthony Martin   Tel: (940) 325-2341   %FO: 100
    Bus: *Sales of base statin antennas.*   Fax: (940) 325-4377

    ZAXUS, DIV. THALES E-SECURITY INC.
    1601 N. Harrison Pkwy., Ste. 100, Sunrise, FL   33323-2899
    CEO: Phil Naybour   Tel: (954) 846-4700   %FO: 100
    Bus: *Provides e-business, security*   Fax: (954) 846-3935
    solutions.

● **THAMES WATER PLC**
14 Cavendish Place, London W1M 9DJ, UK
CEO: Bill Alexander, CEO   Tel: 44-207-636-8686   Rev: $2,177
Bus: *Supplies drinking water and*   Fax: 44-207-833-6137   Emp: 12,000
environmental and waste management www.thames-water.com
products.

F. B. LEOPOLD COMPANY INC.
227 South Division Street, Zelienpole, PA   16063-1313-
CEO: Michael J. Ulizio, Gen. Mgr.   Tel: (724) 452-6300   %FO: 100
Bus: *Supplies drinking water and*   Fax: (724) 452-1377
environmental and waste
management products.

● **THE THOMAS COOK GROUP LTD.**
45 Berkeley Street, London W1A 1EB, UK
CEO: Johannes Ringel, Chmn.   Tel: 44-207-499-4000   Rev: $1,820
Bus: *Tour operator, traveler's checks and* Fax: 44-207-408-4299   Emp: 14,000
travel services.   www.thomascook.com

THOMAS COOK CURRENCY SERVICES INC.
29 Broadway, New York, NY   10006
CEO: John Donaldson, Dir.   Tel: (212) 363-6206   %FO: 100
Bus: *Currency and traveler's checks*   Fax: (212) 809-7983
services.

● **TIBBETT & BRITTEN GROUP PLC**
Ross House, Windmill Hill, Enfield, Middlesex EN2 6SB, UK
CEO: John A. Harvey, Chmn. & CEO   Tel: 44-208-367-9955   Rev: $2,112
Bus: *Engaged in logistic solutions and*   Fax: 44-208-366-7042   Emp: 32,000
services.   www.tibbett-britten.com

TIBBETT & BRITTEN GROUP
1031 Highway 22 West, Ste. 301, Bridgewater, NJ   08807
CEO: Mike Sprague, CEO   Tel: (908) 203-1961   %FO: 100
Bus: *Engaged in logistic solutions and*   Fax: (908) 203-1962   Emp: 2,500
services.

● **TOMKINS PLC**
East Putney House, 84 Upper Richmond Road, London SW15 2ST, UK
CEO: David Newlands, Chmn. & CEO   Tel: 44-208-871-4544   Rev: $8,722
Bus: *Industrial management services. Mfr.* Fax: 44-208-877-9700   Emp: 70,040
garden/leisure products, food, baking,   www.tomkins.co.uk
milling products, industrial products
and handguns.

AIR SYSTEM COMPONENTS
1401 North Plano Road, Richardson, TX   75081
CEO: Terry O'Halloran, Pres.   Tel: (972) 680-9126   %FO: 100
Bus: *Mfr. HVAC components.*   Fax: (972) 575-6225

DEARBORN MID-WEST CONVEYOR CO.
20334 Superior Road, Taylor, MI 48180
CEO: Wes Paisley, Pres. Tel: (724) 288-4400 %FO: 100
Bus: *Mfr. heavy duty conveyor equipment, postal and bulk system conveyors.* Fax: (734) 288-1914

DEXTER AXLE COMPANY
PO Box 250, Elkhart, IN 46515
CEO: W. Michael Jones, Pres. Tel: (219) 295-1900 %FO: 100
Bus: *Mfr. axles and wheels for trailers, motor homes and recreational vehicles.* Fax: (219) 295-1069

THE GATES RUBBER COMPANY
900 South Broadway, PO Box 5887, Denver, CO 80217
CEO: Jim Wiggins, CEO Tel: (303) 744-1911 %FO: 100
Bus: *Mfr./distributor auto & industrial rubber products.* Fax: (303) 744-4000

HART & COOLEY, INC.
300 East Eighth Street, Holland, MI 49423
CEO: Gary Henry, Pres. Tel: (616) 392-7855 %FO: 100
Bus: *Mfr. residential heating and ventilating.* Fax: (616) 392-7971

LASCO BATHWARE, INC.
8101 East Kaiser Blvd., Anaheim, CA 92808
CEO: Dave Bienek, Pres. Tel: (714) 993-1220 %FO: 100
Bus: *Mfr. fiberglass showers and tubs.* Fax: (800) 879-3518

LASCO BATHWARE
3255 East Miraloma Avenue, Anaheim, CA 92806
CEO: Dave Blenek, Pres. Tel: (714) 993-1220 %FO: 100
Bus: *Mfr. fibreglass & acrylic baths & whirlpools.* Fax: (714) 572-0998

LASCO COMPOSITES LP
8015 Dixon Drive, Florence, KY 41042
CEO: Jim Amundson, Pres. Tel: (606) 371-7720 %FO: 100
Bus: *Mfr. construction fibreglass panels.* Fax: (606) 371-8466

LASCO FITTINGS INC.
414 Morgan Street, Brownsville, TN 38012
CEO: Jack McDonald, Pres. Tel: (901) 772-3180 %FO: 100
Bus: *Mfr. PVC pipe.* Fax: (901) 772-0835

LAU INDUSTRIES
4509 Springfield Street, Dayton, OH   45431
CEO: Will Jones, Pres.   Tel: (937) 476-6500   %FO: 100
Bus: *Mfr. centrifugal fans & propellers.*   Fax: (937) 254-9519

MAYFRAN INTERNATIONAL, INC.
650 Beta Drive, Cleveland, OH   44143
CEO: Bruce Terry, Pres.   Tel: (440) 461-4100   %FO: 100
Bus: *Mfr. industrial machinery;*   Fax: (440) 461-5565
     conveyors for waste recovery &.
     metalworking.

PENN VENTILATION, INC.
1370 Welsh Road, North Wales, PA   19454
CEO: Theodore G. Sharpe, Pres.   Tel: (215) 619-8800   %FO: 100
Bus: *Mfr. residential heating and*   Fax: (215) 591-1916
     ventilation.

PHILIPS PRODUCTS, INC.
3221 Magnum Drive, Elkhart, IN   46516
CEO: W. Michael Jones, Pres.   Tel: (219) 296-0000   %FO: 100
Bus: *Mfr. aluminum/vinyl doors,*   Fax: (219) 296-0147
     windows, hoods, and ventilating
     devices.

RUSKIN COMPANY
3900 Doctor Greaves Road, Grandview, MO   64030
CEO: Tom Edwards, Pres.   Tel: (816) 761-7476   %FO: 100
Bus: *Mfr. air, fire and smoke dampers,*   Fax: (816) 763-8102
     louvers and fibreglass products.

THE SCHRADER GROUP
165 Arlington Heights Road, Ste. 150, Buffalo Grove, IL   60089-7974
CEO: Jim Wiggins, Pres.   Tel: (847) 465-8901   %FO: 100
Bus: *Mfr. auto valves and fittings.*   Fax: (847) 465-8920

SMITH & WESSON CORPORATION
2100 Roosevelt Avenue, PO Box 2208, Springfield, MA   01102-2208
CEO: George C. Colclough, Pres.   Tel: (413) 781-8300   %FO: 100
Bus: *Mfr. handguns, handcuffs and*   Fax: (413) 734-9023
     Identi-Kit systems.

THE STANT GROUP
165 Arlington Heights Road, Ste. 150, Buffalo Grove, IL   60089-7974
CEO: Jim Wiggins, Pres.   Tel: (847) 465-8907   %FO: 100
Bus: *Mfr. auto products.*   Fax: (847) 465-8920

TOMKINS INDUSTRIES INC.

4801 Springfield Street, PO Box 943, Dayton, OH   45401-0943

CEO: Anthony J. Reading, Chmn. Tel: (937) 253-7171 %FO: 100

Bus: *Holding company.* Fax: (937) 253-9822 Emp: 60

TRICO

3255 West Hamlin Road, Rochester Hills, MI   48309

CEO: Don Fletcher, Pres. Tel: (248) 371-8338 %FO: 100

Bus: *Mfr. wiper blades and refills.* Fax: (248) 371-8308

● TREATT PLC

North Way, Bury St. Edmunds, Suffolk IP32 6NL, UK

CEO: Hugo W. Bovill, Mng. Dir. Tel: 44-128-470-2500 Rev: $35

Bus: *Mfg. flavors, fragrances & specialty* Fax: 44-128-470-3809 Emp: 120
chemicals. www.treatt.com

FLORIDA TREATT INC.

PO Box 215, 3100 U.S. Hwy. 17-02 West, Haines City, FL   33845

CEO: Steve Shelton Tel: (863) 421-4708 %FO: 100

Bus: *Mfg. flavors, fragrances &* Fax: (863) 422-5930
specialty chemicals.

● TRIKON TECHNOLOGIES, INC.

Ringland Way, Newport, Gwent NP18 2TA, UK

CEO: Nigel Wheeler, CEO Tel: 44-163-341-4000 Rev: $107

Bus: *Mfg., electronics, semiconductor* Fax: 44-163-341-4141 Emp: 552
equipment & materials. www.trikon.com

TRIKON TECHNOLOGIES, INC.

10540 Talbert Avenue, Suite 100, Fountain Valley, CA   92708

CEO: Scott Brown Tel: (800) 727-5585 %FO: 100

Bus: *Mfg., electronics, semiconductor* Fax: (714) 968-2594
equipment and materials.

● TT ELECTRONICS PLC

Clive House, 12-18 Queens Road, Waybridge, Surrey KT13 9XB, UK

CEO: Sheridan W. A. Comonte, CEO Tel: 44-193-284-1310 Rev: $1,114

Bus: *Engaged in electronics, resistor film* Fax: 44-193-284-6724 Emp: 11,080
systems and industrial engineering. www.ttgrp.com

IRC INC.

4222 South Staples Street, Corpus Christi, TX   78411

CEO: Steve Wade Tel: (361) 992-7900

Bus: *Advanced film division.* Fax: (361) 992-3377

IRC INC.
PO Box 1860, Boone, NC   28607
CEO: Jerry August, Pres. Tel: (828) 264-8861
Bus: *Wire and film technology division.* Fax: (828) 264-8866

MAGNETIC MATERIAL GROUP (MMG NORTH AMERICA)
126 Pennsylvania Avenue, Paterson, NJ   07503-2512
CEO: Tom Carr, Pres. Tel: (973) 345-8900
Bus: *Mfr. magnetic materials, including* Fax: (973) 345-1172
iron core products and permanent magnetics.

• TTP COMMUNICATIONS PLC
Melbourn Science Park, Cambridge Road, Melbourn Royston, Hertfordshire SG8 6EE, UK
CEO: Anthony J. Milbourn, Mng. Dir. Tel: 44-176-326-6266 Rev: $30
Bus: *Telecommunications equipment.* Fax: 44-176-326-1216 Emp: 184
www.ttpcom.com

TTPCOM LTD.
PO Box 461, Suwanee, GA   30024-0461
CEO: Tim Link Tel: (770) 614-8689 %FO: 100
Bus: *Telecommunications equipment.* Fax: (678) 714-1287

• THE TUSSAUDS GROUP LIMITED
Maple House, 149 Tottenham Ct. Rd., London W1P 0DX, UK
CEO: Michael Jolly, Chmn. & CEO Tel: 44-207-312-1131
Bus: *Entertainment attractions.* Fax: 44-207-465-0864
www.tussauds.com

MADAME TUSSAUDS
234 West 42nd Street, New York, NY   10036
CEO: Robert Rochester Tel: (212) 512-9600 %FO: 100
Bus: *Entertainment attractions.* Fax: (212) 719-9440

• UMECO PLC
Concorde House, 24 Warwick New Road, Leamington Spa, Warwickshire CV32 5JG, UK
CEO: Clive J. Snowdon, CEO Tel: 44-192-633-1800 Rev: $165
Bus: *Aerospace and defense products.* Fax: 44-192-631-2680 Emp: 663
www.umeco.co.uk

ABSCOA INDUSTRIES, INC.
2000 Robotics Place, Ft. Worth, TX   76118
CEO: Gary North, Pres. Tel: (817) 284-4449 %FO: 100
Bus: *Aerospace and defense products.* Fax: (817) 595-1554

RICHMOND AIRCRAFT PRODUCTS
13503 Pumice Street, Norwalk, CA 90650

CEO: J. Hubl, CEO   Tel: (562) 404-2440   %FO: 100

Bus: *Aerospace and defense products.*   Fax: (562) 404-9011

● UNILEVER PLC
Unilever House, PO Box 68, London EC4P 4BQ, UK

CEO: Niall W.A. FitzGerald, Chmn.   Tel: 44-207-822-5252   Rev: $43,490

Bus: *Soaps and detergents, foods, chemicals, personal products (J/V of UNILEVER NV, Netherlands).*   Fax: 44-207-822-5511   Emp: 255,000

www.unilever.com

CALVIN KLEIN COSMETICS COMPANY
725 Fifth Avenue, New York, NY 10022

CEO: Paulanne Mancuso, Pres.   Tel: (212) 759-8888   %FO: 100

Bus: *Mfr. perfumes, cosmetics.*   Fax: (212) 755-8792

DIVERSEY LEVER
255 East Fifth Street, Cincinnati, OH 45202

CEO: Don Saunders, Pres.   Tel: (513) 762-6000   %FO: 100

Bus: *Mfr. specialty chemicals.*   Fax: (513) 762-6601

DIVERSEY LEVER
14496 Sheldon Road, Plymouth, MI 48170

CEO: Arwin Hughes, Pres.   Tel: (734) 414-1725   %FO: 100

Bus: *Mfr. specialty chemicals.*   Fax: (734) 414-3364

ELIZABETH ARDEN
1345 Avenue of the Americas, New York, NY 10105

CEO: Peter England, Pres.   Tel: (212) 261-1000   %FO: 100

Bus: *Mfr. cosmetics and perfumes.*   Fax: (212) 261-1350

HELENE CURTIS
325 North Wells Street, Chicago, IL 60610

CEO: Ronald J. Gidwitz, Pres.   Tel: (312) 661-0222   %FO: 100

Bus: *Mfr. cosmetics and fragrances.*   Fax: (312) 836-0125

LEVER BROTHERS COMPANY
390 Park Avenue, New York, NY 10022

CEO: John W. Rice, Pres.   Tel: (212) 688-6000   %FO: 100

Bus: *Mfr. soaps and detergents.*   Fax: (212) 906-4411

LIPTON
800 Sylvan Avenue, Englewood Cliffs, NJ 07632

CEO: Richard Goldstein, Pres.   Tel: (201) 567-8000   %FO: 100

Bus: *Mfr. tea, seasonings and food products.*   Fax: (201) 871-8280

SLIM FAST FOODS COMPANY
PO Box 3625, West Palm Beach, FL   33402

CEO: Marc Covent, Pres.	Tel: (561) 833-9920	%FO: 100
Bus: *Mfr. weight loss and weight maintenance food products.*	Fax: (561) 822-2876	

UNILEVER HPC USA
33 Benedict Place, Greenwich, CT   06830

CEO: Robert M. Phillips, Chmn.	Tel: (203) 661-2000	%FO: 100
Bus: *Mfr. home and personal care products. (Formerly Cheseborough-Pond's)*	Fax: (203) 625-1602	

UNILEVER US, INC
390 Park Avenue, New York, NY   10022-4698

CEO: Richard A. Goldstein, Pres.	Tel: (212) 888-1260	%FO: 100
Bus: *Holding company.*	Fax: (212) 318-3800	Emp: 25,000

• UNITED BISCUITS HOLDINGS PLC
Church Road, West Drayton, Middlesex UB7 7PR, UK

CEO: Malcolm Ritchie, Chmn. & CEO	Tel: 44-189-543-2100	Rev: $1,600
Bus: *Mfr. cookies, crackers and snacks.*	Fax: 44-189-543-2201	Emp: 21,000
	www.unitedbiscuits.co.uk	

KEEBLER FOODS COMPANY
677 Larch Avenue, Elmhurst, IL   60126

CEO: Robert P. Crozer, Chmn.	Tel: (630) 833-2900	%FO: JV
Bus: *Mfr./sales/distribution of Keebler and Sunshine cooker and Carr's crackers. (JV with Flowers Industries Baking Co.)*	Fax: (630) 530-8733	

• UNITED BUSINESS MEDIA PLC
Ludgate House, 245 Blackfriars Road, London SE1 9UY, UK

CEO: Clive Hollick, CEO	Tel: 44-207-921-5000	Rev: $2,953
Bus: *Publishes trade and consumer magazines/newspapers.*	Fax: 44-207-921-2728	Emp: 15,000
	www.unm.com	

PR NEWSWIRE ASSOC INC.
810 Seventh Avenue, 35th Floor, New York, NY   10019

CEO: Charles H. Morin, CEO	Tel: (212) 596-1500	%FO: 100
Bus: *News gathering/dissemination.*	Fax: (212) 596-1516	

UNITED ADVERTISING PUBLICATIONS INC.
15400 Knoll Trail, Ste. 400, Dallas, TX   75248

CEO: Nigel Donaldson, Pres. & CEO	Tel: (972) 701-0244	%FO: 100
Bus: *Real estate publications.*	Fax: (972) 701-0244	

● **UNITED UTILITIES PLC**
Birchwood Blvd., Birchwood, Warrington, Cheshire WA3 7WB, UK
CEO: John Roberts, CEO
Bus: *Engaged in water and wastewater operations.*
Tel: 44-192-528-5000
Fax: 44-192-528-5199
www.unitedutillities.com
Emp: 10,350

    US WATER LTD.
    3434 Route 22 West, Somerville, NJ 08876
    CEO: Gordon Waters, Pres.
    Bus: *Engaged in water and wastewater operations.*
    Tel: (908) 707-4545
    Fax: (908) 707-8887
    %FO: 100

    US WATER LTD.
    400 Massasoit Avenue, Ste. 108, East Providence, RI 02914
    CEO: Gordon Waters, Pres.
    Bus: *Engaged in water and wastewater operations.*
    Tel: (401) 438-4600
    Fax: (401) 435-1489
    %FO: 100

    US WATER LTD.
    184 Shuman Boulevard, Naperville, IL 60563
    CEO: Gordon Waters, Pres.
    Bus: *Engaged in water and wastewater operations.*
    Tel: (630) 717-2884
    Fax: (630) 717-2885
    %FO: 100

● **VEOS PLC**
10 Greycoat Place, London SW1P 1SB, UK
CEO: Peggy S. Czyak-Danenbaum, CEO
Bus: *Engaged in innovative, reproductive healthcare products for women.*
Tel: 44-207-960-6066
Fax: 44-207-960-6696
www.veos.com

    VEOS USA INC.
    PO Box 331, Lake Forest, IL 60045
    CEO: Paul Lever
    Bus: *Engaged in innovative, reproductive healthcare products for women.*
    Tel: (847) 735-0003
    Fax: (847) 735-0070
    %FO: 100

● **VINTEN BROADCAST LTD.**
Western Way, Bury Street, Edmund, Suffolk IP33 3SP, UK
CEO: Robin Howe, EVP
Bus: *Mfr./designs camera supports and dimensional animation.*
Tel: 44-128-475-2121
Fax: 44-128-475-0560
www.vinton.com

VINTEN INC.
709 Executive Boulevard, Valley Cottage, NY   10989
CEO: Mike De Nicola, Pres.   Tel: (845) 268-0100   %FO: 100
Bus: *Sales/distribution of camera*   Fax: (845) 268-0113
supports.

VINTEN INC.
709 Executive Boulevard, Valley Cottage, NY   10989
CEO: Michael DeNicola, Pres.   Tel: (845) 268-0100   %FO: 100
Bus: *Mfr. camera supports.*   Fax: (845) 268-0113

● **VIRGIN GROUP LTD.**
120 Campden Hill Road, London W8 7AR, UK
CEO: Richard C .N. Branson, Chmn.   Tel: 44-207-229-1282   Rev: $5,200
Bus: *Holding company: travel, hotels,*   Fax: 44-207-727-8200   Emp: 30,000
communications, cinemas, radio, retail,   www.virgin.com
financial services & investments..

VIRGIN ATLANTIC AIRWAYS LTD.
747 Belden Avenue, Norwalk, CT   06850
CEO: David Tait, EVP   Tel: (203) 750-2000   %FO: 100
Bus: *International commercial air*   Fax: (203) 750-6490   Emp: 500
transport services.

VIRGIN ATLANTIC CARGO
1963 Marcus Avenue, Lake Success, NY   11042
CEO: Angelo Pasateri, Pres.   Tel: (516) 775-2600   %FO: 100
Bus: *International commercial air*   Fax: (516) 354-3760
transport services.

VIRGIN GAMES INC., VIRGIN INTERACTIVE ENTERTAINMENT, INC.
18061 Fitch Avenue, Irvine, CA   92714
CEO: Martin Alper, Pres.   Tel: (714) 833-8710   %FO: 100
Bus: *Design/mfr. interactive video*   Fax: (714) 833-8717
games.

● **VITALOGRAPH LTD.**
Maids Moreton House, Buckingham MK18 1SW, UK
CEO: Bernard Garbe, Pres.   Tel: 44-128-082-7110
Bus: *Mfr. spirometry and peak flow*   Fax: 44-128-082-3302   Emp: 160
measuring equipment for the diagnosis   www.vitalograph.co.uk
and treatment of respiratory diseases.

VITALOGRAPH MEDICAL INSTRUMENTATION, INC.

8347 Quivira Road, Lenexa, KS   66215

CEO: Bernard Garbe, Pres.	Tel: (913) 888-4221	%FO: 100
Bus: *Pulmonary function testing equipment.*	Fax: (913) 888-4259	

● VODAFONE GROUP PLC

The Courtyard, 2-4 London Road, Newbury Berkshire RG14 1JX, UK

CEO: Christopher Gent, CEO	Tel: 44-163-533-251	Rev: $12,545
Bus: *Mobile phone carrier.*	Fax: 44-163-555-0779	Emp: 29,465
	www.vodafone.com	

VERIZON WIRELESS

180 Washington Valley Road, Bedminster, NJ   07921

CEO: Denny F. Strigl, Pres. & CEO	Tel: (908) 306-7000	%FO:
Bus: *Mobile phone carrier.*	Fax: (908) 306-6927	

● VOLEX GROUP PLC

Dornoch House, Kelvin Close, Birchwood Science Park, Warrington, Cheshire WA3 7JX, UK

CEO: Dominick J. Molloy, CEO	Tel: 44-192-583-0101	Rev: $600
Bus: *Mfr. electronic and optical fibre cable assemblies.*	Fax: 44-192-583-0141	Emp: 11,500
	www.volex.com	

VOLEX INC.

1123 Industrial Drive SW, Conover, NC   28613

CEO: Tony Kalaijakis	Tel: (828) 464-4546	%FO: 100
Bus: *Mfr. fibre optic assemblies.*	Fax: (828) 464-8465	

VOLEX INC.

One Batterymarch Park, Quincy, MA   01269

CEO: Dominick J. Molloy, Pres.	Tel: (617) 376-0555	%FO: 100
Bus: *Sales electronic and optical fibre cable assemblies.*	Fax: (617) 376-0590	

VOLEX INC.

1664 Industrial Boulevard, Chula Vista, CA   91911

CEO: Gus Kamburis	Tel: (619) 423-8200	%FO: 100
Bus: *Mfr. fibre optic assemblies.*	Fax: (619) 423-8255	

VOLEX INC.

44250 Osgood Road, Fremont, CA   94539

CEO: Gus Kamburis	Tel: (510) 360-5250	%FO: 100
Bus: *Mfr. fibre optic assemblies.*	Fax: (510) 354-0850	

VOLEX INC.
30A Upton Drive, Wilmington, MA   01887
CEO: Jack Leary, VP   Tel: (978) 988-1250   %FO: 100
Bus: *Mfr. electronic and optical fibre*   Fax: (978) 988-1264
    cable assemblies.

VOLEX INC.
5250 Lakeview Pkwy. South Drive, Ste. D, Indianapolis, IN   46268
CEO: Jeff DeLoughery, Mgr.   Tel: (800) 246-2673   %FO: 100
Bus: *Mfr. electronic and optical fibre*   Fax: (800) 429-2498
    cable assemblies.

● **VOSPER THORNYCROFT HOLDING PLC**
Victoria Road, Woolston, Southampton SO19 9RR, UK
CEO: Martin Jay, CEO   Tel: 44-238-042-6000   Rev: $437
Bus: *Mfr. military and commercial vessels.*   Fax: 44-238-042-6010   Emp: 800
                                                   www.vosperthornycroft.co.uk

    MARITIME DYNAMICS INC.
    21001 Great Mills Road, Lexington Park, MD   20653
    CEO: Martin Jay, Pres.   Tel: (301) 863-0254   %FO: 100
    Bus: *Mfr. military and commercial*   Fax: (301) 863-0254
        vessels.

● **ROBERT WALTERS PLC**
55 Strand, London WC2N 5LR, UK
CEO: Robert C. Walters, CEO   Tel: 44-207-379-3333   Rev: $323
Bus: *Engaged in outsourcing and recruitment.*   Fax: 44-207-915-8714   Emp: 725
                                                   www.robertwalters.com

    ROBERT WALTERS USA INC.
    1500 Broadway, Ste. 1801, New York, NY   10036
    CEO: Kurt Kraeger   Tel: (212) 704-9900   %FO: 100
    Bus: *Engaged in recruitment.*   Fax: (212) 704-4312

● **WHATMAN PLC**
Whatman House, St. Leonard's Road, 10 Maidstone, Kent ME16 OSL, UK
CEO: David Smith, CEO   Tel: 44-162-267-6670   Rev: $158
Bus: *Mfr. lab filtration and chromatography*   Fax: 44-162-267-7011
    products.   www.whatman.co.uk

    WHATMAN INC.
    9 Bridewell Place, Clifton, NJ   07014
    CEO: James M. Stuvdevant, VP   Tel: (973) 773-5800   %FO: 100
    Bus: *Sales/distribution of lab filtration*   Fax: (973) 472-6949
        and chromatography products.

● **WILLIAMS PLC**
Pentagon House, Sir Frank Whittle Road, Derby DE21 4XA, UK
CEO: Roger M. Carr, CEO Tel: 44-332-202-020 Rev: $4,100
Bus: *Holding company: paints & allied* Fax: 44-332-384-402 Emp: 42,000
products, aircraft parts, consumer www.williams-plc.com
products, security devices/systems and
fire detection systems.

AFAC INC.
West Second Avenue, Ranson, WV 25438
CEO: John Hittson, Pres. Tel: (304) 725-9721
Bus: *Mfr./sales automatic sprinkler* Fax: (304) 728-5270
systems.

ANGUS FIRE ARMOUR
1000 Junny Road, State Road 1501, Angier, NC 27501
CEO: John Hittson, Pres. Tel: (919) 639-6151 %FO: 100
Bus: *Mfr. fire hoses and related* Fax: (919) 639-8519
hardware.

BADGER FIRE PROTECTION
4251 Seminole Trail, Charlottesville, VA 22911
CEO: Victor M. Modic, Pres. Tel: (804) 973-4361 %FO: 100
Bus: *Mfr. commercial fire protection* Fax: (804) 973-7620
products.

DETECTOR ELECTRONICS CORPORATION
6901 W. 110th Street, Minneapolis, MN 55438
CEO: Gerald F. Slocum, Pres. Tel: (612) 941-5665 %FO: 100
Bus: *Fire & safety devices & systems.* Fax: (612) 829-8745 Emp: 200

FENWAL SAFETY SYSTEMS
700 Nickerson Road, Marlborough, MA 01752
CEO: John E. Sullivan, Pres. Tel: (508) 481-5800
Bus: *Mfr. fire detection systems.* Fax: (508) 480-6455

FIREYE, INC.
3 Manchester Road, Derry, NH 03038
CEO: Robert D. Downin, Pres. Tel: (603) 432-4100 %FO: 100
Bus: *Fire & safety devices & systems.* Fax: (603) 432-1570

FORNEY CORPORATION
3405 Wiley Post Road, Carrollton, TX 75006
CEO: Jack Satterfield, Pres. Tel: (214) 458-6100
Bus: *Mfr./distribution of commercial* Fax: (214) 458-6106
burner management systems.

FYRNETICS

1055 Stevenson Court, Ste.102 W, Roselle, IL   30172

CEO: Thomas Russo, Pres.   Tel: (630) 893-4592   %FO: 100

Bus: *Mfr. smoke and carbon monoxide*   Fax: (630) 893-7102
    detectors.

KIDDE TECHNOLOGIES INC.

2500 Airport Drive, Wilson, NC   27893

CEO: Douglas J. Vaday, Pres.   Tel: (252) 237-7004

Bus: *Mfr. fire detection and*   Fax: (252) 237-8533
    suppression systems and devices.

KIDDE-FENWAL, INC.

400 Main Street, Ashland, MA   01721

CEO: Richard H. DeMarle, Pres.   Tel: (508) 881-2000   %FO: 100

Bus: *Fire & safety devices & systems.*   Fax: (508) 881-6729

NATIONAL FOAM, INC.

150 Gordon Drive, Exton, PA   19341

CEO: John Hittson, Pres.   Tel: (610) 363-1400

Bus: *Mfr. fire suppression foam.*   Fax: (610) 363-2980

SANTA BARBARA DUAL SPECTRUM

163 Aero Camino, Goleta, CA   93117

CEO: Vincent Rowe, Pres.   Tel: (805) 961-0555

Bus: *Mfr. fire detection systems.*   Fax: (805) 685-8227

TESA ENTRY SYSTEMS INC.

2100A Nancy Hanks Drive, Norcross, GA   30017

CEO: Robert Aquilino, Pres.   Tel: (770) 447-4105

Bus: *Mfr. commercial door closures.*   Fax: (770) 266-8649

WALTER KIDDE AEROSPACE

4200 Airport Drive NW, Wilson, NC   27896

CEO: Brent Ehmke, Pres.   Tel: (252) 237-7004   %FO: 100

Bus: *Mfr. fire detection systems.*   Fax: (252) 237-4814

WALTER KIDDE PORTABLE EQUIPMENT, INC.

1394 South Third Street, Mebane, NC   27302

CEO: Michael W. Apperson, Pres.   Tel: (919) 563-5911   %FO: 100

Bus: *Fire & safety devices & systems.*   Fax: (919) 563-3954

WILLIAMS US INC.

700 Nickerson Road, Marlborough, MA   01752-4602

CEO: John F. Hannon, Pres.   Tel: (508) 481-0700   %FO: 100

Bus: *U.S. headquarters for holding*   Fax: (508) 624-0579
    company.

• WILLIS GROUP HOLDINGS LIMITED

Ten Trinity Square, London EC3P 3AX, UK

CEO: Joseph J. Plumeri, Chmn.

Bus: *Provides insurance and reinsurance brokerage and financial planning.*

Tel: 44-23-7488-8111
Fax: 44-23-7488-8223
www.willis.com

Rev: $1,305
Emp: 10,470

PUBLIC PROGRAM MANAGEMENT, INC.

26 Century Boulevard, Nashville, TN 37214-3695

CEO: Lloyd Kelley, Pres.

Bus: *Insurance and reinsurance services.*

Tel: (615) 872-3000
Fax: (615) 872-3091

%FO: 100

STEWART SMITH GROUP INC.

88 Pine Street, 17th Fl., New York, NY 10005

CEO: Mark M. Smith, CEO

Bus: *Insurance and reinsurance services.*

Tel: (212) 509-2700
Fax: (212) 509-3051

%FO: 100

WILLIS ADMINISTRATIVE SERVICES CORP.

Murfreesboro Road, Ste. 600, Nashville, TN 37217

CEO: Fred Massa, CEO

Bus: *Insurance and reinsurance services.*

Tel: (615) 360-4560
Fax: (615) 360-2885

%FO: 100

WILLIS AEROSPACE

Seven Hanover Square, New York, NY 10004

CEO: Charles Laible, CEO

Bus: *Aerospace insurance services.*

Tel: (212) 344-8888
Fax: (212) 163-5358

%FO: 100

WILLIS CONSTRUCTION INC.

35 Waterview Boulevard, 2nd Fl., Parsippany, NJ 07054

CEO: Mark E. Reagan, Chmn. & CEO

Bus: *Engaged in construction services.*

Tel: (973) 541-3280
Fax: (973) 541-3280

%FO: 100

WILLIS GLOBAL PROPERTY AND CASUALTY

Seven Hanover Square, New York, NY 10004

CEO: Sandy Vietor, Chmn.

Bus: *Insurance and reinsurance services.*

Tel: (212) 837-0780
Fax: (212) 344-8442

%FO: 100

WILLIS MARINE NORTH AMERICA

Seven Hanover Square, New York, NY 10004

CEO: Daniel J. Donahue, CEO

Bus: *Insurance and reinsurance services.*

Tel: (212) 344-8888
Fax: (212) 344-8442

%FO: 100

WILLIS NORTH AMERICA, INC.
26 Century Boulevard, Nashville, TN   37214-3695
CEO: Brian D. Johnson, CEO   Tel: (615) 872-3000   %FO: 100
Bus: *Insurance and reinsurance*   Fax: (615) 872-3091
     services.

WILLIS RE INC.
88 Pine Street, 4th Fl., New York, NY   10005
CEO: Peter Pruitt, Chmn.   Tel: (212) 344-7000   %FO: 100
Bus: *Insurance and reinsurance*   Fax: (323) 344-0586
     services.

WILLIS RISK SOLUTIONS
Seven Hanover Square, New York, NY   10004
CEO: John McCaffrey, Chmn.   Tel: (212) 344-8888   %FO: 100
Bus: *Insurance and risk solutions.* Fax: (212) 344-8442

• GEORGE WIMPEY PLC
3 Shortlands, London W6 8EX, UK
CEO: Dennis G. Brant, CEO   Tel: 44-208-846-2000   Rev: $2,540
Bus: *Engaged in homebuilding.*   Fax: 44-208-846-3121   Emp: 4,617
                                    www.wimpey.co.uk

MORRISON HOMES, INC.
3700 Mansell Road, Ste. 300, Alpharetta, GA   30022
CEO: Stewart M. Cline, Pres.   Tel: (770) 998-9044   %FO: 100
Bus: *Home building.*   Fax: (770) 998-8114

• WINN & COALES DENSO LTD.
Denso House, Chapel Road, London SE27 OTR, UK
CEO: David Winn, Chmn.   Tel: 44-208-670-7511
Bus: *Mfr. tapes, pastes, mastics and protal*   Fax: 44-208-761-2456
     coatings.   www.denso.net

DENSO NORTH AMERICA
18211 Chisholm Trail, Houston, TX   77060
CEO: Lucian Williams, Pres.   Tel: (281) 821-3355   %FO: 100
Bus: *Distribution mastics, pastes, portal* Fax: (281) 821-0304   Emp: 5
     coatings, sea shield systems.

• WOLSELEY PLC
Vines Ln., PO Box 18, Droitwich Spa, Worcestershire WR9 8ND, UK
CEO: Charles A. Bank, CEO   Tel: 44-190-577-7200   Rev: $9,597
Bus: *Mfr. plumbing/heating supplies and*   Fax: 44-190-577-7219   Emp: 33,385
     equipment.   www.wolseley.com

FERGUSON ENTRPRISES

2750 South Towne Avenue, Pomona, CA   91766

CEO: Steve Grosslight, Pres.   Tel: (909) 364-0871   %FO: 100

Bus: *U. S. headquarters office.*   Fax: (909) 364-0726
    Sales/distribution of plumbing and
    heating supplies and equipment.

FERGUSON SIERRA CRAFT INC.

18825 East San Jose Avenue, City of Industry, CA   91748-1326

CEO: Lee Klein, VP   Tel: (626) 964-2395

Bus: *Distribution and fabrication of*   Fax: (626) 964-1471
    plumbing products.

LINCOLN PRODUCTS

17788 East Rowland Street, City of Industry, CA   91748

CEO: Brad Blakeley, Mgr.   Tel: (626) 912-4056

Bus: *Distribution and sales of plumbing*   Fax: (626) 964-1471
    products.

● WPP GROUP PLC

27 Farm Street, London W1X 6RD, UK

CEO: Martin S. Sorrell, CEO   Tel: 44-207-408-2204   Rev: $4,457

Bus: *Media and non-media marketing*   Fax: 44-207-493-6819   Emp: 55,000
    services group.   www.wpp.com

J. WALTER THOMPSON COMPANY

466 Lexington Avenue, 6th Fl., New York, NY   10017

CEO: Charlotte Beers, Chmn.   Tel: (212) 210-7000   %FO: 100

Bus: *International advertising agency.*   Fax: (212) 210-7078   Emp: 7,000

KNOWLTON, INC.

466 Lexington Avenue, New York, NY   10017

CEO: Howard Paster, Chmn. & CEO   Tel: (212) 885-0300   %FO: 100

Bus: *International public relations*   Fax: (212) 885-0570   Emp: 1,200
    agency.

OGILVY & MATHER WORLDWIDE

309 West 49th Street, 12th Fl., New York, NY   10019

CEO: Shelly Lazarus, Chmn.   Tel: (212) 237-4000   %FO: 100

Bus: *International advertising agency.*   Fax: (212) 237-5123   Emp: 6,000

UNIWORLD GROUP, INC.

100 Avenue of the Americas, New York, NY   10013

CEO: Byron E. Lewis, CEO   Tel: (212) 219-1600   %FO: JV

Bus: *International advertising agency.*   Fax: (212) 941-0650   Emp: 160

WPP GROUP USA, INC.
309 West 49th Street, 14th Fl., New York, NY   10019

CEO: Sir Martin Sorrell, CEO   Tel: (212) 632-2200   %FO: 100
Bus: *Engaged in media and non-media*   Fax: (212) 632-2222   Emp: 80
advertising, marketing services,
public relations, market research,
communications, including: J.
Walter Thompson Co; Ogilvy &
Mather Worldwide; Hill &
Knowlton; Carl Byoir Associates;
Cole & Weber; The Futures Group.

YOUNG & RUBICAM, INC.
285 Madison Avenue, New York, NY   10017

CEO: Michael J. Dolan, CEO   Tel: (212) 210-3000   %FO: 100
Bus: *International advertising agency.*   Fax: (212) 490-9073   Emp: 15,000

● **XANSA PLC**
Campus 300, Maylands Avenue, Hemel Hempstead, Hertfordshire HP2 7TQ, UK

CEO: Jo Connell, Dir.   Tel: 44-144-223-3339   Rev: $563
Bus: *Management consulting and business*   Fax: 44-144-243-4241   Emp: 5,120
technology services.   www.xansa.com

XANSA USA INC.
255 Old New Brunswick Road, Piscataway, NJ   08854

CEO: Jo Connell, Pres.   Tel: (732) 981-1212   %FO: 100
Bus: *Management consulting and*   Fax: (732) 981-1212
business technology services.

XANSA USA INC.
520 White Plains Road, Tarrytown, NY   10571

CEO: Jo Connell, Pres.   Tel: (914) 467-7810   %FO: 100
Bus: *Management consulting and*   Fax: (914) 467-7811
business technology services.

● **XYRATEX**
Langstone Road, Havant, Hampshire PO9 1SA, UK

CEO: Ken Wilkie, CEO   Tel: 44-239-249-6000
Bus: *Mfr. computer hardware.*   Fax: 44-239-249-6001
www.xyratex.co.uk

LOGIC INNOVATIONS, INC.
6205 Lusk Boulevard, San Diego, CA   92121

CEO: Michael Krans   Tel: (858) 455-7200   %FO: 100
Bus: *Sales of digital broadcast*   Fax: (858) 455-7273
transmissions systems.

XYRATEX USA INC.
840 Embarcadero Drive, Ste. 80, West Sacramento, CA 95691
CEO: M. Dinha, COO　　　　　Tel: (916) 375-8181　　　%FO: 100
Bus: *Mfr. high performance network*　Fax: (916) 375-8488
　　storage systems.

● **YULE CATTO & CO. PLC**
Temple Fields, Harlow, Essex CM20 2BH, UK
CEO: Alex Walker, CEO　　　　　Tel: 44-127-944-2791　　Rev: $707
Bus: *Mfr. chemicals.*　　　　　　Fax: 44-127-964-1360　Emp: 4,200
　　　　　　　　　　　　　　www.yulecatto.com

　　OXFORD ORGANICS INC.
　　1160 Mciester Street, Elizabeth, NJ 07201
　　CEO: Alex Walker, Pres.　　　Tel: (908) 351-0002　　%FO: 100
　　Bus: *Mfr./sales chemicals.*　　Fax: (908) 351-0007

● **ZEN RESEARCH PLC**
7th Fl., Augustine House, 6A Austin Friars, London EC2N 2HD, UK
CEO: Davidi Gilo　　　　　　　Tel: 44-207-382-0470
Bus: *Mfr. computer hardware.*　Fax: 44-207-588-6330
　　　　　　　　　　　　　　www.zenresearch.co.uk

　　ZEN RESEARCH, INC.
　　20400 Stevens Creek Blvd., Cupertino, CA 95014
　　CEO: Steven Mulhall, VP　　　Tel: (408) 863-2700　　%FO: 100
　　Bus: *Mfr./sales computer hardware.*　Fax: (408) 863-2772

● **ZENITH MEDIA**
Bridge House, 63-65 North Wharf Road, London W2 1LA, UK
CEO: John Perriss, Chmn.　　　Tel: 44-207-224-8500　　Rev: $8,200
Bus: *Provides global media planning and*　Fax: 44-207-706-2650
　　buying services. (JV Saatchi & Saatchi)　www.zenithmedia.com

　　ZENITH MEDIA SERVICES INC.
　　6600 North Andrews Avenue, Ste. 355, Ft. Lauderdale, FL 33309
　　CEO: Jayne McMahon, VP　　　Tel: (954) 229-0998　　%FO: JV
　　Bus: *Provides media planning services.*　Fax: (954) 229-0494

　　ZENITH MEDIA SERVICES INC.
　　299 West Houston Street, 10th Fl., New York, NY 10014
　　CEO: Richard Hamilton, CEO　Tel: (212) 859-5100　　%FO: JV
　　Bus: *Provides media planning services.*　Fax: (212) 727-9495

ZENITH MEDIA SERVICES INC.
3490 Piedmont Road NE, Ste. 420, Atlanta, GA   30325
CEO: Lowery Ferguson, VP   Tel: (404) 467-5250   %FO: JV
Bus: *Provides media planning services.*   Fax: (404) 467-5251

ZENITH MEDIA SERVICES INC.
735 Battery Street, Ste. 200, San Francisco, CA   94111
CEO: Scott Symonds   Tel: (415) 296-6063   %FO: JV
Bus: *Provides media planning services.*   Fax: (415) 391-8209

ZENITH MEDIA SERVICES INC.
875 North Michigan Avenue, Ste. 2130, Chicago, IL   60611
CEO: Jill Larson, VP   Tel: (312) 266-8043   %FO: JV
Bus: *Provides media planning services.*   Fax: (312) 266-9261

ZENITH MEDIA SERVICES INC.
8400 East Prentice Avenue, Ste. 1110, Englewood, CO   80111
CEO: Linda Vorenkamp   Tel: (303) 793-0734   %FO: JV
Bus: *Provides media planning services.*   Fax: (303) 721-1788

ZENITH MEDIA SERVICES INC.
5285 SW Meadows Road, Ste. 232, Lake Oswego, OR   97035
CEO: Linda Graham   Tel: (503) 598-4648   %FO: JV
Bus: *Provides media planning services.*   Fax: (503) 639-3595

• ZEUS TECHNOLOGY LIMITED
Cambridge Business Park, Cambridge CB4 0WZ, UK
CEO: Adam Twiss, Chmn.   Tel: 44-122-352-5000   Rev: $2
Bus: *Mfr. computer software.*   Fax: 44-122-352-5100   Emp: 35
                                 www.zeustechnology.com

ZEUS TECHNOLOGY
5201 Great America Parkway, Ste. 340, Santa Clara, CA   95054
CEO: John Paterson, CEO   Tel: (408) 350-9400   %FO: 100
Bus: *Mfr./sales computer software*   Fax: (408) 350-9408
     products.

Finland

• A. AHLSTROM CORPORATION

PO Box 329, FIN-00101 Helsinki, Finland

CEO: Juha Rantanen, Pres. & CEO   Tel: 358-9-503-911   Rev: $2,180

Bus: *Mfr. fiber based materials and flexible*   Fax: 358-9-503-9709   Emp: 9,000
     packaging.   www.ahlstrom.com

AHLSTROM DEVELOPMENT CORPORATION

4350 La Jolla Village Drive, San Diego, CA   92122

CEO: Gerald C. Mayers, Pres.   Tel: (619) 550-7020   %FO: 100

Bus: *Development services.*   Fax: (619) 458-9591

AHLSTROM ENGINE FILTRATION, LLC

PO Box 1708, Madisonville, KY   42431

CEO: Dennis Molle   Tel: (270) 821-0140   %FO: 100

Bus: *Mfr. fiber based materials and*   Fax: (270) 824-1526
     flexible packaging.

AHLSTROM ENGINE FILTRATION, LLC

PO Box 680, Taylorville, IL   62568

CEO: Terry Dolence   Tel: (217) 824-9611   %FO: 100

Bus: *Engaged in life science and*   Fax: (217) 824-9514
     filtration process.

AHLSTROM ENGINE FILTRATION, LLC

Two Elm Street, Windsor Locks, CT   06096

CEO: Y. Mosio, CEO   Tel: (860) 654-8300   %FO: 100

Bus: *Mfr. wet-formed, nonwoven*   Fax: (860) 654-8301
     materials.

AHLSTROM ENGINE FILTRATION, LLC

5600 Brainerd Road, Ste. 100, Chattanooga, TN   37411

CEO: Gary Blevins   Tel: (423) 825-3200   %FO: 100

Bus: *Mfr. specialty papers.*   Fax: (423) 825-3299

AHLSTROM MACHINERY, INC.

Ridge Center, Glens Falls, NY   12801-3686

CEO: Robert C. Neapole, Pres.   Tel: (518) 793-5111   %FO: 100

Bus: *Equipment for pulp & paper*   Fax: (518) 793-1917
     industry.

AHLSTROM PAPER GROUP ATLANTA, INC.
10745 Westside Parkway, Alpharetta, GA   30504
CEO: Anna Maija Leskinen, Pres.   Tel: (770) 640-2679   %FO: 100
Bus: *Mfr. specialty papers.*   Fax: (770) 640-2681

AHLSTROM PAPER GROUP BOSTON INC.
Ste. 200, 55 Ferncroft Road, Danvers, MA   01923
CEO: Scott McLaughlin, Pres. & CEO   Tel: (978) 777-9888   %FO: 100
Bus: *Mfr. specialty papers.*   Fax: (978) 777-9444

AHLSTROM PAPER GROUP INC.
PO Box 2179, Glens Falls, NY   12801
CEO: Edward A. Leines, Pres.   Tel: (518) 745-2900   %FO: 100
Bus: *Mfr. specialty papers.*   Fax: (518) 745-2749

AHLSTROM PUMPS LLC.
155 Ahlstrom Way, Easley, SC   29640
CEO: Dale Libby, Pres.   Tel: (864) 855-9090   %FO: 100
Bus: *Equipment for pulp & paper*   Fax: (864) 855-9095
  industry.

AHLSTROM RECOVERY INC.
10745 Westside Parkway, Alpharetta, GA   30201
CEO: Robert C. Neapole, Pres.   Tel: (770) 640-2500   %FO: 100
Bus: *Equipment for pulp & paper*   Fax: (770) 640-9454
  industry.

AHLSTROM SERVICES INC.
Industrial Park, Cogswell Avenue, Pell City, AL   35125
CEO: Dan Roods, VP   Tel: (205) 338-3331   %FO: 100
Bus: *Mfr. equipment for pulp and paper* Fax: (205) 338-3334
  industry.

AHLSTROM TECHNICAL SPECIALTIES, INC.
122 West Butler Street, Mt. Holly Springs, PA   17065-0238
CEO: Christopher Coates, CEO   Tel: (717) 486-3438   %FO: 100
Bus: *Engaged in life science and*   Fax: (717) 486-4863
  filtration process.

AHLSTROM CAPITAL CORPORATION
3820 Mansell Road, Ste. 200, Alpharetta, GA   30022
CEO: Brian Bezanson, Pres.   Tel: (770) 650-2100   %FO: 100
Bus: *Mfr. pumps and specialty papers.* Fax: (770) 650-2101

TITANIUM FABRICATION CORPORATION

110 Lehigh Drive, Fairfield, NJ   07006-3044

CEO: Brent Willey, Pres.

Tel: (973) 227-5300

%FO: 100

Bus: *Mfr./sale titanium equipment for industry.*

Fax: (973) 227-6541

• AMER GROUP LTD.

Mäkelänkatu 91, PO Box 130, FIN-00601 Helsinki, Finland

CEO: Roger Talermo, CEO

Tel: 358-9-757-7800

Rev: $832

Bus: *Mfr./marketing sporting goods, tobacco products & personnel time planning systems.*

Fax: 358-9-757-8200

www.amer.fi

Emp: 4,225

ATOMIC SKI USA INC.

9 Columbia Drive, Amherst, NH   03031

CEO: Jack Baltz, Pres.

Tel: (603) 880-6143

%FO: 100

Bus: *Marketing ski, snowboarding & skating equipment.*

Fax: (603) 880-6099

Emp: 30

WILSON SPORTING GOODS COMPANY

8700 West Bryn Mawr Avenue, Chicago, IL   60631

CEO: Jim Baugh, Pres.

Tel: (773) 714-6400

%FO: 100

Bus: *Mfr./marketing sporting goods; racquet, golf & team sports equipment & apparel.*

Fax: (773) 714-4565

Emp: 3,049

• DUOPLAN OYJ

Teollisuuskatu 33, FIN-00510 Helsinki, Finland

CEO: Heikki I. Mannisto, Pres.

Tel: 358-9-393-3672

Bus: *Consulting engineering services.*

Fax: 358-9-393-3696

www.duoplan.com

Emp: 10

EKONO INC.

11601 NE 2nd St., Ste.107, Bellevue, WA   98004-6409

CEO: Pertti O. Winter, VP

Tel: (425) 455-5969

%FO: 51

Bus: *Consulting engineering to pulp & paper industry.*

Fax: (425) 455-3091

Emp: 8

• FINNAIR OYJ

Tietotie 11A, Helsinki-Vantaa Airport, Box 15, FIN-01053 Helsinki, Finland

CEO: Keijo Suila, Pres. & CEO

Tel: 358-9-818-8100

Rev: $1,500

Bus: *Passenger and cargo air transport.*

Fax: 358-9-818-4092

www.finnair.fi

Emp: 11,260

FINNAIR

228 East 45th Street, New York, NY 10017

CEO: Pekka Immonen, Dir.	Tel: (212) 499-9000	%FO: 100
Bus: *Passenger & cargo air transport.*	Fax: (212) 499-9036	Emp: 100

• **FISKARS CORPORATION**

PO Box 235, FIN-00101 Helsinki, Finland

CEO: Bertel Langenskiöld, Pres. & CEO	Tel: 358-9-618-861	Rev: $824
Bus: *Mfr. seasonal lawn, garden and recreation furniture and home, office and craft products.*	Fax: 358-9-604-053 www.fiskars.fi	Emp: 5,300

FISKARS CONSUMER PRODUCTS GROUP

636 Science Drive, Madison, WI 53711

CEO: William Denton, Pres. & CEO	Tel: (608) 233-1649	%FO: 100
Bus: *Mfr. consumer products.*	Fax: (608) 233-5321	

FISKARS CONSUMER PRODUCTS GROUP

2219 Eagle Drive, Middleton, WI 53562

CEO: William Denton, Pres. & CEO	Tel: (608) 836-3133	%FO: 100
Bus: *Engaged in research and development.*	Fax: (608) 836-3337	

FISKARS CONSUMER PRODUCTS GROUP

610 South 80th Avenue, Phoenix, AZ 85043

CEO: William Denton, Pres. & CEO	Tel: (608) 643-4389	%FO: 100
Bus: *Mfr. aquapore moisture systems.*	Fax: (609) 643-4812	

FISKARS CONSUMER PRODUCTS INC.

780 Carolina Street, Sauk City, WI 53583

CEO: William Denton, Pres. & CEO	Tel: (608) 643-4389	%FO: 100
Bus: *Mfr. lawn and garden cutting tools.*	Fax: (608) 643-4812	

FISKARS CONSUMER PRODUCTS INC.

8300 Highland Drive, Wausau, WI 54401

CEO: William Denton, Pres. & CEO	Tel: (800) 289-8288	%FO: 100
Bus: *Mfr. power tools.*	Fax: (715) 848-3342	

FISKARS CONSUMER PRODUCTS INC.

5951 East Firestone Boulevard, South Gate, CA 90280

CEO: William Denton, Pres. & CEO	Tel: (562) 928-3381	%FO: 100
Bus: *Mfr. royal floor mats.*	Fax: (562) 927-2972	

FISKARS CONSUMER PRODUCTS INC.

7811 West Stewart Avenue, Wausau, WI 54401

CEO: William Denton, Pres. & CEO	Tel: (715) 842-2091	%FO: 100
Bus: *Mfr. crafts products.*	Fax: (715) 848-3657	

FISKARS CONSUMER PRODUCTS INC.

2220 Hicks Road, Ste. 210, Rolling Meadows, IL   60008

CEO: William Denton, Pres. & CEO   Tel: (847) 590-0500   %FO: 100

Bus: *Mfr. school and office products   Fax: (847) 590-0599
    and craft supplies.*

FISKARS CONSUMER PRODUCTS INC.

3555 Holly Lane, Ste. 30, Plymouth, MN   55447

CEO: William Denton, Pres. & CEO   Tel: (612) 557-0107   %FO: 100

Bus: *Mfr. consumer products.*   Fax: (612) 557-9993

FISKARS HOME LEISURE DIV.

3000 West Orange Avenue, Apopka, FL   32703

CEO: Dave Smith, Mgr.   Tel: (407) 889-5533   %FO: 100

Bus: *Mfr. outdoor leisure products and   Fax: (407) 889-7457
    American designer pottery.*

FISKARS SPECIAL MARKETS

2620 Stewart Avenue, Wausau, WI   54402

CEO: William Denton   Tel: (715) 845-3802   %FO: 100

Bus: *Mfr. outdoor leisure products and   Fax: (715) 848-3342
    American designer pottery.*

GERBER LEDENDARY BLADES

14200 Southwest 72nd Avenue, Portland, OR   97224

CEO: Jim Wehrs, Gen. Mgr.   Tel: (503) 639-6161   %FO: 100

Bus: *Mfr. garden tools and blades.*   Fax: (503) 620-3446

POWER SENTRY, DIV. FISKARS INC.

3555 Holy Lane, Ste. 30, Plymouth, MN   55447

CEO: Tim Walsh, Mgr.   Tel: (612) 557-0107   %FO: 100

Bus: *Mfr. plastic and metal products.*   Fax: (612) 557-9993

SYROCO INC.

83 Pine Street, Peabody, MA   10960

CEO: John Fravel, Pres.   Tel: (978) 536-7444   %FO: 100

Bus: *Mfr. resin and aluminum casual   Fax: (978) 536-2007
    furniture.*

● FORTUM (FORMERLY NESTE)

PO Box 1, Keilaniementie 1, FIN-00048 Espoo Fortum, Finland

CEO: Eero Aittola, Pres. & CEO   Tel: 358-10-4511   Rev: $11,026

Bus: *Engaged in energy.*   Fax: 358-10-4524798   Emp: 16,200
          www.fortum.fi

NESTE CORPORATE HOLDING INC.
4400 Post Oak Parkway, Ste. 1230, Houston, TX   77027
CEO: Gerald B. McKenna, Pres.   Tel: (713) 622-7459   %FO: 100
Bus: *Engaged in energy services.*   Fax: (713) 622-5570

TOPKO TIDELANDS OIL PRODUCTION COMPANY
PO Box 1330, Long Beach, CA   90801
CEO: Bob Wages, EVP   Tel: (562) 436-7114   %FO: 100
Bus: *Engaged in energy services.*   Fax: (562) 435-2818

● **F-SECURE CORPORATION**
Tammasaarenkatu 7, PL 24, FIN-00180 Helsinki, Finland
CEO: Risto Siilasmaa, Pres. & CEO   Tel: 358-9-2520-0700   Rev: $39
Bus: *Mfr. Internet security and encryption*   Fax: 358-9-2520-5001   Emp: 300
     software.   www.f-secure.com

   F-SECURE, INC.
   5007 Lincoln Avenue, Ste. 310, Lisle, IL   60532
   CEO: Kurt Mills   Tel: (630) 810-8901   %FO: 100
   Bus: *Mfr./sales Internet security and*   Fax: (630) 810-8904
        encryption software.

   F-SECURE, INC.
   1800 Century Blvd., Ste. 1248, Atlanta, GA   30345
   CEO: Mark Kiyosaki   Tel: (404) 329-3073   %FO: 100
   Bus: *Mfr./sales Internet security and*   Fax: (404) 329-3076
        encryption software.

   F-SECURE, INC.
   320 Decker Drive, Ste. 100, Irving, TX   75062
   CEO: Gary Strom   Tel: (972) 767-2740   %FO: 100
   Bus: *Mfr./sales Internet security and*   Fax: (972) 767-2742
        encryption software.

   F-SECURE, INC.
   255 Bear Hill Road, Waltham, MA   02451
   CEO: Bob Ghoman   Tel: (781) 890-2455   %FO: 100
   Bus: *Mfr./sales Internet security and*   Fax: (781) 890-2465
        encryption software.

   F-SECURE, INC.
   60 East 42nd Street, Ste. 1341, New York, NY   10165
   CEO: Chris Vargas   Tel: (212) 953-2160   %FO: 100
   Bus: *Mfr./sales Internet security and*   Fax: (212) 953-2168
        encryption software.

F-SECURE, INC.
211 North Union Street, Ste. 100, Alexandria, VA   22314
CEO: Steve Trebbe   Tel: (703) 519-1201   %FO: 100
Bus: *Mfr./sales Internet security and*   Fax: (703) 519-1203
     encryption software.

F-SECURE, INC.
PO Box 11086, Marina Del Rey, CA   90295
CEO: Dave Moore   Tel: (714) 272-6627   %FO: 100
Bus: *Mfr./sales Internet security and*   Fax: (714) 272-6627
     encryption software.

F-SECURE, INC.
675 N. First Street, 5th Fl., San Jose, CA   95112
CEO: Mike Devere, VP   Tel: (408) 938-6700   %FO: 100
Bus: *Mfr./sales Internet security and*   Fax: (408) 938-6701
     encryption software.

● **HUHTAMAKI OYJ**
Länsituulentie 7, FIN-02100 Espoo, Finland
CEO: Timo Peltola, CEO   Tel: 358-9-686-881   Rev: $3,115
Bus: *Engaged in consumer packaging;*   Fax: 358-9-660-622   Emp: 23,100
     plastic, paper and disposable tableware.   www.huhtamaki.com

HUHTAMAKI PLASTICS INC.
275 Ferris Avenue, East Providence, RI   02916
CEO: Hein Onkenhout, Pres.   Tel: (401) 438-3410   %FO: 100
Bus: *Mfr. of industrial and consumer*   Fax: (401) 438-5975
     packaging containers and
     materials.

HUHTAMAKI PLASTICS INC.
402 N. 44th Avenue, Ste. A, Phoenix, AZ   85043
CEO: Mark Staton, EVP   Tel: (602) 353-9620   %FO: 100
Bus: *Mfr. plastics.*   Fax: (602) 353-0044

HUHTAMAKI PLASTICS INC.
100 State Street, Fulton, NY   13069
CEO: Mark Staton, COE   Tel: (315) 593-5311   %FO: 100
Bus: *Fruit packaging business unit.*   Fax: (315) 593-5345

HUHTAMAKI PLASTICS INC.
8540 Gerber Road, Sacramento, CA   95828
CEO: Hein Onkenhout, Pres.   Tel: (916) 689-2020   %FO: 100
Bus: *Consumer business unit.*   Fax: (916) 689-1013

SEALRIGHT, DIV. HUHTAMAKI
4209 East Noakes Street, Los Angeles, CA   90023
CEO: Cragi Schuning   Tel: (323) 269-0151   %FO: 100
Bus: *Engaged in consumer packaging;*   Fax: (323) 269-3566
plastic, paper and disposable
tableware.

SEALRIGHT, DIV. HUHTAMAKI
9201 Packaging Drive, Desoto, KS   66018
CEO: Mark Staton, CEO   Tel: (913) 583-3025   %FO: 100
Bus: *Engaged in consumer packaging;*   Fax: (913) 583-8756
plastic, paper and disposable
tableware.

● **JAAKKO PÖYRY GROUP OYJ (FINVEST)**
Jaakonktau 3, PO Box 4, FIN-01621 Vantaa, Finland
CEO: Niilo Pellonmaa, Pres. & CEO   Tel: 358-9-8947-1   Rev: $305
Bus: *Forest industry consulting.*   Fax: 358-9-878-1818   Emp: 4,000
www.poyry.com

     JAAKKO PÖYRY CONSULTING (NORTH AMERICA), INC.
     580 White Plains Road, 3rd Fl., White Plains, NY   10591-5183
     CEO: Heikki Melinen, Pres.   Tel: (914) 332-4000   %FO: 100
     Bus: *Engaged in management*   Fax: (914) 332-4411   Emp: 36
     consulting.

     MARATHON LLC
     2323 East Capital Drive, Appleton, WI   54913-8028
     CEO: Chris Cox, Pres.   Tel: (920) 954-2000   %FO: 100
     Bus: *Engaged in forest industry*   Fax: (920) 954-2020
     engineering and consulting.

● **KONE CORPORATION**
PO Box 8, FIN-00331 Helsinki, Finland
CEO: Antti Herlin, CEO   Tel: 358-20-475-1   Rev: $2,452
Bus: *Mfr. elevators, rail-mounted cranes,*   Fax: 358-20-475-4496   Emp: 22,975
cargo handling and access equipment.   www.kone.com

     CURTIS ELEVATOR CORPORATION
     47-36 36th Street, Long Island City, NY   11101
     CEO: Neil P. Mullane, Pres.   Tel: (718) 361-7200   %FO: 100
     Bus: *Mfr. hydraulic and traction*   Fax: (718) 361-0074
     elevators and escalators.

FLYNN HILL ELEVATOR

47-36 36th Street, Long Island City, NY   11101

CEO: Neil P. Mullane, Pres.	Tel: (718) 361-7200	%FO: 100
Bus: *Mfr. hydraulic and traction elevators and escalators.*	Fax: (718) 361-0074	

KONE, INC.

One Kone Court, Moline, IL   61265

CEO: James G. Claassen, Pres.	Tel: (309) 764-6771	%FO: 100
Bus: *Mfr. hydraulic and traction elevators and escalators.*	Fax: (309) 757-1469	Emp: 4,200

● **METRA CORPORATION**

John Stenbergin ranta 2, Postilokero 230, FIN-00101 Helsinki, Finland

CEO: Georg Ehrnrooth, Pres. & CEO	Tel: 358-9-70951	Rev: $3,061
Bus: *Mfr. diesel engines and security systems.*	Fax: 358-9-762278	Emp: 14,420
	www.metrausa.com	

ENVIROVAC, INC.

1260 Turret Drive, Rockford, IL   6115

CEO: Lon Randol, Dir.	Tel: (815) 654-8300	%FO: 100
Bus: *Mfr. distributor diesel engines and security systems.*	Fax: (815) 654-8306	

● **METSO CORPORATION**

Fabianinkatu 9 A, PO Box 1220, FIN-00101 Helsinki, Finland

CEO: Tor Bergman, CEO	Tel: 358-20-484-100	Rev: $3,665
Bus: *Specializes in automation and information management application networks and systems, fiber and paper machinery, automation and control products for the paper and packaging, construction, and mining industries.*	Fax: 358-20-480-101 www.metsoautomation.com	Emp: 22,000

METSO AUTOMATION INC.

3100 Medlock Bridge Rd, Ste. 250, Norcross, GA   30071

CEO: Antti Kusima, Pres.	Tel: (770) 446-7818	%FO: 100
Bus: *Process automation, integration, distribution and control systems.*	Fax: (770) 446-8794	Emp: 100

METSO AUTOMATION INC.

7000 Hollister, Houston, TX   77040

CEO: Tom Christopher	Tel: (713) 939-9399	%FO: 100
Bus: *Information management and new business solutions.*	Fax: (713) 939-7424	

METSO AUTOMATION INC.
3100 Medlock Bridge Road, Ste. 250, Norcross, GA   30017
CEO: Niel Casale, Pres.   Tel: (704) 588-5530   %FO: 100
Bus: *Mfr. machines.*   Fax: (704) 588-5530

METSO AUTOMATION, INC.
640 Lincoln Street, Worcester, MA   01615
CEO: John Quinlivan, Pres.   Tel: (508) 852-0200   %FO: 100
Bus: *Mfr. valves.*   Fax: (508) 852-8172   Emp: 850

METSO MINERALS, INC.
3073 Chase Avenue, Milwaukee, WI   53207
CEO: Jeff Leonard, Pres.   Tel: (414) 769-4300   %FO: 100
Bus: *Mfr. machinery.*   Fax: (414) 747-1766

METSO PAPER, INC.
15 Allen Street, Hudson Falls, NY   12839-1958
CEO: J. Tiitinen, Mgr.   Tel: (518) 747-3381   %FO: 100
Bus: *Designs and manufactures pulp*   Fax: (518) 747-1541
and paper industry processes,
machinery and equipment.

METSO PAPER, INC.
PO Box 502, Biddeford, ME   04005
CEO: Donald Beaumont, Pres.   Tel: (207) 282-1521   %FO: 100
Bus: *Designs and manufactures pulp*   Fax: (207) 283-0926   Emp: 180
and paper industry processes,
machinery and equipment.

METSO USA
133 Federal Street, Ste. 302, Boston, MA   02110
CEO: Mike Phillips, Pres.   Tel: (617) 369-7850   %FO: 100
Bus: *U.S. headquarters holding*   Fax: (617) 369-7877
company. Mfr./sale metals &
engineering equipment.

● **NOKIA GROUP**
PO Box 226, Keilalandentie 4, FIN-00045 Espoo, Finland
CEO: Jorma Ollila, CEO   Tel: 358-9-18071   Rev: $15,677
Bus: *Telecommunications, mobile phones,*   Fax: 358-9-656388   Emp: 60,000
base stations.   www.nokia.com

NOKIA INC.

6000 Connection Drive, Irving, TX   75039

CEO:K. P. Wilska, Pres.	Tel: (972) 894-5000	%FO: 100
Bus: *Designs, mfr./sales electronics, telecommunications equipment. Telecommunications U.S. headquarters.*	Fax: (972) 491-5888	

NOKIA INTERNET COMMUNICATIONS

313 Fairchild Drive, Mountain View, CA   94043

CEO:Kent Elliot, VP	Tel: (650) 625-5000	%FO: 100
Bus: *Develops IP and internet technologies.*	Fax: (650) 625-5000	

NOKIA MOBILE PHONES

6000 Communication Drive, Irving, TX 75039

CEO:K. P. Wilska, SVP	Tel: (972) 894-5000	%FO: 100
Bus: *Sales of wireless phones and accessories.*	Fax: (972) 894-5000	

● **ORION CORPORATION**

Orionintie 1, FIN-02200 Espoo, Finland

CEO: Jukka Viinanen, CEO	Tel: 358-10-429-4291
Bus: *Engaged in biotechnology.*	Fax: 358-10-429-2801
	www.orion.fi

ORION PHARMA INC.

c/o Target Research, 554 Central Avenue, New Providence, NJ   07974

CEO:Pekka Rautala	Tel: (908) 464-7500	%FO: 100
Bus: *Engaged in biotechnology.*	Fax: (908) 464-3529	

● **OUTOKUMPU OYJ**

Riihitontuntie 7B, FIN-02201 Espoo, Finland

CEO: Jyrki Juusela, CEO	Tel: 358-94211	Rev: $3,477
Bus: *Mfr. base metals, stainless steel and copper products.*	Fax: 358-9421-3888	Emp: 11,930
	www.outokmpu.fi	

AVESTA SHEFFIELD BAR COMPANY

3043 Crenshaw Pkwy., Richburg, SC   29729

CEO:Louis Kern, VP	Tel: (803) 789-5385	%FO: 100
Bus: *Mfr. stainless steel bars.*	Fax: (803) 789-3177	Emp: 14

THE NEUMAYER COMPANY

PO Box 620236, Middleton, WI   53562-0236

CEO:Heinz Hiesbock, Pres.	Tel: (608) 836-6664	%FO: 100
Bus: *Mfr. base metals.*	Fax: (608) 836-9266	

THE NIPPERT COMPANY
801 Pittsburgh Drive, Delaware, OH   43015
CEO: Russell Nippert, Pres.   Tel: (740) 363-1981   %FO: JV
Bus: *Mfr. base metals.*   Fax: (740) 363-3847

OUTOKUMPU COPPER AMERICAS, INC.
PO Box 981, Buffalo, NY   14240-0981
CEO: Warren Bartel, Pres.   Tel: (716) 879-6700   %FO: 100
Bus: *Mfr. brass products.*   Fax: (716) 879-6735

OUTOKUMPU COPPER FRANKLIN INC.
PO Box 539, Franklin, KY   42135
CEO: Gene Drape, Pres.   Tel: (502) 586-8201   %FO: 100
Bus: *Mfr. copper products.*   Fax: (502) 586-7404

OUTOKUMPU COPPER USA, INC.
129 Fairfield Way, Bloomington, IL   60108
CEO: Uls Anvin, Pres.   Tel: (630) 980-8400   %FO: 100
Bus: *Mfr./sale copper products.*   Fax: (630) 980-8891

OUTOKUMPU MINTEC USA INC.
109 Inverness Drive East, Englewood, CO   80112
CEO: Jaho Makinen   Tel: (303) 792-3110   %FO: 100
Bus: *Mfr. base metals; stainless steel*   Fax: (303) 799-6892
    and copper products.

OUTOKUMPU TECHNOLOGY, INC.
109 Inverness Drive East, Suite F, Englewood, CO   80112
CEO: David Green, Pres.   Tel: (303) 792-3110   %FO: 100
Bus: *Mfr. base metals; stainless steel*   Fax: (303) 799-6862
    and copper products.

OUTOKUMPU TECHNOLOGY, INC., CARPCO DIV.
1310-1 Tradeport Drive, Jacksonville, FL   32218
CEO: David Green, Pres.   Tel: (904) 353-3681   %FO: 100
Bus: *Design and distribute gravity,*   Fax: (904) 353-8705
    magnetic and electrostatic
    separation equipment.

PRINCETON GAMMA-TECH, INC.
PO Box CN863, Princeton, NJ   08542-0863
CEO: Douglas Skinner, Pres.   Tel: (609) 924-7310   %FO: 100
Bus: *Mfr. high-tech equipment.*   Fax: (609) 924-1729

VALLEYCAST

PO Box 1714, Appleton, WI   54912

CEO: Charles McClay, Pres. Tel: (920) 749-3820 %FO: 100

Bus: *Mfr. base metals; stainless steel* Fax: (920) 749-3830
and copper products.

● **PARTEK AB, OYJ**

Sörnäisten rantatie 23/25, PO Box 61, FIN-00501 Helsinki, Finland

CEO: Christoffer Taxell, Pres. & CEO Tel: 358-204-55-4261 Rev: $2,500

Bus: *Materials handling, minerals, insulation.* Fax: 358-204-55-4844 Emp: 12,000
www.partek.fi

KALMAR INDUSTRIES CORP.

415 East Dundee Street, Ottawa, KS   66067

CEO: Jorma Tirkkonen, Pres. Tel: (785) 242-2200 %FO: 100

Bus: *Mfr. container handling equipment.* Fax: (785) 242-6117

KALMAR, INC.

777 Brickell Avenue, Suite 640, Miami, FL   33121-2803

CEO: K. Holmroos, Pres. Tel: (305) 379-6200 %FO: 100

Bus: *Materials handling, minerals,* Fax: (305) 379-8822
forest products, insulation.

KALMAR, INC.

21 Engelhard Drive, Cranberry, NJ   08512

CEO: Jorma Tirkonnen, Pres. Tel: (609) 860-0150 %FO: 100

Bus: *Materials handling, minerals,* Fax: (609) 850-0224
forest products, insulation.

KALTEX, INC.

2310 Peachtree Road, Atlanta, GA   30338

CEO: Warwick Johnston, Exec.VP Tel: (770) 457-8795 %FO: 100

Bus: *Materials handling, minerals,* Fax: (770) 454-7908
forest products, insulation.

PARTEK FOREST

103 North 12th St., PO Box 401, Gladstone, MI   49837-0401

CEO: K. Lannenpaa, Pres. Tel: (906) 428-4800 %FO: 100

Bus: *Mfr. forest machines.* Fax: (906) 428-3922

● **RAUTARUUKKI OYJ**

PO Box 217, FIN-90101, Oulu, Finland

CEO: Mikko Kivimaki, Chmn. Tel: 358-8-88360 Rev: $3,034

Bus: *Mfr. hot and cold rolled steel sheets,* Fax: 358-8-8836450 Emp: 13,250
pipes and tubes. www.rautaruukki.fi

FINNSTEEL INC.
Five Revere Drive, Ste. 502, Northbrook, IL   60062
CEO: Tage L. Lindholm, Pres.   Tel: (847) 480-0420
Bus: *Wholesale hot and cold rolled*   Fax: (847) 480-9466
steel sheets, pipes and tubes.

● **SAMPO PLC (FORMLERLY LEONIA BANK PLC)**
Yliopistonkatu 27, Sampo-Leonia, FIN-20075 Turku, Finland
CEO: Björn Wahlroos, Chmn. & CEO   Tel: 358-10-515-10   Rev: $5,213
Bus: *Commercial banking services.*   Fax: 358-10-514-1811   Emp: 9,185
www.leonia.fi

    LEONIA BANK PLC
    60 East 42nd Street, Ste. 2544, New York, NY   10165
    CEO: Jukka Hakila, Rep.   Tel: (212) 949-6787   %FO: 100
    Bus: *International banking services.*   Fax: (212) 949-6791

● **SONERA CORPORATION**
Teollisuuskatu 15, FIN-00051 Helsinki Sonera, Finland
CEO: Aimo Eloholma, CEO   Tel: 358-204-01   Rev: $1,937
Bus: *Engaged in wireless*   Fax: 358-2040-60025   Emp: 9,000
telecommunications.   www.sonera.fi

    SONERA CORPORATION
    440 Route 22 East, Grand Commons, Bridgewater, NJ   08807
    CEO: Steve Fleischer, VP   Tel: (908) 203-8500   %FO: 100
    Bus: *Wireless telecommunications.*   Fax: (908) 203-8500

● **STORA ENSO OYJ FINLAND**
Kanavaranta 1, FIN-00160 Helsinki, Finland
CEO: Jukka Harmala, CEO   Tel: 358-9-2046-131   Rev: $12,260
Bus: *Mfr. forest products/paper.*   Fax: 358-9-2046-21471   Emp: 40,226
www.storaenso.com

    CONSOLIDATED PAPERS, INC.
    231 First Avenue North, Wisconsin Rapids, WI   54495
    CEO: George W. Mead, Chmn.   Tel: (715) 422-3111   %FO: 100
    Bus: *Mfr. coated and supercalendered*   Fax: (715) 422-3469   Emp: 6,800
    printing papers for brochures and
    magazines.

STORA ENSO NORTH AMERICA CORPORATION
Two Landmark Square, 3rd Fl., Stamford, CT 06901-2792
CEO: Kal Korhonen, SVP Tel: (203) 356-2300 %FO: JV
Bus: *Distribution forest products; pulp,* Fax: (203) 356-2340 Emp: 100
papers, packaging paper and
board and building materials.

● **SUUNTO OYJ**
Juvan Teollisuuskatu 8, FIN-02920 Espoo, Finland
CEO: Dan W. Colliander, Pres. Tel: 358-9-847033
Bus: *Mfr. marine field compasses,* Fax: 358-9-8438108 Emp: 600
professional instruments. www.suunto.fi

SUUNTO USA
2151 Las Palmas Dr, Ste. G, Carlsbad, CA 92009
CEO: Henri Syvanen, Pres. Tel: (760) 931-6788 %FO: 100
Bus: *Distribution/sale compasses,* Fax: (760) 931-9875 Emp: 18
professional instruments, camping
equipment.

● **TAMFELT CORPORATION**
PO Box 427, FIN-33101 Tampere, Finland
CEO: Risto Hautamaki , Pres. & CEO Tel: 358-3-363-9111 Rev: $117
Bus: *Mfr. industrial textiles.* Fax: 358-3-356-0120 Emp: 1,350
www.tamfelt.fi

TAMFELT, INC.
PO Box 9115, Canton, MA   02021
CEO: Risto Hautamaki, Pres. Tel: (781) 828-3350 %FO: 100
Bus: *Mfr. industrial textiles.* Fax: (781) 828-0848

● **UPM KYMMENE GROUP**
Etelaeslanad 12, FIN-00101 Helsinki, Finland
CEO: Juha Niemelä, Pres. & CEO Tel: 358-204-15111 Rev: $9,841
Bus: *Mfr. forest industries and related* Fax: 358-204-15110 Emp: 32,350
products. www.upm-kymmene.com

BLANDIN PAPER COMPANY
115 Southwest First Street, Grand Rapids, MN 57744
CEO: Kevin Lyden, Pres. & CEO Tel: (218) 327-6200 %FO: 100
Bus: *Mfr. lightweight coated paper.* Fax: (218) 327-6212

ROSENLEW INC.
1812 Brittmoore Road, Houston, TX 77043
CEO: Lauri Haapkyla, Pres. Tel: (713) 461-0840
Bus: *Paper packaging.* Fax: (713) 461-0654

UPM-KYMMENE USA
9 Rockefeller Plaza, 4th Floor, New York, NY   10020
CEO: Bengt Shoblom, Pres.   Tel: (212) 246-9373   %FO: 100
Bus: *Distribution printing and writing*   Fax: (212) 765-0869   Emp: 12
      papers.

● **VAISALA OYJ**
Postilokero 26, FIN-00421 Helsinki, Finland
CEO: Pekka Ketonen, Pres.   Tel: 358-9-89491   Rev: $129
Bus: *Mfr. meteorological instruments.*   Fax: 358-9-49227   Emp: 750
                                         www.vaisala.com

   VAISALA, INC.
   100 Commerce Way, Woburn, MA   01801-1068
   CEO: Steven H. Chansky, Pres.   Tel: (781) 933-4500   %FO: 100
   Bus: *Mfr. meteorological instruments.*   Fax: (781) 933-8029   Emp: 80

   VAISALA, INC.
   1288 Reamwood Avenue, Sunnyvale, CA   94089-2233
   CEO: Steven H. Chansky, Pres.   Tel: (408) 734-9640   %FO: 100
   Bus: *Mfr. meteorological instruments.*   Fax: (408) 734-9640

● **VALMET AUTOMOTIVE, DIV. METSO CORPORATION**
PO Box 4, FIN-23501 Uusikaupunki, Finland
CEO: Tapio Kuisma, Pres. & CEO   Tel: 358-20-484-180
Bus: *Contract manufacturer of premium*   Fax: 358-20-484-181   Emp: 13,000
      specialty cars.   www.valmet.com

   VALMET AUTOMOTIVE, DIV. METSO USA
   133 Federal Street, Ste. 302, Boston, MA   02110
   CEO: Mike Phillips, Pres.   Tel: (617) 369-7850   %FO: 100
   Bus: *US headquarters office.*   Fax: (617) 369-7877

France

● **ACCOR S.A.**
Tour Maine Montparnasse, 33 avenue du Maine, F-75755 Paris Cedex 15, France

CEO: Jean-Marc Espalioux, Pres. & CEO	Tel: 33-1-4538-8600	Rev: $6,534
Bus: *Hotel owner/manager and catering; Sofitel, Motel 6 and retirement homes.*	Fax: 33-1-4538-7134 www.accor.com	Emp: 128,850

ACCOR NORTH AMERICA CORPORATION
245 Park Avenue, 26th Fl., New York, NY   10167

CEO: Jean-Francois Maljean, Pres.	Tel: (212) 949-5700	%FO: 100
Bus: *Management of hotels (Sofitel, Motel 6) and restaurants.*	Fax: (212) 490-0499	

● **ACTIVCARD S.A.**
24-28 Avenue de General de Gaulle, F-92156 Suresnes Cedex, France

CEO: Jean-Gerard Galvez, CEO	Tel: 33-1-4204-8400	Rev: $18
Bus: *Designs smart cards and security software for network servers.*	Fax: 33-1-4204-8484 www.activcard.com	Emp: 113

ACTIVCARD, INC.
6623 Dumbarton Circle, Fremont, CA   94555

CEO: Victor Cebollero	Tel: (510) 574-0100	%FO: 100
Bus: *Designs smart cards and security software for network servers.*	Fax: (510) 574-0101	

● **AEROSPATIALE**
37 blvd. de Montmorency, F-75781 Paris Cedex 16, France

CEO: Philippe Camus, Chmn.	Tel: 33-1-4224-2424	Rev: $9,770
Bus: *Design/mfr. aircraft, aircraft engines and parts.*	Fax: 33-1-4224-5414 www.aerospatiale.fr	Emp: 36,650

AEROSPATIALE, INC.
1101 15th Street, N.W., Washington, DC   20005

CEO: Gregory Bradford, Pres.	Tel: (202) 293-0650	%FO: 100
Bus: *U.S. headquarters for Aerospatiale SNL.*	Fax: (202) 429-0638	

● **AGENCE FRANCE-PRESSE**
13, place de la Bourse, F-75002 Paris, France

CEO: Bertrand Eveno, Chmn. & CEO	Tel: 33-1-4041-4646	Rev: $310
Bus: *Worldwide news agency.*	Fax: 33-1-4240-4632 www.afp.com	Emp: 3,400

AGENCE FRANCE-PRESSE
1015 15th Street NW, 5th Fl., Washington, DC   20005
CEO: Dan Kobermann, Mgr.   Tel: (202) 289-0700   %FO: 100
Bus: *International news agency.*   Fax: (202) 414-0634

● **AIR FRANCE COMPAGNIE NATIONALE**
45, rue de Paris, F-95747 Roissy CDG Cedex, France
CEO: Jean-Cyril Spinetta, Chrm.   Tel: 33-1-4156-7800   Rev: $10,705
Bus: *Commercial airline and catering*   Fax: 33-1-4156-8419   Emp: 55,200
services.   www.airfrance.com

    AIR FRANCE
    125 West 55th Street, New York, NY   10019
    CEO: Jean-Louis Pinson, EVP   Tel: (212) 830-4000   %FO: 100
    Bus: *International air transport*   Fax: (212) 830-4244   Emp: 70
    services.

● **AIR LIQUIDE GROUP SA**
75 quai d'Orsay, F-75321 Paris Cedex 07, France
CEO: Alain Joly, CEO   Tel: 33-1-4062-5555   Rev: $8,100
Bus: *Specializes in industrial and medical*   Fax: 33-1-4555-5876   Emp: 30,000
gases and related services.   www.airliquide.com

    AIR LIQUIDE AMERICA CORPORATION
    13546 N. Central Expressway, Dallas, TX   75243
    CEO: Pierre Dufour, Pres. & CEO   Tel: (972) 995-2709   %FO: 100
    Bus: *Engineering/construction services,*   Fax: (972) 995-3204
    welding, diving and medical
    equipment.

    AIR LIQUIDE AMERICA CORPORATION
    2700 Post Oak Blvd., Ste. 1800, Houston, TX   77056
    CEO: Pierre Dufour, Pres. & CEO   Tel: (713) 624-8000   %FO: 100
    Bus: *Engineering/construction services,*   Fax: (713) 624-8030
    welding, diving and medical
    equipment.

    AIR LIQUIDE PROCESS & CONSTRUCTION, INC.
    2700 Post Oak Blvd., Ste. 1800, Houston, TX   7056
    CEO: Pierre Dufour, Pres. & CEO   Tel: (877) 855-9533   %FO: 100
    Bus: *Engaged in engineering and*   Fax: (713) 624-8030
    construction.

    AQUA-LUNG AMERICA
    2340 Cousteau Court, Vista, CA   92083
    CEO: Pierre Dufour, Pres. & CEO   Tel: (760) 597-5000   %FO: 100
    Bus: *Mfr. diving equipment.*   Fax: (760) 597-4900

CALGAZ, DIV. AIR LIQUIDE
821 Chesapeake Drive, Cambridge, MD   21613
CEO: Emerson Todd, Pres.   Tel: (800) 638-1197   %FO: 100
Bus: *Mfr. calibration gas mixtures and*   Fax: (410) 228-4251
    related equipment.

MEDAL LP
305 Water Street, Newport, DE   19804
CEO: Pierre Dufour, Pres. & CEO   Tel: (302) 999-6130   %FO: 100
Bus: *Engaged in research and*   Fax: (302) 999-6131
    development.

RANSOME COMPANY
3511 West 12th Street, Houston, TX   77008
CEO: J. P. Jurgielewicz   Tel: (713) 438-6400   %FO: 100
Bus: *Mfr. welding materials.*   Fax: (713) 438-6810

RANSOME COMPANY
5153 Westminster Place, St. Louis, MO   63108
CEO: Steve Gray, Mgr.   Tel: (314) 361-2405   %FO: 100
Bus: *Mfr. welding materials.*   Fax: (314) 753-8594

US DIVERS, INC.
PO Box 25018, Santa Ana, CA   92799-8010
CEO: Pierre Dufour, Pres. & CEO   Tel: (714) 540-8010   %FO: 100
Bus: *Mfr. diving equipment.*   Fax: (714) 432-9340

● **AIRBUS INDUSTRIE**
1 Rond Point Maurice Bellonte, F-31707 Blagnac Cedex, France
CEO: Manfred Bishoff, Chmn.   Tel: 33-5-6193-3431   Rev: $13,000
Bus: *Mfr. aircraft.*   Fax: 33-5-6193-4955   Emp: 2,290
                          www.airbus.com

    AIRBUS INDUSTRIE OF NORTH AMERICA, INC.
    198 Van Buren Street, Herndon, VA   20170
    CEO: Clyde Kizer, Pres.   Tel: (703) 834-3400
    Bus: *Provides after sales support for*   Fax: (703) 834-3340
      commercial aircraft.

    AIRBUS INDUSTRIE OF NORTH AMERICA, INC.
    198 Van Buren Street, Herndon, VA   20170
    CEO: Henri Courpron, CEO   Tel: (703) 834-3400   %FO: JV
    Bus: *Mfr./sales aircraft.*   Fax: (703) 834-3340

• ALCATEL

54 rue La Boétie, F-75008 Cedex 8 Paris, France
CEO: Serge Tchuruk, Chrm.   Tel: 33-1-4076-1010   Rev: $25,007
Bus: *Develops/produces/distributes*   Fax: 33-1-4076-1400   Emp: 118,300
telecommunications equipment and   www.alcatel.com
systems and manufactures equipment for
electric power generation.

ALCATEL INTERNETWORKING

26801 West Agoura Road, Calabasas, CA   91301
CEO: Patrick Liot, Pres.   Tel: (818) 880-3500   %FO: 100
Bus: *Mfr. high bandwidth switching*   Fax: (818) 880-3505
systems.

ALCATEL NA CABLE SYSTEMS, INC.

39 Second Street NW, PO Box 900, Hickory, NC   28601
CEO: C J. Phillips, Pres.   Tel: (828) 323-1120   %FO: 100
Bus: *Supplies cable and*   Fax: (828) 328-6339
telecommunications equipment.

ALCATEL TELECOMMUNICATIONS CABLE

2512 Penny Road, PO Box 39, Claremont, NC   28610
CEO: John Steen, Pres.   Tel: (828) 459-9787   %FO: 100
Bus: *Supplies cable and*   Fax: (828) 459-9312
telecommunications equipment.

ALCATEL USA, INC.

1000 Coit Road, Plano, TX   75075-5813
CEO: Mike Quigley, Pres.   Tel: (972) 519-3000   %FO: 100
Bus: *Engaged in telecommunications.*   Fax: (972) 519-2203

ALCATEL USA, INC.

44983 Knoll Square, Ashburn, VA   20147
CEO: Jean-Luc Abaziou, SVP   Tel: (703) 654-8000   %FO: 100
Bus: *Provides network communications.*   Fax: (703) 724-2156

BERK-TEL, DIV. ALCATEL

132 Oak Road, New Holland, PA   17557
CEO: Kevin St. Cyr, Pres.   Tel: (717) 354-6200   %FO: 100
Bus: *Telecommunications and cable*   Fax: (717) 354-7944
systems.

GENESYS TELECOMMUNICATIONS INC.

1155 Market Street, 11th Fl., San Francisco, CA   94103
CEO: Orl Sasson, Pres.   Tel: (415) 437-1100   %FO: 100
Bus: *Telecommunications and cable*   Fax: (415) 437-1260
systems.

● **ALDES AERAULIQUE**

20 Blvd. Joliot-Curie, F-69694 Venissieux, France

CEO: Bruno Lacroix, CEO   Tel: 33-4-7877-1515

Bus: *Mfr. ventilation, fire protection*   Fax: 33-4-7876-1597   Emp: 500
    equipment & metal stamping.   www.aldes.com

   AMERICAN ALDES VENTILATION CORPORATION

   4537 Northgate Court, Sarasota, FL 34234-2124

   CEO: Dwight R. Shackelford, EVP   Tel: (941) 351-3441   %FO: 100

   Bus: *Distribution ventilation products.*   Fax: (941) 351-3442   Emp: 6

● **ALSTOM SA**

25, Avenue Kléber, F-75795 Paris Cedex 16, France

CEO: Pierre Bilger, Chmn. & CEO   Tel: 33-1-4755-2000   Rev: $22,000

Bus: *Engaged in in power generation, power*   Fax: 33-1-4755-2861   Emp: 120,675
   transmission, distribution and power   www.alstom.com
   conversion; and in transport through its
   activities in rail and marine.

   ALSTOM AUTOMATION SCHILLING ROBONICS, INC.

   201 Cousteau Place, Davis, CA 95616

   CEO: Tyler Schilling, Pres.   Tel: (530) 753-6718   %FO: 100

   Bus: *Hydraulic equipment.*   Fax: (530) 753-8092

   ALSTOM DRIVES & CONTROLS, INC.

   301 Alpha Drive, Pittsburgh, PA 15238

   CEO: Frank C. Volker, Pres.   Tel: (412) 967-0765   %FO: 100

   Bus: *Electrical engineering.*   Fax: (412) 967-7660

   ALSTOM ESCA CORPORATION

   11120 Northeast 33rd Place, Bellevue, WA 98004

   CEO: Alain Steven, Pres. & CEO   Tel: (425) 822-6800   %FO: 100

   Bus: *Develops/designs computer*   Fax: (425) 889-1700
    software for the electrical utility
    industry.

   ALSTOM ENERGY SYSTEMS

   1550 Lehigh Drive, Easton, PA 18042

   CEO: Alfred Brady, Pres. & CEO   Tel: (610) 250-1000   %FO: JV

   Bus: *Condensers & dampers.*   Fax: (610) 250-1005

   ALSTOM T&D EQUIPMENT

   1128 Mansfield Avenue, Indiana, PA 15701

   CEO: Patrick E. Pries, Mgr.   Tel: (724) 349-6332

   Bus: *Mfr. T&D equipment for industrial*   Fax: (724) 349-8201
    markets.

ALSTOM T&D EQUIPMENT

11767 Katy Freeway, Ste. 900, Houston, TX   77079

CEO: Frank Reyna, Mgr.   Tel: (281) 496-9449

Bus: *Mfr. T&D equipment for the oil*   Fax: (281) 589-8330
and gas industry.

ALSTOM USA

132A Osigian Blvd., Warner Robins, GA   31088

CEO: Jeff Loewen, Mgr.   Tel: (912) 971-4005

Bus: *Medium voltage contactor and*   Fax: (912) 971-4008
service unit.

ALSTOM USA

11120 NE 33rd Place, Bellevue, WA   98004

CEO: J. D. Hammerly, VP   Tel: (425) 822-6800

Bus: *Generators, motors, controls,*   Fax: (425) 889-1700
valves, pumps, transportation and
marine equipment.

ALSTOM USA

907 Audelia Road, Richardson, TX   75081

CEO: Ken Milligan, Mgr.   Tel: (972) 497-9992

Bus: *Generators, motors, controls,*   Fax: (972) 497-9857
valves, pumps, transportation and
marine equipment.

ALSTOM USA

1000 Show Creek, Normal, IL   61761

CEO: Jim Kriter, Mgr.   Tel: (309) 452-5628

Bus: *Generators, motors, controls,*   Fax: (309) 452-6801
valves, pumps, transportation and
marine equipment.

ALSTOM USA

600 West Germantown Pike, Ste. 131, Plymouth Meeting, PA   19462

CEO: John Valosky, Mgr.   Tel: (610) 832-8840

Bus: *Generators, motors, controls,*   Fax: (610) 825-3269
valves, pumps, transportation and
marine equipment.

ALSTOM USA

11693 San Vincente Blvd., Ste. 152, Los Angeles, CA   90049

CEO: Fadi Aghnatios, Mgr.   Tel: (310) 476-8147

Bus: *Generators, motors, controls,*   Fax: (310) 476-2837
valves, pumps, transportation and
marine equipment.

ALSTOM USA

300 West Antelope Road, Medford, OR   97503

CEO: Tom Steeber, Mgr.   Tel: (724) 483-7308

Bus: *Medium voltage contactor and*   Fax: (724) 483-7771
     service unit.

ALSTOM USA

9400 Ravenwood Circle, Knoxville, TN   37922

CEO: Karl Poelti, Mgr.   Tel: (865) 670-9646

Bus: *Generators, motors, controls,*   Fax: (865) 670-9647
     valves, pumps, transportation and
     marine equipment.

ALSTOM USA INC.

4 Skyline Drive, Hawthorne, NY   10532

CEO: Paul J. Jancek, Pres.   Tel: (914) 345-5137   %FO: 20

Bus: *Generators, motors, controls,*   Fax: (914) 345-5114
     valves, pumps, transportation and
     marine equipment.

● **AMYOT**

1 rue Denis Papin, F-25303 Pontarlier, France

CEO: Michel Amyot, Pres.   Tel: 33-3-8146-2930

Bus: *Mfr. drill chucks and accessories.* Fax: 33-3-8139-6249   Emp: 100

    LFA INDUSTRIES INC.

    PO Box 127, Brookfield, IL   60513

    CEO: Sigmund Travis   Tel: (708) 485-6610   %FO: 50

    Bus: *Mfr./distribution drill chucks and* Fax: (708) 485-6610   Emp: 8
        accessories.

● **APEM SA**

Centre d'Affaires Paris-Nord, Tour Continental, P 200, F-93153 Le Blanc Mesnil Cedex, France

CEO: Georges Ranson, CEO   Tel: 33-1-4814-9265   Rev: $959

Bus: *Mfr. switches, keyboards and*   Fax: 33-1-4814-9284   Emp: 378
     assemblies.   www.apem.fr

    APEM WORLDWIDE

    PO Box 8288, Haverhill, MA   01835-0788

    CEO: Sid Hooper   Tel: (978) 372-1602   %FO: 100

    Bus: *Mfr. switches, keyboards and*   Fax: (978) 372-3534
        assemblies.

- **VERRERIE CRISTALLERIE D'ARQUES, J G DURAND & CIE**

Av. Charles de Gaulle, F-62510 Arques, France

CEO: Philippe Durand, Pres.   Tel: 33-3-21-2193-0000

Bus: *Mfr. lead crystal and glass dinner, stem,*   Fax: 33-3-21-2138-0623   Emp: 13,000
bar, cook/serve and giftware.   www.arc-international.com

    ARC INTERNATIONAL/DURAND GLASS

    Wade Boulevard, Millville, NJ   08332

    CEO: Fred Dohn, CEO   Tel: (609) 825-5620   %FO: 100

    Bus: *Mfr./sales lead crystal and glass*   Fax: (609) 696-3442   Emp: 850
    dinner, stem, bar, cook/serve and
    giftware.

    ARC INTERNATIONAL/DURAND GLASS

    500 Davis Street, Ste. 512, Evanston, IL   60201

    CEO: Fred Dohn, CEO   Tel: (847) 733-0091   %FO: 100

    Bus: *Mfr./sales lead crystal and glass*   Fax: (847) 733-0092
    dinner, stem, bar, cook/serve and
    giftware.

    ARC INTERNATIONAL/DURAND GLASS

    660 South Figueroa St., Ste. 1950, Los Angeles, CA   90017

    CEO: Fred Dohn, CEO   Tel: (213) 624-2609   %FO: 100

    Bus: *Mfr./sales lead crystal and glass*   Fax: (213) 624-3817
    dinner, stem, bar, cook/serve and
    giftware.

    ARC INTERNATIONAL/DURAND GLASS

    230 Spring Street, Ste. 933, Atlanta, GA   30303

    CEO: Fred Dohn, CEO   Tel: (404) 688-5021   %FO: 100

    Bus: *Mfr./sales lead crystal and glass*   Fax: (404) 688-4004
    dinner, stem, bar, cook/serve and
    giftware.

    ARC INTERNATIONAL/DURAND GLASS

    41 Madison Avenue, 20th Fl., New York, NY   10010

    CEO: Fred Dohn, CEO   Tel: (212) 684-3680   %FO: 100

    Bus: *Mfr./sales lead crystal and glass*   Fax: (212) 532-8640
    dinner, stem, bar, cook/serve and
    giftware.

- **ARIANESPACE SA**

Boulevard de l'Europe, B P 177, F-91006 Evry Cedex, France

CEO: Jean Marie Luton, Chmn. & CEO   Tel: 33-1-6087-6000   Rev: $1,254

Bus: *Production/marketing/sales operations*   Fax: 33-1-6087-6247   Emp: 320
for launch services worldwide.   www.arianespace.com

ARIANESPACE, INC.
601 13th Street NW, Ste. 710, Washington, DC   20005
CEO: Leo Mondale, Pres.   Tel: (202) 628-3936   %FO: 100
Bus: *Satellite launching services.*   Fax: (202) 628-3949   Emp: 6

● **ARKOPHARMA**
Zone Industrielle de Carros, 1 re avenue 2079M, F-06511 Carros, France
CEO: Colette Rober, CEO   Tel: 33-4-9329-1128   Rev: $138
Bus: *Mfr. nutritional supplements and herbal* Fax: 33-4-9329-1162   Emp: 1,025
medicines.   www.arkopharma.com

ARKOPHARMA INC.
19 Crosby Drive, Bedford, MA   01730
CEO: Christian Seyrig, VP   Tel: (781) 276-0505   %FO: 100
Bus: *Mfr. nutritional supplements and*   Fax: (781) 276-7335
herbal medicines.

● **ATOS ORIGIN**
3, place de la Pyramide, F-92067 Paris La Défense Cedex, France
CEO: Bernard Bourigeaud, Chmn.   Tel: 33-1-4900-9000   Rev: $2,800
Bus: *Provides information technology and e-*   Fax: 33-1-4773-0763   Emp: 27,000
business solutions.   www.atos-group.com

ATOS ORIGIN
1764-A New Durham Road, South Plainfield, NJ   07080-2328
CEO: Kim Cameron, Pres.   Tel: (972) 861-1700   %FO: 100
Bus: *Provides information technology*   Fax: (972) 861-1994
and e-business solutions.

● **ATOS ORIGIN B.V., DIV. PHILIPS ELECTRONICS**
Immeuble Ile-de-France 3, place de la Pyramide, F-92067 Paris La Défense Cedex France
CEO: Bernard Bourigeaud, CEO   Tel: 33-1-4900-9000   Rev: $2,400
Bus: *Provides information technology*   Fax: 33-1-4773-0763   Emp: 27,000
development.   www.atosorigin.com

ATOS ORIGIN TECHNOLOGY IN BUSINESS INC.
1764-A New Durham Road, South Plainfield, NJ   07080-2328
CEO: Ken Cameron   Tel: (732) 572-4900   %FO: 100
Bus: *Provides information technology*   Fax: (732) 572-4998
development.

● **AUCHAN**
40 Avenue de Flandre, BP 139, F-59964 Croix Cedex, France
CEO: Gerard Mulliez, Pres.   Tel: 33-3-2081-6800   Rev: $24,500
Bus: *Retail supermarkets.*   Fax: 33-3-2081-6909   Emp: 107,000
                                       www.auchan.com

AUCHAN USA, INC.
8800 W. Sam Houston Pkwy South, Houston, TX   77099
CEO: Gerard Gallet, Pres.   Tel: (281) 530-9855   %FO: 100
Bus: *Retail supermarkets.*   Fax: (281) 530-2533   Emp: 500

● **AUDAX INDUSTRIES**
2 rue de Tours, F-72500 Chateau du Loir, France
CEO: Dominique de Gelis, CEO   Tel: 33-1-344-0235
Bus: *Mfr. loudspeaker components.*   Fax: 33-1-344-1202
                                       www.audax.fr

    AUDAX OF AMERICA
    6 New England Executive Park, Ste. 455, Burlington, MA   01803
    CEO: Ralph Nichols, Gen. Mgr.   Tel: (781) 229-7355   %FO: 100
    Bus: *Distribution loudspeaker*   Fax: (781) 229-7356   Emp: 6
        components.

● **AVENTIS PHARMA**
F-67917 Strasbourg Cedex 9 Strasbourg, France
CEO: Jürgen Dormann, Chmn. & CEO   Tel: 33-3-8899-1100   Rev: $21,006
Bus: *Engaged in pharmaceuticals and animal* Fax: 33-3-8899-1101   Emp: 92,500
    health products.   www.aventis.com

    ASTRO ARC POLYSOUDE, INC.
    W133 N5138 Campbell Drive, Menomonee Falls, WI   53051
    CEO: William Heller, VP   Tel: (262) 783-2732   %FO: 100
    Bus: *Mfr. pharmaceuticals.*   Fax: (262) 783-2732

    AVENTIS BEHRING
    1020 First Avenue, King of Prussia, PA   19406
    CEO: Joseph N. Pugliese   Tel: (610) 878-4000   %FO: 100
    Bus: *Mfr. pharmaceuticals, vitamins* Fax: (610) 878-4009
        and feed enzymes.

    AVENTIS CROP SCIENCE
    Two TW Alexander Drive, Research Triangle Park, NC   27709
    CEO: Maurice Delage, Pres.   Tel: (919) 549-2000   %FO: 100
    Bus: *Mfr. insecticides and herbicides.* Fax: (919) 549-2000

    AVENTIS PASTEUR INC.
    Discovery Drive, Swiftwater, PA   18370
    CEO: David J. Williams, Pres.   Tel: (570) 839-4267   %FO: 100
    Bus: *Mfr. vaccines.*   Fax: (570) 839-7235

AVENTIS PHARMACEUTICALS
500 Arcola Road, Collegeville, PA   19426
CEO: Michel de Rosen, Pres. Tel: (610) 454-8000 %FO: 100
Bus: *Mfr. pharmaceuticals.* Fax: (610) 454-2121

AVENTIS PHARMACEUTICALS
399 Interpace Parkway, Parsippany, NJ   07054
CEO: Gerald P. Belle, Pres. Tel: (973) 394-6000 %FO: 100
Bus: *Mfr. pharmaceuticals.* Fax: (973) 394-6000

AVENTIS PHARMACEUTICALS, INC.
PO Box 6800, Bridgewater, NJ   08807-0800
CEO: Richard J. Markham, CEO Tel: (908) 231-4000 %FO: 100
Bus: *Mfr. pharmaceuticals.* Fax: (908) 231-5932

MESSER ADVANCED GAS SYSTEMS
Five Great Valley Parkway, Ste. 150, Malvern, PA   19355
CEO: Thomas Jeffers, Pres. Tel: (610) 695-7410 %FO: 100
Bus: *Gas systems.* Fax: (610) 695-7617

WACKER SILICONES CORP.
3301 Sutton Road, Adrian, MI   49221
CEO: Dr. Matthias Wolfgruber, Pres. Tel: (517) 264-8500 %FO: 100
Bus: *Mfr. silicones.* Fax: (517) 264-8246

● AXA SA
25 ave. Matignon, F-75008 Paris, France
CEO: Claude Bébéar, Chmn. Tel: 33-1-4075-5700 Rev: $83,069
Bus: *Global financial services; insurance,* Fax: 31-1-4075-4792 Emp: 130,000
merchant banking, securities www.axa.com
broker/dealer, investment advisory
services.

ALLIANCE CAPITAL MANAGEMENT CORPORATION
1345 Avenue of the Americas, New York, NY   10105
CEO: Christopher M. Condon, CEO Tel: (212) 969-1000 %FO: 36
Bus: *Investment advisory services.* Fax: (212) 969-1255 Emp: 17,600

AXA ADVISORS
1415 West 22nd Street, Ste. 550, Oak Brook, IL   60523
CEO: Clifford Cadle Tel: (630) 954-3355 %FO: 100
Bus: *Investment advisory services.* Fax: (630) 954-4097 Emp: 8

AXA ADVISORS
101 Fieldcrest Road, Ste. 601, Edison, NJ   08837
CEO: John F. Krahnert, Pres. Tel: (732) 417-2500 %FO: 100
Bus: *Investment advisory services.* Fax: (732) 417-2500

AXA FINANCIAL EQUITABLE INC.
1290 Avenue of the Americas, 13th Fl., New York, NY   10104
CEO: Christopher M. Condon, CEO   Tel: (212) 554-1234   %FO: 60
Bus: *Insurance, investment & real*   Fax: (212) 554-2320
    estate management services.

AXA NORDSTERN ART INSURANCE CORP.
4 West 58th Street, 8th Fl., New York, NY   10019
CEO: Dr. D. von Frank, CEO   Tel: (212) 415-8400   %FO: 100
Bus: *Insurance for fine art and*   Fax: (212) 415-8400
    collectibles.

AXA ROSENBERG INVESTMENT MANAGEMENT
4 Orinda Way, Bldg. E, Orinda, CA   94563
CEO: Nicolas Moreau, CEO   Tel: (925) 254-6464   %FO: 100
Bus: *Engaged in investment*   Fax: (925) 254-0213
    management.

AXA SOLUTIONS, INC.
17 State Street, New York, NY   10004
CEO: Robert Lippencott, CEO   Tel: (212) 493-9300   %FO: 100
Bus: *Reinsurance services.*   Fax: (212) 425-2914

SANFORD C. BERNSTEIN & CO. INC.
One North Lexington Avenue, White Plains, NY   10601-1785
CEO: Louis A. Friedrich, Mng. Dir.   Tel: (914) 993-2300   %FO: 100
Bus: *Manages portfolios for private and* Fax: (914) 993-3145
    institutional investors and
    provides investment research.

SANFORD C. BERNSTEIN & CO. INC.
777 South Flagler Drive, West Palm Beach, FL   33401-6135
CEO: Hans P. Ziegler, Mng. Dir.   Tel: (561) 820-2100   %FO: 100
Bus: *Manages portfolios for private and* Fax: (561) 820-2133
    institutional investors and
    provides investment research.

SANFORD C. BERNSTEIN & CO. INC.
800 Connecticut Avenue NW, Washington, DC   10006-2720
CEO: Mark E. Yadgaroff, Mng. Dir.   Tel: (202) 261-6700   %FO: 100
Bus: *Manages portfolios for private and* Fax: (202) 261-6880
    institutional investors and
    provides investment research.

SANFORD C. BERNSTEIN & CO. INC.

601 Union Street, Ste. 4650, Seattle, WA 98101-4050

CEO: Eric P. Gies, Mng. Dir. Tel: (206) 342-1300 %FO: 100

Bus: *Manages portfolios for private and* Fax: (206) 342-1330
institutional investors and
provides investment research.

SANFORD C. BERNSTEIN & CO. INC.

1999 Avenue of the Stars, Los Angeles, CA 90067-6123

CEO: Daryl L. Deke, Mng. Dir. Tel: (310) 286-6000 %FO: 100

Bus: *Manages portfolios for private and* Fax: (310) 286-6080
institutional investors and
provides investment research.

SANFORD C. BERNSTEIN & CO. INC.

767 Fifth Avenue, New York, NY 10153-0185

CEO: Alan R. Feld, Mng. Dir. Tel: (212) 486-5800 %FO: 100

Bus: *Manages portfolios for private and* Fax: (212) 756-4043
institutional investors and
provides investment research.

SANFORD C. BERNSTEIN & CO. INC.

227 West Monroe Street, Chicago, IL 60606-5016

CEO: Richard B. Bindler, Mng. Dir. Tel: (312) 696-7800 %FO: 100

Bus: *Manages portfolios for private and* Fax: (312) 696-7833
institutional investors and
provides investment research.

● AZUR-GMF GROUP

76 rue de Prony, F-75857 Paris, France

CEO: Christian Sastre, Chmn. Tel: 33-1-4754-1010 Rev: $2,000

Bus: *Insurance services.* Fax: 33-1-4754-1009 Emp: 11,000
www.cnp.fr

CSE INSURANCE GROUP

PO Box 8041, Walnut Creek, CA 94546-3572

CEO: Pierre Bize, Pres. Tel: (925) 817-6300 %FO: 100

Bus: *Provides insurance services.* Fax: (925) 287-9380 Emp: 340

● BACCARAT, DIV. TAITTINGER SA

Rue des Cristalleries, PB 31, F-54120 Baccarat, France

CEO: Anne Clare Tattinger, Pres. & CEO Tel: 33-3-8376-6006 Rev: $117

Bus: *Mfr./sale and distribution of fine crystal* Fax: 33-3-8376-6006 Emp: 1,125
products. www.baccarat.fr

BACCARAT
Galleria - 5085 Westheimer, Houston, TX   77056
CEO: Leslie Nelson, Mgr.   Tel: (713) 572-4001   %FO: 100
Bus: *Sales/distribution of fine crystal.*   Fax: (713) 572-9573

BACCARAT
441 East Hopkins Avenue, Aspen, CO   81611
CEO: Kates Voiles, Mgr.   Tel: (970) 925-9299   %FO: 100
Bus: *Sales/distribution of fine crystal.*   Fax: (970) 925-8909

BACCARAT
343 Powell Street, San Francisco, CA   94102
CEO: Penelope Francis, Mgr.   Tel: (415) 291-0600   %FO: 100
Bus: *Sales/distribution of fine crystal.*   Fax: (415) 291-9039

BACCARAT
625 Madison Avenue, New York, NY   10021
CEO: Elysa Dunster, Mgr.   Tel: (212) 826-4100   %FO: 100
Bus: *Sales/distribution of fine crystal.*   Fax: (212) 826-5043

● **BACOU DALLOZ SA**
63 bis, Boulevard Bessières, F-75017 Paris, France
CEO: Claude-Henri Balleyguier, CEO   Tel: 33-1-5311-1900   Rev: $903
Bus: *Mfr. personal protective equipment and*   Fax: 33-1-5311-1910   Emp: 7,000
safety products; eye and ear protection,   www.bacou.com
footwear and protective garments and
gloves for the workplace.

BACOU DALLOZ USA INC.
10 Thurber Blvd., Smithfield, RI   02917
CEO: Walter Stepan, Pres.   Tel: (401) 233-0333   %FO: 100
Bus: *Sales/distribution of safety*   Fax: (401) 232-1830
eyewear.

● **BANQUE FRANÇAISE DU COMMERCE EXTERIEUR**
21 blvd. Haussmann, F-75009 Paris, France
CEO: François Gavois, Pres.   Tel: 33-1-4800-4800
Bus: *Commercial banking services.*   Fax: 33-1-4800-4151
www.nxpb.fr

BANQUE FRANCAISE DU COMMERCE EXTERIEUR
645 Fifth Avenue, New York, NY   10022
CEO: Jean Richard, Mgr.   Tel: (212) 872-5000   %FO: 100
Bus: *Banking services.*   Fax: (212) 872-5045   Emp: 80

● **BÉGHIN-SAY S.A.**

12 rue Joseph Béghin, F-59239 Thumeries, France

CEO: Jérôme de Pelleport, CEO

Bus: *Agribusiness dealing in the manufacture and distribution of food consumer products, animal feed and oil refining.*

Tel: 33-1-4143-0145
Fax: 33-1-4143-1156
www.beghin-say.com

Rev: $1,864
Emp: 4,150

    SCA NUTRITION, SUB. AKEY, DIV. BÉGHIN-SAY

    2957 Highway 13, Marion, IA 52302

    CEO: Nigel Lecuas, Mgr.

    Bus: *Consumer food products.*

    Tel: (319) 447-0599
    Fax: (319) 447-0901

    %FO: 100

● **BÉNÉTEAU S.A.**

Zone Industrielle des Mares BP 66, F-85270 Saint-Hilaire-de-Riez, France

CEO: Anette Roux, Pres.

Bus: *Engaged in building of sailboats and yachts.*

Tel: 33-5-1555-000
Fax: 33-5-1558-910
www.beneteau.com

Rev: $365
Emp: 2,000

    BÉNÉTEAU USA INC.

    24 North Market Street, Ste. 201, Charleston, SC 29401

    CEO: Wayne Burdick, EVP

    Bus: *Sales of yachts.*

    Tel: (843) 805-5000
    Fax: (843) 805-5010

    %FO: 100

● **SOCIÉTÉ BIC S.A.**

14 rue Jeanne d'Asnières, F-92611 Clichy Cedex, France

CEO: Bruno Bich, CEO

Bus: *Mfr. writing instruments, correction fluids, shavers and lighters.*

Tel: 33-1-4519-5200
Fax: 33-1-4519-5299
www.bic.fr

Rev: $1,342
Emp: 9,766

    BIC CORPORATION

    500 Bic Drive, Milford, CT 06460

    CEO: Raymond Winter, Pres.

    Bus: *Mfr./distributor writing instruments, shavers, and lighters.*

    Tel: (203) 783-2000
    Fax: (203) 763-2108

    %FO: 100
    Emp: 1,500

● **BNP PARIBAS GROUP**

16, boulevard des Italiens, F-75009 Paris Cedex 09, France

CEO: Michel Pébereau, Chmn. & CEO

Bus: *Engaged in commercial and investment banking, and securities and asset management services.*

Tel: 33-1-4014-4546
Fax: 33-1-4214-7546
www.bnpgroup.com

Rev: $49,045
Emp: 77,475

BANC WEST CORPORATION
999 Bishop Street, Honolulu, HI   96813
CEO: Walter A. Dods Jr., Chmn.   Tel: (808) 525-7000   %FO: 100
Bus: *General commercial banking*   Fax: (808) 525-5798
services.

BANK OF THE WEST
180 Montgomery Street, 25th Fl., San Francisco, CA   94104
CEO: Donald J. Mc Grath, CEO   Tel: (925) 765-4800   %FO: 100
Bus: *General commercial banking*   Fax: (925) 399-9118
services.

BNP PARIBAS CORPORATE FINANCE
499 Park Avenue, New York, NY   10022
CEO: Elsa Berry, EVP   Tel: (212) 418-8200   %FO: 100
Bus: *Merchant banking & investment*   Fax: (212) 838-7590
advisory services.

FIRST HAWAIIAN BANK
999 Bishop Street, Honolulu, HI   96813
CEO: Walter A. Dods Jr., CEO   Tel: (808) 525-7000   %FO: 100
Bus: *General commercial banking*   Fax: (808) 525-5798
services.

● **BOIRON**
20 rue de la Liberation, F-69110 Ste-Foy-les-Lyon, France
CEO: Christian Boiron, CEO   Tel: 33-4-7216-4000   Rev: $231
Bus: *Mfr./distribution homeopathic*   Fax: 33-4-7859-6916   Emp: 2,400
pharmaceuticals.   www.boison.fr

BOIRON BORNEMAN INC.
6 Campus Blvd., Newton Square, PA   19073
CEO: Thierry Boiron, Pres.   Tel: (610) 325-7464   %FO: 100
Bus: *Mfr./distribution homeopathic*   Fax: (610) 325-7480   Emp: 64
medicines.

● **BONGRAIN S.A.**
42 rue Rieussec, Cedex, F-78223 Viroflay, France
CEO: Bernard Lacan, Pres.   Tel: 33-1-34-58-6300   Rev: $2,200
Bus: *Produces/distributes dairy products and*   Fax: 33-1-30-24-0383   Emp: 9,800
gourmet foods.   www.bongrain.com

BONGRAIN CHEESE USA
400 South Custer Avenue, New Holland, PA   17557
CEO: James Williams, Pres.   Tel: (717) 355-8500   %FO: 100
Bus: *Mfr. yogurt, imported and*   Fax: (717) 355-8561
     domestic cheeses and dairy
     products.

EAST SMITHFIELD FARMS INC.
150 West Jackson Street, New Holland, PA   17557
CEO: Clifford R. Marquart, Pres.   Tel: (717) 354-4411
Bus: *Produces milk and dairy products.*   Fax: (717) 355-8671

MAJOR SMITH INC.
158 West Jackson Street, New Holland, PA   17557
CEO: J. Darryl Springer, Pres.   Tel: (717) 355-8667
Bus: *Mfr./distributes cheese sauces,*   Fax: (717) 355-8671
     puddings and beverages.

● **BULL**
68 route de Versailles, F-78430 Louveciennes, France
CEO: Guy de Panafieu, CEO   Tel: 33-1-3966-6060   Rev: $3,055
Bus: *Mfr. network management software and* Fax: 33-1-3966-6062   Emp: 17,200
     computer products.   www.bull.com

   BULL HN INFORMATION SYSTEMS INC.
   300 Concord Road, Billerica, MA   01821
   CEO: Don Zereski, Pres.   Tel: (978) 294-6000   %FO: 100
   Bus: *Mfr. network management*   Fax: (978) 294-6418
        software and computer products.

   BULL HN INFORMATION SYSTEMS INC.
   13430 North Black Canyon Hwy., Phoenix, AZ   85029-1310
   CEO: Barry Iselin   Tel: (602) 862-5029   %FO: 100
   Bus: *Mfr. network management*   Fax: (602) 862-6914
        software and computer products.

● **BURELLE SA**
1 rue Du Parc, F-92593 Levallois-Perret, France
CEO: Jean Burelle, Chmn.   Tel: 33-1-4087-6400   Rev: $1,479
Bus: *Mfr. plastic parts for automobiles,* Fax: 33-2-4087-0619   Emp: 8,193
     playground equipment and road signs.

   PLASTIC OMNIUM AUTO, INC.
   5100 Old Pearman Dairy Road, Anderson, SC   29625
   CEO: John Pendleton, Mgr.   Tel: (864) 260-0000   %FO: 100
   Bus: *Mfr. plastic parts for automobiles.* Fax: (864) 231-7537

PLASTIC OMNIUM INDUSTRIES INC.

2610 Bond Street, Rochester Hills, Mi   48309

CEO: R. Salamon, Pres. Tel: (248) 853-0088 %FO: 100

Bus: *Mfr. plastic parts for automobiles,* Fax: (248) 853-6973
playground equipment and road
signs.

● BUSINESS OBJECTS, SA

1 Square Chaptal, F-92300 Lavollois-Perret, France

CEO: Bernard Liautaud, CEO Tel: 33-1-4125-2121 Rev: $349

Bus: *mfr. business software.* Fax: 33-1-4125-3100 Emp: 1,888

www.businessobjects.com

BUSINESS OBJECTS AMERICAS

3030 Orchard Parkway, San Jose, CA   95134

CEO: Jon Temple, SVP Tel: (408) 953-6000 %FO: 100

Bus: *Mfr. software programs for* Fax: (408) 953-6001
corporate executives.

● CAISSE DES DEPOTS ET CONSIGNATIONS

56 rue de Lille, F-75356 Paris, France

CEO: Daniel Lebègue, Chmn. & CEO Tel: 33-1-4049-5678 Rev: $10,413

Bus: *Financial services companies.* Fax: 33-1-4049-8899 Emp: 35,000

www.caissedesdepots.fr

CAISSE DES DEPOTS SECURITIES INC.

9 West 57th Street, 36th Fl., New York, NY   10019

CEO: Luc de Clapiers, Pres. & CEO Tel: (212) 891-6250 %FO: 100

Bus: *Brokerage government securities,* Fax: (212) 527-1426 Emp: 6
corporate equities.

CDC ASSET MANAGEMENT NORTH AMERICA, INC.

399 Boylston Street, Boston, MA   02116

CEO: Peter S. Voss, Pres. & CEO Tel: (617) 578-3500 %FO: 100

Bus: *Provides investment management* Fax: (617) 247-1447 Emp: 1,585
services.

CDC CAPITAL INC.

9 West 57th Street, 36th Fl., New York, NY   10019

CEO: Luc de Clapiers, Pres. & CEO Tel: (212) 891-6100 %FO: 100

Bus: *Fin trading, investment.* Fax: (212) 891-6295 Emp: 52

CDC INVESTMENT MANAGEMENT CORPORATION

9 West 57th Street, 36th Fl., New York, NY   10019

CEO: Luc de Clapiers, Pres. & CEO Tel: (212) 891-6150 %FO: 100

Bus: *Invest management services.* Fax: (212) 891-6294 Emp: 26

CDC NORTH AMERICA INC.
9 West 57th Street, 36th Fl., New York, NY 10019
CEO: Daniel Roth, Chmn.　　　　Tel: (212) 891-6137　　%FO: 100
Bus: *Provides financial services.*　Fax: (212) 891-6118　　Emp: 3

● **CANAL PLUS SA**
85-89 Quai Andre Citroen, F-75015 Paris, France
CEO: Pierre Lescure, Chmn.　　　Tel: 33-1-4425-1000　　Rev: $2,900
Bus: *International telecommunications, TV*　Fax: 33-1-4425-1234　　Emp: 3,800
　　entertainment production and TV　　www.cplus.fr
　　station management. (34% ownership
　　by Vivendi SA)

　　CANAL PLUS US
　　301 N. Canon Drive, Ste. 228, Beverly Hills, CA 90210
　　CEO: Richard Garzilli, EVP　　Tel: (310) 247-0994　　%FO: 100
　　Bus: *Film production and*　　　Fax: (310) 247-0998
　　　　telecommunications.

● **CAP GEMINI ERNST & YOUNG SA**
Place de l'Etoile,11 rue de Tilsitt, F-75017 Paris, France
CEO: Serge Kampf, Exec. Chmn.　　Tel: 33-1-4754-5000　　Rev: $4,652
Bus: *Engaged in management consulting,*　Fax: 33-1-4227-3211　　Emp: 38,340
　　computer services and information　www.capgemini.com
　　technology.

　　CAP GEMINI ERNST & YOUNG LLC
　　3 Paragon Way, Freehold, NJ 07728
　　CEO: Laurie Yeager, Mgr.　　　Tel: (732) 358-8900　　%FO: 100
　　Bus: *Computer services and*　　Fax: (732) 358-8803
　　　　management consulting.

　　CAP GEMINI ERNST & YOUNG LLC
　　One Bala Plaza, Ste. 515, Bala Cynwyd, PA 19004
　　CEO: Michael Meyer, Pres. & CEO　Tel: (610) 668-4626　　%FO: 100
　　Bus: *Computer services and*　　Fax: (610) 668-9914
　　　　management consulting.

　　CAP GEMINI ERNST & YOUNG LLC
　　233 South Wacker Drive, 14th Fl., Chicago, IL 60606
　　CEO: Sarah Hoel　　　　　　　Tel: (312) 879-6700
　　Bus: *Computer services and*　　Fax: (312) 879-6130
　　　　management consulting.

CAP GEMINI ERNST & YOUNG LLC
One North Charles Street, Baltimore, MD 21201

CEO: Sue Welch, Mgr.	Tel: (410) 783-3800	%FO: 100
Bus: *Computer services and management consulting.*	Fax: (410) 783-3801	

CAP GEMINI ERNST & YOUNG LLC
10055 Red Run Blvd., Ste. 100, Owings Mills, MD 21117

CEO: Brian Sullivan, Mgr.	Tel: (410) 581-5022	%FO: 100
Bus: *Computer services and management consulting.*	Fax: (410) 581-7815	

CAP GEMINI AMERICA
5151 Edina Industrial Blvd., Ste. 600, Edina, MN 55434

CEO: Greg Fouks, Mgr.	Tel: (952) 830-6969	%FO: 100
Bus: *Computer services and management consulting.*	Fax: (952) 830-6994	

CAP GEMINI ERNST & YOUNG LLC
101 North Tryon Street, Ste. 1000, Charlotte, NC 28246

CEO: John Sequeira, Mgr.	Tel: (704) 331-1900	%FO: 100
Bus: *Computer services and management consulting.*	Fax: (704) 331-2071	

CAP GEMINI ERNST & YOUNG LLC
4445 Lake Forest Drive, Ste. 550, Cincinnati, OH 45242

CEO: John Rogan, Mgr.	Tel: (513) 563-6622	%FO: 100
Bus: *Computer services and management consulting.*	Fax: (513) 563-6774	

CAP GEMINI ERNST & YOUNG LLC
275 Grove Street, Newton, MA 01466

CEO: Judy Burns, Mgr.	Tel: (617) 928-7600	%FO: 100
Bus: *Computer services and management consulting.*	Fax: (617) 928-7622	

CAP GEMINI ERNST & YOUNG LLC
1114 Avenue of the Americas, 29th Fl., New York, NY 10036

CEO: Dale L. Wartluft, CEO	Tel: (212) 944-6464	%FO: 100
Bus: *Computer services and management consulting.*	Fax: (212) 710-5346	Emp: 3,200

CAP GEMINI AMERICA
14755 Preston Road, Ste. 310, Dallas, TX 75240

CEO: Larry Wolf, Mgr.	Tel: (972) 776-5600	%FO: 100
Bus: *Computer services and management consulting.*	Fax: (972) 776-5607	

CAP GEMINI AMERICA

115 Perimeter Center Place, Ste. 1000, Atlanta, GA   30346

CEO: J.Yann, Mgr.   Tel: (770) 677-3520   %FO: 100

Bus: *Computer services and*   Fax: (770) 677-3521
     management consulting.

● **GROUPE CARBONE-LORRAINE**

Immeuble La Fayette, 2-3 Place, des Vosges, La défense 5, F-92400 Paris, France

CEO: Claude Cocozza, CEO   Tel: 33-1-4691-5400   Rev: $695

Bus: *Mfr. graphite brushes, permanent*   Fax: 33-1-4691-5401   Emp: 7,800
     magnets and electrical protection   www.carbonelorraine.com
     devices for automobiles and machinery.

CARBONE LORRAINE NA

14 Eastmans Road, Parsippany, NJ   07054

CEO: Michelle Consiglio, Pres.   Tel: (973) 503-0600   %FO: 100

Bus: *Mfr./sales/distribution of graphite*   Fax: (973) 503-0335   Emp: 6
     brushes, permanent magnets and
     electrical protection devices.

CARBONE OF AMERICA, CHEMICAL EQUIPMENT DIV.

PO Box 1189, 540 Branch Drive, Salem, VA   24153

CEO: Michelle Consiglio, Pres.   Tel: (540) 389-7535   %FO: 100

Bus: *Chemical equipment division.*   Fax: (540) 389-7538

CARBONE OF AMERICA, GRAPHITE MATERIALS DIV.

215 Stackpole Street, St. Marys, PA   15857-1488

CEO: Ed Stumpff, VP   Tel: (814) 781-1234   %FO: 100

Bus: *Mfr. distribution of graphite*   Fax: (814) 781-8570
     brushes.

CARBONE OF AMERICA, ULTRA CARBON DIV.

900 Harrison Street, Bay City, MI   48708

CEO: Gary A. Mulcahy   Tel: (517) 894-2911   %FO: 100

Bus: *Mfr. ultra carbon.*   Fax: (517) 895-7740

FERRAZ SHAWMUT, DIV. CARBONE-LORRAINE

374 Merrimac Street, Newburyport, MA   01950

CEO: Ken Hooper, SVP   Tel: (978) 465-4203   %FO: 100

Bus: *Mfr. circuit protection equipment.*   Fax: (978) 462-7934

FERRAZ SHAWMUT, DIV. CARBONE-LORRAINE

545 Indian Creek, Trophy Club, TX   76262

CEO: Doyle Anderson, Mgr.   Tel: (817) 430-9112   %FO: 100

Bus: *Mfr. circuit protection equipment.*   Fax: (817) 491-6779

FERRAZ SHAWMUT, DIV. CARBONE-LORRAINE
2262 Parkview Court, West Linn, OR   97068
CEO: Adrian Scott, Mgr.   Tel: (503) 635-9488   %FO: 100
Bus: *Mfr. circuit protection equipment.*   Fax: (503) 635-9499

FERRAZ SHAWMUT, DIV. CARBONE-LORRAINE
112 Williams Street, Monroe, GA   30655
CEO: Stephen Reynolds, Mgr.   Tel: (770) 267-4258   %FO: 100
Bus: *Mfr. circuit protection equipment.*   Fax: (770) 267-8542

FERRAZ SHAWMUT, DIV. CARBONE-LORRAINE
112 Old Settlers Court, Woodstock, GA   30189
CEO: James Thompson, Mgr.   Tel: (770) 516-7766   %FO: 100
Bus: *Mfr. circuit protection equipment.*   Fax: (770) 516-1333

FERRAZ SHAWMUT, DIV. CARBONE-LORRAINE
1135 Arya Drive, Roswell, GA   30076
CEO: Mike Lang, Mgr.   Tel: (770) 740-1315   %FO: 100
Bus: *Mfr. circuit protection equipment.*   Fax: (770) 740-0647

● **CASINO GUICHARD-PERRACHON**
BP 306, 24 rue de la Montat, F-42008 Saint-Etienne Cedex 2, France
CEO: Christian P. Couvreux, CEO   Tel: 33-4-7745-3131   Rev: $17,959
Bus: *Operates warehouse supermarkets.*   Fax: 33-4-7721-8515   Emp: 73,450
                                           www.casine.fr

SMART & FINAL INC.
600 Citadel Drive, Commerce, CA   90040
CEO: Ross E. Roeder, Pres. & CEO   Tel: (323) 869-7608   %FO: 50
Bus: *Operates warehouse-style grocery*   Fax: (323) 869-7858   Emp: 5,300
     chain.

● **CEDRAT SA**
10 Chemin du Pre Carre-Zirst, F-38240 Meylan, France
CEO: Bruno Ribard   Tel: 33-4-7690-5045
Bus: *CAD/CAM element analysis*   Fax: 33-4-7690-1609   Emp: 40
     engineering, agricultural planification.   www.cedrat.com

MAGSOFT CORPORATION
1223 Peoples Avenue, Troy, NY   12180
CEO: Sheppard J. Salon, Pres.   Tel: (518) 271-1352   %FO: 30
Bus: *Engaged in engineering*   Fax: (518) 276-6380   Emp: 10
     CAD/CAM software and
     electromagnetic software solutions.

● **CEGOS**

11 rue René Jacques, F-92798 Issy-les-Moulineaux, Cedex 9 France

CEO: Marc Bossert — Tel: 33-1-5500-9000

Bus: *Consulting.* — Fax: 33-1-5500-9992 — Emp: 2,000

www.cegos.fr

> **CEGMARK INTL INC.**
>
> 1350 Avenue of the Americas, New York, NY 10019
>
> CEO: Ronald R. Mullins, Pres. — Tel: (212) 541-7010 — %FO: 49
>
> Bus: *Marketing consulting services.* — Fax: (212) 581-9819 — Emp: 20

● **CEREOL, DIV. MONTEDISON**

14, boulevard du Général Leclerc, F-92200 Neuilly-sur-Seine, France

CEO: Carl Hausmann, Chmn. & CEO — Tel: 33-1-4143-1550 — Rev: $4,493

Bus: *Engaged in agribusiness.* — Fax: 33-1-4143-1551 — Emp: 7,000

www.cereolworld.com

> **CENTRAL SOYA**
>
> PO Box 1400, Fort Wayne, IN 46802
>
> CEO: Carl Hausmann, CEO — Tel: (219) 425-5100 — %FO: 100
>
> Bus: *Processors of oilseed and related food products.* — Fax: (219) 425-5330

● **CERESTAR INTERNATIONAL, DIV. ERIDANIA BEGHIN-SAY**

14 boulevard du Général Leclerc, F-92572 Neuilly-sur-Seine, France

CEO: Stefano Meloni, Chmn. — Tel: 33-1-4143-1924 — Rev: $1,594

Bus: *Mfr. starch products and derivatives.* — Fax: 33-1-4143-1974 — Emp: 3,900

www.cerestar.com

> **CENTRAL SOYA COMPANY**
>
> 110 West Berry Street, Ste. 1500, Fort Wayne, IN 46802
>
> CEO: Jim P. McCarthy — Tel: (219) 425-5100 — %FO: 100
>
> Bus: *Processor of soya beans to produce raw materials and goods for agricultural, food and industrial markets.* — Fax: (219) 425-5330

> **CERESTAR USA**
>
> 1100 Indianapolis Boulevard, Hammond, IN 46320
>
> CEO: Thad Jones, Pres. — Tel: (219) 659-2000 — %FO: 100
>
> Bus: *Engaged in processing of starch and derivatives.* — Fax: (219) 473-6600

● **CHANEL SA**

135 Avenue Charles de Gaulle, F-92521 Neuilly-sur-Seine Cedex, France

CEO: Ms. Francoise Montenay, Pres. & CEO   Tel: 33-1-4643-4000

Bus: *Mfr. ladies fashions, cosmetics, watches*   Fax: 33-1-4747-6034
and jewelry.   www.chanel.com

    CHANEL USA INC.

    9 East 57th Street, New York, NY 10022

    CEO: Arie Kopelman, Pres.   Tel: (212) 355-5050   %FO: 100

    Bus: *Mfr. ladies fashions, cosmetics,*   Fax:
    watches and jewelry.

● **CHANTIERS BENETEAU SA**

Zone Industrielle des Mares, BP 66, F-85270 Saint-Hilaire-de-Riez, France

CEO: Madame Anette Roux, Pres.   Tel: 33-2-5160-5000

Bus: *Mfr. sailboats and yachts.*   Fax: 33-2-5160-5010
   www.beneteau.fr

    BENETEAU MANUFACTURERS

    PO Drawer 1218, Marion, SC 29571

    CEO: Wayne Burdick, EVP   Tel: (843) 423-4201   %FO: 100

    Bus: *Mfr. sailboats.*   Fax: (843) 423-4912   Emp: 125

    BENETEAU USA INC.

    24 North Market Street, Ste. 201, Charleston, SC 29401

    CEO: Wayne Burdick, EVP   Tel: (843) 805-5000   %FO: 100

    Bus: *Sales/distribution of sailboats and*   Fax: (843) 805-5010   Emp: 12
    yachts.

● **CIMENTS FRANCAIS**

22 Tour Ariane, F-92088 Paris La Défense, France

CEO: Yves-Rene Nanot, Chmn.   Tel: 33-1-4291-7500   Rev: $2,387

Bus: *Mfr./sale cement, ready mixed concrete*   Fax: 33-1-4774-1135   Emp: 12,865
and aggregates.   www.cimfra.fr

    ESSROC CORPORATION

    3251 Bath Pike, Nazareth, PA 18064

    CEO: Robert M. Rayner, Pres.   Tel: (610) 837-6725   %FO: 100

    Bus: *Cement and construction materials.*   Fax: (610) 837-9614

● **CIS BIO INTERNATIONAL**

BP 6, F-91192 Gif-sur-Yvette, France

CEO: Charles Penneciere, CEO   Tel: 33-1-6985-7070   Rev: $198

Bus: *Engaged in biomedical technology.*   Fax: 33-1-6985-7516   Emp: 1,100
(60% JV of Schering AG).   www.cisbiointernational.fr

CIS-US INC.
10 DeAngelo Drive, Bedford, MA   01730
CEO: Glenn Alto, CEO
Bus: *Radio pharmaceuticals: RIA laboratory products, radiation therapy equipment.*
Tel: (781) 275-7120
Fax: (781) 275-2634
%FO: 100
Emp: 50

● **CITEL**
12 Blvd. Des Iles, F-92441 Issy-les-Moulineaus, France
CEO: Francois Guichard, Pres.
Bus: *Mfr. surge and lightning protectors.*
Tel: 33-1-4123-5023
Fax: 33-1-4123-5009
www.citel2cp.com
Rev: $22
Emp: 180

CITEL AMERICA INC.
1111 Parkcentre Blvd., Ste. 340, Miami, FL   33169
CEO: Fabrice Larmier, EVP
Bus: *Distributes surge protectors.*
Tel: (305) 621-0022
Fax: (305) 621-0766
%FO: 100
Emp: 3

● **CLARINS S.A.**
BP 174, F-92203 Neuilly-sur-Seine Cedex, France
CEO: Jacques Courtin-Clarins, Chmn.
Bus: *Produces/distributes skin care products and perfume.*
Tel: 33-1-4738-1212
Fax: 33-1-4745-5576
www.clarins.fr
Rev: $720
Emp: 4,066

CLARINS USA INC
135 East 57th Street, 15th Fl., New York, NY   10022
CEO: J. M. Horowitz, Pres.
Bus: *Distribution/sales of skin care and perfume products.*
Tel: (212) 980-1800
Fax: (212) 308-1448
%FO: 100

● **CLUB MÉDITERRANÉE SA**
11, rue de Cambrai, F-75019 Paris Cedex, France
CEO: Philippe Bourguignon, Pres.
Bus: *Own and operate vacation resorts, hotels, ships, planes.*
Tel: 33-1-5335-3553
Fax: 33-1-5335-3616
www.clubmed.com
Rev: $1,890
Emp: 3,700

CLUB MED INC.
75 Valencia Drive, Coral Gables, FL   33134
CEO: John Vanderslice, CEO
Bus: *Sales and management, vacation hotel, resorts, cruise ships.*
Tel: (305) 925-9000
Fax: (305) 443-9659
%FO: 100

CLUB MED SANDPIPER
3500 Morningside Blvd. SE, Port Saint Lucie, FL   34952
CEO: Lionel Benzoni, Mgr.
Bus: *Resort hotel.*
Tel: (561) 335-4400
Fax: (561) 398-5101
%FO: 100

● **COFACE**

12 COURS Michelet, La défense 10, F-92800 Puteaux, France

CEO: Francois David, CEO   Tel: 33-1-4902-2000   Rev: $872

Bus: *Provides credit information and short-*   Fax: 33-1-4902-2741   Emp: 3,200
term credit insurance.   www.coface.com

    COFACE NORTH AMERICA

    *121 Withney Avenue, New Haven, CT   06510

    CEO: Robert Frewen, Pres.   Tel: (203) 781-3800   %FO: 100

    Bus: *Provides credit information and*   Fax: (203) 781-3833
    short-term credit insurance.

    JI INTERNATIONAL

    699 Terryville Avenue, Bristol, CT   06011-0022

    CEO: Ben Boylan, Pres.   Tel: (860) 589-1698   %FO: 100

    Bus: *Provides credit information and*   Fax: (860) 589-9117
    short-term credit insurance.

    VERITAS BUSINESS INFORMATION

    121 Whitney Avenue, New Haven, CT   06510

    CEO: Recky Oroh   Tel: (203) 781-3800   %FO: 100

    Bus: *Commercial credit, strategic and*   Fax: (203) 781-3833
    financial reports

● **COFLEXIP STENA OFFSHORE SA**

23, avenue de Neuilly, F-75116 Paris, France

CEO: Pierre Marie Valentin, Chmn.   Tel: 33-1-4067-6000   Rev: $1,340

Bus: *Engineering/mfr./offshore installation*   Fax: 33-1-4067-6003   Emp: 4,000
flexible pipe.   www.coflexipstenaoffshore.com

    COFLEXIP STENA OFFSHORE INC.

    7660 Woodway, Ste. 390, Houston, TX   77063

    CEO: Daniel Twiddy, Mgr.   Tel: (713) 789-8540   %FO: 100

    Bus: *Engineering/mfr./offshore*   Fax: (713) 789-7367   Emp: 50
    installation flexible pipe.

    DUCO INC.

    16661 Jacintroport Blvd., Houston, TX   77015

    CEO: John McManus, Mgr.   Tel: (281) 457-9900   %FO: 100

    Bus: *Mfr./design umbilical systems.*   Fax: (281) 457-1537

    PERRY SLINGSBY SYSTEMS, INC

    821 Jupiter Park Drive, Jupiter, FL   33458

    CEO: Allen Leatt, CEO   Tel: (561) 743-7000   %FO: 100

    Bus: *Engineering/mfr./offshore*   Fax: (561) 743-1313
    installation flexible pipe.

● **COGEMA**

2 rue Paul-Dautier, BP 4, F-78141 Velizy-Villacoublay, France

CEO: Anne Lauvergeon, CEO

Tel: 33-1-3926-3000

Rev: $5,090

Bus: *Engaged in fuel products and recycling* Fax: 33-1-3926-2700 Emp: 19,600
services and mines uranium. www.cogema.fr

   COGEMA INC.

   7401 Wisconsin Avenue, Bethesda, MD 20814

   CEO: Michael McMurphy, Pres.

Tel: (301) 986-8585

%FO: 100

   Bus: *Nuclear fuel products & services.* Fax: (301) 652-5690

● **COLAS SA**

7place Rene Clair, F-92653 Boulogne-Billancourt Cedex, France

CEO: Alain Dupont, CEO

Tel: 33-1-4761-7500

Rev: $5,332

Bus: *Engaged in building and paving of* Fax: 33-1-3761-7600 Emp: 43,550
roads. www.colas.fr

   DELTA COMPANIES INC.

   114 South Silver Spring Road, PO Box 880, Cape Girardeau, MO 63702-0880

   CEO: Troy Ward, Controller

Tel: (573) 334-5261

%FO: 100

   Bus: *Engaged in construction and* Fax: (573) 334-9576
building and paving of roads.

   HRI INC.

   7150 West College Avenue, State College, PA 16804-1055

   CEO: John R. Kulka, Pres.

Tel: (814) 238-5071

%FO: 100

   Bus: *Engaged in construction and* Fax: (814) 238-0131
building and paving of roads.

   IA CONSTRUCTION CORPORATION

   PO Box 8, Concordville, PA 19331

   CEO: George Searle, Pres.

Tel: (610) 459-3136

%FO: 100

   Bus: *Engaged in construction and* Fax: (610) 459-2086
building and paving of roads.

   REEVES CONSTRUCTION COMPANY

   844 Spring Street, PO Box 547, Americus, GA 31709

   CEO: Roger Dill, Chmn.

Tel: (912) 924-7574

%FO: 100

   Bus: *Engaged in construction and* Fax: (912) 924-8336
building and paving of roads.

● **COMPAGNIE FINANCIÈRE SUCRES ET DENRÉES SA**

20/22 rue de la Ville L'Eveque, F-75008 Paris, France

CEO: Serge Varsano, Chmn. & CEO

Tel: 33-1-5330-1234

Bus: *International sugar trading.* Fax: 33-1-5330-1212

AMEROP SUGAR CORPORATION
701 Brickell Avenue, Suite 2200, Miami, FL 33131

CEO: Thierry J. Songeur, CEO   Tel: (305) 374-4440   %FO: 100

Bus: *International sugar trading.*   Fax: (305) 374-4330

● COMPAGNIE GENERALE DE GEOPHYSIQUE (CGG)
1 rue Leon Migaux, F-91341 Massy, France

CEO: Robert Brunck, Pres. & CEO   Tel: 33-6-4473-000   Rev: $510

Bus: *Provides geophysical exploration and*   Fax: 33-6-4473-970   Emp: 3,400
data processing.   www.cgg.com

CGG AMERICAS INC.
16430 Park Ten Place, Houston, TX 77084

CEO: Bert Chenin   Tel: (281) 646-2400   %FO: 100

Bus: *Provides geophysical exploration*   Fax: (281) 646-2660
and data processing services.

DATA TRANSCRIPTION SERVICES
19416 Park Row, Ste. 110, Houston, TX 77084

CEO: Mike Simons   Tel: (281) 599-1010   %FO: 100

Bus: *Provides data processing services.*   Fax: (281) 599-7535

SERCEL INC.
17200 Park Row, Houston, TX 77218-5935

CEO: Mike Simons   Tel: (281) 492-6688   %FO: 100

Bus: *Provides equipment*   Fax: (281) 492-6910
manufacturing, sales and service.

● CRÉDIT AGRICOLE INDOSUEZ CHEUVREUX
9, Quai du Président Paul Doumer, F-92400 Coubevoie, France

CEO: Jean Laurent, Dir.   Tel: 33-1-4189-0000   Rev: $14,800

Bus: *Engaged in commercial and Investment*   Fax: 33-1-4189-2956   Emp: 86,000
banking services.   www.credit-agricole.fr

CRÉDIT AGRICOLE INDOSUEZ
1211 Avenue of the Americas, 7th Fl., New York, NY 10036

CEO: Bernard Chauvel, Senior Country   Tel: (212) 278-2000   %FO: 100
    Officer

Bus: *Commercial and Investment*   Fax: (212) 278-2444
banking services.

CRÉDIT AGRICOLE INDOSUEZ
101 California Street, Ste. 4390, San Francisco, CA 94111

CEO: Marcy Lyons, Mgr.   Tel: (415) 391-0810   %FO: 100

Bus: *Commercial and Investment*   Fax: (415) 986-4116
banking services.

CRÉDIT AGRICOLE INDOSUEZ

55 East Monroe Street, Ste. 4700, Chicago, IL   60603

CEO: Jean-Yves Klein, Mgr.	Tel: (312) 372-9200	%FO: 100
Bus: *Commercial and Investment banking services.*	Fax: (312) 372-3724	

CRÉDIT AGRICOLE INDOSUEZ SECURITIES, INC.

520 Madison Avenue, 3rd Fl., New York, NY   10022

CEO: Pascal Viornery, CEO	Tel: (212) 593-9320	%FO: 100
Bus: *Securities dealer/broker.*	Fax: (212) 593-9330	

● CRÉDIT COMMERCIAL DE FRANCE SA (CCF)

103 ave. des Champs Elysees, F-75008 Paris, France

CEO: Charles-Henri Filippi, ceo	Tel: 33-1-4070-7040	Rev: $6,999
Bus: *General commercial banking.*	Fax: 33-1-4720-2372	Emp: 13,650
	www.ccf.fr	

CCF INTERNATIONAL FINANCE CORPORATION

590 Madison Avenue, 25th Fl., New York, NY   10022

CEO: Jean Jacques Salomon, Mgr.	Tel: (212) 836-4400	%FO: 100
Bus: *International commercial banking services.*	Fax: (212) 688-7532	

CCF INTERNATIONAL FINANCE CORPORATION

590 Madison Avenue, 25th Fl., New York, NY   10022

CEO: Tom Higgins, Mgr.	Tel: (212) 486-3080	%FO: 100
Bus: *International commercial banking services.*	Fax: (212) 832-7469	Emp: 75

CHARTERHOUSE INC.

590 Madison Avenue, 27th Fl., New York, NY   10022-1112

CEO: George Michas, Mng. Dir.	Tel: (212) 888-0020	%FO: 100
Bus: *Engaged in corporate finance.*	Fax: (212) 644-5145	

● CREDIT INDUSTRIEL ET COMMERCIAL DE PARIS (CIC)

6 avenue de Provence, F-75009 Paris, France

CEO: Michel Lucas, Chmn. & CEO	Tel: 33-1-4596-9696	Rev: $9,339
Bus: *Provides retail, private and investment banking services.*	Fax: 33-1-4596-9666	Emp: 21,500
	www.cic-banques.fr	

CREDIT INDUSTRIEL ET COMMERCIAL DE PARIS

520 Madison Avenue, New York, NY   10022

CEO: Serge Bellanger, EVP	Tel: (212) 715-4400	%FO: 100
Bus: *Provides banking and investment services.*	Fax: (212) 715-4400	

- **CRÉDIT LYONNAIS S.A.**
  19, blvd. des Italiens, F-75002 Paris, France
  CEO: Dominique Ferrero, CEO   Tel: 33-1-4295-7000   Rev: $14,198
  Bus: *General commercial banking, asset*   Fax: 33-1-4295-0095   Emp: 40,550
  management, securities trading &   www.creditlyonnais.fr
  insurance services.

  ### CRÉDIT LYONNAIS - Los Angeles
  515 South Flower St., Ste. 2200, Los Angeles, CA   90071
  CEO: Diane Scott, Mgr.   Tel: (213) 362-5900   %FO: 100
  Bus: *International banking services.*   Fax: (213) 623-3437   Emp: 15

  ### CRÉDIT LYONNAIS - New York
  1301 Avenue of the Americas, New York, NY   10019
  CEO: Gina Harth-Cryde, Mgr.   Tel: (212) 261-7000   %FO: 100
  Bus: *International banking services.*   Fax: (212) 459-3170   Emp: 600

  ### CRÉDIT LYONNAIS - Chicago
  224 West Monroe Street, Ste. 3800, Chicago, IL   60606
  CEO: Sandra Horowitz, Mgr.   Tel: (312) 641-0500   %FO: 100
  Bus: *International banking services.*   Fax: (312) 641-0527   Emp: 27

  ### CRÉDIT LYONNAIS - Dallas
  2200 Ross Avenue, Dallas, TX   75201
  CEO: Sam Hill, Mgr.   Tel: (214) 220-2300   %FO: 100
  Bus: *International banking services.*   Fax: (214) 220-2323   Emp: 20

  ### CRÉDIT LYONNAIS SECURITIES
  1301 Avenue of the Americas, New York, NY   10019
  CEO: Jerome Brunel, CEO   Tel: (212) 261-7000   %FO: 100
  Bus: *U.S. headquarters.*   Fax: (212) 459-3170

- **DANFOSS SOCLA SA**
  1 rue Paul Sabatier, BP 273, F-71107 Shalon sur Saone Cedex, France
  CEO: Jaques Chaise, Pres.   Tel: 33-3-8546-3034   Rev: $200
  Bus: *Mfr. and sales of wholesale valves.*   Fax: 33-3-8597-4269   Emp: 520
      www.socla.com

  ### FLOMATIC CORPORATION
  145 Murray Street, Glens Falls, NY   12801-4424
  CEO: Bo Andersson, Pres.   Tel: (518) 761-9797   %FO: JV
  Bus: *Mfr./wholesale valves.*   Fax: (518) 761-9798   Emp: 50

  ### SAUER-DANFOSS INC.
  2800 East 13th Street, Ames, IA   50010
  CEO: David L. Pfeifle, CEO   Tel: (515) 239-6000
  Bus: *Mfr./wholesale valves.*   Fax: (515) 239-6318

• GROUPE DANONE SA

7, rue de Téhéran, F-75008 Paris Cedex, France

CEO: Franck Riboud, Chmn. Tel: 33-1-4435-2020 Rev: $13,415
Bus: *Production and distribution of dairy* Fax: 33-1-4225-6716 Emp: 75,965
and other branded food and beverage www.danonegroup.com
products worldwide.

THE DANNON COMPANY

120 White Plains Road, Tarrytown, NY 10591-5536

CEO: Thomas Kunz, Pres. & CEO Tel: (914) 366-9700 %FO: 100
Bus: *Production and distribution of* Fax: (914) 366-2805 Emp: 130
dairy products.

GREAT BRANDS/DANONE INTERNATIONAL

208 Harbor Drive, Stamford, CT 06902

CEO: Pedro Medina, CEO Tel: (203) 425-1700 %FO: 100
Bus: *Sales/distribution of biscuits and* Fax: (203) 425-1900
bottled water.

LEA & PERRINS INC.

15-01 Pollitt Drive, Fair Lawn, NJ 07410

CEO: Ralph Abrams, Pres. Tel: (201) 791-1600 %FO: 100
Bus: *Mfr./sales/distribution of sauces.* Fax: (201) 791-8945 Emp: 120

MCKESSON WATER PRODUCTS COMPANY

3280 East Foothill Blvd., Ste. 400, Pasadena, CA 91107

CEO: Charles A. Norris, Pres. Tel: (626) 585-1000 %FO: 100
Bus: *Mfr. bottled water.* Fax: (626) 585-8433

• DASSAULT AVIATION

9, Rond-Point des Champs-Elysees, Marcel Dassault, F-75008 Paris, France

CEO: M. Charles Edelstenne, CEO Tel: 33-1-5376-9300 Rev: $3,296
Bus: *Mfr. military aircraft.* Fax: 33-1-5376-9320 Emp: 11,600
www.dassault-aviation.fr

DASSAULT FALCON JET CORPORATION

Teterboro Airport, PO Box 2000, S. Hackensack, NJ 07606

CEO: Jean Rosanvallon, Pres. Tel: (201) 440-6700 %FO: 100
Bus: *Aircraft assembly, sales and* Fax: (201) 967-4469 Emp: 180
service.

DASSAULT SYSTEMES OF AMERICA

6320 Canoga Avenue, 3rd Fl., Woodland Hills, CA 91367-2526

CEO: Philippe Forestier, CEO Tel: (818) 999-2500 %FO: 100
Bus: *Develops CAD/CAM software for* Fax: (818) 999-3535
aerospace and automotive
industries.

DELMIA CORPORATION
5501 New King Street, Troy, MI   48098
CEO: Robert Brown, Pres.　　　　　Tel: (248) 267-9696　　　%FO: 100
Bus: *Produces software for digital*　Fax: (248) 267-8585
manufacturing, robotics, NC
verification & virtual prototyping.

ENOVIA CORPORATION
10926 David Taylor Drive, Charlotte, NC   28262
CEO: Joel R. Lemke, CEO　　　　　Tel: (704) 944-8800　　　%FO: 100
Bus: *Provides software solutions to*　Fax: (704) 944-8888
address the product development
management market.

SOLIDWORKS CORPORATION
300 Bake Avenue, Concord, MA   01742
CEO: Jon K. Hirschtick, CEO　　　　Tel: (978) 371-5111　　　%FO: 100
Bus: *Provides modeling solutions for*　Fax: (978) 371-5088
mechanical engineers.

● **DE DIETRICH & CIE, DIV. ABN AMRO**
Chateau de Reichshoffen, F-67891 Niederbronn Cedex, France
CEO: Regis Bello, CEO　　　　　　Tel: 33-3-8880-2600　　　Rev: $735
Bus: *Mfr. glass-lined containers, heating*　Fax: 33-3-8880-2699　　Emp: 6,100
equipment and railway products and　www.dedietrich.com
services.

DE DIETRICH USA, CIN.
PO Box 345, Union, NJ   07083
CEO: Craig Compoli　　　　　　　Tel: (908) 689-4839　　　%FO: 100
Bus: *Sales of glass-lined equipment for*　Fax: (908) 689-0891
the chemical industry.

DE DIETRICH USA, CIN.
PO Box 3121, Glen Ellyn, IL   60138-3121
CEO: Tom Kvinge　　　　　　　　Tel: (630) 858-7182　　　%FO: 100
Bus: *Sales of glass-lined equipment for*　Fax: (630) 858-7183
the chemical industry.

DE DIETRICH USA, CIN.
Po Box 856, Bridgeton, MO   63044
CEO: Kurt Lehman　　　　　　　　Tel: (314) 344-3453　　　%FO: 100
Bus: *Sales of glass-lined equipment for*　Fax: (314) 344-3316
the chemical industry.

- **DECLEOR PARIS**

  31 rue Henri Rochefort, F-75017 Paris, France
  CEO: Herve Lesieur, Chmn.   Tel: 33-1-4212-7373
  Bus: *Aromatherapy and phytotherapy skin*   Fax: 33-1-4212-0241
  care products.   www.decleor.com

  ### DECLEOR U.S.A., INC.

  18 East 48th Street, 21st Fl., New York, NY   10017
  CEO: Mary Leber, VP   Tel: (212) 838-1771   %FO: 100
  Bus: *Distribution and sale of*   Fax: (212) 838-8817
  aromatherapy and phytotherapy
  skin care products.

- **DOLLFUS MIEG & CIE (DMC)**

  10 ave Lefru-Rollin, F-75579 Paris, France
  CEO: Jacques Boubal, Pres. & CEO   Tel: 33-1-4928-1000
  Bus: *Mfr. apparel fabrics and craft supplies.*   Fax: 33-1-4342-5654   Emp: 4,254
                                       www.dmc-cw.com

  ### THE DMC CORP

  10 Port Kearny, South Kearny, NJ   07032
  CEO: Nicholas F. Wallaert, CEO   Tel: (973) 589-0606   %FO: 100
  Bus: *Distributor embroidery threads.*   Fax: (973) 589-8931   Emp: 40

- **DOSATRON INTL SA**

  Rue Pascal, B.P. 6, Tresses, F-33370 Bordeaux, France
  CEO: John D. Kelly, Pres.   Tel: 33-5-5797-1111   Rev: $14
  Bus: *Mfr. non-electric proportional liquid*   Fax: 33-5-5797-1129   Emp: 120
  dispensers.   www.dosatron.com

  ### DOSATRON INTERNATIONAL INC.

  2090 Sunnydale Blvd., Clearwater, FL   34625
  CEO: Eddy Kelly, Pres.   Tel: (813) 443-5404   %FO: 99
  Bus: *Sale/distribution hydraulic*   Fax: (813) 447-0591   Emp: 12
  injectors.

- **EDITIONS QUO VADIS**

  14, rue du Nouveau Bele, F-44470 Carquefour, France
  CEO: Johnny Komnata, Pres.   Tel: 33-2-4030-4816
  Bus: *Mfr. appointment books and diaries.*   Fax: 33-2-4030-4844   Emp: 250
                                       www.quovadis.fr

QUO VADIS PUBLICATIONS
120 Elmview Avenue, Hamburg, NY 14075

CEO: Joseph P. Mead III, Mgr.	Tel: (716) 648-2601	%FO: 100
Bus: *Mfr./sales appointment books and diaries.*	Fax: (716) 648-2607	

• ELA MEDICAL SA, DIV. SANOFI-SYNTHELABO
Casse la Boursidiere, F-92357 La Plessis-Robinson, France

CEO: Mark Diran Boehm	Tel: 33-1-4601-3333	
Bus: *Mfr. cardiac pacemakers and medical equipment.*	Fax: 33-1-4601-3458	Emp: 250
	www.elamedical.com	

ELA MEDICAL INC.
2950 Xenium Lane North, Plymouth, MN 55441

CEO: Lois Riesgraf, Mgr.	Tel: (763) 519-9400	%FO: 90
Bus: *Cardiac pacemakers, medical equipment.*	Fax: (763) 519-9440	Emp: 30

• ÉLECTRICITÉ DE FRANCE (EDF)
2 rue Louis-Murat, F-75384 Paris, France

CEO: François Roussely, CEO	Tel: 33-1-4042-2222	Rev: $32,278
Bus: *Generation/distribution electricity.*	Fax: 33-1-4042-6200	Emp: 132,550
	www.edf.fr	

ÉLECTRICITÉ DE FRANCE INTERNATIONAL NORTH AMERICA, INC.
1730 Rhode Island Avenue, NW, Washington, DC 20036

CEO: Catherine Gaujacq, Pres.	Tel: (202) 429-2527	%FO: 100
Bus: *U.S. headquarters of EDF; an energy generator and distributor.*	Fax: (202) 429-2532	Emp: 10

• ENTRELEC GROUP SA
20 rue Childebert, F-69002 Lyon, France

CEO: Pierre Bauer, CEO	Tel: 33-4-7277-2737	Rev: $211
Bus: *Mfr. industrial connection and control products.*	Fax: 33-4-7277-2718	Emp: 1,450
	www.entrelec.com	

ENTRELEC INC.
1950 Hurd Drive, Irving, TX 75038-4312

CEO: Francis Leynaert, EVP	Tel: (972) 550-9025	%FO: 100
Bus: *Mfr./sales industrial connection and control products.*	Fax: (972) 550-9215	

● **ERAMET**

Tour Maine-Montparnasse 33, ave. du Maine, F-75755 Paris Cedex 15, France

CEO: Yves Rambaud, CEO	Tel: 33-1-4538-4242	Rev: $2,153
Bus: *Mfr. specialty steels and superalloys.*	Fax: 33-1-4538-7425	Emp: 13,250
	www.eramet.fr	

ERAMET NORTH AMERICA, INC.

333 Rouser Road, PO Box 1198, Corapolis, PA   15108

CEO: Stephen Wilkinson	Tel: (412) 262-6200	%FO: 100
Bus: *Mfr. specialty steels and superalloys.*	Fax: (412) 262-8761	

● **EULER**

1 rue Euler, F-75008 Paris, France

CEO: Jean Lanier, CEO	Tel: 33-1-4070-5050	Rev: $1,084
Bus: *Provides credit insurance.*	Fax: 33-1-4070-5017	Emp: 3,520
	www.eulergroup.com	

EULER ACI

100 East Pratt Street, Baltimore, MD   21202-1008

CEO: Daniel North, VP	Tel: (410) 554-0700	%FO: 100
Bus: *Engaged in account receivable insurance, including credit insurance policies.*	Fax: (410) 554-0631	

EULER ACI

*100 East Pratt Street, Baltimore, MD   21202-1008

CEO: Doug Brunner, Pres. & CEO	Tel: (410) 554-0700	%FO: 100
Bus: *Engaged in account receivable insurance, including credit insurance policies.*	Fax: (410) 554-0811	

● **EUROCOPTER SA**

Aeroport International de Marseille, F-13725 Marignane Cedex, France

CEO: Patrick Gavin, Chmn.	Tel: 33-4-4285-8585	Rev: $1,954
Bus: *Mfr. helicopters.*	Fax: 33-4-4285-8500	Emp: 9,682
	www.eurocopter.com	

AMERICAN EUROCOPTER CORPORATION

2701 Forum Drive, Grand Prairie, TX   75052-7099

CEO: Rudy Palladina	Tel: (972) 641-0000	%FO: 100
Bus: *Assembly/sale helicopters.*	Fax: (972) 641-3761	Emp: 250

- **EUROP ASSISTANCE**

1 Promenade de la Bonnette, F-92633 Gennevilliers, France
CEO: Yves Galland, Chmn.   Tel: 33-1-4185-8585
Bus: *Travel assistance services & emergency*   Fax: 33-1-4185-8571
services.   www.europassistance.com

EUROP ASSISTANCE WORLDWIDE SERVICES
1133 15th St. NW, Ste. 400, Washington, DC 20005
CEO: Emmanuel Legeron, CEO   Tel: (202) 331-1609   %FO: 100
Bus: *Travel assistance, travel*   Fax: (202) 331-1588
emergency network.

- **EUROPEAN AERONAUTIC DEFENCE AND SPACE COMPANY EADS NV**

37 Boulevard de Montmorency, F-75016 Paris, France
CEO: Rainer Hertrich, CEO   Tel: 33-1-4224-2424   Rev: $18,290
Bus: *Engaged in aerospace.*   Fax: 33-1-4224-2424   Emp: 88,880
                                 www.eads-nv.com

BARFIELD INSTRUMENTS CORPORATION
4101 NW 29th Street, Miami, FL 33142
CEO: Curtis Lamb   Tel: (305) 876-2367   %FO: 100
Bus: *Sales, distribution, maintenance*   Fax: (305) 876-2392
and repair of all types of aviation
instrumentation.

CASA AIRCRAFT USA INC.
3810 Concorde Pkwy., Ste. 1000, Chantilly, VA 20151-1128
CEO: Douglas A. Balo, CEO   Tel: (703) 802-1000   %FO: 100
Bus: *Provides marketing and integrated* Fax: (703) 802-1025
customer support services.

EADS AEROFRAME SERVICES
PO Box 16574, Lake Charles, LA 70516
CEO: Eric Schulz   Tel: (337) 421-2920   %FO: 100
Bus: *Engaged in repair, maintenance*   Fax: (337) 421-2939
and overhaul of large commercial
aircraft.

EADS, INC.
815 Connecticut Avenue NW, Ste. 700, Washington, DC 20006
CEO: Dr. Manfred von Nordheim   Tel: (202) 776-0988   %FO: 100
Bus: *Engaged in aerospace.*   Fax: (202) 776-9080

• FACOM SA

6, rue Gustave Eiffel, F-91420 Morangis, France

CEO: Alain Gomez, CEO   Tel: 33-1-6454-4545   Rev: $630
Bus: *Mfr. hand tools.*   Fax: 33-1-6909-6093   Emp: 4,000
                                               www.facom.fr

FACOM TOOLS

3535 West 47th Street, Chicago, IL   60632

CEO: Bernard Roussel, Pres.   Tel: (773) 523-1300   %FO: 100
Bus: *Mfr. hand tools.*   Fax: (773) 523-2210

• FAIVELEY SA

143 Blvd. Anatole France, Carrefour Pleyel F-93285 Saint-Denis Cedex, France

CEO: Francois Faiveley, CEO   Tel: 33-1-4813-6500   Rev: $260
Bus: *Mfr. railroad equipment.*   Fax: 33-1-4813-6647   Emp: 1,800
                                               www.faiveley.com

FAIVELEY RAIL INC.

213 Welsh Pool Road, Extron, PA   19341

CEO: Robert Joyeux, Mng. Dir.   Tel: (610) 524-9110   %FO: 100
Bus: *Mfr. railroad equipment.*   Fax: (610) 524-9190   Emp: 280

• FAURECIA

276 rue Louis Bleriot, F-92641 Boulogne Cedex, France

CEO: Armand Batteaux   Tel: 33-1-4122-7000   Rev: $4,291
Bus: *Engaged in manufacture of automotive*   Fax: 33-1-4122-7010   Emp: 31,800
     seating and components and exhaust   www.faurecia.com
     systems.

FAURECIA

2380 Meijer Drive, Troy, MI   48084-7146

CEO: Bob Scales, VP   Tel: (248) 288-1000   %FO: 100
Bus: *Mfr. automobile seating and*   Fax: (248) 288-1074
     exhaust systems.

• FIMALAC SA

97 rue de Lille, F-75007 Paris, France

CEO: Marc Ladreit de Lachamère, CEO   Tel: 33-1-4753-6150   Rev: $1,260
Bus: *Mfr. garage equipment and hand tools*   Fax: 33-1-4553-6163   Emp: 7,150
     and produce furniture and storage of   www.fimalac.fr
     liquid chemical products.

CASSINA USA INC.
155 East 56th Street, New York, NY   10022
CEO: Tom Boland   Tel: (212) 245-2121   %FO: 100
Bus: *Mfr. and sales of high quality,*   Fax: (212) 245-1340
     durable furniture products.

LBC PETRO UNITED INC.
11666 Port Road, Seabrook, TX   77586
CEO: D. W. Knowles, Mgr.   Tel: (281) 474-4433   %FO: 100
Bus: *Terminal facility for storage of*   Fax: (281) 291-3428
     liquid chemical products.

LBC PETRO UNITED INC.
PO Box 487, Sunshine, LA   70780
CEO: Ed Varn, Mgr.   Tel: (225) 642-8335   %FO: 100
Bus: *Terminal facility for storage of*   Fax: (225) 642-7767
     liquid chemical products.

LBC PETRO UNITED INC.
11666 Port Road, Seabrook, TX   77586
CEO: J. Hugh Roff Jr., Pres.   Tel: (291) 281-3440   %FO: 100
Bus: *Engaged in storage of liquid*   Fax: (291) 281-3429
     chemical products.

● FLAMEL TECHNOLOGIES SA
33 avenue du Docteur Georges Levy, F-69693 Venissieux Cedex, France
CEO: Gerard Soula, CEO   Tel: 33-4-7276-3434   Rev: $11
Bus: *Mfr. oral drug delivery systems.*   Fax: 33-4-7276-3435   Emp: 137
                                         www.flamel-technologies.com

FLAMEL USA INC.
2121 K Street NW, Washington, DC   20037
CEO: Steve Willard, EVP   Tel: (202) 862-8400   %FO: 100
Bus: *Mfr. oral drug delivery systems.*   Fax: (202) 862-3933

● FRAMATOME SA
1, place de la Coupole, Tour Fiat, F-92084 Paris La Défense, France
CEO: Dominique Vignon, Chmn. & CEO   Tel: 33-1-4796-1414
Bus: *Nuclear power engineering services.* Fax: 33-1-4796-3031   Emp: 14,850
     (JV with Alcatel-Alsthom SA)   www.framatome.com

CLEXTRAL, INC.
14450 Carlson Circle, Tampa, FL   33626
CEO: Henri Fournand, Gen. Mgr.   Tel: (813) 854-4434   %FO: 100
Bus: *Mfr. electronic/electrical*   Fax: (813) 855-7818
     connectors & connection devices.

FRAMATOME CONNECTORS USA, INC.

PO Box 9507, Manchester, NH   03108

CEO: Robert B. Smart, Pres.
Bus: *Mfr. electronic/electrical connectors & connection devices.*
Tel: (603) 647-5000
Fax: (603) 647-6465
%FO: 100
Emp: 1,300

FRAMATOME TECHNOLOGIES, INC.

3315 Old Forest Road, Lynchburg, VA   24506-0935

CEO: Lyle Bohn, Pres.
Bus: *Provides outage solutions for nuclear plants.*
Tel: (804) 832-3000
Fax: (804) 832-3663
%FO: 100

FRAMATOME USA, INC.

1911 North Fort Myer Drive, Ste. 705, Rosslyn, VA   22209

CEO: Robert B. Smart, Pres.
Bus: *U.S. headquarters. Nuclear power engineering services.*
Tel: (703) 527-4747
Fax: (703) 527-7973
%FO: 100

OPC DRIZO, INC.

12777 Jones Road, Ste. 185, Houston, TX   77070

CEO: Steve Wormald, VP
Bus: *Mfr. electronic/electrical connectors & connection devices.*
Tel: (281) 469-4925
Fax: (281) 894-1024
%FO: 100

PACKINOX, INC.

50 Briar Hollow Lane, Ste. 540E, Houston, TX   77017

CEO: Francois Reverdy, VP
Bus: *Mfr. electronic/electrical connectors & connection devices.*
Tel: (713) 840-1151
Fax: (713) 840-1165
%FO: 100

● FRANCE TELECOM

6 place d'Alleray, F-75505 Paris Cedex 15, France

CEO: Michel Bon, Chrm.
Bus: *International telecommunications carrier.*
Tel: 33-1-4444-2222
Fax: 33-1-4444-0146
www.francetelecom.fr
Rev: $31,704
Emp: 174,265

FRANCE TELECOM NORTH AMERICA INC.

1270 Avenue of the Americas, 28th Fl,, New York, NY   10020

CEO: Marc Dandelot, Pres.
Bus: *International telecommunications carrier.*
Tel: (212) 332-2100
Fax: (212) 245-8605
%FO: 100
Emp: 30

GLOBECAST NORTH AMERICA

3872 South Keystone Avenue, Culver City, CA   90232

CEO: Robert Baher, Pres.
Bus: *Video service.*
Tel: (310) 845-3900
Fax: (310) 845-3901
%FO: 100

QUESTEL ORBIT
8000 Westpart Drive, Ste. 130, McLean, VA   22101
CEO: Michael Wilkes, VP   Tel: (703) 442-0900   %FO: 100
Bus: *Video service.*   Fax: (703) 893-4632

● **FROMAGERIES BEL**
4, rue d'Anjou, F-75008 Paris, France
CEO: Bertrand Dufort, Pres. & CEO   Tel: 33-1-4007-7250   Rev: $1,521
Bus: *Mfr. dairy products.*   Fax: 33-1-4007-7230   Emp: 8,040
                                      www.fromageries-bel.fr

    BEL KAUKAUNA CHEESE USA, INC.
    PO Box 1974, Kaukauna, WI   54130
    CEO: Robert Gilbert, Pres.   Tel: (920) 788-3524   %FO: 100
    Bus: *Sales/distribution of dairy* Fax: (920) 788-9725
        products.

● **GAZ DE FRANCE**
23 rue Philibert Delorem, Cedex 17, F-75840 Paris, France
CEO: Pierre Gadonneix, Pres.   Tel: 33-1-4754-2020   Rev: $9,165
Bus: *Imports and distributes natural gas.* Fax: 33-1-4754-3858   Emp: 31,100
                                      www.gazdefrance.com

    SOFREGAZ US INC.
    200 Westlake Park Blvd., Ste. 1100, Houston, TX   77079
    CEO: Norbert Heltmann, Pres.   Tel: (281) 531-5685   %FO: JV
    Bus: *Provides engineering services for* Fax: (281) 531-5686
        underground storage development
        and procurement of gas and crude
        oil..

    SURFACE PRODUCTION SYSTEMS, INC.
    2550 Greay Falls, Ste. 300, Houston, TX   77077
    CEO: David R. Luetchford, Pres.   Tel: (281) 589-1808   %FO: JV
    Bus: *Engaged in the engineering &* Fax: (281) 589-2638
        transportation of oil & gas.

● **GENSET SA**
24 rue Royale, F-75008 Paris, France
CEO: Andre G. Pernet, CEO   Tel: 33-1-5504-5900   Rev: $28
Bus: *Provides tailored genomics information* Fax: 33-1-5504-5929   Emp: 540
to the pharmaceutical industry.   www.genxy.com

GENSET CORPORATION

10665 Sorrento Valley Road, San Diego, CA   92121

CEO: Sheila Reed, HR Tel: (858) 597-2600 %FO: 100

Bus: *Provides tailored genomics* Fax: (858) 597-2601 Emp: 75
information to the pharmaceutical
industry.

● GROSFILLEX SARL

BP 2, Arbent F-01107 Oyonnaux, France

CEO: Raymond Grosfillex, Pres. Tel: 33-1-7473-3030

Bus: *Mfr./sales furniture and home products.* Fax: Emp: 1,200
www.grosfillex.com

GROSFILLEX, INC.

230 Old West Penn Avenue, Robesonia, PA   19551

CEO: Carel Harmsen, CEO Tel: (610) 693-5835 %FO: 100

Bus: *Mfr./sales furniture and home* Fax: (610) 693-5414 Emp: 180
products and plastics.

● GROUPE AB S.A.

144 avenue du President Wilson, F-93213 La Plaine Saint Denis, France

CEO: Denis Bortot, COO Tel: 33-1-4922-2001 Rev: $131

Bus: *Engaged in pay cable television,* Fax: 33-1-4922-2235 Emp: 467
including movies, history, science and
health.

ARTS & ENTERTAINMENT (A&E) NETWORK

235 East 45th Street, 9th Fl., New York, NY   10017

CEO: Nicholas Devatzes Tel: (212) 210-1400 %FO: 100

Bus: *Cable television, history and* Fax: (212) 210-9755
entertainment.

● GROUPE BULL

68, Route de Versailles, F-78430 Louveciennes, France

CEO: Guy de Panafieu, Chmn. & CEO Tel: 33-1-3966-6060 Rev: $4,500

Bus: *Design/mfr. computer systems and* Fax: 33-1-4696-9092 Emp: 20,600
networks, including PC's, mainframes, www.bull.com
smart cards, contract manufacturing
services, systems integration and
software.

BULL HN INFORMATION SYSTEMS, INC.

2801 4th Avenue South, 2nd Fl., Minneapolis, MN   55408

CEO: Sam Stolis, Mgr. Tel: (612) 870-2300 %FO: 100

Bus: *Sales/distribution of computer* Fax: (612) 870-5247
systems & networks, including
PC's, mainframes and smartcards.

BULL HN INFORMATION SYSTEMS, INC.

300 Concord Road, Billerica, MA 01821

CEO: Don Zereski, CEO   Tel: (978) 294-6000   %FO: 100

Bus: *U.S. headquarters; computer*   Fax: (978) 294-3635
systems & networks, including
PC's, mainframes and smartcards.

BULL HN INFORMATION SYSTEMS INC.

1225 North Loop West, Ste. 208, Houston, TX 77008

CEO: George McNeil, Pres.   Tel: (713) 865-9500   %FO: 100

Bus: *Sales/distribution of computer*   Fax: (713) 865-9563
systems & networks, including
PC's, mainframes and smartcards.

BULL HN INFORMATION SYSTEMS INC.

12755 Olive Boulevard, Ste. 101, St. Louis, MO 63141

CEO: Tom Pierce, Mgr.   Tel: (314) 205-8900   %FO: 100

Bus: *Sales/distribution of computer*   Fax: (314) 205-8917
systems & networks, including
PC's, mainframes and smartcards.

BULL HN INFORMATION SYSTEMS INC.

925 Keynote Circle, Cleveland, OH 44131

CEO: Keith Baker, Mgr.   Tel: (216) 661-2999   %FO: 100

Bus: *Sales/distribution of computer*   Fax: (216) 661-3881
systems & networks, including
PC's, mainframes and smartcards.

BULL INFORMATION SYSTEMS INC.

7600 Leesburg Pike, Falls Church, VA 22043

CEO: Richard Day, Mgr.   Tel: (571) 633-1811   %FO: 100

Bus: *Sales/distribution of computer*   Fax: (571) 633-1816
systems & networks, including
PC's, mainframes and smartcards.

● **GROUPE CASINO**

24 rue de la Montat, PB 306, F-42008 St-Etienne Cedex 2, France

CEO: Christian Couvreux, Pres   Tel: 33-7-7453-131   Rev: $15,748

Bus: *Engaged in operation of supermarkets,*   Fax: 33-7-7218-515   Emp: 73,470
convenience stores, real estate and   www.casino.fr
restaurant holdings.

CASINO USA INC.
269 Beverly Drive, Beverly Hills, CA   90212
CEO: Andre Delolmo, Pres.   Tel: (310) 552-7881   %FO: 100
Bus: *Operates warehouse grocery*   Fax:
     stores, restaurants & specialty
     retail stores.

SMART & FINAL
600 Citadel Drive, City of Commerce, CA   90040
CEO: Ross E. Roeder, Chmn. & CEO   Tel: (323) 869-7500   %FO: 51
Bus: *Warehouse grocery store*   Fax: (323) 869-7858
     operations.

● **GROUPE DES ASSURANCES NATIONALES SA**
2, rue Pillet Will, F-75448 Paris 9, France
CEO: Didier Pfeiffer, Chmn.   Tel: 33-1-4247-5000   Rev: $11,450
Bus: *Engaged in insurance and financial*   Fax: 33-1-4247-3528   Emp: 33,000
     services.   www.gangroup.com

     GAN NATIONAL INSURANCE CO.
     120 Wall Street, New York, NY   10005
     CEO: Roy Lever, Dir.   Tel: (212) 709-1800   %FO: 100
     Bus: *Engaged in insurance and*   Fax: (212) 709-1840
     financial services.

● **GROUPE INGENICO**
9 Quai de Dion Bouton, F-92816 Puteaux Cedex, France
CEO: Jean-Jacques Poutrel, CEO   Tel: 33-1-4625-8200   Rev: $238
Bus: *Mfr. electronic payment and credit*   Fax: 33-1-4772-5695   Emp: 750
     authorization systems.   www.igenico.fr

     IVI CHECKMATE CORP.
     1033 Mansell Road, Roswell, GA   30076
     CEO: L. Barry Thomson, CEO   Tel: (770) 594-6000   %FO: 100
     Bus: *Mfr. electronic payment hardware*   Fax: (770) 594-6020   Emp: 400
     and software.

● **GROUPE LACTALIS**
10, rue Adolphe Beck, F-53089 Laval Cedex 9, France
CEO: Marcel Urion, Dir.   Tel: 33-2-4359-4259   Rev: $4,877
Bus: *Produces/distributes dairy products.*   Fax: 33-2-4349-4263   Emp: 16,000
     www.lactalis.com

LACTALIS USA INC.
950 Third Avenue, 22nd Fl., New York, NY   10022
CEO: Paul Bensabat, CEO   Tel: (212) 758-6666   %FO: 100
Bus: *Mfr. cheese and dairy products.*   Fax: (212) 758-6678

● **GROUPE LIMAGRAIN HOLDING**
BP 1 Chapes, F-63720 Ennezat, France
CEO: Alain Catala, CEO   Tel: 33-4-7363-4000   Rev: $5,964
Bus: *Production and sales of seeds.*   Fax: 33-4-7363-4044   Emp: 4,780
                                             www.limagrain.com

    FERRY-MORSE SEED COMPANY
    PO Box 1620, Fulton, KY   42041
    CEO: Jack Simpson, Pres.   Tel: (270) 472-3400   %FO: 100
    Bus: *Sales/distribution of seeds.*   Fax: (270) 472-3402

    HARRIS MORAN SEED COMPANY
    PO Box 4938, Modesto, CA   95352
    CEO: Bruno Carette, COO   Tel: (209) 579-7333   %FO: 100
    Bus: *Sales/distribution of seeds.*   Fax: (209) 527-5312

    LIMAGRAIN GENETICS CORP.
    4001 North War Memorial Drive, Peoria, IL   61614
    CEO: Craig Anderson, Mgr.   Tel: (309) 681-0300   %FO: 100
    Bus: *Sales/distribution of seeds.*   Fax: (309) 681-0386

    LIMAGRAIN GENETICS CORP.
    RR 1, Box 203, St. Francisville, IL   62460-9989
    CEO: Roger Kemper   Tel: (618) 943-5776   %FO: 100
    Bus: *Sales/distribution of seeds.*   Fax: (618) 943-7333

    VILMORIN INC.
    PO Box 707, Empire, CA   95319
    CEO: Mario Sanchez, Mgr.   Tel: (209) 529-6000   %FO: 100
    Bus: *Sales/distribution of seeds.*   Fax: (209) 529-5848

● **GROUPE SCHNEIDER SA**
64-70, Avenue Jean-Baptiste Clement, F-92646 Boulogne-Billancourt Cedex, France
CEO: Henri Lachmann, Chmn.   Tel: 33-1-4699-7000   Rev: $8,971
Bus: *Industrial equipment, electromechanical* Fax: 33-1-4699-7456   Emp: 60,800
    engineering, general contracting,   www.schneider-electric.com
    engineering and construction.

GROUPE SCHNEIDER
1415 Roselle Road, Palatine, IL   60067
CEO: Charles W. Denny, Pres. & CEO   Tel: (847) 397-2600   %FO: 98
Bus: *Power distribution &*   Fax: (847) 925-7500   Emp: 16,000
    electric/electronic industry control
    equipment.

● **GROUPE STERIA SCA**
12 rue Paul Dautier, BP 58, F-78142 Velizy Villacoublay Cedex, France
CEO: Gerard Guyodo, CEO   Tel: 33-1-3488-6000   Rev: $366
Bus: *Engaged in information technology.*   Fax: 33-1-3488-6262   Emp: 4,220
    www.steria.com

   STERIA USA INC.
   580 California Street, Ste. 500, San Francisco, CA   94104
   CEO: Yves Rouilly, Dir.   Tel: (415) 283-3232   %FO: 100
   Bus: *Engaged in information*   Fax: (415) 283-3382
      technology.

● **GUERLAIN SA**
125 rue de President Wilson, F-92593 Levallois-Perret Cedex, France
CEO: Thibault Ponroy, CEO   Tel: 33-1-4127-3100
Bus: *Mfr. fragrances, cosmetics and skin*   Fax: 33-1-4127-3107
    products.   www.guerlain.com

   GUERLAIN, INC.
   1045 Centennial Avenue, Piscataway, NJ   08854
   CEO: Marjorie Wollan, CEO   Tel: (732) 981-2500   %FO: 100
   Bus: *Mfr./distribute fragrances and*   Fax: (732) 981-2580   Emp: 100
      cosmetics.

   GUERLAIN, INC.
   19 East 57th Street, New York, NY   10022
   CEO: Marjorie Wollan, CEO   Tel: (212) 931-2400   %FO: 100
   Bus: *Mfr./distribute fragrances and*   Fax: (212) 931-2445   Emp: 175
      cosmetics.

● **GUIRAUDIE-AUFFEVE SA**
24 rue Georges Picot, BP 4366, F-31030 Toulouse, France
CEO: Rene Soum, Pres.   Tel: 33-5-6114-4000
Bus: *Engaged in real estate, general*   Fax: 33-5-6152-9196   Emp: 7
    contracting and specialty concrete
    systems.

AMEGA CORPORATION
8989 North Loop East, Houston, TX   77029
CEO: James E. Stubbs, Pres.   Tel: (713) 672-8989   %FO: 100
Bus: *Land development & investments.*   Fax: (713) 675-2461   Emp: 4

● **HACHETTE FILIPACCHI MEDIAS**
149-151 rue Anatol France, F-92300 Levallois-Perret, France
CEO: Gerald de Roquemaurel   Tel: 33-1-4134-6000   Rev: $2,300
Bus: *Publisher of culture and fashion*   Fax: 33-1-4134-7777   Emp: 8,590
magazines, including Home,   www.hachette-filipacchi.com
Metropolitan Home, Popular
Photography, Woman's Day, Premier
and Road and Track.

   HFNM (HACHETTE FILIPACCHI)
   1633 Broadway, New York, NY   10019
   CEO: Jean Paul Denfert-Rochereau   Tel: (212) 767-6418   %FO: 100
   Bus: *Magazine publisher.*   Fax: (212) 767-5785

   WOMAN'S DAY MAGAZINE
   1633 Broadway, New York, NY   10019
   CEO: Ben Tatta, COO   Tel: (212) 767-6418   %FO: 100
   Bus: *Magazine publisher.*   Fax: (212) 767-5785

● **HAMON RESEARCH-COTTRELL**
116-118 rue Jules-Guesde, F-92303 Levallois Perret, France
CEO: Francis Lambilliotte, CEO   Tel: 33-1-4519-3705
Bus: *Engaged in air pollution control and* Fax: 33-1-4519-3777
equipment.   www.hamon.com

   HAMON RESEARCH-COTTRELL INC.
   58-72 East Main Street, Somerville, NJ   08876
   CEO: Jonathan Lagarenne   Tel: (908) 685-4000
   Bus: *Air pollution and control*   Fax: (908) 333-2165
   equipment.

● **HAVAS ADVERTISING**
84 rue de Villers, F-92683 Levallois-Perret Cedex, France
CEO: Alain de Pouzilhac, Chmn.   Tel: 33-1-4134-3000   Rev: $1,216
Bus: *International advertising agency. (Sub* Fax: 33-1-4134-1248   Emp: 12,000
of Havas SA)   www.havas.fr

   EURO RSCG TATHAM
   36 East Grand Avenue, Chicago, IL   60611
   CEO: Gary C. Epstein, Pres.   Tel: (312) 337-4400   %FO: 100
   Bus: *International advertising agency.* Fax: (312) 337-8855   Emp: 292

EURO RSCG WORLDWIDE
350 Hudson Street, 6th Fl., New York, NY   10014

CEO: Robert Schmetterer, CEO	Tel: (212) 886-2000	%FO: 100
Bus: *International communications group of companies. Advertising; audiovisual; publishing; travel & recreation.*	Fax: (212) 886-2016	Emp: 1,083

HAVAS ADVERTISING
410 Park Avenue, Ste. 1520, New York, NY   10022

CEO: Patrick Lemarchand, CEO	Tel: (212) 753-1410	%FO: 100
Bus: *International communications group of companies. Advertising; audiovisual; publishing; travel & recreation.*	Fax: (212) 753-1409	

LALLY, McFARLAND & PANTELLO/EURO RSCG
200 Madison Avenue, New York, NY   10016

CEO: Ronald G. Pantello, Chmn.	Tel: (212) 532-1000	%FO: 100
Bus: *International advertising agency.*	Fax: (212) 213-0449	Emp: 200

MESSNER VETERE BERGER McNAMEE SCHMETTERER/EURO RCG
350 Hudson Street, New York, NY   10014

CEO: Louise McNamee, Pres.	Tel: (212) 886-4100	%FO: 100
Bus: *International advertising agency.*	Fax: (212) 886-4415	Emp: 360

ROBERT A. BECKER EURO RSCG
1633 Broadway, New York, NY   10010

CEO: Sander A. Flaum, Chmn.	Tel: (212) 399-2002	%FO: 100
Bus: *Medical advertising agency.*	Fax: (212) 399-9074	Emp: 172

● HERMES INTERNATIONAL SA
24, rue du Faubourg-Saint-Honore, F-75008 Paris, France

CEO: Jean-Louis Dumas, Chmn.	Tel: 33-1-4017-4920	Rev: $934
Bus: *Men's and women's apparel, including leather handbags, silk scarves and ties.*	Fax: 33-1-4017-4921 www.hermesinternational.com	Emp: 4,240

HERMES PARIS
123 South Onizuka Street, Los Angeles, CA   90012

CEO: Laurent Mommeja, Pres.	Tel: (213) 626-3391	%FO: 100
Bus: *Men's and women's apparel, including leather handbags, silk scarves and ties.*	Fax: (213) 689-4340	

HERMES PARIS

11 East 57th Street, New York, NY   10021

CEO: Laurent Mommeja, Pres.　　　Tel: (212) 751-3181　　　%FO: 100

Bus: *Men's and women's apparel,*　Fax: (212) 826-2540
including leather handbags, silk
scarves and ties.

HERMES PARIS

745 Fifth Avenue, New York, NY   10151

CEO: Laurent Mommeja, Pres.　　　Tel: (212) 759-7585　　　%FO: 100

Bus: *Men's and women's apparel,*　Fax: (212) 644-2132
including leather handbags, silk
scarves and ties.

● **IER SA**

3 rue Salomon de Rothschild, F-92156 Suresnes Cedex, France

CEO: Charles Schulman, Pres.　　　Tel: 33-4-138-6000

Bus: *Designs, manufactures & markets*　Fax: 33-4-138-6200　　　Emp: 450
custom intelligent work stations &　www.ier.fr
systems for transportation networks.

　IER INCORPORATED

　4004 Beltline Road, Ste. 140, Addison, TX   75001

　CEO: Bernard Sanguinetti, VP　　Tel: (972) 991-2292

　Bus: *Designs, manufactures & markets*　Fax: (972) 991-1044
　custom intelligent work stations &
　systems for transportation
　networks.

● **ILOG SA**

9 rue de Verdun, F-94253 Gentilly, France

CEO: Pierre Haren, CEO　　　　　Tel: 33-1-4908-3500　　　Rev: $80

Bus: *Mfr. pre-built software component and*　Fax: 33-1-4908-3510　　Emp: 500
related software.　　　　　　　www.ilog.com

　ILOG, INC.

　889 Alder Avenue, Incline Village, NV   89451

　CEO: Todd Lowe, Pres.　　　　Tel: (775) 831-7744　　　%FO: 100

　Bus: *Mfr. software.*　　　　　Fax: (775) 831-7755

　ILOG, INC.

　4250 North Fairfax Drive, Ste. 800, Arlington, VA   22203-1619

　CEO: Pierre Dowd　　　　　　Tel: (703) 351-6969　　　%FO: 100

　Bus: *Mfr. software.*　　　　　Fax: (703) 351-6969

ILOG, INC.
144 Turnpike Road, Ste. 130, Southborough, MA 01772
CEO: K. Napolitano   Tel: (508) 485-8155   %FO: 100
Bus: *Mfr. software.*   Fax: (508) 485-8155

ILOG, INC.
1080 Linda Vista Avenue, Mountain View, CA 94043
CEO: Patrick Albert, COO   Tel: (650) 567-8000   %FO: 100
Bus: *Mfr. software.*   Fax: (650) 567-8001

● **IMERYS**
Tour Maine-Montparnasse, 33 avenue de Maine, F-75755 Paris Cedex 15, France
CEO: Patrick Kron, Pres. & CEO   Tel: 33-1-4538-4848   Rev: $2,633
Bus: *Produces building materials and* Fax: 33-1-4538-7478   Emp: 11,950
industrial minerals.   www.imerys.com

    C-E MINERALS
    901 East Eighth Avenue, King of Prussia, PA 19406
    CEO: Timothy J. McCarthy, Pres.   Tel: (610) 265-6880   %FO: 100
    Bus: *Mfr. industrial minerals.*   Fax: (610) 337-7163

● **IMPRIMERIE NORTIER**
78/80 rue de Docteur Bauer, F-93400 Saint Ouen, France
CEO: Bertrand Gintz, Dir.   Tel: 33-1-4921-1190
Bus: *Mfr./sales of folding boxes.* Fax: 33-1-49-21-1199
                                    www.nortier.fr

    NORTIER INC.
    54 Riverside Drive, Ste. 15AA, New York, NY 10024
    CEO: Paula J. Hauser-Coburn, Mgr.   Tel: (212) 496-0439   %FO: 100
    Bus: *Sales/distribution of folding boxes.* Fax: (212) 712-0340

● **INFOGRAMES ENTERTAINMENT, SA**
82-84 rue du 1er Mars 1943, F-69628 Villeurbanne Cedex, France
CEO: Bruno Bonnell, CEO   Tel: 33-4-7265-5000   Rev: $500
Bus: *Developer, publisher and distributor of* Fax: 33-4-7265-5001   Emp: 2,150
interactive entertainment software www.infogrames.com
games.

    INFOGRAMES, INC.
    417 Fifth Avenue, New York, NY 10016
    CEO: Denis Guyennot, Pres.   Tel: (212) 726-6500   %FO: 1
    Bus: *Publisher and distributor of* Fax: (212) 726-4222   Emp: 800
    interactive entertainment software
    games.

- **INFOVISTA SA**

6 rue de la Terre de Feu, Courtaboeuf, F-91952 Les Ulis Cedex, France

CEO: Alain Tingaud, CEO   Tel: 33-1-6486-7900   Rev: $10

Bus: *Mfr. software to monitor performance of*   Fax: 33-1-6486-7979   Emp: 35
computer networks.   www.infovista.com

INFOVISTA CORP.

12950 Worldgate Drive, Ste. 250, Herndon, VA   20170

CEO: John A. Vidal, Pres.   Tel: (703) 435-2435   %FO: 100

Bus: *Mfr. software to monitor*   Fax: (703) 435-5122
performance of computer networks.

INFOVISTA CORP.

1250 Oakmead Pkwy., Ste. 316, Sunnyvale, CA   94086

CEO: Paul Frazier   Tel: (408) 774-2960   %FO: 100

Bus: *Mfr. software to monitor*   Fax: (408) 774-2966
performance of computer networks.

INFOVISTA CORP.

521 Fifth Avenue, Ste. 2101, New York, NY   10175

CEO: Dan Magnas, Sales   Tel: (212) 972-5305   %FO: 100

Bus: *Mfr. software to monitor*   Fax: (212) 972-5279
performance of computer networks.

INFOVISTA CORP.

10440 Little Patuxent Pkwy., 4th Fl., Columbia, MD   21044

CEO: John A. Vidal, Pres.   Tel: (410) 997-4470   %FO: 100

Bus: *Mfr. software to monitor*   Fax: (410) 997-4607
performance of computer networks.

- **IPSOS SA**

99 rue de l'Abbé Groult, F-75739 Paris Cedex 15, France

CEO: Jean-Marc Lech, Co-Chmn.   Tel: 33-1-5368-2828   Rev: $310

Bus: *Engaged in market research.*   Fax: 33-1-5366-0162   Emp: 2,440
                                           www.ipsos.fr

IPSOS REID

1700 Broadway, Ste. 902, New York, NY   10019

CEO: Tom Neri, EVP   Tel: (212) 265-3200   %FO: 100

Bus: *Engaged in market research.*   Fax: (212) 625-3790

IPSOS-ASI, INC.

301 Merritt 7, Norwalk, CT   06851

CEO: Jim Thompson, CEO   Tel: (203) 840-3400   %FO: 100

Bus: *Engaged in market research.*   Fax: (203) 840-3450

IPSOS-ASI, INC.
100 Charles Lindbergh Blvd., Uniondale, NY   11553
CEO: Rupert Walters   Tel: (516) 507-3000   %FO: 100
Bus: *Engaged in market research.*   Fax: (516) 607-3300

IPSOS-ASI, INC.
130 North Brand Blvd., Ste. 300, Glendale, CA   91203
CEO: Jim Thompson, CEO   Tel: (818) 637-5600   %FO: 100
Bus: *Engaged in market research.*   Fax: (818) 637-5615

● **JEANTET & ASSOCIES**
87 ave. Kleber, F-75784 Paris Cedex 16, France
CEO: Ferbabd-Charles Jeantet, Mng. Ptnr.   Tel: 33-1-4505-8080
Bus: *International law firm.*   Fax: 33-1-4704-2041
                                     www.icclaw.com

JEANTET & ASSOCIES
152 West 57th Street, Ste. 26C, New York, NY   10019
CEO: Elie Kleiman, Mng. Ptnr.   Tel: (212) 314-9499   %FO: 100
Bus: *International law firm.*   Fax: (212) 582-3806

● **JOUAN SA**
Rue Bobby Sands, F-44805 St. Herblain, France
CEO: Marcel Victorri, Pres.   Tel: 33-2-4016-8000
Bus: *Mfr. laboratory equipment.*   Fax: 33-2-4094-7016   Emp: 200
                                     www.jouan.com

JOUAN, INC.
170 Marcel Drive, Winchester, VA   22602
CEO: Lyle E. Cady, Jr., Pres.   Tel: (540) 869-8623   %FO: 80
Bus: *Mfr. laboratory equipment.*   Fax: (540) 869-8626   Emp: 110

● **LAFARGE, S.A.**
61 rue de Belles Feuilles, F-75782, Paris, Cedex 16, France
CEO: Bertrand P. Collomb, Chmn.   Tel: 33-1-4434-1111   Rev: $12,200
Bus: *Mfr. cement, concrete and aggregates,*   Fax: 33-1-4434-1200   Emp: 65,700
     gypsum and specialty products. (JV   www.lafarge.fr
     Blue Circle)

LAFARGE CORPORATION
300 East Joppa Road, Ste. 200, Towson, MD   21286
CEO: Ronald Heckel   Tel: (410) 847-3300   %FO: 100
Bus: *Mfr./sales/distribution of*   Fax: (410) 847-3308
     construction materials including
     cement, block and pipe concrete
     products and gypsum wallboard.

LAFARGE CORPORATION
11130 Sunrise Valley Drive, Ste. 300, Reston, VA   20191
CEO: John M. Piecuch, Pres. & CEO   Tel: (703) 264-3600   %FO: 53
Bus: *Mfr./sales/distribution of*   Fax: (703) 264-0634   Emp: 10,500
construction materials including
cement, block and pipe concrete
products and gypsum wallboard.

● **LAGARDÈRE GROUPE**
4 rue de Presbourg, F-75116 Paris, France
CEO: Jean-Luc Lagardère, CEO   Tel: 33-1-4069-1600   Rev: $12,576
Bus: *Industrial publishing conglomerate;*   Fax: 33-1-4723-0192   Emp: 49,960
space, defense & transportation,   www.lagardere.fr
communications & media.

HACHETTE FILIPACCHI INC.
1633 Broadway, New York, NY   10019
CEO: Jack Kliger, Pres. & CEO   Tel: (212) 767-6000   %FO: 100
Bus: *Magazine publishing.*   Fax: (212) 767-5600

LAGARDÈRE GROUP NORTH AMERICA, INC.
1633 Broadway, 45th Fl., New York, NY   10019
CEO: Alain Lemarchand, Pres.   Tel: (212) 767-6000   %FO: 100
Bus: *U.S. headquarters. Industrial*   Fax: (212) 767-5635
publishing conglomerate; space,
defense and transportation,
communications and media.

● **LAZARD LLC**
121 blvd. Haussmann, F-75382 Paris Cedex 08, France
CEO: Michel David-Weill, Chmn.   Tel: 33-1-4413-0111
Bus: *Investment banking services.*   Fax: 33-1-4413-0100
www.lazard.com

LAZARD FRÈRES COMPANY
30 Rockefeller Plaza, New York, NY   10020
CEO: Michele David-Weill, Chmn.   Tel: (212) 632-6000   %FO: 100
Bus: *Investment banking services.*   Fax: (212) 632-6060   Emp: 650

LAZARD FRÈRES COMPANY
200 West Madison Street, Chicago, IL   60606
CEO: Michele David-Weill, Chmn.   Tel: (312) 407-6600   %FO: 100
Bus: *Investment banking services.*   Fax: (312) 407-6620

● **LE DOMAINES BARONS DE ROTHSCHILD (LAFITE)**

33 rue de la Baume, F-75008 Paris, France

CEO: W. Philip Woodward, Chmn. Tel: 33-1-5389-7800

Bus: *Distributes imported wines and* Fax: 33-1-5389-7801
domestic products. (JV with Chalone www.caluacom.fr
Wine Group, US)

  CHALONE WINE GROUP LTD.

  621 Airpark Road, Napa, CA 94559

  CEO: Thomas B. Selfridge, Pres. & Tel: (707) 254-4200 %FO: JV
   CEO

  Bus: *Produces premium table wines and* Fax: (707) 254-4201
  distributes imported wines. (Owns
  20% of the Chateau Duhart-Milon
  estate in France.)

● **LECTRA SYSTEMES SA**

16-18 rue Chalgri, F-75016 Paris, France

CEO: Daniel Harari, CEO Tel: 33-1-5364-4200 Rev: $215

Bus: *Mfr. software and equipment for* Fax: 33-1-5364-4300 Emp: 1,517
apparel and textile manufacturers. www.lectra.com

  LECTRA INC.

  889 Franklin Road, Marietta, GA 30067

  CEO: David Siegelman, Pres. & CEO Tel: (770) 422-8050 %FO: 100

  Bus: *Sales software and equipment for* Fax: (770) 422-1503
  apparel industry.

  LECTRA INC.

  10200 Pioneer Blvd., Santa Fe Springs, CA 90670

  CEO: David Siegelman, Pres. & CEO Tel: (562) 903-1340 %FO: 100

  Bus: *Sales software and equipment for* Fax: (562) 903-1346
  apparel industry.

  LECTRA INC.

  2880 East Beltline NE, Grand Rapids, MI 49525

  CEO: David Siegelman, Pres. & CEO Tel: (616) 361-1139 %FO: 100

  Bus: *Sales software and equipment for* Fax: (616) 361-5679
  apparel industry.

  LECTRA INC.

  119 West 40th Street, 3rd Fl., New York, NY 10018

  CEO: David Siegelman, Pres. & CEO Tel: (212) 704-4004 %FO: 100

  Bus: *Sales software and equipment for* Fax: (212) 704-0751
  apparel industry.

• **LEGRAND SA**
128 ave du Marechal de Lattre, F-87045 Limoges Cedex, France
CEO: Francois Grapotte, Pres.　　　　　Tel: 33-5-5506-8787　　　　Rev: $2,316
Bus: *Mfr. electric wiring devices.*　　　Fax: 33-5-5506-8888　　　　Emp: 23,000
　　　　　　　　　　　　　　　　　　www.legrand.fr

　　　PASS & SEYMOUR/LEGRAND
　　　50 Boyd Avenue, PO Box 4822, Syracuse, NY 13209-4822
　　　CEO: Tom Edmonds, Pres.　　　　　Tel: (315) 468-6211　　　%FO: 100
　　　Bus: *Mfr. electric wiring devices.*　Fax: (315) 463-6296　　　Emp: 500

• **LEGRIS INDUSTRIES**
74 rue de Paris, BP 70411, F-35704 Rennes Cedex, France
CEO: Pierre-Yves Legris, CEO　　　　Tel: 33-2-9925-5500　　　　Rev: $675
Bus: *Mfr. and sales of fluid controls.*　Fax: 33-2-9925-5598　　　　Emp: 5,697
　　　　　　　　　　　　　　　　　　www.legris.com

　　　LEGRIS USA INC.
　　　7205 East Hampton Avenue, Mesa, AZ 85208
　　　CEO: Pierre-Yves Legris, Pres.　　Tel: (480) 830-0216　　　%FO: 100
　　　Bus: *Sales of fluid controls.*　　Fax: (480) 839-7556

• **L'OREAL SA**
41, rue Martre, F-92117 Clichy, France
CEO: Lindsay Owen-Jones, Chmn. & CEO　Tel: 33-1-4756-7000　　　Rev: $11,930
Bus: *Mfr. cosmetics, fragrances, hair care*　Fax: 33-1-4756-8002　　　Emp: 42,160
　　products, fashion publishing.　　　www.loreal.com

　　　L'OREAL
　　　575 Fifth Avenue, New York, NY 10017
　　　CEO: Guy Peyrelonuge, Pres. & CEO　Tel: (212) 818-1500　　　%FO: 100
　　　Bus: *Mfr./sale cosmetics, fragrances,*　Fax: (212) 984-4999　　　Emp: 6,000
　　　　hair care products.

　　　MAYBELLINE INC.
　　　575 Fifth Avenue, New York, NY 10017
　　　CEO: Guy Peyrelonuge, Pres. & CEO　Tel: (212) 818-1500　　　%FO: 100
　　　Bus: *Mfr./sale cosmetics and fragrances.*　Fax: (212) 984-4564

　　　SOFT SHEEN PRODUCTS, INC.
　　　1000 East 87th Street, Chicago, IL 60619
　　　CEO: Terry Gardner, Pres.　　　　Tel: (773) 978-0700　　　%FO: 100
　　　Bus: *Mfr. ethnic hair care products.*　Fax: (773) 978-2297

• **LOUIS DREYFUS & CIE**
87 ave. de la Grande Armee, F-75782 Paris Cedex 16, France
CEO: William Louis-Dreyfus, Chmn.   Tel: 33-1-4066-1111
Bus: *Wholesalers of cereals, grains;*   Fax: 33-1-4066-1612
    shipowners.   www.louisdreyfus.com

    LOUIS DREYFUS CORPORATION
    Ten Westport Road, Wilton, CT 06897
    CEO: William Louis-Dreyfus, Chmn.   Tel: (203) 961-0602   %FO: 100
    Bus: *Supplier of grains, cereals and*   Fax: (203) 964-8275
    seeds.

• **LTM SA**
57 rue Salvador Allende, F-95870 Bezons, France
CEO: Karin Eliescaud, Pres.   Tel: 33-1-3996-4848
Bus: *Mfr./distribution motion picture and TV*   Fax: 33-1-3996-4849   Emp: 30
    lighting equipment.   www.ltmlighting.com

    LTM CORP OF AMERICA
    7755 Haskell Avenue, Van Nuys, CA 91406
    CEO: Herb Breltling, VP   Tel: (818) 780-9828   %FO: 100
    Bus: *Sale/rental motion picture & TV*   Fax: (818) 780-9848   Emp: 30
    lighting equipment.

• **LVMH MOËT HENNESSY LOUIS VUITTON SA**
30 ave. Hoche, F-75008 Paris, France
CEO: Bernard J. Arnault, Chmn.   Tel: 33-1-4413-2222   Rev: $10,900
Bus: *Holding co. produces/ retails;*   Fax: 33-1-4413-2223   Emp: 38,280
    wines/liquors; designer clothing;   www.lvmh.fr
    cosmetics/fragrances; shoes,
    luggage/leather goods.

    DFS GROUP LTD.
    525 Market Street, San Francisco, CA 94105-2708
    CEO: Ed Brennan, CEO   Tel: (415) 977-2700
    Bus: *Operators of duty free shops in*   Fax: (415) 977-2956
    international air terminals.

    DOMAINE CHANDON
    One California Drive, Yountville, CA 94599
    CEO: Frederick Cumenal, Pres.   Tel: (707) 944-8844   %FO: 100
    Bus: *Restaurateur and producer of*   Fax: (707) 944-1123
    sparkling wines.

EBEL, INC., DIV. LVMH GROUP
750 Lexington Avenue, New York, NY   10022
CEO: Ronald L. Wolfgang, Pres. & CEO Tel: (212) 888-3235   %FO: 100
Bus: *Sales/distribution of watches.*   Fax: (212) 888-6719   Emp: 55

LOUIS VUITTON USA INC.
19 East 57th Street, New York, NY   10022
CEO: Thomas O'Neill, Pres.   Tel: (212) 931-2000   %FO: 100
Bus: *Handbags, leather goods, luggage.* Fax: (212) 753-7199

● **MANITOU BF SA**
430 rue de l'Aubiniere, BP 249, F-44158 Ancenia Cedex, France
CEO: Marcel Braud, Chmn.   Tel: 33-2-4009-1011   Rev: $618
Bus: *Mfr. industrial vehicles.*   Fax: 33-2-4083-3688   Emp: 2,000
                                     www.manitou.com

KD MANITOU INC.
3120 Gholson Road, Waco, TX   76705-0547
CEO: Serge Bosche, Dir.   Tel: (254) 799-0232   %FO: 100
Bus: *Mfr./sales industrial vehicles.*   Fax: (254) 799-4433

● **MARTEK POWER**
10 rue Jean Jaurés, F-92800 Puteaux, France
CEO: Marcel Katz, Chmn.   Tel: 33-1-4900-1423
Bus: *Mfr. semi-custom and custom power*   Fax: 33-1-4717-0252   Emp: 1,400
    supplies.   www.martekpower.com

MARTEK POWER ABBOTT, INC.
2727 South La Cienega Blvd., Los Angeles, CA   90034
CEO: H. Emami, Pres.   Tel: (310) 202-8820   %FO: 100
Bus: *Mfr. electronic power supplies.*   Fax: (310) 836-1027

MARTEK POWER, INC.
4115 Spencer Street, Torrance, CA   90503
CEO: Loman Rensink, Pres.   Tel: (310) 542-8561   %FO: 100
Bus: *Mfr. electronic power supplies.*   Fax: (310) 371-6331   Emp: 740

MARTEK POWER, INC.
15 Jonathan Drive, Brockton, MA   02402
CEO: S. W. Forrester, Pres.   Tel: (508) 559-0880   %FO: 100
Bus: *Mfr. electronic power supplies.*   Fax: (508) 588-1962

● **MAYDREAM SA**

18-20 rue Jacques, Dulud, F-92200 Neuilly Sur Seine, France

CEO: Herve C. deClerk, CEO

Bus: *Engaged in marketing and public relations.*

Tel: 33-1-2423-7193
Fax: 33-1-4637-3382
www.adforum.com

    ADFORUM MAYDREAM INC.

    8 Marine View Plaza, Hoboken, NJ   07030

    CEO: Phil Guerinet, Pres.

    Bus: *Engaged in marketing and public relations.*

    Tel: (201) 792-3007
    Fax: (201) 792-7234

    %FO: 100

● **MEDASYS DIGITAL SYSTEMS**

Le Mercury, Espace Technologique de St. Aubin, F-91193 Gif sur Yvette Cedex, France

CEO: Jean-Marie Lucani, Pres.

Bus: *Mfr. computer software.*

Tel: 33-1-6933-7300
Fax: 33-1-6933-7301
www.medasys-digital-systems.fr

Rev: $27
Emp: 210

    MEDASYS USA INC.

    5301 Blue Lagoon Drive, Ste. 600, Miami, FL   33128

    CEO: P. Serafino

    Bus: *Mfr. computer software.*

    Tel: (305) 261-6025
    Fax: (305) 261-9765

    %FO: 100

● **MEGTEC SYSTEMS SA**

32-34 rue des Malines, F-91000 Lisses-Evry, France

CEO: John Dangelmaier, Pres.

Bus: *Mfr. press auxiliary equipment.*

Tel: 33-1-6989-4793
Fax: 33-1-6497-7414
www.megtec.com

Emp: 300

    MEGTEC SYSTEMS COMPANY INC.

    830 Prosper Road, DePere, WI   54115

    CEO: Alan Fiers, Pres.

    Bus: *Mfr. equipment for printing, web coating, packaging, paper & tissue, and other industrial markets.*

    Tel: (920) 336-5715
    Fax: (920) 336-3404

    %FO: 100
    Emp: 18

● **MERIDIEN GESTION SA**

171 blvd Haussmann, F-75008 Paris, France

CEO: Alair Eman, Pres.

Bus: *Luxury hotels owners and operators.*

Tel: 33-1-4068-3131
Fax: 33-1-4068-3131
www.lemeridien-paris.com

FORTE & LE MERIDIEN HOTELS & RESORTS

420 Lexington Avenue, Suite 1718, New York, NY   10170

CEO: Fran Brasseux, SVP   Tel: (212) 805-5000   %FO: 100

Bus: *Luxury hotels owners and*   Fax: (212) 805-5047
operators.

PARKER MERIDIEN HOTELS INC

119 West 56th Street, New York, NY   10019

CEO: Steven Pipes, Gen. Mgr.   Tel: (212) 245-5000   %FO: 100

Bus: *Luxury hotels owners and*   Fax: (212) 307-1878
operators.

● MGP FINANCE, SA

6, rue Piccini, F-75116 Paris, France

CEO: Philippe Destenbert, CEO   Tel: 33-1-7657-6060

Bus: *Mfr. and sale of radio protection*   Fax: 33-1-9059-5518   Emp: 280
instrumentation.

MGP INSTRUMENTS, INC.

5000 Highlands Parkway, Ste. 150, Smyrna, GA   30082

CEO: Michael S. Wilson, COO   Tel: (770) 432-2744   %FO: 100

Bus: *Mfr./sale radioprotection*   Fax: (770) 432-9179   Emp: 35
instrumentation.

● MICHELIN & CIE (GROUP MICHELIN)

12 cours Sablon, F-63040 Clermont-Ferrand 9, France

CEO: François Michelin, Mng. Ptr.   Tel: 33-4-7398-5900   Rev: $14,885

Bus: *Mfr./distributes tires and rubber*   Fax: 33-4-7398-5904   Emp: 128,122
products.   www.michelin.fr

MICHELIN NORTH AMERICA, INC.

PO Box 19001, Greenville, SC   29602-9001

CEO: James Micali, Pres.   Tel: (864) 458-5000   %FO: 100

Bus: *Sales/distribution of passenger,*   Fax: (864) 458-6359
light-truck, commercial-truck and
earth-mover tires.

MICHELIN TIRE CORPORATION, NORTH AMERICA

One Parkway South, Greenville, SC   29615

CEO: James Micali, Pres.   Tel: (864) 458-5000   %FO: 100

Bus: *Sales/distribution of tires and*   Fax: (864) 458-6359   Emp: 26,000
rubber products.

UNIROYAL GOODRICH TIRE COMPANY
One Parkway South, Greenville, SC 29615

CEO: James Micali, Pres.	Tel: (864) 458-5000	%FO: 100
Bus: *Sales/distribution of passenger, light-truck, commercial-truck and earth-mover tires.*	Fax: (864) 458-6359	

● **NATEXIS BANQUES POPULAIRES S.A.**
45 rue Saint-Dominique, F-75700 Paris, France

CEO: Francis Gavois, Pres.	Tel: 33-1-4550-9000	Rev: $4,160
Bus: *Engaged in real estate, corporate lending and equity financing.*	Fax: 33-1-4555-6896	Emp: 3,200
	www.natexis.com	

ASSET BACKED MANAGEMENT CORP.
712 Fifth Avenue, 17th Fl., New York, NY 10019

CEO: Daniel Lescop, Dir.	Tel: (212) 314-9500	%FO: 100
Bus: *Engaged in real estate, corporate lending, capital markets and equity financing.*	Fax: (212) 314-9555	

NEXTEXIS BANQUES POPULAIRES
1251 Sixth Avenue, 34th Fl., New York, NY 10020

CEO: Jean Y. Richard, Mgr.	Tel: (212) 872-5000	%FO: 100
Bus: *International banking services.*	Fax: (212) 872-5045	

● **NETVALUE SA**
8 rue de l'Hotel de Ville, F-92200 Neuilly sur Seine, France

CEO: Lennart Brag, CEO	Tel: 33-1-4291-1900	Rev: $3
Bus: *Engaged in market research.*	Fax: 33-1-4291-1901	Emp: 88
	www.netvalue.com	

NETVALUE USA INC.
427 Broadway, 4th Fl., New York, NY 10013

CEO: Bernard Ochs	Tel: (917) 237-0530	%FO: 100
Bus: *Engaged in market research.*	Fax: (917) 237-0531	

● **NOUVELLES FRONTIERES**
87 blvd de Grenelle, F-75738 Paris, France

CEO: Jacques Maillot, Chmn.	Tel: 33-1-4568-7000	Rev: $1,200
Bus: *Travel services, tour operator.*	Fax: 33-1-4568-7003	Emp: 3,600
	www.nouvelles-frontieres.com	

NEW FRONTIERS INC.
6 East 46th Street, 2nd Fl., New York, NY 10017

CEO: Theresa lambert, Mgr.	Tel: (212) 986-6006	%FO: 100
Bus: *Tour operator.*	Fax: (212) 986-3343	

NEW FRONTIERS INC.
5757 West Century Blvd., Ste. 650, Los Angeles, CA   90045
CEO: Renatre Fedi, Mgr.   Tel: (310) 670-7318   %FO: 100
Bus: *Tour operator.*   Fax: (310) 677-7707

● **OBERTHUR CARD SYSTEMS ZAE CAPNORD**
3 bis, rue du Docteur Quignard, F-21000 Dijon, France
CEO: Jean Pierre Savare, Pres.   Tel: 33-3-8060-4300   Rev: $451
Bus: *Engaged in supply of MasterCard, Visa,*   Fax: 33-3-8070-0892   Emp: 1,200
   e-commerce and pay-TV.   www.oberthur.com

   OBERTHUR CARD SYSTEMS, INC.
   523 James Hance Court, Exton, PA   19341
   CEO: Michel Aime   Tel: (610) 524-2410   %FO: 100
   Bus: *Currency handling and security*   Fax: (610) 524-2410
      systems.

   OBERTHUR GAMING TECHNOLOGIES CORP.
   1100 Northeast Loop, San Antonio, TX   78209
   CEO: Francois Charles Oberthur   Tel: (210) 509-9999   %FO: 100
   Bus: *Printing and supplying lottery*   Fax: (210) 824-6044
      tickets.

● **ONDEO DEGREMONT SA, SUB. SUEZ**
183 ave. de 18 Juin 1940, F-92508 Rueil-Malmaison, France
CEO: Jean-Louis Chaussade Chmn. & CEO   Tel: 33-1-4625-6000   Rev: $902
Bus: *Water and wastewater treatment*   Fax: 33-1-4204-1699   Emp: 3,600
   equipment.   www.degremont.fr

   ONDEO DEGREMONT INC.
   550 Kinderkamack Road, Oradell, NJ   07649
   CEO: Joel Pionnié, Pres.   Tel: (201) 225-1140   %FO: 100
   Bus: *Engaged in design/build contracts.*   Fax: (201) 225-1145

   ONDEO DEGRÉMONT INC.
   PO Box 71390, Richmond, VA   23255-1390
   CEO: Vernon D. Lucy III, Pres.   Tel: (804) 756-7600   %FO: 100
   Bus: *Water & wastewater treatment*   Fax: (804) 759-7643   Emp: 180
      equipment.

   ONDEO NALCO COMPANY
   One Nalco Center, Naperville, IL   60563-1198
   CEO: Christian Maurin, CEO   Tel: (630) 305-1000   %FO: 100
   Bus: *Mfr. specialty chemicals.*   Fax: (630) 305-2900

● **OST SA**

B P 158, rue du Bas Village, F-35515 Cesson-Sevigne, France
CEO: Thao Lane, CEO   Tel: 33-2-99-9932-5050
Bus: *Mfr. data communications equipment.*   Fax: 33-2-99-9941-7175   Emp: 300

> **OST INC.**
> 405 Glen Drive, Ste. 5D, Sterling, VA   20164
> CEO: T. Lane, CEO   Tel: (703) 404-5546   %FO: 100
> Bus: *Engineer support office for*   Fax: (703) 404-7230   Emp: 9
>   *sales/service data communications*
>   *equipment.*

● **PECHINEY GROUP SA**

10 place des Vosges, La défense 5, F-92400 Courbevoie, France
CEO: Jean Pierre Rodier, Chmn. & CEO   Tel: 33-4-76-4691-4691   Rev: $11,800
Bus: *Mfr. packaging, aluminum, engineered*   Fax: 33-4-76-4691-4646   Emp: 33,000
     products, ferroalloys, carbon products. www.pechiney.com

> **PECHINEY PLASTIC PACKAGING INC.**
> 155 Western Avenue, Neenah, WI   54956
> CEO: Carol Constantine, PR   Tel: (920) 727-6000   %FO: 100
> Bus: *Mfr. plastic packaging.*   Fax: (920) 727-6227

> **PECHINEY PLASTIC PACKAGING INC.**
> 2450 Alvarado Street, San Leandro, CA   94577
> CEO: Carol Constantine, PR   Tel: (510) 352-2262   %FO: 100
> Bus: *Mfr. plastic packaging.*   Fax: (510) 352-9510

> **PECHINEY PLASTIC PACKAGING INC.**
> 19700 Fairchild Road, Irvine, CA   92612
> CEO: Carol Constantine, PR   Tel: (949) 862-0155   %FO: 100
> Bus: *Mfr. plastic packaging.*   Fax: (949) 862-0156

> **PECHINEY PLASTIC PACKAGING INC.**
> 1972 Akron Peninsula Road, Akron, OH   44313
> CEO: Carol Constantine, PR   Tel: (330) 923-5281   %FO: 100
> Bus: *Mfr. plastic packaging.*   Fax: (330) 923-9637

> **PECHINEY PLASTIC PACKAGING INC.**
> 3600 Alabama Avenue, St. Louis Park, MN   55416
> CEO: Carol Constantine, PR   Tel: (612) 924-1600   %FO: 100
> Bus: *Mfr. plastic packaging.*   Fax: (612) 924-1623

> **PECHINEY PLASTIC PACKAGING INC.**
> 6313 Chenot Drive, Amarillo, TX   79109
> CEO: Michael Schmitt, VP   Tel: (806) 467-0570   %FO: 100
> Bus: *Mfr. plastic packaging.*   Fax: (806) 467-0812

PECHINEY ROLLED PRODUCTS INC.
PO Box 68, Ravenswood, WV   26164
CEO: Carol Constantine, PR   Tel: (304) 273-7000   %FO: 100
Bus: *Mfr. rolled products.*   Fax: (304) 273-6320

PECHINEY SALES CORPORATION
333 Ludlow Street, Stamford, CT   06902
CEO: Gilles Auffret, Chmn.   Tel: (203) 541-9000   %FO: 100
Bus: *Precision castings for aerospace*   Fax: (203) 541-9191   Emp: 50
& industrial gas turbine
applications.

PECHINEY WORLD TRADE (USA) INC.
333 Ludlow Street, Stamford, CT   06902
CEO: Bruno Poux-Guillaume, Chmn.   Tel: (203) 541-9000   %FO: 100
Bus: *International trading, sales*   Fax: (203) 541-9191
agency, metal distribution.

PENCHINEY CHEMICAL DIV.
333 Ludlow Street, 6th Fl., Stamford, CT   06902
CEO: Tom Sliker, Pres.   Tel: (203) 541-9000   %FO: 100
Bus: *Mfr. specialty chemicals.*   Fax: (203) 541-9383

PENCHINEY GROUP NORTH AMERICA, INC.
8770 West Bryn Mawr Avenue, Chicago, IL   60631
CEO: Ilene Gordon, Pres.   Tel: (773) 399-8000   %FO: 100
Bus: *Mfr. flexible packaging,*   Fax: (773) 399-8099
aluminum, engineered products,
ferroalloys and carbon products.

• PERNOD RICARD SA
142 blvd. Haussmann, F-75359 Paris, France
CEO: Patrick Ricard, Chmn.   Tel: 33-1-4076-7778   Rev: $4,143
Bus: *Mfr. spirits, liquors and wines.*   Fax: 33-1-4225-9566   Emp: 14,000
      www.pernod-ricard.fr

AUSTIN NICHOLS & COMPANY, INC.
156 East 46th Street, New York, NY   10017
CEO: Michael Bord, Pres.   Tel: (212) 455-9400
Bus: *Distiller and distributor of wines*   Fax: (212) 455-9431
and spirits.

• BIO MERIEUX PIERRE FABRE

376 Chemin Orme, F-69280 Marcy l'Étoile, France

CEO: François Guinot, CEO

Tel: 33-4-7887-2000

Rev: $550

Bus: *Mfr./markets reagents and automated systems designed for medical analyses and product quality control in the agri-food, cosmetics and pharmaceutical industries.*

Fax: 33-4-7887-2128

www.biomerieux.fr

Emp: 3,700

BIO MERIEUX, INC.

595 Anglum Road, Hazelwood, MO 63042-2320

CEO: Bob Bokerman

Tel: (314) 731-8500

%FO: 100

Bus: *Mfr./markets reagents and automated systems designed for medical analyses and product quality control in the agri-food, cosmetics and pharmaceutical industries.*

Fax: (314) 731-8700

• PINAULT-PRINTEMPTS REDOUTE GROUP

18 Place Henri Bergson, F-75008 Paris, France

CEO: Serge Weinberg, Chmn.

Tel: 33-1-4490-6323

Rev: $19,042

Bus: *Manages department stores, specialty stores and distributes, sells and rents construction equipment.*

Fax: 33-1-4490-6225

www.pprgroup.com

Emp: 78,540

BYRLANE INC.

463 Seventh Avenue, New York, NY 10018

CEO: Russell Stravitz, CEO

Tel: (212) 613-9500

%FO: 100

Bus: *Specialty catalog company.*

Fax: (212) 613-9500

CHADWICK'S OF BOSTON, LTD.

35 United Drive, West Bridgewater, MA 02379

CEO: Kevin Doyle, EVP

Tel: (508) 583-8110

%FO: 100

Bus: *Women's apparel catalog company.*

Fax: (508) 583-8110

GUCCI AMERICA, INC.

685 Fifth Avenue, New York, NY 10022

CEO: Tom Ford

Tel: (212) 826-2600

%FO: 100

Bus: *Sales/distribution of designer clothing and leather goods. (JV w/LVMH, France)*

Fax: (212) 230-0894

REXEL INC.
6700 LBJ Freeway, Ste. 3200, Dallas, TX   75240
CEO: Gilles Guinchard, Pres. & CEO   Tel: (972) 387-3600   %FO: 100
Bus: *Sales/distribution of electrical*   Fax: (972) 934-2056
supplies.

● **PIX TECH, INC.**
Avenue Olivier Perroy, F-13790 Rousset, France
CEO: Dieter Mezger, CEO   Tel: 33-4-4229-1000   Rev: $6
Bus: *Mfr. field emission displays for*   Fax: 33-4-4229-0509   Emp: 200
computers.   www.pixtech.com

　　PIX TECH, INC.
　　2700 Augustine Drive, Ste. 255, Santa Clara, CA   95054
　　CEO: Dave Cathey   Tel: (408) 986-8868   %FO: 100
　　Bus: *Mfr. field emission displays for*   Fax: (408) 986-9896
　　computers.

　　PIX TECH, INC.
　　3000 S. Denvery Way, Boise, ID   83705
　　CEO: Lillian B. Armstrong, VP   Tel: (208) 333-7500   %FO: 100
　　Bus: *Mfr. field emission displays for*   Fax: (208) 333-7505
　　computers.

● **PORCHER INDUSTRIES**
F-38300 Badinieres, France
CEO: Robert Porcher, Chmn.   Tel: 33-4-7443-1010   Rev: $400
Bus: *Mfr. fabrics for technical applications.*   Fax: 33-4-7492-1407   Emp: 4,200
                    www.porcher-ind.com

　　BELMONT OF AMERICA, DIV. BGF INDUSTRIES
　　97 Huger Street, Cheraw, SC   29520
　　CEO: Marion Berry   Tel: (843) 537-9982   %FO: 100
　　Bus: *Reinforcement division.*   Fax: (843) 537-4169

　　BGF INDUSTRIES, INC.
　　3802 Robert Porcher Way, Greensboro, NC   27410
　　CEO: Bob Frank   Tel: (336) 545-0011   %FO: 100
　　Bus: *Glass fabrics for technical*   Fax: (336) 545-0233   Emp: 1,150
　　applications and non-woven
　　fabrics.

● **PROTEX SA**
B P 177, F-92305 Levallois Perret Cedex, France
CEO: Robert Moor, Chmn.   Tel: 33-1-4757-7400
Bus: *Mfr. specialty chemicals.*   Fax: 33-1-4757-6928   Emp: 350
www.protex.ch

     SYNTHRON INC.
     305 Amherst Road, Morganton, NC   28655
     CEO: Raymond Pinard, Pres.   Tel: (828) 437-8611   %FO: 100
     Bus: *Mfr. specialty chemicals.*   Fax: (828) 437-4126   Emp: 20

● **PROVIMI, DIV. ERIDANIA BEGHIN-SAY**
9-11 avenue Arago, F-78190 Trappes, France
CEO: Willem Troost, CEO   Tel: 33-1-4143-1150   Rev: $1,217
Bus: *Engaged in animal nutrition; fish, pet*   Fax: Emp: 6,000
and young animal feeds.   www.provimi.com

     AKEY, INC.
     6531 St. Rt. 503, C.S. 5002, Lewisburg, OH   45338
     CEO: Dwight Armstrong, Pres.   Tel: (937) 962-2661   %FO: 100
     Bus: *Engaged in animal nutrition*   Fax: (937) 962-4753
     solutions; fish, pet and young
     animal feeds.

● **PSA PEUGEOT CITROËN SA**
75 ave de la Grande-Armée, F-75116 Paris, France
CEO: Jean Martin Folz, Chmn.   Tel: 33-1-4066-5511   Rev: $39,450
Bus: *Mfr. automobiles, parts and accessories.*   Fax: 33-1-4066-5414   Emp: 156,000
www.psa-peugeot-citroen.com

     COVISINT, INC.
     25800 Northwestern Hwy., Southfield, MI   48075
     CEO: Kevin W. English, CEO   Tel: (248) 827-6000   %FO: 100
     Bus: *Global solutions provider*   Fax: (248) 827-6345
     partnering with the automotive
     industry.

     PEUGEOT MOTORS OF AMERICA, INC.
     150 Clove Road, Little Falls, NJ   07424-2138
     CEO: Peter S. Paine Jr., Pres.   Tel: (973) 812-4444   %FO: 100
     Bus: *Distribution/service automobiles.*   Fax: (973) 812-2148   Emp: 178

● **PUBLICIS GROUP S.A.**

133 ave. des Champs Elysées, F-75008 Paris Cedéx, France

CEO: Maurice Lévy, CEO	Tel: 33-1-4443-7300	Rev: $1,667
Bus: *Advertising and public relations agencies, media direct mail services and drugstores.*	Fax: 33-1-4443-7553 www.publicis.fr	Emp: 8,700

   BURRELL COMMUNICATIONS GROUP

   20 North Michigan Avenue, Chicago, IL   60602

CEO: Thomas J. Burrell, CEO	Tel: (312) 443-8600	%FO:
Bus: *Advertising agency.*	Fax: (312) 443-0974	

   PUBLICIS & HAL RINEY INC.

   2001 Embarcadero Avenue, San Francisco, CA   94133

CEO: Hal Riney, Chmn.	Tel: (415) 293-2001	%FO: 100
Bus: *Advertising agency.*	Fax: (415) 293-2619	

   PUBLICIS HAL RINEY & PARTNERS

   2001 The Embarcadero, San Francisco, CA   94133

CEO: Hal Riney, Chmn.	Tel: (415) 293-2001	%FO: 100
Bus: *Advertising agency.*	Fax: (415) 293-2619	Emp: 360

   PUBLICIS HAL RINEY & PARTNERS

   224 South Michigan Ave., Ste. 700, Chicago, IL   60604

CEO: Barry Krause, Pres.	Tel: (312) 697-5700	%FO: 100
Bus: *Advertising agency.*	Fax: (312) 697-5770	

   PUBLICIS BLOOM INC.

   304 East 45th Street, New York, NY   10017

CEO: Robert H. Bloom, Chmn.	Tel: (212) 370-1313	%FO: 100
Bus: *Advertising agency.*	Fax: (212) 984-1695	Emp: 100

   ROWLAND WORLDWIDE INC.

   375 Hudson Street, New York, NY   10014

CEO: Mark Weiss, CEO	Tel: (212) 527-8800
Bus: *Provides public relations consulting services.*	Fax: (212) 527-8912

● **RADIALL SA**

101 rue Philibert Hoffmann, F-93116 Rosny-sous-Bois, France

CEO: Pierre Gattaz, Pres.	Tel: 33-1-4935-3535	Rev: $240
Bus: *Mfr. coaxial connectors, microwave devices and fiber optic connectors.*	Fax: 33-1-4854-6363 www.radiall.com	Emp: 1,110

RADIALL, INC.
260 Hathaway Drive, Stratford, CT 06497
CEO: Etienne Lamairesse, Pres. Tel: (203) 380-9800 %FO: 100
Bus: *Mfr. coaxial connectors, microwave devices and fiber optic connectors.* Fax: (203) 375-3808 Emp: 120

RADIALL-JERRIK
102 West Julie Drive, Tempe, AZ 85283
CEO: Andre Hernandez, Pres. Tel: (480) 730-5700 %FO: 100
Bus: *Mfr. and markets connectors and cables.* Fax: (480) 730-5800

● RALLYE SA
32 rue de Ponthieu, F-75008 Paris, France
CEO: Andre Crestey, CEO Tel: 33-1-4471-1470 Rev: $18,777
Bus: *Owns and manages retail hypermarkets and supermarkets.* Fax: 33-1-4471-1380 Emp: 119,000
www.rallye.fr

THE ATHLETE'S FOOT GROUP INC.
1950 Vaughn Road, Kennesaw, GA 30144
CEO: Robert J. Corliss, CEO Tel: (770) 514-4500 %FO: 100
Bus: *Sales and distribution of footwear.* Fax: (770) 514-4903

● REMY COINTREAU
152, ave. des Champs-Elysees, F-75008 Paris, France
CEO: Dominique Heriard-Dubreuil, Chmn. Tel: 33-1-4413-4413 Rev: $755
Bus: *Mfr. cognac and spirits.* Fax: 33-1-4225-6030 Emp: 1,150
www.remy-cointreau.com

REMY COINTREAU AMERICA, INC.
1350 Avenue of the Americas, 7th Fl., New York, NY 10019
CEO: David Meyers, Pres. Tel: (212) 399-4200 %FO: 100
Bus: *Mfr. cognac and spirits.* Fax: (212) 399-6909

● RENAULT, SA
13-15 Quai Le Gallo, F-92100 Boulogne-Billancourt Cedex, France
CEO: Louis Schweitzer, Chmn. & CEO Tel: 33-1-4104-0404 Rev: $37,850
Bus: *Mfr. Renault & Mack vehicles; cars, trucks, tractors.* Fax: 33-1-4104-5149 Emp: 159,600
www.renault.com

MACK TRUCKS INC.
2100 Mack Blvd., PO Box M, Allentown, PA 18105-5000
CEO: Michel Gigou, Pres. Tel: (610) 709-3121 %FO: 100
Bus: *Mfr./sale Mack trucks.* Fax: (610) 709-3364 Emp: 5,250

● **REXEL GROUP SA**

25, rue de Clichy, F-75009 Paris, France

CEO: Alain Redheuil, ceo Tel: 33-1-4285-8500 Rev: $5,826

Bus: *Mfr./distributes electrical parts and* Fax: 33-1-4526-2583 Emp: 16,300
supplies. www.rexel.com

   REXEL CALCON INC.

   150 Alhambra Circle, Ste. 900, Coral Gables, FL 33134

   CEO: Gilles Guinchard, SVP Tel: (305) 446-8000 %FO: 100

   Bus: *Distributes electrical parts and* Fax: (305) 446-8128
   supplies.

   REXEL CALCON INC.

   PO Box 6001, Meridian, MS 39305

   CEO: Gilles Guinchard, SVP Tel: (601) 693-4141 %FO: 100

   Bus: *Distributes electrical parts and* Fax: (601) 482-5770
   supplies.

   REXEL CALCON INC.

   5135 Naiman Parkway, Solon, OH 44139-1047

   CEO: Gilles Guinchard, SVP Tel: (440) 248-3800 %FO: 100

   Bus: *Distributes electrical parts and* Fax: (440) 248-3228
   supplies.

● **RHODIA SA**

25 Quai Paul Doumer, F-92408 Courbevoie Cedex, France

CEO: Jean-Pierre Tirouflet, Chmn. Tel: 33-1-4768-2020 Rev: $6,987

Bus: *Mfr. specialty chemicals and water* Fax: 33-1-4768-1911 Emp: 24,800
treatment systems. www.rhodia.com

   RHODIA INC.

   259 Prospect Plains Road, Cranbury, NJ 08512-7500

   CEO: Myron Galuskin, Pres. Tel: (609) 860-4000 %FO: 100

   Bus: *Mfr. specialty chemicals.* Fax: (609) 860-4900

   RHODIA VSI

   405 Jordan Road, Troy, NY 12180

   CEO: John Blanc, Dir. Tel: (518) 285-6300 %FO: 100

   Bus: *Mfr. specialty chemicals.* Fax: (518) 285-6346

● **SAGEM SA**

6 avenue d' lena, F-75783 Paris Cedex 16, France

CEO: Mario Colaiacovo, Chmn. Tel: 33-1-4770-6363 Rev: $3,434

Bus: *Mfr. navigation, guidance and vehicle* Fax: 33-1-4720-3946 Emp: 15,600
control equipment, data processing and www.sagem.com
communications systems, industrial
equipment.

SAGEM CORPORATION
1145 Broadway Plaza, Ste. 200, Tacoma, WA   98402

CEO: Tim N. Ruggles, VP	Tel: (253) 383-3617	%FO: 100
Bus: *Mfr./distributor industrial and auto equipment.*	Fax: (253) 591-8856	Emp: 14

● COMPAGNIE DE SAINT-GOBAIN
Les Miroirs, 18 Avenue d'Alsace, F-92096 Paris La Défense Cedex, France

CEO: Jean-Louis Beffa, Chmn. & CEO	Tel: 33-1-4762-3000	Rev: $23,110
Bus: *Processor of high performance polymer products, including fluoropolymers, silicones, and high-temperature thermoplastics.*	Fax: 33-1-4762-5207 www.saint-gobain.com	Emp: 165,000

BALL-FOSTER GLASS CONTAINER COMPANY
1509 South Macedonia Avenue, Muncie, IN   47302

CEO: Bruce H. Cowgill, CEO	Tel: (765) 741-7000	%FO: 100
Bus: *Mfr. glass containers.*	Fax: (765) 741-7601	

CALMAR INC.
333 South Turnbull Canyon Road, City of Industry, CA   91745

CEO: Eugene F. Dorsch, CEO	Tel: (626) 937-2600	%FO: 100
Bus: *Mfr. plastic pumps and sprayers.*	Fax: (626) 937-2758	

CERTAIN TEED CORPORATION
750 East Swedesford Road, Valley Forge, PA   19482

CEO: Jean-Francois Phelizon, CEO	Tel: (610) 341-7000	%FO: 100
Bus: *Mfr. plastic pumps and sprayers.*	Fax: (610) 341-7797	

MEYER INTERNATIONAL INC.
11465 Johns Creek Pkwy., Ste. 380, Duluth, GA   30097

CEO: H. Fedden, CEO	Tel: (678) 475-9506	%FO: 100
Bus: *Mfr./sales fluid systems, extruded/molded silicone components, assemblies, glass and building materials.*	Fax: (678) 475-9507	

MEYER LAMINATES INC.
51 Concord Street, North Reading, MA   01864

CEO: Larry Blanch, Mgr.	Tel: (978) 664-5775	%FO: 100
Bus: *Mfr. glass and building materials.*	Fax: (978) 664-5321	

MEYER LAMINATES INC.
19-22 45th Street, Astoria, NY   11105

CEO: Peter Zbytniewski, Mgr.	Tel: (718) 726-8000	%FO: 100
Bus: *Mfr. glass and building materials.*	Fax: (718) 956-1009	

MEYER LAMINATES INC.
2414 Gelman Place, Tampa, FL   33619
CEO: Terry Miller, Pres.   Tel: (813) 247-2502   %FO: 100
Bus: *Mfr. glass and building materials.*   Fax: (813) 247-1247

NORTON COMPANY
One New Bond Street, Worcester, MA   01615-0008
CEO: Dennis Baker, HR   Tel: (508) 795-5000   %FO: 100
Bus: *Mfr. glass and building materials.*   Fax: (508) 795-5741

SAINT-GOBAIN CORPORATION
750 East Swedesford Road, Valley Forge, PA   19482
CEO: Jean-Francois Phelizon, CEO   Tel: (610) 341-7000   %FO: 100
Bus: *Mfr./sales fluid systems,*   Fax: (610) 341-7797
  extruded/molded silicone
  components and assemblies.

SAINT-GOBAIN PERFORMANCE PLASTICS
20245 West 12 Mile Road, Ste. 115, Southfield, MI   48076
CEO: Mike Hitch   Tel: (248) 355-2672   %FO: 100
Bus: *Mfr./sales precision products,*   Fax: (248) 355-2677
  Norglide® Bearings, specialty
  elastomers, foam tapes and
  gaskets.

SAINT-GOBAIN PERFORMANCE PLASTICS
7301 Orangewood Avenue, Garden Grove, CA   92841
CEO: Dan Tolles, Operations Mgr.   Tel: (714) 630-5818   %FO: 100
Bus: *Mfr./sales engineered components*   Fax: (714) 238-1300
  and high performance seals.

SAINT-GOBAIN PERFORMANCE PLASTICS
407 East Street, New Haven, CT   06511
CEO: Woody Swift, Plant Mgr.   Tel: (203) 777-3631   %FO: 100
Bus: *Mfr./sales advanced film products.*   Fax: (203) 787-1725

SAINT-GOBAIN PERFORMANCE PLASTICS
1150 East Allanson Road, Mundelein, IL   60060
CEO: Greg Kamen, Plant Mgr.   Tel: (847) 949-0850   %FO: 100
Bus: *Mfr./sales machined and molded*   Fax: (847) 949-0198
  components.

SAINT-GOBAIN PERFORMANCE PLASTICS
PO Box 3600, Akron, OH   44309
CEO: John Vancse, Mgr.   Tel: (330) 798-9240   %FO: 100
Bus: *Mfr./sales fluid systems and tubing.*   Fax: (330) 798-6968

SAINT-GOBAIN PERFORMANCE PLASTICS
14 McCaffrey Street, Hoosick Falls, NY   12090
CEO: Phil Guy, Plant Mgr.   Tel: (518) 686-7301   %FO: 100
Bus: *Mfr./sales advanced film products*   Fax: (518) 686-4840
     and tapes and fabrics.

SAINT-GOBAIN PERFORMANCE PLASTICS
One Sealant Park, Granville, NY   12832
CEO: Bob Searer, Mgr.   Tel: (518) 642-2200   %FO: 100
Bus: *Mfr./sales specialty elastomers,*   Fax: (518) 642-2793
     foam sealants, tapes and gasketing.

SAINT-GOBAIN PERFORMANCE PLASTICS
1395 Danner Drive, Aurora, OH   44202
CEO: Lee Wilson, Mgr.   Tel: (330) 995-1600   %FO: 100
Bus: *Mfr./sales fluid systems and*   Fax: (330) 995-1699
     macromeric products.

SAINT-GOBAIN PERFORMANCE PLASTICS
150 Dey Road, Wayne, NJ   07470
CEO: Robert C. Ayotte, CEO   Tel: (973) 696-4700   %FO: 100
Bus: *Mfr./sales advanced film products*   Fax: (973) 696-4056   Emp: 50
     and fluid products.

SAINT-GOBAIN PERFORMANCE PLASTICS
1199 South Chillcothe Road, Aurora, OH   44202
CEO: Phil Corvo   Tel: (330) 562-9111   %FO: 100
Bus: *Mfr./sales fluid systems and*   Fax: (330) 562-5717
     transportation hose and tubing.

SAINT-GOBAIN PERFORMANCE PLASTICS
717 Plantation Street, Worcester, MA   01605
CEO: Mark Cosenza, Plant Mgr.   Tel: (508) 852-3072   %FO: 100
Bus: *Mfr./sales advanced film products*   Fax: (508) 852-3759
     and specialty films.

SAINT-GOBAIN PERFORMANCE PLASTICS
3910 Industrial Drive, Beaverton, MI   48612
CEO: Jerry Theiff, Plant Mgr.   Tel: (517) 435-9533   %FO: 100
Bus: *Mfr./sales fluid systems,*   Fax: (517) 435-2355
     extruded/molded silicone
     components and assemblies.

SAINT-GOBAIN PERFORMANCE PLASTICS
40 White Lake Road, Sparta, NJ 07871
CEO: John McKernan, Pres.   Tel: (973) 988-4876   %FO: 100
Bus: *Mfr./sales fluid systems, sanitary*   Fax: (973) 579-3908
     flexible hose and assemblies.

SAINT-GOBAIN PERFORMANCE PLASTICS
I-295 and Harmony Road, Mickleton, NJ 08056
CEO: Gary Garwood, Plant Mgr.   Tel: (856) 423-6630   %FO: 100
Bus: *Mfr./sales engineered components,*   Fax: (856) 423-8182
     tubing, fluoropolymer roll covers.

● SALANS HERTZFELD HEILBRONN HRK
9 rue Boissy d'Anglas, F-75008 Paris, France
CEO: Jeffrey M. Hertzfeld   Tel: 33-1-4268-4800
Bus: *Multi-national law firm.*   Fax: 33-1-4268-1545   Emp: 350
     www.salans.com

SALANS HERTZFELD HEILBRONN CHRISTY & VIENER
620 Fifth Avenue, New York, NY 10020-2457
CEO: John D. Viener   Tel: (212) 632-5500   %FO: 100
Bus: *Multinational law firm.*   Fax: (212) 632-5555

● SAMT-DEVELOPPEMENT
10 rue de la Forge, F-68720 Tagolsheim, France
CEO: Jean-Paul Heuchel, Dir.   Tel: 33-8-9255-999
Bus: *Mfr./sale/service weaving machinery*   Fax: 33-8-9254-303
     and accessories, spare parts.

SACM TEXTILE INC.
PO Box Drawer 547, Lyman, SC 29365
CEO: Amy Comolli, Mgr.   Tel: (864) 877-1886   %FO: 100
Bus: *Distribute spare parts and*   Fax: (864) 877-4171
     accessories for weaving machines

● SANOFI-SYNTHELABO, S.A.
174 avenue de France, F-75635 Paris Cedex 13, France
CEO: Herve Guerin, Chmn.   Tel: 33-1-5377-4000   Rev: $5,387
Bus: *Mfr./marketing healthcare, skincare,*   Fax: 33-1-5377-4133   Emp: 29
     fragrances, clothing and household   www.sanofi-synthelabo.fr
     linens.

SANOFI DIAGNOSTICS PASTEAUR INC.
6565 185th Avenue, NE, Redmond, WA 98052
CEO: Don Diamond, Pres.   Tel: (425) 881-8300
Bus: *Mfr. tests for auto immune and*   Fax: (425) 861-5011
     infectious diseases.

SANOFI-SYNTHELABO, INC.
90 Park Avenue, New York, NY 10016-2499

CEO: Gordon Proctor, Chmn.	Tel: (212) 551-4000	%FO: 100
Bus: *Sales/distribution of healthcare, skincare, fragrances, clothing and household linens.*	Fax: (212) 551-4900	

● SANSHA (FRANCE) SARL
52 rue de Clichy, F-75009 Paris, France

CEO: Franck Raoul-Duval, Pres. Tel: 33-1-4526-0138
Bus: *Mfr. ballet shoes.* Fax: 33-1-4526-0439
www.russiansteppes.com

SANSHA USA, INC.
1717 Broadway, 2nd Fl., New York, NY 10019

CEO: Phillippe Saint-Paul, Mgr.	Tel: (212) 246-6212	%FO: 100
Bus: *Wholesale & retail ballet shoes.*	Fax: (212) 956-7052	

● SCHNEIDER ELECTRIC SA
6470 avenue Jeane-Baptiste Clement, F-926 Boulogne-Billancourte, France

CEO: Henri Lachmann, CEO Tel: 33-1-4690-7000
Bus: *Mfr. voltage power distribution equipment and electronmechanical industrial control components and specializes in electrical contracting.* Fax: 33-1-4699-7100
www.schneiderelectric.com

EFI ELECTRONICS CORP.
1751 South 4800 West, Salt Lake City, UT 84104

CEO: Terry O'Neal, Pres. & CEO	Tel: (801) 977-9009	%FO: 100
Bus: *Supplies consumer, business and industrial power protection products.*	Fax: (801) 977-0200	

SQUARE D SCHNEIDER ELECTRIC INC.
1415 South Roselle Road, Palatine, IL 60067

CEO: Chris C. Richardson, CEO	Tel: (847) 397-2600	%FO: 100
Bus: *Mfr. electrical distribution equipment and systems.*	Fax: (847) 925-7500	

● SCOR SA
Immeuble Scor, 1 ave. de President Wilson, Ladéfense Cedex, F-92074 Paris, France

CEO: Jacques Blondeau, Chmn.	Tel: 33-1-4698-7000	Rev: $2,800
Bus: *Reinsurance services.*	Fax: 33-1-4767-0409	Emp: 1,180
	www.scor.com	

COMMERICAL RISK SERVICES INC.
1300 Mount Kemble Avenue, Morristown, NJ   07962
CEO: Bill Harris, Mgr.   Tel: (973) 425-1322
Bus: *Engaged in reinsurance.*   Fax: (973) 425-1315

SCOR REINSURANCE
101 California Street, Suite 2700, San Francisco, CA   94111
CEO: Jerome Karter, Pres.   Tel: (415) 765-1200   %FO: 100
Bus: *Property & casualty reinsurance*   Fax: (415) 397-8390
    services.

SCOR REINSURANCE COMMERICIAL RISK RE-INSURANCE
177 Broad Street, Stamford, CT   06912
CEO: Paul Bendarz, Mgr.   Tel: (203) 356-3440   %FO: 100
Bus: *Property & casualty reinsurance*   Fax: (203) 356-3480
    services.

SCOR REINSURANCE COMPANY
One Pierce Place, Suite 600, Itasca, IL   60143-4049
CEO: Jim Butridge, Mgr.   Tel: (630) 775-7300   %FO: 100
Bus: *Property & casualty reinsurance*   Fax: (630) 775-0846
    services.

SCOR REINSURANCE COMPANY
15305 Dallas Parkway Suite 700, Dallas, TX   75001
CEO: Yves Corcos, CEO   Tel: (972) 560-9500   %FO: 100
Bus: *Property & casualty reinsurance*   Fax: (972) 560-9535
    services.

SCOR REINSURANCE COMPANY
1401 Brickell Avenue, Ste. 910, Miami, FL   33131-3501
CEO: Maria Bazquez, Mgr.   Tel: (305) 679-9951   %FO: 100
Bus: *Property & casualty reinsurance*   Fax: (305) 679-9963
    services.

SCOR U.S. CORPORATION
*199 Water Street, New York, NY   10038-3526
CEO: Jerome Karter, Pres.   Tel: (212) 480-1900   %FO: 100
Bus: *Property & casualty reinsurance*   Fax: (212) 480-1328   Emp: 258
    services.

● **SCRIPTA, SA**
7 passage Turquetil, F-75011 Paris, France
CEO: Eugene Wayolle, Pres.   Tel: 33-1-4370-2200
Bus: *Mfr. engraving, copy milling and die*   Fax: 33-1-4370-5636   Emp: 375
    sinking machines, cutter grinders and
    bevelers.

SCRIPTA MACHINE TOOL CORPORATION

7 Kulick Road, Fairfield, NJ   07004-3307

CEO: Eugene Wayolle, Pres.	Tel: (973) 575-1950	%FO: 100
Bus: *Distribution engraving, copy milling and die sinking mach, cutter grinders and bevelers.*	Fax: (973) 575-0151	Emp: 5

● **SEB S.A.**

Chemin de Petit-Bois, BP 172, F-69132 Ecully Cedex, France

CEO: Thierry de la Tour, CEO	Tel: 33-4-7218-1818	Rev: $2,050
Bus: *Mfr./market electrical cooking and home care appliances.*	Fax: 33-4-7218-1655 www.seb.fr	Emp: 14,200

ROWENTA INC.

196 Boston Avenue, 4th Fl., Medford, MA   02155

CEO: Paul Pofcher, Gen. Mgr.	Tel: (781) 396-0600	%FO: 100
Bus: *U.S. headquarters for sales/distribution of electrical cooking and personal care appliances and household equipment and supplies.*	Fax: (781) 396-1313	

T-FAL CORPORATION

25 Riverside Drive, Pine Brook, NJ   07058

CEO: Gregers Infeld, Pres. & CEO	Tel: (973) 575-1060	%FO: 100
Bus: *Sales/distribution of cooking equipment and household goods.*	Fax: (973) 575-7522	

T-FAL CORPORATION

2121 Eden Road, Milville, NJ   08332

CEO: Camille Hebert, Mgr.	Tel: (856) 825-6300	%FO: 100
Bus: *Sales/distribution of cooking equipment and household goods.*	Fax: (856) 825-0222	

● **SEDIVER SA**

79 ave Francois Arago, F-92017 Nanterre Cedex, France

CEO: S. Mancuso, Chmn.	Tel: 33-1-4614-1516	Rev: $178
Bus: *Mfr. hi-volt electric insulators for overhead power lines.*	Fax: 33-1-4097-9433 www.sediver.fr	Emp: 1,500

SEDIVER INC.

7801 Park Place Road, York, SC   29712

CEO: John Ray George, Pres.	Tel: (803) 684-4208	%FO: 100
Bus: *Mfr. hi-volt electric insulators for overhead power lines.*	Fax: (803) 684-4940	Emp: 200

● **SEFAC EQUIPMENT**

BP 101-1 rue Andre Compain, F-0880 Montherme, France

CEO: John Paul Planteuin, Pres.   Tel: 33-1-2453-0182

Bus: *Mfr. heavy duty lifts and garage*   Fax:
     equipment.   www.sefac.com

> **SEFAC LIFT & EQUIPMENT CORPORATION**
>
> 1615 Bush Street, Baltimore, MD   21230
>
> CEO: Buck Storck, VP   Tel: (410) 539-5616   %FO: 100
>
> Bus: *Distribution/sale maintenance*   Fax: (410) 539-8195   Emp: 22
>   *heavy duty lifts and garage*
>   *equipment.*

● **SIDEL SA**

Ave. de la Patrouille-de-France, Octeville-Sur-Mer, BP 204, F-76053 La Havre Cedex, France

CEO: Francis Olivier, Chmn. & CEO   Tel: 33-2-3285-8687   Rev: $965

Bus: *Mfr. packaging machines for water and*   Fax: 33-2-3285-8100   Emp: 4,050
     beverages.   www.sidel.com

> **SIDEL INC.**
>
> 5600 Sun Court, Norcross, GA   30092
>
> CEO: Philippe Bartissol, EVP   Tel: (770) 221-3000   %FO: 100
>
> Bus: *Mfr. packaging machines for*   Fax: (770) 447-0084
>   *water and beverages.*

● **SKIS DYNASTAR SA**

1412 ave de Geneve, BP 3, F-74701 Sallanches, France

CEO: Jean Yves Pachoud, Pres.   Tel: 33-4-5091-2930

Bus: *Mfr. snow skis and poles.*   Fax: 33-4-5058-4903   Emp: 500
                                                   www.dynastar.com

> **SKIS DYNASTAR INC.**
>
> Hercules Drive, PO Box 25, Colchester, VT   05446-0025
>
> CEO: David J. Provost, Exec.VP   Tel: (802) 655-2400   %FO: 100
>
> Bus: *Snow skis, poles, boots &*   Fax: (802) 655-4329   Emp: 38
>   *accessories.*

● **SKIS ROSSIGNOL SA**

Le Menon, BP 329, F-38509 Voiron, France

CEO: Jacques H. Rodet, CEO   Tel: 33-4-7666-6565   Rev: $430

Bus: *Mfr. skis, snowboards and in-line*   Fax: 33-4-7665-6751   Emp: 2,700
     skating products.   www.skirossignol.com

ROSSIGNOL SKI CO NC.
PO Box 298, Williston, VT 05495

CEO: Hugh Harley, Pres.	Tel: (802) 863-2511	%FO: 100
Bus: *Mfr. skis, snowboards and in-line skating products*	Fax: (802) 658-1843	

● SNECMA SA
2 Boulevard Martial Valin, F-75015 Paris, France

CEO: Jean-Paul Béchat, CEO	Tel: 33-1-4060-8088	
Bus: *Mfr. aircraft engines and parts.*	Fax: 33-1-4060-8147	
	www.snecma.com	

SNECMA INC.
111 Merchant Street, PO Box 15667, Cincinnati, OH 45246

CEO: Luc Bramy, COO	Tel: (513) 552-3345	
Bus: *Mfr. aircraft engines.*	Fax: (513) 552-3290	Emp: 50

● SOCIÉTÉ DU LOUVRE
58 Boulevard Gouvion Saint Cyr, F-75858 Paris Cedex, France

CEO: Anne-Claire Taittinger, CEO	Tel: 33-1-5805-5000	
Bus: *Luxury hotel group.*	Fax: 33-1-4068-5345	Emp: 695
	www.societedulouvre.fr	

BACCARAT CRYSTAL
625 Madison Avenue, New York, NY 10022

CEO: Corrine Combe, Pres.	Tel: (212) 826-4100	%FO: 100
Bus: *Sales of hand-cut crystal.*	Fax: (212) 826-5043	

BACCARAT CRYSTAL
73-111 El Paseo, Palm Desert, CA 92260

CEO: Joyce Shampeny, Mgr.	Tel: (760) 346-6805	%FO: 100
Bus: *Sales of hand-cut crystal.*	Fax: (760) 346-8498	

BACCARAT CRYSTAL
3333 Bristol Street, Costa Mesa, CA 92626

CEO: Mark Hersh, Mgr.	Tel: (714) 435-9600	%FO: 100
Bus: *Sales of hand-cut crystal.*	Fax: (714) 435-0703	

BACCARAT CRYSTAL
238 Greenwich Avenue, Greenwich, CT 06830

CEO: Jennifer Dunn, Mgr.	Tel: (203) 618-0900	%FO: 100
Bus: *Sales of hand-cut crystal.*	Fax: (203) 618-9086	

BACCARAT CRYSTAL
441 East Hopkins Avenue, Aspen, CO 81611

CEO: Kates Voiles, Mgr.	Tel: (970) 925-9299	%FO: 100
Bus: *Sales of hand-cut crystal.*	Fax: (970) 925-8909	

BACCARAT CRYSTAL
343 Powell Street, San Francisco, CA   94102
CEO: Penelope Francis, Mgr.   Tel: (415) 291-0600   %FO: 100
Bus: *Sales of hand-cut crystal.*   Fax: (415) 291-9039

BACCARAT CRYSTAL
Galleria at 3350 North Dallas Parkway, Ste. 1295, Dallas, TX   13350
CEO: Doug Moss, Mgr.   Tel: (972) 386-4100   %FO: 100
Bus: *Sales of hand-cut crystal.*   Fax: (972) 386-7422

THE COLONNADE HOTEL
120 Huntington Avenue, Boston, MA   02118
CEO: David Colella, Mgr.   Tel: (617) 424-7000   %FO: 100
Bus: *Luxury hotel.*   Fax: (617) 424-1717

THE DYLAN HOTEL
52 East 41st Street, New York, NY   10017
CEO: Debra Griffith Goode, Mgr.   Tel: (212) 338-0500   %FO: 100
Bus: *Luxury hotel.*   Fax: (212) 338-0569

THE HELMSLEY PARK LANE HOTEL
36 Central Park South, New York, NY   10019
CEO: Philip Grose, Mgr.   Tel: (212) 371-4000   %FO: 100
Bus: *Luxury hotel.*   Fax: (212) 319-9065

THE NEW YORK HELMSLEY
212 East 42nd Street, New York, NY   10017
CEO: Carol Conrad   Tel: (212) 490-8900   %FO: 100
Bus: *Luxury hotel.*   Fax: (212) 986-4762

• SOCIÉTÉ GÉNÉRALE
29 blvd. Haussman, F-75009 Paris, France
CEO: Daniel Bouton, CEO   Tel: 33-1-4214-2000   Rev: $31,400
Bus: *General commercial banking.*   Fax: 33-1-4214-7555   Emp: 58,500
    www.socgen.com

FIMAT USA INC
181 West Madison, Ste. 3450, Chicago, IL   60602
CEO: Cynthia Zeltwanger, COO   Tel: (312) 578-5200   %FO: 100
Bus: *Securities broker/dealer.*   Fax: (312) 578-5299   Emp: 41

SG COWEN SECURITIES CORPORATION
1221 Avenue of the Americas, New York, NY   10020
CEO: Kim Fenebresque, CEO   Tel: (212) 495-6000   %FO: 50
Bus: *International commercial banking*   Fax: (212) 480-8212   Emp: 45
    services.

SOCIETE GENERALE ASSET MANAGEMENT
560 Lexington Avenue, New York, NY   10022
CEO: William Church   Tel: (212) 278-7500   %FO: 100
Bus: *Investment management.*   Fax: (212) 278-4582

SOCIÉTÉ GÉNÉRALE ENERGIE
1221 Avenue of the Americas, 8th Floor, New York, NY   10020
CEO: Philippe Aymericol, COO   Tel: (212) 278-5600   %FO: 100
Bus: *Leasing and financing services.*   Fax: (212) 956-5099   Emp: 34

● SODEXHO ALLIANCE
3 ave. Newton, F-78180 Montigngle Bretonneus, France
CEO: Pierre Bellon, Chmn. & CEO   Tel: 33-1-3085-7500   Rev: $7,866
Bus: *Engaged in food and management*   Fax: 33-1-3043-0958   Emp: 232,600
   services.   www.sodexho.com

SODEXHO MARRIOTT SERVICES, INC.
9801 Washingtonian Blvd., Gaithersburg, MD   20878
CEO: Michel Landel, CEO   Tel: (391) 987-4330
Bus: *Provides food and facilities*   Fax:
   management services.

SPIRIT CRUISES
5700 Lakewright Drive, Ste. 203, Norfolk, VA   23502
CEO: Francois Vincent, Pres.   Tel: (757) 627-2900
Bus: *Operates cruise, dining and*   Fax: (757) 640-9315
   entertainment ships.

● SODIAAL SA
170 bis blvd. du Montparnasse, F-75680 Paris, France
CEO: Jean-Claude Dorbec, CEO   Tel: 33-1-4410-9010   Rev: $3,195
Bus: *Mfr. milk ingredients for the food*   Fax: 33-1-4321-6299   Emp: 7,700
   industry.   www.sodiaal.fr

SODIALL NORTH AMERICA CORPORATION
832 Harleysville Pike, Harleysville, PA   19438
CEO: Jean-Michel Duval, Dir.   Tel: (215) 256-3193
Bus: *Sales/distribution of dairy*   Fax: (215) 256-9352
   products.

● SOMMER ALLIBERT, SA
2 rue de l'Egalité, F-92748 Nanterre Cedex, France
CEO: Marc Assa, Chmn.   Tel: 33-1-4120-4040   Rev: $3,480
Bus: *Design/mfr./market textile/plastic*   Fax: 33-1-4120-4909   Emp: 23,225
   products; consumer goods, auto   www.sommer-alibert.com
   components, home furnishings, and
   cosmetics & fragrances.

PRIMINTER INC.
760 Route 10, Whippany, NJ 07981
CEO: Mark Bellard, Pres.
Bus: *Mfr. floor and wall coverings.*
Tel: (973) 781-1200
Fax: (973) 781-1211
%FO: 100

QUALIPAC CORPORATION
130 Algonquin Parkway, Whippany, NJ 07981
CEO: Mark Bellard, Pres.
Bus: *Mfr. plastic bottles for fragrance/cosmetic industry.*
Tel: (973) 503-1199
Fax: (973) 503-1210
%FO: 100

SAI AUTOMOTIVE, INC.
101 International Boulevard, Fountain Inn, SC 29044
CEO: Freddy Balle, Pres.
Bus: *U.S. headquarters. Design/mfr./market textile/plastic products; consumer goods, auto components, home furnishings, and cosmetics & fragrances.*
Tel: (864) 862-1900
Fax: (864) 862-7700
%FO: 100

● **SOPREMA SA**
14 rue de St Nazaire, BP 121, F-67025 Strasbourg, France
CEO: Pierre E. Bindscheidler, Pres.
Bus: *Mfr./sale SBS modified roofing membranes.*
Tel: 33-3-8879-8400
Fax: 33-3-8879-8401
www.soprema.fr
Emp: 3,535

SOPREMA INC
310 Quadral Drive, PO Box 471, Wadsworth, OH 44281-0471
CEO: Gilbert Lorenzo, VP
Bus: *Mfr./sale SBS-modified roofing membranes.*
Tel: (330) 334-0066
Fax: (330) 334-4289
%FO: 100
Emp: 50

● **SOTHYS**
14 rue de L'Hotel de Ville, F-19100 Brive, France
CEO: Bernard Mas, Pres.
Bus: *Skin care products.*
Tel: 33-1-5517-4500
Fax: 33-1-5523-2888
www.sothys.com
Emp: 200

SOTHYS USA INC.
1500 NW 94th Avenue, Miami, FL 33172
CEO: Christian Garces, Pres.
Bus: *Skin care products.*
Tel: (305) 594-4222
Fax: (305) 592-5785
%FO: 100
Emp: 20

● **SPOT IMAGE SA**

5 rue des Satellites, F-31030 Toulouse Cedex, France

CEO: Jacques Mouysset, Pres. Tel: 33-5-6219-4040

Bus: *Satellite imagery provider.* Fax: 33-5-6219-4011 Emp: 200

www.spotimage.fr

    SPOT IMAGE CORPORATION

    1897 Preston White Drive, Reston, VA 22091-4368

    CEO: Gene Colabatistto, Pres. Tel: (703) 715-3100 %FO: 100

    Bus: *Satellite imagery provider.* Fax: (703) 648-1813 Emp: 45

● **ST MICROELECTRONICS N.V.**

Technoparc de Pays de Gex, BP 112, 165 rue Edouard Branly, F-01630 Saint Genis Pouilly, France

CEO: Pasquale Pistorio, Pres. Tel: 33-4-5040-2640 Rev: $7,813

Bus: *French-Italian JV semiconductor* Fax: 33-4-5040-2860 Emp: 42,000
company. www.us.st.com

    ST MICROELECTRONICS, INC.

    1000 East Bell Road, Phoenix, AZ 85002

    CEO: Richard Pieranunzi, VP Tel: (602) 485-6100 %FO: 100

    Bus: *Sales/marketing of semi-* Fax: (602) 485-6102
conductors.

    ST MICROELECTRONICS, INC.

    1310 Electronics Drive, Carrollton, TX 75006-5039

    CEO: Jack Mendenhall, Plant Mgr. Tel: (972) 466-6000 %FO: 100

    Bus: *Mfr. semi-conductors.* Fax: (972) 466-8130

● **STRAT-X SA**

193-197 rue de Bercy, F-75582 Paris Cedex 12, France

CEO: L. Bonnier, Mng. Ptrn. Tel: 33-1-5346-6900

Bus: *Management development programs,* Fax: 33-1-5346-6901 Emp: 21
strategic planning and results- oriented www.stratx.fr
consulting services.

    STRAT-X INTERNATIONAL

    222 Third Street, Ste. 3210, Cambridge, MA 02142

    CEO: Debra Lavender, Mng. Tel: (617) 494-8282 %FO: 100

    Bus: *Management development* Fax: (617) 494-1421 Emp: 6
programs, strategic planning,
results oriented consulting
services.

● SUEZ (FORMERLY SUEZ LYONNAISE DES EAUX)

1, rue D'Astorg, F-75008 Paris, France
CEO: Gérard Mestrallet, CEO   Tel: 33-1-4006-6400   Rev: $32,595
Bus: *Water treatment, energy technology,*   Fax: 33-1-4006-6640   Emp: 222,000
    waste management, mortuary services,   www.suez.fr
    communications, health care, leisure
    services, construction.

AQUASOURCE LLC

PO Box 70295, Richmond, VA   23255
CEO: Michael McLaughlin, Pres.   Tel: (804) 627-8160   %FO: 100
Bus: *Markets ultrafiltration membrane*   Fax: (804) 672-8135
    systems.

HUBBARD CONSTRUCTION COMPANY

1936 Lee Road, Winter Park, FL   32789
CEO: Jean Marc Allard, CEO   Tel: (407) 645-5500   %FO: 100
Bus: *Engaged in highway and road*   Fax: (407) 623-3985
    contracting.

OZONIA NORTH AMERICA

PO Box 455, Elmwood Park, NJ   07407
CEO: Joe Giannone, Pres.   Tel: (201) 794-3100   %FO: 100
Bus: *Supplies ozone generating systems.*   Fax: (201) 794-3358

TRIGEN BIO POWER INC.

9140 Arrow Point Blvd., Ste. 370, Charlotte, NC   28273
CEO: Jim Henslee, Pres.   Tel: (704) 525-5819   %FO: 100
Bus: *Develops energy systems.*   Fax:

TRIGEN ENERGY CORPORATION

One Water Street, White Plains, NY   01601
CEO: Richard E. Kessel, CEO   Tel: (914) 286-6600   %FO: 100
Bus: *Develops energy systems.*   Fax: (914) 948-9157   Emp: 850

TRIGEN ENERGY FEDERAL PROJECTS DIVISION

One North Charles Street, Baltimore, MD   21201
CEO: James J. Abromitis, Pres.   Tel: (410) 649-2200   %FO: 100
Bus: *Operates energy systems.*   Fax: (410) 649-2200

TRIGEN EWING POWER INC.

161 Industrial Blvd., Turners Falls, MA   01376
CEO: Lynn B. DiTullio, Pres.   Tel: (413) 863-3500   %FO: 100
Bus: *Operates energy systems.*   Fax: (413) 863-3500

UNITED WATER RESOURCES INC.

200 Old Hook Road, Harrington Park, NJ   07640

CEO: Donald L. Correll, CEO — Tel: (201) 767-9300 — %FO: 100

Bus: *Management of water and* — Fax: (201) 767-2082
wastewater treatment plant
operation.

● TAITTINGER SA

9 Place Saint-Nicaise, F-51100 Rheims, France

CEO: Claude Taittinger, CEO — Tel: 33-3-2685-4535

Bus: *Producer of champagne.* — Fax: 33-3-2685-4439 — Emp: 7,000
www.taittinger.com

DOMAINE CARNEROS

1240 Duhi Road, Napa, CA   94559

CEO: Claude Taittinger, Pres. — Tel: (707) 257-0101 — %FO: 100

Bus: *Sales/distribution of champagne.* — Fax: (707) 253-3020

● TECHNIP

170 Place Henri Regnault, F-92973 Paris La défense 6, France

CEO: Daniel Valot, CEO — Tel: 33-1-4778-2121 — Rev: $2,798

Bus: *Engaged in engineering and* — Fax: 33-1-4778-3340 — Emp: 9,800
construction. — www.technip.com

TECHNIP USA INC

650 Cienega Avenue, San Dimas, CA   91773

CEO: Volker Krateat — Tel: (909) 592-4455 — %FO: 100

Bus: *Engaged in engineering and* — Fax: (909) 592-6920
construction.

TECHNIP USA INC

1990 Post Oak Blvd., Ste. 200, Houston, TX   77056-3846

CEO: Larry D. J. Pope, Pres. — Tel: (281) 531-7661 — %FO: 100

Bus: *Engaged in engineering and* — Fax: (281) 531-6280
construction.

● TELEVISION FRANCAISE 1, SA

33 rue Vaugelas, F-5015 Paris, France

CEO: Patrick Lelay, Pres. — Tel: 33-1-4141-1234 — Rev: $1,956

Bus: *Privately owned television network.* — Fax: 33-1-4141-1589 — Emp: 2,200
www.tf1.fr

TELEVISION FRANCAISE 1

2100 M Street, NW, Washington, DC   20032

CEO: Ulysse Gosset, Bureau Chief — Tel: (202) 223-3642 — %FO: 100

Bus: *News agency.* — Fax: (202) 223-2196 — Emp: 12

● **THALES (FORMERLY THOMSON-CSF SA)**
173 blvd. Haussmann, F-75414 Paris Cedex 08, France
CEO: Denis Ranque, Pres. & CEO   Tel: 33-1-5377-8000   Rev: $8,098
Bus: *Engaged in aerospace, defense, and*   Fax: 33-1-5377-8300   Emp: 48,900
information technology.   www.thalesgroup.com

   AIRSYS ATM INC.
   23501 West 84th Street, Shawnee, KS   66227
   CEO: Benjamin Sandzer-Bell, CEO   Tel: (913) 422-2600   %FO: 100
   Bus: *Mfr. navigation aids, landing*   Fax: (913) 422-2917
     systems, air traffic control
     equipment.

   AUXILEC INC.
   3920 Park Avenue, Edison, NJ   08820
   CEO: Alain Galy, Pres.   Tel: (732) 494-1010   %FO: 100
   Bus: *Sale/service aeronautical*   Fax: (732) 494-1421
     equipment.

   CETIA, INC.
   8 New England Executive Park, Burlington, MA   01803
   CEO: Richard Goodell, CEO   Tel: (781) 229-7930   %FO: 100
   Bus: *Mfr. computer & data processing* Fax: (781) 229-6926
     systems for air space industry.

   DASSAULT A.T. OF AMERICA
   53 Perimeter Center East, Ste. 175, Atlanta, GA   30346
   CEO: William Peet, Pres.   Tel: (770) 393-2311   %FO: 100
   Bus: *Engaged in aerospace, defense*   Fax: (770) 393-2177
     and information technology.

   THALES
   99 Canal Center Plaza, Ste. 450, Alexandria, VA   22314
   CEO: John White, Pres.   Tel: (703) 838-9685   %FO: 100
   Bus: *Thomson-CSF, US headquarters.*   Fax: (703) 838-1688
     Marketing electronics for civilian
     and defense applications.

   THALES COMMUNICATIONS
   395 Oakhill Road, Mountaintop, PA   18707
   CEO: Jerry Chase, Pres.   Tel: (570) 474-6751   %FO: 100
   Bus: *Mfr. microwave transmitters &*   Fax: (570) 474-5469
     systems.

THALES COMMUNICATIONS
601 North Fairfax Street, Ste. 450, Alexandria, VA   22314
CEO: Mark Richer, VP   Tel: (703) 838-5655
Bus: *Mfr. digital TV transmitters.*   Fax: (703) 838-1687

THOMSON COMPONENTS & TUBES.
40 G Commerce Way, PO Box 540, Totowa, NJ   07511
CEO: Ernest L. Stern, CEO   Tel: (973) 812-9000   %FO: 100
Bus: *Marketing cathode ray tubes.*   Fax: (973) 812-9050

THALES CONSUMER ELECTRONICS INC
10330 North Meridian Street, Indianapolis, IN   46290-1024
CEO: James Meyer, VP   Tel: (317) 587-3000   %FO: 100
Bus: *Mfr./distribution consumer*   Fax: (317) 587-6703
   electronic products.

THALES TRAINING & SIMULATION, INC.
2000 East Lamar Blvd., Ste. 3000, Arlington, TX   76606-7337
CEO: Alex Nick, CEO   Tel: (817) 543-5800   %FO: 100
Bus: *Mfr. aircraft and ground*   Fax: (817) 543-5813
   simulation equipment.

● **THIEFFRY ET ASSOCIÉS**
23 ave. Hoche, F-75008 Paris, France
CEO: PatrickThieffry, Mng. Ptnr.   Tel: 33-1-4562-4554
Bus: *International law firm.*   Fax: 33-1-4225-8007
                                        www.thieffry.com

THIEFFRY ET ASSOCIÉS
630 Fifth Avenue, Ste. 2518, New York, NY   10111
CEO: J. Patrick DeLince, Mng. Assoc.   Tel: (212) 698-4550   %FO: 100
Bus: *International law firm.*   Fax: (212) 698-4551

● **THOMSON MULTIMEDIA SA**
46 Quai Alphonse Le Gallo, F-92100 Boulogne, France
CEO: Thierry Breton, CEO   Tel: 33-1-4186-5000   Rev: $7,735
Bus: *Mfr. consumer electronics.*   Fax: 33-1-4186-5859   Emp: 67,000
                                        www.thomson-multimedia.com

TECHNICOLOR ENTERTAINMENT SERVICES
2913 N. Ontario Street, Burbank, CA   91504
CEO: Timothy C. Maurer, Pres.   Tel: (818) 562-8304   %FO: 100
Bus: *Mfr. consumer electronics.*   Fax: (818) 562-8304

TECHNICOLOR ENTERTAINMENT SERVICES
202 Rochester Avenue, Ontario, CA   91761
CEO: David R. Elliott, CEO   Tel: (909) 974-2222   %FO: 100
Bus: *Mfr. consumer electronics.*   Fax: (909) 974-2251

TECHNICOLOR PACKAGED MEDIA GROUP
39000 West Seven Mile Road, Livonia, MI   48152
CEO: Mike Carroll   Tel: (734) 591-1555   %FO: 100
Bus: *Mfr. consumer electronics.*   Fax: (734) 591-6020

THOMSON BROADCAST SYSTEMS INC.
PO Box 5266, Indianapolis, IN   46290
CEO: Enrique Rodriguez, SVP   Tel: (317) 587-5071   %FO: 100
Bus: *Mfr. consumer electronics.*   Fax: (317) 587-9991

THOMSON MULTIMEDIA INC.
10330 North Meridian Street, Indianapolis, IN   46290-1976
CEO: Larry Chapman, Pres.   Tel: (317) 587-3000   %FO: 100
Bus: *Mfr. consumer electronics.*   Fax: (317) 587-6765

THOMSON MULTIMEDIA INC.
PO Box 2001, Marion, In   46952-8401
CEO: Thierry Breton, CEO   Tel: (765) 662-5000   %FO: 100
Bus: *Mfr. consumer electronics.*   Fax: (765) 662-5354

THOMSON MULTIMEDIA INC.
7225 Winton Drive, PO Box 1976, Indianapolis, IN   46268
CEO: Thierry Breton, CEO   Tel: (317) 415-3900   %FO: 100
Bus: *Mfr. consumer electronics.*   Fax: (317) 415-3900

● TOTAL FINA ELF S.A.
2 Place De La Coupole, La défense 6, F-92400 Courbevoie, France
CEO: M. Thierry Desmarest, Chmn.   Tel: 33-1-4744-4546   Rev: $107,890
Bus: *Exploration, development and   Fax: 33-1-4744-7878   Emp: 135,000
     production of crude oil and gas and   www.totalfinaelf.com
     petro-chemicals.*

COOK COMPOSITES AND POLYMERS
PO Box 419389, Kansas City, MO   64141
CEO: Brent Baker   Tel: (816) 391-6000   %FO: 100
Bus: *Mfr. coatings and resins.*   Fax: (816) 391-6159

ELF LUBRICANTS NORTH AMERICA
Five North Stiles Street, Linden, NJ   07036-4208
CEO: Anthony Soriano, Pres.   Tel: (908) 862-9300   %FO: 100
Bus: *Mfr. lubricants.*   Fax: (908) 862-9300

SARTOMER CHEMICAL, DIV. TOTAL FINA ELF

502 Thomas Jones Way, Exton, PA 19341

CEO: Brian Bellew Tel: (330) 665-3432 %FO: 100

Bus: *Engaged in manufacture of resins* Fax: (330) 665-3433
and coatings and petro chemicals.

TOTAL FINA ELF SERVICES, INC.

444 Madison Avenue, 42nd Fl., New York, NY 10022

CEO: Otto Takken, CEO Tel: (212) 922-3065 %FO: 100

Bus: *Exploration of crude oil and* Fax: (212) 922-3074
natural gas.

• TRANSGENE S.A.

11, rue de Molsheim, F-67082 Strasbourg Cedex, France

CEO: Gilles Bélanger, CEO Tel: 33-3-8827-9121 Rev: $4

Bus: *Biotechnology gene therapy R&D.* Fax: 33-3-8827-9111 Emp: 197
www.transgene.fr

TRANSGENE, INC.

800 Hingham Street, Suite 207, Rockland, MA 02370-1052

CEO: Gilles Bélanger, Pres. Tel: (781) 871-2935 %FO: 100

Bus: *Biotechnology gene therapy R&D.* Fax: (781) 871-4192

• TRIANON INDUSTRIES CORP.

1 rue Thomas Edison, Quartier des Chenes, F-78056 Saint-Quentin-en-Yvelines, France

CEO: Francis Barge Tel: 33-1-3941-2000

Bus: *Mfg. metal fabrication.* Fax: 33-1-3048-5391
www.aetna-ind.com

AETNA INDUSTRIES, INC.

Plants1-5 & 10, 24331 Sherwood Avenue, Centerline, MI 48015

CEO: Ueli Spring Tel: (810) 759-2200 %FO: 100

Bus: *Mfg. metal fabrication.* Fax: (810) 759-2200

• UBI SOFT ENTERTAINMENT S.A.

28, rue Armand Carrel, F-93108 Montreuil-sous-Bois, France

CEO: Yves Guillermot, Pres. & CEO Tel: 33-1-4818-5000 Rev: $125

Bus: *Computer software & services, games &* Fax: 33-1-4857-0741 Emp: 50
entertainment software. www.ubisoft.com

UBI SOFT ENTERTAINMENT, INC.

625 Third Street, 3rd Floor, San Francisco, CA 94107

CEO: Laurent Detoc, Mng. Dir. Tel: (415) 547-4000 %FO: 100

Bus: *Computer software & services,* Fax: (415) 547-4001
games & entertainment software.

● **UGINE, SA**
11-13 cours Valmy, TSA 30003, F-92070 La Défense 7 Cedex, France
CEO: Guy Dollé, Chmn.   Tel: 33-1-4125-6020
Bus: *Mfr. stainless steel products, including*   Fax: 33-1-4125-8717   Emp: 64,000
bar stock, wire and wire rod.   www.ugine.fr

 J&L SPECIALTY STEEL INC.
 PO Box 3373, Pittsburgh, PA   15230
 CEO: Jacques Chabanier   Tel: (412) 338-1600   %FO: 100
 Bus: *Mfr. stainless steel products.*   Fax: (412) 338-1614

 UGINE STAINLESS & ALLOYS, INC.
 2975 Advance Lane, Colmar, PA   18915
 CEO: Dan O'Donnell, Pres.   Tel: (215) 822-1348   %FO: 100
 Bus: *Mfr. stainless steel products.*   Fax: (215) 822-1717

 UGINE STAINLESS & ALLOYS, INC.
 370 Franklin Turnpike, Mahwah, NJ   07430
 CEO: Dan O'Donnell, Pres.   Tel: (201) 529-5800   %FO: 100
 Bus: *Mfr. stainless steel products.*   Fax: (201) 529-5698

 UGINE STAINLESS & ALLOYS, INC.
 184 Strawberry Lane, Perkasie, PA   18944
 CEO: Patrick Mullaney, Mgr.   Tel: (215) 258-5027   %FO: 100
 Bus: *Mfr. stainless steel products.*   Fax: (215) 258-5028

 UGINE STAINLESS & ALLOYS, INC.
 11 Salem Road, East Brunswick, NJ   08816
 CEO: Mike Kleiman, Mgr.   Tel: (732) 390-7676   %FO: 100
 Bus: *Mfr. stainless steel products.*   Fax: (732) 390-7677

 UGINE STAINLESS & ALLOYS, INC.
 38 West Avenue, Fairport, NY   14450
 CEO: Tom Garlipp, Mgr.   Tel: (716) 223-2334   %FO: 100
 Bus: *Mfr. stainless steel products.*   Fax: (716) 223-2386

● **USINOR SA**
Immeuble Pacific, 11-13 Cours Valmy, F-92070 Paris La défense 7 Cedex, France
CEO: Francis Mer, Pres. & CEO   Tel: 33-1-41-258000   Rev: $11,265
Bus: *Mfr. steel.*   Fax: 33-1-41-255675   Emp: 48,450
                                       www.usinor.com

 J&L SPECIALTY STEEL, INC.
 One PPG Place, 18th Fl., Pittsburgh, PA   15222
 CEO: Jacques Chabanier, Pres. & CEO   Tel: (412) 338-1600   %FO: 54
 Bus: *Mfr. stainless steel.*   Fax: (412) 338-1614   Emp: 1,300

TECHALLOY COMPANY INC.
370 Franklin Avenue, Box 604, Mahwah, NJ 07430-2224
CEO: Phililppe Maitrepierre, Pres. & Tel: (201) 529-0900 %FO: 100
   CEO
Bus: *Sales/distribution of specialty steel* Fax: (201) 529-1074
   products.

USINOR AUTO
18915 West 12 Mile Road, Lathrup Village, MI 48076
CEO: Eric Lamm, Mgr. Tel: (248) 552-9614 %FO: 100
Bus: *Sales/distribution of specialty steel* Fax: (248) 552-9630
   products.

USINOR STEEL CORPORATION
430 Blackburn Avenue, Downers Grove, IL 6051
CEO: Daniel J. Carroll Tel: (630) 968-1409 %FO: 100
Bus: *Sales/distribution of specialty steel* Fax: (630) 960-9614
   products.

USINOR STEEL CORPORATION
2011 West TC Jester Boulevard, Houston, TX 77008
CEO: Henri Olivier, Mgr. Tel: (713) 880-4100 %FO: 100
Bus: *Sales/distribution of specialty steel* Fax: (713) 880-4277
   products.

USINOR STEEL CORPORATION
1705 Old Farm Drive, Loveland, OH 45140
CEO: Louis Spizzerri, Mgr. Tel: (513) 774-7530 %FO: 100
Bus: *Sales/distribution of specialty steel* Fax: (513) 774-7531
   products.

USINOR STEEL CORPORATION
1010 Huntcliff, Ste.1350, Atlanta, GA 30350
CEO: John Wilder, Mgr. Tel: (404) 804-2272 %FO: 100
Bus: *Sales/distribution of specialty steel* Fax: (404) 804-4596
   products.

● **VALEO SA**
43 rue Bayen, F-75848 Paris Cedex 17, France
CEO: Thierry Morin, Chmn. & CEO Tel: 33-1-4055-2020 Rev: $8,587
Bus: *Mfr. automotive components.* Fax: 33-1-4055-2171 Emp: 75,000
   www.valeo.com

VALEO CLUTCHES & TRANSMISSIONS
37564 Amrheim, Livonia, MI 48150
CEO: Christina Evans, Mgr. Tel: (734) 432-7304 %FO: 100
Bus: *Mfr. automotive components.* Fax: (734) 591-7623 Emp: 200

VALEO ELECTRICAL SYSTEMS, INC.
3000 North Atlantic Blvd., Auburn Hills, MI   48326
CEO: James Neville, Mgr.   Tel: (248) 340-3852   %FO: 100
Bus: *Mfr. automotive components.*   Fax: (248) 340-4340

VALEO ELECTRONICS, INC.
4100 North Atlantic Blvd., Auburn Hills, MI   48326
CEO: Sam Papazian, Sales Dir.   Tel: (248) 209-8447   %FO: 100
Bus: *Mfr. automotive components.*   Fax: (248) 209-8284

VALEO ENGINE COOLING
4100 North Atlantic Blvd., Auburn Hills, MI   48326
CEO: Dave Siaman, Mgr.   Tel: (248) 209-8332   %FO: 100
Bus: *Mfr. automotive components.*   Fax: (248) 209-8287

VALEO ENGINE COOLING
2258 Allen Street, Jamestown, NY   14701
CEO: Michael Kamsickas, Mgr.   Tel: (716) 665-2620   %FO: 100
Bus: *Heat transfer products, heaters*   Fax: (716) 665-7105   Emp: 3,500
  and coolers.

VALEO FRICTION MATERIALS
37584 Amrheim, Livonia, MI   48326
CEO: Earl Bloom, Dir.   Tel: (734) 432-7372   %FO: 100
Bus: *Mfr. automotive components.*   Fax: (743) 591-0351

VALEO FRICTION MATERIALS, INC.
37584 Amrheim, Livonia, MI   48150
CEO: Earl Bloom, Mng.Dir.   Tel: (734) 432-7389   %FO: 100
Bus: *Mfr. automotive components.*   Fax: (734) 591-7626

VALEO INC.
4100 North Atlantic Blvd., Auburn Hills, MI   48326
CEO: Edward K. Planchon, VP   Tel: (248) 340-3000   %FO: 100
Bus: *U.S. headquarters, holding*   Fax: (248) 209-8280   Emp: 2,500
  company. Mfr. automotive
  components.

VALEO SECURITY SYSTEMS, INC.
4100 North Atlantic Blvd., Auburn Hills, MI   48326
CEO: Francois Feugler, Mgr.   Tel: (248) 209-8253   %FO: 100
Bus: *Mfr. automotive components.*   Fax: (248) 209-8280

VALEO SYLVENIA
1231 Avenue North, Seymour, IN   47274
CEO: Jim Johnson, Mng. Dir.   Tel: (812) 529-5365   %FO: 100
Bus: *Mfr. automotive components.*   Fax: (812) 529-5865

● **VALLOUREC SA**

130 rue de Silly, F-92100 Boulogne-Billancourt Cedex, France
CEO: Jean-Claude Cabre, CEO   Tel: 33-1-4909-3624
Bus: *Production of steel tubing.*   Fax: 33-1-4909-3694
                                        www.vallourec.fr

    VALLOUREC INC.

    414 Allegheny River Blvd., Oakmont, PA   15139
    CEO: Jean-Claude Cabre, CEO   Tel: (412) 828-7520   %FO: 100
    Bus: *Production of steel tubing.*   Fax: (412) 828-4386

    VALLOUREC INC.

    3 Post Oak Boulevard, Houston, TX   77056-3813
    CEO: Jean-Claude Cabre, CEO   Tel: (713) 961-2468   %FO: 100
    Bus: *Production of steel tubing.*   Fax: (713) 961-4316

    VALTIMET INC.

    5501 Air Park Boulevard, Morristown, TN   37813
    CEO: Jean-Claude Cabre, CEO   Tel: (423) 585-4215   %FO: 100
    Bus: *Production of steel tubing.*   Fax: (423) 585-4215

● **VALTECH**

Immeuble Lovoisier 4, place es Vosges, F-92052 Paris Cedex 64, France
CEO: Jean-Yves Hardy, CEO   Tel: 33-1-4188-2300   Rev: $81
Bus: *Engaged in e-commerce applications.*   Fax: 33-1-4188-2301   Emp: 950
                                        www.valtech.com

    VALTECH INC.

    780 Third Avenue, 15th Fl., New York, NY   10021
    CEO: Jennifer Willison   Tel: (212) 688-9900   %FO: 100
    Bus: *Engaged in e-commerce*   Fax: (212) 755-3368
        applications.

    VALTECH INC.

    1200 Smith Street, 16th Fl., Houston, TX   77002
    CEO: Curtis Hite   Tel: (713) 659-3100   %FO: 100
    Bus: *Engaged in e-commerce*   Fax: (713) 353-4601
        applications.

    VALTECH INC.

    4610 South Ulster Street, Denver, CO   80202
    CEO: Barry Rogers   Tel: (720) 529-6100   %FO: 100
    Bus: *Engaged in e-commerce*   Fax: (720) 489-5000
        applications.

VALTECH INC.
5080 Spectrum Drive, Ste. 1010 West, Dallas, TX 75240
CEO: Martin Santora | Tel: (972) 789-1200 | %FO: 100
Bus: *Engaged in e-commerce applications.* | Fax: (972) 789-1340

● **VAREL INTERNATIONAL, INC., DIV. OAKBAY BV**
Route de Pau, BP No. 1, F-64521 Cedex Tarbes, France
CEO: Jim Nixon, CEO | Tel: 33-5-5927-6199
Bus: *Mfr. of roller cone rock bits for use in oil, gas and construction utilities drilling.* | Fax: 33-5-6290-0500
www.varelintl.com

VAREL INTERNATIONAL, INC.
1434 Patton Place, Ste. 106, Carrollton, TX 75007
CEO: Jim Nixon, Pres. & CEO | Tel: (972) 242-8770 | %FO: 100
Bus: *Mfr. of roller cone rock bits for use in oil, gas and construction utilities drilling.* | Fax: (972) 242-1160

VAREL INTERNATIONAL, INC.
2608 Industrial Lane, Conroe, TX 77301
CEO: Jim Nixon, Pres. & CEO | Tel: (936) 539-5500 | %FO: 100
Bus: *Mfr. of roller cone rock bits for use in oil, gas and construction utilities drilling.* | Fax: (936) 539-5500

VAREL INTERNATIONAL, INC.
16630 Imperial Valley, Ste. 147, Houston, TX 77060
CEO: Jim Nixon, Pres. & CEO | Tel: (281) 447-2046 | %FO: 100
Bus: *Mfr. of roller cone rock bits for use in oil, gas and construction utilities drilling.* | Fax: (281) 447-2311

● **VERRERIES BROSSE ET CIE**
39 blvd. Bourdon, F-75004 Paris, France
CEO: Rene Barre, Pres. | Tel: 33-1-4272-7977
Bus: *Distribution cosmetic and pharmaceuticals glassware.* | Fax: 33-1-4272-9088 | Emp: 85
www.doultonfragrances.com

BROSSE USA, INC.
150 East 58th Street, 17th Fl., New York, NY 10155
CEO: Emanuel Mazzei, Pres. | Tel: (212) 832-1622 | %FO: 100
Bus: *Mfr. /distribution glass containers for cosmetic/fragrance industry.* | Fax: (212) 838-1995 | Emp: 8

● **VILMORIN CLAUSE & CIE**
4 quai de la Megisserie, F-75001 Paris, France
CEO: Pierre Lefebvre, CEO Tel: 33-4-7363-4195 Rev: $360
Bus: *Producers of vegetable and flower seeds.* Fax: 33-4-7363-4180 Emp: 2,413
www.vilmorinclause.com

    FERRY MORSE
    PO Box 488, Fulton, KY 42041-0488
    CEO: Scott Witehouse Tel: (800) 283-3400 %FO: 100
    Bus: *Sales/distribution of vegetable and* Fax: (800) 283-2700
        flower seeds.

    HARRIS MORAN
    PO Box 4938, Modesto, CA 95352
    CEO: Sherry Horton Tel: (800) 320-4672 %FO: 100
    Bus: *Sales/distribution of vegetable and* Fax: (800) 320-4672
        flower seeds.

● **VINCI**
1 Cours Ferdinand-de-Lesseps, F-92851 Rueil-Malmaison Cedex, France
CEO: Bernard Huvelin, Mng. Dir. Tel: 33-1-4716-3500 Rev: $13,880
Bus: *Engaged in construction.* Fax: 33-1-4751-9102 Emp: 120,000
www.groupe-vinci.com

    HUBBARD CONSTRUCTION COMPANY
    1936 Lee Road, Winter Park, FL 32789
    CEO: Jean-Marc Allard, CEO Tel: (407) 645-5500 %FO: 100
    Bus: *Engaged in construction.* Fax: (407) 623-3865

● **VIRBAC SA**
13th rue LID, F-06511 Carros Cedex, France
CEO: Eric Maree, CEO Tel: 33-4-9208-7100 Rev: $278
Bus: *Mfr. pharmaceuticals.* Fax: 33-4-9208-7165 Emp: 1,950
www.virbac.com

    VIRBAC CORPORATION
    3200 Meacham Boulevard, Ft. Worth, TX 76137
    CEO: Pierre Pages Tel: (817) 831-5030 %FO: 100
    Bus: *Mfr. pharmaceuticals.* Fax: (817) 831-8327

● **VIVENDI ENVIRONNEMENT SA, SUB. VIVENDI UNIVERSAL**
42 avenue de Friedland, F-75380 Paris Cedex 08, France
CEO: Henri Proglio Tel: 33-1-7171-1000 Rev: $24,952
Bus: *Water company engaging in waste* Fax: 33-1-7171-1545 Emp: 275,000
    management, energy, and www.vivendienvironnement.com
    transportation operations.

KRUGER INC.
401 Harrison Oaks Blvd., Ste. 100, Cary, NC   27513
CEO: Terry Mah, Pres.   Tel: (919) 677-8310   %FO: 100
Bus: *Services waste water treatment*   Fax: (919) 677-0082
  plants.

SCALTECH, INC., DIV. U.S. FILTER
87 Oates Road, Building 1, Houston, TX   77013
CEO: Jim Gentry, VP   Tel: (713) 672-8004   %FO: 100
Bus: *Provides hazardous and non-*   Fax: (713) 672-8209
  hazardous refinery and
  petrochemical sludge processing.

U.S. FILTER
181 Thornhill Road, Warrendale, PA   15086
CEO: Andrew D. Seidel, Pres. & CEO   Tel: (724) 772-0044   %FO: 100
Bus: *Technical design and service*   Fax: (724) 772-1202
  water process systems.

U.S. FILTER CORPORATION
40-004 Cook Street, Palm Desert, CA   92211
CEO: Andrew D. Seidel, Pres. & CEO   Tel: (760) 340-0098   %FO: 100
Bus: *Technical design and service*   Fax: (760) 341-9368   Emp: 22,000
  water process systems.

VIVENDI AMERICA INC.
800 Third Avenue, New York, NY   10022
CEO: Michelle Avenas, Pres. & CEO   Tel: (212) 753-2000   %FO: 100
Bus: *Service water treatment plants.*   Fax: (212) 753-9301

● **VIVENDI UNIVERSAL SA**
42 ave. de Friedland, F-75380 Paris Cedex 08, France
CEO: Jean-Marie Messier, Pres. & CEO   Tel: 33-1-7171-1000   Rev: $39,965
Bus: *Engaged in media and*   Fax: 33-1-7171-1545   Emp: 290,000
  telecommunications.   www.vivendi.com

HOUGHTON MIFFLIN COMPANY
222 Berkeley Street, Boston, MA   02116
CEO: Nader F. Darehshori, Pres. & CEO Tel: (617) 351-5000   %FO: 100
Bus: *Publisher of educational books*   Fax: (617) 351-5113
  and materials.

LAROUSEE KINGFISHER CHAMBERS INC.
95 Madison Avenue, Ste. 1205, New York, NY   10016
CEO: Tim Gillette   Tel: (212) 686-1060   %FO: 100
Bus: *Book publishing, including*   Fax: (212) 686-1082
  bilingual publications.

THE RIVERSIDE PUBLISHING COMPANY
425 Spring Lake Drive, Itasca, IL   60143

CEO: John Laramy, Pres. & CEO Tel: (630) 467-7000 %FO: 100
Bus: *Provides professional testing* Fax: (630) 467-7192
products and services.

USA NETWORKS, INC.
152 West 57th Street, New York, NY   10019

CEO: Barry Diller, CEO Tel: (212) 314-7300 %FO: 100
Bus: *Owns Ticketmaster and Home* Fax: (212) 314-7309 Emp: 20,780
Shopping Network.

VIVENDIA INTERACTIVE PUBLISHING INC.
19840 Pioneer Avenue, Torrance, CA   90503

CEO: Christopher K. McLeod, CEO Tel: (310) 793-0600 %FO: 100
Bus: *Mfr. interactive CD-ROM* Fax: (310) 793-0601
products.

● VIVENTURES PARTNERS SA
Tour Cedre - 20e etage, 7 allee de l'Arche, F-92677, Paris Cedex, France

CEO: Jean-Pascal Tranie, CEO Tel: 33-1-7108-2059
Bus: *Engaged in venture capital.* Fax: 33-1-7108-2073 Emp: 25
www.viventures.com

VIVENTURES PARTNERS INC.
301 Howard Street, Ste. 1040, San Francisco, CA   94105

CEO: Edward Colby Tel: (415) 615-6900 %FO: 100
Bus: *Venture capital.* Fax: (415) 615-6945

● VRANKEN MONOPOLE
17 Avenue de Champagne, F-51200 Epernay, France

CEO: Paul-Francois Vranken, Pres. Tel: 33-3-2659-5050 Rev: $119
Bus: *Production and distribution of* Fax: 33-3-2652-1965 Emp: 800
champagne. www.vranken.net

VRANKEN AMERICA
45 West 45th Street, Ste. 905, New York, NY   10036

CEO: Paul-Francois Vranken, Pres. Tel: (212) 921-1215 %FO: 100
Bus: *Sales and distribution of* Fax: (212) 921-0204
champagne.

● WAVECOM SA
39 rue du Gouverneur General Eboue, F-92442 Issy-les-Moulineaux, France

CEO: Ara Hekimian, CEO Tel: 33-1-4629-0800
Bus: *Mfr. hardware and software for wireless* Fax: 33-1-4629-0808 Emp: 320
communications. www.wavecom.com

WAVECOM INC.
610 West Ash Street, Ste. 1400, San Diego, CA   92101
CEO: Hany Neoman, COO   Tel: (619) 235-9702   %FO: 100
Bus: *Mfr./sales hardware and software*   Fax: (619) 235-9844
     for wireless communications.

● **XRT-CERG**
Tour Eve, Place Sud., La défense 9, F-92806 Puteaux Cedex, France
CEO: Eric Blot-Lefevre, CEO   Tel: 33-1-4692-6000   Rev: $40
Bus: *Mfr. software.*   Fax: 33-1-4694-6060   Emp: 470
                                      www.xrtcerg.com

   XRT USA INC.
   1150 First Avenue, 10th Fl., King of Prussia, PA   19406
   CEO: Stephan Hagelauer   Tel: (610) 290-0300   %FO: 100
   Bus: *Mfr./sales software.*   Fax: (610) 290-0308

● **GROUPE ZODIAC SA**
2, rue Maurice Mallet, F-92137 Cedex Issy les Moulineaux, France
CEO: Jean-Louis Gerondeau, Chmn.   Tel: 33-1-4123-2323   Rev: $1,154
Bus: *Mfr. leisure marine inflatable products,*   Fax: 33-1-4648-7524   Emp: 6,915
     aerospace safety products.   www.zodiac.fr

   ZODIAC OF NORTH AMERICA INC.
   540 Thompson Creek Road, PO Box 400, Stevensville, MD   21666
   CEO: Jean-Jacques Marie, Pres.   Tel: (410) 643-4141   %FO: 100
   Bus: *Sales/distribution of leisure*   Fax: (410) 643-4491   Emp: 26
        marine inflatable products and
        aerospace safety products.

Germany

● **ACLA-WERKE GMBH**
Frankfurter Strasse 142-190, D-51065 Cologne, Germany
CEO: Gerhard Kieffer, CEO   Tel: 49-221-697121
Bus: *Mfr. polyurethane molded parts.*   Fax: 49-221-699980   Emp: 600
www.acla-werke.de

    ACLA USA INC.
    109 Thomson Park Drive, Cranberry Township, PA   16066
    CEO: Andrew P. McIntyre, Pres.   Tel: (412) 776-0099   %FO: 100
    Bus: *Sale/distribution polyurethane*   Fax: (412) 776-0477   Emp: 5
       molded parts.

● **ACO SEVERIN AHLMANN GMBH**
Postfach 3-20, AM Ahlmannkai, D-24755 Rendsburg, Germany
CEO: Hans-Julius Ahlmann, Chmn.   Tel: 49-4331-354242
Bus: *Polymer concrete, fiberglass and*   Fax: 49-4331-354357   Emp: 2,200
polypropylene trench drain systems and   www.acousa.com
building products.

    ACO POLYMER PRODUCTS, INC.
    12080 Ravenna Road, Chardon, OH   44024
    CEO: Maarten Fleurke, Pres.   Tel: (440) 285-7000   %FO: 100
    Bus: *Sales/distribution of polymer*   Fax: (440) 285-7005   Emp: 70
       concrete, fiberglass and
       polypropylene trench drain
       systems and building products.

    ACO POLYMER PRODUCTS, INC.
    750 Freeport Boulevard, Sparks, NV   89431
    CEO: Maarten Fleurke, Pres.   Tel: (775) 355-1178   %FO: 100
    Bus: *Sales/distribution of polymer*   Fax: (775) 355-7221
       concrete, fiberglass and
       polypropylene trench drain
       systems and building products.

● **ADIDAS-SALOMON AG**
Adi-Dassler-Str.1-2, Postfach 11 20, D-91074 Herzogenaurach, Germany
CEO: Herbert Hainer, Chmn. & CEO   Tel: 49-9132-842471   Rev: $5,800
Bus: *Mfr. footwear, sporting and athletic*   Fax: 49-9132-843127   Emp: 12,430
clothing and equipment.   www.adidas.com

ADIDAS AMERICA, INC.
9605 SW Nimbus Avenue, Beaverton, OR   97008

CEO:Ross McMullin, CEO	Tel: (503) 972-2300	%FO: 100
Bus: *Athletic clothing, shoes.*	Fax: (503) 797-4935	Emp: 800

• ADVA AG OPTICAL NETWORKING
Fraunhoferstrasse 11, D-82152 Martinsried, Germany

CEO: Stephan Offermanns, COO	Tel: 49-8989-577-577	Rev: $24
Bus: *Mfr. optical communications products.*	Fax: 49-8989-577-477	Emp: 132
	www.advaoptical.com	

ADVA OPTICAL NETWORKING INC.
19 Spear Road, Ste. 104, Ramsey, NJ   07446

CEO:Brian P. McCann, Mgr.	Tel: (201) 995-0080	%FO: 100
Bus: *Marketing of optical communications products.*	Fax: (201) 995-0081	

• AEG ELEKTROFOTOGRAFIE GMBH
Emil-Siepmann-Strasse 40, D-59581 Warstein-Belecke, Germany

CEO: Ernst Georg Stoeckl, Chmn.	Tel: 49-2-9028-61359	
Bus: *Mfr. drums and photoconductors for a variety of the imaging and printing markets.*	Fax: 49-2-9028-61350	Emp: 59,000
	www.aeg-photoconductor.com	

AEG PHOTOCONDUCTOR CORPORATION
27 Kiesland Court, Hamilton, OH   45015

CEO:Manfred Richard Wagner, Pres.	Tel: (513) 874-4939	%FO: 100
Bus: *Mfr. photo-receptor drums.*	Fax: (513) 874-5082	Emp: 27

• AERZENER MASCHINENFABRIK GMBH
28 Reherweg, D-31855 Aerzen, Germany

CEO: M. Heller, Pres.	Tel: 49-5154-810	
Bus: *Mfr. blowers and compressors.*	Fax: 49-5154-81191	
	www.aerzener.de	

AERZEN USA CORPORATION
645 Sands Court, Coatsville, PA   19320

CEO:Pierre Noack, Pres.	Tel: (610) 380-0244	%FO: 100
Bus: *Sales/distribution of blowers and compressors.*	Fax: (610) 380-0278	Emp: 17

• ALFRED KARCHER GMBH & CO.
Alfred-KarcherStrasse 28-40, D-71349 Winnenden, Germany

CEO: Johannes Karcher, Pres.	Tel: 49-7195-140	
Bus: *Manufacturer of cleaning equipment.*	Fax: 49-7195-142-212	
	www.karcheruk.co.uk	

ALFRED KARCHER INC.

PO Box 6910, Somerset, NJ   08875

CEO: Peter Powell   Tel: (732) 873-5002   %FO: 100

Bus: *Sales and support for high*   Fax: (732) 873-5003
     pressure washing products.

ALFRED KARCHER INC.

PO Box 3900, Rancho Cucamonga, CA   91729

CEO: Bernd Stockburger, EVP   Tel: (909) 481-4331   %FO: 100

Bus: *High pressure washers.*   Fax: (909) 481-4330   Emp: 150

● **ALLIANZ AG**

Koeniginstrasse 28, D-80802 Munich, Germany

CEO: Dr. Henning Schulte-Noell, Chmn.   Tel: 49-8-9380-00   Rev: $70,028

Bus: *Engaged in insurance; property and*   Fax: 49-8-93499-41   Emp: 113,580
     casualty insurance, life and health   www.allianz.de
     insurance,

ALLIANZ INSURANCE COMPANY

3400 Riverside Drive, Suite 300, Burbank, CA   91505-4669

CEO: Dr. Wolfgang Schlink, Chmn.   Tel: (818) 972-8000   %FO: 100

Bus: *Insurance services*   Fax: (818) 972-8466

ALLIANZ LIFE INSURANCE COMPANY OF NORTH AMERICA

1750 Hennepin Avenue, Minneapolis, MN   55403-2195

CEO: Lowell C. Anderson, Chmn. &   Tel: (952) 347-6500   %FO: 100
     Pres.

Bus: *Insurance services*   Fax: (952) 347-6657

ALLIANZ OF AMERICA CORPORATION

55 Greens Farms Road, PO Box 5160, Westport, CT   06881-5160

CEO: David P. Marks, CEO   Tel: (203) 221-8500   %FO: 100

Bus: *Insurance services*   Fax: (203) 221-8529

THE AMERICAN INSURANCE COMPANY

777 San Marin Drive, Novato, CA   94998

CEO: Joe L. Stinnette, Jr., Pres.   Tel: (415) 899-2000   %FO: 100

Bus: *Property/casualty insurance.*   Fax: (415) 899-3600   Emp: 10,000

CADENCE CAPITAL MANAGEMENT CORP.

Exchange Place, 29th Fl., Boston, MA   02109

CEO: David B. Breed, Mng. Dir.   Tel: (617) 367-7400   %FO: 100

Bus: *Insurance services.*   Fax: (617) 367-7393

FIREMAN'S FUND INSURANCE
1101 Connecticut Avenue, NW, Washington, DC   20036
CEO: Peter Larkin, VP   Tel: (202) 785-3575   %FO: 100
Bus: *Government affairs rep office.*   Fax: (202) 785-3023

NICHOLAS-APPLEGATE CAPITAL MANAGEMENT
600 West Broadway, San Diego, CA   92101
CEO: Marna Whittington, Pres.   Tel: (619) 687-8000   %FO: 100
Bus: *Manages for individual and*   Fax: (619) 687-2979
institutional investors, including
corporate and government
retirement plans, foundations,
endowments and mutual fund
families.

PARAMETRIC PORTFOLIO ASSOCIATES
701 Fifth Avenue, Ste. 7310, Seattle, WA   98104-7090
CEO: William E. Cornelius, Dir.   Tel: (206) 386-5575   %FO: 100
Bus: *Insurance services.*   Fax: (206) 386-5581

PIMCO ADVISERS
800 Newport Center Drive, Newport Beach, CA   92660
CEO: William S. Thompson Jr., Pres.   Tel: (949) 219-2200   %FO: 100
Bus: *Insurance services.*   Fax: (949) 759-7055

PIMCO EQUITY ADVISORS
33 Maiden Lane, New York, NY   10038
CEO: Michael F. Gaffney, Dir.   Tel: (212) 208-2852   %FO: 100
Bus: *Insurance services.*   Fax: (212) 208-2889

PIMCO FUNDS DISTRIBUTORS
2187 Atlantic Street, Stamford, CT   06902
CEO: Stephen J. Treadway, CEO   Tel: (800) 628-1237   %FO: 100
Bus: *Insurance services.*   Fax:

PREFERRED LIFE INSURANCE COMPANY
152 West 57th Street, 18th Fl., New York, NY   10019
CEO: Eugene K. Long, VP   Tel: (212) 586-7733   %FO: 100
Bus: *Insurance services.*   Fax: (212) 586-6949

● **ALSTOM ABB ENERGY SYSTEMS SHG GMBH**
Ellenbacher Strasse 10, D-34123 Kassel, Germany
CEO: H. Herrmann, Mng. Dir.   Tel: 49-561-9527-115
Bus: *Mfr. waste heat recovery equipment;*   Fax: 49-561-9527-109   Emp: 150
recuperators, boilers, heat exchangers.   www.power.alstom.com
(JV of Alstom and ABB)

ALSTOM POWER

31 Inverness Center Pkwy., Ste. 400, Birmingham, AL 35243

CEO: James Sullivan, District Mgr.　　Tel: (205) 991-2832　　%FO: 100

Bus: *Engineering and air quality*　　Fax: (205) 995-5380　　Emp: 125
　　control.

ALSTOM POWER

Andover Road, PO Box 372, Wellsville, NY 14895-0372

CEO: Edward J. Bysiek, Pres.　　Tel: (716) 593-2700　　%FO: 100

Bus: *Designs, manufactures and installs*　Fax: (716) 593-2721
　　the Combu-Charger recuperative
　　thermal oxidizers.

ALSTOM POWER

5309 Commonwealth Center Pkwy., Midlothian, VA 23112

CEO: Werner Lieberherr, Pres.　　Tel: (804) 763-2000　　%FO: 100

Bus: *Power engineering services.*　　Fax: (804) 763-2019

ALSTOM POWER ENERGY RECOVER, INC.

PO Box 1395, Wexford, PA 15090-1395

CEO: Greg Homoki, Pres.　　Tel: (724) 935-5725　　%FO: 100

Bus: *Mfr. waste heat recovery*　　Fax: (724) 935-6580　　Emp: 30
　　equipment; recuperates, boilers,
　　heat exchangers.

● **ALTANA AG**

Gunther-Quant-Haus, Seedammweg 55, D-61352 Bad Homburg v.d. Hoehe, Germany

CEO: Nikolaus Schweickart, CEO　　Tel: 49-6172-404-0

Bus: *Mfr. pharmaceuticals, dietetics and*　Fax: 49-6172-404338
　　infant foods.　　www.altana.com

ALTANA/BLYK-GUDEN

60 Baylis Road, Melville, NY 11747

CEO: George Cole, Pres.　　Tel: (516) 454-7677　　%FO: 100

Bus: *Mfr. dietetics, infant food and*　　Fax: (516) 454-1572
　　pharmaceuticals.

● **ATB ANTRIEBSTECHNIK AG**

Silcherstrasse 74, D-73642 Welzheim, Germany

CEO: Dr. Bernhard Ebner, Chmn.　　Tel: 49-7182-141　　Rev: $144

Bus: *Mfr. electrical and mechanical motors*　Fax: 49-7182-2887　　Emp: 1,373
　　and electrical equipment.　　www.atb.de

LOHER DRIVE SYSTEMS, INC.
1050 Northfield Court, Roswell, GA   30076
CEO: Mark Watson, Pres.   Tel: (770) 521-7500   %FO: 100
Bus: *Mfr. standard motors for*   Fax: (770) 521-7519
unregulated drive applications.

● **AUTOKUEHLER GMBH**
Postfach 1346, D-34363 Hofgeismar, Germany
CEO: Dirk Pietzoker, Chmn. & Pres.   Tel: 49-5671-8830   Rev: $140
Bus: *Mfr. heat exchangers.*   Fax: 49-5671-3582   Emp: 1,400
                                      www.akg-gruppe.de

    AKG OF AMERICA, INC.
    7315 Oakwood Street Extension, PO Box 365, Mebane, NC   27302
    CEO: Heinrich Kuehne, VP   Tel: (919) 563-4286   %FO: 100
    Bus: *Mfr./distribution heat exchangers.*   Fax: (919) 563-6060   Emp: 90

● **AXEL SPRINGER-VERLAG AG**
Axel-Springer-Strasse 65, D-10888 Berlin, Germany
CEO: August A. Fischer, Chmn.   Tel: 49-30-25-910   Rev: $2,800
Bus: *Publishing science, technical, medical*   Fax: 49-30-25-160-71   Emp: 12,000
books, journals & electronic media.   www.asv.de

    SPRINGER-VERLAG NEW YORK INC.
    175 Fifth Avenue, New York, NY   10010
    CEO: Rüdiger Gebauer, Pres. & CEO   Tel: (212) 460-1500   %FO: 100
    Bus: *Science technical books, journals.*   Fax: (212) 473-6272   Emp: 250

● **AZO GMBH & COMPANY**
Postfach 1120, D-74701 Osterburken, Germany
CEO: Rainer Zimmermann, CEO   Tel: 49-6291-8920
Bus: *Ingredient automation systems.*   Fax: 49-6291-8928   Emp: 767
                                      www.azo.de

    AZO INC.
    4445 Malone Road, Memphis, TN   38118
    CEO: Bob Moore, Pres.   Tel: (901) 794-9480   %FO: 100
    Bus: *Mfr. ingredient automation*   Fax: (901) 794-9934   Emp: 93
    systems.

● **BABCOCK BORSIG AG**
Dulsburger Strasse 375, D-46049 Oberhausen, Germany
CEO: Dr. Klaus G. Lederer, CEO   Tel: 49-208-2-8330   Rev: $7,043
Bus: *Designs and builds power generation*   Fax: 49-208-2-6091   Emp: 43,620
plants and manufactures finishing   www.babcockborsig.de
machines for the textile industry.

BABCOCK BORSIG CAPITAL CORP.

PO Box 15040, Worcester, MA   01606

CEO: Kenneth Fischer, Pres.   Tel: (508) 854-4036   %FO: 100

Bus: *Engaged in financial services.*   Fax: (508) 856-7025

D.B. RILEY USA INC.

Po Box 150 40, Worchester, MA   01615

CEO: John J. Halloran, Pres.   Tel: (508) 852-7100   %FO: 100

Bus: *Mfr. boilers and fuel firing*   Fax: (508) 852-7548
    equipment.

LOHER DRIVE SYSTEMS

1050 Northfield Court, Ste. 400, Roswell, GA   30076

CEO: Mark Watson, Dir.   Tel: (770) 521-7500   %FO: 100

Bus: *Mfr. gears and motors and drive*   Fax: (770) 521-7519
    systems.

SCHUMAG-KIESERLING MACHINERY, INC.

PO Box 419, Norwood, NJ   07648

CEO: Axel Justus, VP   Tel: (201) 767-6850   %FO: 100

Bus: *Sales of wire drawing and turning,* Fax: (201) 767-3341
    tube drawing and point grinding
    machinery.

VITS AMERICA, INC.

200 Corporate Drive, Blauvelt, NY   10913

CEO: Ton Tinnemans, Pres.   Tel: (914) 353-5000   %FO: 100

Bus: *Mfr. products for the printing and* Fax: (914) 365-1227
    converting industries.

● **BABCOCK TEXTILMASCHINEN GMBH**

Seevetal, Postfach 3148, D-20209 3-Maschen Hamburg, Germany

CEO: Dr. Reinsberg, Pres.   Tel: 49-4105-8110

Bus: *Mfr. textile machinery.*   Fax: 49-4105-811231
                                   www.babcock.de

   BABCOCK TEXTILE MACHINERY, INC.

   11024 Nations Ford Road, Pineville, NC   28134

   CEO: W. Craig Newsome, VP   Tel: (704) 588-2780

   Bus: *Mfr. textile machinery.*   Fax: (704) 588-2651

● **BAHLSEN GMBH & CO. KG**

Podbielskistrasse 289, D-30655 Hanover, Germany

CEO: Werner M. Bahlsen, Chmn.   Tel: 49-511-960-0   Rev: $532

Bus: *Mfr. biscuits and snacks.*   Fax: 49-511-960-2749   Emp: 4,000
                                   www.bahlsen.de

BAHLSEN GMBH & CO.
1335 North Fairfax Avenue, Ste. 6, West Hollywood, CA   90046
CEO: Norbert Maas   Tel: (323) 850-7093   %FO: 100
Bus: *Mfr. biscuits and snacks.*   Fax: (323) 850-6693

● **BARMAG AG, DIV. SAURER GROUP**
Box 11 02 40, D-42862 Remscheid-Lennep, Germany
CEO: Klaus K. Moll, Chmn.   Tel: 49-2191-67-0   Rev: $672
Bus: *Mfr. of machinery and equipment for*   Fax: 49-2191-67-1204   Emp: 3,150
the man made fiber industry.   www.barmag.com

   AMERICAN BARMAG CORPORATION
   1101 Westinghouse Blvd., Charlotte, NC   28241
   CEO: Mike Collins, Pres.   Tel: (704) 588-0072   %FO: 100
   Bus: *Sales/service of machinery &*   Fax: (704) 588-2047   Emp: 115
   equipment for the man made fiber
   industry.

● **BASF AG**
Carl-Bosch Strasse 38, D-67056 Ludwigshafen, Germany
CEO: Dr. Jürgen F. Strube, Chmn.   Tel: 49-621-60-4-3263   Rev: $32,400
Bus: *Oil and gas, petrochemicals,*   Fax: 49-621-60-2-2500   Emp: 105,000
agricultural, plastics and fibers,   www.basf.de
chemicals, dyestuffs, finishing, and
consumer products.

   BASF BIORESEARCH CORPORATION
   100 Research Drive, Worcester, MA   01605
   CEO: Robert Kamen, Pres.   Tel: (508) 849-2500   %FO: 100
   Bus: *Bioscience research facility.*   Fax: (508) 756-8506

   BASF CARPET CENTER
   475 Reed Road NW, Dalton, GA   30720
   CEO: Walter W. Hubbard, Grp. VP   Tel: (706) 259-1200   %FO: 100
   Bus: *Mfr./sales nylon carpet products.*   Fax: (706) 259-1424

   BASF- DISPERSIONS
   11501 Steele Creek Road, Charlotte, NC   28273
   CEO: Klaus E. Loeffler, Grp. VP   Tel: (704) 588-5280   %FO: 100
   Bus: *Mfr./sales dispersion and acrylic*   Fax: (704) 588-7903
   polymer chemicals.

   BASF R&D
   100 Sand Hill Road, Enka, NC   28728
   CEO: Otto Ilg, VP   Tel: (828) 667-7110   %FO: 100
   Bus: *U.S. R&D facility.*   Fax: (828) 667-7110

BASF REFINISH TECHNOLOGIES, INC.

26701 Telegraph Road, Southfield, MI   48034

CEO: James M. Kendall, VP   Tel: (248) 827-4670   %FO: 100

Bus: *Coatings and colorants division.*   Fax: (248) 827-2727

BASF TEXTILE PRODUCTS

4824 Parkway Plaza Blvd., Charlotte, NC   28217

CEO: Walter W. Hubbard, Grp. VP   Tel: (704) 423-2377   %FO: 100

Bus: *Mfr./sales nylon textile products.*   Fax: (704) 423-2101

KNOLL PHARMACEUTIAL COMPANY

3000 Continental Drive North, Mount Olive, NJ   07828-1234

CEO: Carter H. Eckert, Pres.   Tel: (973) 426-2600   %FO: 100

Bus: *Holding company; chemicals,*   Fax: (973) 426-2610   Emp: 15,350
coatings & colorants, consumer
product & life science, fiber
products, polymers, & plastic
materials.

MICRO FLO CO.

530 Oak Court Drive, Memphis, TN   38117

CEO: Brian Wilson, Pres.   Tel: (901) 432-5000   %FO: 100

Bus: *Mfr. crop protection products and*   Fax: (901) 432-5100
systems.

ULTRAFORM COMPANY

4201 Degussa Road, Theodore, AL   36582

CEO: Gerhard Heinz, Mgr.   Tel: (334) 443-1600   %FO: 100

Bus: *Engaged in plastics and fibers.*   Fax: (334) 443-1613

• **BATTENFELD MASCHINEN-FABRIKEN GMBH**

Scherl 10, D-58540 Meinerzhagen, Germany

CEO: Dr. Helmut Eschwey, Chmn.   Tel: 49-23-540-20

Bus: *Mfr. plastics process machinery.*   Fax: 49-23540-72442

www.battenfeld.com

BATTENFELD GLOUCESTER ENGINEERING COMPANY INC.

Blackburn Ind. Park, PO Box 900, Gloucester, MA   01930

CEO: Harold Wrede, Pres.   Tel: (978) 281-1800   %FO: 100

Bus: *Mfr. film and sheet extrusion*   Fax: (978) 282-9111   Emp: 500
machinery.

• **CHRISTIAN BAUER GMBH & CO.**

Schorndorffstrasse, D-73642 Welzheim/Wuertt, Germany

CEO: Helmut Hutt, Gen Dir.   Tel: 49-7-1821-21

Bus: *Mfr. precision disc springs.*   Fax: 49-7-1821-2315   Emp: 536

www.bauersprings.com

BAUER SPRINGS INC
509 Parkway View Drive, Pittsburgh, PA 15205
CEO: Helmut Hutt, Pres. Tel: (412) 787-7930 %FO: 100
Bus: *Engineering/distribution disc* Fax: (412) 787-3882 Emp: 4
springs.

● **BAYER AG**
Bayerwerk, D-51368 Leverkusen, Germany
CEO: Dr. Manfred Schneider, Chmn. Tel: 49-2-1430-8992 Rev: $32,900
Bus: *Holding company for healthcare,* Fax: 49-2-1430-81146 Emp: 145,000
imaging technologies, agricultural, www.bayer.com
industrial products, chemicals, polymer
industries.

BAYER CONSUMER CARE
36 Columbia Road, PO Box 1910, Morristown, NJ 07962-0910
CEO: Gary S. Balkema, Pres. Tel: (973) 254-5000 %FO: 100
Bus: *Consumer products division.* Fax: (973) 408-8000

BAYER CORPORATION (US)
100 Bayer Road, Pittsburgh, PA 15205-9741
CEO: Helge H .Wehmeier, CEO Tel: (412) 777-2000 %FO: 100
Bus: *Headquarters US. Chemicals,* Fax: (412) 777-2447 Emp: 23,000
healthcare, imaging technologies,
agricultural, industrial products,
chemicals, polymer industries.

BAYER CORPORATION AG DIV
8400 Hawthorne Road, Kansas City, MO 64120-2306
CEO: Emil E. Lansu, Pres. Tel: (816) 242-2000 %FO: 100
Bus: *Mfr./sale agricultural products.* Fax: (816) 242-2526

BAYER CORPORATION POLYMERS
100 Bayer Road, Pittsburgh, PA 15205-9741
CEO: Mike Foote, Pres. Tel: (412) 777-2000 %FO: 100
Bus: *Mfr./sales industrial chemicals.* Fax: (412) 777-4959

BAYER - Diagnostics Division
511 Benedict Avenue, Tarrytown, NY 10591-5097
CEO: Rolf A. Classson, Pres. Tel: (914) 631-8000 %FO: 100
Bus: *Healthcare diagnostics division.* Fax: (914) 524-2132

BAYER PHARMACEUTICAL DIV.
400 Morgan Lane, West Haven, CT 06516-4175
CEO: David Ebsworth, Pres. Tel: (203) 812-2000 %FO: 100
Bus: *R&D/mfr./sales ethical* Fax: (203) 812-5554
pharmaceuticals.

BAYER POLYMERS

2401 Walton Boulevard, Auburn Hills, MI   48326-1957

CEO: Dr. Joseph Backes, VP	Tel: (248) 475-7700	%FO: 100
Bus: *Design/mfr./sale automotive products.*	Fax: (248) 475-7700	

CHEM DESIGN CORPORATION

99 Development Road, Fitchburg, MA   01420-6000

CEO: Volker Mirgel, Pres.	Tel: (978) 345-9999	%FO: 100
Bus: *Chemicals.*	Fax: (978) 392-9769	

DEERFIELD URETHANE INC.

PO Box 186, South Deerfield, MA   01373-0186

CEO: Richard C. Baxendell, Pres.	Tel: (413) 665-7016	%FO: 100
Bus: *Mfr. polyurethane films.*	Fax: (413) 665-7159	

RHEIN CHEMIE CORPORATION

1014 Whitehead Road Extension, Trenton, NJ   08638-2495

CEO: Wolfgang Kober, Pres.	Tel: (609) 771-9100	%FO: 100
Bus: *Mfr. chemical additives.*	Fax: (609) 771-0409	

H.C. STARK INC.

45 Industrial Place, Newton, MA   02161-1951

CEO: Lawrence F. McHugh, Pres.	Tel: (617) 630-5800	%FO: 100
Bus: *Mfr. tantalum & niobium products.*	Fax: (617) 630-4888	

WOLFF WALSRODE

15 West 700 South Frontage Road, Burr Ridge, IL   60521-7544

CEO: Timothy M. McDivit, Pres.	Tel: (708) 789-8440	%FO: 100
Bus: *Bayer AG, US subsidiary.*	Fax: (708) 789-8489	

● **BAYERISCHE HYPO-UND VEREINSBANK AG**

Am Tucheerpark 16, D-80538 Munich, Germany

CEO: Dr. Albrecht Schmidt, Chmn.	Tel: 49-8-9378-0	Rev: $30,750
Bus: *General commercial banking services.*	Fax: 49-89-3782-4083	Emp: 46,170
	www.hypovereinsbank.de	

BAYERISCHE VEREINSBANK

800 Wilshire Blvd., Ste. 1600, Los Angeles, CA   90017-2620

CEO: Christine Taylor, Mgr.	Tel: (213) 629-1821	%FO: 100
Bus: *International commercial banking services.*	Fax: (213) 622-6341	Emp: 30

BAYERISCHE VEREINSBANK
150 East 42nd Street, New York, NY   10017
CEO: Stephan W. Bub, CEO   Tel: (212) 672-6000   %FO: 100
Bus: *International commercial banking*   Fax: (212) 210-0330   Emp: 220
    services.

● BAYERISCHE LANDESBANK GIROZENTRALE
Briennerstrasse 20, D-80277 Munich, Germany
CEO: Heinrich Schmidhuber, Chmn.   Tel: 49-8-9217-101   Rev: $12,940
Bus: *General commercial banking services.*   Fax: 49-8-9217-13579   Emp: 5,450
    www.bib.de

BAYERISCHE LANDESBANK GIROZENTRALE
560 Lexington Avenue, New York, NY   10022
CEO: Wilfried Freudenberger, EVP   Tel: (212) 310-9800   %FO: 100
Bus: *International commercial banking*   Fax: (212) 310-9841   Emp: 170
    services.

● BEHR INDUSTRIETECHNIK GMBH & CO.
Heilbronner Strasse 380, D-70469 Stuttgart, Germany
CEO: Horst Geidel, Chmn.   Tel: 49-711-896-3073   Rev: $17,100
Bus: *Engine cooling, air conditioning for*   Fax: 49-711-896-3075   Emp: 11,400
    automotive industry.   www.behr.de

BEHR AMERICA INC.
4500 Leeds Avenue, Charleston, SC   29405
CEO: Hans-Joachim Lange, Pres.   Tel: (843) 745-1233   %FO: 100
Bus: *Engine cooling and air*   Fax: (843) 745-1285   Emp: 950
    conditioning for automotive
    industry.

BEHR AMERICA, INC.
850 Ladd Road, Bldg. A, Walled Lake, MI   48390-3026
CEO: Joseph Kern   Tel: (248) 624-7020   %FO: 100
Bus: *Engine cooling and air*   Fax: (248) 624-9111
    conditioning for automotive
    industry.

BEHR CLIMATE SYSTEMS, INC.
5020 Augusta Drive, Ft. Worth, TX   76106
CEO: Ed Dietz   Tel: (817) 624-7273   %FO: 100
Bus: *Engine cooling and air*   Fax: (817) 624-3328
    conditioning for automotive
    industry.

BEHR HEAT TRANSFER SYSTEMS, INC.

47920 Fifth Street, Canton, SD   57013-5802

CEO: Dennis Coull, Mgr.

Bus: *Engine cooling and air conditioning for automotive industry.*

Tel: (605) 764-2347

Fax: (605) 764-1283

%FO: 100

• BEIERSDORF AG

Unnastrasse 48, D-20253 Hamburg, Germany

CEO: Dr. Rolf Kunisch, Chmn.

Bus: *Mfr. toiletries, pharmaceuticals, medical products, tapes.*

Tel: 49-40-4909-0

Fax: 49-40-4909-3434

www.beiersdorf.com

Rev: $3,664

Emp: 15,850

BEIERSDORF JOBST, INC.

5825 Carnegie Boulevard, Charlotte, NC   28209

CEO: Claus Von Wiegel, Pres.

Bus: *U.S. headquarters. Mfr. toiletries, pharmaceuticals, medical products, tapes.*

Tel: (704) 554-9933

Fax: (704) 553-5853

%FO: 100

BEIERSDORF, INC.

187 Danbury Road, Wilton, CT   06897

CEO: James Kenton, Pres.

Bus: *Mfr. toiletries, medical products. Nivea & Eucerin brand products.*

Tel: (203) 563-5800

Fax: (203) 563-5895

%FO: 100

Emp: 400

TESA TAPE INC.

5825 Carnegie Boulevard, Charlotte, NC   28209

CEO: Torston Shermer, Pres.

Bus: *Mfr. pressure sensitive tape.*

Tel: (704) 554-0707

Fax: (704) 553-5853

%FO: 100

Emp: 100

• BEITEN BURKHARDT MITTL & WEGENER

Leopoldstraße 236, D-80807 Munich, Germany

CEO: Dr. Jack Schiffer

Bus: *International law firm.*

Tel: 49-89-350-6500

Fax: 49-89-350-65123

www.bbmw.de

BEITEN BURKHARDT MITTL & WEGENER

215 East 73rd Street, New York, NY   10021

CEO: Michael Stever

Bus: *International law firm.*

Tel: (212) 570-2141

Fax: (212) 734-7011

%FO: 100

● **BENTELER AUTOMOTIVE GMBH & CO.**

An der Talle 27-31, D-33104 Paderborn, Germany

CEO: Hubertus Benteler, Pres.   Tel: 49-5251-408346   Rev: $2,500

Bus: *Automotive parts, steel tubing, machine* Fax: 49-5254-81-0   Emp: 12,000
     tooling and steel distribution.   www.benteler.de

    BENTELER AUTOMOTIVE CORPORATION

    50 Monroe Avenue, NW, Ste. 500, Grand Rapids, MI 49503

    CEO: Walter E. Frankiewicz, Pres.   Tel: (616) 247-3936   %FO: 100

    Bus: *Mfr. of metal fabricated products:* Fax: (616) 732-1697   Emp: 1,800
       chassis, front exhaust, impact
       management, and stamping
       systems.

    BENTELER AUTOMOTIVE CORPORATION

    17197 North Laurel Park, Ste. 501, Livonia, MI 48152

    CEO: Walter E. Frankiewicz, Pres.   Tel: (734) 432-6740   %FO: 100

    Bus: *US sales office.*   Fax: (734) 462-2626

● **BERTELSMANN AG**

Carl-Bertelsmann-Strasse 270, Postfach 111, D-33311 Gütersloh, Germany

CEO: Dr. Thomas Middelhoff, CEO   Tel: 49-52-41-800   Rev: $12,700

Bus: *International communications holding* Fax: 49-52-41-75166   Emp: 57,800
    company. Publishing, printing, books, www.bertelsmann.de
    magazines, music, computer, TV and
    radio.

    ARISTA RECORDS INC.

    6 West 57th Street, New York, NY 10019-3913

    CEO: Antonio Reid, Pres.   Tel: (212) 489-7400   %FO: 100

    Bus: *Sales of music/recordings.*   Fax: (212) 830-2322

    BALLANTINE DELL PUBLISHING GROUP

    1540 Broadway, New York, NY 10036

    CEO: Irwyn Applebaum, Pres.   Tel: (212) 751-9600   %FO: 100

    Bus: *Book publishing.*   Fax: (212) 302-7985

    BARNES & NOBLE.COM

    76 Ninth Avenue, 11th Fl., New York, NY 10011

    CEO: Steve Riggio, VC   Tel: (212) 414-6000   %FO: 100

    Bus: *On-line book retailer.*   Fax: (212) 414-6120

BERTELSMANN INDUSTRY SERVICES

28210 North Avenue Stanford, Valencia, CA 91355-1111

CEO: Peter Schmitz, Pres.   Tel: (661) 257-0584   %FO: 100

Bus: *Holding company. International*   Fax: (661) 257-3867   Emp: 300
communications holding company; publishing & printing. Books, Magazines, music, computer, TV & radio.

BMG DIRECT MARKETING INC.

1540 Broadway, 24th Fl., New York, NY 10036-4098

CEO: George McMillan, CEO   Tel: (212) 930-4000   %FO: 100

Bus: *Sales of music/recordings.*   Fax: (212) 930-4015

BMG ENTERTAINMENT

1540 Broadway, 24th Fl., New York, NY 10036

CEO: William Duffy   Tel: (212) 930-4000   %FO: 100

Bus: *Distributor/marketing music and*   Fax: (212) 930-4015   Emp: 1,500
video.

CDNOW, INC.

1005 Virginia Drive, Fort Washington, PA 19034

CEO: Michael S. Krupit, CEO   Tel: (215) 619-9900   %FO: 100

Bus: *Online retailer of music and music*   Fax: (215) 619-9525
reviews.

CROWN PUBLISHING

299 Park Avenue, New York, NY 10171

CEO: Chip Gibson, Pres.   Tel: (212) 751-2600   %FO: 100

Bus: *Book publishing.*   Fax: (212) 751-8700

DOUBLEDAY BROADWAY PUBLISHING GROUP

1540 Broadway, New York, NY 10036

CEO: Stephen Rubin, Pres.   Tel: (212) 782-9000   %FO: 100

Bus: *Engaged in fiction, non fiction and*   Fax: (212) 302-7985
trade paperback publishing.

GET MUSIC LLC

11 West 19th Street, 3rd Fl., New York, NY 10011

CEO: Andrew Nibley, Pres. & CEO   Tel: (917) 464-0600   %FO: 100

Bus: *Sale of music on-line.*   Fax: (917) 464-0500

GRUNER+JAHR USA

375 Lexington Avenue, New York, NY 10017

CEO: Daniel B. Brewster Jr., Pres.   Tel: (212) 499-2000   %FO: 100

Bus: *Magazine publisher.*   Fax: (212) 499-2263

KNOPF PUBLISHING GROUP
299 Park Avenue, New York, NY 10071
CEO: Sonny Mehta, Pres.   Tel: (212) 751-2600   %FO: 100
Bus: *Book publishing.*   Fax: (212) 751-8700

OFFSET PAPERBACK MANUFACURERS INC.
PO Box N, Route 309, Dallas, PA 18612
CEO: Michael J. Gallagher, Pres.   Tel: (570) 675-5261   %FO: 100
Bus: *Provides commercial printing and*   Fax: (570) 675-8714
markets digest-size, paperback
books.

RANDOM HOUSE CHILDREN'S PUBLISHING
1540 Broadway, New York, NY 10036
CEO: Craig Virden, Pres.   Tel: (212) 782-9000   %FO: 100
Bus: *Book publishing.*   Fax: (212) 302-7985

RANDOM HOUSE DIVERSIFIED/ AUDIO PUBLISHING
1540 Broadway, 24th Fl., New York, NY 10036
CEO: Jenny Frost, Pres.   Tel: (212) 782-9000   %FO: 100
Bus: *Book publishing in diversified*   Fax: (212) 302-7985   Emp: 60
formats, including audio and CD
formats.

RANDOM HOUSE TRADE PUBLISHING
299 Park Avenue, New York, NY 10171
CEO: Ann Godoff, Pres.   Tel: (212) 751-2600   %FO: 100
Bus: *Book publishing.*   Fax: (212) 751-8700

RANDOM HOUSE, INC.
1540 Broadway, New York, NY 10036
CEO: Erik Engstrom, Pres. & CEO   Tel: (212) 751-2600   %FO: 100
Bus: *Book publishing.*   Fax: (212) 751-8700

RCA MUSIC GROUP
1400 South 18th Avenue, Nashville, TN 37203
CEO: Joseph Gallante, Chmn.   Tel: (615) 301-4300   %FO: 100
Bus: *Sales of music/recordings.*   Fax: (615) 301-4347

RCA RECORDS USA
1540 Broadway, New York, NY 10036
CEO: Robert Jamieson, Pres.   Tel: (212) 930-4936   %FO: 100
Bus: *Sales of music/recordings.*   Fax: (212) 930-4449

SONOPRESS INC.
108 Monticello Road, Weaverville, NC   28787-9441
CEO: Robert Spiller, Pres.   Tel: (704) 658-2000   %FO: 100
Bus: *Sales of music/recordings.*   Fax: (704) 782-7668

SPRINGER-VERLAG NEW YORK INC.
175 Fifth Avenue, New York, NY   10010
CEO: Rüdiger Gebauer, Pres. & CEO   Tel: (212) 460-1500
Bus: *Publishing.*   Fax: (212) 473-6272

● **BHF-BANK AKTIENGESELLSCHAFT**
Bockenheimer Landstrasse 10, D-60323 Frankfurt am Main, Germany
CEO: Ernst Michel Kruse, Mng. Dir.   Tel: 49-69-718-0   Rev: $2,803
Bus: *Manages commercial and mortgage*   Fax: 49-69-718-2296   Emp: 2,900
banks, financing companies and   www.bhf-bank.de
investment banking companies.

BHF SECURITIES CORPORATION
590 Madison Avenue, 28th Fl., New York, NY   10022-2540
CEO: Burkhard Frankenberger, Dir.   Tel: (212) 756-2800
Bus: *Investment banking services.*   Fax: (212) 756-2729   Emp: 70

● **BHK-HOLZU KUNSTSTOFF KG**
Industriegebiet-West, D-33142 Buren, Germany
CEO: Heinz Kottmann, Chmn.   Tel: 49-295-16040
Bus: *Mfr. vinyl-wrapped drawer components,*   Fax: 49-295-17588   Emp: 500
wall and ceiling paneling systems,   www.bhk.de
flooring and decorative moldings.

BHK OF AMERICA INC.
11 Bond Street, Central Valley, NY   10917
CEO: Reiner Kamp, Pres.   Tel: (845) 928-6200   %FO: 70
Bus: *Mfr./sale vinyl-wrapped and wood*   Fax: (845) 928-2287   Emp: 100
drawer components, furniture
components.

BHK OF AMERICA INC.
3045 Philpott Road, Boston, MA   24592
CEO: Reiner Kamp, Pres.   Tel: (804) 572-5500
Bus: *Mfr./sale vinyl-wrapped and wood*   Fax: (804) 572-5503   Emp: 100
drawer components, furniture
components.

● BILFINGER + BERGER BAU AG

Carl-Reiss-Platz 1-5, Postfach 100562, D-68165 Mannheim, Germany

CEO: Herbert Bodner, Chmn.	Tel: 49-621-4590	Rev: $3,680
Bus: *Construction/engineering services.*	Fax: 49-621-459-2366	Emp: 41,650
	www.bilfingerberger.de	

FRU-CON CONSTRUCTION CORPORATION

15933 Clayton Road, PO Box 100, Ballwin, MO 63022-0100

CEO: Peter F. Sanderson   Tel: (636) 391-6700

Bus: *Provides engineering, construction*   Fax: (636) 391-4513
and project development.

FRU-CON DEVELOPMENT CORP

15933 Clayton Road, PO Box 100, Ballwin, MO 63022-0100

CEO: Paul Sauer, Pres.	Tel: (636) 391-6700	%FO: 100
Bus: *Real estate development of retail*	Fax: (636) 391-4513	Emp: 12
& commercial complexes. (Sub. of		
Fru-con Construction Corp.)		

FRU-CON ENGINEERING INC.

15933 Clayton Road, PO Box 100, Ballwin, MO 63022-0100

CEO: Shawn G. Kelly, Pres.	Tel: (636) 391-6700	%FO: 100
Bus: *Consulting & design services.*	Fax: (636) 391-4513	Emp: 400
*(*Sub of Fru-con Construction*		
Corp.)		

FRU-CON HOLDING CORPORATION

15933 Clayton Road, PO Box100, Ballwin, MO 63022-0100

CEO: Bruce A. Frost, Dir.	Tel: (636) 391-6700	%FO: 100
Bus: *Full-service engineering*	Fax: (636) 391-4513	Emp: 2,000
construction.		

FRU-CON TECHNICAL SERVICES INC

15933 Clayton Road, PO Box 100, Ballwin, MO 63022-0100

CEO: Shawn G. Kelly, Pres.	Tel: (636) 391-6700	%FO: 100
Bus: *Full-service technical resource for*	Fax: (636) 391-4513	Emp: 131
*construction industry. (*Sub of*		
Fru-con Construction Corp.)		

H.E.SARGENT, INC.

101 Bennoch Road, Stillwater, ME 04489

CEO: John I. Simpson, Pres.	Tel: (207) 827-4435	%FO: 100
Bus: *Full-service engineering*	Fax: (207) 827-6150	Emp: 131
*construction. (*Sub of Fru-con*		
Construction Corp.)		

● **BAYERISCHE MOTOREN WERKE AG (BMW AG)**

BMW Haus, Petuelring 130, D-80788 Munich, Germany

CEO: Joachim Milberg, Chmn.   Tel: 49-89-3822-4272   Rev: $34,650

Bus: *Mfr. motor vehicles, motorbikes &*   Fax: 49-89-3822-4418   Emp: 114,875
engines.   www.bmw.com

BMW FINANCIAL SERVICES

300 Chestnut Ridge Road, Woodcliff Lake, NJ   07675-1227

CEO: Stefan Krause, Pres.   Tel: (201) 307-4000   %FO: 100

Bus: *Financial services for BMW NA.*   Fax: (201) 307-4000

BMW MANUFACTURING CORPORATION

1400 Hwy. 101 South, Greer, SC   29651

CEO: Dr. Helmut Leube, Pres.   Tel: (864) 968-6000   %FO: 100

Bus: *Manufacturing facility.*   Fax: (864) 968-6000

BMW OF NORTH AMERICA, INC.

PO Box 1227, Westwood, NJ   07675

CEO: Gene Donnelly, VP   Tel: (201) 307-4000   %FO: 100

Bus: *Import/distribution automobiles,*   Fax: (201) 307-4095   Emp: 910
motorcycles, parts & service.

● **BOEHRINGER INGELHEIM GMBH**

Bingerstrasse 173, D55216 Ingelheim, Germany

CEO: Rolf Krebs, Chmn.   Tel: 49-6132-770   Rev: $5,827

Bus: *Mfr. prescription and veterinary drugs.*   Fax: 49-6132-77-3000   Emp: 27,325
www.boehringer-ingelheim.com

BEN VENUE LABORATORIES, INC.

300 Northfield Road, Bedford, OH   44146

CEO: Peter Hansbury, Mgr.   Tel: (440) 232-3320   %FO: 100

Bus: *Mfr. prescription and over-the-*   Fax: (440) 439-6398
counter drugs.

BOEHRINGER INGELHEIM CORP.

900 Ridgebury Road, Ridgefield, CT   06877-0368

CEO: James Heins, Mgr.   Tel: (203) 798-9988   %FO: 100

Bus: *Mfr. prescription and veterinary*   Fax: (203) 791-6234
drugs.

ROXANE LABORATORIES, INC.

1809 Wilson Road, Columbus, OH   43228

CEO: Werner Gerstenberg, Pres. & CEO   Tel: (614) 276-4000   %FO: 100

Bus: *Engaged in palliative care and*   Fax: (614) 308-0236   Emp: 900
pain management products.

● **ROBERT BOSCH GMBH**

Robert Bosch Platz 1, Postfach 10 60 50, D-70049 Stuttgart, Germany

CEO: Hermann Scholl, Chmn.　　　　　Tel: 49-711-8110　　　　　Rev: $28,100

Bus: *Mfr. auto components, communications*　Fax: 49-711-8116630　　　Emp: 196,000
　　　technology, consumer and capital goods.　www.bosch.com

ASSOCIATED FUEL PUMP SYSTEMS CORPORATION

1100 Scotts Bridge Road, Anderson, SC　29622

CEO: Masayuki Iyoda, Pres.　　　　　Tel: (864) 224-0012　　　　%FO: JV

Bus: *Mfr./sale auto electric gasoline*　　Fax: (864) 224-2927
　　　pumps.

AUTECS INC.

Hwy 81 at I-85, Anderson, SC　29621

CEO: Wolfgang Simon, VP　　　　　Tel: (864) 224-0012　　　　%FO: JV

Bus: *Mfr. electronic controls for gas*　　Fax: (864) 224-2927
　　　injection systems & auto
　　　transmissions, mass airflow meters

AUTOMOTIVE LIGHTING CORP.

47000 Liberty Drive, Wixom, MI　48393

CEO: Peter A. Cirulis, Pres.　　　　　Tel: (248) 668-3600　　　　%FO: JV

Bus: *Mfr. automotive lighting.*　　　Fax: (248) 668-3601

BOSCH AUTOMATION PRODUCTS, INC.

816 East Third Street, Buchanan, MI　49107

CEO: A. Benz, VP　　　　　　　Tel: (616) 695-0151　　　　%FO: 100

Bus: *Provides custom solutions to*　　Fax: (616) 695-5363
　　　maximize factory floor
　　　productivity, including conveyors,
　　　aluminum framing and
　　　workstations.

BOSCH BRAKING SYSTEMS

401 North Bendix Drive, South Bend, IN　46634-4001

CEO: Hans Weckerle, Pres.　　　　　Tel: (219) 237-2000　　　　%FO: 100

Bus: *Develop/mfr./sale braking systems.*　Fax: (219) 237-3242

ROBERT BOSCH CORPORATION

2800 South 25th Avenue, Broadview, IL　60153

CEO: Knut Bendixen, Pres.　　　　　Tel: (708) 865-5200　　　　%FO: 100

Bus: *Administrative offices.*　　　　Fax: (708) 865-6430

ROBERT BOSCH CORPORATION

38000 Hills Tech Drive, Farmington Hills, MI   48331-3417

CEO: Robert S. Oswald, Pres.   Tel: (248) 553-9000   %FO: 100

Bus: *Develop/mfr./distribution equipment for cars and trucks.*   Fax: (248) 553-1309

BOSCH REXROTH CORP.

7505 Durand Avenue, Sturtevant, WI   53177

CEO: Bill Widen, Mgr.   Tel: (262) 554-8595   %FO: 100

Bus: *Provides custom solutions to maximize factory floor productivity, including industrial hydraulics, mobile hydraulics and pneumatics.*   Fax: (262) 554-7117

BOSCH ROBERT SURFTRAN DIV.

30250 Stephenson Hwy., Madison Heights, MI   48071

CEO: Eden Diver, Pres.   Tel: (248) 547-8103   %FO: 100

Bus: *Mfr. metal deburring/finishing system, computer controls, servo drives.*   Fax: (248) 547-0206

DETECTION SYSTEMS, INC.

130 Perinton Pkwy., Fairport, NY   14450-9199

CEO: Karl H. Kostusiak, CEO   Tel: (716) 223-4060   %FO: 100

Bus: *Mfr. electronic detection and communications equipment.*   Fax: (716) 223-9180   Emp: 1,200

ROBERT BOSCH FLUID POWER CORPORATION

7505 Durand Avenue, Racine, WI   53406

CEO: Mike Hadfield, Pres.   Tel: (414) 554-7100   %FO: 100

Bus: *Mfr. hydraulic/pneumatic products.*   Fax: (414) 554-7117

ROBERT BOSCH CORPORATION PACKAGING MACHINERY DIV.

9850 Red Arrow Hwy., Bridgman, MI   49106

CEO: Peter Loveland, Pres.   Tel: (616) 465-6986   %FO: 100

Bus: *Mfr. integrated manufacturing systems.*   Fax: (616) 465-3400

TL SYSTEMS BOSCH CORPORATION

8700 Wyoming Avenue North, Brooklyn Park, MN   55445-1840

CEO: Don DeMorett, Pres.   Tel: (763) 493-6770   %FO: 100

Bus: *Mfr./sales packaging machinery for pharmaceuticals.*   Fax: (763) 493-6711

VERMONT AMERICAN CORPORATION
101 South Fifth Street, Ste. 2300, Louisville, KY   40202
CEO: Timothy T. Shea, Pres. & CEO   Tel: (502) 625-2000   %FO: JV
Bus: *Mfr. cutting tools, hand tools &*   Fax: (502) 625-2122
 accessories, lawn garden
 products, closet organizers.

● **GEOBRA BRANDSTATTER GMBH & CO KG**
Brandstätter Str. 2-10, D-90513 Zirndorf, Germany
CEO: Horst Brandstatter, Pres.   Tel: 49-911-966-60   Rev: $216
Bus: *Mfr. toys.*   Fax: 49-911-966-6120   Emp: 2,190
 www.playmobil.com

PLAYMOBIL FUNPARK
8031 North Military Trail, Palm Beach Gardens, FL   33410
CEO: Jamie Gallagher, Pres.   Tel: (561) 691-9577   %FO: 100
Bus: *Funpark.*   Fax: (561) 691-9577   Emp: 10

PLAYMOBIL USA INC.
PO Box 877, Dayton, NJ   08810
CEO: Jamie Gallagher, Pres.   Tel: (609) 395-5566   %FO: 100
Bus: *Sale/distribution toys.*   Fax: (609) 409-1288   Emp: 40

PLAYMOBIL USA INC.
26 Commerce Drive, Cranbury, NJ   08512
CEO: John Thorpe, Pres.   Tel: (609) 395-5566   %FO: 100
Bus: *Sale/distribution toys.*   Fax: (609) 409-1288

● **BRENNTAG AG, DIV. STINNES**
Humboldtring 15, D-45472 Mulheim an der Ruhr, Germany
CEO: Dr. Klaus Engel   Tel: 49-208-7828-0   Rev: $650
Bus: *Engaged in distribution and logistics of*   Fax: 49-208-7828-698   Emp: 4,300
 industrial and specialty chemicals.   www.brenntag.com

BRENNTAG, INC.
PO Box 13786, Reading, PA   19612-3786
CEO: Robert L. Moser Jr., VP   Tel: (610) 926-6100   %FO: 100
Bus: *Mfr. specialty chemicals.*   Fax: (610) 926-0420

CROWN CHEMICAL
1888 Nirvana Avenue, Chula Vista, CA   92011
CEO: William E. Huttner Jr., Pres.   Tel: (619) 421-6601   %FO: 100
Bus: *Distribution of chemicals.*   Fax: (619) 421-1127

DELTA DISTRIBUTORS INC.
610 Fisher Road, Longview, TX   75604
CEO: Kevin Kessing, Pres.   Tel: (903) 759-7151   %FO: 100
Bus: *Distribution of chemicals.*   Fax: (903) 759-7548

PB&S CHEMICAL
PO Box 20, Henderson, KY   42419
CEO: Thomas M. McFarland, Pres.   Tel: (270) 830-1200   %FO: 100
Bus: *Distribution of chemicals.*   Fax: (270) 827-4767

SOCO-LYNCH CHEMICAL CORPORATION
10747 Patterson Place, Santa Fe Springs, CA   90670
CEO: Anthony J. Gerace, Pres.   Tel: (562) 903-9626   %FO: 100
Bus: *Distribution of chemicals.*   Fax: (562) 903-9622

SOUTHCHEM
PO Box 1491, Durham, NC   27702
CEO: Gil Steadman, Pres.   Tel: (919) 596-0681   %FO: 100
Bus: *Distribution of chemicals.*   Fax: (919) 596-6438

WHITTAKER CLARK & DANIELS
1000 Coolidge Street, South Plainfield, NJ   07080
CEO: Bob Przybylowski   Tel: (908) 561-6100   %FO: 100
Bus: *Distribution of chemicals.*   Fax: (908) 757-3488

● BROKAT INFOSYSTEMS
industriestrasse 3, D-70565 Stuttgart, Germany
CEO: Stefan Rover, CEO   Tel: 49-71-178-8440   Rev: $113
Bus: *Mfr. e-commerce software.*   Fax: 49-71-178-8440777   Emp: 800
                                       www.brokat.com

BROKAT INFOSYSTEMS INC.
150 Almaden Boulevard, San Jose, CA   95113
CEO: Gary Shroyer, Pres.   Tel: (408) 275-6900   %FO: 100
Bus: *Mfr. e-commerce software.*   Fax: (408) 535-1776

INTEGRIS AMERICAS TELCO SERVICES
300 Concord Road, Billerica, MA   01821
CEO: Michael Kayat, VP   Tel: (978) 294-6201   %FO: 100
Bus: *Mfr. e-commerce software.*   Fax: (978) 294-5164

● **BSN MEDICAL GMBH & CO.**

Quickbornstrasse 24, D-20253 Hamburg, Germany

CEO: Graham Siddle, CEO   Tel: 49-404-909-909

Bus: *Engaged in woundcare, casting,*   Fax: 49-404-909-6666   Emp: 3,000
     bandaging and phlebology. (JV of Smith   www.smith-nephew.com
     & Nephew UK and Beiersdorf AG
     Germany).

   BSN MEDICAL INC.

   5285 Carnegie Blvd., Charlotte, NC   28209

   CEO: Ron Sparks, Pres.   Tel: (704) 554-9933   %FO: JV

   Bus: *Engaged in woundcare, casting,*   Fax: (704) 551-8585
        bandaging and phlebology.

   BSN MEDICAL INC.

   1450 Brooks Road, Memphis, TN   38116

   CEO: Larry Papasan, Pres.   Tel: (901) 396-2121   %FO: JV

   Bus: *Engaged in woundcare, casting,*   Fax: (901) 399-6189
        bandaging and phlebology.

● **BUEHLER MOTOR GMBH**

Anne-Frank-Strasse 33, D-90459 Nuremberg, Germany

CEO: Michael Schumann, Mgr.   Tel: 49-911-45040

Bus: *Mfr. sub-fractional motors, gear motors*   Fax: 49-911-454626
     and fans.   www.buehlermotor.de

   BUEHLER MOTOR INC.

   PO Box 5069, Cary, NC   27512

   CEO: L. P. LaFreniere, Mgr.   Tel: (919) 469-8522   %FO: 49

   Bus: *Mfr. sub-fractional motors, gear*   Fax: (919) 469-8522   Emp: 750
        motors & fans

● **BYK-GUDEN LOMBERG CHEMISCH FABRIK GMBH**

Byk-Gulden-Strasse 1, D-78467 Konstanz, Germany

CEO: Heinz W. Bull, Pres.   Tel: 49-7531-840

Bus: *Pharmaceutical products.*   Fax: 49-7531-842474   Emp: 2,500

   ALTANA/BLYK-GUDEN

   60 Baylis Road, Melville, NY   11747

   CEO: Art Dulik   Tel: (516) 454-7677   %FO: 76

   Bus: *Mfg./sales/distribution of*   Fax: (516) 454-6389   Emp: 470
        pharmaceuticals and chemicals.

● **CARGOLIFTER AG**

Potsdamer Platz 10, D-10785 Berlin, Germany

CEO: Carl-Heinrich von Gablenz, Chmn.   Tel: 49-30-726-10-3920

Bus: *Engaged in cargo shipment.*   Fax: 49-30-726-39-2099   Emp: 250

www.cargolifter.com

    CARGOLIFTER USA

    4600 Marriott Drive, Ste. 225, Raleigh, NC 27612

    CEO: Tom Boyle   Tel: (919) 788-0613   %FO: 100

    Bus: *Engaged in cargo shipment.*   Fax: (919) 788-0614

● **CELANESE AG, DIV. HOECHST GROUP**

Industriepark Hochst, Bldg. F-821, D-65926 Frankfurt, Germany

CEO: Claudio Sonder, Chmn.   Tel: 49-69-305-1400   Rev: $4,100

Bus: *Mfr. chemicals and pharmaceuticals.*   Fax: 49-69-305-4888   Emp: 10,700

www.celanese.com

    CELANESE CHEMICALS

    1601 West LBJ Freeway, Dallas, TX 75234

    CEO: Rick N. Shaw, EVP   Tel: (972) 443-4000

    Bus: *Mfr. commodity chemicals and*   Fax: (972) 443-4000
        acetate products.

    CELANESE INC.

    1601 West LBJ Freeway, Dallas, TX 75234-6034

    CEO: David Weidman, CEO   Tel: (972) 443-4000   %FO: 45

    Bus: *Mfr. chemicals.*   Fax: (972) 443-2060

    TICONA

    86 Morris Avenue, Summit, NJ 07901

    CEO: Edward Munoz, CEO   Tel: (908) 598-4000

    Bus: *Mfr. high performance technical*   Fax: (908) 598-4165
        polymers.

● **CEYONIQ GMBH**

Herforder Straße 155a, D-33609 Bielefeld, Germany

CEO: Jürgen Brintrup, COO   Tel: 49-521-93-18-01   Rev: $88

Bus: *Provides software and services for*   Fax: 49-521-93-18-111   Emp: 650
    document management.   www.ce-ag.com

    CEYONIQ INC.

    13900 Lincoln Park Drive, Ste. 300, Herndon, VA 20171

    CEO: Steve Wood   Tel: (703) 478-2260   %FO: 100

    Bus: *Provides innovative content*   Fax: (703) 481-6920
        lifecycle management solutions for
        businesses.

- **CHIRON-WERKE GMBH & CO KG**
Talstraße 23, D-78532 Tuttlingen, Germany
CEO: Hans H. Winkler, Pres.   Tel: 49-74-61-9400
Bus: *CNC vertical machining centers.* Fax: 49-75-61-3159   Emp: 650
               www.chiron-werke.de

   CHIRON AMERICA INC.
   14201-G South Lakes Drive, Charlotte, NC 28273
   CEO: William M. Carr, Pres. Tel: (704) 587-9526 %FO: 100
   Bus: *CNC vertical machining centers.* Fax: (704) 587-0485 Emp: 42

- **CHRISTIAN BAUER GMBH & COMPANY**
49 Schorndorfer Strasse, D-73642 Welzheim/Württ, Germany
CEO: Helmut Hutt, Gen. Dir.   Tel: 49-7182-121
Bus: *Mfr. precision disc springs.* Fax: 49-7182-12315

   BAUER SPRINGS, INC.
   509 Pkwy View Drive, Pittsburgh, PA 15205
   CEO: Ms. Ute Tell, Mgr. Tel: (412) 787-7930 %FO: 100
   Bus: *Mfr./distribution precision disc* Fax: (412) 787-3882
     springs.

- **CLAAS KGAA**
Muensterstrasse 33, D-33428 Harsewinkel, Germany
CEO: Dr. Eckart Kottkamp, CEO Tel: 49-5247-120
Bus: *Mfr./assembly harvesting equipment.* Fax: 49-5247-121927
              www.claas.de

   CLAAS OF AMERICA INC.
   3030 Norcross Drive, PO Box 3008, Columbus, IN 47202-3008
   CEO: Roger Parker, Dir. Tel: (812) 342-4441 %FO: 100
   Bus: *Mfr./assembly harvesting* Fax: (812) 342-3525 Emp: 19
     equipment.

- **COMMERZBANK AG**
Kaiserplatz, D-60261 Frankfurt, Germany
CEO: Klaus-Peter Müller, Chmn. Tel: 49-69-136-20 Rev: $21,425
Bus: *Commercial and investment banking* Fax: 49-69-285-389 Emp: 39,460
   services.   www.commerzbank.com

   COMMERZ FUTURES
   311 South Wacker Drive, Ste. 5800, Chicago, IL 60606
   CEO: Colleen Baer, Pres. Tel: (312) 408-6995 %FO: 100
   Bus: *Engaged in clearing and execution* Fax: (312) 360-1176 Emp: 25
     for financial futures and non-
     financial futures such as metals.

COMMERZBANK - New York Branch

2 World Financial Center, 225 Liberty Street, New York, NY   10281-1050

CEO: Hermann Burger, Gen. Mgr.   Tel: (212) 266-7200   %FO: 100

Bus: *International commercial and*   Fax: (212) 266-7235   Emp: 300
    investment banking services.

MONTGOMERY ASSET MANAGEMENT

101 California Street, 34th Fl., San Francisco, CA   94111

CEO: R. Stephen Doyle, CEO   Tel: (415) 248-6000   %FO: 100

Bus: *Engaged in asset management*   Fax: (415) 248-6100
    services.

● CONTACT GMBH ELEKTRISCHE BAUELEMENTE

Gewerbstrasse 30, D-7000 Stuttgart, Germany

CEO: U. A. Lapp, Pres.   Tel: 49-711-783803

Bus: *Mfr. environmentally protected*   Fax: 49-711-7838366
    industrial connectors, electrical   www.contactelectronics.com
    connectors & cable harnessing.

CONTACT ELECTRONICS INC.

38 Fairfield Place, West Caldwell, NJ   07004

CEO: John Ciccone, Pres.   Tel: (973) 575-7660   %FO: 100

Bus: *Distribution industrial and*   Fax: (973) 575-7208   Emp: 25
    electrical connectors & harnessing.

● CONTINENTAL AG

Vahrenwalder Strasse 9, Postfach 169, D-30165 Hannover, Germany

CEO: Dr. Stephan Kessel, CEO   Tel: 49-511-93801   Rev: $9,196

Bus: *Mfr. tires and industrial rubber*   Fax: 49-511-9382766   Emp: 62,155
    products, including brands Continental,   www.conti.de
    Uniroyal and General.

CONTINENTAL GENERAL TIRE INC.

1800 Continental Boulevard, Charlotte, NC   28278

CEO: Bernd Frangenberg, Pres.   Tel: (704) 583-3900   %FO: 100

Bus: *Mfr./sales and distribution of tires.*   Fax: (704) 583-8698   Emp: 8,000

● COPERIAN WAESCHLE GMBH (FORMERLY WAESCHLE MASCHINENFABRIK GMBH)

Niederbregerstrasse 9, D-88250 Weingarten, Germany

CEO: Michael J. Kenny, CEO   Tel: 49-751-4080

Bus: *Bulk solids handling conveyor systems.*   Fax: 49-750-408200   Emp: 700
    www.ecom.waeschle.de

WAESCHLE, INC.
1420 N. Sam Houston Pkwy. East, Ste. 120, Houston, TX   77032

CEO: Heinz W. Schneider, Pres. Tel: (281) 449-9944 %FO: 100
Bus: *Sales office for bulk solids* Fax: (281) 449-4599
handling conveyor systems.

WAESCHLE, INC.
230 Covington Drive, Bloomingdale, IL   60108

CEO: Heinz W. Schneider, Pres. Tel: (630) 539-9100 %FO: 100
Bus: *Bulk solids handling conveyor* Fax: (630) 539-9196 Emp: 60
systems.

● CYBIO AG
Goeschwitzer Strasse 40, D-07745 Jena, Germany

CEO: Heinz Daugart, CEO Tel: 49-3641-351-0
Bus: *Engaged in biotechnology and* Fax: 49-3641-351-409
laboratory automation. www.cybio-ag.de

CYBIO, INC.
500 West Cummings Park, Woburn, MA   01801

CEO: M. Matus, Pres. Tel: (781) 376-9899 %FO: 100
Bus: *Engaged in biotechnology and* Fax: (781) 376-9897
laboratory automation.

● DAIMLER-CHRYSLER AG
Epplestrasse 225, Postfach 800230, D-70546 Stuttgart, Germany

CEO: Jüergen E. Schrempp, CEO Tel: 49-711-179-2287 Rev: $152,446
Bus: *Mfr. cars, trucks, commercial vehicles,* Fax: 49-711-179-4022 Emp: 466,940
aircraft engines, electronics. www.daimlerchrysler.com

MERCEDES-BENZ CREDIT CORPORATION
201 Merritt 7, Ste. 700, Norwalk, CT   06856

CEO: Greg Galetta, Pres. Tel: (203) 847-4500 %FO: JV
Bus: *Leasing and financing services.* Fax: (203) 847-9245 Emp: 521

DAIMLER-BENZ RESEARCH & TECHNOLOGY
1510 Page Mill Road, Palo Alto, CA   94304

CEO: Paul Mehring, Pres. & CEO Tel: (650) 845-2500 %FO: JV
Bus: *Conducts transportation services* Fax: (650) 845-2555
related to research.

DAIMLER-CHRYSLER NORTH AMERICA
1000 Chrysler Drive, Auburn Hills, MI   48326

CEO: Dieter Zetsche, Pres. & CEO Tel: (248) 576-5741 %FO: JV
Bus: *Mfr. car, trucks, commercial* Fax: (248) 512-5143
vehicles.

DETROIT DIESEL CORPORATION

13400 Outer Drive West, Detroit, MI 48239-4001

CEO: Roger S. Penske, Chmn. Tel: (313) 592-5990 %FO: 100
Bus: *Mfr. diesel, alternative fuel, and* Fax: (313) 592-5887 Emp: 6,300
automotive engines and engine
parts

DETROIT DIESEL CORPORATION

169 Old New Brunswick Road, Piscataway, NJ 08854

CEO: Charles McClure, Pres. Tel: (732) 926-9622 %FO: 100
Bus: *Mfr. diesel, alternative fuel, and* Fax: (732) 926-8522
automotive engines and engine
parts

FREIGHTLINER CORPORATION

4747 North Channel Avenue, Portland, OR 97217

CEO: James L. Hebe, Pres. & CEO Tel: (503) 735-8000 %FO: JV
Bus: *Mfr. heavy-duty trucks.* Fax: (503) 735-8192

KASSBOHRER OF NORTH AMERICA INC.

PO Box 1270, Grey, ME 04039-1270

CEO: Christoph von der Osten, CEO Tel: (207) 657-2455 %FO: JV
Bus: *Mfr. heavy-duty trucks.* Fax: (207) 657-3395

MERCEDES-BENZ ADVANCED DESIGN OF N.A., INC.

17742 Cowan Street, Irvine, CA 92614

CEO: Karlheinz Bauer, Pres. Tel: (949) 476-8300 %FO: JV
Bus: *Designs/develops new vehicles.* Fax: (949) 476-2366 Emp: 12

MERCEDES-BENZ LATINA, INC.

1221 Brickell Avenue, Ste. 1140, Miami, FL 33131

CEO: Echart Mayer, Pres. Tel: (305) 755-8888 %FO: JV
Bus: *Sales/distribution of cars and* Fax: (305) 575-5887
trucks.

MERCEDES-BENZ OF NORTH AMERICA, INC.

One Mercedes Drive, Montvale, NJ 07645

CEO: Paul Halata, CEO Tel: (201) 573-0600 %FO: JV
Bus: *Sales/distribution of cars and* Fax: (201) 573-0117
trucks.

MERCEDES-BENZ US INTERNATIONAL INC.

One Mercedes Drive, Vance, AL 35490

CEO: William Taylor, Pres. & CEO Tel: (205) 507-3300 %FO: JV
Bus: *Sales/distribution of cars and* Fax: (205) 507-3700
trucks.

SETRA/KASSBOHRER OF NORTH AMERICA, INC.

PO Box 1270, Gary, ME 04039-1270

CEO: Christoph van der Osten, Pres.   Tel: (207) 657-2455   %FO: JV

Bus: *Sales/service of luxury motor*   Fax: (207) 657-3395   Emp: 19
     coaches. Sub of EvoBus GmbH,
     Div. of Daimler-Benz AG

● DBT DEUTSCHE BERGBAU-TECHNIK GMBH

Postfach 100269, D-24002 Wuppertal, Germany

CEO: Jurgen Tonn   Tel: 49-202-7590-0

Bus: *Engaged in design and manufacture of*   Fax: 49-202-7590-421
     mining equipment and captive-guided   www.dbt.de
     transport systems for underground
     mining operations.

DBT AMERICA INC.

PO Box 1287, Craig, CO 81625

CEO: Stuart Rhodes, Mgr.   Tel: (970) 824-3240   %FO: 100

Bus: *Mfr./service of mining, hauling*   Fax: (970) 824-8851   Emp: 25
     and transportation equipment.

DBT AMERICA INC.

2045 West Pike Street, Houston, PA 15342

CEO: William Tate, CEO   Tel: (724) 743-1200   %FO: 100

Bus: *Mfr./service of mining, hauling*   Fax: (724) 743-1201   Emp: 25
     and transportation equipment.

DBT AMERICA INC.

255 Berry Road, Washington, PA 15301

CEO: Harry Martin, VP   Tel: (724) 225-4049   %FO: 100

Bus: *Mfr./service of mining, hauling*   Fax: (724) 228-2177   Emp: 25
     and transportation equipment.

DBT AMERICA INC.

1814 North 1500 West, Price, UT 84501

CEO: Dan Espinoza, Mgr.   Tel: (435) 637-3930   %FO: 100

Bus: *Mfr./service of mining, hauling*   Fax: (435) 637-9754   Emp: 25
     and transportation equipment.

● WALTER DE GRUYTER & CO

Postfach 303421, D-10728 Berlin, Germany

CEO: Reinhold Tokar, CEO   Tel: 49-30-260050

Bus: *Publisher of scholarly and scientific*   Fax: 49-30-26005251   Emp: 270
     books and journals.   www.degruyter.com

WALTER DE GRUYTER, INC.
200 Saw Mill River Road, Hawthorne, NY   10532
CEO: Eckart A. Scheffler, VP   Tel: (914) 747-0110   %FO: 100
Bus: *Publisher; scholarly and scientific*   Fax: (914) 747-1326   Emp: 18
      books and journals.

● **DEGUSSA AG**
Weissfrauenstraße 9, D-60287 Frankfurt am Main, Germany
CEO: Dr. Uwe-Ernst Bufe, CEO   Tel: 49-69-218-01   Rev: $17,135
Bus: *Precious metals, chemical,*   Fax: 49-69-218-3218   Emp: 62,940
      pharmaceuticals, colors, plastics.   www.degussa.com

  CREANOVA INC.
  220 Davidson Avenue, Somerset, NJ   08873
  CEO: Hans-Christoph Porth, VP   Tel: (732) 560-6800   %FO: 100
  Bus: *Fine chemicals.*   Fax: (732) 560-6950

  DEGUSSA CORPORATION - CHEMICAL PIGMENT GROUP
  65 Challenger Road, Ridgefield Park, NJ   07660
  CEO: Andrew J. Burke, Pres. & CEO   Tel: (201) 641-6100   %FO: 100
  Bus: *Chemicals, electronics, pigments.*   Fax: (201) 807-3183

  DEGUSSA CORPORATION - MOBILE PLANT
  PO Box 868, Mobile, AL   36601
  CEO: Dr. Wolfgang Buder, Mgr.   Tel: (334) 443-4000   %FO: 100
  Bus: *Chemicals, electronics.*   Fax: (334) 443-4000

  DEGUSSA CORPORATION - METAL AND DENTAL GROUP
  3900 South Clinton Avenue, So. Plainfield, NJ   07080
  CEO: Craig Benson, VP   Tel: (908) 561-1100   %FO: 100
  Bus: *Metal, dental products.*   Fax: (908) 668-7896

  DEGUSSA-NEY DENTAL, INC.
  65 West Dudley Town Road, Bloomfield, CT   06002
  CEO: Hoger Meinike, Pres.   Tel: (860) 242-6188   %FO: 100
  Bus: *Dental products.*   Fax: (860) 769-5050

  PHENOLCHEMIE INC.
  5 Concourse Parkway, Atlanta, GA   30328
  CEO: Peter Bickert, Pres.   Tel: (770) 804-6500   %FO: 100
  Bus: *Specialty chemicals.*   Fax: (770) 804-6503

  SILIKAL RESIN SYSTEMS
  173 Interstate Lane, Waterbury, CT   06705
  CEO: Wilfred Riesterer   Tel: (203) 754-8373   %FO: 100
  Bus: *Mfr. resins.*   Fax: (203) 754-8791

• DEPFA DEUTSCHE PFANDBRIEF BANK AG

Paulinenstrasse 15, D-65189 Wiesbaden, Germany

CEO: Thilo Köpfler, CEO

Bus: *Engaged in property financing.*

Tel: 49-611-3480

Fax: 49-611-348-2549

www.depfa.de

Rev: $540

Emp: 2,475

DEPFA USA INC.

570 Lexington Avenue, 39th Fl., New York, NY   10022

CEO: Fulvio Dobrich, Pres. & CEO

Bus: *Engaged in property financing.*

Tel: (212) 682-6474

Fax: (212) 867-7810

%FO: 100

• DEUTSCHE BABCOCK AG

Duisburger Strasse 375, D-46041 Oberhausen, Germany

CEO: Klaus Lederer, CEO

Bus: *Mfr./markets conveyor equipment and woodworking machinery and provides engineering services.*

Tel: 49-2-08-8330

Fax: 49-2-08-26091

www.deutschebabock.de

BABCOCK BORSIG POWER, INC.

Five Neponset Street, Worcester, MA   01606

CEO: W. John Halloran, Pres.

Bus: *Mfr. boilers for utility and industrial use.*

Tel: (508) 852-7100

Fax: (508) 852-7548

%FO: 100

SCHUMAG-KIESERLING MACHINERY, INC.

PO Box 419, Norwood, NJ   07648

CEO: Axel Justus, VP Sales

Bus: *Mfr. machinery for turning, point grinding and cutting.*

Tel: (201) 767-6850

Fax: (201) 767-3341

%FO: 100

VITS AMERICA INC.

200 Corporate Drive, Blauvelt, NY   10913

CEO: Tom Tinnemans, VP

Bus: *Sales/distribution of hardware machinery.*

Tel: (845) 353-5000

Fax: (845) 365-1227

%FO: 100

• DEUTSCHE BANK AG

Taunusanlage 12, D-60262 Frankfurt, Germany

CEO: Dierk Hartwig

Bus: *Commercial, private, investment and merchant banking services.*

Tel: 49-69-910-43800

Fax: 49-69-910-34227

www.info.deutsche-bank.de

Rev: $27,024

Emp: 98,300

DEUTSCHE BANC ALEX BROWN INC.

One South Street, Baltimore, MD   21202

CEO: Christine Cortezi, Mgr.

Bus: *Provides investment banking services.*

Tel: (410) 895-3418

Fax: (410) 895-3424

%FO: 100

Emp: 2,600

DEUTSCHE BANK NORTH AMERICA

31 West 52nd Street, New York, NY   10019

CEO: Rohini Pragasam	Tel: (212) 469-4516	%FO: 100
Bus: *New York branch of Deutsche Bank AG.*	Fax: (212) 469-7456	Emp: 100

DEUTSCHE BANK SECURITIES INC.

31 West 52nd Street, New York, NY   10019

CEO: James Edward Virtue, Pres.	Tel: (212) 469-5000	%FO: 100
Bus: *Securities broker/dealer, investment banking & asset management services.*	Fax: (212) 469-4133	Emp: 200

● **DEUTSCHE BUNDESBANK**

Wilhelm-Spstein Strausse 14-6, Postfach 10602, D-60006 Frankfurt, Germany

CEO: Ernst Welteke, Pres.	Tel: 49-69-9566-1
Bus: *General banking services.*	Fax: 49-69-9566-3077
	www.bundesbank.de

DEUTSCHE BUNDESBANK

499 Park Avenue, New York, NY   10022

CEO: Dr. Hermann Naust, Rep.	Tel: (212) 688-3680	%FO: 100
Bus: *General banking services.*	Fax: (212) 688-4274	

● **DEUTSCHE GELATINE FABRIKEN STOESS AG**

Gammelsbacher Strasse 2, D-69412 Eberbach/Baden, Germany

CEO: Jorg Siebert, Pres.	Tel: 49-6271-8401
Bus: *Mfr. gelatin.*	Fax: 49-6271-8427000
	www.dynagel.com

DGF STOESS, INC.

2445 Port Neal Industrial Road, Sergeant Bluff, IA   51054

CEO: Charles Markham, CEO	Tel: (712) 943-1670	%FO: 100
Bus: *Mfr. gelatin.*	Fax: (712) 943-1644	

DYNAGEL INC.

Ten Wentworth Avenue, Calumet City, IL   60409

CEO: George Risenfeld, Pres.	Tel: (708) 891-8400	%FO: JV
Bus: *Mfr. gelatin. (JV with Leiner Davis Gelatin, Australia).*	Fax: (708) 891-8432	Emp: 63

KIND & KNOX GELATINE, INC.

PO Box 927, Sioux City, IA   51102

CEO: Charles Markham, CEO	Tel: (712) 943-5516	%FO: 100
Bus: *Mfr. gelatin.*	Fax: (712) 943-3372	

● **DEUTSCHE LUFTHANSA AG**
Von-Gablenz-Strasse 2-6, D-50679 Cologne, Germany
CEO: Jürgen Weber, Chmn.   Tel: 49-221-826-2444   Rev: $14,313
Bus: *International air transport services.*   Fax: 49-221-826-2286   Emp: 69,550
                                             www.lufthansa.de

    LUFTHANSA USA
    680 Fifth Avenue, 17th Fl., New York, NY   10019
    CEO: William C. Yanson   Tel: (212) 479-8800   %FO: 100
    Bus: *International air transport*   Fax: (212) 479-0795   Emp: 2,000
        services.

    LUFTHANSA USA - EAST
    1640 Hempstead Turnpike, East Meadow, NY   11554
    CEO: Uwe Hinrichs, SVP   Tel: (516) 296-9200   %FO: 100
    Bus: *International air transport*   Fax: (516) 296-9639   Emp: 700
        services.

    LUFTHANSA USA - WEST
    703 Market Street, San Francisco, CA   94103
    CEO: Uwe Hinrichs, SVP   Tel: (415) 995-7300   %FO: 100
    Bus: *International air transport*   Fax: Emp: 200
        services.

● **DEUTSCHE MESSE AG**
Messegelaende, D-30521 Hannover, Germany
CEO: Klaus E. Goehrman, Chrm.   Tel: 49-511-890
Bus: *Trade fairs operators.*   Fax: 49-511-8932626   Emp: 550
                                           www.messe.de

    HANNOVER FAIRS USA INC.
    103 Carnegie Center, Ste.207, Princeton, NJ   08540
    CEO: Joachim Schafer, Pres.   Tel: (609) 987-1202   %FO: 100
    Bus: *Trade fairs management &*   Fax: (609) 987-0092   Emp: 32
        promotion.

● **DEUTSCHE TELEKOM AG**
Friedrich-Ebert-Allee 140, D-53113 Bonn, Germany
CEO: Dr. Ron Sommer, Chmn.   Tel: 49-228-181-0   Rev: $41,000
Bus: *Provides telephone service, internet* Fax: 49-228-181-8872   Emp: 226,000
    access and digital mobile   www.telekom.de
    communications services.

    DEUTSCHE TELEKOM, INC.
    280 Park Avenue, 26th Fl., New York, NY   10017
    CEO: Paul B. Grosse, CEO   Tel: (212) 424-2900   %FO: 100
    Bus: *Engaged in telecommunications.*   Fax: (212) 424-2989

- **DEUTZ AG**

Deutz-Muelheimer Strasse 147-149, D-51057 Cologne, Germany

CEO: Gordon Riske, CEO

Bus: *Mfr. diesel engines and industrial plant systems.*

Tel: 49-221-8220
Fax: 49-221-8222-004
www.deutz.de

Rev: $1,269
Emp: 6,700

DEUTZ CORPORATION

3883 Steve Reynolds Boulevard, Norcross, GA 30093

CEO: Robert T. Mann, CEO

Bus: *Mfr. diesel engines and industrial plant systems.*

Tel: (770) 564-7100
Fax: (770) 564-7272

%FO: 100

HUMBOLDT WEDAG, INC.

400 Technology Parkway, Norcross, GA 20092

CEO: Kenneth M. Hitcho, Pres.

Bus: *Provides design & product support in the area of industrial engineering.*

Tel: (770) 810-7300
Fax: (770) 810-7343

%FO: 100

- **DG BANK**

Am Platz der Republik, D-60325 Frankfurt, Germany

CEO: Wolfgang Grüger, Chmn.

Bus: *International banking services.*

Tel: 49-69-7447-2382
Fax: 49-69-7447-1685
www.dgbank.de

Rev: $11,447
Emp: 12,350

DG BANK ATLANTA

303 Peachtree Street NE, Ste. 2900, Atlanta, GA 30308

CEO: John Somers, Mgr.

Bus: *General banking services.*

Tel: (404) 524-3966
Fax: (404) 524-4006

%FO: 100

DG BANK NEW YORK

609 Fifth Avenue, New York, NY 10017-1021

CEO: Hans W. Meyers, SVP

Bus: *General banking services.*

Tel: (212) 745-1400
Fax: (212) 745-1550

%FO: 100

DG SECURITIES

609 Fifth Avenue, New York, NY 10017

CEO: Oliver Guminsky, Pres.

Bus: *Engaged in broker services.*

Tel: (212) 745-1600
Fax: (212) 745-1616

%FO: 100

- **DG BANK (DEUTSCHE GENOSSENSCHAFTSBANK)**

Am Platz der Republik, D-60325 Frankfurt am Main, Germany

CEO: Ingrid Altwicker

Bus: *Commercial banking services.*

Tel: 49-69-7447-2050
Fax: 49-69-7447-7374
www.dgbank.de

Emp: 5,104

DG BANK - New York Branch
609 Fifth Avenue, New York, NY   10017-1021
CEO: Hans W. Meyers, SVP, Gen. Mgr.   Tel: (212) 745-1400   %FO: 100
Bus: *Commercial banking services.*   Fax: (212) 745-1550

DG EUROPEAN SECURITIES
609 Fifth Avenue, New York, NY   10017-1021
CEO: Oliver D'Oelsnitz   Tel: (212) 745-1600   %FO: 100
Bus: *Securities broker/dealer.*   Fax: (212) 745-1616

● **DIALOG SEMICONDUCTOR PLC**
Neus Strasse 95, D-73230 Kirchheim-Nabern, Germany
CEO: Roland Pudelko, Pres. & CEO   Tel: 49-7021-805-0   Rev: $202
Bus: *Develops integrated circuits for wireless* Fax: 49-7021-805-100   Emp: 270
communications.   www.diasemi.com

DIALOG SEMICONDUCTOR
54 Old Highway 22, Clinton, NJ   08809
CEO: Andrea Habrunner   Tel: (908) 238-0200   %FO: 100
Bus: *Develops integrated circuits for*   Fax: (908) 238-0201
wireless communications.

● **DIA-NIELSEN GMBH**
Postfach 100452, D-52304 Dueren, Germany
CEO: Norbert Klinke, Pres.   Tel: 49-2421-59010
Bus: *Mfr. marking systems for recording*   Fax: 49-2421-590179   Emp: 250
instruments.   www.dia-nielsen.com

DIA NIELSEN USA INC.
41 Twosome Drive, Ste. 5, Moorestown, NJ   08057
CEO: Wayne Connelly, Mgr.   Tel: (856) 642-9700   %FO: 100
Bus: *Supplier marking systems for*   Fax: (856) 642-9709   Emp: 9
recording instruments.

● **FRIEDR. DICK GMBH**
Postfach 1173, D-73777 Deizisau, Germany
CEO: Wilhem Leuze, CEO   Tel: 49-715-38170
Bus: *Mfr. tools, machines and cutlery for*   Fax: 49-715-38170   Emp: 300
food industry.   www.fdick.com

FRIEDR. DICK CORPORATION
33 Allen Boulevard, Farmingdale, NY   11735
CEO: William E. Colwin, Gen. Mgr.   Tel: (516) 454-6955   %FO: 100
Bus: *Distribution/sale cutlery.*   Fax: (516) 454-6184   Emp: 6

● **DIE NORDDEUTSCHE LANDESBANK**

Georgsplatz 1, D-30151 Hannover, Germany

CEO: Dr. Manfred Bodin, Chmn.   Tel: 49-511-3610

Bus: *Commercial banking services.*   Fax: 49-511-3612501   Emp: 6,089

www.nordlb.de

    NORDDEUTSCHE LANDESBANK GIROZENTRALE

    1114 Ave. of the Americas, 37th Fl., New York, NY   10036

    CEO: Dr. Jens A .Westrick, EVP   Tel: (212) 398-7300   %FO: 100

    Bus: *International commercial banking*   Fax: (212) 812-6860   Emp: 30
        services.

● **DIENES-WERKE**

D-51491 Overath-Vilerath, Germany

CEO: Bernd Supe Dienes, Pres.   Tel: 49-2206-6050

Bus: *Sales/distribution of slitting tools and*   Fax: 49-2206-605111   Emp: 250
   compressor valves.   www.dienes.de

    DIENES CORPORATION

    Spencer Corporate Park, Spencer, MA   01562-2498

    CEO: George Benson, Mgr.   Tel: (508) 885-6301   %FO: 100

    Bus: *Mfr. slitting tools and replacement*   Fax: (508) 885-3452   Emp: 55
        parts for compressors.

● **ALOYS F. DORNBRACHT GMBH & CO. KG**

PO Box 1454, D-58584 Iserlohn, Germany

CEO: Andreas Dornbracht, Chmn. & CEO   Tel: 49-2371-4330

Bus: *Mfr. design fittings and accessories for*   Fax: 49-2371-433135
   bath and kitchens.   www.dornbracht.de

    DORNBRACHT USA, INC.

    1700 Executive Drive, Ste. 600, Duluth, GA   30096

    CEO: Jon Spector, Dir.   Tel: (770) 564-3599   %FO: 100

    Bus: *Mfr. design fittings and*   Fax: (770) 638-3316
        accessories for bath and kitchens.

● **DOUGLAS HOLDING AG**

Kabeler Strasse 4, D-58099 Hagen, Germany

CEO: Henning Kreke, Chmn.   Tel: 49-2331-690362   Rev: $2,015

Bus: *Perfume retailer.*   Fax: 49-2331-690690   Emp: 18,670

www.douglas-holding.com

    PARFUMERIE DOUGLAS

    156 Kings Highway North, Westport, CT   06880

    CEO: Monika Burg, HR   Tel: (203) 226-2233   %FO: 100

    Bus: *Full-service, retail perfume store.*   Fax: (203) 226-2233

● **DRÄGERWERK AG**

Moislinger Allee 53/55, D-23542 Luebeck, Germany

CEO: Theo Dräeger, Pres.   Tel: 49-451-882-2977   Rev: $1,095

Bus: *Aerospace, diving and medical*   Fax: 49-451-882-3703   Emp: 9,200
technology equipment manufacturer.   www.draeger.com

DRÄEGER MEDICAL, INC.

3135 Quarry Road, Telford, PA   18969

CEO: Wesley J. Kenneweg, Pres.   Tel: (215) 721-5400   %FO: 100

Bus: *Mfr. medical devices.*   Fax: (215) 723-5973

DRÄEGER SAFETY, INC.

101 Technology Drive, PO Box 120, Pittsburgh, PA   15230-0128

CEO: Wesley J. Kenneweg, Pres.   Tel: (412) 787-8383   %FO: 100

Bus: *Mfr. safety equipment, respiratory*   Fax: (412) 787-2207   Emp: 200
protection products and gas
detection products.

● **DRESDNER BANK AG, DIV. ALLIANZ GROUP**

Jüergen-Ponto-Platz 1, D-60301 Frankfurt/Main, Germany

CEO: Bernd Fahrholz, Chmn. & CEO   Tel: 49-692--630   Rev: $21,910

Bus: *General banking services.*   Fax: 49-692-63-4831   Emp: 50,660
www.dresdner-bank.de

DRESDNER BANK AG

75 Wall Street, New York, NY   10005

CEO: George N. Fugelsang   Tel: (212) 429-2000   %FO: 100

Bus: *International commercial banking*   Fax: (212) 429-2127   Emp: 50
services.

DRESDNER BANK AG

190 South LaSalle Street, Chicago, IL   60603

CEO: John Schaus, SVP   Tel: (312) 444-1300   %FO: 100

Bus: *International commercial banking*   Fax: (312) 444-1305
services.

DRESDNER BANK AG

333 South Grand Avenue, Los Angeles, CA   90017

CEO: Guity Javid, SVP   Tel: (213) 630-5400   %FO: 100

Bus: *International commercial banking*   Fax: (213) 627-3819
services.

DRESDNER KLEINWORT BENSON

75 Wall Street, 35th Fl., New York, NY   10005

CEO: George N. Fugelsang, CEO   Tel: (212) 429-2000   %FO: 100

Bus: *International commercial banking*   Fax: (212) 429-2127
services.

DRESDNER RCM GLOBAL INVESTORS

Four Embarcadero Center, Ste. 3000, San Francisco, CA 94111-4189

CEO: William L. Price, CEO

Tel: (415) 954-5400

%FO: 100

Bus: *Institutional asset management.*

Fax: (415) 954-8200

● **DUERKOPP ADLER AG**

Postdamer Strasse 190, D-33719 Bielefeld, Germany

CEO: Dr. H. Forberich, Pres.

Tel: 49-521-925-01

Bus: *Mfr. industrial sewing equipment.*

Fax: 49-521-925-2458

Emp: 2,800

www.duerkopp-adler.com

DUERKOPP ADLER AMERICA INC.

3025 Northwoods Pkwy, Norcross, GA 30071

CEO: John Couch, Pres.

Tel: (770) 446-8162

%FO: 100

Bus: *Sales/service industrial sewing
equipment.*

Fax: (770) 448-1545

Emp: 100

● **DÜRKOPP ADLER AG, DIV. FAG KUGELFISCHER GROUP**

Postdamer Strasse 190, D-33719 Bielefeld, Germany

CEO: Dr. H. Forberich, Chmn.

Tel: 49-521-925-01

Bus: *Mfr. industrial sewing equipment.*

Fax: 49-521-925-2435

Emp: 2,700

www.duerkopp-adler.com

DÜRKOPP ADLER AMERICA INC.

3025 Northwoods Parkway, Norcross, GA 30071

CEO: Winslow Wise, Pres.

Tel: (770) 446-8162

%FO: 100

Bus: *Mfr./distribution of sewing
equipment.*

Fax: (770) 448-1545

● **DURR AG**

Otto-Dürr-Straße 8, D-70435 Stuttgart Zuffenhausen, Germany

CEO: Hans Dieter Pötsch, CEO

Tel: 49-711-1361-095

Rev: $1,799

Bus: *Paint finishing systems, industrial
cleaning systems and automation and
conveyor systems.*

Fax: 49-711-1361-455

Emp: 11,558

www.durr.com

DURR INDUSTRIES INC.

40600 Plymouth Road, Plymouth, MI 48170-4297

CEO: Dave Ciuffoletti, Mgr.

Tel: (734) 459-6800

%FO: 100

Bus: *Paint finishing systems.*

Fax: (734) 459-5837

● **DYCKERHOFF AG**

Biebricher Straße 69, D-65203 Wiesbaden, Germany

CEO: Peter Rohde, Chmn.

Tel: 49-611-6760

Rev: $2,305

Bus: *Mfr. cement and concrete products.*

Fax: 49-611-676-1040

Emp: 10,100

www.dyckerhoff.de

GLENS FALLS LEHIGH CEMENT CO.
PO Box 440, Glens Falls, NY   12801-0440

CEO: Michael B. Clarke, Pres.   Tel: (518) 792-1137   %FO: 50
Bus: *Mfr. cement.*   Fax: (518) 792-0731

LONESTAR INDUSTRIES, INC.
PO Box 120014, Stamford, CT   06912-0014

CEO: David W. Wallace   Tel: (203) 969-8600   %FO: 100
Bus: *Sales cement and concrete*   Fax: (203) 969-8600
    products.

LONESTAR INDUSTRIES, INC.
10401 North Meridian Street, Ste. 400, Indianapolis, IN   46290

CEO: William Roberts, PR   Tel: (317) 706-3300   %FO: 100
Bus: *Mfr. cement and concrete products.* Fax:

● E.ON AG
Bennigsenplatz 1, D-40474 Düsseldorf, Germany

CEO: Ulrich Hartmann, CEO   Tel: 49-211-4579-1   Rev: $72,400
Bus: *Holding company engaged in energy* Fax: 49-211-4579-501   Emp: 213,411
    and specialty chemicals.   www.eon.com

E.ON NORTH AMERICA, INC.
405 Lexington Avenue, New York, NY   10174

CEO: Wilhelm Simson   Tel: (646) 658-1962   %FO: 100
Bus: *Engaged in energy and specialty* Fax: (212) 557-5189
    chemicals.

INSIGHT ELECTRONICS INC.
9980 Huennekens Street, San Diego, CA   92121

CEO: Greg Provenzano, Pres.   Tel: (619) 587-1100   %FO: 100
Bus: *Technical distributor of semi-* Fax: (619) 677-3151
    conductors.

MEMC INC.
6414 Highway 75 South, Sherman, TX   75090

CEO: Klaus von Hörde   Tel: (903) 868-5930   %FO: 100
Bus: *Mfr. semiconductors.*   Fax: (903) 868-7539

MEMC Inc.
3000 North South Street, Pasadena, TX   77503

CEO: Klaus von Hörde   Tel: (713) 740-1420   %FO: 100
Bus: *Mfr. semiconductors.*   Fax: (713) 740-1774

MILLER AND COMPANY LLC

6400 Shafer Court, Ste. 500, Rosemont, IL   60018

CEO: William A. Henning, VP   Tel: (847) 696-2400   %FO: 100

Bus: *Supplies raw materials to the*   Fax: (847) 696-2419
ferrous foundry and steel
industries.

● **EDEL MUSIC AG**

Wichmannstrasse 4, Haus 2, D-22607 Hamburg, Germany

CEO: Michael Haentjes, CEO   Tel: 49-40-890-850   Rev: $570

Bus: *Distribution of music publishing,*   Fax: 49-40-890-85-310   Emp: 1,550
recordings and DVD manufacturing.   www.edel.com

   SPITFIRE RECORDS INC.

   101 Bay Avenue, Hicksville, NY   11801

   CEO: Paul Bibeau, Pres.   Tel: (516) 942-7729   %FO: 100

   Bus: *Rock music publisher; record*   Fax: (516) 942-7729
   label.

● **EDUARD LOEHLE SEN GMBH**

Stöch Strasse 11, D-70190 Stuttgart, Germany

CEO: Thomas Pfisterer, CEO   Tel: 49-711-282041

Bus: *Provides international packing, moving*   Fax: 49-711-2868329
& shipping.   www.loehle.de

   KNOPF & LOEHLE INC.

   7259 Cross Park Drive, North Charleston, SC   29418

   CEO: Siegfried J. Zarwel, Pres.   Tel: (843) 760-2501   %FO: 100

   Bus: *Provides international packing,*   Fax: (843) 760-2503
   moving & shipping.

● **EISELE GMBH & CO**

Nuertinger Strasse, D-7316 Koengen, Germany

CEO: Ralph Dietrich, Pres.   Tel: 49-7102-800169

Bus: *Mfr. machine tools.*   Fax: 49-7102-800171
   www.eiseleusa.com

   EISELE CORPORATION

   1500-C Higgins Road, Elk Grove Village, IL   60007

   CEO: Ralph Dietrich, Pres.   Tel: (847) 364-1335   %FO: 100

   Bus: *Sale/distribution machine tools.*   Fax: (847) 364-1336   Emp: 6

● **ELEKTRO-PHYSIK KOLN GMBH & CO. KG**

Pasteurstrasse 15, D-50735 Cologne, Germany

CEO: Klaus E. Steingroever, Dir.　　　　Tel: 49-221-752040

Bus: *Mfr. coating thickness testing gauges*　Fax: 49-221-7520467
　　　for quality control & corrosion　　www.thomasregister.com
　　　prevention.

　　ELECTRO-PHYSIK USA INC.

　　770 West Algonquin Road, Arlington Heights, IL　60005

　　CEO: Aivars Friedenfelds, Mgr.　　Tel: (847) 437-6616　　　%FO: 100

　　Bus: *Distribution/service coating*　Fax: (847) 437-0053
　　　　thickness gauges.

● **EM.TV & MERCHANDISING AG**

Betastrasse 11, D-85774 Unterfohring, Germany

CEO: Werner Klatten, CEO　　　　　Tel: 49-89-995-000　　　Rev: $43

Bus: *Distributes and produces cartoons and*　Fax: 49-89-995-0011　Emp: 173
　　　related television merchandising.　www.em-ag.de

　　THE JIM HENSON COMPANY, INC.

　　1416 North La Brea Avenue, Hollywood, CA　90028

　　CEO: Charles H. Rivkin, Pres.　　Tel: (323) 802-1500　　　%FO: 100

　　Bus: *multimedia production company;*　Fax: (323) 802-1825
　　　　character licensors, publisher of
　　　　children's books and Jim Henson
　　　　TV.

● **ERICH NETZSCH GHMB & CO.**

Gebrueder-Netzsch-Strasse 19, D-95100 Selb, Bavaria, Germany

CEO: Thomas Netzsch, Chmn.　　　Tel: 49-9287-75202

Bus: *Mfr. filter presses and dispersion pumps*　Fax:
　　　and equipment.　　　www.netzsch.com

　　NETZSCH INCORPORATED

　　119 Pickering Way, Exton, PA　19341-1393

　　CEO: Tilo Stahl, Pres. & CEO　　Tel: (610) 363-8010　　　%FO: 100

　　Bus: *Mfr./sales/distribution of filter*　Fax: (610) 363-0971
　　　　presses & dispersion equipment &
　　　　pumps.

● **ESCADA AG**

Margaretha-Ley-Ring 1, D-85609 Aschheim bei Munchen, Germany

CEO: Wolfgang Ley, CEO　　　　　Tel: 49-899-944-0　　　Rev: $819

Bus: *Design and manufacture of upscale*　Fax: 49-988-944-1111　Emp: 4,200
　　　women's apparel, accessories and　www.escada.com
　　　fragrances.

ESCADA BOUTIQUE

259 Post Street, San Francisco, CA   94108

CEO: Wolfgang Ley, Pres. & CEO	Tel: (415) 391-3500	%FO: 100
Bus: *Design and manufacture of upscale women's apparel, accessories and fragrances.*	Fax: (415) 391-4329	

ESCADA BOUTIQUE

34 Highland Park Village, Dallas, TX   75205

CEO: Wolfgang Ley, Pres. & CEO	Tel: (214) 521-2882	%FO: 100
Bus: *Design and manufacture of upscale women's apparel, accessories and fragrances.*	Fax: (214) 521-2994	

ESCADA BOUTIQUE

222 Worth Avenue, Palm Beach, FL   33480

CEO: Wolfgang Ley, Pres. & CEO	Tel: (561) 835-9700	%FO: 100
Bus: *Design and manufacture of upscale women's apparel, accessories and fragrances.*	Fax: (561) 835-4503	

ESCADA BOUTIQUE

7 East 57th Street, New York, Ny   10022

CEO: Wolfgang Ley, Pres. & CEO	Tel: (212) 755-2200	%FO: 100
Bus: *Design and manufacture of upscale women's apparel, accessories and fragrances.*	Fax: (212) 759-4169	

ESCADA BOUTIQUE

9502 Wilshire Boulevard, Beverly Hills, CA   90212

CEO: Wolfgang Ley, Pres. & CEO	Tel: (310) 285-0330	%FO: 100
Bus: *Design and manufacture of upscale women's apparel, accessories and fragrances.*	Fax: (310) 285-0165	

ESCADA BOUTIQUE

1302 Fifth Avenue, Seattle, WA   98101

CEO: Robin Scheer Ettinger, VP	Tel: (206) 223-9433	%FO: 100
Bus: *Design and manufacture of upscale women's apparel, accessories and fragrances.*	Fax: (206) 223-9433	

● EURO LLOYD REISEBÜRO GMBH

Neumarkt 35-37, D-50667 Cologne, Germany

CEO: Rudolf Aenis, Dir.	Tel: 49-221-2028100	
Bus: *Travel agency.*	Fax: 49-221-2028125	Emp: 900
	www.eurolloyd.com	

EURO LLOYD TRAVEL INC.
350 Fifth Avenue, New York, NY   10118
CEO: Juergen Weinroth, EVP   Tel: (212) 629-5470   %FO: 100
Bus: *U.S. headquarters. Travel agency*   Fax: (212) 643-0223
    and tour operators.

EURO LLOYD TRAVEL INC.
125 State Street, Hackensack, NJ   07601
CEO: Sophie Sbaschnik, Mgr.   Tel: (201) 489-0711   %FO: 100
Bus: *Travel agency.*   Fax: (201) 489-8614

EURO LLOYD TRAVEL INC.
Haywood Plaza, 30 Orchard Park Drive, Ste. 3, Greenville, SC   29615
CEO: Ursula Rhine, Mgr.   Tel: (864) 627-8001   %FO: 100
Bus: *Travel agency.*   Fax: (864) 627-8003

EURO LLOYD TRAVEL INC.
1910 Fairview Avenue East, Ste. 301, Seattle, WA   98102
CEO: Theresa Studer, Mgr.   Tel: (206) 860-0715   %FO: 100
Bus: *Travel agency.*   Fax: (206) 860-0821

EURO LLOYD TRAVEL INC.
3384 Peachtree Road, NE, Atlanta, GA   30326
CEO: Klaus van Keiser, Mgr.   Tel: (404) 231-0704   %FO: 100
Bus: *Travel agency.*   Fax: (404) 231-5078

EURO LLOYD TRAVEL INC.
220 Sansome Street, San Francisco, CA   94104
CEO: James Sugden, Mgr.   Tel: (415) 391-9011   %FO: 100
Bus: *Travel agency.*   Fax: (415) 391-9378

EURO LLOYD TRAVEL INC.
1640 Hempstead Turnpike, East Meadow, NY   11554
CEO: Regina Higgins, Mgr.   Tel: (516) 228-4970   %FO: JV
Bus: *Travel agency.*   Fax: (516) 228-8258   Emp: 80

● A.W. FABER-CASTELL GMBH
Numberger Strasse 2, D-90546 Stein, Germany
CEO: Wolfgang Graf von Faber-Castell, CEO Tel: 49-911-9965-0   Rev: $350
Bus: *Mfr. of pencils, fountain and roller pens* Fax: 49-911-9965-760   Emp: 5,000
    and cosmetic products.   www.faber-castell.de

A. W. FABER-CASTELL COSMETICS, INC.
420 Jericho Turnpike, Jericho, NY   11753
CEO: Patricia Shephard   Tel: (516) 433-4064   %FO: 100
Bus: *Mfr. cosmetic products.*   Fax: (516) 433-4031

A. W. FABER-CASTELL USA, INC.
1802 Central Avenue, Cleveland, OH 44115

CEO: Christopher Wiedenmayer, CEO	Tel: (216) 589-4800	%FO: 100
Bus: *Mfr. pencils, fountain and roller pens.*	Fax: (216) 589-4800	

● FAG KUGELFISCHER GEORG SCHAFER AG
Georg-Schafer-Strasse 30, Postfach 1260, D-97421 Schweinfurt, Germany

CEO: Peter-Juergen Kreher, Pres.	Tel: 49-9721-910	Rev: $2,015
Bus: *Mfr./wholesale anti-friction bearings.*	Fax: 49-9721-913435 www.fag.com	Emp: 16,200

FAG BEARINGS CORPORATION
200 Park Avenue, Danbury, CT 06810

CEO: Dieter Kuetemeier, Pres.	Tel: (203) 790-5474	%FO: 100
Bus: *Mfr./distribution/sale bearings.*	Fax: (203) 830-8105	Emp: 1,600

LACEY MANUFACTURING COMPANY, INC.
1146 Barnum Avenue, Bridgeport, CT 06610

CEO: Robert A. Werner, Pres.	Tel: (203) 336-0121	%FO: 100
Bus: *Mfr./distribution/sale of disposable surgical instruments.*	Fax: (203) 336-6425	

POPE CORPORATION
261 River Street, Haverhill, MA 01832

CEO: Jeffrey Pfeiffer, CEO	Tel: (978) 373-5678	%FO: 100
Bus: *Mfr./design sprindle assemblies for machine tools.*	Fax: (978) 373-6386	

● WILHELM FETTE GMBH
Grabauer Strasse 24, D-2053 Schwarzenbek, Germany

CEO: Eugene Valerius, CEO	Tel: 49-4151-120	
Bus: *Mfr. of precision metalwork cutters.*	Fax: 49-4151-12511 www.fette.de	Emp: 1,200

LMT - FETTE INC.
18013 Cleveland Parkway, Ste. 180, Cleveland, OH 44135

CEO: Robert J. Rubenstahl, Pres.	Tel: (216) 377-6130	%FO: 100
Bus: *Mfr./distribution Hob's (gear generating tools), HSS End-Mills and indexable milling cutter's & insert's; general cutting tools.*	Fax: (216) 377-0787	Emp: 17

- **FIRMA AUGUST BILSTEIN GMBH & CO**

Postfach 1151, D-58256 Ennepetal, Germany

CEO: F. Riemenschneider, Pres.

Bus: *Mfr. shock absorbers, window hardware, car jacks.*

Tel: 49-23-337920

Fax: 49-23-3379-2253

www.bilstein.de

Emp: 1,900

KRUPP BILSTEIN CORPORATION

8845 Rehco Road, San Diego, CA 92121

CEO: Reinhard Schomburg, Pres.

Bus: *Assembly/distribute shock absorbers.*

Tel: (858) 453-7723

Fax: (858) 453-0770

%FO: 100

Emp: 60

- **FLEISSNER GMBH & CO**

Wolfsgartenstrasse 6, D-63329 bei Frankfurt/Main, Germany

CEO: Gerold Fleissner, Pres.

Bus: *Mfr. fiber, textile, non-woven, finishing equipment*

Tel: 49-6103-4010

Fax: 49-6103-401440

www.fleissner.de

Emp: 800

FLEISSNER INC.

12301 Moores Chapel Road, Charlotte, NC 28214

CEO: Don B. Gillespie, VP

Bus: *Sale fiber, textile, non-woven finishing equipment.*

Tel: (704) 394-3376

Fax: (704) 393-2637

%FO: 100

Emp: 6

- **FLUX GERAETE GMBH**

Postfach 49, D-75429 Maulbronn, Germany

CEO: Klaus Hann, Pres.

Bus: *Mfr./distribution drum and container chemical transfer pumps.*

Tel: 49-7043-10141

Fax: 49-7043-10133

www.chemforum.ru

FLUX PUMPS CORPORATION

4330 Commerce Circle, Atlanta, GA 30336

CEO: Michael T. O'Toole, Gen. Mgr.

Bus: *Mfr./distribution drum & container chemical transfer pumps.*

Tel: (404) 691-6010

Fax: (404) 691-6314

%FO: 100

- **FRANCOTYP-POSTALIA AG & CO.**

Triftweg 21-26, D-16542 Birkenwerder, Germany

CEO: Ulrich Fehlauer, CEO

Bus: *Mfr. postage meters, mail & shipping room systems.*

Tel: 49-3303-525-0

Fax: 49-3303-525-799

www.fpusa.net

FRANCOTYP-POSTALIA INC.

140 North Mitchell Court, Ste. 200, Addison, IL 60101

CEO: William R. Pesch, Pres.	Tel: (630) 519-2600	%FO: 100
Bus: *Distribution postage meters, mailing machines, office equipment.*	Fax: (630) 519-2499	Emp: 50

● FRANKL & KIRCHNER GMBH & CO. KG

Scheffelstrasse 73, D-68723 Schwetzingen, Germany

CEO: Lotte Wiest, Pres.	Tel: 49-6-202 2020
Bus: *Electronic positioning motors for industrial sewing equipment.*	Fax: 49-6-202 202115
	www.efka.germany.net

EFKA OF AMERICA INC.

3715 Northcrest Rd, Ste. 10, Atlanta, GA 30340

CEO: J. D. Price, VP	Tel: (770) 457-7006	%FO: 100
Bus: *Sale/service electronic positioning motors for industrial sewing equipment*	Fax: (770) 458-3899	Emp: 12

● FRANZ HANIEL & CIE GMBH

Franz-Haniel-Platz 1, D-47119 Duisburg, Germany

CEO: Dieter Schadt, Chmn.	Tel: 49-203-806-0	Rev: $16,360
Bus: *Engaged in pharmaceuticals, stainless-steel recycling and trading, disaster recovery and property restoration.*	Fax: 49-203-806-622	Emp: 40,075
	www.haniel.de	

BELFOR USA

2425 Blue Smoke Court South, Ft. Worth, TX 76105

CEO: Kirk Lively, CEO	Tel: (817) 535-6793	%FO: 100
Bus: *Engaged in property restoration.*	Fax:	

BELFOR USA

4835 Forder Oaks Court, St. Louis, MO 63129

CEO: Robert Peetz	Tel: (314) 892-2315	%FO: 100
Bus: *Engaged in property restoration.*	Fax: (314) 892-2312	

ELG METALS, INC.

PO Box 369, McKeesport, PA 15134

CEO: Friedrich Teroerde, Chmn.	Tel: (412) 672-9200	%FO: 100
Bus: *Engaged in recycling of raw materials for stainless steel industry.*	Fax: (412) 672-0824	

- **FRANZ HERMLE & SOHN**

Bahnhofstrasse 6, D-78559 Gosheim, Germany

CEO: Rolf Hermle, Pres.   Tel: 49-7426-6010

Bus: *Mfr. of clocks and clock movements.*   Fax: 49-7426-601333   Emp: 300

www.hermle-clocks.com

HERMLE BLACK FOREST CLOCKS

PO Box 670, Amherst, VA   24521

CEO: Helmut Mangold, Mgr.   Tel: (804) 946-7751   %FO: 100

Bus: *Mfr. of clocks & clock movements,*   Fax: (804) 946-7747   Emp: 50
*clock kits, Swiss screw machine
parts.*

- **FRESENIUS MEDICAL CARE AG**

Else-Krönerstrasse 1, D-61352 Badhomburg, Germany

CEO: Gerd Krick, Chmn.   Tel: 49-6172-609-0   Rev: $3,299

Bus: *Healthcare operations in dialysis/renal*   Fax: 49-6172-609-2488   Emp: 29,318
services, dialysis products and   www.fmc-ag.com
homecare.

FRESENIUS MEDICAL CARE N.A.

2 Ledgemont Ctr., 95 Hayden Avenue, Lexington, MA   02173

CEO: Dr. Ben J. Lipps, Pres. & CEO   Tel: (781) 402-9000   %FO: 100

Bus: *Healthcare operations in*   Fax: (781) 402-9006
*dialysis/renal services, dialysis
products and homecare.*

- **FREUDENBERG & CO**

Leibeitzstrass, 2-4, D-69469 Weinheim, Germany

CEO: Dr. Peter Bettermann, Chmn.   Tel: 49-6201-80-5808

Bus: *Mfr. seals, rubber, polymer, foam*   Fax: 49-6201-88-3430   Emp: 29,667
products and leather.   www.freudenberg.com

FREUDENBERG NONWOVENS

2975 Pembroke Road, Hopkinsville, KY   42240

CEO: Lee Sullivan, Pres.   Tel: (502) 885-9420   %FO: 100

Bus: *Sales/distribution filters.*   Fax: (502) 886-5878

FREUDENBERG NONWOVENS

3400 Industrial Drive, Durham, NC   27704

CEO: Lee J. Sullivan, Pres. & CEO   Tel: (919) 620-3900   %FO: 100

Bus: *Technical products division; mfr.*   Fax: (919) 620-3909
nonwoven fabrics.

FREUDENBERG NONWOVENS VITECH LTD.

221 Jackson Street, Lowell, MA   01852

CEO: Lee Sullivan, Pres. Tel: (978) 454-0461 %FO: 100

Bus: *Mfr. seals, rubber/polymer/foam products & leather.* Fax: (978) 454-0461

FREUDENBERG NORTH AMERICA, LTD.

Route 104, PO Box 2001, Bristol, NH   03222-2001

CEO: Joseph C. Day, Pres. Tel: (603) 744-2281 %FO: 100

Bus: *Mfr. seals, rubber/polymer/foam products, leather.* Fax: (603) 744-8722

FREUDENBERG SPUNWEB COMPANY

PO Box 15910, 3500 Industrial Dr., Durham, NC   27704

CEO: Lee Sullivan, Pres. Tel: (919) 471-2582 %FO: 100

Bus: *Mfr. polyester spunbond fabric.* Fax: (919) 477-1165

FREUDENBERG-NOK GENERAL PARTNERSHIP

47690 East Anchor Court, Plymouth, MI   48170

CEO: Joseph C. Day, Pres. Tel: (734) 451-0020 %FO: 100

Bus: *Mfr. seals, molded rubber & plastic components, vibration control systems, aftermarket rebuild kits.* Fax: (734) 451-2245

KLUEBER LUBRICATION NA INC.

54 Wentworth Avenue, Londonderry, NH   03053

CEO: Ewald Stralucke, Pres. Tel: (603) 434-7704 %FO: 100

Bus: *Mfr. industrial lubricants.* Fax: (603) 434-8046

SUMMIT INDUSTRIAL PRODUCTS INC.

PO Box 131359, 9010 Country Road, Tyler, TX   75707

CEO: Fred Pate, Mgr. Tel: (903) 534-8021 %FO: 100

Bus: *Mfr. of synthetic lubricants, lime-scale dissolvers, and oil/water separators.* Fax: (903) 581-4376

● FUCHS PETROLUB AG

Friesenheimer Strasse 17, D-68169 Mannheim, Germany

CEO: Dr. Manfred Fuchs, Pres. Tel: 49-621-38-02105 Rev: $834

Bus: *Mfr. industrial lubricants.* Fax: 49-621-38-02190 Emp: 3,890

www.fuchs-oil.de

CENTURY LUBRICANTS COMPANY

2140 South 88th Street, Kansas City, KS   66111-8701

CEO: Mike Ryan Tel: (913) 422-4022 %FO: 100

Bus: *Mfr. industrial lubricants.* Fax: (913) 422-2333

CENTURY LUBRICANTS CO.
613 Industrial Road, Helper, UT   84526
CEO: Lynne Thomas   Tel: (435) 472-8708   %FO: 100
Bus: *Mfr. industrial lubricants.*   Fax: (435) 472-8735

CENTURY LUBRICANTS CO.
15556 Highway 216, Brookwood, AL   35444
CEO: Norm Hall   Tel: (205) 633-3526   %FO: 100
Bus: *Mfr. industrial lubricants.*   Fax: (205) 633-3527

CENTURY LUBRICANTS CO.
PO Box 450, Waynesburg, PA   15370
CEO: Keith McClure   Tel: (724) 627-3200   %FO: 100
Bus: *Mfr. industrial lubricants.*   Fax: (724) 852-2351

CENTURY LUBRICANTS CO.
PO Box 73, Corbin, KY   40734
CEO: Jack Yates, Mgr.   Tel: (606) 528-9706   %FO: 100
Bus: *Mfr. industrial lubricants.*   Fax: (606) 528-9708

CENTURY LUBRICANTS CO.
PO Box 161, 501 North Carbon St., Marion, IL   62959
CEO: Mike Green   Tel: (618) 997-2302   %FO: 100
Bus: *Mfr. industrial lubricants.*   Fax: (618) 997-2119

CENTURY LUBRICANTS CO.
PO Box 9367, Huntington, WV   25704
CEO: Jack Yates   Tel: (304) 523-3716   %FO: 100
Bus: *Mfr. industrial lubricants.*   Fax: (304) 523-3751

FUCHS LUBRICANTS CO.
160 Weldon Parkway, Maryland Heights, MO   63043
CEO: Tim Swearingen   Tel: (314) 997-4200   %FO: 100
Bus: *Mfr. industrial lubricants.*   Fax: (314) 997-6704

FUCHS LUBRICANTS CO.
17050 Lathrop Avenue, Harvey, IL   60426
CEO: Phil DeSanto   Tel: (708) 333-8900   %FO: 100
Bus: *Mfr. industrial lubricants.*   Fax: (708) 333-9180

FUCHS LUBRICANTS CO.
2601 New Cut Road, Spartanburg, SC   29303
CEO: Dave Spagnola   Tel: (864) 574-9300   %FO: 100
Bus: *Mfr. industrial lubricants.*   Fax: (864) 574-1591

FUCHS LUBRICANTS CO.
1001 Oakmead Drive, Arlington, TX   76011
CEO: Keith Brewer   Tel: (817) 640-0200   %FO: 100
Bus: *Mfr. industrial lubricants.*   Fax: (817) 649-8141

FUCHS LUBRICANTS CO.
281 Silver Sands Road, East Haven, CT   06512
CEO: Marty Wisnieski   Tel: (203) 469-2336   %FO: 100
Bus: *Mfr. industrial lubricants.*   Fax: (203) 467-3223

FUCHS LUBRICANTS CO.
1700 South Caton Avenue, Baltimore, MD   21227
CEO: Ed Peres   Tel: (410) 368-5000   %FO: 100
Bus: *Mfr. industrial lubricants.*   Fax: (410) 368-5019

FUCHS LUBRICANTS CO.
8802 Bash Street, Ste. G, Indianapolis, IN   46258
CEO: Dave Reinhold   Tel: (317) 570-1800   %FO: 100
Bus: *Mfr. industrial lubricants.*   Fax: (317) 570-9042

FUCHS LUBRICANTS CO.
105 Eighth Street, Emlenton, PA   16373
CEO: Tim Russell   Tel: (724) 867-5000   %FO: 100
Bus: *Mfr. industrial lubricants.*   Fax: (724) 867-1182

FUCHS LUBRICANTS CO.
17191 Chrysler Freeway, Detroit, MI   48203
CEO: Bob Cassidy   Tel: (313) 891-3700   %FO: 100
Bus: *Mfr. industrial lubricants.*   Fax: (313) 891-1450

FUCHS LUBRICANTS CO.
250 SW 14th Avenue, Pompano Beach, FL   33069
CEO: Rick Nachenberg   Tel: (954) 782-9300   %FO: 100
Bus: *Mfr. industrial lubricants.*   Fax: (954) 781-5809

FUCHS LUBRICANTS CO.
11400 Grooms Road, Blue Ash, OH   45242
CEO: Rick Klann   Tel: (513) 489-8378   %FO: 100
Bus: *Mfr. industrial lubricants.*   Fax: (513) 489-8379

FUCHS LUBRICANTS CO.
8036 Bavaria Road, Twinsburg, OH   44087
CEO: Jerry Brillhart   Tel: (330) 963-0400   %FO: 100
Bus: *Mfr. industrial lubricants.*   Fax: (330) 963-2995

FUCHS LUBRICANTS CO.
760 36th Street SE, Grand Rapids, MI   49548
CEO: Mike Messer   Tel: (616) 247-0363   %FO: 100
Bus: *Mfr. industrial lubricants.*   Fax: (616) 247-4856

● **FUCHS SYSTEMTECHNIK GMBH**
Reithallenstrasse 1, D-77731 Willstatt-Legelshurst, Germany
CEO: Gerhard Fuchs, Pres.   Tel: 49-785-24100
Bus: *Mfr. electric, ladle and shaft furnaces,*   Fax: 49-785-241141
current conducting electrode arms and   www.fuchs-co.de
equipment for the steel industry.

    FUCHS SYSTEMS, INC.
    812 West Innes Street, PO Box 379, Salisbury, NC   28144
    CEO: Manfred Haissig, Pres.   Tel: (704) 633-2141   %FO: 100
    Bus: *Mfr. furnaces (electric arc, ladle,*   Fax: (704) 633-6103   Emp: 141
    shaft), current conducting
    electrode arms, equipment for
    steel industry.

● **GAUSS INTERPRISE AG**
Himmelstrasse 12-16, D-22299 Hamburg, Germany
CEO: Heino Buchner, CEO   Tel: 49-40-3250-0   Rev: $33
Bus: *Mfr. software to manage content.*   Fax: 49-40-3250-1990   Emp: 325
                                          www.gaussinterprise.de

    GAUSS INTERPRISE USA INC.
    8717 Research Drive, Irvine, CA   92618
    CEO: Ron Vangell, Pres.   Tel: (949) 784-8000   %FO: 100
    Bus: *Mfr./sales software to manage*   Fax: (949) 784-8200
    content.

● **GEOBRA BRANDSTATTER GMBH & CO. KG**
Brandstatter Strasse2-10, D-90513 Zirndorf, Germany
CEO: Horst Brandstatter, Mng. Dir.   Tel: 49-9119-6660   Rev: $216
Bus: *Mfr. Playmobil plastic toys and*   Fax: 49-9119-66120   Emp: 2,190
figurines.   www.playmobil.de

    PLAYBOBIL USA, INC.
    PO Box 877, Dayton, NJ   08810
    CEO: James Gallagher, Pres.   Tel: (609) 395-5566   %FO: 100
    Bus: *Mfr. Playmobil plastic toys and*   Fax: (609) 409-1288
    figurines.

- **GEORG VON HOLTZBRINCK GMBH**

Gaensheidestrasse 26, D-70184 Stuttgart, Germany

CEO: Dieter von Holtzbrinck, CEO   Tel: 49-711-2150-0   Rev: $2,150

Bus: *Engaged in magazine, book and*   Fax: 49-711-210-269   Emp: 11,500
newspaper publishing.   www.spektrum-verlag.com

    FARRAR, STRAUS & GIROUX, INC.

    19 Union Square West, New York, NY   10003

    CEO: Roger W. Straus Jr., Pres.   Tel: (212) 741-6900   %FO: 100

    Bus: *Book publishing.*   Fax: (212) 663-3938

    W. H. FREEMAN & COMPANY

    41 Madison Avenue, New York, NY   10010

    CEO: Elizabeth Widdicombe, Pres.   Tel: (212) 576-9400   %FO: 100

    Bus: *Publishes trade and professional*   Fax: (212) 689-2383
books.

    HENRY HOLT & COMPANY

    115 West 18th Street, 6th Fl., New York, NY   10011

    CEO: John Sterling, Pres.   Tel: (212) 886-9200   %FO: 100

    Bus: *Trade and professional book*   Fax: (212) 355-6245
publisher.

    SCIENTIFIC AMERICAN

    415 Madison Avenue, New York, NY   10010

    CEO: Joachim P. Rosler, Pres.   Tel: (212) 754-0550   %FO: 100

    Bus: *Magazine and book publisher.*   Fax: (212) 754-1138

    ST. MARTIN'S PRESS, INC.

    175 Fifth Avenue, New York, NY   10010

    CEO: Sally Richardson, Pres.   Tel: (212) 674-5151   %FO: 100

    Bus: *Book publishing.*   Fax: (212) 420-9314

    WORTH PUBLISHER INC.

    33 Irving Place, 10th Fl., New York, NY   10003

    CEO: Susan Driscoll, Pres.   Tel: (212) 475-6000   %FO: 100

    Bus: *Publishes trade books.*   Fax: (212) 505-9570

- **GERLING-KONZERN VERSICHERUNGS-BETEILIGUNGS AG**

lm Klapperhof 13-15, D-50670 Cologne, Germany

CEO: Jürgen Zech, CEO   Tel: 49-221-144-7318   Rev: $8,809

Bus: *Insurance holding company.*   Fax: 49-221-144-3319   Emp: 12,000
    www.gerling.de

GERLING GLOBAL REINSURANCE CORPORATION
717 Fifth Avenue, New York, NY   10022
CEO: Gerhard Niebubr, Chmn.   Tel: (212) 754-7500   %FO: 100
Bus: *Reinsurance products & services.*   Fax: (212) 826-5645

● **GILDEMEISTER AG**
Gildemeisterstraße 60, D-33689 Bielefeld, Germany
CEO: Rüdiger Kapitza, CEO   Tel: 49-5205-74-3001   Rev: $870
Bus: *Mfr. machine and cutting tools.*   Fax: 49-5205-74-3061   Emp: 4,640
                                       www.gildemeister.com

   DMG, INC.
   1665 Penny Lane, Schaumburg, IL   60173
   CEO: Harry Domnik   Tel: (847) 781-0277   %FO: 100
   Bus: *Mfr. machine and cutting tools.*   Fax: (847) 781-0388

   DMG, INC.
   13509 S. Point Blvd., Charlotte, NC   28273-6759
   CEO: Harry Domnik   Tel: (704) 583-1193   %FO: 100
   Bus: *Mfr. machine and cutting tools.*   Fax: (704) 583-1149

   DMG, INC.
   3880 East Eagle Drive, Anaheim, CA   92807
   CEO: Harry Domnik   Tel: (714) 237-9976   %FO: 100
   Bus: *Mfr. machine and cutting tools.*   Fax: (714) 237-9978

   DMG, INC.
   757 Kenrick, Ste. 108, Houston, TX   77060
   CEO: Harry Domnik   Tel: (281) 999-3641   %FO: 100
   Bus: *Mfr. machine and cutting tools.*   Fax: (281) 999-1279

● **GIRMES AG**
Johannes-Girmes Strasse 27, D-47929 Grefrath-Oedt, Germany
CEO: Dr. Dirk Busse, CEO   Tel: 49-2158-301
Bus: *Mfr. textiles and textile products.*   Fax: 49-2158-30433   Emp: 2,500
                                       www.girmes.de

   J. L .DE BALL OF AMERICA LTD.
   111 West 40th Street, Ste. 414, New York, NY   10018
   CEO: Bill Trienekens, Pres.   Tel: (212) 575-8613   %FO: 100
   Bus: *Marketing/trading textiles.*   Fax: (212) 575-8616   Emp: 6

- **GPC BIOTECH AG**

Fraunhoferstrasse 20, D-82152 Munich, Germany

CEO: Bernd R. Seizinger, CEO   Tel: 49-89-85-65-2600

Bus: *Engaged in research and technology.*   Fax: 49-89-85-65-2610

www.gpc-biotech.com

GPC BIOTECH INC.

One Deer Park Drive, Ste. O, Monmouth Junction, NJ   08852

CEO: Sebastian Meier-Ewert, SVP   Tel: (732) 355-1222   %FO: 100

Bus: *Engaged in research and technology.*   Fax: (732) 355-1225

GPC BIOTECH INC.

610 Lincoln Street, Waltham, MA   02451

CEO: Sebastian Meier-Ewert, SVP   Tel: (781) 890-9007   %FO: 100

Bus: *Engaged in research and technology.*   Fax: (781) 890-9005

- **GROB WERKE GMBH & CO KG**

Postfach 1257, Industriestasse 4, D-87712 Mindelheim, Germany

CEO: Karl Rehm, Pres.   Tel: 49-8261-9960

Bus: *Mfr. machine tools and assembly equipment.*   Fax: 49-8261-996268   Emp: 2,300

www.grob.de

GROB SYSTEMS, INC.

1070 Navajo Drive, Bluffton, OH   45817

CEO: Michael Hutecker, Pres.   Tel: (419) 358-9015   %FO: 100

Bus: *Mfr. machine tools & assembly equipment.*   Fax: (419) 358-3660   Emp: 100

- **GROZ-BECKERT K.G.**

Postfach 10 02 49, D-72423 Albstadt, Germany

CEO: Dr. Thomas Linder, CEO   Tel: 49-74-31-100

Bus: *Mfr. industrial knitting, sewing, felting & tufting needles.*   Fax: 49-74-31-102776   Emp: 6,000

www.groz-beckert.de

GROZ-BECKERT USA INC.

PO Box 7131, Charlotte, NC   29715

CEO: Henry Tio, Pres.   Tel: (803) 548-0334   %FO: 100

Bus: *Service and sales of industrial knitting, sewing, felting and tufting needles.*   Fax: (800) 354-8880

• **GRUNER + JAHR AG & CO.**

Druck-und Verlagshaus, D-20444 Hamburg, Germany

CEO: Bernd Kundrun, CEO

Bus: *Magazine and newspaper publishing.*

Tel: 49-40-37030
Fax: 49-40-37035653
www.guj.de

Rev: $2,800
Emp: 12,130

CHILD MAGAZINE

375 Lexington Avenue, New York, NY 10017

CEO: Miriam Arond, Editor

Bus: *Magazine on child development and advice.*

Tel: (212) 499-2000
Fax: (212) 499-1987

%FO: 100

FAMILY CIRCLE MAGAZINE

375 Lexington Avenue, New York, NY 10017

CEO: Susan Ungaro, Editor

Bus: *Family magazine.*

Tel: (212) 499-2000
Fax: (212) 499-1987

%FO: 100

FITNESS MAGAZINE

375 Lexington Avenue, New York, NY 10017

CEO: Diane Bulmer Newman, Pub.

Bus: *Fitness magazine.*

Tel: (212) 499-2000
Fax: (212) 463-1170

GRUNER + JAHR BUSINESS INFORMATION GROUP

375 Lexington Avenue, New York, NY 10017

CEO: Daniel B. Brewster, Pres. & CEO

Bus: *Web publications.*

Tel: (212) 499-2000
Fax: (212) 499-1987

%FO: 100

PARENTS MAGAZINE

375 Lexington Avenue, 10th Fl., New York, NY 10017

CEO: John Heins, Pres.

Bus: *Magazine for parents.*

Tel: (212) 499-2000
Fax: (212) 499-2063

ROSIE MAGAZINE

375 Lexington Avenue, New York, NY 10017

CEO: Rosie O'Donnell

Bus: *Women's magazine.*

Tel: (212) 463-1462
Fax: (212) 463-1403

YM YOUNG & MODERN MAGAZINE

375 Lexington Avenue, New York, NY 10017

CEO: Axel Ganz, Pres.

Bus: *Teen/young adult magazine.*

Tel: (212) 499-2000
Fax: (212) 499-2000

• GUNOLD + STICKMA GMBH

Obernburger Strasse 125, D-63811 Stockstadt, Germany

CEO: Christoph Gunold, Dir.

Tel: 49-60 272008

Bus: *Distributor machine embroidery supplies, CAD computer systems, punching services for designs and consulting for embroidery industry.*

Fax: 49-60 273243

www.gunold.de

Emp: 110

GUNOLD + STICKMA OF AMERICA, INC.

980 Cobb Blvd, Ste. 130, Kennesaw, GA 30144

CEO: Ole Prior, Pres.

Tel: (770) 421-0300

%FO: 100

Bus: *Wholesale/distribution machine embroidery supplies, CAD computer system, punching services for designs, letter & appliqués cutting.*

Fax: (770) 421-0505

Emp: 50

• HACOBA-TEXTILMASCHINEN GMBH & CO KG

Postfach 200751, D-42207 Wuppertal, Germany

CEO: Peter Boden, Pres.

Tel: 49-202 709101

Bus: *Textile machinery and parts.*

Fax: 49-02 7091214

www.hacoba.com

HACOBA TEXTILE MACHINERY LP

11024 Nations Ford Road, Pineville, NC 28134

CEO: Craig Newsome, VP

Tel: (704) 588-2493

%FO: 100

Bus: *Sale/service textile machines.*

Fax: (704) 588-4798

Emp: 2,516

• HAFELE GMBH & CO.

Postfach 12 37, D-72192 Nagold, Germany

CEO: Hans Nock, Pres.

Tel: 49-7452-95328

Bus: *Distribution of European furniture and cabinet hardware.*

Fax: 49-7452-95402

www.hafele.de

Emp: 1,600

HAFELE AMERICA COMPANY

3901 Cheyenne Drive, PO Box 4000, Archdale, NC 27263

CEO: John Hossil, Pres.

Tel: (336) 889-2322

%FO: 100

Bus: *Distribution European furniture cabinet hardware.*

Fax: (336) 431-3831

Emp: 200

• HAMBURG-SÜD

Postfach 11 15 33, D-20457 Hamburg, Germany

CEO: Dr. Klaus Meves, Chrm.

Tel: 49-40-3705-0

Bus: *Engaged in marine transport and logistics management.*

Fax: 49-40-3705-2400

www.hamburg-sued.de

Emp: 2,670

COLUMBUS LINE USA INC.
465 South Street, Morristown, NJ   07960

CEO: Juergen Pump, SVP	Tel: (973) 775-5300	%FO: 100
Bus: *Containerized shipping to Australia, New Zealand, South America and Eastern Mediterranean.*	Fax: (973) 775-5315	Emp: 250

COLUMBUS LINE USA INC.
Curtis Center, Ste.1075 West, Philadelphia, PA   19106

CEO: Steve George, Mgr.	Tel: (215) 923-6900	%FO: 100
Bus: *Containerized shipping to Australia, New Zealand, South America and Eastern Mediterranean.*	Fax: (215) 625-9810	

COLUMBUS LINE USA INC.
1245 Diehl Road, Ste. 305, Naperville, IL   60563

CEO: Lynn Ennis, Mgr.	Tel: (630) 955-9700	%FO: 100
Bus: *Containerized shipping to Australia, New Zealand, South America and Eastern Mediterranean.*	Fax: (630) 955-0772	

COLUMBUS LINE USA INC.
5255 NW 87th Avenue, Ste. 101, Miami, FL   33176

CEO: Juergen Pump, SVP	Tel: (305) 470-2294	%FO: 100
Bus: *Containerized shipping to Australia, New Zealand, South America and Eastern Mediterranean.*	Fax: (305) 470-2761	

COLUMBUS LINE USA INC.
249 East Ocean Boulevard, Ste. 200, Long Beach, CA   90802

CEO: Gail Searing	Tel: (562) 590-9021	%FO: 100
Bus: *Containerized shipping to Australia, New Zealand, South America and Eastern Mediterranean.*	Fax: (562) 436-0404	

● **HANNOVER RUECKVERSICHERUNGS AG (HANNOVER RE)**
Karl-Wiechert-Allee 50, Postfach 610369, D-30625 Hannover, Germany

CEO: Wilhelm Zeller, Chmn.	Tel: 49-511-56040	Rev: $4,900
Bus: *Reinsurance.*	Fax: 49-511-5604188	Emp: 1,500
	www.hannover-rueck.de	

CLARENDON NSURANCE GROUP

1177 Ave. of the Americas, Ste. 4500, New York, NY 10036

CEO: Robert D. Ferguson, Pres.   Tel: (212) 805-9700   %FO: 100

Bus: *Provides property and casualty*   Fax: (212) 805-9800
    insurance.

HANNOER FINANCE, INC.

1177 Ave. of the Americas, Ste. 4500, New York, NY 10036

CEO: Anders Larsson, CEO   Tel: (212) 805-9700   %FO: 100

Bus: *Reinsurance services.*   Fax: (212) 805-9790

HANNOVER USA

1901 North Roselle Road, Ste. 1040, Schaumburg, Il 60195

CEO: Anders Larsson, CEO   Tel: (847) 310-3854   %FO: 100

Bus: *Reinsurance services.*   Fax: (847) 310-3856

INSURANCE CORP OF HANNOVER

3435 Wilshire Blvd., Ste. 700, Los Angeles, CA 90010

CEO: John F. Sullivan, Pres. & CEO   Tel: (213) 380-8822   %FO: 100

Bus: *Reinsurance services.*   Fax: (213) 386-2062   Emp: 58

REASSURNCE COMPANY OF HANNOVER

800 North Magnolia Ave., Ste. 1000, Orlando, FL 32803

CEO: William W. Walker, Pres.   Tel: (407) 649-8411   %FO: 100

Bus: *Reinsurance services.*   Fax: (407) 649-8322

● HAPAG-LLOYD CONTAINER LINE GMBH

Ballindamm 25, Postfach 102626, D-20095 Hamburg, Germany

CEO: Bernd Wrede, Chmn.   Tel: 49-40-30010   Rev: $7,831

Bus: *Freight container shipping, cruise line*   Fax: 49-40-336432   Emp: 17,775
    and travel.   www.hapag-lloyd.com

HAPAG-LLOYD (AMERICA) INC.

399 Hoes Lane, Piscataway, NJ 08854

CEO: Rudiger Mack, Pres.   Tel: (732) 562-1800   %FO: 100

Bus: *Ocean freight forwarding.*   Fax: (732) 885-3730   Emp: 450

● HAVER & BOECKER

Carl Haver Platz 3, D-59302 Oelde/Westfalen, Germany

CEO: Reinhold Festge, Mgr.   Tel: 49-25-22300

Bus: *Mfr./engineering/sale/service individual*   Fax: 49-25-2230403   Emp: 1,350
    packaging systems.   www.haverboecker.com

HAVER FILLING SYSTEMS INC.

PO Box 80937, Conyers, GA   30013

CEO: Thomas Reckersdrees, VP	Tel: (770) 760-1130	%FO: 100
Bus: *Engineering/sale/service individual packaging systems.*	Fax: (770) 760-1181	Emp: 8

• HEIDELBERGER DRUCKMASCHINEN AG

Kurfursten Anlage 52-60, D-69115 Heidelberg, Germany

CEO: Bernhard Schreier, Chmn.	Tel: 49-62-21-92-00	Rev: $4,600
Bus: *Mfr. printing presses and cutting, folding and binding machines.*	Fax: 49-62-21-92-6999 www.heidelberg.com	Emp: 24,170

HEIDELBERG INC.

4665 Paris Street, Ste. C-350, Denver, CO   80239

CEO: Niels M. Winther, Pres.	Tel: (303) 371-7870	%FO: 100
Bus: *Sales printing presses.*	Fax: (303) 371-5212	

HEIDELBERG INC.

121 Broadway, Dover, NH   03820-3290

CEO: Vernon Albrecht, Pres.	Tel: (603) 749-6600	%FO: 100
Bus: *Research, development and manufacturing of web offset printing presses.*	Fax: (603) 743-5467	Emp: 600

HEIDELBERG INC.

18711 Broadwick Street, Rancho Dominguez, CA   90220

CEO: Niels M. Winther, Pres.	Tel: (310) 761-1500	%FO: 100
Bus: *Sales printing presses.*	Fax: (310) 761-1539	

HEIDELBERG INC.

625 Slawin Court, Mt. Prospect, IL   60056

CEO: Niels M. Winther, Pres.	Tel: (847) 390-8900	%FO: 100
Bus: *Sales printing presses.*	Fax: (847) 390-6914	

HEIDELBERG INC.

250 East Grand Avenue, Ste. 35, South San Francisco, CA   94080

CEO: Niels M. Winther, Pres.	Tel: (650) 873-0490	%FO: 100
Bus: *Sales printing presses.*	Fax: (650) 873-2054	

HEIDELBERG INC.

10250 Valley View Road, Ste. 129, Eden Prairie, MN   55344

CEO: Hans Peetz-Larsen, CEO	Tel: (612) 942-6100	%FO: 100
Bus: *Sales printing presses.*	Fax: (612) 942-8892	

HEIDELBERG INC.
9104 Guilford Road, Columbia, MD   21046
CEO: Hans Peetz-Larsen, CEO   Tel: (301) 483-0304   %FO: 100
Bus: *Sales printing presses.*   Fax: (301) 483-0506

HEIDELBERG INC.
77 Accord Park Drive, Ste. B-10, Norwell, MA   02061
CEO: Hans Peetz-Larsen, CEO   Tel: (781) 871-3328   %FO: 100
Bus: *Sales printing presses.*   Fax: (781) 878-3685

HEIDELBERG INC.
21 Commerce Drive, Cranbury, NJ   08512
CEO: Hans Peetz-Larsen, CEO   Tel: (609) 395-9600   %FO: 100
Bus: *Sales printing presses.*   Fax: (609) 395-0021

HEIDELBERG INC.
1000 Gutenberg Drive, Kennesaw, GA   30144
CEO: Hans Peetz-Larsen, CEO   Tel: (770) 419-6500   %FO: 100
Bus: *Sales printing presses.*   Fax: (770) 419-6912

HEIDELBERG INC.
1801 Royal Lane, Ste. 1012, Dallas, TX   75229
CEO: Hans Peetz-Larsen, CEO   Tel: (972) 506-7000
Bus: *Production of side frames, drums*   Fax: (972) 506-0476   Emp: 120
    and bearings.

HEIDELBERG INC.
24500 Northline Road, Taylor, MI   48180
CEO: Niels M. Winther, Pres.   Tel: (734) 946-7050   %FO: 100
Bus: *Sales printing presses.*   Fax: (734) 946-4493

● **DR. JOHANNES HEIDENHAIN GMBH**
Dr.-Johannes-Heidenhain-Straße 5, D-83301 Traunreut, Germany
CEO: Ludwig Wagatha, Chmn.   Tel: 49-8669-310
Bus: *Mfr. optical rotary encoders.*   Fax: 49-8669-5061
    www.heidenhain.de

    HEIDENHAIN CORPORATION
    333 E. State Parkway, Schaumburg, IL   60173
    CEO: Rick Corte, CEO   Tel: (847) 490-1191   %FO: 100
    Bus: *Mfr./sales optical rotary encoders.*   Fax: (847) 490-3931

    HEIDENHAIN CORPORATION
    226 Airport Parkway, Suite 620, San Jose, CA   95110
    CEO: Aya Hoban   Tel: (406) 437-1663   %FO: 100
    Bus: *Mfr./sales optical rotary encoders.*   Fax: (408) 437-1676

HEIDENHAIN CORPORATION
333 State Parkway, Schaumburg, IL   60173-5337
CEO: Rick Korte   Tel: (847) 490-1191   %FO: 100
Bus: *Mfr./sales optical rotary encoders.*   Fax: (847) 490-3931

HEIDENHAIN CORPORATION
5862 Bolsa Avenue, Ste. 105, Huntington Beach, CA   92648
CEO: Rick Korte   Tel: (714) 901-0029   %FO: 100
Bus: *Mfr./sales optical rotary encoders.*   Fax: (714) 901-2907

● **THOMAS JOSEF HEIMBACH GMBH**
An Gut Nazareth 73, D-52353 Düren, Germany
CEO: Otto G.I. Merckens   Tel: 49-24-218-020
Bus: *Mfr. specialty fabrics for paper industry.*   Fax: 49-24-218-02700   Emp: 800
                                          www.heimbach-group.com

ASTENJOHNSON, INC.
1145 Battle Creek Road, Jonesboro, GA   30236
CEO: Garry Kirby, Pres.   Tel: (770) 471-0660   %FO: 100
Bus: *Mfr. specialty fabrics for paper*   Fax: (770) 471-1365
   industry.

● **HEINRICH LIEBIG STAHLDUBEL-WERKE GMBH**
Wormser Strasse 23, Postfach 1309, D-64319 Pfungstadt, Germany
CEO: Heinrich Liebig, CEO   Tel: 49-6157 2027
Bus: *Mfr./sales of concrete expansion,*   Fax: 49-6157 2020   Emp: 200
   undercut, self-undercut anchors, wedge   www.liebig,profitbolt.com
   anchors and chemical anchors.

LIEBIG INTERNATIONAL INC.
1545 Avon Street Extension, Charlottesville, VA   22902
CEO: Heinrich Liebig, Pres.   Tel: (804) 979-7115   %FO: 100
Bus: *Mfr./sales of concrete expansion,*   Fax: (804) 979-7117   Emp: 4
   undercut, self-undercut anchors,
   wedge anchors and chemical
   anchors.

● **HEINZ KETTLER METALLWARENFABRIC GMBH & CO.**
Postfach 1020, Hauptstrasse, D-59463 Ense-Parsit, Germany
CEO: Heinz Kettler, CEO   Tel: 49-2938-810
Bus: *Mfr. children's bicycles and bicycle*   Fax: 49-2938-2022   Emp: 3,500
   seats, patio furniture, table tennis and   www.heinz-kettler.de
   exercise equipment and juvenile
   products.

KETTLER INTERNATIONAL INC.

PO Box 2747, Virginia Beach, VA   23450-2747

CEO: Ludger Busche, VP

Bus: *Mfr. children's bicycles and bicycle seats, patio furniture, table tennis and exercise equipment and juvenile products.*

Tel: (757) 427-2400
Fax: (757) 427-0183

%FO: 100
Emp: 20

● **HELLA KG HUECK & CO.**

Rixbecker Strasse 75, D-59552 Lippstadt, Germany

CEO: Juergen Behrend, Chrm.

Bus: *Mfr. lamps and lighting equipment, pumps, control modules.*

Tel: 49-2941-387549
Fax: 49-2941-387133
www.hella.de

Emp: 21,100

HELLA NORTH AMERICA, INC.

43811 Plymouth Oaks Blvd., Plymouth, MI   48170

CEO: Joseph V. Borruso, CEO

Bus: *Mfr. automotive relays & flashers for OEM marketing.*

Tel: (734) 414-0910
Fax: (734) 414-0911

%FO: 100

HELLA NORTH AMERICA INC.

201 Kelly Drive, PO Box 2665, Peachtree City, GA   30269

CEO: Mitch Williams, Pres.

Bus: *Sale/distribution automotive lighting & accessories.*

Tel: (770) 631-7500
Fax: (770) 631-7575

%FO: 100

● **HELLMANN WORLDWIDE LOGISTICS GMBH**

Elbestrasse, D-49090 Osnatrück, Germany

CEO: Klaus Hellmann, Mng. Dir.

Bus: *Provides freight forwarding, logistics, customs brokerage and warehousing services.*

Tel: 49-541-605-1253
Fax: 49-541-605-1664

HELLMANN WORLDWIDE LOGISTICS, INC.

10450 Doral Blvd., Miami, FL   33178

CEO: Karl Weyeneth, Pres.

Bus: *Provides freight forwarding, logistics, customs brokerage and warehousing services.*

Tel: (305) 406-4500
Fax: (305) 406-4519

%FO: 100

● **HELM AG**

Nordkanalstrasse 28, D-20097 Hamburg, Germany

CEO: Dieter Schnabel, Chmn. & CEO

Bus: *Trading/distribution, warehousing, service functions of medical, pharmaceuticals, chemicals, plastics, steel, etc.*

Tel: 49-40-23750
Fax: 49-40-2375-1845
www.helmag.com

Rev: $797
Emp: 1,194

HELM NEW YORK INC.
1110 Centennial Avenue, Piscataway, NJ   08855-1333

CEO: Christian Torske, EVP & Gen.Mgr.	Tel: (732) 981-1160	%FO: 100
Bus: *Import export/distribution pharmaceuticals, veterinary, raw materials, feed & food additives, essential oils, aroma chemicals.*	Fax: (732) 981-0528	Emp: 14

● **HELMUT MAUELL GMBH**
Am Rosenhuegel 1-7, D-42553 Velbert, Germany
CEO: Helmut Mauell, CEO   Tel: 49-2-053-13432
Bus: *Control and display systems.*   Fax: 49-2-053-13653   Emp: 550
                                        www.mauell.com

MAUELL CORPORATION
31 Old Cabin Hollow Road, Dillsburg, PA   17019-0339
CEO: Gary Suchy, Mgr.   Tel: (717) 432-8686   %FO: 100
Bus: *Mosaic display panels.*   Fax: (717) 432-8688   Emp: 25

● **HENGELER MUELLER WEITZEL WIRTZ**
Kurfürstendamm 54/55, D-10707 Berlin, Germany
CEO: Dr. Hasselmann, Mng. Ptnr.   Tel: 49-30-885-7190
Bus: *International law firm.*   Fax: 49-30-882-7144

HENGELER MUELLER WEITZEL WIRTZ
712 Fifth Avenue, New York, NY   10019
CEO: Dr. Böhlhoff, Mng. Ptnr.   Tel: (212) 586-4600   %FO: 100
Bus: *International law firm.*   Fax: (212) 586-4481

● **HENKEL KGAA**
Henklestrasse 67, D-40191 Düsseldorf, Germany
CEO: Dr. Ulrich Lehner, CEO   Tel: 49-211-797-3533   Rev: $11,441
Bus: *Branded detergents, personal care products and chemical products.*   Fax: 49-211-798-4040   Emp: 55,943
                                        www.henkel.de

HENKEL CORPORATION
1615 Johanson Road, NW, Atlanta, GA   30092
CEO: Rick Luedecke, Plant Mgr.   Tel: (404) 799-1292
Bus: *Mfr. specialty chemicals.*   Fax: (404) 799-3292

HENKEL CORPORATION
2200 Renaissance Blvd., Ste. 200, Gulph Mills, PA   19406

CEO: Robert A. Lurcott, Pres. Tel: (610) 270-8100 %FO: 100

Bus: *U.S. headquarters operation for* Fax: (610) 270-8291 Emp: 2,500
manufacture of specialty
chemicals.

HENKEL CORPORATION CHEMICALS GROUP
300 Brookside Avenue, Ambler, PA   19002

CEO: James Lee, EVP Tel: (215) 628-1000 %FO: 100

Bus: *Mfr. specialty chemicals for paper,* Fax: (215) 628-1200
coatings, textile, leather, and
cosmetics markets.

HENKEL CORPORATION CHEMICALS GROUP
5051 Este Creek Drive, Cincinnati, OH   45232

CEO: Robert T. Betz, Chmn. Tel: (513) 482-3000 %FO: 100

Bus: *Mfr. specialty chemicals for paper,* Fax: (513) 482-5508
coatings, textile, leather, and
cosmetics markets.

HENKEL CORPORATION SURFACE TECHNOLOGIES
140 Germantown Pike, Ste. 150, Plymouth Meeting, PA   19462

CEO: Robert A. Lurcott, Pres. Tel: (248) 683-9300

Bus: *Patent division.* Fax: (248) 583-2976

HENKEL CORPORATION SURFACE TECHNOLOGIES
5555 Triangle Parkway, Ste. 470, Norcross, GA   30092

CEO: Robert A. Lurcott, Pres. Tel: (770) 446-7308

Bus: *Mfr. specialty chemicals.* Fax: (770) 446-8141

HENKEL SURFACE TECHNOLOGIES
32100 Stephenson Hwy., Madison Heights, MI   48071

CEO: James W. Harrison, Pres. Tel: (248) 583-9300 %FO: 100

Bus: *Mfr. metal pretreatment chemicals.* Fax: (248) 583-2976

LOCTITE CORPORATION
1001 Trout Brook Crossing, Rocky Hill, CT   06067

CEO: Helnrich Gunn, CEO Tel: (860) 571-5100 %FO: 100

Bus: *Mfr. adhesives.* Fax: (860) 571-5465 Emp: 4,500

SCHWARZKOPF & DEP INC.
2101 East Via Arado, Rancho Dominguez, CA   90220
CEO: Robert Berglass, Pres. & Chmn.   Tel: (310) 604-0777
Bus: *Mfr. personal care products,*   Fax: (310) 537-4098   Emp: 300
including Dep styling hair gel,
Lavoris mouthwash and Porcelana
skin products.

● **HERAEUS HOLDING GMBH**
Heracusstrasse 12-14, D-63450 Hanau, Germany
CEO: Horst Heidsieck, CEO   Tel: 49-6181-35-5100   Rev: $4,800
Bus: *Holding company for mfr./distribution*   Fax: 49-6181-35-4242   Emp: 9,500
of metals, chemicals, sensors & glass.   www.heraeus.de

HERAEUS AMERSIL
3473 Satellite Boulevard, Duluth, GA   30136-5821
CEO: Dr. Peter Schultz, Pres.   Tel: (770) 623-6000   %FO: 100
Bus: *Production of quartz glass*   Fax: (770) 623-5640
products for fiber optic, optical,
semiconductor & industrial
applications.

HERAEUS ELECTRO-NITE COMPANY
9901 Blue Grass Road, Philadelphia, PA   19114
CEO: Michael Midash, Pres.   Tel: (215) 464-4200   %FO: 100
Bus: *Production of industrial*   Fax: (215) 698-7793
temperature sensors.

HERAEUS INC. CERMALLOY DIV.
24 Union Hill Rd. PO Box 306, Conshohocken, PA   19428
CEO: Thomas Lorandeau, Mgr.   Tel: (610) 825-6050   %FO: 100
Bus: *Production of film and solder*   Fax: (610) 825-7061
paste products.

HERAEUS PRECIOUS METALS MANAGEMENT INC.
65 Euclid Avenue, Newark, NJ   07105
CEO: John Carroll, VP   Tel: (201) 817-7878   %FO: 100
Bus: *Precious metals trading.*   Fax: (201) 578-2786

HERAEUS KULZER, INC.
4315 South Lafayette Blvd., South Bend, IN   46614-2517
CEO: Gerrit Steen, Pres.   Tel: (219) 291-0661   %FO: 100
Bus: *Sales/distribution of dental*   Fax: (219) 291-0720
equipment & dental products.

HERAEUS PRECIOUS METALS MANAGEMENT, INC.

540 Madison Avenue, New York, NY   10022

CEO: John Burdsall, Pres.   Tel: (212) 752-2180   %FO: 100

Bus: *Trades precious metals.*   Fax: (212) 752-7141

HERAEUS SYSTEMS, INC.

540 Madison Avenue, 16th Fl., New York, NY   10022

CEO: John Burdsall, Pres.   Tel: (212) 752-2705   %FO: 100

Bus: *U.S. headquarters.*   Fax: (212) 752-4686

J. F. JELELENKO & COMPANY

99 Business Park Drive, Armonk, NY   10504

CEO: Horst Becker, Pres.   Tel: (914) 273-8600   %FO: 100

Bus: *Sales/distribution of dental* Fax: (914) 273-4413
  equipment.

L&N METALLURGICAL PRODUCTS CO.

Three Fountain Avenue, Ellwood City, PA   16117

CEO: David Aranelcka, Pres.   Tel: (724) 758-4541   %FO: 100

Bus: *Mfr./sales expendable process* Fax: (724) 758-4832
  control sensors for steel mills and
  foundries.

● **HERMANN FINCKH MASCHINENFABRIK GMBH & CO.**

Marktstrasse 185, D-72793 Pfullingen, Germany

CEO: Hagen Hutzler, Pres.   Tel: 49-7121-2750

Bus: *Processing equipment for pulp and* Fax: 49-7121-275237   Emp: 200
  paper industry.

FINCKH MACHINERY CORPORATION

2302 Columbia Circle, PO Box 912, Merrimack, NH   03054

CEO: Maurice Lindsay, VP   Tel: (603) 424-4148   %FO: 100

Bus: *Sales/service processing*   Fax: (603) 429-0540   Emp: 4
  equipment for pulp & paper
  industry.

● **DR. ERWIN HETTICH GMBH & CO. / ANTON HETTICH GMBH & CO.**

Vahrenkampstrasse 12-16, D-32278 Kirchlengern, Germany

CEO: Hans-Dieter Jähler, Pres.   Tel: 49-5223-770   Rev: $400

Bus: *Mfr./distribution furniture fittings and* Fax: 49-5223-771202   Emp: 4,000
  furniture accessories.   www.hettich.com

HETTICH AMERICA LP

6225 Shiloh Road, Alpharetta, GA   30005

CEO: Ben Burks, Pres.   Tel: (770) 887-3733   %FO: 100

Bus: *Mfr./distribution quality furniture* Fax: (770) 887-0752   Emp: 70
  hardware.

● **HIRSCHMANN ELECTRONICS GMBH & CO.**
Stuttgarter Str. 45-51, D-72654 Neckartenzlingen, Germany
CEO: Reinhard Sitzmann, Pres. & CEO   Tel: 49-7127-140
Bus: *Mfr. mobile antenna systems stationary*   Fax: 49-7127-141214   Emp: 2,000
receiving system, telecommunication   www.hirschmann.de
equipment, connectors.

HIRSCHMANN ELECTRONICS
30 Hook Mountain Road, Ste. 201, Pinebrook, NJ   07058
CEO: Klaus Egert, Pres.   Tel: (973) 830-2000   %FO: 100
Bus: *Distributor mobile antenna*   Fax: (973) 830-1470   Emp: 45
systems, telecommunication
technology, connectors.

● **HOCHTIEF, AG**
Opernplatz 2, D-45128 Essen, Germany
CEO: Hans-Peter Keitel, CEO   Tel: 49-201-824-0   Rev: $5,125
Bus: *Engaged in design and construction.*   Fax: 49-201-824-2777   Emp: 37,350
www.hochtief.de

THE TURNER CORPORATION
250 West Court Street, Ste. 300 West, Cincinnati, OH   45202
CEO: Roger Baldwin, Mgr.   Tel: (513) 721-4224
Bus: *Engaged in design and*   Fax: (513) 542-8801
construction.

THE TURNER CORPORATION
565 Marriott Drive, Ste. 200, Nashville, TN   37214
CEO: Russ Burns, Pres.   Tel: (615) 231-6300
Bus: *Engaged in design and*   Fax: (615) 231-6301
construction.

THE TURNER CORPORATION
265 Davidson Avenue, Somerset, NJ   08873
CEO: Cliff Tanzler   Tel: (723) 627-8300
Bus: *Engaged in design and*   Fax: (723) 356-1861
construction.

THE TURNER CORPORATION
440 Wheelers Farm Road, Ste. 301, Milford, CT   06460
CEO: John Coutsouridis   Tel: (203) 783-8800
Bus: *Engaged in design and*   Fax: (203) 783-8899
construction.

THE TURNER CORPORATION

555 West Fifth Street, 37th Fl., Los Angeles, CA   90013

CEO: Bill Cody, Mgr.   Tel: (213) 891-3000

Bus: *Engaged in design and*   Fax: (213) 486-9857
     construction.

THE TURNER CORPORATION

100 State Street, Albany, NY   12207

CEO: Carl Stewart, Mgr.   Tel: (518) 432-0277

Bus: *Engaged in design and*   Fax: (518) 432-0279
     construction.

THE TURNER CORPORATION

901 Main St., Ste. 4900, Dallas, TX   75202

CEO: Robert E. Fee, CEO   Tel: (214) 915-9600

Bus: *Engaged in design and*   Fax: (214) 915-9700
     construction.

● **HOERMANN GMBH**

Hauptstrasse 45-47, D-85614 Kirchseeon, Munich, Germany

CEO: Hans Hoermann, Pres.   Tel: 49-8091-520

Bus: *High power warning systems, electric*   Fax: 49-8091-52200
     engineering, swim pools, building   www.hoermann-gmbh.de
     facades.

RAYTEK INC.

PO Box 1820, 1201 Shaffer Road, Santa Cruz, CA   95060-1820

CEO: Cliff Warren, Pres.   Tel: (831) 458-1110   %FO: 50

Bus: *Thermometers and calibration*   Fax: (831) 458-1239
     instruments. (50% ownership).

● **MATTH. HOHNER GMBH**

Postfach 1260, D-78647 Trossingen, Germany

CEO: Dr. Horst Bräuning, CEO   Tel: 49-7425-200

Bus: *Mfr. musical instruments, amplifiers*   Fax: 49-7425-20249
     and accessories.   www.hohner.de

HOHNER INC.

PO Box 15035, Richmond, VA   23227-5035

CEO: Robert W. Cotton, Pres.   Tel: (804) 550-2700   %FO: 100

Bus: *Sale/service musical instruments,*   Fax: (804) 550-2670   Emp: 40
     amplifiers and accessories.

- **H. HOLTKAMP GMBH & CO., KG**
Blumenstrassa 27, Rees 4, D-46459 Haffen, Germany
CEO: Thomas Holtkamp, Pres.   Tel: 49-28-57 2991
Bus: *Produce African violets.*   Fax: 49-28-57 2442   Emp: 450
                                      www.optimara.com

   HOLTKAMP GREENHOUSES INC.
   1501 Lischey Avenue, Nashville, TN   37207
   CEO: Reinhold Holtkamp Sr., Pres.   Tel: (615) 228-2683   %FO: 100
   Bus: *Produce/wholesale African violets.* Fax: (615) 228-5831   Emp: 120

- **PHILIPP HOLZMANN GROUP AG**
Taunusanlage 1, D-60299 Frankfurt am Main, Germany
CEO: Konrad Hinrichs, Chmn.   Tel: 49-69-2621   Rev: $5,496
Bus: *Construction services; architecture,*   Fax: 49-69-262433   Emp: 22,900
engineering, consulting, property   www.philipp-hotzmann.de
management, real estate development
and financing.

   J. A. JONES CONSTRUCTION COMPANY
   7800 Southland Blvd., Ste. 154, Orlando, FL   32809
   CEO: Susan Tosco   Tel: (407) 251-0551   %FO: 100
   Bus: *Engaged in engineering and*   Fax: (407) 251-0554
   construction.

   J. A. JONES CONSTRUCTION COMPANY
   6 East 43rd Street, 6th Fl., New York, NY   10017
   CEO: Alfred T. McNeill, Chmn.   Tel: (212) 916-8900   %FO: 100
   Bus: *Engaged in engineering and*   Fax: (212) 916-8888
   construction.

   J. A. JONES CONSTRUCTION COMPANY
   1395 South Marietta Pkwy., Ste. 910, Marietta, GA   30067
   CEO: Carl Frinzi, Div. Mgr.   Tel: (770) 428-4999   %FO: 100
   Bus: *Engaged in engineering and*   Fax: (770) 428-8930
   construction.

   J. A. JONES INC.
   6060 J. A. Jones Drive, Charlotte, NC   28287
   CEO: Charles T. Davidson, Pres. & CEO Tel: (704) 553-3036   %FO: 100
   Bus: *Project finance.*   Fax: (704) 553-3037   Emp: 13

   J. A. JONES CONSTRUCTION CO
   6000 Fairview at J. A. Jones Drive, Charlotte, NC   28287
   CEO: Charles T Davidson, Pres.   Tel: (704) 553-3000   %FO: 100
   Bus: *Construction.*   Fax: (704) 553-3524   Emp: 1,400

J. A. JONES ENVIRONMENTAL SERVICES

6135 Park South Drive, Ste. 104, Charlotte, NC   28287

CEO: Vald Heiberg III, Pres.　　　Tel: (704) 553-3595　　　%FO: 100

Bus: *Provides Life Cycle Advantage TM* Fax: (704) 553-3599　　　Emp: 100
　　solutions in development,
　　engineering, construction,
　　integrated facility-management,
　　and environmental services.

LOCKWOOD GREENE

11595 North Meridian Street, Ste. 600, Carmel, IN   46032

CEO: J. Austin Hurley　　　Tel: (317) 571-3292　　　%FO: 100

Bus: *Engaged in engineering and*　　　Fax: (317) 571-3292
　　construction.

LOCKWOOD GREENE

PO Box 491, Spartanburg, SC   29304

CEO: Doug Hamer, VP　　　Tel: (864) 578-2000　　　%FO: 100

Bus: *Engaged in engineering and*　　　Fax: (864) 599-4117
　　construction.

LOCKWOOD GREENE ENGINEERS, INC.

PO Box 491, Spartanburg, SC   29304

CEO: Fred M. Brune, CEO　　　Tel: (864) 578-2000　　　%FO: 80

Bus: *Engineering, architecture,*　　　Fax: (864) 599-0436　　　Emp: 1,500
　　consulting.

METRIC CONSTRUCTORS, INC.

6000 Fairview Road, Charlotte, NC   28287

CEO: Timothy Minahan, Pres.　　　Tel: (704) 554-1415　　　%FO: 100

Bus: *Engaged in construction.*　　　Fax: (704) 553-3373

PPM INC.

1127 South Main Street, Society Hill, SC   29593

CEO: Henry B. Moree, Pres.　　　Tel: (843) 378-4700　　　%FO: 100

Bus: *Engaged in contract mechanical*　　　Fax: (843) 378-4339
　　maintenance.

QUEENS PROPERTIES INC.

J. A. Jones Drive, Charlotte, NC   28287

CEO: Richard M. Porter, Pres.　　　Tel: (704) 553-3293　　　%FO: 100

Bus: *Engaged in real estate and*　　　Fax: (704) 553-3286
　　development.

REA CONSTRUCTION
PO Box 32487, Charlotte, NC   28210
CEO: Carey Tate, Pres.   Tel: (704) 553-6500   %FO: 100
Bus: *Engaged in pavement contracting.*   Fax: (704) 553-6598

REGENT PARTNERS
3340 Peachtree Road, Ste. 1500, Atlanta, GA   30326
CEO: David B. Allman, Pres.   Tel: (404) 364-1400   %FO: 100
Bus: *Real estate acquisition and*   Fax: (404) 364-1420   Emp: 30
development, property
management.

VIRTUAL ESI
6100 Fairview Road, Ste. 860, Charlotte, NC   26210
CEO: Dr. Johannes A. Ohlinger, Pres.   Tel: (704) 553-4550   %FO: 100
Bus: *Engaged in engineering and*   Fax: (704) 553-4599
construction.

● HUGO BOSS AG
Dieselstrasse 12, D-72555 Metzingen, Germany
CEO: Werner Baldessarini, Chmn.   Tel: 49-7123-940   Rev: $758
Bus: *Mfr./distribution of designer men's*   Fax: 49-7123-942014   Emp: 2,518
fashions.   www.hugoboss.de

HUGO BOSS USA, INC.
601 West 26th Street, 8th Fl., New York, NY   10001
CEO: Marty Staff, Pres.   Tel: (212) 940-0600   %FO: JV
Bus: *Mfr./distribution of designer men's*   Fax: (212) 840-0615   Emp: 509
fashions.

● HYPO VEREINS BANK
Am Tucherpark 12, D-80311 Munich, Germany
CEO: Dr. Albrecht Schmidt, Chmn.   Tel: 49-89-378-0   Rev: $30,754
Bus: *International commercial and*   Fax: 49-89-378-24083   Emp: 46,170
investment banking and asset   www.hypoverinsbank.de
management services.

HYPO VEREINS BANK
Two Greenwich Plaza, 4th Fl., Greenwich, CT   06830
CEO: Wolfgang Schoellkopf, CEO   Tel: (203) 861-6464   %FO: 100
Bus: *International commercial and*   Fax: (203) 861-6430
investment banking and asset
management services.

HYPO VEREINS BANK
150 East 42nd Street, 32nd Fl., New York, NY 10017
CEO: Stephan Bub, Mng. Dir.   Tel: (212) 672-5311   %FO: 100
Bus: *International commercial and*   Fax: (212) 672-5310   Emp: 100
investment banking and asset
management services.

● **IKA WERKE STAUFEN**
Neumagen Str 27, D-79219 Staufen, Germany
CEO: Rene Steigelmann, CEO   Tel: 49-7633-83198
Bus: *Mfr. laboratory equipment.*   Fax: 49-7633-8310   Emp: 300
www.ika.net

     IKA-WORKS INC.
     2635 North Chase Pkwy., SE, Wilmington, NC 28405
     CEO: Rene Steigelmann, Pres.   Tel: (910) 452-7059   %FO: 100
     Bus: *Mfr./sale lab/process equipment.*   Fax: (910) 452-7693   Emp: 18

● **IKB DEUTSCHE INDUSTRIEBANK AG**
Wilhelm Bötzkes-Straß 1, D-40474 Düsseldorf, Germany
CEO: Alexander von Tippelskirch, CEO   Tel: 49-211-8221-0   Rev: $2,400
Bus: *Provides long-term financing and*   Fax: 49-211-8221-2559   Emp: 1,150
consulting services.   www.ikb.de

     IKB CAPITAL CORPORATION
     555 Madison Avenue, New York, NY 10022
     CEO: Daniel O'Connell   Tel: (212) 485-3600   %FO: 100
     Bus: *Supplies long-term financing and*   Fax: (212) 583-8800
consulting services.

● **IM INTERNATIONALMEDIA AG**
Cuvilliesstrasse 25, D-81679 Munich, Germany
CEO: Antoinette Hiebeler-Hasne, CEO   Tel: 49-89-9810-7100   Rev: $141
Bus: *Engaged in motion picture development*   Fax: 49-89-9810-7199   Emp: 90
and financing.   www.internationalmedia.com

     INTERMEDIA INC.
     8490 Sunset Blvd., 7th Fl., West Hollywood, CA 90069
     CEO: Bill Curbishley   Tel: (310) 777-0007   %FO: 100
     Bus: *Engaged in motion picture*   Fax: (310) 777-0008
development and financing.

• **IMI NORGREN HERION FLUIDTRONIC GMBH & CO.**

Stuttgarter Strasse 120, D-70736 Fellbach, Germany

CEO: Dr. Krumholz, Mgr.   Tel: 49-711-520-9447

Bus: *Mfr. pneumatics, hydraulics,*   Fax: 49-711-520-9532   Emp: 2,500
     automatics, pressure and temperature www.norgren-herion.de
     devices, electric fluid power products,
     process valves.

   HERION USA INC.

   176 Thorn Hill Road, Warrendale, PA   15086

   CEO: Kenneth H. Foster, Pres.   Tel: (724) 776-5577   %FO: 90

   Bus: *Fluid power products, process*   Fax: (724) 776-0310   Emp: 45
     valves; pneumatics, hydraulics,
     automatics, pressure and
     temperature devices.

   NORGREN, INC.

   5400 South Delaware Street, Littleton, CO   80120

   CEO: Terry Weeber   Tel: (303) 794-2611   %FO: 100

   Bus: *Fluid power products, process*   Fax: (303) 794-4871
     valves; pneumatics, hydraulics,
     automatics, pressure and
     temperature devices.

• **INDEX-WERKE GMBH & CO KG HAHN & TESSKY**

Plochinger Strasse 92, D-73730 Esslingen, Germany

CEO: K. Frick, Dir.   Tel: 49-711-31910

Bus: *Mfr. metalworking mach tools, turning* Fax: 49-711-3191587   Emp: 1,200
     automatics.

   INDEX CORPORATION

   829 Bridgeport Avenue, PO Box 233, Shelton, CT   06484

   CEO: Gary Sihler, CEO   Tel: (203) 926-0323   %FO: 100

   Bus: *Sales/service metalworking*   Fax: (203) 926-0476   Emp: 30
     machine tools, turning automatics.

• **INFINEON TECHNOLOGIES AG**

St. Martin Strasse 53, D-81669 Munich, Germany

CEO: Dr. Ulrich Schumacher, CEO   Tel: 49-89-9221-4086   Rev: $4,000

Bus: *Mfr. semiconductors.*   Fax: 49-89-9221-2071   Emp: 25,000
                                            www.infineon.com

   INFINEON TECHNOLOGIES INC.

   1730 North First Street, San Jose, CA   95112

   CEO: Jan du Preez, Pres. & CEO   Tel: (408) 501-6000   %FO: 100

   Bus: *Mfr. semiconductors.*   Fax: (408) 501-6000

• INSTITUT DR. FÖRSTER

Postfach 1564, D-72705 Reutlingen, Germany

CEO: Martin Förster, Chrm.   Tel: 49-7121-140281

Bus: *Mfr. non-destructive testing equipment.*   Fax: 49-7121-140357   Emp: 500

www.foerstergroup.com

FÖRSTER INSTRUMENTS, INC.

140 Industry Drive, RIDC Park West, Pittsburgh, PA   15275-1028

CEO: Robert Shaffer, Pres.   Tel: (412) 788-8976   %FO: 90

Bus: *Mfr./distribution/service non-destructive testing equipment.*   Fax: (412) 788-8984   Emp: 50

• INTERTAINMENT AG

49 Widenmayerstrasse, D-80538 Munich, Germany

CEO: Rudiger Baeres, CEO   Tel: 49-89-21699-211   Rev: $83

Bus: *Engaged in film making and merchandising of movies.*   Fax: 49-89-21699-211   Emp: 30

www.intertainment-ag.de

SIGHT SOUND TECHNOLOGIES, INC.

733 Washington Road, Ste. 400, Mount Lebanon, PA   15228

CEO: Scott Sander, Pres. & CEO   Tel: (412) 341-1001   %FO: 100

Bus: *Engaged in film making and merchandising of movies.*   Fax: (412) 341-2442

• IXOS SOFTWARE AG

Technopark Neukeferloh, Bretonischer Ring 12, D-85630 Grasbrunn, Germany

CEO: Robert Hoog, CEO   Tel: 49-89-46005-0   Rev: $99

Bus: *Mfr. business document management software.*   Fax: 49-89-46005-199   Emp: 970

www.ixos.de

IXOS SOFTWARE, INC.

901 Mariner's Island Blvd., Ste.725, San Mateo, CA   94404

CEO: Rick Pitts   Tel: (650) 294-5800   %FO: 100

Bus: *Mfr. business document management software.*   Fax: (650) 294-5836

• JAGENBERG AG

Postfach 101123, D-40002 Düsseldorf, Germany

CEO: Dieter Niederste-Werbeck, Chmn.   Tel: 49-2131-9901

Bus: *Mfr. machinery for paper mills and paper converting industry.*   Fax: 49-2131-2900   Emp: 2,000

www.jagenberg.com

JAGENBERG INC.

175 Freshwater Blvd., PO Box 1250, Enfield, CT   06083-1250

CEO: Volker Rose, CEO

Tel: (860) 741-2501

%FO: 100

Bus: *Mfr./sale machinery for paper mills & paper converting industry.*

Fax: (860) 741-2508

Emp: 200

• M K JUCHHEIM GMBH & CO

Moltkestrasse 13-31, D-36039 Fulda, Germany

CEO: Bernard Juchheim, Pres.

Tel: 49-661-6003-206

Bus: *Mfr. temperature, pressure and humidity sensors, transmitters, controls and recorders.*

Fax: 49-661-6003-500
www.jumo.de

Emp: 1,900

JUMO PROCESS CONTROL INC.

735 Fox Chase, Coatesville, PA   19320

CEO: Haubold vom Berg, Pres.

Tel: (610) 380-8002

%FO: 100

Bus: *Sale/service temperature, pressure & humidity sensors, transmitters, controls & recorders.*

Fax: (610) 380-8009

Emp: 10

• JUNGHEINRICH AG

Friedrich-Eberrt-Damm 129, D-22047 Hamburg, Germany

CEO: Cletus von Pichler, Chmn.

Tel: 49-40-6948-1228

Rev: $30

Bus: *Mfr. material handling equipment.*

Fax: 49-40-6948-1308
www.jungheinrich.de

Emp: 9,250

JUNGHEINRICH LIFT TRUCK CORP. USA

5701 Eastport Boulevard, Richmond, VA   23231

CEO: Cletus von Pichler, CEO

Tel: (804) 737-6084

%FO: 100

Bus: *Mfr./sales material handling equipment.*

Fax: (804) 737-6136

• KALENBORN KALPROTECT

Postfach 31, D-53558 Vettelschoss, Germany

CEO: Michael W. Rokitta, Dir.

Tel: 49-2645-180

Bus: *Mfr. abrasion and corrosion-resistant linings and pipelines.*

Fax: 49-2645-18180
www.kalenborn.de

Emp: 220

ABRESIST CORPORATION

5541 N. State Road 13, PO Box 38, Urbana, IN   46990

CEO: Joe Accetta, Pres.

Tel: (219) 774-3327

%FO: 100

Bus: *Mfr./sale/service abrasion and corrosion-resistant linings and pipelines.*

Fax: (219) 774-8188

Emp: 35

● **KAMPF GMBH & CO MASCHINENFABRIK**

Meuhlenerstrasse 36-42, D-51674 Wiehl, Germany

CEO: H. Merch, CEO   Tel: 49-2262 810

Bus: *Mfr./sale machines for paper, film and*   Fax: 49-2262 81208   Emp: 550
foil converting industry.

KAMPF MACHINERY CORP. OF AMERICA

175 Freshwater Boulevard, Enfield, CT   06083

CEO: Peter Hoelzel, Div. Mgr.   Tel: (860) 253-9660   %FO: 100

Bus: *Sale/service machines for paper,*   Fax: (860) 253-9662   Emp: 50
film & foil converting industry.

● **KISTERS MACHINENBAU GMBH**

Boschstrasse 1-3, D-47533 Kleve, Germany

CEO: Jean Marti, Mng. Dir.   Tel: 49-28-215030

Bus: *Mfr. packaging equipment.*   Fax: 49-28-2126110   Emp: 500

www.kisters.com

KISTERS KAYAT INC.

4100 US Highway 1 South, Edgewater, FL   32141

CEO: Andrew Neagle, Pres.   Tel: (904) 424-0101   %FO: 100

Bus: *Sales, service and spare parts for*   Fax: (904) 424-0266   Emp: 10
packaging equipment.

● **C. KLINGSPOR GMBH**

Huettenstrasse 36, D-35708 Haiger, Germany

CEO: Walter Klingspor, Chmn.   Tel: 49-2773-9220

Bus: *Mfr. coated & bonded abrasives.*   Fax: 49-2773-816186

www.klingspor.de

KLINGSPOR ABRASIVES INC.

2555 Tate Blvd., SE, Hickory, NC   28602-1445

CEO: Christoph Klingspor, Pres.   Tel: (828) 322-3030   %FO: 100

Bus: *Mfr. coated & bonded abrasives.*   Fax: (828) 322-6060   Emp: 150

● **KLOCKNER & CO. AG, SUB. E.ON AG**

Neudorfer Strasse 3-5, D-47057 Duisburg, Germany

CEO: Erhard Schipporeit, Chmn.   Tel: 49-203-307-0   Rev: $5,000

Bus: *Distributes steel and metal products.*   Fax: 49-203-307-5000   Emp: 11,300

www.kloeckner.de

NAMASCO CORPORATION

3212 East 19th Court, Des Moines, IA   50313

CEO: Dave Doty   Tel: (515) 265-5351   %FO: 100

Bus: *Distributes steel and metal*   Fax: (515) 265-3933
products.

NAMASCO CORPORATION
5775-C Glenridge Drive, Ste. 110, Atlanta, GA 30328

CEO: Barney O'Brien   Tel: (404) 267-8800   %FO: 100

Bus: *Distributes steel and metal*   Fax: (404) 267-8870
products.

● KLÖCKNER MERCATOR MASCHINENBAU GMBH
KlöcknerstraBe 299, D-47057 Duisburg, Germany

CEO: Klöckner Werke, Chrm.   Tel: 49-203-396

Bus: *Mfr. pharmaceutical and food*   Fax: 49-203-396-3535
equipment, print/stationary materials,   www.klockner.com
packaging materials/equipment.

KLÖCKNER-PENTAPLAST OF AMERICA, INC.
Klöckner Road, PO Box 500, Gordonsville, VA 22942

CEO: Tom Goeke, Pres.   Tel: (540) 832-3600   %FO: 100

Bus: *Sales/distribution of*   Fax: (540) 832-5656   Emp: 700
pharmaceutical and food
equipment, print/stationary
materials, packaging
materials/equipment.

● KLOCKNER-WERKE AG
Klöcknerstraße 29, D-47057 Duisburg, Germany

CEO: Dr. Heinz-Ludwig Schmitz, Chmn.   Tel: 49-203-396-3245   Rev: $4,702

Bus: *Mfr. automotive supplier, rigid films,*   Fax: 49-203-396-3535   Emp: 11,500
filming and packaging technology.   www.kloecknerwerke.de

KLOCKNER CAPITAL CORPORATION
PO Box 750, Gordonsville, VA 22942

CEO: Harry van Beek, Pres.   Tel: (540) 832-3400   %FO: 100

Bus: *Mfr. fineblanked precision*   Fax: (540) 832-7000
components and assemblies.

● KLOECKNER INDUSTRIE-ANLAGEN GMBH
Neudorfer Strasse 3-5, D-4100 Duisburg, Germany

CEO: Hans Kathage, Mng. Dir.   Tel: 49-203-309-0

Bus: *Engaged in flue-gas cleaning and water*   Fax: 49-203-309-2028
treatment.   www.kloeckner-ina.com

KLOCKNER INA INDUSTRIAL INSTALLATIONS INC.
775 Park Avenue, Ste. 320, Huntington, NY 11743

CEO: Klaus Brosig, VP   Tel: (516) 271-3160   %FO: 100

Bus: *General contractor for turnkey*   Fax: (516) 271-3465
industrial plants.

● **KLÜBER LUBRICATION MUNCHEN KG**

Geisenhausenerstr. 7, D-81379 Munich, Germany

CEO: Hanno D. Wentzler, Pres. & CEO   Tel: 49-89-7876-0   Rev: $235

Bus: *Mfr. of synthetic lubricants, lime-scale*   Fax: 49-89-7876-333   Emp: 1,350
dissolvers, and oil/water separators.   www.kluber.com

    KLUBER LUBRICATION NORTH AMERICA, INC.

    54 Wentworth Avenue, Londonderry, NH   03053

    CEO: Bernard Greene   Tel: (603) 434-7704   %FO: 100

    Bus: *Mfr. of synthetic lubricants, lime-*   Fax: (603) 434-8046
    scale dissolvers, and oil/water
    separators.

    KLUBER LUBRICATION NORTH AMERICA, INC.

    512 West Burlington Ave., Ste. 208, LaGrange, IL   60525

    CEO: Steve Vidmer   Tel: (708) 482-9730   %FO: 100

    Bus: *Mfr. of synthetic lubricants, lime-*   Fax: (708) 482-9407
    scale dissolvers, and oil/water
    separators.

    KLUBER LUBRICATION NORTH AMERICA, INC.

    572 East Green Street, Suite 208, Pasadena, CA   91101

    CEO: Burt Smith   Tel: (626) 795-5455   %FO: 100

    Bus: *Mfr. of synthetic lubricants, lime-*   Fax: (626) 795-6064
    scale dissolvers, and oil/water
    separators.

    KLUBER LUBRICATION NORTH AMERICA, INC.

    233 North Main Street, Ste. 300A, Greenville, SC   29601

    CEO: Ed Wiseman   Tel: (864) 380-2522   %FO: 100

    Bus: *Mfr. of synthetic lubricants, lime-*   Fax: (864) 467-0740
    scale dissolvers, and oil/water
    separators.

    SUMMIT INDUSTRIAL PRODUCTS INC.

    PO Box 131359, Tyler, TX   75707

    CEO: Joe Garrett   Tel: (903) 534-8021   %FO: 100

    Bus: *Mfr. of synthetic lubricants, lime-*   Fax: (903) 581-4376
    scale dissolvers, and oil/water
    separators.

● **KOLBUS GMBH + CO. KG**

Osnabrücker Strasse 77, D-32363 Rahden, Germany

CEO: Oliver Buchmann   Tel: 49-5771-710

Bus: *Mfr. bookbinding machinery.*   Fax: 49-5771-71333   Emp: 1,000
                    www.kolbus.com

KILBUS AMERICA, INC.
PO Box 510, Wykoff, NJ 07481

CEO: B. Shafer   Tel: (201) 848-8300   %FO: 100

Bus: *Sales/distribution of bookbinding machinery.*   Fax: (201) 848-0368   Emp: 50

● KOMET PRÄZISIONSWERKZEUGE ROBERT BREUNING GMBH
Postfach 13 61, D-74351 Besigheim, Germany

CEO: Peter Höger, CEO   Tel: 49-7143-37-30   Rev: $133

Bus: *Mfr. cutting tools.*   Fax: 49-7143-37-32-33   Emp: 1,370

www.komet.de

KOMET OF AMERICA, INC.
6804 19 1/2 Mile Road, Sterling Heights, MI 48314-1404

CEO: Tom Kowalec, Mgr.   Tel: (810) 997-0588

Bus: *Mfr./sales cutting tools.*   Fax: (810) 997-0859

KOMET OF AMERICA, INC.
2050 Mitchell Boulevard, Schaumburg, IL 60193

CEO: Erik Koik, Pres. & CEO   Tel: (847) 923-8400   %FO: 100

Bus: *Mfr./sales cutting tools.*   Fax: (847) 923-0638   Emp: 250

● KONTRON EMBEDDED COMPUTERS AG
Oskar-von-Miller-Straße 1, D-85386 Eching, Germany

CEO: Hannes Niederhauser, Pres. & CEO   Tel: 49-81-65-77-666   Rev: $119

Bus: *Provides embedded computing solutions.*   Fax: 49-81-65-77-333   Emp: 865

www.kontron.com

FIELDWORKS
7631 Anagram Drive, Eden Prairie, MN 55344

CEO: Pierre McMaster   Tel: (952) 974-7000   %FO: 100

Bus: *Provides embedded computing solutions.*   Fax: (952) 949-2791

KONTRON MOBILE COMPUTING INC.
7631 Anagram Drive, Eden Prairie, MN 55344

CEO: Thomas Sparrvik, Pres.   Tel: (952) 974-7000   %FO: 1

Bus: *Provides embedded computing solutions.*   Fax: (952) 949-2791

● KRAUSS-MAFFEI KUNSTSTOFFTECHNIK GMBH
Krauss-Maffei-Straße 2, D-80997 Munich, Germany

CEO: Dr. Hans Wobbe   Tel: 49-89-88-990   Rev: $418

Bus: *Mfr. plastics machinery, process equipment, armored tanks, locomotives, high-speed trains.*   Fax: 49-89-88-99-3092   Emp: 2,036

www.krauss-maffei.de

KRAUSS-MAFFEI CORPORATION
7095 Industrial Road, PO Box 6270, Florence, KY 41022-6270

CEO: Sandra Winter, EVP	Tel: (859) 283-0200	%FO: 100
Bus: *Mfr./assembly/sale/service plastics machinery, process equipment.*	Fax: (859) 283-9631	Emp: 115

• H KRIEGHOFF GMBH
Postfach 2610, Boschstrasse 22, D-89016 Ulm, Germany

CEO: Walter Brass, Pres.	Tel: 49-731-401820	
Bus: *Mfr. hunting and sporting firearms.*	Fax: 49-731-4018270	Emp: 95
	www.krieghoff.de	

KRIEGHOFF INTL, INC.
PO Box 549, 7528 Easton Road, Ottsville, PA 18942

CEO: Jim Hollingsworth, Pres.	Tel: (610) 847-5173	%FO: JV
Bus: *Importer/distributor hunting and sporting firearms.*	Fax: (610) 847-8691	Emp: 13

• KROHNE MESSTECHNIK GMBH & CO KG
Ludwig-Krohne-Strasse 5, D-47058 Duisburg, Germany

CEO: Kristian Dubbick, Chmn.	Tel: 49-203-3011	
Bus: *Mfr. electromechanical & electronic flow and liquid level measurement equipment.*	Fax: 49-203-301380 www.krohne.com	

KROHNE AMERICA INC.
7 Dearborn Road, Peabody, MA 01960

CEO: Jack Evans, Pres.	Tel: (978) 535-6060	%FO: 100
Bus: *Mfr. electromechanical and electronic flow and liquid level measurement equipment.*	Fax: (978) 535-1720	Emp: 70

• KRONE AG
Beeskowdamm 3-11, D-14167 Berlin, Germany

CEO: W. Schnider, Chmn.	Tel: 49-30-8453-1729	Rev: $600
Bus: *Mfr. telecommunications equipment.*	Fax: 49-30-8453-1355 www.krone.com	Emp: 3,300

KRONE, INC.
6950 S. Tucson Way, Suite R, Englewood, CO 80112

CEO: Klaus Remy, VP & Gen. Mgr.	Tel: (303) 790-2619	%FO: 100
Bus: *Mfr. telecommunications equipment.*	Fax: (303) 790-2117	Emp: 130

● **KRONES AG**

Böhmerwaldstraße 5,D-93068 Neutraubling, Germany

CEO: Volker Kronseder, CEO — Tel: 49-9401-70-0 — Rev: $1,015

Bus: *Mfr. labeling, bottle-filling and packaging equipment.* — Fax: 49-9401-702488 — Emp: 8,000
www.krones.de

   KRONES INC.

   9600 S. 58th Street, PO Box 32100, Franklin, WI 53132-0100

   CEO: Bernhard Baumgartner, CEO — Tel: (414) 421-5650 — %FO: 100

   Bus: *Labeling, bottle-filling and packaging equipment.* — Fax: (414) 421-2222

● **KRUPP BILSTEIN GMBH & CO., DIV. THYSSEN KRUPP**

August-Bilstein, Strasse 4, PO Box 1151, D-58240 Ennepetal, Germany

CEO: Hans Bohlman, Pres. — Tel: 49-23-339870

Bus: *Mfr. shock absorbers, car jacks and window hardware.* — Fax: 49-23-3398-77253 — Emp: 1,900
www.bilstein.de

   KRUPP BILSTEIN OF AMERICA INC.

   8845 Rehco Road, San Diego, CA 92121

   CEO: Micke Poucher, CEO — Tel: (619) 453-7723 — %FO: 100

   Bus: *Sales/distribution of shock absorbers.* — Fax: (619) 453-0770

● **KRUPP POLYSIUS AG, DIV. THYSSEN KRUPP**

Graf-Galen-Strase 17, D-59269 Beckum, Germany

CEO: Tyark Allers, Chmn. — Tel: 49-2525-99-0

Bus: *Mfr. cement machinery and equipment.* — Fax: 49-2525-99-2100
www.krupp.com

   KRUPP POLYSIUS CORPORATION

   180 Interstate North Parkway, Atlanta, GA 30339-2194

   CEO: Ron Parks, Mgr. — Tel: (770) 955-3660 — %FO: 100

   Bus: *Mfr. cement machinery and equipment.* — Fax: (770) 955-8789

● **KTR KUPPLUNGSTECHNIK GMBH**

Postfach 1763, D-48407 Rheine, Germany

CEO: Rainer Reichert, CEO — Tel: 49-5971-798445

Bus: *Mfr. mechanical power transmission equipment.* — Fax: 49-5971-798450 — Emp: 350
www.ktr.com

KTR CORPORATION

PO Box 9065, 122 Anchor Road, Michigan City, IN   46361

CEO: James C. Scott, Pres.	Tel: (219) 872-9100	%FO: 100
Bus: *Sale mechanical power transmission equipment.*	Fax: (219) 872-9150	Emp: 20

● LAMBDA PHYSIK AG

Hans-Böckler-Straße 12, D-37079 Göttingen, Germany

CEO: Dirk Basting	Tel: 49-551-69-38-0	Rev: $88
Bus: *Mfr. lasers for industrial, scientific, and medical applications.*	Fax: 49-551-68-69-1 www.lambdaphysik.com	Emp: 330

LAMBDA PHYSIK USA INC.

3201 West Commercial Blvd., Ft. Lauderdale, FL   3309

CEO: Mike Heglin	Tel: (954) 486-1500	%FO: 100
Bus: *Sales of lasers for industrial, scientific, and medical applications.*	Fax: (954) 486-1501	

● LANDESBANK BADEN-WURTTEMBERG

Am Hauptbahnhof 2, D-70173 Stuttgart, Germany

CEO: Werner Schmidt, Chmn.	Tel: 49-711-127-0	Rev: $15,524
Bus: *International commercial bank.*	Fax: 49-711-127-3278 www.landesbank-bw.de	Emp: 9,465

LANDESBANK BADEN-WURTTEMBERG

535 Madison Avenue, 6th Fl., New York, NY   10022

CEO: Franz Waas, Mgr.	Tel: (212) 584-1700	%FO: 100
Bus: *International commercial bank.*	Fax: (212) 584-1700	

● LANDESBANK HESSEN-THÜRINGEN GIROZENTRALE

Neue Mainzer Strasse 52-58, D-60311 Frankfurt am Main, Germany

CEO: Walter Scharfer, Chmn.	Tel: 49-69-913201	
Bus: *International commercial banking services*	Fax: 49-69-291517 www.helaba.de	

LANDESBANK HESSEN-THÜRINGEN

420 Fifth Avenue, 24th Fl., New York, NY   10018

CEO: Hans-Christian Ritter, EVP	Tel: (212) 703-5200	%FO: 100
Bus: *International commercial banking services.*	Fax: (212) 703-5256	Emp: 30

- **LANGENSCHEIDT KG**
Neusser Strasse 3, D-80807 Munich, Germany
CEO: Andreas Langenscheidt, Chmn.   Tel: 49-89-36-0960
Bus: *Publisher of maps.*   Fax: 49-89-36-096258   Emp: 900
                                           www.langenscheidt.de

  ADC MAPS INC.
  6440 General Green Way, Alexandria, VA   22312
  CEO: Mark Turcotte, EVP   Tel: (703) 750-0510   %FO: 100
  Bus: *Mfr./sale/distribution maps.*   Fax: (703) 750-3092   Emp: 100

  AMERICAN MAP CORPORATION
  46-35 54th Road, Maspeth, NY   11378
  CEO: Richard Strug, Dir.   Tel: (718) 784-0055   %FO: 100
  Bus: *Mfr./sale/distribution maps.*   Fax: (718) 784-0640   Emp: 50

  ARROW MAP INC.
  50 Scotland Blvd., Bridgewater, MA   02324
  CEO: Thomas Folkers, VP   Tel: (508) 279-1177   %FO: 100
  Bus: *Mfr./sale/distribution maps.*   Fax: (508) 279-0073   Emp: 15

  CREATIVE SALES CORPORATION
  780 West Belden, Ste. A, Madison, IL   60101
  CEO: Paula Bregman, VP   Tel: (630) 458-1500   %FO: 100
  Bus: *Publishers.*   Fax: (630) 458-1511   Emp: 10

  HAGSTROM MAP COMPANY, INC.
  46-35 54th Road, Maspeth, NY   11378
  CEO: Richard Strug, Mgr.   Tel: (718) 784-0055   %FO: 100
  Bus: *Mfr./sale/distribution maps.*   Fax: (718) 784-0640   Emp: 30

  LANGENSCHEIDT PUBLISHERS INC.
  46-35 54th Road, Maspeth, NY   11378
  CEO: Stuart Dolgins, Pres.   Tel: (718) 784-0055   %FO: 100
  Bus: *Publishers.*   Fax: (718) 784-0640   Emp: 15

  TRAKKER MAP INC. NATIONWIDE DISTRIBUTORS INC.
  12027 SW 117th Court, Miami, FL   33186
  CEO: Jim Moyer, VP   Tel: (305) 255-4485   %FO: 100
  Bus: *Mfr./sale/distribution maps.*   Fax: (305) 232-5257   Emp: 20

- **LECHLER GMBH & CO KG**
Ulmerstrasse 128, Postfach 1323, D-72555 Metzingen, Germany
CEO: Walter Lechler, Pres.   Tel: 49-7123-9620
Bus: *Mfr. industrial nozzles and spray*   Fax: 49-7123-962444   Emp: 200
    equipment.   www.lechler.de

LECHLER INC.
445 Kautz Road, St. Charles, IL   60174-5301
CEO: Ralph Fish, Pres.   Tel: (630) 377-6611   %FO: 100
Bus: *Mfr./distribution industrial nozzles* Fax: (630) 377-6657   Emp: 60
      & spray equipment.

● **LEHMANN & VOSS & CO**
Alsterufer 19, D-20354 Hamburg, Germany
CEO: Dr. Dirk Thomsen, CEO   Tel: 49-40 441-970
Bus: *Mfr./distribution specialty chemicals.* Fax: 49-40 441-97219
                                            www.lehvoss.de

    LEHVOSS CORP OF AMERICA
    700 Canal Street, Stamford, CT   06902
    CEO: Joachim Hogenow, Pres.   Tel: (203) 328-3736   %FO: 100
    Bus: *Distributor/service sourcing for*   Fax: (203) 328-3738
       parent company, technology
       transfer.

● **LEICA CAMERA, INC.**
Oskar Barnack, Strasse 11, D-35606 Solms, Germany
CEO: H. P. Cohn, Chmn.   Tel: 49-6442-208-450   Rev: $180
Bus: *Manufacturer of high quality camera* Fax: 49-6442-208-455   Emp: 1,600
      equipment and supplies.   www.leica-camera.com

    LEICA CAMERA INC.
    156 Ludlow Avenue, Northvale, NJ   07647
    CEO: David Elwell   Tel: (201) 767-7500   %FO: 100
    Bus: *Sales, distribution and parts for* Fax: (201) 767-8666
       Leica camera equipment.

● **GEBR LEITZ GMBH & CO**
Leitzstrasse 2, Postfach 1229, D-73443 Oberkochen, Germany
CEO: Dieter Brucklacher, CEO   Tel: 49-7364-9500
Bus: *Mfr. woodworking tooling.*   Fax: 49-7364-950662   Emp: 2,400
                                            www.leitz.org

    LEITZ TOOLING SYSTEMS INC.
    4301 East Paris Avenue SE, Grand Rapids, MI   49512
    CEO: Terry Jacks, Pres.   Tel: (616) 698-7010   %FO: 100
    Bus: *Mfr./sale/service woodworking*   Fax: (616) 698-9270   Emp: 70
       tooling.

• LINDE AG

Abraham-Lincoln-Strasse 21, D-65189 Wiesbaden, Germany

CEO: Gerhard Full, Chmn.

Bus: *Holding company. engineering & contracting; material handling, refrigeration, and industrial gases.*

Tel: 49-611-770-0
Fax: 49-611-770-269
www.linde.de

Rev: $7,957
Emp: 47,000

HOLOX, INC.

1500 Indian Trail Road, Ste. C, Norcross, GA   30093-6100

CEO: Brian Haley, Pres.

Bus: *Pyrolysis, steam reforming and refinery, furnaces for the chemical, petrochemical and refining industries.*

Tel: (770) 925-4640
Fax: (770) 925-4966

%FO: 100

LINDE HYDRAULICS CORPORATION

5089 Western Reserve Road, Ste. C, Canfield, OH   44406-0082

CEO: Louis Kasper, Pres.

Bus: *Mfr. forklift trucks.*

Tel: (330) 533-6801
Fax: (330) 533-6893

%FO: 100

LINDE LIFT TRUCK CORP.

2450 West Fifth North Street, Summerville, SC   29483

CEO: Mitch Milovich, Pres.

Bus: *Pyrolysis, steam reforming and refinery, furnaces for the chemical, petrochemical and refining industries.*

Tel: (843) 875-8000
Fax: (843) 875-8329

%FO: 100

LOTEPRO CORPORATION

115 Stevens Avenue, Valhalla, NY   10595

CEO: Dr. Hans Kistenmacher, Pres.

Bus: *Engineering services, pyrolysis, steam reforming and refinery, furnaces for the chemical, petrochemical and refining industries.*

Tel: (914) 747-3500
Fax: (914) 747-3422

%FO: 100
Emp: 130

THE PRO-QUIP CORPORATION

8522 East 61st Street, Tulsa, OK   74133

CEO: John Brandon, Pres.

Bus: *Design/manufacture industrial gas systems.*

Tel: (918) 250-8522
Fax: (918) 250-6915

%FO: 100

SCIENTIFIC DESIGN COMPANY, INC.
49 Industrial Avenue, Little Ferry, NJ   07643

CEO: Joseph V. Procelli, Pres. & CEO	Tel: (201) 641-0500	%FO: 100
Bus: *Design/manufacture industrial gas systems.*	Fax: (201) 641-6986	

SELES FLUID PROCESSING CORPORATION
5 Sentry Pkwy East, Ste. 204, Blue Bell, PA   19422

CEO: Steve Bertone, Pres.	Tel: (610) 834-0300	%FO: 100
Bus: *Pyrolysis, steam reforming and refinery, furnaces for the chemical, petrochemical and refining industries.*	Fax: (610) 834-0473	Emp: 90

● LION BIOSCIENCE AG
Im Neuenheimer Feld 515-157, D-69120 Heidelberg, Germany

CEO: Klaus J. Sprockamp, COO	Tel: 49-6221-4038-0	Rev: $21
Bus: *Engaged in biotechnology for drug development.*	Fax: 49-6221-4038-301 www.lionbioscience.com	Emp: 440

LION BIOSCIENCE INC.
9880 Campus Point Drive, San Diego, CA   92121

CEO: Dr. Rudolph Potenzone, CEO	Tel: (858) 410-6500	%FO: 100
Bus: *Engaged in biotechnology for drug development.*	Fax: (858) 410-6501	

LION BIOSCIENCE INC.
141 Portland Street, 10th Fl., Cambridge, MA   02139

CEO: Dr. Reinhard Schneider, CEO	Tel: (617) 245-5400	%FO: 100
Bus: *Engaged in biotechnology for drug development.*	Fax: (617) 245-5401	

● LISEGA GMBH
PO Box 1357, D-27393 Zeven, Germany

CEO: Hans Hardtke, Pres.	Tel: 49-42-8171-3240	
Bus: *Mfr. equipment, piping supports, hangers.*	Fax: 49-42-8171-3214 www.lisega.de	Emp: 450

LISEGA USA INC.
375 Lisega Boulevard, Newport, TN   37821

CEO: James R. Curran	Tel: (423) 625-2000	%FO: 100
Bus: *Sale/service equipment, piping supports, hangers.*	Fax: (423) 625-9009	Emp: 90

- **EDUARD LOEHLE SEN GMBH**
Stoeckachstrasse 11, D-70191 Stuttgart, Germany
CEO: Thomas Pfisterer, Mng. Dir.   Tel: 49-711-282041
Bus: *International moving, crating, shipping.* Fax: 49-711-2868329   Emp: 45

> **KNOPF & LOEHLE INC.**
> 3211 Industry Drive, North Charleston, SC 29418
> CEO: Siegfried J. Zarwell, Pres.   Tel: (843) 760-2501   %FO: JV
> Bus: *International moving, crating,*   Fax: (843) 760-2503   Emp: 5
> *shipping.*

- **LTS LOHMANN THERAPEI SYSTEME AG, SUB. LOHMANN GROUP**
Lohmannstr. 2, D-56626 Andernach, Germany
CEO: Dr. Peter Barth, Mng. Dir.   Tel: 49-2632-99-0   Rev: $500
Bus: *Engaged in development and production* Fax: 49-2632-99-2200   Emp: 3,000
of transdermal therapeutic systems.   www.ltslohmann.de

> **LOHMANN THERAPY SYSTEMS, INC.**
> 21 Henderson Drive, West Caldwell, NJ 07006
> CEO: Patrick Walters, CEO   Tel: (973) 575-5170   %FO: 100
> Bus: *Engaged in development and*   Fax: (973) 575-5174
> *production of transdermal*
> *therapeutic systems.*

- **LTU GROUP**
Flughafen Düsseldorf, Halle 8 D-40474 Düsseldorf, Germany
CEO: Peter Frankhauser, CEO   Tel: 49-211-941-8888   Rev: $493
Bus: *Commercial air transport services.*   Fax: 49-211-941-8881   Emp: 826
www.ltu.com

> **LTU CARGO c/o DITCO PACIFIC**
> 6033 West Century Blvd., Ste. 1190, Los Angeles, CA 90045
> CEO: Mark Waldner   Tel: (310) 645-7551   %FO: 100
> Bus: *International commercial air*   Fax: (310) 645-0727
> *transport services.*

> **LTU CARGO DIAMOND AIR FREIGHT**
> PO Box 521935, Miami, FL 33152
> CEO: Carole Lozano   Tel: (305) 870-9555   %FO: 100
> Bus: *International commercial air*   Fax: (305) 870-0880
> *transport services.*

• THE MAN GROUP GMBH

Ungererstraße 69, D-80805 Munich, Germany

CEO: Dr. E. H. Rudolf Rupprecht, Chmn.	Tel: 49-89-36098-272	Rev: $7,524
Bus: *Mfr. commercial vehicles, industrial services and equipment, printing machines and diesel engines.*	Fax: 49-89-36098-453 www.man.de	Emp: 76,604

FERROSTAAL INC.

16510 North Chase Drive, Houston, TX   77060

CEO: Wilfried Von Bulow, Pres.	Tel: (281) 999-9995	%FO: 100
Bus: *Engaged in construction and contracting, industrial equipment and systems and steel trading and logistics.*	Fax: (281) 878-0767	

MAN CAPITAL CORPORATION

17 State Street, 18th Fl., New York, NY   10004

CEO: Claus Windelev, Pres.	Tel: (212) 509-4549	%FO: 100
Bus: *U.S. holding company engaged in corporate and financial services.*	Fax: (212) 269-2854	Emp: 1,500

MAN ROLAND INC.

800 East Oak Hill Drive, Westmont, IL   60559

CEO: Heigl Schmidt-Liermann, CEO	Tel: (630) 920-2000	%FO: 100
Bus: *Mfr. printing presses.*	Fax: (630) 920-2457	

• MANNESMANN AG, SUB. VODAFONE

Mannesmannufer 2, Postfach 103641, D-40027 Düsseldorf, Germany

CEO: Julian Michael Horn-Smith, Chmn.	Tel: 49-211-820-0	Rev: $23,428
Bus: *Provides digital mobile phones, industrial machinery, plant construction, automotive assemblies, pumps, instruments, construction equipment, & printers.*	Fax: 49-211-820-1846 www.mannesmann.com	Emp: 130,860

DEMAG CORP.

9871 Highway 78, Ladson, SC   29456

CEO: Art Gilford, Mgr.	Tel: (843) 572-9311	%FO: 100
Bus: *Mfr. mobile cranes.*	Fax: (843) 569-0944	

DEMAG DELAVAL TURBOMACHINERY CORP.

840 Nottingham Way, Trenton, NJ   05650

CEO: Donal Maloney, Pres.	Tel: (609) 890-5000	%FO: 100
Bus: *Mfr. turbo machinery compressors.*	Fax: (609) 890-9180	

KRAUSS-MAFFEI CORPORATION

7095 Industrial Road, PO Box 6270, Florence, KY   41042-6270

CEO: Sandra Winter, EVP   Tel: (606) 283-0200   %FO: 100

Bus: *Plastics technology, process plant*   Fax: (606) 283-0291
and equipment, transport
engineering. Surface treatment
technology. automation
technology and defense
engineering.

MANNESMANN CORP

450 Park Avenue, 24th Floor, New York, NY   10022-2669

CEO: Peter Prinz Wittgenstein, Pres.   Tel: (212) 826-0040   %FO: 100

Bus: *Holding company, U.S.*   Fax: (212) 826-0074   Emp: 6,000
headquarters.

MANNESMANN DEMAG CORP.

Airport Office Park, Bldg. 5, Corapolis, PA   15108-4744

CEO: Keith Ascough, Pres.   Tel: (412) 269-5600   %FO: 100

Bus: *Mfr. cranes and components.*   Fax: (412) 269-5526

MANNESMANN DEMATIC RAPISTAN CORPORATION

507 Plymouth Avenue NE, Grand Rapids, MI   49505

CEO: Pete Metros, Pres.   Tel: (616) 451-6200   %FO: 100

Bus: *Mfr. conveyor systems, automated*   Fax: (616) 451-6425
guided vehicles and materials
handling equipment.

MANNESMANN PIPE & STEEL CORPORATION

1990 Post Oak Blvd, 18th Fl., Houston, TX   77056

CEO: Murat Askin, Mgr.   Tel: (713) 960-1900   %FO: 100

Bus: *Mfr. rolled steel products for*   Fax: (713) 960-1063
industry.

MANNESMANN REXROTH CORPORATION

5150 Prairie Stone Parkway, Hoffman Estates, IL   60192

CEO: John Kowal, Mgr.   Tel: (847) 645-3600   %FO: 100

Bus: *Mfr. hydraulic and pneumatic*   Fax: (847) 645-6201
system and equipment.

NETSTAL MACHINERY, INC.

20 Authority Drive, Fitchburg, MA   01420-6017

CEO: Werner Christinger, Pres.   Tel: (978) 345-9400   %FO: 100

Bus: *Plastics technology services.*   Fax: (978) 345-6153

SACHS NORTH AMERICA

909 Crocker Road, Westlake, OH   44145

CEO: John Edwards, Pres. Tel: (440) 871-4890 %FO: 100

Bus: *Distributes auto parts: clutches* Fax: (440) 871-6904
and shock absorbers.

STABILUS

1201 Tulip Drive, Gastonia, NC   28052

CEO: David Rigneson, Pres. Tel: (704) 865-7444 %FO: 100

Bus: *Mfr. industrial machinery; gas* Fax: (704) 810-3651
springs.

VDO NORTH AMERICA CORPORATION

789 Chicago Road, Troy, MI   48083

CEO: Ronald L. Marsiglio, Pres. Tel: (248) 583-1234 %FO: 100

Bus: *Mfr. control/information* Fax: (248) 593-2391
systems/sensors for auto industry.

● **MASCHINENFABRIK NIEHOFF GMBH & CO KG**

Postfach 1289, D-91124 Schwabach, Germany

CEO: Heinz Rockenhaeuser, Pres. Tel: 49-9122-9770

Bus: *Mfr. machinery and equipment for non-* Fax: 49-9122-977155 Emp: 580
ferrous wire and cable industry. www.niehoff.de

NIEHOFF ENDEX, INC.

One Mallard Court, Swedesboro, NJ   08085

CEO: Helmut Berthold, Pres. Tel: (609) 467-4884 %FO: 100

Bus: *Sale/service machinery &* Fax: (609) 467-0584 Emp: 12
equipment for non-ferrous wire &
cable industry, distribution
machinery & equipment for steel
wire & cable industry.

● **KARL MAYER TEXTILMASCHINENFABRIK GMBH**

Bruhlstrasse 25, D-63179 Obertshausen, Germany

CEO: Karl Mayer Tel: 49-6104-4020

Bus: *Mfr. warp knitting machinery and parts,* Fax: 49-6104-43574 Emp: 3,000
warping equipment. www.karlmayer.de

MAYER TEXTILE MACHINE CORPORATION

310 North Chimney Rock Road, Greensboro, NC   27409

CEO: M. Burke Tel: (336) 294-1572 %FO: 100

Bus: *Mfr./distribution warp knitting* Fax: (336) 854-0251
machinery, parts and warping
equipment.

MAYER TEXTILE MACHINE CORPORATION
310 Brighton Road, PO Box 1240, Clifton, NJ 07012

CEO: E. Dombrowsky	Tel: (973) 773-3350	%FO: 100
Bus: *Mfr./distribution warp knitting machinery, parts and warping equipment.*	Fax: (973) 473-3463	Emp: 140

● **MELITTA BENTZ KG**
Marienstrasse 88, D-54310 Minden, Germany

CEO: J. Bentz, Chmn.	Tel: 49-571-40460	Rev: $1,050
Bus: *Mfr./marketing coffee & coffee related products; food preparation/preservation products; convenient products.*	Fax: 49-571-4046499 www.melitta.de	Emp: 4,588

EUROPEAN COFFEE CLASSICS, INC.
1401 Berlin Road, Cherry Hill, NJ 08003

CEO: Victor Altadonna, VP	Tel: (609) 428-7202	%FO: 100
Bus: *Produces/sell Melitta brand coffee & operates Coffee World retail stores.*	Fax: (609) 795-7543	

MELITTA NORTH AMERICA INC.
13925 58th Street North, Clearwater, FL 33760

CEO: Mike Modzelewski, SVP	Tel: (727) 535-2111	%FO: 100
Bus: *U.S. holding company.*	Fax: (727) 535-7376	Emp: 175

MELITTA USA INC.
13925 58th Street North, Clearwater, FL 33760

CEO: Marty Miller, EVP	Tel: (727) 535-2111	%FO: 100
Bus: *Mfr./sales/distribution of filter paper and coffee systems.*	Fax: (727) 535-7376	

● **MERCK KGAA**
6100 Frankfurter Strasse 250, D-64293 Darmstadt, Germany

CEO: Bernhard Scheuble, Chmn. & CEO	Tel: 49-6151-727-426	Rev: $6,350
Bus: *Mfr. pharmaceuticals, chemicals and laboratory preparations.*	Fax: 49-6151-728-793 www.merck.de	Emp: 33,500

CN BIOSCIENCES, INC.
10394 Pacific Center Court, San Diego, CA 92121

CEO: Stellos B. Papadopoulos, CEO	Tel: (858) 450-5500	%FO: 100
Bus: *Mfr./sales pharmaceuticals.*	Fax: (858) 450-5522	

DEY LABORATORIES, INC.
2751 Napa Valley Corporate Drive, Napa, CA 94558

CEO: Don Hume	Tel: (707) 224-3200	%FO: 100
Bus: *Mfr./sales pharmaceuticals.*	Fax: (707) 224-3235	

EM INDUSTRIES, INC.
7 Skyline Drive, Hawthorne, NY   10566

CEO: Dr. Peter A. Wriede, Pres. & CEO   Tel: (914) 592-4660   %FO: 100

Bus: *Mfr. pharmaceuticals and organic*   Fax: (914) 592-9469   Emp: 850
     and inorganic chemicals.

EM INDUSTRIES, INC.
PO Box 1206, Savannah, GA   31402

CEO: Dr. Peter A. Wriede, Pres. & CEO   Tel: (912) 964-9050   %FO: 100

Bus: *Mfr. pharmaceuticals and organic*   Fax: (912) 966-1891
     and inorganic chemicals.

EM SCIENCE
2909 Highland Avenue, Cincinnati, OH   45212

CEO: Thomas Colclough, VP   Tel: (513) 631-0445   %FO: 100

Bus: *Mfr./sales pharmaceuticals.*   Fax: (513) 631-0164

EM SCIENCE
480 South Democrat Road, Gibbstown, NJ   08027

CEO: Thomas Colclough, VP   Tel: (856) 423-6300   %FO: 100

Bus: *Mfr./sales pharmaceuticals,*   Fax: (856) 423-4891
     chemicals and laboratory
     preparations.

EMD PHARMACEUTICALS, INC.
3211 Shannon Road, Ste. 500, Durham, NC   27707

CEO: Nancy Wysenski, CEO   Tel: (919) 401-7100   %FO: 100

Bus: *Mfr./sales pharmaceuticals.*   Fax: (919) 401-7180

LEXIGEN PHARMACEUTICAL
125 Hartwell Avenue, Lexington, MA   02421

CEO: Stephen Gillies, Pres.   Tel: (781) 861-5300   %FO: 100

Bus: *Mfr./sales pharmaceuticals.*   Fax: (781) 861-5301

LIPHA PHARMACEUTICALS, INC.
1114 Avenue of the Americas, 41st Fl, New York, NY   10036-7703

CEO: Anita M. Goodman, COO   Tel: (212) 398-4602   %FO: JV

Bus: *Develops pharmaceutical products.* Fax: (212) 398-5026

LIPHA TECH INC.
3101 West Custer Avenue, Milwaukee, WI   53209-4827

CEO: Al Smith   Tel: (414) 351-1476   %FO: 100

Bus: *Mfr. pharmaceuticals and organic*   Fax: (414) 462-7186
     and inorganic chemicals.

VWR SCIENTIFIC PRODUCTS
1310 Goshen Parkway, West Chester, PA   19380
CEO: Jerrold B. Harris, CEO   Tel: (610) 431-1700   %FO: 100
Bus: *Mfr./sales pharmaceuticals.*   Fax: (610) 436-1760

• MERO SYSTEME GMBH & CO
Postfach 6169, D-97064 Wurzburg, Germany
CEO: Roland Klose, Dir.   Tel: 49-931-66700
Bus: *Mfr. spaceframes, special*   Fax: 49-931-6670547   Emp: 1,000
structures/raised floors, exhibits and   www.mero.de
displays.

MERO STRUCTURES INC.
N112 W18810 Mequon Road, PO Box 610, Germantown, WI   53022
CEO: Ian Collins, Pres.   Tel: (414) 255-5561   %FO: 100
Bus: *Space frames, special structures,*   Fax: (414) 255-6932   Emp: 30
exhibits and displays.

• MESSE DÜSSELDORF GMBH
Stockumer Kirchstrasse 61, D-40474 Düsseldorf, Germany
CEO: Karlheinz Wismer, CEO   Tel: 49-211-4560-01
Bus: *Organizes trade shows for medical,*   Fax: 49-211-4560-668   Emp: 700
fashion and service industries.   www.messe-duesseldorf.de

MESSE DÜSSELDORF NORTH AMERICA
150 N. Michigan Avenue, Ste. 2920, Chicago, IL   60601
CEO: Wolfgang Marzin, Pres.   Tel: (312) 781-5180   %FO: 100
Bus: *Promotes trade show program of*   Fax: (312) 781-5188   Emp: 7
Messe Dusseldorf in the USA.

• LUCAS MEYER GMBH & COMPANY
Postfach 262665, D-20506 Hamburg, Germany
CEO: Lucas Meyer III, Pres.   Tel: 49-40-7895-50
Bus: *Mfr. lecithin.*   Fax: 49-40-7893-29   Emp: 100

LUCAS MEYER INC.
765 East Pythian Avenue, Decatur, IL   62526
CEO: Peter Rohde, Pres.   Tel: (217) 875-3660   %FO: 100
Bus: *Mfr. lecithin.*   Fax: (217) 877-5046   Emp: 18

• MG TECHNOLOGIES AG (METALLGESELLSCHAFT)
Bockenheimer Landstrasse 73-77, D-60271 Frankfurt am Main, Germany
CEO: Karl J. Neukirchen, CEO   Tel: 49-69-71199-0   Rev: $7,735
Bus: *Develops and produces non-ferrous*   Fax: 49-69-71199-100   Emp: 38,400
metals, chemicals, explosives and offers   www.mg-ag.de
services for transportation and
engineering.

GEA ECOFLEX INC.

7150 Distribution Drive, Louisville, KY 40258

CEO: Terry Snell

Bus: *Mfr. fluid heat exchangers.*

Tel: (502) 935-3539

Fax: (502) 326-3539

%FO: 100

GEA POWER COOLING SYSTEMS, INC.

5355 Mira Sorrento Place, Ste. 600, San Diego, CA 92121

CEO: Gerhard Hesse, Pres.

Bus: *Engaged in heat rejection technology.*

Tel: (858) 457-0086

Fax: (858) 457-0570

%FO: 100

MG NORTH AMERICA HOLDINGS INC.

520 Madison Avenue, 28th Fl., New York, NY 10022

CEO: Karlheinz Hornung, CEO

Bus: *Sales/distribution of non-ferrous metals, chemicals, and offers services for transportation and engineering.*

Tel: (212) 715-5200

Fax: (212) 715-5291

%FO: 100

NIRO INC.

9165 Rumsey Road, Columbia, MD 21045

CEO: Steven Kaplan, Pres.

Bus: *Mfr. liquid and powder processing equipment.*

Tel: (410) 997-8700

Fax: (410) 997-5021

%FO: 100

WESTFALIA SEPARATOR, INC.

100 Fairway Court, Northvale, NJ 07647

CEO: Clement O'Donnell, Pres.

Bus: *Mfr. spare parts and centrifuges and systems.*

Tel: (201) 767-3900

Fax: (201) 767-3416

%FO: 100

WESTFALIA-SURGE, INC.

1880 Country Farm Drive, Naperville, IL 60563-1000

CEO: Dirk Hejnal, CEO

Bus: *Mfr. dairy equipment.*

Tel: (630) 369-8100

Fax: (630) 369-9875

%FO: 100

● MIELE & CIE GMBH

Can-Miele-Straße 29, D-33325 Gütersloh, Germany

CEO: Nick Lord, Pres. & CEO

Bus: *Mfr. commercial equipment and fitted kitchens, built-in appliances, including washing machines, tumble dryers, dishwashers, microwave ovens and vacuum cleaners.*

Tel: 49-52-41-890

Fax: 49-52-41-892090

www.miele.de

Emp: 14,800

MIELE, INC.
9 Independence Way, Princeton, NJ   08540
CEO: Nick Lord, Pres.   Tel: (609) 419-9898   %FO: 100
Bus: *Mfr. commercial equipment, fitted*   Fax: (609) 419-1794
     kitchens and built-in appliances.

MIELE, INC.
3100 West Dundee Road, Ste. 901, Northbrook, IL   60062
CEO: James Golan, Mgr.   Tel: (847) 714-9433   %FO: 100
Bus: *Mfr. commercial equipment, fitted*   Fax: (847) 714-9434
     kitchens and built-in appliances.

MIELE, INC.
680 Eighth Street, Ste. 168, San Francisco, CA   94103
CEO: Steve Evans, Mgr.   Tel: (415) 241-6820   %FO: 100
Bus: *Mfr. commercial equipment, fitted*   Fax: (415) 241-6822
     kitchens and built-in appliances.

MIELE, INC.
189 North Robertson Blvd., Beverly Hills, CA   90211
CEO: Nick Lord, Pres.   Tel: (310) 855-9470   %FO: 100
Bus: *Showroom for Miele products.*   Fax: (310) 358-0238

● **MOELLER-WEDEL GMBH, DIV. HAAG-STREIT AG**
Rosengarten 10, D-22880 Wedel, Germany
CEO: Wolfgang Blome, Mng. Dir.   Tel: 49-4103-709-01
Bus: *Mfr. operating microscopes and eye*   Fax: 49-4103-709-355   Emp: 7,500
     examination equipment.   www.moeller-wedel.com

   HS RELIANCE INTERNATIONAL, INC.
   3535 Kings Mill Road, Mason, OH   45040-2303
   CEO: Dennis Imwalle, Pres.   Tel: (513) 398-3937   %FO: 100
   Bus: *Mfr./sales of ophthalmologic*   Fax: (513) 398-0356
        chairs and stands.

   MOELLER ELECTRIC CORPORATION
   25 Forge Parkway, Franklin, MA   02038
   CEO: Nicolas Dudas, Pres.   Tel: (508) 520-7080   %FO: 100
   Bus: *Mfr./distribution industrial*   Fax: (508) 520-7084   Emp: 225
        electrical electronic controls and
        systems.

● **MUNICH REINSURANCE COMPANY**
Köeniginstrasse 107, D-80791 Munich, Germany
CEO: Dr. Hans-Jurgen Schinzler, Chmn.   Tel: 49-89-3891-3900   Rev: $35,464
Bus: *Engaged in reinsurance services.*   Fax: 49-89-3990-56   Emp: 33,250
                                           www.munichre.com

AMERICAN RE CORPORATION

555 College Road East, Princeton, NJ   08543-5241

CEO:Edward J. Noonan, Pres. & CEO	Tel: (609) 243-4200	%FO: 100
Bus: *Reinsurance services.*	Fax: (609) 243-4257	Emp: 1,600

● **MWG BIOTECH AG**

Anzinger Strasse 7a, D-85560 Ebersberg, Germany

CEO: Michael Weichselgartner, CEO   Tel: 49-8092-82890

Bus: *Engaged in biotechnology.*   Fax: 49-8092-11084

www.mwgbiotech.com

MWG BIOTECH, INC.

4170 Mendenhall Oaks Pkwy., High Point, NC   27265

CEO:Michael Weichselgartner, Pres.	Tel: (336) 812-9995	%FO: 100
Bus: *Engaged in biotechnology.*	Fax: (336) 812-9983	

● **GEBRUDER NETZSCH MASCHINENFABRIK GMBH & CO.**

Gebrüder-Netzsch-Straße 19, D-95100 Selb, Germany

CEO: Thomas Netzsch, Mng. Dir.   Tel: 43-732-7705-91-0

Bus: *Mfr. specialized industrial equipment.*   Fax: 43-732-7705-9131   Emp: 1,800

www.netzsch.com/f

NETZSCH INC.

421 Glan Tai Drive, Manchester, MO   63011

CEO:Tilo Stahl, Pres. & CEO	Tel: (636) 394-7733	%FO: 100
Bus: *Sales/service machinery for ceramic industry, filter presses, grinding and dispersion equipment, pumps.*	Fax: (636) 527-0715	

NETZSCH INC.

6711-225 South Yale Avenue, Tulsa, OK   74136

CEO:Tim Otton	Tel: (918) 481-1808	%FO: 100
Bus: *Sales/service machinery for ceramic industry, filter presses, grinding and dispersion equipment, pumps.*	Fax: (918) 481-8740	

NETZSCH INC.

3308 Preston Road, Ste. 350-131, Plano, TX   75093

CEO:Tilo Stahl, Pres. & CEO	Tel: (972) 599-0716	%FO: 100
Bus: *Sales/service machinery for ceramic industry, filter presses, grinding and dispersion equipment, pumps.*	Fax: (972) 599-1737	

NETZSCH INC.
37 Industrial Blvd., Sec. D, Paoli, PA   19301
CEO: Tilo Stahl, Pres. & CEO   Tel: (610) 722-0520   %FO: 100
Bus: *Sales/service machinery for*
ceramic industry, filter presses,   Fax: (610) 722-0522
grinding and dispersion
equipment, pumps.

NETZSCH INC.
3812 NE 100th Court, Vancouver, WA   98662
CEO: Tilo Stahl, Pres. & CEO   Tel: (360) 882-4018   %FO: 100
Bus: *Sales of pumps.*   Fax: (360) 882-4020

NETZSCH INC.
2729 Kozy Court, Marietta, GA   30066
CEO: Wally Phenegar   Tel: (770) 977-5360   %FO: 100
Bus: *Sales of pumps.*   Fax: (770) 578-1770

NETZSCH INC.
84 North Eastwood, Ste. 3031, Woodstock, IL   60098
CEO: Tilo Stahl, Pres. & CEO   Tel: (815) 648-1301   %FO: 100
Bus: *Sales of grinding and dispersion*   Fax: (815) 337-0848
equipment.

NETZSCH INC.
128 Deer Run Lane, Elgin, IL   60120
CEO: Bill McGraw   Tel: (847) 622-3960   %FO: 100
Bus: *Sales/service machinery for*   Fax: (847) 622-3961
ceramic industry, filter presses,
grinding and dispersion
equipment, pumps.

NETZSCH INC.
119 Pickering Way, Exton, PA   19341-1393
CEO: Robert E. Fisher   Tel: (610) 363-8010   %FO: 100
Bus: *Mfr./service machinery for*   Fax: (610) 363-0971   Emp: 123
ceramic industry, filter presses,
grinding and dispersion
equipment, pumps.

NETZSCH INC.
12123 Shellbyville Road, Box 174, Louisville, KY   40243
CEO: Tim Otton   Tel: (502) 245-6964   %FO: 100
Bus: *Sales/service machinery for*   Fax: (502) 245-4993
ceramic industry, filter presses,
grinding and dispersion
equipment, pumps.

NETZSCH THERMAL ANALYSIS, DIV. NETZSCH INC.

PO Box 995, Huntersville, NC   28070-0995

CEO:Tilo Stahl, Pres. & CEO	Tel: (704) 948-9534	%FO: 100
Bus: *Sales/service machinery for ceramic industry, filter presses, grinding and dispersion equipment, pumps.*	Fax: (704) 948-9535	

NETZSCH THERMAL ANALYSIS, DIV. NETZSCH INC.

PO Box 4469, Estes Park, CO   80517

CEO:Tilo Stahl, Pres. & CEO	Tel: (970) 577-0840	%FO: 100
Bus: *Sales/service machinery for ceramic industry, filter presses, grinding and dispersion equipment, pumps.*	Fax: (970) 577-1224	

● **NEUE HERBOLD MACHINEN UND ANLAGENBAU GMBH**

Wiefenstrasse 34, D-74889 Sinshiem Reihen, Germany

CEO: Peter Abraham, Pres.	Tel: 49-7261-92480	
Bus: *Mfr. recycling equipment.*	Fax: 49-7261-924800	Emp: 70
	www.neue-herbold.com	

NEW HERBOLD INC.

12C John Road, Sutton, MA   01590

CEO:Edward J. Ronca, Pres.	Tel: (508) 865-7355	%FO: 100
Bus: *Mfr./distribution of recycling equipment.*	Fax: (508) 865-9975	Emp: 5

● **OETKER GROUP**

Lutterstrasse 14, D-33617 Bielefeld, Germany

CEO: Rudolf August Oetker, Chmn.	Tel: 49-521-1550	
Bus: *Mfr. food products, wine, beer and soft drinks.*	Fax: 49-521-2995	
	www.oetker.de	

GALLARD-SCHLESINGER INDUSTRIES INC.

777 Zeckerndorf Blvd., Garden City, NY   11530

CEO:Sheldon Silbiger, Pres.	Tel: (516) 229-4000
Bus: *Imports/distributes chemicals.*	Fax: (516) 229-4015

● **OPTIMA MASCHINENFABRIK**

Steinbeisweg 20, Postfach 100520, D-74523 Schwaebisch Hall, Germany

CEO: Hans Buehler, Pres. & CEO	Tel: 49-79-791-5060	
Bus: *Mfr. and sales of packaging and filling machinery.*	Fax: 49-79-791-51835	Emp: 400
	www.optima-ger.com	

OPTIMA MACHINERY CORPORATION
1330 Contract Drive, PO Box 28173, Green Bay, WI   54304-0173

CEO: Thomas Seifert, EVP	Tel: (920) 339-2222	%FO: 100
Bus: *Mfr. and sales of packaging machinery.*	Fax: (920) 339-2233	Emp: 25

• OTTO VERSAND GMBH & CO.
Wandsbeker Strasse 3-7, D-22172 Hamburg, Germany

CEO: Michael Otto, Chmn. & ceo	Tel: 49-40-6461-0	Rev: $21,480
Bus: *Engaged in mail order businesses.*	Fax: 49-40-6461-8571	Emp: 65,000
	www.otto.de	

CRATE & BARREL
725 Landwehr Road, Northbrook, IL   60062

CEO: Michael Otto, Pres.	Tel: (847) 272-2888	%FO: 100
Bus: *Housewares chain store.*	Fax: (847) 272-5276	

SPIEGEL
3500 Lacey Road, Downers Grove, IL   60515

CEO: Michael Otto, Pres.	Tel: (630) 986-8800	%FO: 100
Bus: *Catalog company.*	Fax: (630) 769-2012	

• PANDATEL AG
Fasanenweg 25, D-22145 Hamburg, Germany

CEO: Henrik Foderer, CEO	Tel: 49-40-664-140	Rev: $35
Bus: *Mfr. optical telecommunication transmission equipment.*	Fax: 49-40-664-5792	Emp: 100
	www.pandatel.de	

PANDATEL INC.
1095 Cranbury South River Road, Ste. 24, Jamesburg, NJ   08831

CEO: Frank Mauritz	Tel: (732) 271-8680	%FO: 100
Bus: *Mfr./sales optical telecommunication transmission equipment.*	Fax: (732) 271-8689	

PANDATEL INC.
7200 Corporate Center Drive, Ste. 304, Miami, FL   33126

CEO: Frank Mauritz	Tel: (305) 471-0050	%FO: 100
Bus: *Mfr./sales optical telecommunication transmission equipment.*	Fax: (305) 471-0049	

● **PEPPERL+FUCHS GMBH**

Koenigsberger Allee 87, D-68307 Mannheim, Germany

CEO: Dr. W. Kegel, Pres. & CEO

Bus: *Mfr. proximity sensors & electronic controls.*

Tel: 49-621-7760

Fax: 49-621-7761000

www.pepperl-fuchs.com

Emp: 2,500

    PEPPERL+FUCHS INC.

    1600 Enterprise Pkwy., Twinsburg, OH 44087

    CEO: Wolfgang Mueller, Pres.

    Bus: *Mfr. proximity sensors and electronic controls.*

    Tel: (330) 425-3555

    Fax: (330) 425-4607

    %FO: 100

    Emp: 125

● **PERI GMBH**

PO Box 1264, D-89259 Weissenhorn, Germany

CEO: Artur Schworer, Pres.

Bus: *Concrete formwork and scaffolding.*

Tel: 49-7309-9500

Fax: 49-7309-950176

www.peri.de

Emp: 1,500

    PERI FORMWORK INC.

    7272 Park Circle Drive, Ste. 200, Hanover, MD 21076

    CEO: Harvey Evans, VP

    Bus: *Distribution/sale/service concrete formwork and scaffolding.*

    Tel: (410) 712-7225

    Fax: (410) 712-7080

    %FO: 100

    Emp: 100

● **PFEIFFER VACUUM TECHNOLOGY AG**

Emmeliusstrasse 33, D-35614 Asslar, Germany

CEO: Wolfgang Dondorf, Chmn.

Bus: *Mfr. turbomolecular pumps and markets components for vacuum technology.*

Tel: 49-6441-802-314

Fax: 49-6441-802-365

www.pfeiffer-vacuum.de

Rev: $174

Emp: 790

    PFEIFFER VACUUM TECHNOLOGY INC.

    24 Trafalgar Square, Nashua, NH 03063-1988

    CEO: Roland Hellmer, EVP

    Bus: *Sales/distribution of turbomolecular pumps and marketing of components for vacuum technology.*

    Tel: (603) 578-6500

    Fax: (603) 578-6500

● **PHOENIX AG**

Hannoversche Straße 88, D-21079 Hamburg, Germany

CEO: Konrad Ellegast, CEO

Bus: *Mfr. acoustic systems and rubber products for the auto industry.*

Tel: 49-40-7667-01

Fax: 49-40-7667-2211

www.phoenix-ag.com

Rev: $915

Emp: 9,850

PHOENIX NORTH AMERICA, INC.
720 King Georges Post Road, Ste. 3J, Fords, NJ 08863

CEO: Burkhard Meister

Bus: *Mfr./sales acoustic systems and rubber products for the auto industry.*

Tel: (732) 346-5353
Fax: (732) 346-3355

%FO: 100

• CARL AUG PICARD GMBH
Hasteraue 9, D-42857 Remscheid, Germany

CEO: Klaus Picard, CEO

Bus: *Precision grinding, wear parts & heat treating.*

Tel: 49-2191-8930
Fax: 49-2191-893111
www.capicard.com

Emp: 350

C. A . PICARD INC.
305 Hill Brady Road, Battle Creek, MI 49015

CEO: Gunter Schramm, Pres.

Bus: *Tooling for printed circuit board industry.*

Tel: (616) 962-2231
Fax: (616) 962-4916

%FO: 100
Emp: 50

• PORSCHE AG
Porschestrasse 42, Postfach 400640, D-70435 Stuttgart, Germany

CEO: Dr. Wendelin Wiedeking, Pres.

Bus: *Mfr. and sales automobiles, engines and components.*

Tel: 49-711-8270
Fax: 49-711-827-5777
www.porsche.com

PORSCHE CARS OF NORTH AMERICA INC.
980 Hammond Drive, Ste. 1000, Atlanta, GA 30328

CEO: Fredrick J. Schwab, Pres. & CEO

Bus: *Sales/distribution of automobiles.*

Tel: (770) 290-3500
Fax: (770) 290-3700

%FO: 100

• PREUSSAG AG
4 Karl-Wiechert-Allee, D-30625 Hannover, Germany

CEO: Dr. Michael H. Frenzel, Chmn.

Bus: *Holding company engaged in steel and nonferrous metals production, trading, transport, information technology, energy and commodities.*

Tel: 49-511-566-00
Fax: 49-511-566-1901
www.preussag.de

Rev: $18,739
Emp: 57,675

AMALGAMET INC.
55 Railroad Avenue, Greenwich, CT 06830

CEO: C. J. Moreton, SVP

Bus: *Sales non-ferrous metals, chemicals and essential oils.*

Tel: (203) 629-4400
Fax: (203) 863-0700

DELTA STEEL, INC.

5599 San Felipe, Ste. 600, Houston, TX   77252

CEO: Robert Embry, Pres.   Tel: (713) 585-7117   %FO: 100

Bus: *Sales/distribution of steel and*   Fax: (713) 960-0655
nonferrous metals.

FERALLOY CORPORATION

8755 West Higgins Road, Ste. 970, Chicago, IL   60631

CEO: Frank M. Walker, Pres.   Tel: (312) 380-1500   %FO: 100

Bus: *Sales/distribution of steel and*   Fax: (312) 380-1535
nonferrous metals.

NOELL INC.

55 Railroad Avenue, Greenwich, CT   06830

CEO: Ron Kaye, CEO   Tel: (203) 629-4400   %FO: 100

Bus: *Engaged in construction.*   Fax: (203) 863-0700

PREUSSAG INTERNATIOAL STEEL CORP

400 Northridge Road, Ste. 850, Atlanta, GA   30350

CEO: Dr. Hartmut Nolte, Pres.   Tel: (770) 641-6460   %FO: 100

Bus: *Engaged in steel and nonferrous*   Fax: (770) 641-6495
metals production.

PREUSSAG NORTH AMERICA INC.

55 Railroad Avenue, Greenwich, CT   06830

CEO: Chris Moreton   Tel: (203) 629-4400   %FO: 100

Bus: *Engaged in steel & nonferrous*   Fax: (203) 863-0700
metals production, trading &
transport, information technology
& energy & commodities.

TR METRO CHEMICALS INC.

36 Mileed Way, Avenel, NJ   07001

CEO: J. J. Sette, Pres.   Tel: (732) 382-2100

Bus: *Mfr. chemicals.*   Fax: (732) 499-7799

VOTG NORTH AMERICA, INC.

1234 West Chester Pike, West Chester, PA   19382

CEO: Leon van Bergen, Dir.   Tel: (215) 429-5440

Bus: *Mfr. industrial chemicals.*   Fax: (215) 429-5448

● PROMINENT DOSIERTECHNIK GMBH

Im Schuhmachergewann 7, D-69123 Heidelberg, Germany

CEO: Viktor Dulger, Pres.   Tel: 49-6221-8420

Bus: *Mfr. of chemical metering pumps,*   Fax: 49-6221-842-419   Emp: 300
controllers, sensors and pre-packaged   www.prominent.de
and custom chemical feed systems.

PROMINENT FLUID CONTROLS INC.

136 Industry Drive, RIDC Park West, Pittsburgh, PA   15275-1014

CEO: Sandy Chu, VP Tel: (412) 787-2484 %FO: 100

Bus: *Mfr. of chemical metering pumps,* Fax: (412) 787-0704 Emp: 65
controllers, sensors and pre-
packaged and custom chemical
feed systems.

● **PTR PRAEZISIONSTECHNIK GMBH (FORMERLY INTEGRAL HYDRAULIK)**

Am Spitzen Sand 1, D-63477 Maintal, Germany

CEO: Ingo Kloss, Pres. Tel: 49-6181-40940

Bus: *Electron beam welders and electron* Fax: 49-6181-409413
beam job shop services. www.ptreb.com

PTR - PRECISION TECHNOLOGIES, INC.

120 Post Road, Enfield, CT   06082-5625

CEO: D. E. Powers Tel: (860) 741-2281 %FO: 100

Bus: *Electron beam welders, laser* Fax: (860) 745-7932 Emp: 50
beam systems, electron beam job
shop services.

● **PUMA AG**

Wurzburgerstrasse 13, D-91074 Herzogenaurach, Germany

CEO: Jochen Zeitz, CEO Tel: 49-9132-810 Rev: $435

Bus: *Mfr. athletic apparel and sports shoes.* Fax: 49-9132-8122-46 Emp: 1,525
 www.puma.com

PUMA NORTH AMERICA, INC.

5 Lyberty Way, Westford, MA   01886

CEO: Amber Friedman Tel: (978) 698-1000 %FO: 100

Bus: *Mfr./sales athletic apparel and* Fax: (978) 698-1050
sports shoes.

● **A. RACKE GMBH & CO.**

Postfach 1653, D-55386 Bingen, Germany

CEO: Marcus Moller-Racke, Chmn. Tel: 49-6-721-1881

Bus: *Production/marketing of wines & spirits.* Fax: 49-6-721-188220
 www.racke.de

BUENA VISTA WINERY, INC./RACKE USA

PO Box 182, Sonoma, CA   95476

CEO: Harry Parsley, Pres. & CEO Tel: (707) 252-7117 %FO: 100

Bus: *Production & marketing of·wine.* Fax: (707) 252-0392 Emp: 80

● **RACO ELEKTRO MASCHINEN GMBH**

Jesinghauserstrasse 56-64, D-58332 Schwelm, Germany

CEO: R. Wilke, Pres.   Tel: 49-23-3640-090

Bus: *Mfr. electric actuators and cylinders.*   Fax: 49-23-3640-0910

                                        www.raco.de

    RACO INTL INC.

    3350 Industrial Blvd., PO Box 151, Bethel Park, PA   15102

    CEO: Reinhard Wilke, Pres.   Tel: (412) 835-5744   %FO: 100

    Bus: *Mfr. electric actuators and*   Fax: (412) 835-0338

      cylinders.

● **RAG AKTIENGESELLSCHAFT**

Rellinghauser Strasse 1-11, D-45128 Essen, Germany

CEO: Georg Kowalczyk, CEO   Tel: 49-201-177-01   Rev: $13,950

Bus: *Engaged in mining, energy and*   Fax: 49-201-177-3475   Emp: 92,700

  technology.   www.rag.de

    RAG AMERICAN COAL HOLDING INC.

    999 Corporate Boulevard, Linthicum Heights, MD   21090-2227

    CEO: John Tellmann   Tel: (410) 689-7500   %FO: 100

    Bus: *Mining, energy and technology.*   Fax: (410) 689-7652

    RAG AMERICAN COAL HOLDING INC.

    PO Box 144, Kennsburg, IL   62852

    CEO: William A. Kelly   Tel: (618) 298-2394   %FO: 100

    Bus: *Mining, energy and technology.*   Fax: (618) 298-2620

● **REALAX SOFTWARE AG**

Am Sandfeld 15a, D-76149 Karlsruhe, Germany

CEO: Wolfgang Störzer, CEO   Tel: 49-721-66-396-0

Bus: *Develops and manufactures software*   Fax: 49-721-66-396-66

  and digital prototyping.   www.realax.com

    REALAX CORPORATION

    1540 Broadway, Ste. 29H, New York, NY   10036

    CEO: Marcel Kreutler, Pres.   Tel: (212) 782-5292   %FO: 100

    Bus: *Mfr. software.*   Fax: (212) 782-5291

● **REEMTSMA CIGARETTENFABRIKEN GMBH**

Parkstrasse 51, Postfach 520653, D-22596 Hamburg, Germany

CEO: Thierry Paternot, Chmn.   Tel: 49-40-8220-0   Rev: $2,493

Bus: *Mfr. cigarettes and fine tobacco*   Fax: 49-40-8220-1645   Emp: 11,818

  products.   www.reemtsma.de

WEST PARK TOBACCO USA, INC.
13293 Rivers Bend Boulevard, Chester, VA   23836
CEO: Cheryl Ligon, Mgr.   Tel: (804) 530-0031   %FO: 100
Bus: *Mfr./distributor cigarettes and fine*   Fax: (804) 530-9921
     tobacco products.

● **REICH SPEZIALMASCHINEN GMBH**
Plochinger Strasse 65, D-72622 Nuertingen, Germany
CEO: Wulf W. Reich, CEO   Tel: 49-7022-7020
Bus: *Mfr. industrial woodworking machines.*   Fax: 49-7022-702101
                                        www.holzher.de   Emp: 400

HOLZ-HER US, INC.
5120 Westinghouse Boulevard, Charlotte, NC   28273
CEO: Richard C. Hannigan, VP   Tel: (704) 587-3400   %FO: 100
Bus: *Industrial woodworking machines.*   Fax: (704) 587-3412   Emp: 51

● **REIFENHAUSER GMBH & CO. MASCHINENFABRIK**
Spicher Strasse 46-48, Postfach 1664, D-53839 Troisdorf, Germany
CEO: Ulrich Reifenhauser, Chmn.   Tel: 49-22-41-4810
Bus: *Mfr. plastic extrusion equipment.*   Fax: 49-22-41-408778

REIFENHAUSER, INC.
Two Washington Street, Ipswich, MA   01938
CEO: Richard Dexter, Mgr.   Tel: (978) 412-9700   %FO: 100
Bus: *Sale/service & spare parts*   Fax: (978) 412-9715   Emp: 10
     distribution plastic extrusion
     equipment.

● **RENFERT GMBH & CO**
Industrial Area, D-78247 Hilzingen, Germany
CEO: Klaus U. Rieger, Pres.   Tel: 49-77-31-8208
Bus: *Mfr. dental laboratory equipment.*   Fax: 49-77-31-820830   Emp: 100
                                        www.renfert.com

RENFERT USA INC.
3718 Illinois Avenue, St. Charles, IL   60174
CEO: Richard Jakus, EVP   Tel: (630) 762-1803   %FO: 100
Bus: *Distribution/service dental*   Fax: (630) 762-9787   Emp: 5
     laboratory equipment.

● **RENK AG, DIV. OF MAN GROUP**
Gögginger Straße 73, D-86159 Augsburg, Germany
CEO: Norbert Schulze   Tel: 49-821-5700-250
Bus: *Mfr./distributes industrial gears and*   Fax: 49-821-5700-640   Emp: 1,510
     vehicle transmissions.   www.renk.de

RENK CORPORATION
304 Tucapau Road, Duncan, SC   29344
CEO: Klaus I. Bock, VP   Tel: (864) 433-0069   %FO: 100
Bus: *Mfr./distributes industrial gears*   Fax: (864) 433-0636
and vehicle transmissions.

● **RITTAL-WERK, GMBH**
Rudolf Loh Gmbh & Co. KG, Postfach 1662, D-35726 Herborn, Germany
CEO: Friedhelm Loh, CEO   Tel: 49-2772-5051
Bus: *Mfr. electric/electronic enclosures.*   Fax: 49-2772-505319   Emp: 3,500
www.rittal.com

RITTAL CORPORATION
One Rittal Place, Springfield, OH   45504
CEO: Hans J. Wagner, Pres.   Tel: (937) 399-0500   %FO: 100
Bus: *Mfr. electric/electronic enclosures.* Fax: (937) 390-5599   Emp: 280

● **ROEDIGER ANLAGENBAU GMBH**
Kinzigheimer Weg 104, D-63450 Hanau/Main, Germany
CEO: Robert Huth, Dir.   Tel: 49-6181-3090
Bus: *Engineering/design/construct waste*   Fax: 49-6181-309111   Emp: 400
water treatment plants, mfr. related
equipment.

ROEDIGER PITTSBURGH INC.
3812 Route 8, Allison Park, PA   15101
CEO: Dr. Marcus Roediger, Pres.   Tel: (412) 487-6010   %FO: 100
Bus: *Engineering/design/mfr. waste*   Fax: (412) 487-6005   Emp: 40
water treatment equipment.

● **ROHDE & SCHWARZ GMBH & CO.**
Muhldorfstraße 15, D-81671 Munich, Germany
CEO: Friedrich Schwarz, CEO   Tel: 49-89-41-290   Rev: $800
Bus: *Mfr. test and measurement equipment.* Fax: 49-89-41-2912164   Emp: 5,000
www.rohde-schwarz.com

ROHDE & SCHWARZ
7150 Riverwood Drive, Columbia, MD   21046
CEO: Reinhard Bruckner, Pres.   Tel: (410) 910-7818   %FO: 100
Bus: *Mfr. test and measurement*   Fax: (410) 910-7819
equipment.

ROHDE & SCHWARZ
3 Meeting Rock Drive, Atkinson, NH   03811
CEO: Reinhard Bruckner, Pres.   Tel: (603) 362-5749   %FO: 100
Bus: *Mfr. test and measurement*   Fax: (603) 362-6179
equipment.

ROHDE & SCHWARZ
811 Aberdeen Way, Southlake, TX   76092
CEO: Reinhard Bruckner, Pres.   Tel: (972) 915-0294   %FO: 100
Bus: *Mfr. test and measurement*   Fax: (972) 719-9195
      equipment.

ROHDE & SCHWARZ
5510 E. Coralite Street, Long Beach, CA   90808
CEO: Reinhard Bruckner, Pres.   Tel: (562) 425-1037   %FO: 100
Bus: *Mfr. test and measurement*   Fax: (562) 425-1037
      equipment.

● **ROSENTHAL AG**
Wittelsbacher Strasse 43, D-95100 Selb/Bayern, Germany
CEO: Ottmar Küsel, Pres.   Tel: 49-92-87-72300
Bus: *Manufacturer of china, crystal and*   Fax: 49-92-87-72225
      flatware.   www.rosenthalchina.com

    ROSENTHAL USA LTD.
    355 Michele Place, Carlstadt, NJ   07072
    CEO: Georg Simon, Pres.   Tel: (201) 804-8000   %FO: 100
    Bus: *Wholesale distributor of imported*   Fax: (201) 804-9300
       china, crystal and flatware

● **ROVEMA VERPACKUNGSMASCHINEN GMBH**
Industriestrasse 1, D-35463 Fernwald, Germany
CEO: Walter Baur, Pres.   Tel: 49-641-409-0
Bus: *Mfr. packaging machinery.*   Fax: 49-641-409212
    www.rovema.com

    ROVEMA PACKAGING MACHINES, INC.
    650 Hurricane Shoals Road, NW, Lawrenceville, GA   30045
    CEO: William Brown, Sales   Tel: (770) 513-9604   %FO: 100
    Bus: *Sale/service packaging machinery.*   Fax: (770) 513-0814

● **RUETGERSWERKE AG**
Mainzer Landstrasse 217, D-60326 Frankfurt/Main, Germany
CEO: Eberhardt von Persall, Pres.   Tel: 49-69 75921
Bus: *Mfr. coal tar based intermediates.*   Fax: 49-69 7592488   Emp: 15,000
    www.ruetgers-organics-corp.com

    RUETGERS ORGANICS CORPORATION
    201 Struble Road, State College, PA   16801
    CEO: Peter Keyser   Tel: (814) 238-2424   %FO: 100
    Bus: *Mfr. detergent intermediates,*   Fax: (814) 238-1567   Emp: 200
       custom organic synthesis

● **RUHRGAS AG**

Huttropstrasse 60, D-45138 Essen, Germany

CEO: Friedrich Späth, Chmn.

Bus: *Supplies natural gas.*

Tel: 49-201-184-3857

Fax: 49-201-184-3171

www.ruhrgas.de

Rev: $7,334

Emp: 8,875

> ### AMERICAN METER COMPANY
>
> 300 Welsh Road, Horsham, PA 19044-2234
>
> CEO: Harry I. Skilton, CEO
>
> Bus: *Mfr. and market gas measurement and control products.*
>
> Tel: (215) 830-1800
>
> Fax: (215) 830-1890
>
> %FO: 100

● **RÜTGERS AG**

Rellinghauser Strabe 3, D-45128 Essen, Germany

CEO: Dr. Eberhard von Perfall, Chmn. & CEO

Bus: *Mfr. specialty chemicals, coal tar-based intermediates and plastics for road construction.*

Tel: 49-201-177-02

Fax: 49-201-177-20-50

www.ruetgers.de

> ### ISOLA USA INC.
>
> 401 Whitney Place, Fremont, CA 94539
>
> CEO: Ted Becker, Pres.
>
> Bus: *Mfr. base material for the manufacture of industrial laminated plastics and printed circuits.*
>
> Tel: (510) 683-3100
>
> Fax: (510) 657-8855

> ### RÜTGERS ORGANICS CORPORATION
>
> 201 Struble Road, State College, PA 16801
>
> CEO: David S. Johnson, Pres.
>
> Bus: *Mfr. detergent intermediates.*
>
> Tel: (814) 238-2424
>
> Fax: (814) 238-1567

● **RWE AKTIENGESELLSCHAFT**

Opernplatz 1, D-45128 Essen, Germany

CEO: Dietmar Kuhnt, Pres. & CEO

Bus: *Holding company: production/distribution of power, petroleum, mining, water, waste management, engineering and construction services.*

Tel: 49-201-1200

Fax: 49-201-1215-265

www.rwe.de

Rev: $45,618

Emp: 155,700

> ### AMERICAN WATER WORKS COMPANY, INC.
>
> PO Box 1770, 1025 Laurel Oak Road, Voorhees, NJ 08043
>
> CEO: J. James Barr, Pres. & CEO
>
> Bus: *Provides water services.*
>
> Tel: (856) 346-8203
>
> Fax: (856) 346-8229
>
> %FO: 100
>
> Emp: 5,000

CONDEA VISTA COMPANY
900 Treadneedle, Houston, TX   77079
CEO: Charles F. Putnik, CEO   Tel: (281) 588-3000   %FO: 100
Bus: *U. S. headquarters office.*   Fax: (281) 588-3236

CONSOL ENERGY INC.
1800 Washington Road, Pittsburgh, PA   15241
CEO: J. Brett Harvey, CEO   Tel: (412) 831-4000
Bus: *Production of bituminous coal for*   Fax: (412) 831-4571
utilities.

THE LATHROP COMPANY, INC.
460 West Dussel Drive, Maumee, OH   43537
CEO: Robert L. Maxwell, CEO   Tel: (419) 893-7000   %FO: 100
Bus: *Engaged in construction.*   Fax: (419) 893-1741

SERVICE BUILDING PRODUCTS, INC.
460 West Dussel Drive, Maumee, OH   43537
CEO: William L. Venn, Pres.   Tel: (419) 897-0708   %FO: 100
Bus: *Engaged in construction.*   Fax: (419) 897-0938

TURNER CONSTRUCTION INTERNATIONAL LLC
375 Hudson Street, New York, NY   10014
CEO: Nicholas E. Billotti, Pres. & CEO   Tel: (212) 229-6388   %FO: 100
Bus: *Engaged in construction.*   Fax: (212) 229-6418

THE TURNER CORPORATION
901 Main Street, Ste. 4900, Dallas, TX   75202
CEO: Robert E. Fee, CEO   Tel: (214) 915-9600   %FO: 100
Bus: *Engaged in construction.*   Fax: (214) 915-9700

UNIVERSAL CONSTRUCTION COMPANY
336 James Record Road, Huntsville, AL   35806
CEO: Russell L. Burns, Pres.   Tel: (256) 461-0568   %FO: 100
Bus: *Engaged in construction.*   Fax: (256) 461-6731

● **SAP AG**
Neurottstrasse 16, D-69190 Walldorf, Germany
CEO: Hasso Plattner, Co-Chmn.   Tel: 49-6227-74-7474   Rev: $5,900
Bus: *Develop, manufacture, sales and service*   Fax: 49-6227-75-7575   Emp: 24,175
of applications software.   www.sap.com

SAP AMERICA INC.
3999 West Chester Pike, Newtown Square, PA   19073
CEO: Wolfgang Kemna, CEO   Tel: (610) 355-2500   %FO: 100
Bus: *Developer/mfr./distributor/service*   Fax: (610) 355-2501   Emp: 500
applications software.

• CARL SCHENCK AG, DIV. DURR GROUP

Landwehrstrasse 55, D-64273 Darmstadt, Germany

CEO: Dr. G. Wiedemeyer, Pres. Tel: 49-6151-320

Bus: *Engineering/mfr./instruments for* Fax: 49-6151-893686   Emp: 7,000
weighing balancing machines and   www.carlschenck.com
testing systems.

SCHENCK ACCURATE AND WEIGHING SYSTEMS

746 E. Milwaukee Street, Whitewater, WI 53190

CEO: Gregory F. Fream, Pres. Tel: (262) 473-2441   %FO: 100

Bus: *Mfr. metering and weighing* Fax: (262) 473-2232   Emp: 135
devices.

SCHENCK CORPORATION

535 Acorn Street, Deer Park, NY 11729

CEO: Blaise Sarcone, Pres. Tel: (631) 242-4010   %FO: 100

Bus: *Holding company.* Fax: (631) 242-4308

SCHENCK MOTORAMA, INC.

34300 West Nine Mile Road, Farmington, MI 48335

CEO: Homer Harrison, Pres. Tel: (248) 478-3500   %FO: 100

Bus: *Design systems for the automotive* Fax: (248) 478-7114
business.

SCHENCK PEGASUS CORPORATION

2890 John R. Road, Troy, MI 48083

CEO: F. Schuppenies, Pres. Tel: (248) 689-9000   %FO: 100

Bus: *Mfr. materials testing,* Fax: (248) 689-8978   Emp: 130
dynamometer system.

SCHENCK TREBEL CORPORATION

394 Branch Avenue, Little Silver, NJ 07739

CEO: B. Dittmar, CEO Tel: (732) 741-0164   %FO: 100

Bus: *Sales of balancing machines and* Fax: (732) 741-0151
vibration equipment.

SCHENCK TREBEL CORPORATION

3070 SE Galt Circle, Port St. Lucie, FL 34984

CEO: B. Dittmar, CEO Tel: (802) 253-7191   %FO: 100

Bus: *Sales of balancing machines and* Fax: (802) 253-7191
vibration equipment.

SCHENCK TREBEL CORPORATION

10 Alder Place, The Woodlands, TX 77380

CEO: B. Dittmar, CEO Tel: (281) 367-7232   %FO: 100

Bus: *Sales of balancing machines and* Fax: (281) 292-2477
vibration equipment.

SCHENCK TREBEL CORPORATION
1357 Stowe Hollow Road, Stowe, VT   05672
CEO: B. Dittmar, CEO   Tel: (802) 253-7191   %FO: 100
Bus: *Sales of balancing machines and* Fax: (802) 253-7097
      vibration equipment.

SCHENCK TREBEL CORPORATION
535 Acorn Street, Deer Park, NY   11729
CEO: Blaise Sarcone, Pres.   Tel: (631) 242-4010   %FO: 100
Bus: *Mfr. industry balancing machine* Fax: (631) 242-4308   Emp: 72
      and related equipment.

SCHENCK TREBEL CORPORATION
251 Winslow Way, Lake Hills, IL   60156
CEO: B. Dittmar, CEO   Tel: (847) 669-6974   %FO: 100
Bus: *Sales of balancing machines and* Fax: (847) 669-6981
      vibration equipment.

SCHENCK TURNER INC.
100 Kay Drive, Lake Orion, MI   48035
CEO: Blaise Sarcone, Pres.   Tel: (810) 377-2100   %FO: 100
Bus: *Mfr. automated balancing system.* Fax: (810) 377-2744

SCHENCK WEIGHING SYSTEMS
81 Two Bridges Road, Fairfield, NJ   07004
CEO: Gregory F. Fream, Pres.   Tel: (973) 882-4650   %FO: 100
Bus: *Mfr. weighing components.*   Fax: (973) 882-3796

● **SCHENKER AG, DIV. STINNES**
Alfredstrasse 81, D-45130 Essen, Germany
CEO: Dr. Hans v. Dewall   Tel: 49-2-01-87810   Rev: $5,900
Bus: *Provides logistics solutions; land* Fax: 49-2-01-8781-8495   Emp: 29,000
      transport, sea and air.   www.schenker.com

SCHENKER USA INC.
3 D Gill Street, Woburn, MA   01801
CEO: Arthur Imbriano, Mgr.   Tel: (781) 729-6300   %FO: 100
Bus: *Provides customs brokerage and*   Fax: (781) 729-3030
      logistics solutions.

SCHENKER USA INC.
380 Littlefield Avenue, So. San Francisco, CA   94080
CEO: Frank Engels, Mgr.   Tel: (650) 875-2000   %FO: 100
Bus: *Provides customs brokerage and*   Fax: (650) 742-0669
      logistics solutions.

SCHENKER USA INC.
150 Albany Avenue, Freeport, NY 11520
CEO: Peter Mandt, Mgr.   Tel: (516) 377-3000   %FO: 100
Bus: *Provides customs brokerage and*   Fax: (516) 377-3100
   logistics solutions.

SCHENKER USA INC.
775 Atlanta South Parkway, College Park, GA 30349
CEO: Frank Szewczyk, Mgr.   Tel: (404) 768-1800   %FO: 100
Bus: *Provides customs brokerage and*   Fax: (404) 768-0577
   logistics solutions.

SCHENKER USA INC.
1390 Donaldson Drive Center, Ste. H, Erlanger, KY 41018
CEO: Bob Bishopp, Mgr.   Tel: (859) 525-8432   %FO: 100
Bus: *Provides customs brokerage and*   Fax: (859) 525-0108
   logistics solutions.

SCHENKER USA INC.
600 East Dallas Road, Ste. 100, Grapevine, TX 76051
CEO: Earl Williams, Mgr.   Tel: (817) 329-0050   %FO: 100
Bus: *Provides customs brokerage and*   Fax: (817) 488-7501
   logistics solutions.

SCHENKER USA INC.
28825 East Goddard Road, Romulus, MI 48174
CEO: Nancy Johnson, Mgr.   Tel: (734) 941-4650   %FO: 100
Bus: *Provides customs brokerage and*   Fax: (734) 941-5559
   logistics solutions.

SCHENKER USA INC.
123 Sivert Court, Bensenville, IL 60106
CEO: Mike Meierkort, Mgr.   Tel: (630) 595-0095   %FO: 100
Bus: *Provides customs brokerage and*   Fax: (630) 860-9166
   logistics solutions.

SCHENKER USA INC.
10813 NW 30th Street, Ste. 115, Miami, FL 33172
CEO: Christian Finnern, Mgr.   Tel: (305) 592-6377   %FO: 100
Bus: *Provides customs brokerage and*   Fax: (305) 593-0161
   logistics solutions.

● **SCHERING AG**
Müllerstrasse 178, D-13342 Berlin, Germany
CEO: Dr. Giuseppe Vita, Chmn.   Tel: 49-30-4681-2838   Rev: $3,860
Bus: *Mfr. pharmaceuticals.*   Fax: 49-30-4681-5305   Emp: 21,800
    www.schering.de

BERLEX LABORATORIES, INC.

300 Fairfield Road, Wayne, NJ   07470

CEO: Lutz Lingnau, Chmn.　　　　Tel: (973) 694-4100　　　　%FO: 100

Bus: *Sales/distribution of*　　　　Fax: (973) 694-4100
pharmaceuticals.

BERLEX LABORATORIES, INC.

340 Changebridge Road, PO Box 1000, Montville, NJ   07045-1000

CEO: Lutz Lingnau, Chmn.　　　　Tel: (973) 276-2000　　　　%FO: 100

Bus: *U.S. holding company: ethical*　　　　Fax: (973) 276-2006
pharmaceuticals, agrochemicals.

BERLICHEM INC.

PO Box 1000, Montville, NJ   07045-1000

CEO: Jorge Engel, Pres.　　　　Tel: (973) 276-2000　　　　%FO: 100

Bus: *Sales/distribution of*　　　　Fax:
pharmaceuticals and chemicals.

MEDRAD INC.

One Medrad Drive, Indianola, PA   15051

CEO: John P. Friel, Pres. & CEO　　　　Tel: (412) 767-2400　　　　%FO: 100

Bus: *Engaged in medical technology.*　　　　Fax: (412) 767-2400

SCHERING BERLIN

300 Fairfield Road, Wayne, NJ   07470-7358

CEO: John Nicholson　　　　Tel: (973) 276-2000　　　　%FO: 100

Bus: *Engaged in equity investments.*　　　　Fax: (973) 305-3532

● **SCHLEICHER & SCHUELL KG & COMPANY**

Postfach 4, D-37586 Dassel, Germany

CEO: Dr. Werner Specht, Pres.　　　　Tel: 49-5564-7910

Bus: *Engaged in life sciences and*　　　　Fax: 49-5564-72743
manufacture of paper products.　　　　www.s-und-s.de

DIA-NIELSEN USA

PO Box 865, Moorestown, NJ   08057-0865

CEO: Wayne Connelly, Pres.　　　　Tel: (609) 829-9441　　　　%FO: 100

Bus: *Mfr. accessories for recording and*　Fax: (609) 829-8814
control.

HAHNEMUHLE USA

41 Twosome Drive, Moorestown, NJ   08057

CEO: Wayne Connelly, Pres.　　　　Tel: (856) 642-9700　　　　%FO: 100

Bus: *Mfr. paper products.*　　　　Fax: (856) 642-9709

S&S BIOPATH INC.
2611 Mercer Avenue, West Palm Beach, FL   33401
CEO: Joe Small

Tel: (561) 655-2302

%FO: 100

Bus: *Engaged in life sciences.*

Fax: (561) 655-2302

SCHLEICHER & SCHUELL INC.
10 Optical Avenue, Keene, NH   03431
CEO: Gary Henricksen

Tel: (603) 352-3810

%FO: 100

Bus: *Mfr. filtration, paper products.*

Fax: (603) 352-3627

Emp: 150

● **SCHMALBACH-LUBECA AG**
Kaiserswertherstrasse 115, PO Box 10 12 57, D-40880 Ratingen, Germany
CEO: Hanno C. Fiedler, CEO

Tel: 49-2101-130

Bus: *Mfr. tinplate, aluminum, plastic packaging, bottle stoppers and closures.*

Fax: 49-2102-130-130

www.schmalbach.com

Emp: 8,438

WHITE CAP INC.
1140 31st Street, Downers Grove, IL   60515
CEO: Roy Torres, CEO

Tel: (630) 515-8383

%FO: 100

Bus: *Mfr. plastic packaging, bottle stoppers and closures.*

Fax: (630) 515-0943

● **ADOLF SCHNORR GMBH & CO KG**
Postfach 60 01 62, D-71050 Sindelfingen, Germany
CEO: D. Jentsch, Pres.

Tel: 49-70-313-3020

Bus: *Mfr. disc springs & safety washers.*

Fax: 49-70-313-82600

www.schnorr.de

SCHNORR CORPORATION
4355 Varsity Drive, Ste. A, Ann Arbor, MI   48108
CEO: Gerhard Schremmer, Pres.

Tel: (734) 677-2683

%FO: 100

Bus: *Sales/distribution disc springs & safety washers.*

Fax: (734) 975-0408

● **FELIX SCHOELLER JR. PAPIERFABRIKEN GMBH**
D-49026 Burg Gretesch, Germany
CEO: Hans Michael Gallenkamp, Chmn.

Tel: 49-38001

Bus: *Holding company.*

Fax: 49-3800425

www.felix-schoeller.com

FELIX SCHOELLER TECHNICAL PAPERS INC.
PO Box 250, Pulaski, NY   13142
CEO: Donald H. Schnackel, Pres.

Tel: (315) 298-5133

%FO: 100

Bus: *Photographic base papers and technical paper products*

Fax: (315) 298-4337

● **SCHOTT GLAS**

Hattenbergstrasse 10, D-55122 Mainz, Germany

CEO: Leopold von Helmendahl, Chmn.	Tel: 49-6131-66-0	Rev: $1,349
Bus: *Mfr. specialty glass and fiber optic lighting components.*	Fax: 49-6131-66-2000 www.schott-group.com	Emp: 18,300

BARON INDUSTRIES CORP.

1401 Tunnel Hill Varnell Road, Dalton, GA   30720

CEO: Juergen Ausborn, Pres.	Tel: (706) 694-2950	%FO: 100
Bus: *Develops wet seal application and adhesive assembly process technology.*	Fax: (706) 694-2951	

GEMTRON CORPORATION

615 Highway 68, Sweetwater, TN   37874

CEO: Douglas Roberts, Pres.	Tel: (423) 337-3522
Bus: *Mfr. specialty glass for technical applications.*	Fax: (423) 337-7979

SCHOTT CORPORATION

Three Odell Plaza, Yonkers, NY   10701

CEO: Guy De Coninck, Pres. & CEO	Tel: (914) 968-1400	%FO: 100
Bus: *Mfr./marketing specialty glass.*	Fax: (914) 968-8585	Emp: 2,000

SCHOTT DONNELLY LLC

4545 East Fort Lowell Road, Tucson, AZ   85712

CEO: Stephan Hansen, Pres.	Tel: (520) 321-7680	%FO: JV
Bus: *Designs and manufactures electrochromic glass windows.*	Fax: (520) 322-5635	

SCHOTT ELECTRONIC PACKAGING

1500 West Park Drive, Westborough, MA   01581

CEO: Joe Hale, Mgr.	Tel: (508) 389-9310	%FO: 100
Bus: *Electronic packaging.*	Fax: (508) 389-9390	

SCHOTT FIBER OPTICS INC.

122 Charleston Street, Southbridge, MA   01550

CEO: Don Miller, Pres.	Tel: (508) 765-9744
Bus: *Mfr. specialty glass for technical applications.*	Fax: (508) 764-6273

SCHOTT GLASS TECHNOLOGIES INC.

400 York Avenue, Duryea, PA   18642

CEO: Bruce Jennings, Pres.	Tel: (570) 457-7485
Bus: *Mfr. specialty glass for technical applications.*	Fax: (570) 457-6960

SCHOTT PHARMACEUTICAL PACKAGING, INC.
150 North Grant Street, Cleona, PA   17042

CEO: Wolfram Weiss, Pres.	Tel: (717) 228-4200	%FO: 100
Bus: *Mfr. pharmaceuticals.*	Fax: (717) 273-4730	

SCHOTT SCIENTIFIC GLASS, INC.
1624 Staunton Avenue, Parkersburg, WV   26101

CEO: Reinhard Maenni, Pres.	Tel: (304) 424-8900	%FO: 100
Bus: *Mfr. glass tubing and blownware.*	Fax: (304) 424-8907	

SCHOTT-FOSTEC LLC
62 Columbus Street, Auburn, NY   13021

CEO: John Smith, Pres.	Tel: (315) 255-2791	%FO: JV
Bus: *Mfr. and supplies standard and custom fiber optic lighting components for the lighting market.*	Fax: (315) 255-2695	

• SCHUMAG AG
Nerscheider Weg 170, D-52076 Aachen, Germany

CEO: Dr. Ing. Klaus F. Erkes, Chmn.	Tel: 49-2408-120	
Bus: *Mfr. of cold drawing, grinding, bar turning, bar straightening, progressive cold forming machines and precision parts.*	Fax: 49-2408-12256 www.schumag.de	Emp: 1,000

SCHUMAG-KIESERLING MACHINERY, INC.
155 Hudson Avenue, Norwood, NJ   07648-0419

CEO: Dr. Erkes, Pres.	Tel: (201) 767-6850	%FO: 100
Bus: *Sales/service of cold drawing, grinding, bar turning, bar straightening machines and manufacturer of spare parts.*	Fax: (201) 767-3341	Emp: 16

• SCHUNK GROUP GMBH
Postfach 100951, D-35339 Giessen, Germany

CEO: Dr. Dagobert Kotzur, Pres.	Tel: 49-641-608-0	
Bus: *Holding company: carbon and sintered metal technology; engineering ceramics, bearing and seal technology.*	Fax: 49-641-608-1223 www.schunk-group.com	Emp: 3,860

CERCOM, INC.
991 Park Center Drive, Vista, CA   92083

CEO: Richard Palicka, Pres.	Tel: (760) 727-6200	%FO: 100
Bus: *Engaged in technology for the manufacturing of advanced materials.*	Fax: (760) 727-6209	

HOFFMANN CARBON INC.
PO Box 357, Bradford, PA   16701
CEO: Thomas Hoffman, CEO　　　　Tel: (814) 362-5588　　　　%FO: 100
Bus: *Mfr. carbon/graphite products for*　Fax: (814) 362-5590
　　　purification and coating.

SCHUNK GRAPHITE TECHNOLOGY, INC.
West 146 N9300 Held Drive, Menomonee Falls, WI   53051
CEO: Heinz Volk, Pres.　　　　　Tel: (414) 253-8720　　　　%FO: 100
Bus: *Mfr. carbon/graphite products for*　Fax: (414) 255-1391　　　Emp: 105
　　　purification and coating.

SCHUNK INEX, INC.
9229 Olean Road, Holland, NY   14080
CEO: Michael Kasprzyk, Pres.　　Tel: (716) 537-2270　　　　%FO: 100
Bus: *Mfr. carbon/graphite products for*　Fax: (716) 537-3218
　　　purification and coating.

SCHUNK QUARTZ, INC.
101 Inner Loop Road, Georgetown, TX   78626
CEO: Wim van Velzen, Pres.　　　Tel: (512) 863-0033　　　　%FO: 100
Bus: *Manufacturing facility.*　　　Fax: (512) 863-7376

STAPLA ULTRASONICS CORPORATION
375 Ballardvale Street, Wilmington, MA   01887
CEO: M. Mogaban, CEO　　　　　Tel: (978) 658-9400　　　　%FO: 100
Bus: *Mfr. carbon/graphite products for*　Fax: (978) 658-6550
　　　purification and coating.

WEISS ENVIRONMENTAL TECHNOLOGY INC.
West 146 N 9300 Held Drive, Menomonee Falls, WI   53051
CEO: Heinz Volk, Pres.　　　　　Tel: (262) 253-8720　　　　%FO: 100
Bus: *Mfr. carbon/graphite products for*　Fax: (262) 255-1391
　　　purification and coating.

● SCHWARZ PHARMA AG
10 Alfred Nobelstrasse, D-40789 Monheim, Germany
CEO: Patrick Schwarz-Schüette, Chmn.　Tel: 49-2173-480　　　　Rev: $736
Bus: *Mfr./distribution ethical pharmaceutical*　Fax: 49-2173-481608　　Emp: 1,288
　　　products.　　　　　　　　www.schwarzpharma.com

SCHWARZ PHARMA INC.
6140 Executive Drive, Mequon, WI   53092
CEO: Klaus Veitinger　　　　　Tel: (414) 238-5450　　　　%FO: 100
Bus: *Gastrointestinal, cardiovascular*　Fax: (414) 242-1641
　　　and pharmaceutical products.

SCHWARZ PHARMA INC.
PO Box 2038, Milwaukee, WI 53201

CEO: Ron Stratton, Pres.	Tel: (414) 238-5704	%FO: 100
Bus: *Gastrointestinal, cardiovascular and pharmaceutical products.*	Fax: (414) 238-0611	Emp: 160

SCHWARZ PHARMA INC.
1101 C Avenue, West Seymour, IN 47274

CEO: Leo Katalinas, Mng.	Tel: (812) 523-5468	%FO: 100
Bus: *Gastrointestinal, cardiovascular and pharmaceutical products.*	Fax: (812) 523-1887	

● **SEMIKRON INTL GMBH & CO**
Sigmundstrasse 200, D-90431 Nuremberg, Germany

CEO: Peter Martin, Pres.	Tel: 49-911-65590
Bus: *Mfr. power semiconductors.*	Fax: 49-911-6559262
	www.semikron.com

SEMIKRON INTL INC.
24456 Silver Spur Lane, Laguna Niguel, CA 92677

CEO: Dennis Isaac	Tel: (949) 362-3965	%FO: 100
Bus: *Mfr. power semiconductors.*	Fax: (949) 362-3559	

SEMIKRON INTL INC.
11 Executive Drive, PO Box 66, Hudson, NH 03051

CEO: Tom Rantala, Mgr.	Tel: (603) 883-8102	%FO: 100
Bus: *Mfr. power semiconductors.*	Fax: (603) 883-8021	

SEMIKRON INTL INC.
13920 Quail Oval, North Royalton, OH 44133

CEO: Andy Camardo	Tel: (440) 237-7095	%FO: 100
Bus: *Mfr. power semiconductors.*	Fax: (440) 237-1557	

SEMIKRON INTL INC.
8027 Eaglecreek Court, Sylvania, OH 43560

CEO: Gregg Vining	Tel: (419) 885-3124	%FO: 100
Bus: *Mfr. power semiconductors.*	Fax: (419) 882-8374	

SEMIKRON INTL INC.
20356 41st Place, Denver, CO 80249

CEO: Arthur Connolly	Tel: (303) 307-1286	%FO: 100
Bus: *Mfr. power semiconductors.*	Fax: (303) 981-8343	

SEMIKRON INTL INC.
561 Yarmouth Road, Elk Grove Village, IL 60007

CEO: Don Vogt	Tel: (847) 437-8886	%FO: 100
Bus: *Mfr. power semiconductors.*	Fax: (847) 437-9899	

SEMIKRON INTL INC.
6123 N. Cobb Road, Elkhorn, WI   53121
CEO: David Ahler   Tel: (262) 743-1367   %FO: 100
Bus: *Mfr. power semiconductors.*   Fax: (262) 743-1368

● **SER SYSTEMS AG**
Innovationspark Rahms, D-53577 Neustadt/Wied, Germany
CEO: Gert J. Reinardt, CEO   Tel: 49-2683-984-361   Rev: $175
Bus: *Mfr. software.*   Fax: 49-2683-984-222   Emp: 1,250
                                www.ser.com

   SER SOLUTIONS, INC.
   555 Herndon Parkway, Herndon, VA   20170
   CEO: Carl E. Mergele, Pres.   Tel: (703) 478-9808   %FO: 100
   Bus: *Mfr./sales software.*   Fax: (703) 787-6720

● **SGL CARBON AG**
Rheingaustrasse 182, D-65203 Wiesbaden, Germany
CEO: Robert J. Koehler, CEO   Tel: 49-611-962-73   Rev: $1,190
Bus: *Mfr. graphite and carbon products.*   Fax: 49-611-962-73   Emp: 8,000
                                    www.sglcarbon.com

   CARBON & CERAMIC TECHNOLOGY, INC.
   59 Beachwood Drive, Madison, CT   06643
   CEO: Mark Kokosinski   Tel: (203) 421-0655   %FO: 100
   Bus: *Mfr. graphite and carbon products.*   Fax: (203) 421-0655

   SGL ACOTEC INC.
   8320 Hempstead Highway, Houston, TX   77270
   CEO: Mark Kokosinski   Tel: (713) 867-8400   %FO: 100
   Bus: *Mfr. graphite and carbon products.*   Fax: (713) 867-8433

   SGL ACOTEC INC.
   6611 West Snowvile Road, Brecksville, OH   44141
   CEO: Mark Kokosinski   Tel: (440) 717-7037   %FO: 100
   Bus: *Mfr. graphite and carbon products.*   Fax: (440) 717-7466

   SGL CARBON CORPORATION
   800 Theresa Street, St. Marys, PA   15857
   CEO: Mark Kokosinski   Tel: (814) 781-2698   %FO: 100
   Bus: *Mfr. graphite and carbon products.*   Fax: (814) 781-2611

   SGL CARBON CORPORATION
   PO Box 563960, Charlotte, NC   28256
   CEO: Mark Kokosinski   Tel: (704) 593-5243   %FO: 100
   Bus: *U.S. headquarters location; mfr.*   Fax: (704) 593-5117
      graphite and carbon products.

SGL TECHNIC INC.

21945 Drake Road, Strongsville, OH   44136

CEO: Mark Kokosinski

Bus: *Mfr. graphite and carbon products.*

Tel: (410) 572-9570

Fax: (410) 572-3600

%FO: 100

● **SIEMENS AG**

Wittelsbacherplatz 2, D-80333 Munich, Germany

CEO: Dr. Heinrich von Pierer, Pres.

Bus: *Design/development/mfr. electrical and electronic system for industry.*

Tel: 49-89-636-3300

Fax: 49-89-636-4242

www.siemens.com

Rev: $68,918

Emp: 430,200

ADB

977 Gahanna Pkwy, PO Box 30829, Columbus, OH   43230-0829

CEO: Steve Rauch, Pres.

Bus: *Mfr. airfield lighting products, design/mfr. airport automation systems.*

Tel: (614) 861-1304

Fax: (614) 864-2069

%FO: 100

CRYSTAL TECHNOLOGY, INC.

1040 East Meadow Circle, Palo Alto, CA   94303-4230

CEO: George Eberharter, Pres.

Bus: *Design/mfr. electronic components and system or automotive industry.*

Tel: (650) 856-7911

Fax: (650) 424-8806

%FO: 100

SIEMENS NIXDORF INFORMATION SYSTEMS, INC.

1730 North First Street, San Jose, CA   95134

CEO: Bharat Dave, CEO

Bus: *Develops, integrates and services computer hardware and software solutions.*

Tel: (408) 428-9000

Fax: (408) 428-8320

%FO: 100

MOODY PRICE, INC.

PO Box 260044, Baton Rouge, LA   70826-0044

CEO: Dan Daniel, Pres.

Bus: *Instrumentation, filtration and heat transfer products.*

Tel: (225) 767-7755

Fax: (225) 763-6005

%FO: 100

NSW CORPORATION

530 Gregory Avenue, Roanoke, VA   24016

CEO: Lawrence E. Ptaschek, Pres.

Bus: *Plastic packaging and industrial nets, filtration covers/sleeves/nets, plastic belts; waste water filters.*

Tel: (540) 981-0362

Fax: (540) 345-8421

%FO: 100

OSRAM SYLVANIA INC.
100 Endicott Street, Danvers, MA   01923-3623

CEO: Dean Langford, Pres.	Tel: (978) 777-1900	%FO: 100
Bus: *Mfr./marketing lighting products, precision materials and components for consumers and industry.*	Fax: (978) 750-2152	

SIEMENS APPLIED AUTOMATION, INC.
Pawhuska Road, Barlesville, OK   74005

CEO: Gary Waugh, Pres.	Tel: (918) 662-7000	%FO: 100
Bus: *Mfr. process automation equipment and related services.*	Fax: (918) 662-7810	

SIEMENS AUTOMOTIVE CORPORATION
2400 Executive Hills Drive, Auburn Hills, MI   48326-2980

CEO: John Sanderson, CEO	Tel: (248) 253-1000	%FO: JV
Bus: *Design/mfr. electronic components and system or automotive industry.*	Fax: (248) 253-2999	

SIEMENS BUILDING TECHNOLOGY
1000 Deerfield Parkway, Buffalo Grove, IL   60089

CEO: John J. Grad, Pres.	Tel: (847) 215-1000	%FO: 100
Bus: *Utility services.*	Fax: (847) 215-1093	

SIEMENS BUSINESS COMMUNICATION SYSTEMS, INC.
4900 Old Ironsides Dr., PO Box 58075, Santa Clara, CA   95052-8075

CEO: Fred Fromm, Pres.	Tel: (408) 492-2000	%FO: 100
Bus: *Mfr./marketing/support private telecommunications system.*	Fax: (408) 492-3430	

SIEMENS CORPORATION
153 East 53rd Street, New York, NY   10022

CEO: Gerhard Schulmeyer, CEO	Tel: (212) 258-4000	%FO: 100
Bus: *Holding company: electrical and electronic systems.*	Fax: (212) 258-4370	Emp: 33,400

SIEMENS CORPORATION
701 Pennsylvania Avenue, NW, Washington, DC   20004

CEO: Jermiah L. Murphy, VP	Tel: (202) 434-4800	%FO: 100
Bus: *Government relations Washington office.*	Fax: (202) 347-4015	

SIEMENS CORPORATE RESEARCH INC.
755 College Road East, Princeton, NJ   08540-6632

CEO: Thomas Grandke, Pres.	Tel: (609) 734-6500	%FO: 100
Bus: *Exploratory and applied research.*	Fax: (609) 734-6565	

SIEMENS ENERGY & AUTOMATION INC.

405 Brookview Drive, Ste. 204, Evansville, IN   47711

CEO: Scott Gartner   Tel: (812) 867-0920   %FO: 100

Bus: *Metals process technology solutions.*   Fax: (812) 867-0922

SIEMENS ENERGY & AUTOMATION INC.

1700 Ridge Avenue, Corapolis, PA   15108

CEO: Pat Gilmore   Tel: (412) 788-8076   %FO: 100

Bus: *Metals process technology solutions.*   Fax: (412) 788-1334

SIEMENS ENERGY & AUTOMATION INC.

5313 Campbells Run Road, Ste. 100, Pittsburgh, PA   15205

CEO: Bill Kavel   Tel: (724) 446-0349   %FO: 100

Bus: *Metals process technology solutions.*   Fax: (724) 446-0359

SIEMENS ENERGY & AUTOMATION INC.

101 Creek Road, Churchville, PA   18966

CEO: Jim Hugo   Tel: (215) 953-8755   %FO: 100

Bus: *Metals process technology solutions.*   Fax: (215) 953-8756

SIEMENS ENERGY & AUTOMATION INC.

333 Old Milton Parkway, Alpharetta, GA   30005

CEO: Richard C. Buzun, Pres. & CEO   Tel: (770) 751-2000   %FO: 100

Bus: *Mfr./markets a wide variety of electrical and electronic equipment and systems in the industrial and construction market segments.*   Fax: (770) 740-2534

SIEMENS ENERGY & AUTOMATION INC.

7135 Pine Grove Lane, Two Rivers, WI   54241

CEO: Bob Lockington   Tel: (920) 794-8701   %FO: 100

Bus: *Metals process technology solutions.*   Fax: (920) 794-7198

SIEMENS ENERGY & AUTOMATION, INC.

100 Technology Drive, Alpharetta, GA   30005

CEO: Peter Cobb   Tel: (770) 751-3372   %FO: 100

Bus: *Metals process technology solutions.*   Fax: (770) 740-3294

SIEMENS FINANCIAL SERVICES

200 Somerset Corporate Boulevard, Bridgewater, NJ   08807

CEO: William T. Zadrozny, CEO

Tel: (908) 429-6000

%FO: 100

Bus: *Provides sales and investment financing.*

Fax: (908) 429-6072

SIEMENS HEARING INSTRUMENTS, INC.

10 Constitution Avenue, Piscataway, NJ   08855-1397

CEO: John Krauter, VP

Tel: (732) 562-6600

%FO: 100

Bus: *Sales/mfr. hearing instruments.*

Fax: (732) 562-6696

SIEMENS INFORMATION & COMMUNICATION NETWORKS, INC.

900 Broken Sound Pkwy., Boca Raton, FL   33487-3587

CEO: Dieter Diehn, EVP

Tel: (561) 955-5000

%FO: 100

Bus: *Design/develop/mfr. systems and equipment for network communications (see joint parent: The General Electric Co. Plc.)*

Fax: (561) 955-8014

SIEMENS MEDICAL SYSTEMS, INC.

186 Wood Avenue South, Iselin, NJ   08830

CEO: Thomas N. McCausland, CEO

Tel: (732) 205-2200

%FO: 100

Bus: *Products and services related to rail transport and technology.*

Fax: (732) 603-7379

SIEMENS MOORE PROCESS AUTOMATION

Sumneytown Pike, Spring House, PA   19477

CEO: William B. Moore, Pres.

Tel: (215) 646-7400

%FO: 100

Bus: *Mfr. process control instruments.*

Fax: (215) 646-2621

Emp: 1,147

SIEMENS POWER CORPORATION

155 108th Avenue NE, Bellevue, WA   98004-5901

CEO: Robert Stephenson, Pres.

Tel: (425) 453-4300

%FO: 100

Bus: *Power generation equipment, nuclear fuel, power plant services, photovoltaic modules and lasers.*

Fax: (425) 453-4446

SIEMENS POWER CORPORATION

1040 South 70th Street, Milwaukee, WI   53214

CEO: Baird Stephenson, Pres.

Tel: (414) 475-3600

%FO: 100

Bus: *Engaged in nuclear power generation products and services.*

Fax: (414) 475-4040

SIEMENS POWER TRANSMISSION & DISTRIBUTION

7000 Siemens Road, Wendell, NC   27591-8309

CEO: Jan Van Dokkum, CEO   Tel: (919) 365-2200   %FO: 100

Bus: *Mfr. power transmission and*   Fax: (919) 365-2315
   distribution equipment.

SIEMENS SOLAR INDUSTRIES, LP

4650 Adohr Lane, Camarillo, CA   93012-8508

CEO: Gernot Oswald, Pres.   Tel: (805) 482-6800   %FO: 100

Bus: *Supplier of photovoltaic (solar)*   Fax: (805) 388-6395
   cells and panels.

SIEMENS TRANSPORTATION SYSTEMS

1700 Tribute Road, Ste. 200, Sacramento, CA   95815

CEO: Roelof van Ark, Pres.   Tel: (916) 646-2300   %FO: 100

Bus: *Engaged in transportation.*   Fax: (916) 646-2375

SIEMENS WESTINGHOUSE POWER CORPORATION

4400 Alafaya Trail, Orlando, FL   32826-2399

CEO: Randy Zwirn, CEO   Tel: (407) 281-2000   %FO: 100

Bus: *Supplies power generation*   Fax: (407) 736-5045
   equipment, plants and services.

VACUUMSHMEIZE CORPORATION

4027 Will Rogers Parkway, Oklahoma City, OK   73108-2035

CEO: Don Lenord, Pres.   Tel: (405) 943-9651   %FO: 100

Bus: *Engaged in magnetic assemblies.*   Fax: (405) 949-2967

• SMS DEMAG AG (FORMERLY SMS SCHLOEMANN-SIEMAG AG)

Eduard-Schloemann-Strasse 4, D-40237 Düsseldorf, Germany

CEO: Michael Hanisch, CEO   Tel: 49-211-8810   Rev: $2,500

Bus: *Mfr. rolling mills and casters for the*   Fax: 49-211-8814902   Emp: 3,300
   steel and aluminum industries.   www.sms-ag.de

SMS DEMAG, HOT ROLLING MILL DIV.

345 Rouser Road, Bldg. 5, Pittsburgh, PA   15108-4744

CEO: Michael Mullen, VP   Tel: (412) 231-2100   %FO: 100

Bus: *Mfr. rolling mills.*   Fax: (412) 231-4919

SMS DEMAG, METALLURGY DIV.

345 Rouser Road, Bldg. 5, Pittsburgh, PA   15108-4744

CEO: Joe Dzierzawski, VP   Tel: (412) 231-2100   %FO: 100

Bus: *Engineering and sales of*   Fax: (412) 231-4919   Emp: 40
   equipment for the steel industry;
   electric arc furnaces, ladle
   furnaces, bofs, etc.

- **SOFTWARE AG**

Uhlandstrasse 12, D-64297 Darmstadt, Germany

CEO: Erwin W. Konigs, CEO | Tel: 49-6151-920 | Rev: $392
Bus: *Mfr. software.* | Fax: 49-6151-92-1933 | Emp: 2,800
| www.softwareag.com |

SOFTWARE AG INC.

11190 Sunrise Valley Drive, Reston, VA 20191

CEO: Gary M. Voight, CEO | Tel: (703) 860-5050 | %FO: 100
Bus: *Sales/distribution of software.* | Fax: (703) 391-6975 |

- **SOLO KLEINMOTOREN GMBH**

Stuttgarter Strasse 41, D-71069 Sindelfingen, Germany

CEO: Hans Emmerich, Pres. | Tel: 49-7013-3010 |
Bus: *Mfr. chain saws, water pumps,* | Fax: 49-7013-301149 |
lawnmowers, sprayers and trimmers. | www.solo-germany.com |

SOLO, INC.

5100 Chestnut Avenue, PO Box 5030, Newport News, VA 23605

CEO: James Dunne, Pres. | Tel: (757) 245-4228 | %FO: 100
Bus: *Mfr. chain saws, sprayers &* | Fax: (757) 245-0800 | Emp: 72
trimmers. | |

- **SPHERETEX GMBH**

Eller Straße 101 Geb.: A3, D-40721 Hilden, Germany

CEO: Klaus Koelzer, Pres. | Tel: 49-2103-58993 |
Bus: *High-tech core materials for fiberglass* | Fax: 49-2103-54901 | Emp: 20
sandwich laminates. | www.spheretex.com |

SPHERETEX AMERICA INC.

985 11th Avenue South, Jacksonville Beach, FL 32250

CEO: Klaus Koelzer, Pres. | Tel: (904) 273-0708 | %FO: 100
Bus: *Sale/service high-tech core* | Fax: (904) 273-0709 |
materials. | |

- **SRS WORLDHOTELS - STEIGENBERGER RESERVATION SERVICE**

Lyoner Strasse 40, D-60528 Frankfurt am Main, Germany

CEO: Reinhard Przybilski, Chmn. | Tel: 49-69-6056-405 |
Bus: *Hotel representation & reservation* | Fax: 49-69-6656-4545 | Emp: 100
services. | www.srs-worldhotels.com |

SRS WORLDHOTELS

152 West 57th Street, 33rd Fl., New York, NY 10019-3301

CEO: Edward N. Brill, VP | Tel: (212) 956-0200 | %FO: 100
Bus: *Hotel representation &* | Fax: (212) 956-2555 | Emp: 20
reservation. | |

● **STAEDTLER MARS GMBH & CO.**

Schreib-und Zeichengeräte-Fabriken, Moosäckerstraße 3, D-90427 Nürnberg, Germany

CEO: Oskar Reutter, Mng. Dir.   Tel: 49-911-93650

Bus: *Mfr. writing and drafting materials.*   Fax: 49-911-9365400   Emp: 3,700

www.staedtler.de

STAEDTLER, INC.

21900 Plummer Street, Chatsworth, CA 91311

CEO: Sal R. Elia, Pres.   Tel: (818) 882-6000   %FO: 100

Bus: *Mfr. writing & drafting materials.*   Fax: (818) 882-0036   Emp: 60

● **R. STAHL GMBH, DIV. HEIDELBERG GROUP**

Bergstraße 2, D-74653 Künzelsau, Germany

CEO: Dr. Peter Völker   Tel: 49-7940-17326   Rev: $228

Bus: *Mfr. electronic switchgear, intrinsic*   Fax: 49-7940-17333   Emp: 2,088
      safety interface systems.   www.stahl.de

R. STAHL INC.

45 Northwestern Drive, Salem, NH 03079

CEO: Wolfgang Zaers, Pres.   Tel: (603) 870-9500   %FO: 100

Bus: *Suppliers of apparatus and*   Fax: (603) 870-9290   Emp: 25
      systems for instrumentation,
      energy distribution and lighting in
      hazardous areas.

● **STEAG HAMA TECH AG**

Ferdinand-von-Steinbeis-Ring 10, D75447 Stemenfels/Wurtlemberg, Germany

CEO: Stephan W. Mohren, CEO   Tel: 49-7045-41-219   Rev: $203

Bus: *Mfr. of optical disk machinery and*   Fax: 49-7045-41-119   Emp: 500
      equipment.   www.steag-hamatech.com

STEAG HAMA TECH, INC.

PO Box 70, Saco, ME 04072

CEO: Francis Watts   Tel: (207) 282-4698   %FO: 100

Bus: *Mfr./sales of optical disk*   Fax: (207) 282-9884
      machinery and equipment.

● **ANDREAS STIHL**

Badstrasse 115, D-71336 Waiblingen, Germany

CEO: Hans-Peter Stihl, CEO   Tel: 49-7151-260

Bus: *Mfr. outdoor power equipment.*   Fax: 49-7151-261140   Emp: 3,000

www.stihl.com

STIHL INC.
536 Viking Drive, Virginia Beach, VA   23450
CEO: F. J. Whyte, Pres.   Tel: (757) 486-9100   %FO: 100
Bus: *Sales/distribution of outdoor*   Fax: (757) 486-9324
power equipment.

● STINNES AG, SUB. E.ON
Humboldtring 15, D-45472 Mulheim an der Rurh, Germany
CEO: Dr. Wulf H. Bernotat, Chmn.   Tel: 49-208-494-0   Rev: $11,843
Bus: *Mfr./distributes metals, minerals,*   Fax: 49-208-494-698   Emp: 43,800
chemicals and industrial products.   www.stinnes.de

BRENNTAG INC.
PO Box 13786, Reading, PA   19612
CEO: Stephen R. Clark, Pres.   Tel: (610) 926-6100   %FO: 100
Bus: *Distribution of metals, minerals,*   Fax: (610) 926-3070
chemicals and industrial products.

CROWN CHEMICAL CORPORATION
1888 Nirvana Avenue, Chula Vista, CA   92011-6197
CEO: William E. Huttner Jr., Pres.   Tel: (619) 421-6601   %FO: 100
Bus: *Distribution of metals, minerals,*   Fax: (619) 421-1127
chemicals and industrial products.

DELTA DISTRIBUTORS, INC.
610 Fisher Road, Longview, TX   75604
CEO: Kevin Kessing, Pres.   Tel: (903) 759-7151   %FO: 100
Bus: *Distribution of metals, minerals,*   Fax: (903) 759-7548
chemicals and industrial products.

EASTECH CHEMICAL INC.
5700 Tacony Street, Philadelphia, PA   19135
CEO: Lawrence J. Kelly, Pres.   Tel: (215) 537-1000   %FO: 100
Bus: *Distribution of metals, minerals,*   Fax: (215) 537-8575
chemicals and industrial products.

MILSOLV CORPORATION
8100 West Florist Street, Milwaukee, WI   53218
CEO: Chester J. Lukeszewicz, Pres.   Tel: (262) 252-3550   %FO: 100
Bus: *Distribution of metals, minerals,*   Fax: (262) 252-5250
chemicals and industrial products.

P.B.&S. CHEMICAL COMPANY, INC.
PO Box 20, Henderson, KY   42420-0020
CEO: Thomas M. McFarland, Pres.   Tel: (270) 827-3545   %FO: 100
Bus: *Distribution of metals, minerals,*   Fax: (270) 826-1486
chemicals and industrial products.

SCHENKER INTERNATIONAL, INC.

150 Albany Avenue, Freeport, NY   11520

CEO: Hartmut Luehr, Pres.   Tel: (516) 377-3000   %FO: 100

Bus: *Engaged in logistics and*   Fax: (516) 377-3100
distribution of industrial products.

SOCO-LYNCH CHEMICAL CO.

10747 Patterson Place, Santa Fe Springs, CA   90670

CEO: William E. Huttner Jr., Pres.   Tel: (562) 903-9626   %FO: 100

Bus: *Distribution of metals, minerals,*   Fax: (562) 903-9622
chemicals and industrial products.

SOUTHCHEM, INC.

2000 East Pettigrew, Durham, NC   27703

CEO: Gil Steadman, Pres.   Tel: (919) 596-0681   %FO: 100

Bus: *Distribution of metals, minerals,*   Fax: (919) 596-6438
chemicals and industrial products.

STINNES CORPORATION

120 White Plains Road, Tarrytown, NY   10591

CEO: Dr. Hans-Henning Maier, CEO   Tel: (914) 366-7200   %FO: 100

Bus: *Distribution of metals, minerals,*   Fax: (914) 366-8226
chemicals and industrial products.

TEXTILE CHEMICAL CORP.

Pottsville Pike & Huller Lane, Reading, PA   19605

CEO: Anthony Gerace, Pres.   Tel: (610) 926-4151   %FO: 100

Bus: *Distribution of metals, minerals,*   Fax: (610) 926-4160
chemicals and industrial products.

WHITTAKER, CLARK & DANIELS, INC.

1000 Coolidge Street, South Plainfield, NJ   07080

CEO: Michael C. Argyelan, Pres.   Tel: (908) 561-6100   %FO: 100

Bus: *Distribution of metals, minerals,*   Fax: (908) 258-5041
chemicals and industrial products.

● **SÜD-CHEMIE AG**

Lenbachplatz 6, D-80333 Munich, Germany

CEO: Jürgen F. Kammer, CEO   Tel: 49-89-5100-0   Rev: $735

Bus: *Mfr. chemicals, bleaching products and*   Fax: 49-89-5110-375   Emp: 5,175
thickening agents.   www.sued-chemie.com

SUD-CHEMIE PERFORMANCE PACKAGING, INC.

PO Box 610, Colton, CA   92324

CEO: Mel Bernett, VP   Tel: (909) 825-1793   %FO: 100

Bus: *Manufacturing plant.*   Fax: (909) 825-6271

SUD-CHEMIE PERFORMANCE PACKAGING, INC.
101 Christine Drive, Belen, NM   87002
CEO: Mel Bernett, VP   Tel: (505) 864-6691   %FO: 100
Bus: *Manufacturing plant.*   Fax: (505) 864-9296

SUD-CHEMIE PROTOTECH, INC.
32 Fremont Street, Needham, MA   02494
CEO: Dr. Amiram Bar-llan, Pres.   Tel: (781) 444-5188   %FO: 100
Bus: *Mfr. chemicals for oxidation*   Fax: (781) 444-0130
     systems.

SUD-CHEMIE RHEOLOGICALS
PO Box 32370, Louisville, KY   40232
CEO: Dr. Amiram Bar-llan, Pres.   Tel: (502) 634-7500   %FO: 100
Bus: *Mfr. rheological additives.*   Fax: (502) 634-7727

• SUPFINA GRIESHABER GMBH & CO.
Rippoldsauer Strasse 49, D-77776 Bad Rippoldsau-Schapbach, Germany
CEO: W. Kera-Barz, CEO   Tel: 49-78-3989-200   Rev: $20
Bus: *Mfr. superfinishing machines &*   Fax: 49-78-3989-0   Emp: 200
     attachments.   www.supfina.com

SUPFINA MACHINE COMPANY
181 Circuit Drive, North Kingstown, RI   01852
CEO: Wolfgang Auschner, Pres.   Tel: (401) 294-6600   %FO: 100
Bus: *Mfr. superfinishing machines &*   Fax: (401) 294-6262   Emp: 35
     attachments.

• SUSE LINUX AG
Schanzaeckerstrasse 10, D-90443 Nuremberg, Germany
CEO: Roland Dyroff, CEO   Tel: 49-911-74053-31   Rev: $10
Bus: *Mfr. software.*   Fax: 49-911-74177-55   Emp: 130
                                 www.suse.com

SUSE LINUX, INC.
580 Second Street, Ste. 210, Oakland, CA   94607
CEO: Holger Dyroff, Sales   Tel: (510) 628-3380   %FO: 100
Bus: *Mfr. software.*   Fax: (510) 628-3381

• TARKETT SOMMER AG
Nachtweideweg 1-7, D-67227 Frankenthal, Germany
CEO: Marc Assa, CEO   Tel: 49-623-3810   Rev: $1,281
Bus: *Mfr. hardwood flooring.*   Fax: 49-623-3811-648   Emp: 7,215
                                 www.tarkett-sommer.com

HARRIS-TARKETT INC.
2225 Eddie Williams Road, PO Box 300, Johnson City, TN 37601-0300
CEO: Wayne Anderson   Tel: (423) 928-3122   %FO: 100
Bus: *Mfr./sales hardwood flooring.*   Fax: (423) 928-9445

● **TENGELMANN GROUP**
Wissollstrasse 5-43, D-54486 Mulheim/Ruhr, Germany
CEO: Erivan k. Haub, Chmn.   Tel: 49-208-5806-662   Rev: $30,800
Bus: *Retail food chain.*   Fax: 49-208-5806-6401   Emp: 200,000
                                   www.tengelmann.de

    GREAT ATLANTIC & PACIFIC TEA COMPANY INC. (A&P)
    2 Paragon Drive, Montvale, NJ 07645
    CEO: Christian W. E. Haub, CEO   Tel: (201) 573-9700   %FO: 53
    Bus: *Retail food chain.*   Fax: (201) 930-4079   Emp: 90,000

● **TERROT STRICKMASCHINEN GMBH**
Postfach 501129, D-70341 Stuttgart, Germany
CEO: Werner Bohringer, Pres.   Tel: 49-711-5531-0
Bus: *Mfr. large diameter circular knitting* Fax: 49-711-5531-111   Emp: 700
  machines.   www.terrot.de

    TERROT KNITTING MACHINES INC.
    4808 Persimmon Court, Monroe, NC 28110
    CEO: Gerhard A. Kuhn, VP   Tel: (704) 283-9434   %FO: 100
    Bus: *Sale/service large diameter*   Fax: (704) 289-9812   Emp: 5
      knitting machines.

● **THIES GMBH & CO.**
Borkener Strasse 155, D-48653 Coesfeld, Germany
CEO: Erich Thies, Pres.   Tel: 49-2541-7331
Bus: *Mfr. textile dyeing equipment.*   Fax: 49-2541-733299   Emp: 500
                                   www.thiesgmbh.de

    THIES CORPORATION
    PO Box 36010, Rock Hill, SC 29732-0500
    CEO: Ronald Schrell, Pres.   Tel: (803) 366-4174   %FO: 100
    Bus: *Sale/service textile dyeing*   Fax: (803) 366-8103   Emp: 10
      equipment.

● **THYSSEN KRUPP AG**

August-Thyssen-Strasse 1, D-40211 Düsseldorf, Germany

CEO: Dr. Ekkehard Schulz, Chmn. Tel: 49-211-824-0 Rev: $32,710

Bus: *Mfr. industrial materials, systems and components, including production of steel and manufacture of elevators and escalators.* Fax: 49-211-824-36000 Emp: 193,300

www.thyssenkruppelevator.com

THE BUDD COMPANY

3155 West Big Beaver Road, Troy, MI 48084

CEO: Albert F. Kovach, CEO Tel: (248) 643-3500 %FO: 100

Bus: *U.S. headquarters. Mfr. sheet metal stampings, assemblies, auto body panels, prototypes and products for auto industry.* Fax: (248) 643-3593 Emp: 9,600

GIDDINGS & LEWIS INC.

142 Doty Street, PO Box 590, Fond du Lac, WI 54936-0590

CEO: Stephen M. Peterson, CEO Tel: (920) 921-4100

Bus: *Sales of industrial automation products and machine tools.* Fax: (920) 929-4334

POLYSIUS/KRUPP USA

180 Interstate North Parkway, Atlanta, GA 30339-2194

CEO: Daniel R. Fritz, Pres. Tel: (770) 995-3660 %FO: 100

Bus: *Logistics, air freight, overseas shipping.* Fax: (770) 955-8789 Emp: 270

THYSSE KRUPP

400 Renaissance Center, Ste. 1700, Detroit, MI 48243

CEO: Kenneth J. Graham, Pres. Tel: (313) 567-5600 %FO: 100

Bus: *Mfr./process steel.* Fax: (313) 567-5667 Emp: 350

THYSSEN KRUPP ELEVATOR

30984 Santana Street, Hayward, CA 94544

CEO: Kenneth J. Graham, Pres. Tel: (510) 476-1900 %FO: 100

Bus: *Mfr./sale/service elevators.* Fax: (510) 476-1919

THYSSEN KRUPP ELEVATOR

2260 Northwest Parkway, Suite E, Marietta, GA 30067

CEO: Kenneth J. Graham, Pres. Tel: (770) 916-0555 %FO: 100

Bus: *Mfr./sale/service elevators.* Fax: (770) 988-9547

THYSSEN KRUPP ELEVATOR

2801 SW 15th Street, Pompano Beach, FL 33069

CEO: Kenneth J. Graham, Pres. Tel: (954) 971-6500 %FO: 100

Bus: *Mfr./sale/service elevators.* Fax: (954) 974-0668

THYSSEN KRUPP ELEVATOR

15141 East Whittier Blvd, Ste. 505, Whittier, CA   90603

CEO: John Brant, Pres. — Tel: (562) 693-9491 — %FO: 100

Bus: *Mfr./sales/service elevators.* — Fax: (562) 693-0028

THYSSEN KRUPP ELEVATOR CO.

665 Concord Avenue, Cambridge, MA   02138

CEO: Kenneth J. Graham, Pres. — Tel: (617) 547-9000 — %FO: 100

Bus: *Mfr./sale/service elevators.* — Fax: (617) 876-3167 — Emp: 180

THYSSEN SPECIALTY STEELS INC.

365 Village Drive, Carol Stream, IL   60188-1828

CEO: James Peters, Mgr. — Tel: (630) 682-3900 — %FO: 100

Bus: *Sale specialty steels.* — Fax: (630) 682-4587 — Emp: 140

● **ALFRED TRONSER GMBH**

Postfach 63, D-75329 Engelsbrand, Germany

CEO: Michael Tronser, Pres. — Tel: 49-7082-798-0

Bus: *Design and manufacture of Air Variable* — Fax: 49-7082-798155 — Emp: 110
Capacitors for professional electronics. — www.tronser.com

TRONSER, INC.

2763 Route 20 East, PO Box 315, Cazenovia, NY   13035

CEO: James Dowd, VP — Tel: (315) 655-9528 — %FO: 100

Bus: *Mfr. capacitors, microwave tuning* — Fax: (315) 655-2149 — Emp: 20
elements

● **TRUMPF GMBH & CO**

Johann-Maus-Strasse 2, D-71254 Ditzingen, Germany

CEO: Berthold Leibinger, Pres. — Tel: 49-7156-303-0

Bus: *Mfr. sheetmetal fabricating equipment,* — Fax: 49-7156-303-309
punch presses, laser processing centers, — www.trumpf.com
portable power tools.

HUETTINGER ELECTRONIC INC.

11 Hyde Road, Farmington, CT   06032

CEO: Paul A. Oranges, VP Sales — Tel: (860) 677-9730 — %FO: 100

Bus: *Provides DC Power Supplies,* — Fax: (860) 678-8345
Medium Frequency Generators
and RF Generators for industrial
and scientific applications.

TRUMPF AMERICA INC.

11 Hyde Road, Farmington, CT   06032

CEO: Peter Leibinger, CEO — Tel: (860) 677-9741 — %FO: 100

Bus: *Mfr. machine tools.* — Fax: (860) 674-5341

● **HANS TURCK GMBH & CO. KG**

Witzlebenstrasse 7, D-45472 Mulheim an der Ruhr, Germany

CEO: Ulrich Turck, Mng. Dir.   Tel: 49-208-49520

Bus: *Mfr./sales sensors for automation:*   Fax: 49-208-4952-264   Emp: 3,000
inductive, capacitive, ultrasonic,   www.turck-globe.com
inductive magnetic; flow controls, auto
controls.

   TURCK, INC.

   3000 Campus Drive, Minneapolis, MN   55441

   CEO: William A. Schneider, Pres.   Tel: (612) 553-7300   %FO: 90

   Bus: *Mfr./distribution inductive,*   Fax: (612) 553-0708   Emp: 300
   capacitive, ultrasonic, inductive
   magnetic proximity sensors;
   cordsets, intrinsically safe sensors,
   controls and flow switches,
   junction boxes and bus products.

● **TUV RHEINLAND/BERLIN-BRANDENBURG EV**

Am Grauen Stein, D-51105 Cologne, Germany

CEO: Prof. Dr. Bruno O. Braun, Pres. & CEO   Tel: 49-221-8060   Rev: $285

Bus: *International product safety testing and* Fax: 49-221-8061760   Emp: 7,000
certification services.   www.de.tuv.com

   TUV RHEINLAND OF NORTH AMERICA, INC.

   12 Commerce Road, Newtown, CT   06470

   CEO: Stephan Schmitt, Pres.   Tel: (203) 426-0888   %FO: 100

   Bus: *International product safety*   Fax: (203) 270-8883   Emp: 125
   testing and certification services.

   TUV RHEINLAND OF NORTH AMERICA, INC.

   1279 Quarry Lane, Ste. A, Pleasanton, CA   94566

   CEO: Andreas Eberhard   Tel: (925) 249-9123   %FO: 100

   Bus: *International product safety*   Fax: (925) 249-9124
   testing and certification services.

   TUV RHEINLAND OF NORTH AMERICA, INC.

   762 Park Avenue, Youngsville, NC   27596-9470

   CEO: Louis A. Feudi   Tel: (919) 872-3316   %FO: 100

   Bus: *International product safety*   Fax: (919) 872-9356
   testing and certification services.

   TUV RHEINLAND OF NORTH AMERICA, INC.

   10260 SW Nimbus, Ste. M-11, Portland, OR   97223

   CEO: Jim Mohr   Tel: (503) 620-0418   %FO: 100

   Bus: *International product safety*   Fax: (503) 620-6490
   testing and certification services.

TUV RHEINLAND OF NORTH AMERICA, INC.
2170 W. State Rd. 434, Ste. 160, Longwood, FL   32779
CEO: Eli Orsoff   Tel: (407) 774-1222   %FO: 100
Bus: *International product safety*   Fax: (407) 774-1033
  testing and certification services.

TUV RHEINLAND OF NORTH AMERICA, INC.
1815 Aston Avenue, Ste. 104, Carlsbad, CA   92008
CEO: Korina A. Ortiz   Tel: (760) 929-1780   %FO: 100
Bus: *International product safety*   Fax: (760) 929-1781
  testing and certification services.

TUV RHEINLAND OF NORTH AMERICA, INC.
32553 Schoolcraft, Ste. 100, Livonia, MI   48150
CEO: Rick Grumski   Tel: (734) 261-8881   %FO: 100
Bus: *International product safety*   Fax: (734) 261-8929
  testing and certification services.

TUV RHEINLAND OF NORTH AMERICA, INC.
1945 Techny Road, Unit 4, Northbrook, IL   60062-5357
CEO: Matthew Fielding   Tel: (847) 562-9888   %FO: 100
Bus: *International product safety*   Fax: (847) 562-0688
  testing and certification services.

TUV RHEINLAND OF NORTH AMERICA, INC.
182 Turnpike Road, Ste. 91, Westborough, MA   01851
CEO: Robert Parsons   Tel: (508) 836-3366   %FO: 100
Bus: *International product safety*   Fax: (508) 836-3601
  testing and certification services.

TUV RHEINLAND OF NORTH AMERICA, INC.
2324 Ridgepoint Drive, Ste. E, Austin, TX   78754-5214
CEO: Mike Flicinski   Tel: (512) 927-0070   %FO: 100
Bus: *International product safety*   Fax: (512) 927-0080
  testing and certification services.

TUV TELECOM SERVICES, INC.
1775 Old Hwy. 8, Ste. 107-108, St. Paul, MN   55112-1891
CEO: Gary Hojan   Tel: (651) 639-0775   %FO: 100
Bus: *International product safety*   Fax: (651) 639-0873
  testing and certification services.

● **UNIVERSAL MASCHINENFABRIK DR RUDOLPH SCHIEBER GMBH & CO**
Postfach 20, D-73461 Westhausen, Germany
CEO: Richard Geitner, Pres.   Tel: 49-7363 880
Bus: *Mfr. computerized flat sweater, collar &*   Fax: 49-7363 88230   Emp: 1,000
  trimming machines.   www.universal.de

EXU KNITTING MACHINES
820 Grand Boulevard, Deer Park, NY   11729
CEO: Alfred Stojda, EVP   Tel: (516) 242-2323   %FO: 84
Bus: *Distribution/sale/service knitting*   Fax: (516) 242-2276   Emp: 10
      machines.

● VARTA AG
Am Leineufer 51, D-30419 Hanover, Germany
CEO: Georg Prilhofer, Chmn.   Tel: 49-511-79-03-0   Rev: $1,048
Bus: *Mfr. of batteries and plastics.*   Fax: 49-511-79-03-7-66   Emp: 7,800
      www.varta.de

VARTA BATTERIES, INC.
300 Executive Blvd., Elmsford, NY   10523-1202
CEO: Thomas G. Broderick, Pres.   Tel: (914) 592-2500
Bus: *Mfr./sales of batteries and plastics.*   Fax: (914) 592-2667

● VAW ALUMINUM AG
Georg-vo-Boeselagerstrasse 25, D-53117 Bonn, Germany
CEO: Helmut Burmester, CEO   Tel: 49-49-228-552-02   Rev: $3,485
Bus: *Mfr. rolled aluminum products.*   Fax: 49-49-228-552-2268   Emp: 15,900
      www.vaw.de

HALCO MINING COMPANY
20 Stanwix Street, 10th Fl., Pittsburgh, PA   15222
CEO: Helmut Burmester, CEO   Tel: (412) 467-3236   %FO: 100
Bus: *Mfr. primary materials.*   Fax: (412) 467-3255

VAW OF AMERICA, INC.
171 Industrial Boulevard, Fayetteville, TN   37334
CEO: Mark Casadevall   Tel: (931) 438-0850   %FO: 100
Bus: *Mfr. aluminum extrusions.*   Fax: (931) 438-4124

VAW OF AMERICA, INC.
9 Aluminum Drive, Ellenville, NY   12428
CEO: Al Styring, Pres. & CEO   Tel: (845) 647-7510   %FO: 100
Bus: *Mfr. aluminum extrusions.*   Fax: (845) 647-7535

VAW OF AMERICA, INC.
101 East Town Place, Ste. 800, St. Augustine, FL   32092
CEO: Al Styring, Pres. & CEO   Tel: (904) 794-2003   %FO: 100
Bus: *Mfr. aluminum extrusions.*   Fax: (904) 940-1535

● **VERLAGSGRUPPE GEORG VON HOLTZBRINCK GMBH**

Gansheidestraße 26, D-70184 Stuttgart, Germany

CEO: Stefan von Holtzbrinck, CEO   Tel: 49-711-2150-0   Rev: $2,214

Bus: *Engaged in publishing.*   Fax: 49-711-2150-100   Emp: 12,600

www.holtzbrinck.com

     HENRY HOLT AND COMPANY, INC.

     115 West 18th Street, New York, NY   10011

     CEO: Audrey D. Melkin   Tel: (212) 886-9200   %FO: 100

     Bus: *Book publishing.*   Fax: (212) 633-0748

● **VILLEROY & BOCH AG**

Postfach 10140, D-66693 Mettlach, Saarland, Germany

CEO: Wendelin von Boch-Galhau, Chmn.   Tel: 49-6864-81-1293   Rev: $1,657

Bus: *Mfr. tableware, ceramic tiles, plumbing*   Fax: 49-6864-81-2692   Emp: 11,000
     fixtures.   www.villeroy-boch.de

     VILLEROY & BOCH TABLEWARE LTD.

     5 Vaughn Drive, Ste. 303, Princeton, NJ   08540

     CEO: Bernard Reuter, Pres.   Tel: (609) 734-7800   %FO: 100

     Bus: *Wholesale china dinnerware,*   Fax: (609) 734-7840   Emp: 300
     crystal stemware and gifts.

● **WILLY VOGEL AG**

Motzener Strasse 35/37, D-12277 Berlin, Germany

CEO: Manfred Neubert, Chmn.   Tel: 49-30-720020

Bus: *Mfr. lubrication equipment and devices*   Fax: 49-30-72002111   Emp: 843
     for industry, fluid transfer pumps.   www.vogel-ag.de

     VOGEL LUBRICATION INC.

     1008 Jefferson Avenue, Newport News, VA   23607

     CEO: Joe Ahrens, Pres.   Tel: (757) 380-8585   %FO: 100

     Bus: *Sale/service lubrication system &*   Fax: (757) 380-0709   Emp: 65
     equipment, fluid transfer pumps.

● **J M VOITH GMBH**

St. Pöltener Str. 43, PO Box 2000, D-89522 Heidenheim, Germany

CEO: Hermut Kormann, CEO   Tel: 49-7321-37-0   Rev: $2,228

Bus: *Hydroelectric turbines, paper*   Fax: 49-7321-37-7000   Emp: 16,000
     machinery, power transmission engines,   www.voith.de
     propellers and special drives and
     machine tools.

APPLETON FABRICS

PO Box 1899, Appleton, WI   54913

CEO: Ivan Fernhead, Pres.   Tel: (920) 734-9876   %FO: 100

Bus: *Installation of stock preparation equipment.*   Fax: (920) 734-1444

VOITH SIEMENS HYDRO POWER

PO Box 712, East Berlin Road, York, PA   17405

CEO: Wolfgang Heine, EVP   Tel: (717) 792-7000   %FO: JV

Bus: *Mfr. hydroelectric turbines, digital & electro-hydraulic governors.*   Fax: (717) 792-7263   Emp: 550

VOITH TRANSMISSIONS, INC.

25 Winship Road, York, PA   17402

CEO: David M. Calveley, Pres.   Tel: (717) 767-3200   %FO: 100

Bus: *Sales/distribution of power transmission engines.*   Fax: (717) 767-3210

VOITH-SLZER PAPER

2620 East Glendale Avenue, Appleton, WI   54193

CEO: Werner Kade, Pres.   Tel: (920) 731-7724   %FO: 100

Bus: *Machine and paper technology.*   Fax: (920) 731-0240

● VOLKSWAGEN AG

Brieffach 1848-2, D-38436 Wolfsburg, Germany

CEO: Dr. Ferdinand Piëch, Chrm.   Tel: 49-53-61-90   Rev: $80,553

Bus: *Mfr. automobiles and parts.*   Fax: 49-53-61-928282   Emp: 324,400

www.2.vw-online.de

COSWORTH TECHNOLOGY INC.

4100 Vincenti Court, Novi, MI   48375-1921

CEO: Mitch Wetzler, CEO   Tel: (248) 471-5000

Bus: *Research and technology.*   Fax: (248) 471-3680

ROLLS-ROYCE MOTOR CARS, INC. - NORTHERN REGION

140 East Ridgewood Avenue, 5th Fl., Paramus, NJ   07652

CEO: A. Stewart, Mng. Dir.   Tel: (201) 967-9100   %FO: 100

Bus: *Import/distribution/service motor vehicles.*   Fax: (201) 967-2070

ROLLS-ROYCE MOTOR CARS, INC.

5136 Commerce Avenue, Moorpark, CA   93020

CEO: A. Stewart, Mng. Dir.   Tel: (310) 750-8381   %FO: 100

Bus: *Import/distribution/service motor vehicles.*   Fax: (310) 750-8421

ROLLS-ROYCE MOTOR CARS, INC.
CENTRAL REGION

303 East Army Trail Road, Ste. 108, Bloomingdale, IL 60108

CEO: A. Stewart, Mng. Dir.   Tel: (630) 529-5330   %FO: 100

Bus: *Import/distribution/service motor*   Fax: (630) 529-9841
     vehicles.

ROLLS-ROYCE MOTOR CARS, INC. - SOUTHERN REGION

900 N. Federal Highway, #360, Boca Raton, FL 33432

CEO: Gustavo Velazute, Reg. Dir.   Tel: (561) 750-8381   %FO: 100

Bus: *Import/distribution/service motor*   Fax: (561) 750-8421
     vehicles.

VOLKSWAGEN OF AMERICA

3800 Hamlin Road, Auburn Hills, MI 48326

CEO: Gerd Klauss, CEO   Tel: (248) 340-5000   %FO: 100

Bus: *Import/marketing automobiles.*   Fax: (248) 340-4930   Emp: 1,143

VORELCO INC.

3800 Hamlin Road, Auburn Hills, MI 48326

CEO: William H. Devine, Gen.Mgr.   Tel: (248) 340-5000   %FO: 100

Bus: *Commercial and industrial*   Fax: (248) 340-5525   Emp: 40
     building operator.

● VOLLMER WERKE MASCHINENFABRIK GMBH

Ehinger Str 34, D-88400 Biberach, Germany

CEO: Douglas Downs, Pres.   Tel: 49-7351-5710

Bus: *Mfr. saw sharpening machines and*   Fax: 49-7351-571130
     systems.

VOLLMER OF AMERICA

105 Broadway Avenue, Carnegie, PA 15106

CEO: Douglas Downs, Pres.   Tel: (412) 278-0655   %FO: 100

Bus: *distribution/service saw*   Fax: (412) 278-0520
     sharpening machines and systems.

● VON ARDENNE GMBH

OT Dresden Weißig, Am Hahnweg 16, D-01328 Dresden-Weißig, Germany

CEO: Dr. Peter Lenk, Pres.   Tel: 49-35126-37-300

Bus: *Mfr. equipment, machinery and*   Fax: 49-35126-37-308   Emp: 200
     technology for vacuum coatings and   www.ardenne-at.de
     materials treatment.

INTERTURBINE INC.
One International Place, Ste. 8, Boston, MA   02110
CEO: Gordon Walsh, Pres. & CEO   Tel: (617) 439-8808   %FO: 100
Bus: *U.S. headquarters location;*   Fax: (617) 439-8808
    specialized honeycomb fabrication.

● **VOSSLOH AG**
Vosslohstrasse 4, D-58791 Werdohl, Germany
CEO: Burkhard Schuchmann, CEO   Tel: 49-2392-520   Rev: $805
Bus: *Mfr. and sales of railway products.*   Fax: 49-2392-52-219   Emp: 5,590
    www.vossloh.com

    VOSSLOH-SCHWABE, INC.
    55 Mayview Road, Lawrence, PA   15055
    CEO: Burkhard Schuchmann, CEO   Tel: (724) 743-4770   %FO: 100
    Bus: *Mfr. and sales of railway products.*   Fax: (724) 743-4771

● **WACKER WERKE**
Preussenstrasse 41, D-80809 Munich, Germany
CEO: Dieter Stelter   Tel: 49-89-35402
Bus: *Mfr. light machinery.*   Fax: 49-89-35402-390   Emp: 3,000

    WACKER CORPORATION
    N92 W. 15000 Anthony Avenue, Menomonee Falls, WI   53052
    CEO: Christopher Barnard, Pres.   Tel: (262) 255-0500   %FO: 100
    Bus: *Mfr. light machinery.*   Fax: (262) 255-0550   Emp: 515

● **WALTER AG**
Postfach 20 49, D-72010 Tubingen, Germany
CEO: Franco Mambretti, Chmn.   Tel: 49-70-7170-1530   Rev: $251
Bus: *Mfr. tool machines.*   Fax: 49-70-7170-1645   Emp: 1,780
    www.walter-ag.de

    WALTER GRINDERS, INC.
    5160 Lad Land Drive, Fredericksburg, VA   22407
    CEO: Franco Mambretti, CEO   Tel: (540) 898-3700   %FO: 1
    Bus: *Sale of grinding and measuring*   Fax: (540) 898-2811
    machines.

    WALTER WAUKESHA INC.
    1111 Sentry Drive, Waukesha, WI   53186
    CEO: Franco Mambretti, CEO   Tel: (262) 542-4426   %FO: 100
    Bus: *Sale of carbide tools.*   Fax: (262) 542-9178

- **WEIDMULLER INTERFACE INTERNATIONAL GMBH**
Paderborner Strasse 175, D-38444 Detmold, Germany
CEO: W. Schubl, Pres.   Tel: 49-52-3114-0
Bus: *Mfr. terminal blocks and connectors.*   Fax: 49-52-3114-1175
                                         www.weidmuller.de

  WEIDMULLER INC.
  821 Southlake Boulevard, Richmond, VA   23236
  CEO: David Brooks, Pres.   Tel: (804) 794-2877   %FO: 100
  Bus: *Mfr./sale terminal blocks &*   Fax: (804) 794-0252   Emp: 50
  connectors.

- **WELLA AG**
Berliner Allee 65, D-64274 Darnstadt, Germany
CEO: Heiner Gurtler, Chmn.   Tel: 49-6151-340
Bus: *Mfr. hair care products.*   Fax: 49-6151-342981
                                         www.wella.de

  WELLA CORPORATION
  12 Mercedes Drive, Montvale, NJ   07645
  CEO: Steve Goddard, CEO   Tel: (201) 930-1020   %FO: 100
  Bus: *Mfr./sale hair care products.*   Fax: (201) 505-5200   Emp: 100

- **WERZALIT AG & CO**
Gronauer Strasse 70, D-71720 Oberstenfeld, Germany
CEO: Dr. Gunter Heddemann, Chmn.   Tel: 49-7062-500
Bus: *Mfr. molded wood products and veneers.* Fax: 49-7062-50208   Emp: 600
                                         www.werzalit.com

  WERZALIT OF AMERICA INC.
  PO Box 373, 40 Holly Avenue, Bradford, PA   16701
  CEO: Robert H. Sefton, Pres.   Tel: (814) 362-3881   %FO: 100
  Bus: *Mfr. molded wood parts.*   Fax: (814) 362-4237   Emp: 100

- **WESTDEUTSCHE LANDESBANK GIROZENTRALE**
PO Box 40199, Herzogstrasse 15, D-40217 Düsseldorf, Germany
CEO: Hans Henning Offen, VC   Tel: 49-211-82601   Rev: $22,732
Bus: *Commercial and investment banking* Fax: 49-211-8266126   Emp: 14,367
services.   www.westpac.com.au

  WESTDEUTSCHE LANDESBANK GIROZENTRALE
  653 West Fifth Street, Ste. 6750, Los Angeles, CA   90017
  CEO: Robert Edmonds, Mng. Dir.   Tel: (213) 623-0009   %FO: 100
  Bus: *International commercial banking* Fax: (213) 623-4700
  services.

WESTDEUTSCHE LANDESBANK GIROZENTRALE
1211 Avenue of the Americas, 24th Fl., New York, NY 10036-8701
CEO: Dirk H. Koerner, Mng. Dir.   Tel: (212) 852-6000   %FO: 100
Bus: *International commercial banking* Fax: (212) 921-7655
    services.

WESTDEUTSCHE LANDESBANK GIROZENTRALE
233 South Wacker Drive, Ste. 5210, Chicago, IL 60606
CEO: Mark Worley, Mng. Dir.   Tel: (312) 930-9200   %FO: 100
Bus: *International commercial banking* Fax: (312) 930-9281
    services.

● **ERNST WINTER & SOHN, DIV. SAINT GOBAIN**
Osterstrasse 58/2, D-22359 Hamburg, Germany
CEO: Hans Robert Meyer, CEO   Tel: 49-40-52580
Bus: *Mfr. diamond cutting tools, grinding* Fax: 49-40-4905102
    wheels, sawblades.   www.winter-dtcbn.de

    SAINT GOBAIN WINTER INC.
    21 Saddleback Cove, PO Box 1006, Travelers Rest, SC 29690
    CEO: Mark J. Dion, Pres.   Tel: (864) 834-4145   %FO: 100
    Bus: *Mfr./sale diamond cutting tools.* Fax: (864) 834-3730   Emp: 120

● **RICHARD WOLF GMBH**
Postfach 1164, D-75434 Knittlingen, Germany
CEO: Ms. I. Burkhard, Mng. Dir.   Tel: 49-7043-350
Bus: *Produces endoscopes and modular* Fax: 49-7043-35300   Emp: 1,000
    system solutions for all medical fields. www.richard-wolf.com

    RICHARD WOLF MEDICAL INSTRUMENT CORPORATION
    353 Corporate Woods Pkwy., Vernon Hills, IL 60061
    CEO: Ed Troichie, Mgr.   Tel: (847) 913-1113   %FO: 100
    Bus: *Mfr./distribution of surgical* Fax: (847) 913-1490   Emp: 170
    instruments.

● **PETER WOLTERS GMBH**
Busumer Strasse 96-104, D-24768 Rendsburg, Germany
CEO: G. Morsch   Tel: 49-4331-458-271
Bus: *Mfr. of tools for lapping, polishing and* Fax: 49-4331-458-290   Emp: 75
    fine-grinding.   www.peter-wolters.com

    PETER WOLTERS OF AMERICA, INC.
    14 High Street, Plainville, MA 02762
    CEO: Katie Faiella, CEO   Tel: (508) 695-7151   %FO: 100
    Bus: *Mfr. and sales of tools for lapping,* Fax: (508) 695-7154   Emp: 2
    polishing and fine-grinding.

• WÜRTH GROUP

Reinhold-Würth-Str. 12-16, D-74653 Künzelsau-Gaisbach, Germany

CEO: Rainer Bürkert	Tel: 49-79-40-15-0	Rev: $4,833
Bus: *Mfr. of fasteners and assembly technology.*	Fax: 49-79-40-15-10-00 www.wuerth.com	Emp: 36,100

ACTION BOLT & TOOL COMPANY, INC.

PO Box 10864, Riviera Beach, FL 33404

CEO: Robert L. Muller, Pres.	Tel: (561) 845-8800	%FO: 100
Bus: *Mfr. industrial fasteners and tools.*	Fax: (561) 845-0255	

BAER SUPPLY COMPANY, INC.

909 Forest Edge Drive, Vernon Hills, IL 60016-3149

CEO: Allen Baer, Pres.	Tel: (847) 913-2237	%FO: 100
Bus: *Mfr. decorative and functional hardware for woodworking industry.*	Fax: (847) 913-2048	

THE HARDWOOD GROUP INC.

PO Box 668005, Charlotte, NC 28266-8005

CEO: Robert H. Stolz, Pres.	Tel: (704) 394-9479	%FO: 100
Bus: *Mfr. hardwood flooring, moulding, lumber, plywood and decorative hardware.*	Fax: (704) 398-2182	

MEPLA-ALFIT, INC.

PO Box 1666, Lexington, NC 27293

CEO: Doug Rex, Pres.	Tel: (336) 956-4600	%FO: 100
Bus: *Mfr. of functional hardware for cabinetry and furniture.*	Fax: (336) 956-4750	Emp: 100

MEPLA-ALFIT INC.

761 N. Edgewood Avenue, Wood Dale, IL 60191

CEO: Mark Schmitt	Tel: (630) 860-1331	%FO: JV
Bus: *Mfr. European-type furniture and cabinet hardware; serving furniture and kitchen cabinet industries.*	Fax: (630) 860-7544	

WURTH USA INC.

93 Grant Street, Ramsey, NJ 07446

CEO: Eric Robibero, Mgr.	Tel: (800) 526-5228	%FO: 100
Bus: *Purchasing and distribution.*	Fax: (201) 825-3706	

WURTH USA INC.
8501 Parkline Boulevard, Orlando, FL   32809
CEO: Terry Heard, Mgr.   Tel: (800) 346-4198   %FO: 100
Bus: *Distribution center.*   Fax: (407) 856-8391

WURTH USA INC.
1486 East Cedar Street, Ontario, CA   91787
CEO: Tony King, Mgr.   Tel: (800) 346-4198   %FO: 100
Bus: *Distribution center.*   Fax: (909) 947-9793

● **CARL ZEISS**
Postfach 13 69, Carl-Zeiss-Strasse 2-60, D-73446 Oberkochen, Germany
CEO: Dr. Peter H. Grassman, Chmn.   Tel: 49-7364-2000
Bus: *Mfr. precision optical/mechanical,*   Fax: 49-7364-6808
electrical instruments and products.   www.zeiss.de

CARL ZEISS INC.
One Zeiss Drive, Thornwood, NY   10594
CEO: James Kelly, Pres.   Tel: (914) 747-1800   %FO: 100
Bus: *Mfr. precision optical,*   Fax: (914) 682-8296
mechanical, electric instruments
and products.

CARL ZEISS INC., SURGICAL PRODUCTS DIV.
One Zeiss Drive, Thornwood, NY   10594
CEO: Eric Timko, Pres.   Tel: (914) 747-1800   %FO: 100
Bus: *Mfr. optical and surgical products.*   Fax: (914) 682-8296

● **ZF FRIEDRICHSHAFEN AG**
Loewentaler Strasse 100, D-88038 Friedrichshafen, Germany
CEO: Klaus Peter Bleyer, CEO   Tel: 49-7541-770   Rev: $5,208
Bus: *Mfr. axles, transmission and steering*   Fax: 49-7541-7790-8000   Emp: 33,393
products for on/off highway and marine   www.zf-group.de
markets.

ZF GROUP NORTH AMERICA
7310 Turfway Road, Ste. 450, Florence, KY   41042
CEO: James C. Orchard, Pres. & CEO   Tel: (859) 282-4300   %FO: 100
Bus: *U.S. headquarters.*   Fax: (859) 282-4311

● **ZIMMERMANN & JANSEN GMBH**
Bahnstrasse 52, D-52355 Düren, Germany
CEO: Ekkehard Brzoska, Pres.   Tel: 49-2421-6910
Bus: *Mfr. petrochemicals and glass*   Fax: 49-2421-691200
manufacturing equipment.   www.zjgmbh.de

ZIMMERMANN & JANSEN, INC.
PO Box 3365, Humble, TX   77347-3365
CEO: James Adams, Pres.   Tel: (281) 446-8000   %FO: 100
Bus: *Mfr. petrochemicals and glass*   Fax: (281) 446-8126
    manufacturing equipment.

Greece

- **NATIONAL BANK OF GREECE**
  86 Eolou, GR-102 32 Athens, Greece
  CEO: Gov. Theordora Karatzas, Pres.   Tel: 30-1-334-1521   Rev: $5,138
  Bus: *State-controlled, commercial banking*   Fax: 30-13-25-11-33   Emp: 15,200
      services.   www.ethniki.gr

  ### ATLANTIC BANK
  33 State Street, 3rd Fl, Boston, MA   02109
  CEO: Robert Bender, Mgr.   Tel: (617) 557-0364   %FO: 100
  Bus: *Banking services.*   Fax: (617) 557-0364

  ### ATLANTIC BANK OF NEW YORK
  960 Ave. of the Americas, 14th Fl., New York, NY   10001
  CEO: T. Sipple   Tel: (212) 695-5400   %FO: 100
  Bus: *Commercial banking services.*   Fax: (212) 563-2729   Emp: 350

  ### NATIONAL BANK OF GREECE
  168 North Michigan Avenue, Chicago, IL   60601
  CEO: Jack Steinmetz, Mgr.   Tel: (312) 641-6600   %FO: 100
  Bus: *Banking services.*   Fax: (312) 263-4195   Emp: 25

- **OLYMPIC AIRWAYS SA**
  96 Syngrou, GR-117 41 Athens, Greece
  CEO: Dionyslos Kalofonos, CEO   Tel: 30-1-926-9111   Rev: $964
  Bus: *Commercial air transport services.*   Fax: 30-1-926-7154   Emp: 8,500
      www.olympicair.com

  ### OLYMPIC AIRWAYS
  645 Fifth Avenue, New York, NY   10022
  CEO: Kostas Stynias, Dir.   Tel: (212) 735-0200   %FO: 100
  Bus: *Commercial air transport services.*   Fax: (212) 735-0215   Emp: 103

- **ROYAL OLYMPIC CRUISES, LTD. (ROC)**
  Akti Miaouli 87, GR-18538 Piraeus, Greece
  CEO: John Pantazis, CEO   Tel: 30-1-429-1000   Rev: $130
  Bus: *Shipping line specializing in cruises to*   Fax: 30-1-429-0862   Emp: 1,600
      historical and religious sites.   www.royalolympiccruises.com

ROYAL OLYMPIC CRUISES, INC. (ROC USA)

805 Third Avenue, New York, NY   10022-7513

CEO: Vasilios Kapetanakos, Pres. & CEO

Bus: *Operates cruises specializing in historical and religious sites.*

Tel: (212) 397-6400

Fax: (212) 688-2304

%FO: 100

Guatemala

● **LA GOTEX (LIZTEX)**

KM 30.5, Carretera Alpacifico, Amatitlan, Guatemala

CEO: Al Dinunzio, Pres.　　　　　　　　Tel: 502-597-6757

Bus: *Mfr. cotton and cotton blend fabrics,*　Fax: 502-633-5808
including yarn dyes, wovens, knits,　www.novatextiles.com
denims and woven terry.

NOVA TEXTILES, INC. (LIZTEX)

1359 Broadway, Ste. 1018, New York, NY　10018

CEO: Al Dinunzio, Pres.　　　　　　　Tel: (212) 643-1200　　　　%FO: 100

Bus: *U.S. sales office representing*　　Fax: (212) 643-9444
textile mills in sales of cotton and
cotton blend fabrics.

Hong Kong

● **THE BANK OF EAST ASIA, LIMITED**
10 Des Voeux Road, 19th Fl., Central, Hong Kong

CEO: Kwok Po Li, Chmn. & CEO	Tel: 852-2842-3200	Rev: $1,409
Bus: *Provides commercial and retail banking services.*	Fax: 852-2842-9333 www.hkbea.com	Emp: 3,800

    THE BANK OF EAST ASIA, LIMITED
    600 Wilshire Boulevard, Ste. 1550, Los Angeles, CA 90017

CEO: Victor Li Man-Fong, Gen. Mgr.	Tel: (213) 892-1572	%FO: 100
Bus: *International commercial banking services.*	Fax: (213) 892-1004	

    THE BANK OF EAST ASIA, LIMITED
    202 Canal Street, New York, NY 10013

CEO: Tang Peng-Wah, VP & Gen. Mgr.	Tel: (212) 233-8833	%FO: 100
Bus: *International commercial banking services.*	Fax: (212) 219-8299	Emp: 60

● **CATHAY PACIFIC AIRWAYS**
2 Pacific Place, 88 Queensway, Hong Kong

CEO: David Turnbull, CEO	Tel: 852-2747-5210	Rev: $4,425
Bus: *Commercial air transport services.*	Fax: 852-2810-6563 www.cathaypacific-air.com	Emp: 14,300

    CATHAY PACIFIC AIRWAYS
    300 Continental Blvd., Ste. 500, El Segundo, CA 90245

CEO: Tom Wright, Pres.	Tel: (310) 615-1113	%FO: 100
Bus: *U.S. headquarters.*	Fax: (310) 615-0042	

    CATHAY PACIFIC AIRWAYS
    590 Fifth Avenue, New York, NY 10036

CEO: Tom Wright, Pres.	Tel: (212) 819-0210	%FO: 100
Bus: *Commercial air transport services.*	Fax: (212) 944-6519	Emp: 6

● **CHINA PATENT AGENT (HK) LTD.**
22/F. Great Eagle Centre, 23 Harbour Rd, Wanchai, Hong Kong

CEO: Songyu Zheng, Chrm.	Tel: 852-2828-4688	
Bus: *Intellectual property service; consultants, representatives & other legal services.*	Fax: 852-2827-1018 www.cptausa.com	Emp: 250

CHINA PATENT & TRADEMARK AGENT (USA) LTD.
*One World Trade Center, Ste. 2957, New York, NY   10048

CEO: Yansheng Yu, VP	Tel: (212) 912-1870	%FO: 100
Bus: *Intellectual property service; consultants, representatives & other legal services.*	Fax: (212) 912-1873	Emp: 3

● **CHINA PEARL HONG KONG**
Room 1209, Tower 1, Silvercord, 30 Canton Road, Tsimshatsui Kowloon, Hong Kong

CEO: Hung Lam, Pres.	Tel: 852-2736-0038
Bus: *Mfr./distribution ceramics and chinaware.*	Fax: 852-2735-3298
	www.chinapearl.com

CCA INTERNATIONAL, INC.
328 Thomas Street, Newark, NJ   07114

CEO: Hung Lam, Pres.	Tel: (973) 817-8337	%FO: 100
Bus: *Distribution/sale ceramics and porcelain dinnerware.*	Fax: (973) 817-8552	

● **CITIC KA WAH BANK LTD.**
232 Des Voeux Road, Central, Hong Kong

CEO: Kong Dan, Chmn.	Tel: 852-2545-7131	Rev: $541
Bus: *General banking services.*	Fax: 852-2287-6899	Emp: 1,035
	www.citickawahbank.com	

CITIC KA WAH BANK LTD.
323 West Valley Boulevard, Alhambra, CA   91803

CEO: Aaron K F Cheung, VP	Tel: (626) 282-9820
Bus: *General banking services.*	Fax: (626) 282-9399

CITIC KA WAH BANK LTD.
11 East Broadway, 3rd Fl., New York, NY   10038

CEO: Peter Zhao, EVP	Tel: (212) 732-8868	%FO: 100
Bus: *General banking services.*	Fax: (212) 791-3776	

● **DAH CHONG HONG GROUP, DIV. CITIC PACIFIC GROUP**
8/F, 20 Kai Cheung Road, Kowloon Bay, Kowloon, Hong Kong

CEO: Karl Kwok, Chrm.	Tel: 852-2768-3388	Rev: $254
Bus: *Department stores, real estate, and automobile dealerships.*	Fax: 852-2768-8838	Emp: 2,000
	www.dch.co.hk	

DCH GROUP OF COMPANIES
362 Fifth Avenue, New York, NY   10001

CEO: Sha-Wai Lam, Pres.	Tel: (212) 947-6860	%FO: 100
Bus: *Import/export trading company.*	Fax: (212) 244-1457	Emp: 1,300

HUNTER ENGINEERING COMPANY

11250 Hunter Drive, Bridgeton, MO 63044

CEO: Ronald C. May

Bus: *Tire equipment and wheel alignment services.*

Tel: (314) 731-3020

Fax: (314) 731-0132

%FO: 100

● **DSG INTERNATIONAL LIMITED**

17th Fl. Watson Centre, 16-22 Kung Yip Street, Kwai Chung, Hong Kong

CEO: Brandon S.L. Wang, Pres. & CEO

Bus: *Mfr. personal care products.*

Tel: 852-2484-4820

Fax: 852-2480-4491

www.dsgil.com

Rev: $215

Emp: 1,415

ASSOCIATED HYGIENIC PRODUCTS LLC

205 East Highland Drive, Oconto Falls, WI 54154

CEO: John Dickenson, Plant Mgr.

Bus: *Sales/distribution of personal care products.*

Tel: (920) 846-8444

Fax: (920) 846-3026

%FO: 100

ASSOCIATED HYGIENIC PRODUCTS LLC

4455 River Green Parkway, Duluth, GA 30096

CEO: George H. Jackson III, CEO

Bus: *Sales/distribution of personal care products.*

Tel: (770) 497-9800

Fax: (770) 623-8887

%FO: 100

● **FIRST ECOM.COM, INC.**

8/F Henley Bldg., 5 Queen's Road, Central Hong Kong

CEO: Gregory M. Pek, CEO

Bus: *Global provider of electronic payment processing.*

Tel: 852-2801-5181

Fax: 852-2801-5939

www.firstecom.com

FIRST ECOM.COM, INC.

50 West Liberty Street, Ste. 880, Reno, NE 89501

CEO: Ken Telford

Bus: *Global provider of electronic payment processing.*

Tel: (888) 305-8233

Fax: (888) 305-8233

%FO: 100

GASCO ENERGY

14 Inverness Dr. E., Suite 236-H, Englewood, CO 80112

CEO: Mark A. Erickson, Pres. & CEO

Bus: *Acquires and explores petroleum and natural gas properties in the US.*

Tel: (303) 483-0044

Fax: (303) 483-0011

%FO: 100

● **FIRST NATIONAL TRADING, LTD.**

2/F Block C Startex Ind. Bldg. 14, Tai Yau Street, San Po Kong, Kowloon, Hong Kong

CEO: Michael Chen, Pres.

Bus: *Import/export trading company.*

Tel: 852-2322-2231

Fax:

FIRST NATIONAL TRADING, COMPANY, INC.
503 Chancellor Avenue, New York, NY   10001
CEO: Paul Shen, Pres.   Tel: (212) 695-1097   %FO: 100
Bus: *Import/export trading company.*   Fax: (212) 695-2867

● **FIRST PACIFIC COMPANY LIMITED**
2 Exchange Square, 24th Fl., 8 Connaught Place, Hong Kong
CEO: Ronald A. Brown   Tel: 852-2842-4388   Rev: $2,900
Bus: *Provides personal and commercial*   Fax: 852-2845-9243   Emp: 30,700
banking services.   www.firstpacco.com

UNITED COMMERCIAL BANK
711 Van Nees Avenue, San Francisco, CA   94102
CEO: James C. Ng, Exec. Dir.   Tel: (415) 929-6070   %FO: 100
Bus: *Provides personal and commercial* Fax: (415) 885-5248
banking services.

● **GLOBAL SOURCES LTD.**
23/F Vita Tower A, 29 Wong Chuk Hang Road, Hong Kong
CEO: Merle A. Hinrichs, CEO   Tel: 852-2555-4777   Rev: $105
Bus: *On-line import and export company*   Fax: 852-2553-0398   Emp: 570
providing e-commerce services.   www.globalsources.com

GLOBAL SOURCES USA, INC.
14901 N. Scottsdale Road, Ste. 201, Scottsdale, AZ   85254
CEO: James Strachan   Tel: (480) 951-4400   %FO: 100
Bus: *Engaged in on-line marketing.*   Fax: (480) 951-4405

TRADE SOURCES, INC.
901 Sneath Lane, San Bruno, CA   94066
CEO: Chuck Armitage   Tel: (650) 742-7900   %FO: 100
Bus: *Engaged in on-line marketing.*   Fax: (650) 742-7962

WORDRIGHT ENTERPRISES, INC.
2859 Central Street, Ste. 111, Evanston, IL   60201
CEO: Judy Trusdell   Tel: (847) 869-3740   %FO: 100
Bus: *Engaged in e-commerce.*   Fax: (847) 869-3755

● **HECNY TRANSPORTATION INC.**
111 Wai Yip Street, Kwun Tong Kowloon, Hong Kong
CEO: Charlie Lee, Pres. & CEO   Tel: 852-2751-4304
Bus: *Engaged in freight forwarding.*   Fax: 852-2789-7719
                                            www.hecny.com

HECNY TRANSPORATION INC.
147-39 175th Street, Jamaica, NY 11434
CEO: Jim Georgakis, VP   Tel: (718) 656-5537   %FO: 100
Bus: *Engaged in freight forwarding.*   Fax: (718) 632-8491

● **TOMMY HILFIGER CORPORATION**
6/F, Precious Industrial Centre, 18 Cheung Yue Street, Cheung Sha Wan, Kowloon, Hong Kong
CEO: Silas K. F. Chou, Co -Chair   Tel: 852-2745-7798   Rev: $1,637
Bus: *Design/mfr. clothing and accessories.*   Fax: 852-2312-1368   Emp: 1,881
(JV with Tommy Hilfiger USA)   www.hilfiger.com

    TOMMY HILFIGER CORPORATION
    25 West 39th Street, New York, NY 10018
    CEO: Joel J. Horowitz, CEO   Tel: (212) 840-8888   %FO: 100
    Bus: *Sales/distribution of clothing and*   Fax: (212) 302-8718
    accessories.

    TOMMY HILFIGER CORPORATION
    466 North Rodeo Drive, Beverly Hills, CA 90210
    CEO: Corin Garrahan, Gen. Mgr.   Tel: (310) 888-0132   %FO: 100
    Bus: *Sales/distribution of clothing and*   Fax: (310) 888-0142
    accessories.

● **HONG KONG & SHANGHAI HOTELS, LIMITED**
St. George's Building, 2 Ice House Street, 8th Floor, Hong Kong
CEO: Pierre R. Boppe, CEO   Tel: 852-2840-7788   Rev: $392
Bus: *Owns and manages hotel properties.*   Fax: 852-2868-4770   Emp: 6,000
www.irasia.com

    QUAIL LODGE
    8205 Valley Greens Drive, Carmel, CA 93923
    CEO: Pierre R. Boppe, Mng. Dir.   Tel: (831) 624-2888
    Bus: *Hotel property.*   Fax: (831) 624-3726

    THE PENINSULA HOTEL
    9882 Little Santa Monica Blvd., Beverly Hills, CA 90212
    CEO: Pierre R. Boppe, Mng. Dir.   Tel: (310) 551-2888   %FO: 100
    Bus: *Hotel property.*   Fax: (310) 788-2319

● **HONG KONG TRADE DEVELOPMENT COUNCIL**
38th Fl., Office Tower, Convention Plaza, 1 Harbour Road, Wanchai, Hong Kong
CEO: Victor Fung   Tel: 852-2584-4333
Bus: *Trade development for the Chinese*   Fax: 852-2824-0249
mainland and the wider region.   www.tdc.org.hk

HONG KONG TRADE DEVELOPMENT COUNCIL
219 East 46th Street, New York, NY   10017
CEO: Joyce Hui, Dir.　　　　Tel: (212) 838-8688　　　%FO: 100
Bus: *Trade development for the Chinese*　Fax: (212) 838-8941
　　　mainland and the wider region.

HONG KONG TRADE DEVELOPMENT COUNCIL
130 Montgomery Street, San Francisco, CA   94104
CEO: Marian Lam, Dir.　　　Tel: (415) 677-9038　　　%FO: 100
Bus: *Trade development for the Chinese*　Fax: (415) 982-7268
　　　mainland and the wider region.

HONG KONG TRADE DEVELOPMENT COUNCIL
601 Brickell Drive, Ste. 509, Miami, FL   33131
CEO: Carmen Bruno, Dir.　　Tel: (305) 577-0414　　　%FO: 100
Bus: *Trade development for the Chinese*　Fax: (305) 572-9142
　　　mainland and the wider region.

HONG KONG TRADE DEVELOPMENT COUNCIL
333 North Michigan Avenue, Ste. 2028, Chicago, IL   60601
CEO: Kelly Ngan, Mgr.　　　Tel: (312) 726-4515　　　%FO: 100
Bus: *Trade development for the Chinese*　Fax: (312) 726-2441
　　　mainland and the wider region.

HONG KONG TRADE DEVELOPMENT COUNCIL
350 South Figueroa Street, Ste. 282, Los Angeles, CA   90017-1386
CEO: Tony Wong, Dir.　　　Tel: (213) 622-3194　　　%FO: 100
Bus: *Trade development for the Chinese*　Fax: (213) 613-1490
　　　mainland and the wider region.

● **HUTCHISON WHAMPOA LIMITED**
Hutchison House, 10 Harcourt Road, 22nd Fl, Hong Kong
CEO: Canning K. N. Fok, CEO　　Tel: 852-2128-1188　　Rev: $7,310
Bus: *Engaged in food processing and*　Fax: 852-2128-1705　　Emp: 50,000
　　　distribution and hotel management.　www.hutchison-whampoa.com

HUTCHISON WHAMPOA AMERICAS LIMITED
10900 NE 8th Street, Ste. 1488, Bellevue, WA   98004
CEO: Jean Johnson, VP　　　Tel: (425) 709-8888　　　%FO: 100
Bus: *Engaged in food processing and*　Fax: (425) 709-8899
　　　distribution and hotel management.

- **JARDINE MATHESON HOLDINGS LTD.**

Jardine House, 48th Fl., Connaught Road, GPO Box 70, Central, Hong Kong

CEO: Henry Keswick, Chmn.	Tel: 852-845-8388	Rev: $10,400
Bus: *Engaged in engineering, construction,*	Fax: 852-845-9005	Emp: 160,000
financial services, marketing,	www.jardines.com	
distribution, real estate, transportation		
services and food service.		

    JARDINE MOTORS BEVERLY HILLS LTD.

    9250 Beverly Boulevard, Beverly, CA   90210

CEO: Gary Wassel, Pres.	Tel: (310) 659-4286	%FO: 100
Bus: *Import/sales/service automobiles.*	Fax: (310) 659-4286	

    THEO H. DAVIES, EUROMOTORS, LTD.

    124 Wiwoole Street, Hilo, HI   96720

CEO: James Crawley, VP	Tel: (808) 961-6087	%FO: 100
Bus: *Import/sales/service automobiles.*	Fax: (808) 935-4949	

    THEODAVIES EUROMOTORS, LTD.

    818 Kapiolani Boulevard, Honolulu, HI   96813

CEO: Gary Wassel, Pres.	Tel: (808) 592-5600	%FO: 100
Bus: *Property development, insurance,*	Fax: (808) 592-5619	
freight forwarding, investment		
advisory.		

- **KING FOOK FINANCE COMPANY**

30-32 Des Voeux Road, Central, Hong Kong

CEO: Mr. Yeung, Pres.	Tel: 852-2523-5111
Bus: *Export jewelry, arts, crafts and antiques.*	Fax:

    KING FOOK NY COMPANY, LTD.

    673 Fifth Avenue, New York, NY   10022

CEO: M. Wong, Mgr.	Tel: (212) 355-3636	%FO: 100
Bus: *Imp/retail jewelry, arts, crafts and*	Fax: (212) 688-1081	
antiques.		

- **KYCE ENTERPRISE (HK) LTD.**

Merit Industrial Centre 94 Tokwawan Road To Kwa Wan, Kowloon, Hong Kong

CEO: Yuk Yun-Kit, Dir.	Tel: 852-3764-7255
Bus: *Mfr. watches and consumer electronics.*	Fax: 852-3764-1401
	www.sinutex.com

    KYCE, INC.

    4801 Metropolitan Avenue, Ridgewood, NY   11385

CEO: Y. K. Yuk, Pres.	Tel: (718) 628-6282	%FO: 100
Bus: *Import watches and consumer*	Fax: (718) 628-1038	
electronics.		

● **LIU CHONG HING BANK, LTD.**
24 Des Voeux Road, Central, Hong Kong
CEO: Lit Man Liu, Pres   Tel: 852-2-841-7417   Rev: $365
Bus: *Commercial banking services.*   Fax: 852-2-845-9134

    LIU CHONG HING BANK LTD.
    601 California Street, San Francisco, CA   94108
    CEO: Ki Hong Chan, VP   Tel: (415) 433-6404   %FO: 100
    Bus: *International banking services.*   Fax: (415) 433-0686

● **MANDARIN ORIENTAL INTERNATIONAL LIMITED**
281 Gloucester Road, PO Box 30632, Causeway Bay, Hong Kong
CEO: Edouard Ettedgui, CEO   Tel: 852-2895-9288   Rev: $227
Bus: *Manages high-end hotels.*   Fax: 852-2837-3500   Emp: 9,000
                                  www.mandarinoriental.com

    MANDARIN ORIENTAL
    509 Madison Avenue, Ste. 1800, New York, NY   10022
    CEO: Wolfgang Hultner, CEO   Tel: (212) 207-8880   %FO: 100
    Bus: *Manages high-end hotels.*   Fax: (212) 207-8886

    MANDARIN ORIENTAL
    500 Brickell Key Drive, Miami, FL   33131
    CEO: Jorge Gonzalez   Tel: (305) 913-8288   %FO: 100
    Bus: *Manages high-end hotels.*   Fax: (305) 913-8300

● **ORIENT OVERSEAS CONTAINER LINES, LTD.**
31 Harbour Centre, 25 Harbour Road, Hong Kong
CEO: Tung Chee Chen, Pres. & CEO   Tel: 852-5833-3838   Rev: $1,832
Bus: *International steamship transport,*   Fax: 852-5833-3777   Emp: 3,940
    freight forwarding.   www.oocl.com

    OOCL (USA), INC.
    PO Box 5100, San Ramon, CA   94583
    CEO: C.L. Ting, Pres.   Tel: (925) 358-6625   %FO: 100
    Bus: *International steamship transport,*   Fax: (925) 358-6625
      freight forwarding.

    OOCL (USA), INC.
    88 Pine Street, 8th Fl., New York, NY   10005
    CEO: C.L. Ting, Pres.   Tel: (212) 428-2200   %FO: 100
    Bus: *International steamship transport,*   Fax: (212) 428-2297   Emp: 60
      freight forwarding.

OOCL (USA), INC.
111 West Ocean Blvd., Ste. 1800, Long Beach, CA   90802
CEO: Philip Chow, Pres.   Tel: (562) 499-2600   %FO: 100
Bus: *International steamship transport,*   Fax: (562) 435-2750
    freight forwarding.

● **P.E. INTERNATIONAL PLC**
5th Floor, Kaiseng Commercial Centre, 4-6 Hankow Road, Tsimshatsui, Kowloon, Hong Kong
CEO: Bill Cox   Tel: 852-2576-7382   Rev: $140
Bus: *Management consulting services to*   Fax: 852-2576-6835   Emp: 500
    public and private sectors.   www.pehwhk.com

   P.E. HANDLEY WALKER INC.
   6000 Freedom Square Drive, Cleveland, OH   44141
   CEO: Charles R. Brown, Pres.   Tel: (216) 524-2200   %FO: 100
   Bus: *Management consultants services*   Fax: (216) 524-1488   Emp: 25
       to public and private sectors.

● **PACIFIC CENTURY CYBERWORKS LIMITED**
PCCW Tower, 39th Fl., TaiKoo Place, 979 King's Road, Quarry Bay, Hong Kong
CEO: Peter To   Tel: 852-2888-2888   Rev: $935
Bus: *Engaged in telecommunications.*   Fax: 852-2877-8877   Emp: 15,000
                                       www.pccw.com

   PCCW PACIFIC INC.
   50 California Street, Ste. 3325, San Francisco, CA   94111
   CEO: Tin Fan Yuen   Tel: (415) 834-4602   %FO: 100
   Bus: *Engaged in telecommunications.*   Fax: (415) 834-4603

   PCCW PACIFIC INC.
   44 Wall Street, 12th Fl. Unit 1231, New York, NY   10005
   CEO: Tin Fan Yuen   Tel: (212) 461-2382   %FO: 100
   Bus: *Engaged in telecommunications.*   Fax: (212) 461-2381

● **THE PENINSULA GROUP**
8/F St. George Building, 2 Ice House Street, Central District, Hong Kong
CEO: Pierre Boppe, CEO   Tel: 852-2840-7488
Bus: *Operates hotels, tourism industry.* Fax: 852-2845-5508
                                       www.peninsula.com

   THE PENINSULA GROUP
   333 N. Michigan Avenue, Ste.1120, Chicago, IL   60601
   CEO: Glordia S. Flowers, Mgr.   Tel: (312) 263-6069   %FO: 100
   Bus: *Sales; hotels, tourism industry.*   Fax: (312) 263-3744

● **PENINSULA KNITTERS, LIMITED**
538 Castle Peak Road, Cheung Shajuan Kowloon, Hong Kong
CEO: Henry Tang, Pres.   Tel: 852-372-19498
Bus: *Engaged in production of textiles and*   Fax:
    apparel.

    BELFORD INC.
    1441 Broadway, Ste. 2401, New York, NY   10018
    CEO: Jack Fok, Pres.   Tel: (212) 944-2020   %FO: 100
    Bus: *Mfr. knitwear for men and women.* Fax: (212) 944-0202

● **RADICA GAMES LTD.**
2-12 Au Pui Wan Street, Ste. R, 6th Fl., Fo Tan, Hong Kong
CEO: Patrick S. Feely, CEO   Tel: 852-2693-2238   Rev: $100
Bus: *Mfr. hand held electronic and*   Fax: 852-2695-9657   Emp: 4,000
    mechanical games.   www.radicagames.com

    RADICA USA, INC.
    13628-A, Ste. A, Beta Road, Dallas, TX   75244
    CEO: David Lau, Pres. & CEO   Tel: (972) 490-4247
    Bus: *Sales/distribution of hand held* Fax: (972) 490-0765
    electronic and mechanical games.

● **SHANGHAI COMMERCIAL BANK LTD.**
12 Queen's Road, Central, Hong Kong
CEO: John Yan, Gen. Mgr.   Tel: 852-841-5415
Bus: *Commercial banking services.*   Fax: 852-810-4623   Emp: 1,000
                                  www.shanghaibank.com.hk

    SHANGHAI COMMERCIAL BANK LTD.
    231 Sansome Street, San Francisco, CA   94104
    CEO: Phillip Lee, VP   Tel: (415) 433-6700   %FO: 100
    Bus: *International commercial banking* Fax: (415) 433-0210   Emp: 26
    services.

    SHANGHAI COMMERCIAL BANK LTD.
    125 East 56th Street, New York, NY   10022
    CEO: Timothy Chan, VP   Tel: (212) 699-2800   %FO: 100
    Bus: *International commercial banking* Fax: (212) 699-2818   Emp: 15
    services.

● **SINA.COM**
Vicwood Plaza, Units 01-03, 18th Fl., 199 Dex Voeux Road, Central Hong Kong
CEO: Daniel Mao, CEO   Tel: 852-2155-8800   Rev: $27
Bus: *Operates Chinese Web portals.*   Fax: 852-2295-3630   Emp: 625
                                  www.sina.com

SINA.COM
1313 Geneva Drive, Sunnyvale, CA   94089
CEO: Hurst Lin, VP   Tel: (408) 548-0000   %FO: 100
Bus: *Operates Chinese Web portals.* Fax: (408) 548-0068

• SUNBASE ASIA, INC.
19/F, First Pacific Bank Centre, 51-57 Gloucester Road, Wanchai, Hong Kong
CEO: Gunter Gao, Pres. & Chmn.   Tel: 852-2865-1511   Rev: $57
Bus: *Mfr. ball bearings for aircraft, auto,*   Fax: 852-2865-4293   Emp: 11,700
    machine tool and appliance industries.

SOUTHWEST PRODUCTS COMPANY
PO Box 1028, Monrovia, CA   91017-1028
CEO: William McKay   Tel: (626) 358-0181   %FO: 100
Bus: *Mfr. ball bearings for aircraft,*   Fax: (626) 303-6141
    auto, machine tool and appliance
    industries.

• SUNHAM & COMPANY, LTD.
14 On Lan Street, Hong Kong
CEO: A. Yung, Pres.   Tel: 852-2522-8388
Bus: *Mfr. linens.*   Fax:

SUNHAM & COMPANY
308 Fifth Avenue, New York, NY   10001
CEO: Howard Yung, Pres.   Tel: (212) 695-1218   %FO: 100
Bus: *Sale/distribution of linens.* Fax: (212) 947-4793

• SWIRE PACIFIC LIMITED
Rm. 423, Swire House, No. 9 Connaught Road, Central Hong Kong
CEO: J. W. J. Hughes-Hallett, CEO   Tel: 852-2840-8098   Rev: $1,929
Bus: *Holding company; commercial air and*   Fax: 852-2526-9365   Emp: 60,000
    sea transport, beverages, real estate   www.swire.com
    development and investment, petroleum
    exploration , entertainment media, food
    distribution, trading & financial
    services.

SWIRE COCA-COLA, USA
875 South West Temple, Salt Lake City, UT   84101
CEO: Jack Pelo, Pres.   Tel: (801) 816-5300   %FO: 100
Bus: *Bottler/distributor of beverages.*   Fax: (801) 530-5342

● **TAI FOOK SECURITIES GROUP LTD. (FORMERLY SUN HUNG KAI & CO LTD.)**

16-18 Queen's Road Central, 25th Fl. New World Tower, Hong Kong

CEO: Peter S. H. Wong, Mng. Dir.   Tel: 852-2848-4333

Bus: *Engaged in securities, margin*   Fax: 852-2845-0537
     financing, corporate finance, futures,   www.taifook.com
     options, insurance brokerage and fund
     management.

     TAI FOOK SECURITIES (U.S.) INC.

     *One World Trade Center, Ste. 3915, New York, NY   10048

     CEO: K. C. Poon, Pres.   Tel: (212) 321-1929   %FO: 100

     Bus: *Stock brokerage.*   Fax: (212) 321-1940

● **TAI PING CARPETS INTERNATIONAL LTD.**

261F, Tower A Regent Centre, 63 Wo Yi Hop Road, Kwai Chung, Hong Kong

CEO: Mr. Kent Yeh, CEO   Tel: 852-2818-7668

Bus: *Mfr. custom carpet and area rugs.*   Fax: 852-2845-9363
                                   www.taipingcarpets.com

     OPTIONS TAI PING CARPETS INC.

     715 Curtis Parkway SE,, Calhoun, GA   30701

     CEO: Steven Brandon, Pres.   Tel: (706) 625-8905   %FO: JV

     Bus: *U.S. subsidiary; sale/distribution*   Fax: (706) 625-8719
        of carpets.

● **VARITRONIX INTERNATIONAL LIMITED**

22 Chun Cheong Street, Tseung Kwan O Industrial Estates, Tseung Kwan O, Hong Kong

CEO: Chang Chu Cheng, Chmn.   Tel: 852-219-76000

Bus: *Mfr. electronics.*   Fax: 852-234-39555
                               www.varitronix.com

     VL ELECTRONICS, INC.

     3250 Wilshire Boulevard, Los Angeles, CA   90010

     CEO: Susie Scott   Tel: (213) 738-8700   %FO: 100

     Bus: *Sales and distribution of*   Fax: (213) 738-5340
        electronics.

● **VTECH HOLDINGS LIMITED**

57 Ting Kok Road, Tai Po, New Territories, Hong Kong

CEO: Allan C. Y. Wong, Chmn. & CEO   Tel: 852-2680-1000   Rev: $1,046

Bus: *Mfr. electronic learning games, toys,*   Fax: 852-2665-5099   Emp: 27,000
     pre-computer educational games and   www.vtech.com.hk
     cordless phones.

VTECH COMMUNICATIONS, INC.
8770 SW Nimbus Avenue, Beaverton, OR 97005
CEO: Bruce Garfield, Pres. Tel: (503) 626-1918 %FO: 100
Bus: *Sales/distribution of Vtech* Fax: (503) 644-9887
cordless phones.

VTECH INDUSTRIES
2350 Ravine Way, Ste. 100, Glenview, IL 60025
CEO: Bruce Garfield, Pres. Tel: (847) 400-2600 %FO: 100
Bus: *Sales/distribution of Vtech* Fax: (847) 400-2601
cordless phones.

VTECH INDUSTRIES, LLC
101 East Palatine Road, Wheeling, IL 60090
CEO: Emil Heidkamp, Pres. Tel: (847) 215-9700 %FO: 100
Bus: *Sales/distribution of electronic* Fax: (847) 215-9710
toys and games.

VTECH TELECOM, LLC
545 Concord Avenue, Ste. 12, Cambridge, MA 02140
CEO: Rolf Seichter, Mgr. Tel: (617) 576-3300 %FO: 100
Bus: *Engaged in contract* Fax: (617) 576-7753 Emp: 2
manufacturing services.

VTECH WIRELESS, INC.
One Corporate Park Drive, Ste. 100, Irvine, CA 92606
CEO: Thomas Ludwig, Pres. Tel: (949) 752-0312 %FO: 100
Bus: *Sales/distribution of wireless data* Fax: (949) 752-5014
communication products.

VTECHSOFT, INC.
3002 Dow Avenue, Ste. 104, Tustin, CA 92780
CEO: Thomas Ludwig, Pres. Tel: (714) 734-4800 %FO: 100
Bus: *Sales/distribution of educational* Fax: (714) 734-4801
software products.

● WING LUNG BANK LTD.
45 Des Voeux Road, Central Hong Kong
CEO: Michael Po-Ko Wu, Chmn. Tel: 852-2826-8333 Rev: $611
Bus: *Commercial banking services.* Fax: 852-2810-0592 Emp: 1,250
www.winglungbank.com.hk

WING LUNG BANK LTD.
445 South Figueroa St., Ste. 2270, Los Angeles, CA 90070
CEO: Anthony Yip, VP Tel: (213) 489-4193 %FO: 100
Bus: *International banking services.* Fax: (213) 489-3545

• ZINDART LIMITED

Flat C&D, 2/F Blk. 1, Tai Ping Industrial Centre, 57 Ting Kok Road, Tai Po NT Hong Kong

CEO: Alexander M. K. Ngan, Pres. & CEO	Tel: 852-2665-6992	Rev: $136
Bus: *Mfr. die-cast and injection-molded toys and collectibles, pop-up books, puzzles and board games.*	Fax: 852-2664-7066 www.zindart.com	Emp: 12,500

CORGI CLASSIC LTD.

430 West Erie, Suite 205, Chicago, IL   60610

CEO: Len Kalkun	Tel: (800) 800-2674	%FO: 100
Bus: *sales/distribution of die-cast and injection-molded toys and collectibles, pop-up books, puzzles and board games.*	Fax: (312) 302-9959	

ZINDART LTD., C/O CHINA VEST

10 Sansome Street, 18th Fl., San Francisco, CA   94104

CEO: Robert A. Theleen, Pres.	Tel: (415) 276-8888	%FO: 100
Bus: *U.S rep office for sales/distribution of die-cast and injection-molded toys and collectibles, pop-up books, puzzles and board games.*	Fax: (415) 276-8885	

ZINDART, C/O WILLIAM DUNK PARTNERS INC.

PO Box 3687, Chapel Hill, NC   27515-3687

CEO: Debbie Passik, Mgr.	Tel: (919) 929-4100	%FO: 100
Bus: *U.S rep office for sales/distribution of die-cast and injection-molded toys and collectibles, pop-up books, puzzles and board games.*	Fax: (919) 929-1186	

Hungary

● **GRAPHISOFT NV**
Graphisoft Park 1, H-1031 Budapest, Hungary
CEO: Gabor Bojar, CEO   Tel: 36-1-437-3000
Bus: *Develops engineering software.*   Fax: 36-1-437-3099
                                   www.graphisoft.com

    DRAWBASE SOFTWARE INC.
    One Gateway Center, Ste. 302, Newton, MA   02458-2802
    CEO: David Connors   Tel: (617) 641-2827   %FO: 100
    Bus: *Mfr. software.*   Fax: (617) 641-2801

    GRAPHISOFT US INC.
    224 Mississippi Street, San Francisco, CA   94107
    CEO: Al Moulton, Pres.   Tel: (415) 703-9777   %FO: 100
    Bus: *Mfr. software.*   Fax: (415) 703-9770

● **HEREND**
8440 Herend, Kossuth Lajor Str. 140, Budapest, Hungary
CEO: Peter Akos Bod, Chmn.   Tel: 36-8-852-3100
Bus: *Mfr. hand-painted, porcelain figurines*   Fax: Emp: 1,550
    and china.   www.herend.com

    MARTIN'S HEREND IMPORTS INC.
    21440 Pacific Boulevard, Sterling, VA   20167
    CEO: Tori Richardson-Hill   Tel: (703) 450-1601
    Bus: *Mfr. hand-painted, porcelain*   Fax: (703) 450-1605
    figurines and china.

● **MALEV HUNGARIAN AIRLINES**
Roosevelt Ter #2, H-1051 Budapest, Hungary
CEO: Ferenc Kovacs, CEO   Tel: 36-1-235-3888
Bus: *International airline carrier.*   Fax: 36-1-266-6009
                                     www.malev.hu

    MALEV HUNGARIAN AIRLINES
    630 Fifth Avenue, Suite 1900, New York, NY   10111
    CEO: G. Kucsma, Mgr.   Tel: (212) 757-6480   %FO: 100
    Bus: *International airline carrier.*   Fax: (212) 459-0675

Hungary

● **NAGY ÉS TRÓCSÁNYI**
Pálya Utca 9, H-1012 Budapest, Hungary
CEO: Peter Nagy, Mng. Ptnr.   Tel: 36-1-212-0444
Bus: *International law firm.*   Fax: 36-1-212-0443

   NAGY & TRÓCSANYI LLP.
   1114 Avenue of the Americas, New York, NY   10036
   CEO: Andre H. Friedman, Mng. Ptnr.   Tel: (212) 626-4206   %FO: 100
   Bus: *International law firm.*   Fax: (212) 626-4208

Iceland

- **THE ICELAND STEAMSHIP COMPANY LTD.**

  Pósthússtraeti 2, IS-101 Reykjavik, Iceland

  CEO: Höróur Sigurgestsson, Mng. Dir. Tel: 354-525-7000 Rev: $165

  Bus: *Engaged in transportation and* Fax: 354-525-7009 Emp: 1,100
  investment. www.eimskip.is

  ### EIMSKIP USA INC.

  109 E. Main Street, PO Box 3698, Norfolk, VA   23514

  CEO: Pam Jennings Tel: (757) 627-4444 %FO: 100

  Bus: *Fully integrated transportation,* Fax: (757) 622-7936
  ground operation, warehousing,
  coastal service, trucking and
  intermodal transportation.

- **ICELANDAIR**

  Reykjavik Airport, IS-101 Reykjavik, Iceland

  CEO: Sigurdur Helgason, Pres. & CEO Tel: 354-505-0300 Rev: $183

  Bus: *International passenger air carrier.* Fax: 354-505-0350 Emp: 1,280
  www.icelandair.is

  ### ICELANDAIR

  5950 Symphony Woods Road, Ste. 410, Columbia, MD   21044

  CEO: Gunnar Eklund, Dir. Tel: (410) 715-5110 %FO: 100

  Bus: *International passenger air carrier.* Fax: (410) 715-3547 Emp: 120

- **ICELANDIC FREEZING PLANTS CORP. LTD.**

  Aoalstraeti 6, IS-101 Reykjavik, Iceland

  CEO: Gunnar Svavarsson Tel: 354-560-7800 Rev: $360

  Bus: *Importers and processors of frozen and* Fax: 354-562-1252
  fresh fish. www.icelandic.is

  ### COLDWATER SEAFOOD CORPORATION

  60 Commercial Street, Everett, MA   02149

  CEO: Rick Gordon, Mgr. Tel: (617) 387-2050 %FO: 100

  Bus: *Dock and warehouse facilities for* Fax: (617) 387-2249
  imported fish products.

COLDWATER SEAFOOD CORPORATION
133 Rowayton Avenue, Rowayton, CT   06853
CEO: M. Gustaffson, Pres.   Tel: (203) 852-1600   %FO: 100
Bus: *Sales/distribution of Icelandic &*   Fax: (203) 866-4871
SeaStar frozen and fresh fish
products.

● **MAREL HF**
Höfobakki 9, IS-110 Reykjavik, Iceland
CEO: Hordur Arnarson, CEO   Tel: 354-563-8000   Rev: $28
Bus: *Mfr. of automation systems for the food*   Fax: 354-563-8001   Emp: 240
industry; weighing and vision   www.marel.is
equipment and systems automatic
portioning machines for fish and meat
industry.

MAREL USA
5801 14th Avenue, NW, Seattle, WA   98107
CEO: Gunnar Johennesson, Mgr.   Tel: (206) 789-4577   %FO: 100
Bus: *Sales/distribution of weighing and*   Fax: (206) 781-8657
portioning machines for fish and
meat industry.

MAREL USA
9745 Widmer Road, Lenexa, KS   66215
CEO: Noel Whitten   Tel: (913) 888-9110   %FO: 100
Bus: *Sales/distribution of weighing and*   Fax: (913) 888-8124
portioning machines for fish and
meat industry.

● **ÖSSUR HF**
Grjótháls 5, IS-110 Reykjavik, Iceland
CEO: Jón Sigurosson, CEO   Tel: 354-515-1300
Bus: *Develop and manufacture prosthetic*   Fax: 354-515-1366   Emp: 100
aids.   www.ossur.is

ÖSSUR USA INC.
27412 Laguna Hills Drive, Aliso Viejo, CA   92656
CEO: Ms. Siw Schalin, Dir.   Tel: (949) 362-3883   %FO: 100
Bus: *Sales/distribution of prosthetic*   Fax: (949) 362-3888
aids.

● **OZ.COM**
Snorrabraut 54, IS-105 Reykjavik, Iceland
CEO: Skuli Mogensen   Tel: 354-535-0035   Rev: $8
Bus: *Software company.*   Fax: 354-535-0055   Emp: 165
                                                   www.oz.com

OZ.COM

9820 Towne Centre Drive, San Diego, CA   92121

CEO: Fredrik Torstensson, EVP   Tel: (858) 320-3850   %FO: 100

Bus: *Software company.*   Fax: (858) 320-3851   Emp: 10

● **SIF GROUP PLC (FORMERLY ICELAND SEAFOOD)**

Fornubudir 5, PO Box 20222, Hafnarfjordur, Iceland

CEO: Gunnar Orn Kristjansson, Pres. & CEO   Tel: 354-569-8000   Rev: $250

Bus: *Provides sourcing, marketing and*   Fax: 354-588-8001   Emp: 78
distribution of frozen quality seafood.   www.is.is

SIF ICELAND SEAFOOD CORPORATION

190 Enterprise Drive, Newport News, VA   23603

CEO: Benedikt Sveinsson, Pres.   Tel: (757) 820-4000   %FO: 100

Bus: *Sales, marketing and processing*   Fax: (757) 888-6250   Emp: 280
plant for seafood products.

India

● **AIR-INDIA LTD.**
Air-India Bldg., Nariman Point, Mumbai 400 021, India
CEO: Ravindra Gupta, Chmn.   Tel: 91-22-202-4142
Bus: *Commercial air transport services.*   Fax: 91-22-283-1210
                                         www.airindia.com

   AIR-INDIA
   570 Lexington Avenue, 15th Fl., New York, NY   10022
   CEO: P. Goregaoker, Dir.   Tel: (212) 407-1300   %FO: 100
   Bus: *International commercial air*   Fax: (212) 838-9533
     transport services.

● **BANK OF BARODA**
3 Walchand Hirachand, Mumbai 400 038, India
CEO: Shri P. S. Shenoy, Chmn.   Tel: 91-22-261-0341   Rev: $1,269
Bus: *Commercial banking services.*   Fax: Emp: 45,900
                                         www.bankofbaroda.com

   BANK OF BARODA
   One Park Avenue, New York, NY   10016
   CEO: M.Balachandran, CEO   Tel: (212) 578-4550   %FO: 100
   Bus: *Banking services.*   Fax: (212) 578-4565

● **BANK OF INDIA**
Madame Cama Road, Mumbai 400 021, India
CEO: Shri G. G. Vaidya, Chmn.   Tel: 91-22-202-2426   Rev: $502
Bus: *Commercial banking services.*   Fax: 91-22-202-8808   Emp: 239,650
                                         www.bankofindia.com

   BANK OF INDIA
   277 Park Avenue, New York, NY   10172
   CEO: R. M. Desal, CEO   Tel: (212) 753-6100   %FO: 100
   Bus: *International banking services.*   Fax: (212) 980-0052   Emp: 55

● **BHARAT ELECTRONICS LTD.**
25 MG Road, 2nd Fll, Bangalore 560 001, India
CEO: Dr. V. K. Koshy, Chmn.   Tel: 91-80-559-5001
Bus: *Mfr. semiconductor devices,*   Fax: 91-80-558-4911   Emp: 16,000
  communication and radar systems.   www.bel-india.com

BHARAT ELECTRONICS LTD.
53 Hilton Avenue, Garden City, NY   11530
CEO: V.V.R. Sastry, Gen. Mgr. Tel: (516) 248-4020 %FO: 100
Bus: *Procurement of electronic* Fax: (516) 741-5894 Emp: 7
components and export to India
for in-house use.

● **DCM LTD.**
Vikrant Towers, 4 Rajendra Place, New Delhi 110 008, India
CEO: Sumant Bharat Ram Tel: 91-11-5719967
Bus: *Software programming service; mfr.* Fax: 91-11-5755731 Emp: 800
computers and related equipment, www.dcmds.com
software products and service.

DCM DATA SYSTEMS, LTD.
111F The Orchard, Cranbury, NJ   08512
CEO: Mosit Rasdogi, Mgr. Tel: (609) 448-0207 %FO: 100
Bus: *Software programming service.* Fax: (609) 448-0207

DCM DATA SYSTEMS, LTD.
39675 Cedar Boulevard, Suite 220, Newark, CA   94560
CEO: A. R. Choudhury, VP Tel: (510) 687-1669 %FO: 100
Bus: *Software programming service.* Fax: (510) 687-1667 Emp: 68

● **INFOSYS TECHNOLOGIES LIMITED**
Plot No. 44 & 97A, Electronics City, Hosur Road, Bangalore 561 229, India
CEO: N. R. Narayana Murthy, CEO Tel: 91-80-852-0261 Rev: $414
Bus: *Develops software products and* Fax: 91-80-852-0362 Emp: 9,850
provides software services. www.inf.com

INFOSYS INC.
2300 Cabot Drive, Ste. 250, Lisle, IL   60532
CEO: Manish Verma Tel: (630) 482-5000 %FO: 100
Bus: *Develops software products and* Fax: (630) 501-9144
provides software services.

INFOSYS INC.
Two Adams Place, Quincy, MA   02169
CEO: Ashok Vemuri Tel: (781) 356-3105 %FO: 100
Bus: *Develops software products and* Fax: (781) 356-3150
provides software services.

INFOSYS INC.
10900 NE 4th Street, Ste. 2300, Bellevue, WA   98004
CEO: Pradeep Prabhu Tel: (425) 990-1028 %FO: 100
Bus: *Develops software products and* Fax: (425) 990-1029
provides software services.

INFOSYS INC.

1950 Spectrum Circle, Ste. 400, Marietta, GA 30067

CEO: Ankush Patel

Bus: *Develops software products and provides software services.*

Tel: (770) 857-4428

Fax: (770) 857-7225

%FO: 100

INFOSYS INC.

100 Liberty Center, Ste. 200, Troy, MI 48084

CEO: Srinath Kashyap

Bus: *Develops software products and provides software services.*

Tel: (248) 524-0320

Fax: (248) 524-0321

%FO: 100

INFOSYS INC.

34760 Campus Drive, Fremont, CA 94555

CEO: Prasad Tadimeti

Bus: *Develops software products and provides software services.*

Tel: (510) 742-3000

Fax: (510) 742-3090

%FO: 100

INFOSYS INC.

2 Connell Drive, Ste. 4100, Berkeley Heights, NJ 07922

CEO: Shobha Meera

Bus: *Develops software products and provides software services.*

Tel: (908) 286-3100

Fax: (908) 286-3125

%FO: 100

INFOSYS INC.

10851 N. Black Canyon Fwy., Ste. 830, Phoenix, AZ 85029

CEO: Sanjay Dutt

Bus: *Develops software products and provides software services.*

Tel: (602) 944-4855

Fax: (602) 944-4879

%FO: 100

INFOSYS INC.

15305 Dallas Pkwy., Ste. 210, Addison, TX 75001

CEO: T. P. Prasad

Bus: *Develops software products and provides software services.*

Tel: (972) 770-0450

Fax: (972) 770-0490

%FO: 100

● **SKHEMA TECHNOLOGIES LTD.**

33/1 Lalbagh Road, Bangalore 560 027, India

CEO: Anant R. Koppar, CEO

Bus: *Mfr. computer software.*

Tel: 91-80-299-5115

Fax: 91-80-227-2933

www.kshema.com

KSHEMA TECHNOLOGIES

10 Pidgeon Hill Drive, Ste. 100, Sterling, VA 20165

CEO: Raj Rajkumar, SVP

Bus: *Mfr. computer software.*

Tel: (703) 259-2160

Fax: (703) 433-9175

%FO: 100

KSHEMA TECHNOLOGIES
12820 Greenwood Forest Drive, Houston, TX   77066

CEO: Raj Rajkumar, SVP	Tel: (832) 484-1602	%FO: 100
Bus: *Mfr. computer software.*	Fax: (832) 484-1602	

• OBEROI GROUP OF HOTELS
7 Sham Nath Marg, Delhi 110 054, India

CEO: P. R. S. Oberol, Chmn.	Tel: 91-11-2525464	Rev: $700
Bus: *Develops and manages hotel properties.*	Fax: 91-11-2929800	Emp: 12,000
	www.oberoihotels.com	

OBEROI GROUP OF HOTELS
509 Madison Avenue, Ste. 1906, New York, NY   10017

CEO: Caroline Wilson-Kent, Mgr.	Tel: (212) 223-8800	%FO: 100
Bus: *Develop and manage hotel properties.*	Fax: (212) 223-8500	Emp: 4

• DR. REDDY'S LABORATORIES LIMITED
7-1-27 Ameerpet, Hyderabad, Andhra Pradesh 500 016, India

CEO: G. V. Prasad, CEO	Tel: 91-40-373-1946	Rev: $112
Bus: *Develops and manufactures generic and branded pharmaceuticals.*	Fax: 91-40-373-1955	Emp: 4,440
	www.drreddys.com	

REDDY CHEMINOR INC
66 South Maple Avenue, Ridgewood, NJ   07450

CEO: Cameron Reid	Tel: (201) 444-4424	%FO: 100
Bus: *Develops and manufactures generic and branded pharmaceuticals.*	Fax: (201) 444-1456	

• SATYAM COMPUTER SERVICES LTD.
Mayfair Center, 1-8 303/36, SP Road, Secunderabad, Andhra Pradesh 500 003, India

CEO: B. Rama Raju, Mng. Dir.	Tel: 91-40-784-3222	Rev: $165
Bus: *Provides information technology services.*	Fax: 91-40-781-3166	Emp: 6,000
	www.satyam.com	

SATYAM COMPUTER SERVICES
8500 Leesburg Pike, Ste. 202, Vienna, VA   22182

CEO: B. Rama Raju	Tel: (703) 734-2100	%FO: 100
Bus: *Provides information technology services.*	Fax: (703) 734-2110	

SATYAM COMPUTER SERVICES
1000 Windward Concourse, Ste. 540, Alpharetta, GA 30005
CEO: Jonathan Watkins Tel: (770) 442-3111 %FO: 100
Bus: *Provides information technology* Fax: (770) 442-3913
services.

SATYAM COMPUTER SERVICES
One Tower Lane, Ste. 2600, Oakbrook Terrace, IL 60181
CEO: Jaison Thomas Tel: (630) 928-0700 %FO: 100
Bus: *Provides information technology* Fax: (630) 928-0701
services.

SATYAM COMPUTER SERVICES
3945 Freedom Circle, Ste. 720, Santa Clara, CA 95054
CEO: Richard Grehalva, SVP Tel: (408) 988-3100 %FO: 100
Bus: *Provides information technology* Fax: (408) 988-3876
services.

SATYAM COMPUTER SERVICES
One Gatehall Drive, Ste. 301, Parsippany, NJ 07054
CEO: Joseph Abraham Tel: (973) 656-0650 %FO: 100
Bus: *Provides information technology* Fax: (973) 656-0653
services.

VISION COMPASS INC.
1301 Fifth Avenue, Ste. 1400, Seattle, WA 98101
CEO: Ravi Chaturbhuja, Pres. Tel: (206) 770-2800 %FO: 100
Bus: *Provides information technology* Fax: (206) 770-2828
services.

● **SILVERLINE TECHNOLOGIES LTD.**
Unit 121, SDF IV, Seepz, Andheri, Mumbai 400-096, India
CEO: Shankar Iyer, CEO Tel: 91-22-829-1950 Rev: $28
Bus: *Engaged in software development and* Fax: 91-22-829-0199 Emp: 2,600
integration. www.silverline.com

SILVERLINE TECHNOLOGIES, INC.
691 North Squirrel Road, Ste. 140, Auburn Hills, MI 48326
CEO: Ravi Singh, CEO Tel: (248) 475-1282 %FO: 100
Bus: *Engaged in software development* Fax: (248) 475-4858
and integration.

SILVERLINE TECHNOLOGIES, INC.
145 West 57th Street, New York, NY 10019
CEO: Ravi Singh, CEO Tel: (212) 489-9288 %FO: 100
Bus: *Engaged in software development* Fax: (212) 489-8821
and integration.

SILVERLINE TECHNOLOGIES, INC.
53 Knightsbridge Road, Piscataway, NJ 08854
CEO: Ravi Singh, CEO   Tel: (732) 584-5300   %FO: 100
Bus: *Engaged in software development* Fax: (732) 584-5500
    and integration.

SILVERLINE TECHNOLOGIES, INC.
950 Tower Lane, Ste. 300, Foster City, CA 94404
CEO: Ravi Singh, CEO   Tel: (650) 358-6400   %FO: 100
Bus: *Engaged in software development* Fax: (650) 358-6414
    and integration.

SILVERLINE TECHNOLOGIES, INC.
2809 Butterfield Road, Ste. 340, Oakbrook, IL 60523
CEO: Ravi Singh, CEO   Tel: (630) 571-5555   %FO: 100
Bus: *Engaged in software development* Fax: (630) 571-5609
    and integration.

SILVERLINE TECHNOLOGIES, INC.
9399 West Higgins Road, Ste. 810, Rosemont, IL 60018
CEO: Ravi Singh, CEO   Tel: (847) 292-8060   %FO: 100
Bus: *Engaged in software development* Fax: (847) 292-1965
    and integration.

SILVERLINE TECHNOLOGIES, INC.
1681 Old Henderson Road, Columbus, OH 43220
CEO: Ravi Singh, CEO   Tel: (614) 457-5544   %FO: 100
Bus: *Engaged in software development* Fax: (614) 457-5540
    and integration.

• SINGHANIA & COMPANY
G107, Himalaya House, 23 Kasdurda Gandhi, New Delhi, India
CEO: T. P. Radhakrishnan, Ptrn.   Tel: 91-11-331-8300
Bus: *International law firm.*   Fax: 91-11-331-4413
                     www.singhania.com

SINGHANIA & COMPANY
375 Park Avenue, Ste. 1606, New York, NY 10152
CEO: Vabi Singhania, Mng. Ptnr.   Tel: (212) 563-1222   %FO: 100
Bus: *International law firm.*   Fax: (212) 563-1444

• STATE BANK OF INDIA
Madam Cama Road, Mumbai 400 021, India
CEO: V. Kamesam, Mng. Dir.   Tel: 91-22-202-2426   Rev: $5,486
Bus: *Commercial banking services.*   Fax: 91-22-204-0073   Emp: 239,650
                     www.statebankofindia.com

STATE BANK OF INDIA
2001 Pennsylvania Avenue, NW, Ste. 625, Washington, DC   20006
CEO: O. P. Bhatt, Rep.   Tel: (202) 223-5579   %FO: 100
Bus: *International banking services.*   Fax: (202) 785-3739

STATE BANK OF INDIA
19 South LaSalle Street, Ste. 200, Chicago, IL   60603
CEO: K. Rajagopaian, CEO   Tel: (312) 621-1200   %FO: 100
Bus: *International banking services.*   Fax: (312) 321-0740

STATE BANK OF INDIA
707 Wilshire Blvd., Ste.11995, Los Angeles, CA   90017
CEO: B. D. Sumitra, CEO   Tel: (213) 623-7250   %FO: 100
Bus: *International banking services.*   Fax: (213) 622-2069

STATE BANK OF INDIA
460 Park Avenue, 2nd Fl., New York, NY   10022
CEO: S. Sundar, Pres.   Tel: (212) 521-3200   %FO: 100
Bus: *International banking services.*   Fax: (212) 521-3364   Emp: 200

● **STATE TRADING CORP. OF INDIA LTD.**
Jawawar Vyapar Shawan, Tolstoy Marg, New Delhi 110 001, India
CEO: S. M. Dewan, Chmn.   Tel: 91-11-332-3002   Rev: $900
Bus: *General commodities including*   Fax: 91-11-332-6459
   chemicals, rice, wheat, tea, coffee, oils,   www.rajindia.com
   textile/leather/sporting goods & medical
   disposables

STATE TRADING CORP OF INDIA
350 Fifth Avenue, Ste. 1124, New York, NY   10018
CEO: N.A N. Jeyakumar, Mgr.   Tel: (212) 244-3317   %FO: 100
Bus: *Trading company; organizes all*   Fax: (212) 224-3319   Emp: 5,000
   products from India.

● **THE TATA IRON AND STEEL COMPANY LIMITED**
Bombay House, 24 Homi Mody Street, Mumbai 400 001, India
CEO: Ratan N. Tata, Chmn.   Tel: 91-22-204-9131   Rev: $1,192
Bus: *Mfr. steel and iron products.*   Fax: 91-22-204-9522   Emp: 52,167
                                          www.tatasteel.com

TATA INC.

101 Park Avenue, New York, NY   10178

CEO: Ashok Mehta, Pres.	Tel: (212) 557-7979	%FO: 100
Bus: *U.S. headquarters, diversified conglomerate, engineering & locomotive, mfr. commercial vehicles, computer software, tea production, hotels, (US: Lexington Hotel, NY; Executive Plaza, Chicago; Hampshire Hotel, D.C.)*	Fax: (212) 557-7987	Emp: 10

● **VOLTAS LTD.**

19 JN Heredia Marg, Ballard Estate, Mumbai 400 001, India

CEO: A. H. Tobaccowala, Chmn.	Tel: 91-22-261-8131	Rev: $206
Bus: *Mfr. divers consumer and industrial products and equipment.*	Fax: 91-22-261-8504 www.tata.com/voltas	Emp: 10,020

VOLTAS LTD.

655 Yonkers Avenue, Yonkers, NY   10704

CEO: Amal Merhi, Mgr.	Tel: (914) 965-4988	%FO: 100
Bus: *Import/export engineering equipment, granite products, contracting projects, technology transfers*	Fax: (914) 965-6730	Emp: 15

● **WIPRO LIMITED**

Doddakannelli, Sarjapur Road, Bangalore, Karnataka 560 035, India

CEO: Azim H. Premji, CEO	Tel: 91-80-844-0011	Rev: $661
Bus: *Engaged in in information technology and software engineering.*	Fax: 91-80-844-0054 www.wiproindia.com	

WIPRO TECHNOLOGIES

1995 El Camino Real, Ste. 200, Santa Clara, CA   95050

CEO: Soumitro Ghosh, VP	Tel: (408) 249-6345	%FO: 100
Bus: *Engaged in in information technology and software engineering.*	Fax: (408) 615-7174	

WIPRO TECHNOLOGIES

15455 NW Greenbrier Parkway, Beaverton, OR   98004

CEO: Soumitro Ghosh, VP	Tel: (503) 439-0825	%FO: 100
Bus: *Engaged in in information technology and software engineering.*	Fax: (503) 439-8426	

Indonesia

- **BANK BNI (BANK NEGARA INDONESIA)**
  Jalan Jendral Sudirnan Kavi, Jakarta-Kota 10220, Indonesia
  CEO: Widigdo Sukarman, Pres.   Tel: 62-21-251-1946   Rev: $1,702
  Bus: *International banking services.*   Fax: 62-21-570-0980   Emp: 14,000
  www.bni.co.id

  BANK BNI
  55 Broadway, 26th Fl., New York, NY   10006
  CEO: Maruli Pohan, Gen. Mgr.   Tel: (212) 943-4750   %FO: 100
  Bus: *International banking services.*   Fax: (212) 344-5723

- **BANK CENTRAL ASIA**
  J. L. Jendral, Sudirman Kav 22-23, Jakarta 12920, Indonesia
  CEO: Soedono Salim, Chmn.   Tel: 62-21-520-8650
  Bus: *Commercial banking services.*   Fax: 62-21-571-0928
  www.bca.co.id

  BANK CENTRAL ASIA
  641 Lexington Avenue, 15th Fl., New York, NY   10022
  CEO: Wee Beng Aw, Gen. Mgr.   Tel: (212) 888-3300   %FO: 100
  Bus: *International banking services.*   Fax: (212) 223-1333

- **BANK INDONESIA**
  Jalan M. H. Thamrin No. 2, Jakarta 10010, Indonesia
  CEO: Shiomo Braun, SVP   Tel: 62-21-231-0108
  Bus: *Government banking activities.*   Fax: 62-21-231-0592
  www.bii.co.id

  BANK INDONESIA
  *One Liberty Plaza, 165 Broadway, 31st Fl., New York, NY   10006
  CEO: Aslim Tadjuddin, Rep.   Tel: (212) 732-1958   %FO: 100
  Bus: *Government banking activities.*   Fax: (212) 732-4003

- **PT DJAKARTA LLOYD**
  Sangga Buana Bldg., Jalan Senan Raya No.44, Jakarta 10410, Indonesia
  CEO: Dr. Faisal J. Manoppo, Pres.   Tel: 62-21-345-6208
  Bus: *International steamship ocean transport*   Fax: 62-21-380-2545
  services.   www.dlloyd.co.id

DJAKARTA LLOYD INC.

50 Broad Street, Ste. 815, New York, NY   10004

CEO: Jerry Granberg, VP	Tel: (212) 344-0426	%FO: 100
Bus: *Steamship agents.*	Fax: (212) 363-4176	Emp: 5

● **LIPPO BANK**

Menara Asia 8th Floor, Jalan Diponegoro No. 101, Lippo Karawaci, Tangerang 15810, Indonesia

CEO: Ian B. Clyne, Pres. & CEO	Tel: 62-21-546-0191	Rev: $540
Bus: *International banking services and*	Fax: 62-21-546-0259	
investments.	www.lippobank.co.id	

LIPPO BANK

100 East San Clara Street, San Jose, CA   95113

CEO: James Per Lee, Pres.	Tel: (408) 286-1888	%FO: 100
Bus: *International banking services.*	Fax: (408) 286-9521	

LIPPO BANK

711 West College Street, Los Angeles, CA   90012

CEO: James Per Lee, Pres.	Tel: (213) 625-1888	%FO: 100
Bus: *International banking services.*	Fax: (213) 680-9725	Emp: 30

LIPPO BANK

1001 Grant Avenue, San Francisco, CA   94133

CEO: James Per Lee, Pres.	Tel: (415) 982-3572	%FO: 100
Bus: *International banking services.*	Fax: (415) 986-1919	Emp: 50

Iran

● DR. ALEXANDER AGHAYAN & ASSOCIATES, INC.

149 Sarhang Sakhaee Avenue, Tehran 11354, Iran

CEO: Robert Martin CEO

Bus: *Engaged in patent and trademark law.*

Tel: 98-21-670-5056

Fax: 98-21-670-4858

www.aghayan.com

DR. ALEXANDER AGHAYAN & ASSOCIATES, INC.

666 Fifth Avenue, 37th Fl., New York, NY   10103

CEO: Alexander Aghayan, CEO

Bus: *Engaged in patent and trademark law.*

Tel: (212) 586-7272

Fax: (212) 504-7951

%FO: 100

● BANK MELLI IRAN

Ferdoesi Avenue, Tehran 11354, Iran

CEO: Asadollah Amirsiani, Chmn.

Bus: *Banking services.*

Tel: 98-21-3231

Fax: 98-21-302813

Emp: 32,000

BANK MELLI IRAN

767 Fifth Avenue, 44th Floor, New York, NY   10153

CEO: Gholamreza Rahi, Chief Rep.

Bus: *International banking services.*

Tel: (212) 759-4700

Fax: (212) 759-4704

%FO: 100

● BANK SADERAT IRAN

43 Somayeh Street, PO Box 15745-631, Tehran, Iran

CEO: Mr. Razavi, Chmn.

Bus: *Commercial banking services.*

Tel: 98-21-832699

Fax: 98-21-880-9539

www.bank-saderat-iran.com

Emp: 30,000

BANK SADERAT IRAN

120 East 56th Street, Suite 410, New York, NY   10022

CEO: Ali Eliassi, Gen. Mgr.

Bus: *International banking services.*

Tel: (212) 753-6400

Fax: (212) 223-3726

%FO: 100

Emp: 2

● BANK SEPAH-IRAN

Iman Khomeini Square, Tehran, Iran

CEO: A. Seif, Chmn.

Bus: *Commercial banking services.*

Tel: 98-21-311-12718

Fax: 98-21-311-2138

www.edbi-iran.com

BANK SEPAH-IRAN
650 Fifth Avenue, New York, NY   10022
CEO: Hassan Kosari, Mgr.   Tel: (212) 974-1777   %FO: 100
Bus: *International commercial banking*   Fax: (212) 541-4347
   services.

Ireland

• A&L GOODBODY SOLICITORS

International Financial Services Centre, North Wall Quay, Dublin 1, Ireland

CEO: Frank O'Riordan, Mng.Prtn.   Tel: 353-1-649-2000

Bus: *International law firm.*   Fax: 353-1-649-2649   Emp: 450

www.algoodbody.ie

A & L GOODBODY

10 Rockefeller Plaza, Ste. 816, New York, NY   10020

CEO: John Coman, Prtn.   Tel: (212) 582-4499   %FO: 100

Bus: *International law firm.*   Fax: (212) 333-5126

A & L GOODBODY

One Financial Center, Ste. 3800, Boston, MA   02111

CEO: Aidan Browne   Tel: (617) 348-1800   %FO: 100

Bus: *International law firm.*   Fax: (617) 348-3018

• AER LINGUS GROUP PLC

PO Box 180, Dublin Airport, Dublin, Ireland

CEO: Michael Foley, CEO   Tel: 353-1-886-2222   Rev: $1,216

Bus: *Commercial air transport services.*   Fax: 353-1-886-3833   Emp: 7,000

www.aerlingus.ie

AER LINGUS

538 Broadhollow Road, Melville, NY   11747

CEO: Jack Foley, SVP   Tel: (516) 577-5700   %FO: 100

Bus: *International air transport*   Fax: (516) 752-3600   Emp: 350
    services.

• ALLIED IRISH BANKS, PLC

Bankcentre, Ballsbridge, Dublin 4, Ireland

CEO: Michael Buckley, CEO   Tel: 353-1-660-0311   Rev: $6,060

Bus: *Commercial banking services.*   Fax: 353-1-660-9137   Emp: 26,265

www.aib.ie

ALLFIRST FINANCIAL CENTER

499 Mitchell Street, Millsboro, DE   19966

CEO: Bernard M. Cregg, Pres.   Tel: (302) 934-9232   %FO: 100

Bus: *Commercial banking and trust*   Fax:
    services.

ALLFIRST ANNUITIES AGENCY

25 South Charles Street, P.O.Box 1596, Baltimore, MD 21203

CEO: Mark A. Mullican, Pres.   Tel: (410) 244-4000   %FO: 100

Bus: *Insurance services.*   Fax: (410) 244-3751

ALLFIRST FINANCIAL INC.

25 South Charles Street, PO Box 1596, Baltimore, MD 21203

CEO: Susan C. Keating, CEO   Tel: (410) 244-4830   %FO: 100

Bus: *Commercial and consumer credit services.*   Fax: (410) 244-4459

ALLFIRST TRUST COMPANY

8601 Westwood Center Drive, Vienna, VA 22182

CEO: Rick A. Gold, Pres.   Tel: (410) 244-3987   %FO: 100

Bus: *Commercial banking and trust services.*   Fax: (410) 244-3987

ALLIED IRISH BANKS

601 South Figueroa Street, Los Angeles, CA 90017-2513

CEO: Warren J. Guinane   Tel: (213) 622-4900

Bus: *Commercial banking and trust services.*   Fax: (213) 622-4900

ALLIED IRISH BANKS

405 Park Avenue, New York, NY 10022

CEO: Brian M. Leeney, EVP   Tel: (212) 339-8000   %FO: 100

Bus: *International commercial banking services.*   Fax: (212) 339-8008   Emp: 100

ZIRKIN-CUTLER INVESTMENTS INC.

3 Bethesda Metro Center, Ste. 840, Bethesda, MD 20811

CEO: Harold Zirkin, Pres.   Tel: (301) 961-9000

Bus: *Commercial banking and trust services.*   Fax: (301) 961-9000

● BANK OF IRELAND

Lower Baggot Street, Dublin 2, Ireland

CEO: Maurice A. Keane, CEO   Tel: 353-1-661-5933   Rev: $3,731

Bus: *Banking services.*   Fax: 353-1-661-5671   Emp: 13,365

www.boi.ie

BANK OF IRELAND ASSET MANAGEMENT (U.S.)

75 Holly Hill Lane, Greenwich, CT 06830-6327

CEO: Denis Curran, Pres.   Tel: (203) 869-0111   %FO: 100

Bus: *Investment advisory services.*   Fax: (203) 869-0268

● **ARTHUR COX SOLICITORS**
Earlsfort Centre, Earlsfort Terrace, Dublin 2, Ireland
CEO: Pádraig Ó Ríordáin   Tel: 353-1-618-0000
Bus: *International law firm.*   Fax: 353-1-618-0618   Emp: 100
                                            www.arthurcox.ie

   ARTHUR COX
   570 Lexington Avenue, 28th Fl., New York, NY   10022
   CEO: John Matson, Mng. Ptnr.   Tel: (212) 759-0808   %FO: 100
   Bus: *International law firm.*   Fax: (212) 688-3237

● **CRH PLC**
Belgard Castle, Clondalkin, Dublin 22, Ireland
CEO: W. Liam O'Mahoney, CEO   Tel: 353-1-404-1000   Rev: $8,195
Bus: *Building materials manufacture and* Fax: 353-1-404-1415   Emp: 36,665
   distribution.   www.crh.cie

   OLDCASTLE, INC.
   375 Northridge Road, Ste. 350, Atlanta, GA   30350
   CEO: John Wittstock, CEO   Tel: (770) 804-3360   %FO: 100
   Bus: *Mfr./distribution of building*   Fax: (770) 673-2400
     materials.

   THOMPSON-MCCULLY CO.
   5905 Belleville Road, Belleville, MI   48111
   CEO: Bob Thompson, CEO   Tel: (734) 397-2050   %FO: 100
   Bus: *Mfr. integrated aggregates.*   Fax: (734) 397-1290

   TILCON INC.
   642 Black Rock Avenue, New Britain, CT   06052
   CEO: Joseph A. Abate, CEO   Tel: (860) 223-3651   %FO: 100
   Bus: *Mfr. building materials.*   Fax: (860) 225-1865

● **EIRCOM PLC**
114 St. Stephen's Green West, Dublin 2, Ireland
CEO: Alfie Kane, CEO   Tel: 353-1-671-4444
Bus: *Engaged in telecommunications.*   Fax: 353-1-671-6916
                                            www.eircom.com

   EIRCOM U.S. LTD.
   One Landmark Square, Ste. 1105, Stamford, CT   06901
   CEO: Eamonn Condon, Mgr.   Tel: (203) 363-7171   %FO: 100
   Bus: *Engaged in telecommunications.*   Fax: (203) 363-7176

EIRCOM U.S. LTD.
2055 Gateway Place, Ste. 400, San Jose, CA 95110
CEO: Brad Montano, Mgr.   Tel: (408) 467-3863   %FO: 100
Bus: *Engaged in telecommunications.*   Fax: (408) 441-9076

● **ELAN CORPORATION PLC**
Lincoln Home, 2 Lincoln Place, Dublin 2, Ireland
CEO: Donal J. Geaney, CEO   Tel: 353-1-709-4000   Rev: $710
Bus: *Mfr. and research pharmaceuticals.*   Fax: 353-1-662-4949   Emp: 2,600
                                   www.elancorp.com

CARNRICK LABORATORIES, INC.
45 Horsehill Road, Cedar Knolls, NJ 07927
CEO: Edmond Bergeron, Pres.   Tel: (973) 267-2670   %FO: 100
Bus: *Mfr. pharmaceuticals.*   Fax: (973) 267-2289

ELAN CORPORATION
1140 Connecticut Avenue NW, Ste. 350, Washington, DC 20036
CEO: Paul Goddard, Pres.   Tel: (202) 872-7800   %FO: 100
Bus: *Mfr. pharmaceuticals.*   Fax: (202) 872-7808

ELAN DIAGNOSTICS
231 North Puente, Brea, CA 92821
CEO: Paul Goddard, Pres.   Tel: (714) 871-8360   %FO: 100
Bus: *Mfr. pharmaceuticals.*   Fax: (714) 871-2439

ELAN DIAGNOSTICS
2 Thurber Boulevard, Smithfield, RI 02917
CEO: Dr. Thomas M. Jackson   Tel: (401) 233-3526   %FO: 100
Bus: *Mfr. diagnostics instruments.*   Fax: (401) 233-6480

ELAN PHARMA INC.
345 Park Avenue, 8th Fl., New York, NY 10154
CEO: Paul Goddard, Pres.   Tel: (212) 407-5740   %FO: 100
Bus: *Mfr. pharmaceuticals.*   Fax: (212) 755-1043

ELAN PHARMACEUTICAL RESEARCH CORPORATION
4 Biotech Park, 377 Plantation South, Worcester, MA 01605
CEO: Izzy Tsals, Pres.   Tel: (508) 756-2886   %FO: 100
Bus: *Mfr./research pharmaceuticals*   Fax: (508) 798-7121
     specializing in pain medication.

ELAN PHARMACEUTICAL RESEARCH CORPORATION & ELAN HOLDINGS, INC.
1300 Gould Drive, SW, Gainesville, GA 30504
CEO: Hal Herring, VP   Tel: (770) 534-8239   %FO: 100
Bus: *Mfr./research pharmaceuticals.*   Fax: (770) 534-8247   Emp: 70

ELAN PHARMACEUTICALS
3760 Haven Avenue, Menlo Park, CA   94025
CEO: Paul Goddard, Pres.   Tel: (650) 853-1500   %FO: 100
Bus: *Mfr./research pharmaceuticals*   Fax: (650) 853-1538
    specializing in pain medication.

ELAN PHARMACEUTICALS
800 Gateway Blvd., South San Francisco, CA   94080
CEO: Michael Coffee, Pres.   Tel: (650) 877-0900   %FO: 100
Bus: *Mfr./research pharmaceuticals.* Fax: (650) 877-8370

ELAN TRANSDERMAL TECHNOLOGIES
3250 Commerce Parkway, Miramar, FL   33025
CEO: Manuel Gonzalez, Pres.   Tel: (954) 430-3340   %FO: 100
Bus: *Mfr./research pharmaceuticals*   Fax: (954) 430-3390
    specializing in pain medication.

● THE FITZPATRICK HOTEL GROUP
14 Windsor Terrace, Dun Laoghaire, Dublin, Ireland
CEO: Paddy Fitzpatrick, Chmn.   Tel: 353-1-284-5656
Bus: *Family owned and operated hotel group.* Fax: 353-1-284-5655
    www.fitzpatrickhotels.com

FITZPATRICK CHICAGO HOTEL
166 E. Superior Street, Chicago, IL   60611
CEO: Michael Baker, Mgr.   Tel: (312) 787-6000   %FO: 100
Bus: *Hotel.*   Fax: (312) 787-6133

FITZPATRICK GRAND CENTRAL HOTEL
141 East 44th Street, New York, NY   10017
CEO: Sean Holmes, Gen. Mgr.   Tel: (212) 351-6800   %FO: 100
Bus: *Hotel.*   Fax: (212) 818-1747

FITZPATRICK MANHATTAN HOTEL
687 Lexington Avenue, New York, NY   10021
CEO: Hilda Garvey, Gen. Mgr.   Tel: (212) 355-0100   %FO: 100
Bus: *Hotel.*   Fax: (212) 308-5166

● GLANBIA PLC
Glanbia House, Kilkenny, Ireland
CEO: Thomas Corcoran, Chmn. & CEO   Tel: 353-5-672-200   Rev: $2,262
Bus: *Dairy products.*   Fax: 353-5-672-222   Emp: 7,400
    www.glanbia.com

GLANBIA FOODS, INC.
1572 East Highway 26, Richfield, ID   83349
CEO: Ed Bastian   Tel: (208) 487-2545   %FO: 100
Bus: *Dairy products.*   Fax: (208) 487-2545

GLANBIA FOODS, INC.
1373 Fillmore Street, Twin Falls, ID   83301
CEO: David Thomas, Pres.   Tel: (208) 733-7555   %FO: 100
Bus: *Dairy products.*   Fax: (208) 733-9222

● **GORANN LTD.**
25/26 Great Strand Street, Dublin 1, Ireland
CEO: Philipp Matuschka, CEO   Tel: 353-1-874-8188
Bus: *Engaged in company start-up, product*   Fax: 353-1-289-1236
introduction and management   www.gorann.com
consulting for the Irish consumer
market.

    GORANN INC.
    350 Fifth Avenue, Ste. 5809, New York, NY   10188
    CEO: Pat Plunkett, Chmn.   Tel: (212) 404-7500   %FO: 100
    Bus: *Engaged in management*   Fax: (212) 656-1866
    consulting; start-up to successful
    global organizations.

● **IONA TECHNOLOGIES PLC**
The IONA Bldg., Shelbourne Road, Ballsbridge, Dublin 4, Ireland
CEO: Barry Morris, CEO   Tel: 353-1-637-2000   Rev: $154
Bus: *Mfr. Web development software.*   Fax: 353-1-637-2888   Emp: 770
                                   www.iona.com

    IONA TECHNOLOGIES INC.
    1117 Perimeter Center West, Ste. 500E, Atlanta, GA   30338
    CEO: Barry Morris, Pres.   Tel: (770) 392-3300   %FO: 100
    Bus: *Sales Web development software.*   Fax: (770) 392-0320

    IONA TECHNOLOGIES INC.
    200 West Street, 4th Fl., Waltham, MA   02451
    CEO: Barry Morris, Pres.   Tel: (781) 902-8000   %FO: 100
    Bus: *Sales Web development software.*   Fax: (781) 902-8001

    IONA TECHNOLOGIES INC.
    1902 Wright Place, Ste. 200, Carlsbad, CA   92009
    CEO: Barry Morris, Pres.   Tel: (760) 918-5628   %FO: 100
    Bus: *Sales Web development software.*   Fax: (760) 918-5629

IONA TECHNOLOGIES INC.
15301 Spectrum Drive, 4th Fl., Addison, TX   75001
CEO: Barry Morris, Pres.   Tel: (972) 789-2920   %FO: 100
Bus: *Sales Web development software.*   Fax: (972) 789-2927

IONA TECHNOLOGIES INC.
10 South Riverside Plaza, 18th Fl., Chicago, IL   60606
CEO: Barry Morris, Pres.   Tel: (312) 474-6066   %FO: 100
Bus: *Sales Web development software.*   Fax: (312) 474-6067

● IRISH LIFE & PERMANENT PLC
Irish Life Centre, 1 Lower Abbey Street, Dublin 1, Ireland
CEO: David Went, CEO   Tel: 353-1-704-2000   Rev: $4,456
Bus: *Engaged in insurance, investment*   Fax: 353-1-704-1900   Emp: 4,500
   management and financial services.   www.irishlifepermanent.ie

FIRST VARIABLE LIFE INSURANCE COMPANY
10 Post Office Square, Boston, MA   02109
CEO: Diane M. McMullin, VP   Tel: (617) 457-6700
Bus: *Engaged in insurance and*   Fax: (617) 457-6760
   investment management.

INTERSTATE ASSURANCE COMPANY
PO Box 1907, Des Moines, IA   50306
CEO: Ronald Butkiewicz, Pres. & CEO   Tel: (515) 440-3330   %FO: 100
Bus: *Manufacturer and marketer of*   Fax: (515) 440-3345
   personal financial products, with
   an emphasis on life insurance and
   information.

IRISH LIFE FINANCIAL SERVICES
2122 York Road, Oak Brook, IL   60523
CEO: Norman A. Fair, VP   Tel: (630) 586-5000   %FO: 100
Bus: *Engaged in insurance, investment*   Fax: (630) 586-1005
   management and financial
   services.

IRISH LIFE OF NORTH AMERICA INC.
2211 York Road, Ste. 202, Oak Brook, IL   60523
CEO: Norman A. Fair, VP   Tel: (630) 571-4562   %FO: 100
Bus: *Engaged in insurance and*   Fax: (630) 571-4578
   investment management.

TRI-MERICA SECURITIES CORPORATION
1206 Mulberry Street, Des Moines, IA   50309
CEO: Thomas D. Gualdoni, Pres.   Tel: (515) 283-2501
Bus: *Engaged in financial services.*   Fax: (515) 282-3250

• JEFFERSON SMURFIT GROUP PLC

Beech Hill, Clonskeagh, Dublin 4, Ireland
CEO: Michael W.J. Smurfit, Chmn.   Tel: 353-1-202-7000   Rev: $4,300
Bus: *Corrugated paper and board, print,*   Fax: 353-1-269-4481   Emp: 40,225
  packaging and newsprint.   www.smurfit.ie

SMURFIT STONE CONTAINER CORPORATION

PO Box 2200, Flemington, NJ   08822
CEO: Frank Lucard, Gen. Mgr.   Tel: (908) 782-0505   %FO: 100
Bus: *Mfr. paper and paperboard*   Fax: (908) 782-0583
  packaging.

SMURFIT STONE CONTAINER CORPORATION

8182 Maryland Avenue, Clayton, MO   63105
CEO: Roger W. Stone, Pres. & CEO   Tel: (314) 746-1100   %FO: 50
Bus: *Mfr. paper and paperboard*   Fax: (314) 746-1259   Emp: 20,000
  packaging.

SMURFIT STONE CONTAINER CORPORATION

150 North Michigan Avenue, Chicago, IL   60601
CEO: Raymond M. Curran, Pres.   Tel: (312) 346-6600   %FO: 100
Bus: *U.S. headquarters.*   Fax: (312) 580-4919

SMURFIT STONE CONTAINER CORPORATION

600 Wissahickon Avenue, Cedartown, GA   30125
CEO: Benjamin Bonham, Mgr.   Tel: (770) 748-3520   %FO: 100
Bus: *Mfr. paper and paperboard*   Fax: (770) 749-0863
  packaging.

SMURFIT STONE CONTAINER CORPORATION

9600 South Harlem Avenue, Bridgeview, IL   60455
CEO: Roger W. Stone, Pres. & CEO   Tel: (708) 499-2600   %FO: 100
Bus: *Mfr. paper and paperboard*   Fax: (708) 499-1750
  packaging.

SMURFIT STONE CONTAINER CORPORATION

1501 Indiana Avenue, Saint Charles, IL   60174
CEO: Cindy Anderson, Operations Mgr.   Tel: (630) 584-2900   %FO: 100
Bus: *Mfr. paper and paperboard*   Fax: (630) 584-8521
  packaging.

SMURFIT STONE CONTAINER CORPORATION

5000 Flat Rock Road, Philadelphia, PA   19127
CEO: Rusty Miller, Gen. Mgr.   Tel: (215) 984-7000   %FO: 100
Bus: *Mfr. paper and paperboard*   Fax: (215) 984-7044
  packaging.

SMURFIT STONE CONTAINER CORPORATION
8080 North Point Blvd., Winston-Salem, NC   27106

CEO: Mike Maloney, Gen. Mgr.   Tel: (336) 759-7821   %FO: 100

Bus: *Mfr. paper and paperboard*   Fax: (336) 759-8900
packaging.

SMURFIT STONE INFORMATION TECHNOLOGY
401 Alton Street, Alton, IL   62002

CEO: James A. Hayssen, VP   Tel: (618) 463-6000   %FO: 100

Bus: *Mfr. paper and paperboard*   Fax: (618) 463-6320
packaging.

SMURFIT STONE MBI
7393 Shawnee Road, North Tonawanda, NY   14120

CEO: Paul Tracey, Gen. Mgr.   Tel: (716) 694-1000   %FO: 100

Bus: *Mfr. paper and paperboard*   Fax: (716) 694-1035
packaging.

SMURFIT STONE MBI
51 Robinson Street, North Tonawanda, NY   14120

CEO: Gregory Sommer   Tel: (716) 692-6510   %FO: 100

Bus: *Mfr. paper and paperboard*   Fax: (716) 694-9262
packaging.

SMURFIT-STONE CORP.
8182 Maryland Avenue, St. Louis, MO   63105

CEO: Timothy J.P. McKenna, VP   Tel: (314) 746-1100   %FO: 100

Bus: *Mfr. paper and paperboard*   Fax: (314) 746-1331
packaging.

• JURYS DOYLE HOTEL GROUP PLC
146 Pembroke Road, Ballsbridge, Dublin 4, Ireland

CEO: Patrick A. McCann, CEO   Tel: 353-1-607-0070

Bus: *Hotel group.*   Fax: 353-1-667-2370

www.jurys.com

JURYS WASHINGTON COURTYARD
1900 Connecticut Avenue NW, Washington, DC   20036

CEO: Niall Geoghegan, Dir.   Tel: (202) 332-9300   %FO: 100

Bus: *Hotel group.*   Fax: (202) 319-1793

JURYS WASHINGTON HOTEL
1500 New Hampshire Avenue NW, Washington, DC   20036

CEO: Niall Geoghegan, Dir.   Tel: (202) 483-6000   %FO: 100

Bus: *Hotel group.*   Fax: (202) 328-3265

• KINGSPAN GROUP PLC

Dublin Road, Kingscourt, County Caven, Ireland
CEO: Eugene Murtagh, CEO
Tel: 353-42-969-8000
Rev: $606
Bus: *Mfr. raised flooring.*
Fax: 353-42-966-7501
Emp: 500
www.kingspan.com

TATE ACCESS FLOORS INC.

7510 Montevideo Road, Jessup, MD 20794
CEO: Russell Shiels, CEO
Tel: (410) 799-4200
%FO: 100
Bus: *Mfr./sales raised flooring.*
Fax: (410) 799-4207

• OAKHILL GROUP PLC

Oakhill House, Rowan Avenue, Stillorgan Industrial Park, Dublin 18, Ireland
CEO: Alan Jordan, COO
Tel: 353-1-240-1400
Bus: *Engaged in printing and packaging.*
Fax: 353-1-240-1450
www.oakhillplc.ie

ELITE COLOR GROUP

233 Georgia Avenue, Providence, RI 01905
CEO: Kevin Reilly, Mgr.
Tel: (401) 941-5990
%FO: 100
Bus: *Printing.*
Fax: (401) 941-5995

MERIDIAN PRINTING, INC.

1538 South County Trail, PO Box 1160, East Greenwich, RI 02818
CEO: Fern Malouin, Pres. & CEO
Tel: (401) 885-4882
%FO: 100
Bus: *Printing.*
Fax: (401) 885-1350

• PARTHUS TECHNOLOGIES PLC

32-34 Harcourt Street, Dublin 2, Ireland
CEO: Brian Long, CEO
Tel: 353-1-402-5700
Rev: $32
Bus: *Designs semiconductors, circuits and software.*
Fax: 353-1-402-5711
Emp: 370
www.parthus.com

PARTHUS INC.

12365 Riata Trace Parkway, Bldg. 2-150, Austin, TX 78727
CEO: William McLean, Pres.
Tel: (512) 249-2330
%FO: 100
Bus: *Mfr./sales semiconductors, circuits and software.*
Fax: (512) 249-5357

PARTHUS INC.

2033 Gateway Place, Ste. 150, San Jose, CA 95110-1002
CEO: Richard Martin
Tel: (408) 514-2900
%FO: 100
Bus: *Mfr./sales semiconductors, circuits and software.*
Fax: (408) 514-2995

PARTHUS INC.
100 Rialto Place, Ste. 815, Melbourne, FL   32901
CEO: William McLean, Pres.   Tel: (321) 733-1991   %FO: 100
Bus: *Mfr./sales semiconductors, circuits*   Fax: (321) 733-1991
    and software.

● **RIVERDEEP GROUP PLC**
Styne House 3rd Fl., Upper Hatch Street, Dublin 2, Ireland
CEO: Barry O'Callaghan, CEO   Tel: 353-1-670-7570   Rev: $52
Bus: *Mfr. web-based, educational software*   Fax: 353-1-670-7570   Emp: 159
    products.   www.riverdeep.net

    RIVERDEEP INC.
    125 Cambridge Park Drive, Cambridge, MA   02140
    CEO: William H. Burke   Tel: (617) 995-1000   %FO: 100
    Bus: *Sales of web-based, educational*   Fax: (617) 491-5855
        software products.

● **TRINITY BIOTECH PLC**
Bray Business Park, Bray, Wicklow, Ireland
CEO: Ronan O'Caoimh, Chmn.   Tel: 353-1-276-9800   Rev: $23
Bus: *Biotech company engaged in*   Fax: 353-1-276-9888   Emp: 190
    manufacture of saliva and blood-based   www.trinitybiotech.com
    medical tests.

    TRINITY BIOTECH USA, INC.
    PO Box 1059, Jamestown, NY   14702-1059
    CEO: Brendan Farrell, Pres.   Tel: (716) 483-3851   %FO: 100
    Bus: *Mfr./sales of medical tests.*   Fax: (716) 488-1990

● **TRINTECH GROUP PLC**
Trintech House, South County Business Park, Leopardstown, Dublin 18, Ireland
CEO: John F. McGuire   Tel: 353-1-207-4000   Rev: $49
Bus: *Computer hardware and business*   Fax: 353-1-207-4190   Emp: 623
    equipment.   www.trintech.com

    TRINTECH INC.
    9606 North Mopac, Suite 800, Austin, TX   78759
    CEO: John McGuire, CEO   Tel: (512) 427-7820   %FO: 100
    Bus: *Computer hardware and business*   Fax:
        equipment.

    TRINTECH INC.
    2755 Campus Drive, Suite 220, San Mateo, CA   94403
    CEO: Kevin Shea   Tel: (650) 227-7000   %FO: 100
    Bus: *Computer hardware and business*   Fax: (650) 227-7100
        equipment.

TRINTECH INC.
6205 Blue Lagoon Drive, Suite 130, Miami, FL   33126

CEO: John McGuire, CEO   Tel: (786) 388-1950   %FO: 100

Bus: *Computer hardware and business*   Fax: (786) 388-1956
equipment.

TRINTECH INC.
15851 Dallas Pkwy., Suite 940, Addison, TX   75001

CEO: John McGuire, CEO   Tel: (800) 416-0075   %FO: 100

Bus: *Computer hardware and business*   Fax: (972) 701-9337
equipment.

TRINTECH INC.
5 Independence Way, Suite 170, Princeton, NJ   08540

CEO: John McGuire, CEO   Tel: (609) 919-6000   %FO: 100

Bus: *Computer hardware and business*   Fax: (609) 720-1020
equipment.

TRINTECH INC.
600 W. Germantown Pike. Suite 210, Plymouth Meeting, PA   19462

CEO: John McGuire, CEO   Tel: (610) 825-0550   %FO: 100

Bus: *Computer hardware and business*   Fax: (610) 825-7676
equipment.

• WATERFORD WEDGWOOD PLC
1-2 Upper Hatch Street, Dublin 2, Ireland

CEO: Anthony J. F. O'Reilly, Chmn.   Tel: 353-1478-1855   Rev: $888

Bus: *Manufacturing and marketing of lead*   Fax: 353-1478-4863   Emp: 4,944
crystal and china.   www.fitzwilton.ie

WATERFORD WEDGWOOD USA INC
1330 Campus Parkway, Wall, NJ   07719

CEO: Christopher J. Mc Gillivary, CEO   Tel: (732) 938-5800   %FO: 100

Bus: *Marketing of crystal and china.*   Fax: (732) 938-7108

Israel

● **ACS-TECH80 LTD.**
PO Box 5668, Migdal Ha'Emek 10500, Israel
CEO: Ze'ev Kirshenboim, CEO   Tel: 972-6-654-6440   Rev: $17
Bus: *Mfr. programmable motion control*   Fax: 972-6-654-6443   Emp: 50
     products for automated systems.   www.acs-motion-control.com

     ACS-TECH80 INC.
     7351 Kirkwood Lane North, Ste. 130, Maple Grove, MN   55369
     CEO: Jonathon Summers   Tel: (763) 493-4080   %FO: 100
     Bus: *Mfr. programmable motion control*   Fax: (763) 493-4089
     products for automated systems.

● **ALADDIN SOFTWARE SECURITY INC.**
15 Bein Oved Street, Tel Aviv 61110, Israel
CEO: Yanki Margalit, Chmn. & CEO   Tel: 972-3-636-2222   Rev: $36
Bus: *Sales, installation and service of*   Fax: 972-3-537-5796   Emp: 280
     software for security systems.   www.aks.com

     ALADDIN KNOWLEDGE SYSTEMS, INC.
     2920 N. Arlington Heights Road, Arlington Heights, MI   60004
     CEO: Ami Dar, Pres.   Tel: (847) 808-0300   %FO: 100
     Bus: *Develop/sales/installation/service*   Fax: (847) 808-0313
     software for security systems.

     ALADDIN KNOWLEDGE SYSTEMS, INC.
     350 Fifth Avenue, Suite 6614, New York, NY   10118
     CEO: Ami Dar, Pres.   Tel: (212) 564-5678   %FO: 100
     Bus: *Develop/sales/installation/service*   Fax: (212) 564-3377   Emp: 18
     software for security systems.

● **ALLIANCE TIRE COMPANY**
PO Box 48, Hadera 38100, Israel
CEO: A. Esroni, Pres.   Tel: 972-6-624-0520   Rev: $123
Bus: *Mfr. tires.*   Fax:
     www.alliance.co.il

     ALLIANCE TIRE COMPANY
     204 Eaglerock Avenue, Roseland, NJ   07068
     CEO: Ms. Leslie Gurland, Gen. Mgr.   Tel: (973) 364-5100   %FO: 100
     Bus: *Tire distribution.*   Fax: (973) 364-8177   Emp: 10

• AMERICAN ISRAELI PAPER MILLS LTD.

PO Box 142, Industrial Zone, Hadera 38101, Israel

CEO: Yaacov Yerushalmi, CEO	Tel: 972-6-634-9349	Rev: $349
Bus: *Mfr. paper and paper products.*	Fax: 972-6-633-9740	Emp: 2,000
	www.aipm.co.il	

GREEN LIND & McNULTY, INC.

1435 Morris Avenue, Union, NJ   07083

CEO: Philip Y. Sardoff, SVP	Tel: (908) 686-7500	%FO: 100
Bus: *Investor relations consultant to American Israeli Paper mills, a mfr. of paper and paper products.*	Fax: (908) 686-4757	

• AUDIOCODES LTD.

4 Hahoresh Street, Yehud 60256, Israel

CEO: Shabtai Adlersberg, CEO	Tel: 972-3-539-4000	Rev: $71
Bus: *Mfr. voice compression products for network use.*	Fax: 972-3-539-4040	Emp: 150
	www.audiocodes.com	

AUDIOCODES, INC.

Deerfoot Office Park 257, Turnpike Road Ste. 320, Southborough, MA   01772

CEO: David McGillivray, VP Sales	Tel: (508) 787-3800	%FO: 100
Bus: *Mfr. voice compression products for network use.*	Fax: (508) 357-2043	

AUDIOCODES, INC.

2890 Zanker Road, San Jose, CA   95134

CEO: Bruce Gellman, Pres.	Tel: (408) 577-0488	%FO: 100
Bus: *Mfr. voice compression products for network use.*	Fax: (408) 577-0492	

AUDIOCODES, INC.

101 West Renner Road, Ste. 220, Richardson, TX   75081

CEO: John D'Annunzio	Tel: (972) 238-7976	%FO: 100
Bus: *Mfr. voice compression products for network use.*	Fax: (972) 238-8038	

AUDIOCODES, INC.

8700 West Bryn Mawr, Ste. 755-S, Chicago, IL   60606

CEO: Ben Rabinowitz	Tel: (847) 579-0398	%FO: 100
Bus: *Mfr. voice compression products for network use.*	Fax: (847) 579-0398	

- **BANK HAPOALIM BM**
50 Rothschild Blvd., Tel Aviv 61000, Israel
CEO: Amiram Sivan, CEO   Tel: 972-3-567-3333   Rev: $1,690
Bus: *Commercial banking services.*   Fax: 972-3-560-7028   Emp: 2,500
                               www.bankhapoalim.co.il

    BANK HAPOALIM
    1177 Avenue of the Americas, 14th Fl., New York, NY 10036
    CEO: Shiomo Braun, SVP   Tel: (212) 782-2000   %FO: 100
    Bus: *Commercial banking branch office.* Fax: (212) 782-2007   Emp: 200

- **BANK LEUMI LE ISRAEL B.M.**
24-32 Yehuda, Halevi Street, Tel Aviv 65546, Israel
CEO: Galia Maor, Pres. & CEO   Tel: 972-3-514-8111   Rev: $4,292
Bus: *Commercial banking services.*   Fax: 972-3-566-1872   Emp: 12,200
                               www.bankleumi.co.il

    BANK LEUMI LE ISRAEL - Beverly Hills Branch
    8383 Wilshire Blvd., Ste. 400, Beverly Hills, CA 90211
    CEO: Dr. Zalman Segal, Pres.   Tel: (323) 966-4700   %FO: 100
    Bus: *International commercial banking* Fax: (323) 653-9608   Emp: 60
       services.

    BANK LEUMI LE ISRAEL
    800 Brickell Avenue, Ste. 1400, Miami, FL 33131
    CEO: Ofer Koren, Mgr.   Tel: (305) 377-6500   %FO: 100
    Bus: *Commercial banking services.*   Fax: (305) 377-6540

    BANK LEUMI LE ISRAEL - Chicago Branch
    100 North Lasalle Street, Chicago, IL 60602
    CEO: Shlomo Osher, Mgr.   Tel: (312) 781-1800   %FO: 100
    Bus: *International commercial banking* Fax: (312) 781-1946   Emp: 35
       services.

    BANK LEUMI LE ISRAEL
    579 Fifth Avenue, 2nd Fl., New York, NY 10173
    CEO: Dr. Zalman Segal, Pres.   Tel: (212) 343-5000   %FO: 100
    Bus: *U.S. agency headquarters;*   Fax: (212) 226-5628   Emp: 50
       commercial banking services.

    BANK LEUMI LEASING CORPORATION
    562 Fifth Avenue, New York, NY 10036
    CEO: Dr. Zalman Segal, Chmn.   Tel: (212) 626-1321   %FO: 100
    Bus: *Commercial banking services.*   Fax: (212) 626-1271

BANK LEUMI TRUST COMPANY OF NY

579 Fifth Avenue, New York, NY   10017

CEO: Aaron Kacarginsky

Bus: *NY Branch banking office.*

Tel: (212) 407-4400

Fax: (212) 407-4411

%FO: 100

Emp: 340

● **BATM ADVANCED COMMUNICATIONS LTD.**

22 Hamelacha Street, Bldg. 4, Rosh Ha'ayin 48091, Israel

CEO: Zvi Marom, CEO

Bus: *Mfr. networking and connectivity hardware.*

Tel: 972-3-938-6888

Fax: 972-3-938-6896

www.batm.com

Rev: $27

Emp: 133

TELCO SYSTEMS, INC.

63 Nahatan Street, Norwood, MA   01062

CEO: David A. LeBeau, CEO

Bus: *Mfr. networking and connectivity hardware.*

Tel: (781) 551-0300

Fax: (781) 551-0538

%FO: 100

● **CHECK POINT SOFTWARE TECHNOLOGIES LTD.**

3A Jabotinsky Street, Diamond Tower, Ramat Gan 52520, Israel

CEO: Gil Shwed, CEO

Bus: *Mfr. virus protection software.*

Tel: 972-3-753-4555

Fax: 972-3-575-9256

www.checkpoint.com

Rev: $425

Emp: 1,100

CHECK POINT SOFTWARE TECHNOLOGIES LTD.

2505 North Highway 360, Ste. 800, Grand Prairie, TX   75050

CEO: Kenneth Casey, VP Sales

Bus: *Mfr. virus protection software.*

Tel: (817) 606-6600

Fax: (817) 652-9373

%FO: 100

CHECK POINT SOFTWARE TECHNOLOGIES LTD.

Three Lagoon Drive, Ste. 400, Redwood City, CA   94065

CEO: Asheem Chandna, VP

Bus: *Mfr. virus protection software.*

Tel: (650) 628-2000

Fax: (650) 654-4233

%FO: 100

● **CLICKSOFTWARE TECHNOLOGIES LTD.**

34 Habarzel Street, Tel Aviv 69710, Israel

CEO: Moshe BenBassat, CEO

Bus: *Mfr. ClickSchedule software for corporations.*

Tel: 972-3-765-9400

Fax: 972-3-765-9401

www.clicksoftware.com

Rev: $16

Emp: 200

CLICKSOFTWARE, INC.

655 Campbell Technology Pkwy., Campbell, CA   95008

CEO: Amit Bendov

Bus: *Mfr. ClickSchedule software for corporations.*

Tel: (408) 377-6088

Fax: (408) 377-9088

%FO: 100

CLICKSOFTWARE, INC.
70 Blanchard Road, Burlington, MA   01830
CEO: Janet Zipes, Mgr.   Tel: (781) 272-5903   %FO: 100
Bus: *Mfr. ClickSchedule software for*   Fax: (781) 272-6409
  corporations.

● THE CLOCKWORK GROUP
8 Maskit, Herzliyya, 46120 Israel
CEO: Chaim Forst, CEO   Tel: 972-9-952-6890
Bus: *Engaged in software development for*   Fax: 972-9-952-6895
  management technology solutions.   www.clockwork-group.com

CLOCKWORK SOLUTIONS, INC.
3432 Greystone Drive, Ste. 202, Austin, TX   78731
CEO: Mike Strobel, VP   Tel: (512) 338-1945   %FO: 100
Bus: *Engaged in software development*   Fax: (512) 338-1946
  for management technology
  solutions.

CLOCKWORK SOLUTIONS, INC.
1127 Benfield Road, Suites E-J, Millersville, MD   21108
CEO: Dr. Paula deWitte, Pres.   Tel: (410) 729-5680   %FO: 100
Bus: *Engaged in software development*   Fax: (410) 729-5681
  for management technology
  solutions.

● COMPUGEN LTD.
72 Pinchas Rosen Street, Tel Aviv 69512, Israel
CEO: Dr. Mor Amitai, CEO   Tel: 972-3-765-8585   Rev: $7
Bus: *Develops gene technology.*   Fax: 972-3-765-8555   Emp: 130
          www.cgen.com

COMPUGEN, INC.
7 Centre Drive, Ste. 7, Jamesburg, NJ   08831
CEO: Eli Mintz, Pres.   Tel: (609) 655-5105   %FO: 100
Bus: *Develops gene technology.*   Fax: (609) 655-5114

● COMSOFT TECHNOLOGIES LTD., DIV. FORMULA SYSTEMS
3 Hagalim Boulevard, PO box 2016, Herzliyya 46120, Israel
CEO: Iris Agam   Tel: 972-9-959-8954
Bus: *Provides advanced data-driven*   Fax: 972-9-959-8980
  solutions, services and products for e-   www.comsoft.co.il
  commerce and business solutions.

XTIVIA TECHNOLOGIES, INC.
2035 Lincoln Highway, Ste. 2150, Edison, NJ   08817
CEO: Dennis Robinson, Pres.   Tel: (732) 248-9399   %FO: 100
Bus: *Provides advanced data-driven*   Fax: (732) 248-5522
   solutions, services and products
   for e-commerce and business
   solutions.

● **CONNECT ONE, LTD.**
2 Hanagar Street, Kfar Saba 44425, Israel
CEO: Amir Friedman, CEO   Tel: 972-9-760-0456
Bus: *Mfr. chips, software, and hardware that*   Fax: 972-9-766-0461
   enable manufacturers of industrial,   www.connectone.com
   commercial and consumer devices to
   reduce the time, cost and complexity of
   connecting devices to the Internet.

CONNECT ONE SEMICONDUCTORS, INC.
4677 Old Ironsides Drive, Ste. 280, Santa Clara, CA   95054
CEO: Alan Singer, VP   Tel: (408) 968-9602   %FO: 100
Bus: *Mfr. chips, software, and*   Fax: (408) 968-9604
   hardware that enable
   manufacturers of industrial,
   commercial and consumer devices
   to reduce the time, cost and
   complexity of connecting devices
   to the Internet.

● **CRYSTAL SYSTEMS SOLUTIONS LTD.**
6 Maskit Street, Herzliyya 46733, Israel
CEO: Gad Goldstein   Tel: 972-9-952-6100   Rev: $49
Bus: *Mfr. software.*   Fax: 972-9-952-6111   Emp: 500
   www.crystal-sys.com

CRYSTAL AMERICA INC.
132 West 31st Street, Ste. 1602, New York, NY   10001
CEO: R. Frank, Pres.   Tel: (212) 947-5802   %FO: JV
Bus: *Mfr. software.*   Fax: (212) 714-2228

● **CUBITAL LTD.**
24 Amal Street, Afek Industrial Park, Rosh-Ha'Ayin 48091, Israel
CEO: Yanir Farber   Tel: 972-3-903-6569
Bus: *Mfr. rapid prototyping equipment.*   Fax: 972-3-903-6596   Emp: 50
   www.cubital.com

CUBITAL AMERICA, INC.

10501 Haggerty Street, Dearborn, MI 48126

CEO: Udi Avrahami, Gen. Mgr.	Tel: (313) 846-7885	%FO: 100
Bus: *Customer support office; sales/distribution of rapid prototyping equipment.*	Fax: (313) 846-7884	Emp: 6

● DELTA-GALIL INDUSTRIES LTD.

2 Kaufman Street, Tel Aviv 68012, Israel

CEO: Arnon Tiberg, CEO	Tel: 972-3-519-3636	Rev: $434
Bus: *Mfr. private label and licensed underwear.*	Fax: 972-5-519-3705 www.deltagalil.com	

DELTA TEXTILES LTD.

347 Fifth Avenue, Ste. 503, New York, NY 10016

CEO: Este Maoz, Mgr.	Tel: (212) 481-3550	%FO: 100
Bus: *Mfr. private label and licensed underwear.*	Fax: (212) 481-3881	

● ECI TELECOM LTD.

30 Hasivim Street, Petah Tikva 49133, Israel

CEO: Doron Inbar, CEO	Tel: 972-3-926-6555	Rev: $1,170
Bus: *Mfr. telecom equipment.*	Fax: 972-3-926-6711 www.ecitele.com	Emp: 6,170

ECI TELECOM, INC.

6021 142nd Avenue North, Clearwater, FL 34620

CEO: Jeff Hale	Tel: (727) 523-0000	%FO: 100
Bus: *Mfr./sales telecom equipment.*	Fax: (727) 523-0010	

ECI TELECOM, INC.

12950 Worldgate Drive, Herndon, VA 20170

CEO: Mark Vida	Tel: (703) 456-3400	%FO: 100
Bus: *Mfr./sales telecom equipment.*	Fax: (703) 456-3410	

ECI TELECOM, INC.

39 Headquarters Plaza North, Ste. 1417, Morristown, NJ 07960

CEO: Douglas Dean	Tel: (973) 401-6405	%FO: 100
Bus: *Mfr./sales telecom equipment.*	Fax: (973) 401-6406	

● EDUSOFT LTD.

16 Hamelacha Street, Afek Industrial Park, Rosh Ha'ain 48091, Israel

CEO: Roberto Chernitsky, CEO	Tel: 972-3-900-2400	
Bus: *Mfr. multimedia educational software.*	Fax: 972-3-900-2401 www.edusoft.co.il	Emp: 80

EDUSOFT INC.
590 Herndon Parkway, Herndon, VA   20170
CEO: Stuart Holtz, Pres.   Tel: (703) 708-9250   %FO: 100
Bus: *Multimedia educational software.*   Fax: (703) 708-9355

● **EL AL ISRAEL AIRLINES LTD.**
Ben Gurion Airport, Tel Aviv 70110, Israel
CEO: Joseph Clechanover, Chmn.   Tel: 972-3-971-6111   Rev: $1,246
Bus: *International air transport services.*   Fax: 972-3-972-1442   Emp: 3,500
www.elal.co.il

EL AL ISRAEL AIRLINES
120 West 45th Street, New York, NY   10036-9998
CEO: Michael Mayer, Gen.Mgr.   Tel: (212) 852-0600   %FO: 100
Bus: *International air transport*   Fax: (212) 768-9440
services.

● **ELECTRONICS LINE LTD.**
58 Amal Street, Petah Tikva 49513, Israel
CEO: Gad Krubiner, Mgr.   Tel: 972-3-921-1110
Bus: *Mfr. wireless and wired burglar alarm*   Fax: 972-3-922-0831
systems.   www.elecline.com

ELECTRONICS LINE USA INC.
1640 Range Street, Boulder, CO   80301
CEO: Gad Krubiner   Tel: (800) 683-6835   %FO: 100
Bus: *Mfr. wireless and wired burglar*   Fax: (303) 938-8062
alarm systems.

● **ELRON ELECTRONIC INDUSTRIES LTD.**
Three Azrieli Center, 42nd Fl., Tel Aviv 67023, Israel
CEO: Ami Erel, CEO   Tel: 972-3-607-5555   Rev: $40
Bus: *Develops internet applications and*   Fax: 972-3-607-5556   Emp: 525
telecommunications software.   www.elron.com

CHIP EXPRESS CORPORATION
2323 Owen Street, Santa Clara, CA   95054
CEO: Stephen McMinn, CEO   Tel: (408) 988-2445   %FO: 100
Bus: *Develops internet applications and*   Fax: (408) 988-2449
telecommunications software.

ELRON TELESOFT INC.
7 New England Executive Park, Burlington, MA   01803
CEO: Ray Boelig, CEO   Tel: (781) 744-6000   %FO: 100
Bus: *Develops internet applications and*   Fax: (781) 744-6222
telecommunications software.

MEDIAGATE INC.
1245 S. Winchester Blvd., Ste. 108, San Jose, CA   95128
CEO: Jonathan Taylor   Tel: (408) 248-9495   %FO: 100
Bus: *Develops internet applications and*   Fax: (408) 248-8552
telecommunications software.

● **EMBLAZE SYSTEMS LTD.**
1 Corazin Street, Givatayim 53583, Israel
CEO: Eli Reifman, CEO   Tel: 972-3-572-2111   Rev: $31
Bus: *Provides streaming video solutions over*   Fax: 972-3-572-2100   Emp: 250
Wireless and IP networks; encoding and   www.emblaze.com
playback of live and on-demand video
messages.

WEBRADIO.COM, INC.
21110 Oxnard Street, Woodland Hills, CA   91367
CEO: Hamid Kohan, Pres.   Tel: (818) 703-8436   %FO: 100
Bus: *Radio broadcasting.*   Fax: (818) 703-8654

● **ESC SHARPLAN MEDICAL SYSTEMS**
PO Box 240, Yokneam Industrial Park, Yokneam, Israel
CEO: Yacha Sutton, Pres. & CEO   Tel: 972-4-959-9000   Rev: $143
Bus: *Mfr./sales of medical lasers.*   Fax: 972-4-959-9050   Emp: 730
                                        www.escmed.com

ESC MEDICAL SYSTEMS
100 Morse Street, Norwood, MA   02062
CEO: Raffi Werner, CEO   Tel: (781) 278-7600   %FO: 100
Bus: *Sales/distribution of medical*   Fax: (781) 278-7700
lasers.

ESC MEDICAL SYSTEMS
22011 30th Avenue SE, Bothell, WA   98021
CEO: I. David, Mgr.   Tel: (425) 483-4142   %FO: 100
Bus: *Sales/distribution of medical*   Fax: (425) 483-6844
lasers.

SHARPLAN LASERS INC.
One Pearl Court, Allendale, NJ   07401
CEO: Avi Farbstein, Mgr.   Tel: (201) 327-1666   %FO: 100
Bus: *Sales/distribution of medical*   Fax: (201) 445-4048
lasers.

- **E-SIM LTD.**
  Kiryat Mada 5, Jerusalem 91450, Israel
  CEO: Marc Belzberg, CEO   Tel: 972-2-587-0770   Rev: $9
  Bus: *Mfr. software to prototype and test*   Fax: 972-2-587-0773   Emp: 65
      products.   www.e-sim.com

      E-SIM INC.
      301North Lake Avenue, Ste. 1002, Pasadena, CA   91101
      CEO:Ken Dixon   Tel: (626) 584-7810   %FO: 100
      Bus: *Mfr. software to prototype and test*   Fax: (626) 584-7175
        products.

- **EXENT TECHNOLOGIES LTD.**
  10 Granit Street, Petah Tikva 49125, Israel
  CEO: Zvi Levgoren, CEO   Tel: 972-3-924-3828
  Bus: *Develops Applications-on-Demand*   Fax: 972-3-924-3930
      (AoD) technology to deliver computer   www.exent.com
      software programs over IP networks in
      real time.

      EXENT TECHNOLOGIES INC.
      1999 S. Bascom Avenue, Ste. 700, Campbell, CA   950000
      CEO:Yizhar Ganov, VP   Tel: (408) 879-2370   %FO: 100
      Bus: *Sales of Applications-on-Demand*   Fax: (408) 904-4539
        (AoD) technology to deliver
        computer software programs over
        IP networks in real time.

      EXENT TECHNOLOGIES INC.
      6903 Rockledge Drive, Ste. 1500, Bethesda, MD   20817
      CEO:Avi Horwitz, VP Sales   Tel: (301) 581-5900   %FO: 100
      Bus: *Sales of Applications-on-Demand*   Fax: (301) 581-5925
        (AoD) technology to deliver
        computer software programs over
        IP networks in real time.

- **FORMULA SYSTEMS**
  3 Hagalim Boulevard, Herzliya 46120, Israel
  CEO: Gad Goldstein, CEO   Tel: 972-9-959-8888   Rev: $406
  Bus: *Engaged in information technology and*   Fax: 972-9-959-8877   Emp: 4,000
      proprietary software.   www.formula.co.il

      CRYSTAL SYSTEMS AMERICA, INC.
      132 West 31st Street, Ste. 1602, New York, NY   10001
      CEO:Gad Goldstein, Pres.   Tel: (212) 947-5802   %FO:
      Bus: *Software systems.*   Fax: (212) 714-2228

INTERSYSTEMS INC.
6675 South Kenton Street, Ste. 116, Englewood, CO   80111
CEO: Nimrod Halfon, Pres.   Tel: (303) 858-1000   %FO: 1
Bus: *Software development.*   Fax: (303) 858-1100

● **FORSOFT LTD., SUB. FORMULA SYSTEMS**
3 Hagalim Boulevard, Herzliyya 46120, Israel
CEO: Emanuel Cohen, CEO   Tel: 972-9-959-8840   Rev: $65
Bus: *Provides information technology and*   Fax: 972-9-959-8844   Emp: 850
software for industrial industries.   www.forsoft.co.il

   FORSOFT INC.
   462 Seventh Avenue, 4th Fl., New York, NY   10018
   CEO: Joe Musacchio, Pres.   Tel: (212) 736-5870   %FO: 100
   Bus: *Provides information technology*   Fax: (212) 736-9046
   and software for industrial
   industries.

● **GILAT SATELLITE NETWORKS LTD.**
21 Yegia Kapayim Street, Kiryat Arie, Petah Tikva 49130, Israel
CEO: Yoel Gat, CEO   Tel: 972-3-925-2000   Rev: $505
Bus: *Mfr. satellite systems for data*   Fax: 972-3-925-2222   Emp: 1,400
transmittal.   www.gilat.com

   SPACENET, INC.
   1750 Old Meadow Road, McLean, VA   22102
   CEO: David Shiff, VP   Tel: (703) 848-1000   %FO: 100
   Bus: *Mfr. satellite systems for data*   Fax: (703) 848-1010
   transmittal.

● **GIVEN IMAGING LTD.**
2 Hacarmel Street, New Industrial Park PO Box 258, Yoqneam 26902, Israel
CEO: Dr. Gavriel D. Meron, Pres. & CEO   Tel: 972-4-909-7777
Bus: *Mfr. minimally-invasive, disposable*   Fax: 972-4-959-2466   Emp: 75
imaging capsule for diagnosing small   www.givenimaging.com
intestine disorders and diseases.

   GIVEN IMAGING, INC.
   5555 Oakbrook Parkway, Ste. 355, Norcross, GA   30093
   CEO: Mark Gilreath, Pres.   Tel: (770) 662-0870   %FO: 100
   Bus: *Mfr. minimally-invasive,*   Fax: (770) 662-0510
   disposable imaging capsule for
   diagnosing small intestine
   disorders and diseases.

● **GOTTEX MODELS LTD.**

1 Yoni Netanyahu Street, New Industrial Zone Or, Yeuda 60200 , Israel

CEO: Uzi Evron, CEO   Tel: 972-3-538-7777

Bus: *Mfr. swimwear.*   Fax: 972-3-533-3423

www.main.aquanet.co.il

GOTTEX INDUSTRIES, INC.

1411 Broadway, 29th Fl., New York, NY   10018

CEO: Uzi Evron, CEO   Tel: (212) 354-1240   %FO: 100

Bus: *Mfr. swimwear.*   Fax: (212) 302-3851

● **HAMAT ISRAEL**

41 Hayozma Street, North Industrial Area, Asdod 77164, Israel

CEO: Jsoeph Ohayan, Dir.   Tel: 972-8-851-3888

Bus: *Mfr./sale decorative bathroom fixtures.*   Fax: 972-8-856-7164

HAMAT USA, INC. C/O SPC VOLTA

100 Bomont Place, Totowa, NJ   07512

CEO: Roger Martin, Mgr.   Tel: (973) 785-1700

Bus: *Sales/distribution of decorative*   Fax: (973) 785-9899
      hardware.

● **IAI ISRAEL AIRCRAFT INDUSTRIES LTD.**

Ben-Gurion International Airport, Tel Aviv 70100 Israel

CEO: Moshe Keret, Pres. & CEO   Tel: 972-3-935-3433   Rev: $2,181

Bus: *Engaged in aerospace.*   Fax: 972-3-935-8278   Emp: 14,000

www.iai.co.il

ISRAEL AIRCRAFT INDUSTRIES INTERNATIONAL INC.

3003 West Casino Road, Everett, WA   98203

CEO: Y. Kimmel   Tel: (425) 717-7782   %FO: 100

Bus: *Mfr. aircraft.*   Fax: (425) 717-7422

ISRAEL AIRCRAFT INDUSTRIES INTERNATIONAL INC.

50 West 23rd Street, New York, NY   10010

CEO: Moshe Keret, Pres.   Tel: (212) 620-4400   %FO: 100

Bus: *Mfr. aircraft.*   Fax: (212) 620-1799

ISRAEL AIRCRAFT INDUSTRIES INTERNATIONAL INC.

1700 N-Moore Street, Ste. 1210, Arlington, VA   22209

CEO: I. Sharon   Tel: (703) 875-3729   %FO: 100

Bus: *Mfr. aircraft.*   Fax: (703) 875-3770

● **IDE TECHNOLOGIES, LTD.**
13 Zarchin Road, P.O.Box 591, Raanana 43104, Israel
CEO: Gustavo Kronenberg   Tel: 972-9-747-9777
Bus: *Water desalinization plants and water*   Fax: 972-9-747-9715
     solutions.   www.ide-tech.com

    AMBIENT TECHNOLOGIES, INC.
    2999 N.E. 191st Street, Suite 407, Aventura, FL   33180
    CEO: Ezra Barkai, Pres.   Tel: (305) 937-0610   %FO: 100
    Bus: *Install/service water desalinization*   Fax: (305) 937-2137
        plants.

● **ISRAEL AIRCRAFT INDUSTRIES LTD.**
Ben Gurion International Airport, Tel Aviv 70100, Israel
CEO: Moshe Keret, Pres.   Tel: 972-3-935-3111   Rev: $1,690
Bus: *Mfr. business jet aircraft, electronic*   Fax: 972-3-935-3131   Emp: 13,700
     systems, unmanned space vehicles;   www.ibc.co.il
     upgrade civilian & military aircraft.

    IAI INTERNATIONAL, INC.
    1700 North Moore Street, Arlington, VA   22032
    CEO: Marvin Klemow, VP   Tel: (703) 875-3723   %FO: 100
    Bus: *Marketing, product support;*
        business jet aircraft, electronic   Fax: (703) 875-3740
        systems, unmanned space vehicles;
        upgrade civilian & military
        aircraft.

    IAI INTERNATIONAL, INC.
    50 West 23rd Street, New York, NY   10010
    CEO: David Onn, Pres.   Tel: (212) 620-4404   %FO: 100
    Bus: *Marketing, product support;*   Fax: (212) 620-1799   Emp: 15
        business jet aircraft, electronic
        systems, unmanned space vehicles;
        upgrade civilian & military
        aircraft.

● **ISRAEL DISCOUNT BANK LTD.**
27 Yehuda Halevi Street, Tel Aviv 65136, Israel
CEO: Arie Mientkavich, Chmn.   Tel: 972-3-514-5555   Rev: $2,367
Bus: *Commercial banking services.*   Fax: 972-3-514-5346   Emp: 7,700
                                          www.israel-discount-bank.co.il

    ISRAEL DISCOUN BANK LTD.
    2875 Northeast 191st Street, Aventura, FL   33180
    CEO: Menachem Ben Bassat, SVP   Tel: (305) 682-3700   %FO: 100
    Bus: *Commercial banking services.*   Fax: (305) 682-3777

ISRAEL DISCOUN BANK LTD.
206 North Beverly Drive, Beverly Hills, CA   90210
CEO: Yoav Peled, SVP   Tel: (310) 275-1411   %FO: 100
Bus: *Commercial banking services.*   Fax: (310) 859-1021

ISRAEL DISCOUNT BANK OF NY
511 Fifth Avenue, New York, NY   10017
CEO: Arie Sheer, Pres. & CEO   Tel: (212) 551-8500   %FO: 100
Bus: *Commercial banking services.*   Fax: (212) 370-9623   Emp: 530

● **KOOR INDUSTRIES LTD.**
Platinum House, 21 Ha'arba'a Street, Tel Aviv 64739, Israel
CEO: Jonathan Kolber, CEO   Tel: 972-3-623-8333   Rev: $2,571
Bus: *Diversified industries; electronics,*   Fax: 972-3-623-8334   Emp: 20,000
telecommunications, agrochemicals,   www.koor.co.il
food, construction, steel, tourism &
international trade.

    ELISRA GROUP
    10 East 53rd Street, New York, NY   10022
    CEO: Israel Adan, Pres.   Tel: (212) 751-3600   %FO: 100
    Bus: *Liaison and corporate*   Fax: (212) 751-5181
    development.

● **LANOPTICS LTD.**
Ramat Gabriel Industrial Park, Migdal Haemek 10551, Israel
CEO: Meir Burstin, CEO   Tel: 972-6-644-9944   Rev: $3
Bus: *Engaged in computer hardware and*   Fax: 972-6-654-0124   Emp: 100
networking communication.   www.lanoptics.com

    LANOPTICS INC.
    2201 Midway Road, Ste. 312, Carrollton, TX   75006
    CEO: Jack Behar   Tel: (972) 503-8030   %FO: 100
    Bus: *Mfr. computer hardware.*   Fax: (972) 503-7600

● **LIRAZ SYSTEMS LTD.**
5 Hazoref Street, Holon 55856, Israel
CEO: Mot Gutman, Mng. Dir.   Tel: 972-3-557-3434
Bus: *Mfr. computer software.*   Fax: 972-3-559-8822
     www.liraz.co.it

    LEVEL 8 INC.
    8000 Regency Parkway, Cary, NC   27511
    CEO: Anthony Pizi, CEO   Tel: (919) 380-5000   %FO: 100
    Bus: *Mfr./sales computer software.*   Fax: (919) 469-1910

● **MAGAL SECURITY STSTEMS LTD.**

Industrial Zone, PO Box 70, Yahud 56100, Israel

CEO: Jacob Even-Ezra, Chmn.　　　Tel: 972-3-539-1444　　　Rev: $32

Bus: *Mfr. security, video motion detection*　Fax: 972-3-536-6245　　　Emp: 190
systems to detect explosives in sealed　www.magal-ssl.com
packages and boxes.

PERIMETER PRODUCTS, INC.

43180 Osgood Road, Fremont, CA　94539

CEO: Martha Lee, Pres.　　　Tel: (510) 249-1450　　　%FO: 100

Bus: *Sales security systems.*　　Fax: (510) 249-1540

SENSTAR-STELLAR CORP.

6504 Hickory Hill Drive, Temperance, MI　48182

CEO: Brian G. Rich, Pres.　　　Tel: (734) 854-2228　　　%FO: 100

Bus: *Mfr. security, video motion*　　Fax: (734) 854-2228
detection systems to detect
explosives in sealed packages and
boxes.

SENSTAR-STELLAR CORP.

1223 Innsbruck Drive, Sunnyvale, CA　94089

CEO: Eleanor Hodgson, VP　　　Tel: (408) 734-3000　　　%FO: 100

Bus: *Mfr. security, video motion*　　Fax: (408) 734-8099
detection systems to detect
explosives in sealed packages and
boxes.

● **MAGIC SOFTWARE ENTERPRISES LTD.**

5 Haplada Street, Or Yehuda 60218, Israel

CEO: Menachem Hasfari, CEO　　　Tel: 972-3-538-9292　　　Rev: $90

Bus: *Software applications and development*　Fax: 972-3-583-9333　　　Emp: 1,500
systems and training.　　www.magicsoftware.com

CORE TECH CONSULTING GROUP, INC.

1040 First Avenue, King of Prussia, PA　19406

CEO: Doug Nohe　　　Tel: (800) 220-3337　　　%FO: 100

Bus: *Provides e-business professional*　Fax: (800) 649-1814
services.

CORE TECH CONSULTING GROUP, INC.

132 West 31st Street, Ste. 1602, New York, NY　10002-3406

CEO: Richard Gengenbach　　　Tel: (212) 714-2240　　　%FO: 100

Bus: *Software applications and*　　Fax: (212) 736-9046
development systems and training.

MAGIC SOFTWARE ENTERPRISES, INC.

1642 Keyser, Irvine, CA   92614

CEO: Nancy Barr | Tel: (949) 250-1718 | %FO: 100
Bus: *Software applications and development systems and training.* | Fax: (949) 250-7404 | Emp: 50

MAGIC SOFTWARE ENTERPRISES, INC.

132 West 31st Street, Ste. 1602, New York, NY   10002-3406

CEO: Rami Meluban | Tel: (212) 714-2240 | %FO: 100
Bus: *Software applications and development systems and training.* | Fax: (212) 736-9046

● MENTERGY, LTD.

21/D Yegia Kapayim Street, Petah Tikva 49130, Israel

CEO: Shlomo Tirosh, CEO | Tel: 972-3--925-5000 | Rev: $74
Bus: *Provides e-learning products and services.* | Fax: 972-3-925-5005 | Emp: 1,000
| www.mentergy.com |

ALLEN COMMUNICATION

5 Triad Center, 5th Fl., Salt Lake City, UT   84180

CEO: Bill Byron Concevitch | Tel: (601) 537-7600 | %FO: 100
Bus: *Provides e-learning products and services.* | Fax: (601) 537-7805

LEARNL INC.

385 Jordan Road, Troy, NY   12160

CEO: Donna Bonacquisti | Tel: (518) 286-7000 | %FO: 100
Bus: *Provides e-learning products and services.* | Fax: (518) 286-2439

MENTERGY

2000 River Edge Pkwy., Ste. 850, Atlanta, GA   30328

CEO: Ron Zamir, SVP | Tel: (770) 612-9129 | %FO: 100
Bus: *Provides e-learning products and services.* | Fax: (770) 859-9110

● MER TELEMANAGEMENT SOLUTIONS LTD.

10 Hakison Street, Bnei-Brak 51203, Israel

CEO: Shai Levanon, CEO | Tel: 972-3-577-5777 | Rev: $11
Bus: *Mfr. software.* | Fax: 972-3-618-4458 | Emp: 75
| www.mtsint.com |

MTS INTEGRATRAK

12600 SE 38th Street, Ste. 250, Bellevue, WA   98006-5232

CEO: Amir Rosenzweig, CEO | Tel: (425) 401-1000 | %FO: 100
Bus: *Mfr. software.* | Fax: (425) 401-1700

- **MIND CTI LTD.**

Industrial Park, Bldg. 7, Yoqneam 20692, Israel

CEO: Monica Eisinger, CEO	Tel: 972-4-993-6666	Rev: $16
Bus: *Mfr. software.*	Fax: 972-4-993-7776	Emp: 180
	www.mindcti.com	

    MIND CTI INC.

    777 Terrace Avenue, Hasbrouck Heights, NJ 07604

CEO: Ilan melamed, VP	Tel: (201) 288-3900	%FO: 100
Bus: *Mfr./sales software.*	Fax: (201) 288-4590	

- **M-SYSTEMS FLASH DISK PIONEERS LTD.**

Central Park 2000, 7 Atir Yeda Street, Kfar Saba 44425, Israel
7 Atir Yeda Street, Kfar Saba 44425, Israel

CEO: Dov Moran, CEO	Tel: 972-3-764-5000	Rev: $16
Bus: *Mfr. flash memory products and software.*	Fax: 972-3-548-8666	Emp: 85
	www.m-sys.com	

    M-SYSTEMS INC.

    8371 Central Avenue, Ste. A, Newark, CA 94560

CEO: Dov Moran, CEO	Tel: (510) 494-2090
Bus: *Mfr. flash memory products and software.*	Fax: (510) 494-5545

- **MYSTICOM LTD.**

6 Hazoran Street, PO Box 8364, Netanya 42504, Israel

CEO: David Almagor, CEO	Tel: 972-9-863-6465	
Bus: *Engaged in data communications and computer chips.*	Fax: 972-9-863-6466	Emp: 80
	www.mysticom.com	

    MYSTICOM INC.

    1804 N. Shoreline Blvd., Ste. 240, Mountain View, CA 94043

CEO: Rich Seifert	Tel: (650) 210-8080	%FO: 100
Bus: *Engaged in data communications and computer chips.*	Fax: (650) 210-9030	

- **NESS TECHNOLOGIES INC.**

Ness Tower, Atidim Bldg. 4, Tel Aviv 61580, Israel

CEO: Raviv Zoller, Pres. & CEO	Tel: 972-3-766-6800	Rev: $180
Bus: *Provides information technology.*	Fax: 972-3-766-6809	Emp: 2,200
	www.ness.com	

    NESS TECHNOLOGIES INC.

    4812 Auburn Avenue, Bethesda, MD 20814

CEO: Rina Levy, Mng. Dir.	Tel: (301) 986-0996	%FO: 100
Bus: *Provides information technology.*	Fax: (301) 465-0426	

● **NETAFIM**

Kibutz Hatzerim, M P Hanegev 85420, Israel

CEO: Yigal Stav, Pres.　　　　　　　　Tel: 972-7-674-3111　　　　Rev: $220

Bus: *Mfr./distribution micro-irrigation*　Fax: 972-7-642-0038　　　　Emp: 420
　　　components.　　　　　　　　　　www.netafim.com

　　　NETAFIM USA INC.

　　　5470 East Home Avenue, Fresno, CA　93727

　　　CEO: Zvi E. Sella, Pres.　　　　　　Tel: (209) 453-6800　　　　%FO: 100

　　　Bus: *Mfr./distribution micro-irrigation*　Fax: (209) 453-6803　　　Emp: 69
　　　　　components, filters, micro-
　　　　　sprinklers.

● **NEXUS TELOCATION SYSTEMS LTD.**

1 Korazin Street, Givatayim 53583, Israel

CEO: Shiomo Sadowsky, CEO　　　　Tel: 972-3-572-3111　　　　Rev: $6

Bus: *Mfr. location-based management and*　Fax: 972-3-571-9698　　　　Emp: 60
　　　security systems.　　　　　　　www.nexus.telocation.com

　　　NGK METALS CORPORATION

　　　150 Tuckerton Road, PO Box 13367, Reading, PA　19612-3367

　　　CEO: Allen Kohl　　　　　　　　Tel: (610) 921-5000　　　　%FO: 100

　　　Bus: *Mfr. and sales of location-based*　Fax: (610) 921-5000
　　　　　management and security systems.

　　　NGK-LOCKE POLYMER INSULATORS, INC.

　　　1609 Diamond Springs Road, Virginia Beach, VA　23455

　　　CEO: M. McClure　　　　　　　　Tel: (757) 460-3649　　　　%FO: 100

　　　Bus: *Mfr. and sales of location-based*　Fax: (757) 460-3649
　　　　　management and security systems.

　　　OPTOBAHN CORPORATION

　　　970 Knox Street, Ste. A, Torrance, CA　90502

　　　CEO: Toshikazu Uchida, CEO　　　Tel: (310) 768-2900　　　　%FO: 100

　　　Bus: *Mfr. and sales of location-based*　Fax: (310) 768-2900
　　　　　management and security systems.

● **NICE SYSTEMS LTD.**

8 Hapnina Street, PO Box 690, Ra'anana 43107, Israel

CEO: Haim Shani, CEO　　　　　　Tel: 972-9-775-3777　　　　Rev: $153

Bus: *Mfr. computer telephony integration*　Fax: 972-9-743-4282　　　　Emp: 900
　　　systems.　　　　　　　　　　www.nice.com

NICE SYSTEMS, INC.
717 17th Street, Ste. 1900, Denver, CO   80202
CEO: Richard Ott, CEO   Tel: (720) 264-4000   %FO: 100
Bus: *Mfr. computer telephony*   Fax: (720) 264-4010
     integration systems.

NICE SYSTEMS, INC.
PO Box 61089, Sunnyvale, CA   94089
CEO: Richard Ott, CEO   Tel: (408) 743-8959   %FO: 100
Bus: *Mfr. computer telephony*   Fax: (408) 743-8970
     integration systems.

NICE SYSTEMS, INC.
12626 High Bluff Drive, Ste. 240, San Diego, CA   92126
CEO: Richard Ott, CEO   Tel: (858) 792-0273   %FO: 100
Bus: *Mfr. computer telephony*   Fax: (858) 792-5199
     integration systems.

NICE SYSTEMS, INC.
200 Plaza Drive, 4th Fl., Secaucus, NJ   07094
CEO: Richard Ott, CEO   Tel: (201) 617-8800   %FO: 100
Bus: *Mfr. computer telephony*   Fax: (201) 617-9898
     integration systems.

● **NUR MACROPRINTERS LTD.**
12 Abba Hilel Silver Street, PO Box 1281, Lod 7111, Israel
CEO: Erez Shachar, CEO   Tel: 972-8-921-5555   Rev: $122
Bus: *Mfr. digital/color printers.*   Fax: 972-8-921-1220   Emp: 525
                                       www.nur.com

  NUR AMERICA, INC.
  4671 Highway 90 West, San Antonio, TX   78237
  CEO: Rick Clarke, Pres.   Tel: (210) 431-8500   %FO: 100
  Bus: *Mfr. and sales of digital/color* Fax: (214) 318-8501
       printers.

● **OPHIR OPTRONICS LTD.**
PO Box 45021, Jerusalem 91450, Israel
CEO: Jacov Zerem, Pres.   Tel: 972-2-258-4444
Bus: *Mfr. laser power energy*   Fax: 972-2-258-2338   Emp: 70
     instrumentation, FLIR & IR optical www.ophiropt.com
     components.

OPHIR OPTRONICS INC.
9 Electronics Avenue, Danvers, MA   01923
CEO: Carl G. Burns, Mgr.   Tel: (978) 774-8200   %FO: 100
Bus: *Sale/service laser power energy*   Fax: (978) 774-8202
   instrumentation.

● **OPTIBASE LTD.**
7 Shenkar Street, Herzliyya 46120, Israel
CEO: Jack Krooss, Dir.   Tel: 972-9-970-9288   Rev: $30
Bus: *Mfr. hardware and software products.*   Fax: 972-9-958-6099   Emp: 200
                                     www.optibase.com

   OPTIBASE INC.
   3031 Tisch Way Plaza West, Ste. 1, San Jose, CA   95128
   CEO: Robert DeFeo, CEO   Tel: (408) 260-6760   %FO: 100
   Bus: *Mfr. hardware and software*   Fax: (408) 244-0545
      products.

   OPTIBASE INC.
   156 Andover Street, Ste. 210, Danvers, MA   01923
   CEO: Robert DeFeo, CEO   Tel: (978) 774-5766   %FO: 100
   Bus: *Mfr. hardware and software*   Fax: (978) 774-5766
      products.

   OPTIBASE INC.
   1250 Space Park Way, Mountain View, CA   94040
   CEO: Robert DeFeo, CEO   Tel: (650) 903-4900   %FO: 100
   Bus: *Mfr. hardware and software*   Fax: (650) 969-6388
      products.

● **ORBOTECH LTD.**
New Industrial Zone, PO Box 215, Yavne 81102, Israel
CEO: Yochai Richter, Pres.   Tel: 972-8-942-3533   Rev: $372
Bus: *Automated optical inspection*   Fax: 972-3-943-8769   Emp: 1,395
   equipment, CAD/CAM systems.   www.orbotech.com

   ORBOTECH INC.
   44 Manning Road, Billerica, MA   01821
   CEO: Shabtai Shaanani, CEO   Tel: (978) 667-6037   %FO: 100
   Bus: *Mfr./sale automated optical*   Fax: (978) 667-9969   Emp: 180
      inspection equipment, CAD/CAM
      systems, pre-press image setters.

● **ORCKIT COMMUNICATIONS LTD.**
126 Yig'al Allon Street, Tel Aviv 67443, Israel
CEO: Eric Paneth, CEO   Tel: 972-3-696-2121   Rev: $130
Bus: *Mfr. high-speed digital modems.*   Fax: 972-3-696-5678   Emp: 585
                                         www.orckit.com

    ORCKIT COMMUNICATIONS
    110 Blue Ravine Road, Ste. 160, Folsom, CA   95630
    CEO: Jim Szeliga, Gen. Mgr.   Tel: (916) 351-5600
    Bus: *Sales/distribution high-speed   Fax: (916) 351-5700
       digital modems.*

    ORCKIT COMMUNICATIONS
    574 Heritage Road, Southbury, CT   06488
    CEO: Jim Szeliga, Gen. Mgr.   Tel: (203) 267-1000
    Bus: *Sales/distribution high-speed   Fax: (203) 267-1003
       digital modems.*

    ORCKIT COMMUNICATIONS, INC.
    125 Half Mile Road, Ste. 200, Red Bank, NJ   07701
    CEO: Dan Arazi, EVP   Tel: (732) 933-2640   %FO: 100
    Bus: *DSL technology.*   Fax: (732) 463-0187

● **ORMAT INDUSTRIES LTD.**
New Industrial Area, PO Box 68, Yavne 70650, Israel
CEO: Lucien Bronicki, Chmn.   Tel: 972-8-943-3777
Bus: *Mfr. geothermal equipment.*   Fax: 972-8-943-9901   Emp: 200
                                         www.ormat.com

    ORMAT SYSTEMS INC.
    980 Greg Street, Sparks, NV   89431
    CEO: Dita Bronicki, Pres.   Tel: (775) 356-9029   %FO: 100
    Bus: *Mfr./sale geothermal equipment.*   Fax: (775) 356-9039   Emp: 7

● **PRECISE SOFTWARE SOLUTIONS LTD.**
1 Hashikma Street, PO Box 88, Savyon 56518, Israel
CEO: Shimon Alon, CEO   Tel: 972-3-635-2566   Rev: $27
Bus: *Mfr. software.*   Fax: 972-3-635-2599   Emp: 260
                                         www.precisesoft.com

    PRECISE SOFTWARE SOLUTIONS IN
    2050 Center Avenue, Ste. 200, Fort Lee, NJ   07024
    CEO: Shimon Alon, CEO   Tel: (201) 242-5500   %FO: 100
    Bus: *Mfr. software.*   Fax: (201) 461-9598

PRECISE SOFTWARE SOLUTIONS IN
303 Twin Dolphin Drive, Redwood Shores, CA   94065
CEO: Michael Killoran, VP   Tel: (650) 342-5066   %FO: 100
Bus: *Mfr. software.*   Fax: (413) 520-9040

PRECISE SOFTWARE SOLUTIONS IN
22305 Savona Street, Laguna Hills, CA   92653
CEO: Michael Killoran, VP   Tel: (949) 215-5679   %FO: 100
Bus: *Mfr. software.*   Fax: (949) 215-5679

PRECISE SOFTWARE SOLUTIONS IN
12200 E. Briarwood Ave., Ste. 260, Englewood, CO   80112-6702
CEO: Michael Killoran, VP   Tel: (303) 790-1959   %FO: 100
Bus: *Mfr. software.*   Fax: (303) 790-2816

PRECISE SOFTWARE SOLUTIONS IN
690 Canton Street, Westwood, MA   02090
CEO: Shimon Alon, CEO   Tel: (781) 461-0700   %FO: 100
Bus: *Mfr. software.*   Fax: (781) 461-0460

PRECISE SOFTWARE SOLUTIONS IN
210 Interstate North Parkway, Ste. 700, Atlanta, GA   30339
CEO: Shimon Alon, CEO   Tel: (770) 980-6716   %FO: 100
Bus: *Mfr. software.*   Fax: (770) 980-6719

PRECISE SOFTWARE SOLUTIONS IN
6430 Rockledge Drive, Ste. 402, Bethesda, MD   20817
CEO: Shimon Alon, CEO   Tel: (301) 581-0500   %FO: 100
Bus: *Mfr. software.*   Fax: (301) 581-0590

PRECISE SOFTWARE SOLUTIONS IN
2838 East Long Lake Road, Troy, Mi   48098
CEO: Shimon Alon, CEO   Tel: (248) 689-2574   %FO: 100
Bus: *Mfr. software.*   Fax: (248) 689-2581

● **RADA ELECTRONIC INDUSTRIES LIMITED**
7 Giborei Israel Street, Netanya, Israel
CEO: Herzle Bodinger, CEO   Tel: 972-9-892-1111   Rev: $19
Bus: *Mfr. avionics and automatic test*   Fax: 972-9-8855885   Emp: 140
  equipment.   www.rada.com

RADA USA INC.
8361 NW 64th Street, Miami, FL   33166
CEO: Zvi Alon, COO   Tel: (305) 591-9562   %FO: 100
Bus: *Mfr. avionics and automatic test*   Fax: (305) 591-9320
  equipment.

- **RADCOM LTD.**
12 Hanechoshet Street, Tel Aviv 69710, Israel
CEO: Arnon Toussia-Cohen, CEO   Tel: 972-3-645-5055   Rev: $31
Bus: *Mfr. test equipment and software.*   Fax: 972-3-647-4681   Emp: 170
     www.radcom-inc.com

     RADCOM EQUIPMENT, INC.
     6 Forest Avenue, Paramus, NJ 07652
     CEO: Terri Griffin, VP   Tel: (201) 518-0033   %FO: 100
     Bus: *Mfr./sales test equipment and*   Fax: (201) 556-9030
     software.

- **RADWARE LTD.**
22 Raoul Wallenberg Street, Tel Aviv 69710, Israel
CEO: Roy Zisapel, CEO   Tel: 972-3-766-8666   Rev: $38
Bus: *Mfr. internet traffic hardware and*   Fax: 972-3-766-8655   Emp: 225
software.   www.radware.com

     RADWARE, INC.
     575 Corporate Drive, Ste. 205, Mahwah, NJ 07430
     CEO: Mike Long, VP   Tel: (201) 512-9771   %FO: 100
     Bus: *Mfr./sales internet traffic*   Fax: (201) 512-9774
     hardware and software.

- **RETALIX LTD.**
10 Zarhin Street, Corex House, Ra'anana 43000, Israel
CEO: Barry Shaked, CEO   Tel: 972-9776-6677   Rev: $36
Bus: *Mfr. software for grocery industry.*   Fax: 972-9740-0470   Emp: 450
     www.retalix.com

     RETALIX USA INC.
     8081 Royal Ridge Pkwy., Ste. 100, Irving, TX 75063
     CEO: Avinoam Bloch, EVP   Tel: (972) 827-1001   %FO: 100
     Bus: *Sales/distribution of software.*   Fax: (972) 827-1038

     RETALIX USA INC.
     7220 Aveinda Encinas, Ste. 206, Carlsbad, CA 92009
     CEO: Lawrence L. Allman, EVP   Tel: (760) 931-6940   %FO: 100
     Bus: *Sales/distribution of software.*   Fax: (760) 931-6978

- **RIT TECHNOLOGIES LTD.**
24 Raoul Wallenberg Street, Tel Aviv 69719, Israel
CEO: Liam Galin, CEO   Tel: 972-3-645-5151   Rev: $39
Bus: *Mfr. hardware and software to track*   Fax: 972-3-647-4115   Emp: 599
network computer cable connections.   www.rittech.com

RIT TECHNOLOGIES, INC.
900 Corporate Drive, Mahwah, NJ   07430
CEO: Mark Gross, VP   Tel: (201) 512-1970   %FO: 100
Bus: *Sales/distribution of hardware and*   Fax: (201) 512-1286
    software products.

RIT TECHNOLOGIES, INC.
22661 Lambert Street, Ste. 200-201, Lake Forest, CA   92630
CEO: Mark Gross, VP   Tel: (949) 380-7088   %FO: 100
Bus: *Sales/distribution of hardware and*   Fax: (949) 380-7005
    software products.

• SAPIENS INTERNATIONAL CORPORATION NV
Yitzhak Rabin Science Park, PO Box 4011, Rehovot 76120, Israel
CEO: Yitzhak Sharir, CEO   Tel: 972-8-938-2777   Rev: $73
Bus: *Mfr. software.*   Fax: 972-8-938-2730   Emp: 800
    www.sapiens.com

SAPIENS AMERICAS
2000 Centre Green Way, Ste. 240, Cary, NC   27513
CEO: Yitzhak Sharir, CEO   Tel: (919) 405-1500   %FO: 100
Bus: *Mfr./sales of software.*   Fax: (919) 405-1700

• SCITEX CORPORATION LTD.
Hamada Street, Industrial Park, PO Box 330, Herzlia B 46103, Israel
CEO: Yoav Z. Chelouche, Pres. & CEO   Tel: 972-9-597-222   Rev: $640
Bus: *Mfr. digital information systems.*   Fax: 972-9-502-922   Emp: 3,200
    www.scitex.com

CREO SCITEX AMERICA, INC.
Eight Oak Park Drive, Bedford, MA   01730
CEO: Dr. Shlomo Shamir, Pres.   Tel: (781) 275-5150   %FO: 100
Bus: *Mfr. equipment for graphic*   Fax: (781) 275-3420
    communications.

• SILICOM LIMITED
8 Hanagar Street, PO Box 2164, Kfar-Sava 44000, Israel
CEO: Avi Eizenman, Pres. & CEO   Tel: 972-9-764-4555   Rev: $6
Bus: *Mfr. PC cards for portable and laptop*   Fax: 972-9-765-1977   Emp: 50
    computers.   www.silicom.co.il

SILICOM LTD.
575 Corporate Drive, Mahwah, NJ   07430
CEO: Ran Rachlin, Pres.   Tel: (201) 529-1121
Bus: *Mfr. PC cards for portable and*   Fax: (201) 529-0906
    laptop computers.

● **SMARTEAM CORPORATION**
5 Hagavish Street, Kfar Saba 44422, Israel
CEO: Avinoam Nowogrodski, CEO   Tel: 972-9-764-4000
Bus: *Computer software services.*   Fax: 972-9-764-4001
                                         www.smarteam.com

    SMARTEAM CORPORATION
    900 Cummings Center, Ste. 307T, Beverly, MA   01915
    CEO: Andrew Rodger, VP   Tel: (978) 524-1950   %FO: 100
    Bus: *Engaged in computer software*   Fax: (978) 524-1951
      services.

    SMARTEAM CORPORATION
    Bank One Towers 8044 Montgomery Road, Cincinnati, OH   45236
    CEO: Andrew Rodger, VP   Tel: (513) 792-2953   %FO: 100
    Bus: *Engaged in computer software*   Fax: (513) 792-2954
      services.

    SMARTEAM CORPORATION
    26400 Lahser Road, Ste. 310, Southfield, MI   48034
    CEO: Andrew Rodger, VP   Tel: (248) 784-6060   %FO: 100
    Bus: *Engaged in computer software*   Fax: (248) 784-6061
      services.

    SMARTEAM CORPORATION
    9820 Willow Creek Road, Ste. 420, San Diego, CA   92131
    CEO: Andrew Rodger, VP   Tel: (858) 536-5155   %FO: 100
    Bus: *Engaged in computer software*   Fax: (858) 549-8679
      services.

● **TAT INDUSTRIES LTD.**
PO Box 80, Gedera 70750, Israel
CEO: Shlomo Ostersetzer, Chmn.   Tel: 972-8-859-5411   Rev: $18
Bus: *Mfr. aircraft equipment for major*   Fax: 972-8-859-2831   Emp: 200
  aviation and aerospace companies.   www.tat.co.il

    LIMCO AIREPAIR INC.
    5304 South Lawton Avenue, Tulsa, OK   74107
    CEO: Shaul Menachem, Pres.   Tel: (918) 446-4300   %FO: 100
    Bus: *Mfr. aircraft equipment for major*   Fax: (918) 446-2988
      aviation and aerospace companies.

• TECNOMATIX TECHNOLOGIES LTD.

Delta House, 16 Hagalim Ave., Herzliyya 46733, Israel

CEO: Harel Beit-On, Pres. & CEO	Tel: 972-9-9594777	Rev: $89
Bus: *Computer software services.*	Fax: 972-9-9544402	Emp: 600
	www.tecnomatix.com	

TECNOMATIX-UNICAM, INC.

4010 Moorpark Ave., Suite 200, San Jose, CA 95117

CEO: Israel Levy, CEO	Tel: (408) 985-7530	%FO: 100
Bus: *Computer software services.*	Fax: (408) 985-7341	

TECNOMATIX-UNICAM, INC.

16253 Laguna Canyon Road, Suite 100, Irvine, CA 92618

CEO: Israel Levy, CEO	Tel: (949) 754-1765	%FO: 100
Bus: *Computer software services.*	Fax: (949) 754-1788	

TECNOMATIX-UNICAM, INC.

2 International Drive, Suite 150, Portsmouth, NH 03801

CEO: Israel Levy, CEO	Tel: (603) 431-9411	%FO: 100
Bus: *Computer software services.*	Fax: (603) 431-9516	

• TELRAD NETWORKS

8 Modeen Street, PO Box 50, Lod 71100, Israel

CEO: Rubin Avital, Pres. & CEO	Tel: 972-8-927-3634	
Bus: *Mfr. central office switching equipment, key systems, PBXs, ACDs, voice mail systems.*	Fax: 972-8-977-4190 www.telrad.co.il	Emp: 2,100

TELRAD NETWORKS INC.

135 Crossways Park Drive, Woodbury, NY 11797

CEO: Israel Ronn, Pres.	Tel: (516) 921-8300	%FO: 100
Bus: *Mfr./distribution/service business telecommunications products, voice mail systems, ISDN terminals & devices.*	Fax: (516) 921-8064	Emp: 90

• TEVA PHARMACEUTICALS IND LTD.

5 Basel Street, PO Box 3190, Petach Tikva 49131, Israel

CEO: Eli Hurvitz, Pres. & CEO	Tel: 972-3-926-7267	Rev: $1,750
Bus: *Mfr. pharmaceuticals, medical and veterinary supplies.*	Fax: 972-3-923-4050 www.tevapharma.com	Emp: 6,360

PLANTEX INC.
482 Hudson Terrace, Englewood Cliffs, NJ   07632
CEO: George Svokos, Pres.   Tel: (201) 567-1010   %FO: 100
Bus: *Mfr. pharmaceutical and raw*   Fax: (201) 567-7994   Emp: 40
     materials.

TEVA NEUROSCIENCE
10236 Marion Park Drive, Kansas City, MO   64133-1405
CEO: Judy Katterhenrich, Mgr.   Tel: (816) 966-4254   %FO: 100
Bus: *Engaged in innovative*   Fax: (816) 966-4113
     pharmaceuticals.

TEVA PHARMACEUTICALS USA
1090 Horsham Road, PO Box 1090, North Wales, PA   19454
CEO: William Fletcher, Pres.   Tel: (215) 591-3000   %FO: 100
Bus: *Mfr./sale pharmaceuticals.*   Fax: (215) 591-8600

● **TIOGA TECHNOLOGIES LTD.**
32 Nahalat Yitzhak Street, Tel Aviv 67448, Israel
CEO: Douglas D. Goodyear, CEO   Tel: 972-3-649-1444   Rev: $15
Bus: *Designs computer chips.*   Fax: 972-3-649-1445   Emp: 150
                                  www.tiogatech.com

TIOGA TECHNOLOGIES INC.
828 Crane Drive, Coppell, TX   75019
CEO: Douglas D. Goodyear, Pres.   Tel: (972) 304-9669   %FO: 100
Bus: *Sales/distribution semiconductors.*   Fax: (972) 304-6246

TIOGA TECHNOLOGIES INC.
2195 Zanker Road, San Jose, CA   95131
CEO: Douglas D. Goodyear, Pres.   Tel: (408) 434-5300   %FO: 100
Bus: *Sales/distribution semiconductors.*   Fax: (408) 434-5310

● **TOWER SEMICONDUCTOR LTD.**
Ramat Gavriel Industrial Zone, PO Box 619, Migdal Haemek 23105, Israel
CEO: Rafael M. Levin, CEO   Tel: 972-4-650-6611   Rev: $104
Bus: *Mfr. computer chips.*   Fax: 972-4-654-7788   Emp: 930
                              www.towersemi.com

TOWER SEMICONDUCTOR USA, INC.
4300 Stevens Creek Blvd., Ste. 175, San Jose, CA   95129
CEO: Doron Simon   Tel: (408) 551-6500   %FO: 100
Bus: *Mfr. computer chips.*   Fax: (408) 551-6509

- **TTI TEAM TELECOM INTERNATIONAL LTD.**

7 Martin Gahl Street, Kiryat Arie, Petah Tikva 49512, Israel

CEO: Meir Lipshes, CEO	Tel: 972-3-926-9700	Rev: $43
Bus: *Computer software and services.*	Fax: 972-3-926-9849	Emp: 400
	www.tti.co.il	

    TTI TEAM TELECOM INTERNATIONAL LTD.

    2 Hudson Place, 6th Fl., Hoboken, NJ 07030

| CEO: Bill Archer | Tel: (201) 425-1183 | %FO: 100 |
| Bus: *Computer software & services.* | Fax: (201) 795-3920 | |

- **TTR TECHNOLOGIES, INC.**

2 Hanagar Street, Kfar Saba 44425, Israel

CEO: Marc D. Tokayer, Chmn. & CEO	Tel: 972-9-766-2393	Rev: $
Bus: *Computer software & services.*	Fax: 972-9-766-2394	Emp: 8
	www.ttrtech.com	

    TTR TECHNOLOGIES, INC.

    575 Lexington Avenue, Suite 400, New York, NY 10022

| CEO: Matthew L. Cohen, EVP | Tel: (212) 527-7599 | %FO: 100 |
| Bus: *Computer software & Services.* | Fax: (530) 690-7812 | |

- **UNITED MIZRAHI BANK LTD.**

13 Rothschild Blvd., Tel Aviv 65121, Israel

CEO: Victor Medina, Mng. Dir.	Tel: 972-3-567-9211	
Bus: *Commercial banking services.*	Fax: 972-3-560-4780	Emp: 3,400
	www.mizrahi.co.il	

    UNITED MIZRAHI BANK LTD. - LA Branch

    611 Wilshire Blvd., Ste. 500-700, Los Angeles, CA 90017

| CEO: Jacob Wintner, SVP & Gen.Mgr. | Tel: (213) 362-2999 | %FO: 100 |
| Bus: *International commercial banking services.* | Fax: (213) 488-9783 | Emp: 33 |

- **VALOR COMPUTERIZED SYSTEMS**

11 Faran, Bldg. 4, Yavne 70600, Israel

CEO: Schmuel E. Dolberg, CEO	Tel: 972-8-943-2430	
Bus: *Computer software and services.*	Fax: 972-8-943-2429	
	www.valor.com	

    VALOR COMPUTERIZED SYSTEMS, INC.

    25341 Commercentre Drive, Ste. 2, Lake Forest, CA 92630

| CEO: Schmuel E. Dolberg, CEO | Tel: (949) 586-5969 | %FO: 100 |
| Bus: *Computer software and services.* | Fax: (949) 586-1343 | |

● **VERISITY LTD.**

8 Hamelacha Street, Rosh Ha'ain 48091, Israel

CEO: Moshe Gavnelov, CEO   Tel: 972-3-900-4000   Rev: $22

Bus: *Development of software.*   Fax: 972-3-900-4001   Emp: 140

www.verisity.com

    VERISITY INC.

    2041 Landings Drive, Mountain View, CA   94043

    CEO: Ziv Binyamini, VP   Tel: (650) 934-6800   %FO: 100

    Bus: *Sales software.*   Fax: (650) 934-6801

    VERISITY INC.

    1700 West Park Drive, Ste. 290, Westborough, MA   01581

    CEO: Erik Panu   Tel: (508) 870-9733   %FO: 100

    Bus: *Sales software.*   Fax: (508) 870-9733

● **VIRYANET LTD.**

5 Kiryat Hamada Street, Science Based Industries Campus, Har Hotzvim Jerusalem 91230, Israel

CEO: Winfried A. Burke, CEO   Tel: 972-2-581-1462   Rev: $27

Bus: *Mfr. application software.*   Fax: 972-2-581-5507   Emp: 200

www.viryanet.com

    VIRYANET USA LTD.

    2 Willow Street, Ste. 100, Southboro, MA   01745

    CEO: John Leary   Tel: (800) 661-7096   %FO: 100

    Bus: *Mfr./sales application software.*   Fax: (508) 490-8666

● **VOCALTEC COMMUNICATIONS LTD.**

2 Masket Street, Herzliyya 46733, Israel

CEO: Elon A. Ganor, CEO   Tel: 972-9-970-7777   Rev: $42

Bus: *Develops and manufactures voice and*   Fax: 972-9-956-1867

fax hardware.   www.vocaltec.com

    VOCALTEC INC.

    One Executive Drive, Ste. 320, Fort Lee, NJ   07024-3393

    CEO: Bob Van Sickle, VP Sales   Tel: (201) 228-7000   %FO: 100

    Bus: *Mfr./sales voice and fax hardware.*   Fax: (201) 363-8986

● **ZAG INDUSTRIES LTD.**

Ha'Melacha Street, New Industrial Zone, Rosh Ha'ayin 48091, Israel

CEO: Zvi Yemini, CEO   Tel: 972-3-902-0200

Bus: *Mfr. office products, lawn products and*   Fax: 972-3-902-0222

tool products.   www.zag.co.il

ZAG USA, INC.
Two Executive Drive, Fort Lee, NJ   07020
CEO: Zvi Yemini, CEO   Tel: (201) 242-1470   %FO: 100
Bus: *Sales office products, lawn*   Fax: (201) 242-1460
     products and tool products.

● **ZIM ISRAEL NAVIGATION CO LTD.**
7-9 Pal Yam Avenue, PO Box 1723, Haifa 31000, Israel
CEO: Dr. Yoram Sebba, Pres.   Tel: 972-4-865-2111   Rev: $1,600
Bus: *Ship owner and operator.*   Fax: 972-4-865-2956
                                  www.zim.co.il

B&R AGENCY, DIV. ZIM
4080 Woodcock Drive, Ste. 135, Jacksonville, FL   32207
CEO: Tom Haeussner, Mgr.   Tel: (904) 399-5693   %FO: 100
Bus: *Ship owners and operators.* Fax: (904) 399-5577

ZIM-AMERICAN ISRAEL SHIPPING CO INC.
Maher Terminal 4010, Tripoli Street, Elizabeth, NJ   07201
CEO: P. Honrath, Mgr.   Tel: (908) 527-9641   %FO: 100
Bus: *Ship owners and operators.* Fax: (908) 527-8336

ZIM-AMERICAN ISRAEL SHIPPING CO INC.
321 St. Charles Avenue, Ste. 700, New Orleans, LA   70130
CEO: T. O'Hara, Mgr.   Tel: (504) 524-1184   %FO: 100
Bus: *Ship owners and operators.* Fax: (504) 525-8451

ZIM-AMERICAN ISRAEL SHIPPING CO INC.
1939 Harrison Street, Ste. 412, Oakland, CA   94612
CEO: Hollie Palabay, Mgr.   Tel: (510) 465-7110   %FO: 100
Bus: *Ship owners and operators.* Fax: (510) 465-7112

ZIM-AMERICAN ISRAEL SHIPPING CO INC.
1900 North Loop West, Ste. 600, Houston, TX   77018
CEO: William Corrow, Mgr.   Tel: (713) 688-7447   %FO: 100
Bus: *Ship owners and operators.* Fax: (713) 688-2180

ZIM-AMERICAN ISRAEL SHIPPING CO INC.
5801 Lake Wright Drive, Norfolk, VA   23502
CEO: Shaul Cohen-Mintz, Pres.   Tel: (757) 228-1300
Bus: *Ship owners and operators.* Fax: (757) 228-1400

ZIM-AMERICAN ISRAEL SHIPPING CO INC.
222 West Oglethorpe, Ste. 202, PO Box 2807, Savannah, GA   31401
CEO: Walter Mitchell, Mgr.   Tel: (912) 236-4263   %FO: 100
Bus: *Ship owners and operators.* Fax: (912) 238-5011

ZIM-AMERICAN ISRAEL SHIPPING CO INC.
9950 West Lawrence Avenue, Ste. 409, Chicago, IL   60176
CEO: Ken Hundert, Mgr.   Tel: (847) 671-7999   %FO: 100
Bus: *Ship owners and operators.*   Fax: (847) 671-7444

ZIM-AMERICAN ISRAEL SHIPPING CO INC.
4 Concourse Parkway, Ste. 155, Atlanta, GA   30325
CEO: Tom Bresnan, Mgr.   Tel: (770) 395-3790   %FO: 100
Bus: *Ship owners and operators.*   Fax: (770) 395-3791

ZIM-AMERICAN ISRAEL SHIPPING CO INC.
1521 Pier "C" Straw, Long Beach, CA   90813
CEO: Capt. K. Lemke, Mgr.   Tel: (562) 506-2820   %FO: 100
Bus: *Ship owners and operators.*   Fax: (562) 506-2860

Italy

- **3V GROUP ITALIA S.p.A.**
  Box 219, Via Tasso 58, I-24100 Bergamo, Italy
  CEO: Dr. Antonio Seccomandi, Chmn.   Tel: 39-035-212274
  Bus: *Mfr. specialty chemicals and process*   Fax: 39-035-239569
  equipment.   www.3v.com

  ### 3V INC.
  1500 Harbor Boulevard, Weehawken, NJ   07087
  CEO: Giorgio Ferraris, EVP   Tel: (201) 865-3600   %FO: 100
  Bus: *Mfr./sale specialty chemicals and*   Fax: (201) 865-1892
  process equipment.

  ### 3V INC., COGEIM EQUIPMENT DIVISION
  9140 Arrowpoint Boulevard, Ste. 120, Charlotte, NC   28273
  CEO: Gary Matthews   Tel: (704) 523-5252   %FO: 100
  Bus: *Mfr./sale specialty chemicals and*   Fax: (704) 522-1763
  process equipment.

- **AGUSTA S.p.A.**
  Via Giovanni Agusta 520, I-21017 Cascina Costa di Samarato (VA), Italy
  CEO: Anedeo Catoraletti, Pres.   Tel: 39-0331-229111
  Bus: *Manufacturer of helicopters and fixed-*   Fax: 39-0331-229605   Emp: 6,000
  wing aircraft.   www.augusta.it

  ### AGUSTA AEROSPACE CORPORATION
  3050 Red Lion Road, Philadelphia, PA   19114
  CEO: Dr. Robert J. Budica, CEO   Tel: (215) 281-1400   %FO: 100
  Bus: *Helicopter marketing, sales &*   Fax: (215) 281-0441   Emp: 100
  after-sale support.

- **ALITALIA S.p.A.**
  Centro Direzionale, Via Alessandro Marchetti 111, I-00148 Rome, Italy
  CEO: Domenico Cempella, CEO   Tel: 39-06-6562-1   Rev: $5,439
  Bus: *Commercial air transport services.*   Fax: 39-06-6562-7800   Emp: 18,700
  www.alitalia.com

  ### ALITALIA AIRLINES
  666 Fifth Avenue, New York, NY   10103
  CEO: Paolo Rubino   Tel: (212) 903-3300   %FO: 100
  Bus: *International commercial air*   Fax: (212) 903-3331   Emp: 334
  transport services.

● **GIORGIO ARMANI SPA**
Via Borgonuovo 11, I-20121 Milan, Italy
CEO: Pino Brusone, Mng. Dir.   Tel: 39-02-723-181   Rev: $973
Bus: *Men's/women's clothing, eyewear and*   Fax: 39-02-723-18-452   Emp: 3,835
accessories.   www.giorgioarmani.com

     GIORGIO ARMANI
     114 Fifth Avenue, New York, NY   10011
     CEO: Andrew Grossman, COO   Tel: (212) 366-9720   %FO: 100
     Bus: *Men's and women's clothing,*   Fax: (212) 727-3240
     eyewear and accessories.

● **ARQUATI SPA**
Localit Castellaro, I-43038 Sala Baganza, Italy
CEO: Franco Arquati, CEO   Tel: 39-02-0521-6321   Rev: $140
Bus: *Mfr. curtains, sun awnings, patio*   Fax: 39-02-0521-8366-82   Emp: 2,000
covers, picture frame moldings and   www.arquati.it
furnishings.

     ARQUATI USA INC.
     1433 W. Franckford Road, Ste. 100, Carrollton, TX   75007
     CEO: Alberto Tanzi, Pres.   Tel: (972) 466-0721   %FO: 100
     Bus: *Mfr. curtains, sun awnings,*   Fax: (800) 778-7329
     screens, patio covers, picture
     frame moldings and furnishings.

● **ASSICURAZIONI GENERALI, S.p.A.**
Piazza Duca degli Abruzzi 2, Casella Poste 538, I-34132 Trieste, Italy
CEO: Gianfranco Gutty, Pres. & CEO   Tel: 39-040-671-400   Rev: $52,084
Bus: *General insurance services.*   Fax: 39-040-671-600   Emp: 56,593
   www.generali.com

     BUSINESS MEN'S ASSURANCE CO. OF AMERICA
     PO Box 419458, BMA Tower, Kansas City, MO   64141
     CEO: Robert Rakich, CEO   Tel: (816) 753-8000
     Bus: *General insurance services*   Fax: (816) 531-5967

     GENERALI GLOBAL
     100 Brickell Avenue Suite 803, Miami, FL   33131
     CEO: Dario Picco, Pres.   Tel: (305) 381-7772   %FO: 100
     Bus: *General insurance services.*   Fax: (305) 381-7768

     GENERALI US
     *One Liberty Plaza, 37th Floor, New York, NY   10006
     CEO: Christopher J. Carnicelli, CEO   Tel: (212) 602-7600   %FO: 100
     Bus: *General insurance services.*   Fax: (212) 587-9537   Emp: 60

● **AUSIMONT S.p.A., DIV. MONTEDISON GROUP**
V.le Lombardia, 20, 1-20021 Bollate Milan, Italy
CEO: Carlo Cogliati   Tel: 39-02-38351
Bus: *Engaged in sale of fluorochemicals and*   Fax: 39-0-2-3835-2110   Emp: 2,000
    polymers.   www.ausimont.it

> **AUSIMONT USA INC.**
> 10 Leonards Lane, Thorofare, NJ   08086
> CEO: Michael T. Lacey, Pres.   Tel: (609) 853-8119   %FO: 100
> Bus: *Engaged in sale of specialty*   Fax: (609) 853-6405
>   *chemicals and polymers.*

● **AUTOGRILL SPA**
Via Caldera 21, I-20153 Milan, Italy
CEO: Paolo Prota Giurleo, CEO   Tel: 39-02-4826-3224   Rev: $2,662
Bus: *Provides restaurant concessions at*   Fax: 39-02-4527-4443   Emp: 12,310
    airports, train stations and malls.   www.autogrill.it

> **HMS HOST CORPORATION**
> 6600 Rockledge Drive, Bethesda, MD   20817
> CEO: John J. McCarthy, CEO   Tel: (240) 694-4100   %FO: 100
> Bus: *Provides restaurant and retail*   Fax: (240) 694-4100
>   *services.*

● **BANCA DI ROMA S.p.A.**
Vialle Tupini, 180, I-00144 Rome, Italy
CEO: Cesare Geronzi, Chmn.   Tel: 39-06-654-45   Rev: $5,622
Bus: *Commercial banking services.*   Fax: 39-06-544-52-879   Emp: 18,300
                                        www.bancaroma.it

> **BANCA DI ROMA**
> 34 East 51st Street, New York, NY   10022
> CEO: Alexander Voller, Mgr.   Tel: (212) 407-1600   %FO: 100
> Bus: *Commercial banking services.*   Fax: (212) 407-1677   Emp: 104

> **BANCA DI ROMA**
> 225 W. Washington St., Ste. 1200, Chicago, IL   60606
> CEO: Luigi Rocchi, Mgr.   Tel: (312) 368-8855   %FO: 100
> Bus: *Commercial banking services.*   Fax: (312) 726-3058

● **BANCA MONTE DEI PASCHI DI SIENA S.p.A. (BMPS)**
Via Dell' Abbadia, 5, I-53100 Siena, Italy
CEO: Divo Gronchi, CEO   Tel: 39-0577-294494   Rev: $7,590
Bus: *Commercial banking services.*   Fax: 39-0577-294313   Emp: 28,050

BANCA MONTE DEI PASCHI DI SIENA SPA.
55 East 59th Street, 9th Fl., New York, NY   10022-1112

CEO: Guilio Natalicchi, Mgr.   Tel: (212) 891-3600   %FO: 100

Bus: *Wholesale corporate banking;*   Fax: (212) 891-3661   Emp: 33
    U.S. branch.

• BANCA NAZIONALE DEL LAVORO
Via Vittorio Veneto 119, I-00187 Rome, Italy

CEO: David Croff, Chmn.   Tel: 39-06-47021   Rev: $9,026

Bus: *Commercial banking services.*   Fax: 39-06-47032-665   Emp: 23,800
                                  www.bnl.it

BANCA NAZIONALE DEL LAVORO
25 West 51st Street, New York, NY   10019

CEO: Alessandro DiGiovanni, EVP   Tel: (212) 581-0710   %FO: 100

Bus: *International banking services.* Fax: (212) 246-3192   Emp: 122

BANCA NAZIONALE DEL LAVORO
55 West Monroe Street, Chicago, IL   60603

CEO: Stefano Carsetti, Rep.   Tel: (312) 444-9250   %FO: 100

Bus: *International banking services.* Fax: (312) 444-9410

BANCA NAZIONALE DEL LAVORO
660 South Figueroa Street, Los Angeles, CA   90017

CEO: Filippo Cattaneo, Rep.   Tel: (213) 622-1400   %FO: 100

Bus: *International banking services.* Fax: (213) 622-5050

• BANCA NAZIONALE DELL'AGRICOLTURA
Via Salaria 231, I-00199 Rome, Italy

CEO: Dino Marchiorello, Chmn.   Tel: 39-06-8588-1   Rev: $1,542

Bus: *Commercial banking services.*   Fax: 39-06-8588-3419   Emp: 5,430
                                  www.bna.it

BANCA NAZONALE DELL' AGRICOLTURA
17 State Street, 21st Fl., New York, NY   10004

CEO: Giuseppe Magaletti, EVP   Tel: (212) 412-9600   %FO: 100

Bus: *Commercial banking services.*   Fax: (212) 412-9609

• BANCA POPOLARE DI MILANO
Piazza F Meda 4, I-20121 Milan, Italy

CEO: Paolo Bassi, Chmn.   Tel: 39-02-7700-1   Rev: $2,134

Bus: *Commercial banking services.*   Fax: 39-02-7700-2280   Emp: 6,800
                                  www.bpm.it

BANCA POPOLARE DI MILANO
375 Park Avenue, 9th Fl., New York, NY   10152
CEO: Anthony Franco, EVP   Tel: (212) 758-5040   %FO: 100
Bus: *Commercial banking services.*   Fax: (212) 838-1077   Emp: 27

• BANCA POPOLARE DI NOVARA
Via Negroni 12, I-28100 Novara, Italy
CEO: Siro Lombardini, Chmn.   Tel: 39-0321-662211   Rev: $1,800
Bus: *Commercial Banking services.*   Fax: 39-0321-662100   Emp: 7,120
www.bpn.it

BANCA POPOLARE DI NOVARA
645 Fifth Avenue, Olympic Tower, 3rd Fl., New York, NY   10022
CEO: Salvatore Catalano, Rep.   Tel: (212) 755-1300   %FO: 100
Bus: *Commercial banking services.*   Fax: (212) 486-0458   Emp: 2

• BANCO DI NAPOLI SPA
Via Toledo 177-178, I-80132 Naples, Italy
CEO: Giuseppe Falcone, Chmn.   Tel: 39-081-792-1111   Rev: $2,977
Bus: *Commercial banking services.*   Fax: 39-081-792-4400   Emp: 10,500
www.bancodinapoli.it

BANCO DI NAPOLI
4 East 54th Street, New York, NY   10022
CEO: Vito Spada, EVP   Tel: (212) 872-2400   %FO: 100
Bus: *Commercial banking services.*   Fax: (212) 872-2426   Emp: 65

• BANCO DI SICILIA S.p.A
Via Generale Magliocco 1, I-90141 Palermo, Italy
CEO: Cesare Caletti, Mgr.   Tel: 39-091-608111
Bus: *Commercial banking services.*   Fax: 39-091-6085964   Emp: 8,523
www.bancodisicilia.it

BANCO DI SICILIA
250 Park Avenue, 8th Floor, New York, NY   10177
CEO: Carlo Cracolici, SVP   Tel: (212) 692-4300   %FO: 100
Bus: *Commercial banking services.*   Fax: (212) 370-5790   Emp: 34

• BARALAN INTL SPA
Baralan Building, Via Copernico, I-20090 Trezzano, Italy
CEO: Roland Baranes, Pres.   Tel: 39-02-484-4961
Bus: *Mfr. cosmetic packaging.*   Fax: 39-02-484-2719   Emp: 100

ARROWPAK INC.

1016 Burgrove Avenue, Carson, CA   90746

CEO: James J. Slowey, VP   Tel: (310) 636-0211   %FO: 100

Bus: *Sales/distribution cosmetic*   Fax: (310) 635-1959   Emp: 7
packaging.

ARROWPAK INC.

120-19 89th Avenue, Richmond Hill, NY   11418

CEO: Luisa Kamelhar, VP   Tel: (718) 849-1600   %FO: JV

Bus: *Sales/distribution cosmetic*   Fax: (718) 849-1383   Emp: 50
packaging.

● **BARILLA G & R RATELLI SPA**

Via Mantova 166, I-43100 Parma, Italy

CEO: Guido Maria Barilla, Chmn.   Tel: 39-0-521-2621   Rev: $2,140

Bus: *Mfr. pasta, break sticks, crackers and*   Fax: 39-0-521-270-621   Emp: 8,500
cookies.   www.barilla.it

BARILLA AMERICA INC.

200 Tri State International, Lincolnshire, IL   60069-4443

CEO: Gianluigi Zenti, VP   Tel: (847) 405-7500   %FO: 100

Bus: *Mfr. pasta, break sticks, crackers*   Fax: (847) 948-8791
and cookies.

● **BENETTON GROUP, SPA**

Via Villa Minelli 1, I-31050 Ponzano Veneto Treviso, Italy

CEO: Luciano Benetton, Chmn.   Tel: 39-0422-4491   Rev: $1,995

Bus: *Mfr. fashion apparel and accessories.*   Fax: 39-0422-449930   Emp: 6,585
   www.benetton.com

BENETTON USA CORPORATION

597 Fifth Avenue, 11th Fl., New York, NY   10017

CEO: Carlo Tunioli, Mgr.   Tel: (212) 593-0290   %FO: 100

Bus: *Mfr./sale of fashion apparel and*   Fax: (212) 371-1438
accessories.

● **PIETRO BERETTA S.P.A.**

Via Pietro Beretta 18, I-25063 Gardone Val Trompia Brescia, Italy

CEO: Ugo Gussalli Beretta, Pres.   Tel: 39-030-83411   Rev: $125

Bus: *Mfr. shotguns.*   Fax: 39-030-8341421   Emp: 1,000
   www.beretta.il

BERETTA USA CORPORATION
17601 Beretta Drive, Accokeek, MD   20607
CEO: Robert Bonaventure, EVP   Tel: (301) 283-2191   %FO: 100
Bus: *Sales of hunting and sporting*   Fax: (301) 283-0990
        arms/guns.

● **BIESSE S.p.A.**
16 Via della Meccanica, I-61100 Pesaro, Italy
CEO: Roberto Selci, Pres.   Tel: 39-0721-439100
Bus: *Mfr. woodworking equipment for* Fax: 39-0721-439499   Emp: 1,550
        furniture industry.   www.biesse.it

   BIESSE GROUP AMERICA INC.
   4477 East Paris Avenue SE, Grand Rapids, MI   49512
   CEO: Federico Broccoli, CEO   Tel: (616) 554-0990
   Bus: *Distribution/service woodworking* Fax: (616) 554-9880
           equipment.

   BIESSE GROUP AMERICA INC.
   4110 Meadow Oak Lane, Charlotte, NC   28219-9849
   CEO: Federico Broccoli, CEO   Tel: (704) 357-3131   %FO: 80
   Bus: *Distribution/service woodworking* Fax: (704) 357-3130   Emp: 45
           equipment.

● **BONDIOLI & PAVESI S.p.A.**
Via 23 Aprice 35/A, I-46029 Suzzara, Italy
CEO: Edi Bondioli, Pres.   Tel: 39-037-65141
Bus: *Mfr. drive shafts, gear boxes, hydraulics.* Fax: 39-037-6531382
                                       www.bypy.it

   BONDIOLI & PAVESI INC.
   10252 Sycamore Drive, Ashland, VA   23005-9401
   CEO: Franco Laghi, Pres.   Tel: (804) 550-2224   %FO: 100
   Bus: *Distributor drive shafts, gear* Fax: (804) 550-2837
           boxes, and hydraulics

● **BREMBO SPA**
Via Brembo 25, I-24035 Bergamo, Italy
CEO: Alberto Bombassei, Chmn.   Tel: 39-035-605-111   Rev: $355
Bus: *Mfr. braking components and*   Fax: 39-035-605-400   Emp: 2,000
        components for autos.   www.brembo.it

BREMBO NORTH AMERICA, INC.
1585 Sunflower Avenue, Costa Mesa, CA 92626

CEO: Cristina Bombassei	Tel: (714) 641-0104	%FO: 100
Bus: *Mfr. braking components and components for autos.*	Fax: (714) 641-5827	

• BULGARI SPA
Lungotevere Marzio 11, I-00186 Rome, Italy

CEO: Francesco Trapani, CEO	Tel: 39-06-688-10477	Rev: $637
Bus: *Mfr. and sales of contemporary Italian jewelry and leather goods.*	Fax: 39-06-688-10401 www.bulgari.it	Emp: 1,575

BULGARI
605 East Cooper Street, Aspen, CO 81611

CEO: Nicole Bulgari, Pres.	Tel: (970) 925-6225	%FO: 100
Bus: *Retail store; sales of contemporary Italian jewelry and leather goods.*	Fax: (970) 925-4418	

BULGARI
909 North Michigan Avenue, Chicago, IL 60611

CEO: Nicole Bulgari, Pres.	Tel: (312) 255-1313	%FO: 100
Bus: *Retail store; sales of contemporary Italian jewelry and leather goods.*	Fax: (312) 255-1326	

BULGARI
730 Fifth Avenue, New York, NY 10019

CEO: Nicole Bulgari, Pres.	Tel: (212) 315-9000	%FO: 100
Bus: *Retail store; sales of contemporary Italian jewelry and leather goods.*	Fax: (212) 462-4001	

BULGARI
9700 Collins Avenue, Bal Harbour, FL 33154

CEO: Nicole Bulgari, Pres.	Tel: (305) 861-8898	%FO: 100
Bus: *Retail store; sales of contemporary Italian jewelry and leather goods.*	Fax: (305) 861-5718	

BULGARI
201 North Rodeo Drive, Beverly Hills, CA 90210

CEO: Nicole Bulgari, Pres.	Tel: (310) 858-9216	%FO: 100
Bus: *Retail store; sales of contemporary Italian jewelry and leather goods.*	Fax: (310) 858-9226	

● **CARRARO SPA**
Via Olmo 37, I-35011 Campodarsego Padua, Italy
CEO: Mario Carraro, Chmn. & CEO — Tel: 39-0-49-921-9111 — Rev: $324
Bus: *Mfr. components for cars and* — Fax: 39-0-49-928-9111 — Emp: 2,000
machinery, including axles, — www.carraro.com
transmissions, tractors and forklifts.

> **CARRARO NORTH AMERICA, INC.**
> 2118 US 41 Southeast, Calhoun, GA   30701
> CEO: Tomaso Carraro, Pres. — Tel: (706) 625-2460 — %FO: 100
> Bus: *Mfr. agricultural and construction* — Fax: (706) 625-3321 — Emp: 17
> *equipment axles and transmissions.*

● **CASSA DI RISPARMIO DI FIRENZE**
Via Bufalini 6, I-50122 Florence, Italy
CEO: Giovanni Fossi — Tel: 39-055-261-2900
Bus: *Commercial banking services.* — Fax: 39-055-261-2298 — Emp: 3,500
www.carifirenze.it

> **CASSA DI RISPARMIO DI FIRENZE**
> 375 Park Avenue, New York, NY   10152-0054
> CEO: Paolo G. Palli, U.S. Rep. — Tel: (212) 421-6010 — %FO: 100
> Bus: *International banking services.* — Fax: (212) 759-6785 — Emp: 3

● **CEMBRE SPA**
Via Serenissima 9, I-25135 Brescia, Italy
CEO: Carlo Rosani, Chmn. — Tel: 39-030-369-21 — Rev: $45
Bus: *Mfr. electrical connectors.* — Fax: 39-030-336-5766
www.cembre.com

> **CEMBRE**
> 70 Campus Plaza II, Edison, NJ   08837
> CEO: Carlo Rosani, CEO — Tel: (732) 225-7415 — %FO: 100
> Bus: *Mfr. electrical connectors.* — Fax: (732) 225-7414

● **DAVIDE CENCI & MGT SRL**
Via Campo Marzio 4/7, I-00186 Rome, Italy
CEO: Paolo Cenci, Pres. — Tel: 39-06-699-0681
Bus: *Design/mfr. wearing apparel.* — Fax: 39-06-379-5900 — Emp: 65
www.davidecenci.com

> **DAVIDE CENCI INC.**
> 801 Madison Avenue, New York, NY   10021
> CEO: David Cenci, VP — Tel: (212) 628-5910 — %FO: 100
> Bus: *Retail men's wear.* — Fax: (212) 439-1650 — Emp: 13

● **COMPAGNIA ITALIANA DEI JOLLY HOTELS SPA**
Via Bellini 6, I-36078 Valdagno, Italy
CEO: Vittorio Zanusa, Chmn.　　　　Tel: 39-0-445-410-000　　　Rev: $180
Bus: *Hotel chain.*　　　　　　　　　　Fax: 39-0-445-411-472　　　Emp: 2,250
　　　　　　　　　　　　　　　　　　www.jollyhotels.it

　　　HOTEL JOLLY
　　　22 East 38th Street, New York, NY　10016
　　　CEO: Walter Paier, Mgr.　　　　　Tel: (212) 802-0600　　　%FO: 100
　　　Bus: *Hotel.*　　　　　　　　　　Fax: (212) 447-0747

● **COSTA CROCIERE**
Via XII, Ittobre 2, I-16121 Genoa, Italy
CEO: Nicola Costa, Chmn.　　　　　　Tel: 39-01-548-31
Bus: *Shipping/cruise line.*　　　　　　Fax: 39-010-548-3290　　　Emp: 1,661
　　　　　　　　　　　　　　　　　　www.costacruises.com

　　　COSTA CRUISE LINES NV
　　　80 SW 8th Street, Miami, FL　33130-3097
　　　CEO: Dino Schibuola, Pres.　　　Tel: (305) 358-7325　　　%FO: 100
　　　Bus: *Cruise line.*　　　　　　　Fax: (305) 375-0676　　　Emp: 140

● **DE LONGHI SPA**
Via L. Seitz 47, I-31100 Treviso, Italy
CEO: Silvano Gatto, CEO　　　　　　Tel: 39-0422-4131
Bus: *Mfr. small, household appliances.*　Fax: 39-0422-412420
　　　　　　　　　　　　　　　　　　www.delonghi.com

　　　DE LONGHI AMERICA, INC.
　　　Park 80 West Plaza One, 4th Fl., Saddle Brook, NJ　07663
　　　CEO: Jim McCusker, Pres.　　　　Tel: (201) 909-4000　　　%FO: 100
　　　Bus: *Mfr. household, air-conditioning,*　Fax: (201) 909-8550
　　　　　air-treatment and heating
　　　　　appliances.

● **DELLE VEDOVE LEVIGATRICI S.p.A.**
Viale Treviso 13A, I-33170 Pordenone, Italy
CEO: Gaetano Delle Vedove, Pres.　　Tel: 39-0434-572-277
Bus: *Mfr. woodworking machinery.*　　Fax: 39-0434-572-775　　　Emp: 45
　　　　　　　　　　　　　　　　　　www.delllevedove.com

　　　DELLE VEDOVE USA INC.
　　　6031 Harris Technology Blvd., Charlotte, NC　28269
　　　CEO: Vittorio Belluz, CEO　　　　Tel: (704) 598-0020　　　%FO: 70
　　　Bus: *Sale/service woodworking*　　Fax: (704) 598-3950　　　Emp: 6
　　　　　equipment & abrasives.

● **DEROMA SPA**
Via Pasubio 17, I-36034 Malo Vicenza, Italy
CEO: Giovanni Franco Masello, Dir.   Tel: 39-01-4450595311
Bus: *Mfr. terra cotta pots.*   Fax: 39-01-4455955322
          www.deroma.it

> **MARSHALL POTTERY INC.**
> 4901 Elysean Field, Marshall, TX   75670
> CEO: Giovanni Masello, Pres.   Tel: (903) 927-5400   %FO: 100
> Bus: *Mfr. terra cotta pots.*   Fax: (903) 935-1654

● **DIESEL S.p.A.**
Via Dell Industria 7, I-73606 Molvena, Italy
CEO: Renzo Rosso, CEO   Tel: 39-0424-477-555   Rev: $450
Bus: *Mfr. high-fashion clothing and*   Fax: 39-0424-708-061   Emp: 1,000
    accessories.   www.diesel.com

> **DIESEL INC.**
> 770 Lexington Avenue, New York, NY   10021
> CEO: Armin Broger, COO   Tel: (212) 308-0055   %FO: 100
> Bus: *Sales/distribution of high-fashion*   Fax:
>   *clothing and accessories.*

● **DOLCE & GABBANA**
Via Santa Cecilia 7, I-20122 Milan, Italy
CEO: Stafano Gabbana, Chmn.   Tel: 39-02-7742-71   Rev: $120
Bus: *Mfr. men's and women's upscale,*   Fax: 39-02-7601-0600
    designer clothing, fragrances and   www.dolcegabbana.it
    eyewear.

> **DOLCE & GABBANA**
> 825 Madison Avenue, New York, NY   10021
> CEO: Domenico Dolce   Tel: (212) 249-4100   %FO: 100
> Bus: *Sales of men's and women's*   Fax: (212) 249-4100
>   *upscale, designer clothing,*
>   *fragrances and eyewear.*

● **DUCATI MOTOR HOLDING SPA**
Via A. Cavalieri Ducati 3, Bologna I-40132, Italy
CEO: Carlo Di Biagio, Chmn.   Tel: 39-051-641-3111   Rev: $387
Bus: *Mfr. luxury, high-speed motorcycles and* Fax: 39-051-641-3223   Emp: 945
    sport touring bikes.   www.ducati.it

DUCATI NORTH AMERICA, INC.
237 West Parkway, Pompton Plains, NJ 07444-1028
CEO: Federico Minoli, CEO   Tel: (973) 839-2600   %FO: 100
Bus: *Sales/distribution of luxury, high-speed motorcycles and sport touring bikes.*   Fax: (973) 839-2331

● **ENI SPA**
Piazzale E Mattei 1, I-00144 Rome, Italy
CEO: Vittorio Mincato, CEO   Tel: 39-06-59-821   Rev: $45,103
Bus: *Energy related product and services.*   Fax: 39-06-59-822-141   Emp: 72,025
www.eni.it

AGIP PETROLEUM COMPANY INC.
2950 North Loop West, Ste. 300, Houston, TX 77092
CEO: Alberto Pagani, CEO   Tel: (713) 688-6281   %FO: 100
Bus: *Oil exploration/products, crude oil trading.*   Fax: (713) 688-6091

ENI REPRESENTATIVE FOR THE AMERICAS
666 Fifth Avenue, New York, NY 10103
CEO: Enzo Viscusi, Rep.   Tel: (212) 887-0330   %FO: 100
Bus: *Group activity coordination.*   Fax: (212) 246-0009

SAIPEM, INC.
15950 Park Row, Houston, TX 77084
CEO: Bruce C. Gilman, CEO   Tel: (281) 552-5700   %FO: 100
Bus: *Onshore/offshore drilling and pipelines.*   Fax: (281) 552-5915

SNAMPROGETTI USA
1200 Smith Street, Ste. 2880, Houston, TX 77002
CEO: Alessandro Serpetti, CEO   Tel: (713) 655-7071   %FO: 100
Bus: *Technology sales/service.*   Fax: (713) 655-7764

SONSUB INC.
15950 Park Row, Houston, TX 77084
CEO: Aldo Gebbia, Pres. & CEO   Tel: (281) 552-5600   %FO: 100
Bus: *Sub-sea engineering services.*   Fax: (281) 552-5910

● **GRUPPO ERMENEGILDO ZEGNA**
5 Via Forcella, I-20144 Milan, Italy
CEO: Angelo Zegna, Chmn.   Tel: 39-02-58-103-787   Rev: $530
Bus: *Mfr. menswear and sportswear.*   Fax: 39-02-58-103-901   Emp: 3,800
www.zegnaermenegildo.com

ERMENEGILDO ZEGNA
743 Fifth Avenue, New York, NY   10022
CEO: Richard Cohen, CEO   Tel: (212) 421-4488   %FO: 100
Bus: *Sales/distribution of menswear*   Fax: (212) 421-4488
     and sportswear.

ERMENEGILDO ZEGNA
39 Newbury Street, Boston, MA   02116
CEO: Richard Cohen, CEO   Tel: (617) 424-9300   %FO: 100
Bus: *Sales/distribution of menswear*   Fax: (617) 424-9300
     and sportswear.

● **ESAOTE SPA**
Via Siffredi 58, I-16153 Genoa, Italy
CEO: Carlo Castellano, Chmn.   Tel: 39-01-654-71   Rev: $1,000
Bus: *Develops and manufactures ultrasound*   Fax: 39-010-6547-275   Emp: 214
     imaging (MRI).   www.esaote.com

   BIOSOUND ESAOTE INC.
   8000 Castleway Drive, PO Box 50858, Indianapolis, IN   46250
   CEO: Fabrizio Landi, Chmn.   Tel: (317) 849-1793   %FO: 100
   Bus: *Develops and manufactures*   Fax: (317) 841-8616
        ultrasound imaging (MRI).

● **SALVATORE FERRAGAMO ITALIA SPA**
Via del Tornabuoni 2, I-50123 Florence, Italy
CEO: Ferruccio Ferragamo, CEO   Tel: 39-05-533-601   Rev: $600
Bus: *Mfr. clothing, belts, ties, handbags and*   Fax: 39-05-533-60215
     scarves.   www.salvatoreferragamo.it

   FERRAGAMO STORES
   661 Fifth Avenue, New York, NY   10022
   CEO: Ferruccio Ferragamo, CEO   Tel: (212) 759-3822   %FO: 100
   Bus: *Sales of clothing, belts, ties,*   Fax: (212) 308-4493
        handbags and scarves.

● **FERRERO SPA**
Piazzale Pietro Ferrero, I-12051 Alba Cuneo, Italy
CEO: M. DeBona, Pres.   Tel: 39-01-73-2951   Rev: $91
Bus: *Mfr. confectionery products, including*   Fax: 39-0173-363034   Emp: 14,000
     Nutella Hazelnut Spread, Rocher   www.ferrerousa.com
     chocolates and Tic Tac Breath Mints.

FERRERO USA INC.
600 Cottontail Lane, Somerset, NJ   08873

CEO: Michael F. Gilmore, CEO	Tel: (732) 764-9300	%FO: 100
Bus: *Mfr./repackaging sale confectionery goods.*	Fax: (732) 764-2700	Emp: 154

● FIAT S.p.A.
Corso Marconi 20, I-10125 Turin, Italy

CEO: Paolo Cantarella, CEO	Tel: 39-01-686-1111	Rev: $53,866
Bus: *Diversified industrial conglomerate: autos; commercial, industrial, agricultural and construction equipment.*	Fax: 39-01-686-3400 www.fiat.com	Emp: 220,550

ALFA ROMEO DISTRIBUTORS INC.
7505 Exchange Drive, Orlando, FL   32809

CEO: Riccardo Brugnoli, Mgr.	Tel: (407) 856-5000	%FO: 100
Bus: *Sale/service automobiles.*	Fax: (407) 438-0804	

COFAP OF AMERICA, INC.
PO Box 5955, Kingsport, TN   37663

CEO: Jose Luiz Siqueira, Mgr.	Tel: (423) 279-6306	%FO: 100
Bus: *Mfr. shock absorbers.*	Fax: (423) 279-7123	

FERRARI NORTH AMERICA, INC.
250 Sylvan Avenue, Englewood Cliffs, NJ   07632

CEO: Stuart Robinson, Pres.	Tel: (201) 816-2600	%FO: 100
Bus: *Sale/service automobiles.*	Fax: (201) 816-2626	

FIAT AVIO, INC.
270 Sylvan Avenue, Englewood Cliffs, NJ   07632

CEO: Edmund R. Dobak, COO	Tel: (201) 816-2720	%FO: 100
Bus: *Design/mfr. airplane engines.*	Fax: (201) 816-2740	Emp: 15

FIAT U.S.A, INC.
375 Park Avenue, Suite 2703, New York, NY   10152

CEO: Daniele G. Rulli, Pres.	Tel: (212) 355-2600	%FO: 100
Bus: *Diversified industrial conglomerate: autos; commercial, industrial, agricultural, and construction equipment; transportation systems; engineering, chemicals, and financial services.*	Fax: (212) 308-2968	Emp: 16

IVECO TRUCKS OF NORTH AMERICA, INC.
3433 Progress Drive, Bensalem, PA   19020-8527
CEO: John Sherlock, Pres. & CEO   Tel: (215) 244-2250   %FO: 100
Bus: *Sales/distribution of trucks.*   Fax: (215) 639-0962

MAGNETI MARELLI U.S.A., INC.
2101 Nash Street, Sanford, NC   27331
CEO: Fred Gopal, Pres.   Tel: (919) 776-4111   %FO: 100
Bus: *Mfr. auto engines.*   Fax: (919) 775-6337

TEKSID ALUMINUM FOUNDRY, INC.
1635 Old Columbia Road, Dickson, TN   37055
CEO: Paolo Maccario, Pres.   Tel: (615) 446-8110   %FO: 100
Bus: *Mfr. aluminum automotive parts.*   Fax: (615) 446-2460

TEKSID, INC.
14901 Galleon Court, Plymouth, MI   48170
CEO: Massimo Fracchia, Pres.   Tel: (734) 456-5600   %FO: 100
Bus: *Aluminum manufacturing*   Fax: (734) 456-5678
    equipment & systems consulting.

● **FILA HOLDINGS S.p.A.**
26 Viale Cesare Battisti, I-13051 Biella, Italy
CEO: Dr. Michele Scannavini, Chmn.   Tel: 39-01-5350-6246   Rev: $1,104
Bus: *Sales/distribution of sports footwear* Fax: 39-01-5350-6347   Emp: 2,830
    and clothing.   www.fila.com

FILA U.S.A., INC.
14114 York Road, Sparks, MD   21152
CEO: Jon Epstein, Pres. & CEO   Tel: (410) 773-3000   %FO: 100
Bus: *Mfr./sales sports footwear &*   Fax: (410) 773-4967   Emp: 200
    clothing.

● **CESARE FIORUCCI S.p.A.**
Santa Palomba, I-00040 Rome, Italy
CEO: Ferrucio Fiorucci, Pres.   Tel: 39-06-911-93639
Bus: *Mfr. Italian specialty meats.*   Fax: 39-06-911-93639
                                          www.fiorucci.com

FIORUCCI FOODS INC.
1800 Ruffin Mill Road, Colonial Heights, VA   23834
CEO: Claudio Colmignoli, Pres.   Tel: (804) 520-7775   %FO: 100
Bus: *Sales/distribution of Italian*   Fax: (804) 520-7180
    specialty meats.

● **GEORGE FUNARO & ASSOCIATES**
7, Largo Augusto, Milan I-20121, Italy
CEO: George Funaro   Tel: 39-02-784267
Bus: *Financial consultants and certified*   Fax: 39-02-783652   Emp: 50
    public accountants.   www.funaro.com

    GEORGE FUNARO & ASSOCIATES
    One Penn Plaza, Ste. 3515, New York, NY   10119
    CEO: Sheldon Satlin, Pres.   Tel: (212) 947-3333   %FO: JV
    Bus: *Accounting and financial services.*   Fax: (212) 947-4725   Emp: 40

● **CARLO GAVAZZI HOLDING AG**
Via Milano 13, I-20020 Lainate, Italy
CEO: Dr. Leonardo E. Vannotti, Chmn.   Tel: 39-02-931-761   Rev: $260
Bus: *Mfr./design and marketing of system*   Fax: 39-02-931-76402   Emp: 2,240
    integration products and control   www.carlogavazzi.com/us
    components for the industrial
    automation markets.

    CARLO GAVAZZI INC.
    740 East Glendale Avenue, Sparks, NV   89431
    CEO: Chris Boutilier, Mgr.   Tel: (775) 331-8283   %FO: 100
    Bus: *Design/mfr./marketing of system*   Fax: (775) 331-8004
    integration products.

    CARLO GAVAZZI INC.
    750 Hasting Lane, Buffalo Groves, IL   60089-6904
    CEO: Fred Shirzadi, Pres.   Tel: (847) 465-6100   %FO: 100
    Bus: *Sales of control components for*   Fax: (847) 465-7373
    the industrial automation market.

    CARLO GAVAZZI INC.
    10 Mupac Drive, PO Box 3099, Brockton, MA   02401
    CEO: Caryn A. Banks   Tel: (508) 588-6110   %FO: 100
    Bus: *Design/mfr./marketing of system*   Fax: (508) 588-0498
    integration products.

● **GENNY MODA S.p.A.**
Via Bella Spiga 30, I-20121 Milan, Italy
CEO: Donatella Girombelli, Pres.   Tel: 39-02-762-731
Bus: *Mfr. designer clothing.*   Fax: 39-02-784-161   Emp: 400
                                              www.genny.com

    GENNY USA
    650 Fifth Avenue, 18th Fl., New York, NY   10017
    CEO: R. Farro, Pres.   Tel: (212) 245-4860   %FO: 100
    Bus: *Import/sales designer clothing.*   Fax: (212) 969-9396   Emp: 23

● **GIANFRANCO FERRE SPA, DIV. IT HOLDING**
Via S. Andrea 18, I-20121 Milan, Italy
CEO: Franco Mattioli, CEO — Tel: 39-02-784-460
Bus: *Mfr. clothing, yarns and fabrics.* — Fax: 39-02-781-485
www.gianfrancoferre.com

    MARZOTTA USA CORPORATION
    650 Fifth Avenue, 17th Fl., New York, NY 10019
    CEO: Graziano de Boni, Pres. — Tel: (212) 641-1600 — %FO: 100
    Bus: *Sales/distribution of menswear.* — Fax: (212) 641-1630

● **GIULIANI, IGMI S.p.A.**
Via del Lavoro 7, Quarto Inferiore, I-40050 Bologna, Italy
CEO: Tomaso Tarozzi, CEO — Tel: 39-051-603-7811
Bus: *Mfr. standard and customized machine* — Fax: 39-051-603-7933
tools for the global security industry. — www.giulianaco.com

    GIULIANA, DIV. IGMI USA INC.
    252 Brenner Drive, Congers, NY 10920
    CEO: Evasio Asepsi, EVP — Tel: (845) 267-2290 — %FO: 100
    Bus: *Sales/distribution of machinery for* — Fax: (845) 267-2276
    the lock industry.

● **GROVE DRESSER ITALIA S.p.A.**
11 Via Italo Betto, I-27058 Voghera (Pavia), Italy
CEO: Salvatore Ruggeri, Pres. — Tel: 39-0383-6911
Bus: *Mfr. valves and regulators for oil and* — Fax: 39-0383-367-166 — Emp: 350
gas industry. — www.grove.it

    DRESSER FLOW CONTROL
    11100 West Airport Blvd., Stafford, TX 77477
    CEO: Stewart P. Yee — Tel: (281) 568-2211 — %FO: 100
    Bus: *Mfr. valves/regulators for oil and* — Fax: (281) 568-6731 — Emp: 145
    gas industry.

● **GRUPPO CERAMICHE RICCHETTI SPA**
Via Radici in Piano 428, I-41049 Sassuolo Modena, Italy
CEO: R. Arletti, Chmn. — Tel: 39-0536-86-511 — Rev: $380
Bus: *Mfr. glazed ceramic and stoneware tile.* — Fax: 39-0536-80-7355 — Emp: 2,762
www.ricchetti.it

    RICCHETTI CERAMIC, INC.
    200 S. Harbor City Blvd., Ste. 403, Melbourne, FL 32901
    CEO: William Johnson — Tel: (407) 984-0505 — %FO: 100
    Bus: *Mfr. glazed ceramic and* — Fax: (407) 984-0503
    stoneware tile.

RICCHETTI CERAMIC, INC.
37 Beech Hill Avenue, Manchester, NH   03103
CEO: Ken Cloud   Tel: (603) 644-7662   %FO: 100
Bus: *Mfr. glazed ceramic and*   Fax: (603) 669-9698
stoneware tile.

RICCHETTI CERAMIC, INC.
2200 Park Newport, Ste. 404, Newport Beach, CA   92660
CEO: Cecilia Chiossi   Tel: (949) 759-4850   %FO: 100
Bus: *Mfr. glazed ceramic and*   Fax: (949) 759-4850
stoneware tile.

● **GRUPPO GFT**
Corso Emilia 6, I-10152 Torino, Italy
CEO: Dr. Roberto Jorio Fili, Pres.   Tel: 39-01-1-23971
Bus: *Mfr./distributes wearing apparel.*   Fax: 39-011-2397319   Emp: 10,000
www.sahza.it

GFT USA INC.
11 West 42nd Street, New York, NY   10036
CEO: Wayne M. Markowitz, EVP   Tel: (212) 302-8877   %FO: 100
Bus: *Marketing/distribute wearing*   Fax: (212) 302-8889
apparel.

● **GRUPPO RCS EDITORI SPA**
Via Mecensate A1, I-20138 Milan, Italy
CEO: Giorgio Fattori, Chmn.   Tel: 39-02-5095-2584
Bus: *Bookstores engaged in publishing.*   Fax:
www.rcs.it

RCS RIZZOLI CORPORATION
300 Park Avenue South, New York, NY   10010
CEO: Antonio Polito, Chmn.   Tel: (212) 387-3400   %FO: 100
Bus: *Engaged in bookstores and*   Fax: (212) 387-3535
publishing.

● **HOLDING DI PARTECIPAZIONI INDUSTRIALI S.p.A.**
Via Turati 16/18, I-20121 Milan, Italy
CEO: Nicolo Nefri, Chmn.   Tel: 39-02-622-91   Rev: $3,710
Bus: *Holding company for fashion and*   Fax: 39-02-6229-301   Emp: 12,700
publishing industries.   www.valentino.it

VALENTINO COUTURE
600 Madison Avenue, New York, NY   10021
CEO: Angela Istok, EVP   Tel: (212) 355-0554   %FO: 100
Bus: *Sales of couture clothing and*   Fax: (212) 628-0554
     accessories.

● **I PELLETTIERI D'ITALIA S.p.A.**
Via Andrea Maffei 2, I-20122 Milan, Italy
CEO: Patrizio Bertelli, CEO   Tel: 39-02-254-6701   Rev: $1,554
Bus: *Mfr. clothing line and leather goods.*   Fax: 39-02-254-6701   Emp: 2,000
                                     www.prada.com

   IPI USA (PRADA)
   50 West 57th Street, New York, NY   10019
   CEO: Connie Darrow, Pres.   Tel: (212) 307-9300   %FO: 100
   Bus: *Sales/distribution of Prada clothes*   Fax: (212) 974-2186
        and leather goods.

● **IFI ISTITUTO FINANZIARIO INDUSTRIALE SPA**
Corso Matteotti 26, I-10121 Turin, Italy
CEO: Umberto Agnelli, Mng. Dir.   Tel: 39-01-509-0266   Rev: $63,100
Bus: *Holding company engaged in car*   Fax: 39-01-535-6000   Emp: 244,500
     manufacture, food production,
     packaging and insurance.

   RIVERWOOD INTERNATIONAL PACKAGING, INC.
   3350 Riverwood Pkwy., Ste. 1400, Atlanta, GA   30339
   CEO: Thomas M. Gannon, COO   Tel: (770) 644-3000   %FO:
   Bus: *Paperboard and packaging*   Fax: (770) 644-2927   Emp: 4,000
        machinery manufacturing for the
        beverage and consumer products
        market.

● **IGMI SPA**
Via del Lavoro 7, Quarto Inferiore, I-40050 Bologna, Italy
CEO: Saverio Gellini, Mgr.   Tel: 39-051-603-7811
Bus: *Mfr. machinery for lock industry and*   Fax: 39-051-03-7933
     transfer machines.   www.giulianoco.com

   IGM USA INC.
   252 Brenner Drive, Congers, NY   10920
   CEO: Manfred Sprenger, EVP   Tel: (845) 267-2290   %FO: 100
   Bus: *Mfr. standard and customized*   Fax: (845) 267-2276
        machine tools for the global
        security industry.

● **IMPREGILO SPA**

Viale Italia 1, Sesto S. Giovanni, I-20099 Milan, Italy

CEO: Pier Giorgio Romiti, CEO   Tel: 39-02-244-22111   Rev: $2,008

Bus: *Engaged in construction of dams, water*   Fax: 39-02-244-22293   Emp: 29,150
      systems and transportation   www.impregilo.it
      infrastructures.

    S. A. HEALY COMPANY

    1910 South Highland Avenue, Ste. 300, Lombard, IL   601486192

    CEO: Fulvio Castaldi, Pres.   Tel: (630) 679-3110   %FO: 100

    Bus: *Sales of heavy equipment.*   Fax: (630) 678-3130

    S. A. HEALY COMPANY

    9300 NW 25th Street, Miami, FL   33172

    CEO: Fulvio Castaldi, Pres.   Tel: (305) 477-1494   %FO: 100

    Bus: *Sales of heavy equipment.*   Fax: (305) 477-2874

● **IMT INTERMATO SRL**

Via Carego 14, I-21020 Crosio della Valle, Italy

CEO: C. Caprioli, Pres.   Tel: 39-0332-966110

Bus: *Mfr. equipment for machining alloy*   Fax: 39-0332-966033   Emp: 85
      aluminum wheels.   www.imtintermato.com

    IMT AMERICA INC

    18341 Sherman Way, Ste. 204, Reseda, CA   91335

    CEO: Francesco Chinaglia, Pres.   Tel: (818) 705-1741   %FO: JV

    Bus: *Distributes equipment for*   Fax: (818) 705-0462   Emp: 10
      machining light alloy aluminum
      parts.

● **INDUSTRIA MACCHINE AUTOMATICHE SPA**

Via Tosarelli 184, I-40055 Castenaso Bologna, Italy

CEO: Alberto Vacchi, Dir.   Tel: 39-05-1783-111   Rev: $283

Bus: *Mfr. packaging machines for*   Fax: 39-05-1784-422   Emp: 1,800
      pharmaceuticals.   www.ima.it

    IMA NORTH AMERICA, INC.

    211 Sinclair Street, Bristol, PA   19007

    CEO: Alberto Vacchi, Pres.   Tel: (215) 826-0400   %FO: 100

    Bus: *Mfr. packaging machines for*   Fax: (215) 826-0400
      pharmaceuticals.

● **INDUSTRIE NATUZZI S.p.A.**
47 Via Lazzitiello, I-70029 Santeramo in Colle Bari, Italy

CEO: Guiseppe Desantis, CEO	Tel: 39-0-80-882-0111	Rev: $648
Bus: *Mfr. of leather furniture.*	Fax: 39-0-80-882-0555	Emp: 3,465
	www.natuzzi.com	

    NATUZZI AMERICAS
    130 West Commerce Street, High Point, NC   27260

CEO: Dino Lorusso, Pres.	Tel: (336) 884-4234	%FO: 100
Bus: *Sales/distribution of leather furniture.*	Fax: (336) 887-8500	

● **INTERPUMP GROUP SPA**
Via E. Fermi 25, I-42040 Calerno di S. Illario d'Enza, Reggio, Italy

CEO: Sergio Erede, Chmn.	Tel: 39-052-290-4311	Rev: $388
Bus: *Mfr. high-pressure water plunger pumps.*	Fax: 39-052-290-4444	Emp: 1,200
	www.interpumpgroup.it	

    MUNCIE POWER PRODUCTS, INC.
    PO Box 548, Muncie, IN   47308-0548

CEO: Terry Walker	Tel: (765) 284-7721	%FO: 100
Bus: *Sales high-pressure water plunger pumps.*	Fax: (765) 284-6991	

● **INTESABCI SPA (FORMERLY BANCA COMMERCIALE ITALIANA)**
Piazza Paolo Ferrari, 10, I-20121 Milan, Italy

CEO: Giovanni Bazoli, Chmn.	Tel: 39-02-8844-1	Rev: $111,685
Bus: *International banking.*	Fax: 39-02-8844-3638	Emp: 28,600
	www.bancaintesa.it	

    INTESABCI SPA
    One William Street, New York, NY   10004

CEO: Claudio Marchiori, SVP	Tel: (212) 607-3500	%FO: 100
Bus: *International banking services.*	Fax: (212) 809-2124	Emp: 150

    INTESABCI SPA
    One Embarcadero Center, San Francisco, CA   94111

CEO: Joseph Raffetto	Tel: (415) 439-6780
Bus: *International banking services.*	Fax: (415) 439-6780

● **ITALDESIGN S.p.A.**
Via A Grandi 11, I-10024 Moncalieri, Turin, Italy

CEO: Giorgetto Giugiaro, Chmn.	Tel: 39-01-689-1611	Rev: $85
Bus: *Automotive research and construction.*	Fax: 39-01-647-0858	Emp: 750
	www.italdesign.it	

I.D.C. ITALDESIGN CALIFORNIA, INC.
6481 Oak Canyon Road, Irvine, CA   92620

CEO: Dr. Renato Sconfienza, Pres. & CEO	Tel: (949) 654-0070	%FO: 100
Bus: *Automotive engineering, models and prototype building.*	Fax: (949) 654-0077	Emp: 50

• IVECO SPA
Via Puglia 35, I-10156 Turin, Italy

CEO: Giancarlo Boschetti, Pres.	Tel: 39-01-6872111	Rev: $6,000
Bus: *Manufacturer of industrial vehicles.*	Fax: 39-01-2482180	Emp: 32,200
	www.iveco.com	

IVECO TRUCKS OF NORTH AMERICA
3433 Progress Drive, PO Box 8527, Bensalem, PA   19020-0407

CEO: John J. Sherlock, Mgr.	Tel: (215) 639-9696	%FO: 100
Bus: *Distributor of spare parts.*	Fax: (215) 639-0962	Emp: 20

• KINOMAT SPA
Via Enrico Fermi 635, I-21042 Caronno P, Italy

CEO: Antonio Rivara, Pres.	Tel: 39-02-9645-1154	
Bus: *Mfr. coil winding equipment and automation systems.*	Fax: 39-02-9645-1173	Emp: 80
	www.kinomat.com	

EPM CORPORATION
8866 Kelso Drive, Baltimore, MD   21221

CEO: Kumar Rajasekhara, Pres.	Tel: (410) 686-7800	%FO: 100
Bus: *Mfr. coil winding equipment and automation systems.*	Fax: (410) 686-4662	Emp: 40

• LOMBARDINI MOTORI S.p.A.
Via F.lli Manfredi 6, I-42100 Reggio Emilia, Italy

CEO: Dr. Gianni Borghi, Gen Mgr.	Tel: 39-0522-5801	
Bus: *Mfr. industrial diesel engines.*	Fax: 39-0522-580295	Emp: 1,300
	www.lombardini.it	

LOMBARDINI USA INC.
2150 Boggs Rd., Bldg 300, Ste. 300, Duluth, GA   30136

CEO: Jim McPherson, Pres.	Tel: (770) 623-3554	%FO: 100
Bus: *Distribute industrial diesel engines.*	Fax: (770) 623-8833	Emp: 20

● **LUIGI LAVAZZA SPA**

Corso Novara 59, I-10154 Turin, Italy

CEO: Robert Consonni, CEO — Tel: 39-01-123-981 — Rev: $666

Bus: *Producer of coffee beans.* — Fax: 39-01-123-98324 — Emp: 500

www.lavazza.it

> **LAVAZZA PREMIUM COFFEES CORP.**
>
> 3 Park Avenue, 35th Fl., New York, NY   10016
>
> CEO: Ennio Ranaboldo, Mgr. — Tel: (212) 725-8800 — %FO: 100
>
> Bus: *Producer of coffee beans.* — Fax: (212) 725-9475

● **LUXOTTICA GROUP, S.p.A.**

Via Vacozzena, 10, I-32021 Agordo Belluno, Italy

CEO: Leonardo Del Vecchio, Pres. — Tel: 39-0437-63746 — Rev: $2,275

Bus: *Mfr. eyeglass frames, retail eyecare and* — Fax: 39-0437-63840 — Emp: 19,400
clothing stores. — www.luxottica.it

> **AVANT GARDE OPTICS INC.**
>
> 44 Harbor Park Drive, Port Washington, NY   11050
>
> CEO: Claudio Del Vecchio, Pres. — Tel: (516) 484-3800 — %FO: 100
>
> Bus: *Distribution, eyeglass frames.* — Fax: (516) 484-4481 — Emp: 326

> **LENSCRAFTERS INC.**
>
> 8650 Governor's Hill Drive, Cincinnati, OH   43068
>
> CEO: Cliff Bartow, COO — Tel: (513) 583-6000 — %FO: 100
>
> Bus: *Eyeglass frames, eyecare retail* — Fax: (513) 583-6388 — Emp: 12,800
> *stores.*

● **MANFREDI**

Via Pietro Verri 4, I-20121 Milan, Italy

CEO: Giulio Manfredi, Pres. — Tel: 39-02-760-22001

Bus: *Mfr. jewelry.* — Fax: 39-02-760-21984 — Emp: 110

www.manfredi.it

> **MANFREDI**
>
> 737 Madison Avenue, New York, NY   10021
>
> CEO: Michelle Sober, Mgr. — Tel: (212) 734-8710 — %FO: 100
>
> Bus: *Distributor/sale jewelry.* — Fax: (212) 734-4741 — Emp: 16

● **MANULI RUBBER INDUSTRIES SPA**

Viale Lombardia 51, I-20047 Brugherio Milan, Italy

CEO: Aldo Occan, Mng. Dir. — Tel: 39-039-212-31 — Rev: $350

Bus: *Mfr. of rubber components and systems* — Fax: 39-039-212-3382 — Emp: 3,050
for transmitting fluids. — www.manulirubber.com

MANULI OIL & MARINE USA INC.
2788 East Oakland Park Blvd., Ft. Lauderdale, FL   3306
CEO: Dardanio Manuli   Tel: (954) 561-3777   %FO: 100
Bus: *Mfr. of rubber components and*   Fax: (954) 563-0644
    systems for transmitting fluids.

● **MARAZZI GRUPPO CERAMICHE SPA**
V.le Regina Pacis 39, I-41049, Sassuoto, Italy
CEO: Filippo Marazzi, Chmn.   Tel: 39-0536-860111   Rev: $700
Bus: *Mfr. ceramic tile.*   Fax: 39-0536-860644   Emp: 4,000
    www.marazi.it

    AMERICAN MARAZZI INC.
    359 Clay Road, Sunnyvale, TX   75182
    CEO: Daniel J. Lasky, Pres.   Tel: (972) 226-0110   %FO: 100
    Bus: *Mfr. ceramic tile.*   Fax: (972) 226-2265

    MONARCH CERAMIC TILE INC., DIV. AMERICAN MARAZZI
    834 Rickwood Road, PO Box 999, Florence, AL   35631
    CEO: Daniel J. Lasky, Pres.   Tel: (256) 764-6181   %FO: 100
    Bus: *Mfr. ceramic tile.*   Fax: (256) 760-8686

● **MARCOLIN SPA**
Localita Villanova 4, I-32013 Longarone Belluno, Italy
CEO: Cirillo Marcolin, CEO   Tel: 39-04-3777-7111   Rev: $113
Bus: *Mfr. designer eyewear.*   Fax: 39-04-3777-7282   Emp: 1,100
    www.marcolin.com

    MARCOLIN USA INC.
    1407 Coral Way, Miami, FL   33145-2876
    CEO: Thora Thoroddsen   Tel: (888) 627-2654   %FO: 100
    Bus: *Mfr./sales designer eyewear.* Fax: (888) 627-2671

● **ANGELA MISSONI**
Via L. Rossi 52, I-21040 Sumirago, Italy
CEO: Angela Missoni, CEO   Tel: 39-0331-988-000
Bus: *Women's wear.*   Fax: 39-0331-909-955
    www.missoni.com

    MISSONI STORES
    821 Madison Avenue, New York, NY   10021
    CEO: Angela Missoni, CEO   Tel: (212) 980-7691   %FO: 100
    Bus: *Women's wear.*   Fax: (212) 980-7691

● **MONTEDISON SPA**

3 Piazzetta Maurilio Bossi, I-20121 Milan, Italy

CEO: Luigi Lucchini, Chmn.

Bus: *Holding company for agribusiness, chemicals, electric power, oil and gas.*

Tel: 39-02-6270-1
Fax: 39-02-6270-4610
www.montedisongroup.com

Rev: $14,300
Emp: 32,978

   AUSIMONT USA INC.

   10 Leonards Lane, Thorofare, NJ   08086

   CEO: Michael Coates, Pres.

   Bus: *Mfr. specialty chemicals.*

   Tel: (609) 853-8119
   Fax: (609) 853-3929

   %FO: 100

   ERIDANIA BEGHIN-SAY AMERICA

   110 West Berry Street, Fort Wayne, IN   46802

   CEO: Carl Hausmann, CEO

   Bus: *Engaged in agribusiness.*

   Tel: (219) 425-5100
   Fax: (219) 425-5330

   %FO: 100

   TECNIMONT, INC.

   3122 North Braeswood Blvd., Houston, TX   77025

   CEO: Christine Aringo

   Bus: *Engaged in engineering and construction.*

   Tel: (713) 666-4783
   Fax: (713) 664-0253

   %FO: 100

● **OLIVETTI GROUP**

Via Jervis 77, I-10015 Ivrea, Italy

CEO: Enrico Bondi, CEO

Bus: *Mfr. office automation systems date processing products.*

Tel: 39-0125-5200
Fax: 39-0125-522524
www.olivetti.it

Rev: $28,350
Emp: 120,975

   OLIVETTI USA, INC.

   765 US Highway 202, PO Box 6945, Bridgewater, NJ   08807

   CEO: Salomon Suwalsky, Pres. & CEO

   Bus: *Sales/marketing computers, office machinery, products and supplies.*

   Tel: (908) 526-8200
   Fax: (908) 526-8405

   %FO: 100

● **OTIM S.p.A.**

Via Porro Lambertenghi, 9, Milan, Italy

CEO: Mario Carniglia, Pres.

Bus: *International freight forwarder.*

Tel: 39-02-699121
Fax: 39-02-69912245
www.otim.it

Rev: $5,976
Emp: 39,350

   OTIM USA INC.

   476 Broadway, 5th Fl., New York, NY   10013

   CEO: Mayra Villamil, Mgr.

   Bus: *International freight forwarder.*

   Tel: (212) 941-1122
   Fax: (212) 941-1919

   %FO: 100

● **PARMALAT FINANZIARIA S.p.A.**
Piazza Ercules 9, I-20122 Milan, Italy
CEO: Stefano Tanzi, CEO   Tel: 39-02-806-8801   Rev: $6,900
Bus: *Produces milk and dairy products.*   Fax: 39-02-869-3863   Emp: 38,300
www.parmalat.com

    PARMALAT USA CORPORATION
    520 Main Street, Wallington, NJ 07057
    CEO: Aido Uva, CEO   Tel: (973) 777-2500   %FO: 100
    Bus: *Mfr. milk and dairy products.*   Fax: (973) 777-7648

● **PELUSO & ASSOCIATI**
Via Panama 74, I-00198 Rome, Italy
CEO: Giovanni Peluso, Partner   Tel: 39-06-884-0881
Bus: *International law firm.*   Fax: 39-06-884-1717   Emp: 35

    GIOVANNI PELUSO & ASSOCIATES
    375 Park Avenue, 2nd Fl., New York, NY 10152
    CEO: Giovanni Peluso, Partner   Tel: (212) 980-3368   %FO: JV
    Bus: *International law firm.*   Fax: (212) 980-3378   Emp: 5

● **FABIO PERINI S.p.A.**
Via per Mugnano, I-55100 Lucca, Italy
CEO: Uwe Langfeld, CEO   Tel: 39-0538-9725
Bus: *Mfr./sales tissue converting equipment.*   Fax: 39-0583-972610   Emp: 450
www.fabio-perini.it

    PERINI AMERICA, INC.
    3060 South Ridge Road, Green Bay, WI 54304
    CEO: Michael Drage, Pres. & CEO   Tel: (920) 336-5000   %FO: 100
    Bus: *Sales/distribution of tissue*   Fax: (920) 337-0363
           converting equipment.

● **PERLIER SPA**
Corso Monforte 36, I-20122 Milan, Italy
CEO: Maria Elena Giraudi, Mng. Dir.   Tel: 39-02-76-008-125   Rev: $23
Bus: *Develops bath and body treatments and*   Fax: 39-02-76-009-207   Emp: 300
cosmetic products.

    PERLIER KELEMATA
    436 West Broadway, New York, NY 10012
    CEO: Marie Elena Giraudi   Tel: (212) 737-5353   %FO: 100
    Bus: *Develops bath and body*   Fax: (212) 925-8088
           treatments and cosmetic products.

● **PIAGGIO SPA**

25 Viale Rinaldo Piaggio, I-56025 Pontedera, Italy

CEO: Stefano Rosselli Del Turco, CEO	Tel: 39-587-27-2111	Rev: $976
Bus: *Mfr. Vespa scoters.*	Fax: 39-587-27-2274	Emp: 500
	www.piaggio.com	

   PIAGGIO USA, INC.

   20003 South Rancho Way, Rancho Dominguez, CA   90220

CEO: Giancario Fantappie, Pres.	Tel: (310) 604-3980	%FO: 100
Bus: *Mfr. Vespa scooters.*	Fax: (310) 604-3989	

● **PIRELLI S.p.A.**

Viale Sarca, 222, I-20126 Milan, Italy

CEO: Marco Tronchetti Provera, CEO	Tel: 39-02-64421	Rev: $6,459
Bus: *Mfr. tires, rubber products and plastics. (49% JV with Société Internationale Pirelli SA, Basel, Switzerland).*	Fax: 39-02-6442-3300 www.pirelli.com	Emp: 38,210

   PIRELLI ARMSTRONG TIRE CORPORATION

   500 Sargent Drive, New Haven, CT   06536

CEO: Carlo Bianconi, Pres.	Tel: (860) 784-2200	%FO: 100
Bus: *Mfr. tires, tubes, rubber products.*	Fax: (860) 784-2408	Emp: 3,300

   PIRELLI CABLE CORPORATION

   700 Industrial Drive, Lexington, SC   29072

CEO: Kevin E. Riddett, Pres.	Tel: (803) 951-4000	%FO: 100
Bus: *Mfr. tires, tubes, rubber products.*	Fax: (803) 951-1069	Emp: 100

● **POLIFORM, S.p.A.**

Via Montessanto No. 28, Inverigo, Italy

CEO: Alberto Spinelli, Chmn.	Tel: 39-031-69951	
Bus: *Mfr./sales of premium closet systems, wall units, beds and dining room furniture.*	Fax: 39-031-699444 www.poliform.it	

   POLIFORM CHICAGO

   1379 The Merchandise Mart, Chicago, IL   60654

CEO: David Yarom, Pres.	Tel: (312) 321-9600	%FO: 100
Bus: *Sales/distribution of premium closet systems, wall units, beds and dining room furniture.*	Fax: (312) 321-9797	

POLIFORM LOS ANGELES

8687 Melrose Avenue, Ste. G-280, West Hollywood, CA   90069

CEO: David Yarom, Pres.

Bus: *Sales/distribution of premium closet systems, wall units, beds and dining room furniture.*

Tel: (310) 360-1451

Fax: (310) 360-1453

%FO: 100

POLIFORM MANHASSET

1492 Northern Boulevard, Manhasset, NY   11030

CEO: David Yarom, Pres.

Bus: *Sales/distribution of premium closet systems, wall units, beds and dining room furniture.*

Tel: (516) 869-6600

Fax: (516) 869-6565

%FO: 100

POLIFORM USA, INC.

150 East 58th Street, New York, NY   10155

CEO: David Yarom, Pres.

Bus: *Sales/distribution of premium closet systems, wall units, beds and dining room furniture.*

Tel: (212) 421-1220

Fax: (212) 421-1600

%FO: 100

● RAI INTERNATIONAL, SUB. OF IRI SPA

Via V. Veneto, I-00187 Rome, Italy

CEO: Roberto Morrione, Dir.

Bus: *Government owned; engaged in television and radio broadcasting.*

Tel: 39-06-33-17-2269

Fax: 39-06-33-17-0767

www.rai.it

RAI CORPORATION

1350 Avenue of the Americas, 21st Fl., New York, NY   10019

CEO: Marina Giordano

Bus: *Global connections television.*

Tel: (212) 468-2500

Fax: (212) 956-3174

%FO: 100

● RATTI SPA

Via Madonna 30, Guanzate Como, Italy

CEO: Francois Baufume, CEO

Bus: *Mfr. printed silk fabrics.*

Tel: 39-031-3-5351

Fax: 39-031-3-535351

www.ratti.it

Rev: $132

Emp: 1,000

RATTI USA INC.

8 West 40th Street, New York, NY   10018

CEO: Donatella Ratti

Bus: *Mfr. printed silk fabrics.*

Tel: (212) 391-2191

Fax: (212) 391-0115

%FO: 100

● **RCS EDITORI S.p.A.**
Via A Rizzoli 2, I-20132 Milan, Italy
CEO: Giorgio Fattori, Chmn. Tel: 39-02-22584
Bus: *Publishing, printing and operation of* Fax: 39-02-5065390 Emp: 6,900
bookstores. www.rcs.it

  RCS RIZZOLI CORPORATION
  300 Park Avenue South, New York, NY 10010
  CEO: Antonio Polito, Chmn. & Pres. Tel: (212) 387-3400 %FO: 100
  Bus: *Publishers; bookstores.* Fax: (212) 387-3535 Emp: 280

● **RECORDATI SPA**
Via Matteo Civitali 1, I-20148 Milan, Italy
CEO: Giovanni Recordati, CEO Tel: 39-02-4878-71 Rev: $335
Bus: *Mfr. pharmaceuticals and generic drugs.* Fax: 39-02-4007-3747 Emp: 1,700
  www.recordati.com

  RECORDATI CORPORATION
  110 Commerce Drive, Allendale, NJ 07401
  CEO: Jim Alexander Tel: (201) 236-9000 %FO: 100
  Bus: *Sales and distribution of generic* Fax: (201) 236-9404
  drugs.

● **RITRAMA, S.p.A**
Via della Guerrina 108, I-20052 Monza Milan, Italy
CEO: Tomas Rink, CEO Tel: 39-03-983-9215
Bus: *Mfr. graphic art supplies and pressure* Fax: 39-03-983-4718
sensitive film. www.ritrama.it

  RITRAMA DURAMARK, INC.
  341 Eddy Road, Cleveland, OH 44108
  CEO: Daryl Hanzel, Pres. Tel: (216) 851-2300 %FO: 100
  Bus: *Sales/distribution of graphic art* Fax: (216) 851-1938 Emp: 159
  supplies and pressure sensitive
  film and self adhesive materials.

● **SAES GETTERS SPA**
Viale Italia 77, I-0020 Lainate Milan, Italy
CEO: Paolo della Porta, CEO Tel: 39-02-931781 Rev: $162
Bus: *Mfr. industrial equipment and* Fax: 39-02-93178320 Emp: 1,200
components. www.saesgetters.com

FST CONSULTING
4175 Santa Fe Road, San Luis Obispo, CA   93401
CEO: Giulio Canale, Mng. Dir.   Tel: (805) 783-1155
Bus: *Mfr. industrial equipment and*   Fax: (805) 786-1155
  components.

GETTER CORPORATION OF AMERICA
5604 Valley Belt Road, Cleveland, OH   44102
CEO: Giulio Canale, Mng. Dir.   Tel: (216) 661-8488
Bus: *Mfr. industrial equipment and*   Fax: (216) 661-8796
  components.

SAES GETTERS USA INC.
1122 E. Cheyenne Mountain Blvd., Colorado Springs, CO   80906
CEO: Giulio Canale, Mng. Dir.   Tel: (719) 576-3200
Bus: *Mfr. industrial equipment and*   Fax: (719) 576-5025
  components.

SAES PURE GAS, INC
4175 Santa Fe Road, San Luis Obispo, CA   93401
CEO: Giulio Canale, Mng. Dir.   Tel: (805) 541-9299   %FO: 100
Bus: *Mfr. industrial equipment and*   Fax: (805) 541-9399
  components.

TRACE ANALYTICAL
3617 A. Edison Way, Menlo Park, CA   94025
CEO: Giulio Canale, Mng. Dir.   Tel: (650) 364-6885
Bus: *Mfr. industrial equipment and*   Fax: (650) 364-6887
  components.

• SAFILO SPA
Zona Industriale, VII Strada 15, I-35129 Padua, Italy
CEO: Vittorio Tabacchi, CEO   Tel: 39-049-698-5111   Rev: $646
Bus: *Mfr. eyeglass frames, sunglasses and*   Fax: 39-049-869-9875   Emp: 3,375
  goggles.   www.safilo.com

CARRERA SPORT INC.
111 Lewis Street, Ketchum, ID   83340
CEO: Vittorio Tabacchi, Pres.   Tel: (208) 726-6542   %FO: 100
Bus: *Mfr./sales goggles, sunglasses,*   Fax: (208) 727-6576
  helmets and headgear

SAFILO USA INC.
801 Jefferson Road, Parsippany, NJ   07054-3753
CEO: Claudio Gottardi, Pres. & CEO   Tel: (972) 952-2800   %FO: 100
Bus: *Mfr./sales eyeglass frames,*   Fax: (973) 560-1598
  sunglasses and goggles.

● **SAIPEM SPA**

Via Martiridi Cefalonia 67, San Donato Milanese, I-20097 Milan, Italy

CEO: Pietro Fracno Tali, CEO   Tel: 39-02-5201

Bus: *Provides drilling and construction*   Fax: 39-02-5203-3460   Emp: 10,700
services to the oil and gas industries.   www.saipem.it

     SAIPEM USA INC.

     15950 Park Row, Houston, TX   77084

     CEO: Hugh O'Donnell, COO   Tel: (281) 552-5700   %FO: 100

     Bus: *Provides drilling and construction*   Fax: (281) 552-5915
     services to the oil and gas
     industries.

● **SAN PAOLO IMI**

Corso Galileo Ferraris 54/A, I-10129 Torino, Italy

CEO: Luigi Arcuti, Chmn.   Tel: 39-01-5551000

Bus: *Banking and financial services.*   Fax: 39-01-555-6650   Emp: 1,400
     www.sanpaolo.it

     SAN PAOLO BANK USA INC.

     444 South Flower Street, Ste. 4550, Los Angeles, CA   90071

     CEO: Donald W. Brown   Tel: (213) 489-3100   %FO: 100

     Bus: *Engaged in banking and financial*   Fax: (213) 622-2514
     services

     SAN PAOLO BANK USA INC.

     245 Park Avenue, Suite 3500, New York, NY   10021

     CEO: Daniela Giberti, Mng..Dir.   Tel: (212) 326-1114   %FO: 100

     Bus: *Engaged in banking and financial*   Fax: (212) 326-1179
     services

● **SAN PELLEGRINO S.p.A.**

17-23 Via Castelvetro, I-20154 Milan, Italy

CEO: Dr. Paolo Luni, Pres.   Tel: 39-02-319-7275

Bus: *Sale and distribution of beverages.*   Fax: 39-02-319-7294   Emp: 1,000
     www.sanpellegrino.it

     SAN PELLEGRINO c/o PERRIER GROUP

     777 West Putnam Avenue, Greenwich, CT   06836

     CEO: Kim Jeffrey   Tel: (203) 863-0200   %FO: 100

     Bus: *Sale and distribution of beverages.*   Fax: (203) 863-0200

- **SANPAOLO IMI SPA**

Piazza San Carlo 156, I-10121 Turin, Italy
CEO: Luigi Maranzana, Mng. Dir.   Tel: 39-01-5551
Bus: *Engaged in banking.*   Fax: 39-01-513826
                                         www.sanpaolo.it

> **SANPAOLO IMI BANK**
>
> 245 Park Avenue, New York, NY   10167
> CEO: Giuseppe Cuccurese, EVP   Tel: (212) 692-3000   %FO: 100
> Bus: *Banking services.*   Fax: (212) 599-5303

- **SASIB SPA**

Via la Spezia, 241/A, I-43040 Parma, Italy
CEO: Alberto Piaser   Tel: 39-0521-999-1   Rev: $582
Bus: *Mfr. labeling and bottling machines.*   Fax: 39-0521-959-009   Emp: 3,100
                                         www.sasib.com

> **SASIB NORTH AMERICA, INC.**
>
> 808 Stewart Avenue, Plano, TX   75074
> CEO: Greg Harris   Tel: (972) 424-5041   %FO: 100
> Bus: *Mfr. labeling and bottling*   Fax: (972) 424-5041
>   *machines.*

- **SEAT PAGINE GIALLE SPA**

Via A. Saffi 18, I-10138 Turin, Italy
CEO: Paolo Dal Pino, CEO   Tel: 39-011-435-2600   Rev: $1,270
Bus: *Mfr. bicycle parts.*   Fax: 39-011-435-2722   Emp: 2,450
                                         www.seat.it

> **NET CREATIONS, INC.**
>
> 379 W. Broadway, Ste. 202, New York, NY   10012
> CEO: Rosalind B. Resnick, CEO   Tel: (212) 625-1370   %FO: 100
> Bus: *Mfr./sales bicycle parts.*   Fax: (212) 274-9266

- **SMW AUTOBLOK SPA**

Via Duca d'Aosta 24, I-10040 Capri-Torino, Italy
CEO: Walter Bronzino, Sales Dir.   Tel: 39-0963-2020
Bus: *Mfr. power chucks.*   Fax: 39-0963-2288   Emp: 250
                                         www.smwautoblok.com

> **SMW AUTOBLOK CORPORATION**
>
> 285 Egidi Drive, Wheeling, IL   60090
> CEO: Sidney N. Roth, Pres.   Tel: (847) 215-0591   %FO: 100
> Bus: *Sale/service power chucks,*   Fax: (847) 215-0594   Emp: 21
>   *hydrotating cylinders, steady rests.*

- **SOGEFI SPA**
Via Ulisse Barbieri 1, I-46100 Mantova, Italy
CEO: Emanuele Bosio, Mgr.   Tel: 39-0376-2031   Rev: $635
Bus: *Mfr. auto parts, including air and oil*   Fax: 39-0376-374-733   Emp: 5,150
filters and mufflers and horns.   www.sogefi.it

     ANSA AUTOMOTIVE PARTS DISTRIBUTORS INC.
     PO Box 10215, Macon, GA   31297
     CEO: Emanuele Bosio, Mgr.   Tel: (912) 788-6653   %FO: 100
     Bus: *Mfr./sales auto parts, including air*   Fax: (912) 784-1694
     and oil filters and mufflers and
     horns.

     ANSA AUTOMOTIVE PARTS DISTRIBUTORS INC.
     6079 Rickenbacker Road, Commerce, CA   90040
     CEO: Emanuele Bosio, Mgr.   Tel: (800) 841-1916   %FO: 100
     Bus: *Mfr./sales auto parts, including air*   Fax: (800) 841-1916
     and oil filters and mufflers and
     horns.

- **STARHOTELS SPA**
Viale Belfiore 27, I-50144 Florence, Italy
CEO: Ferruccio Fabri, Pres. & CEO   Tel: 39-055-36921
Bus: *Four-star hotel chain.*   Fax: 39-055-36924   Emp: 1,000
          www.starhotels.it

     THE MICHELANGELO HOTEL (STARHOTELS)
     152 West 51 Street, New York, NY   10019
     CEO: Elisabetta Fabri, Pres.   Tel: (212) 765-1900   %FO: 100
     Bus: *178 room, 4-star hotel.*   Fax: (212) 581-7618   Emp: 100

- **STUDIO LEGALE BISCONTI**
Via Bissolati, 76, I-00187 Rome, Italy
CEO: Giuseppe Bisconti, Mng. Ptnr.   Tel: 39-06-479-881
Bus: *International law firm.*   Fax: 39-06-487-2070

     STUDIO LEGALE BISCONTI
     730 Fifth Avenue, New York, NY   10019
     CEO: Andre Bisconti, Mng. Ptnr.   Tel: (212) 956-9400   %FO: 100
     Bus: *International law firm.*   Fax: (212) 956-9405

- **TARGETTI SANKEY, SPA**
Via Pratese, 164, I-50145 Florence, Italy
CEO: Paolo Targetti, Chmn.   Tel: 39-055-379-11   Rev: $99
Bus: *Mfr. specialty lighting and related*   Fax: 39-055-379-1266   Emp: 575
products.   www.targetti.it

TARGETTI-TIVOLI, INC.
1513 E. St. Gertrude Place, Santa Ana, CA   92705
CEO: Terrence C. Walsh, CEO   Tel: (714) 957-6101   %FO: 100
Bus: *Mfr. specialty lighting and related*   Fax: (714) 957-6101
products.

● TELECOM ITALIA S.p.A.
34 Via Bertola, I-20122 Turin, Italy
CEO: Roberto Colaninno, Chmn.   Tel: 39-01-1551-41   Rev: $27,223
Bus: *Telecommunication services.*   Fax: 39-01-1532-269   Emp: 114,670
                                        www.telecomitalia.it

TELECOM ITALIA
499 Park Avenue, 23rd Fl., New York, NY   10022-1240
CEO: Giulio Senni, Pres.   Tel: (212) 755-5280   %FO: 100
Bus: *Telecommunications services.*   Fax: (212) 755-5766   Emp: 20

● TREVI-FINANZIARIA INDUSTRIALE SpA
201 via Largo, I-7023 Cesena, Italy
CEO: Davide Trevisani, Chmn, & Pres.   Tel: 39-0547-319300
Bus: *International engineering and*   Fax: 39-0547-319313
architectural services.   www.trevispa.com

TREVI - ICOS CORPORATION
250 Summer Street - 4th Floor, Boston, MA   02210
CEO: Nino Catalano, CEO   Tel: (617) 345-9955   %FO: 100
Bus: *International engineering and*   Fax: (617) 345-0041
architectural services.

● UNI CREDITO ITALIANO S.p.A.
Piazza Cordusio 2, I-20123 Milan, Italy
CEO: Alessandro Profumo, CEO   Tel: 39-02-8862-1   Rev: $3,530
Bus: *Commercial banking services.*   Fax: 39-02-8862-3034   Emp: 13,580
                                        www.credit.it

BANCA CRT SPA
500 Park Avenue, New York, NY   10022
CEO: Giorgio Cuccolo, EVP   Tel: (212) 980-0690   %FO: 100
Bus: *International banking services.*   Fax: (212) 980-0809   Emp: 2

CREDITO ITALIANO - Chicago Agency
2 Prudential Pl., 180 N. Stetson St., Ste. 1310, Chicago, IL   60601-6713
CEO: Paolo Garlanda, VP & Rep.   Tel: (312) 946-1111   %FO: 100
Bus: *International commercial banking* Fax: (312) 946-1112   Emp: 4
services.

CREDITO ITALIANO

375 Park Avenue, 2nd Fl., New York, NY   10152-0099

CEO: Carmelo Mazza, Sr.VP & Gen.Mgr.   Tel: (212) 546-9600   %FO: 100

Bus: *International commercial banking services.*   Fax: (212) 546-9675   Emp: 63

CREDITO ITALIANO - Los Angeles Agency

500 South Grand Avenue, Ste. 1600, Los Angeles, CA   90071

CEO: Riccardo Gallo, VP & Rep.   Tel: (213) 622-2787   %FO: 100

Bus: *International commercial banking services.*   Fax: (213) 623-3799   Emp: 3

UNI CREDITO ITALIANO SPA

500 Park Avenue, New York, NY   10022

CEO: Carmelo Mazza, SVP   Tel: (212) 980-0690   %FO: 100

Bus: *International banking services.*   Fax: (212) 980-0809

● **GIANNI VERSACE**

Via Manzoni 38, I-20121 Milan, Italy

CEO: Santo Versace, Chmn.   Tel: 39-02-760-931   Rev: $425

Bus: *Design/mfr./sale clothing, perfume, ceramics and tiles for home furnishings.*   Fax: 39-02-760-93823   Emp: 1,500
www.versace.it

PRATO VERDE

645 Fifth Avenue, New York, NY   10022

CEO: Giuseppe Celio, Pres.   Tel: (212) 753-8002   %FO: 100

Bus: *Design/mfr./distribute fashion clothing, fragrances and retail boutiques.*   Fax: (212) 752-6072   Emp: 200

VERSACE COMPANY

1200 Morris Turnpike, Ste. 123, Short Hills, NJ   07078

CEO: Donatella Versace   Tel: (973) 379-9871   %FO: 100

Bus: *Design/mfr./sale clothing, perfume, ceramics and tiles for home furnishings.*   Fax: (973) 379-9875

VERSACE COMPANY

60 Post Street, San Francisco, CA   94109

CEO: Donatella Versace   Tel: (415) 616-0604   %FO: 100

Bus: *Design/mfr./sale clothing, perfume, ceramics and tiles for home furnishings.*   Fax: (415) 732-7058

VERSACE COMPANY
One Premium Outlets 265, Wrentham, MA   02093
CEO: Donatella Versace   Tel: (508) 384-2254   %FO: 100
Bus: *Design/mfr./sale clothing,*   Fax: (508) 384-2390
      perfume, ceramics and tiles for
      home furnishings.

VERSACE COMPANY
125 Westchester Avenue, Ste. 1210, White Plains, NY   10604
CEO: Donatella Versace   Tel: (914) 684-1394   %FO: 100
Bus: *Design/mfr./sale clothing,*   Fax: (914) 684-1295
      perfume, ceramics and tiles for
      home furnishings.

VERSACE COMPANY
11211 120th Avenue, Ste. 6, Pleasant Prairie, WI   53158
CEO: Donatella Versace   Tel: (262) 857-4511   %FO: 100
Bus: *Design/mfr./sale clothing,*   Fax: (262) 857-4331
      perfume, ceramics and tiles for
      home furnishings.

VERSACE COMPANY
1866 94th Drive, Vero Beach, FL   32960
CEO: Donatella Versace   Tel: (561) 794-7622   %FO: 100
Bus: *Design/mfr./sale clothing,*   Fax: (561) 794-7590
      perfume, ceramics and tiles for
      home furnishings.

VERSACE COMPANY
160 North Gulph Road, Unit 5217, King of Prussia, PA   19405
CEO: Donatella Versace   Tel: (610) 337-4774   %FO: 100
Bus: *Design/mfr./sale clothing,*   Fax: (610) 332-4780
      perfume, ceramics and tiles for
      home furnishings.

VERSACE JEANS COUTURE
755 Washington Avenue, Miami, FL   33131
CEO: Donatella Versace   Tel: (305) 532-5993   %FO: 100
Bus: *Sales of women's clothing.*   Fax: (305) 672-4606

● **WAM S.p.A.**
Via Cavour 338-1, I-41030 Pontemotta-Cavezzo, Italy
CEO: Valner Marchesini, Pres.   Tel: 39-0535-618111
Bus: *Mfr. industrial and bulk handling*   Fax: 39-0535-618226   Emp: 850
      equipment.   www.wam.it

WAM CORPORATION OF AMERICA

75 Boulderbrook Circle, Lawrenceville, GA 30045

CEO: Massimo Magnani, Pres.	Tel: (770) 339-6767	%FO: JV
Bus: *Mfr. dust collectors and screw conveyors; distribute industrial and bulk handling equipment.*	Fax: (770) 339-4727	Emp: 15

● **ZAMBON GROUP, S.p.A.**

Via Lillo del Duca 10, I-20091 Bresso, Italy

CEO: Roberto Rettani, CEO	Tel: 39-02-66-5241	Rev: $380
Bus: *Prescription/pharmaceutical products, fine chemicals and home health products.*	Fax: 39-02-66-524534 www.zambongroup.com	Emp: 2,600

ZAMBON CORPORATION

150 Meadowlands Pkwy., Secaucus, NJ 07094

CEO: George Griffiths, Gen. Mgr.	Tel: (201) 422-9000	%FO: 100
Bus: *Prescription and OTC pharmaceutical product development and licensing.*	Fax: (201) 422-9000	Emp: 17

Japan

- **ACHILLES CORPORATION**

  22 Daikyo-machi, Shinjuku-ku, Tokyo 160-8885, Japan

  CEO: Takeshi Yagi, Pres.   Tel: 81-3-3322-2170   Rev: $990

  Bus: *Manufacture plastic film and roll*   Fax: 81-3-3225-4013   Emp: 2,444
  products and inflatable boat products.   www.achillesusa.com

  ### ACHILLES USA INC.

  10230 Norwalk Blvd., Santa Fe Springs, CA 90670

  CEO: M. Kuwashima, Mgr.   Tel: (562) 944-4560   %FO: 100

  Bus: *Manufacture plastic film and*   Fax: (562) 944-0511
  sheeting and inflatable boat
  products..

  ### ACHILLES USA INC.

  355 Murray Hill Parkway, East Rutherford, NJ 07073

  CEO: M. Higashizono, Mgr.   Tel: (201) 438-6400   %FO: 100

  Bus: *Manufacture plastic film and*   Fax: (201) 438-2618
  sheeting and inflatable boat
  products..

  ### ACHILLES USA INC.

  1407 80th Street SW, Everett, WA 98203

  CEO: Hideo Nishikimi, Pres.   Tel: (425) 353-7000   %FO: 100

  Bus: *Manufacture plastic film and*   Fax: (425) 347-5785   Emp: 185
  sheeting.

- **ADVANTEST CORPORATION**

  4-1, Nishi-Shinjuku-ku 2 chome, Tokyo 163-0880, Japan

  CEO: Hiroshi Oura, Pres.   Tel: 81-3-3342-7500   Rev: $1,443

  Bus: *Research and development of electronic*   Fax: 81-3-3342-7510   Emp: 4,317
  measurement and testing devices.   www.advantest.co.jp

  ### ADVANTEST AMERICA CORPORATION

  1100 Busch Parkway, Buffalo Grove, IL 60089-4503

  CEO: Hiroj Agata, Pres.   Tel: (847) 634-2552   %FO: 100

  Bus: *Research and development of*   Fax: (847) 520-4717
  electronic measurement and
  testing devices.

ADVANTEST AMERICA INC.
3201 Scott Blvd., Santa Clara, CA 95054
CEO: Nick Konidaris, Pres.   Tel: (408) 988-7700   %FO: 100
Bus: *Sales/distribution of electronic*   Fax: (408) 987-0691
      measurement and testing devices.

● **AISIN SEIKI CO. LTD.**
2-1, Asahi-machi 2 chome, Kariya City, Aichi 448-8650, Japan
CEO: Kanshiro Toyoda, Pres.   Tel: 81-5-6624-8801   Rev: $8,152
Bus: *Mfr./sales automotive components and*   Fax: 81-5-6624-8894   Emp: 11,061
      home industrial equipment.   www.aisin.co.jp

AISIN USA MFG., INC.
1700 East Fourth Street, Seymour, IN 47274
CEO: Tsutomo Yasui, Pres.   Tel: (812) 523-1969   %FO: 100
Bus: *Sales/distribution of auto*   Fax: (812) 523-1984
      components and home industrial
      equipment.

AISIN WORLD CORPORATION OF AMERICA
24330 Garnier Street, Torrance, CA 90505
CEO: M. Yasui, Pres.   Tel: (310) 326-8581   %FO: 100
Bus: *Sales/distribution of auto*   Fax: (310) 533-8271
      components and home industrial
      equipment.

AMRA AMERICA, INC
1044 Woodridge Avenue, Ann Arbor, MI 48105
CEO: Takashi Omitsu, Pres.   Tel: (734) 930-2560   %FO: 100
Bus: *R&D automotive technology.*   Fax: (734) 930-9957

● **AIWA CO., LTD.**
2-11, Ikenohata 1-chome, Taito-ku Tokyo 110-8710, Japan
CEO: Kozo Ohsone, CEO   Tel: 81-3-3827-2420   Rev: $3,000
Bus: *Mfr. audio, video and computer*   Fax: 81-3-3827-2888   Emp: 10,885
      equipment.   www.aiwa.co.jp

AIWA AMERICA INC.
800 Corporate Drive, Mahwah, NJ 07430
CEO: Hideki Tafuku, Pres. & CEO   Tel: (201) 512-3600   %FO: 100
Bus: *Mfr. audio, video and computer*   Fax: (201) 512-3705   Emp: 172
      equipment.

● **AJINMOTO COMPANY, INC.**

15-1 Kyobashi 1-chome, Chuo-ku Tokyo 104, Japan

CEO: Kunio Egashira, Pres.   Tel: 81-3-5250-8111   Rev: $7,315

Bus: *Seasonings, amino acids, oil products*   Fax: 81-3-5250-8293   Emp: 16,991
      and other foodstuffs and specialty   www.ajinomoto.co.jp
      chemicals.

    AJINMOTO USA INC.

    1251 Ave. of the Americas, Ste. 2320, New York, NY   10020

    CEO: Hiroshi Kurihari, Pres.   Tel: (212) 899-4765   %FO: 100

    Bus: *Mfr. food products, amino acids*   Fax: (212) 899-4794
        and specialty chemicals.

● **ALL NIPPON AIRWAYS CO., LTD.**

510, Hanedakuko 3-chome, Ohta-ku Tokyo 144-0041, Japan

CEO: Kichisaburo Nomura, Pres. & CEO   Tel: 81-3-5756-5665   Rev: $8,600

Bus: *Commercial air transport and hotel*   Fax: 81-3-3592-3069   Emp: 14,640
      services.   www.ana.co.jp

    ALL NIPPON AIRWAYS COMPANY, LTD.

    1251 Avenue of the Americas, 8th Fl., New York, NY   10111

    CEO: Jiro Miyake, VP   Tel: (212) 840-3700   %FO: 100

    Bus: *International air transport*   Fax: (212) 840-3704   Emp: 50
        services.

● **ALPINE ELECTRONICS INC.**

1-1-8 Nishi-Gotanda, Shinagawa-ku, Tokyo 141-8501, Japan

CEO: Seizo Ishiguro, Pres.   Tel: 81-3-3494-1101

Bus: *Mfr. audio, visual, navigation and*   Fax: 81-3-3494-1109
      security products for the mobile   www.alpine.co.jp
      environment.

    ALPINE ELECTRONICS MANUFACTURING OF AMERICA INC.

    421 North Emerson Avenue, Greenwood, In   46142

    CEO: Bernie Pierce, Pres.   Tel: (317) 881-7700   %FO: 100

    Bus: *Mfr. high-performance mobile*   Fax: (317) 887-2415
        electronics.

    ALPINE ELECTRONICS OF AMERICA, INC.

    19145 Gramercy Place, Torrance, CA   90501

    CEO: Boone Sugimura, Pres.   Tel: (310) 326-8000   %FO: 100

    Bus: *Mfr. high-performance mobile*   Fax: (310) 533-0369
        electronics.

● **ALPS ELECTRIC CO., LTD.**

1-7 Yukigaya-otsuka-cho, Ota-Ku, Tokyo 145, Japan

CEO: Masataka Kataoka, Pres.   Tel: 81-3-3726-1211   Rev: $4,979

Bus: *Mfr. electric component and switches*   Fax: 81-3-3728-1741   Emp: 28,077
      and communications devices.   www.alps.co.jp

     ALPS AUTOMOTIVE, INC.

     1500 Atlantic Blvd.,, Auburn Hills, MI   48326

     CEO: John Keegan, Pres. & CEO   Tel: (248) 391-2500   %FO: 100

     Bus: *Design, develop, and mfr. custom*   Fax: (248) 391-2847
        switches, remote keyless entry
        systems, communication bus
        products, clocksprings, sensors,
        and standard components for
        automotive applications.

     ALPS ELECTRIC USA, INC.

     5295 Hellyer Avenue, San Jose, CA   95138

     CEO: Tak Sato, Pres. & CEO   Tel: (408) 432-6400   %FO: 100

     Bus: *Sales/distribution of computers,*   Fax: (408) 226-7301
        computer peripherals and
        components.

● **AMADA LTD.**

200 Ishida-shi, Kanagawa 259-1196, Japan

CEO: E. Emori, Chmn.   Tel: 81-463-96-1111   Rev: $1,020

Bus: *Engineering/machinery production.*   Fax: 81-463-93-1323   Emp: 2,360
                              www.amada.co.jp

     AMADA AMERICA, INC.

     7025 Firestone Blvd., Buenos Park, CA   90621

     CEO: Takashi Hirate, Pres.   Tel: (714) 739-2111   %FO: 100

     Bus: *Mfr./sales machine tools.*   Fax: (714) 739-4099

     AMADA CUTTING TECHNOLOGIES INC.

     14849 East Northam Street, La Mirada, CA   90638

     CEO: Toshi Ichimure, Pres.   Tel: (714) 670-1704   %FO: 100

     Bus: *Mfr. metal cutting machines.*   Fax: (714) 670-2017

     AMADA ENGINERING & SERVICE CO., INC.

     14921 East Northam Street, La Mirada, CA   90638

     CEO: Y. Kageyama, Pres.   Tel: (714) 670-2111   %FO: 100

     Bus: *Provides services to the sheet*   Fax: (714) 690-3204
        metal fabrication industry.

• ANRITSU CORPORATION

5-10-27 Minamiazabu, Minato-ku, Tokyo 106, Japan

CEO: Yasuo Nakagawa, Pres.	Tel: 81-3-3446-1111	Rev: $1,017
Bus: *Mfr./sales optical and electronic measuring instruments, communications systems and computer peripherals.*	Fax: 81-3-3442-0235 www.anritsu.co.jp	Emp: 2,666

ANRITSU COMPANY

1155 East Collins Blvd., Ste. 100, Richardson, TX   75081

CEO: Phil Bowen, Pres.	Tel: (972) 644-1777	%FO: 100
Bus: *Mfr./sales electronic test instruments, systems and components.*	Fax: (972) 644-3416	

ANRITSU COMPANY

312 West First Street, Ste. 300, Sanford, FL   32771

CEO: John Lewis	Tel: (407) 321-5130	%FO: 100
Bus: *Engaged in sales and service of electronic test instruments, systems and components.*	Fax: (407) 330-2018	

ANRITSU COMPANY

490 Jarvis Drive, Morgan Hill, CA   95037

CEO: Mark Evans, Pres.	Tel: (408) 778-2000	%FO: 100
Bus: *Mfr./sales electronic test instruments, systems and components.*	Fax: (408) 277-8408	

ANRITSU COMPANY

10 New Maple Avenue, Ste. 305, Pine Brook, NJ   07058-0836

CEO: Jack Landau	Tel: (973) 227-8999	%FO: 100
Bus: *Engaged in sales and service of electronic test instruments, systems and components.*	Fax: (973) 575-0092	

ANRITSU COMPANY

4625 Alexander Drive, Alpharetta, GA   30022

CEO: Mark R. Evans, Pres.	Tel: (678) 566-0454	%FO: 100
Bus: *Engaged in sales and service of electronic test instruments, systems and components.*	Fax: (678) 566-1776	

• AOZORA BANK (FORMERLY THE NIPPON CREDIT BANK, LTD.)

13-10, Kudan-kita 1-chome, Chiyoda-ku, Tokyo 102-8660, Japan

CEO: Yoshinobu Kotera, Dir.	Tel: 81-3-3263-1111	Rev: $6,164
Bus: *Credit banking, financing and investment banking.*	Fax: 81-3-3264-7025 www.ncb.co.jp	Emp: 2,290

AOZORA BANK
101 East 52nd Street, New York, NY 10022
CEO: Kkihiro Yamasaki, Rep.   Tel: (212) 751-7330   %FO: 100
Bus: *Financial banking services.*   Fax: (212) 751-0987

● **ARAKAWA CHEMICAL INDUSTRIES LTD.**
3-7 Hiranomachi, 1-chome Chuo-ku, Osaka 541, Japan
CEO: Shuhei Ishibe, Pres.   Tel: 81-6 209 8580
Bus: *Mfr./supplier rosin ester, absorbents,*   Fax: 81-6-209-8542   Emp: 684
hydrocarbon and special resins.   www.arakawahem.co.jp

    ARAKAWA CHEMICAL USA, INC.
    625 North Michigan Ave., Ste.1700, Chicago, IL 60611
    CEO: Mack M. Harashima, Pres.   Tel: (312) 642-1750   %FO: 100
    Bus: *Distributor/supplier rosin ester,*   Fax: (312) 642-0089   Emp: 21
    absorbents, hydrocarbon and
    special resins.

● **ASACA CORPORATION**
3-2-28 Asahigaoka, Hino-shi, Tokyo 191-0086, Japan
CEO: Nobunori Shigezaki, Pres.   Tel: 81-42-583-1211
Bus: *Mfr. tape and disc storage disc systems* Fax: 81-42-586-9000
and audio and video equipment. (JV of www.asaca.co.jp
ShibaSoku Co.)

    ASACA/SHIBA SOKU CORP.
    400 Corporate Circle, Ste. G, Golden, CO 80401
    CEO: Noboru Note, VP   Tel: (303) 278-1111   %FO: JV
    Bus: *Sales and services of professional* Fax: (303) 278-0303
    color monitors.

● **THE ASAHI BANK, LTD.**
1-2 Otemachi 1-chome, Chiyoda-ku, Tokyo 100-8106, Japan
CEO: Yukiuo Yanase, Pres.   Tel: 81-3-3287-2111   Rev: $8,847
Bus: *International banking services.*   Fax: 81-3-3212-3484   Emp: 12,688
www.asahibank.co.jp

    THE ASAHI BANK, LTD.
    *c/o Showa Leasing Inc., 405 Park Avenue 8th Fl., New York, NY 10022
    CEO: Minoru Takahashi, Mgr.   Tel: (212) 909-4444   %FO: 100
    Bus: *International banking services.*   Fax: (212) 909-4441

    THE ASAHI BANK, LTD.
    190 South LaSalle Street, Ste. 2350, Chicago, IL 60603
    CEO: Kenichi Nakabayashi, Mgr.   Tel: (312) 606-1000   %FO: 100
    Bus: *International banking services.*   Fax: (312) 606-1010

THE ASAHI BANK, LTD.
350 South Grand Avenue, Ste. 3800, Los Angeles, CA 90017
CEO: Naoke Ogake Tel: (213) 473-3300 %FO: 100
Bus: *International banking services.* Fax: (213) 624-0172

● **ASAHI BREWERIES, LTD.**
23-1 Azumabashi 1 chome, Sumida-ku, Tokyo 130-8602, Japan
CEO: Shigeo Fukuchi, Pres. Tel: 81-3-5608-5126 Rev: $8,113
Bus: *Engaged in production and marketing* Fax: 81-3-5608-7121 Emp: 4,195
of alcoholic beverages and soft drinks. www.asahibeer.co.jp

ASAHI BEER USA INC.
20000 Mariner Avenue, Ste. 300, Torrance, CA 90503
CEO: Yoshiteru Aso, Pres. Tel: (310) 921-4000 %FO: 100
Bus: *Market and sales of Asahi beer.* Fax: (310) 921-4001

● **ASAHI GLASS COMPANY, LTD.**
12-1, Yurakucho 1-chrome Chiyoda-ku, Tokyo 100-8405, Japan
CEO: Shinya Ishizu, Pres. & CEO Tel: 81-3-3218-5408 Rev: $11,915
Bus: *Mfr. flat and fabricated glass, chemicals* Fax: 81-3-3218-7805 Emp: 43,217
and ceramics and produces optical www.agc.co.jp
lenses.

AA GLASS CORPORATION
3050 East Victoria Street, Compton, CA 90221
CEO: T. Ichkawa, Pres. Tel: (310) 631-1123 %FO: 100
Bus: *Distributor auto safety glass parts.* Fax: (310) 632-7272

AG SODA CORPORATION
2201 Water Ridge Parkway, Ste. 400, Charlotte, NC 28217
CEO: Hiroyki Okuno, Pres. Tel: (704) 329-7610 %FO: 100
Bus: *Production facility.* Fax: (704) 357-6308

AGA CHEMICALS, INC.
2201 Water Ridge Pkwy., Ste. 400, Charlotte, NC 28217
CEO: Tashiaki Hayashi, Pres. Tel: (704) 329-7600 %FO: 100
Bus: *Marketing/sales for chemical* Fax: (704) 357-6308
products.

AMA GLASS
1400 Lincoln Street, PO Box 929, Kingsport, TN 37662
CEO: Alan Hunt Tel: (423) 229-7200 %FO: 100
Bus: *Mfr. mirrors and double glazing* Fax: (423) 229-7211
glass.

AP TECHNOGLASS

350 Magnolia Drive, Mt. Pleasant, TN   38474

CEO: Jay Strong, Pres.   Tel: (615) 379-0124   %FO: 100

Bus: *Mfr. automotive glass.*   Fax: (615) 379-0930

AP TECHNOGLASS COMPANY

PO Box 819, Bellefontaine, OH   43311

CEO: Takaaki Yamaguchi, Pres.   Tel: (513) 599-3131   %FO: 100

Bus: *Sale/distribution of augo safety*   Fax: (513) 599-3322
    glass.

ASAHI GLASS AMERICA, INC.

2201 Water Ridge Pkwy., Ste. 400, Charlotte, NC   28217

CEO: Joseph Cafaro Sr., Pres. & CEO   Tel: (704) 357-1106   %FO: 100

Bus: *U.S. headquarters office.*   Fax: (704) 357-6328

BELLTECH

700 West Lake Avenue, Bellefontaine, OH   43311

CEO: Takaaki Yamaguchi, Pres.   Tel: (513) 599-3774   %FO: 100

Bus: *Mfr. automotive glass.*   Fax: (513) 599-5478

● **ASAHI KASEI CORPORATION**

Hibiya-Mitsui Bldg., 1-2, Yurakucho, 1-chome, Chiyoda-ku, Tokyo 100, Japan

CEO: Dr. Kazumoto Yamamoto, Pres.   Tel: 81-3-3507-2060   Rev: $10,000

Bus: *Mfr. chemicals, medical products,*   Fax: 81-3-3507-2495   Emp: 27,792
    plastics, fibers, textiles and construction   www.asahi-kasei.co.jp
    materials.

ASAHI KASEI AMERICA, INC.

535 Madison Avenue, 33rd Fl., New York, NY   10022-4212

CEO: Yoshihisa Iwasaki, Pres.   Tel: (212) 371-9900   %FO: 100

Bus: *Sales/distribution of chemicals,*   Fax: (212) 371-9050
    medical products and housing and
    construction materials.

● **ASAHI MUTUAL LIFE INSURANCE COMPANY**

7-3 Nishi-Shinjuku 1-chome, Shinjuku-ku, Tokyo 163-8611, Japan

CEO: Yuzuru Fujita, Pres.   Tel: 81-3-3342 3111   Rev: $11,002

Bus: *Life insurance.*   Fax: 81-3-3346-9397   Emp: 12,150
    www.asahi-life.co.jp

ASAHI AMERICA INC.

400 Park Avenue, 20th Fl., New York, NY   10022

CEO: Shinji Koma, Pres.   Tel: (212) 752-0202   %FO: 100

Bus: *Investment research.*   Fax: (212) 752-0419   Emp: 13

● **ASAHI OPTICAL COMPANY, LTD.**

11-1 Nagata-cho 1-chome, Chiyoda-ku, Tokyo 100, Japan

CEO: Tohru Matsumoto, Pres.	Tel: 81-3-3960-5151	Rev: $1,150
Bus: *Mfr. Pentax cameras, binoculars,*	Fax: 81-3-3960-5151	Emp: 2,363
lenses, photo, video components and	www.pentax.co.jp	
accessories.		

   PENTAX CORPORATION

   35 Inverness Drive East, Englewood, CO   80112

CEO: Andy Fukano, Pres.	Tel: (303) 799-8000	%FO: 100
Bus: *Sales/distribution of cameras,*	Fax: (303) 790-1131	
binoculars, lenses, etc.		

   PENTAX PRECISION INSTRUMENTS CORP.

   30 Ramland Road, Orangeburg, NY   10962

CEO: Ed Cochrane, Mgr.	Tel: (845) 365-0708	%FO: 100
Bus: *Mfr. video and fiber endoscopy*	Fax: (845) 365-0822	
equipment.		

   PENTAX TECHNOLOGIES CORP.

   100 Technology Drive, Ste. 200, Broomfield, CO   80021

CEO: Flip Dalfonso, VP	Tel: (303) 460-1600	%FO: 100
Bus: *Sales/distribution of cameras,*	Fax: (303) 460-1628	
binoculars, lenses, etc.		

● **ASATSU INC.**

7-16-12 Ginza, Chuo-ku, Tokyo 104-8172, Japan

CEO: Tsuromu Takeda, Pres. & COO	Tel: 81-3-3547-2111	Rev: $263
Bus: *International advertising agency.*	Fax: 81-3-3547-2345	Emp: 2,038
	www.asatsu-dk.co.jp	

   ASATSU AMERICA

   420 Lexington Avenue, 7th Fl., New York, NY   10017

CEO: Shinya Miyata, Pres.	Tel: (212) 210-6100	%FO: 100
Bus: *International advertising agency.*	Fax: (212) 210-6100	

   ASATSU AMERICA

   1411 West 190th Street, Suite 570, Gardena, CA   90248

CEO: Shinya Miyata, Pres.	Tel: (310) 630-3600	%FO: 100
Bus: *International advertising agency.*	Fax: (310) 630-3620	Emp: 23

● **ASICS CORPORATION JAPAN**

1-1 Minatojima-Nakamachi, 7-chome, Chuo-ku, Kobe 650-8555, Japan

CEO: Yoshiyuki Takahashi, Pres. & CEO	Tel: 81-78-303-6888	Rev: $631
Bus: *Mfr. sporting goods & health related*	Fax: 81-78-303-2244	Emp: 1,481
products.	www.asics.co.jp	

ASICS TIGER CORPORATION
16275 Laguna Canyon Road, Irvine, CA   92618
CEO: Richard Bourne, EVP | Tel: (949) 453-8888 | %FO: 100
Bus: *Mfr./sale/promotion athletic* | Fax: (949) 453-0292 | Emp: 186
footwear, apparel, accessories &
skiwear.

● ASO PHARMACEUTICAL COMPANY, LTD.
91 Tsukure, Kikuyo, Kikuchi, Kumamoto 869-11, Japan
CEO: Yakushi Kuki, Pres. | Tel: 81-96-232-2131
Bus: *Mfr. health care and first aid products.* | Fax: 81-96-232-2137 | Emp: 300
www.aso-pharm.co.jp

ASO CORPORATION
300 Sarasota Center Blvd., Sarasota, FL   34240
CEO: John D. Macaskill, CEO | Tel: (941) 379-0300 | %FO: 100
Bus: *Mfr. first aid products and* | Fax: (941) 378-9040 | Emp: 40
adhesive bandages.

● BANK OF JAPAN
2-1-1, Hongoku-cho, Nihonbashi, Chuo-ku, CPO 203, 100-91 Tokyo, Japan
CEO: Akira Nagashima, Deputy Governor, | Tel: 81-3-3279-1111
Int'l
Bus: *Government; central bank.* | Fax: 81-3-3245-0538 | Emp: 1,300
www.boj.or.jp

BANK OF JAPAN
One Chase Manhattan Plaza, New York, NY   10005
CEO: I. Horii, Mgr. | Tel: (212) 269-6566 | %FO: 100
Bus: *Government; central bank.* | Fax: (212) 269-6127 | Emp: 5

● BANK OF TOKYO MITSUBISHI, LTD.
2-7-1 Marunouchi 2-chome, Chiyoda-ku, Tokyo 100, Japan
CEO: Satoru Kishi, Pres. | Tel: 81-3-3240-1111 | Rev: $31,198
Bus: *Wholesale and retail banking.* | Fax: 81-3-3240-4197 | Emp: 18,000
www.btm.co.jp

BANK OF TOKYO MITSUBISHI, LTD.
1251 Avenue of the Americas, New York, NY   10022
CEO: Keizo Iijma, Pres. | Tel: (212) 782-4000 | %FO: 100
Bus: *International banking services.* | Fax: (212) 782-6439 | Emp: 1,300

BTM CAPITAL CORPORATION
125 Summer Street, Boston, MA   02110
CEO: David E. Hale, Pres. | Tel: (617) 573-9000 | %FO: 100
Bus: *Financial services.* | Fax: (617) 345-5688

BTM INFORMATION SERVICES INC.
Harborside Financial Center, Plaza III, 5th Fl., Jersey City, NJ   07311
CEO: Masahiro Wasa, Pres.   Tel: (201) 413-8150
Bus: *Financial services.*   Fax: (201) 413-8980

BTM LEASING AND FINANCE, INC.
1251 Avenue of the Americas, New York, NY   10020
CEO: Sabro Sano, Pres.   Tel: (212) 782-4496   %FO: 100
Bus: *Financial services.*   Fax: (212) 782-4006   Emp: 18

● THE BANK OF YOKOHAMA, LTD.
1-1, Minatomirai 3-chome, Nishi-ku, Yokohama 220, Japan
CEO: Sadaaki Hirasawa, Pres.   Tel: 81-45-225-1111   Rev: $4,200
Bus: *General commercial banking services.*   Fax: 81-45-225-1160   Emp: 6,000
                                           www.boy.co.jp

BANK OF YOKOHAMA, LTD
*c/o City of Yokohama, NY Rep. Off., 1251 Ave of Americas Ste. 4850, New York, NY
10020
CEO: Yasuhiro Ohashi, Rep.   Tel: (212) 575-9106   %FO: 100
Bus: *International commercial banking*   Fax: (212) 575-9153   Emp: 43
  services.

● BRIDGESTONE CORPORATION
10-1 Kyobashi 1-chome, Chuo-ku, Tokyo 104-8340, Japan
CEO: Yoichiro Kaizaki, Pres. & CEO   Tel: 81-3-3567-0111   Rev: $18,020
Bus: *Mfr. rubber tires, chemical and*   Fax: 81-3-3535-2553   Emp: 101,490
  industrial products, sporting goods and   www.bridgestone.co.jp
  marine equipment.

AMERICAN TIRE AND SERVICE COMPANY
2550 West Golf Road, Rolling Meadows, IL   60008
CEO: Larry Magee, Pres.   Tel: (847) 981-2200   %FO: 100
Bus: *Mfr. tires.*   Fax: (847) 981-2351

BRIDGESTONE AIRCRAFT TIRE
7775 Northwest 12th Street, Miami, FL   33126
CEO: Den Bucher, Pres.   Tel: (305) 592-3530   %FO: 100
Bus: *Mfr. tires.*   Fax: (305) 592-0485

BRIDGESTONE APM COMPANY
1800 Industrial Drive, Findlay, OH   45839
CEO: Bob Creamer, Pres.   Tel: (419) 423-9552   %FO: 100
Bus: *Mfr. vibration isolating rubber for*   Fax: (419) 423-1232
  autos.

BRIDGESTONE METALPHA INC.

1200 Industrial Park Road, Clarksville, TN 37040

CEO: Tora Toraiwa, Pres. Tel: (931) 552-2112 %FO: 100
Bus: *Mfr. tires.* Fax: (931) 920-4585

BRIDGESTONE SPORTS

15320 Industrial Park Boulevard NE, Covington, GA 30019

CEO: M. Moteki, Pres. Tel: (770) 787-7400 %FO: 100
Bus: *Mfr. tires.* Fax: (770) 786-6416

BRIDGESTONE/FIRESTONE

50 Century Boulevard, Nashville, TN 37214

CEO: John Lampe, CEO Tel: (615) 872-5000 %FO: 100
Bus: *Mfr./sales commercial truck tires.* Fax: (615) 872-1599 Emp: 45,000

BRIDGESTONE/FIRESTONE

One Town Square, Ste. 1470, Southfield, MI 48076

CEO: Art Stuart, Pres. Tel: (248) 208-3600 %FO: 100
Bus: *Sales of tires to original* Fax: (248) 208-3635
 equipment auto manufacturers.

BRIDGESTONE/FIRESTONE OFF ROAD TIRE COMPANY

565 Marriott Drive, Ste. 600, Nashville, TN 37214

CEO: Manny Cicero, Pres. Tel: (615) 231-5700 %FO: 100
Bus: *Mfr./sales tires for construction* Fax: (615) 231-5796
 and mining industries.

BRIDGESTONE/FIRESTONE RESEARCH

1200 Firestone Parkway, Akron, OH 44317

CEO: Itsuo Miyake, Pres. Tel: (330) 379-7570 %FO: 100
Bus: *Engaged in research and* Fax: (330) 379-7530
 development.

FIRESTONE AGRICULTURAL TIRE COMPANY

730 East Second Street, Des Moines, IA 50309

CEO: Chuck Ramsey, Pres. Tel: (515) 283-1440 %FO: 100
Bus: *Mfr. tires for agricultural* Fax: (515) 283-1610
 equipment.

FIRESTONE BUILDING PRODUCTS COMPANY

525 Congressional Blvd., Carmel, IN 46032

CEO: David Grass, Pres. Tel: (317) 575-7000 %FO: 100
Bus: *Mfr. building products.* Fax: (317) 575-7100

FIRESTONE FIBERS & TEXTILES COMPANY
PO Box 1369, Kings Mountain, NC   28086

CEO: Jaggy Anand, Pres.	Tel: (704) 734-2100	%FO: 100
Bus: *Mfr. industrial fibers and textiles.*	Fax: (704) 734-2104	

FIRESTONE INDUSTRIAL PRODUCTS COMPANY
12650 Hamilton Crossing Blvd., Carmel, IN   46032-5400

CEO: Gary Reynolds, Pres.	Tel: (317) 818-8600	%FO: 100
Bus: *Mfr. air springs.*	Fax: (317) 818-8645	

FIRESTONE POLYMERS COMPANY
381 West Wilbeth Road, Akron, OH   44319

CEO: John Schremp, Pres.	Tel: (330) 379-7781	%FO: 100
Bus: *Mfr. rubber products.*	Fax: (330) 379-4422	

FIRESTONE TUBE COMPANY
2700 East Main Street, Russellville, AR   72802

CEO: David Moore, Mgr.	Tel: (501) 968-1443	%FO: 100
Bus: *Mfr. tire tubes.*	Fax: (501) 964-0266	

• BROTHER INDUSTRIES LTD.
15-1 Nae Shiro-cho, Mizuho-ku, Nagoya 467, Japan

CEO: Yoshihiro Yasui, Pres.	Tel: 81-52-824-2511	Rev: $2,656
Bus: *Mfr. typewriters, microwave ovens, facsimile machines, home & industrial sewing machinery.*	Fax: 81-52-824-3398 www.brother.com	Emp: 3,674

BROTHER INTERNATIONAL CORPORATION
100 Somerset Corporate Blvd., Bridgewater, NJ   08807-0911

CEO: Toshikazu Koike, Pres.	Tel: (908) 704-1700	%FO: 49
Bus: *U.S. headquarters. Sales/marketing parent company products.*	Fax: (908) 704-8235	Emp: 600

• CANON, INC.
30-2 Shimomaruko 3-chome, Ohta-ku, Tokyo 146-8501, Japan

CEO: Fujio Mitarai, Pres. & CEO	Tel: 81-3-3758-2111	Rev: $24,400
Bus: *Mfr. office equipment, cameras, video, audio, medical & broadcast equipment.*	Fax: 81-3-5482-5130 www.canon.co.jp	Emp: 79,800

AFFILIATED BUSINESS SOLUTIONS, INC.
300 Commerce Square Boulevard, Burlington, NJ   08016

CEO: Dennis Uhniat, Pres.	Tel: (609) 387-8700	%FO: 100
Bus: *Mfr. business machines.*	Fax: (609) 387-8700	

AMBASSADOR BUSINESS SOLUTIONS, INC.
425 North Martingale Road, Ste. 1400, Schaumburg, IL   60173
CEO: Emily Reynolds, Pres.   Tel: (847) 706-3400   %FO: 100
Bus: *Sales business machines.*   Fax: (847) 706-3400

ASTRO BUSINESS SOLUTIONS, INC.
110 West Walnut Street, Gardena, CA   90248
CEO: Ollie Hatch Jr., Pres.   Tel: (310) 217-3000   %FO: 100
Bus: *Sales business machines.*   Fax: (310) 715-7050

CANON COMPUTER SYSTEMS, INC.
2995 Red Hill Avenue, Costa Mesa, CA   92626
CEO: Hiro Goto, VP   Tel: (714) 438-3000   %FO: 100
Bus: *Mfr. computer peripherals.*   Fax: (714) 438-3099

CANON FINANCIAL SERVICES, INC.
200 Commerce Square Boulevard, Burlington, NJ   08016
CEO: Albert Smith, Pres.   Tel: (609) 387-8555   %FO: 100
Bus: *Financial services.*   Fax: (609) 386-5181

CANON LATIN AMERICA, INC.
6505 Blue Lagoon Drive, Ste. 325, Miami, FL   33126
CEO: Nobuo Ijichi, Pres.   Tel: (305) 260-7400   %FO: 100
Bus: *Sales of cameras and office*   Fax: (305) 260-7409
     equipment.

CANON RESEARCH CENTER AMERICA, INC.
3300 North First Street, San Jose, CA   95134
CEO: Vataka Hirai, Pres.   Tel: (408) 468-2810   %FO: 100
Bus: *Research of computer systems and*   Fax: (408) 468-2810
     software.

CANON USA, INC.
One Canon Plaza, Lake Success, NY   11042
CEO: Kinya Uchida, Pres. & CEO   Tel: (516) 488-6700   %FO: 100
Bus: *Mfr./distributor office equipment,*   Fax: (516) 328-5069   Emp: 8,200
     cameras, video, audio, medical &
     broadcast equipment.

CANON USA, INC.
2110 Washington Blvd., Ste. 150, Arlington, VA   22204
CEO: Kinya Uchida, Pres. & CEO   Tel: (703) 807-3400   %FO: 100
Bus: *Mfr./distributor office equipment.*   Fax: (703) 807-3029

CANON, INC.
12000 Canon Boulevard, Newport News, VA 23606
CEO: Kenji Mori, Pres.   Tel: (757) 881-6000   %FO: 100
Bus: *Mfr. copy machines, printers and*   Fax: (757) 881-9507
toner.

MCS BUSINESS SOLUTIONS, INC.
125 Park Avenue, New York, NY 10017
CEO: Wayne Frahn, Pres.   Tel: (212) 557-2400   %FO: 100
Bus: *Markets business machines.*   Fax: (212) 557-2400

SINTAKS
408 East Fourth Street, Bridgeport, PA 19405
CEO: Timothy Wenhold, Pres.   Tel: (610) 277-1750   %FO: 100
Bus: *Provides information technology*   Fax: (610) 270-0951
sales and support.

SOUTH TECH, INC.
PO Box 126, Tappahannock, VA 22560
CEO: Naoki Iwami, Pres.   Tel: (804) 443-8000   %FO: 100
Bus: *Mfr. molded and pressed parts for*   Fax: (804) 443-1000
office equipment.

● **CASIO COMPUTER COMPANY, LTD.**
6-2 Honmachi, 1-Shinjuku-ku, Tokyo 151-8543, Japan
CEO: Kazuo Kashio, Pres.   Tel: 81-3-5334-4111   Rev: $3,860
Bus: *Mfr. electronic consumer products;*   Fax: 81-3-5334-4887   Emp: 17,800
calculators, watches,   www.casio.co.jp
telecommunications equipment, cameras
and computers.

CASIO INC.
570 Mt. Pleasant Avenue, Dover, NJ 07801
CEO: Gary Rado, Pres.   Tel: (973) 361-5400   %FO: 100
Bus: *Mfr./distribution electronic*   Fax: (973) 361-3819
consumer products; calculators,
watches, telecommunications
equipment, cameras and
computers.

● **CBC CO. LTD. (FORMERLY CHUGAI BOYEKI CO LTD.)**
2-15-13 Tsukishima, Chuo-ku, Tokyo 104-0052, Japan
CEO: U. Doi Shoten, Pres.   Tel: 81-3-3536-4500
Bus: *International trading and manufacturer*   Fax: 81-3-3536-4780
and distribution in optical and   www.cbc.co.jp
electronics markets.

CBC CO. AMERICA

55 Mall Drive, Commack, NY   11725

CEO: Ron Johnson   Tel: (631) 864-9700   %FO: 100

Bus: *International trading and*   Fax: (631) 864-9710
manufacturer and distribution in
optical and electronics markets.

CBC CO. AMERICA

20521 Earl Street, Torrance, CA   90503

CEO: Ron Johnson   Tel: (310) 793-1500

Bus: *International trading and*   Fax: (310) 793-1506
manufacturer and distribution in
optical and electronics markets.

● **CENTRAL JAPAN RAILWAY COMPANY**

1-1-4, Meieki, Nakamura-ku, Nagoya, Aichi 450-8610, Japan

CEO: Yoshiyuki Kasai   Tel: 81-3-3274-9727   Rev: $11,580

Bus: *Passenger railway.*   Fax: 81-3-5255-6780   Emp: 22,075
www.jr-central.co.jp

CENTRAL JAPAN RAILWAY COMPANY

300 South Grand Avenue, Ste. 3830, Los Angeles, CA   90071

CEO: Katsuhiko Ichikawa, Mgr.   Tel: (213) 617-7353   %FO: 100

Bus: *Representative office for*   Fax: (213) 617-7464
passenger railway.

● **THE CHIBA BANK, LTD.**

1-2 Chiba-Minato, Chuo-ku, Chiba 260, Japan

CEO: Takashi Tamaki, Chmn. & CEO   Tel: 81-43-3245-1111   Rev: $2,276

Bus: *General commercial banking services.*   Fax: 81-43-3242-1735   Emp: 4,771
www.chibabank.co.jp

THE CHIBA BANK, LTD.

1133 Avenue of the Americas, New York, NY   10036

CEO: Keiji Yoshioka, Gen. Mgr.   Tel: (212) 354-7777   %FO: 100

Bus: *International commercial banking*   Fax: (212) 354-8575   Emp: 18
services.

● **CHORI COMPANY, LTD.**

4-7 Kawaramachi 2-chome, Chuo-ku, Osaka 540-8603, Japan

CEO: Hisao Nakamura, Pres.   Tel: 81-6-228-5071   Rev: $5,000

Bus: *Textiles, chemical products and*   Fax: 81-6-228-5611   Emp: 1,218
machinery.   www.chori.co.jp

CHORI AMERICA INC
1180 Avenue of the Americas, New York, NY   10119-5498
CEO: Shumpei Iuchi, Pres.   Tel: (212) 563-3264   %FO: 100
Bus: *Textiles, chemical products and*   Fax: (212) 736-6392
machinery

● **CHUBU ELECTRIC POWER CO. INC.**
1 Higashi-shinmachi, Higashi-ku, Nagoya 461-8680, Japan
CEO: Hiroji Ota, Pres. & CEO   Tel: 81-52-951-8211   Rev: $20,545
Bus: *Supplies electricity.*   Fax: 81-52-962-4624   Emp: 19,785
www.chuden.co.jp

CHUBU ELECTRIC POWER COMPANY INC.
900 17th Street NW, Ste. 1220, Washington, DC   20006
CEO: Kazunori Kuze, Rep.   Tel: (202) 775-1960   %FO: 100
Bus: *Supplies electric power.*   Fax: (202) 331-9256

● **CHUGAI PHARMACEUTICAL CO., LTD.**
1-9 Kyobashi 2-chome, Chuo-ku, Tokyo 104-8301, Japan
CEO: Osamu Nagayama, Pres. & CEO   Tel: 81-3-3281-6611   Rev: $1,702
Bus: *Mfr. pharmaceuticals for bone and* Fax: 81-3-3281-2828   Emp: 4,800
blood disorders and infectious diseases. www.chugai-pharm.co.jp

CHUGAI PHARMA USA INC.
444 Madison Avenue, 12th Fl., New York, NY   10022
CEO: Yuji Suzawa, Pres.   Tel: (212) 486-7780   %FO: 100
Bus: *Mfr. pharmaceuticals for bone and* Fax: (212) 355-3253
blood disorders and infectious
diseases.

GEN-PROBE INCORPORATED
10210 Genetic Center Drive, San Diego, CA   92121
CEO: Henry L. Nordhoff, Pres. & CEO   Tel: (858) 410-8000   %FO: 100
Bus: *Engaged in DNA probe technology.* Fax: (858) 410-8000

● **CHUGOKU BANK LTD.**
15-20 Marunouchi 1-chome, Okayama 700, Japan
CEO: Akira Nagashima, Pres.   Tel: 81-86-223-3111   Rev: $1,220
Bus: *International banking services.* Fax: 81-86-234-6582   Emp: 3,578
www.chugin.co.jp

CHUGOKU BANK LTD.
*One World Trade Center, Ste. 9007, New York, NY   10048
CEO: Kozo Nakamura, Gen. Mgr.   Tel: (212) 321-3111   %FO: 100
Bus: *General banking services.*   Fax: (212) 321-3367

● THE CHUO MITSUI TRUST & BANKING CO., LTD.

7-1 Kyobashi 1-chome, Chuo-ku, Tokyo 104-8345, Japan

CEO: Hisao Muramoto, Chmn.　　Tel: 81-3-3562-6900　　Rev: $1,480

Bus: *Engaged in securities transactions, real*　Fax: 81-3-3562-6902　　Emp: 5,279
estate brokerage and appraisal services.　www.chuotrust.co.jp

THE CHUO MITSUI TRUST & BANKING COMPANY LTD.

*Two World Trade Center, Ste. 8322, New York, NY　10048

CEO: Hideki Iwakami, Pres.　　Tel: (212) 938-0100　　%FO: 100

Bus: *Engaged in securities*　　Fax: (212) 466-1140
transactions, real estate brokerage
and appraisal services.

● CITIZEN WATCH COMPANY, LTD.

6-1-12,Tanashi-cho, Nishi Tokyo-shi, Tokyo 188-8511, Japan

CEO: Hiroshi Haruta, Pres.　　Tel: 81-3-42466-1231　　Rev: $3,250

Bus: *Mfr. wrist-watches, information and*　Fax: 81-3-42466-1280　　Emp: 17,530
electronic equipment and industrial　www.citizen.co.jp
equipment and instruments.

CITIZEN AMERICA CORPORATION

831 South Douglas Drive, Ste. 121, El Segundo, CA　90245

CEO: Tetsuo Kasahara, Pres.　　Tel: (310) 643-9825　　%FO: 100

Bus: *Information equipment and*　　Fax: (310) 643-9825　　Emp: 35
service/repair of watches.

CITIZEN SERVICE HDQRTS.

1000 West 190th Street, Torrance, CA　90502

CEO: M. Maruyama, Pres.　　Tel: (310) 215-9660　　%FO: 100

Bus: *Manufactures calculators and*　　Fax: (310) 781-9157
electronic equipment.

CITIZEN WATCH COMPANY OF AMERICA

1200 Wall Street West, Lyndhurst, NJ　07071

CEO: Laurence Grunstein, Pres.　　Tel: (201) 438-8150　　%FO: 100

Bus: *U.S. headquarters office.*　　Fax: (201) 438-4161

MARUBENI CITIZEN-CINCOM, INC.

90 Boroline Road, Allendale, NJ　07401

CEO: Tony Nakamura, Pres.　　Tel: (201) 818-0100　　%FO: 100

Bus: *Manufactures precision industrial*　Fax: (201) 818-1877　　Emp: 25
machinery.

● **CLARION COMPANY, LTD.**
22-3 Shibuya 2-chome, Shibuya-ku, Tokyo 150-8335, Japan
CEO: Ichizo Ishitsubo, Pres.   Tel: 81-3-3400-1121   Rev: $1,818
Bus: *Mfr. mobile electronics.*   Fax: 81-3-3400-8505   Emp: 2,231
                                       www.clarion.co.jp

    CLARION CORPORATION OF AMERICA
    661 West Redondo Beach Blvd., Gardena, CA 90247
    CEO: Jim Minarik, Pres.   Tel: (310) 327-9100   %FO: 100
    Bus: *Mfr./sale/service mobile*   Fax: (310) 327-1999   Emp: 500
        electronics.

● **CORONA CORPORATION**
7-7 Higashi Shinbo, Sanjo City, Niigata Prefect 955, Japan
CEO: Tsutomu Uchida, Pres.   Tel: 81-256-32-2111   Rev: $621
Bus: *Mfr. kerosene heaters and air*   Fax: 81-256-35-6892   Emp: 2,173
    conditioners.   www.corona.co.jp

    CORONA USA CORPORATION
    2050 Center Avenue, Ste. 4501, Fort Lee, NJ 07024
    CEO: Jiro Kataoka, Pres.   Tel: (201) 592-0123   %FO: 100
    Bus: *Sales/distribution of kerosene* Fax: (201) 592-8848
        heaters and air conditioners.

● **COSMO OIL CO. LTD.**
Toshiba Bldg., 1-1 Shibaura 1-chome, Minato-ku, Tokyo 105, Japan
CEO: Keichiro Okabe, Pres. & CEO   Tel: 81-3-3798-3200   Rev: $15,000
Bus: *Oil exploration, refining and sales.* Fax: 81-3-3798-3237 Emp: 2,050
                                       www.cosmo-oil.co.jp

    COSMO OIL OF USA INC.
    150 East 52nd Street, 22nd Fl., New York, NY 10022
    CEO: Koji Hashimoto, Pres.   Tel: (212) 486-3700   %FO: 100
    Bus: *Engineering and biotechnology.* Fax: (212) 486-4715

● **CSK CORPORATION**
2-6-1- Nishi-Shinjuku, Shinjuku-ku, Tokyo 160-0227, Japan
CEO: Masahiro Aozono   Tel: 81-3-3344-1811   Rev: $3,335
Bus: *Engaged in information services;* Fax: 81-3-5321-3939   Emp: 4,850
    computer equipment, publishing and www.csk.co.jp
    telemarketing.

CSK SOFTWARE NA, INC.
40 Broad Street, 4th Fl., New York, NY 10004
CEO: Jim Ryan   Tel: (212) 504-0200   %FO: 100
Bus: *Mfr./sales software and computer*   Fax: (212) 504-0300
  equipment.

● **DAI NIPPON PRINTING CO LTD.**
1-1 Ichigaya-Kagacho 1-chome, Shijuku-ku, Tokyo 162-8001, Japan
CEO: Yoshitoshi Kitajima, Pres.   Tel: 81-3-5225-8220   Rev: $12,195
Bus: *Engaged in printing services.*   Fax: 81-3-5225-8239   Emp: 35,350
                                          www.dnp.co.jp

    DNP AMERICA, INC.
    335 Madison Avenue, 3rd Fl., New York, NY   10017
    CEO: Yoji Yamakawa, Pres.   Tel: (212) 503-1060   %FO: 100
    Bus: *Printing sales.*   Fax: (212) 286-1501

● **DAIDO STEEL CO INC**
11-18 Nishiki l-chome, Naka-ku, Nagoya 460, Japan
CEO: Tsuyoshi Takayama, Pres.   Tel: 81-52-201-5111   Rev: $3,040
Bus: *Specialty steel products.*   Fax: 81-52-221-9268   Emp: 5,911
                                          www.daido.co.jp

    DAIDO STEEL (AMERICA), INC.
    2200 East Devon Ave., Ste. 314, Des Plaines, IL   60018
    CEO: Yoshiro Kumaki, Pres.   Tel: (847) 699-9066   %FO: 100
    Bus: *Import and export steel.*   Fax: (847) 699-9067   Emp: 10

    INTERNATIONAL MOLD STEEL
    6796 Powerline Drive, Florence, KY   41042
    CEO: Yoshiro Kumaki, Pres.   Tel: (859) 342-6000   %FO: 100
    Bus: *Engaged in processing and selling*   Fax: (859) 342-6006
      steel for plastic molding.

    OHIO STAR FORGE COMPANY
    4000 Mahoning Avenue, Warren, OH   44483
    CEO: Yoshiro Kumaki, Pres.   Tel: (330) 847-6360   %FO: 100
    Bus: *Mfr./sales small precision forgings.* Fax: (330) 847-6368

    OOZX USA INC.
    10101 Caneel Drive, Knoxville, TN   37931
    CEO: Yoshiro Kumaki, Pres.   Tel: (423) 691-4000   %FO: 100
    Bus: *Mfr. automobile parts.*   Fax: (423) 539-9950

- **DAIDO TSUSHO CO LTD.**

1-6 Kyobashi 1-chome, Chuo-ku, Tokyo 104, Japan

CEO: Koki Ogawa, Pres.　　　　　　　　　Tel: 81-3-273-2451

Bus: *Imp/export power transmission*　Fax: 81-3-255-6615　　　Emp: 100
products, electronic control devices,　www.daidocorp.com
tools, surveying & measuring
instruments.

DAIDO CORPORATION

615 Pierce St., PO Box 6739, Somerset, NJ　08875-6739

CEO: Keiji Omata, Pres.　　　　　　　　Tel: (732) 805-1900　　　%FO: 100

Bus: *Distribution/sale power*　　　　Fax: (732) 805-0122　　　Emp: 140
transmission products, power
tools, general merchandise.

- **DAIDOH, LTD.**

1-16 Sotokanda 3-chome, Chiyoda-ku, Tokyo 101, Japan

CEO: Isamu Takei, Pres.　　　　　　　　Tel: 81-3-3257-5050　　　Rev: $286

Bus: *Mfr. worsted fabrics and yarns; men's*　Fax: 81-3-3257-5051　　Emp: 588
and women's apparel.

DAIDO INTERNATIONAL INC.

25 West 42nd Street, Ste. 1007, New York, NY　10036

CEO: Fumitaka Saito, Pres.　　　　　　Tel: (212) 581-8255　　　%FO: 100

Bus: *Import/export textile, apparel and*　Fax: (212) 541-5120　　　Emp: 3
furnishings.

- **THE DAIEI, INC.**

4-1-1, Minatojima Nakamachi, Chuo-ku, Kobe 650-0046, Japan

CEO: Kunio Takagi, CEO　　　　　　　Tel: 81-78-302-5001　　　Rev: $25,883

Bus: *Retail food and chain store operator.*　Fax: 81-78-302-5572　　Emp: 13,775
www.daiei.co.jp

D INTERNATIONAL, INC.

2601 Elliott Avenue, Ste. 3301, Seattle, WA　98121

CEO: Nobuyoshi Mizoguchi, Mgr.　　　Tel: (206) 269-7438　　　%FO: 100

Bus: *Retail food and chain store*　　Fax: (206) 269-7447
operator.

DAIEI USA, INC.

801 Kahake Street, Honolulu, HI　96814

CEO: Takashi Ichikawa, CEO　　　　　Tel: (808) 973-6600　　　%FO: 100

Bus: *Retail food and chain store*　　Fax: (808) 941-6457
operator.

• DAIHATSU MOTOR CO., LTD.

1-1 Daihatsu-cho, Ikeda, Osaka 563-8651, Japan

CEO: Takaya Yamada, Pres.   Tel: 81-727-51-8811   Rev: $8,005

Bus: *Mfr./sales passenger cars and*   Fax: 81-727-53-6880   Emp: 11,259
     commercial vehicles.   www.daihatsu.co.jp

DAIHATSU AMERICA INC.

20 Center Point Drive, Ste. 120, La Palma, CA   90623

CEO: Mitsuhiko Okuda, CEO   Tel: (714) 690-4700   %FO: 100

Bus: *Sales/distribution of cars and*   Fax: (714) 690-4720
     commercial vehicles.

• DAIICHI CHUO KK

3-5-15 Nihonbashi, Chuo-ku, Tokyo 103-8271, Japan

CEO: Shozo Inada, Pres.   Tel: 81-3-3278-6800   Rev: $537

Bus: *Engaged in the transportation of bulk*   Fax: 81-3-3278-6831   Emp: 200
     cargo.

DAIICHI CHUO SHIPPING AMERICA, INC.

450 Lexington Avenue, New York, NY   10017

CEO: J. Kohashi, Pres.   Tel: (212) 972-6080   %FO: 100

Bus: *Shipping agents and brokers.*   Fax: (212) 370-0831   Emp: 11

• THE DAI-ICHI KANGYO BANK LIMITED, DIV. MIZUHO FINANCIAL GROUP

1-5 Uchisaiwai-cho l-chome, Chiyoda-ku, Tokyo 100, Japan

CEO: Katsuyuki Sugita, Pres. & CEO   Tel: 81-3-3596-1111   Rev: $17,500

Bus: *General commercial banking services.*   Fax: 81-3-3596-5098   Emp: 17,100
     www.dkb.co.jp

DAI-ICHI KANGYO BANK - NEW YORK

*95 Christopher Columbus Drive, 18th Fl., Jersey City, NJ   07302-2927

CEO: Keiji Toril, Mgr.   Tel: (201) 200-6100   %FO: 100

Bus: *International commercial banking*   Fax: (201) 200-6122   Emp: 400
     services.

DAI-ICHI KANGYO BANK OF CALIFORNIA

555 West Fifth Street, Los Angeles, CA   90013

CEO: Takuo Yoshida, Chmn.   Tel: (213) 612-2700   %FO: 100

Bus: *International commercial banking*   Fax: (213) 612-2875   Emp: 125
     services.

DKB DATA SERVICES INC.

95 Christopher Columbus Drive, 18th Fl., Jersey City, NJ   07302-2927

CEO: Riichi Ito, Pres.   Tel: (201) 200-6100   %FO: 100

Bus: *International commercial banking*   Fax: (201) 200-6122
     services.

DKB FINANCIAL FUTURES CORPORATION
10 South Wacker Drive, Ste. 1835, Chicago, IL   60606
CEO: Akira Watanabe, Pres.　　　Tel: (312) 466-1700　　　%FO: 100
Bus: *International commercial banking* 　Fax: (312) 466-8623
services.

● DAIICHI PHARMACEUTIAL CO. LTD.
14-10 Nihonbashi 3-chome, Chuo-ku, Tokyo 103, Japan
CEO: Tadashi Suzuki, Chmn. & CEO　　Tel: 81-3-3272-0611　　Rev: $2,849
Bus: *Research and distributes ethical* 　Fax: 81-3-3272-7348　　Emp: 6,945
pharmaceuticals and veterinary 　www.daiichipharm.co.jp
products.

DAIICHI FINE CHEMICALS INC.
820 Forest Edge Drive, Corporate Woods, IL   60016
CEO: Timothy Jacobson, Pres.　　　Tel: (847) 634-7251　　　%FO: 100
Bus: *Markets anti-cancer and wound* 　Fax: (847) 634-7257
healing agents.

DAIICHI PHARMACEUTICAL CORPORATION
11 Philips Parkway, Montvale, NJ   07645
CEO: Masatoshi Sakamoto, CEO　　Tel: (201) 573-7000　　　%FO: 100
Bus: *Markets anti-cancer and wound* 　Fax: (201) 573-7650
healing agents.

● DAIKIN INDUSTRIES, LTD.
Umeda Center Bldg., 4-12 Nakazaki-Nishi 2-chome, Kita-ku Osaka 530, Japan
CEO: Noriyuki Inoue, Pres.　　　Tel: 81-6-373-4351　　　Rev: $4,170
Bus: *Mfr. industrial pumps and refrigeration* 　Fax: 81-6-373-4388　　Emp: 7,775
equipment, air-conditioning systems, 　www.daikin.co.jp
medical equipment and fluorochemicals.

DAIKIN AMERICA INC.
20 Olympic Drive, Orangeburg, NY   10962
CEO: T. K. Sakanoue, Pres.　　　Tel: (914) 365-9500　　　%FO: 100
Bus: *Mfr. commercial/industrial air* 　Fax: (914) 365-9515
conditioning systems.

DAIKIN U.S. CORPORATION, INC.
375 Park Avenue, New York, NY   10152
CEO: Yoshihiro Mineno, Pres.　　　Tel: (212) 935-4890　　　%FO: 100
Bus: *Mfr. commercial/industrial air* 　Fax: (212) 935-4895　　Emp: 25
conditioning systems.

● **DAINICHISEIKA COLOUR & CHEMICALS MFR. CO., LTD.**

7-6, Bakurocho 1-chome, Nihonbashi, Chuo-ku Tokyo 103-8383, Japan

CEO: Osamu Takahashi, Pres.　　　　　Tel: 81-3-3662-7111　　　Rev: $1,227

Bus: *Mfr. pigments and coloring agents for*　Fax: 81-3-3669-3936　　　Emp: 1,644
plastics and printing ink.　　　　　　www.daicolor.co.jp

ADVANCED POLYMER INC.

400 Paterson Plank Road, Carlstadt, NJ　07072

CEO: J. David Sagurton　　　　　　Tel: (201) 933-0600

Bus: *Mfr./sales/distribution of pigments*　Fax: (201) 933-8442
and dispersions.

DAICOLOR-POPE, INC.

33 Sixth Avenue, Paterson, NJ　07524

CEO: Akira Ishizaka, Pres. & CEO　　　Tel: (973) 278-5170　　　%FO: 100

Bus: *Mfr./sales/distribution of pigments*　Fax: (973) 279-1256
and dispersions.

HI-TECH COLOR, INC.

1721 Midway Road, Odenton, MD　21113

CEO: Akira Ishizaka, Pres. & CEO　　　Tel: (410) 551-9871

Bus: *Mfr./sales/distribution of pigments*　Fax: (410) 672-3002
and dispersions.

● **DAINIPPON INK & CHEMICALS INC.**

7-20 Nihonbashi 3-chome, Chuo-Ku, Tokyo 103, Japan

CEO: Takemitsu Takahashi, Pres.　　　Tel: 81-3-3272-4511　　　Rev: $8,902

Bus: *Printing inks, supplies, machinery,*　Fax: 81-3-3278-8558　　　Emp: 30,975
chemicals, imaging reprographic　　www.dic.co.jp
products, resins, plastics,
petrochemicals, building materials.

DIC AMERICAS, INC.

222 Bridge Plaza South, Fort Lee, NJ　07024

CEO: Tsuguo Tomiyama, Pres.　　　　Tel: (201) 592-5100　　　%FO: 100

Bus: *Sales of DIC products.*　　　　Fax: (201) 592-8232

DYNARIC INC.

500 Frank W. Burr Blvd., Teaneck, NJ　07666

CEO: Joseph Martinez, Pres.　　　　Tel: (201) 692-7700　　　%FO: 100

Bus: *Mfr. plastic strapping material.*　Fax: (201) 692-7757

EARTHRISE FARMS

113 East Hooher Roads, Calipatria, CA　92233

CEO: Yoshimichi Ota, Pres.　　　　Tel: (760) 348-5027

Bus: *Mfr./sale printing inks and*　　Fax: (760) 348-2895
organic chemicals.

REICHHOLD CHEMICALS, INC.
2400 Ellis Road, Durham, NC   27703-5543
CEO: Yoshi Kawashima, CEO   Tel: (919) 990-7500   %FO: 100
Bus: *Mfr. synthetic resins and adhesives.* Fax: (919) 990-7711

SUN CHEMICAL CORPORATION
222 Bridge Plaza South, Fort Lee, NJ   07024
CEO: Henri Dyner, Pres. & CEO   Tel: (201) 224-4600   %FO: 100
Bus: *Mfr./sale printing inks and*   Fax: (201) 224-4512
      organic chemicals.

● **DAIO PAPER CORPORATION**
2-60 Kamiya-cho, Iyomishima 799-04, Japan
CEO: Tamotsu Osawa, Pres.   Tel: 81-89-623-3300   Rev: $2,697
Bus: *Mfr. pulp and paper.*   Fax: 81-89-623-3300   Emp: 3,600
                                      www.daio-paper-co.jp

CALIFORNIA WOODFIBER CORPORATION
1890 Parkway Blvd., PO Box 753, West Sacramento, CA   95691
CEO: Elichiro Kubo, Pres.   Tel: (916) 371-3682   %FO: 80
Bus: *Mfr. woodchips for pulp.*   Fax: (916) 371-5060   Emp: 18

● **DAISHOWA INTL CO LTD.**
1-1-7 Nihonbashi Tyuo-ku, Tokyo 103-0027, Japan
CEO: Kazumoto Sogo, Pres.   Tel: 81-3 3242-6123   Rev: $2,792
Bus: *Import woodchips.*   Fax: 81-3 3245-0133   Emp: 3,657
                                      www.daishowa.co.jp

DAISHOWA AMERICA COMPANY, LTD.
1815 Marine Drive, Port Angeles, WA   98363
CEO: David Tamaki, Pres.   Tel: (360) 457-4474   %FO: 100
Bus: *Sales woodchips & manufacture*   Fax: (360) 452-9004   Emp: 320
      telephone directory paper.

DAISHOWA SALES LIMITED
3675 Crestwood Parkway, Ste. 400, Duluth, GA   30136
CEO: Paul Gordon, VP   Tel: (770) 279-8808   %FO: 100
Bus: *Sales/distribution of*   Fax: (770) 279-2690
      woodchips/paper.

● **DAIWA HOUSE INDUSTRY CO. LTD.**
5-16 Awaza 1-chome, Nishi-ku, Osaka 0550, Japan
CEO: Kelichi Uemura, Pres.   Tel: 81-6-538-5111   Rev: $8,046
Bus: *Construction of residential, non-*   Fax: Emp: 12,900
      residential and pre-fabricated homes   www.daiwahouse.co.jp
      and metal buildings.

LA TOUR WILSHIRE DEVELOPMENT COMPANY INC.
2082 Business Center Drive, Ste. 170, Irvine, CA   92715
CEO: Katsuya Terada, Pres.   Tel: (949) 955-0992   %FO: 100
Bus: *Construction of residential, non-*   Fax:
residential & pre-fabricated
homes & metal buildings.

• DAIWA SB INVESTMENTS LTD.
7-9 Nihodbashi 2-chome, Chuo-ku, Tokyo 103-0027, Japan
CEO: Minoru Mori   Tel: 81-3-3243-2915
Bus: *Engaged in investment management.*   Fax: 81-3-3274-2328   Emp: 175
www.ir.daiwa.co.jp

DAIWA SB INVESTMENTS LTD.
380 Madison Avenue, 23rd Fl., New York, NY   10017
CEO: Kiyotaka Hoshino, Pres.   Tel: (212) 983-4600   %FO: 100
Bus: *Investment management.*   Fax: (212) 983-4647

• DAIWA SECURITIES GROUP INC.
6-4, Otemachi 2-chome, Chiyoda-ku, Tokyo 100-8101, Japan
CEO: Akira Kiyota, Pres.   Tel: 81-3-3243-2100   Rev: $6,205
Bus: *Engaged in wholesale securities.*   Fax: 81-3-3242-0955   Emp: 11,415
www.daiwa.co.jp

DAIWA SECURITIES AMERICA INC.
32 Old Slip, Financial Square, New York, NY   10005
CEO: Ikuo Mori, Pres.   Tel: (212) 612-7000   %FO: 100
Bus: *Investment banking and securities*   Fax: (212) 612-7100   Emp: 400
broker.

DAIWA SECURITIES TRUST CO.
One Evertrust Plaza, Jersey City, NJ   07302
CEO: Hidaki Matsuura, Pres.   Tel: (201) 333-7300   %FO: 100
Bus: *Investment banking and securities*   Fax: (201) 333-7726
broker.

• DENKI KAGAKU KOGYO KK
4-1 Yuraku-ho 1-chome, Chiyoda-ku, Tokyo 100, Japan
CEO: Tsuneo Yano, Pres.   Tel: 81-3-3507-5124   Rev: $2,429
Bus: *Chemical and cement products.*   Fax: 81-3-3507-5126   Emp: 3,135
www.denka.co.jp

DENKA CORPORATION
780 Third Avenue, 32nd Fl., New York, NY   10017
CEO: Mike Yamamoto, VP   Tel: (212) 688-8700   %FO: 100
Bus: *Service chemical products.*   Fax: (212) 688-8727   Emp: 3

• DENSO CORPORATION

1-1 Showa-cho, Kariya Aichi 448, Japan
CEO: Hiromu Okabe, Pres. & CEO
Bus: *Mfr. automotive components and systems technology.*

Tel: 81-566-25-5511
Fax: 81-566-25-4522
www.denso.co.jp

Rev: $17,851
Emp: 81,000

AMERICAN INDUSTRIAL MANUFACTURING SERVICES, INC.
41673 Corning Place, Murrieta, CA 92562
CEO: Hisashi Matsunobu, Pres.
Bus: *Mfr. automotive components.*

Tel: (909) 698-3379
Fax: (909) 698-1379

%FO: 100
Emp: 90

DENSO INTERNATIONAL, INC.
PO Box 5133, Southfield, MI 48086-5133
CEO: Shuichi "Chad" Kosuge, Pres.
Bus: *Mfr. automobile systems.*

Tel: (248) 350-7500
Fax: (248) 350-7772

%FO: 100

DENSO MANUFACTURING INC.
1720 Robert C. Jackson Drive, Maryville, TN 37801-3748
CEO: Kunitaka Ozeki, Pres.
Bus: *Mfr. auto starters and alternators.*

Tel: (865) 982-7000
Fax: (865) 981-5250

%FO: 100

DENSO MANUFACTURING MICHIGAN, INC.
One Denso Road, Battle Creek, MI 49015-1083
CEO: Takeshi Tsubol, Pres.
Bus: *Mfr./sales of heaters, air conditioners and automotive components.*

Tel: (616) 965-3322
Fax: (616) 965-8399

%FO: 100
Emp: 6,000

DENSO SALES CALIFORNIA, INC.
3900 Via Oro Avenue, Long Beach, CA 90810
CEO: Roy Nakaue, EVP
Bus: *Automotive component supplier.*

Tel: (310) 834-6352
Fax: (310) 513-7319

%FO: 100
Emp: 400

DENSO WIRELESS SYSTEMS INC.
3250 Business Park Drive, Vista, CA 92083
CEO: Teruaki Toyoda, Pres.
Bus: *Mfr. cellular handsets.*

Tel: (760) 734-4600
Fax: (760) 734-4685

%FO: 100

MICHIGAN AUTOMOTIVE COMPRESSOR, INC.
2400 North Dearing Road, Parma, MI 49269
CEO: Kimio Kato, Pres.
Bus: *Mfr./sale compressors & clutches.*

Tel: (517) 531-5500
Fax: (517) 531-5680

%FO: JV

PURODENSO COMPANY
PO Box 1887, Jackson, TN 38302-1887
CEO: Masafumi Suzuki, Pres.
Bus: *Mfr./sale oil filters & detergents.*

Tel: (901) 427-4774
Fax: (901) 424-4733

%FO: 100
Emp: 330

• DENTSU INC.

1-11-10 Tsukiji, Chuo-ku, Tokyo 104-8426, Japan

CEO: Yutaka Narita, Pres.
Tel: 81-3-5511-5111
Rev: $2,462

Bus: *Advertising and communications services.*
Fax: 81-3-5511-2013
Emp: 10,840
www.dentsu.co.jp

BCOM3 GROUP

35 West Wacker Drive, Chicago, IL 60601

CEO: Roger A. Haupt
Tel: (312) 220-5959
%FO:

Bus: *Advertising & communications services.*
Fax: (312) 220-3299

DCA ADVERTISING, INC.

666 Fifth Avenue, 9th Fl., New York, NY 10103

CEO: Tetsuo Machida, Pres.& CEO
Tel: (212) 397-3333
%FO: 100

Bus: *Advertising & communications services.*
Fax: (212) 261-4238
Emp: 99

DENTSU COMMUNICATIONS

666 Fifth Avenue, 9th Fl., New York, NY 10103

CEO: Yuki Hattori, Pres.
Tel: (212) 261-2650
%FO: 100

Bus: *Engaged in public relations.*
Fax: (212) 261-4288

DENTSU USA

2001 Wiltshire Blvd., Santa Monica, CA 90403

CEO: Hiroaki Sano, SVP
Tel: (310) 586-5600
%FO: 100

Bus: *Advertising & communications services.*
Fax: (310) 586-5890
Emp: 37

THE LORD GROUP

20 Cooper Square, 3rd Fl., New York, NY 10003

CEO: Roger Chiocchi, CEO
Tel: (212) 780-5400
%FO: 100

Bus: *Advertising & communications services.*
Fax: (212) 780-1663
Emp: 193

RENEGADE MARKETING GROUP

75 Ninth Avenue, 4th Fl., New York, NY 10011

CEO: Andrew Neisser, Pres.
Tel: (646) 486-7700
%FO: 100

Bus: *Engaged in marketing.*
Fax: (646) 486-7800

• DESCENTE LTD.

1-11-3 Dogashiba, Tennoji-ku, Osaka 543, Japan

CEO: Yozo Iida, Pres. & CEO
Tel: 81-6-774-0365
Rev: $775

Bus: *Mfr./distributes active sportswear.*
Fax: 81-6-779-0453
Emp: 1,046
www.descente.co.jp

DESCENTE AMERICA INC.
7367 South Revere Parkway, Bldg. 2A, Englewood, CO   80112
CEO: Guy Christie, Pres.   Tel: (303) 790-1155   %FO: 100
Bus: *Mfr./distributes sports apparel.*   Fax: (303) 790-2149

● **DEVELOPMENT BANK OF JAPAN**
9-1 Otemachi 1-chome, Chiyoda-ku, Tokyo 100-0004, Japan
CEO: Masami Kogayu, Gov.   Tel: 81-3-3244-1770
Bus: *Government financial institution.*   Fax: 81-3-3245-1938

    DEVELOPMENT BANK OF JAPAN
    1101 17th Street NW, Ste. 1001, Washington, DC   20036
    CEO: Haruhisa Kawashita   Tel: (202) 331-8696   %FO: 100
    Bus: *Banking and loans.*   Fax: (202) 029-3932

    DEVELOPMENT BANK OF JAPAN
    1251 Avenue of the Americas, Ste. 830, New York, NY   10020
    CEO: Tsutomu Kishino, Rep.   Tel: (212) 221-0708   %FO: 100
    Bus: *Banking and loans.*   Fax: (212) 221-6138

    DEVELOPMENT BANK OF JAPAN
    601 South Figueroa Street, Ste. 2190, Los Angeles, CA   90017
    CEO: Kaoya Kitamura, Rep.   Tel: (213) 362-2980   %FO: 100
    Bus: *Banking and loans.*   Fax: (213) 362-2982

● **EAST JAPAN RAILWAY COMPANY**
2-2, Yoyogi 2-chome, Shibuya-ku, 151-8578 Tokyo, Japan
CEO: Mutsutake Otsuka, Pres.   Tel: 81-3-5334-1310   Rev: $23,725
Bus: *National railway system.*   Fax: 81-3-5334-1297   Emp: 82,750
                                      www.jreast.co.jp

    EAST JAPAN RAILWAY COMPANY
    One Rockefeller Plaza, Ste. 1622, New York, NY   10020
    CEO: Shunsaku Inoue, Dir.   Tel: (212) 332-8686   %FO: 100
    Bus: *Information and liaison office for*   Fax: (212) 332-8690   Emp: 5
    East Japan Railway Company
    (non-commercial).

● **EBARA CORPORATION**
11-1 Haneda Asahi-cho, Ohta-ku, Tokyo 144-8510, Japan
CEO: Masatoshi Yoda, Pres.   Tel: 81-3-37436111   Rev: $4,310
Bus: *Mfr. water and air transportation*   Fax: 81-3-37453356   Emp: 13,445
systems, precision machinery and   www.ebara.co.jp
communications systems.

AIRVAC, INC.
PO Box 528, Rochester, IN 46975
CEO: Shinichi Hirano, CEO   Tel: (219) 223-3980   %FO: 100
Bus: *Mfr./sales valves for vacuum*   Fax: (219) 223-5566
sewage systems.

EBARA AMERICA CORPORATION
45 East Plumeria Drive, San Jose, CA 95134
CEO: Mitsuhiro Kochi, Pres.   Tel: (408) 571-2250   %FO: 100
Bus: *Mfr./sales water and air transport*   Fax: (408) 571-2259
systems and precision machinery.

EBARA INTERNATIONAL CORPORATION
350 Salomon Circle, Sparks, NV 89434
CEO: Everett H. Hylton, CEO   Tel: (775) 356-2796   %FO: 100
Bus: *Mfr. standard pumps and motors.*   Fax: (775) 356-2884

EBARA SOLAR, INC.
1801 Route 51, Jefferson Hills, PA 15025
CEO: R. Rosey, Pres.   Tel: (412) 382-1250   %FO: 100
Bus: *Mfr. solar cells.*   Fax: (412) 382-1251

EBARA TECHNOLOGIES INC.
51 Main Avenue, Sacramento, CA 95838
CEO: John Aldeborgh, CEO   Tel: (916) 920-5451   %FO: 100
Bus: *Mfr. vacuum pumps.*   Fax: (916) 925-6654

EBARA TECHNOLOGIES INC.
323 Sinclair Frontage Road, Milpitas, CA 95035
CEO: Ibrahim Arnaout, Pres.   Tel: (408) 934-2888   %FO: 100
Bus: *Sales/markets vacuum pumps.*   Fax: (408) 934-2801

MATSUBO COMPANY, INC.
226 Airport Parkway, Ste. 440, San Jose, CA 95110
CEO: Kijuo Ito, Mgr.   Tel: (408) 467-1280   %FO: 100
Bus: *Engaged in machinery trading.*   Fax: (408) 467-1286

MULTI PLANAR TECHNOLOGIES INC.
45 East Plumeria Drive, San Jose, CA 95134
CEO: Masayoshi Hirose, Pres.   Tel: (408) 571-2270   %FO: 100
Bus: *Development of machinery for*   Fax: (408) 571-2002
semi-conductor industry.

● **EIKI INDUSTRIAL COMPANY, LTD.**
CPO Box 1229, Osaka 530-91, Japan
CEO: Mr. Imai, Pres.   Tel: 81-6-364-5691
Bus: *Mfr. film projectors and VCRs.*   Fax:
                                               www.eiki.com

    EIKI INTERNATIONAL INC.
    26794 Vista Terrace Drive, Lake Forest, CA   92630-8113
    CEO: R. Fujishige, Mgr.   Tel: (949) 457-0200   %FO: 100
    Bus: *Film projectors and VCRs.*   Fax: (949) 457-7878

● **EISAI CO., LTD.**
4-6-10 Koishikawa, Bunkyo-ku, Tokyo 112-8088, Japan
CEO: Haruo Naito, Chmn. & CEO   Tel: 81-3-3817-5011   Rev: $2,558
Bus: *Mfr. cosmetics and toiletries,*   Fax: 81-3-3811-3305   Emp: 4,372
    pharmaceuticals and diagnostic drugs,   www.eisai.co.jp
    vet products and chemicals.

    EISAI CORPORATION OF NORTH AMERICA
    500 Frank W. Burr Blvd., Teaneck, NJ   07666
    CEO: Soichi Matsuno, Pres.   Tel: (201) 692-1100   %FO: 100
    Bus: *Mfr./distributes pharmaceutical*   Fax: (201) 692-1804
        products.

    EISAN RESEARCH INSTITUTE OF BOSTON, INC.
    Four Corporate Drive, Andover, MA   01810-2441
    CEO: Hiroshi Yamauchi, Pres.   Tel: (978) 794-1117   %FO: 100
    Bus: *Pharmaceutical research.*   Fax: (978) 794-4910

    EISAI USA INC.
    5555 San Felipe Road, Ste. 690, Houston, TX   77056
    CEO: Yutaka Hosegawa, Pres.   Tel: (713) 621-9030   %FO: 100
    Bus: *Mfr./sales vitamins & chemicals.*   Fax: (713) 621-9095

● **ELMO COMPANY, LTD.**
6-14 Meizen-cho, Mizuho-ku, Nagoya-shi Aichi 467, Japan
CEO: Hachiro Nagao, Mgr.   Tel: 81-52-811-5143
Bus: *Mfr. electronic imaging equipment.*   Fax: 81-52-811-5243   Emp: 500
                                               www.elmo-corp.com

    ELMO MANUFACTURING CORPORATION
    1478 Old Country Road, Plainview, NY   11803
    CEO: Vince Giovinco, EVP   Tel: (516) 501-1400   %FO: 100
    Bus: *Sale/service audio-visual,*   Fax: (516) 501-0429   Emp: 30
        electronic imaging and CCTV
        products.

● **FANUC LTD.**

3580 Shibokusa Aza-Komanba, Oshino-mura, Minamitsuru-gun, Yamanashi Perfecture 401-05, Japan

CEO: Dr. Seluemon Inaba, Pres.	Tel: 81-555-84-5555	Rev: $1,898
Bus: *Researches/produces industrial equipment.*	Fax: 81-555-84-5512	Emp: 6,000
	www.fanuc.co.jp	

FANUC AMERICA

1800 Lakewood Boulevard, Hoffman Estates, IL 60195

CEO: Ken Matsuo, Pres.	Tel: (847) 898-6000	%FO: 100
Bus: *Sales/distribution of industrial equipment.*	Fax: (847) 898-6001	

FANUC ROBOTICS OF NA, INC.

3900 West Hamlin Road, Rochester Hills, MI 48309-3253

CEO: Rick Schneider, CEO	Tel: (248) 377-7000	%FO: 100
Bus: *Sales/distribution of industrial equipment.*	Fax: (248) 377-7366	

● **THE FUJI BANK LTD., DIV. MIZUHO FINANCIAL GROUP**

5-5 Otemachi 1-chome, Chiyoda-ku, Tokyo 100, Japan

CEO: Yashiro Yamamoto, Pres.	Tel: 81-3 3216-2211	Rev: $21,580
Bus: *Commercial banking services.*	Fax: 81-3 3216-2211	Emp: 14,000
	www.fujibank.co.jp	

THE FUJI BANK & TRUST COMPANY - NY Agency

*Two World Trade Center, 79-82 Fls., New York, NY 10048

CEO: Kenichiro Tanaka, Pres. & CEO	Tel: (212) 898-2400	%FO: 100
Bus: *Commercial banking services.*	Fax: (212) 321-9408	Emp: 1,000

THE FUJI BANK LTD.

*Two World Trade Center , 82nd Fl., New York, NY 10048

CEO: Michio Ueno, Mng. Dir.	Tel: (212) 898-2000	%FO: 100
Bus: *Commercial banking services.*	Fax: (212) 898-2770	

THE FUJI BANK LTD. - LA Agency

333 South Hope Street, Los Angeles, CA 90071

CEO: M. Kamyo, Gen. Mgr.	Tel: (213) 680-9855	%FO: 100
Bus: *Commercial banking services.*	Fax: (213) 253-4198	

THE FUJI BANK LTD. - Chicago Agency

225 West Wacker Drive, Ste. 2000, Chicago, IL 60606

CEO: Peter Chinici, Mgr.	Tel: (312) 621-0500	%FO: 100
Bus: *Commercial banking services.*	Fax: (312) 621-0539	

FUJI CAPITAL MARKETS CORPORATION
*Two World Trade Center, 80th Fl., New York, NY   10048

CEO: Michio Tani, Pres. & CEO	Tel: (212) 898-2657	%FO: 100
Bus: *Engaged in derivatives products.*	Fax: (212) 488-9415	

FUJI MARINE CORPORATION
*Two World Trade Center, 79th Fl., New York, NY   10048

CEO: Kenichiro Tanaka, VP	Tel: (212) 898-2000	%FO: 100
Bus: *Marine division.*	Fax: (212) 321-9407	

HELLER FINANCIAL, INC.
500 West Monroe Street, 16th Fl., Chicago, IL   60661

CEO: Dennis P. Lockhart, Pres.	Tel: (312) 441-7000	%FO: 100
Bus: *Commercial finance services. (JV with Fuji Bank, Japan.)*	Fax: (312) 441-7499	Emp: 1,200

HELLER FIRST CAPITAL CORPORATION
500 West Monroe Street, 16th Fl., Chicago, IL   60661

CEO: Richard J. Almeida, CEO	Tel: (312) 441-7404	%FO: 100
Bus: *Financial services.*	Fax: (312) 441-7499	

HELLER REAL ESTATE FINANCIAL SERVICES
500 West Monroe Street, 16th Fl., Chicago, IL   60661

CEO: John Petrovski, Pres.	Tel: (312) 441-6700	%FO: 100
Bus: *Real estate and financial services.*	Fax: (312) 346-7119	

● FUJI ELECTRIC COMPANY, LTD.
Gate City Osaka East Tower, 11-2 Osaki 1-chome, Shinagawa-ku Tokyo 141-0032, Japan

CEO: Kunihiko Sawa, Pres.	Tel: 81-3-5435-7206	Rev: $8,074
Bus: *Mfr. electric and electronic devices, industrial/consumer electronics and specialty appliances.*	Fax: 81-3-5435-7486 www.fujielectric.co.jp	Emp: 27,640

FUJI ELECTRIC CORPORATION OF AMERICA, INC.
Park 80 West, Plaza 2, Saddle Brook, NJ   07663

CEO: Masao Takahashi, Pres.	Tel: (201) 712-0555	%FO: 100
Bus: *Sales/marketing of electric and electronic products & information processing systems.*	Fax: (201) 368-8258	Emp: 30

FUJI HI-TECH, INC.
47520 Westinghouse Drive, Fremont, CA   94538

CEO: Minoru Yamamoto, Pres.	Tel: (510) 651-0811	%FO: 100
Bus: *Sales/distribution of industrial and consumer electronics.*	Fax: (510) 651-9070	

● **FUJI HEAVY INDUSTRIES LTD.**

Subaru Bldg, 7-2 Nishishinjuku 1-chome, Shinjuku-ku, Tokyo 160, Japan

CEO: Takeshi Tanaka, Pres. Tel: 81-3-3347-2111 Rev: $12,607

Bus: *Mfr. SUV automobiles, buses, railcars,* Fax: 81-3-3347-2338 Emp: 26,915
aircraft components, engines, and www.fhi.co.jp
garbage trucks.

FUJI HEAVY INDUSTRIES INC.

3003 West Casino Road, Everett, WA   98203

CEO: Yasuo Watanabe, Mgr. Tel: (206) 342-7643 %FO: 100

Bus: *Mfr. motor vehicles, engines,* Fax: (206) 294-2556
machinery & aircraft parts.

SUBARU OF AMERICA

Subaru Plaza, PO Box 6000, Cherry Hill, NJ   08034-6000

CEO: Takao Saito, CEO Tel: (856) 488-8500 %FO: 100

Bus: *Sale/marketing/service cars, parts* Fax: (856) 488-3274 Emp: 656
& accessories.

SUBARU RESEARCH & DESIGN

3995 Research Park Drive, Ann Arbor, MI   48108

CEO: Tatsuo Kakai, Pres. Tel: (734) 623-0075 %FO: JV

Bus: *Research & design of motor* Fax: (734) 623-0076
vehicles.

● **FUJI PHOTO FILM CO., LTD.**

26-30 Nishiazabu 2-chome, Minato-ku, Tokyo 106, Japan

CEO: Shigetaka Komori, Pres. & CEO Tel: 81-33-406-2111 Rev: $13,658

Bus: *Mfr. photographic, reprographic,* Fax: 81-33-406-2173 Emp: 37,150
micrographic, audio and visual, x-ray www.fujifilm.co.jp
and graphic art supplies.

ANCHOR LITH KEM KO

50 Industrial Loop North, Orange Park, FL   32073

CEO: Albert Aerts, Pres. Tel: (904) 264-3500 %FO: 100

Bus: *Mfr. floppy disks.* Fax: (904) 269-3841

FUJI HUNT PHOTO. CHEMICALS, INC.

Country Club Pl., Bldg. 1F, W. 115 Century Road, Paramus, NJ   07652

CEO: Albert Aerts, Pres. Tel: (201) 967-7500 %FO: 100

Bus: *Photographic chemicals.* Fax: (201) 967-9299

FUJI MEDICAL SYSTEMS USA, INC.

419 West Avenue, Stamford, CT   06902

CEO: John Weber, CFO Tel: (203) 324-2000 %FO: 100

Bus: *Distribution/service x-ray film and* Fax: (203) 353-0926
equipment.

FUJI PHOTO FILM HAWAII, INC.
1650 Kalakaua Avenue, Honolulu, HI   96826
CEO: H. Okutsu, Pres.   Tel: (808) 942-9400   %FO: 100
Bus: *Distribution photo and magnetic*   Fax: (808) 946-7071
    products.

FUJI PHOTO FILM, INC.
211 Pucketts Ferry Road, Greenwood, SC   29649
CEO: Harry Watanabe, Pres.   Tel: (864) 223-2888   %FO: 100
Bus: *Mfr. photo film.*   Fax: (864) 223-8181

FUJI PHOTO FILM USA, INC.
555 Taxter Road, Elmsford, NY   10523
CEO: Yasuo Tanaka   Tel: (914) 789-8100   %FO: 100
Bus: *Marketing/distribution photo and* Fax: (914) 789-8514   Emp: 8,000
    magnetic products.

● FUJIKURA LTD.
5-1 Kiba 1-chome, Koto-ku, Tokyo 135-8512, Japan
CEO: Akira Tsujijawa, CEO   Tel: 81-3-5606-1030   Rev: $3,080
Bus: *Mfr. wire and cable.*   Fax: 81-3-5606-1502   Emp: 20,800
                           www.fujijura.co.jp

FUJIKURA AMERICA INC.
2121 Newmarket Pkwy. SE, Ste. 100, Marietta, GA   30067-9309
CEO: Toshi Takahashi   Tel: (770) 956-7200   %FO: 100
Bus: *Mfr. wire and cable.*   Fax: (770) 956-9854

FUJIKURA AMERICA INC.
3001 Oakmead Village Drive, Santa Clara, CA   95051-0811
CEO: Mitusuji Hashimoto   Tel: (408) 748-6991   %FO: 100
Bus: *Mfr. wire and cable.*   Fax: (408) 727-3415

FUJIKURA AMERICA INC.
17150 Via del Campo Suite 301, San Diego, CA   92127
CEO: Toru Hamasuna   Tel: (858) 613-6600   %FO: 100
Bus: *Mfr. wire and cable.*   Fax: (858) 613-6610

● FUJISAWA PHARMACEUTICAL COMPANY, LTD.
4-7 Doshomachi, 3-chome, Chuo-ku, Osaka 541-8514, Japan
CEO: Akira Fujiyama, Pres. & CEO   Tel: 81-6-202-1141   Rev: $2,355
Bus: *Mfr./sale healthcare products.*   Fax: 81-6-206-7925   Emp: 5,144
                           www.fujisawa.co.jp

FUJISAWA HEALTHCARE, INC.
3 Parkway North, Deerfield, IL   60015
CEO: Noboru Maeda, Pres.   Tel: (847) 317-8800   %FO: 100
Bus: *Healthcare products.*   Fax: (847) 317-7296

● **FUJITA CORPORATION**
4-6-15 Sendagaya, Shibuya-ku, Tokyo 151-8570, Japan
CEO: Hiroaki Tamura, Pres.   Tel: 81-3-3402-1911   Rev: $5,125
Bus: *Engaged in engineering and* Fax: 81-3-3402-9815   Emp: 4,200
construction.   www.fujita.co.jp

    FUJITA CORPORATION USA, INC.
    PO Box 1607, Santa Monica, CA   90406
    CEO: Tatsuo Fujlil, Pres.   Tel: (310) 393-0787   %FO: 100
    Bus: *Engineering and construction.* Fax: (310) 395-8130

● **FUJITEC COMPANY LTD.**
28-10 Shoh 1-chome, Ibaraki, Osaka 567-8510, Japan
CEO: Kenji Otani, Pres.   Tel: 81-726-22-8151   Rev: $750
Bus: *Mfr./installation/service of elevators* Fax: Emp: 1,393
and escalators.   www.fujitec.co.jp

    FUJITEC AMERICA, INC.
    401 Fujitec Drive, Lebanon, OH   45036
    CEO: Kirk Feuerbach, EVP   Tel: (513) 932-8000   %FO: 100
    Bus: *Mfr. /installation/service of* Fax: (513) 933-5504   Emp: 276
    elevators, escalators and
    autowalks.

● **FUJITSU LTD.**
Marunouchi Center Bldg, 6-1 Marunouchi 1-chome, Chiyoda-ku, Tokyo 100-8211, Japan
CEO: Naoyuki Akikusa, CEO   Tel: 81-3-3216-3211   Rev: $49,800
Bus: *Mfr. computer systems,*   Fax: 81-3-3216-9365   Emp: 188,000
telecommunications equipment,   www.fujitsu.com
electrical components and
semiconductors.

    AMDAHL CORPORATION
    1250 East Arques Avenue, Sunnyvale, CA   94086
    CEO: Yasushi Tajiri, EVP   Tel: (408) 746-6000   %FO: 44
    Bus: *Mfr. mainframe computer systems* Fax: (408) 746-6233   Emp: 7,700
    and consulting services.

DMR CONSULTING GROUP, INC.
333 Thornall Street, Edison, NJ   08837-2220
CEO: Michael J. Poehner, CEO   Tel: (408) 998-2112   %FO: 100
Bus: *Provider of e-consulting services*   Fax: (408) 998-2151
and business solutions.

FUJITSU AMERICA, INC.
3055 Orchard Drive, San Jose, CA   95134
CEO: Motoyasu Matsuzaki, COO   Tel: (408) 432-1300   %FO: 100
Bus: *Corporate administration.*   Fax: (408) 432-1318   Emp: 4,800

FUJITSU BUSINESS COMMUNICATION SYSTEMS, INC.
3190 Miraloma Avenue, Anaheim, CA   92806
CEO: Takuhito Kojima, Pres.   Tel: (714) 630-7721   %FO: 100
Bus: *Mfr./sale/maintenance PBX*   Fax: (714) 630-2991
switching systems.

FUJITSU COMPOUND SEMICONDUCTOR, INC.
3811 Zanker Road, Bldg. 8A, San Jose, CA   95134-1402
CEO: Kinji Yano, Pres.   Tel: (408) 232-9500   %FO: 100
Bus: *R&D mainframe computers.*   Fax: (408) 428-9111

FUJITSU COMPUTER PRODUCTS OF AMERICA, INC.
2904 Orchard Pkwy., San Jose, CA   95134
CEO: Larry Sanders, Pres.   Tel: (408) 432-6333   %FO: 100
Bus: *R&D/mfr. /sale electronic*   Fax: (408) 894-1709
equipment.

FUJITSU LTD.
733 Third Avenue, 20th Fl., New York, NY   10010
CEO: Korendo Shiotsuki, Gen. Mgr.   Tel: (212) 599-9800   %FO: 100
Bus: *Sales/distribution of computers.*   Fax: (212) 599-4129

FUJITSU MEDIA DEVICES OF AMERICA
1731 Technology Drive, Ste. 800, San Jose, CA   95110
CEO: Tatsuo Shirakawa, Pres.   Tel: (408) 437-8900   %FO: 100
Bus: *Markets electronic components.*   Fax: (408) 437-0700

FUJITSU MICROELECTRONICS, INC.
3545 North First Street, San Jose, CA   95134-1804
CEO: Ryusuke Hoshikawa, Pres.   Tel: (408) 922-9000   %FO: 100
Bus: *R&D/mfr./sale semiconductors.*   Fax: (408) 432-9044

FUJITSU NETWORK COMMUNICATIONS, INC.
1000 Saint Albans Drive, Raleigh, NC   27609
CEO: Harry Kanzaki, EVP Tel: (919) 790-2211 %FO: 100
Bus: *Sale/maintenance* Fax: (919) 790-8376
   telecommunications equipment.

FUJITSU NETWORK COMMUNICATIONS, INC.
2801 Telecom Pkwy., Richardson, TX   75082
CEO: Akira Kokimasa, Pres. Tel: (972) 690-6000 %FO: 100
Bus: *Mfr./sale telecommunications* Fax: (972) 467-6991
   equipment.

FUJITSU PC CORPORATION
598 Gibraltar Drive, Milpitas, CA   95035
CEO: Chiaki Ito, Chmn. Tel: (408) 935-8800 %FO: 100
Bus: *Mfr. notebook computers.* Fax: (408) 935-1501

FUJITSU PERSONAL SYSTEMS, INC.
5200 Patrick Henry Drive, Santa Clara, CA   95054
CEO: Louis Panetta, Pres. Tel: (408) 982-9500 %FO: 100
Bus: *Design/sale portable computers.* Fax: (408) 496-0575

FUJITSU TAKAMISAWA AMERICA, INC.
250 East Caribbean Drive, Sunnyvale, CA   94089
CEO: Naoyuki Akikusa, Pres. Tel: (408) 745-4900 %FO: 100
Bus: *Mfr. electronic components.* Fax: (408) 745-4970

FUJITSU-ICL SYSTEMS, INC.
5429 LBJ Freeway, Dallas, TX   75240
CEO: Austen Mulinder, Pres. & CEO Tel: (972) 716-8300 %FO: 100
Bus: *Computer systems.* Fax: (972) 716-8586

● FUJITSU TEN LTD.
1-2-28 Gosho Dori, Hyogo-ku, Kobe 652, Japan
CEO: Takamitsu Tsuchimoto, Pres. Tel: 81-78-671-5081
Bus: *Mfr. car stereos, two-way radios and* Fax: 81-78-671-5325 Emp: 2,200
   audio equipment. www.fujitsu-ten.co.jp

FUJITSU TEN CORP OF AMERICA
616 Conrad Harcourt Way, Rushville, IN   46173
CEO: Richard Marks, EVP Tel: (765) 938-5555 %FO: 100
Bus: *Mfr. car stereos.* Fax: (765) 932-3257 Emp: 50

● **FUKUDA DENSHI CO., LTD.**
3-39-4 Hongo, Bunkyo-ku, Tokyo 113, Japan
CEO: Kotaro Fukuda, Pres.   Tel: 81-3 38152121
Bus: *Mfr. medical equipment.*   Fax: 81-3 56841577   Emp: 1,500
                                            www.fukuda.co.jp

>   **FUKUDA DENSHI AMERICA CORP**
>   17725 NE 65th Street, Redmond, WA   98052
>   CEO: Noboru Yamamoto   Tel: (425) 881-7737   %FO: 100
>   Bus: *Sales/service medical equipment.*   Fax: (425) 869-2018   Emp: 35

● **FURUKAWA ELECTRIC COMPANY LTD.**
6-1, Marunouchi 2 chome, Chiyoda-Ku, Tokyo 100-8322, Japan
CEO: Junnosuke Furukawa, Pres.   Tel: 81-3-3286-3001   Rev: $6,602
Bus: *Mfr. electric wire and optical fiber* Fax: 81-3-3286-3747   Emp: 9,300
     cables and non-ferrous metals.   www.furukawa.co.jp

>   **FITEL TECHNOLOGIES, INC.**
>   PO Box 5027, Clinton, NJ   08809
>   CEO: Dr. John Pilitsis, Pres.   Tel: (908) 713-3525
>   Bus: *Engineering/business services.*   Fax: (908) 713-3515

>   **FURUKAWA ELECTRIC NORTH AMERICA, INC.**
>   900 Lafayette Street, Ste. 509, Santa Clara, CA   95050
>   CEO: Masato Sakamoto, Pres. & CEO   Tel: (408) 248-4884
>   Bus: *Administrative sales office.*   Fax: (408) 249-3094

● **GC DENTAL CORPORATION**
76-1 Hasunuma-cho, Itabashi-ku, Tokyo 174, Japan
CEO: Makoto Nakao, Pres.   Tel: 81-3-3965-0127
Bus: *Mfr. professional dental products.*   Fax: 81-3-3965-1567
                                            www.gcasia.com

>   **GC AMERICA INC.**
>   3737 West 127th Street, Alsip, IL   60803
>   CEO: Ken Sletcher, Pres.   Tel: (708) 597-0900   %FO: 100
>   Bus: *Sales and distribution of dental*   Fax: (708) 371-5148
>   *products.*

● **GRAPHTEC CORPORATION**
503-10, Shinano-cho, Totsuka-ku, Yokohoma 244-8503, Japan
CEO: Masahika Katahira, Pres.   Tel: 81-3-45-8256250   Rev: $111
Bus: *Mfr. analog recorders and digital pen* Fax: 81-3-45-8256396   Emp: 378
     plotters, scanners and printers.   www.graphteccorp.com

GRAPHTEC CORPORATION
14 Chrysler, Irvine, CA   92618
CEO: K. Minejima, Pres.   Tel: (949) 855-9407   %FO: 52
Bus: *Mfr./sales of analog recorders and* Fax: (949) 855-8601   Emp: 65
  digital pen plotters, scanners and
  printers.

● **THE GUNMA BANK, LTD.**
194 Motosojamachi, Maebashi, Gunma 371-8611, Japan
CEO: Kyoza Yoshida, Pres.   Tel: 81-272-52-1111   Rev: $1,713
Bus: *Financial banking services.*   Fax: 81-272-52-9721   Emp: 3,862
                                 www.gunmabank.co.jp

  THE GUNMA BANK, LTD.
  245 Park Avenue, New York, NY   10167
  CEO: Toshinori Fukasawa, Gen. Mgr. Tel: (212) 949-8690   %FO: 100
  Bus: *Provides financial banking*   Fax: (212) 867-1081
    services.

● **THE HACHIJUNI BANK LTD.**
178-8 Okada, Nagano 380-8682, Japan
CEO: Minoru Chino, Pres.   Tel: 81-26-3227-1182   Rev: $1,455
Bus: *Commercial banking services.* Fax: 81-26-3277-0146   Emp: 4,000
                                 www.82bank.co.jp

  THE HACHIJUNI BANK LTD.
  280 Park Avenue, West Bldg., 28th Fl., New York, NY   10022
  CEO: Hiroshi Miyashita, CEO   Tel: (212) 557-1182   %FO: 100
  Bus: *International commercial banking* Fax: (212) 557-8026   Emp: 13
    services.

● **HAKUHODO, INC.**
Gran Park Tower, 3-4-1 Shibaura, Minato-ku, Tokyo 108-8088, Japan
CEO: Toshio Miyagawa, Pres. & CEO Tel: 81-3-5446-6161   Rev: $850
Bus: *Advertising and communications* Fax: 81-3-5446-6166   Emp: 3,260
  services.   www.hakuhodo.co.jp

  HAKUHODO ADVERTISING AMERICA, INC.
  475 Park Avenue South, 18th Fl., New York, NY   10020
  CEO: Kolchiro Yabuki, Pres. & CEO Tel: (212) 684-7000   %FO: 100
  Bus: *Advertising agency.*   Fax: (212) 684-2801   Emp: 21

● **HAMADA PRINTING PRESS MFG CO LTD.**

2-15-28 Mitejima 2-chome, Nishi Yodogawa-ku, Osaka 555, Japan

CEO: Takeshi Kajitani, Pres.   Tel: 81-6-472-6200   Rev: $129

Bus: *Mfr. printing machinery and equipment.*   Fax: 81-6-472-6267   Emp: 389

www.hamada.co.jp

    HAMADA OF AMERICA,INC.

    110 Arovista Circle, Brea, CA   92621

    CEO: Ken Ichi Yokoe, EVP   Tel: (714) 990-1999   %FO: 100

    Bus: *Sheet-fed offset printing presses.*   Fax: (714) 990-1930

● **HAMAMATSU PHOTONICS KK**

325-6 Sunayama-Cho, Hamamatsu City, Shizuoka 430-8587, Japan

CEO: Teruo Hiruma, Pres.   Tel: 81-53-452-2141   Rev: $410

Bus: *Photosensitive devices and systems.*   Fax: 81-53-452-7889   Emp: 1,847

www.hamamatsu.com

    HAMAMATSU CORPORATION

    360 Foothill Road, PO Box 6910, Bridgewater, NJ   08807

    CEO: Jay Ralph Eno, Pres.   Tel: (908) 231-0960   %FO: 100

    Bus: *Holding company.*   Fax: (908) 231-1218

    INSPEX, INC.

    47 Manning Road, Billerica, MA   01821-3900

    CEO: Akira Hiruma, VP   Tel: (978) 667-5500   %FO: 100

    Bus: *Mfr. photosensitive devices &*   Fax: (978) 663-0011
        systems.

● **HANKYU CORPORATION**

8-8 Kakuda-cho, Kita-ku, Osaka 0530, Japan

CEO: Motohiro Sugai, Pres.   Tel: 81-6-373-5088   Rev: $3,607

Bus: *Provides railroad and line-haul*   Fax: Emp: 4,841
    operations.   www.hankyu.co.jp

    HANKYU EXPRESS

    2222 Kalakaua Avenue, Honolulu, HI   96815-2524

    CEO: Katsuya Mihashi, Pres.   Tel: (808) 922-5061   %FO: 100

    Bus: *Operates travel agencies.*   Fax:

    HANKYU INTERNATIONAL TRANSPORT INC.

    5353 West Imperial Highway, Ste. 100, Los Angeles, CA   90045

    CEO: Takaaki Yagi, Pres.   Tel: (310) 665-1400   %FO: 100

    Bus: *Provides freight forwarding*   Fax:
        services.

● **HANWA CO., LTD.**

1-13-10 Tsukiji, Chuo-ku, Tokyo 104-8429, Japan

CEO: Shuji Kita, Pres.   Tel: 81-3-3544-2171   Rev: $5,000

Bus: *Trades in steel and stainless products,*   Fax: Emp: 1,250
     petroleum products and foodstuffs.   www.hanwa.co.jp

     HANWA AMERICAN CORPORATION

     400 Kelby Street, 6th Fl., Fort Lee, NJ   07024

     CEO: S. Yuchi, Pres.   Tel: (201) 363-4500   %FO: 100

     Bus: *U.S. headquarters.*   Fax: (201) 346-9890

● **HARADA INDUSTRY CO LTD.**

17-13 Minami Ohi 4-chome, Shinagawa, Tokyo, Japan

CEO: Suichi Harada, Chmn.   Tel: 81-33-765-4321

Bus: *Mfr. auto and communication antennas,*   Fax: 81-33-763-0130   Emp: 1,800
     electric equipment, automotive access,   www.harada.co.jp
     household health appliances.

     HARADA INDUSTRY OF AMERICA ,INC.

     22925 Venture Drive, Novi, MI   48375

     CEO: Chris Hiyama, Pres.   Tel: (248) 374-9000   %FO: 100

     Bus: *Sales/distribution of auto antennas.*   Fax: (248) 374-0300   Emp: 102

● **HASEKO CORPORATION**

32-1 Shiba 2-chome, Minato-ku, Tokyo 105-8507, Japan

CEO: Toshihisa Dake, Pres.   Tel: 81-3-3456-3901   Rev: $3,400

Bus: *Engaged in construction, land*   Fax: 81-3-3452-6399   Emp: 2,250
     development and engineering.   www.haseko.co.jp

     HASEKO CORPORATION

     350 South Figueroa Street, Ste. 255, Los Angeles, CA   90017

     CEO: Toru Nagayama, Pres.   Tel: (213) 620-7100   %FO: 100

     Bus: *Provides construction & land*   Fax: (213) 680-4181
     development services.

     HASEKO HAWAII INC.

     820 Mililani Street, Ste. 820, Honolulu, HI   96813

     CEO: Toru Nagayama, Pres.   Tel: (808) 536-3771   %FO: 100

     Bus: *Develops high-rise condominiums,*   Fax: (808) 538-7654
     office buildings, hotels & shopping
     centers.

● **HAZAMA CORPORATION**
2-5-8 Kita-Aoyama Minato-ku, Tokyo 107, Japan
CEO: Fumiya Yamato, Pres.   Tel: 81-3-3405-1111   Rev: $3,746
Bus: *General construction contractors.*   Fax: 81-3-3405-1568   Emp: 4,810
                                   www.hazama.co.jp

> **HAZAMA CORPORATION**
> 6465 Reflections Drive, Ste. 240, Dublin, OH   43017
> CEO: Kenji Hosaka, Mgr.   Tel: (614) 792-8206   %FO: 100
> Bus: *Construction/engineering services.* Fax: (614) 792-8209

> **HAZAMA CORPORATION**
> 1045 W. Redondo Beach Blvd., Ste. 211, Gardena, CA   90247
> CEO: Toshihiko Kitano, Mgr.   Tel: (310) 352-3070   %FO: 100
> Bus: *Construction/engineering services.* Fax: (310) 352-3077   Emp: 30

> **HAZAMA CORPORATION**
> 2320 Paseo de Las Americas, Ste. 212, San Diego, CA   92154
> CEO: Toshihiko Kitano, Mgr.   Tel: (619) 661-8390   %FO: 100
> Bus: *Construction/engineering services.* Fax: (619) 661-8392

● **HINO MOTORS, LTD.**
1-1 Hinodai 3-chome, Hino-shi, Tokyo 191-8860, Japan
CEO: Hiroshi Yuasa, Pres.   Tel: 81-3-5419-9320   Rev: $6,192
Bus: *Mfr./markets diesel trucks and buses.*   Fax: 81-3-5419-9363   Emp: 9,074
                                   www.hino.co.jp

> **HINO DIESEL TRUCKS USA, INC.**
> 25 Corporate Drive, Orangeburg, NY   10962
> CEO: E. Ishizu, Pres.   Tel: (845) 365-1400   %FO: 100
> Bus: *Sales/distribution of diesel trucks*   Fax: (845) 365-1409
>   *and buses.*

● **HIRANO & ASSOCIATES**
8-12-7 Fukazawa, Setagaya-ku, Tokyo 158-8555, Japan
CEO: Tetsuyuki Hirano, Pres. & CEO   Tel: 81-3-704-3111
Bus: *Engaged in industrial design and*   Fax: 81-3-704-3200   Emp: 80
  architecture.   www.hd-group.co.jp

> **HIRANO DESIGN INTL INC.**
> 875 North Michigan Ave., Ste.3443, Chicago, IL   60611
> CEO: Hiroshi Ariyama, VP   Tel: (312) 335-0090   %FO: 100
> Bus: *Industrial and graphic design and*   Fax: (312) 335-0093   Emp: 8
>   *marketing.*

● **THE HIROSHIMA BANK LTD.**
3-8 Kamiyaa-cho 1-chome, Naka-ku, Hiroshima 730-8588, Japan
CEO: Makoto Uda, Pres.   Tel: 81-82-247-5151   Rev: $1,154
Bus: *Commercial banking services.*   Fax: 81-82-240-7698   Emp: 4,000
                                 www.hirogin.co.jp

    THE HIROSHIMA BANK LTD.
    444 Madison Avenue, Ste. 3502, New York, NY   10022
    CEO: Hiroshi Mizunoue, Rep.   Tel: (212) 644-8555   %FO: 100
    Bus: *Commercial banking services.*   Fax: (212) 644-0905   Emp: 15

● **HITACHI KOKI CO., LTD.**
Nippon Bldg., 2-6-2 Ohtemachi, Chiyoda-ku, Tokyo 100-0004, Japan
CEO: Hiroshi Gommori, Chmn.   Tel: 81-3-3270-6130   Rev: $1,295
Bus: *Mfr. electric tools and line printers for*   Fax: 81-3-3245-1777   Emp: 3,092
    computers & scientific instruments.   www.hitachi-koki.com.jp

    HITACHI KOKI IMAGING SOLUTIONS, INC.
    1757 Tapo Canyon Road, Simi Valley, CA   93063
    CEO: Yasuo Kikuchi, CEO   Tel: (805) 578-4000   %FO: 100
    Bus: *Mfr. computer printers and printer*   Fax: (805) 578-4001
      supplies.

    HITACHI KOKI USA LTD.
    3950 Steve Reynolds Blvd., Norcross, GA   30093
    CEO: Shintaro Shingyoji, Pres.   Tel: (770) 925-1774   %FO: 100
    Bus: *Sales/distribution of power tools.*   Fax: (770) 564-7003

● **HITACHI LTD.**
6 Kanda-Surugadai 4-chome, Chiyoda-ku, Tokyo 101-8010, Japan
CEO: Tsutomu Kanai, Chmn.   Tel: 81-3-3258-1111   Rev: $77,950
Bus: *Information systems and electronics,*   Fax: 81-3-3258-2375   Emp: 337,900
    power and industrial systems, consumer   www.hitachi.co.jp
    products and materials.

    HITACHI AMERICA, LTD.
    2000 Sierra Point Parkway, Brisbane, CA   94005
    CEO: Tomoharu Shimayama, Pres.   Tel: (650) 589-8300   %FO: 100
    Bus: *Manufactures electronics and*   Fax:
      electrical products.

HITACHI AMERICA, LTD.
50 Prospect Avenue, Tarrytown, NY   10591-4698
CEO: Tomoharu Shimayama, Pres.   Tel: (914) 332-5800   %FO: 100
Bus: *Information systems and*   Fax: (914) 332-5555   Emp: 1,000
electronics, power and industrial
systems, consumer products and
materials.

HITACHI COMPUER PRODUCTS AMERICA, INC.
1800 East Imhjoff Road, Norman, OK   73071
CEO: G. Kato, Pres.   Tel: (405) 360-5500   %FO: 100
Bus: *Mfr./sales of computer products.*   Fax: (405) 573-1299

HITACHI DATA SYSTEMS CORPORATION
750 Central Expressway, Santa Clara, CA   95050
CEO: Steve West, Pres.   Tel: (408) 970-1000   %FO: 100
Bus: *Manufactures electronics and*   Fax: (408) 727-8036
electrical products.

HITACHI INSTRUMENTS
3100 North First Street, San Jose, CA   95134
CEO: Mark McDonald, Pres.   Tel: (408) 432-0520   %FO: 100
Bus: *Sales/distribution of instruments.*   Fax: (408) 432-0704

HITACHI LEASING AMERICA INC.
400 Park Avenue, 8th Fl., New York, NY   10022
CEO: S. Shunzo, Pres.   Tel: (212) 888-2170   %FO: 100
Bus: *Leasing division.*   Fax: (212) 980-9296

HITACHI, LTD.
2029 Century Park East, Ste. 3940, Los Angeles, CA   90067
CEO: Tsutomu Gomibuchi, Mgr.   Tel: (310) 286-0243   %FO: 100
Bus: *Manufactures electronics and*   Fax: (310) 286-0230
electrical products.

HITACHI, LTD.
1900 K Street NW, Ste. 800, Washington, DC   20006
CEO: Takashi Chiba, Dir.   Tel: (202) 828-9272   %FO: 100
Bus: *Manufactures electronics and*   Fax:
electrical products.

● HITACHI METALS LTD.
Chiyoda Bldg., 1-2 Marunouchi 2-chome, Chiyoda-ku, Tokyo 100, Japan
CEO: Yoshimi Tokuda, Chmn.   Tel: 81-3-3284-4511   Rev: $3,874
Bus: *Mfr. custom metal products and*   Fax: 81-3-3287-1956   Emp: 24,500
specialty steel.   www.hitachimetals.com

AAP ST. MARY'S CORPORATION
1100 McKinley Avenue, St. Mary's, OH   44885

CEO: Martin Bando, Pres. Tel: (419) 394-7840 %FO: 100

Bus: *Mfg. aluminum wheels for automobiles.* Fax: (419) 394-4776 Emp: 340

HI SPECIALTY AMERICA, INC.
PO Box 442, Arona Road, Irwin, PA   15642

CEO: David Spehar, Pres. Tel: (412) 864-2370 %FO: 100

Bus: *Mfr. of cold-drawn special steel products.* Fax: (412) 864-0366 Emp: 25

HITACHI MAGNETICS CORPORATION
7800 Neff Road, Edmore, MI   48829

CEO: Kurt Miyairi, Pres. Tel: (517) 427-5151 %FO: 100

Bus: *Mfr. magnets.* Fax: (517) 427-5571 Emp: 500

HITACHI METALS AMERICA LTD.
One Hitachi Metals Drive, China Grove, NC   28023

CEO: Masanobu Sakae Tel: (704) 855-2800 %FO: 100

Bus: *Mfr./sale custom metal products, magnetic products, specialty steel.* Fax: (704) 855-2750

HITACHI METALS AMERICA, LTD.
2400 Westchester Avenue, Purchase, NY   10577

CEO: Mark Sakae, Pres. Tel: (914) 694-9200 %FO: 100

Bus: *Mfr./sale custom metal products, magnetic products, specialty steel.* Fax: (914) 694-9279 Emp: 2,500

HITACHI METALS AMERICA, LTD.
475 Hillside Avenue, Needham, MA   02494

CEO: Mark Sakae, CEO Tel: (781) 444-6533 %FO: 100

Bus: *Mfr./sale custom metal products, magnetic products, specialty steel.* Fax: (781) 444-8775

HITACHI METALS AMERICA, LTD.
745 South Church Street, Ste. 501, Murfreesboro, TN   37130

CEO: Mark Sakae, CEO Tel: (615) 849-6900 %FO: 100

Bus: *Mfr./sale custom metal products, magnetic products, specialty steel.* Fax: (615) 849-8492

HITACHI METALS AMERICA, LTD.
3020 Old Ranch Pkway., Ste. 270, Seal Beach, CA   90740

CEO: Mark Sakae, CEO Tel: (562) 493-8822 %FO: 100

Bus: *Mfr./sale custom metal products, magnetic products, specialty steel.* Fax: (562) 493-8520

HITACHI METALS AMERICA, LTD.

2151 O'Toole Avenue, Ste. B, San Jose, CA 95131

CEO: Arindam Saha, Mgr.   Tel: (408) 383-1780   %FO: 100

Bus: *Mfr./sale custom metal products,*   Fax: (408) 383-1762
magnetic products, specialty steel.

HITACHI METALS AMERICA, LTD.

2101 South Arlington Heights Road, Arlington Heights, IL 60005

CEO: Masanobu Sakae   Tel: (708) 364-7200   %FO: 100

Bus: *Mfr./sale custom metal products,*   Fax: (708) 364-7279
magnetic products, specialty steel.

HITACHI METALS AMERICA, LTD.

4601 Charlotte Park Drive, Ste. 210, Charlotte, NC 28217

CEO: Robert Kaminski, Mgr.   Tel: (704) 525-4136   %FO: 100

Bus: *Mfr./sale custom metal products,*   Fax: (704) 522-7189
magnetic products, specialty steel.

HITACHI METALS AMERICA, LTD.

41800 West Eleven Mile Road, Ste. 100, Novi, MI 48375

CEO: Mark Sakae, CEO   Tel: (248) 465-6400   %FO: 100

Bus: *Mfr./sale custom metal products,*   Fax: (248) 465-6020
magnetic products, specialty steel.

NEWPORT PRECISION

400 Cherry Street, Newport, TN 37821

CEO: P. Smith   Tel: (423) 623-3445   %FO: 100

Bus: *Mfr./sale vanes for power steering*   Fax: (423) 623-3449
pumps.

WARD MANUFACTURING CORPORATION

115 Gulick St., PO Box 9, Blossburg, PA 16912

CEO: Doyne Chartrau, CEO   Tel: (717) 638-2131   %FO: 100

Bus: *Mfr. pipe fittings & cast iron parts*   Fax: (717) 638-3410   Emp: 1,000
for automobiles.

• HITACHI SEIKI COMPANY, LTD.

1 Abiko City, Chiba 270-1195, Japan

CEO: Mutsushi Okamoto, Pres.   Tel: 81-3-471-84-1111   Rev: $385

Bus: *Mfr. metal cutting machine tools.*   Fax: 81-3-471-84-1511   Emp: 917
www.hitachiseiki.co.jp

HITACHI SEIKI USA, INC.

250 Brenner Drive, Congers, NY 10920

CEO: Masauki Izuchi, Chmn.   Tel: (845) 268-4124   %FO: 100

Bus: *Mfr./distribution/service machine*   Fax: (845) 268-7304   Emp: 100
tools.

● **HITACHI ZOSEN CORPORATION**
7-89 Nankokita 1-chome, Suminoe-ku, Osaka 559-0034, Japan
CEO: Isoh Minami, Pres.   Tel: 81-6-6569-0001   Rev: $4,505
Bus: *Environmental systems and industrial*   Fax: 81-6-6569-0002   Emp: 10,867
    plants, shipbuilding and offshore   www.hitachizosen.co.jp
    structures, steel structures, construction
    machinery, and logistics systems and
    machinery.

    HITACHI ZOSEN USA LTD.
    767 Third Avenue, 17th Fl., New York, NY   10017
    CEO: Kiyokazu Uehara, Pres.   Tel: (212) 355-5650   %FO: 100
    Bus: *Sales/liaison shipbuilding repair*   Fax: (212) 308-4937   Emp: 20
       offshore equipment.

    HITACHI ZOSEN USA LTD.
    1699 Wall Street, Ste. 425, Mt. Prospect, IL   60056
    CEO: Ken Inoue, Mgr.   Tel: (847) 532-9611   %FO: 100
    Bus: *Sales/liaison shipbuilding repair*   Fax: (847) 532-9533
       offshore equipment.

    HITACHI ZOSEN USA LTD.
    10777 Westheimer Road , Ste. 1075, Houston, TX   77042
    CEO: Kuniaki Furuya, Mgr.   Tel: (713) 532-9611   %FO: 100
    Bus: *Sales/liaison shipbuilding repair*   Fax: (713) 532-9533
       offshore equipment.

● **HOCHIKI CORPORATION**
2-10-43 Kami-ohsaki 2-chome, Shinagawa-ku, Tokyo 141-8660, Japan
CEO: Eiichi Okada, Pres.   Tel: 81-3 3444-4111   Rev: $502
Bus: *Mfr./install fire alarms and TV*   Fax: 81-3 3444-4555   Emp: 1,200
    equipment.   www.hochiki.co.jp

    HOCHIKI AMERICA CORPORATION
    5415 Industrial Drive, Huntington Beach, CA   92649
    CEO: Shunichi Shoji, CEO   Tel: (714) 898-0795   %FO: 100
    Bus: *Mfr./distribution fire alarms.*   Fax: (714) 892-2809   Emp: 80

● **THE HOKURIKU BANK, LTD.**
2-10, Nihonbashi Muro-machi 3-chome, Chuo-ku Tokyo 103, Japan
CEO: Shinichiro Inushima, Pres. & CEO   Tel: 81-3-3241-7771   Rev: $1,383
Bus: *Provides banking and financial services.*   Fax: 81-3-3241-5948   Emp: 4,000

THE HOKURIKU BANK LTD.
*780 Third Avenue, 28th Floor, New York, NY   10017
CEO: Shuichi Nakagawa, Rep.   Tel: (212) 355-3883   %FO: 100
Bus: *Provides banking and financial*   Fax: (212) 355-3887
    services.

● **HOKURIKU ELECTRIC INDUSTRY CO. LTD.**
7-89, Nanko-kita 1-chome, Suminoe-ku, Osaka 559-0034, Japan
CEO: Yoshihiro Fujii, Chmn. & CEO   Tel: 81-6-6569-0001   Rev: $4,505
Bus: *Mfr. film resistors and variable and*   Fax: 81-6-6569-0002   Emp: 10,870
    high-voltage resistors and sensor   www.rikuden.co.jp
    components.

    HOKURIKU USA COMPANY, LTD.
    2995 B Wall Triana Highway, Huntsville, AL   35824
    CEO: Scott Wilhelm, VP   Tel: (256) 772-9620   %FO: 100
    Bus: *Sales/distribution of film resistors*   Fax: (256) 772-3475
        and variable and high-voltage
        resistors.

● **HONDA MOTOR CO LTD.**
2-1-1 Minami-Aoyama 2-chome, Minato-ku, Tokyo 107, Japan
CEO: Hiroyuki Yoshino, Pres. & CEO   Tel: 81-3-3423-1111   Rev: $52,400
Bus: *Mfr. automobiles, motorcycles & power*   Fax: 81-3-3423-0217   Emp: 112,200
    products.   www.honda.co.jp

    AMERICAN HONDA MOTOR COMPANY, INC.
    1919 Torrance Blvd., Torrance, CA   90501-2746
    CEO: Koichi Amemiya, EVP   Tel: (310) 783-2000   %FO: 100
    Bus: *Sales, marketing, import/export*   Fax: (310) 783-3900   Emp: 12,000
        cars, motorcycles & power
        equipment.

    HONDA OF AMERICA MFG., INC.
    2400 Honda Parkway, Marysville, OH   43040
    CEO: K. Hirashima, Pres.   Tel: (937) 642-5000   %FO: 100
    Bus: *Mfr. automobiles, engines and*   Fax: (937) 644-6543
        motorcycles.

    HONDA R&D NORTH AMERICA ,INC.
    1900 Harpers Way, Torrance, CA   90501
    CEO: Hiro Watanabe, Pres.   Tel: (310) 781-5500   %FO: 100
    Bus: *Design/engineer motor products.*   Fax: (310) 781-5768

HONDA TRADING AMERICA INC.
700 Van Ness Avenue, Torrance, CA 90501
CEO: Y. Saito, Pres.   Tel: (310) 781-4065   %FO: 100
Bus: *Import/export/marketing services*   Fax: (310) 781-4776
for U.S. operations.

● **HORIBA LTD.**
2, Miyanohigashi-cho, Kisshoin, Minami-ku, Kyoto-shi, 601-8305, Japan
CEO: Masao Horiba, Chrm.   Tel: 81-75-312-9938   Rev: $607
Bus: *Mfr. analyzer systems.*   Fax: 81-75-312-9936   Emp: 995
                                www.horiba.co.jp

    HORIBA STEC INC.
    5900 Hines Drive, Ann Arbor, MI 48108
    CEO: Rex Tapp, VP   Tel: (734) 213-6555   %FO: 100
    Bus: *Mfr. analyzer systems.*   Fax: (734) 213-6525

    HORIBA STEC INC.
    2520 South Industrial Park Drive, Tempe, AZ 85282
    CEO: L. Dolley   Tel: (602) 967-2283   %FO: 100
    Bus: *Mfr. analyzer systems.*   Fax: (602) 967-2283

    HORIBA STEC INC.
    17671 Armstrong Avenue, Irvine, CA 92714
    CEO: Neal Harvey, CEO   Tel: (949) 250-4811   %FO: 100
    Bus: *Mfr. analyzer systems.*   Fax: (949) 250-0924   Emp: 120

● **HOSOKAWA MICRON GROUP**
Midosuji-Hommachi Bldg, 5-7 Mommachi 3-chome, Osaka 541, Japan
CEO: Masuo Hosokawa, Chmn.   Tel: 81-6-263-2555   Rev: $577
Bus: *Powder processing equipment and*   Fax: 81-6-263-2552   Emp: 421
systems, environmental protection, filter   www.hosokawamicron.com
media, plastics processing equipment.

    HOSOKAWA BEPEX, INC.
    333 NE Taft Street, Minneapolis, MN 55413
    CEO: Bruce Chambers   Tel: (612) 331-4370   %FO: 100
    Bus: *Mfr. powder processing equipment*   Fax: (612) 627-1458
    and systems.

    HOSOKAWA MANUFACTURING
    150 Todd Road, Santa Rosa, CA 95402
    CEO: Masuo Hosokawa, Chmn.   Tel: (707) 586-6000   %FO: 100
    Bus: *Mfr. powder processing equipment*   Fax: (707) 585-2478
    and systems.

HOSOKAWA MICRON POWDER SYSTEMS, INC.

10 Chatham Road, Summit, NJ   07901

CEO: Ralph Imholt	Tel: (908) 273-6360	%FO: 100
Bus: *Mfr. powder processing equipment and systems.*	Fax: (908) 273-7432	Emp: 150

HOSOKAWA POLYMER SYSTEMS

63 Fuller Way, Berlin, CT   06037

CEO: Masuo Hosokawa, Chmn.	Tel: (860) 828-0541	%FO: 100
Bus: *Mfr. powder processing equipment and systems.*	Fax: (860) 829-1313	

● THE HYAKUJUSHI BANK LTD.

5-1 Kamei-cho, Takamatsu, Kagawa 760-8574, Japan

CEO: Kyosuke Matsumoto, Chmn.	Tel: 81-87-831-0114	Rev: $858
Bus: *Provides commercial banking services.*	Fax: 81-87-836-3693	Emp: 2,490
	www.bank-ir.ne.jp	

THE HYAKUJUSHI BANK, LTD.

2 Wall Street, 11th Fl., New York, NY   10005

CEO: Hiroyuki Fujita, Rep.	Tel: (212) 513-0114	%FO: 100
Bus: *Commercial banking services.*	Fax: (212) 619-0757	Emp: 16

● IBIDEN CO., LTD.

2-1 Kanda-machi, Ogaki, Gifu 503-8604, Japan

CEO: Yoshifumi Iwata, Pres.	Tel: 81-584-81-3111	Rev: $1,830
Bus: *Mfr. chemicals.*	Fax: 81-584-81-4676	Emp: 4,554
	www.ibiden.co.jp	

IBIDEN USA CORP.

2350 Mission College Blvd., Ste. 975, Santa Clara, CA   95054

CEO: Takeshi Sugimoto	Tel: (408) 986-4343	%FO: 100
Bus: *Mfr. chemicals.*	Fax: (408) 986-4343	

IBIDEN USA CORP.

1600 West Chandler Blvd, Ste. 260, Chandler, AZ   85224

CEO: Takeshi Sugimoto	Tel: (602) 726-8701	%FO: 100
Bus: *Mfr. chemicals.*	Fax: (602) 726-8701	

IBIDEN USA CORP.

875 Toll Gate Road, Elgin, IL   60123

CEO: Takeshi Sugimoto	Tel: (847) 608-4800	%FO: 100
Bus: *Mfr. chemicals.*	Fax: (847) 608-4800	

- **IDEMITSU KOSAN CO., LTD.**

1-1 Marunouchi 3-chome, Chiyoda-ku, Tokyo, Japan

CEO: Akira Idemitsu, Chmn.	Tel: 81-3-3213-3115	Rev: $20,725
Bus: *Refines crude oil and markets and distributes petroleum products.*	Fax: 81-3-3213-9354 www.idemitsu.co.jp	Emp: 3,875

IDEMITSU APOLLO CORPORATION

1270 Avenue of the Americas, Ste. 420, New York, NY   10020

CEO: Toshimichi Kono, Pres.	Tel: (212) 332-4820	%FO: 100
Bus: *Sales/distribution of petroleum products.*	Fax: (212) 322-4819	

- **IKEGAI CORPORATION**

80 Shinmei 1-chome, Saiwai-ku, Kawasaki-shi Kanagawa-ken 210-0922, Japan

CEO: Shoji Inagawa, Pres.	Tel: 81-44-544-3561	Rev: $174
Bus: *CNC machine tool lathe and machine centers.*	Fax: 81-44-544-3707 www.ikegai.co.jp	Emp: 478

IKEGAI AMERICA CORPORATION

100 High Grove Boulevard, Glendale Heights, IL   60139

CEO: Yasushi Inagawa, Pres.	Tel: (630) 924-0641	%FO: 100
Bus: *CNC machine tool related parts and service.*	Fax: (630) 924-1779	Emp: 10

- **INDUSTRIAL BANK OF JAPAN LTD. (SUB. MIZUHO HOLDINGS)**

3-3 Marunouchi 1-chome, Chiyoda-ku, Tokyo 100-8210, Japan

CEO: Masao Nishimura, Pres. & CEO	Tel: 81-3-3214-1111	Rev: $28,430
Bus: *Wholesale banking and long-term credit facilities.*	Fax: 81-3-3201-7643 www.lbjbank.co.jp	Emp: 7,395

IBJ WHITEHALL BANK & TRUST COMPANY

One State Street, New York, NY   10004

CEO: Dennis G. Buchert, CEO	Tel: (212) 858-2000	%FO: 100
Bus: *Wholesale banking, corporate and private banking, trust and investment advisory services.*	Fax: (212) 425-0542	

IBJ WHITEHALL BUSINESS CREDIT CORP.

One State Street, New York, NY   10004

CEO: Edward J. Fanning, CEO	Tel: (212) 858-2000	%FO: 100
Bus: *Wholesale banking, corporate and private banking, trust and investment advisory services.*	Fax: (212) 425-0542	Emp: 500

IBJS CAPITAL CORPORATION
One State Street, New York, NY   10004
CEO: Lawrence S. Zilavy, CEO   Tel: (212) 858-2546   %FO: 100
Bus: *Wholesale banking, long-term*   Fax: (212) 858-2768
      credit facilities.

INDUSTRIAL BANK OF JAPAN TRUST COMPANY
1251 Avenue of the Americas, New York, NY   10020
CEO: Shoji Noguchi, Chmn.   Tel: (212) 282-3000   %FO: 100
Bus: *Wholesale banking, long-term*   Fax: (212) 282-4252   Emp: 500
      credit facilities.

INNOVEST CAPITAL MANAGEMENT INC.
One State Street, New York, NY   10004
CEO: Noboru Nagata, VC   Tel: (212) 858-2595   %FO: 100
Bus: *Engaged in asset management.*   Fax: (212) 858-3613

● **ISETAN COMPANY, LTD.**
14-1 Shinjuku 3-chome, Shinjuku-ku, Tokyo 160-8001, Japan
CEO: Kazumasa Koshiba, Pres.   Tel: 81-3-3352-1111   Rev: $5,432
Bus: *Manages and operates department* Fax: 81-3-5273-5321   Emp: 5,100
      stores.   www.isetan.co.jp

   ISETAN COMPANY, LTD.
   1411 Broadway, 25th Fl., New York, NY   10018
   CEO: Tai Ogata, Rep.   Tel: (212) 767-0300   %FO: 100
   Bus: *Manages/operates department* Fax: (212) 767-0307   Emp: 6
         stores.

● **ISHIKAWAJIMA-HARIMA HEAVY INDUSTRIES COMPANY, LTD.**
2-1 Ohtemachi, 2-chome, Chiyoda-ku, Tokyo 100-8182, Japan
CEO: Kosaku Inaba, Chmn. & CEO   Tel: 81-3-3244-5111   Rev: $9,431
Bus: *Shipbuilding and repair, mfr.*   Fax: 81-3-3244-5131   Emp: 12,795
      machinery, diesels, boilers, bridges, etc. www.ihi.co.jp

   IHI, INC.
   280 Park Avenue, 30th Fl. West Bldg, New York, NY   10017
   CEO: Yuji Hiruma, Pres.   Tel: (212) 599-8100   %FO: 100
   Bus: *Shipbuilding and repair technical* Fax: (212) 599-8111
         consultants; sale of ship-building
         material.

IHI, INC.
755 West Bog Beaver Rd., Ste. 420, Troy, MI   48084
CEO: M. Yamada, Mgr. Tel: (248) 244-9370 %FO: 100
Bus: *Shipbuilding and repair technical* Fax: (248) 244-9062
consultants; sale of ship-building
material.

• ISUZU MOTORS LTD.
26-1 Minami-oi 6-chome, Shinagawa-ku, Tokyo 140-8722, Japan
CEO: Kazuhira Seki, Chmn. Tel: 81-3 5471-1141 Rev: $14,280
Bus: *Mfr. motor vehicles, parts and* Fax: 81-3-5471-1042 Emp: 12,965
accessories. www.isuzu.com

AMERICAN ISUZU MOTORS, INC.
13340 183rd Street, Suite 6007, Cerritos, CA   90703-8748
CEO: Norihiko Oda, CEO Tel: (562) 229-5000 %FO: 100
Bus: *Sale/service trucks, sport utility* Fax: (562) 926-5174
vehicles.

ISUZU AUTOMOTIVE, INC.
PO Box 5689, Lafayette, IN   47903
CEO: Masayoshi Nagano, Pres. Tel: (765) 449-1111 %FO: 49
Bus: *Mfr. motor vehicles.* Fax: (765) 449-6269 Emp: 1,900

ISUZU MOTORS AMERICA
16323 Shoemaker Avenue, Cerritos, CA   90703
CEO: Norihiko Oda, CEO Tel: (562) 229-7000
Bus: *Mfr. motor vehicles.* Fax: (562) 404-1099

ISUZU MOTORS AMERICA, INC.
16323 Shoemaker Avenue, Cerritos, CA   90703
CEO: Hiroo Majima, COO Tel: (562) 949-0320 %FO: 100
Bus: *Distribute light-duty motor* Fax: (562) 404-9046
vehicles.

• ITOCHU CORPORATION
5-1 Kita Aoyama 2 chome, Minato-ku, Tokyo 107-8077, Japan
CEO: Uicharo Niwa, Pres. & CEO Tel: 81-3-3497-2121 Rev: $115,100
Bus: *General international trading activities;* Fax: 81-3-3497-4141 Emp: 5,300
construction, research, science and air www.itochu.co.jp
lease divisions.

HELMITIN INC.
11110 Airport Road, Olive Branch, TN   38654
CEO: Larry Droski, Pres. Tel: (601) 895-4565 %FO: 100
Bus: *Mfr./sales/distribution of* Fax: (601) 895-4583
adhesives.

ITOCHU COTTON INC.

777 South Figueroa Street, Ste. 4500, Los Angeles, CA   90017

CEO: Mark Lewkowitz | Tel: (213) 623-4001 | %FO: 100

Bus: *General international trading activities in cotton.*   Fax: (213) 623-4005

ITOCHU INTERNATIONAL INC.

1300 Post Oak Boulevard, Ste. 900, Houston, TX   77056

CEO: Taijiro Sakagami, Mgr. | Tel: (713) 843-6500 | %FO: 100

Bus: *General international trading activities.*   Fax: (713) 843-6620

ITOCHU INTERNATIONAL INC.

1155 21st Street NW, Ste. 710, Washington, DC   20036

CEO: Takeshi Kondo, SVP | Tel: (202) 822-9082 | %FO: 100

Bus: *General international trading activities.*   Fax: (202) 822-9233

ITOCHU INTERNATIONAL INC.

26622 Woodward Avenue, Ste. 200, Royal Oak, MI   48067

CEO: Mark Kanada, Mgr. | Tel: (248) 399-6440 | %FO: 100

Bus: *General international trading activities.*   Fax: (248) 399-9680

ITOCHU INTERNATIONAL INC.

100 East River Center Boulevard, Covington, KY   41011

CEO: Nick Yanni, Mgr | Tel: (859) 581-1555 | %FO: 100

Bus: *General international trading activities.*   Fax: (859) 581-5636

ITOCHU INTERNATIONAL INC.

50 California Street, Ste. 50, San Francisco, CA   94111

CEO: T. Hosokawa, Mgr. | Tel: (415) 399-3700 | %FO: 100

Bus: *General international trading activities.*   Fax: (415) 398-4648

ITOCHU INTERNATIONAL INC.

2333 North Waukegan Road, Bannockburn, IL   60015

CEO: M. Hayashi, Mgr. | Tel: (847) 948-8400 | %FO: 100

Bus: *General international trading activities.*   Fax: (847) 948-7780

ITOCHU INTERNATIONAL INC.

4000 Embassy Parkway, Ste. 320, Akron, OH   43333

CEO: N. Sasaki, Mgr. | Tel: (330) 670-1116 | %FO: 100

Bus: *General international trading activities.*   Fax: (330) 670-1120

ITOCHU INTERNATIONAL INC.
One SW Street, Ste. 730, Portland, OR   97258
CEO: H. Masuda, Mgr.   Tel: (503) 227-6694   %FO: 100
Bus: *General international trading*   Fax: (503) 226-3054
      activities.

ITOCHU INTERNATIONAL INC.
335 Madison Avenue, 22-24 Fls., New York, NY   10017
CEO: Jay W. Chai, Chmn. & CEO   Tel: (212) 818-8000   %FO: 100
Bus: *General international trading*   Fax: (212) 818-8361   Emp: 460
      activities.

ITOCHU INTERNATIONAL INC.
900 Fourth Avenue, Ste. 1275, Seattle, WA   98164
CEO: Taka Ichimura, Mgr.   Tel: (206) 623-3764   %FO: 100
Bus: *General international trading*   Fax: (206) 623-0730
      activities.

● **ITO-YOKADA COMPANY, LTD.**
1-4 Shibakoen, 4-chome, Minato-ku, Tokyo 105-8571, Japan
CEO: Toshifumi Suzuki, Pres. & CEO   Tel: 81-3-3459-2111   Rev: $29,308
Bus: *Operates convenience stores (7-Eleven)*   Fax: 81-3-3434-8378   Emp: 116,636
      and specialty stores, department stores   www.itoyokada.iyg.co.jp
      and supermarkets.

   7-ELEVEN, INC.
   2711 North Haskell Avenue, Dallas, TX   75204
   CEO: Masatoshi Ito, Chmn.   Tel: (214) 828-7011   %FO: 100
   Bus: *Operates convenience stores.*   Fax: (214) 828-7848   Emp: 32,000

● **IWATANI INTERNATIONAL CORPORATION**
4-8, Hommachi 3-chome, Chuo-ku Osaka 541-0053, Japan
CEO: Akiji Makino, Pres.   Tel: 81-6-6267-3355   Rev: $5,543
Bus: *Mfr./sales consumer products,*   Fax: 81-6-6267-3350   Emp: 1,442
      agricultural and medical products,   www.iwatani.co.jp
      industrial gases/materials and
      construction.

   IWATANI INTERNATIONAL CORPORATION OF AMERICA
   1701 Golf Road, Ste. 1106, Rolling Meadows, IL   60008
   CEO: Shuji Nakamura, Pres.   Tel: (847) 290-0300   %FO: 100
   Bus: *Sales of consumer products,*   Fax: (847) 290-0350
      agricultural/medical products,
      industrial gases/materials and
      construction.

IWATANI INTERNATIONAL CORPORATION OF AMERICA
1025 West 190th Street, Gardena, CA   90248
CEO: John Wooden, Mgr.   Tel: (310) 324-9174   %FO: 100
Bus: *Sales of consumer products,*   Fax: (310) 324-9177
agricultural/medical products,
industrial gases/materials and
construction.

IWATANI INTERNATIONAL CORPORATION OF AMERICA
2050 Center Avenue, Ste. 425, Fort Lee, NJ   07024
CEO: Sadao Yasumi, Pres.   Tel: (201) 585-2442   %FO: 100
Bus: *U.S. headquarters operation.*   Fax: (201) 585-2369

● **THE IYO BANK LTD.**
1 Minami-Horibata-cho, Matsuyama 790, Japan
CEO: Gizo Mizuki, Chmn.   Tel: 81-89-941-1141   Rev: $937
Bus: *Commercial banking services.*   Fax: 81-89-946-9101   Emp: 3,500
www.iyobank.co.jp

THE IYO BANK LTD.
780 Third Avenue, 18th Fl., New York, NY   10017
CEO: Eiji Shigematsu, Rep.   Tel: (212) 688-6031   %FO: 100
Bus: *Commercial banking services.*   Fax: (212) 688-6420

● **JAFCO CO., LTD.**
1-8-2 Marunochi, Chiyoda-ku, Tokyo 100-005, Japan
CEO: Mitsumasa Murase, Pres.   Tel: 81-3-5223-7536
Bus: *Engaged in capital ventures.*   Fax: 81-3-5223-7561
www.jafco.co.jp

JAFCO AMERICA VENTURES, INC.
One Boston Place, Boston, MA   02108
CEO: Andy Goldfarb, Dir.   Tel: (617) 367-3510   %FO: 100
Bus: *Engaged in capital ventures.*   Fax: (617) 367-3532

JAFCO AMERICA VENTURES, INC.
505 Hamilton Avenue, Ste. 310, Palo Alto, CA   94301
CEO: Barry Schiffman, Pres.   Tel: (650) 463-8800   %FO: 100
Bus: *Engaged in capital ventures.*   Fax: (650) 463-8801

● **JAPAN AIRLINES COMPANY, LTD.**
4-11 Higashi Shinagawa, Shinagawa-ku, Tokyo 140, Japan
CEO: Isao Kaneko, Pres.   Tel: 81-3-5460-3121   Rev: $17,860
Bus: *International airline, hotels/catering.*   Fax: 81-3-5460-5913   Emp: 14,064
www.japanair.com

JAPAN AIR LINES (USA) Ltd.
655 Fifth Avenue, New York, NY   10022
CEO: Kazunari Yashiro, CEO   Tel: (212) 310-1318   %FO: 100
Bus: *International air transport*   Fax: (212) 310-1238   Emp: 200
    services.

● **JAPAN AVIATION ELECTRONICS INDUSTRY LTD.**
21-2 Dogenzaka 1-chome, Shibuya-ku, Tokyo 150, Japan
CEO: Masami Shinozaki, Pres.   Tel: 81-3-3780-2711   Rev: $765
Bus: *Mfr. connectors and switches.* Fax: 81-3-3780-2733   Emp: 1,974
                                     www.jae.co.jp

    JAE ELECTRONICS INC.
    142 Technology Drive, Ste.100, Irvine, CA   92718-2401
    CEO: Yasuo Takagi, Pres.   Tel: (949) 753-2600   %FO: 100
    Bus: *Distribution/sale switches and* Fax: (949) 753-2699
        connectors.

● **JAPAN BANK FOR INTERNATIONAL CORP.**
4- Ohtemachi 1-chome, Chiyoda-ku, Tokyo 100-8144, Japan
CEO: Hiroshi Yasuda, Gov.   Tel: 81-3-3287-9106
Bus: *Government bank providing foreign* Fax: 81-3-3287-9101
    interchange, capital contributions and www.japanexim.go.jp
    guarantees.

    THE EXPORT-IMPORT BANK OF JAPAN
    601 South Figueroa Street, Ste. 4590, Los Angeles, CA   90017
    CEO: Kazuo Yokoyama, Rep.   Tel: (213) 627-3500   %FO: 100
    Bus: *Government bank providing*   Fax: (213) 627-3900
        foreign interchange, capital
        contributions and guarantees.

    THE EXPORT-IMPORT BANK OF JAPAN
    2000 Pennsylvania Avenue NW, Ste. 3350, Washington, DC   20006
    CEO: Toru Tokuhisa, Rep.   Tel: (202) 331-8547   %FO: 100
    Bus: *Government bank providing*   Fax: (202) 775-1990
        foreign interchange, capital
        contributions and guarantees.

    JAPAN BANK FOR INTERNATIONAL CORP. (JBIC)
    520 Madison Avenue, 40th Fl., New York, NY   10022
    CEO: Shigeki Yoshida, Rep.   Tel: (212) 888-9500   %FO: 100
    Bus: *Government bank providing*   Fax: (212) 888-9503
        foreign interchange, capital
        contributions and guarantees.

- **JAPAN ENERGY CORPORATION**
10-1 Toranomon 2-chome, Minato-ku, Tokyo 105-8407, Japan
CEO: Akihiko Nomiyama, CEO   Tel: 81-3-5573-6100   Rev: $18,400
Bus: *Electronic and petroleum refining, oil*   Fax: 81-3-5573-6784   Emp: 13,295
     exploration/development, specialty   www.j-energy.co.jp
     metals, pharmaceuticals and
     biotechnology.

     AMERICAN MICROSYSTEMS, INC.
     2300 Buckskin Road, Pocatello, ID   83201
     CEO: Gene Patterson, Pres.   Tel: (208) 233-4690   %FO: 100
     Bus: *Mfr./sales semiconductors.*   Fax: (208) 234-6795

     GOULD ELECTRONICS INC.
     34929 Curtis Boulevard, Eastlake, OH   44095-4001
     CEO: C. David Ferguson, Pres. & CEO   Tel: (440) 953-5000   %FO: 100
     Bus: *Mfr./sales electro-deposited*   Fax: (440) 953-5050
       copper foil and other electronic
       materials.

     IRVINE SCIENTIFIC SALES COMPANY INC.
     2511 Daimler Street, Santa Ana, CA   92705-5588
     CEO: Michael J. Kelly, Pres.   Tel: (949) 261-7800   %FO: 100
     Bus: *Mfr./sales serum and media for*   Fax: (949) 261-6522
       biotechnology.

     NIMTEC INC.
     125 North Price Road, Chandler, AZ   85224
     CEO: Robert Combs, Pres.   Tel: (480) 732-9857   %FO: 100
     Bus: *Mfr./sales of semiconductors.*   Fax: (480) 899-0779

- **JAPAN RADIO COMPANY, LTD.**
17-22 Akasaka 2-chome, Minato-ku, Tokyo 107, Japan
CEO: Hiroshi Yokomizo, Pres.   Tel: 81-3-3584-8743   Rev: $2,481
Bus: *Mfr. marine/land radio and navigation*   Fax: Emp: 3,964
     equipment.   www.jre.co.jp

     JAPAN RADIO COMPANY, LTD.
     1011 Southwest Klicktat Way, Seattle, WA   98134
     CEO: Shunichi Hasama, Mgr.   Tel: (206) 654-5644   %FO: 100
     Bus: *Sale marine/land radio and*   Fax: (206) 654-7030   Emp: 7
       navigation equipment.

• **THE JAPAN STEEL WORKS, LTD.**
Hibiya Mitsui Bldg., 1-2 Yuraku-cho, 1-chome, Chiyoda-ku, Tokyo 100-006, Japan
CEO: Keizo Ohnishi, Pres.   Tel: 81-3-3501-6111   Rev: $1,186
Bus: *Produces defense equipment, steel*   Fax: 81-3-3504-0727   Emp: 2,890
products and industrial machinery.   www.jsw.co.jp

  JAPAN STEEL WORKS AMERICA INC.
  200 Park Avenue, Ste. 3920, New York, NY   10166
  CEO: I. Oguri, Pres.   Tel: (212) 878-9700   %FO: 100
  Bus: *Mfr. steel products and industrial*   Fax: (212) 490-2575
  machinery.

  JAPAN STEEL WORKS AMERICA INC.
  9801 Westheimer, Ste. 702, Houston, TX   77042
  CEO: I. Oguri, Pres.   Tel: (713) 953-9151   %FO: 100
  Bus: *Mfr. steel products and industrial*   Fax: (713) 953-1439
  machinery.

  JAPAN STEEL WORKS AMERICA INC.
  5801 East Slauson Avenue, Ste. 205, Los Angeles, CA   90040
  CEO: I. Oguri, Pres.   Tel: (323) 725-3143   %FO: 100
  Bus: *Mfr. steel products and industrial*   Fax: (323) 725-6662
  machinery.

• **JAPAN STORAGE BATTERY CO LTD.**
1 Inobanba-cho Nishinosho, Kisshoin, Minami-ku, Kyoto 601-8520, Japan
CEO: Mitsuo Iwai, Pres.   Tel: 81-75-316-3100   Rev: $1,233
Bus: *Mfr. storage batteries, rectifiers and*   Fax: 81-75-326-3101   Emp: 2,356
lighting equipment.   www.nippondenchi.co.jp

  GS BATTERY (USA) INC.
  17253 Chestnut Street, City of Industry, CA   91748
  CEO: Hiroshi Hatano, Pres.   Tel: (626) 964-8348   %FO: 100
  Bus: *Distribution of batteries and*   Fax: (626) 810-9438   Emp: 16
  chargers.

• **JAPAN TOBACCO INC.**
2-1 Toranomon, 2-chome, Minato-ku, Tokyo 105-8411, Japan
CEO: Katsuhiko Honda, Pres.   Tel: 81-3-3582-3111   Rev: $41,430
Bus: *Mfr. tobacco, salt, food and*   Fax: 81-3-5572-1441   Emp: 16,235
pharmaceutical products.   www.jti.co.jp

JAPAN TOBACCO INC.
375 Park Avenue, Ste. 1307, New York, NY   10152
CEO: Shuji Kondo, Mng. Dir.   Tel: (212) 319-8990   %FO: 100
Bus: *Mfr. tobacco, salt, food and*   Fax: (212) 319-8993   Emp: 4
pharmaceutical products.

JT INTL, INC.
2441 205th Street, C-102, Torrance, CA   90501
CEO: Masayuki Hamada, Pres.   Tel: (310) 212-6416   %FO: 100
Bus: *Mfr. tobacco, salt, food and*   Fax: (310) 533-8027   Emp: 9
pharmaceutical products.

● JEOL LTD.
1-2 Musashino 3-chome, Akishima Tokyo 196-8558, Japan
CEO: Takashi Takeuchi, Pres.   Tel: 81-42-542-2187   Rev: $680
Bus: *Mfr. scientific instruments, including*   Fax: 81-42-546-5757   Emp: 1,116
electron optics and semiconductor and   www.jeol.co.jp
medical equipment.

JEOL USA, INC.
600 North Bell Avenue, Carnegie, PA   15106
CEO: John Dombroski, Mgr.   Tel: (412) 279-7791   %FO: 100
Bus: *Distribute/service scientific*   Fax: (412) 276-4676
instruments.

JEOL USA, INC.
9501 West Devon Avenue, Ste. 500, Rosemont, IL   60018
CEO: Terry McGrath, Mgr.   Tel: (847) 823-0306   %FO: 100
Bus: *Distribute/service scientific*   Fax: (847) 692-5164
instruments.

JEOL USA, INC.
3446 Bridgeland Drive, Bridgeton, MO   63044
CEO: Randy Cripe, Mgr.   Tel: (314) 739-8433   %FO: 100
Bus: *Distribute/service scientific*   Fax: (314) 291-8595
instruments.

JEOL USA, INC.
11 Dearborn Road, Peabody, MA   01960
CEO: Gary L. Cogswell, CEO   Tel: (978) 535-5900   %FO: 100
Bus: *Distribute/service scientific*   Fax: (978) 535-7741   Emp: 270
instruments.

JEOL USA, INC.
9870 Highway 92, Ste. 310, Woodstock, GA 30188
CEO: Mike Maguire, Mgr.   Tel: (770) 592-6443   %FO: 100
Bus: *Distribute/service scientific*   Fax: (770) 592-5622
    instruments.

● **JIJI PRESS LTD.**
1-3 Hibiya Park, Chiyoda-ku, Tokyo 100-8568, Japan
CEO: Matsatoshi Murakami, Pres. & CEO   Tel: 81-3-3591-1111
Bus: *News syndicate providing news services*   Fax: 81-3-3591-1111   Emp: 1,400
    for newspapers, TV and radio stations,   www.jiji.co.jp
    and news agencies in Japan and abroad.

   JIJI PRESS AMERICA, LTD.
   120 West 45th Street, 14th Fl., New York, NY 10036
   CEO: Hiroshi Kanashige, Pres.   Tel: (212) 575-5830   %FO: 100
   Bus: *News agency.*   Fax: (212) 764-3951   Emp: 16

● **THE JOYO BANK LTD.**
5-5 Minami-machi 2-chome, Mito City, Ibaraki 310-8604, Japan
CEO: Toranosuke Nishino, Pres.   Tel: 81-292-312151   Rev: $2,270
Bus: *Commercial banking services.*   Fax: 81-3-3274-3626   Emp: 4,583
                                         www.jojobank.co.jp

   THE JOYO BANK LTD.
   150 East 52nd Street, 6th Fl., New York, NY 10022-6017
   CEO: Hiroaki Yokochi, Mgr.   Tel: (212) 752-2500   %FO: 100
   Bus: *Commercial banking services.*   Fax: (212) 752-6900   Emp: 20

● **JTB, INC. (JAPAN TRAVEL BUREAU, INC.)**
2-3-11 Higashi-Shinagawa, Shinagawa-ku, Tokyo 100-0005, Japan
CEO: Ryuichi Funayama, Pres.   Tel: 81-3-3284-7502   Rev: $2,742
Bus: *Travel services.*   Fax: 81-3-3284-7050   Emp: 12,400
                                         www.jtb.co.jp

   JTB INC.
   777 S. Figueroa Street, Ste. 3900, Los Angeles, CA 90017
   CEO: Fujo Kato, Pres.   Tel: (213) 553-6500   %FO: 100
   Bus: *Travel services.*   Fax: (213) 553-6555   Emp: 410

   JTB INC.
   810 Seventh Avenue, New York, NY 10019
   CEO: M. Noguchi, Mgr.   Tel: (212) 246-8030   %FO: 100
   Bus: *Travel services.*   Fax: (212) 265-7234   Emp: 400

- **JUSCO CO., LTD./ AEON GROUP**

5-1-1 Nakase, Mihama-ku, Chiba 261-8515, Japan
CEO: Tohiji Tokiwa, Chmn. & CEO Tel: 81-43-212-6093 Rev: $22,042
Bus: *Operates specialty store chains and* Fax: 81-43-212-6805 Emp: 45,000
general merchandising stores. (Sub of www.jusco.co.jp
AEON Group)

JUSCO (U.S.A.), INC.

520 Madison Avenue, 24th Fl., New York, NY   10022
CEO: Isao T. Tsuruta, SVP Tel: (212) 821-9100 %FO: 100
Bus: *Retail holding company.* Fax: (212) 838-0469 Emp: 7

REVMEN INDUSTRIES INC.

1211 Avenue of the Americas, New York, NY   10036
CEO: Richard Roman, Pres. & CEO Tel: (212) 278-0300 %FO: 100
Bus: *Wholesales home furnishing* Fax: (212) 840-8446
products.

TALBOTS, INC.

175 Beal Street, Hingham, MA   02043
CEO: Arnold Zetcher, CEO Tel: (781) 749-7600 %FO: 100
Bus: *Operates retail clothing chain* Fax: (781) 749-0845 Emp: 1,000
stores.

- **KAJIMA CORPORATION**

2-7 Motoakasaka 1-chome, Minato-ku, Tokyo 107-8388, Japan
CEO: Sadao Umeda, Pres. & CEO Tel: 81-3-3404-3311 Rev: $16,375
Bus: *Engaged in general contracting,* Fax: 81-3-3470-1444 Emp: 11,665
architectural and engineering services. www.kajima.co.jp

KAJIMA U.S.A. INC.

1251 Avenue of the Americas, 9th Fl., New York, NY   10020
CEO: Shoichi Kajima, Pres. & CEO Tel: (212) 355-4571 %FO: 100
Bus: *Real estate investment &* Fax: (212) 355-4576 Emp: 25
development and general
contracting, architectural &
engineering services.

- **KANEBO, LTD.**

20-20 Kaigan, 3-chome, Minato-ku, Tokyo 108, Japan
CEO: Masatoshi Takeda, Pres. Tel: 81-3-5446-3002 Rev: $4,350
Bus: *Produces cosmetics and textiles.* Fax: 81-3-5446-3003 Emp: 4,160
www.kanebo.co.jp

KANEBO, LTD.
693 Fifth Avenue, 17th Fl., New York, NY   10022
CEO: Hiroshi Yuki, Pres.   Tel: (212) 750-3650   %FO: 100
Bus: *Sales/distribution of cosmetics and* Fax: (212) 750-3600
  textiles.

• KANEKA CORPORATION
Asahi-Shimbun Bldg., 3- 2-4 Nakanoshima Kita-ku, Osaka 530-8288, Japan
CEO: Takeshi Furuta, Pres.   Tel: 81-6-6226-5169   Rev: $3,080
Bus: *Mfr. performance polymers, plastic*   Fax: 81-6-6226-5177   Emp: 3,419
  products, food products, electronic   www.kaneka.co.jp
  equipment, pharmaceuticals and
  medical devices.

KANEKA AMERICA CORPORATION
65 East 55th Street, New York, NY   10022
CEO: Kazuo Kuruma, Pres.   Tel: (212) 705-4340   %FO: 100
Bus: *U.S. headquarters office.*   Fax: (212) 705-4350

KANEKA TEXAS HIGHTECH MATERIALS, CORPORATION
6161 Underwood Road, Pasadena, TX   77507
CEO: Kiyoshi Nagal, Pres.   Tel: (281) 474-7084   %FO: 100
Bus: *Plant site.*   Fax: (281) 474-9307

• KANEMATSU CORPORATION
2-1, Shibaura 1-chome, Minato-ku, Tokyo 105-8005, Japan
CEO: Tadashi Kurachi, Pres.   Tel: 81-3-5440-8111   Rev: $13,344
Bus: *International trading company engaged* Fax: 81-3-5440-6504   Emp: 1,000
  in petroleum, machinery, textiles,   www.kanematsu.co.jp
  metals and food products.

KANEMATSU (USA) INC
114 West 47th Street, 23rd Fl., New York, NY   10036
CEO: Ikufumi Sakata, Pres.   Tel: (212) 704-9400   %FO: 100
Bus: *Engaged in the trade of petroleum,*   Fax: (212) 704-9483
  machinery, textiles, metals & food
  products.

KANEMATSU (USA) INC
13220 Moore Street, Cerritos, CA   90703
CEO: Ikufumi Sakata, Pres.   Tel: (562) 802-3330
Bus: *Engaged in the trade of petroleum,*   Fax: (562) 802-3330
  machinery, textiles, metals & food
  products.

● **THE KANSAI ELECTRIC POWER COMPANY, INC.**
3-22 Nakanoshima 3-chome, Kita-ku, Osaka 530-8270, Japan
CEO: Yoshihisa Akiyama, Chmn. & CEO — Tel: 81-6-441-8821 — Rev: $24,533
Bus: *Electric utility.* — Fax: 81-6-441-0743 — Emp: 33,000
www.kepco.co.jp

　　THE KANSAI ELECTRIC POWER COMPANY, INC.
　　2001 L Street, NW, Washington, DC　20036
　　CEO: Motohisa Fujita, Mgr. — Tel: (202) 659-1138 — %FO: 100
　　Bus: *Electric utility.* — Fax: (202) 457-0272

　　THE KANSAI ELECTRIC POWER COMPANY, INC.
　　375 Park Avenue, Ste. 2607, New York, NY　10152
　　CEO: Yozo Miyazaki, Mgr. — Tel: (212) 758-3505 — %FO: 100
　　Bus: *Electric utility.* — Fax: (212) 832-3253

● **KAO CORPORATION**
14-10 Nihonbashi Kayabacho 1-chome, Chuo-ku, Tokyo 103-8210, Japan
CEO: Takuya Goto, Pres. — Tel: 81-3-3660-7111 — Rev: $8,027
Bus: *Mfr./sales personal care products,* — Fax: 81-3-3660-7044 — Emp: 15,900
detergents/chemical products and — www.kao.co.jp
information technology products.

　　THE ANDREW JERGENS COMPANY
　　2535 Spring Grove Avenue, Cincinnati, OH　45214
　　CEO: William Gentner, Pres. — Tel: (513) 421-1400 — %FO: 100
　　Bus: *Mfr. personal care products.* — Fax: (513) 421-1590

　　DAO SPECIALTIES LLC
　　243 Woodbine Street, PO Box 2316, High Point, NC　27261
　　CEO: Harvey L. Lowd, Pres. & CEO — Tel: (336) 884-2214 — %FO: 100
　　Bus: *Mfr./sales chemicals.* — Fax: (336) 884-8975

　　GOLDWELL COSMETICS INC.
　　981 Corporate Boulevard, Linthicum Heights, MD　21090
　　CEO: Philip L. Hester, CEO — Tel: (410) 850-7555 — %FO: 100
　　Bus: *Mfr. hair care products through* — Fax: (410) 850-7622
　　salons.

　　HIGH POINT TEXTILE AUXILARIES
　　PO Box 2316, High Point, NC　27261
　　CEO: Harvey L. Lowd, CEO — Tel: (336) 884-2214 — %FO: 100
　　Bus: *Mfr./sales chemicals.* — Fax: (336) 884-8975

● **C.I. KASEI CO., LTD.**
No. 18-1, 1-Chome, Kyobashi, Chuo-ku, Tokyo 104, Japan
CEO: H. Ishigai, Pres. & CEO   Tel: 81-3-3535-4547   Rev: $420
Bus: *Mfr. plastics.*   Fax: 81-3-3535-4542   Emp: 1,400

   BONSET AMERICA CORPORATION
   6107 Corporate Park Drive, Brown Summit, NC   27214
   CEO: Mark Reed, EVP   Tel: (336) 375-0234   %FO: 100
   Bus: *Mfr. plastic shrink film.* Fax: (336) 375-6129   Emp: 60

● **KAWAI MUSICAL INSTRUMENTS MFG. CO., LTD.**
200 Terajima-cho, Hamamatsu, Shizuoka 430-8665, Japan
CEO: Hirotaka Kawai, Pres.   Tel: 81-53-457-1291   Rev: $827
Bus: *Mfr./sales pianos, electronic pianos and* Fax: 81-53-457-1884   Emp: 1,929
   organs.   www.kawai.co.jp

   KAWAI AMERICA CORPORATION
   2055 East University Drive, Compton, CA   90220
   CEO: Jun Ando, EVP   Tel: (310) 631-1771   %FO: 100
   Bus: *Mfr./sales pianos, electronic* Fax: (310) 604-6913
       pianos and organs.

● **KAWASAKI HEAVY INDUSTRIES, LTD.**
Kobe Crystal Tower, 1-3, Higashikawasaki-cho 1-chome, Chuo-ku Kobe 650-8680, Japan
CEO: Toshio Kamei, Pres.   Tel: 81-78-371-9530   Rev: $10,900
Bus: *Mfr. heavy machinery and large-scale* Fax: 81-78-371-9568   Emp: 26,100
   equipment for transportation, aerospace www.khi.co.jp
   and industry.

   KAWASAKI CONSTRUCTION MACHINERY CORPORATION
   2140 Barrett Park Drive, Ste. 1010, Kennesaw, GA   30144
   CEO: Mack Kodera, Pres.   Tel: (770) 449-7000   %FO: 100
   Bus: *Mfr./sale heavy machinery.* Fax: (770) 421-6842

   KAWASAKI HEAVY INDUSTRIES USA, INC.
   599 Lexington Ave, Ste. 3901, New York, NY   10022
   CEO: Hiroshi Noda, Pres.   Tel: (212) 759-4950   %FO: 100
   Bus: *Mfr./sale industrial equipment.* Fax: (212) 759-6421   Emp: 11

   KAWASAKI HEAVY INDUSTRIES, LTD.
   333 Clay Street, Ste. 4480, Houston, TX   77002
   CEO: Hiroshi Noda, Pres.   Tel: (713) 654-8981   %FO: 100
   Bus: *Mfr. machinery.*   Fax: (713) 654-8187

KAWASAKI MOTOR CORPORATION, U.S.A.
9950 Jeronimo Road, PO Box 25252, Irvine, CA 92799-5252
CEO: Masatoshi Tsurutani, Pres.   Tel: (949) 770-0400   %FO: 100
Bus: *Mfr./sale motorcycles.*   Fax: (949) 460-5600

KAWASAKI MOTOR MANUFACTURING CORPORATION
6600 North West 27th Street, Lincoln, NE 68524
CEO: S. Tamba, Pres.   Tel: (402) 476-6600   %FO: 100
Bus: *Mfr./sale heavy machinery.*   Fax: (402) 476-6672

KAWASAKI RAIL CAR, INC.
29 Wells Avenue, Bldg. 4, Yonkers, NY 10701
CEO: Sotaro Yamada, Pres.   Tel: (914) 376-4700   %FO: 100
Bus: *Mfr./sale transportation equipment.* Fax: (914) 376-4779

KAWASAKI ROBOTICS INC.
28059 Center Oaks Court, Wixom, MI 48393
CEO: Mitsuo Miyamoto, Pres.   Tel: (248) 305-7610   %FO: 100
Bus: *Mfr./sale industrial equipment.*   Fax: (248) 305-7618

KAWASAKI ROBOTICS USA
49113 Wixom Tech Drive, Wixom, MI 48393
CEO: Tim Henrickson   Tel: (248) 926-3480   %FO: 100
Bus: *Operates training center.*   Fax: (248) 926-3485

KAWASAKI ROBOTICS USA
2726 River Green Circle, Louisville, KY 40206
CEO: James Ritter   Tel: (502) 893-3889   %FO: 100
Bus: *Mfr. machinery.*   Fax: (502) 893-3830

● KAWASAKI KISEN KAISHA LTD.
Hibiya Central Bldg, 2-9 Nishi Shinbashi 1-chome, Minato-ku, Tokyo 105, Japan
CEO: Isao Shintani, Pres.   Tel: 81-3 3595-5063   Rev: $4,603
Bus: *Steamship company; cargo and cruise*   Fax: 81-3 3595-5001   Emp: 750
    sea transport.   www.kline.co.jp

INTL TRANSPORTATION SERVICE INC. (ITS)
1281 Pier J Avenue, Long Beach, CA 90802
CEO: S. Ishitobi, Pres.   Tel: (562) 435-7781   %FO: 100
Bus: *Steamship & shipping agency;*   Fax: (562) 499-0460
    cargo and cruise sea transport.

K LINE AMERICA, INC.
301 Concourse Blvd., Ste. 300, Glen Allen, VA 23060
CEO: Yoshio Iinuma, CEO   Tel: (804) 935-3100   %FO: 100
Bus: *Steamship & shipping agency;*   Fax:
    cargo and cruise sea transport.

K LINE INTERNATIONAL (U.S.A.), INC.
Three Park Avenue, 28th Fl., New York, NY   10016

CEO: Nigel J.Hawkins, Pres.	Tel: (212) 447-1947	%FO: 100
Bus: *Steamship & shipping agency; cargo and cruise sea transport.*	Fax: (212) 447-1843	Emp: 4

• KAWASAKI STEEL CORPORATION
Hibiya Kokusai Bldg, 2-2-3 Uchisaiwai-cho, Chiyoda-ku, Tokyo 100, Japan

CEO: Kanji Emoto, Pres.	Tel: 81-3-3597-3111	Rev: $11,918
Bus: *Mfr. steel, chemicals, semi-conductors and new materials.*	Fax: 81-3-3597-4868 www.kawasaki-steel.co.jp	Emp: 10,200

KAWASAKI STEEL AMERICA, INC.
350 Park Avenue, 27th Fl., New York, NY   10022

CEO: Masakazu Kurushima, Pres.	Tel: (212) 310-9320	%FO: 100
Bus: *Liaison office; information and technical services for steel customers.*	Fax: (212) 308-9292	Emp: 14

KAWASAKI STEEL AMERICA, INC.
600 Travis Street, Ste. 6375, Houston, TX   77002

CEO: Kazutaka Nakanishi, Mgr.	Tel: (713) 654-0031	%FO: 100
Bus: *Liaison office; information and technical services for steel customers.*	Fax: (713) 654-9089	

• KAWASHO CORPORATION
2-7-1 Otemachi Chiyoda-ku, Tokyo 100-8070, Japan

CEO: Mitsuru Shiokawa, Pres.	Tel: 81-3-5203-5055	Rev: $12,124
Bus: *General trading company; heavy machinery and construction building materials.*	Fax: 81-3-5203-5290 www.kawasho.co.jp	Emp: 1,800

AMERICAN SOY PRODUCTS, INC.
1474 North Woodland Drive, Saline, MI   48176

CEO: Ron Roller, Pres.	Tel: (734) 429-2310	%FO: 100
Bus: *General trading company activities.*	Fax: (734) 429-2112	

KAWASHO INTL (USA), INC.
45 Broadway, 18th Fl., New York, NY 1006

CEO: Tatsuji Togawa, Pres.	Tel: (212) 841-7400	%FO: 100
Bus: *General trading company activities.*	Fax: (212) 841-7465	Emp: 50

VEST INC.
6023 Alcoa Avenue, Los Angeles, CA   90058
CEO: Iwaki Sugiyama, Pres.   Tel: (213) 581-8823   %FO: 100
Bus: *General trading company*   Fax: (213) 581-3465
     activities.

● **KAYABA INDUSTRY COMPANY, LTD.**
PO Box 3, World Trade Center Bldg., Minato-ku, Tokyo 105-6111, Japan
CEO: Kiyoshi Hosomi, Pres.   Tel: 81-3-3435-3580   Rev: $1,665
Bus: *Mfr. marine, aircraft, auto, hydraulic*   Fax: 81-3-3435-3580   Emp: 5,847
     and construction parts and components.   www.kyb.co.jp

　　　KYB CORPORATION OF AMERICA
　　　140 North Mitchell Court, Addison, IL   60101
　　　CEO: Kiyoshi Hosomi, Pres.   Tel: (630) 620-5555   %FO: 100
　　　Bus: *Import/distribute auto shock*   Fax: (630) 620-8133   Emp: 34
　　　 absorbers, industrial hydraulic
　　　 motors and components.

　　　KYB INDUSTRIES, INC.
　　　2625 N. Morton, PO Box 490, Franklin, IN   46131
　　　CEO: T. Koshiyama, Dir.   Tel: (317) 736-7774   %FO: 100
　　　Bus: *Mfr./sales automobile shock*   Fax: (317) 736-4618
　　　 absorbers.

● **KDDI CORPORATION**
3-2, Nishi-Shinjuku 2-chome, Shinjuku-ku Tokyo 163-8003, Japan
CEO: Yusai Okuyama, Pres. & CEO   Tel: 81-3-3222-9676   Rev: $14,463
Bus: *Engaged in telecommunications.*   Fax: 81-3-3221-9696   Emp: 2,586
                                        www.kddi.com

　　　KDDI AMERICA, INC.
　　　1953 Gallows Road, Ste. 200, Vienna, VA   22182
　　　CEO: Satoru Manabe, Dir.   Tel: (703) 714-6262   %FO: 100
　　　Bus: *Telecommunications.*   Fax: (703) 714-6260

　　　KDDI AMERICA, INC.
　　　1350 Bayshore Hwy., Ste. 580, Burlingame, CA   94010
　　　CEO: Akio Oril, Mgr.   Tel: (650) 558-0005   %FO: 100
　　　Bus: *Telecommunications.*   Fax: (650) 401-3290

　　　KDDI AMERICA, INC.
　　　600 Wilshire Blvd., Ste. 1460, Los Angeles, CA   90017
　　　CEO: Susumu Fujioka, VP   Tel: (213) 996-4080   %FO: 100
　　　Bus: *Telecommunications.*   Fax: (213) 489-5446

KDDI AMERICA, INC.

375 Park Avenue, 7th Fl., New York, NY 10152

CEO: Akio Nozaka, Chmn.   Tel: (212) 702-3720   %FO: 100

Bus: *Telecommunications.*   Fax: (212) 702-3765

TELECOMET INC.

375 Park Avenue, 7th Fl., New York, NY 10152

CEO: Akio Nozaka, Chmn.   Tel: (212) 521-1100   %FO: 100

Bus: *Telecommunications.*   Fax: (212) 557-0140

● **KENWOOD CORPORATION**

14-6, Dogenzaka 1-chome, Shibuya-ku, Tokyo 150-8501, Japan

CEO: Kaku Sakaida, Pres.   Tel: 81-3-5457-7111   Rev: $2,600

Bus: *Mfr. audio and communications*   Fax: 81-3-5457-7110   Emp: 2,615
  equipment and test & measurement   www.kenwoodcorp.com
  instruments.

    KENWOOD COMMUNICATIONS CORPORATION

    PO Box 22745, Long Beach, CA 90801-5745

    CEO: Joe Richter, Pres.   Tel: (310) 639-9000   %FO: 100

    Bus: *Sales/service land mobile radio*   Fax: (310) 604-4488
      and marine radio test equipment.

    KENWOOD TECHNOLOGIES INC.

    1701 Junction Court, Ste. 100, San Jose, CA 95112

    CEO: Hitoshi Nagamatsu, Pres.   Tel: (408) 467-7900   %FO: 100

    Bus: *Distributes CD-ROM drives and*   Fax: (408) 451-1150
      speakers for computers.

● **KEYENCE CORPORATION**

1-3-14 Higashi-Nakajima, Higashi-Yodogawa-ku, Osaka 533, Japan

CEO: Takemitsu Takizaki, Pres.   Tel: 81-6-379-2211   Rev: $750

Bus: *Mfr. sensors and instruments to measure*   Fax: 81-6-379-2131   Emp: 1,600
  electricity and industrial instruments to   www.keyence.co.jp
  measure display/control process
  variables.

    KEYENCE CORP. OF AMERICA

    50 Tice Boulevard, Woodcliff Lake, NJ 07675-7654

    CEO: Ken Noami, VP   Tel: (201) 930-0100   %FO: 100

    Bus: *Mfr. sensors and measuring*   Fax: (201) 930-0099
      equipment.

● **KIKKOMAN CORPORATION**
250 Noda Noda-shi, Chiba 278-8601, Japan
CEO: Yuzaburo Mogi, Pres.   Tel: 81-471-23-5111   Rev: $2,169
Bus: *Mfr. soy related sauces, wine and*   Fax: 81-471-23-5200   Emp: 2,825
    pharmaceuticals.   www.kikkoman.co.jp

    JFC INTERNATIONAL, INC.
    540 Forbes Blvd., San Francisco, CA   94080-2018
    CEO: Nobuyuki Enokido, Pres.   Tel: (650) 871-1660   %FO: 100
    Bus: *Sales/distribution of soy and*   Fax: (650) 952-3272
        related sauces and food products.

    KIKKOMAN FOODS, INC.
    6 Corner Road, PO Box 69, Walworth, WI   53184
    CEO: Hiro Takamatsu, EVP   Tel: (262) 275-6181   %FO: 100
    Bus: *Mfr. soy and related sauces.*   Fax: (262) 275-9452   Emp: 130

    KIKKOMAN INTERNATIONAL, INC.
    PO Box 420784, San Francisco, CA   94111
    CEO: Masaki Miki, Pres.   Tel: (415) 956-7750   %FO: 100
    Bus: *Mfr. soy and related sauces.*   Fax: (415) 956-7760

● **KINOKUNIYA COMPANY, LTD.**
3-17-7 Shinjuku 3-chome, Shinjuku-ku, Tokyo 160-09, Japan
CEO: Osamu Matsubara, Pres.   Tel: 81-3 3354-0131
Bus: *Sales/distribution of books, magazines,*   Fax: 81-3-3354-2719
    printed and electronic publications.   www.kinokuniya.com

    KINOKUNIYA BOOKSTORES COMPANY, LTD.
    123 Weller Street, Ste.106, Los Angeles, CA   90012
    CEO: Tom Miyashita, Mgr.   Tel: (213) 687-4480   %FO: 100
    Bus: *Distribution books and*   Fax: (213) 621-4456
        periodicals, related services.

    KINOKUNIYA BOOKSTORES OF AMERICA COMPANY, LTD.
    1581 Webster Street, San Francisco, CA   94115
    CEO: Tomoshige Okazaki, Pres.   Tel: (415) 567-7625   %FO: 100
    Bus: *Books, magazines, printed and*   Fax: (415) 567-4109   Emp: 95
        electronic publication.

    KINOKUNIYA PUBLICATIONS SERVICE OF NEW YORK COMPANY, LTD.
    Ten West 49th Street, New York, NY   10020
    CEO: Shigeharu Ono, VP   Tel: (212) 765-7766   %FO: 100
    Bus: *Distribution books and*   Fax: (212) 541-9355
        periodicals, related services.

• KINTETSU GROUP

1-6-1 Ohtemachi, Chiyoda-ku, Tokyo 100-04, Japan

CEO: Toshio Kumokawa, Pres.	Tel: 81-3-3201-2580	Rev: $31,500
Bus: *Holding company engaged in international freight forwarding and customs brokerage, e-business solutions, rail, ocean, travel, hotel, restaurants and real estate.*	Fax: 81-3-3201-2666 www.kwe.com	Emp: 82,000

GS XXI, INC.

100 Jericho Quadrangle, Ste. 144, Jericho, NY   11753

CEO: Robert Rice, Mgr.	Tel: (516) 433-4300	%FO: 100
Bus: *Provides e-business solutions.*	Fax: (516) 433-4419	

GS XXI, INC.

6498 Weathers Place, Ste. 100, San Diego, CA   92121

CEO: Kevin Jackson, Mgr.	Tel: (858) 623-5868	%FO: 100
Bus: *Provides e-business solutions.*	Fax: (800) 584-2007	

GS XXI, INC.

8551 Kintetsu Way, Miami, FL   33122

CEO: Robert Rice, Mgr.	Tel: (305) 592-6746	%FO: 100
Bus: *Provides e-business solutions.*	Fax: (305) 592-2065	

GS XXI, INC.

1811 Adrian Road, Burlingame, CA   94010

CEO: Kevin Jackson, Mgr.	Tel: (650) 692-3400	%FO: 100
Bus: *Provides e-business solutions.*	Fax: (650) 692-3763	

GS XXI, INC.

1221 North Mittel Blvd., Wood Dale, IL   60191

CEO: Robert Rice, Mgr.	Tel: (630) 787-5100	%FO: 100
Bus: *Provides e-business solutions.*	Fax: (630) 787-5150	

KINTETSU FLEXIPAK INC.

PO Box 10357, Houston, TX   77206

CEO: Roger Goose, Pres.	Tel: (713) 862-2232	%FO: 100
Bus: *Mfr. flexitanks for portable transportation of bulk liquids.*	Fax: (713) 862-2343	

• KIRIN BREWERY COMPANY, LTD.

10-1-Shinkawa 2-chome, Chuo-ku, Tokyo 104-8288, Japan

CEO: Yasuhiro Satoh, Pres.	Tel: 81-3-5540-3411	Rev: $8,860
Bus: *Brewery.*	Fax: 81-3-5540-3547 www.kirin.co.jp	Emp: 7,000

KIRIN USA, INC.
2400 Broadway, Suite 240, Santa Monica, CA   90404
CEO: Keiji Iijimi   Tel: (310) 829-2400   %FO: 100
Bus: *Import/distribution beer.*   Fax: (310) 829-0424   Emp: 22

● **KITZ CORPORATION**
1-10-1 Nakase, Mihama-ku, Chiba 261-8577, Japan
CEO: Yusuke Shimizu, Pres.   Tel: 81-43-299-0111
Bus: *Mfr. fluid control equipment.*   Fax: 81-43-299-1740
                                               www.kitz.co.jp

   KITZ CORPORATION OF AMERICA
   10750 Corporate Drive, Stafford, TX   77477
   CEO: Steve Twellman, Pres.   Tel: (281) 491-7333   %FO: 100
   Bus: *Mfr./sales fluid control equipment.*   Fax: (281) 491-9402

● **KOBE STEEL LTD.**
9-12, Kita-Shinagawa 5-chome, Shinagawa-ku, Tokyo 141-8688, Japan
CEO: Koshi Mizukoshi, Pres. & CEO   Tel: 81-3-5739-6000   Rev: $11,875
Bus: *Mfr. aluminum and copper products,*   Fax: 81-3-5739-6903   Emp: 10,580
   steel, industrial and construction   www.kobelco.co.jp
   machinery and welding/cutting tools.

   KOBE STEEL USA INC.
   535 Madison Avenue, New York, NY   10022
   CEO: Haruhisa Sato, Pres.   Tel: (212) 751-9400   %FO: 100
   Bus: *U.S. headquarters. Liaison &*   Fax: (212) 355-5564   Emp: 60
      development.

   KOBE STEEL USA, INC.
   1000 Town Center, Ste. 2450, Southfield, MI   48075
   CEO: Tadashi Takeuchi, VP   Tel: (248) 827-7757   %FO: 100
   Bus: *Mfr. steel and related materials.*   Fax: (248) 827-7759

● **KODANSHA INTL, LTD.**
2-12-21 Otowa, Bunkyo-ku, Tokyo 112-8001, Japan
CEO: Sawako Noma, Pres.   Tel: 81-3-3945-1111   Rev: $1,855
Bus: *Publisher of books and magazines.*   Fax: 81-3-3944-9915   Emp: 1,142
                                               www.kodansha.co.jp

   KODANSHA AMERICA, INC.
   114 Fifth Avenue, 18th Fl., New York, NY   10011
   CEO: Jiro Onoda, Mgr.   Tel: (212) 727-6460   %FO: 100
   Bus: *Publishing.*   Fax: (212) 727-9177   Emp: 25

● **KOMATSU, LTD.**

2-3-6 Akasaka, Minato-ku, 2-chome, Tokyo 107-8414, Japan

CEO: Satoru Anzaki, Pres.	Tel: 81-3 5561-2687	Rev: $100,005
Bus: *Mfr. construction equipment, industrial machines & presses.*	Fax: 81-3 3561-4763 www.komatsu.com	Emp: 28,525

KOMATSU AMERICAN INTL CORPORATION

440 North Fairway Drive, Vernon Hills, IL   60061-8112

CEO: Karl Hoshino, Pres.	Tel: (847) 970-4100	%FO: 100
Bus: *Distribution heavy equipment.*	Fax: (847) 970-4189	Emp: 50

KOMATSU CUTTING TECHNOLOGIES, INC.

265 Ballardvale Street, Wilmington, MA   01887

CEO: Tak Ishihara, Pres.	Tel: (978) 658-1650	%FO: 100
Bus: *Mfr. Rasor plasma cutting systems for production of precision metal parts*	Fax: (978) 658-1655	Emp: 50

● **KONICA CORPORATION**

26-2 Nishi Shinjuku 1-chome, Shinjuku-ku, Tokyo 163-0512, Japan

CEO: Tomiji Uematsu, Pres. & CEO	Tel: 81-3-3349-5251	Rev: $4,846
Bus: *Photographic films, papers, chemicals, photo equipment, business machines, cameras & accessories, magnetic products.*	Fax: 81-3-3349-5250 www.konica.co.jp	Emp: 17,840

KONICA BUSINESS TECHNOLOGIES, INC.

500 Day Hill Road, Windsor, CT   06095

CEO: Teruo Nakazawa, Pres.	Tel: (860) 683-2222	%FO: 100
Bus: *Photo copiers and copier consumables, facsimile terminals, computer terminal printers.*	Fax: (860) 688-0700	

KONICA COMPUTER SOLUTIONS, INC.

7710 Kenamar Court, San Diego, CA   92121

CEO: Brent Wellman	Tel: (858) 549-2199	%FO: 100
Bus: *Photo copiers and copier consumables, facsimile terminals, computer terminal printers.*	Fax: (858) 549-2199	

KONICA COMPUTER SOLUTIONS, INC.

2100 Main Street, Ste. 100, Irvine, CA   92614

CEO: Brent Wellman	Tel: (949) 476-2448	%FO: 100
Bus: *Photo copiers and copier consumables, facsimile terminals, computer terminal printers.*	Fax: (949) 476-2448	

KONICA FINANCE USA CORPORATION
225 Corporate Blvd, Ste. 206, Newark, DE 19702-3312

CEO: Y. Shibanuma, Pres.   Tel: (302) 737-9293   %FO: 100
Bus: *Group financial services.*   Fax: (302) 737-3349

KONICA GRAPHIC IMAGING INC.
71 Charles Street, Glen Cove, NY 11542-9001

CEO: Stepehn Schuster, Pres.   Tel: (516) 674-2500   %FO: 100
Bus: *Graphic arts equipment, film, paper and chemicals.*   Fax: (516) 676-4124

KONICA MANUFACTURING USA, INC.
6900 Konica Drive, Whitsett, NC 27377

CEO: Robert L. Harris, Pres.   Tel: (910) 449-8000   %FO: 100
Bus: *Mfr. photographic color paper.*   Fax: (910) 449-7554

KONICA MEDICAL CORPORATION
411 Newark Pompton Turnpike, Wayne, NJ 07470

CEO: Wayne Thompson, Pres.   Tel: (973) 633-1500   %FO: 100
Bus: *Medical film processor, medical imaging systems, film and accessories, clinical analysis equipment.*   Fax: (973) 523-7408

KONICA PHOTO IMAGING INC
71 US Route 1, Scarborough, ME 04074

CEO: Tom Meyer, Mgr.   Tel: (207) 883-7376   %FO: 100
Bus: *Wholesale photofinishing.*   Fax: (207) 883-3009

KONICA PHOTO IMAGING INC.
440 Sylvan Avenue, Englewood Cliffs, NJ 07632

CEO: Richard Carter, Pres.   Tel: (201) 568-3100   %FO: 100
Bus: *Photographic color film and paper, photofinishing equipment, cameras, video tape.*   Fax: (201) 816-9541

KONICA SUPPLIES MFG USA, INC.
1000 Konica Drive, Elkton, MD 21921

CEO: Takashi Hogi, Pres.   Tel: (410) 398-7371   %FO: 100
Bus: *Mfr. photocopier consumables.*   Fax: (410) 392-4626

KONICA TECHNOLOGY, INC.
490 Potrero Avenue, Sunnyvale, CA 94086

CEO: Chao King, Pres.   Tel: (408) 773-9551   %FO: 100
Bus: *Research and development.*   Fax: (408) 720-9288

• KOYO SEIKO COMPANY, LTD.

5-8 Minamisemba 3-chome, Chuo-Ku, Osaka 542, Japan

CEO: Hiroshi Inoue, Pres. Tel: 81-6 245-6087 Rev: $3,422

Bus: *Mfr. ball and roller bearings, auto* Fax: 81-6 244-0814 Emp: 6,975
steering gear, machine tools, industry www.koyo-seiko.co.jp
furnaces and seals.

KOYO CORPORATION OF USA, SALES DIV.

PO Box 45028, Westlake, OH 44145

CEO: Shinobu Tohara, Pres. Tel: (440) 835-1000 %FO: 100

Bus: *Mfr./distribution anti-friction* Fax: (440) 835-9347 Emp: 115
bearings and bearing units.

KOYO CORPORATION OF USA, MFR. DIV.

Highway 601, PO Drawer 967, Orangeburg, SC 29116

CEO: Ralph Kraus, VP Tel: (803) 536-6200 %FO: 100

Bus: *Mfr. bearings.* Fax: (803) 534-0599 Emp: 701

KOYO MACHINERY USA, INC.

47771 Halyard, Plymouth, MI 48170

CEO: T. Masuda, Pres. Tel: (734) 454-6627 %FO: 100

Bus: *Sale machinery.* Fax: (734) 454-4265 Emp: 5

• KUBOTA CORPORATION

2-47 Shikitsuhigashi 1-chome, Naniwa-ku, Osaka 556-8601, Japan

CEO: Yoshikuni Dobashi, Chmn. & CEO Tel: 81-6-648-2111 Rev: $9,252

Bus: *Mfr. tractors and farm machinery,* Fax: 81-6-648-2398 Emp: 14,600
ductile iron pipe, roofing and building www.kubota.co.jp
materials.

AUBURN CONSOLIDATED INDUSTRIES, INC.

2100 South J Street, PO Box 350, Auburn, NE 68305-0350

CEO: Philip Hamilton, Pres. Tel: (402) 274-4911 %FO: 100

Bus: *Mfr./distribution tractors and farm* Fax: (402) 274-5031
machinery, ductile iron pipe,
roofing and building materials.

KUBOTA AMERICAN CORPORATION

320 Park Avenue, 23rd Fl., New York, NY 10022

CEO: H. Takahashi, Pres. Tel: (212) 355-2440 %FO: 100

Bus: *Mfr./distribution tractors and farm* Fax: (212) 355-2124
machinery, ductile iron pipe,
roofing and building materials.

KUBOTA CREDIT CORPORATION
3401 Del Amo Boulevard, Torrance, CA   90509-2992

CEO: Mori Hayashi, Pres.
Bus: *Corporate financial and
administrative services.*

Tel: (310) 370-3370
Fax: (310) 370-2370

%FO: 100

KUBOTA MFG, OF AMERICA CORPORATION
2715 Ramsey Road, Gainesville, GA   30501

CEO: John Shiraishi, Pres.
Bus: *Mfr./distribution tractors and farm
machinery, ductile iron pipe,
roofing and building materials.*

Tel: (770) 532-0038
Fax: (770) 532-9057

%FO: 100

KUBOTA TRACTOR CORP.
6665 East Hardaway Road, Stockton, CA   95215

CEO: Russ Cobb, Mgr.
Bus: *Sales of tractors.*

Tel: (209) 931-5051
Fax: (209) 931-5541

%FO: 100

KUBOTA TRACTOR CORP.
2626 Port Road, Columbus, OH   43217

CEO: Ted Pederson, Mgr.
Bus: *Sales of tractors.*

Tel: (614) 492-1100
Fax: (614) 492-1101

%FO: 100

KUBOTA TRACTOR CORP.
1025 Northbrook Pkwy., Suwanee, GA   30174

CEO: Larry Fischer, Mgr.
Bus: *Sales of tractors.*

Tel: (770) 995-8855
Fax: (770) 962-0221

%FO: 100

KUBOTA TRACTOR CORP.
14855 FAA Blvd., Ft. Worth, TX   76155

CEO: Mike Broeker, Mgr.
Bus: *Sales of tractors.*

Tel: (817) 571-0900
Fax: (817) 571-0910

%FO: 100

● KUMAGAI GUMI COMPANY, LTD.
2-1 Tsukudo-cho, Shinjuku-ku, Tokyo 162, Japan

CEO: Kazutoshi Torikai, Pres.
Bus: *General contractor and real estate
developer.*

Tel: 81-3-3260-2111
Fax: 81-3-3235-3308
www.kumagaigumi.co.jp

Rev: $7,574
Emp: 6,573

KG LAND NEW YORK CORPORATION
1177 Avenue of the Americas, New York, NY   10036

CEO: Kazuo Kimata, Pres.
Bus: *Real estate development.*

Tel: (212) 391-8500
Fax: (212) 891-8550

%FO: 100

● **KURARAY CO., LTD.**
Shin-Hankyu Bldg., 1-12-39 Umeda, Kita-ku, Osaka 530-8611, Japan
CEO: Hiroto Matsuo, Chmn. Tel: 81-6-6348-2111 Rev: $3,000
Bus: *Mfr. synthetic fibers.* Fax: 81-6-6348-2165 Emp: 7,433
  www.kuraray.co.jp

  KURARAY AMERICA, INC.
  200 Park Avenue, 30th Fl., New York, NY   10166
  CEO: Hiroyuki Yonekura Tel: (212) 986-2230 %FO: 100
  Bus: *Mfr. synthetic fibers.* Fax: (212) 867-3543

● **KUROI ELECTRIC COMPANY, LTD.**
27 Yawata-cho Nishishichijyo, Shimogyo-ku, Kyoto 600, Japan
CEO: T. Matsuura, Pres. Tel: 81-75-313-5191
Bus: *Mfr. lighting products and electronics.* Fax: 81-75-314-1766 Emp: 750

  KUROI INTL CORPORATION
  497 Pini Road, Watsonville, CA   95076
  CEO: Sumio Yonemoto, Pres. Tel: (831) 761-8977 %FO: 100
  Bus: *Mfr. lighting products and* Fax: (831) 761-3043 Emp: 5
   agricultural products.

● **KYOCERA CORPORATION**
6, Takeda Tobadono-cho, Fushimi-ku, Kyoto 612-8501, Japan
CEO: Kensuke Itoh, Chmn. & CEO Tel: 81-75-604-3500 Rev: $10,200
Bus: *Mfr. integrated ceramic packages for* Fax: 81-75-604-3501 Emp: 14,660
 computers. www.kyocera.co.jp

  AVX CORPORATION
  PO Box 867, Myrtle Beach, SC   29578
  CEO: John S. Gilbertson, CEO Tel: (843) 448-9411 %FO: 100
  Bus: *Mfr. passive electronic* Fax: (843) 448-7139 Emp: 18,000
   components.

  KYOCERA INDUSTRIAL CERAMICS CORPORATION
  5713 East Fourth Plain Blvd., Vancouver, WA   98661
  CEO: R. Osmun, Pres. Tel: (360) 696-8950 %FO: 100
  Bus: *Mfr. structural ceramic* Fax: (360) 696-9804
   components for industrial and
   auto applications.

  KYOCERA INTERNATIONAL INC.
  8611 Balboa Avenue, San Diego, CA   92123-1580
  CEO: Rodney Lanthorne, Pres. Tel: (619) 576-2600 %FO: 100
  Bus: *U.S. headquarters.* Fax: (619) 492-1456

KYOCERA OPTICS INC.
2301 Cottontail Lane, Somerset, NJ   08873
CEO: William Heuer, Pres.   Tel: (732) 560-3400   %FO: 100
Bus: *Mfr. cameras.*   Fax: (732) 560-8380   Emp: 50

KYOCERA SOLAR, INC.
7812 East Acoma Drive, Scottsdale, AZ   85260
CEO: Doug Allday, Pres.   Tel: (480) 951-6330   %FO: 100
Bus: *Mfr. solar electric generating*   Fax: (480) 951-6329
    systems.

● **KYOCERA MITA CORPORATION, DIV. KYOCERA GROUP**
2-28, 1-Chome, Tamatsukuri, Chuo-ku, Osaka, 540-8585, Japan
CEO: Koji Seki, Pres.   Tel: 81-75-604-3500
Bus: *Mfr. copiers, network-ready,*   Fax: 81-75-604-3501
    multifunctional document imaging   www.kyoceramita.com
    systems and computer peripherals.

KYOCERA MITA AMERICA, INC.
225 Sand Road, Fairfield, NJ   07004-0008
CEO: Shichiro Noda, Pres.   Tel: (973) 808-8444   %FO: 100
Bus: *Mfr. digital copiers.*   Fax: (973) 882-4421

● **KYODO NEWS**
2-2-5 Toranomon, Minato-ku, Tokyo 105, Japan
CEO: Ichiro Saita, Pres.   Tel: 81-3-5573-8000   Rev: $370
Bus: *News wire service (news media).*   Fax: 81-3-5573-8018   Emp: 1,970
                                          www.kyodo.co.jp

KYODO NEWS AMERICA, INC.
50 Rockefeller Plaza, Ste. 816, New York, NY   10020
CEO: Takaji Hamashima, EVP   Tel: (212) 603-6600   %FO: 100
Bus: *Wire service (news media).*   Fax: (212) 603-6621   Emp: 35

● **THE KYOEI MUTUAL FIRE & MARINE INSURANCE COMPANY**
18-6 Shimbashi 1-chome, Minato-ku, Tokyo 105-8604, Japan
CEO: Wataru Ozawa, Pres.   Tel: 81-3-504-2336   Rev: $12,500
Bus: *Insurance services.*   Fax: 81-3-508-7680   Emp: 16,800
                                          www.sam.hi-ho.ne.jp

THE KYOEI MUTUAL FIRE & MARINE INSURANCE COMPANY
420 Lexington Avenue, Ste. 2058, New York, NY   10170
CEO: Yoshiaki Toyonaga, Rep.   Tel: (212) 490-0710   %FO: 100
Bus: *Representative office: insurance*   Fax: (212) 692-9362
    services.

● **KYOWA HAKKO KOGYO CO., LTD.**

1-6-1 Ohtemachi, Chiyoda-ku, Tokyo 100-8185, Japan

CEO: Tadashi Hirata, Pres.	Tel: 81-3-3282-0007	Rev: $3,229
Bus: *Develops, markets and manufactures pharmaceuticals, chemicals, food products and alcoholic beverages.*	Fax: 81-3-3284-1968 www.kyowa.co.jp	Emp: 5,044

    BIOKYOWA, INC.

    5469 Nash Road, PO Box 1550, Cape Girardeau, MO   63702-1550

CEO: Kohta Fujiwara, Pres.	Tel: (573) 335-4849	%FO: 100
Bus: *Sales/distribution of chemical products.*	Fax: (573) 335-1466	

    KYOWA HAKKO USA, INC.

    599 Lexington Avenue, Ste. 4103, New York, NY   10022

CEO: Toshi Asada, Pres.	Tel: (212) 319-5353	%FO: 100
Bus: *U.S. headquarters.*	Fax: (212) 421-1283	

    KYOWA PHARMACEUTICAL

    104 Carnegie Center, Ste. 301, Princeton, NJ   08540

CEO: Dr. Tesushi Inada, Pres.	Tel: (609) 919-1100	%FO: 100
Bus: *Sales of pharmaceutical products.*	Fax: (609) 919-1111	

    NUTRI-QUEST, INC.

    1400 Elbridge Payne Road, Ste. 110, Chesterfield, MO   63017

CEO: Kohta Fujiwara, Pres.	Tel: (314) 537-4057	%FO: 100
Bus: *Sales/distribution of food products.*	Fax: (314) 532-1710	

● **MABUCHI MOTOR CO LTD.**

430 Matsuhidia, Matsudo-shi, Chiba-ken 270-2280, Japan

CEO: Takaichi Mabuchi, Pres.	Tel: 81-47-384-1111	Rev: $1,015
Bus: *Mfr. DC motors for home electric appliances, precision machinery, auto machinery and supplies printers and power tools.*	Fax: 81-47-385-2026 www.mabuchi-motor.co.jp	Emp: 60,500

    MABUCHI MOTOR AMERICAN CORPORATION

    3001 West Big Beaver Rd., Ste. 520, Troy, MI   48084

CEO: Mitsuyoshi Hamada, EVP	Tel: (248) 816-3100	%FO: 100
Bus: *Produces and distributes DC motors for home electric appliances, precision machinery, auto machinery and supplies printers and power tools.*	Fax: (248) 816-3242	

● **MAKINO MILLING MACHINE COMPANY, LTD.**
3-19 Nakane 2-chome, Meguro-ku, Tokyo 152-8578, Japan

CEO: Jiro Makino, Pres.	Tel: 81-3-3717-1151	Rev: $539
Bus: *Machine centers, mfr. systems, electric machinery, copy mills, engine lathes.*	Fax: 81-3-3724-2105 www.makino.co.jp	Emp: 700

    MAKINO
    7680 Innovation Way, Mason, OH 45040-9695

CEO: Don Lane, Pres.	Tel: (513) 573-7200	%FO: 100
Bus: *Mfr./distribution machine tools and systems.*	Fax: (513) 573-7360	Emp: 300

● **MAKITA CORPORATION**
13-11-8 Sumiyoshi-cho 3-chome, Anjo Aichi 446-8502, Japan

CEO: Masahiko Goto, Pres.	Tel: 81-5-6698-1711	Rev: $1,695
Bus: *Portable electric power tools and accessories.*	Fax: 81-5-6698-6021 www.makita.co.jp	Emp: 7,900

    MAKITA USA INC.
    14930-C Northam Street, La Mirada, CA 90638-5753

CEO: Gary Morikawa, Pres.	Tel: (714) 522-8088	%FO: 100
Bus: *Portable electric power tools & accessories.*	Fax: (714) 522-8133	Emp: 700

● **MARUBENI CORPORATION**
4-2 Ohtemachi 1-chome, Chiyoda-ku, Tokyo 100-8088, Japan

CEO: Tohru Tsuji, Pres. & CEO	Tel: 81-3-3282-2111	Rev: $95,796
Bus: *Import/export metals, machinery, chemicals, textiles, general merchandise, petroleum, agricultural and marine products.*	Fax: 81-3-3282-7456 www.marubeni.co.jp	Emp: 7,700

    MARUBENI AMERICA CORPORATION
    450 Lexington Avenue, New York, NY 10017-3984

CEO: N. Watanabe, Pres. & CEO	Tel: (212) 450-0100	%FO: 100
Bus: *Import/export metals, machinery, chemicals, textiles, general merchandise, petroleum, agricultural & marine products.*	Fax: (212) 450-0710	Emp: 400

    MARUBENI INTERNATIONAL ELECTRONICS CORPORATION
    790 Lucerne Drive, Sunnyvale, CA 94086

CEO: Y. Miyagi, Mgr.	Tel: (408) 727-8447	%FO: 100
Bus: *Engaged in high tech electronics trading.*	Fax: (408) 245-4816	

MARUBENI METAL BLANKING INC.
1460 West McPherson Park Drive, Howell, MI   48833
CEO: M. Ohama, CEO   Tel: (517) 552-0181   %FO: 100
Bus: *Mfr. high-quality configured*   Fax: (517) 545-8643
blanked sheets.

MARUBENI PROJECT INVESTMENT COMPANY
515 South Figueroa Street, Ste. 2000, Los Angeles, CA   90071
CEO: M. Takayanagi, Mgr.   Tel: (213) 972-2758   %FO: 100
Bus: *Provides consulting services to*   Fax: (213) 972-2809
foreign investors for real estate
and development projects.

MARUBENI STEEL PROCESSING, INC.
104 Western Avenue, Portland, TN   37148
CEO: Moto Hirai, Pres.   Tel: (615) 325-5454   %FO: 100
Bus: *Mfr. precision slit steel for*   Fax: (615) 315-4815
automotive business.

MARUBENI TUBULARS, INC.
7500 San Felipe, Ste. 950, Houston, TX   77063
CEO: Shigeru Steve Ohta, Pres.   Tel: (713) 780-5600   %FO: 100
Bus: *Mfr. tubular products for oil and*   Fax: (713) 780-7922
gas industry.

VECTANT
111 West 57th Street, Ste. 100, New York, NY   10019
CEO: M. Pagos, Pres.   Tel: (212) 636-4900   %FO: 100
Bus: *Engaged in data and e-commerce*   Fax: (212) 636-4905
networking.

WESTERN METAL LATH
6510 General Drive, Riverside, CA   92509
CEO: George Kitano, Pres.   Tel: (909) 360-3500   %FO: 100
Bus: *Mfr. high quality, light gauge steel*   Fax: (909) 360-3131
construction products.

● MARUHA CORPORATION
1-2 Otemachi, 1-chome, Chiyoda-ku, Tokyo 100-8608, Japan
CEO: Keijiro Nakabe, Pres.   Tel: 81-3-3216-0821   Rev: $8,922
Bus: *Provides refrigerated and cold storage*   Fax: 81-3-3216-0342   Emp: 18,500
services, food processing and plant   www.maruha.co.jp
management and engineering services.

REEFER EXPRESS LINES LTD.
5 Becker Farm Road, 4th Fl., Roseland, NJ   07068
CEO: Byron M. Sugahara, Pres. & CEO   Tel: (973) 740-0740   %FO: 100
Bus: *Provides refrigerated and cold*   Fax: (973) 740-0449
    storage services for food
    processing.

WESTERN ALASKA FISHERIES, INC.
1111 Third Avenue, Ste. 2200, Seattle, WA   98101
CEO: Kazuyoshi Kawai, CEO   Tel: (206) 382-0640   %FO: 100
Bus: *Sales/distribution of marine*   Fax: (206) 625-0089
    product; aquaculture, fish feed.

WESTWARD SEAFOODS INC.
1111 Third Avenue, Ste. 2200, Seattle, WA   98101
CEO: Greg Baker, Pres.   Tel: (206) 682-5949   %FO: 100
Bus: *Sales/distribution of marine*   Fax: (206) 682-1825
    product; aquaculture, fish feed.

● **MARUKAI CORPORATION KK**
18-5 Kyomachibori, l-chome, Nishi-ku, Osaka 550, Japan
CEO: Junzo Matsu, Pres.   Tel: 81-6-443-0071
Bus: *Import/export general merchandise.*   Fax: 81-6-443-2182   Emp: 50
                          www.marukai.co.jp

MARUKAI CORPORATION
1420 S Azusa Ave, West Covina, CA   91791-4121
CEO: Y. Sugiyam   Tel: (626) 918-0825   %FO: 100
Bus: *Department store engaged in sale*   Fax: (626) 918-0825
    of oriental goods.

MARUKAI CORPORATION
1740 West Artesia Blvd., Gardenia, CA   90247
CEO: Hidejiro Matsu, Pres.   Tel: (310) 660-6300   %FO: 100
Bus: *Sale/distribution of retail oriental*   Fax: (310) 660-6301
    goods.

MARUKAI CORPORATION
2310 Kamehameha Hwy., Honolulu, HI   96819
CEO: Hidejiro Matsu, Pres.   Tel: (808) 845-5051   %FO: 100
Bus: *Sale/distribution of retail oriental*   Fax: (808) 841-2379   Emp: 260
    goods.

● **MATSUSHITA COMMUNICATION INDUSTRIAL CO. LTD., DIV. MATSUSHITA ELECTRIC IND.**

3-1, Tsunashima-Higashi, 4-chome, Kohoku-ku, Yokohama 223, Japan

CEO: Takashi Kawada, Pres.	Tel: 81-45-531-1231	Rev: $6,450
Bus: *Mfr. Panasonic brand pagers, cell phones, network systems and surveillance equipment.*	Fax: 81-45-544-3285 www.mcl.panasonic.co.jp	Emp: 7,900

MATSUSHITA ELECTRIC CORPORATION OF AMERICA

1225 Northbrook Pkwy., Ste. 2330, Suwanee, GA   30024

CEO: Yoshinori Kobe, Pres.	Tel: (770) 338-6000	%FO: 100
Bus: *Mfr. electronic/electrical products for consumer, business and industry.*	Fax: (770) 338-6001	Emp: 23,000

● **MATSUSHITA ELECTRIC INDUSTRIAL COMPANY, LTD.**

1006 Oaza Kadoma, Kadoma-shi, Osaka 571-8501, Japan

CEO: Yoichi Morishita, Chmn.	Tel: 81-6-6908-1121	Rev: $71,118
Bus: *Mfr. electronic and electric products for consumer, business and industry.*	Fax: 81-6-6908-2351 www.mei.co.jp	Emp: 290,450

AMERICAN MATSUSHITA ELECTRONICS COMPANY

1400 West Market Street, Troy, OH   45373

CEO: Mike Nakamoto, Pres.	Tel: (937) 339-6300	%FO: 100
Bus: *Mfr. color TV picture tubes.*	Fax: (937) 440-6149	

MATSUSHITA AVIONICS SYSTEMS CORPORATION

22333 29th Drive SE, Bothell, WA   98021

CEO: Takashi Mizuma, Pres.	Tel: (425) 486-2684	%FO: 100
Bus: *Supplies in-flight entertainment systems.*	Fax: (425) 485-6175	

MATSUSHITA ELECTRIC CORPORATION OF AMERICA

One Panasonic Way, Secaucus, NJ   07094

CEO: Don Iwatani, Chmn. & CEO	Tel: (201) 348-7000	%FO: 100
Bus: *Mfr. electronic/electrical products for consumer, business and industry.*	Fax: (201) 348-8378	Emp: 23,000

PANASONIC BROADCAST SYSTEMS COMPANY

Two Panasonic Way, Secaucus, NJ   07094

CEO: Milton Landau, Pres.	Tel: (201) 348-7000	%FO: 100
Bus: *Mfr. electronic products.*	Fax: (201) 348-7372	

PANASONIC COMPANY

One Panasonic Way, Secaucus, NJ   07094

CEO: Yoshinori Kobe, CEO   Tel: (201) 348-7000   %FO: 100

Bus: *Mfr./wholesale consumer and*   Fax: (201) 271-3092   Emp: 1,100
    industrial electronic products.

PANASONIC FACTORY AUTOMATION COMPANY

9377 West Grand Avenue, Franklin Park, IL   60131

CEO: Nori Tsuchiya, CEO   Tel: (847) 288-4400   %FO: 100

Bus: *Mfr. factory automation assembly*   Fax: (847) 288-4564
    systems.

● **MATSUSHITA ELECTRIC WORKS LTD.**

1048 Kadoma, Osaka 571-8686, Japan

CEO: Kazushige Nishida, Pres.   Tel: 81-6-6908-1131   Rev: $9,200

Bus: *Mfr. electrical fixtures, equipment,*   Fax: 81-6-6909-1860   Emp: 39,000
    appliances, building products, electrical   www.mew.co.jp
    & plastic materials.

    AROMAT CORPORATION

    629 Central Avenue, New Providence, NJ   07974-1526

    CEO: Tim Teroka, CEO   Tel: (908) 464-3550

    Bus: *Sales/distribution of residential*   Fax: (908) 771-5658
        fixtures, home appliances, lighting
        and building products.

    MATSUSHITA ELECTRIC WORKS, R&D LABORATORY INC

    1975 West El Camino Real, Ste. 102, Mountain View, CA   94040

    CEO: Takashi Ozone, CEO   Tel: (650) 938-6639   %FO: 100

    Bus: *Research & development facility.*   Fax: (650) 938-6629   Emp: 10

● **MATSUZAKAYA CO LTD.**

16-1 Sakae 3-chome, Naka-ku, Nagoya 460-8430, Japan

CEO: Kunihiko Okada, Pres.   Tel: 81-52-251-1111   Rev: $3,750

Bus: *Department stores.*   Fax: 81-52-264-7140   Emp: 6,000
         www.matsuzakaya-dept.co.jp

    MATSUZAKAYA AMERICA, INC.

    460 East Third Street, Los Angeles, CA   90013

    CEO: Koji Okamoto, Pres.   Tel: (213) 626-0133   %FO: 100

    Bus: *Department stores.*   Fax: (213) 626-7936   Emp: 42

● **MAZDA MOTOR CORPORATION**

3-1 Shinchi, Fucho-cho, Aki-Gun, Hiroshima 730-19, Japan

CEO: Mark Fields, Pres.   Tel: 81-82-282-1111   Rev: $20,487

Bus: *Mfr. automobiles, machine tools and*   Fax: 81-82-287-5190   Emp: 23,550
    rock drills.   www.mazda.co.jp

MAZDA MOTOR MFG USA, CORPORATION

7755 Irvine Center Drive, Irvine, CA   97218-2922

CEO: Charles R. Hughes, Pres. & CEO   Tel: (949) 727-1990   %FO: 100

Bus: *Mfr. automobiles, machine tools*   Fax: (949) 727-6101   Emp: 3,105
and rock drills.

• MEIJI LIFE INSURANCE COMPANY

1-1, Marunouchi 2-chome, Chiyoda-ku, Tokyo 100-005, Japan

CEO: Ryotaro Kaneko, Pres.   Tel: 81-3-3283-9211   Rev: $26,000

Bus: *Life insurance services.*   Fax: 81-3-3215-8123   Emp: 40,000
www.meiji-life.co.jp

PACIFIC GUARDIAN LIFE INS. COMPANY LTD.

1440 Kapiolani Blvd., Ste. 1700, Honolulu, HI   96814

CEO: Hideaki Hattori, Pres.   Tel: (808) 955-2236   %FO: 100

Bus: *Life insurance services.*   Fax: (808) 942-1280

• MEIJI SEIKA KAISHA LTD.

4-16, Kyobashi 2-chome, Chuo-ku, Tokyo 104-8002, Japan

CEO: Ichiro Kitasato, Pres. & CEO   Tel: 81-3-3272-6511   Rev: $3,444

Bus: *Mfr. foods, confectionery,*   Fax: 81-3-3274-4063   Emp: 4,970
pharmaceuticals and machinery.   www.meiji.co.jp

MEIJI SEIKA (USA), INC.

150 East 52nd Street, 17th Fl., New York, NY   10022

CEO: Kenji Saito, Gen. Mgr.   Tel: (212) 813-1886   %FO: 100

Bus: *Sale/distribution of confections*   Fax: (212) 813-9805
and pharmaceuticals.

• MEIKO TRANS COMPANY, LTD.

4-6 Irifune 2-chome, Nagoya City, Aichi Pref 455-8650, Japan

CEO: Jiro Takahasai, Pres.   Tel: 81-52-661-8111   Rev: $376

Bus: *Wholesale, trucking, stevedoring,*   Fax: 81-52-661-6125   Emp: 847
freight forwarding, customs house   www.cgc.co.jp/meiko
broker and air cargo agent.

MEIKO AMERICA, INC.

2160 East Dominguez Street, Long Beach, CA   90810

CEO: Koichiro Murakami, Pres.   Tel: (310) 549-3371   %FO: 100

Bus: *Warehousing, trucking, freight*   Fax: (310) 834-0383
forwarding, customs house broker
and air cargo agent.

- **MIKIMOTO**
4-5-5 Ginza Chuo-ku, Tokyo 104, Japan
CEO: Toyohiko Mikimoto, Pres.   Tel: 81-3-3535-4611
Bus: *Mfr. and sales of pearls and pearl*   Fax: 81-3-3535-4620
     jewelry.   www.mikimoto.co.jp

  MIKIMOTO
  40 West 57th Street, New York, NY   10019
  CEO: Kikuichiro Ishii, Pres.   Tel: (212) 457-4500   %FO: 100
  Bus: *U.S. corporate office.*   Fax: (212) 457-4525

  MIKIMOTO
  730 Fifth Avenue, New York, NY   10019
  CEO: Kikuichiro Ishii, Pres.   Tel: (212) 457-4600   %FO: 100
  Bus: *Retail store for sales of pearls and*   Fax: (212) 457-4605
       pearl jewelry.

- **MIKUNI CORPORATION**
13-11 Sotokanda 6-chome, Chiyoda-ku, Tokyo, Japan
CEO: Masaki Ikuta, Pres.   Tel: 81-3-3833-0392   Rev: $609
Bus: *Mfr. motor vehicle parts.*   Fax: 81-3-3836-4210   Emp: 1,404
      www.mikuni.co.jp

  MIKUNI AMERICAN CORPORATION
  8910 Mikuni Avenue, Northridge, CA   91324
  CEO: Masaki Ikuta, Pres.   Tel: (818) 885-1242   %FO: 100
  Bus: *Distribution of motor vehicle parts.*   Fax: (818) 993-7387

- **MINEBEA CO., LTD.**
1-8-1 Shimo-Meguro, 19th Fl, Meguro-ku, Tokyo 153-8662, Japan
CEO: Tsugio Yamamoto, Pres.   Tel: 81-3-5434-8611   Rev: $2,699
Bus: *Mfr. miniature and instrument ball*   Fax: 81-3-5434-8601   Emp: 42,400
     bearings and components for aerospace,   www.minebea.co.jp
     telecommunications and personal
     computers.

  HANSEN CORPORATION
  901 South First Street, Princeton, IN   47670
  CEO: William K. Poyner, Pres.   Tel: (812) 385-3415   %FO: 100
  Bus: *Mfr./sales of motors.*   Fax: (812) 386-6387

  IMC MAGNETICS CORPORATION
  1900 East Fifth Street, Tempe, AZ   85281
  CEO: Dave Davidson, Pres.   Tel: (480) 968-4441   %FO: 100
  Bus: *Mfr./sales of solenoid valves and*   Fax: (480) 968-5026
       motors.

NEW HAMPSHIRE BALL BEARINGS INC.
9727 DeSoto Avenue, Chatsworth, CA   91311
CEO: Gary C. Yomantas, Pres. & CEO   Tel: (818) 993-4100   %FO: 100
Bus: *Mfr./sales of ball bearings.*   Fax: (818) 407-5020

NMB CORPORATION
9730 Independence Avenue, Chatsworth, CA   91311
CEO: Masayoshi Yamanaka, Pres.   Tel: (818) 341-0820   %FO: 100
Bus: *Sales/distribution of miniature and*   Fax: (818) 709-0387
instrument ball bearings and
components for aerospace,
telecommunications and personal
computers.

● **MINOLTA CO LTD.**
3-13 Azuchi-machi 2-chome, Chuo-ku, Osaka 541-8556, Japan
CEO: Yoshikatsu Ota, Pres.   Tel: 81-6-271-2251   Rev: $4,595
Bus: *Mfr. office equipment, cameras and*   Fax: 81-6-266-1010   Emp: 4,881
lenses, optical products, radiometric   www.minolta.com
instruments, office equipment and
facsimile and copy machines.

MINOLTA BUSINESS SYSTEMS, INC.
One International Blvd., 9th Fl., Mahwah, NJ   07495
CEO: Joseph Villanella, Pres.   Tel: (201) 512-5800   %FO: 100
Bus: *Distribution business machines.*   Fax: (201) 529-0622

MINOLTA CORPORATION (USA), INC>
101 Williams Drive, Ramsey, NJ   07446
CEO: Hiroshi Fujii, Pres. & CEO   Tel: (201) 825-4000   %FO: 100
Bus: *Distribution/service office*   Fax: (201) 825-7605   Emp: 2,000
machinery, photo and
micrographic equipment.

MINOLTA-QMS, INC.
One Magnum Pass, Mobile, AL   36618
CEO: Edward E. Lucente, Pres.   Tel: (334) 633-4300   %FO: 100
Bus: *Mfr. printing solutions.*   Fax: (334) 633-4866

● **MISUMI CORPORATION**
4-43 Toyo 2-chome, Koto-ku, Tokyo 135-8458, Japan
CEO: Hiroshi Taguchi, Chmn. & CEO   Tel: 81-3-647-7116   Rev: $351
Bus: *Mfr. press die, plastic mold and*   Fax: 81-3-647-7125   Emp: 390
automatic machine components.   www.misumi.co.jp

MISUMI OF AMERICA INC.
1039 Hawthorn Drive, Itasca, IL   60143
CEO: Hiroshi Taguchi, Pres.   Tel: (630) 773-3244   %FO: 100
Bus: *Sale press die, plastic mold and*   Fax: (630) 773-3284   Emp: 12
  automatic machine components.

● MITSUBISHI CABLE INDUSTRIES, LTD.
4-1 Marunouchi 3-chome, Chiyoda-ku, Tokyo 100, Japan
CEO: Harunosuke Fuji, Pres.   Tel: 81-3-3216-1551   Rev: $1,180
Bus: *Mfr. cables and fiber optics.*   Fax: 81-3-3201-2239   Emp: 2,000
  www.mitsubishi-cable.co.jp

MITSUBISHI CABLE AMERICA, INC.
411 Hackensack Avenue, Hackensack, NJ   07610
CEO: Masahiko Hori, CEO   Tel: (201) 343-1818   %FO: 100
Bus: *Sales/service silica and plastic*   Fax: (201) 343-6113   Emp: 10
  optical fibers, opti-electronic
  products, medical angiograms,
  automatic connectors, special
  gaskets.

● MITSUBISHI CHEMICAL CORPORATION
5-2 Marunouchi 2-chome, Chiyoda-ku, Tokyo 100, Japan
CEO: Kanji Shono, CEO   Tel: 81-3-3283-6531   Rev: $13,000
Bus: *Mfr./markets carbon products,*   Fax: 81-3-3283-6658   Emp: 12,000
  inorganic chemicals and   www.m-kagaku.co.jp
  pharmaceuticals.

MITSUBISHI CHEMICAL AMERICA, INC.
One North Lexington Avenue, White Plains, NY   10601
CEO: Dr. Yoshitomi, Pres.   Tel: (914) 286-3600   %FO: 100
Bus: *Sales/distribution of carbon*   Fax: (914) 681-0760
  products, inorganic chemicals and
  pharmaceuticals.

● MITSUBISHI CORP
6-3 Marunouchi 2-chome, Chiyoda-ku, Tokyo 100-8086, Japan
CEO: Mikio Sasaki, Pres. & CEO   Tel: 81-3 3210-2121   Rev: $122,883
Bus: *Trading company: raw materials,*   Fax: 81-3 3210-8051   Emp: 11,650
  chemicals, general merchandise.   www.mitsubishi.or.jp

MITSUBISHI INTERNATIONAL CORPORATION
520 Madison Avenue, New York, NY   10022
CEO: Hironori Alhara, Pres.   Tel: (212) 605-2000   %FO: 100
Bus: *Import/export; raw materials,*   Fax: (212) 605-2597
  chemicals, general merchandise.

- **MITSUBISHI ELECTRIC CORPORATION**

Mitsubishi Denki Bldg., 2-3 Marunouchi 2-chome, Chiyoda-ku Tokyo 100-8310, Japan

CEO: Ichiro Taniguchi, Pres. Tel: 81-3-3218-2111 Rev: $35,775

Bus: *Mfr. electronics and electrical* Fax: 81-3-3218-2431 Emp: 116,580
    appliances. www.mitsubishielectric.com

MITSUBISHI CONSUMER ELECTRONICS AMERICA, INC.

1001 Cherry Drive, Braselton, GA   30517

CEO: Harutsugu Okada, Pres. Tel: (706) 654-3011 %FO: 100

Bus: *Sales/distribution of cellular* Fax: (706) 654-3940
    mobile phones.

MITSUBISHI DIGITAL ELECTRONICS AMERICA

9351 Jeronimo Avenue, Irvine, CA   92618

CEO: Yogi Otani, CEO Tel: (949) 465-6000 %FO: 100

Bus: *Sales/distribution of audio and* Fax: (949) 465-6037
    video equipment.

MITSUBISHI ELECTRIC AMERICA INC.

PO Box 6007, Cypress, CA   90630-0007

CEO: Akira Katayama, Chmn. & CEO Tel: (714) 220-2500 %FO: 100

Bus: *Sales/distribution of electronics* Fax: (714) 229-6576
    and electrical appliances.

MITSUBISHI ELECTRIC AUTOMATION, INC.

500 Corporate Wood Parkway, Vernon Hills, IL   60061

CEO: Yusuke Ishita, Pres. & CEO Tel: (847) 478-2100 %FO: 100

Bus: *Sales/distribution of electronics* Fax: (847) 478-0328
    and electrical appliances.

MITSUBISHI ELECTRIC FINANCE AMERICA, INC.

5665 Plaza Drive, Cypress, CA   90639

CEO: Hiroki Yoshimatsu, Pres. Tel: (714) 220-2500 %FO: 100

Bus: *Sales/distribution of electronics* Fax: (714) 229-6543
    and electrical appliances.

MITSUBISHI ELECTRIC INFORMATION TECHNOLOGY CENTER AMERICA, INC.

201 Broadway, 8th Fl., Cambridge, MA   02139

CEO: Dr. Richard Waters, CEO Tel: (617) 621-7500 %FO: 100

Bus: *Research center for computer* Fax: (617) 621-7548
    electronics.

MITSUBISHI ELECTRIC MANUFACTURING CINCINNATI, INC.
4773 Bethany Road, Mason, OH   45040

CEO: Takeo Sasaki, Pres.
Tel: (513) 398-2220
%FO: 100

Bus: *Mfr./sales of alternators and starters.*
Fax: (513) 398-1121

MITSUBISHI ELECTRIC POWER PRODUCTS, INC.
512 Keystone Drive, Warrendale, PA   15086

CEO: Roger Barna, Pres.
Tel: (724) 772-2555
%FO: 100

Bus: *Mfr./sales of electric power products.*
Fax: (724) 772-2146

● MITSUBISHI ESTATE COMPANY, LTD.
7-3, Marunouchi 1-chome, Chiyoda-ku, Tokyo 100, Japan

CEO: Takeshi Fukuzawa, Pres.
Tel: 81-3-3287-5100
Rev: $4,125

Bus: *Engaged in real estate development and hotel and resort management.*
Fax: 81-3-3214-7036
www.mec.co.jp
Emp: 1,960

CALIFORNIA MEC, INC.
777 South Figueroa Street, Ste. 4050, Los Angeles, CA   90017

CEO: Yutaka Yanaglsawa, Pres.
Tel: (213) 236-3924
%FO: 100

Bus: *Engaged in real estate development and hotel and resort management.*
Fax: (213) 236-3933

MEC FINANCE USA INC.
1105 North Market Street, Ste. 1300, Wilmington, DE   19801

CEO: E. Tan, Pres.
Tel: (302) 427-8974
%FO: 100

Bus: *Engaged in real estate development and hotel and resort management.*
Fax:

ROCKEFELLER GROUP INC.
1221 Avenue of the Americas, 39th Fl., New York, NY   10020

CEO: Lorian Mariantes, CEO
Tel: (212) 282-2000
%FO: 100

Bus: *Engaged in real estate development and hotel and resort management.*
Fax: (212) 757-0515

WEST MEC INC.
777 South Figueroa Street, Ste. 4050, Los Angeles, CA   90017

CEO: Yutaka Yanagisawa, Pres.
Tel: (213) 236-3924
%FO: 100

Bus: *Engaged in real estate development and hotel and resort management.*
Fax: (213) 236-3933

- **MITSUBISHI HEAVY INDUSTRIES LTD.**

5-1 Marunouchi 2-chome, Chiyoda-ku, Tokyo 100-8315, Japan

CEO: Nobuyuki Masuda, Chmn.	Tel: 81-3-3212-3111	Rev: $27,250
Bus: *Machinery and plants, aerospace*	Fax: 81-3-3201-9800	Emp: 40,300
system, shipbuilding and steel	www.mhi.co.jp	
structures, R&D.		

MITSUBISHI CATERPILLAR FORKLIFT AMERICA, INC.

2011 W. Sam Houston Pkwy. N., Houston, TX 77043-2421

CEO: Yoichiro Okazaki, Pres.	Tel: (713) 467-1234	%FO: 100
Bus: *Mfr. forklifts.*	Fax: (713) 467-3232	

MITSUBISHI ENGINE NORTH AMERICA, INC.

1250 Greenbriar Drive, Ste. E, Addison, IL 60101-1065

CEO: Yoshiaki Koga, Pres.	Tel: (630) 268-0750	%FO: 100
Bus: *Sales/distribution of offroad*	Fax: (630) 268-9293	
engines and parts.		

MITSUBISHI HEAVY INDUSTRIES AMERICAS, INC.

630 Fifth Avenue, Ste. 3155, New York, NY 10111

CEO: Hideo Egawa, Pres.	Tel: (212) 969-9000	%FO: 100
Bus: *Industrial machinery and systems.*	Fax: (212) 262-3301	

MITSIBISHI LITHOGRAPHIC PRESSES, INC.

600 Barclay Blvd., Lincolnshire, IL 60069

CEO: Wilson F. Buchanan, Pres.	Tel: (847) 634-9100	%FO: 100
Bus: *Sales lithographic presses.*	Fax: (847) 634-9109	

- **MITSUBISHI LOGISTICS CORPORATION**

1-19-1 Nihonbashi, Chuo-ku, Tokyo 103-0027, Japan

CEO: Tsuyoshi Miyazaki, Chmn.	Tel: 81-3-3278-6611
Bus: *Engaged in sea and air freight*	Fax: 81-3-3278-6694
forwarding.	www.mitsubishi-logistics.co.jp

MITSUBISHI LOGISTICS AMERICA CORP.

One Penn Plaza, Ste. 1908, New York, NY 10119

CEO: Tadashi Okayama, CEO	Tel: (212) 695-8552	%FO: 100
Bus: *Engaged in sea and air freight*	Fax: (212) 967-6491	
forwarding.		

MITSUBISHI LOGISTICS AMERICA CORP.

400 West Artesia Boulevard, Compton, CA 90220

CEO: Tadashi Okayama, CEO	Tel: (310) 661-3560	%FO: 100
Bus: *Engaged in sea and air freight*	Fax: (310) 631-7834	
forwarding.		

MITSUBISHI LOGISTICS AMERICA CORP.
3040 East Victoria Street, Rancho Dominguez, CA 90221
CEO: Tadashi Okayama, CEO   Tel: (310) 886-5500   %FO: 100
Bus: *Engaged in sea and air freight*   Fax: (310) 604-1552
forwarding.

● **MITSUBISHI MATERIALS CORPORATION**
1-5-1, Marunouchi, Chiyoda-ku, Tokyo 101-8117, Japan
CEO: Masaya Fujimura, Chmn.   Tel: 81-3-5252-5201   Rev: $8,260
Bus: *Non-ferrous metals, fabricated metals,*   Fax: 81-3-5252-5271   Emp: 7,060
electronic material, aluminum cans,   www.mmc.co.jp
golden jewelry and semi-conductors.

DIAMET CORPORATION
1751 Arcadia Drive, Columbus, IN 47201
CEO: Koji Yamada, Pres.   Tel: (812) 379-4606   %FO: 100
Bus: *Production/sales of powder*   Fax: (812) 379-1216
metallurgical products.

HEISEI MINERALS CORPORATION
399 Park Avenue, 38th Fl., New York, NY 10022
CEO: Shuji Hagino, SVP   Tel: (212) 319-0954   %FO: 100
Bus: *Copper mining and production of*   Fax: (212) 319-0972
copper concentrate.

KAMAYA, INC.
6407 Cross Creek Boulevard, Fort Wayne, IN 46818
CEO: Mike Liebing, Sales   Tel: (219) 489-1533   %FO: 100
Bus: *Sales/distribution of semi-*   Fax: (219) 489-2261
conductors and surface mount chip
resistors.

MITSUBISHI CEMENT CORPORATION
3633 Inland Empire Blvd., Ste. 900, Ontario, CA 91764-4922
CEO: Ysuguo Yoshida, Chmn.   Tel: (909) 466-5900   %FO: 100
Bus: *Production and sales of cement.*   Fax: (909) 466-5910

MITSUBISHI MATERIALS CORPORATION
399 Park Avenue, 38th Fl., New York, NY 10022
CEO: C. P. Brauch, Chmn.   Tel: (212) 688-9550   %FO: 100
Bus: *Sales/distribution of metal*   Fax: (212) 688-9616
products.

MITSUBISHI SILICON AMERICA

2445 Faber Place, Ste. 100, PO Box 10445, Palo Alto, CA   94303

CEO: Chet Brauch, CEO

Tel: (415) 853-5019

%FO: 100

Bus: *Marketing headquarters: mfr./sale* Fax: (415) 853-5080
polished and epitaxial silicon
wafers for semiconductor industry.

MITSUBISHI SILICON AMERICA

3990 Fairview Industrial Drive SE, Salem, OR   97302

CEO: Robert Swor, SVP

Tel: (503) 391-0678

%FO: 100

Bus: *Mfr. polished and epitaxial silicon* Fax: (503) 315-6551
wafers for semiconductor industry.

MITSUBISHI SILICON AMERICA

17304 N. Preston Road, Ste. 800, Dallas, TX   75252-5645

CEO: Joe Baranowski

Tel: (972) 733-6878

%FO: 100

Bus: *Sales office for sale of polished &* Fax: (972) 233-6938
epitaxial silicon wafers for
semiconductor industry.

Emp: 2

MITSUBISHI SILICON AMERICA

1351 Tanden Avenue NE, PO Box 7748, Salem, OR   97303

CEO: Neil Nelson, VP

Tel: (503) 371-0041

%FO: 100

Bus: *Mfr. polished and epitaxial silicon* Fax: (503) 361-3409
wafers for semiconductor industry.

Emp: 1,200

MITSUBISHI SILICON AMERICA

2141 East Broadway Road, Ste. 215, Tempe, AZ   85292

CEO: Shinichi Kamizuma

Tel: (480) 929-6380

%FO: 100

Bus: *Marketing headquarters: mfr./sale* Fax: (480) 449-3550
polished and epitaxial silicon
wafers for semiconductor industry.

MITSUBISHI SILICON AMERICA

2445 Faber Place, Palo Alto, CA   94303-0912

CEO: Shinichi Kamizuma

Tel: (650) 853-5090

%FO: 100

Bus: *Mfr./sale polished and epitaxial* Fax: (650) 853-5080
silicon wafers for semiconductor
industry.

MMC ELECTRONICS AMERICA INC.

1365 Wiley Road, Ste. 149, Schaumburg, IL   60173

CEO: Akira Nishikawa, Pres.

Tel: (847) 490-0222

%FO: 100

Bus: *Provides technical and sales* Fax: (847) 490-0218
support.

MMC ELECTRONICS AMERICA INC.
45 East Plumeria Drive, San Jose, CA   95134
CEO: Akira Nishikawa, Pres.   Tel: (408) 571-2001   %FO: 100
Bus: *Provides technical and sales*   Fax: (408) 571-2099
    support.

● **MITSUBISHI MOTORS CORPORATION**
5-33-8 Shiba, Minato-ku, Tokyo 108-8410, Japan
CEO: Takashi Sonobe, Pres.   Tel: 81-3-3456-1111   Rev: $31,609
Bus: *Mfr./sales of cars, diesel truck and*   Fax: 81-3-5232-7731   Emp: 25,850
    buses.   www.mitsubishi-motors.co.jp

MITSUBISHI FUSO TRUCK OF AMERICA, INC.
100 Center Square Road, Bridgeport, NJ   08014-0464
CEO: Kazushige Kinoshita, Pres.   Tel: (856) 467-4500   %FO: 100
Bus: *Sales/distribution of trucks.*   Fax: (856) 467-4695

MITSUBISHI MOTOR MFG. OF AMERICA, INC.
100 North Mitsubishi Motorway, Normal, IL   61761
CEO: Richard Gilligan, COO   Tel: (309) 888-8000   %FO: 100
Bus: *Sales/distribution of motor*   Fax: (309) 888-8154
    vehicles.

MITSUBISHI MOTOR SALES OF AMERICA, INC.
6400 Katella Avenue, Cypress, CA   90630-0064
CEO: Pierre Gagnon, Pres. & CEO   Tel: (714) 372-6000   %FO: 100
Bus: *Sales/distribution of motors.*   Fax: (714) 373-1020

MITSUBISHI MOTORS AMERICA, INC.
3000 Town Center, Ste. 1960, Southfield, MI   48075
CEO: Kazushige Kinoshita, Pres.   Tel: (248) 353-5444   %FO: 100
Bus: *Sales/distribution of motor*   Fax: (248) 649-0630
    vehicles.

● **MITSUBISHI RAYON COMPANY, LTD.**
1-6-41 Kounan, Minato-ku, Tokyo 108-8506, Japan
CEO: Yoshiyuki Sumeragi, Pres. & CEO   Tel: 81-3-5495-3088   Rev: $2,975
Bus: *Mfr. synthetic fibers, films, resins,*   Fax: 81-3-5495-3227   Emp: 4,385
    medical devices.   www.mrc.co.jp

MITSUBISHI RAYON AMERICA, INC.
520 Madison Avenue, 17th Fl., New York, NY   10022
CEO: Makoto Gonda, Pres.   Tel: (212) 759-5605   %FO: 100
Bus: *Synthetic, optical & carbon fibers,*   Fax: (212) 355-7994
    resins, medical devices.

● **MITSUBISHI TRUST & BANKING CORPORATION**

4-5 Marunouchi 1-chome, Chiyoda-ku, Tokyo 100-0005, Japan

CEO: Hiroshi Hayashi, Chmn.	Tel: 81-3-3212-1211	Rev: $8,300
Bus: *General banking services.*	Fax: 81-3-3211-1267	Emp: 5,800
	www.mitsubishi-trust.co.jp	

    MITSUBISHI TRUST & BANKING CORPORATION

    520 Madison Avenue, 39th Fl., New York, NY 10022

CEO: M. Tsuji	Tel: (212) 891-8500	%FO: 100
Bus: *International banking services.*	Fax: (212) 935-3508	

    MITSUBISHI TRUST & BANKING CORPORATION

    311 South Wacker Drive, Chicago, IL 60606

CEO: Naoya Nishimura, Gen. Mgr.	Tel: (312) 408-6000	%FO: 100
Bus: *International banking services.*	Fax: (312) 663-0863	

    MITSUBISHI TRUST & BANKING CORPORATION

    801 South Figueroa Street, Ste. 500, Los Angeles, CA 90017

CEO: Kazuaki Kido, Gen. Mgr.	Tel: (213) 488-9003	%FO: 100
Bus: *International banking services.*	Fax: (213) 687-4631	

● **MITSUBOSHI BELTING, LTD.**

Kobe Harborland Center Bldg., 3-3 Higashi 1-chome, Kawasaki-cho, Chuo-ku, Kobe 650, Japan

CEO: Norio Nishikawa, Pres.	Tel: 81-78-360-5939	Rev: $613
Bus: *Mfr. power transmission and conveyor belts, auto comps, structural foam, waterproofing materials, tires/tubes, engineering. plastics.*	Fax: 81-78-360-5991 www.mitsuboshi.co.jp	Emp: 1,693

    MBL (USA) CORPORATION

    601 Dayton Road, Ottawa, IL 61350

CEO: Keiji Murata, Pres.	Tel: (815) 434-1282	%FO: 98
Bus: *Mfr. industrial/auto power transmission belts, polyurethane precision belts and molded products.*	Fax: (815) 434-2897	Emp: 270

● **MITSUI & COMPANY, LTD.**

CPO Box 822, Tokyo 100-8631, Japan

CEO: Shigeji Ueshima, Chmn. & CEO	Tel: 81-3-3285-1111	Rev: $123,706
Bus: *General trading company and administrative services for Mitsui Group.*	Fax: 81-3-3285-9819 www.mitsui.co.jp	Emp: 10,600

MITSUI & COMPANY, (USA) INC.

200 East Randolph Drive, Suite 5200, Chicago, IL   60601

CEO: Shozaburo Maruyama, SVP   Tel: (312) 540-4000   %FO: 100

Bus: *Mfr. steel, machinery and general*   Fax: (312) 540-4001
     merchandise.

MITSUI & COMPANY, (USA) INC.

200 Park Avenue, 36th Fl., New York, NY   10166-0130

CEO: Shinjiro Shimizu, Pres. & CEO   Tel: (212) 878-4000   %FO: 100

Bus: *General trading company:*   Fax: (212) 878-4800   Emp: 750
     export/import, finance, investment,
     transportation and technology
     transfer.

MITSUI & COMPANY, (USA) INC.

1000 Town Center, Ste. 1900, Southfield, MI   48075

CEO: Masazumi Shibata, SVP   Tel: (248) 357-3300   %FO: 100

Bus: *Mfr. steel and machinery for the*   Fax: (248) 355-3572
     auto industry.

MITSUI & COMPANY, (USA) INC.

2500 Windy Ridge Pkwy., Ste. 1500, Atlanta, GA   30339

CEO: Masayuki Hirose, SVP   Tel: (770) 859-0700   %FO: 100

Bus: *Mfr. steel, machinery and general*   Fax: (770) 859-0520
     merchandise.

MITSUI & COMPANY, (USA) INC.

1701 Pennsylvania Ave. NW, Ste. 500, Washington, DC   20006

CEO: Yuji Takagi, Mgr.   Tel: (202) 861-0660   %FO: 100

Bus: *Mfr. steel, machinery and general*   Fax: (202) 861-0437
     merchandise.

MITSUI & COMPANY, (USA) INC.

25 Century Boulevard, Nashville, TN   37214

CEO: Shinjiro Shimizu, Pres. & CEO   Tel: (615) 885-5318   %FO: 100

Bus: *Mfr. steel, machinery and general*   Fax: (615) 885-5321
     merchandise.

MITSUI & COMPANY, (USA) INC.

200 Public Square, Cleveland, OH   44114

CEO: M. Matsumoto, Mgr.   Tel: (216) 696-8710   %FO: 100

Bus: *Mfr. steel, machinery and general*   Fax: (216) 696-8574
     merchandise.

● **MITSUI CHEMICALS, INC.**

2-5 Kasumigaseki 3-chome, Chiyoda-ku, Tokyo 100-6070, Japan

CEO: Shigenori Koda, Chmn.   Tel: 81-3-3592-4060   Rev: $8,373

Bus: *Mfr./sales chemical, pharmaceutical*   Fax: 81-3-3592-4211   Emp: 11,480
    and electronic materials and products.   www.mitsui-chem.co.jp

    MITSUI CHEMICALS AMERICA, INC.

    2500 Windy Ridge Pkwy., Ste.1500, Atlanta, GA   30339

    CEO: Junichi Shibuta, Mgr.   Tel: (770) 859-0700   %FO: 100

    Bus: *Mfr. chemicals and plastics.*   Fax: (770) 859-0520

    MITSUI CHEMICALS AMERICA, INC.

    2500 Westchester Avenue, Ste.110, Purchase, NY   10577

    CEO: Manabu Fujise, Pres.   Tel: (914) 253-0777   %FO: 100

    Bus: *Sales/distribution of chemical,*   Fax: (914) 253-0790
    pharmaceutical and electronic
    materials and products.

● **MITSUI ENGINEERING & SHIPBUILDING CO., LTD.**

6-4 Tsukiji 5-chome, Chuo-ku, Tokyo 104-8439, Japan

CEO: Toshimichi Okano, Pres.   Tel: 81-3-3544-3147   Rev: $4,328

Bus: *Engaged in system engineering,*   Fax: 81-3-3544-3050   Emp: 3,931
    shipbuilding, medical equipment,   www.mes.co.jp
    industrial machinery and pollution
    control plants.

    MITSUI ZOSEN USA INC.

    405 Park Avenue, Ste. 501, New York, NY   10022

    CEO: Elji Moriwaki, Pres.   Tel: (212) 308-3350   %FO: 100

    Bus: *Engaged in system engineering,*   Fax: (212) 308-3358
    shipbuilding, medical equipment,
    industrial machinery and pollution
    control plants.

● **MITSUI FUDOSAN CO., LTD.**

Mitsui Fudosan, 1-1 Nihonbashi, Muromachi 2-chome, Chuo-ku, Tokyo 103-0022, Japan

CEO: Hiromichi Iwasa, Pres. & CEO   Tel: 81-3-3246-3435   Rev: $11,485

Bus: *Engaged in real estate development,*   Fax: 81-3-3246-3543   Emp: 13,485
    construction and financing.   www.mitsuifudosan.co.jp

    MITSUI FUDOSAN, INC.

    601 South Figueroa Street, Ste. 2625, Los Angeles, CA   90017

    CEO: Shuhei Okuda, Chmn.   Tel: (213) 683-1757   %FO: 100

    Bus: *Engaged in real estate*   Fax: (213) 624-5857
    development, construction and
    financing.

MITSUI FUDOSAN, INC.

1251 Avenue of the Americas, Ste. 4800, New York, NY   10020

CEO: Hitoshi Sata, Pres. & CEO

Bus: *Engaged in real estate development, construction and financing.*

Tel: (212) 302-6331

Fax: (212) 302-6594

%FO: 100

● MITSUI MARINE & FIRE INSURANCE CO., LTD.

3-9 Kanda-Surugadai, Chiyoda-ku, Tokyo 101-11, Japan

CEO: Takeo Inokuchi, CEO

Bus: *Non-life insurance services, including fire, personal accident and auto insurance.*

Tel: 81-3-3259-3111

Fax: 81-3-3291-5466

www.mitsuimarine.co.jp

Rev: $7,150

Emp: 7,400

MITSUI MARINE & FIRE INSURANCE COMPANY OF AMERICA

33 Whitehall Street, 26th Fl., New York, NY   10004-2112

CEO: Akira Tomeda, Pres.

Bus: *Non-life insurance services, including fire, personal accident and auto insurance.*

Tel: (212) 480-2550

Fax: (212) 480-1127

%FO: 100

Emp: 24

MITSUI MARINE & FIRE INSURANCE COMPANY OF AMERICA

601 South Figueroa Street, Ste. 1390, Los Angeles, CA   90017

CEO: Noriaki Hamanaka, SVP

Bus: *Non-life insurance services, including fire, personal accident and auto insurance.*

Tel: (213) 612-0123

Fax: (213) 612-0028

%FO: 100

● MITSUI MINING & SMELTING COMPANY, LTD.

11-1 Osaki 1-chrome, Shinagawa-ku, Tokyo 141-8584, Japan

CEO: Shimpei Miyamura, Pres.

Bus: *Mfr. non-ferrous metals.*

Tel: 81-3-5437-8028

Fax: 81-3-5437-8029

www.mitsui-kinzoku.co.jp

Rev: $3,741

Emp: 10,000

ALLIED SIGNAL OAK-MITSUI, INC.

80 First Street, PO Box 99, Hoosick Falls, NY   12090

CEO: Steve Hochhauser, Pres.

Bus: *Mfr./sale copper foil for print circuit.*

Tel: (518) 686-4961

Fax: (518) 686-4980

%FO: 50

Emp: 230

GECOM CORPORATION

1025 Barachel Lane, Greensburg, IN   47240

CEO: M. Nagashima, CEO

Bus: *Mfr./sale automobile door locks.*

Tel: (812) 663-2270

Fax: (812) 663-2230

%FO: 100

Emp: 642

MITSUI MINING & SMELTING COMPANY, (USA) INC.

461 Fifth Avenue, New York, NY   10017

CEO: Nobuo Abe, Pres.   Tel: (212) 679-9300   %FO: 100

Bus: *Import/export non-ferrous metals*   Fax: (212) 679-9303
    and products, research and service.

● MITSUI OSK LINES LTD.

1-1 Toranomon 2-chome, Minato-ku, Tokyo 105-8688, Japan

CEO: Masaharu Ikuta, Chmn.   Tel: 81-3-3587-7111   Rev: $8,358

Bus: *International transport, sea, land and*   Fax: 81-3-3587-7734   Emp: 7,465
    rail carriers, terminals, cruise ships and   www.mol.co.jp
    resorts, and real estate development.

AMT FREIGHT, INC.

2500 Logistics Drive, Battle Creek, MI   49015

CEO: Isao Okada, Pres.   Tel: (616) 965-0054   %FO: 100

Bus: *International freight forwarding*   Fax: (616) 965-2040
    services.

MCS LTD.

Harborside Financial Center, Plaza III, Ste. 601, Jersey City, NJ   07311

CEO: Dennis Sheehan, AVP   Tel: (201) 200-5200   %FO: 100

Bus: *Marine transportation services.*   Fax: (201) 200-5396   Emp: 415

MITSUI OSK BULK SHIPPING INC.

Harborside Financial Center, Plaza III, Ste. 601, Jersey City, NJ   07311

CEO: Yoshiaki Takagi, Pres.   Tel: (201) 200-5200   %FO: 100

Bus: *Bulk shipping transportation.*   Fax: (201) 200-5297

MITSUI OSK LINES (America) LTD.

2300 Clayton Road, Ste. 1500, Concord, CA   94520

CEO: James C. Galligan   Tel: (925) 688-2600   %FO: 100

Bus: *Marine transportation services.*   Fax: (925) 688-2604

● MITSUI-SOKO CO., LTD.

1-13-12 Nibonbashi Kayabacho, Chuo-ku, Tokyo 103-025, Japan

CEO: Goro Hara, CEO   Tel: 81-3-3667-5331   Rev: $856

Bus: *Provides warehouse storage.*   Fax: 81-3-3639-5055   Emp: 900
                                          www.mitsui-soko.co.jp

MITSUI-SOKO CO., LTD.

1320 Greenway Drive, Ste. 610, Irving, TX   75038

CEO: Yoshie Sugawara   Tel: (972) 518-1933   %FO: 100

Bus: *Provides warehouse storage.*   Fax: (972) 550-0117

MITSUI-SOKO CO., LTD.
20974 South Santa Fe Avenue, Carson, CA   90810-1131
CEO: Katsumi Namiki, Pres.   Tel: (310) 639-3060   %FO: 100
Bus: *Provides warehouse storage.*   Fax: (310) 639-4060

MITSUI-SOKO CO., LTD.
875 Mahler Road, Ste. 201, Burlingame, CA   94010
CEO: Sean Chen   Tel: (650) 652-1510   %FO: 100
Bus: *Provides warehouse storage.*   Fax: (650) 652-1515

MITSUI-SOKO CO., LTD.
3 Butterfield Trail, Ste. 122, El Paso, TX   79906
CEO: Yuzo Yamashita   Tel: (915) 772-3540   %FO: 100
Bus: *Provides warehouse storage.*   Fax: (915) 772-3728

MITSUI-SOKO CO., LTD.
101 Mark Street, Ste. A, Wood Dale, IL   60191
CEO: Hiroyuki Hamano   Tel: (630) 616-0990   %FO: 100
Bus: *Provides warehouse storage.*   Fax: (630) 616-0996

MITSUI-SOKO CO., LTD.
101 Hudson Street, Ste. 2601, Jersey City, NJ   07302
CEO: Norihiko Kakuta   Tel: (201) 435-5500   %FO: 100
Bus: *Provides warehouse storage.*   Fax: (201) 435-6487

● **MITSUKOSHI, LTD.**
1-4-1 Muromachi-Nihonbashi, 1-chome, Chuo-ku, Tokyo 103-8001, Japan
CEO: Kazuo Inoue, Pres.   Tel: 81-3-241-3311   Rev: $8,075
Bus: *Operates retail department stores.*   Fax: 81-3-3274-8795   Emp: 10,100
                                    www.mitsukoshi.co.jp

   MITSUKOSHI USA, INC.
   12 East 49 Street, 17th Fl., New York, NY   10017
   CEO: Yutaka Tetsuyama, Pres.   Tel: (212) 753-5580   %FO: 100
   Bus: *Sale/service restaurants, retail,*   Fax: (212) 355-7161   Emp: 215
     exporting and interior decoration.

● **MIURA CO LTD.**
7 Horie-cho, Matsuyama Ehime 799-2966, Japan
CEO: Shozo Shiraishi, Pres.   Tel: 81-899-791-111   Rev: $440
Bus: *Mfr. steam and hot water boilers and*   Fax: 81-899-782-321   Emp: 1,670
food machines.   www.miura.co.jp

   MIURA BOILER USA, INC.
   600 Northgate Pkwy, Ste. M, Wheeling, IL   60090-3201
   CEO: Mark Utzinger, VP   Tel: (847) 465-0001   %FO: 100
   Bus: *Sales and service of boilers.*   Fax: (847) 465-0011   Emp: 10

MIURA BOILER USA, INC.
1945 South Myrtle Avenue, Monrovia, CA   91016-4854
CEO: David Miyauchi, Pres.   Tel: (626) 305-6622   %FO: 100
Bus: *Sales and service of boilers.*   Fax: (626) 305-6624

• MIYACHI TECHNOS CORPORATION
Koyosha Bldg, 8/F, 5-48-5 Higashinippori, Arakawa-ku, Tokyo 116, Japan
CEO: Keiji Nishizawa, Pres.   Tel: 81-6-891-2211
Bus: *Mfr. welding controls, power supplies*   Fax: 81-6-891-7887   Emp: 250
    and industrial laser systems.   www.miyachitechnos.co.jp

UNITEC MIYACHI CORPORATION
1820 South Myrtle Avenue, Monrovia, CA   91017-7133
CEO: R. Patterson Jackson, CEO   Tel: (626) 303-5676   %FO: 100
Bus: *Sales/service of welding controls,*   Fax: (626) 358-8048
    power supplies and monitors.

• MIZUNO CORPORATION
1-12-35 Nanko-kita, Suminoe-ku, Osaka 559-8510, Japan
CEO: Setsuo Yoshimatsu, Mng. Dir.   Tel: 81-6-6614-8467   Rev: $1,213
Bus: *Mfr. sporting goods.*   Fax: 81-6-6614-8493   Emp: 3,800
    www.mizuno.com

MIZUNO CORPORATION
5125 Peachtree Industrial Boulevard, Norcross, GA   30092
CEO: Robert Puccini, CEO   Tel: (800) 966-1211   %FO: 100
Bus: *Mfr./sales sporting goods.*   Fax: (770) 448-3234

• MORI SEIKI CO., LTD.
362 Idono-cho, Yamatokoriyama-shi, Nara 639-1183, Japan
CEO: Masahiko Mori, Pres.   Tel: 81-7-43-53-1121   Rev: $878
Bus: *Manufacturer of machine tools.*   Fax: 81-7-43-52-8713   Emp: 1,737
    www.moriseki.co.jp

MORI SEIKI USA, INC.
9001 Currency Street, Irving, TX   75063
CEO: M. Hamabe, Mgr.   Tel: (972) 929-8321   %FO: 100
Bus: *Sales/distribution of machine tools.*   Fax: (972) 929-8226

• J. MORITA CORPORATION
33-18 Tarumi-cho, 3-chome, Suita City 564, Japan
CEO: Haruo Morita, CEO   Tel: 81-6-380-1521   Rev: $351
Bus: *Mfr./distributor of dental equipment and*   Fax: 81-6-380-0585   Emp: 880
    supplies.   www.morita.co.j

J. MORITA USA, INC.
Nine Mason Street, Irvine, CA 92618
CEO: Junichi Miyata, Pres.   Tel: (949) 581-9600   %FO: 100
Bus: *Mfr./distribution of furniture and*   Fax: (949) 581-9688   Emp: 25
dental instruments/equipment.

● **MURATA MACHINERY, LTD. (MURATEC)**
136, Takeda-Mukaishiro-cho, Fushimitu Kyoto 612, Japan
CEO: Junichi Murata, Pres. & CEO   Tel: 81-75-672-8138   Rev: $122,000
Bus: *Mfr./distribution of textile machinery,*   Fax: 81-75-672-8691   Emp: 3,000
material handling equipment and   www.muratec.co.jp
machine tools.

    MURATA AUTOMATED SYSTEMS, INC.
    2120 I-85 South, PO Box 668887, Charlotte, NC 28266-8887
    CEO: Hideki Ichikawa, Pres.   Tel: (704) 394-6900   %FO: 100
    Bus: *Sales/distribution of textile*   Fax: (704) 394-2001
    machinery, material handling
    equipment and machine tools.

    MURATEC AMERICA, INC.
    6400 International Parkway, Ste.1500, Plano, TX 75093
    CEO: Hideki "Henry" Mori, Pres. &   Tel: (972) 364-3300   %FO: 100
    CEO
    Bus: *Mfr. fax and copy machines.*   Fax: (972) 364-3311

● **MURATA MANUFACTURING COMPANY, LTD.**
26-10 Tenjin 2-chome, Nagaokakyo, Kyoto 617-8555, Japan
CEO: Yasutaka Murata, Pres.   Tel: 81-75-951-9111   Rev: $3,296
Bus: *Mfr. electronic components.*   Fax: 81-75-954-7720   Emp: 4,489
    www.murata.co.com

    MURATA ELECTRONICS NORTH AMERICA, INC.
    2200 Lake Park Drive SE, Smyrna, GA 30080
    CEO: Takeshi Iishi, Pres.   Tel: (770) 436-1300   %FO: 100
    Bus: *Mfr./sale electronic components.*   Fax: (770) 436-3030   Emp: 1,700

● **NAGASE & CO. LTD.**
5-1 Nihonbashi Kobunacho, Chuo-ku, Tokyo 103-8355, Japan
CEO: Hiroshe Nagase, CEO   Tel: 81-3-3665-3022   Rev: $5,386
Bus: *Development, production, sale and*   Fax: 81-3-3665-3030   Emp: 1,166
import and export of dyestuffs,   www.nagase.co.jp
chemicals, plastics, and biochemical
products.

NAGASE AMERICA CORPORATION
34119 West Twelve Mile Road, Ste. 205, Farmington Hills, MI   48331
CEO: M. Mitsuhashi, Pres.   Tel: (248) 324-1467   %FO: 100
Bus: *Engaged in development and*   Fax: (248) 324-4471
      manufacture of chemicals.

NAGASE AMERICA CORPORATION
546 Fifth Avenue, 16th Fl., New York, NY   10036
CEO: M. Mitsuhashi, Pres.   Tel: (212) 703-1340   %FO: 100
Bus: *Engaged in development and*   Fax: (212) 398-0687
      manufacture of chemicals.

NAGASE CALIFORNIA CORPORATION
125 East Baker Street, Ste. 207, Costa Mesa, CA   92626
CEO: M. Mitsuhashi, Pres.   Tel: (714) 557-7038
Bus: *Engaged in development and*   Fax: (714) 557-8575
      manufacture of chemicals.

NAGASE CALIFORNIA CORPORATION
710 Lakeway, Ste. 135, Sunnyvale, CA   94086
CEO: M. Mitsuhashi, Pres.   Tel: (408) 773-0700
Bus: *Engaged in development and*   Fax: (408) 773-9567
      manufacture of chemicals.

NAGASE KISHO ELECTRONICS INC.
710 Lakeway, Ste. 135, Sunnyvale, CA   94086
CEO: M. Mitsuhashi, Pres.   Tel: (408) 773-0700
Bus: *Mfr. of electronics.*   Fax: (408) 773-9567

● **NAMBA PRESS WORKS COMPANY, LTD.**
8-3-8 Kojima-Ogawa, Kurashiki, Okayama 711, Japan
CEO: Shigezo Namba, Pres.   Tel: 81-86-473-3111
Bus: *Original equipment auto seating and*   Fax: 81-86-473-4774
      related products.

BLOOMINGTON-NORMAL SEATING COMPANY
2031 Warehouse Road, Normal, IL   61761
CEO: Nobuhiro Morimoto, Chmn.   Tel: (309) 452-7878   %FO: JV
Bus: *Mfr. automotive seating systems.*   Fax: (309) 452-2312   Emp: 150

● **NEC CORPORATION**
NEC Building, 7-1 Shiba 5-chome, Minato-ku, Tokyo 108-01, Japan
CEO: Koji Nishigaki, Pres.   Tel: 81-3-3454-1111   Rev: $42,823
Bus: *Communication systems and equipment,*   Fax: 81-3-3798-1510   Emp: 154,785
      computers, industrial electronic   www.nec.com
      systems, electronic devices.

DCM SOLUTIONS, INC.
100 Decker Court, Ste. 120, Irving, TX   75062

CEO: Troy Richards, Pres.   Tel: (972) 541-1730   %FO: 100

Bus: *Mfr./sales of demand chain*   Fax: (972) 541-1732
management solutions.

NEC AMERICA, INC.
6555 N. State Highway 161, Irving, TX   75039

CEO: Noboru Norose   Tel: (214) 262-2000   %FO: 100

Bus: *Mfr. advanced wireless*   Fax: (214) 262-6800
communications products.

NEC COMPUTER SYSTEMS INC
2890 Scott Boulevard, Ste. 300, Santa Clara, CA   98052-8155

CEO: Susumu Sato, SVP   Tel: (408) 844-1100   %FO: 100

Bus: *Mfr. ICs and electronic devices.*   Fax: (408) 844-1208

NEC COMPUTERS
15 Business Park Way, Sacramento, CA   95828

CEO: Steve Boogar, COO   Tel: (916) 388-0101   %FO: 100

Bus: *Mfr. and sales of computer*   Fax: (916) 388-5292
peripheral products.

NEC ELECTRONICS, INC.
2880 Scott Boulevard, Santa Clara, CA   95050-2454

CEO: Hirokazu Hashimoto, Pres.   Tel: (408) 588-6000   %FO: 100

Bus: *Mfr. electronic devices.*   Fax: (408) 588-6130   Emp: 2,400

NEC ELUMINANT TECHNOLOGIES, INC.
14700 Avion Parkway, Chantilly, VA   20151

CEO: Kunitetsu Makino, Pres.   Tel: (703) 834-4000   %FO: 100

Bus: *Design of transmission access*   Fax: (703) 437-7178
systems.

NEC INDUSTRIES, INC.
101 East 52nd Street, New York, NY   10022

CEO: M. Miwa, Pres.   Tel: (212) 326-2400   %FO: 100

Bus: *Financing for U.S. subsidiaries.*   Fax: (212) 326-2419   Emp: 7,000

NEC INDUSTRIES, INC.
10 East 50th Street, 25th Fl., New York, NY   10022

CEO: Kaoru Yano, Pres.   Tel: (212) 702-7000   %FO: 100

Bus: *Engaged in financial services.*   Fax: (212) 702-7020

NEC RESEARCH INSTITUTE, INC.
4 Independence Way, Princeton, NJ   08540
CEO: C. William Gear, Pres.   Tel: (609) 520-1555   %FO: 100
Bus: *Engaged in research.*   Fax: (609) 951-2961

NEC SYSTEMS, INC.
110 Rio Robles, San Jose, CA   95134
CEO: S. Tashiro, Pres.   Tel: (408) 434-7100   %FO: 100
Bus: *Marketing research services.*   Fax: (408) 434-7119

NEC TECHNOLOGIES, INC.
1250 N. Arlington Heights Rd., Ste. 500, Itasca, IL   60143-1248
CEO: Mike Piehl, Mgr.   Tel: (630) 775-7900   %FO: 100
Bus: *Mfr. computers and related*   Fax: (630) 775-7901
     systems.

NEC USA, INC.
8 Corporate Center Drive, Melville, NY   11747
CEO: Yoji Shikama   Tel: (631) 753-7000   %FO: 100
Bus: *Holding company. Communication*   Fax: (631) 753-7434
     systems and equipment,
     computers, industrial electronic
     systems, electronic devices.

NORTH COAST LOGIC, INC.
4100 Holiday Street, Ste. 200, Canton, OH   44178
CEO: Gregory Moore, Pres.   Tel: (330) 492-4499   %FO: 100
Bus: *Mfr. telecommunications software*   Fax: (330) 492-4489
     for telephones switches.

SUPLICITY CORPORATION
305 Foster Street, Littleton, MA   01460
CEO: David Wiedmer, Pres.   Tel: (978) 742-4690   %FO: 100
Bus: *Marketing of supercomputers.*   Fax: (978) 742-4689

VIBREN TECHNOLOGIES, INC.
80 Central Street, Boxborough, MA   01719
CEO: Tom DeSisto, VP   Tel: (978) 929-5500   %FO: 100
Bus: *Engineering and development*   Fax: (978) 635-6378
     services for computer and network
     technology products.

● **NEW JAPAN SECURITIES COMPANY, LTD.**
3-11 Kanda Surugadai, Tokyo 101-8003, Japan
CEO: Tadashi Kawaguchi, Pres.   Tel: 81-3-3219-1111   Rev: $680
Bus: *Securities broker/dealer.*   Fax: 81-3-3292-6937   Emp: 3,045
                                         www.shinnihon.co.jp

NEW JAPAN SECURITIES INTL, INC.
*One World Trade Center Ste. 9133, New York, NY   10048
CEO: Kenshiro Oshima, CEO   Tel: (212) 839-0001   %FO: 100
Bus: *Securities broker/dealer.*   Fax: (212) 938-1580   Emp: 30

● **THE NEW OTANI COMPANY, LTD.**
4-1 Kioi-cho, Chiyoda-ku, Tokyo 102, Japan
CEO: Kazuhiko Otani, Pres.   Tel: 81-3-3265-1111
Bus: *Hotels management services.*   Fax: 81-3-3221-2619   Emp: 1,300
                                    www.newotani.co.jp

HOTEL KAIMANA, INC.
2863 Kalakaua Avenue, Honolulu, HI   96813
CEO: Steven Boyle, Gen. Mgr.   Tel: (808) 923-1555   %FO: 100
Bus: *Hotels management services.*   Fax: (808) 922-9404   Emp: 150

THE NEW OTANI HOTEL & GARDEN
120 South Los Angeles Street, Los Angeles, CA   90012
CEO: Kenji Yoshimoto, Pres.   Tel: (213) 629-1200   %FO: 100
Bus: *Hotels management services.*   Fax: (213) 622-0980   Emp: 350

● **NEWLONG MACHINE WORKS, LTD.**
14-14 Matsugaya 1-chome, Tait-ku, Tokyo 111-0036, Japan
CEO: Y. Cho, Pres.   Tel: 81-3-3843-0258   Rev: $300
Bus: *Mfr. automated/semi-automated, heavy-*   Fax: 81-3-3843-9963   Emp: 1,500
   duty bag   www.newlong.com
   packaging/closing/filling/making
   equipment, and printing machines.

AMERICAN - NEWLONG, INC.
5310 South Harding Street, Indianapolis, IN   46217
CEO: Gary L. Wells, VP & Gen. Mgr.   Tel: (317) 787-9421   %FO: 100
Bus: *Mfr. automated/semi-automated,*   Fax: (317) 786-5225   Emp: 17
   heavy-duty bag
   packaging/closing/filling/making
   equipment, and printing machines.

AMERICAN - NEWLONG, INC.
1485 Enea Court, Ste. 1330, Concord, CA   94520
CEO: Gary L. Wells, VP & Gen. Mgr.   Tel: (925) 674-3696   %FO: 100
Bus: *Mfr. automated/semi-automated,*   Fax: (925) 798-3077
   heavy-duty bag
   packaging/closing/filling/making
   equipment, and printing machines.

- **NGK INSULATORS, LTD.**

2-56 Suda-Cho, Mizho-ku, Nagoya 467-8530, Japan

CEO: Toshihito Kohara, Chmn.   Tel: 81-52-872-7111   Rev: $2,992

Bus: *Mfr. surge arresters, air/water filters,*   Fax: 81-52-872-7690   Emp: 11,940
noise absorption panels, sewage   www.ngk.co.jp
treatment systems and beryllium-copper
products.

NGK LOCKE POLYMERS INSULATORS, INC.

1609 Diamond Springs Road, Virginia Beach, VA   23455

CEO: Masaharu Shibata, Pres.   Tel: (757) 460-3649   %FO: 100

Bus: *Produces silicone polymer*   Fax: (757) 460-3550
insulators for transmission lines.

NGK LOCKE POLYMERS INSULATORS, INC.

2525 Insulator Drive, Baltimore, MD   21230

CEO: Eddy Ozawa, Pres.   Tel: (410) 347-1700   %FO: 100

Bus: *Mfr. high voltage polymer*   Fax: (410) 347-1724
insulators for electric utilities.

NGK LOCKE POLYMERS INSULATORS, INC.

21250 Hawthorne Blvd., Ste. 110, Torrance, CA   90503

CEO: Masaharu Shibata, Pres.   Tel: (310) 316-3323   %FO: 100

Bus: *Mfr. high voltage polymer*   Fax: (310) 316-3944
insulators for electric utilities.

- **THE NICHIDO FIRE AND MARINE INSURANCE CO. LTD.**

5-3-16 Ginza Chuo-ku, Tokyo 104-0061, Japan

CEO: Ikuo Egashira, Chmn.   Tel: 81-3-3571-5141   Rev: $5,495

Bus: *Insurance underwriter.*   Fax: 81-3-3574-0823   Emp: 7,700
    www.nichido.co.jp

THE NICHIDO FIRE AND MARINE INSURANCE COMPANY LTD.

777 South Figueroa Street, 14th Fl., Los Angeles, CA   90017

CEO: Hikaru Ono, Rep.   Tel: (213) 689-3965   %FO: 100

Bus: *Insurance underwriter for marine,*   Fax: (213) 689-3965
fire, personal accident and auto.

THE NICHIDO FIRE AND MARINE INSURANCE COMPANY LTD.

70 Pine Street, 57th Street, New York, NY   10270

CEO: Masahiro Kondo, Rep.   Tel: (212) 770-6200   %FO: 100

Bus: *Insurance underwriter for marine,*   Fax: (212) 425-1092
fire, personal accident and auto.

- **NICHIEI COMPANY, LTD.**

33-1 Tsurumi-chu 4-chome, Tsurumi-ku, Yokohama 231-8571, Japan

CEO: Koichiro Hirata, Pres.   Tel: 81-45-521-6161   Rev: $1,975

Bus: *Wholesale housing materials, real*   Fax: 81-45-502-3446   Emp: 1,125
estate development and importer of   www.nichiei.co.jp
lumber.

> **NICE INTERNATIONAL AMERICA CORPORATION**
>
> 10220 SW Greenburg Road, Ste.220, Portland, OR 97223
>
> CEO: Katsuo Todoroki, Pres.   Tel: (503) 245-9910   %FO: 100
>
> Bus: *Export lumber; real estate*   Fax: (503) 245-9907   Emp: 14
> *development.*

- **NICHIMEN CORPORATION**

1-23, Shiba 4-chome, Minato-ku, Tokyo 108, Japan

CEO: Akira Watari, Pres.   Tel: 81-3-5446-1111   Rev: $27,125

Bus: *Wholesale textiles, food, machines,*   Fax: 81-3-5446-1010   Emp: 1,415
metals and chemicals.   www.nichimen.co.jp

> **NICHIMEN AMERICA, INC.**
>
> 1345 Avenue of the Americas, 23rd Fl., New York, NY 10105
>
> CEO: Hioshi Yoshikawa, Pres.   Tel: (212) 698-5000   %FO: 100
>
> Bus: *Wholesale textiles, food,*   Fax: (212) 698-5200
> *machines, metals and chemicals.*

- **NICHIREI CORPORATION**

Nichirei Higashi-Ginza Bldg., 6-19-20 Tsukiji, Chuo-ku, Tokyo 104, Japan

CEO: Tadashi Teshima, Pres.   Tel: 81-3-3248-2245   Rev: $5,398

Bus: *Produces and distributes frozen food*   Fax: 81-3-3248-2189   Emp: 5,950
and operates warehouses.   www.nichirei.co.jp

> **NICHIREI FOODS INC.**
>
> 2033 Sixth Avenue, Ste. 900, Seattle, WA 98121
>
> CEO: Masatoshi Toyama, Pres.   Tel: (206) 448-7800   %FO: 100
>
> Bus: *Produces and distributes frozen*   Fax: (206) 443-5800
> *food and operates warehouses;*
> *engages in real estate,*
> *biotechnology and information*
> *services.*

> **SUN-HUSKER FOODS INC.**
>
> 4611 West Adams Street, Lincoln, NE 68529
>
> CEO: Takashi Asano, Pres.   Tel: (402) 470-4300   %FO: 100
>
> Bus: *Processes beef and chicken*   Fax: (402) 470-4380
> *products.*

TENGU COMPANY INC.
446 Towne Avenue, Los Angeles, CA   90013
CEO: Masatoshi Toyama, Pres.   Tel: (213) 622-4261   %FO: 100
Bus: *Processes and sells beef jerky and*   Fax: (213) 622-7250
other beef products.

● **NICHIRO CORPORATION**
Shinyurakucho Bldg, 1-12-1 Yurakucho, Chiyoda-ku, Tokyo 100-0006, Japan
CEO: Keinosuke Hisai, Pres.   Tel: 81-3-3240-6211   Rev: $2,295
Bus: *Seafood products.*   Fax: 81-3-5252-7966   Emp: 925
                                      www.nichiro.co.jp

PETER PAN SEAFOODS, INC.
2200 Sixth Avenue, Ste.1000, Seattle, WA   98121
CEO: Barry Collier, Pres.   Tel: (206) 728-6000   %FO: 100
Bus: *Seafood distributor.*   Fax: (206) 441-9090

● **NIDEC CORPORATION**
10 Tsutsumisoto-cho, Nishikyogoku, Ukyo-ku, Kyoto 615-0854, Japan
CEO: Shigenobu nagamori, CEO   Tel: 81-75-316-1771   Rev: $1,313
Bus: *Mfr. spindle motors to service computer*   Fax: 81-75-316-1781   Emp: 38,000
hard disk drives.   www.nidec.co.jp

NIDEC AMERICA CORPORATION
1823 Sunset Place, Ste. C, Longmont, CO   80501
CEO: Tetsuji Arita, Mng. Dir.   Tel: (303) 631-1025   %FO: 100
Bus: *R&D for small high-precision*   Fax: (303) 651-6816
motors, mid-size motors and
production engineering.

NIDEC AMERICA CORPORATION
152 Will Drive, Canton, MA   02021
CEO: Tetsuji Arita, Mng. Dir.   Tel: (781) 828-6216   %FO: 100
Bus: *Mfr., research and development of*   Fax: (781) 830-1155
power supplies, fans and small
high-precision DC motors.

NIDEC AMERICA CORPORATION
1001 Cross Timbers Road, Ste. 1310, Flower Mound, TX   75028
CEO: Tetsuji Arita, Mng. Dir.   Tel: (972) 691-1119   %FO: 100
Bus: *R&D for small high-precision*   Fax: (972) 691-1319
motors, mid-size motors and
production engineering.

NIDEC AMERICA CORPORATION

318 Industrial Lane, Torrington, CT   06790

CEO: Tetsuji Arita, Mng. Dir. Tel: (860) 482-4422 %FO: 100

Bus: *R&D for small high-precision* Fax: (860) 489-7201
motors, mid-size motors and
production engineering.

NIDEC AMERICA CORPORATION

6860 Shingle Creek Parkway, Ste. 111, Minneapolis, MN   55430-1451

CEO: Tetsuji Arita, Mng. Dir. Tel: (763) 561-6000 %FO: 100

Bus: *R&D for small high-precision* Fax: (763) 561-4500
motors, mid-size motors and
production engineering.

NIDEC AMERICA CORPORATION

2160 Lundy Avenue, Ste. 230, San Jose, CA   95131-1852

CEO: Tetsuji Arita, Mng. Dir. Tel: (408) 432-9140 %FO: 100

Bus: *R&D for small high-precision* Fax: (408) 432-9621
motors, mid-size motors and
production engineering.

NIDEC AMERICA CORPORATION

500 N. Meridian, Ste. 205, Oklahoma City, OK   73107

CEO: Tetsuji Arita, Mng. Dir. Tel: (405) 946-1511 %FO: 100

Bus: *R&D for small high-precision* Fax: (405) 946-1577
motors, mid-size motors and
production engineering.

● NIHON KEIZAI SHIMBUN, INC.

1-9-5 Otemachi, Chiyoda-ku, Tokyo 100-66, Japan

CEO: Takuhiko Tsuruta, Pres. Tel: 81-3-270-0251

Bus: *Newspaper publisher, data bank* Fax: Emp: 4,400
services, broadcasting and exhibitions. www.nni.nikkei.co.jp

NIHON KEIZAI SHIMBUN AMERICA, INC.

1325 Avenue of the Americas, Ste. 2500, New York, NY   10019

CEO: Kazuhiko Mitsumori, Pres. Tel: (212) 261-6200 %FO: 100

Bus: *Newspaper publisher, data bank* Fax: (212) 261-6209
services and research.

● NIIGATE ENGINEERING CO., LTD.

10-1 Kamatahoncho 1-chome, Ohta-ku, Tokyo 144-8639, Japan

CEO: Yoshihiro Muramatsu, Pres. Tel: 81-357-107-700 Rev: $1,797

Bus: *Engaged in engineering services and* Fax: 81-357-104-750 Emp: 2,100
manufacture of industrial machinery. www.niigate-eng.co.jp

NIIGATA MACHINERY CO., INC.
8 Remington Road, Schaumburg, IL   60173-3705
CEO: Mark Fitch   Tel: (847) 839-1000   %FO: 100
Bus: *Engaged in engineering services*   Fax: (847) 839-1088
and manufacture of industrial
machinery.

● NIKKO CORDIAL SECURITIES INC.
3-1 Margnouchi 3-Chome, Chiyoda-Ku Tokyo 103-8225, Japan
CEO: Masashi Kaneko, Pres.   Tel: 81-3-5644-4541   Rev: $4,162
Bus: *Investment banking and brokerage.*   Fax: 81-3-56444555   Emp: 7,675
                                     www.nikko.co.jp

NIKKO SECURITIES COMPANY INTL, INC.
*489 Fifth Avenue, New York, NY   10017
CEO: Masao Matsuda, CEO   Tel: (212) 599-0300   %FO: 100
Bus: *Investment banking/brokerage.*   Fax: (212) 599-4640   Emp: 275

NIKKO GLOBAL ASSET MANAGEMENT
489 Fifth Avenue, New York, NY   10017
CEO: Yoichi Kuwata, Pres.   Tel: (212) 599-0300   %FO: 100
Bus: *Investment advisors.*   Fax: (212) 599-4640

● NIKON CORPORATION
Fuji Bldg, 2-3 Marunouchi 3-chome, Chiyoda-ku, Tokyo 100-8331, Japan
CEO: Shoichiro Yoshida, Pres.   Tel: 81-3-3214-5311   Rev: $3,523
Bus: *Industrial equipment, imaging and*   Fax: 81-3-3201-5856   Emp: 6,675
information, health and medical   www.nikon.com
equipment and services.

NIKON EYEWEAR, INC.
1300 Walt Whitman Road, Melville, NY   11747
CEO: Masaki Hanagata, Pres.   Tel: (516) 547-4200   %FO: 100
Bus: *Mfr. eyeglass frames.*   Fax: (516) 547-0299

NIKON INSTRUMENTS INC.
1300 Walt Whitman Road, Melville, NY   11747
CEO: Takeshi Hirai, Pres.   Tel: (516) 547-4200   %FO: 100
Bus: *Mfr. microscopes, measuring*   Fax: (516) 547-0299
instruments, inspection
instruments and survey
instruments.

NIKON PRECISION, INC.

1399 Shoreway Road, Belmont, CA   94002-4107

CEO: David Huchital, Pres.   Tel: (650) 508-4674   %FO: 100

Bus: *Service/support semiconductor*   Fax: (650) 508-4600   Emp: 280
and manufacturing equipment.

NIKON RESEARCH COMPANY OF AMERICA

1399 Shoreway Road, Belmont, CA   94002

CEO: Gil Varnell, Pres.   Tel: (650) 508-4674   %FO: 100

Bus: *Engaged in research of*   Fax: (650) 508-4600
semiconductor equipment.

NIKON, INC.

19601 Hamilton Avenue, Torrance, CA   90502

CEO: William Gardner, Mgr.   Tel: (310) 516-7124   %FO: 100

Bus: *Service/support semiconductor*   Fax: (310) 516-7751
and manufacturing equipment.

NIKON, INC.

1300 Walt Whitman Road, Melville, NY   11747

CEO: Hideo Fukuchi, Pres.   Tel: (516) 547-4200   %FO: 100

Bus: *U.S. headquarters.*   Fax: (516) 547-0299

● NINTENDO COMPANY, LTD.

11-1 Hokotate-cho, Kamitoba, Minami-ku, Kyoto 601-8501, Japan

CEO: Hiroshi Yamauchi, Pres.   Tel: 81-75-541-6112   Rev: $5,279

Bus: *Develop/mfr. video games and video* Fax: 81-75-541-6127   Emp: 1,000
equipment.   www.nintendo.co.jp

NINTENDO OF AMERICA, INC.

4820 150th Avenue, NE, Redmond, WA   98052-9733

CEO: Minoru Arakawa, Pres.   Tel: (425) 882-2040   %FO: 100

Bus: *Develop/mfr./distribution video*   Fax: (425) 882-3585   Emp: 850
games and video equipment.

● NIPPON CHEMICAL INDUSTRIAL CO., LTD.

9-11-1 Kameido, Koto-ku, Tokyo 136-8515, Japan

CEO: Junichi Tanahashi, Pres. & CEO   Tel: 81-3-3636-8111   Rev: $425

Bus: *Mfr. industrial chemicals.*   Fax: 81-3-3636-6817   Emp: 750
                                          www.nippon-chem.com

JCI USA INC.

30 Rockefeller Plaza, Ste. 1914, New York, NY   10020

CEO: Nobuyuki Muramatsu   Tel: (212) 632-4870   %FO: 100

Bus: *Sales of industrial chemicals.*   Fax: (212) 632-4865

JCI USA INC.
1311 Mamaroneck Avenue, Ste. 145, White Plains, NY   10605
CEO: Nobuyuki Muramatsu   Tel: (914) 761-6555   %FO: 100
Bus: *Sales of industrial chemicals.*   Fax: (914) 761-6940

● **NIPPON COLUMBIA COMPANY, LTD.**
5-1 Minato-cho Kawasaki-ku, Kawasaki Kanagawa 210, Japan
CEO: Hiroshi Takano, Pres.   Tel: 81-44-211-7529   Rev: $830
Bus: *Mfr. audio and video products.*   Fax: 81-44-211-7529   Emp: 1,287
                                        www.elec.donon.co.jp

    DENON CORPORATION
    1640 West 190th Street, Torrance, CA   90501
    CEO: Hideo Kushida, Pres.   Tel: (310) 974-1010   %FO: 100
    Bus: *Distributes audio and video*   Fax: (310) 974-1003
        products.

    DENON CORPORATION
    19 Chapin Road, Pinebrook, NJ   07058
    CEO: Hideo Kushida, Pres.   Tel: (973) 396-0810   %FO: 100
    Bus: *Distributes audio and video*   Fax: (973) 396-7459
        products.

● **NIPPON EXPRESS COMPANY, LTD.**
3-12-9, Sotokanda, Chiyoda-ku, Tokyo 101-8617, Japan
CEO: Masahiko Okabe, Pres.   Tel: 81-3-3253-1111   Rev: $15,523
Bus: *Leasing, finance, import/export, real*   Fax: 81-3-5294-5129   Emp: 51,500
   estate, equipment sales.   www.nittsu.co.jp

    NIPPON EXPRESS TRAVEL USA, INC.
    720 Market Street, 7th Fl., San Francisco, CA   94102
    CEO: H. Nagano, Pres.   Tel: (415) 421-1822   %FO: 100
    Bus: *Travel services.*   Fax: (415) 421-1809

    NIPPON EXPRESS USA, INC.
    590 Madison Avenue, Suite 2401, New York, NY   10022
    CEO: Toru Irie, Pres.   Tel: (212) 758-6100   %FO: 80
    Bus: *Freight forwarding, air/ocean*   Fax: (212) 758-2595   Emp: 1,000
        cargo, household goods moving.

● **NIPPON EXPRESS CORPORATION**
Sotokanda 3-12-9, Chiyoda-ku, Tokyo 101-8617, Japan
CEO: Masahiko Okabe, CEO   Tel: 81-3-3253-1111
Bus: *Travel agency.*   Fax: 81-3-3289-5466   Emp: 40,000
                                        www.nittsu.co.jp

NIPPON EXPRESS HAWAII, INC.
2270 Kalakaua Avenue, Honolulu, HI   96815-2561
CEO: Yoshiharu Kamel, Pres.   Tel: (808) 922-5795   %FO: 100
Bus: *Travel agency services.*   Fax: (808) 922-5795

NIPPON EXPRESS TRAVEL USA, INC.
590 Madison Avenue, Ste. 2401, New York, NY   10022
CEO: T. Hashimoto, Pres.   Tel: (212) 758-6100   %FO: 100
Bus: *Travel agency services.*   Fax: (212) 758-9001

NIPPON EXPRESS TRAVEL USA, INC.
26111 Evergreen Rd., Ste. 306, Southfield, MI   48076
CEO: Osamu Hagiwara, EVP   Tel: (248) 357-6555   %FO: 100
Bus: *Travel agency services.*   Fax: (248) 357-6559

● **NIPPON FLOUR MILLS CO., LTD.**
5-27-5, Sendagaya, Shibuya-ku, Tokyo 151-8537, Japan
CEO: Koichiro Hayakawa, Mng. Dir.   Tel: 81-333-502-311   Rev: $1,536
Bus: *Sales of flour and flour products for*   Fax: 81-352-669-320
industrial and food service.   www.nippn.co.jp

PASTA MONTANA INC.
One Pasta Place, Great Falls, MT   59401
CEO: Joe DeFrancisci, Pres. & CEO   Tel: (406) 761-1516   %FO: 100
Bus: *Sales of flour and flour products*   Fax: (406) 761-1516
for industrial and food service.

● **NIPPON KAYAKU CO., LTD.**
Tokyo Fujimi Bldg., 11-2 Fujimi 1-chome, Chiyoda-ku, Tokyo 102-8172, Japan
CEO: Teruo Nakamura, Pres. & CEO   Tel: 81-3-3237-5111   Rev: $1,060
Bus: *Mfr. pharmaceuticals, agri chemicals*   Fax: 81-3-3237-5085   Emp: 2,143
and pesticides.   www.nipponkayaku.co.jp

NIPPON KAYAKU AMERICA, INC.
711 Westchester Avenue, 2nd Fl., White Plains, NY   10604
CEO: Koichiro Shimada, Mng. Dir.   Tel: (914) 686-6800   %FO: 100
Bus: *Mfr. pharmaceuticals, agri*   Fax: (914) 686-6800
chemicals and pesticides.

● **NIPPON LIFE INSURANCE COMPANY**
2-2 Yurakucho 1-chome, Chiyoda-ku, Tokyo 100-8444, Japan
CEO: Ikuo Uno, Pres.   Tel: 81-3-3507-1421   Rev: $65,850
Bus: *Life insurance.*   Fax: 81-3-5510-7340   Emp: 78,000
                                     www.2nissay.co.jp

NIPPON LIFE INSURANCE OF AMERICA, INC.
757 Third Avenue, 26th Fl., New York, NY 10017
CEO: Takashi Oyama, VP   Tel: (212) 682-3000   %FO: 100
Bus: *Engaged in life insurance.*   Fax: (212) 909-9899

NIPPON LIFE INSURANCE OF AMERICA, INC.
190 South LaSalle Street, Ste. 1680, Chicago, IL 60603
CEO: Takayuki Murai, VP   Tel: (312) 807-1100   %FO: 100
Bus: *Engaged in life insurance.*   Fax: (312) 807-1110

NIPPON LIFE INSURANCE OF AMERICA, INC.
450 Lexington Avenue, Ste. 3200, New York, NY 10017
CEO: Koichi Toyomaru, CEO   Tel: (212) 682-3000   %FO: 100
Bus: *Engaged in life insurance.*   Fax: (212) 682-3002   Emp: 10

NIPPON LIFE INSURANCE OF AMERICA, INC.
445 South Figueroa Street, Ste. 3700, Los Angeles, CA 90017
CEO: Tsutomu Nakamura, VP   Tel: (213) 955-9520   %FO: 100
Bus: *Engaged in life insurance.*   Fax: (213) 955-9539

NLI INTERNATIONAL INC.
1251 Avenue of the Americas, Ste. 5210, New York, NY 10020
CEO: Kiyoshi Ujihara, Pres.   Tel: (212) 403-3400   %FO: 100
Bus: *Engaged in research, investment*   Fax: (212) 764-9773
and asset management.

NLI PROPERTIES CENTRAL, INC.
190 South LaSalle Street, Ste. 1660, Chicago, IL 60603
CEO: Takuya Sawabe, Pres.   Tel: (312) 516-2100   %FO: 100
Bus: *Engaged in real estate investment.*   Fax: (312) 516-0116

NLI PROPERTIES EAST INC.
1251 Avenue of the Americas, Ste. 5230, New York, NY 10020-1191
CEO: Katsumi Nakamura, Pres.   Tel: (212) 403-3456   %FO: 100
Bus: *Engaged in real estate investment.*   Fax: (212) 764-3235

NLI PROPERTIES WEST, INC.
445 South Figueroa Street, Ste. 2850, Los Angeles, CA 90017
CEO: Naoto Kojima, Pres.   Tel: (213) 623-9307   %FO: 100
Bus: *Engaged in real estate investment.*   Fax: (213) 623-9263

PAN AGORA ASSET MANAGEMENT, INC.
260 Franklin Street, 22nd Fl., Boston, MA 02110
CEO: William J. Poutstaka, CEO   Tel: (617) 439-6300   %FO: JV
Bus: *Engaged in asset management.*   Fax: (617) 439-6675

• **NIPPON MEAT PACKERS INC.**
6-14 Minami-Honmachi 3-chome, Chuo-ku, Osaka 541-0054, Japan
CEO: Yoshinori Okoso, Chmn.   Tel: 81-6-282-3031   Rev: $8,356
Bus: *Engaged in meat processing and*   Fax: 81-6-282-1056   Emp: 3,425
     services.   www.nipponham.co.jp

    DAY-LEE FOODS INC.
    13055 East Molette Street, Santa Fe Springs, CA   90670-5593
    CEO: Takahito Okoso, Pres.   Tel: (562) 802-6800   %FO: 100
    Bus: *Sales/distribution of frozen foods.*   Fax: (562) 926-0646

    REDONDO'S INC.
    94-140 Leokane Street, Waipahu, HI   96797
    CEO: Yoshi Shintani, EVP   Tel: (808) 671-5444   %FO: 100
    Bus: *Manages and operates meat*   Fax: (808) 676-7009
         factories.

• **NIPPON METAL INDUSTRY COMPANY, LTD.**
Shinjuku Mitsui Bldg. 1-1, Nishi-Shinjuku 2-chome, Shinjuku-ku, Tokyo 163-0470, Japan
CEO: R. Kimura, Pres. & CEO   Tel: 81-3-3345-5588   Rev: $770
Bus: *Mfr. stainless steel.*   Fax: 81-3-3345-5592   Emp: 1,300
                                     www.nikkinko.co.jp

    NIPPON METAL INDUSTRY USA, INC.
    276 Fifth Avenue, New York, NY   10020
    CEO: Ikuya Fujimaki, Pres.   Tel: (212) 725-0991   %FO: 100
    Bus: *Sale stainless steel.*   Fax: (212) 725-8316   Emp: 3

• **NIPPON MITSUBISHI OIL CORPORATION**
3-12, Nishi Shimbashi 1-chome, Minato-ku, Tokyo 105-8412, Japan
CEO: Fumiaki Watari, Pres. & CEO   Tel: 81-3-3502-1135   Rev: $34,073
Bus: *Engaged in oil import and distribution.*   Fax: 81-3-3502-9352   Emp: 15,965
                                         www.nmoc.co.jp

    NIPPON OIL EXPLORATION LTD.
    5847 San Felipe, Ste. 2800, Houston, TX   77057
    CEO: Kazuo Sawada, Pres.   Tel: (713) 260-7400   %FO: 100
    Bus: *Engaged in oil import and*   Fax: (713) 978-7800
         distribution.

    NIPPON OIL LIMITED
    280 Park Avenue, 35th Fl., New York, NY   10017
    CEO: Naoaki Tsuchiya, Pres.   Tel: (212) 986-7835   %FO: 100
    Bus: *Engaged in oil import and*   Fax: (212) 599-2628
         distribution.

● **NIPPON PAINT COMPANY, LTD.**

1-2, Oyodo-kita, 2-chome, Kita-ku, Osaka 531-8511, Japan

CEO: Hiroshi Fujii, Pres.

Bus: *Mfr. and sales of powder coatings, automotive coatings, pre-treatment chemicals and paint protection film.*

Tel: 81-6-458-1111
Fax: 81-6-6455-9261
www.npacorp.com

Rev: $1,777
Emp: 2,688

NPA COATINGS

11110 Berea Road, Cleveland, OH   44102

CEO: Tatsuo Takeda, Pres.

Bus: *Mfr. and sales of powder coatings, automotive coatings, pre-treatment chemicals and paint protection film.*

Tel: (216) 651-5900
Fax: (216) 651-5902

%FO: 100

NPA COATINGS

500 Frank W. Burr Blvd., Teaneck, NJ   07666

CEO: Kenji Mitsushio, Pres.

Bus: *Mfr. and sales of powder coatings, automotive coatings, pre-treatment chemicals and paint protection film.*

Tel: (201) 692-1111
Fax: (201) 692-0555

%FO: 100

● **NIPPON PAPER INDUSTRIES CO., LTD.**

Shin-Yuraku-cho Bldg., 12-1 Yuraku-cho 1 -chome, Chiyoda-ku, Tokyo 100, Japan

CEO: Takeshiro Miyashita, Chmn.

Bus: *Mfr. paper and paper products.*

Tel: 81-3-3218-8000
Fax: 81-3-3216-4753
www.npaper.co.jp

Rev: $7,800
Emp: 7,175

NORTH PACIFIC PAPER CORPORATION

3001 Industrial Way, Longview, WA   98632-2069

CEO: William Baird, VP

Bus: *Mfr./sales/distribution of paper and paper products.*

Tel: (360) 636-6400
Fax: (360) 423-1514

%FO: 100

● **NIPPON SANSO CORP**

16-7 Nishi-Shinbashi 1-chome, Minato-ku, Tokyo 105-8442, Japan

CEO: Hiroshi Taguchi, CEO

Bus: *Mfr. industrial gases and industrial gas equipment.*

Tel: 81-3-3581-8313
Fax: 81-3-5482-9138
www.sanso.co.jp

Rev: $2,275
Emp: 1,745

THE THERMOS COMPANY

300 North Martingale Road, Ste.200, Schaumburg, IL   60173

CEO: Y. Satomi, Pres.

Bus: *Mfr. thermos containers, gas grilles, gas-fueled equipment.*

Tel: (847) 240-3150
Fax: (847) 240-3160

%FO: 100

THE THERMOS COMPANY
7360 Northwest 34th Street, Miami, FL 33122
CEO: Jaime Sanchez, Mgr.　　　Tel: (305) 715-9071　　　%FO: 100
Bus: *Mfr./sales thermos containers, gas*　Fax: (305) 715-9544　　　Emp: 2
　　grilles, gas-fueled equipment.

● **NIPPON SHEET GLASS COMPANY, LTD.**
5-11, 3-chome, Doshomachi, Chuo-ku, Osaka 541-8559, Japan
CEO: Yousou Izuhara, Pres.　　　Tel: 81-6-6222-7511　　　Rev: $2,565
Bus: *Mfr. flat and safety glass, glass fiber*　Fax: 81-6-6222-7580　　　Emp: 2,200
　　and fiber optic products.　　　www.nsg.co.jp

　　NSG AMERICA, INC.
　　27 Worlds Fair Drive, Somerset, NJ 08873
　　CEO: Nick Hirayama, Pres.　　　Tel: (732) 469-9650　　　%FO: 100
　　Bus: *Mfr. fiber optic products*　　Fax: (732) 469-9654　　　Emp: 35

● **NIPPON SHINPAN COMPANY, LTD.**
3-33-5 Hongo, Bunkyo-ku, Tokyo 113-91, Japan
CEO: Yoji Yamada, CEO　　　Tel: 81-3-3811-3111　　　Rev: $2,800
Bus: *Consumer finance, credit card and*　Fax: 81-3-3815-6650　　　Emp: 6,640
　　investment services.　　　www.nicos.co.jp

　　NIPPON SHINPAN USA, INC.
　　2222 Kalakaua Avenue, Ste.1500, Honolulu, HI 96815
　　CEO: Takayuki Fukuda, VP　　　Tel: (808) 971-9000　　　%FO: 100
　　Bus: *Consumer finance, credit card and*　Fax: (808) 971-9007　　　Emp: 7
　　　investment services.

● **NIPPON SHUPPAN HANBAI, INC.**
4-3 Kandasurugadai, Chiyoda-ku, Tokyo 101-8710, Japan
CEO: Tetsuo Suga, Pres. & CEO　　　Tel: 81-3-3233-1111　　　Rev: $6,670
Bus: *Book wholesaler.*　　　Fax: 81-3-3233-4106　　　Emp: 2,570

　　NIPPON SHUPPAN HANBAI, INC.
　　605 West 7th Street, Los Angeles, CA 90017
　　CEO: Kazuyoshi Kobayashi, Pres.　　　Tel: (213) 891-9636　　　%FO: 100
　　Bus: *Book wholesaler.*　　　Fax: (213) 687-7400

● **NIPPON SODA COMPANY, LTD.**
Shin-Ohtemachi Bldg., 2-2-1 Ohtemachi, Chiyoda-ku, Tokyo 100-8165, Japan
CEO: Tamitaka Tsukihashi, Pres.　　　Tel: 81-3-3245-6053　　　Rev: $1,375
Bus: *Mfr. chemicals.*　　　Fax: 81-3-3245-6238　　　Emp: 1,500
　　　www.nisso.co.jp

NISSO AMERICA, INC.
220 East 42nd Street, Ste. 3002, New York, NY 10017
CEO: Takenobu Shimtzu, CEO   Tel: (212) 490-0350   %FO: 100
Bus: *Distribution of chemicals.*   Fax: (212) 972-9361   Emp: 4

● **NIPPON STEEL CORPORATION**
2-6-3 Otemachi, Chiyoda-ku, Tokyo 100-8071, Japan
CEO: Takashi Imai, Chmn.   Tel: 81-3-3242-4111   Rev: $25,407
Bus: *Mfr. steel products; engineering and*   Fax: 81-3-3275-5607   Emp: 40,000
    construction activities.   www.nsc.co.jp

    NIPPON STEEL USA, INC.
    10 East 50th Street, New York, NY 10022
    CEO: Kelichiro Shimakawa, CEO   Tel: (212) 486-7150   %FO: 100
    Bus: *Marketing research and liaison*   Fax: (212) 593-3049   Emp: 50
       services.

● **NIPPON SUISAN KAISHA, LTD.**
Nippon Building, 2-6-2 Otemachi, Chiyoda-ku, Tokyo 100-8686, Japan
CEO: Naoya Kakizoe, Pres.   Tel: 81-3-3244-7000   Rev: $4,476
Bus: *Mfr. various food products.*   Fax: 81-3-3244-7426   Emp: 2,050
    www.nissui.co.jp

    NIPPON SUISAN USA, INC.
    15400 NE 90th Street, Redmond, WA 98073-9719
    CEO: Katunori Sasao, Pres.   Tel: (425) 869-1703   %FO: 100
    Bus: *U.S. headquarters.*   Fax: (425) 869-1615

    UNISEA FOODS INC.
    15400 NE 90th Street, Redmond, WA 98073-9719
    CEO: Terry Shaff, CEO   Tel: (425) 881-1919   %FO: 100
    Bus: *Sale/distribution of seafood.*   Fax: (425) 821-8416

    UNISEA FOODS INC.
    15110 NE 90th Street, Redmond, WA 98073
    CEO: Dennis Delaye, Pres.   Tel: (425) 881-8181   %FO: 100
    Bus: *Sale/distribution of seafood.*   Fax: (425) 882-1660

● **NIPPON TELEGRAPH & TELEPHONE CORP. (NTT)**
3-1 Otemachi 2-chome, Chiyoda-ku, Tokyo 100-8116, Japan
CEO: Junichiro Miyazu, Pres.   Tel: 81-3-5205-5111   Rev: $97,956
Bus: *Engaged in telecommunication services.*   Fax: 81-3-5205-5589   Emp: 224,000
    www.ntt.co.jp

NTT AMERICA, INC.
101 Park Avenue, 41st Fl., New York, NY   10178

CEO: Akihiko Okada, CEO	Tel: (212) 661-0810	%FO: 100
Bus: *Telecommunication products and services R&D.*	Fax: (212) 661-1078	Emp: 60

VERIO INC.
8005 South Chester Street, Ste. 200, Englewood, CO   80112

CEO: Justin L. Jaschke, CEO	Tel: (303) 645-1900	%FO: 100
Bus: *Provides internet services.*	Fax: (303) 708-2494	

● **NIPPON TELEVISION NETWORK CORPORATION**
14 Niban-cho, Chiyoda-ku, Tokyo 102-8004, Japan

CEO: Yosoji Kobayashi, CEO	Tel: 81-3-5275-111
Bus: *Provides television broadcast services.*	Fax: 81-3-5275-4012
	www.ntv.co.jp

NTV INTERNATIONAL CORP.
50 Rockefeller Plaza, Ste. 940, New York, NY   10020

CEO: Yoichi Shimada, Pres.	Tel: (212) 489-8390	%FO: 100
Bus: *Provides video production and webcasting.*	Fax: (212) 489-8395	

● **NYK LINE (NIPPON YUSEN KAISHA)**
3-2 Marunouchi 2-chome, Chiyoda-ku, Tokyo 100, Japan

CEO: Takao Kusakari, CEO	Tel: 81-3-3284-5151	Rev: $10,450
Bus: *Steamship operator and international transportation.*	Fax: 81-3-3284-6361	Emp: 2,030
	www.nykroro.com	

CRYSTAL CRUISES, INC.
2049 Century Park East, Ste. 1400, Los Angeles, CA   90067

CEO: Joseph A. Watters, Pres.	Tel: (310) 785-9300	%FO: 100
Bus: *Cruise ship tour operator.*	Fax: (310) 785-0011	

NYK BULKSHIP USA, INC.
150 East 52nd Street, 9th Fl., New York, NY   10022

CEO: Hiromitsu Kuramoto, Pres.	Tel: (212) 935-2490	%FO: 100
Bus: *International marine transport.*	Fax: (212) 935-2498	

NYK LINE NORTH AMERICA, INC.
300 Lighting Way, 5th Fl., Secaucus, NJ   07094-1588

CEO: Tetsufumi Otsuki, Pres.	Tel: (201) 330-3000	%FO: 100
Bus: *International marine transport.*	Fax: (201) 867-9059	Emp: 500

● **NIPPON ZEON COMPANY, LTD.**

2-6-1 Marunouchi, Chiyoda-ku, Tokyo 100-8323, Japan

CEO: Katsuhiko Nakano, Pres.	Tel: 81-3-3216-1775	Rev: $1,530
Bus: *Mfr. specialty elastomers, polymers and specialty chemicals.*	Fax: 81-3-3216-1790 www.zeon.co.jp	Emp: 3,500

ZEON CHEMICALS INCORPORATED

4111 Bells Lane, Louisville, KY   40211

CEO: William Niederst, Pres.	Tel: (502) 775-2043	%FO: 100
Bus: *R&D chemicals, specialty chemicals, equipment. and consumer products; flavors & fragrances.*	Fax: (502) 775-2055	Emp: 5

● **NIPPONKOA INSURANCE COMPANY LIMITED**

2-10 Nihonbashi 2-chome, Chuo-ku, Tokyo 103-8255, Japan

CEO: Ken Matsuzawa, Pres.	Tel: 81-3-3272-8111	Rev: $6,589
Bus: *Engaged in property and casualty insurance.*	Fax: 81-3-5229-3369 www.nipponkoa.co.jp	Emp: 5,735

THE NIPPONKOA MANAGEMENT CORPORATION

14 Wall Street, Ste. 1210, New York, NY   10005

CEO: Takashi Oishi, Pres.	Tel: (212) 566-7100	%FO: 100
Bus: *Engaged in property and casualty insurance.*	Fax: (212) 566-7187	

THE NIPPONKOA MANAGEMENT CORPORATION

Ten Universal City Plaza, Ste. 2630, Universal City, CA   91608

CEO: Jungo Takaishi, SVP	Tel: (818) 509-6220	%FO: 100
Bus: *Engaged in property and casualty insurance.*	Fax: (818) 509-6222	

THE NIPPONKOA MANAGEMENT CORPORATION

190 South LaSalle, Ste. 1620, Chicago, IL   60603

CEO: Akihiko Maruyama, VP	Tel: (312) 368-0574	%FO: 100
Bus: *Engaged in property and casualty insurance.*	Fax: (312) 641-1767	

● **NISHI NIPPON RAILROAD CO., LTD.**

1-11-17 Tenjin, Chuo-ku, Fukuoka 810-8570, Japan

CEO: Hiroyoshi Akashi, Pres.	Tel: 81-92-734-1552	Rev: $2,550
Bus: *Engaged in railway and coach services.*	Fax: 81-92-781-2583 www.nishitetsu.co.jp	Emp: 6,480

NNR AIRCARGO SERVICE (USA), INC.

450 East Devon, Ste. 260, Itasca, IL   60143

CEO: Todoroki Miyashita, CEO   Tel: (630) 773-1490   %FO: 100

Bus: *Freight forwarding and customs*   Fax: (630) 773-1442   Emp: 2
     house broker.

● **NISHIMOTO TRADING COMPANY, LTD.**

5-1-8 Kaigandori 3-chome, Chuo-ku, Kobe 650, Japan

CEO: Tatszo Susaki, Pres.   Tel: 81-78-360-3832

Bus: *Supplies fresh fruits, vegetables and*   Fax: 81-78-360-3923   Emp: 50
     food products.   www.ntcltd.com

NISHIMOTO TRADING COMPANY OF AMERICA, LTD.

2747 South Malt Avenue, Los Angeles, CA   90040

CEO: Richard T. Hashii, Pres.   Tel: (323) 889-4100   %FO: 100

Bus: *Sale/distribution of food products,*   Fax: (323) 888-1601   Emp: 55
     fresh fruits and vegetables.

NISHIMOTO TRADING COMPANY OF AMERICA, LTD.

5522 W. Roosevelt, Suite 6 & 8, Phoenix, AZ   85034

CEO: Richard T. Hashii, Pres.   Tel: (602) 415-0011   %FO: 100

Bus: *Sale/distribution of food products,*   Fax: (602) 415-0011
     fresh fruits and vegetables.

● **NISHI-NIPPON BANK LTD.**

3-6 Hakata-ekimae, 1-chome, Hakata-ku, 812-91 Fukuoka, Japan

CEO: Tsuneo Sindo, Pres.   Tel: 81-92-476-2481   Rev: $1,295

Bus: *General banking and security trading*   Fax: 81-92-476-2736   Emp: 3,560
     services.   www.nishigin.co.jp

THE NISHI-NIPPON BANK LTD.

*One World Trade Center, Ste. 10227, New York, NY   10048

CEO: Minoru Tahara, Mgr.   Tel: (212) 432-7100   %FO: 100

Bus: *General banking and security*   Fax: (212) 432-4010
     trading services.

● **NISSAN CHEMICAL INDUSTRIES, LTD.**

7-1 Kanda Nishiki-cho 3-chome, Chiyoda-ku, Tokyo 101-0054, Japan

CEO: Nobuichiro Fujimoto, Pres. & CEO   Tel: 81-3-3296-8320   Rev: $1,230

Bus: *Mfr. chemical fertilizers.*   Fax: 81-3-3296-8210   Emp: 1,585
     www.nissanchem.co.jp

NISSAN CHEMICAL AMERICA CORPORATION

10777 Westheirmer, Ste. 150, Houston, TX   77042

CEO: Hajime Yoshida, Mgr.   Tel: (713) 532-4745   %FO: 100

Bus: *Mfr. chemical fertilizers.*   Fax: (713) 532-0363

● NISSAN MOTOR COMPANY, LTD.

17-1 Ginza 6-chome, Chuo-ku, Tokyo 104-8023, Japan

CEO: Yoshikazu Hanawa, Pres.   Tel: 81-3-3543-5523   Rev: $56,388

Bus: *Mfr. cars, trucks, diesel and marine*   Fax: 81-3-3546-2669   Emp: 136,400
engines, industrial machinery and   www.global.nissan.co.jp
vehicles, boats. (35% interest by
Renault SA, France)

NISSAN CAPITAL OF AMERICA, INC.

399 Park Avenue, 18th Fl., New York, NY   10022

CEO: Ben Howard, Dir.   Tel: (212) 572-9100   %FO: 100

Bus: *Financial services.*   Fax: (212) 750-6982

NISSAN DESIGN INTERNATIONAL

9800 Campus Point Drive, San Diego, CA   92121

CEO: Tom Semple, Pres.   Tel: (858) 457-4400   %FO: 100

Bus: *Vehicle design.*   Fax: (858) 450-3332

NISSAN FORKLIFT CORPORATION, NA

240 North Prospect Street, Marengo, IL   60152

CEO: Mark Akabori, Pres.   Tel: (815) 568-0061   %FO: 100

Bus: *Production/import/sale forklifts.*   Fax: (815) 568-0179

NISSAN MOTOR ACCEPTANCE CORPORATION

990 West 190th Street, Torrance, CA   90502-1019

CEO: Yoichiro Nagashima, Pres.   Tel: (310) 719-8000   %FO: 100

Bus: *Financial services.*   Fax: (310) 719-8016

NISSAN MOTOR CORP IN HAWAII, LTD.

2880 Kilihau Street, Honolulu, HI   96819

CEO: Eric H. Miyasaki, CEO   Tel: (808) 836-0888   %FO: 100

Bus: *Distribute automotive vehicles.*   Fax: (808) 839-0400

NISSAN MOTOR MFG CORPORATION, USA

983 Nissan Drive, Smyrna, TN   37167

CEO: Jerry L. Benefield, Pres. & CEO   Tel: (615) 459-1400   %FO: 100

Bus: *Mfr. cars and light trucks.*   Fax: (615) 459-1554

NISSAN NORTH AMERICA, INC.

18051 South Figueroa Street, PO Box 191, Gardena, CA   90248-0191

CEO: Jed Connelly, VP   Tel: (310) 532-3111   %FO: 100

Bus: *Sales/distribution of automobiles.*   Fax: (310) 771-3343

NISSAN TECHNICAL CENTER

39001 Sunrise Drive, Farmington Hills, MI   48331

CEO: Shigeo Ishida, Pres.   Tel: (248) 488-4123   %FO: 100

Bus: *Engaged in research and development.*   Fax: (248) 488-3901

NISSAN TRADING CORP.

38505 Country Club Drive, Ste. 200, Farmington Hills, MI   48331

CEO: Tadashi Ukai, Pres.   Tel: (248) 489-5656   %FO: 100

Bus: *Import and export of autos.*   Fax: (248) 489-5660

● NISSEI SANGYO COMPANY, LTD.

24-14 Nishi-Shimbashi, 1-chome, Minato-ku, Tokyo 105, Japan

CEO: Noriaki Higuchi, Pres.   Tel: 81-3-3504-7111   Rev: $6,584

Bus: *Marketing of scientific instruments.*   Fax: 81-3-3504-7123   Emp: 1,408

www.nisseisg.co.jp

NISSEI SANGYO AMERICA, LTD.

2850 East Golf Road, Ste. 200, Rolling Meadows, IL   60008

CEO: Yasuhiko Kobata, Pres.   Tel: (847) 981-8989   %FO: 100

Bus: *Sale electronics and scientific instruments.*   Fax: (847) 364-9052   Emp: 115

● NISSHIN STEEL CO., LTD.

Shinkokusai Bldg., 4-1 Marunouchi 3-chome, Chiyoda-ku Tokyo 100, Japan

CEO: Minoru Tanaka, CEO   Tel: 81-3-3216-5511

Bus: *Mfr. galvanized and aluminized and copper-plated steel sheets and strips.*   Fax: 81-3-3214-1895

www.nisshn-steel.co.jp

NISSHIN HOLDING INC.

375 Park Avenue, Ste. 1005, New York, NY   10152

CEO: Shoichi Ueda, Pres.   Tel: (212) 317-3501   %FO: 100

Bus: *Mfr. galvanized and aluminized steel products.*   Fax: (212) 421-0496

● NISSHINBO INDUSTRIES, INC.

2-13-11, Ningyo-cho, Nihonbashi, Chuo-ku, Tokyo 103-8650, Japan

CEO: Yoshikazu Sashida, CEO   Tel: 81-3-5965-8833   Rev: $2,156

Bus: *Engaged in manufacture of textile products, plastics, automobile brakes, paper and machinery.*   Fax: 81-3-5695-8970   Emp: 8,235

www.nisshinbo.co.jp

NISSHINBO AUTOMOTIVE CORPORATION

43355 Merrill Road, Sterling Heights, MI   48314

CEO: Yukio Hosoya, Dir.   Tel: (810) 997-1000   %FO: 100

Bus: *Mfr./sales of brake linings.*   Fax: (810) 997-1010

● NISSHO IWAI CORPORATION

4-5 Akasaka, 2-chome, Minato-ku, Tokyo 107-0052, Japan

CEO: Shiro Yasutake, Pres. & CEO	Tel: 81-3-3588-2111	Rev: $77,760
Bus: *Import/export/trading; industrial development.*	Fax: 81-3-3588-4136 www.nisshoiwai.co.jp	Emp: 6,240

NISSHO IWAI AMERICAN CORPORATION

1211 Avenue of the Americas, 44th Fl., New York, NY 10036

CEO: Hidetoshi Nishimura, CEO	Tel: (212) 704-6500	%FO: 100
Bus: *Sales/distribution of general commodities and food.*	Fax: (212) 704-6543	Emp: 500

● NISSIN CORPORATION

5 Sanban-cho, Chiyoda-ku, Tokyo 102-8350, Japan

CEO: Hiroshi Tsutsui, Pres.	Tel: 81-3-3238-6663	Rev: $1,457
Bus: *Total transportation service.*	Fax: 81-3-3238-6638 www.nissin-tw.co.jp	Emp: 1,181

NISSIN CUSTOMS SERVICE, INC.

1580 West Carson Street, Long Beach, CA 90810

CEO: Bennett Johnson, VP	Tel: (310) 816-5706	%FO: 100
Bus: *Custom house broker.*	Fax: (310) 816-5716	

NISSIN INTL TRANSPORT USA, INC.

1540 West 190th Street, Torrance, CA 90510

CEO: Kazufumi Yamaguchi, Pres.	Tel: (310) 222-5800	%FO: 100
Bus: *Transportation services.*	Fax: (310) 787-7150	Emp: 300

● NISSIN FOOD PRODUCTS CO., LTD.

1-1 Nishinakajima 4-chome, Yodogawa-ku, Osaka 532, Japan

CEO: Koki Ando, Pres.	Tel: 81-6-305-7711	Rev: $2,372
Bus: *Mfr. food products and pharmaceuticals.*	Fax: 81-6-304-1288 www.nissin-foods.com	Emp: 5,368

NISSIN FOODS COMPANY, INC.

2001 West Rosecrans Avenue, Gardena, CA 90249

CEO: Tsuneaki Tanaka, Pres.	Tel: (323) 321-6453	%FO: 100
Bus: *Sales/distribution of soups, cereals and desserts.*	Fax: (323) 515-3751	

NISSIN MOLECULAR BIOLOGY INSTITUTE

20 Overland Street, 2nd Fl., Boston, MA 02215

CEO: Akira Matsumoto, Pres.	Tel: (617) 262-6899	%FO: 100
Bus: *Sales/distribution of pharmaceuticals.*	Fax: (617) 262-7184	

● **NITTA CORPORATION**

4-4-26 Sakuragawa, Naniwa-ku Osaka 556-0022, Japan

CEO: Seiichi Nitta, Pres. Tel: 81-6-563-1211 Rev: $370

Bus: *Industrial belting, construction* Fax: 81-6-563-1212 Emp: 797
materials, conveyor systems, air www.nitta.co.jp
filtration products, hoses and tubes,
farming and forestry.

NITTA CORPORATION OF AMERICA

3790 Boyd Road, Suwanee, GA   30024

CEO: Ichiro Watanabe, Pres. Tel: (770) 497-0212 %FO: 100

Bus: *Mfr./distribute industrial flat* Fax: (770) 623-1398 Emp: 55
belting.

● **NITTETSU SHOJI COMPANY, LTD.**

1-5-7 Kameido Koto-ku, 1-chome Tokyo 136-8733, Japan

CEO: Kazuhiko Fukuda, Pres. Tel: 81-3-5627-2990 Rev: $7,759

Bus: *Trading company: raw materials, steel* Fax: 81-3-5627-2196 Emp: 624
products, building materials, www.ns-net.co.jp
machinery, non-ferrous metals and
construction.

NITTETSU SHOJI AMERICA, INC.

725 S. Figueroa Street, Ste.1860, Los Angeles, CA   90017

CEO: Osamu Maeda, Pres. Tel: (213) 485-9072 %FO: 100

Bus: *Import/export, metal trading, raw* Fax: (213) 688-7579
materials, steel and aluminum.

● **NITTO BOSEKI COMPANY, LTD.**

1-2-1 Hamacho Nihonbashi, Chuo-ku, Tokyo 103-8489, Japan

CEO: Atsuhiko Sagara, Pres. Tel: 81-3-3865-6613 Rev: $1,103

Bus: *Mfr. textiles, fibers, building materials* Fax: 81-3-3865-6721 Emp: 4,240
and specialty chemicals.

INTERNATIONAL IMMUNOLOGY CORPORATION

25549 Adams Avenue, Murrieta, CA   92562

CEO: Yoshio Nakaamura, Pres. Tel: (909) 677-5629 %FO: 100

Bus: *Mfr./sale biological bulk material* Fax: (714) 677-6752 Emp: 36
for diagnostics industry.

● **NITTO DENKO CORPORATION**

11-8, 2-chome, Ginza, Chuo-ku, Tokyo 104-8112, Japan

CEO: Keigo Takahashi, CEO Tel: 81-33-546-9319 Rev: $375

Bus: *Mfr. industrial and electronic materials,* Fax: 81-33-542-3690 Emp: 510
including ferromanganese. www.nippondenko.co.jp

NITTO DENKO AMERICA INC.
48500 Fremont Boulevard, Fremont, CA 94538
CEO: Ted Nakayama, Pres.   Tel: (510) 445-5400   %FO: 100
Bus: *Mfr. ferromanganese.*   Fax: (510) 445-5480

• NKK CORPORATION
1-1-2 Marunouchi, Chiyoda-ku, Tokyo 100, Japan
CEO: Yoichi Shimogaichi, Pres. & CEO   Tel: 81-3-3212-7111   Rev: $15,975
Bus: *Steel products, shipbuilding,*   Fax: 81-3-3214-8401   Emp: 39,600
engineering, heavy industrial   www.nkk.co.jp
equipment, new material.

NATIONAL STEEL CORPORATION
4100 Edison Lakes Parkway, Mishawaka, IN 46545-3440
CEO: Yutaka Tanaka, Chmn.   Tel: (219) 273-7000   %FO: 70
Bus: *Mfr. sheet flat rolled steel*   Fax: (219) 273-7867   Emp: 12,000
products.

NKK AMERICA, INC.
450 Park Avenue, New York, NY 10022
CEO: Mineo Shimura, CEO   Tel: (212) 826-6250   %FO: 100
Bus: *Marketing research.*   Fax: (212) 826-6358   Emp: 19

• NOF CORPORATION
20-3 Ebisu 4-chome, Shibuya-ku, Tokyo 150-6019, Japan
CEO: Masayasu Uno, Pres. & CEO   Tel: 81-354-246-600   Rev: $1,445
Bus: *Mfr. petroleum-based chemicals and*   Fax: 81-354-246-800   Emp: 2,120
paints for ships and automobiles.   www.nof.co.jp

METAL COATINGS INTERNATIONAL INC.
PO Box 127, Chardon, OH 44024-1083
CEO: Jody Warnke   Tel: (440) 285-2231   %FO: 100
Bus: *Production and sales of special*   Fax: (440) 285-2231
corrosion prevention agents.

NOF AMERICA CORPORATION
200 Park Avenue, New York, NY 10166
CEO: K. Akama, Pres.   Tel: (212) 682-2815   %FO: 100
Bus: *Imports and exports of chemicals.*   Fax: (212) 972-1546

• THE NOMURA SECURITIES CO., LTD.
1-9-1 Nihonbashi, Chuo-ku, Tokyo 103-8011, Japan
CEO: Junichi Ujile, Pres. & CEO   Tel: 81-3-3211-1811   Rev: $10,788
Bus: *International securities broker/dealer,*   Fax: 81-3-3278-0420   Emp: 15,580
investment banking and asset   www.nomura.co.jp
management services.

THE CAPITAL COMPANY OF AMERICA LLC
*15 Corporate Place South, Piscataway, NJ 08854
CEO: Michael Hurdelbrink, CEO   Tel: (732) 465-1600   %FO: 100
Bus: *International securities*   Fax:
   broker/dealer, investment banking
   and asset management services.

NOMURA CORPORATE RESEARCH AND ASSET MGMT. INC.
*15 Corporate Place South, Piscataway, NJ 08854
CEO: Robert A. Levine, Pres.   Tel: (732) 465-1600   %FO: 100
Bus: *Research and asset management*   Fax:
   services.

NOMURA MORTGAGE FUND MANAGEMENT CORP.
*15 Corporate Place South, Piscataway, NJ 08854
CEO: Takashi Tachi, VP   Tel: (732) 465-1600   %FO: 100
Bus: *International securities*   Fax:
   broker/dealer, investment banking
   and asset management services.

NOMURA SECURITIES INTERNATIONAL INC. (US)
311 South Wacker Drive, Ste. 6100, Chicago, IL 60606
CEO: Joseph R. Schmuckler, Co-Pres.   Tel: (312) 408-9500   %FO: 100
Bus: *International securities*   Fax: (312) 408-9555
   broker/dealer, investment banking
   and asset management services.

NOMURA SECURITIES INTERNATIONAL INC. (US)
633 West Fifth Street, 68th Fl., Los Angeles, CA 90071
CEO: Joseph R. Schmuckler, Co-Pres.   Tel: (213) 243-1600   %FO: 100
Bus: *International securities*   Fax: (213) 243-1649
   broker/dealer, investment banking
   and asset management services.

NOMURA SECURITIES INTERNATIONAL INC. (US)
*15 Corporate Place South, Piscataway, NJ 08854
CEO: Joseph R. Schmuckler, Co-Pres.   Tel: (732) 465-1600   %FO: 100
Bus: *International securities*   Fax:
   broker/dealer, investment banking
   and asset management services.

● **NOMURA TRADING COMPANY, LTD.**
4-5 Bingo-machi l-chome, Chuo-ku, Osaka 541, Japan
CEO: Yoshihisa Idesawa, CEO   Tel: 81-6-268-8111
Bus: *Import/export general merchandise.*   Fax: 81-6-268-8268   Emp: 600
   www.nomuratrading.co.jp

NOMURA (AMERICA) CORPORATION
747 Third Avenue, 19th Fl., New York, NY 10017
CEO: Makoto Kamai, CEO   Tel: (212) 935-7151   %FO: 100
Bus: *Import/export general*   Fax: (212) 935-6717   Emp: 20
  merchandise.

NOMURA (AMERICA) CORPORATION
970 West 190th Street, Ste. 970, Torrance, CA   90502
CEO: A. Minamiyama, Mgr.   Tel: (310) 354-0059   %FO: 100
Bus: *Import/export general*   Fax: (310) 354-0079
  merchandise.

NOMURA (AMERICA) CORPORATION
900 Fourth Avenue, Seattle, WA   98164
CEO: Akihiro Uraha, Mgr.   Tel: (206) 343-0882   %FO: 100
Bus: *Import/export general*   Fax: (206) 343-7237
  merchandise.

● **THE NORINCHUKIN BANK**
13-2 Yurakucho 1-chome, Chiyoda-ku, Tokyo 100-8420, Japan
CEO: Hirofumi Ueno, Pres.   Tel: 81-3-32-79-0111   Rev: $15,863
Bus: *Engaged in agricultural banking*   Fax: 81-3-32-18-5174   Emp: 2,858
  services.   www.nochubank.or.jp

THENORINCHUKIN BANK
245 Park Avenue, 29th Fl., New York, NY   10167-0104
CEO: Ken Niyomura, VP   Tel: (212) 697-1717   %FO: 100
Bus: *Agricultural banking services.*   Fax: (212) 697-5754

● **NORITAKE CO., LIMITED**
1-36, Noritake-Shinmachi 3-chome, Nishi-ku, Nagoya 451-8501, Japan
CEO: Takashi Iwasaki , Pres. & CEO   Tel: 81-52-561-7113   Rev: $997
Bus: *Mfr. china, stone and porcelain*   Fax: 81-52-561-9721
  dinnerware.   www.noritake.co.jp

NORITAKE INC.
75 Seaview Drive, Secaucus, NJ   07094
CEO: Noboru Akahane   Tel: (201) 319-0600   %FO: 100
Bus: *Mfr. china, stone and porcelain*   Fax: (201) 319-1962
  dinner wear.

● **NORITSU KOKI COMPANY, LTD.**
579-1 Umeharaa, Wakayamashi 640-8550, Japan
CEO: Kanichi Nishimoto, Pres.   Tel: 81-734-540-345   Rev: $606
Bus: *Mfr. photo finishing equipment.*   Fax: 81-734-540-330   Emp: 1,287
                                www.noritsu.co.jp

NORITSU AMERICA CORPORATION

6900 Noritsu Avenue, Buena Park, CA   90620

CEO: Akihiko Kuwabara, Pres.	Tel: (714) 521-9040	%FO: 100
Bus: *Sales/service of photo finishing equipment*	Fax: (714) 670-2049	Emp: 290

● NSK, LTD.

Nissei Bldg.,1-6-3 Ohsaki 1-chome, Shinagawa-ku, Tokyo 141, Japan

CEO: Tetsuo Seikya, Pres.	Tel: 81-3-3495-8200	Rev: $4,611
Bus: *Mfr. motion technology products.*	Fax: 81-3-3495-8240	Emp: 24,295
	www.nsk.com	

NSK CORPORATION

3861 Research Park Drive, Ann Arbor, MI   48106

CEO: Larry McPherson, Pres. & CEO	Tel: (734) 761-9500	%FO: 100
Bus: *Mfr. anti-friction bearings and related products*	Fax: (734) 761-9510	

● NTN CORPORATION

3-17 Kyomachibori 1-chome, Osaka 550-0003, Japan

CEO: Toyoaki Itoh, Pres.	Tel: 81-6-443-5001	Rev: $2,735
Bus: *Mfr. bearings, joints and precision processing equipment.*	Fax: 81-3-445-8581	Emp: 6,948
	www.ntn.co.jp	

AMERICAN NTN BEARING MFG CORPORATION

9515 Winona Avenue, Schiller Park, IL   60176

CEO: M. Iwano	Tel: (847) 671-5450	%FO: 100
Bus: *Mfr. bearings, wheel units.*	Fax: (847) 681-5298	Emp: 457

NTN BEARING CORP OF AMERICA

1600 East Bishop Court, PO Box 7604, Mt. Prospect, IL   60056-7604

CEO: George Hammond, Pres.	Tel: (847) 298-7500	%FO: 100
Bus: *Engineering/sale anti-friction bearings & constant velocity joints.*	Fax: (847) 699-9745	Emp: 298

NTN BEARINGS

39255 West 12 Mile Road, Farmington Hills, MI   48331

CEO: Tim Brown, VP	Tel: (248) 324-4700	%FO: 100
Bus: *Sales of roller bearings.*	Fax: (248) 324-1103	

NTN BOWER CORPORATION

2086 Military Street South, Hamilton, AL   35570

CEO: Dwight Nixon, Mgr.	Tel: (205) 921-2173	%FO: 100
Bus: *Plant facility.*	Fax: (205) 921-2059	

NTN BOWER CORPORATION
707 North Bower Road, Macomb, IL   61455
CEO: Setsuo Yamaori, Pres.   Tel: (309) 837-0440   %FO: 100
Bus: *Sales of roller bearings.*   Fax: (309) 837-0438

NTN DRIVESHAFT INC.
8251 South International Drive, Columbus, IN   47201
CEO: Komei Sakano, Pres.   Tel: (812) 342-7000   %FO: 100
Bus: *Mfr. constant velocity joints.* Fax: (812) 342-1155   Emp: 458

NTN TECHNICAL CENTER
3980 Research Park Drive, Ann Arbor, MI   48104
CEO: N. Kashino, Pres.   Tel: (734) 761-3610   %FO: 100
Bus: *R&D services.*   Fax: (734) 761-3632   Emp: 27

● **NTT DATA CORPORATION**
3-3-3 Toyosu, Koto-ku, Tokyo 135-6033, Japan
CEO: Toshiharu Aoki, CEO   Tel: 81-3-5546-8202   Rev: $6,875
Bus: *Provides e-commerce solutions.* Fax: 81-3-5546-8145   Emp: 10,500
                                     www.nttdata.co.jp

NTT DATA USA, INC.
95 Christopher Columbus Drive, Jersey City, NJ   07302
CEO: Takeo Kojima, VP   Tel: (201) 413-5400   %FO: 100
Bus: *Provides e-commerce solutions.* Fax: (201) 413-5400

● **NTT DOCOMO, INC .**
11-1 Nagatacho-2-chome, Chiyoda-ku, Tokyo 100-6150, Japan
CEO: Keiji Tachikawa, CEO   Tel: 81-3-5156-1111   Rev: $37,100
Bus: *Provides wireless phone services.* Fax: 81-3-5156-0271   Emp: 10,100
                                     www.nttdocomo.com

NTT USA INC.
700 East El Camino Real, Ste. 200, Mountain View, CA   94040
CEO: Roy Tseng   Tel: (650) 940-6565   %FO: 100
Bus: *Provides wireless phone services.*   Fax: (650) 940-1375

NTT USA INC.
101 Park Avenue, 41st Fl., New York, NY   10178
CEO: Shigehiko Suzuki   Tel: (212) 808-2296   %FO: 100
Bus: *Provides wireless phone services.*   Fax: (212) 661-1078

• **OBAYASHI CORPORATION**

Shinagawa Intercity Tower B, 2-15-2 Konan, Minato-ku Tokyo 108-8502, Japan

CEO: Yoshiro Obayashi, Chmn. & CEO   Tel: 81-3-5769-1111   Rev: $10,730

Bus: *General building contractor.*   Fax: 81-3-5769-1910   Emp: 11,260

www.obayashi.co.jp

     OC AMERICA CONSTRUCTION, INC.

     420 East Third Street, Ste. 600, Los Angeles, CA   90013

     CEO: Takayuki Fujisawa, Pres.   Tel: (213) 687-8700   %FO: 100

     Bus: *General building contractor.*   Fax: (213) 687-3700   Emp: 48

• **OJI PAPER COMPANY, LTD.**

7-5 Ginza, 4-chome, Chuo-ku, Tokyo 104-0061, Japan

CEO: Shoichiro Suzuki, Pres. & CEO   Tel: 81-3-3563-1111   Rev: $10,150

Bus: *Mfr. paper, paperboard, pulp and*   Fax: 81-3-3563-1130   Emp: 12,000
       converted products.   www.ojipaper.co.jp

     KANZAKI SPECIALTY PAPERS

     16306 Bloomfield Avenue, Cerritos, CA   90703

     CEO: Masatsune Ogura, VP   Tel: (562) 924-2438   %FO: 100

     Bus: *Sales/distribution of paper*   Fax: (562) 402-5379
        products.

     OJI PAPER COMPANY, LTD.

     100 Galleria Parkway NW, Ste. 960, Atlanta, GA   30399

     CEO: Eiichi Shibusawa, Pres.   Tel: (770) 226-0012   %FO: 100

     Bus: *Mfr. paper and paperboard*   Fax: (770) 226-0339
        materials.

     OJI PAPER COMPANY, LTD.

     600 University Street, Seattle, WA   98101

     CEO: Shiro Takhata, Gen. Mgr.   Tel: (206) 622-2820   %FO: 100

     Bus: *Mfr. paper and paperboard*   Fax: (206) 292-9798
        materials.

• **OKAMOTO INDUSTRIES INC**

3-27-12 Hongo, Bunkyo-ku, Tokyo, 113-8710, Japan

CEO: Takehiko Okamoto, CEO   Tel: 81-3-3817-4146   Rev: $194

Bus: *Mfr. rubber and plastic products.*   Fax: 81-3-3814-2355   Emp: 1,151

www.okamoto.co.jp

     OKAMOTO USA, INC

     18 King Street, Stratford, CT   06615

     CEO: Mamoru Kobayashi   Tel: (203) 378-0003   %FO: 100

     Bus: *Mfr. and sales of latex rubber*   Fax: (203) 375-2040   Emp: 8
        products.

• OKAMOTO MACHINE TOOL WORKS LTD.

2-7-3 Minowa-cho, Kohoku-ku, Yokohama 223-8533, Japan

CEO: Taizo Hosoda, Pres.
Bus: *Mfr./sale of grinding machines.*

Tel: 81-45-562-3113
Fax: 81-45-562-3122
www.okamoto.co.jp

Rev: $180
Emp: 417

OKAMOTO CORPORATION

1500 Busch Parkway, Buffalo Grove, IL   60089

CEO: Jim Asakawa, VP
Bus: *Mfr./sale/service of grinding machines.*

Tel: (847) 520-7700
Fax: (847) 520-7980

%FO: 100
Emp: 35

• OKAYA & COMPANY, LTD.

2-4-18, Sakae, Naka-ku, Nagoya 460-8666, Japan

CEO: Tokuichi Okaya, Pres.
Bus: *Wholesale iron and steel products, machinery and electrical products.*

Tel: 81-3-3214-8721
Fax: 81-3-3214-8709
www.okaya.co.jp

Rev: $4,367
Emp: 900

OKAYA ELECTRIC AMERICA, INC.

503 Wall Street, Valparaiso, IN   46383

CEO: Hiroshi Yamashita
Bus: *Designs, manufactures and markets LCD modules and panels, plasma panels, and other display products.*

Tel: (219) 477-4488
Fax: (219) 477-4856

%FO: 100

• OKI ELECTRIC INDUSTRY COMPANY, LTD.

7-12, Toranomon 1-chome, Minato-ku, Tokyo 105-8460, Japan

CEO: Katsumasa Shinozuka, Pres. & CEO
Bus: *Mfr. electronic equipment, including microelectronics, office electronics equipment and telecommunications products.*

Tel: 81-3-3501-3111
Fax: 81-3-3581-5522
www.oki.co.jp

Rev: $6,350
Emp: 25,450

OKI NETWORK TECHNOLOGIES, INC.

3 University Plaza, Hackensack, NJ   07601

CEO: Tetsuji Banno, Pres.
Bus: *Engaged in research and marketing of telecommunications systems and equipment.*

Tel: (201) 646-0011
Fax: (201) 646-9229

%FO: 100
Emp: 500

OKI NETWORK TECHNOLOGIES, INC.

1101 Cadillac Court, Milpitas, CA   95035

CEO: Harushige Sugimoto, Pres.
Bus: *Engaged in research and marketing of telecommunications systems and equipment.*

Tel: (408) 935-3331
Fax: (408) 935-3337

%FO: 100

OKI TELECOM, INC.
70 Crestridge Dr., Ste. 150, Suwanee, GA   30024

CEO: Reed Fisher	Tel: (678) 482-9640	%FO: 100
Bus: *Engaged in wireless communication.*	Fax: (678) 482-9142	

OKIDATA, INC.
2000 Bishops Gate Blvd., Mount Laurel, NJ   08054

CEO: Dennis Flanagan, Pres.	Tel: (856) 235-2600	%FO: 100
Bus: *Supplier of computer peripherals for personal and general business computers.*	Fax: (856) 235-2600	Emp: 500

SILICON DYNAMICS, INC.
785 North Mary Avenue, Sunnyvale, CA   94086

CEO: Mike Rosenbaum	Tel: (408) 737-6401	%FO: 100
Bus: *R&D, mfr./sales integrated circuits, semiconductor products, and advanced electronics.*	Fax: (408) 737-6441	

● **OKUMA CORPORATION**
Oguchi-cho, Niwa-gun, Aichi 480-0193, Japan

CEO: Junro Kashiwa, CEO	Tel: 81-587-95-7825	Rev: $875
Bus: *Mfr. machine tools.*	Fax: 81-587-95-6074	Emp: 1,400
	www.okuma.co.jp	

OKUMA CORPORATION
12200 Steele Creek Road, Charlotte, NC   28273

CEO: Kent Shigetomi, CEO	Tel: (704) 588-7000	%FO: 100
Bus: *Mfr. machine tools.*	Fax: (704) 588-6503	

● **OLYMPUS OPTICAL COMPANY, LTD.**
Monolith, 3-1 Nishi-Shinjuku 2-chome, Shinjuku-ku, Tokyo 163-0914, Japan

CEO: Toshiro Shimoyama, CEO	Tel: 81-3-3340-2111	Rev: $4,062
Bus: *Mfr. opto-electronic products, R&D consumer and medical products.*	Fax: 81-3-3340-2098	Emp: 19,000
	www.olympus.co.jp	

OLYMPUS AMERICA, INC.
Two Corporate Center Drive, Melville, NY   11747-3157

CEO: Tom Kikukawa, CEO	Tel: (631) 844-5000	%FO: 100
Bus: *Distribution consumer and scientific products.*	Fax: (631) 844-5265	Emp: 1,600

● **OMRON CORPORATION**

Shiokoji Horikawa, Shimogyo-ku, Kyoto 600-8530, Japan

CEO: Nobuo Tateisi, Chmn.   Tel: 81-75-344-7000   Rev: $5,265

Bus: *Mfr. automation components and*   Fax: 81-75-344-7001   Emp: 24,900
    systems.   www.omron.com

    OMRON ELECTRONICS, INC.

    One East Commerce Drive, Schaumburg, IL 60173

    CEO: Frank Newburn, Pres.   Tel: (847) 843-7900   %FO: 100

    Bus: *Engaged in sales and marketing of* Fax: (847) 843-8568
        automation components and
        systems.

    OMRON HEALTHCARE, INC.

    300 Lakeview Parkway, Vernon Hills, IL 60061

    CEO: Kazuo Saito, Pres.   Tel: (847) 680-6200   %FO: 100

    Bus: *Mfr. electronic healthcare*   Fax: (847) 680-6269
        products.

    OMRON MANUFACTURING OF AMERICA, INC.

    3705 Ohio Avenue, St. Charles, IL 60174

    CEO: Kiyoshi Oka, VP   Tel: (630) 513-0400   %FO: 100

    Bus: *Mfr. of industrial automation*   Fax: (630) 513-1027
        components and systems.

    OMRON OFFICE AUTOMATION PRODUCTS, INC.

    3345 Freedom Circle, Ste. 400, Santa Clara, CA 95054

    CEO: Kazuto Toyoda, EVP   Tel: (408) 727-1444   %FO: 100

    Bus: *Mfr. scanners and modems.*   Fax: (408) 970-1149

● **ONO PHARMACEUTICAL COMPANY, LTD.**

2-1-5 Doshomachi, Chuo-Ku, Osaka 541, Japan

CEO: Toshio Ueno, Pres.   Tel: 81-6-222-5551   Rev: $1,090

Bus: *Mfr. pharmaceuticals.*   Fax: 81-6-222-2381   Emp: 2,113
    www.ono-pharm.co.jp

    ONO PHARMA, INC.

    401 Hackensack Avenue, Hackensack, NJ 07601

    CEO: Katsura Kasahara, Pres.   Tel: (201) 342-8228

    Bus: *Mfr./sales pharmaceuticals.*   Fax: (201) 342-8283

● **ORIENTAL MOTOR CO., LTD.**

6-16-17 Ueno, Taito-ku, Tokyo 110, Japan

CEO: Takao Iwasa, Pres.   Tel: 81-3-3835-0684

Bus: *Mfr./sales small electric motors, drivers* Fax: 81-3-3835-1890   Emp: 2,500
    and fans.   www.orientalmotor.co.jp

ORIENTAL MOTOR USA CORPORATION

2580 West 237th Street, Torrance, CA   90505

CEO: Steve Nomura, Pres.	Tel: (310) 325-0040	%FO: 100
Bus: *Assembly/sale/distribute small motors, fans and drives.*	Fax: (310) 515-2879	Emp: 60

● ORIX CORPORATION

WTC Bldg, 2-4-1, Hamamsatsu-cho, Minato-ku, Tokyo 105-6135, Japan

CEO: Yoshihiko Miyauchi, Chmn. & CEO	Tel: 81-3-3435-6981	Rev: $12,187
Bus: *Engaged in equipment leasing, asset based lending and corporate financing.*	Fax: 81-3-3435-6665 www.orix.co.jp	Emp: 8,203

ORIX REAL ESTATE CAPITAL MARKETS, LLC

1717 Main Street, 14th Fl., Dallas, TX   75201

CEO: James R. Thompson, CEO	Tel: (214) 290-2408	%FO: 100
Bus: *Engaged in servicing loans over commercial properties.*	Fax: (214) 290-4480	

ORIX REAL ESTATE EQUITIES, INC.

100 North Riverside Plaza, Ste. 1400, Chicago, IL   60606

CEO: James H. Purinton, CEO	Tel: (312) 669-6400
Bus: *Engaged in development of industrial and office projects.*	Fax: (312) 669-6464

ORIX USA CORPORATION

300 Lighting Way, Secaucus, NJ   07096-1525

CEO: Jay Holmes, Chmn.	Tel: (201) 601-9000
Bus: *Engaged in financing and leasing of capital equipment.*	Fax: (201) 601-9100

ORIX USA CORPORATION

1177 Avenue of the Americas, 10th Fl., New York, NY   10036-2714

CEO: Yoshio Ono, Chmn.	Tel: (212) 739-1600	%FO: 100
Bus: *Engaged in equipment leasing, corporate financing and asset based lending.*	Fax: (212) 739-1701	

● OSAKA GAS COMPANY, LTD.

4-1-2 Hiranomachi, Chuo-ku, Osaka 541-0046, Japan

CEO: Shinichiro Ryoki, CEO	Tel: 81-6-6202-2221	Rev: $6,588
Bus: *Produces and distributes gas.*	Fax: 81-6-6202-4637 www.osakagas.co.jp	Emp: 9,566

OSAKA GAS COMPANY, LTD.

300 North Lake Avenue, Ste. 920, Pasadena, CA   91101

CEO: Atsumu Mori, Mgr.	Tel: (626) 304-1082	%FO: 100
Bus: *Produces and distributes gas.*	Fax: (626) 304-9327	

OSAKA GAS COMPANY, LTD.
375 Park Avenue, Ste. 2109, New York, NY   10152
CEO: Kunihiko Takahashi, Rep.   Tel: (212) 980-1666   %FO: 100
Bus: *U.S. representative office.*   Fax: (212) 832-0946

● **OTSUKA PHARMACEUTICAL COMPANY, LTD.**
2-9 Kanda Tsukasa-cho, Chiyoda-ku, Tokyo 101-8535, Japan
CEO: Yukio Kobayashi, Pres.   Tel: 81-3-3292-0021   Rev: $3,293
Bus: *Mfr. pharmaceuticals, chemicals,*   Fax: 81-3-3292-0021   Emp: 5,201
     fertilizers, foods, drinks and furniture.   www.otsuka.co.jp

　　OTSUKA AMERICA PHARMACEUTICALS, INC.
　　11517 Fury Lane, Unit 64, El Cajon, CA   92019
　　CEO: Sheri Clonts   Tel: (619) 660-9045
　　Bus: *Mfr. pharmaceuticals.*   Fax: (619) 660-9045

　　OTSUKA AMERICA PHARMACEUTICALS, INC.
　　7799 Leesburg Pike, Ste. 900N, Falls Church, VA   22043
　　CEO: A. Monii, Mgr.   Tel: (703) 847-6810
　　Bus: *Mfr. pharmaceuticals.*   Fax: (703) 847-6809

　　OTSUKA AMERICA, INC.
　　9900 Medical Center Drive, Rockville, MD   20850
　　CEO: Max Yoshitake   Tel: (301) 424-9055
　　Bus: *Engaged in research and*   Fax: (301) 424-9055
　　　　development.

　　OTSUKA AMERICA, INC.
　　One Embarcadero Center, San Francisco, CA   94111
　　CEO: H. Yoshikawa   Tel: (415) 986-5300   %FO: 100
　　Bus: *Pharmaceuticals and chemicals.*   Fax: (415) 986-5300

　　OTSUKA AMERICA, INC.
　　2440 Research Boulevard, Rockville, MD   20850
　　CEO: Joseph Bocchino, VP   Tel: (301) 990-0030
　　Bus: *Mfr. pharmaceuticals.*   Fax: (301) 990-0030

　　OTSUKA CHEMICAL COMPANY
　　747 Third Avenue, 16th Fl., New York, NY   10017
　　CEO: Ken Tanigawa, Pres.   Tel: (212) 826-4374   %FO: 100
　　Bus: *Mfr. pharmaceuticals.*   Fax: (212) 826-5094

● **OYO CORPORATION**
2-6, Kudan-kita 4-chome, Chiyoda-ku, Tokyo 102-0073, Japan
CEO: Satoru Ohya, CEO   Tel: 81-3-3234-0811   Rev: $507
Bus: *Mfr. measurement instruments.*   Fax: 81-3-3262-5169   Emp: 1,400
                                  www.oyo.co.jp

OYO CORPORATION
9777 West Gulf Bank Road, Ste. 5, Houston, TX   77040
CEO: Ernest M. Hall, Pres.   Tel: (713) 849-0804   %FO: 100
Bus: *Mfr. measurement instruments.*   Fax: (713) 849-4915

● PENTA-OCEAN CONSTRUCTION CO., LTD.
2-8, Koraku 2-chome, Bunkyo-ku, Tokyo 112-8576, Japan
CEO: Renpei Mizuno, Chmn.   Tel: 81-3-3817-7181   Rev: $4,398
Bus: *Engaged in construction and marine*   Fax: 81-3-3817-7642   Emp: 3,950
engineering.   www.penta-ocean.co.jp

PENTA-OCEAN CONSTRUCTION COMPANY
450 Park Avenue, New York, NY   10022
CEO: Yasuro Mizuno, EVP   Tel: (212) 421-5400   %FO: 100
Bus: *Engaged in construction and*   Fax: (212) 421-5452
marine engineering.

● PENTEL COMPANY, LTD.
7-2 Nihonbashi Koamicho, Chuo-ku, Tokyo 103, Japan
CEO: Yukio Horie, Pres.   Tel: 81-3-3667-3333
Bus: *Mfr. pens, mechanical pencils,*   Fax: 81-3-3667-3331   Emp: 1,400
industrial machines and computers.   www.pentel.co.jp

PENTEL OF AMERICA, LTD.
2805 Columbia Street, Torrance, CA   90509
CEO: M. Osada, Gen. Mgr.   Tel: (310) 320-3831   %FO: 100
Bus: *Pens, pencils and art materials.*   Fax: (310) 533-0697   Emp: 200

● PILOT CORPORATION (FORMERLY PILOT PEN)
8-1, Nishi-Gotanda 2-chome, Shinagawa-ku, Tokyo 141-8553 Japan
CEO: Akira Tsuneto, Pres.   Tel: 81-3-548-78111   Rev: $680
Bus: *Mfr. writing instruments.*   Fax: 81-3-548-78181   Emp: 1,489
                                      www.pilot.co.jp

PILOT CORPORATION OF AMERICA
60 Commerce Drive, Trumbull, CT   06611
CEO: Ronald G. Shaw, Pres.   Tel: (203) 377-8800   %FO: 100
Bus: *Sales/distribution of writing*   Fax: (203) 377-4024   Emp: 240
instruments

● PIONEER CORPORATION
4-1 Meguro 1-chome, Meguro-ku, Tokyo 153-8654, Japan
CEO: Kaneo Ito, Pres.   Tel: 81-3-3494-1111   Rev: $5,626
Bus: *Mfr. electronics, video, music,*   Fax: 81-3-3495-4428   Emp: 27,415
telecommunications products, consumer   www.pioneer.co.jp
electronics.

PIONEER ELECTRONICS (USA), INC.

PO Box 1760, Long Beach, CA   90810

CEO: Takafumi Asano, Pres.   Tel: (310) 952-2210   %FO: 100

Bus: *Mfr. car stereos and home*   Fax: (310) 952-2402
     electronics.

● **RHEON AUTOMATIC MACHINERY COMPANY, LTD.**

2-3 Nozawa-machi, PO Box 50, Utsunomiya 320, Japan

CEO: Torahiko Hayashi, Pres.   Tel: 81-286-65-1111   Rev: $145

Bus: *Mfr. food processing equipment.*   Fax: 81-286-66-1013   Emp: 728
                                     www.rheon.co.jp

RHEON USA, INC.

13400 Reese Blvd., Huntersville, NC   28078-7925

CEO: Kiyo Kamiyama, Mgr.   Tel: (704) 875-9191   %FO: 100

Bus: *Mfr./sale food processing*   Fax: (704) 875-9595
     equipment.

● **RICOH COMPANY, LTD.**

15-5 Minami-Aoyama 1-chome, Minato-ku, Tokyo 107, Japan

CEO: Hiroshi Hamada, Chmn. & CEO   Tel: 81-3-3479-3111   Rev: $13,715

Bus: *Mfr. and market multi-function digital*   Fax: 81-3-3402-1103   Emp: 67,300
     office automation equipment, thermal   www.ricoh.co.jp
     media and imaging materials.

RICOH CORPORATION

5 Dedrick Place, West Caldwell, NJ   07006

CEO: Katsumi Yoshida, CEO   Tel: (973) 882-2000   %FO: 100

Bus: *Mfr./sale/service copiers,*   Fax: (973) 808-7555   Emp: 3,850
     facsimiles, cameras, scanners,
     printers, optical storage devices.

RICOH ELECTRONICS INC.

2320 Redhill Avenue, Santa Ana, CA   92705

CEO: Yoshihiro Nomura, EVP   Tel: (949) 263-2000   %FO: 100

Bus: *Supply products group.*   Fax: (949) 263-2000

RICOH ELECTRONICS INC.

1125 Hurricane Shoals Road, Lawrenceville, GA   30243

CEO: Jennifer Marinacci   Tel: (770) 338-7200   %FO: 100

Bus: *Manufacturing plant.*   Fax: (770) 338-7200

RICOH ELECTRONICS, INC.
One Ricoh Sq., 1100 Valencia Ave., Tustin, CA   92680
CEO: Lee Gjetley   Tel: (714) 259-1310   %FO: 100
Bus: *Mfr./sale/service copiers,*   Fax: (714) 259-9342
     facsimiles, cameras, scanners,
     printers, optical storage devices.

● RIKEN CORPORATION
1-13-5 Kudan-Kita, Chiyoda-ku, Tokyo 102-8202, Japan
CEO: Kunihiko Oguchi, Pres.   Tel: 81-3-3230-3911
Bus: *Mfr. electronics.*   Fax: 81-3-3230-3431
                                      www.riken.co.jp

RIKEN OF AMERICA INC.
4709 Golf Road, Ste. 807, Skokie, IL   60076
CEO: Don McNulty   Tel: (847) 673-1400   %FO: 100
Bus: *Sales/distribution of electronic* Fax: (847) 673-1457
     products.

● RINGER HUT COMPANY, LTD.
20-3 Mugino, 5-Chomehakata-Ku Fukuoka 816-0082, Japan
CEO: Kazuhide Yonehama, CEO   Tel: 81-92-573-6655   Rev: $283
Bus: *Restaurant chain.*   Fax: 81-92-573-6655   Emp: 475
                                      www.ringer.co.jp

RINGER HUT AMERICA
1072 Saratoga Avenue, San Jose, CA   95133
CEO: Mr. Hideyuki Yamashita   Tel: (408) 259-3101   %FO: 100
Bus: *Restaurant chain and food*   Fax: (408) 259-3297   Emp: 60
     production.

● ROHM COMPANY, LTD.
21 Saiin Mizosaki-cho, Ukyo-ku, Kyoto 615-8585, Japan
CEO: Kenichiro Sato, Pres.   Tel: 81-75-311-2121   Rev: $2,951
Bus: *Mfr. diverse electronic components,* Fax: 81-75-315-0172   Emp: 12,663
     including semiconductors.   www.rohm.co.jp

CREE CORPORATION
4600 Silicon Drive, Durham, NC   27703
CEO: Neal Hunter   Tel: (919) 313-5300   %FO: 100
Bus: *Mfr. semiconductors.*   Fax: (919) 313-5452   Emp: 600

EXAR CORPORATION
48720 Kato Road, Freemont, CA   94538
CEO: Don Ciffone, CEO   Tel: (408) 434-6400   %FO: 100
Bus: *Mfr./sale diverse electronic*   Fax: (408) 943-8245   Emp: 65
components.

ROHM ELECTRONICS
4550 North Point Pkwy., Ste. 360, Alpharetta, GA   30202
CEO: Ken Sykes, VP   Tel: (770) 754-5972   %FO: 100
Bus: *Design/assemble electronic circuit* Fax: (770) 754-0691
boards.

ROHM ELECTRONICS
4550 North Point Parkway, Ste. 360, Alpharetta, GA   30202
CEO: Ken Sykes   Tel: (770) 754-5972   %FO: 100
Bus: *Sales of electronic components.*   Fax: (770) 754-0691

ROHM ELECTRONICS USA
3034 Owen Drive, Nashville, TN   37013
CEO: Dan Sasagawa, Pres.   Tel: (615) 641-2020   %FO: 100
Bus: *Mktg./sale electronic components.* Fax: (615) 641-2022   Emp: 100

ROHM LSI SYSTEMS INC.
10145 Pacific Heights, Ste. 1000, San Diego, CA   92121
CEO: Yoshi Kurahashi, Pres.   Tel: (858) 625-3660   %FO: 100
Bus: *Mfr. electronic components.*   Fax: (858) 625-3690

ROHM LSI SYSTEMS INC.
10145 Pacific Heights, Ste. 1000, San Diego, CA   92121
CEO: Yoshi Kurahashi, Pres.   Tel: (858) 625-3660   %FO: 100
Bus: *Electric components.*   Fax: (858) 625-3690   Emp: 125

XETEL CORPORATION
2105 Gracy Farms Lane, Austin, TX   78758
CEO: Angelo DeCaro, Pres.   Tel: (512) 435-1000   %FO: 100
Bus: *Design/assemble electronic circuit* Fax: (512) 834-1856   Emp: 80
boards.

• ROHTO PHARMACEUTICAL COMPANY
8-1, Tatsumi-nishi 1-chome, Ikuno-ku, Osaka 544-8666, Japan
CEO: Kunio Yamada, CEO   Tel: 81-6-6758-1231   Rev: $528
Bus: *Mfr. eye lotions, gastrointestinal* Fax: 81-6-6757-5155   Emp: 775
medicines and skin care products.   www.rohto.co.jp

THE MENTHOLATUM COMPANY
707 Sterling Drive, Orchard Park, NY   14127
CEO: Akiyoshi Yoshida, CEO   Tel: (716) 677-2500   %FO: 100
Bus: *Mfr. eye lotions, gastrointestinal*   Fax: (716) 674-3696
      medicines and skin care products.

● **ROLAND CORPORATION**
1-4-16 Dojimahama, Kita-ku, Osaka 530-0004, Japan
CEO: Ikutaro Kakehashi, CEO   Tel: 81-6-6345-9800   Rev: $580
Bus: *Mfr. musical instruments and electronic*   Fax: 81-6-6345-9792   Emp: 830
      and pipe organs.   www.roland.co.jp

    ROLAND CORPORATION
    5100 South Eastern Avenue, Los Angeles, CA   90040-2938
    CEO: Dam Katsuyoshi, Pres.   Tel: (323) 890-3700   %FO: 100
    Bus: *Sales and service of musical*   Fax: (323) 890-3701
        instruments.

● **RYOBI LTD.**
762, Mesaki-cho, Fuchu, Hiroshima 726-8628, Japan
CEO: Hiroshi Urakami, Pres   Tel: 81-847-41-111   Rev: $2,180
Bus: *Mfr. die castings, printing machinery,*   Fax: Emp: 5,000
      power tools and fishing tackle.   www.ryobi-group.co.jp

    RYOBI DIE CASTING INC.
    800 West Mausoleum Road, Shelbyville, IN   46176
    CEO: Mark Allen, Mgr.   Tel: (317) 398-3398
    Bus: *Mfr. die castings.*   Fax: (317) 398-2873

● **S&B FOODS INC.**
18-6 Kabuto-cho, Nihonbashi, Chuo-ku, Tokyo 103-0026, Japan
CEO: Masaru Yamasaki, Pres.   Tel: 81-3-6680551   Rev: $849
Bus: *Mfr./import/export food products.*   Fax: Emp: 1,269
                            www.sbfoods.co.jp

    S&B INTERNATIONAL CORPORATION
    23430 Hawthorne Blvd., Ste. 125, Torrance, CA   90505
    CEO: Akira Takahashi, Pres.   Tel: (310) 378-0898   %FO: 100
    Bus: *Mfr. food products, import/export.*   Fax: (310) 378-1868

● **SANDEN INTL CORPORATION**

31-7 Taito, 1-chome Taito-ku, Tokyo 110-8555, Japan

CEO: Masayoshi Ushikubo, Pres.   Tel: 81-3-3833-1211   Rev: $2,080

Bus: *Mfr. auto A/C systems, kerosene*   Fax: 81-3-3833-0796   Emp: 3,261
     heaters, compressors and components,   www.sanden.co.jp
     vending machines and refrigerated
     showcases.

    SANDEN INTL (USA), INC.

    47772 Halyard Drive, Plymouth, MI 48170

    CEO: Seishi Kimura, Pres.   Tel: (734) 459-1900   %FO: 100

    Bus: *Mfr./distribute mobile A/C*   Fax: (734) 459-1902
       compressors and components.

    SANDEN INTL (USA), INC.

    601 South Sanden Blvd., Wylie, TX 75098-4999

    CEO: Seishi Kimura, Pres.   Tel: (972) 442-8400   %FO: 100

    Bus: *Mfr./distribute mobile A/C*   Fax: (972) 442-8700   Emp: 510
       compressors and components.

● **THE SANKO STEAMSHIP CO., LTD.**

2-3 Uchisaiwai-cho, 2-chome, Chiyoda-ku, Tokyo 100-0011, Japan

CEO: S. Kawai, Pres.   Tel: 81-3-3507-8305

Bus: *Ship owner and operator.*   Fax: 81-3-3507-8369

    SANKO KISEN (USA) CORPORATION

    5 River Road, Cos Cob, CT 06807

    CEO: Clifford Jagoe, EVP   Tel: (203) 625-5584   %FO: 100

    Bus: *Ship owner representation.*   Fax: (203) 625-7633   Emp: 13

● **SANKYO CO., LTD.**

5-1 Nihonbashi Hon-cho, 3-chome, Chuo-ku, Tokyo 103-8426, Japan

CEO: Tetsuo Takato, Pres. & CEO   Tel: 81-3-5255-7111   Rev: $5,589

Bus: *Mfr. and markets pharmaceuticals and*   Fax: 81-3-5255-7035   Emp: 6,620
    medical devices.   www.sankyo.co.jp

    SANKYO PHARMA INC.

    780 Third Avenue, New York, NY 10017

    CEO: Kanichi Nakamura, Pres.   Tel: (212) 753-3172   %FO: 100

    Bus: *Mfr. pharmaceuticals.*   Fax: (212) 308-2491

● **SANKYU INC.**

5-23, Kachidoki 6-chome, Chuo-ku, Tokyo 104-0054, Japan

CEO: Kimikazu Nakamura, Pres. & CEO   Tel: 81-3-3536-3939   Rev: $2,465

Bus: *Engaged in marine and air cargo,*   Fax: 81-3-3536-3875   Emp: 11,090
    trucking and shipping.   www.sankyu.co.jp

SANKYU INC.
24700 South Main Street, Carson, CA   90745
CEO: Yoji Kodama, EVP　　　　　　　Tel: (310) 834-2245　　　　%FO: 100
Bus: *Engaged in marine and air cargo,*　Fax: (310) 834-2128　　　　Emp: 44
trucking and shipping and custom
brokerage.

SANKYU INC.
1555 Mittel Blvd., Ste. H, Wood Dale, IL   60191
CEO: Yoji Kodama, EVP　　　　　　　Tel: (630) 595-3009　　　　%FO: 100
Bus: *Engaged in marine and air cargo,*　Fax: (630) 595-8757
trucking and shipping.

● **SANRIO COMPANY, LTD.**
6-1 Osaki 1-chome, Shinagawa-ku, Tokyo 141-8603, Japan
CEO: Shintaro Tsuji, Pres.　　　　　　Tel: 81-3-3779-8111　　　　Rev: $1,095
Bus: *Mfr./distributes character merchandise*　Fax: 81-3-3779-8054　　　　Emp: 965
for children.　　　　　　　　　　www.sanrio.co.jp

　　SANRIO, INC.
　　570 Eccles Avenue, South San Francisco, CA   94080
　　CEO: Peter Gastaldi, VP　　　　　Tel: (650) 952-2880　　　　%FO: 100
　　Bus: *Sales/distribution of children's*　Fax: (650) 872-2513
　　gifts and accessories.

● **SANWA SHUTTER CORPORATION**
2-1-1 Nishi-Shinjuku, Shinjuku-ku, Tokyo 163-04, Japan
CEO: Toshitaka Takayama, Pres.　　　Tel: 81-3-3346-3019　　　　Rev: $2,107
Bus: *Mfr. shutters, doors and window*　Fax: 81-3-3346-3317　　　　Emp: 3,480
products.　　　　　　　　　　　www.sanwa-ss.co.jp

　　OVERHEAD DOOR CORPORATION
　　34 North Lakewood Street, Tulsa, OK   74158
　　CEO: Masat Izu, Pres.　　　　　　Tel: (918) 838-9901　　　　%FO: 100
　　Bus: *Mfr. garage doors and shutters.*　Fax: (918) 838-9674

　　OVERHEAD DOOR CORPORATION
　　PO Box 809046, Dallas, TX   75380
　　CEO: Masat Izu, Pres.　　　　　　Tel: (972) 233-0367　　　　%FO: 100
　　Bus: *Mfr. garage doors and shutters.*　Fax: (972) 233-6611

● **SANYEI CORPORATION**
1-2 Kotobuki 4-chome, Taito-ku, Tokyo 111, Japan
CEO: I. Hori, Pres.　　　　　　　　Tel: 81-3-3847-3500
Bus: *Import/export general merchandise.*　Fax: 81-3-3842-4906　　　　Emp: 300

SANYEI AMERICA CORPORATION
300 Harmon Meadow Blvd., Secaucus, NJ 07094

CEO: N. Kobayashi, Pres.	Tel: (201) 864-4848	%FO: 100
Bus: *Import/export general merchandise.*	Fax: (201) 864-5770	Emp: 8

● SANYO ELECTRIC COMPANY, LTD.
5-5 Keihan-Hondori 2-chome, Moriguchi City, Osaka 570-8677, Japan

CEO: Satoshi Iue, Chmn. & CEO	Tel: 81-6-6991-1181	Rev: $19,000
Bus: *Mfr. audio and video equipment, commercial and consumer electric appliances, semiconductors, batteries, and components.*	Fax: 81-6-6991-6566 www.sanyo.co.jp	Emp: 83,520

SANYO E&E CORPORATION
2055 Sanyo Avenue, San Diego, CA 92173

CEO: Shigeru Otsuka, Pres.	Tel: (619) 661-1134	%FO: 100
Bus: *Mfr./distribution/service audio and video equipment, commercial and consumer electric appliances, semi-conductors, batteries, and components.*	Fax: (619) 661-6795	

SANYO FISHER USA COMPANY
21605 Plummer Street, Chatsworth, CA 91311-2329

CEO: S. Oka, Pres.	Tel: (818) 998-7322	%FO: 100
Bus: *Mfr./distribution/service audio equipment and components.*	Fax: (818) 998-3533	

SANYO MANUFACTURING CORPORATION
3333 Sanyo Road, Forrest City, AR 72335

CEO: N. Nakamura, Pres.	Tel: (870) 633-5030	%FO: 100
Bus: *Manufacturing operation; subsidiary of Sanyo Electric Co., Ltd.*	Fax: (870) 633-0650	

SANYO NORTH AMERICA CORPORATION
2055 Sanyo Avenue, San Diego, CA 92173

CEO: Masafumi Matsunaga, Pres.	Tel: (619) 661-1134	%FO: 100
Bus: *Mfr./distribution/service audio and video equipment, commercial and consumer electric appliances, semi-conductors, batteries, and components.*	Fax: (619) 661-6795	

SANYO NORTH AMERICA CORPORATION
666 Fifth Avenue, 35th Fl., New York, NY   10103

CEO: M. Ando, Pres.   Tel: (212) 315-3232   %FO: 100

Bus: *U.S. headquarters.*   Fax: (212) 315-3263

SOLEC INTERNATIONAL INC
970 East 236th Street, Carson, CA   90745

CEO: Mitsuo Sada, Chmn.   Tel: (310) 834-5800

Bus: *Mfr./sales commercial electrical*   Fax: (310) 834-0728
and electronic equipment.

• SANYO SPECIAL STEEL COMPANY, LTD.
3007 Nakashima, Shikama-ku, Himeji 672-8677, Japan

CEO: Kunihiko Bando, Pres.   Tel: 81-792-380-001   Rev: $764

Bus: *Mfr. specialty steel.*   Fax: Emp: 2,046
www.sanyo-steel.co.jp

SANYO SPECIAL STEEL COMPANY, LTD.
445 Park Avenue, Ste. 2104, New York, NY   10022

CEO: Hank Sakuma, Pres.   Tel: (212) 935-9033   %FO: 100

Bus: *Mfr. specialty steel.*   Fax: (212) 980-8838

• SANYO TRADING COMPANY, LTD.
11 Kandanishiki-cho 2-chome, Chiyoda-ku, Tokyo 101, Japan

CEO: Yoshimitsu Machida, Pres.   Tel: 81-3-3233-5700

Bus: *Import/export rubber, agricultural and*   Fax: 81-3-3233-5777   Emp: 296
chemicals, automotive parts, machinery   www.sanyo-trading.co.jp
materials, agricultural and marine
products and lumber.

SANYO CORPORATION OF AMERICA
529 Fifth Avenue, 17th Fl., New York, NY   10017-4608

CEO: Ryosuke Kawakita, Pres.   Tel: (212) 808-4860   %FO: 100

Bus: *Sale industrial chemicals, plastics*   Fax: (212) 808-4878   Emp: 16
and machinery.

• SAPPORO BREWERIES, LIMITED
20-1 Ebisu 4-chome, Shibuyaku, Tokyo 150-8686, Japan

CEO: Tatushi Iwama, Pres.   Tel: 81-3-5423-2111   Rev: $5,604

Bus: *Mfr. and imports beer soft drinks, wine*   Fax: 81-3-5423-2057   Emp: 5,820
and spirits   www.sapporobeer.co.jp

SAPPORO USA, INC.
18881 Von Karman Ave., Ste. 1175, Irvine, CA   92612-1569

CEO: Yukio Sekine, Pres.   Tel: (949) 553-9733   %FO: 100

Bus: *Import/distribution of beer and*   Fax: (949) 553-9737
production of wine.

SAPPORO USA, INC.

666 Third Avenue, 18th Fl., New York, NY 10017

CEO: Yasuyuki Takahashi, Mgr. Tel: (212) 922-9165 %FO: 100

Bus: *Import/distribution of beer and* Fax: (212) 922-9576 Emp: 30
production of wine.

● SECOM CO., LTD.

5-1, Jingumae 1-chome,, Shibuya-ku, Tokyo 150-0001, Japan

CEO: Toshitaka Sugimachi Tel: 81-3-5770-0780 Rev: $3,908

Bus: *Provides security services and products.* Fax: 81-3-5775-8927 Emp: 12,000
www.secom.co.jp

THE WESTEC SECURITY GROUP, INC.

100 Bayview Circle, Ste. 5000, Newport Beach, CA 92660

CEO: Michael S. Kaye, CEO Tel: (949) 725-6200 %FO: 100

Bus: *Provides security services and* Fax: (949) 725-6690
products.

● SEGA CORPORATION, DIV. CSK

1-2-12 Haneda 1-chome, Ohta-ku, Tokyo 144-8531, Japan

CEO: Hideki Sato, Pres Tel: 81-3-5736-7034 Rev: $3,213

Bus: *Develop/mfr. video games and* Fax: 81-3-5736-7059 Emp: 3,975
equipment. Entertainment facilities. www.sega.co.jp

SEGA CORPORATION, INC.

650 Townsend Street, Ste. 575, San Francisco, CA 94065

CEO: Alan Stone, Pres. Tel: (415) 701-6000 %FO: 100

Bus: *Sale/service video games and* Fax: (415) 701-6001
equipment systems.

SEGA GAMEWORKS LLC

10 Universal City Plaza, Ste. 3300, Universal City, CA 91608

CEO: Ron Benison, CEO Tel: (818) 866-4263 %FO: 100

Bus: *Sale/service video games and* Fax:
equipment systems.

SEGA OF AMERICA DREAMCAST, INC.

650 Townsend Street, Ste. 575, San Francisco, CA 94065

CEO: Peter Moore, Pres. & COO Tel: (415) 701-6000 %FO: 100

Bus: *Sale/service video games and* Fax: (415) 701-6001
equipment systems.

SEGASOFT NETWORKS INC.

650 Townsend Street, San Francisco, CA 94103-4908

CEO: Gary Griffiths, Pres. Tel: (415) 701-6000 %FO: 100

Bus: *Sale/service video games and* Fax: (415) 701-6018
equipment systems.

● **SEIKO CORPORATION**

15-1, Kyobashi 2-chome, Chuo-ku, Tokyo 104-8331, Japan

CEO: Chushichi Inoue, Pres.

Bus: *Mfr./ sales of clocks/watches, eyeglass lenses/frames and golf clubs.*

Tel: 81-3-3563-2111
Fax: 81-3-3563-9556
www.seiko-corp.co.jp

Rev: $2,618
Emp: 900

SEIKO CORPORATION OF AMERICA, INC.

1111 MacArthur Blvd., Mahwah, NJ 07430

CEO: Tsutomu Mitome, Pres.

Bus: *Sales of clocks/watches and golf clubs.*

Tel: (201) 529-5730
Fax: (201) 529-2736

%FO: 100

SEIKO OPTICAL PRODUCTS, INC.

575 Corporate Drive, Mahwah, NJ 07430

CEO: Atsushi Iwasaki, Pres.

Bus: *Sales of eyeglass lenses and frames.*

Tel: (201) 529-9099
Fax: (201) 529-9019

%FO: 100

● **SEIKO EPSON CORPORATION**

3-5 Owa 3-chome, Suwa-Shi, Nagaro-Ken 392-8502, Japan

CEO: Hideaki Yasukawa, Pres.

Bus: *Mfr. printer mechanisms, liquid crystal displays, printers, computers and disk drives.*

Tel: 81-2-6652-3131
Fax: 81-2-6653-4844
www.epson.co.jp

Rev: $10,994
Emp: 42,500

EPSON AMERICA, INC.

3840 Kilroy Airport Way, Long Beach, CA 90806

CEO: Norio Niwa, Pres.

Bus: *Sales desktop and portable computers, printers, scanners and related equipment.*

Tel: (562) 290-4000
Fax: (562) 290-5220

%FO: 100

EPSON PORTLAND INC.

3950 Northwest Aloclek Place, Hillsboro, OR 97124

CEO: Akio Mitsuishi, Pres.

Bus: *Sales desktop and portable computers, printers, scanners and related equipment.*

Tel: (503) 645-1118
Fax: (503) 690-5452

%FO: 100

EPSON RESEARCH & DEVELOPMENT

150 River Oak Parkway, San Jose, CA 95134

CEO: Eiji Momosaki, Pres.

Bus: *Sales desktop and portable computers, printers, scanners and related equipment.*

Tel: (408) 922-0200
Fax: (408) 922-0238

• SEINO TRANSPORTATION COMPANY, LTD.

1 Taguchi-cho, Ogaki-shi, Gifu Pref, Japan

CEO: Yoshikazu Taguchi, Pres.

Bus: *Trucking, moving, air and sea transportation, warehousing and distribution.*

Tel: 81-584-811111
Fax: 81-584-753366
www.seino.co.jp

Rev: $2,827
Emp: 15,800

SEINO AMERICA, INC.

8728 Aviation Blvd., Inglewood, CA   90301

CEO: Norizumi Fuma, Pres. & CEO

Bus: *International freight forwarding, moving, trade consulting and customs broker.*

Tel: (310) 215-0500
Fax: (310) 337-0073

%FO: 99
Emp: 120

• SEKISUI CHEMICAL COMPANY, LTD.

4-4 Nishitenma 2-chome, Kita-ku, Osaka 530-8565, Japan

CEO: Naotake Okubo, Pres.

Bus: *Molded plastic products and residential housing.*

Tel: 81-6-365-4122
Fax: 81-6-365-4370
www.sekisui.co.jp

Rev: $8,720
Emp: 4,850

SEKISUI AMERICA CORPORATION

666 Fifth Avenue, 12th Fl., New York, NY   10103

CEO: Masaoki Hoshina, Pres.

Bus: *Manufacture and marketing of plastic products.*

Tel: (212) 489-3500
Fax: (212) 489-5100

%FO: 100
Emp: 500

• SHARP CORPORATION

22-22 Nagaike-cho, Abeno-ku, Osaka 545-8522, Japan

CEO: Katsuhiko Machida, Pres.

Bus: *Mfr. video and audio systems, appliances, office and information equipment and electronic components.*

Tel: 81-6-6621-1221
Fax: 81-6-6627-1759
www.sharp.co.jp

Rev: $17,580
Emp: 49,750

SHARP ELECTRONICS CORPORATION

Sharp Plaza, Mahwah, NJ   07430-2135

CEO: O. Perry Clay, Pres.

Bus: *Mfr./sale/service video and audio systems, appliances, office and information equipment and electronic components.*

Tel: (201) 529-8200
Fax: (201) 529-8425

%FO: 100

• SHIBA SOKU COMPANY, LTD.

6-8 Shinbashi 4-chome, Minato-ku, Tokyo 105, Japan

CEO: Takashi Shigezaki, Pres.

Bus: *Mfr. audio and video test equipment. (JV of ASACA Corp.)*

Tel: 81-3-5401-3811
Fax: 81-3-5401-3815
www.shibasoku.co.jp

ASACA-SHIBASOKU CORPORATION OF AMERICA
400 Corporate Circle, Suite G, Golden, CO   80401

CEO: Noboru Note, VP	Tel: (303) 278-1111	%FO: JV
Bus: *Sales/service of audio and video test equipment.*	Fax: (303) 278-0303	

● SHIMIZU CORPORATION
Seavans South No, 2-3 Shibaura 1-chome, Minato-ku, Tokyo 105-8007, Japan

CEO: Harusuke Imamura, Pres.	Tel: 81-3-5441-1111	Rev: $14,830
Bus: *Engaged in engineering and construction.*	Fax: 81-3-5441-0520	Emp: 10,717
	www.shimz.co.jp	

SHIMIZU AMERICA CORPORATION
800 Wilshire Blvd., Ste. 800, Los Angeles, CA   90177

CEO: Masao Okamoto, SVP	Tel: (213) 362-7500	%FO: 100
Bus: *General contractor, engineer and design.*	Fax: (213) 362-7511	

SHIMIZU AMERICA CORPORATION
7204 SW Durham Road, Ste. 600, Portland, OR   97224

CEO: Hiroshi Mimura, Pres.	Tel: (503) 620-2965	%FO: 100
Bus: *General contractor, engineer and design.*	Fax: (503) 620-0223	

SHIMIZU AMERICA CORPORATION
1820 Water Place, Ste. 255, Atlanta, GA   30339

CEO: Hideaki Izumi, VP	Tel: (770) 956-1123	%FO: 100
Bus: *General contractor, engineer and design.*	Fax: (770) 956-7575	

SHIMIZU AMERICA CORPORATION
461 Fifth Avenue, 3rd Fl., New York, NY   10017

CEO: Kojiro Shada, Pres.	Tel: (212) 251-0050	%FO: 100
Bus: *General contractor, engineer and design.*	Fax: (212) 251-1052	

HIMIZU INTERNATIONAL FINANCE INC.
461 Fifth Avenue, 3rd Fl., New York, NY   10017

CEO: Yasuhiro Takasaki, SVP	Tel: (212) 251-0050	%FO: 100
Bus: *Engaged in finance.*	Fax: (212) 251-1070	

● SHIN-ETSU CHEMICAL COMPANY, LTD.
Asahi-Tokai Bldg., 6-1-2-chome, Otemachi, Chiyoda-ku, Tokyo 100-0004, Japan

CEO: Chihiro Kanagawa, Pres. & CEO	Tel: 81-3-3246-5111	Rev: $6,434
Bus: *Mfr. specialty chemicals and high-tech materials.*	Fax: 81-3-3246-5350	Emp: 18,750
	www.sinetsu.co.jp	

HERAEUS SHIN-ETSU AMERICA, INC.
4600 NW Pacific Rim Blvd., Camas, WA 98607
CEO: Dr. Katsuhiko Kemmochi, Pres.   Tel: (360) 834-4004   %FO: 100
Bus: *Mfr./sales/marketing of high-*   Fax: (360) 834-3115
     purity quartz glass crucibles.

SHINCOR SILICONES, INC.
1030 Evans Avenue, Akron, OH 44305
CEO: Kaz Kitani, Gen. Mgr.   Tel: (330) 630-9460   %FO: 100
Bus: *Mfr./sales/marketing of fluoro-*   Fax: (330) 630-2857
     silicone and silicone rubber.

SHIN-ETSU BIO INC.
6650 Lusk Blvd., Ste. B-106, San Diego, CA 92121
CEO: Juro Ichimura, Pres.   Tel: (858) 455-8500
Bus: *Mfr./sales/marketing of fluoro-*   Fax: (858) 587-2716
     silicone and silicone rubber.

SHIN-ETSU HANDOTAI AMERICA INC.
4111 Northeast 112th Avenue, Vancouver, WA 98682-6776
CEO: Isao Iwashita, Pres.   Tel: (360) 883-7000
Bus: *Sales/marketing semiconductor*   Fax: (360) 254-6973
     silicon wafers.

SHIN-ETSU MAGNETICS, INC.
2362 Qume Drive, Ste. A, San Jose, CA 95131
CEO: Satoru Iwakwaki, Pres.   Tel: (408) 383-9240   %FO: 100
Bus: *Mfr. rare earth magnets.*   Fax: (408) 383-9245

SHIN-ETSU POLYMER AMERICA, INC.
5600 Mowry School Road, Newark, CA 94500
CEO: Hiroshi Kosaki, Pres.   Tel: (510) 623-1881   %FO: 100
Bus: *Mfr. precision molded products.*   Fax: (510) 623-1603

SHIN-ETSU SILICONES OF AMERICA, INC.
1050 Evans Avenue, Akron, OH 44305
CEO: Nobuyuki Uesugi, CEO   Tel: (330) 630-9860   %FO: 100
Bus: *Mfr./sales/marketing of silicone*   Fax: (330) 630-9855
     rubber compounds.

SHINTECH INC.
24 Greenway Plaza, Ste. 811, Houston, TX 77046
CEO: Chihiro Kanagawa, Pres.   Tel: (713) 965-0713   %FO: 100
Bus: *Mfr. PVC.*   Fax: (713) 965-0629

● **SHINKAWA LTD.**
2-51-1, Inadaira Musashimurayama, Tokyo 208-8585, Japan
CEO: Kenji Fujiyama, Pres.   Tel: 81-42-560-1231
Bus: *Mfr. electronics.*   Fax: 81-42-560-1231
                                      www.shinkawa.com

    SHINKAWA USA INC.
    1930 South Alma School Rd., Ste. 107, Mesa, AZ   85210
    CEO: Kenji Fujiyama   Tel: (480) 831-7988   %FO: 100
    Bus: *Mfr. electronics.*   Fax: (480) 831-9480

● **SHINSEI BANK (FORMERLY LONG-TERM CREDIT BANK)**
1-8 Uchisaiwaicho 2-chome, Chiyoda-ku, Tokyo 100, Japan
CEO: Masamoto Yashiro, Pres. & CEO   Tel: 81-3-5511-5111   Rev: $18,720
Bus: *Commercial banking services.*   Fax: 81-3-5511-5505   Emp: 2,175
                                      www.shinseibank.co.jp

    CAPSTAR PARTNERS, INC.
    40 East 52nd Street, 12th Fl., New York, NY   10022
    CEO: R. Lee Rigney, Pres.   Tel: (212) 339-4200   %FO: 100
    Bus: *Financial services.*   Fax: (212) 339-4225

    SHINSEI BANK
    350 S. Grand Avenue, Los Angeles, CA   90071
    CEO: M. Takemoto, Gen. Mgr.   Tel: (213) 629-5777   %FO: 100
    Bus: *Commercial banking services.*   Fax: (213) 626-1067

    SHINSEI BANK
    2200 Ross Ave., Ste. 4700 West, Dallas, TX   75201
    CEO: Sadao Muraoka, Chief Rep.   Tel: (214) 969-5352   %FO: 100
    Bus: *Commercial banking services.*   Fax: (214) 969-5357

    SHINSEI BANK
    165 Broadway, New York, NY   10006
    CEO: Tetsuo Makabe, CEO   Tel: (212) 335-4400   %FO: 100
    Bus: *Commercial banking services.*   Fax: (212) 608-2303

    SHINSEI BANK
    245 Peachtree Center, Ste. 2801, Atlanta, GA   30303
    CEO: Y. Terai, Gen. Mgr.   Tel: (404) 659-7210   %FO: 100
    Bus: *Commercial banking services.*   Fax: (404) 658-9751

    SHINSEI BANK
    190 S. Lasalle Street, Ste 800, Chicago, IL   60603
    CEO: Tetsuo Makabe, CEO   Tel: (312) 704-1700   %FO: 100
    Bus: *Commercial banking services.*   Fax: (312) 704-8505

SHINSEI BANK
165 Broadway, New York, NY   10006
CEO: John J. Simone, Pres.　　　Tel: (212) 335-4900　　%FO: 100
Bus: *Financial services.*　　　Fax: (212) 608-3081

● **SHINSHO CORPORATION**
6-17 Kitahama 2-Chome Chuo-Ku, Osaka 541-8557, Japan
CEO: Yoshiki Miyaji, Pres.　　　Tel: 81-6-6206-7065　　Rev: $4,518
Bus: *Mfr. steel and metal products.*　　Fax:　　　　Emp: 875
　　　　　　　　　　　　　　www.shinsho.co.jp

　　SHINSHO AMERICAN CORP.
　　1275 Milwaukee Avenue, Ste. 301, Glenview, IL   60025
　　CEO: Y. Kimoto, Pres.　　　Tel: (847) 298-1074　　%FO: 100
　　Bus: *Mfr. steel and metal products.*　Fax: (847) 635-9117

● **SHINTOA CORPORATION**
3-3-1 Marunouchi, Chiyoda-ku, Tokyo 100, Japan
CEO: A. Arai, Pres.　　　　Tel: 81-3-3286-0213
Bus: *Trading company.*　　　Fax: 81-3-3213-2420　　Emp: 600
　　　　　　　　　　　　　www.shintoa.co.jp

　　SHINTOA INTL, INC.
　　333 South Hope Street, Ste. 2603, Los Angeles, CA   90071
　　CEO: Masahiro Ono, Pres.　　Tel: (213) 687-0633　　%FO: 100
　　Bus: *Trading company.*　　　Fax: (213) 586-0755　　Emp: 21

● **SHINWA KAIUN KAISHA, LTD.**
No.5-7. 1-chome, Kameido, Koto-ku, Tokyo 136-8506, Japan
CEO: Yoshikazu Sumi, Pres..　　Tel: 81-3-5627-7511　　Rev: $666
Bus: *Shipping operator and tramp chartering*　Fax: 81-3-5627-2200　　Emp: 1,200
　　and shipping agent.　　　www.shinwa-net.com

　　SHINWA USA, INC.
　　300 Harmon Meadow Blvd., Secaucus, NJ   07094
　　CEO: Hiromoto Nakagawa, Pres.　Tel: (201) 348-2101　　%FO: 100
　　Bus: *Marine transport operations,*　Fax: (201) 319-0305　　Emp: 8
　　　tramp chartering and shipping
　　　agency.

● **SHINYEI KAISHA**
77-1 Kyomachi, Chuo-ku, Kobe 651-0178, Japan
CEO: Yoshiaki Fujioka, Pres.　　Tel: 81-78-392-6800　　Rev: $481
Bus: *Trading: textiles, silk, electronics,*　Fax: 81-78-392-0707　　Emp: 307
　　agricultural & marine products; mfr.　www.shinyei.com
　　electronics.

SHINYEI CORP OF AMERICA
342 Madison Avenue, Ste. 1705, New York, NY 10173
CEO: Kiyoshi Ikeda, Pres.
Bus: *Import/export electric appliances, foodstuff, fish, ball bearings and fasteners.*

Tel: (212) 682-4610
Fax: (212) 286-8426

%FO: 100
Emp: 10

● SHIONOGI & CO., LTD.
1-8, Doshomachi 3-chome, Chuo-ku, Osaka 541-0045, Japan
CEO: Yoshihoko Shiono, Pres.
Bus: *Research, manufacture and marketing of pharmaceuticals and animal health products.*

Tel: 81-6-6202-2161
Fax: 81-6-6229-9596
www.shionogi.co.jp

Rev: $3,794
Emp: 5,718

SHIONOGI & COMPANY, LTD.
PO Box 2217, Rivervale, NJ 07675
CEO: Paul Napier, Mgr.
Bus: *Markets pharmaceutical, animal health products, agrochemicals and industrial chemicals.*

Tel: (201) 342-7776
Fax: (201) 342-7718

%FO: 100

● SHISEIDO COMPANY LTD.
7-5-5, Ginza, Chuo-ku, Tokyo 104-8010, Japan
CEO: Akira Gemma, Chmn.
Bus: *Mfr./market cosmetics and healthcare products.*

Tel: 81-3-3572-5111
Fax: 81-3-3574-8380
www.shiseido.co.jp

Rev: $5,655
Emp: 25,500

DAVLYN INDUSTRIES, INC.
7 Fitzgerald Avenue, Monroe Township, NJ 08831
CEO: Mitsuyuki Yamazaki, Pres.
Bus: *Mfr./marketing cosmetics and healthcare products.*

Tel: (609) 655-5600
Fax: (609) 655-4862

%FO: 100

SHISEIDO COSMETICS (AMERICA) LTD.
900 Third Avenue, 15th Floor, New York, NY 10022
CEO: Isao Isejima, CEO
Bus: *Mfr./marketing cosmetics and healthcare products.*

Tel: (212) 805-2300
Fax: (212) 688-0109

%FO: 100
Emp: 41

SHISEIDO HAWAII, INC.
1516 South King Street, Honolulu, HI 96826
CEO: Masaichi Suglyama, Pres.
Bus: *Mfr./marketing cosmetics and healthcare products.*

Tel: (808) 941-7755
Fax: (808) 946-5482

%FO: 100

SHISEIDO INTERNATIONAL CORPORATION
178 Bauer Drive, Oakland, NJ   07436
CEO: Nobuo Takahashi, Pres.   Tel: (201) 337-3750   %FO: 100
Bus: *Mfr./marketing cosmetics and*   Fax: (201) 337-3862
    healthcare products.

ZOTOS INTERNATIONAL
100 Tokeneke Road, Darien, CT   06820
CEO: Robert Seikl, Pres.   Tel: (203) 656-7999   %FO: 100
Bus: *Mfr./marketing cosmetics and*   Fax: (203) 656-7995
    healthcare products.

● **SHIZUOKA BANK, LTD.**
10 Gofukucho 1-chome, Shizuoka-shi, Shiizuoka 420-0031, Japan
CEO: Yasuo Matsuura, Pres.   Tel: 81-54-254-3111
Bus: *Commercial banking services.*   Fax:
    www.shizuokabank.co.jp

    SHIZUOKA BANK LTD.
    *One World Trade Center, Ste. 8025, New York, NY   10048
    CEO: Hidetoshi Sakai, Mgr.   Tel: (212) 466-0082   %FO: 100
    Bus: *Commercial banking services.*   Fax: (212) 466-0288

● **THE SHOKO CHUKIN BANK**
10-17 Yaesu 2-chome, Chuo-ku, Tokyo 104, Japan
CEO: Yukiharu Kodama, Pres.   Tel: 81-3-3172-6111
Bus: *Commercial banking services.*   Fax: 81-3-3274-1257   Emp: 6,000

    THE SHOKO CHUKIN BANK
    666 Fifth Avenue, 9th Fl., New York, NY   10019
    CEO: Heiji Ueshima, Mgr.   Tel: (212) 581-2800   %FO: 100
    Bus: *Commercial banking.*   Fax: (212) 581-4850   Emp: 20

● **SHOWA DENKO KK**
13-9 Shiba Daimon 1-chome, Minato-ku, Tokyo 105-8518, Japan
CEO: Makoto Murata, Chmn.   Tel: 81-3-5470-3533   Rev: $6,435
Bus: *Chemicals and petrochemicals and*   Fax: 81-3-3431-2625   Emp: 12,475
    ceramic materials.   www.sdk.co.jp

    SHOWA DENKO AMERICA, INC.
    489 Fifth Avenue, Ste. 18F, New York, NY   10017
    CEO: Tetsuzo Ishikawa, CEO   Tel: (212) 687-0773   %FO: 100
    Bus: *Sale/distribution of chemicals.*   Fax: (212) 573-9007   Emp: 15

• **SNOW BRAND MILK PRODUCTS CO. LTD.**
13 Honshio-cho, Shinjuku-ku, Tokyo 160-8575, Japan
CEO: Kohei Nishi, Pres.   Tel: 81-3-3226-2158   Rev: $12,205
Bus: *Mfr. milk and dairy products.*   Fax: 81-3-3226-2150   Emp: 15,125
                                         www.snowbrand.co.jp

    SNOW BRAND AMERICA, INC.
    44 Montgomery Street, Ste. 3350, San Francisco, CA 94104
    CEO: Kazuhiro Harada, EVP   Tel: (415) 677-0914   %FO: 100
    Bus: *Researches food ingredients and*   Fax: (415) 677-0916
       distributes dairy products.

• **SOC CORPORATION**
1-32-13 Shinkoyasu, Kanagawa-ku, Yokohama 221, Japan
CEO: H. Arikawa, Pres. & CEO   Tel: 81-45-432-4141
Bus: *Mfr. electronic fuses and fuse holders.*   Fax: 81-45-432-3976   Emp: 1,900

    SAN-O INDUSTRIAL CORPORATION
    91-3 Colin Drive, Holbrook, NY 11741
    CEO: Neil Sato, Pres.   Tel: (516) 472-6666   %FO: 95
    Bus: *Mfr./sale electronic fuses and fuse*   Fax: (516) 472-6777   Emp: 38
       holders.

• **SOFTBANK CORPORATION**
24-1 Nihonbashi Hakozaki-cho, Chuo-ku, Tokyo 103, Japan
CEO: Masayoshi Son, Pres. & CEO   Tel: 81-3-5642-8000   Rev: $3,144
Bus: *Retailer; computer software and*   Fax: 81-3-5641-3401   Emp: 6,865
   network products. Publisher of hi-tech   www.softbank.co.jp
   magazines and invests in technology
   globally.

    SOFTBANK HOLDINGS, INC.
    1188 Centre Street, Newton Center, MA 02159
    CEO: Ronald Fisher, Vice Chmn.   Tel: (617) 928-9300   %FO: 100
    Bus: *U.S. headquarters. Retailer;*   Fax: (617) 928-9301
       computer software and network
       products. Publisher of hi-tech
       magazines and invests in
       technology globally.

• **SONY CORPORATION**
7-35 Kitashinagawa 6-chome, Shinagawa-ku, Tokyo 141-0001, Japan
CEO: Nobuyuki Idei, CEO   Tel: 81-3-5448-2111   Rev: $58,518
Bus: *Mfr. audio, video, TV equipment,*   Fax: 81-3-5448-2244   Emp: 189,700
   computer peripherals, electronic   www.world.sony.com
   communications; entertainment product.

SONY COMPUTER ENTERTAINMENT AMERICA

919 East Hillsdale Blvd., Foster City, CA 94404

CEO: Estelle DeMuesy, Pres.

Tel: (650) 655-8000

%FO: 100

Bus: *Develop/produce entertainment computers and multimedia software.*

Fax: (650) 655-8001

SONY CORP OF AMERICA

550 Madison Avenue, New York, NY 10022

CEO: Howard Stringer, Pres. & CEO

Tel: (212) 833-6800

%FO: 100

Bus: *U.S. headquarters for electronics and hardware-related products for global entertainment units.*

Fax: (212) 833-6924

Emp: 2,500

SONY MUSIC ENTERTAINMENT INC.

550 Madison Avenue, New York, NY 10022

CEO: Thomas D. Mottola, Pres. & CEO

Tel: (212) 833-8000

%FO: 100

Bus: *Mfr. recorded music and video.*

Fax: (212) 833-7458

Emp: 1,500

SONY PICTURES ENTERTAINMENT

10202 West Washington Blvd, Culver City, CA 90232

CEO: Mel Harris, CEO

Tel: (310) 280-8000

%FO: 100

Bus: *Production/distribution motion pictures & television, including Loews Cineplex Entertainment theater chain, home video, studio operations, new entertainment technologies, & licensed merchandise.*

Fax: (310) 204-1300

Emp: 2,500

SONY RETAIL ENTERTAINMENT

711 Fifth Avenue, 12th Fl., New York, NY 10022

CEO: Stanley (Mickey) Steinberg, Chmn.

Tel: (212) 833-8828

%FO: 100

Bus: *Operate/develop theatrical exhibition sites, location-based entertainment centers and retail stores.*

Fax: (212) 833-8311

• SPC ELECTRONICS CORPORATION

2-1-3 Shibasaki Chofu-shi, Tokyo 182-8602, Japan

CEO: T. Shimada, Mgr.

Tel: 81-3-4248-18518

Rev: $191

Bus: *Satellite/terrestrial communication systems, service. & maintenance industrial equipment, R&D microwave & millimeter wave energy systems.*

Fax: 81-3-4248-18593

www.spc.co.jp

Emp: 1,000

SPC ELECTRONICS AMERICA, INC.
105 Technology Pkwy., Norcross, GA   30092

CEO: Masaru Kuzuhara, Pres.　　Tel: (770) 446-8626　　%FO: 100

Bus: *R&D, service communication units*　Fax: (770) 441-2380　　Emp: 16
　　and systems

• STAR MICRONICS COMPANY, LTD.
20-10 Nakayoshida, Shizuoka 422-8654, Japan

CEO: Shozo Kasuya, Pres. & CEO　　Tel: 81-542-631111　　Rev: $417

Bus: *Mfr. of precision electronic equipment*　Fax: 81-542-631057　　Emp: 722
　　and machine tools.　　www.star-micronics.co.jp

STAR MICRONICS AMERICA INC
1150 King Georges Post Road, Edison, NJ   08837-3729

CEO: Steve Funasho, Pres.　　Tel: (800) 782-7636　　%FO: 100

Bus: *Mfr./sales of precision electronic*　Fax: (732) 623-5590
　　equipment and machine tools.

• SUGINO MACHINE, LTD.
2410 Hongo, Toyama Prefect, Uozu 937-8511, Japan

CEO: Kenji Sugino, Chmn.　　Tel: 81-765-24-5111

Bus: *Mfr. machine tools and jet pumps.*　Fax: 81-765-24-5051　　Emp: 750
　　www.sugino-machine.co.jp

SUGINO CORPORATION
1700 North Penny Lane, Schaumburg, IL   60173

CEO: Tom Sakata, Pres.　　Tel: (847) 397-9401　　%FO: 100

Bus: *Machine tools, pumps and cutting*　Fax: (847) 397-9490　　Emp: 30
　　systems.

• SUMIKIN BUSSAN CORPORATION (DIV. SUMITOMO GROUP)
6-2, Hommachi 3-chome, Chuo-ku, Osaka 541-8544, Japan

CEO: Ryuji Kisada, Pres.　　Tel: 81-6-6244-8001　　Rev: $8,667

Bus: *Mfr. textiles, iron, steel and industrial*　Fax: 81-6-6244-8009　　Emp: 1,350
　　supplies.　　www.sumibinbussan.co.jp.

SUMIKIN BUSSAN INTERNATIONAL CORPORATION
707 Wilshire Blvd., Ste. 4350, Los Angeles, CA   90017

CEO: Norio Takahashi, Pres.　　Tel: (213) 689-4453　　%FO: 100

Bus: *Sales/distribution of iron and steel*　Fax: (213) 627-9450
　　products.

● **SUMITOMO BAKELITE COMPANY, LTD.**

Tennoz Parkside Bldg., 2-5-8 Higashi-Shinagawa, 2-chome, Shinagawa-ku, Tokyo 104-0002, Japan

CEO: Tsuneo Moriya, Pres.	Tel: 81-3-5462-4111	Rev: $1,663
Bus: *Mfr. chemical and plastic products.*	Fax: 81-3-5462-4873	Emp: 2,254
	www.sumibe.co.jp	

    SUMITOMO PLASTICS AMERICA INC.

    900 Lafayette Street, Ste. 510, Santa Clara, CA 95050-4967

CEO: Tadashi Imamura, Pres.	Tel: (408) 243-8402	%FO: 100
Bus: *Mfr./sale chemical and plastic products.*	Fax: (408) 243-8405	

● **SUMITOMO CHEMICAL COMPANY, LTD.**

27-1, Shinkawa, 2-chome, Chuo-ku, Tokyo 104-8260, Japan

CEO: Akio Kosai, Chmn.	Tel: 81-3-5543-5102	Rev: $9,000
Bus: *Mfr. industrial chemicals, fertilizers, fine chemicals, agrochemicals, and pharmaceuticals.*	Fax: 81-3-5543-5901 www.sumitomo-chem.co.jp	Emp: 17,475

    SUMITOMO CHEMICAL AMERICA INC

    335 Madison Avenue, Ste. 830, New York, NY 10017

CEO: Tetsu Wakabayashi, Pres.	Tel: (212) 572-8200	%FO: 100
Bus: *Distribution/sales/service of specialty chemicals.*	Fax: (212) 572-8234	Emp: 27

    SUMITOMO CHEMICAL AMERICA INC

    2350 Mission College Blvd., Ste. 360, Santa Clara, CA 95054

CEO: Alan Kozlowski, Mgr.	Tel: (408) 982-3890	%FO: 100
Bus: *Distribution/sales/service of specialty chemicals.*	Fax: (408) 982-3891	

● **SUMITOMO CORPORATION**

2-2 Hitotsubashi 1-chome, Chiyoda-ku, Tokyo 100-8601, Japan

CEO: Kenji Miyahara, Pres. & CEO	Tel: 81-3 3217-5000	Rev: $100,998
Bus: *Worldwide trading group; administrative services.*	Fax: 81-3 3217-5128 www.sumitomocorp.co.jp	Emp: 8,195

    AUBURN STEEL COMPANY INC.

    PO Box 2008, Qarry Road, Auburn, NY 13021

CEO: Mike Mueller, Pres.	Tel: (315) 253-4561	%FO: 100
Bus: *Sales/distribution of steel.*	Fax: (315) 253-8441	

    AUSTEEL LEMONT COMPANY, INC.

    PO Box 280, Lemont, IL 60439

CEO: Mike Mueller, Pres.	Tel: (630) 243-0012	%FO: 100
Bus: *Sales/distribution of steel.*	Fax: (630) 243-0028	

SUMITOMO CORPORATION OF AMERICA
600 Third Avenue, New York, NY   10016
CEO: Keltaro Yokohata, Pres.   Tel: (212) 207-0700   %FO: 100
Bus: *Trading and investment services.*   Fax: (212) 207-0456   Emp: 500

• SUMITOMO ELECTRIC INDUSTRIES, INC.
5-33 Kitahama 4-chome, Chuo-ku, Osaka 541-0041, Japan
CEO: Norio Okayama, Pres.   Tel: 81-6-220-4141   Rev: $12,403
Bus: *Mfr. electrical wire and cable,*   Fax: 81-6-222-3380   Emp: 66,993
telecommunications cable, specialty   www.sei.co.jp
steel wire and automotive parts.

K&S WIRING SYSTEMS, INC.
1809 Ward Drive, Murfreesboro, TN   37129
CEO: Ryozo Arai, Pres.   Tel: (615) 893-1788
Bus: *Sales/distribution of automotive*   Fax: (615) 867-3407
wiring harnesses.

SEI BRAKES INC.
1650 Kingsview Drive, Lebanon, OH   45036
CEO: Geoffrey Hearsum, Pres.   Tel: (513) 932-7878   %FO: 100
Bus: *Mfr. automotive front disc brake*   Fax: (513) 932-7975
calipers.

SEMIA, INC.
One California Street, Ste. 1500, San Francisco, CA   94111
CEO: Norihisa Wanibe, Pres.   Tel: (415) 765-1129   %FO: 100
Bus: *Sales/distribution of compound*   Fax: (415) 765-1180
semiconductors.

SUMIDEN WIRE PRODUCTS CORP
1412 El Pinal Drive, Stockton, CA   95205
CEO: Rick Yokoyama, Chmn.   Tel: (209) 466-8924   %FO: 80
Bus: *Mfr. specialty steel wire*   Fax: (209) 941-2990   Emp: 78

SUMITOMO ELECTRIC CARBINE INC.
901 N. Business Center Drive, Mt. Prospect, IL   60056
CEO: M. Maeda, Pres.   Tel: (847) 635-0044   %FO: 100
Bus: *Sale powdered metal products.*   Fax: (847) 635-7866   Emp: 54

SUMITOMO ELECTRIC FIBER OPTICS CORPORATION
78 Alexander Drive, PO Box 13445, Research Triangle Park, NC   27709
CEO: H. Horima, Pres.   Tel: (919) 541-8100   %FO: 100
Bus: *U.S. headquarters. Mfr. optical*   Fax: (919) 541-8220   Emp: 288
fiber cable, connectors & data link.

SUMITOMO ELECTRIC FINANCE INC.
65 East 55th Street, 16th Fl., New York, NY 10022
CEO: Satoru Nakahori, Pres.   Tel: (212) 317-7210   %FO: 100
Bus: *Financing.*   Fax: (212) 308-6575

SUMITOMO ELECTRIC INTERCONNECT PRODUCTS INC.
155 C-1 Moffett Park Drive, Sunnyville, CA 94089
CEO: Chris Foeger, Pres.   Tel: (408) 734-8880   %FO: 100
Bus: *Sale heat shrinkable tape.*   Fax: (408) 734-8881   Emp: 20

SUMITOMO ELECTRIC LIGHTWAVE CORPORATION
78 Alexander Drive, PO Box 13667, Research Triangle Park, NC 27709
CEO: Yasuo Sakata, Pres.   Tel: (919) 541-8100   %FO: 49
Bus: *Mfr. optical fiber.*   Fax: (919) 541-8220   Emp: 138

SUMITOMO ELECTRIC MAGNET WIRE COMPANY
909 Industrial Drive, Edmonton, KY 42129
CEO: T. Okuno, Pres.   Tel: (502) 432-2233   %FO: JV
Bus: *Mfr. magnet wire.*   Fax: (502) 432-2838   Emp: 37

SUMITOMO ELECTRIC USA, INC.
65 East 55th Street, 16th Fl., New York, NY 10022
CEO: Ryoji Koyanagi, Pres.   Tel: (212) 317-7210   %FO: 100
Bus: *Sale semiconducting material, new* Fax: (212) 308-6575
    material, optical fiber cable.

SUMITOMO ELECTRIC WIRING SYSTEMS INC.
755 Rochester Street, Morgantown, KY 42262
CEO: Ken Komatsu, Pres.   Tel: (270) 526-5655   %FO: 60
Bus: *Mfr. auto wire harness & parts.*   Fax: (270) 526-6986   Emp: 1,900

SUMITOMO ELECTRIC WIRING SYSTEMS, INC.
PO Box 90031, Bowling Green, KY 42102
CEO: David Jean, VP   Tel: (502) 782-7397   %FO: 100
Bus: *Mfr. wiring harnesses for*   Fax: (502) 793-0603
    automobiles.

SUMITOMO ELECTRIC WIRING SYSTEMS, INC.
3235 Kifer Road, Suite 150, Santa Clara, CA 95051-0815
CEO: David Jean, VP   Tel: (408) 737-8517   %FO: 100
Bus: *Mfr. wiring harnesses for*   Fax: (408) 737-0134
    automobiles.

SUMITOMO WIRING SYSTEMS INC.
3000 Town Center, Ste. 2400, Southfield, MI 48075-1194
CEO: Yoshio Hatsusaka, Pres.   Tel: (248) 262-1393   %FO: 100
Bus: *Sales/distribution of automotive*   Fax: (248) 262-1439
    and motorcycle wiring harnesses.

● SUMITOMO FORESTRY CO., LTD.
6-14-1 Nishi-Shinjuku 6 chome, Shinjuku-ku, Tokyo 160-8360, Japan
CEO: Ryu Yano, Pres.   Tel: 81-3-5322-6666   Rev: $6,653
Bus: *Engaged in the import/sales of timber*   Fax: 81-3-5322-6766   Emp: 3,975
    and construction and marketing of   www.sfc.co.jp
    custom built homes.

SUMITOMO FORESTRY INC.
1000 Second Avenue, Ste. 1220, Seattle, WA 98104
CEO: Akira Ichikawa, VP   Tel: (206) 623-8840   %FO: 100
Bus: *Engaged in exporting lumber.*   Fax: (206) 345-0391

● SUMITOMO HEAVY INDUSTRIES, LTD.
9-11, Kita-Shinagawa 5-chome, Shinagawa-ku, Tokyo 141-8686, Japan
CEO: Yoshio Hinoh, CEO   Tel: 81-3-5488-8335   Rev: $5,370
Bus: *Mfr. industrial machineries, ships,*   Fax: 81-3-5488-8056   Emp: 13,800
    bridges, defense systems, environmental   www.shi.co.jp
    systems and power transmissions.

SHI PLASTICS MACHINERY INC. OF AMERICA
1256 Oakbrook Drive, Ste. D, Norcross, GA 30093
CEO: Koji Shintani, Pres.   Tel: (770) 447-5430   %FO: 100
Bus: *Sale plastics injection molding*   Fax: (770) 441-9168   Emp: 20
    machines.

SUMITOMO CRYOGENICS OF AMERICA INC.
870 Cambridge Drive, Elk Grove, IL 60007
CEO: Isamu Dekiya, Pres.   Tel: (847) 290-5801   %FO: 100
Bus: *Provides maintenance and repair*   Fax: (847) 290-1984
    services for cryocollers.

SUMITOMO HEAVY INDUSTRIES (USA) INC.
666 Fifth Avenue, Ste. 1002, New York, NY 10103-1099
CEO: Tsuneo Nagano, Pres.   Tel: (212) 459-2477   %FO: 100
Bus: *Marketing research.*   Fax: (212) 223-0399   Emp: 12

SUMITOMO MACHINERY CORPORATION OF AMERICA
4200 Holland Blvd., Chesapeake, VA 23323
CEO: Steve King, Pres.   Tel: (757) 485-3355   %FO: 100
Bus: *Mfr. power transmissions,*   Fax: (757) 487-3291   Emp: 300
    variators, gear speed reducers.

● **SUMITOMO MARINE & FIRE INSURANCE COMPANY, LTD.**

2-27-2 Shinkawa, Chuo-ku, Tokyo 104-8252, Japan

CEO: Hiroyuki Uemura, Pres. & CEO   Tel: 81-3-3297-1111   Rev: $8,834

Bus: *Property and casualty insurance.*   Fax: 81-3-3297-6880   Emp: 7,468

                                              www.sumitimo-marine.co.jp

     SUMITOMO MARINE & FIRE INSURANCE COMPANY, LTD.

     *One World Trade Center, Ste. 9035, New York, NY   10048

     CEO: Koji Yoshida, Dir.   Tel: (212) 488-0600   %FO: 100

     Bus: *Engaged in property and casualty*   Fax: (212) 775-1248   Emp: 150
         insurance services.

     SUMITOMO MARINE MANAGEMENT INC.

     15 Independence Blvd., Warren, NJ   07059

     CEO: M. Terada, Mgr.   Tel: (908) 604-2900   %FO: 100

     Bus: *Engaged in property and casualty*   Fax: (908) 604-2991
         insurance services.

● **SUMITOMO METAL INDUSTRIES, LTD.**

5-33 Kitahama 4-chome, Chuo-ku, Osaka 541-0041, Japan

CEO: Hiroshi Shimozuma, Pres. & CEO   Tel: 81-6-220-5111   Rev: $13,498

Bus: *Mfr. steel product; steel mill technology.*   Fax: 81-6-223-0305   Emp: 15,295

                                              www.sumikin.co.jp

     SUMITOMO METAL USA CORPORATION

     8750 West Bryn Mawr Ave., Ste. 1000, Chicago, IL   60631-3508

     CEO: Yasukazu Morooka, Pres.   Tel: (773) 714-8130   %FO: 100

     Bus: *Mfr. steel product; steel mill*   Fax: (773) 714-8183
         technology.

● **SUMITOMO METAL MINING COMPANY, LTD.**

11-3, Shimbashi 5-chome, Minato-ku, Tokyo 105-8716, Japan

CEO: Koichi Fukushima, Pres.   Tel: 81-3-3436-7701   Rev: $3,415

Bus: *Engaged in mining and smelting,*   Fax: 81-3-3436-7734   Emp: 2,495
    electronics and metal fabrication.   www.smm.co.jp

     SUMITOMO METAL MINING INC.

     4055 Calle Platino, Oceanside, CA   92056

     CEO: Tohru Yamasaki, Pres.   Tel: (760) 941-4500   %FO: 100

     Bus: *Produces television frames.*   Fax: (760) 941-0900

● **SUMITOMO MITSUI BANKING CORPORATION (SMBC)**

C-2, Marunouchi, 1-Chome, Chiyoda-ku, Tokyo 100, Japan

CEO: Yoshifumi Nishikawa, Pres. & CEO   Tel: 81-3-3282-5111   Rev: $28,563

Bus: *Commercial banking services.*   Fax: 81-3-5512-4429   Emp: 14,395

                                              www.smbc.co.jp

SMBC

277 Park Avenue, 6th Fl., New York, NY   10172-0002

CEO: Takao Umino   Tel: (212) 224-5100   %FO: 100

Bus: *International commercial banking*   Fax: (212) 224-5111
services.

SMBC CAPITAL MARKETS INC.

277 Park Avenue, 6th Fl., New York, NY   10172-0002

CEO: Peter Fink, Mktg.   Tel: (212) 224-5100   %FO: 100

Bus: *Investment services.*   Fax: (212) 224-5111

● **SUMITOMO REALTY & DEVELOPMENT CO., LTD.**

Shinjuku NS Bldg., 4-1 Nishi-Shinjuku 2-chome, Shinjuku-ku, Tokyo 163-0820, Japan

CEO: Shinichiro Takagi, Chmn.   Tel: 81-3-3346-1054   Rev: $3,494

Bus: *Engaged in construction and*   Fax: 81-3-3346-1149   Emp: 799
development and leasing and managing   www.sumitomo-rd.com
office buildings.

SUMITOMO REALTY & DEVELOPMENT CA, INC.

15707 Rockfield Blvd., Irvine, CA   92718

CEO: Teruhiro Katagiri, Pres.   Tel: (949) 586-1011   %FO: 100

Bus: *Engaged in development and*   Fax: (949) 581-4551
leasing of office buildings.

SUMITOMO REALTY & DEVELOPMENT NY INC.

666 Fifth Avenue, 9th Fl., New York, NY   10103

CEO: Tetsuya Fujita, Pres.   Tel: (212) 582-8010   %FO: 100

Bus: *Engaged in development and*   Fax: (212) 582-8749
leasing of office buildings.

● **SUMITOMO RUBBER INDUSTRIES LTD.**

3-6-9 Wakinohama-cho, Chuo-ku, Kobe 651-0072, Japan

CEO: Mitsuaki Asai, Pres.   Tel: 81-78-265-3000   Rev: $4,981

Bus: *Mfr. golf balls, tennis balls and rubber*   Fax: 81-78-265-3111   Emp: 28,000
tires.   www.sumitomorubber.co.jp

DUNLOP MAXFLI SPORTS CORP.

728 N. Pleasantburg Drive, Greenville, SC   29607

CEO: Mike Rizzo, Pres.   Tel: (864) 241-2200   %FO: JV

Bus: *Mfr. golf balls.*   Fax: (864) 241-2268

DUNLOP TIRE CORPORATION

200 John James Audubon Pkwy., West Amherst, NY   14228

CEO: P.D. Campbell, Pres. & CEO   Tel: (716) 639-5200   %FO: JV

Bus: *Mfr. tires.*   Fax: (716) 639-5515   Emp: 3,300

● **THE SUMITOMO TRUST & BANKING CO., LTD.**
4-4 Marunouchi 1-chome, Chiyoda-ku, Tokyo 100, Japan
CEO: Atsushi Takahashi, Pres. Tel: 81-3-3286-1111 Rev: $8,865
Bus: *Commercial banking services.* Fax: 81-3-3286-8787 Emp: 6,000
  www.sumitomotrust.co.jp

 SUMITOMO TRUST & BANKING COMPANY, USA
 527 Madison Avenue, New York, NY 10022
 CEO: Yukio Aoyama, Mgr. Tel: (212) 303-9200 %FO: 100
 Bus: *Commercial banking.* Fax: (212) 644-3077 Emp: 50

● **SUNTORY, LTD.**
1-40 Dojimahama 2-chome, Kita-ku, Osaka 530-0004, Japan
CEO: Nobutada Saji, Pres. & CEO Tel: 81-6-6346-1131 Rev: $12,640
Bus: *Produces wine, liquors, malt beverages* Fax: 81-6-6345-1169 Emp: 20,000
 and specialty foods. www.suntory.com.

 SUNTORY INTL CORPORATION
 12 East 49th Street, 29th Fl., New York, NY 10017
 CEO: Takashi Nishii, Pres. Tel: (212) 891-6600 %FO: 100
 Bus: *Wines, liquors, malt beverages* Fax: (212) 891-6601
 and bottled water.

● **SUZUKI MOTOR CORPORATION**
300 Takatsuka-cho, Hamamatsu-shi, Shizuoka 432-91, Japan
CEO: Masao Toda, Pres. & COO Tel: 81-53-440-2061 Rev: $11,180
Bus: *Mfr./sale automobiles and motorcycles.* Fax: 81-53-445-2776 Emp: 14,418
  www.suzuki.co.jp

 AMERICAN SUZUKI MOTOR CORPORATION
 3251 East Imperial Hwy., PO Box 1100, Brea, CA 92621-6722
 CEO: Ryosaku Suzuki, Pres. Tel: (714) 996-7040 %FO: 100
 Bus: *Mfr./sale automobiles and* Fax: (714) 524-2512
 motorcycles.

● **SYSMEX CORPORATION**
1-5-1, Wakinohara-Kaigandori, Chuo-ku, Kobe, Hyogo 651-0073, Japan
CEO: Hisashi Ietsugu, CEO Tel: 81-78-265-0500 Rev: $344
Bus: *Manufacturer and developer of* Fax: 81-78-303-5640 Emp: 959
 diagnostic instruments and reagents. www.sysmex.co.jp

 PLUS INTERNATIONAL CORPORATION
 19231 144th Avenue NE, Woodinville, WA 98072
 CEO: Kevin Cumley Tel: (425) 402-4000 %FO: 100
 Bus: *Mfr. diagnostic instruments and* Fax: (425) 424-3633
 reagents.

STRECK LABORATORIES INC.
7002 S. 109 Street, LaVista, NE   68128
CEO: Margaret Nolan, Mgr.   Tel: (402) 333-1982   %FO: 100
Bus: *Mfr. diagnostic instruments and*   Fax: (402) 333-6605
reagents.

SYSMEX INFO SYSTEMS AMERICA INC.
One Wildlife Way, Long Grove, IL   60047
CEO: John Kershaw, Pres. & CEO   Tel: (847) 726-3562   %FO: 100
Bus: *Software developer and consultant*   Fax: (847) 726-3568
for diagnostic laboratories.

● TABUCHI ELECTRIC COMPANY, LTD.
5-4 Technopark, Sanda City 669-1339, Japan
CEO: Teruhisa Tabuchi, Pres.   Tel: 81-795-683211   Rev: $276
Bus: *Mfr. electronic components.*   Fax: 81-795-685851   Emp: 64

TABUCHI ELECTRIC COMPANY OF AMERICA
65 Germantown Court, Ste. 107, Cordova, TN   38018
CEO: Haru Nakagawa, Pres.   Tel: (901) 757-2300   %FO: 100
Bus: *Mfr./sale electronic components.*   Fax: (901) 757-1001   Emp: 19

● TAIHEIYO CEMENT CORPORATION
3-8-1 Nishi-Kanda, Chiyoda-ku, Tokyo 101-8357, Japan
CEO: Michio Kimura, Pres.   Tel: 81-3-5214-1520
Bus: *Mfr. cement and cement products.*   Fax: 81-3-5214-1707
www.taiheiyo-cement.co.jp

TAIHEIYO CEMENT INC.
2025 East Financial Way, Glendora, CA   91741
CEO: Noburu Kasai, Pres.   Tel: (626) 852-6200   %FO: 100
Bus: *Mfr. cement and cement products.*   Fax: (626) 852-6217

● TAISEI CORPORATION
1-25-1, Nishi-Shinjuku, Shinjuku-ku, Tokyo 163-0606, Japan
CEO: Kanji Hayama, Pres.   Tel: 81-3-3348-1111   Rev: $15,935
Bus: *Engaged in general construction and*   Fax: 81-3-3345-0481   Emp: 11,330
civil engineering.   www.taisei.co.jp

TAISEI CONSTRUCTION CO., LTD.
301 East Ocean Boulevard, Ste. 400, Long Beach, CA   90802
CEO: Hiroshi Toride, Pres. & CEO   Tel: (562) 432-5020   %FO: 100
Bus: *Engaged in general construction*   Fax: (562) 435-8151
and civil engineering.

- **TAISHO PHARMACEUTICAL CO., LTD.**
  24-1 Takata 3-chome, Toshima-ku, Tokyo 170-8633, Japan
  CEO: Shoji Uehara, Chmn.   Tel: 81-3-3985-1111   Rev: $2,082
  Bus: *Mfr./market pharmaceutical products*   Fax: 81-3-3985-6485   Emp: 4,733
      and prescription drugs.   www.taisho.co.jp

  ### TIASHO PHARMACEUTICALS CALIFORNIA INC.
  3878 Carson Street, Ste. 216, Torrance, CA 90503
  CEO: Jun Kuroda, Pres.   Tel: (310) 543-2035
  Bus: *Sales/distribution of*   Fax: (310) 543-9636
      pharmaceutical products.

- **TAIYO YUDEN CO., LTD.**
  6-16-20 Ueno Taito-ku, Tokyo 110-0005, Japan
  CEO: Mitsuga Kawada, CEO   Tel: 81-3-3833-5441
  Bus: *Mfr. electronics.*   Fax: 81-3-3635-4752   Emp: 2,740
      www.yuden.co.jp

  ### TAIYO YUDEN USA INC.
  1930 North Thoreau Drive, Ste. 190, Schaumburg, IL 60173
  CEO: Toshi Watanabe, Rep.   Tel: (800) 348-2496   %FO: 100
  Bus: *Mfr./sales electronics.*   Fax: (847) 925-0899

  ### TAIYO YUDEN USA INC.
  1770 La Costa Meadows Drive, San Marcos, CA 92069
  CEO: Tom Brooks   Tel: (760) 510-3200   %FO: 100
  Bus: *Mfr./sales electronics.*   Fax: (760) 471-4021

  ### TAIYO YUDEN USA INC.
  2107 N. First Street, Ste. 370, San Jose, CA 95131
  CEO: Mitsuga Kawada, Pres.   Tel: (800) 368-2496   %FO: 100
  Bus: *Mfr./sales electronics.*   Fax: (408) 573-4151

- **TAKAGI CHOKUKU COMPANY, LTD.**
  1525 Nakanoshima, Wakayama-shi, Japan
  CEO: T. Takagi, Pres.   Tel: 81-734-35205
  Bus: *Engraving for textiles and other*   Fax:
      industries.   www.takagi.co.jp

  ### TKG INTERNATIONALL CORPORATION
  2630 Weaver Road, Macon, GA 31201
  CEO: Manabu Takahira, Pres.   Tel: (912) 738-9700   %FO: 100
  Bus: *Engraved screens for textile and*   Fax: (912) 738-0307   Emp: 50
      printing.

● **TAKARA SHUZO COMPANY, LTD.**
Nissei Bldg., Shijo-Higashinotoin, Shimogyo-ku, Kyoto 600-8688, Japan
CEO: Hisashi Omiya, Pres.   Tel: 81-75-241-5110   Rev: $1,823
Bus: *Mfr./import wines and liquors.*   Fax: 81-75-241-5127   Emp: 2,044
                                              www.takara.co.jp

    AGE INTERNATIONAL INC.
    229 West Main Street, Frankfort, KY   40601
    CEO: Yutaka Takano, Pres.   Tel: (302) 223-9874   %FO: 100
    Bus: *Sales of liquor, including bourbon*   Fax: (302) 223-9877
       and whiskey.

    TAKARA SAKE USA, INC.
    708 Addison Street, Berkeley, CA   94710
    CEO: Teisuke Kainuma, Pres.   Tel: (510) 540-8250   %FO: 100
    Bus: *Mfr. sake and wines.*   Fax: (510) 486-8758

● **TAKASHIMAYA COMPANY, LIMITED**
1-5, Namba 5-chome, Chuo-ku, Osaka 542-8510, Japan
CEO: Tatsuro Tanaka, Pres.   Tel: 81-6-6631-1101   Rev: $10,134
Bus: *Department store and restaurant*   Fax: 81-6-6631-9850   Emp: 10,442
owner/operator, direct marketing and   www.takashimaya.co.jp
design consulting services.

    TAKASHIMAYA CALIFORNIA, INC.
    626 Wilshire Blvd, Ste. 925, Los Angeles, CA   90017
    CEO: Hisao Enomoto, Pres.   Tel: (213) 624-9886   %FO: 100
    Bus: *Department store and restaurant*   Fax: (213) 624-7396
       owner/operator, direct marketing
       and design consulting services.

    TAKASHIMAYA ENTERPRISES, INC.
    401 Old Country Road, Carle Place, NY   11514
    CEO: Tatsuro Tanaka, Pres.   Tel: (516) 997-4770   %FO: 100
    Bus: *U.S. headquarters. Department*   Fax: (516) 997-4772
       store and restaurant
       owner/operator, direct marketing
       and design consulting services.

    TAKASHIMAYA NEW YORK, INC.
    693 Fifth Avenue, New York, NY   10022
    CEO: Tatsuro Tanaka, Pres.   Tel: (212) 350-0592   %FO: 100
    Bus: *Department store and restaurant*   Fax: (212) 350-0192
       owner/operator, direct marketing
       and design consulting services.

● **TAKATA CORPORATION**
25 Mori Bldg., 4-30 Roppongi 1-chome, Minato-ku, Tokyo 106, Japan
CEO: J. Takada, Pres.   Tel: 81-3-582-3222
Bus: *Mfr. industrial hose, lubricants, seat*   Fax: 81-3-505-3022   Emp: 6,000
     belts and air bags.   www.takata.co.jp

     TAKATA FABRICATION CORPORATION
     2500 Takata Drive, Auburn Hills, MI 48326
     CEO: Tim Healy, Pres.   Tel: (248) 873-8040   %FO: JV
     Bus: *Mfr./distribution seat belts.*   Fax: (248) 373-2897

● **TAKEDA CHEMICAL INDUSTRIES, LTD.**
1,1 Doshomachi 4-chome, Chuo-ku, Osaka 541-8645, Japan
CEO: Kunio Takeda, Pres.   Tel: 81-6-204-2111   Rev: $8,749
Bus: *Mfr. pharmaceuticals, bulk vitamins,*   Fax: 81-6-204-2880   Emp: 16,370
     agricultural and environmental   www.takeda.co.jp
     products, agricultural chemicals.

     TAKEDA AMERICA, INC.
     555 Madison Avenue, 11th Fl., New York, NY 10022
     CEO: Shoji Isahaya, EVP   Tel: (212) 421-6950   %FO: 100
     Bus: *U.S. headquarters.*   Fax: (212) 355-5243

     TAKEDA VITAMIN & FOOD INC.
     101 Takeda Drive, Wilmington, NC 28401
     CEO: Yoshihisa Takeda, Pres.   Tel: (910) 762-8666   %FO: 100
     Bus: *Mfr. bulk vitamins, flavor*   Fax: (910) 762-6846   Emp: 160
     enhancers, ascorbic acid and
     thiamin.

     TAKEDA VITAMIN & FOOD INC.
     Park 80 West, Plaza 1, Saddle Brook, NJ 07663
     CEO: Yoshihisa Takeda, Pres.   Tel: (201) 368-2875   %FO: 100
     Bus: *Sale/distribution bulk vitamins,*   Fax: (201) 368-2875   Emp: 50
     flavor enhancers, functional
     ingredients for farm & food
     industries.

     TAP HOLDINGS INC.
     2355 Waukegan Road, Deerfield, IL 60015
     CEO: H. Thomas Watkins, Pres.   Tel: (847) 317-5712   %FO: 50
     Bus: *Mfr. pharmaceuticals.*   Fax: (847) 317-5797   Emp: 850

● **TAKENAKA CORPORATION**
1-13, 4-chome, Hommachi, Chuo-ku, Osaka 541-0053, Japan
CEO: Toichi Takenaka, Pres. & CEO   Tel: 81-6-6252-1201   Rev: $8,877
Bus: *Planners, architects, engineers and*   Fax: 81-6-6271-0398   Emp: 9,300
    builders.   www.takenaka.co.jp

    TAKENAKA (USA) CORPORATION
    555 Pierce Road, Ste. 190, Itasca, IL   60143
    CEO: Shinichi Sawada, Pres.   Tel: (630) 250-3400   %FO: 100
    Bus: *Planners, architects, engineers*   Fax: (630) 250-3433
        and general construction.

    TAKENAKA (USA) CORPORATION
    801 S. Figueroa Street, Ste. 1070, Los Angeles, CA   90017
    CEO: Shinichi Sawada, Pres.   Tel: (213) 489-8900   %FO: 100
    Bus: *Planners, architects, engineers*   Fax: (213) 489-8996   Emp: 90
        and general construction.

● **TAKEUCHI MFG COMPANY, LTD.**
205-3 Uadaira, Sakaki-machi, Hanishina-gun, Nagano 389-07, Japan
CEO: Akio Takeuchi, Pres.   Tel: 81-262-882331
Bus: *Mfr. compact excavators.*   Fax: Emp: 350
          www.takeuchi.co.jp

    TAKEUCHI MFG (USA), LTD.
    1525 Broadmoor Boulevard, Buford, GA   30518
    CEO: W. Scott Rogers, EVP   Tel: (770) 831-0661   %FO: 100
    Bus: *Distribute and service compact*   Fax: (770) 831-9484   Emp: 11
        excavators.

● **TAKISAWA MACHINE TOOL COMPANY, LTD.**
983 Natsukawa, Okayama 701-0164, Japan
CEO: Tadayoshi Takisawa, Pres.   Tel: 81-86-293-1500   Rev: $108
Bus: *Mfr. machine tools.*   Fax: 81-86-293-6111   Emp: 330
          www.takisawa.co.jp

    TAKISAWA USA, INC.
    1571 Barclay Boulevard, Buffalo Grove, IL   60089
    CEO: Tony Todoroki, VP   Tel: (847) 419-0046   %FO: 100
    Bus: *Sale machine tools.*   Fax: (847) 419-0043

● **TAMRON COMPANY, LTD.**

17-11 Takinogawa 7-chome, Kita-ku, Tokyo 114, Japan

CEO: T. Hishikawa, CEO   Tel: 81-3 3916-0131

Bus: *Mfr. photo/video lenses, optical*   Fax: 81-3 3916-1860   Emp: 1,200
components, Broncia medium format   www.tamron.co.jp
cameras.

     TAMRON INDUSTRIES, INC.

     125 Schmitt Blvd., Farmingdale, NY   11735

     CEO: Shoji Kono, Pres.   Tel: (631) 694-8700   %FO: 100

     Bus: *Distribution photo & CCTV*   Fax: (631) 694-1414   Emp: 20
     lenses, optical components.

● **TDK CORPORATION**

1-13-1 Nihonbashi, Chuo-ku, Tokyo 103-8272, Japan

CEO: Hiroshi Sato, Pres.   Tel: 81-3-3278-5111   Rev: $5,280

Bus: *Mfr. electronic materials, components*   Fax: 81-3-3278-5330   Emp: 31,300
and recording media.   www.tdk.co.jp

     DISCOM, INC.

     334 Littleton Road, Westford, MA   01886

     CEO: Mitsukuni Baba, Pres.   Tel: (978) 692-6000   %FO: 100

     Bus: *Mfr./sale deflection yokes and*   Fax: (978) 692-8489   Emp: 80
     high voltage power supply.

     SAKI MAGNETICS, INC.

     9330 Eton Avenue, Chatsworth, CA   91311

     CEO: Richard P. Drake, Pres.   Tel: (818) 775-1145   %FO: 100

     Bus: *Mfr./sale industry magnetic*   Fax: (818) 775-1290   Emp: 40
     recording heads.

     TDK COMPONENTS USA, INC.

     One TDK Blvd., Highway 74 South, Peachtree City, GA   30269

     CEO: K. Mura, Pres.   Tel: (770) 631-0410   %FO: 100

     Bus: *Mfr. multiple layer ceramic*   Fax: (770) 631-0425   Emp: 90
     capacitors.

     TDK CORPORATION OF AMERICA

     1600 Feehanville Drive, Mount Prospect, IL   60056

     CEO: Den Suzuki, Pres.   Tel: (847) 803-6100   %FO: 100

     Bus: *Sale electronic materials and*   Fax: (847) 803-6296   Emp: 200
     components.

     TDK ELECTRONICS CORPORATION

     12 Harbor Park Drive, Port Washington, NY   11050

     CEO: Ken Aoshima, Pres.   Tel: (516) 625-0100   %FO: 100

     Bus: *Sale magnetic recording media.*   Fax: (516) 625-0653   Emp: 150

TDK FERRITES CORPORATION
5900 North Harrison Street, Shawnee, OK 74801
CEO: Mitsukuni Baba, Pres.   Tel: (405) 275-2100   %FO: 100
Bus: *Mfr. hard & soft ceramic magnetic* Fax: (405) 878-0574   Emp: 960
  materials.

TDK SEMICONDUCTOR CORPORATION
2642 Michelle Drive, Tustin, CA 92780-7019
CEO: Den Suzuki, Pres.   Tel: (714) 508-8800   %FO: 100
Bus: *Design/mfr. integrated circuits.* Fax: (714) 508-8877   Emp: 2,000

TDK SYSTEMS, INC.
136 New Mohawk Road, Nevada City, CA 95959
CEO: Erik Viught, Mgr.   Tel: (530) 478-8421   %FO: 100
Bus: *Designs/sales PC modem cards.* Fax: (530) 478-8290

TDK TEXAS CORPORATION
6A Founders Blvd., El Paso, TX 79906
CEO: Ichiro Fujiyama, Pres.   Tel: (915) 778-9971
Bus: *Designs/mfr./distributes ceramic* Fax: (915) 772-1082
  magnets.

TDK USA CORPORATION
12 Harbor Park Drive, Port Washington, NY 11050
CEO: Kuniyoshi Matsui, Pres.   Tel: (516) 625-0100   %FO: 100
Bus: *Holding company.*   Fax: (516) 625-2923   Emp: 25

● **TEAC CORPORATION**
3-7-3 Naka-cho, Musashine City, Tokyo 180, Japan
CEO: Norio Tamura, Pres. & CEO   Tel: 81-422-52-5009   Rev: $1,425
Bus: *Mfr. computer disk drives, data* Fax: 81-422-52-6784   Emp: 1,170
  instrumentation recorders and audio www.teac.co.jp
  recorders.

TEAC AMERICA, INC.
7733 Telegraph Road, Montebello, CA 90640
CEO: Hajime Yamaguchi, Pres.   Tel: (323) 726-0303   %FO: 100
Bus: *Mfr. computer disk drives, data* Fax: (323) 727-7656
  instrumentation recorders and
  audio recorders.

● **TEIJIN LTD.**
6-7 Minami-Honmachi, 1-chome, Chuo-ku, Osaka 541-8587, Japan
CEO: Shosaku Yasui, Pres. & CEO   Tel: 81-6-6268-2132   Rev: $4,570
Bus: *Mfr. synthetic fibers, raw materials for* Fax: 81-6-6268-3205   Emp: 6,150
  chemicals, pharmaceuticals and   www.teijin.co.jp
  medical products.

TEIJIN AMERICA, INC.
10 East 50th Street, New York, NY   10022
CEO: Dr. Yoshinaga Karagawa, Pres.   Tel: (212) 308-8744   %FO: 100
Bus: *U.S. headquarters office; vending*   Fax: (212) 308-8902
      and food services.

● **TIEJIN SEIKI CO. LTD.**
2-4-1 Nishishinjuku, Shinjuku-ku, Tokyo 163-08, Japan
CEO: Yukitaka Tobari, Pres.   Tel: 81-3-3348-1721
Bus: *Mfr. textile machinery, industrial*   Fax: 81-3-3348-1050
      machinery and aircraft parts.

   TEIJIN SEIKI AMERICA INC.
   17770 Northeast 78th Place, Redmond, WA   98052-4960
   CEO: Ken Katada, Pres.   Tel: (425) 702-5757   %FO: 100
   Bus: *Mfr./services aircraft parts.*   Fax: (425) 602-8408

● **TEIJIN SHOJI COMPANY, LTD.**
8-14 Minami-Honmachi 1-chome, Chuo-ku, Osaka 541, Japan
CEO: K. Tsutsumi, Pres.   Tel: 81-6-266-8011
Bus: *Export textiles and raw materials.*   Fax: 81-6-266-8230
      www.teijin.co.jp

   TEIJIN SHOJI USA, INC.
   42 West 39th Street, 6th Fl., New York, NY   10018
   CEO: Noriaki Morimoto, Pres.   Tel: (212) 840-6900   %FO: 100
   Bus: *Import/export textiles, yarns,*   Fax: (212) 719-9656   Emp: 20
      fibers, sleep and sportswear.

● **TERUMO CORPORATION**
44-1, 2-Chome Hatagaya, Shibuya-ku, Tokyo 151-0072, Japan
CEO: Takashi Wachi, Pres. & CEO   Tel: 81-3-3374-8111   Rev: $1,394
Bus: *Mfg. pharmaceuticals and hospital*   Fax: 81-3-3374-8399   Emp: 7,438
      supplies.   www.terumo.co.jp

   TERUMO CARDIOVASCULAR SYSTEMS (TCVS)
   Maryland Factory, West Plant, 125 Blue Ball Road, Elkton, MD   21921
   CEO: S. Ninomiya, Pres.   Tel: (410) 398-8500   %FO: 100
   Bus: *Mfg. pharmaceuticals and hospital* Fax: (410) 392-7171
      supplies.

   TERUMO CARDIOVASCULAR SYSTEMS (TCVS)
   California Factory, 1311 Valencia Avenue, Tustin, CA   92780
   CEO: S. Ninomiya, Pres.   Tel: (714) 258-8001   %FO: 100
   Bus: *Mfg. pharmaceuticals and hospital* Fax: (714) 258-1230
      supplies.

TERUMO CARDIOVASCULAR SYSTEMS (TCVS)
Massachusetts Factory, 28 Howe Street, Ashland, MA   01721
CEO: S. Ninomiya, Pres.   Tel: (508) 881-2250   %FO: 100
Bus: *Mfg. pharmaceuticals and hospital*   Fax: (508) 881-4858
    supplies.

TERUMO MEDICAL CORPORATION
Phoenix Distribution Center, 302 North 45th Ave., Suite 1, Phoenix, AZ   85043
CEO: S. Ninomiya, Pres.   Tel: (602) 484-7842   %FO: 100
Bus: *Mfg. pharmaceuticals and hospital*   Fax: (602) 484-7951
    supplies.

TERUMO MEDICAL CORPORATION
Memphis Distribution Center, 5280 Meltech Drive, Suite 101, Memphis, TN   38118
CEO: S. Ninomiya, Pres.   Tel: (901) 362-6551   %FO: 100
Bus: *Mfg. pharmaceuticals and hospital*   Fax: (901) 794-6043
    supplies.

TERUMO MEDICAL CORPORATION
Corporate Office, 6200 Jackson Road, Ann Arbor, MI   48103-9300
CEO: S. Ninomiya, Pres.   Tel: (734) 663-4145   %FO: 100
Bus: *Mfg. pharmaceuticals and hospital*   Fax: (734) 663-7981
    supplies.

TERUMO MEDICAL CORPORATION
2101 Cottontail Lane, Somerset, NJ   08873
CEO: S. Ninomiya, Pres.   Tel: (732) 302-4900   %FO: 100
Bus: *Mfg. pharmaceuticals and hospital*   Fax: (732) 302-3083
    supplies.

TERUMO MEDICAL CORPORATION
Maryland Factory, East Plant, 950 Elkton Blvd., Elkton, MD   21921
CEO: S. Ninomiya, Pres.   Tel: (410) 398-8500   %FO: 100
Bus: *Mfg. pharmaceuticals and hospital*   Fax: (410) 392-7218
    supplies.

● TOAGOSEI CO. LTD.
1-14-1 Nishi-Shinbashi, Minato-ku, Tokyo 105-8419, Japan
CEO: Bunshiro Fukuzawa, Pres.   Tel: 81-3-3597-7215   Rev: $1,285
Bus: *Mfr. chemicals, industrial coatings and*   Fax: 81-3-3597-7217   Emp: 1,610
    adhesives.   www.toagosei.co.jp

BORDEN-TOAGOSEA CO.
180 East Broad Street, Columbus, OH   43215
CEO: M. Hiyashi, Mgr.   Tel: (614) 225-3471   %FO: 100
Bus: *Mfr. chemicals, industrial coatings*   Fax: (614) 225-3471
    and adhesives.

TOAGOSEI AMERICA INC.
650 Shawan Falls Drive, Suite 205, Columbus, OH   43215
CEO: Sakou Suzuki   Tel: (614) 718-3855   %FO: 100
Bus: *Mfr. chemicals, industrial coatings* Fax: (614) 718-3855
    and adhesives.

● **TODA CORPORATION**
7-1 Kyobashi 1-chome, Chuo-ku, Tokyo 104-8388, Japan
CEO: Moriji Toda, Pres.   Tel: 81-3-3562-6111   Rev: $5,852
Bus: *Engaged in construction and real estate* Fax: 81-3-3564-6713   Emp: 5,215
    development.   www.toda.co.jp

    TODA AMERICA, INC.
    5816 Corporate Avenue, Ste. 160, Cypress, CA   90630
    CEO: Akinori Nakagawa, Pres.   Tel: (714) 220-3141   %FO: 100
    Bus: *Engaged in construction and real* Fax: (714) 220-1360
        estate development.

● **TOHOKU ELECTRIC POWER CO., INC.**
7-1 Ichibancho 3-chome, Aoba-ku, Sendai, Miyagi 980-8550, Japan
CEO: Toshiaki Yashima, Pres.   Tel: 81-22-225-2111   Rev: $14,950
Bus: *Engaged in telecommunication, natural* Fax: 81-22-222-2881   Emp: 13,730
    gas and electricity.   www.tohoku-epco.co.jp

    TOHOKU ELECTRIC POWER COMPANY, INC.
    65 East 55th Street, Ste. 2304, New York, NY   10022
    CEO: Minoru Sata, Mgr.   Tel: (212) 319-6200   %FO: 100
    Bus: *Engaged in telecommunication,* Fax: (212) 319-1836
        natural gas and electricity.

● **THE TOKAI BANK, LTD., DIV. UNITED FINANCIAL OF JAPAN (UFJ)**
21-24 Nishiki 3-chome, Naka-ku, Nagoya 460, Japan
CEO: Hideo Ogasawara, Pres.   Tel: 81-52- 211-1111   Rev: $10,150
Bus: *Commercial banking services.*   Fax: 81-52-203-1207   Emp: 112,000
                                         www.tokai.com

    THE TOKAI BANK LTD
    505 Montgomery Street, San Francisco, CA   94111
    CEO: Sadao Akiyama, Pres.   Tel: (415) 399-0660   %FO: 100
    Bus: *Commercial banking services.*   Fax: (415) 399-9736

    THE TOKAI BANK LTD
    55 East 52nd Street, 11th Fl., New York, NY   10055
    CEO: Sadao Akiyama, Mgr.   Tel: (212) 339-1200   %FO: 100
    Bus: *Commercial banking services.*   Fax: (212) 754-2153

TOKAI BANK OF CALIFORNIA
300 South Grand Avenue, Los Angeles, CA   90017
CEO: Kazunori Nishimoto, CEO   Tel: (213) 972-0200   %FO: 100
Bus: *Commercial banking services.*   Fax: (213) 972-0325

● TOKAI CARBON CO., LTD.
1-2-3- Kita-Aoyama, Minato-ku, Tokyo 107-8636, Japan
CEO: Masahisa Sanmonji, Chmn. & CEO   Tel: 81-337-465-100   Rev: $17
Bus: *Mfr. carbon black for rubber products.*   Fax: 81-334-057-205   Emp: 1,550

TOKAI CARBON CO., INC.
4375 NW 235th Avenue, Hillsboro, OR   97124
CEO: Akio Haioka, Pres.   Tel: (503) 844-3605   %FO: 100
Bus: *Mfr./sales carbon black for car*   Fax: (503) 844-7207
    tires and rubber products.

● TOKINA OPTICAL COMPANY, LTD.
192 Nozuta-machi, Machida-shi, Tokyo 194-01, Japan
CEO: T. Yamanaka, Pres.   Tel: 81-3-42735-3611
Bus: *Mfr. photographic and CCTV lenses*   Fax: Emp: 500
    and security cameras.   www.introphoto.co.uk

THK PHOTO PRODUCTS, INC.
2360 Mira Mar Avenue, Long Beach, CA   90815
CEO: Yusu Suga, Pres.   Tel: (562) 494-9575   %FO: 100
Bus: *Sales/distribution of photographic*   Fax: (562) 494-3375   Emp: 20
    products.

● THE TOKIO MARINE & FIRE INSURANCE CO., LTD
2-1 Marunouchi 1-chome, Chiyoda-ku, Tokyo, Japan
CEO: Koukei Higuchi, Pres.   Tel: 81-3-3212-6211   Rev: $14,304
Bus: *Property, casualty and ocean marine*   Fax: 81-3-5223-3100   Emp: 13,615
    insurance.   www.tokiomarine.co.jp

AXIA SERVICES INC.
101 Park Avenue, New York, NY   10178-0095
CEO: Ramon Padron, Pres.   Tel: (212) 297-6600
Bus: *Property, casualty and ocean*   Fax: (212) 297-6898
    marine insurance.

TOKIO MARINE ASSET MANAGEMENT
101 Park Avenue, New York, NY   10178-0095
CEO: Toshiya Kimura   Tel: (212) 297-6600   %FO: 100
Bus: *Property, casualty and ocean*   Fax: (212) 297-6898
    marine insurance.

TOKIO MARINE MANAGEMENT

101 Park Avenue, New York, NY 10178-0095

CEO: Morio Ishil, Chmn.

Bus: *Property, casualty and ocean marine insurance.*

Tel: (212) 297-6600

Fax: (212) 297-6898

%FO: 100

TOKIO RE CORPORATION

101 Park Avenue, New York, NY 10178-0095

CEO: Kazuo Kawabata, Pres.

Bus: *Property, casualty and ocean marine insurance.*

Tel: (212) 297-6600

Fax: (212) 297-6898

%FO: 100

● TOKYO AIRCRAFT INSTRUMENT COMPANY, LTD.

35-1 Izumi-honcho 1-chome, Komae-shi, Tokyo 201, Japan

CEO: A. Wada, Pres.

Bus: *Mfr. aircraft instruments, business machines and industrial equipment.*

Tel: 81-3-489-1191

Fax: 81-3-488-5521

www.sjac.or.jp

Emp: 800

UNITED INSTRUMENTS, INC.

3625 Comotara Avenue, Wichita, KS 67226

CEO: T. Hanamura, Pres.

Bus: *Mfr. aircraft instruments.*

Tel: (316) 636-9203

Fax: (316) 636-9243

%FO: 100

Emp: 21

● THE TOKYO ELECTRIC POWER COMPANY, INC.

1-3 Uchisaiwai-cho 1-chome, Chiyoda-ku, Tokyo 100, Japan

CEO: Hiroshi Araki, Pres.

Bus: *Electric power generation and distribution.*

Tel: 81-3 3501-8111

Fax: 81-3 3591-4609

www.tepco.co.jp

Rev: $39,600

Emp: 42,000

TOKYO ELECTRIC POWER COMPANY, INC.

1901 L Street NW, Ste. 720, Washington, DC 20036

CEO: Shuya Shibasaki, Dir.

Bus: *Electric power generation and distribution.*

Tel: (202) 457-0790

Fax: (202) 457-0810

%FO: 100

● TOKYO ELECTRON LIMITED

TBS Broadcast Center, 3-6 Akasaka 5-chome, Minato-ku, Tokyo 107-8481, Japan

CEO: Tetsuro Higashi, Pres.

Bus: *Mfr. medical and hospital equipment and industrial machinery.*

Tel: 81-3-5561-7000

Fax: 81-3-5561-7400

www.tel.co.jp

Rev: $4,177

Emp: 8,950

TOKYO ELECRON AMERICA INC.

2400 Grove Boulevard, Austin, TX 78760

CEO: Barry Rapozo, Pres.

Bus: *Mfr. semiconductor manufacturing equipment.*

Tel: (512) 424-1000

Fax: (512) 424-1001

%FO: 100

TOKYO ELECRON AMERICA INC.
2120 West Guadalupe Road, Gilbert, AZ   85233
CEO: Jerry Adomshick, Pres.   Tel: (602) 437-9035   %FO: 100
Bus: *Mfr. semiconductor manufacturing* Fax: (602) 507-9364
  equipment.

TOKYO ELECTRON INC. (MA)
123 Brimbal Avenue, Beverly, MA   01915
CEO: Mike jamison, Pres.   Tel: (978) 921-0031   %FO: 100
Bus: *Mfr. semiconductor manufacturing* Fax: (978) 524-7000
  equipment.

TOKYO ELECTRON INC. (OR)
5350 Northeast Dawson Creek Drive, Hillsboro, OR   97124
CEO: David Matthews, VP   Tel: (503) 615-2100   %FO: 100
Bus: *Mfr. semiconductor manufacturing* Fax: (503) 615-2101
  equipment.

TOKYO ELECTRON INC. (TX)
2400 Grove Boulevard, Austin, TX   78760
CEO: Akira Miura, COO   Tel: (512) 486-4200   %FO: 100
Bus: *Mfr. semiconductor manufacturing* Fax: (512) 486-4201
  equipment.

TOKYO ELECTRON PHOENIX LABORATORIES, INC.
1829 West Drake Drive, Tempe, AZ   85283
CEO: Wayne Johnson, Pres.   Tel: (480) 345-6470   %FO: 100
Bus: *Mfr. semiconductor manufacturing* Fax: (480) 345-0259
  equipment.

● **TOKYO ROPE MANUFACTURING CO., LTD.**
Furukawa Bldg., 2-3-14, Nihonbasi-Muromachi, Chuoku, Tokyo 103-8306, Japan
CEO: Jun Uenishi, Pres.   Tel: 81-3-3211-2851   Rev: $773
Bus: *Mfr. fiber rope and wire.*   Fax: 81-3-3242-7584   Emp: 1,165
                                    www.tokyorope.co.jp

ATR WIRE & CABLE COMPANY INC.
1857 South Danville Bypass, Danville, KY   40422
CEO: Carl Metz, Plant Mgr.   Tel: (606) 236-9220   %FO: 100
Bus: *Mfr. wire and cable.*   Fax: (606) 236-9489

● **TOKYO SEIMITSU COMPANY, LTD.**
9-7-1 Shimotenjaku, Mitaka-shi, Tokyo 181-8515, Japan
CEO: Hideo Ohtsubo, Pres.   Tel: 81-3-4224-81019   Rev: $289
Bus: *Mfr. precision measuring and semi-* Fax: 81-3-4224-97315 Emp: 648
  conductor machinery.   www.tsk.co.jp

TSK AMERICA INC

39205 Country Club Drive, Ste.C-26, Farmington Hills, MI   48331

CEO: Michiaki Koda, Pres.	Tel: (248) 489-5500	%FO: 100
Bus: *Sales and service of measuring instruments.*	Fax: (248) 489-5503	Emp: 10

● **TOKYU CORPORATION**

5-6 Nanpeidai-cho, Shibuya-ku, Tokyo 150-8511, Japan

CEO: Shinobu Shimizu, Chmn.	Tel: 81-3-3477-6180	Rev: $9,433
Bus: *Transportation, development, hotels and recreation, retail distribution.*	Fax: 81-3-3464-6505 www.tokyu.co.jp	Emp: 4,445

MAUNA LANI RESORT INC.

68-1310 Mauna Lani Drive, Kohala Coast, HI   96743

CEO: Kenneth F. Brown, Chmn.	Tel: (808) 885-6677	%FO: 99
Bus: *Resort land development.*	Fax: (808) 885-6375	Emp: 265

SHIROKIYA, INC.

1450 Ala Moana Blvd., Honolulu, HI   96814

CEO: Shuzo Ishikawa, Pres.	Tel: (808) 347-3777	%FO: 100
Bus: *Engaged in retail sales.*	Fax: (808) 943-0483	

TOKYU TRAVEL AMERICA

2222 Kalakaua Avenue, Ste. 701, Honolulu, HI   96815

CEO: Naohumi Katayama, Mgr.	Tel: (808) 922-2315	%FO: 100
Bus: *Travel agency.*	Fax: (808) 945-3942	

● **TOMEN CORPORATION**

14-27 Akasaka 2-chome, Minato-ku, CPO Box 183, Tokyo 100-8623, Japan

CEO: Morihiko Tashiro, Pres.	Tel: 81-3-5288-2111	Rev: $27,175
Bus: *Engaged in general trading including chemicals, textiles, machinery and food.*	Fax: 81-3-5288-9100 www.tomen.co.jp	Emp: 2,774

TOMEN AMERICA INC.

1285 Avenue of the Americas, New York, NY   10019-6028

CEO: Michio Ishidate, Pres.	Tel: (212) 397-4600	%FO: 100
Bus: *General trading company.*	Fax: (212) 397-5797	Emp: 353

● **TOPPAN PRINTING COMPANY, LTD.**

1 Kanda Izumi-cho, Chiyoda-ku, Tokyo 101-0024, Japan

CEO: Naoki Adachi, Pres. & CEO	Tel: 81-3-3835-5741	Rev: $11,725
Bus: *Printing, publishing, packaging, semi-conductors, interior decorating materials, securities.*	Fax: 81-3-3835-0674 www.toppan.co.jp	Emp: 33,380

TOPPAN ELECTRONICS USA, INC.
7770 Miramar Road, San Diego, CA   92126

CEO: Naoki Iwata, Pres.	Tel: (858) 695-2222	%FO: 100
Bus: *Sales/distribution precision electronic components and packaging.*	Fax: (858) 695-6823	

TOPPAN INTERAMERICA INC.
1131 Highway 155 South, McDonough, GA   30253

CEO: Jack Jo, Pres.	Tel: (770) 957-5060	%FO: 100
Bus: *Full service commercial printing.*	Fax: (770) 957-6447	

TOPPAN PRINTING COMPANY OF AMERICA, INC.
666 Fifth Avenue, 7th Fl., New York, NY   10103

CEO: Roy Ariga, Pres.	Tel: (212) 489-7740	%FO: 100
Bus: *Full service commercial printing.*	Fax: (212) 969-9349	Emp: 180

• TOPY INDUSTRIES LIMITED
5-9 Yonban-cho, Chiyoda-ku, Tokyo 102-8448, Japan

CEO: Osami Sugiyama, CEO	Tel: 81-3-3265-0111	Rev: $1,608
Bus: *Mfr. automobile wheels.*	Fax: 81-3-3234-7675	Emp: 4,200

TOPY INDUSTRIES, DIV. NIPPON STEEL
10 East 50th Street, 29th Fl., New York, NY   10022

CEO: Osami Sugiyama, Pres.	Tel: (212) 486-7150	%FO: 100
Bus: *Mfr. automobile wheels.*	Fax: (212) 593-3049	

• TORAY INDUSTRIES INC.
2-1 Nihonbashi Muromachi, Chuo-ku, Tokyo 103-8666, Japan

CEO: Katsuhiko Hirai, Pres. & CEO	Tel: 81-3-3245-5111	Rev: $9,388
Bus: *Mfr. fibers, plastics and chemicals.*	Fax: 81-3-3245-5459	Emp: 9,510
	www.toray.co.jp	

TORAY CARBON FIBERS AMERICA
2030 Highway 20, Decatur, AL   35601

CEO: Kyoichi Kaku, Pres.	Tel: (256) 260-2626	%FO: 100
Bus: *Mfr. polyacrylonitrile-based carbon fiber.*	Fax: (256) 260-2627	

TORAY COMPOSITE (AMERICA), INC.
19002 50th Avenue East, Tacoma, WA   98446

CEO: Ken Nishikawa, Pres.	Tel: (253) 846-1777	%FO: 100
Bus: *Mfr. carbon fiber prepreg products.*	Fax: (253) 846-3897	

TORAY INDUSTRIES (AMERICA), INC.
600 Third Avenue, 5th Fl., New York, NY   10016

CEO: Yoshiomi Onishi, Pres.	Tel: (212) 697-8150	%FO: 100
Bus: *Liaison office, U.S. headquarters.*	Fax: (212) 972-4279	Emp: 20

TORAY MARKETING & SALES (AMERICA), INC.
600 Third Avenue, 5th Fl., New York, NY   10016

CEO: Hideo Maruhashi, Pres.	Tel: (212) 697-8150	%FO: 100
Bus: *Trading, import/export.*	Fax: (212) 972-4279	Emp: 40

TORAY PLASTICS (AMERICA), INC.
50 Belver Avenue, North Kingstown, RI   02852

CEO: Yasuo Abe, Pres.	Tel: (401) 294-4500	%FO: 100
Bus: *Mfr. polypropylene and polyester films.*	Fax: (401) 294-2154	

TORAY RESIN COMPANY
100 East Big Beaver, Ste. 310, Troy, MI   48083-1210

CEO: Toshio Ohshima, Pres.	Tel: (248) 740-2757	%FO: 100
Bus: *Mfr. nylon resin compounds.*	Fax: (248) 740-1150	

TORAY ULTRASUEDE INC.
1450 Broadway, New York, NY   10018

CEO: Andrea Boragno, Pres.	Tel: (212) 382-1590	%FO: 100
Bus: *Mfr. man-made suede products.*	Fax: (212) 382-1551	

● TOSHIBA CORPORATION
1-1 Shibaura 1-chome, Minato-ku, Tokyo 105-8001, Japan

CEO: Tadashi Okamura, CEO	Tel: 81-3-3457-2096	Rev: $54,495
Bus: *Mfr. information and communications systems, information media & consumer products, power systems & industrial equipment, electronic components.*	Fax: 81-3-3457-9202 www.toshiba.co.jp	Emp: 198,000

TOSHIBA AMERICA CONSUMER PRODUCTS, INC.
82 Totowa Road, Ste. 1, Wayne, NJ   07470

CEO: Toshihide Yasui, Pres.	Tel: (973) 628-8000	%FO: 100
Bus: *Mfr./sale consumer products.*	Fax: (973) 628-1875	

TOSHIBA AMERICA ELECTRONIC COMPONENTS, INC.
9775 Toledo Way, Irvine, CA   92718

CEO: Robert Brown, Pres.	Tel: (949) 455-2000	%FO: 100
Bus: *Mfr./sale electronic components.*	Fax: (949) 859-3963	

TOSHIBA AMERICA, INC.
1251 Ave. of the Americas, 41st Fl., New York, NY   10020
CEO: Shunichi Yamashita, Chmn.   Tel: (212) 596-0600   %FO: 100
Bus: *Holding company. U.S.*   Fax: (212) 593-3875
   headquarters.

TOSHIBA AMERICA INFORMATION SYSTEMS, INC.
9740 Irvine Blvd, Irvine, CA   92718
CEO: Atsutoshi Nishida, Pres.   Tel: (949) 583-3000   %FO: 100
Bus: *Mfr./sale of information and*   Fax: (949) 587-6424
   communication equipment.

TOSHIBA AMERICA MEDICAL SYSTEMS, INC.
2441 Michelle Drive, Tustin, CA   92681-2068
CEO: H. Igarashi, Pres.   Tel: (714) 730-5000   %FO: 100
Bus: *Mfr./sale medical equipment.*   Fax: (714) 505-3076

TOSHIBA INTERNATIONAL CORPORATION
13131 West Little York Road, Houston, TX   77041
CEO: Teruyuki Sugizaki, Pres.   Tel: (713) 466-0277   %FO: 100
Bus: *Mfr. industrial motors, adjustable* Fax: (713) 466-8773
   speed drives, and switchgear.

● TOSHIBA MACHINE COMPANY, LTD.
2-11 Ginza 4-chome, Chuo-ku, Tokyo 104, Japan
CEO: Sadao Okano, Pres.   Tel: 81-3-3567-0954   Rev: $792
Bus: *Mfr. machine tools, plastic machinery,* Fax: 81-3-3535-2570   Emp: 2,920
   die casting, printing press, etc.   www.toshiba-machine.co.jp

TOSHIBA MACHINE COMPANY OF AMERICA
755 Greenleaf Avenue, Elk Grove Village, IL   60007
CEO: Mitsunori Otsu, Pres.   Tel: (847) 593-1616   %FO: 100
Bus: *Import/distribution machine tools,* Fax: (847) 593-0897   Emp: 111
   injection molding, print & die-cast
   machinery and system robots.

● TOSOH CORPORATION
3-8-2, Shiba, Minato-ku, Tokyo 105-8623, Japan
CEO: Madoka Tashiro, Pres.   Tel: 81-3-5427-5140   Rev: $3,547
Bus: *Mfr./process chemicals, metals and raw* Fax: 81-3-5427-5208   Emp: 8,000
   materials.   www.tosoh.com

TOSOH USA, INC.
1100 Circle 75 Pkwy, Ste. 600, Atlanta, GA   30339-3097
CEO: Ken Dooley, VP   Tel: (770) 956-1100   %FO: 100
Bus: *Mfr. industrial chemicals and* Fax: (770) 956-7368
   chemical intermediates.

● **TOTO LTD.**

1-1 Nakashima 2-chome, Kokurakita-ku, PO Box 56, Kitakyushu, Fukuoka 802, Japan

CEO: Masatoshi Shigefuchi, Pres. Tel: 81-93-951-2707 Rev: $3,715

Bus: *Mfr. and markets water related products* Fax: 81-93-922-6789 Emp: 10,028
for commercial, residential and public www.toto.co.jp
facilities.

TOTO INDUSTRIES, INC.

1155 Southern Road, Morrow, GA 30260

CEO: Kazuo Narmi, Pres. Tel: (770) 282-8686 %FO: 100

Bus: *Mfr. and markets water related* Fax: (770) 282-8698
products for commercial,
residential and public facilities.

TOTO USA INC.

1155 Southern Road, Morrow, GA 30260

CEO: Toshio Kitano, Pres. Tel: (770) 282-8686 %FO: 100

Bus: *Mfr. and markets water related* Fax: (770) 282-8698
products for commercial,
residential and public facilities.

● **TOYO SUISAN KAISHA, LTD.**

1-3-1 Uchi-Saiwaicho, Chiyoda-ku, Tokyo 100-8522, Japan

CEO: Hirofumi Miki, Pres. Tel: 81-3-3508-2112 Rev: $6,880

Bus: *Mfr./sale glass and plastic containers* Fax: 81-3-3508-2265 Emp: 6,000
and paper packaging products. www.toyo-seikan.co.jp

TOYO SEIKAN

707 Skokie Blvd., Ste. 670, Northbrook, IL 60062

CEO: Hirofumi Mike, Pres. Tel: (847) 509-3080 %FO: 100

Bus: *Sales of glass and plastic* Fax: (847) 509-3080
containers.

● **TOYO TIRE & RUBBER CO., LTD.**

1-17-18 Edobori, Nishi-ku, Osaka 550, Japan

CEO: Shozo Katayama, Pres. & CEO Tel: 81-6-6441-8801 Rev: $2,200

Bus: *Mfr. automobile tires.* Fax: 81-6-6441-1847 Emp: 6,800
www.toyo.com

TOYO TIRE USA CORPORATION

6415 Katella Avenue, Cypress, CA 90630

CEO: Shari Arfons, PR Tel: (714) 236-2080 %FO: 100

Bus: *Mfr. automobile tires.* Fax: (714) 229-6183

● **TOYOBO CO., LTD.**
2-8 Dojima Hama 2-chome, Kita-ku, Osaka 530-8230, Japan
CEO: Junji Tsumura, Pres.   Tel: 81-6-6348-3137   Rev: $3,932
Bus: *Mfr. fiber and textiles.*   Fax: 81-6-6348-9626   Emp: 4,710
                                            www.toyobo.co.jp

    TOYOBO AMERICA, INC.
    40 East 52nd Street, 20th Fl., New York, NY   10022
    CEO: Morio Miyagi, Pres.   Tel: (212) 317-9245   %FO: 100
    Bus: *Mfr. fiber and textile products.*   Fax: (212) 317-9280

● **TOYODA AUTOMATIC LOOM WORKS, LTD.**
2-1, Toyoda-cho, Kariya, Aichi, 448-8671, Japan
CEO: Tadashi Ishikawa, Pres.   Tel: 81-566-22-2511
Bus: *Mfr. textile machinery, industrial*   Fax: 81-566-27-5650
vehicles and engines.   www.toyota-shokki.co.jp

    MICHIGAN AUTOMOTIVE COMPRESSOR, INC.
    2400 North Dearing Road, Parma, MI   49269
    CEO: Akira Imura, Pres.   Tel: (517) 531-5500   %FO: 100
    Bus: *Mfr. textile machinery and*   Fax: (517) 531-5680
    industrial vehicles.

    TOYOTA INDUSTRIAL EQUIPMENT MFG INC.
    5555 Inwood Drive, Columbus, IN   47201
    CEO: Yoshimitsu Ogihara, Pres.   Tel: (812) 342-0060   %FO: 100
    Bus: *Produces industrial vehicles and*   Fax: (812) 342-0064
    parts. (JV with Toyota Motor
    Corp.)

● **TOYODA MACHINE WORKS**
1-1 Asahi-Mamachi, Kariya City, Aichi Prefect 448-8652, Japan
CEO: Yoshio Yunokawa, Pres.   Tel: 81-566-255-170   Rev: $1,714
Bus: *Mfr. and sales of machine tools and* Fax: 81-566-255-470   Emp: 4,272
auto parts.   www.toyoda-kouki.co.jp

    TOYODA MACHINERY USA, INC.
    316 West University Drive, Arlington Heights, IL   60004
    CEO: Howard Michael, Pres. & CEO   Tel: (847) 253-0340   %FO: 100
    Bus: *Mfr./distribute horizontal/vertical*   Fax: (847) 577-4680   Emp: 400
    machining centers, grinders,
    machining cells & systems.

● **TOYOSHIMA SPECIAL STEEL COMPANY, LTD.**

1-6 Sumiyoshi 1-chome, Ikeda 563, Japan
CEO: Susumu Tanabe, Pres.
Tel: 81-722-61-2021
Bus: *Springs, fork arms, earthmover*
equipment and auto spare parts.
Fax: 81-722-61-9619

TOYOSHIMA INDIANA, INC.

735 St. Paul Street, Indianapolis, IN   46203
CEO: M. Fujimoto, Pres.
Tel: (317) 638-3511
%FO: 100
Bus: *Mfr./distribute springs for trucks*
Fax: (317) 631-7729
Emp: 126
and automobiles.

● **TOYOTA MOTOR CORPORATION**

1 Toyota-cho, Toyota City, Aichi Prefecture 471-8571, Japan
CEO: Fujio Cho, Chmn.
Tel: 81-565-282121
Rev: $120,697
Bus: *Mfr. motor vehicles, prefab housing,*
Fax: 81-565-235800
Emp: 214,600
telecommunications products.
www.global.toyota.com

BODINE ALUMINUM, INC.

100 Cherry Blossom Way, Troy, MO   63379
CEO: Robert Lloyd, Pres.
Tel: (636) 462-2200
Bus: *Mfr. aluminum and iron castings.*
Fax: (636) 462-2213

CALTY DESIGN RESEARCH, INC.

2810 Jamboree Road, Newport Beach, CA   92660
CEO: Kazuo Morohoshi, EVP
Tel: (949) 759-1701
%FO: 60
Bus: *Automotive design research.*
Fax: (949) 759-0377
Emp: 50

NEW UNITED MOTOR MFG., INC.

45500 Fremont Boulevard, Fremont, CA   94538
CEO: Kanji Ishii, Pres. & CEO
Tel: (510) 498-5500
%FO: JV
Bus: *Production/sales autos and*
Fax: (510) 770-4010
Emp: 4,800
compact pickup trucks. (JV with
GM).

TABC, INC.

PO Box 2140, Long Beach, CA   90801-2140
CEO: Ted Kajikawa, Pres.
Tel: (562) 428-3604
Bus: *Mfr. truck beds and steering*
Fax: (562) 637-6096
columns.

TOYOTA MOTOR NA INC.

9 West 57th Street, 49th Fl., New York, NY   10019
CEO: Toshiaki Taguchi, Pres.
Tel: (212) 223-0303
%FO: 100
Bus: *Imp./sale motor vehicles.*
Fax: (212) 759-7670

TOYOTA MOTOR CREDIT CORPORATION
19001 South Western Avenue, Torrance, CA 90509

CEO: Yoshimi Inaba, Pres.	Tel: (310) 618-4000	%FO: 100
Bus: *Provides leasing and loan financing.*	Fax: (310) 618-7802	Emp: 2,800

TOYOTA MOTOR MFG. INDIANA, INC.
4000 Tulip Tree Drive, Princeton, IN 47670-4000

CEO: Seizo Okamoto, Pres.	Tel: (812) 387-2000	%FO: 100
Bus: *Mfr. pick-up trucks.*	Fax: (812) 387-2001	Emp: 250

TOYOTA MOTOR MFG, INC.
1001 Cherry Blossom Way, Georgetown, KY 40324

CEO: Masamoto Amuzawa, Pres.	Tel: (502) 868-2000	%FO: 100
Bus: *Mfr./sale automobiles and parts.*	Fax: (502) 868-2008	

TOYOTA MOTOR MFG. WEST VIRGINIA INC.
One Sugar Maple Lane, Buffalo, WV 25033

CEO: Tomoya Toriumi, Pres.	Tel: (304) 937-7000	%FO: 100
Bus: *Mfr. four-cylinder engines*	Fax: (304) 937-7299	

TOYOTA MOTOR SALES USA, INC.
19001 South Western Avenue, Torrance, CA 90509

CEO: Yoshimi Inaba, CEO	Tel: (310) 618-4000	%FO: 100
Bus: *Mktg./distribution motor vehicles.*	Fax: (310) 618-7802	Emp: 3,200

TOYOTA TECHNICAL CENTER USA INC.
1555 Woodridge Avenue, Ann Arbor, MI 48105

CEO: Mike Masaki, Pres.	Tel: (734) 995-2600	%FO: 100
Bus: *Automobile testing, research and information gathering.*	Fax: (734) 995-5139	Emp: 346

● **TOYOTA TSUSHO CORPORATION**
7-23 Meieki 4-chome, Nakamura-ku, Nagoya 450-8575, Japan

CEO: Hiroshi Chiwa, Pres.	Tel: 81-52-584-5000	Rev: $16,061
Bus: *Iron and steel, non-ferrous metals, machinery, vehicles, energy, textiles, general merchandise, chemicals, insurance services and products.*	Fax: 81-52-584-5037 www.toyotsu.co.jp	Emp: 2,362

TOYOTA TSUSHO AMERICA, INC
7300 Turfway Road, Ste. 500, Florence, KY 41042

CEO: Senji Fujita, Pres.	Tel: (859) 746-7800	%FO: 100
Bus: *Import/export and domestic trading.*	Fax: (859) 746-7817	Emp: 250

● **TREND MICRO INC.**

Odakyu Southern Tower, 10th Fl., 2-1, Yoyogi 2-Chome, Shibuya-ku, Tokyo 151-8583, Japan

CEO: Steve Ming-Jang Chang, Chmn. & Pres. & CEO — Tel: 81-3-5334-3650 — Rev: $175

Bus: *Computer software services.* — Fax: 81-3-5334-3651 — Emp: 1,100

www.antivirus.com

    TREND MICRO INC.

    10101 N. De Anza Blvd., Cupertino, CA 95014

    CEO: Charlie Stuart, Dir. Global Alliances — Tel: (408) 257-1500 — %FO: 100

    Bus: *Computer software services.* — Fax: (408) 257-2003

● **TSUBAKIMOTO CHAIN COMPANY**

2-4, Kudan-Kita 3 chome, Chiyoda-ku, Tokyo 102-8186, Japan

CEO: Takashi Fukunaga, Chmn. — Tel: 81-3-3221-5612 — Rev: $996

Bus: *Mfr. chain and power transmission products and material handling systems.* — Fax: 81-3-3221-5639 — Emp: 3,018

www.tsubakimoto.co.jp

    TSUBAKI CONVEYOR OF AMERICA, INC.

    138 Davis Street, PO Box 710, Portland, TN 37148-0710

    CEO: Eishi Haga, Pres. — Tel: (615) 325-9221 — %FO: 100

    Bus: *Mfr. material handling systems.* — Fax: (615) 325-2442 — Emp: 130

● **TSUKAMOTO SOGYO COMPANY, LTD.**

4-2-15 Ginza, Chuo-ku, Tokyo, Japan

CEO: Seishiro Tsukamoto, Pres. — Tel: 81-3-535-3211

Bus: *Steel and iron product trading.* — Fax:

www.tsukamoto.com

    MONTECITO COUNTRY CLUB

    PO Box 1170, Santa Barbara, CA 93102

    CEO: Seishiro Tsukamoto, Pres. — Tel: (805) 969-3216 — %FO: 100

    Bus: *Golf and country club.* — Fax: (805) 565-3906

● **TSUMURA & COMPANY**

2-12-7 Nibancho, Chiyoda-ku, Tokyo 102-8422, Japan

CEO: Hachizaemon Kazama, Pres. — Tel: 81-3-3221-0001 — Rev: $768

Bus: *Mfr. herbal medicines.* — Fax: 81-3-3221-3776 — Emp: 3,113

www.tsumura.co.jp

    TSUMURA & COMPANY

    17870 Skypark Circle, Ste. 250, Irvine, CA 92614

    CEO: Dennis M. Newnham, CEO — Tel: (949) 833-7882 — %FO: 100

    Bus: *Mfr. herbal medicines.* — Fax: (949) 833-7774

TSUMURA & COMPANY
910 Sylvan Avenue, Ste. 100, Englewood Cliffs, NJ 07632
CEO: Dennis M. Newnham, CEO   Tel: (201) 816-6000   %FO: 100
Bus: *Mfr. herbal medicines.*   Fax: (201) 816-8477   Emp: 500

• UBE INDUSTRIES LTD.
1978-96, Kogushi, Ube, Yamaguchi 755-8633, Japan
CEO: Kazumasa Tsunemi, Pres. & CEO   Tel: 81-836-31-1111   Rev: $4,880
Bus: *Petrochemicals, chemicals, cement, construction materials and machinery, coal, and plant engineering services.*   Fax: 81-836-21-2252   Emp: 12,100
www.ube-ind.co.jp

ATC CORPORATION
3607 Trousdale Drive, Nashville, TN 37204
CEO: Nobuyuki Takahashi, Pres.   Tel: (615) 244-8994   %FO: 100
Bus: *Petrochemicals, chemicals, cement, construction materials and machinery, coal, and plant engineering services.*   Fax: (615) 244-8997

UBE INTERNATIONAL INC.
55 East 59th Street, 18th Fl., New York, NY 10022
CEO: Nobuyuki Takahashi, Pres.   Tel: (212) 813-8300   %FO: 100
Bus: *Export of UBE Group products and import of raw materials to Japan.*   Fax: (212) 826-0454   Emp: 12

UBE MACHINERY INC.
5700 South State Street, Ann Arbor, MI 48108
CEO: Toshiaki Kaku, Pres.   Tel: (734) 741-7000   %FO: 100
Bus: *Mfr./sales machinery.*   Fax: (734) 741-7017

• UCHIDA YOKO COMPANY, LTD.
4-7, Shinkawa, 2-chome, Chuo-ku, Tokyo 1304-8282, Japan
CEO: Shinichi Mukai, Pres.   Tel: 81-3-5634-6350   Rev: $1,421
Bus: *Mfr. metal office furniture.*   Fax: Emp: 2,009
www.uchida.co.jp

UCHIDA OF AMERICA CORPORATION
3535 Del Amo Blvd., Torrance, CA 90503
CEO: Andy Fujisawa, Pres. & CEO   Tel: (310) 793-2200   %FO: 100
Bus: *Sales/distribution of metal office furniture.*   Fax: (310) 793-2210

● **UNIDEN CORPORATION**
2-12-7 Hatchobori, Chuo-ku, Tokyo 104-8512, Japan
CEO: Yoshihiko Baba, CEO   Tel: 81-3-5543-2800   Rev: $614
Bus: *Mfr. telephone and radio*   Fax: 81-3-5543-2926   Emp: 11,200
communications equipment.   www.uniden.co.jp

    UNIDEN AMERICA CORPORATION
    4700 Amon Carter Boulevard, Ft. Worth, TX   76155
    CEO: Becky Busker   Tel: (817) 858-3300   %FO: 100
    Bus: *Mfr. telephone and radio*   Fax: (817) 323-2641
    communications equipment.

● **UNISIA JECS CORPORATION**
1370 Onna, Atsugi-shi, Kanagawa-ken 243-8510, Japan
CEO: Koichiro Toda, Pres.   Tel: 81-462-258050   Rev: $1,756
Bus: *Automotive component supplier.*   Fax: 81-462-213326   Emp: 6,473
www.unisiajecs.com

    ZUA AUTOPARTS, INC.
    5750 McEver Road, Oakwood, GA   30566
    CEO: Gary L. Collar, Pres.   Tel: (770) 967-2000   %FO: 100
    Bus: *Mfr. power steering pumps.*   Fax: (770) 967-0827   Emp: 132

● **UNITED FINANCIAL OF JAPAN (FORMERLY SANWA BANK, LTD.)**
1-1-1 Ohtemachi, Ciyoda-Ku, Tokyo 100-8114, Japan
CEO: Kaneo Muromachi, CEO   Tel: 81-3-5252-1111   Rev: $21,100
Bus: *Commercial banking services.*   Fax: 81-3-3214-6470   Emp: 13,000
www.ufj.co.jp

    UNITED FINANCIAL OF JAPAN
    55 East 52nd Street, New York, NY   10055
    CEO: Takashi Mori, Mng. Dir.   Tel: (212) 339-6300   %FO: 100
    Bus: *Commercial banking services.*   Fax: (212) 754-1851

    UNITED FINANCIAL OF JAPAN
    601 Figueroa Street, Los Angeles, CA   90017
    CEO: Isao Matsuura, Chmn.   Tel: (213) 896-7000   %FO: 100
    Bus: *Commercial banking services.*   Fax: (213) 896-7542

● **UNITIKA LTD.**
4-1-3 Kyutaro-machi, Chou-ku, Osaka 541-8566, Japan
CEO: Masaaki Katsu, Pres.   Tel: 81-6-6281-5695   Rev: $2,778
Bus: *Mfr. fibers, textiles, plastics.*   Fax: 81-6-6281-5697   Emp: 3,500
www.unitika.co.jp

UNITIKA AMERICA CORPORATION
1350 Avenue of the Americas, 20th Fl., New York, NY   10019
CEO: Fumio Ohama, Pres.   Tel: (212) 765-3760   %FO: 100
Bus: *Export/import textiles, fibers,*   Fax: (212) 765-3771
     plastics.

● **VICTOR COMPANY OF JAPAN, LIMITED (FORMERLY JVC LTD.)**
12 Moriya-cho 3-Chome, Kanagawa-ku, Yokohama 221-8528, Japan
CEO: Takeo Shuzui, Pres.   Tel: 81-45-450-2837   Rev: $8,248
Bus: *Mfr. electronic audio equipment.*   Fax: 81-45-450-1574   Emp: 35,875
                                   www.jvc-victor.co.jp

    HUGHES-JVC TECHNOLOGY CORPORATION
    2310 Camino Vida Roble, Carlsbad, CA   92009
    CEO: Seizo Watanabe, Pres.   Tel: (760) 929-5300
    Bus: *Mfr./sales of projectors.*   Fax: (760) 929-5708

    JVC AMERICA, INC.
    One JVC Road, Tuscaloosa, AL   35405
    CEO: Brad Springer, VP   Tel: (205) 556-7111   %FO: 100
    Bus: *Mfr. electronic audio equipment.*   Fax: (205) 554-5500

    JVC CORPORATION
    1700 Valley Road, Wayne, NJ   07470
    CEO: Katsuhiko Hattori, Pres.   Tel: (973) 315-5000   %FO: 100
    Bus: *Mfr. electronic audio equipment.*   Fax: (973) 315-5010

    JVC DISC AMERICA COMPANY
    Two JVC Road, Tuscaloosa, AL   35405
    CEO: Henry Hayamizu, Pres.   Tel: (205) 556-7111   %FO: 100
    Bus: *Mfr./sales of audio equipment.*   Fax:

    JVC INDUSTRIAL AMERICA INC.
    2320 Paseo De Las Americas, Ste. 205, San Diego, CA   92173
    CEO: M. Sasaki, Pres.   Tel: (619) 661-5300   %FO: 100
    Bus: *Sales/distribution of audio*   Fax: (619) 661-5333
         equipment.

    JVC LABORATORY OF AMERICA
    3211 Scott Blvd., Ste. 203, Santa Clara, CA   95054
    CEO: Kenny Goto, Pres.   Tel: (408) 988-4515   %FO: 100
    Bus: *Research.*   Fax: (408) 988-2687

JVC PROFESSIONAL COMPUTER PRODUCTS

5665 Corporate Avenue, Cypress, CA 90630

CEO: Richard Young, VP Tel: (714) 816-6500 %FO: 100

Bus: *Production/sales of CD recording* Fax: (714) 816-6519
systems.

JVC SERVICE & ENGINEERING COMPANY

107 Little Falls Road, Fairfield, NJ 07004

CEO: Mike Colicchio, Pres. Tel: (973) 808-2100 %FO: 100

Bus: *Service.* Fax: (973) 808-1370

● **WACOAL CORPORATION**

29, Nakajima-cho, Kisshoin, Minami-ku, Kyoto 601-8530, Japan

CEO: Yoshikata Tsukamoto, Pres. Tel: 81-75-682-5111 Rev: $1,430

Bus: *Mfr. lingerie, hosiery, underwear and* Fax: 81-75-661-5603 Emp: 4,500
outerwear. www.wacoal.com

WACOAL AMERICA INC.

40 Triangle Boulevard, Carlstadt, NJ 07072

CEO: Richard Murray, Pres. Tel: (201) 933-8400

Bus: *Mfr. lingerie, hosiery, underwear* Fax: (201) 933-8296
and outerwear.

● **M. WATANABE & COMPANY, LTD.**

2-16-4 chome, Nihonbashi-Muromachi, Chuo-ku, Tokyo 103-0022, Japan

CEO: Masaki Kusuhara, Pres. Tel: 81-3-3241-9141

Bus: *Mfr. steel and brass tubing.* Fax: 81-3-3241-9170
www.watanabe.co.jp

WACOM CORPORATION

146 Red School House Road, Spring Valley, NY 10977

CEO: Hisao Takahashi, Pres. Tel: (914) 735-1302 %FO: 100

Bus: *Wholesale non-metallic minerals.* Fax: (914) 735-3940

● **YAMAHA CORP**

10-1 Nakazawa-cho, Hamamatsu, Shizuoka-Pref 430, Japan

CEO: Shuji Ito, Pres. Tel: 81-53-460-2211 Rev: $5,003

Bus: *Mfr. musical instruments, audio* Fax: 81-53-460-2525 Emp: 21,600
products, household and sporting goods, www.yamaha.co.jp
metal products, furniture and
recreational equipment.

C&C BOAT MANUFACTURING INC.

6725 Bayline Drive, Panama City, FL 32404

CEO: Tim Leach, Mgr. Tel: (850) 769-0311 %FO: 100

Bus: *Mfr. boats.* Fax: (850) 769-0731

TENNESSEE WATER CRAFTS, INC.
2000 Cobia Drive, Vonore, TN 37885
CEO: Jim Balloni, Mgr.   Tel: (423) 884-6881   %FO: 100
Bus: *Mfr. FRP boats.*   Fax: (423) 884-6393

YAMAHA CORP OF AMERICA
6600 Orangethorpe Avenue, Buena Park, CA 90620
CEO: Mitsuru Umemura, Pres.   Tel: (714) 522-9011   %FO: 100
Bus: *Distribution musical instruments*   Fax: (714) 522-9350   Emp: 425
    and products; pianos, organs and
    computer chips.

YAMAHA MUSIC MANUFACTURING INC.
100 Yamaha Park, Thomason, GA 30286
CEO: Yoshi Ishikawa, Pres.   Tel: (706) 647-9601   %FO: 100
Bus: *Mfr. pianos and organs.*   Fax: (706) 647-8936   Emp: 195

YAMAHA MUSICAL PRODUCTS
PO Box 899, Grand Rapids, MI 49518
CEO: Kenji Sone, EVP   Tel: (616) 940-4900   %FO: 100
Bus: *Mfr. musical instruments.*   Fax: (616) 949-7721   Emp: 190

● **YAMAHA MOTOR CO., LTD.**
2500 Shingai, PO Box 1, Iwata-shi, Shizuoka-ken 438, Japan
CEO: Toru Hasegawa, CEO   Tel: 81-538-32-1145   Rev: $8,313
Bus: *Mfr. motorized vehicles and parts,*   Fax: 81-538-32-1131   Emp: 27,765
    including golf carts and snowmobiles.   www.yamaha-motor.co.jp

SKEETER PRODUCTS INC.
One Skeeter Road, PO Box 230, Kilgore, TX 75662
CEO: Steve Berry, Pres.   Tel: (903) 984-0541
Bus: *Mfr. and sales of boats.*   Fax: (903) 984-7740

YAMAHA MOTOR CORPORATION USA
6555 Katella Avenue, Cypress, CA 90630
CEO: Steve Kato, Pres.   Tel: (714) 761-7300   %FO: 100
Bus: *Distribute/sales Yamaha products.*   Fax: (714) 761-7302

● **YAMAKA SHOTEN LTD.**
Izumi-Cho, Toki-Shi, Gifu Pref, Japan
CEO: Kosuke Kato, Pres.   Tel: 81-61-5725-43111
Bus: *Mfr. dinnerware.*   Fax: Emp: 700

INTERNATIONAL CHINA COMPANY, INC.
131 Seaview Drive, Secaucus, NJ 07094
CEO: Kenichi Kato, Chmn.   Tel: (201) 864-9641   %FO: 100
Bus: *Wholesale/distribute dinnerware.*   Fax: (201) 864-4579   Emp: 50

- **YAMAMOTOYAMA CO LTD.**
5-2 Nihonbashi 2-chome, Chuo-ku, Tokyo 103, Japan
CEO: Kahei Yamamoto, Pres.   Tel: 81-3 3278-4479
Bus: *Tea and dried seaweed.*   Fax: 81-3 3278-0704   Emp: 800
                                              www.yamamotoyama-usa.com

   YAMA MOTO YAMA OF AMERICA, INC.
   122 Voyager Street, Pomona, CA   91768
   CEO: Hisayuki Nakagawa, Pres.   Tel: (909) 594-7356   %FO: 100
   Bus: *Tea, dried seaweed, real estate*   Fax: (909) 595-5849   Emp: 100
        investments.

- **YAMANOUCHI PHARMACEUTICAL CO., LTD.**
3-11 Nihonbashi-Honcho 2 chome, Chuo-ku, Tokyo 103-8411, Japan
CEO: Masayoshi Onoda   Tel: 81-3-3244-3000   Rev: $4,110
Bus: *Mfr./distribution of pharmaceuticals.* Fax: 81-3-5201-7473   Emp: 8,955
                                              www.yamanouchi.co.jp

   BEAR CREEK CORPORATION
   2518 South Pacific Highway, PO Box 299, Medford, OR   97501
   CEO: William H. Williams, Pres.   Tel: (541) 776-2362   %FO: 100
   Bus: *Mail order distribution of*   Fax: (541) 776-2194
        nutritional and personal care
        products.

   SHAKLEE CORPORATION
   1992 Alpine Way, Hayward, CA   94545
   CEO: Charles Orr, Pres. & CEO   Tel: (510) 887-5000   %FO: 100
   Bus: *Sales/distribution of household*   Fax: (510) 887-8583
        and nutritional products.

   SHAKLEE RESEARCH CENTER
   1992 Alpine Way, Hayward, CA   94545
   CEO: Charles Orr, Pres.   Tel: (510) 887-5000   %FO: 100
   Bus: *Research facility.*   Fax: (510) 887-8583

   YAMANOUCHI USA INC.
   Mark Centre IV, 4th Fl. South, 61 Paramus Road, Paramus, NJ   07652
   CEO: Dr. Gensel Kon, Pres.   Tel: (201) 291-2556   %FO: 100
   Bus: *Sales/distribution of*   Fax: (201) 291-7929
        pharmaceuticals.

   YAMONOUCHI PHARMA TECHNOLOGIES, INC.
   1050 Arastradero Road, Palo Alto, CA   94304
   CEO: Dan Green, CEO   Tel: (650) 849-8500
   Bus: *Sales/distribution of*   Fax: (650) 494-6794
        pharmaceuticals.

● **YAMATO TRANSPORT CO.MPANY, LTD.**
16-10 Ginza 2-chome, Chuo-ku, Tokyo 104-8125, Japan
CEO: Keiji Aritomi, Pres.   Tel: 81-3-3541-3411   Rev: $7,700
Bus: *Door-to-door parcel delivery services,*   Fax: 81-3-3542-3887   Emp: 93,425
moving & freight forwarding services.   www.kuronekoyamato.co.jp

> **YAMATO TRANSPORT USA, INC.**
> 80 Seaview Drive, Secaucus, NJ   07094
> CEO: Jun Tsunoda, Pres.   Tel: (201) 583-9706   %FO: 100
> Bus: *Door-to-door parcel delivery*   Fax: (201) 583-9703
> *services, moving and freight*
> *forwarding services.*

● **YAMAZAKI BAKING CO., LTD.**
3-10-1 Iwamoto-cho 3-chome, Chiyoda-ku, Tokyo 101-8585, Japan
CEO: Nobuhiro Iijima, Pres.   Tel: 81-3-3864-3111   Rev: $5,280
Bus: *Wholesale and retail bakery products.*   Fax: 81-3-3864-3109   Emp: 18,900

> **VIE DE FRANCE YAMAZAKI, INC.**
> 2070 Chain Bridge Road, Suite 500, Vienna, VA   22182-2536
> CEO: Nobuhiko Egawa, Pres.   Tel: (703) 442-9205   %FO: 100
> Bus: *Wholesale baked goods and*   Fax: (703) 821-2695   Emp: 1,000
> *bakery, café restaurant operations.*

> **YAMAZAKI BAKING COMPANY LTD.**
> 342 Madison Avenue, Ste. 604, New York, NY   10173
> CEO: Moriyoshi Abe, Rep.   Tel: (212) 490-0055   %FO: 100
> Bus: *Operates bakeries.*   Fax:

● **THE YASUDA FIRE & MARINE INSURANCE COMPANY, LTD.**
26-1 Nishi-Shinjuku 1-chome, Shinjuku-ku, Tokyo 160-8338, Japan
CEO: Hiroshi Hirano, Pres.   Tel: 81-3-3349-3111   Rev: $12,961
Bus: *Engaged in fire insurance and*   Fax: 81-3-3349-4697   Emp: 11,270
property/casualty and auto insurance.   www.yasuda.co.jp

> **YASUDA FIRE & MARINE INSURANCE COMPANY OF AMERICA**
> 777 South Figueroa Street, 48th Fl., Los Angeles, CA   90017
> CEO: K. Yamamoto, Mgr.   Tel: (213) 243-1800   %FO: 100
> Bus: *Insurance services.*   Fax: (213) 243-1855

> **YASUDA FIRE & MARINE INSURANCE COMPANY OF AMERICA**
> 404 BNA Drive, Ste. 101, Nashville, TN   37217
> CEO: Stephanie Bryant, Mgr.   Tel: (615) 366-8610   %FO: 100
> Bus: *Insurance services.*   Fax: (615) 366-8619

YASUDA FIRE & MARINE INSURANCE COMPANY OF AMERICA

225 West Wacker Drive, Ste. 2140, Chicago, IL   60606-1229

CEO: M. Shinohara   Tel: (312) 629-3000   %FO: 100

Bus: *Insurance services.*   Fax: (312) 629-3015

YASUDA FIRE & MARINE INSURANCE COMPANY OF AMERICA

*225 Liberty Street, 2 World Financial Center, 43rd Fl., New York, NY   10281

CEO: T. Uno, Pres.   Tel: (212) 416-1200   %FO: 100

Bus: *Insurance services.*   Fax: (212) 416-1288

YASUDA FIRE & MARINE INSURANCE COMPANY OF AMERICA

6 Concourse Parkway, Ste. 2130, Atlanta, GA   30328

CEO: T. Urata Pres.   Tel: (770) 394-5644   %FO: 100

Bus: *Insurance services.*   Fax: (770) 394-5605

● **YASUDA TRUST & BANKING CO. LTD.**

2-1 Yaesu 1-chome, Chuo-ku, Tokyo 103-8670, Japan

CEO: Hiroaki Etou, Pres. & CEO   Tel: 81-3-3278-8111   Rev: $2,529

Bus: *Commercial banking services.*   Fax: 81-3-3273-6329   Emp: 4,350

www.ytb.co.jp

YASUDA TRUST & BANKING COMPANY, LTD.

666 Fifth Avenue, Ste. 801, New York, NY   10103

CEO: M. Atsunobu, Rep.   Tel: (212) 373-5700   %FO: 100

Bus: *Representative office.*   Fax: (212) 373-5799

● **YKK CORPORATION**

1 Kanda Izumi-cho, Chiyoda-ku, Tokyo 101-8642, Japan

CEO: Tadahiro Yoshida, Pres.   Tel: 81-33-864-2103   Rev: $1,984

Bus: *Mfr. zippers, buttons and clothing fasteners.*   Fax: 81-33-864-2139   Emp: 35,750

www.ykk.com

UNIVERSAL FASTENERS, INC.

302 Factory Avenue, Lawrenceburg, KY   40342

CEO: Scott Kawamoto, Pres.   Tel: (502) 839-6971   %FO: 100

Bus: *Mfr. zippers, buttons and clothing fasteners.*   Fax: (502) 839-6525

YKK CORPORATION OF AMERICA

1251 Valley Brook Avenue, Lyndhurst, NJ   07071

CEO: Jay Takahaski, Pres.   Tel: (201) 935-4200   %FO: 100

Bus: *U.S. operations holding company.*   Fax: (201) 935-4033

● **YOKOGAWA ELECTRIC CORPORATION**
2-9-32 Nakaco, Musashino-shi, Tokyo 180-8750, Japan
CEO: Isao Uchida, CEO   Tel: 81-422-52-5530   Rev: $2,970
Bus: *Mfr. measurement instruments.*   Fax: 81-422-55-6492   Emp: 6,000
                                        www.yokogawa.co.jp

    YOKOGAWA CORP. OF AMERICA
    2 Dart Road, Newnan, GA   30265
    CEO: Isao Uchida, Pres.   Tel: (770) 253-7000   %FO: 100
    Bus: *Mfr./sales measurement equipment.* Fax: (770) 251-2088

● **YOKOHAMA RUBBER COMPANY**
36-11 Shimbashi 5-chome, Minato-ku, Tokyo 105-8685, Japan
CEO: Yasuo Tominaga, Pres.   Tel: 81-3-5400-4531   Rev: $3,717
Bus: *Mfr. automotive/aerospace/industrial* Fax: 81-3-5400-4570 Emp: 13,765
rubber products.   www.yrc.co.jp

    YOKOHAMA TIRE CORPORATION
    601 South Acadia Avenue, Fullerton, CA   92831-5197
    CEO: Daniel Ogden, CEO   Tel: (714) 870-3800   %FO: 100
    Bus: *Wholesale tires.*   Fax: (714) 870-3899   Emp: 1,200

● **YUASA CORPORATION**
2-3-21, Kosobe-cho, Takatsuki, Osaka 569-1115, Japan
CEO: Naruo Otsubo, Pres.   Tel: 81-726-86-6181   Rev: $1,597
Bus: *Mfr. motorcycle batteries.*   Fax: 81-726-86-6345   Emp: 1,875
                                        www.yuasabatteries.com

    YUASA INC.
    2366 Bernville Road, Reading, PA   19605
    CEO: John D. Craig, Pres.   Tel: (610) 208-1991   %FO: 87
    Bus: *Mfr./distribute batteries.*   Fax: (610) 208-1807   Emp: 2,500

● **YUASA TRADING COMPANY, LTD.**
13-10 Nihonbashi-Oden Macho, Chuo-ku, Tokyo 103-8570, Japan
CEO: Teruhisa Yuasa, Pres.   Tel: 81-3-3665-6938   Rev: $4,770
Bus: *Import and export of general*   Fax: 81-3-3665-5967   Emp: 1,545
merchandise.   www.yuasa-jp.com

    YUASA TRADING COMPANY (AMERICA) INC.
    150 East 52nd Street, New York, NY   10022
    CEO: Shugi Inoue, Pres.   Tel: (212) 751-3800   %FO: 100
    Bus: *Import/sales/distribution of* Fax: (212) 751-3831   Emp: 13
    general merchandise.

● **ZERIA PHARMACEUTICAL COMPANY, LTD.**
10-11 Nihonbashi Kobuma-cho, Chuo-Ku, Tokyo 103-8351, Japan
CEO: Sachiaki Ibe, Pres.   Tel: 81-3-3663-2351
Bus: *Mfr. and distribution of*   Fax: 81-3-3663-4503   Emp: 1,550
    pharmaceuticals.   www.zeria.co.jp

    ZERIA USA, INC.
    278 South Healy Avenue, Scarsdale, NY   10583
    CEO: Elio R. Loo, Dir.   Tel: (914) 285-9085   %FO: 100
    Bus: *Sales/distribution of*   Fax: (914) 285-9085   Emp: 2
       pharmaceuticals.

● **ZUKEN INC.**
2-25-1 Edahigashi, Tsuzuki-ku, Yokohama 224-8585, Japan
CEO: Makoto Kaneko, Pres.   Tel: 81-45-942-1511   Rev: $162
Bus: *Mfr. computer software.*   Fax: 81-45-942-1559   Emp: 585
                                             www.zuken.co.jp

    ZUKEN USA INC.
    2055 Gateway Place, Ste. 400, San Jose, CA   95110
    CEO: Eric Bruggeman, Mgr.   Tel: (408) 467-3876   %FO: 100
    Bus: *Mfr./sales computer software.*   Fax: (408) 567-3824

    ZUKEN USA INC.
    238 Littleton Road, Ste. 100, Westford, MA   01886
    CEO: Joanne Lynch, Mgr.   Tel: (978) 692-4900   %FO: 100
    Bus: *Mfr./sales computer software.*   Fax: (978) 692-4725

Jordan

● **ARAB BANK, PLC.**
PO Box 950545, Shmeisani, Amman 11195, Jordan
CEO: Abdulmajeed A. H. Shoman, CEO   Tel: 962-6-560-7231   Rev: $1,470
Bus: *Commercial banking services.*   Fax: 962-6-560-6793
www.arabbank.com

    ARAB BANK PLC
    520 Madison Avenue, 2nd Fl., New York, NY   10022
    CEO: Nofal S. Barbar, EVP   Tel: (212) 715-9700   %FO: 100
    Bus: *Commercial banking services.*   Fax: (212) 593-4632

● **ARAMEX INTERNATIONAL LIMITED**
2 Badr Shaker Alsayyab Street, Um Uthayna, Amman, Jordan
CEO: Fadi Ghandour, CEO   Tel: 962-6-553-4590   Rev: $106
Bus: *Provides freight forwarding, express*   Fax: 962-6-551-6820   Emp: 2,400
package delivery and transportation   www.aramex.com
services.

    ARAMEX INTERNATIONAL
    6201 Leesburg Pike, Falls Church, VA   22044
    CEO: Saadeh Saadeh, Mgr.   Tel: (703) 534-0828   %FO: 100
    Bus: *Provides freight forwarding,*   Fax: (703) 534-1408
    express package delivery and
    transportation services.

    ARAMEX INTERNATIONAL
    165-15 145th Drive, Jamaica, NY   11434
    CEO: Haitham Ajlouni, Mgr.   Tel: (718) 553-8740   %FO: 100
    Bus: *Provides freight forwarding,*   Fax: (718) 244-0462
    express package delivery and
    transportation services.

    ARAMEX INTERNATIONAL, C/O AIRBORNE EXPRESS
    6056 West View, Houston, TX   77055
    CEO: Amer Dajani, Mgr.   Tel: (713) 683-0113   %FO: 100
    Bus: *Provides freight forwarding,*   Fax: (713) 680-2166
    express package delivery and
    transportation services.

ARAMEX INTERNATIONAL, C/O AIRBORNE EXPRESS

5651 West 96th Street, Los Angeles, CA   90045

CEO: Adib Barake, Mgr.   Tel: (310) 642-0414   %FO: 100

Bus: *Provides freight forwarding,*   Fax: (310) 641-1494
express package delivery and
transportation services.

● **ROYAL JORDANIAN AIRLINES**

PO Box 302, Amman 11193, Jordan

CEO: Basel Jardaneh, Chrm. & CEO   Tel: 962-56-07300   Rev: $409

Bus: *Commercial air transport services.* Fax: 962-56-88341   Emp: 5,249
www.rja.com.jo

ROYAL JORDANIAN AIRLINES

6 East 43rd Street, New York, NY   10017

CEO: Taha Abutaha, Reg. Dir.   Tel: (212) 949-0060   %FO: 100

Bus: *International commercial air*   Fax: (212) 949-0488
transport services.

ROYAL JORDANIAN AIRLINES

JFK International Airport Bldg., Jamaica, NY   11430

CEO: S. Khan, Reg. Dir.   Tel: (718) 656-6030   %FO: 100

Bus: *International commercial air*   Fax: (718) 244-1821
transport services.

Kuwait

● **COMMERCIAL BANK OF KUWAIT (CBK)**
Box 2861, Safat 13029, Kuwait
CEO: Jamel Al Muttawa, Gen. Mgr.   Tel: 96-5-241-1001
Bus: *Commercial banking services.*   Fax:
                                            www.banktijari.com

COMMERCIAL BANK OF KUWAIT
1180 Avenue of the Americas, Ste. 2210, New York, NY   10036
CEO: Edwin Birkins, Mgr.   Tel: (212) 398-9600   %FO: 100
Bus: *International banking services.* Fax: (212) 768-7606

● **KUWAIT AIRWAYS CORP.**
International Airport Building, Safat 13004, Kuwait
CEO: Ahmed Al Mishari, Chmn.   Tel: 96-5-434-5555
Bus: *Commercial air transport services.* Fax: 96-5-431-4726   Emp: 5,250
                                        www.kuwait-airways.com

KUWAIT AIRWAYS CORPORATION
350 Park Avenue, New York, NY   10022
CEO: Faisal Alzaid, Reg. Mgr.   Tel: (212) 308-5454   %FO: 100
Bus: *International air transport.*   Fax: (212) 308-0524

● **KUWAIT PETROLEUM CORP**
PO Box 26565, Safat 13126, Kuwait
CEO: Ali Ahmed Al-Baghi, Chmn.   Tel: 96-5-246-9760
Bus: *Integrated petroleum company.*   Fax: 96-5-246-3315   Emp: 15,000
                                        www.bunkerworld.com

SANTA FE INTERNATIONAL CORPORATION
5420 LBJ Freeway, Ste.1100, Dallas, TX   75240
CEO: Sted Garber, Pres.   Tel: (972) 701-7300   %FO: 100
Bus: *Oil drilling services.*   Fax: (972) 701-7777

● **THE NATIONAL BANK OF KUWAIT S.A.K.**
Abdullah Al Salem Street, PO Box 95, Safat 13001, Kuwait
CEO: Ibrahim Dabdoub, Gen. Mgr.   Tel: 96-5-242-2011
Bus: *Commercial banking services.*   Fax: 96-5-242-9442
                                        www.nbk.com

THE NATIONAL BANK OF KUWAIT S.A.K.
299 Park Avenue, 17th Floor, New York, NY   10171
CEO: Muhamad Kamal, Gen. Mgr.   Tel: (212) 303-9800   %FO: 100
Bus: *International banking services.*   Fax: (212) 319-8269

• **THE UNITED BANK OF KUWAIT PLC**
Seven Baker Street, London W1M 1AB, UK
CEO: Adel El-Labban, CEO   Tel: 44-207-487-6500
Bus: *Private banking, asset management,*   Fax: 44-207-487-6808
commercial lending and finance.
(Hdqrts. UK)

THE UNITED BANK OF KUWAIT PLC
126 East 56th Street, 3rd Fl., New York, NY   10022
CEO: Abdulkader Steven Thomas, Mgr.   Tel: (212) 906-8500   %FO: 100
Bus: *International banking services.*   Fax: (212) 319-4762

Lebanon

- **BANK AUDI, SAL**

  Charles Malek Avenue, St. Nicolas Area, PO Box 11, 2560 Beirut, Lebanon

CEO: Raymond W. Audi, Chmn.	Tel: 961-1-200-250	Rev: $87
Bus: *Commercial banking services.*	Fax: 961-1-200-955	
	www.audi.com.lb	

  ### BANK AUDI

  19 East 54th Street, New York, NY   10021

CEO: Lawrence J. Ayoub, VP	Tel: (212) 833-1000	%FO: 100
Bus: *International commercial banking services.*	Fax: (212) 833-1033	Emp: 60

  ### BANK AUDI

  701 North Brand Blvd., Ste. 250, Glendale, CA   91203

CEO: Joseph G. Audi, Pres.	Tel: (818) 550-3999	%FO: 100
Bus: *International commercial banking services.*	Fax: (818) 246-8600	

- **MIDDLE EAST AIRLINES (MEA)**

  PO Box 206, Beirut International Airport, Beirut, Lebanon

CEO: Mohamad A. El-Hout, Chmn. & Pres.	Tel: 961-1-822860	
Bus: *Commercial air transport services.*	Fax: 961-1-629260	
	www.mea.com.lb	

  ### MIDDLE EAST AIRLINES

  Airport Center, 9841 Airport Blvd., Ste. 810, Los Angeles, CA   90045

CEO: Badara Habib, Mgr.	Tel: (310) 338-9124	%FO: 100
Bus: *International air transport.*	Fax: (310) 338-9148	Emp: 3

  ### MIDDLE EAST AIRLINES

  362 Fifth Avenue, New York, NY   10001

CEO: Adib Kassis, Mgr.	Tel: (212) 244-6850	%FO: 100
Bus: *International air transport.*	Fax: (212) 244-6860	Emp: 18

Liechtenstein

● **BALZERS AG, DIV. UNAXIS**
Iramali 18, FL-9496 Balzers, Liechtenstein
CEO: Dr. Hans Schulz, Pres. & CEO   Tel: 49-423-388-4785
Bus: *Mfr. coated tools and film.*   Fax: 49-423-388-5419   Emp: 1,835
                                                                    www.balzers.com

BALZERS, INC.
495 Commerce Drive, Amherst, NY   14228
CEO: Dennis Baer   Tel: (716) 564-8557   %FO: 100
Bus: *Mfr. coated tools.*   Fax: (716) 564-0206

Luxembourg

● **ARBED S.A.**
19, Avenue de la Liberté, L-2930 Grand Duchy of Luxembourg, Luxembourg
CEO: Fernard Wagner, Chmn. & CEO   Tel: 352-4792-1   Rev: $12,400
Bus: *Mfr. iron and steel products.*   Fax: 352-4792-2675   Emp: 41,200
                                            www.arbed.com

   TRADE ARBED INC.
   825 Third Avenue, New York, NY   10022
   CEO: Fred Lamesch, CEO   Tel: (212) 940-8000   %FO: 100
   Bus: *Trading company.*   Fax: (212) 355-2159

   TREFILARBED ARKANSAS INC.
   5100 Industrial Drive South, Pine Bluff, AR   71602
   CEO: Joe Jacqué, Pres.   Tel: (870) 247-2444   %FO: 100
   Bus: *Mfr. of steelcord and reinforcing*   Fax: (870) 247-1622
       wire for tire/hose industry.

● **CEDEL GROUP, DIV. CEDEL INTERNATIONAL**
PO Box 1006, L-1010 Luxembourg
CEO: Martin Brennan, Mgr.   Tel: 352-44-99-21
Bus: *International banking and securities*   Fax: 352-44-99-28210
    transactions.   www.cedelbank.com

   CEDELBANK
   *99 Park Avenue Suite 8F, New York, NY   10016
   CEO: Michael Barrett, Mgr.   Tel: (212) 293-2300   %FO: 100
   Bus: *International banking and*   Fax:
       securities transactions.

● **THE CRONOS GROUP**
16 Allee Marconi, Boite Postale 260, L-2120 Luxembourg
CEO: Dennis J. Tietz   Tel: 352-453-145
Bus: *Engaged in leasing of intermodal*   Fax: 352-453-147
    containers to marine carriers and   www.cronos.com
    transport operators.

   CRONOS CONTAINERS INC.
   517 Route One South, Ste. 1000, Iselin, NJ   08830
   CEO: Tom Lovgren, Mgr.   Tel: (732) 602-0808   %FO: 100
   Bus: *Engaged in leasing of intermodal*   Fax: (732) 602-7722
       containers to marine carriers and
       transport operators.

CRONOS CONTAINERS INC.

444 Market Street, 15th Fl., San Francisco, CA   94111

CEO: Dennis Tietz, Pres.   Tel: (415) 677-8996   %FO: 100

Bus: *Engaged in leasing of intermodal*   Fax: (415) 677-9396
    containers to marine carriers and
    transport operators.

● **ESPIRITO SANTO FINANCIAL GROUP (ESFG)**

231 Val des Bons Malades, L-2121 Lusembourg-Kirchberg, Luxembourg

CEO: Ricardo Salgado, Pres.   Tel: Rev: $3,650

Bus: *General commercial banking services.* Fax: Emp: 8,200

                                        www.esfg.com

    BANCO ESPIRITO SANTO

    320 Park Avenue, 29th Fl., New York, NY   10022-6839

    CEO: Joaquim Guarnecho, Gen. Mgr.   Tel: (212) 702-3400   %FO: 100

    Bus: *Commercial banking services.*   Fax: (212) 980-1777

    ESPIRITO SANTO BANK

    999 Brickell Avenue, Miami, FL   33131

    CEO: Tel: (305) 358-7000

    Bus: Fax: (305) 371-4410

    ESPIRITO SANTO FINANCIAL SERIVCES, INC.

    1350 Connecticut Avenue, NW, Suite 1200, Washington, DC   20036

    CEO: Tel: (202) 785-2938

    Bus: Fax: (202) 785-3479

● **GEMPLUS INTERNATIONAL SA**

Aerogolf Center, 1 Hohenhof, L-2633 Senningerberg, Luxembourg

CEO: Antonio M. Pérez, ceo   Tel: 352-2634-6100   Rev: $1,135

Bus: *Mfr. of magnetic stripe cards (Smart* Fax: 352-2634-6161   Emp: 7,870
    Cards) and software for access.   www.gemplus.com

    GEMPLUS CORPORATION

    3 Lagoon Drive, Ste. 300, Redwood City, CA   94065-1566

    CEO: Gilles Lisimaque, VP   Tel: (650) 654-2900   %FO: 100

    Bus: *Mfr. of magnetic stripe cards and* Fax: (650) 654-2900
       software for access.

    GEMPLUS CORPORATION

    101 Park Drive, Montgomeryville, PA   18936

    CEO: Justin D'Angelo   Tel: (215) 654-8900   %FO: 100

    Bus: *Mfr. of magnetic stripe cards and* Fax: (215) 654-8900
       software for access.

Malaysia

● **BANK MUAMALAT MALAYSIA BERHAD**
21 Jalan Melaka, 50100 Kuala Lumpur, Malaysia
CEO: Tuan Hj Mohd Shukri Hussin, CEO   Tel: 60-3-2698 8787
Bus: *Banking services.*   Fax:
www.muamalat.com.my

    BANK MUAMALAT MALAYSIA BERHAD
    325 West 38th Street, New York, NY   10017
    CEO: Shamsuddin Mahayidin, Mgr.   Tel: (212) 888-9220
    Bus: *Banking services.*   Fax: (212) 888-9220

● **BANK NEGARA MALAYSIA**
Jalan Dato'Onn, (PO Box 10922), 50929 Kuala Lumpur, Malaysia
CEO: Dato' Huang Sin Cheng, Gov.   Tel: 60-3-298-8044
Bus: *Government bank.*   Fax: 60-3-291-2990
www.bnm.gov.my

    BANK NEGARA MALAYSIA
    900 Third Avenue, 18th Fl., New York, NY   10022
    CEO: Soookpeng Tan, Mgr.   Tel: (212) 888-9220   %FO: 100
    Bus: *Government & banking services.*   Fax: (212) 755-4561

● **MALAYAN BANKING BERHAD (MAYBANK)**
Menara Maybank, 100 Jalan Tun Perak, PO Box 12010, 50050 Kuala Lumpur, Malaysia
CEO: Mohamed Basir bin Ahmad, Chmn.   Tel: 60-3-230-8833   Rev: $2,324
Bus: *Commercial banking services.*   Fax: 60-3-230-2600   Emp: 12,000
www.maybank.com.my

    MALAYAN BANKING BERHAD (MAYBANK)
    400 Park Avenue, 9th Fl., New York, NY   10022
    CEO: Baharudin Abd Majid, Gen. Mgr.   Tel: (212) 303-1300   %FO: 100
    Bus: *International banking services.*   Fax: (212) 308-0109   Emp: 30

● **MALAYSIA AIRLINE SYSTEM BERHAD**
MAS Bldg, 33/F, Jalan Sultan Ismail, 50250 Kuala Lumpur, Malaysia
CEO: Wan M. B. Ibrahim, Mng. Dir.   Tel: 60-3-261-0555   Rev: $1,982
Bus: *International commercial air transport.*   Fax: 60-3-261-3472   Emp: 23,075
www.malaysiaairlines.com

—

MALAYSIA AIRLINES

100 North Sepulveda Blvd., Ste. 400, El Segundo, CA   90245

CEO: Ismail Talib, VP	Tel: (310) 535-9288	%FO: 100
Bus: *International commercial air transport services.*	Fax: (310) 535-9088	Emp: 100

MALAYSIA AIRLINES

100 Northeast Third Avenue, Ste. 790, Ft. Lauderdale, FL   33301

CEO: Nicholas Sardana, Sales Mgr.	Tel: (954) 767-0907	%FO: 100
Bus: *International commercial air transport services.*	Fax:	

MALAYSIA AIRLINES

1350 Connecticut Avenue NW, Ste. 405, Washington, DC   20036

CEO: Zeenat Koreshi, Sales Mgr.	Tel: (202) 833-9180	%FO: 100
Bus: *International commercial air transport services.*	Fax: (202) 833-9178	

MALAYSIA AIRLINES

919 North Michigan Avenue, Ste. 2508, Chicago, IL   60611

CEO: Ruth Esparza, Sales Mgr.	Tel: (312) 943-0925	%FO: 100
Bus: *International commercial air transport services.*	Fax: (312) 943-9127	

MALAYSIA AIRLINES

140 East 45th Street, New York, NY   10170

CEO: Fred Siems, Sales Mgr.	Tel: (212) 697-8994	%FO: 100
Bus: *International commercial air transport services.*	Fax: (212) 867-0325	Emp: 100

• MARUICHI MALAYSIAN STEEL TUBE LTD.

B-8-7 Megan Phileo Promenade, 189 Jalan Tun Razak, 50400 Kuala Lumpur, Malaysia

CEO: Azahari Abidin, Chmn.	Tel: 60-3-2161-6322	Rev: $367
Bus: *Mfr. steel pipe and tubing.*	Fax: 60-3-2161-6322	Emp: 720
	www.maruichi.com.my	

MARUICHI AMERICAN CORPORATION

11529 Greenstone Avenue, Santa Fe Springs, CA   90670

CEO: Riichi Soda, Pres.	Tel: (562) 946-1881	%FO: 38
Bus: *Mfr. steel pipe and tubing.*	Fax: (562) 941-0047	Emp: 83

● **O.Y.L. INDUSTRIES, BHD.**

Level 8 Wisma Hong Leong, 18 Jalan Perak, 50450 Kuala Lumpur, Malaysia

CEO: Omar Yoke Lin Ong, Chmn.

Bus: *Investment holding company with subsidiary companies engaged in mfr./mktg./distr./service of heating, ventilation and air conditioning systems and products.*

Tel: 60-3-2164-3000
Fax: 60-3-550-3730
www.oyl.com.my

Rev: $1,167

AMERICAN AIR FILTER AAF INTERNATIONAL

215 Central Avenue, Louisville, KY 40208

CEO: Leese M. Jones, HR

Bus: *Sales/distribution of heating, ventilation and air conditioning systems and products.*

Tel: (502) 637-0011
Fax: (502) 637-0113

%FO: 100

MC QUAY, C/O SCHWAB, VOLLHABER, LUBRATT, INC.

4600 Churchill Street, St. Paul, MN 55126

CEO: Paul Lubratt, Pres.

Bus: *US representative office for sales/distribution of heating, ventilation and air conditioning systems and products.*

Tel: (651) 481-8000
Fax: (651) 481-8621

%FO: 100

Mexico

- **AEROMEXICO**
  Paseo de la Reforma 445, 06500 Mexico DF, Mexico
  CEO: Alfonso Pasquel, Pres.　　　　Tel: 52-5-133-4000
  Bus: *Commercial air transport carrier.*　Fax: 52-5-133-4623
  　　　　　　　　　　　　　　　www.aeromexico.com

  - **AEROMEXICO**
    13405 Northwest Fwy., Ste. 111, Houston, TX　77040
    CEO: Jaime Bernal, Mgr.　　　　Tel: (713) 744-8400　　%FO: 100
    Bus: *International commercial air*　Fax: (713) 460-3334　Emp: 300
    　　transport carrier.

- **AMERICA MOVIL, SA DE CV**
  Lago Alberto 366, Colonia Anahuac, 11320 Mexico DF, Mexico
  CEO: Daniel Hajj Abourmrad, CEO　Tel: 52-5-703-3390　Rev: $1,618
  Bus: *Provides wireless phone service and*　Fax: 52-5-545-5550　Emp: 6,050
  　　telephone cards.　　　　www.americamovil.com

  - **TRACFONE WIRELESS, INC.**
    8390 NW 25th Street, Miami, FL　33122
    CEO: F. J. Pollak, CEO　　　　Tel: (305) 640-2000　　%FO: 100
    Bus: *Provides wireless phone services.*　Fax: (305) 715-6921

- **BANCO INTERNACIONAL, S.A.**
  Paseo de la Reforma 156, 06600 Mexico DF, Mexico
  CEO: Antonio del Valle, CEO　　Tel: 52-5-721-2222
  Bus: *International banking services.*　Fax: 52-5-721-2993　Emp: 13,000
  　　　　　　　　　　　　　　www.banif.pt

  - **BANCO INTERNACIONAL, S.A.**
    437 Madison Avenue, 17th Fl., New York, NY　10022
    CEO: Carlos Martinez, EVP　　Tel: (212) 758-2660　　%FO: 100
    Bus: *International banking services.*　Fax: (212) 758-7552　Emp: 30

- **BANCO NACIONAL DE MEXICO S.A. (BANAMEX)**
  Isabel la Catolica 44, 06089 Mexico DF, Mexico
  CEO: Robert Hernandez, Chmn.　Tel: 52-5-225-5500　Rev: $7,100
  Bus: *International banking services.*　Fax: 52-5-225-5044　Emp: 36,000
  　　　　　　　　　　　　　　www.banamex.com

BANCO NACIONAL DE MEXICO
1000 Louisiana Street, Suite 6920, Houston, TX   77002
CEO: Arturo Ayala, Mgr.   Tel: (713) 651-9091   %FO: 100
Bus: *International banking services.*   Fax: (713) 659-2241

BANCO NACIONAL DE MEXICO
767 Fifth Avenue, 8th Fl., New York, NY   10153
CEO: G. Jiminez, Mgr.   Tel: (212) 751-5090   %FO: 100
Bus: *International banking services.*   Fax: (212) 303-1489   Emp: 60

CALIFORNIA COMMERCE BANK
2029 Century Park East, 42nd Fl., Los Angeles, CA   90017
CEO: Salvador Villar, Pres.   Tel: (310) 203-3401   %FO: 100
Bus: *International banking services.*   Fax: (310) 203-3587

● **BRYAN, GONZALEZ VARGAS Y GONZALEZ BAZ, S.C.**
Temistocles 10, Piso 3, Colonia Polanco, 11560 Mexico DF, Mexico
CEO: Eduardo Ramos Gomez, CEO   Tel: 52-5-282-1155
Bus: *International law firm; Mexican and*   Fax: 52-5-282-0513   Emp: 250
Latin American law.   www.bryanny.com

BRYAN, GONZALEZ VARGAS Y GONZALEZ BAZ, S.C.
405 Lexington Avenue, New York, NY   10174
CEO: Aureliano Gonzalez Baz   Tel: (212) 682-1555   %FO: 100
Bus: *International law firm; Mexican*   Fax: (212) 682-3241
and Latin American law.

● **CEMEX (CEMENTOS MEXICANOS)**
Avenida Constitucion, 444 Poniente, 64000 Monterrey Nuevo Leon, Mexico
CEO: Lorenzo H. Zambrano, CEO   Tel: 52-8-328-3000   Rev: $4,363
Bus: *Mfr. cement and concrete.*   Fax: 52-8-328-2025   Emp: 20,500
                                 www.cemex.com

CEMEX
590 Madison Avenue, 41st Fl., New York, NY   10022
CEO: Lorenzo H. Zambrano, Chmn.   Tel: (212) 317-6000   %FO: 100
Bus: *Mfr./distribution cement &*   Fax: (212) 317-6047
concrete.

CEMEX
One Riverway, Suite 2200, Houston, TX   77056
CEO: Gilberto Perez, Pres. & CEO   Tel: (713) 881-1000   %FO: 100
Bus: *Mfr./distribution cement &*   Fax: (713) 881-1012
concrete.

• CONTROLADORA COMERCIAL MEXICANA, S.A. DE C.V. (CCM)

Ave. Revolución 780 Módulo 2, 03730 Mexico DF, Mexico

CEO: Carlos González Zabalegui, CEO

Bus: *Owns and manages supermarket and general merchandise stores and restaurants.*

Tel: 52-5-371-7312
Fax: 52-5-371-7302
www.comerci.com.mx

Rev: $3,287
Emp: 35,300

COSTCO COMPANIES

999 Lake Drive, Issaquah, WA   98027

CEO: Jim Sinegal, Pres. & CEO

Bus: *Operates Price/Costco warehouse clubs (JV).*

Tel: (425) 313-8100
Fax: (425) 313-8221

%FO: JV

• ELAMEX, S.A. DE C.V.

Avenida Insurgentes No. 4145-B Oriente, 32340 Ciudad Juarez Chihuahua, Mexico

CEO: Eloy S. Vallina, Chmn.

Bus: *Provides shelter, assembly, injection molding, and metal stamping services for industries.*

Tel: 52-16-649-1000
Fax: 52-16-649-1000
www.elamex.com

Rev: $175
Emp: 3,100

ELAMEX USA INC.

220 North Kansas Street, Ste. 566, El Paso, TX   79901

CEO: Hector Raynal, CEO

Bus: *Mfr. printed circuit boards, fiber-optic cables, connectors, outlet strips, smoke detectors, medical products packaging and electronic switches.*

Tel: (915) 774-8369
Fax: (915) 774-8377

• GRUMA, S.A. DE C.V.

Calzada del Valle 407, OrienteSan Pedro Garza Garcia, 66220 Nuevo Leon, Mexico

CEO: Don Roberto Gonzalez Barrera, Chmn.

Bus: *Mfr. milled corn tortillas. (JV with Archer-Daniels-Midland U.S.)*

Tel: 52-8-399-3300
Fax: 52-8-399-3359
www.gruma.com

Rev: $1,400
Emp: 12,380

GRUMA CORPORATION/AZTECA MILLING

122 West Carpenter Pkwy., Ste. 410, Irving, TX   75039

CEO: Martin Ricoy Luviano, Pres. & CEO

Bus: *Mfr. milled corn.*

Tel: (214) 541-0040
Fax:

%FO: 50

GRUMA CORPORATION/MISSION FOODS

5750 Grace Place, PO Box 22034, Los Angeles, CA   90022

CEO: Martin Ricoy Luviano, Pres. & CEO

Bus: *Sales/distribution of tortilla and taco products.*

Tel: (213) 722-8790
Fax: (800) 424-7862

%FO: 50

● **GRUPO BIMBO, SA**

Pro. Paseo de la Reforma 1000, Col. Desarrollo Santa Fe, Del. Alvaro Obregon, 01210 Mexico DF, Mexico

CEO: Daniel Servitje Montull, CEO

Bus: *Commercial bakers of bread, tortillas, cookies and cakes.*

Tel: 52-5-258-6842

Fax: 52-5-258-6847

www.gibsa.com.mx

Rev: $3,035

Emp: 60,000

    BIMBO BAKERIES USA, INC.

    7301 South Freeway, Ft. Worth, TX   76134

    CEO: Juan Muldoon, Pres.

    Bus: *Commercial bakers of bread, tortillas, cookies and cakes.*

    Tel: (817) 293-6230

    Fax: (817) 293-6230

    %FO: 100

    BIMBO BAKERIES USA, INC.

    515 Jones Street, Ft. Worth, TX   76102

    CEO: Juan Muldoon, Pres.

    Bus: *Commercial bakers of bread, tortillas, cookies and cakes.*

    Tel: (817) 212-2000

    Fax: (817) 212-2000

    %FO: 100

● **GRUPO CARSO, S.A. DE C.V.**

Avenida Insurgentes Sur 3500, PB Colonia Pena Pobre, 14060 Mexico DF, Mexico

CEO: Patrick S. Domit, CEO

Bus: *Engaged in mining, cement, paper and telecommunications.*

Tel: 52-5-325-0505

Fax: 52-5-238-0601

www.porcelanite.com

Rev: $4,272

    PORCELANITE INC.

    15918 Midway Road, Addison, TX   75001

    CEO: Alejandro Abormrad, Pres.

    Bus: *Mfr. ceramic tile.*

    Tel: (972) 628-4600

    Fax: (972) 628-4614

    %FO: 100

● **GRUPO CEMENTOS DE CHIHUAHUA, SA DE CV**

Vicente Suarez y Sextra, Colonia Nombre de Dios, 31110 Chihuahua, Mexico

CEO: Federico Terrazas Torres, Chmn.

Bus: *Mfr. cement, cement block and limestone aggregates.*

Tel: 52-14-24-3355

Fax: 52-14-24-3516

www.gcc.com

Rev: $295

    RIO GRANDE PORTLAND CEMENT

    4253 Montgomery NE, Albuquerque, NM   87109

    CEO: Ronald W. Hedrick

    Bus: *Sales of cement and cement products.*

    Tel: (800) 234-2266

    Fax: (505) 281-3353

    %FO: 100

RIO GRANDE PORTLAND CEMENT
11783 State Highway 14S, Tijeras, NM   87059

CEO: Ronald W. Hedrick	Tel: (505) 281-3311	%FO: 100
Bus: *Sales of cement and cement products.*	Fax: (505) 281-9126	

RIO GRANDE PORTLAND CEMENT
112 Close Drive, Ruidoso, NM   88355

CEO: William C. Webb	Tel: (505) 336-4475	%FO: 100
Bus: *Sales of cement and cement products.*	Fax: (505) 257-2464	

RIO GRANDE PORTLAND CEMENT
One South Florida, Alamogordo, NM   88310

CEO: William C. Webb	Tel: (505) 434-1520	%FO: 100
Bus: *Sales of cement and cement products.*	Fax: (505) 434-1507	

RIO GRANDE PORTLAND CEMENT
300 South Walnut, Las Cruces, NM   88001

CEO: William C. Webb	Tel: (505) 524-8692	%FO: 100
Bus: *Sales of cement and cement products.*	Fax: (505) 524-0046	

● GRUPO FINANCIERO BBVA BANCOMER, SA
Montes Urales 424, Col. Lomas de Chapultepec, 11000 Mexico DF, Mexico

CEO: Vitalino M. Nafria Aznar, CEO	Tel: 52-52-01-2000	Rev: $7,577
Bus: *Financial services holding company for international banking services.*	Fax: 52-52-01-2313 www.bancomer.com.mx	Emp: 36,350

BBVA BANCOMER
444 South Flower St., Ste.100, Los Angeles, CA   90071

CEO: Javier de Leon, SVP	Tel: (213) 489-7245	%FO: 100
Bus: *International banking services.*	Fax: (213) 622-8519	

BBVA BANCOMER
430 Park Avenue, 19th Fl., New York, NY   10022

CEO: Bartolo Lopez, SVP	Tel: (212) 759-7600	%FO: 100
Bus: *International banking services.*	Fax: (212) 750-9228	

BBVA BANCOMER
444 South Flower St., Ste. 100, Los Angeles, CA   90071

CEO: Alvaro Meza, VP	Tel: (213) 488-3330	%FO: 100
Bus: *Securities services.*	Fax: (213) 489-9864	

BBVA BANCOMER

430 Park Avenue, 19th Fl., New York, NY 10022

CEO: Volker Mergenthaler, Mgr.	Tel: (212) 759-7600	%FO: 100
Bus: *Financial/securities services.*	Fax: (212) 230-0355	Emp: 3

BBVA BANCOMER

5775 Westheimer Road, Houston, TX 77056

CEO: Hector Chacon, Mgr.	Tel: (713) 341-8208	%FO: 100
Bus: *Financial/securities services.*	Fax: (713) 871-0444	

● **GRUPO FINANCIERO SERFIN S.A.**

Av. Paseo de La Reforma No. 211 Piso 13, Cuauhtemoco, 06500 Mexico DF, Mexico

CEO: C. Gomez Y. Gomez	Tel: 52-5-257-8000	Rev: $3,983
Bus: *Financial services; commercial and investment banking.*	Fax: 52-5-257-8566	Emp: 14,950
	www.serfin.com.mx	

BANCA SERFIN SA

399 Park Ave., 37th Fl., New York, NY 10022

CEO: Alejandro Garcia, Reg. Mgr.	Tel: (212) 572-0617	%FO: 100
Bus: *Commercial banking.*	Fax: (212) 421-5128	Emp: 34

● **GRUPO IMSA, S.A. DE C.V.**

Avenida Batallon de San Patricio 111, San Pedro Dela Garza Garcia, 66269 Nuevo Leon, Mexico

CEO: Eugenio Clariond Reyes-Retano, CEO	Tel: 52-8-153-8300	Rev: $2,206
Bus: *Mfr. steel, automotive and aluminum and construction products.*	Fax: 52-8-153-8400	Emp: 14,500
	www.grupoimsa.com	

DAVIDSON LADDERS INC., DIV. LOUISVILLE LADDERS

700 Swan Drive, Smyrna, TN 37167

CEO: Warren Markwell, Pres.	Tel: (615) 459-6094	%FO: 100
Bus: *Mfr./sales aluminum ladders.*	Fax: (615) 355-4711	

GLASTEEL USA INC.

830 Highway 57 East, Collierville, TN 38017

CEO: Eric Fryer, Gen. Mgr.	Tel: (901) 853-2010	%FO: 100
Bus: *Mfr. steel and plastic products.*	Fax: (901) 853-3908	

LOUISVILLE LADDERS INC.

1163 Algonquin Parkway, Louisville, KY 40208

CEO: Warren Markwell, Pres.	Tel: (502) 636-2811	%FO: 100
Bus: *Mfr./sales aluminum ladders.*	Fax: (502) 636-1014	

METI-SPAN
1497 North Kealy, Lewisville, TX   75057
CEO: Carl Hielscher, CEO   Tel: (877) 585-9969   %FO: 100
Bus: *Mfr. of insulated metal panels for*   Fax: (972) 436-0648
   buildings.

● **GRUPO INDUSTRIAL DURANGO, SA DE CV**
Potasio 150, Ciudad Industrial, 34220 Durango, Mexico
CEO: Miguel Rincon, CEO   Tel: 52-1829-1010   Rev: $632
Bus: *Mfr. packaging products.*   Fax: 52-1814-1275   Emp: 7,770
                                         www.gidusa.com.mx

   DURANGO INC.
   1000 Osborne Street, St. Mary's, GA   31558
   CEO: J. Rincon   Tel: (912) 882-6500   %FO: 100
   Bus: *Mfr. and sales packaging and*   Fax: (912) 882-6500
      paper products.

   DURANGO INC.
   700 Sam Houston Road, Mezquite, TX   75149
   CEO: J. Rincon   Tel: (972) 285-8865   %FO: 100
   Bus: *Mfr. and sales packaging and*   Fax: (972) 288-6255
      paper products.

   DURANGO INC.
   1050 Montgomery Blvd. NE, Albuquerque, NM   87111
   CEO: J. Rincon   Tel: (505) 271-7500   %FO: 100
   Bus: *Mfr. and sales packaging and*   Fax: (505) 271-7575
      paper products.

● **GRUPO INDUSTRIAL MASECA**
Calzada del Valle 407 Ote., San Pedro, 66220 Garza Garcia N.L., Mexico
CEO: Ricardo Alvarez-Tostado Penella, CEO   Tel: 52-8-399-3300   Rev: $497
Bus: *Mfr. ready-mixed corn flour to produce*   Fax: 52-8-399-3359   Emp: 2,975
   corn tortillas, including Mission brand.   www.gruma.com

   MISSION FOODS
   1159 Cottonwood Lane, Ste. 200, Irving, TX   75038
   CEO: Martin Ricoy, Pres.   Tel: (972) 232-5200   %FO: 100
   Bus: *Sales/distribution of Mission*   Fax: (972) 232-5176
      brand corn flour products.

   MISSION FOODS
   2110 Santa Fe Drive, Pueblo, CO   81006
   CEO: Martin Ricoy, Pres.   Tel: (719) 543-4350   %FO: 100
   Bus: *Sales/distribution of Mission*   Fax: (719) 545-3681
      brand corn flour products.

● **GRUPO MEXICO SA DE CV**
Avenida Baja California 200, Colonia Roma Sur, 06760 Mexico DF, Mexico
CEO: Germán Larrea Mota-Velasco, CEO   Tel: 52-5-564-7066   Rev: $3,592
Bus: *Production of copper.*   Fax: 52-5-564-7677   Emp: 30,400
   www.gmexico.com

    ASARCO INCORPORATED
    Box 1230, East Helena, MT 59635
    CEO: Luke N. Downing, Mgr.   Tel: (406) 227-7100   %FO: 100
    Bus: *Copper plant.*   Fax: (406) 227-8849

    ASARCO INCORPORATED
    495 East 51st Avenue, Denver, CO 80216-2098
    CEO: Randy L. Flynn   Tel: (303) 296-5900   %FO: 100
    Bus: *Production of copper.*   Fax: (303) 296-0508

    ASARCO INCORPORATED
    PO Box 1111, El Paso, TX 79999
    CEO: Greg Parham   Tel: (915) 541-1800   %FO: 100
    Bus: *Copper plant.*   Fax: (915) 541-1866

    ASARCO INCORPORATED
    PO Box 460, Strawberry Plains, TN 37871
    CEO: Clifford T. Smith, Mgr.   Tel: (865) 475-2644   %FO: 100
    Bus: *Copper plant.*   Fax: (865) 475-3654

    ASARCO INCORPORATED
    PO Box 30200, Amarillo, TX 79120-0200
    CEO: Lawrence W. Castor, Mgr.   Tel: (806) 468-4000   %FO: 100
    Bus: *Copper plant.*   Fax: (806) 468-4291

    ASARCO INCORPORATED
    PO Box 4767, Corpus Christi, TX 78407
    CEO: Alfonso Benavides, Mgr.   Tel: (361) 289-0300   %FO: 100
    Bus: *Production of copper.*   Fax: (361) 289-6526

    HYDROMETRICS, INC.
    5825 Lazy Lane, Billings, MT 59106
    CEO: Al Hilty, Sr. Mgr.   Tel: (406) 656-1172   %FO: 100
    Bus: *Production of copper.*   Fax: (406) 656-8912

    HYDROMETRICS, INC.
    2727 Airport Road, Helena, MT 59601
    CEO: Tom Aldrich, Pres.   Tel: (406) 443-4150   %FO: 100
    Bus: *Production of copper.*   Fax: (406) 443-4155

- **GRUPO MINSA, SA DE CV**
Prolongacion Toltecas 4, Los Reyes Ixtacala, 54090 Tialnepantla, Mexico
CEO: Juan Gargallo Costa, CEO   Tel: 52-5722-1946
Bus: *Mfr. corn flour.*   Fax: 52-5565-5951
www.minsa.com

  MINSA USA INC.
  RR1, Box 111A, Red Oak, IA   51566
  CEO: Juan Costa, Pres.   Tel: (712) 623-5255   %FO: 100
  Bus: *Manufacturing plant for corn flour.* Fax: (712) 623-5255   Emp: 100

- **GRUPO NACIONAL PROVINCIAL, S.A.**
Ave. Cerro de Las Torres 395, Col. Campestere Churubusco, 04200 Mexico D.F., Mexico
CEO: Clemente Cabello, Pres.   Tel: 52-5-227-3999
Bus: *Engaged in multi-line insurance.*   Fax: 52-5-227-3154   Emp: 5,000
www.gnp.com.mx

  LA PROV CORPORATION
  One Penn Plaza, Ste. 2108, New York, NY   10119
  CEO: Richard M. Murray, Chmn.   Tel: (212) 947-4070   %FO: 100
  Bus: *Insurance services.*   Fax: (212) 947-3090   Emp: 4

- **MEXICANA DE AVIACIÓN SA DE CV**
Xola 535, Colonia del Valle, 03100 Mexico DF, Mexico
CEO: Fernando Flores, Dir. Gen.   Tel: 525-448-3000
Bus: *International commercial air transport*   Fax: 515-669-3342   Emp: 6,422
 services.   www.mexicana.com.

  MEXICANA AIRLINES
  767 Third Avenue, 14th Fl., New York, NY   10017
  CEO: George Edelmann, Mgr.   Tel: (212) 688-6342   %FO: 100
  Bus: *Air transport services.*   Fax: (212) 688-9516   Emp: 500

  MEXICANA AIRLINES
  9841 Airport Boulevard, Suite 200, Los Angeles, CA   90045
  CEO: Linda Mansell, Mgr.   Tel: (310) 646-0401   %FO: 100
  Bus: *Air transport services.*   Fax: (310) 646-0400   Emp: 599

- **NACIONAL FINANCIERA SNC MEXICO**
Ave. Isensurgentest Sur 1971, Torre 4, 13th Fl., Col. Guadalupe Enn, 01020 Mexico DF, Mexico
CEO: Carlos Sales, CEO   Tel: 52-5-325-6700
Bus: *Develops industry through Nafin*   Fax: 52-5-661-8418
 (Nacional Financiera), long-term   www.nafinsa.com
 financing, foreign exchange operation
 and direct investment.

NAFINSA SECURITIES, INC.
21 East 63 Street, New York, NY 10020

CEO: Mark Laedig, Pres.   Tel: (212) 821-0300   %FO: 100

Bus: *Develops industry through Nafin*   Fax: (212) 821-0330
(Nacional Financiera), long-term
financing, foreign exchange
operation and direct investment.

• SANLUIS CORPORACION, SA DE CV
Monte Pelvous 220-8, Colonia Lomas de Chapultepec 11000 Mexico DF, Mexico

CEO: Antonio Madero, CEO   Tel: 52-5-229-5800   Rev: $532

Bus: *Mfr. auto supplies.*   Fax: 52-5-202-6604   Emp: 500

www.sanluiscorp.com

SANLUIS RASSINI INTERNATIONAL INC.
14500 Beck Road, Plymouth, MI 48170

CEO: Pam VanDermoon   Tel: (734) 454-4904   %FO: 100

Bus: *Mfr./sales auto supplies.*   Fax: (734) 454-4914

• SAVIA, SA DE CV, DIV. GRUPO PULSAR
Ave. Batallon de San Patricio No. 111, Col. Valle Oriente, 66269 San Pedro NL, Mexico

CEO: Alfonso Romo Garza   Tel: 52-8-399-0830   Rev: $3,211

Bus: *Diversified holdings including,*   Fax: 52-8-399-0858
property/casualty, life, and health   www.savia.com.mx
insurance and fruit and vegetable seed
supplier and packager.

BIONOVA HOLDING
6701 San Pablo Avenue, Oakland, CA 94608

CEO: Bernardo Jimenez, CEO   Tel: (510) 547-2395   %FO: 100

Bus: *Engaged in biotechnology, genetic*   Fax: (510) 547-2817
engineering and plant science
technologies.

COMERCIAL AMERICAN INS. CO., DIV. SEGCOAM
2700 Post Oak Boulevard, Ste.1110, Houston, TX 77056

CEO: Alfonso Romo Garza   Tel: (713) 960-1214   %FO: JV

Bus: *Engaged in property/casualty, life,*   Fax: (713) 960-1214
health and financial services.

SEMINIS, INC.
2700 Camino del Sol, Oxnard, CA 93030

CEO: Eugenio Najera Solorzano, CEO   Tel: (805) 647-1572   %FO: 100

Bus: *Producer of fruit and vegetable*   Fax: (805) 918-2545   Emp: 3,800
seeds.

- **TAMSA (TUBOS DE ACERO DE MEXICO, S.A.)**
  KM 433.5 Carretera, Mexico-Xalapa, Veracruz, Mexico
  CEO: Gerardo Varela, CFO   Tel: 52-5282-9900   Rev: $713
  Bus: *Manufacture/produce seamless steel*   Fax: 52-2282-9964   Emp: 2,553
  pipe.   www.tamsa.com.mx

  > **DST**
  > 4511 Brittmoore Road, Houston, TX   77041
  > CEO: Alex Di Bagno, Pres.   Tel: (713) 767-4400   %FO: 100
  > Bus: *Sales/distribution of seamless steel*   Fax: (713) 767-4444
  > *pipe.*

- **TELEFONOS DE MEXICO, S.A. DE C.V.**
  Parque Via 190 Colonia Cuauhtemoc, 06599 Mexico, D.F., Mexico
  CEO: Jaime Chico Pardo, CEO   Tel: 52-5-703-3990   Rev: $10,650
  Bus: *Provides local and long-distance*   Fax: 52-5-545-5550   Emp: 72,325
  telephone service.   www.telmex.com.mx

  > **TOPP TELECOM, INC.**
  > 8390 Northwest 25th Street, Miami, FL   33122
  > CEO: F. J. Pollak, CEO   Tel: (305) 640-2000   %FO: 100
  > Bus: *Engaged in telecommunications.*   Fax: (305) 908-2987

- **TRANSMISIONES Y EQUIPOS - MECANICOS SA DE CV**
  Avenida 5 de Febrero 2115, 76120 Queretaro, Mexico
  CEO: Luis Fernandez, Dir.   Tel: 52-42-170-717
  Bus: *Mfr. manual transmissions, gears,*   Fax: 52-42-170-345   Emp: 1,600
  shafts, synchronizers.

  > **TRANSMISSIONS TECHNOLOGY INC.**
  > 23382 Commerce Drive, Farmington Hills, MI   48335
  > CEO: Lee Davis, VP & Mgn Dir   Tel: (248) 471-3200   %FO: 100
  > Bus: *Sale/distribution automotive*   Fax: (248) 471-3722   Emp: 29
  > *manual transmissions, gears,*
  > *shafts, synchronizers.*

- **VECTOR CASA DE BOLSA S.A. de C.V.**
  Avenida Roble 565, Coloina Valle del Compestre, 66265 Garza Garcia, Mexico
  CEO: Pedro Aspe, CEO   Tel: 52-8-318-3500
  Bus: *Securities broker/dealer.*   Fax: 52-8-318-3535   Emp: 350
  www.vector.com.mx

  > **VECTORMEX INC**
  > 535 Madison Avenue, 2nd Fl., New York, NY   10022-4212
  > CEO: Sergio Sanchez, Chmn. & Pres.   Tel: (212) 407-5500   %FO: 100
  > Bus: *Securities broker/dealer.*   Fax: (212) 407-5555   Emp: 25

● **VITRO, SA DE CV**

Av. Ricardo Margain Zozaya 400, Col. Valle del Campestre, 66265 Garza Garcia Nuevo Leon, Mexico

CEO: Federico Sada Gonzalez, CEO   Tel: 52-8-329-1200

Bus: *Producer of glass.*   Fax: 52-8-329-1290   Emp: 33,800

www.vto.com

V. V. P. AMERICA INC.

PO Box 171173, Memphis, TN   38187

CEO: Mark A. Burke, Pres. & CEO   Tel: (901) 767-7111   %FO: 100

Bus: *Engaged in the fabrication, distribution, and installation of glass in the construction, automotive replacement, and furniture markets.*   Fax: (800) 238-6057

Monaco

- **SEA HORSE INTERNATIONAL**
  Chateau d'Azur, Block B, 44, blvd. d'Italie, 98000 Monte Carlo, Monaco
  CEO: Capt. Assem Elbendary, Pres.

  Bus: *Business of managing, mitigating and verifying losses arising from ocean marine claims.*

  Tel: 377-9315-9657
  Fax: 377-9315-9658
  www.shorse.com

  SEA HORSE INTERNATIONAL
  2052 Rockingham Street, McLean, VA   22101
  CEO: Capt. Assem Elbendary, Pres.

  Bus: *Business of managing, mitigating and verifying losses arising from ocean marine claims.*

  Tel: (703) 237-9046
  Fax: (703) 241-7562

  %FO: 100

Morocco

- **ROYAL AIR MAROC**
  Sieje, Casa-Ansa, Casablanca, Morocco
  CEO: Pres. Hassad
  Bus: *Commercial air transport services.*
  Tel: 21-2-231-1122
  Fax: 21-2-236-0520
  www.royalairmaroc.com
  Rev: $590

  ROYAL AIR MAROC
  55 East 59th Street, Ste 17B, New York, NY   10019
  CEO: Pres. Hassad
  Bus: *Commercial air transport services.*
  Tel: (212) 750-5115
  Fax: (212) 754-4215
  %FO: 100

Netherlands

• ACORDIS BV

PO Box 9600, NL-6800 TC, Arnhem, Netherlands

CEO: Folkert Blaisse, CEO

Bus: *Mfr. synthetic and specialty fibers, including acrylic, polyester and nylon.*

Tel: 31-26-366-4444
Fax: 31-26-366-4692
www.acordis.com

Rev: $2,257
Emp: 16,600

ACORDIS CELLULOSIC FIBERS INC.

PO Box 141, Axis, AL   35605

CEO: Glen Smith

Bus: *Mfr./sales cellulosic rayon fibers.*

Tel: (334) 679-2200
Fax: (334) 679-2350

%FO: 100

ACORDIS INDUSTRIAL FIBERS INC.

7526 Akzo Boulevard, Scottsboro, AL   35769-8106

CEO: L. Bevins, Mgr.

Bus: *Plant for manufacture of industrial fibers.*

Tel: (256) 574-7200
Fax: (256) 574-7274

%FO: 100

CLARIFOIL, DIV. ACORDIS ACETATE CHEMICALS LTD.

9 South Virginia Court, Englewood Cliffs, NJ   07632

CEO: Don Taylor

Bus: *Mfr./sales acetate fibers and textiles.*

Tel: (201) 541-2476
Fax: (201) 541-2478

%FO: 100

COLBOND INC., DIV. ACORDIS

PO Box 1057, Enka, NC   28728

CEO: J. von Boldrik, Pres.

Bus: *Mfr./sales geosynthetics.*

Tel: (828) 665-5000
Fax: (828) 665-5065

%FO: 100

TENCEL, DIV. ACORDIS

111 West 40th Street, 34th Street, New York, NY   10019

CEO: David Adkins

Bus: *Manufacturing and sales of textiles.*

Tel: (212) 944-7400
Fax: (212) 944-7406

%FO: 100

• AEGON N.V.

PO Box 202, The Hague NL-2501 CE, Netherlands

CEO: Kees J. Storm, Chmn.

Bus: *Provides insurance and financial services.*

Tel: 31-70-344-3210
Fax: 31-70-344-8445
www.aegon.be

Rev: $19,308
Emp: 24,315

AEGON USA, INC.
1111 North Charles Street, Baltimore, MD   21201
CEO: Donald J. Shepard, Chmn. & Pres.   Tel: (410) 576-4571   %FO: 100
Bus: *Insurance & financial services.*   Fax: (410) 347-8686   Emp: 10,000

AUSA LIFE INSURANCE COMPANY INC.
Four Manhattanville Road, Purchase, NY   10577
CEO: Thomas A. Schlossberg, Pres.   Tel: (914) 697-8000
Bus: *Insurance services.*   Fax: (914) 697-3743

DIVERSIFIED INVESTMENT ADVISORS, INC.
Four Manhattanville Road, Purchase, NY   10577
CEO: Thomas A. Schlossberg, Pres.   Tel: (914) 697-8000   %FO: 100
Bus: *Investment advisory services.*   Fax: (914) 697-3743

FIRST AUSA LIFE INSURANCE CO.
4333 Edgewood Road NE, Cedar Rapids, IA   52499
CEO: Patrick S. Baird, COO   Tel: (319) 398-8660
Bus: *Provides insurance services.*   Fax: (319) 369-2218

LIBERTY INTERNATIONAL UNDERWRITERS
61 Broadway, 32nd Fl., New York, NY   10006
CEO: Victor M. Yerrill, CEO   Tel: (212) 208-4100   %FO: 100
Bus: *Insurance services.*   Fax: (212) 635-3621

MONUMENTAL GENERAL CASUALTY COMPANY
8019 Corporate Drive, Ste. J, Baltimore, MD   21201
CEO: Steven Burkett, Mgr.   Tel: (410) 931-1020
Bus: *Insurance services.*   Fax: (410) 347-8693

MONUMENTAL LIFE INSURANCE COMPANY
1111 North Charles Street, Baltimore, MD   21201
CEO: Henry G. Hagan, Pres.   Tel: (410) 685-2900   %FO: 100
Bus: *Insurance services.*   Fax: (410) 347-8686   Emp: 1,600

TRANSAMERICA BUSINESS CREDIT CORP.
9399 West Higgins Road, Rosemont, IL   60018
CEO: Steven A. Read, CEO   Tel: (847) 292-8900   %FO: 100
Bus: *Engaged in insurance and*   Fax: (847) 685-1140
    financial services.

TRANSAMERICA CORPORATION
4333 Edgewater Road, NE, Cedar Rapids, IA   52499-0010
CEO: Frank C. Herringer, Chmn.   Tel: (415) 983-4000   %FO: 100
Bus: *Insurance services.*   Fax: (415) 983-4234

TRANSAMERICA DISTRIBUTION FINANCE CORP.
1701 Golf Road, Rolling Meadows, IL   60008
CEO: James L. Schoedinger, CEO   Tel: (847) 747-6800   %FO: 100
Bus: *Engaged in insurance and*   Fax: (847) 747-7451
     financial services.

TRANSAMERICA OCCIDENTAL LIFE INSURANCE
1150 South Olive Street, Los Angeles, CA   90015
CEO: Ron F. Wagley, Pres.   Tel: (213) 742-2111   %FO: 100
Bus: *Engaged in insurance and*   Fax: (213) 741-5969
     financial services.

TRANSAMERICA REAL ESTATE TAX SERVICE
1201 Elm Street, Dallas, TX   75270
CEO: Russell T. Charlton, Pres.   Tel: (214) 571-1500   %FO: 100
Bus: *Engaged in real estate tax services.* Fax: (214) 571-2329

● **AKZO NOBEL N.V.**
PO Box 9300, 76 Velperweg, NL-6800 5B, SB Arnhem, Netherlands
CEO: Cees J. A. van Lede, Chmn.   Tel: 31-26-366-4433   Rev: $13,188
Bus: *Mfr. chemicals, man-made fibers, salt,* Fax: 31-26-366-3250   Emp: 68,400
     coatings, pharmaceuticals.   www.akzonobel.com

AKZO NOBEL COATINGS, INC.
PO Box 37230, Louisville, KY   40233
CEO: Robert J. Torba, Pres.   Tel: (502) 375-5452   %FO: 100
Bus: *Mfr. distribution of industrial* Fax: (502) 375-5463   Emp: 60
     coatings.

AKZO NOBEL COATINGS, INC.
PO Box 7062, Troy, MI   48007
CEO: J. Theo Bouwens, Mgr.   Tel: (248) 637-0400   %FO: 100
Bus: *Mfr./sales plastic closures and* Fax: (248) 649-3584
     overcaps.

AKZO NOBEL RESINS
PO Box 1950, Baxley, GA   31515
CEO: Goran Jonsson   Tel: (912) 367-3616   %FO: 100
Bus: *Mfr./sales resins.*   Fax: (912) 367-5754

AKZO NOBEL RESINS
PO Box 37510, Louisville, KY   40233
CEO: Goran Jonsson   Tel: (502) 367-6111   %FO: 100
Bus: *Mfr./sales resins.*   Fax: (502) 375-5477

AKZO NOBEL RESINS
PO Box 638, New Brunswick, NJ 08903
CEO: M. de Haan   Tel: (732) 247-2202   %FO: 100
Bus: *Mfr./sales resins.*   Fax: (732) 247-2287

AKZO NOBEL RESINS & VEHICLES
21625 Oak Street, Matteson, IL 60443
CEO: Ken Malin, Mgr.   Tel: (708) 481-8900   %FO: 100
Bus: *Mfr./sales resins.*   Fax: (708) 481-5978

AKZO NOBEL RESINS & VEHICLES
2904 Missouri Avenue East, St. Louis, IL 62205
CEO: Ken Malin   Tel: (618) 271-6601   %FO: 100
Bus: *Mfr./sales resins.*   Fax: (618) 874-5228

AKZO NOBEL, INC.
300 South Riverside Plaza, Chicago, IL 60606
CEO: Piet P. Kluit, Pres.   Tel: (312) 906-7500   %FO: 100
Bus: *Mfr. salt/basic chemicals,*   Fax: (312) 906-7545
pharmaceuticals & coatings,
plastics.

COURTAULDS FIBERS INC.
PO Box 141, Axis, AL 36505
CEO: David Duthie, CEO   Tel: (334) 679-2200   %FO: 100
Bus: *Mfr./sales of cellulosic fibers,*   Fax: (334) 679-2452
viscose and tencel.

COURTAULDS PACKAGING LAMINATE TUBES N.A.
7850 Foundation Drive, Florence, KY 41042
CEO: Charles Dudgeon, Pres.   Tel: (606) 342-8900   %FO: 100
Bus: *Mfr./sales plastic and laminate*   Fax: (606) 342-8528
tubes and bottle enclosures.

DIOSYNTH, INC.
2136 South Wolf Road, Des Plaines, IL 60018
CEO: Geraldine Roman, Mgr.   Tel: (847) 635-0985   %FO: 100
Bus: *Mfr./sales pharmaceutical raw*   Fax: (847) 635-1320
materials.

FORTAFIL FIBERS INC.
8870 Cedar Springs Lane, Knoxville, TN 37923
CEO: Roger Prescott, Pres.   Tel: (800) 252-3001   %FO: 100
Bus: *Mfr./sales carbon fibers.*   Fax: (865) 694-7547

KNIGHT ENGINEERING AND PLASTIC
1008 Courtaulds Drive, Woodstock, IL 60098
CEO: Steven Cassidy, Pres.   Tel: (815) 334-1240   %FO: 100
Bus: *Mfr./sales plastic closures and*   Fax: (815) 334-1244
  overcaps.

● AMBAC B.V.
Terheydenseweg 169, NL-4800 DH, Breda, Netherlands
CEO: T. Toussaints, Dir.   Tel: 31-76-579-2700
Bus: *Mfr. precision mechanical products.* Fax: 31-76-587-7434

AMBAC INTERNATIONAL
27 Baynard Park Road, Hilton Head Island, SC 29928
CEO: Stewart H. Rodman, CEO   Tel: (843) 363-6470   %FO: 100
Bus: *Sales/distribution of precision*   Fax: (843) 363-6472
  mechanical products.

● AMMERAAL BELTECH BV
PO Box 38, NL-1700 AA, Heerhugowaard Netherlands
CEO: I. A. Roberti, CEO   Tel: 31-72-575-1212
Bus: *Manufacturer of industrial conveyor* Fax: 31-72-571-6455
  belting.   www.ammeraalbeltech.com

AMMERAAL BELTECH, INC.
7501 Saint Louis Avenue, Skokie, IL 60076
CEO: Dieter Jung   Tel: (847) 673-6720   %FO: 100
Bus: *Mfr. and sales of conveyor belting.* Fax: (847) 673-6373

AMMERAAL BELTECH, INC.
3720 Three Mile Road NW, Grand Rapids, MI 49504
CEO: Jim Honeycutt   Tel: (616) 791-0162   %FO: 100
Bus: *Mfr. and sales of conveyor belting.* Fax: (616) 791-1067

● ANKER COAL COMPANY B.V.
Vasteland 4, NL-3000 BK, Rotterdam, Netherlands
CEO: K. Zubli, Mng. Dir.   Tel: 31-10-452-9566   Rev: $250
Bus: *Sales and export of coal.*   Fax: 31-10-452-9073
                                          www.ankercoal.nv

ANKER ENERGY
PO Box 4360, Star City, WV 26504
CEO: Gerald Peacock, Pres.   Tel: (304) 983-8710   %FO: 100
Bus: *Coal mining and preparation.*   Fax: (304) 983-8714

ANKER ENERGY CORPORATION, VANTRANS DIV.
2708 Cranberry Square, Morgantown, WV   26505
CEO: William D. Kilgore   Tel: (304) 594-1616   %FO: 100
Bus: *Sales and export of coal.*   Fax: (304) 594-3695

ANKER WV MINING, SPRUCE FORK DIV.
Route 6, Box 543, Buckhannon, WV   26201
CEO: Gary McCauley, Pres.   Tel: (304) 472-5201   %FO: 100
Bus: *Coal mining and preparation.*   Fax: (304) 472-5223

MARINE COAL SALES COMPANY
645 West Carmel Drive, Ste. 190, Carmel, IN   46032
CEO: Larry Kaelin, Pres.   Tel: (317) 844-6628   %FO: 100
Bus: *Tank storage for liquid bulk*   Fax: (317) 844-6628
    products.

PHILIPPI DEVELOPMENT, INC., SENTINEL MINES
Route 3, Box 146, Philippi, WV   26416
CEO: Gary McCauley, Pres.   Tel: (304) 457-1895   %FO: 100
Bus: *Coal mining and preparation.*   Fax: (304) 457-1005

● **ANSALDO SIGNAL N.V., SUB. FINMECCANICA**
Schiphol Boulevard 267, NL-1118 BH, Schiphol, Netherlands
CEO: Roberto Gagliardi, Chmn.   Tel: 31-20-405-9841   Rev: $355
Bus: *Design, manufacture and service of*   Fax: 31-20-405-9842   Emp: 2,400
    signaling, automation and control   www.switch.com
    equipment and systems for the railroad
    and mass transit industries.

UNION SWITCH & SIGNAL INC.
78 Lake Road, Ballston Lake, NY   12019
CEO: Ken Gaus, Reg. Mgr.   Tel: (518) 371-2410   %FO: 100
Bus: *Sales/distribution of railroad*   Fax: (518) 371-2413
    signal, automation and control
    systems.

UNION SWITCH & SIGNAL INC.
*Two World Trade Center, Ste. 3050, New York, NY   10048
CEO: Kenneth Burk, Pres.   Tel: (212) 839-6806   %FO: 100
Bus: *Sales/distribution of railroad*   Fax: (212) 839-6810
    signal, automation and control
    systems.

UNION SWITCH & SIGNAL INC.

1000 Technology Drive, Pittsburgh, PA   15219

CEO: Kenneth Burk, Pres.   Tel: (412) 688-2400   %FO: 100

Bus: *Sales/distribution of railroad*   Fax: (412) 688-2399
signal, automation and control
systems.

UNION SWITCH & SIGNAL INC.

16 Washington Road, Ste. 722, Princeton, NJ   08550

CEO: Kurt Tamenne, Reg. Mgr.   Tel: (609) 716-9325   %FO: 100

Bus: *Sales/distribution of railroad*   Fax: (609) 716-9441
signal, automation and control
systems.

UNION SWITCH & SIGNAL INC.

645 Russell Street, Batesburg, SC   29006

CEO: Kenneth Burk, Pres.   Tel: (803) 532-4432   %FO: 100

Bus: *Sales/distribution of railroad*   Fax: (803) 532-2940
signal, automation and control
systems.

UNION SWITCH & SIGNAL INC.

455 S. Frontage Road, Ste. 102, Burr Ridge, IL   60521

CEO: Frank Pohle, Reg. Mgr.   Tel: (630) 323-3969   %FO: 100

Bus: *Sales/distribution of railroad*   Fax: (630) 323-3969
signal, automation and control
systems.

● **ARCADIS NV**

PO Box 33, NL-6800 LE, Amhem, Netherlands

CEO: Harrie L. J. Noy, Chmn.   Tel: 31-26-377-8911   Rev: $519

Bus: *Engaged in international consulting,*   Fax: 31-26-351-5235   Emp: 7,750
engineering and contracting.   www.arcadis.nl

   ARCADIS G&M

   3000 Cabot Blvd. West, Ste. 3004, Langhorne, PA   19047

   CEO: Joseph Hastey, CEO   Tel: (215) 752-6840   %FO: 100

   Bus: *Engaged in environmental and*   Fax: (215) 752-6879
   engineering consulting services.

   ARCADIS G&M

   5608 Parkcrest Drive, Ste. 300, Austin, TX   78731

   CEO: Robert Miller, VP   Tel: (512) 451-1188   %FO: 100

   Bus: *Engaged in environmental and*   Fax: (512) 451-2930
   engineering consulting services.

ARCADIS G&M
2849 Paces Ferry Road, Ste. 400, Atlanta, GA   30339
CEO: Joe Wright, Pres.   Tel: (770) 431-8666   %FO: 100
Bus: *Engaged in environmental and*   Fax: (770) 435-2666
engineering consulting services.

ARCADIS G&M
35 East Wacker Drive, Ste. 1000, Chicago, IL   60601
CEO: Phil Hutton, Pres.   Tel: (312) 263-6703   %FO: 100
Bus: *Engaged in environmental and*   Fax: (312) 263-7897
engineering consulting services.

ARCADIS G&M
41511 Eleven Mile Road, Novi, MI   48375
CEO: Kurt Kramer, Pres.   Tel: (248) 305-9400   %FO: 100
Bus: *Engaged in environmental and*   Fax: (248) 305-9401
engineering consulting services.

ARCADIS G&M
630 Plaza Drive, Ste. 200, Denver, CO   80126
CEO: Joseph Hastey, CEO   Tel: (720) 344-3500   %FO: 100
Bus: *U.S. headquarters location for*   Fax: (720) 344-3535
environmental and engineering
consulting services.

ARCADIS G&M
175 Cabot Street, Ste. 503, Lowell, MA   01854
CEO: Charles Castelluccio, Pres.   Tel: (978) 937-9999   %FO: 100
Bus: *Engaged in environmental and*   Fax: (978) 937-7555
engineering consulting services.

ARCADIS G&M
1400 N. Harbor Blvd., Ste. 700, Fullerton, CA   92835-4127
CEO: Steve Figgins, Mgr.   Tel: (714) 278-0992   %FO: 100
Bus: *Engaged in environmental and*   Fax: (714) 278-0051
engineering consulting services.

ARCADIS G&M
1131 Benfield Blvd., Ste. A, Millersville, MD   21108
CEO: John Barron, Mgr.   Tel: (410) 987-0032   %FO: 100
Bus: *Engaged in environmental and*   Fax: (410) 987-4392
engineering consulting services.

ARCADIS G&M

88 Duryea Road, Melville, NY   11747

CEO: Tom Lobasso, Mgr.	Tel: (516) 249-7600	%FO: 100

Bus: *Engaged in environmental and*   Fax: (516) 249-7610
engineering consulting services.

ARCADIS G&M

600 Sandtree Drive, Ste. 106, Palm Beach Gardens, FL   33403

CEO: William Vogelsong, Mng. Dir.   Tel: (561) 694-0300   %FO: 100

Bus: *Engaged in environmental and*   Fax: (561) 622-6379
engineering consulting services.

ARCADIS G&M

11490 Westheimer, Ste. 600, Houston, TX   70777

CEO: William Wozny, CEO   Tel: (281) 496-9737   %FO: 100

Bus: *Engaged in environmental and*   Fax: (281) 496-2936
engineering consulting services.

ARCADIS G&M

2301 Rexwood Drive, Ste. 200, Raleigh, NC   27607

CEO: Mike Ray, Pres.   Tel: (919) 782-5511   %FO: 100

Bus: *Engaged in environmental and*   Fax: (919) 782-5905
engineering consulting services.

ARCADIS G&M

126 N. Jefferson Street, Ste. 400, Milwaukee, WI   53202

CEO: Kathy Niesen, Mgr.   Tel: (414) 276-7742   %FO: 100

Bus: *Engaged in environmental and*   Fax: (414) 276-7603
engineering consulting services.

ARCADIS GIFFELS

PO Box 5025, Southfield, MI   48086

CEO: Douglas J. Sordye   Tel: (248) 936-8000   %FO: 100

Bus: *Engaged in international*   Fax: (248) 936-8111
consulting, engineering and
contracting.

ARCADIS JSA

301 East Ocean Blvd., Ste. 1530, Long Beach, CA   90802

CEO: Brenda Sanders   Tel: (562) 628-1176   %FO: 100

Bus: *Engaged in international*   Fax: (562) 628-1196
consulting, engineering and
contracting.

● **ASM INTERNATIONAL N.V.**

De Run 1110, NL-5500 AH, Veldhoen, Netherlands

CEO: Dougl J. Dunn, Chmn. & CEO	Tel: 31-40-268-4941	Rev: $2,029
Bus: *Mfr. semiconductor lithography equipment.*	Fax: 31-40-268-3635 www.asml.com	Emp: 4,377

ASM AMERICA INC.

86 Pearl Street, Essex Junction, VT   05452

CEO: Daniel Queyssac, Pres.	Tel: (802) 879-5255	%FO: 100
Bus: *Mfr./sales semiconductor equipment.*	Fax: (802) 879-1301	

ASM AMERICA INC.

1018 Bethlehem Pike, Ste. 201B, Spring House, PA   19477

CEO: Daniel Queyssac, Pres.	Tel: (215) 646-7791	%FO: 100
Bus: *Mfr./sales semiconductor equipment.*	Fax: (215) 646-8604	

ASM AMERICA INC.

97 East Brokaw Road, Ste. 100, San Jose, CA   95112-4209

CEO: Doug Traina, Pres.	Tel: (408) 451-0830	%FO: 100
Bus: *Mfr./sales semiconductor equipment.*	Fax: (408) 451-0825	

ASM AMERICA INC.

5446 Highway 290 West, Ste. 107, Austin, TX   78735

CEO: Daniel Queyssac, Pres.	Tel: (512) 892-9062	%FO: 100
Bus: *Mfr./sales semiconductor equipment.*	Fax: (512) 892-9063	

ASM AMERICA INC.

3440 East University Drive, Phoenix, AZ   85034

CEO: Daniel Queyssac, Pres.	Tel: (602) 470-5700	%FO: 100
Bus: *Mfr./sales semiconductor equipment.*	Fax: (602) 437-8497	

ASM PACIFIC ASSEMBLY PRODUCTS INC.

3440 East University Drive, Phoenix, AZ   85034

CEO: Daniel Queyssac, Pres.	Tel: (602) 437-4760	%FO: 100
Bus: *Mfr./sales semiconductor equipment.*	Fax: (602) 437-4630	

SILICON VALLEY GROUP, INC.

101 Metro Drive, Ste. 400, San Jose, CA   95110

CEO: Papken S. Der Torossian, CEO	Tel: (408) 441-6700	%FO: 100
Bus: *Mfr. Automated wafer processing equipment.*	Fax: (408) 467-5828	

● **AVIKO, BV**

Postbus 8, NL-7220 CD, Steenderen, Netherlands

CEO: J. Zikken, Pres. Tel: 31-57-545-8200

Bus: *Engaged in potato processing for* Fax: 31-57-545-8380
retailing and catering trades. www.aviko.com

    AVIKO USA

    PO Box 1980, Jamestown, ND   58402-1980

    CEO: Jerry Decoteau, VP Tel: (701) 252-5222 %FO: 100

    Bus: *Potato processing plant.* Fax: (701) 252-6863

● **BAAN COMPANY N.V., DIV. INVENSYS PLC**

PO Box 143, NL-3770 AC, Barneveld, Netherlands

CEO: Laurens van der Tang, CEO Tel: 31-34-242-8888 Rev: $620

Bus: *Provides business software application* Fax: 31-34-242-8822 Emp: 5,000
and consulting services. www.baan.com

    BAAN USA

    4851 LBJ Freeway, Ste. 200, Dallas, TX   75244

    CEO: Susan Heystee, Pres. Tel: (972) 383-7302 %FO: 100

    Bus: *Sales/distribution of business* Fax: (972) 383-7310
    software application.

    BAAN USA

    2191 Fox Mill Road, 5th Fl., Herndon, VA   20171

    CEO: Susan Heystee, Pres. Tel: (703) 471-8785 %FO: 100

    Bus: *Sales/distribution of business* Fax: (703) 234-6719
    software application.

    BAAN USA

    6000 28th Street SE, Grand Rapids, MI   49546

    CEO: Tony Casciato Tel: (616) 942-7444 %FO: 100

    Bus: *Sales/distribution of business* Fax: (616) 942-8167
    software application.

    BAAN USA

    5100 River Road, 3rd Fl., Schiller Park, IL   60176

    CEO: Ed Walovitch, VP Tel: (847) 928-3600 %FO: 100

    Bus: *Sales/distribution of business* Fax: (847) 678-9450
    software application.

● **BALLAST NEDAM N.V.**

PO Box 500, NL-1180 BE, Amstelveen, Netherlands

CEO: Martin J.F. Weck, Chmn. Tel: 31-20-545-9111 Rev: $2,432

Bus: *Engineering, construction, dredging,* Fax: 31-20-647-3000 Emp: 8,545
excavation, ship-building, project www.ballast-nedam.nl
management.

BALLAST NEDAM CONSTRUCTION, INC.

2800 Biscayne Boulevard, Ste. 730, Miami, FL   33137

CEO:Ger Van Der Schaaf, Gen.Mgr.   Tel: (305) 576-6617   %FO: 100

Bus: *Construction and dredging*   Fax: (305) 576-6890
equipment services.

● BCD HOLDINGS N.V. (BTI/HOGG ROBINSON)

Utrechtseweg 67, NL-3704 HB, Zeist, Netherlands

CEO: John Fentener van Vlissingen   Tel: 31-30-695-8404

Bus: *Engaged in travel management and*   Fax: 31-30-695-9771
corporate travel solutions.   www.bti-worldwide.com

ATLANTA REALTY MANAGEMENT GROUP, INC., DIV. NORO REALTY

2581 Piedmont Road, Ste. A 580, Atlanta, GA   30324

CEO:John W. Sexton, Pres.   Tel: (404) 233-1902   %FO: 100

Bus: *Property management.*   Fax: (404) 261-4283

BCD HOLDINGS N.V.

2060 Mount Paran Road, Ste. 207, Atlanta, GA   30327

CEO:Fred Clemente, CEO   Tel: (404) 264-1000   %FO: 100

Bus: *Holding company.*   Fax: (404) 364-0477

PRIMARY CAPITAL ADVISORS, L.C.

2060 Mount Paran Road, Ste. 101, Atlanta, GA   30327

CEO:William B. Pendleton, Pres.   Tel: (404) 365-9300   %FO: 100

Bus: *Commercial mortgage banking.*   Fax: (404) 266-1448

WORLD TRAVEL / BTI

1055 Lenox Park Boulevard, Atlanta, GA   30319

CEO:Jack C. Alexander, CEO   Tel: (404) 841-6600   %FO: 100

Bus: *Corporate, group, and event travel.* Fax: (404) 814-2983

● BE SEMICONDUCTOR INDUSTRIES N.V.

Marconilaan 4, NL-5151 DR, Drunen, Netherlands

CEO: Richard W. Blickman, CEO   Tel: 31-41-638-4345   Rev: $186

Bus: *Produces integrated systems for*   Fax: 31-416-384-344   Emp: 775
semiconductor equipment industry.   www.besi.nl

FICO AMERICA

15720 Winchester Blvd., Ste. 4, Los Gatos, CA   95030

CEO:Richard W. Blickman, Pres. &   Tel: (408) 399-4580   %FO: 100
CEO

Bus: *Produces integrated systems for*   Fax: (408) 399-4582
semiconductor equipment industry.

FICO AMERICA

3630-1 North Josey Lane, Ste. 100, Carrollton, TX 75007

CEO: Al Stroscher, Mgr. Tel: (214) 395-2106

Bus: *Produces integrated systems for* Fax: (214) 395-2116
semiconductor equipment industry.

FICO AMERICA, INC.

224 E. Chilton Drive, Ste. 9, Chandler, AZ 85225

CEO: M. Melissa, Mgr. Tel: (480) 497-8190 %FO: 100

Bus: *Mfr. high quality production and* Fax: (480) 497-9104
inspection equipment for the
semiconductor industry.

LILOGIX RD AUTOMATION

121 Ethel Road West, Piscataway, NJ 08854

CEO: Steve Bendat Tel: (732) 572-4800 %FO: 100

Bus: *Mfr. high quality production and* Fax: (732) 572-4808
inspection equipment for the
semiconductor industry.

● **BENIER B.V., DIV. KAAK GROUP**

PO Box 2165, NL-5222 BS, 's-Hertogenbosch, Netherlands

CEO: P. C. F. Oud, Dir. Tel: 31-73-621-7225

Bus: *Mfr. of dough processing equipment for* Fax: 31-73-621-5769
baking industries. www.benier.com

BENIER USA INC., DIV. KAAK

213 Thornton Road, Ste. 400, Lithia Springs, GA 30122

CEO: Hans Van Der Maarel, Pres. Tel: (770) 745-2200 %FO: 100

Bus: *Sales, distribution and service of* Fax: (770) 745-0050
machinery for the baking business.

● **BORSTLAP B.V.**

Zevenheuvelenweg 44, NL-5048 AN, Tilburg, Netherlands

CEO: J. M. A. Borstlap, Dir. Tel: 31-13-594-1234

Bus: *Metric fasteners.* Fax: 31-13-594-1212
www.borstlap.com

FABORY USA LTD.

824 East Fairplay Boulevard, Fairplay, SC 29643

CEO: Ken Morrison, Pres. Tel: (864) 972-2170 %FO: 100

Bus: *Import/sales/distribution of metric* Fax: (864) 972-2471
fasteners and hardware.

FABORY USA LTD.
7110 Golden Ring Road, Ste. 105, Baltimore, MD 21221
CEO: Remi Swart, Mgr.   Tel: (410) 780-0311   %FO: 100
Bus: *Import/sales/distribution of metric*   Fax: (410) 780-0384
    fasteners and hardware.

FABORY USA LTD.
6095 Rickenbacker Road, Los Angeles, CA 90040
CEO: Jennifer Moisa, Mgr.   Tel: (323) 726-9944   %FO: 100
Bus: *Import/sales/distribution of metric*   Fax: (323) 726-6718
    fasteners and hardware.

FABORY USA LTD.
2240 29th Street, Grand Rapids, MI 49508
CEO: Ken Morrison, Pres.   Tel: (616) 247-4777   %FO: 100
Bus: *Import/sales/distribution of metric*   Fax: (616) 247-0408
    fasteners and hardware.

FABORY USA LTD.
1360 Donaldson Road, Ste. D, Erlinger, KY 41018
CEO: Ken Morrison, Pres.   Tel: (859) 282-8100   %FO: 100
Bus: *Import/sales/distribution of metric*   Fax: (859) 282-8250
    fasteners and hardware.

● **BUHRMANN N.V.**
Postbus 23456 NL-1100 DZ, Amsterdam, Netherlands
CEO: Frans H. J. Koffrie, Chmn. & CEO   Tel: 31-20-651-1111   Rev: $9,500
Bus: *Mfr. graphic paper, distribute business*   Fax: 31-20-651-1000   Emp: 28,000
    machines & graphic systems, mfr.   www.buhrmann.com
    packaging, distribute paper/office
    products.

ASAP SOFTWARE EXPRESS
850 Asbury Drive, Buffalo Grove, IL 60089
CEO: Paul Jarvee, Pres.   Tel: (847) 465-3700   %FO: 100
Bus: *Sales/support PC software.*   Fax: (847) 465-3734

BT OFFICE PRODUCTS INTERNATIONAL, INC.
6371 Burnt Poplar Road, Greensboro, NC 27409
CEO: Kevin Diamond, Pres.   Tel: (336) 852-3112   %FO: 100
Bus: *Mfr./sales/distribution printing*   Fax: (336) 852-3013
    equipment.

BT OFFICE PRODUCTS INTERNATIONAL, INC.
303 West 10th Street, 4th Fl., New York, NY 10014
CEO: Peter Guala, Pres.
Bus: *Sales/distribution of office products.*
Tel: (212) 242-5300
Fax: (212) 242-3854
%FO: 70

BT OFFICE PRODUCTS INTERNATIONAL, INC.
500 108th Street Ave. NE 800, Bellevue, WA 98004
CEO: Marco Bes, Mgr.
Bus: *Mfr./sales/distribution of specialized packaging equipment.*
Tel: (425) 646-7484
Fax: (425) 646-7483
%FO: 100

BT OFFICE PRODUCTS INTERNATIONAL, INC.
6900 Lindenbergh Blvd., Ste. 200, Philadelphia, PA 19128
CEO: Gary Deblais, Pres.
Bus: *Mfr./sales/distribution printing equipment.*
Tel: (215) 365-2171
Fax: (215) 863-3210
%FO: 100

BT OFFICE PRODUCTS INTERNATIONAL, INC.
79 North Industrial Park, Glenfield, PA 15143
CEO: John R. Kennedy, Pres.
Bus: *Mfr./sales/distribution printing equipment.*
Tel: (412) 741-6494
Fax: (412) 741-8726
%FO: 100

BT OFFICE PRODUCTS INTERNATIONAL, INC.
7301 Pinemont Drive, Houston, TX 77040
CEO: Joe Cox, VP
Bus: *Mfr./sales/distribution printing equipment.*
Tel: (713) 690-8181
Fax: (713) 690-0133
%FO: 100

BT OFFICE PRODUCTS INTERNATIONAL, INC.
5656 West 74th Street, Indianapolis, IN 46278
CEO: Rod Idle, Pres.
Bus: *Mfr./sales/distribution printing equipment.*
Tel: (317) 298-0808
Fax: (317) 328-4970
%FO: 100

BT OFFICE PRODUCTS INTERNATIONAL, INC.
5000 Tremont Avenue, Davenport, IA 52807
CEO: Ford Schick, Pres.
Bus: *Mfr./sales/distribution printing equipment.*
Tel: (319) 386-7600
Fax: (319) 386-4986
%FO: 100

BT OFFICE PRODUCTS INTERNATIONAL, INC.
7340 Alondra Blvd., Paramount, CA 90723
CEO: Steve Stadell, Pres.
Bus: *Sales/distribution of office products.*
Tel: (562) 634-5862
Fax: (562) 634-3845
%FO: 100

BT OFFICE PRODUCTS INTERNATIONAL, INC.
13909 NE Airport Way, Portland, OR   97230
CEO: Brian Macalaufo, Pres.   Tel: (503) 239-4404   %FO: 100
Bus: *Sales/distribution of office*   Fax: (503) 731-6200
      products.

BT OFFICE PRODUCTS INTERNATIONAL, INC.
Six Parkway North, Deerfield, IL   60015
CEO: Richard Dubin, Pres. & CEO   Tel: (847) 444-4000   %FO: 70
Bus: *Holding company of U.S. divisions.* Fax: (847) 444-4040

BT OFFICE PRODUCTS INTERNATIONAL, INC.
700 West Chicago Avenue, Chicago, IL   60610
CEO: Brad Wols, Pres.   Tel: (312) 226-1000   %FO: 100
Bus: *Sales/distribution of commercial*   Fax: (312) 226-7725
      office supplies, printing and
      computer supplies.

BT OFFICE PRODUCTS INTERNATIONAL, INC.
93-01 Logo Drive West, Springdale, MD   20774
CEO: Bob Schectelson, Pres.   Tel: (301) 808-7136   %FO: 100
Bus: *Sales/distribution of office*   Fax: (301) 499-6009
      products.

BT OFFICE PRODUCTS INTERNATIONAL, INC.
6601 Overlake Place, Newark, CA   94560
CEO: D. Parsons, Pres.   Tel: (510) 732-9100   %FO: 100
Bus: *Sales/distribution of office*   Fax: (510) 293-6280
      products.

BT OFFICE PRODUCTS INTERNATIONAL, INC.
1834 Walton Road, St. Louis, MO   63114
CEO: Catherine Adams, Pres.   Tel: (314) 426-7222   %FO: 100
Bus: *Sales/distribution of office*   Fax: (314) 426-3026
      products.

BT OFFICE PRODUCTS INTERNATIONAL, INC.
114 First Avenue, Needham, MA   02194
CEO: Steve Frager, Pres.   Tel: (781) 455-9150   %FO: 100
Bus: *Mfr./sales/distribution printing*   Fax: (781) 455-0377
      equipment.

BT OFFICE PRODUCTS INTERNATIONAL, INC.
9319 Peach Palm Avenue, Tampa, FL   33619
CEO: Robert Berg, Gen. Mgr.   Tel: (813) 623-3229   %FO: 100
Bus: *Sales/distribution of office*   Fax: (813) 623-3503
      products.

BUHRMANN US INC.
One Environmental Way, Broomfield, CO   80021
CEO: Robert King, CEO   Tel: (303) 664-2000   %FO: 100
Bus: *Mfr./sales/distribution of office*   Fax: (303) 664-3622
    and computer supplies.

CORPORATE EXPRESS, INC.
1096 E. Newport Center Dr., Ste. 300, Deerfield Beach, FL   33442
CEO: Robert King, Pres.   Tel: (954) 379-5510   %FO: 100
Bus: *Imaging and graphic supplies.*   Fax: (954) 379-5486

KELLY PAPER, DIV. BT INC.
1441 East 16th Street, Los Angeles, CA   90021
CEO: Edward Pearson, Pres.   Tel: (213) 749-1311   %FO: 100
Bus: *Mfr./sales/distribution printing*   Fax: (213) 749-3637
    equipment.

● **CAMPINA MELKUNIE**
Hogeweg 9, NL-5301 LB, Zaltbommel, Netherlands
CEO: J.J.G.M. Sanders, Chmn.   Tel: 31-41-857-1300   Rev: $12,902
Bus: *Mfr. dairy and condensed powder*   Fax: 31-41-854-0066   Emp: 15,000
    products for the food and   www.campina-melkunie-nl
    pharmaceutical industries.

DMV CAMPINA INC.
1285 Rudy Street, Onalaska, WI   54632
CEO: Dave Lee, Pres.   Tel: (608) 779-7676   %FO: 100
Bus: *Mfr./sales dairy products.*   Fax: (608) 779-7666

DMV INTERNATIONAL
1712 Deltown Plaza, Fraser, NY   13753
CEO: Donald H. Combs, Pres.   Tel: (607) 746-7421   %FO: 100
Bus: *Sales/distribution of condensed*   Fax: (607) 746-7252
    powder.

● **CHICAGO BRIDGE & IRON COMPANY N.V.**
Polarisavenue 31, NL-2132 JH, Hoofddorp, Netherlands
CEO: Gerald M. Glenn, Chmn. & CEO   Tel: 31-23-568-5660   Rev: $370
Bus: *Engaged in engineering and*   Fax: 31-20-568-5661   Emp: 6,500
    construction specializing in bulk liquid www.chicago-bridge.com
    terminals.

CB&I CONSTRUCTORS, INC.
PO Box 41146, Houston, TX   77241-1146

CEO: Gerald M. Glenn, CEO	Tel: (713) 466-1226	%FO: 100
Bus: *Engaged in engineering and construction specializing in bulk liquid terminals.*	Fax: (713) 466-1259	

CB&I CONSTRUCTORS, INC.
PO Box 5650, Norcross, GA   30091-5650

CEO: Stephen P. Crain, VP Sales	Tel: (770) 446-0036	%FO: 100
Bus: *Engaged in engineering and construction specializing in bulk liquid terminals.*	Fax: (770) 449-5206	

CB&I CONSTRUCTORS, INC.
1501 N. Division Street, Plainfield, IL   60544

CEO: Gerald M. Glenn, Pres.	Tel: (815) 439-6000	%FO: 100
Bus: *Engaged in engineering and construction specializing in bulk liquid terminals.*	Fax: (815) 439-6010	

CB&I CONSTRUCTORS, INC.
21660 East Copley Drive, Ste. 250, Diamond Bar, CA   91765

CEO: Gerald M. Glenn, Pres.	Tel: (909) 860-7114	%FO: 100
Bus: *Engaged in engineering and construction specializing in bulk liquid terminals.*	Fax: (909) 860-7128	

CB&I SERVICES, INC.
44 Read's Way, New Castle, DE   19720

CEO: Gerald M. Glenn, Pres.	Tel: (302) 325-8400	%FO: 100
Bus: *Engaged in engineering and construction specializing in bulk liquid terminals.*	Fax: (302) 323-0788	

HOWE-BAKER ENGINEERS, INC.
3102 E. Fifth Street, Tyler, TX   75701

CEO: Ron Brazzel, Pres. & CEO	Tel: (903) 597-0311	%FO: 100
Bus: *Engaged in engineering and construction specializing in bulk liquid terminals.*	Fax: (903) 595-7751	Emp: 450

● **CHN GLOBAL NV**
Schiphol Blvd. 217, 10th Fl. Tower B, NL-118 BH, Schiphol Airport, Netherlands

CEO: Paolo Monferino, Pres. & CEO	Tel: 31-20-446-0429	Rev: $5,717
Bus: *Mfr. agricultural and construction equipment.*	Fax: 31-20-446-0436	Emp: 31,000
	www.newholland.com	

NEW HOLLAND CONSTRUCTION INC. , DIV. CNH GLOBAL

245 East North Avenue, Carol Stream, IL   60188

CEO: James Galddert, Pres.   Tel: (630) 260-4000   %FO: 100

Bus: *Mfr./sales agricultural and*   Fax: (630) 260-4605
construction equipment.

● **CONVEYOR BELTING NV**

Handelsstraat 1, Postbus 38, NL-1700 AA, Heerhugowaard, Netherlands

CEO: J. A. Goud, CEO   Tel: 31-72-575-1212

Bus: *Mfr. conveyor belting.*   Fax: 31-72-574-3364

　AMMERAAL INC.

　3720 Three Mile Road, Grand Rapids, MI   49544

　CEO: Paul Hamilton, Pres.   Tel: (616) 791-0162   %FO: 100

　Bus: *Mfr. conveyor belting.*   Fax: (616) 791-1067

● **COOP VERKOOP & PRODUCTIEV-ERENIGING**

Benedon Oosterdiep 27, NL-9640 AA, Groningen, Netherlands

CEO: Albert de Jonge, Chmn.   Tel: 31-598-669-111

Bus: *Engaged in potato milling, starches and*   Fax:
derivations.   www.adebe.com

　AVEBE AMERICA INC.

　4 Independence Way, Princeton, NJ   08540

　CEO: Fred S. Kaper, Pres.   Tel: (609) 520-1400   %FO: 100

　Bus: *Produces starches/chemicals.*   Fax: (609) 520-1473

● **CORE LABORATORIES**

Herenracht 424, NL-1017 BZ, Amsterdam, Netherlands

CEO: David M. Demshur, Pres. & CEO   Tel: 31-20-420-3191   Rev: $336

Bus: *Provides reservoir management services*   Fax: 31-20-627-9886   Emp: 3,900
and geological and petroleum   www.corelab.com
engineering services.

　CORE LABORATORIES, INC.

　6316 Windfern, Houston, TX   77040

　CEO: Monty L. Davis, COO   Tel: (713) 328-2673   %FO: 100

　Bus: *Provides reservoir management*   Fax: (713) 328-2150
services and geological and
petroleum engineering services.

THE PENCOR GROUP

PO Box 926, Broussard, LA   70518-0926

CEO:Bryan Sonnier, Pres.   Tel: (318) 839-9060   %FO: 100

Bus: *Engaged in design and mfr. of*   Fax: (318) 839-9070
specialty instruments, reservoir
fluid sampling and analysis and
mobile laboratory services.

● **CSM N.V.**

PO Box 349, 1000 AH Amsterdam, Nienoord 13, NL-1112 XE, Diemen, Netherlands

CEO: J. A. J. Vink, Chmn.   Tel: 31-20-590-6911   Rev: $2,420

Bus: *Mfr./distributes cake food products and*   Fax: 31-20-695-1942   Emp: 7,450
ingredients to food processors,   www.csmnv.com
retailers/institutional food service
companies.

HENRY & HENRY INC.

3765 Walden Avenue, Lancaster, NY   14086

CEO:Richard Dahlin, Mgr.   Tel: (716) 685-4000   %FO: 100

Bus: *Mfr. icing products, toppings and*   Fax: (716) 685-0160
fruit fillings for the bakery and ice
cream industries.

WESTCO BAKEMARK INC.

7351 Crider Avenue, Pico Rivera, CA   90660

CEO:Rik Bennett, Mgr.   Tel: (562) 949-1054

Bus: *Mfr. ingredients for bakery*   Fax: (562) 949-1257
products.

● **DE BRAUW BLACKSTONE WESTBROEK, LINKLATERS ALLIANCE**

Tripolis 300, Burgerweeshuispad 301, NL-1076 HR, Amsterdam, Netherlands

CEO: Baron H. Collot d'Escury, Dir.   Tel: 31-20-577-1771

Bus: *International law firm.*   Fax: 31-20-577-1775   Emp: 2,200
www.dbbw.nl

DE BRAUW BLACKSTONE, LINKLATERS ALLIANCE

1345 Avenue of the Americas, New York, NY   10105-0302

CEO:Caird Forbes-Cockell, CEO   Tel: (212) 424-9000   %FO: 100

Bus: *International law firm.*   Fax: (212) 424-9100   Emp: 120

● **DELFT INSTRUMENTS N.V.**

Röntgenweg 1, 2624 BD, PO Box 103, NL-2600 AC, Delft, Netherlands

CEO: E. Van Hooft, Pres.   Tel: 31-15-2601-200   Rev: $203

Bus: *Mfr. instruments for the medical, space,*   Fax: 31-15-2601-222   Emp: 1,194
industrial and scientific industries.   www.delftinstruments.nl

ENRAF INC.
500 Century Plaza Drive, Ste. 120, Houston, TX   77073

CEO: Steve Yon, Pres.	Tel: (281) 443-4291	%FO: 100
Bus: *Sales/service of tank gauge systems.*	Fax: (281) 443-6776	

OLDELFT ULTRASOUND INC.
7080 Columbia Gateway Drive, Columbia, MD   21046

CEO: Tom Maher, Pres.	Tel: (410) 312-4100	%FO: 100
Bus: *Sales/distribution, sales/service of radiation therapy equipment.*	Fax: (410) 312-4195	

• DELI UNIVERSAL
Wijnhaven 65, NL-3011 WJ, Rotterdam, Netherlands

CEO: D. G. Cohen ter Vaert, CEO	Tel: 31-10-402-1700
Bus: *Import, sales/distribution of coffee, dried nuts and fruits, sunflower/birdseed, and agricultural commodities.*	Fax: 31-10-411-7694 www.deli-universal.nl

IMPERIAL COMMODITIES CORPORATION
17 Battery Place, Ste. 636, New York, NY   10004-1101

CEO: Louis Mucciolo, Pres.	Tel: (212) 837-9400	%FO: 100
Bus: *Mfr. polymers.*	Fax: (212) 269-9878	

MOMENTUM TECHNOLOGIES INC.
1507 Boettler Road, Uniontown, OH   44685

CEO: Daniel Salopek, Mgr.	Tel: (330) 896-5900	%FO: 100
Bus: *Laboratory and polymer distribution services.*	Fax: (330) 896-9943	

RED RIVER COMMODITIES INC.
PO Box 3022, Fargo, ND   58102

CEO: Robert Majkrzek, Pres.	Tel: (701) 282-2600	%FO: 100
Bus: *Mfr./sales/distribution/warehousing of processors of sunflower and bird seed*	Fax: (701) 282-5325	

RED RIVER FOODS
PO Box 13328, Richmond, VA   23225

CEO: James Phipts, Pres.	Tel: (804) 320-1800	%FO: 100
Bus: *Import/export, sales/distribution of dried nuts and fruits*	Fax: (804) 320-1896	

● **DOCDATA N.V.**

Helvoirtseweg 9, NL-5261 CA, Vught, Netherlands

CEO: Hans van Gerwen, Pres.   Tel: 31-73-684-7000   Rev: $122

Bus: *Provides e-commerce fulfillment*   Fax: 31-73-684-0122   Emp: 850
services to webshops, retail chains,   www.docdata.com
direct marketing and internet service
providers.

DOCDATA CALIFORNIA INC.

8960 Eton Avenue, Canoga Park, CA   91304

CEO: Robert Pettit, Pres.   Tel: (818) 341-1124   %FO: 100

Bus: *Produces laser system software*   Fax: (818) 341-9131
and audio/ multimedia compact
discs.

DOCDATA NEW ENGLAND INC.

One Eagle Drive, Sanford, ME   04073

CEO: Robert Pettit, Pres.   Tel: (207) 324-1124   %FO: 100

Bus: *Produces laser system software*   Fax: (207) 490-1707
and audio/ multimedia compact
discs.

● **DRAKA HOLDING B.V.**

Rhijnspoorplein 22, NL-1018 TX, Amsterdam, Netherlands

CEO: F. H Fentener van Vlissingen, Chmn.   Tel: 31-20-568-9898   Rev: $829

Bus: *Manufacturer of wire and cables.*   Fax: 31-20-624-5633   Emp: 4,767
                                                 www.draka.com

BIW CABLE SYSTEMS, INC.

22 Joseph E. Warner Blvd., North Dighton, MA   02764

CEO: Henry Huta, Pres.   Tel: (508) 822-5444   %FO: 100

Bus: *Mfr. industrial & specialty cables.*   Fax: (508) 822-1944

BIW CONNECTOR SYSTEMS, INC.

500 Tesconi Circle, Santa Rosa, CA   95401

CEO: Robert Roeser, Pres.   Tel: (707) 523-2300   %FO: 100

Bus: *Mfr. connectors.*   Fax: (707) 523-3567

CHROMATIC TECHNOLOGIES INC

9 Forge Park, Franklin, MA   02038

CEO: Gleason Gallagher, Gen. Mgr.   Tel: (508) 541-7100   %FO: 100

Bus: *Mfr. fiber optic cables.*   Fax: (508) 541-8122

DRAKA CABLES

One Tamaqua Blvd., Schuylkill Haven, PA   17972

CEO: Henry Huta, Pres.   Tel: (570) 385-4381   %FO: 100

Bus: *Mfr. instrumentation cables.*   Fax: (570) 385-1092

DRAKA USA CORPORATION

9 Forge Park, Franklin, MA   02038

CEO: Garo Artinian, Pres. & CEO   Tel: (508) 520-1200   %FO: 100

Bus: *Mfr. industrial cables.*   Fax: (508) 541-6862

HELIX / HITEMP CABLES, INC.

20 Forge Park, Franklin, MA   02038

CEO: William Dungan, Gen. Mgr.   Tel: (508) 541-7100   %FO: 100

Bus: *Mfr. communications & electric cables.*   Fax: (508) 541-8122

● DSM N.V.

Het Overloon 1, NL-6411 TE, Heerlen, Netherlands

CEO: Peter A. Elverding, Chmn.   Tel: 31-45-578-8111   Rev: $7,500

Bus: *Manufacture of chemicals, hydrocarbons, synthetic/crude rubber, and printing resins.*   Fax: 31-45-571-9753   Emp: 22,700

www.dsm.nl

DSM CHEMICALS NORTH AMERICA

PO Box 2451, Augusta, GA   30901

CEO: William Price, Pres.   Tel: (706) 849-6600   %FO: 100

Bus: *Manufacture of chemicals.*   Fax: (706) 849-6999

DSM ELASTOMERS COPOLYMER

5955 Scenic Highway, Baton Rouge, LA   70821

CEO: Steve Nathanson, Dir.   Tel: (225) 267-3400   %FO: 100

Bus: *Specialty petroleum additives.*   Fax: (225) 267-3633

DSM ENGINEERING PLASTICS, INC.

PO Box 3333, Evansville, IN   47732

CEO: Roeland H. Polet, VP   Tel: (812) 424-3831   %FO: 100

Bus: *Compounder of reinforced thermoplastics and additives.*   Fax: (812) 435-7709

DSM FINE CHEMICALS USA, INC.

Park 80 West, Plaza 2, Saddle Brook, NJ   07663-5817

CEO: Richard D. Morford, Pres.   Tel: (201) 845-4404   %FO: 100

Bus: *Powder coating/printing resins.*   Fax: (201) 845-4406

DSM HYDROCARBONS AMERICAS, INC.

16945 Northchase Drive, Ste. 120, Houston, TX   77060

CEO: Ted Cormier, Pres.   Tel: (281) 873-0196   %FO: 100

Bus: *Provides consulting services for DSM affiliates.*   Fax: (281) 873-6121

- **DUTCH SPACE INDUSTRY, FORMERLY FOKKER SPACE BV**

Aviolandalaan 31, NL-4631 RP, Hoogerheide, Netherlands

CEO: Jan Närlinge, Pres. & CEO

Bus: *Specialist in advanced robotics technology supplying solar arrays. (65% JV of Saab Ericsson Space, Sweden and 35% JV of Stock, Netherlands)*

Tel: 31-16-4618000
Fax: 31-164-612018
www.fokkerservices.com

Rev: $100
Emp: 400

FOKKER SPACE, INC.

5169 Southridge Parkway, Ste. 100, Atlanta, GA   30349

CEO: Yolanda Johnson, Office Services Mgr.

Bus: *Mfr./sales/distribution and service of aircraft parts.*

Tel: (770) 991-4373
Fax: (770) 991-4360

%FO: 100
Emp: 22

- **ELSEVIER NV**

Van de Sande Bakhuyzenstraat 4, NL-1061 AG, Amsterdam, Netherlands

CEO: Herman J. Bruggink, Chmn.

Bus: *Publisher of business, educational, legal, and scientific information. (JV of Elsevier NV and Reed Int'l PLC)*

Tel: 31-20-515-9341
Fax: 31-20-683-2617
www.reed-elsevier.com

Rev: $650
Emp: 26,100

MATTHEW BENDER

2 Park Avenue, 7th Fl., New York, NY 10016-5675

CEO: Paul Brown, CEO

Bus: *Publishing.*

Tel: (212) 448-2300
Fax: (212) 448-2196

%FO: JV

CAHNERS TRAVEL GROUP INC.

500 Plaza Drive, Secaucus, NJ   07096

CEO: Kevin Condon, SVP

Bus: *Travel related publishing & services.*

Tel: (201) 902-2000
Fax: (201) 319-1726

%FO: 100

ELSEVIER SCIENCE INC.

655 Avenue of the Americas, New York, NY   10010

CEO: Russell White, Pres.

Bus: *Publisher of science and medical journals.*

Tel: (212) 989-5800
Fax: (212) 633-3990

%FO: 100

LEXIS NEXIS

9393 Springboro Pike, Miamisburg, OH   45342

CEO: Hans Gleskes, Pres. & CEO

Bus: *On-line information service; reference information & databases.*

Tel: (937) 865-7000
Fax: (937) 865-1555

%FO: 100

REED ELSEVIER, INC.

2 Park Avenue, 7th Fl., New York, NY 10016-5675

CEO: H. J. Bruggink, Co-Chrm.   Tel: (212) 448-2300   %FO: 100

Bus: *U.S. headquarters of joint venture*   Fax: (212) 448-2196
holding company; Elsevier NV,
Amsterdam and Reed Int'l plc,
London. Publisher of scientific
information.

SPRINGHOUSE CORPORATION

1111 Bethlehem Pike, Springhouse, PA 19477

CEO: Kevin Hurley, Pres.   Tel: (215) 646-8700   %FO: 100

Bus: *Publishing.*   Fax: (215) 628-3080

● **EQUANT N.V.**

Gatwickstraat 21-23, NL-1043 GL, Amsterdam-Sloterdijk, Netherlands

CEO: Didier J. Delepine, Pres. & CEO   Tel: 31-20-581-8383   Rev: $1,050

Bus: *Operates airline data network systems.*   Fax: 31-20-688-0388   Emp: 2,400
www.equant.com

EQUANT NETWORK SERVICES DIVISION

330 North Wabash Avenue, Ste. 2801, Chicago, IL 60611

CEO: Jim Wilkes, VP   Tel: (312) 321-6400   %FO: 100

Bus: *Operates airline data network*   Fax: (312) 321-4750
systems.

EQUANT NETWORK SERVICES DIVISION

3 Park Avenue, 25th Fl., New York, NY 10016

CEO: Jim Wilkes, VP   Tel: (212) 251-2000   %FO: 100

Bus: *Operates airline data network*   Fax: (212) 251-2197
systems.

EQUANT NETWORK SERVICES DIVISION

400 Galleria Parkway, Tower 400, Atlanta, GA 30339

CEO: Jim Wilkes, VP   Tel: (678) 346-3000   %FO: 100

Bus: *Operates airline data network*   Fax: (678) 346-3636
systems.

EQUANT NETWORK SERVICES DIVISION

8 New England Executive Park, 2 West, Burlington, MA 01803

CEO: Jim Wilkes, VP   Tel: (781) 221-9950   %FO: 100

Bus: *Operates airline data network*   Fax: (781) 221-9955
systems.

EQUANT NETWORK SERVICES DIVISION
4541 East Juana Court, Cave Creek, AZ   85331
CEO: Jim Wilkes, VP   Tel: (623) 473-4766   %FO: 100
Bus: *Operates airline data network*   Fax: (623) 473-4767
    systems.

EQUANT NETWORK SERVICES DIVISION
45 Orville Drive, Bohemia, NY   11716
CEO: Jim Wilkes, VP   Tel: (631) 589-8666   %FO: 100
Bus: *Operates airline data network*   Fax: (631) 589-6395
    systems.

EQUANT NETWORK SERVICES DIVISION
8300 Bonne Blvd., Ste. 200, Vienna, VA   22182
CEO: Jim Wilkes, VP   Tel: (703) 734-2250   %FO: 100
Bus: *Operates airline data network*   Fax: (703) 734-2257
    systems.

EQUANT NETWORK SERVICES DIVISION
KLM Terminal, Bldg. 51, JFK Airport, Jamaica, NY   11372
CEO: Jim Wilkes, VP   Tel: (718) 632-8281   %FO: 100
Bus: *Operates airline data network*   Fax: (718) 632-1116
    systems.

EQUANT NETWORK SERVICES DIVISION
1100 Lee Wagener Blvd., Ste. 206, Ft. Lauderdale, FL   33315
CEO: Jim Wilkes, VP   Tel: (954) 359-8336   %FO: 100
Bus: *Operates airline data network*   Fax: (954) 359-0359
    systems.

EQUANT NETWORK SERVICES DIVISION
1300 SW Fifth Avenue, Portland, OR   97201
CEO: Jim Wilkes, VP   Tel: (503) 471-2830   %FO: 100
Bus: *Operates airline data network*   Fax: (503) 471-2950
    systems.

EQUANT NETWORK SERVICES DIVISION
2020 Front Street, Ste. 201, Cuyahoga Falls, OH   44221
CEO: Jim Wilkes, VP   Tel: (330) 926-5801   %FO: 100
Bus: *Operates airline data network*   Fax: (330) 926-9289
    systems.

EQUANT NETWORK SERVICES DIVISION
900 East Eighth Avenue, Ste.300, King of Prussia, PA   19406
CEO: Jim Wilkes, VP   Tel: (610) 768-2804   %FO: 100
Bus: *Operates airline data network*   Fax: (610) 768-2806
    systems.

EQUANT NETWORK SERVICES DIVISION

277 Coon Rapids Blvd., Ste. 410, Minneapolis, MN   55433

CEO: Jim Wilkes, VP   Tel: (612) 780-0200   %FO: 100

Bus: *Operates airline data network*   Fax: (612) 717-7259
    systems.

EQUANT NETWORK SERVICES DIVISION

26020 Acero Street, Ste. 200, Mission Viejo, CA   92691

CEO: Jim Wilkes, VP   Tel: (949) 470-6300   %FO: 100

Bus: *Operates airline data network*   Fax: (949) 470-6313
    systems.

EQUANT NETWORK SERVICES DIVISION

4801 Woodway Drive, Ste. 300 East, Stafford, TX   77056

CEO: Jim Wilkes, VP   Tel: (713) 964-2786   %FO: 100

Bus: *Operates airline data network*   Fax: (713) 964-2779
    systems.

EQUANT NETWORK SERVICES DIVISION

4600 South Syracuse, Ste. 900, Denver, CO   80237

CEO: Jim Wilkes, VP   Tel: (303) 256-6475   %FO: 100

Bus: *Operates airline data network*   Fax: (303) 256-6479
    systems.

EQUANT NETWORK SERVICES DIVISION

125 East Carpenter Freeway, Ste. 800, Irving, TX   75062

CEO: Jim Wilkes, VP   Tel: (972) 443-2233   %FO: 100

Bus: *Operates airline data network*   Fax: (972) 444-0101
    systems.

EQUANT NETWORK SERVICES DIVISION

12444 Powerscourt Drive, Ste. 300, St. Louis, MO   63131

CEO: Jim Wilkes, VP   Tel: (314) 984-2540   %FO: 100

Bus: *Operates airline data network*   Fax: (314) 957-6329
    systems.

● **ERIKS GROUP N.V.**

Voormeer 33, PO Box 289, NL-1800 BK, Alkmaar, Netherlands

CEO: A. A. Van Dusseldorp, Pres.   Tel: 31-72-514-1217   Rev: $282

Bus: *Technical trading companies.*   Fax: 31-72-514-1115   Emp: 1,574
                                 www.eriks.com

ERIKS AIRSPACE

3002 North Commerce Pkwy., Miramar, FL   33025

CEO: Robert Heinzmann, Pres.   Tel: (954) 447-4700   %FO: 100

Bus: *Sale of aircraft maintenance parts.*   Fax: (954) 447-4800

ERIKS CORPORATION
443 North Main Street, PO Box 220, Grafton, OH   44044
CEO: Nicolas Storm, CFO   Tel: (440) 926-3681   %FO: 100
Bus: *Technical components and systems.* Fax: (440) 926-3519

ERIKS MIDWEST
361 Cleveland Avenue, Aurora, IL   60507
CEO: Mark Yerrick, Pres.   Tel: (630) 859-3606   %FO: 100
Bus: *Sales/distribution of sealing* Fax: (630) 859-8171
    instruments.

ERIKS, INC.
21700 Doral Road, Waukesha, WI   53186
CEO: Mark Yerrick, Pres.   Tel: (262) 785-1333   %FO: 100
Bus: *Sealing elements.*   Fax: (262) 785-1756

ERIKS, INC.
14600 Interuban Avenue, South, Seattle, WA   98168
CEO: Cindy Burnett, Pres.   Tel: (206) 243-9660   %FO: 100
Bus: *Sealing elements.*   Fax: (206) 243-4718

ERIKS, INC.
PO Box 155399, Ft. Worth, TX   76155
CEO: Shun Courtney, Pres.   Tel: (817) 267-8837   %FO: 100
Bus: *Airline industry materials*   Fax: (817) 571-4700

● **FEADSHIP HOLLAND**
Aerdenhoutsduinweg 1, PO Box 70, NL 2110 AB, Aerdenhout, Netherlands
CEO: M. S. DeVries, Pres.   Tel: 31-23-524-7000
Bus: *Mfr./sales of yachts.*   Fax: 31-23-524-8639
                                      www.feadship.nl

FEADSHIP AMERICA INC.
801 Seabreeze Boulevard, Ft. Lauderdale, FL   33316
CEO: Don Kenniston, Pres.   Tel: (954) 761-1830   %FO: 100
Bus: *Sales, distribution and service of* Fax: (954) 761-3412
    yachts.

● **FGH BANK N.V.**
Leidseveer 50, NL-3511 SB, Utrecht, Netherlands
CEO: R. J. Kahlmann, Pres.   Tel: 31-30-233-4572
Bus: *Real estate financing.*   Fax: 31-30-232-3911
                                      www.fgh.nl

REALTY ADVISORS INC.
292 Madison Avenue, 5th Fl., New York, NY   10017
CEO: George McGoey, Pres.   Tel: (212) 251-0101   %FO: 100
Bus: *Real estate financing.*   Fax: (212) 251-0149

● FORTIS (NL)
Archimedeslaan 6, NL-3584 BA, Utrecht, Netherlands
CEO: Jaap Glasz, Chmn.   Tel: 31-30-257-6576   Rev: $1,039
Bus: *Insurance, banking, and financial*   Fax: 31-30-257-7835   Emp: 29,000
    services (JV Fortis AG, Belgium).   www.fortis.com

FIRST FORTIS LIFE INSURANCE COMPANY
308 Maltbie Street, Ste. 200, Syracuse, NY   13204
CEO: Terry J. Kryshak, SVP   Tel: (315) 451-0066   %FO: 100
Bus: *Group long and short-term*   Fax: (315) 453-2343
    disability insurance.

FIRST FORTIS LIFE INSURANCE CO
PO Box 3209, Syracuse, NY   13220
CEO: Terry Kryshak, Pres.   Tel: (315) 451-0066   %FO: 100
Bus: *Life, disability, medical & dental*   Fax: (315) 453-2343
    group insurance.

FORIS INSURANCE/FORTIS HEALTH
501 West Michigan, Milwaukee, WI   53201-2989
CEO: Benjamin M. Cutler, CEO   Tel: (414) 271-3011   %FO: 100
Bus: *Financial services.*   Fax: (414) 271-0879

FORTIS ADVISERS INC.
One Chase Manhattan Plaza, New York, NY   10005
CEO: Gary N. Yalen, Pres.   Tel: (212) 859-7000   %FO: 100
Bus: *Real estate asset management*   Fax: (212) 859-7034
    services.

FORTIS BENEFITS INSURANCE COMPANY
2323 Grand Boulevard, Kansas City, MO   64108
CEO: Michael Peninger, Pres. & CEO   Tel: (816) 474-2345   %FO: 100
Bus: *Insurance services.*   Fax: (816) 881-8646

FORTIS FAMILY INS.
Ten Glenlake Parkway, Ste. 500, Atlanta, GA   30328
CEO: Alan W. Feagin, Pres.   Tel: (800) 801-0800   %FO: 100
Bus: *Provides small life insurance and*   Fax: (770) 206-6381
    pre-need products.

FORTIS PRIVATE CAPITAL, INC.
One Chase Manhattan Plaza, New York, NY   10005

CEO: J. Kerry Clayton, CEO

Tel: (212) 859-7000

%FO: 100

Bus: *Provides specialty insurance and investment products.*

Fax: (212) 859-7010

● GEODIS LOGISTICS VITESSE B.V.
Smirnoff Weg 3, NL-3088 HC, Rotterdam, Netherlands

CEO: Cees Weima, Pres.

Tel: 31-10-428-6666

Bus: *Engaged in warehousing and distribution.*

Fax: 31-10-428-1716
www.geodis.com

Emp: 250

GEODIS VITESSE LOGISTICS INC.
333 North Michigan Avenue, Ste. 1816, Chicago, IL   60601

CEO: Herbert Wennink, Dir.

Tel: (312) 641-2805

%FO: 100

Bus: *European warehousing and distribution.*

Fax: (312) 641-6733

Emp: 3

● GETRONICS NV
Donauweg 10, PO Box 652, NL-1043 AJ, Amsterdam, Netherlands

CEO: Cees G. van Luijk, Pres. & CEO

Tel: 31-20-586-1412

Rev: $3,886

Bus: *Information technology service provider including systems integration, networking, consulting and human resources services.*

Fax: 31-20-586-1568
www.getronics.com

Emp: 34,700

GETRONICS INC.
600 Technology Park Drive, Billerica, MA   01821

CEO: David Goulden, Pres. & CEO

Tel: (978) 967-5000

%FO: 100

Bus: *Information technology service provider.*

Fax: (978) 967-5911

WANG GOVERNMENT SERVICES
7900 Westpark Drive, McLean, VA   22102

CEO: James J. Hogan, Pres.

Tel: (703) 827-3000

%FO: 100

Bus: *Engaged in information technology services for the U.S. federal government.*

Fax: (703) 827-3126

Emp: 2,700

● GRANARIA HOLDINGS B.V
PO Box 233, NL-2501 CE, The Hague, Netherlands

CEO: Joel P. Wyler, Chmn.

Tel: 31-70-312-1100

Rev: $3,400

Bus: *Industry operations include food processing, real estate investment & manufacturing.*

Fax: 31-70-312-1150
www.granaria.nl

Emp: 7,000

EAGLE-PICHER INDUSTRIES, INC.
250 East Fifth Street, Ste. 500, Cincinnati, OH 45202

CEO: Andries Ruljssenaars, Pres.   Tel: (513) 721-7010   %FO: 100

Bus: *Mfr. industrial products for*   Fax: (513) 721-2341
automotive, defense, aerospace &
construction industries.

● GRASSO PRODUCTS N.V.
Parallelweg 27, NL-5201 AG, Hertogenbosch, Netherlands

CEO: F. Buckalew, Dir.   Tel: 31-73-620-3911

Bus: *Holding company; mfr./sales*   Fax: 31-73-621-0310   Emp: 1,400
refrigerator equipment.   www.grasso.nl

GRASSO INC.
PO Box 4799, Evansville, IN 47724

CEO: F. Buckalew, Gen. Mgr.   Tel: (812) 465-6600   %FO: 100

Bus: *Mfr./sale refrigerator equipment.*   Fax: (812) 465-6610   Emp: 40

● GUCCI GROUP N.V.
Rembrandt Tower, Amstelplein 1, NL-1096 HA, Amsterdam, Netherlands

CEO: Domenico DeSole, Pres.. & CEO   Tel: 31-10-20-462-1700   Rev: $1,236

Bus: *Design/mfr. clothing and leather goods.*   Fax: 31-0-20-465-3569   Emp: 3,500
(JV of Pinault-Printemps-Redoute,   www.gucci.com
France and)

GUCCI AMERICA, INC.
685 Fifth Avenue, New York, NY 10022

CEO: Patricia Malone, Pres.   Tel: (212) 826-2600   %FO: 100

Bus: *Sales/distribution of designer*   Fax: (212) 230-0894
clothing and leather goods.

GUCCI AMERICA, INC.
344 North Rodeo Drive, Los Angeles, LA 90210

CEO: Nora Bedrossian, Mgr.   Tel: (310) 278-3451   %FO: 100

Bus: *Sales/distribution of designer*   Fax:
clothing and leather goods.

GUCCI AMERICA, INC.
50 Hartz Way, Secaucus, NJ 07094

CEO: Patricia Malone, Pres.   Tel: (201) 867-8800   %FO: 100

Bus: *Sales/distribution of designer*   Fax: Emp: 200
clothing and leather goods.

● **HAGEMEYER N.V.**

Rijksweg 69, NL-1410 AC, Naarden, Netherlands

CEO: R. ter Haar, CEO   Tel: 31-35-695-7611   Rev: $6,414

Bus: *Gourmet and specialty foods, indoor*   Fax: 31-35-694-7850   Emp: 18,840
plants, ceramics and decorative articles.   www.hagemeyer.nl

    CASE LOGIC, INC.

    6303 Dry Creek Parkway, Longmont, CO   80503

    CEO: Peter Storz, Pres.   Tel: (303) 652-1000   %FO: 100

    Bus: *Develops and distributes audio*   Fax: (303) 652-1094
    and computer accessory products.

● **HEINEKEN N.V.**

Tweede Weteringsplantsoen 21, NL-1017 ZD, Amsterdam, Netherlands

CEO: Karel Vuursteen, Chmn.   Tel: 31-20-523-9239   Rev: $7,627

Bus: *Mfr. Heineken, Buckler and Amstel light* Fax: 31-20-626-3503   Emp: 36,700
beers.   www.heineken.nl

    HEINEKEN U.S.A., INC.

    50 Main Street, White Plains, NY   10606-1955

    CEO: Frank Van der Minne, CEO   Tel: (914) 681-4100   %FO: 100

    Bus: *Import/sales/distribution of*   Fax: (914) 681-1900
    Heineken, Buckler, and Amstel
    light beers.

● **HOLMATRO INDUSTRIAL EQUIPMENT BV**

Zalmweg 30, NL-4941 VX, Raamsdonksveer, Netherlands

CEO: J. Meyers, Pres.   Tel: 31-16-258-9200

Bus: *Mfr. high-pressure hydraulic equipment.* Fax: 31-16-252-2482
www.holmatro.com

    HOLMATRO INC.

    505 McCormick Drive, Glen Burnie, MD   21061-3254

    CEO: William Swayne, Pres.   Tel: (410) 768-9662   %FO: 100

    Bus: *Mfr./sale/distribution/service and* Fax: (410) 768-4878
    warehousing of industrial and
    rescue equipment.

● **HUNTER DOUGLAS N.V.**

Piekstraat 2, NL-3071 EL, Rotterdam, Netherlands

CEO: Ralph Sonnenberg, Pres.   Tel: 31-10-486-9911   Rev: $1,370

Bus: *Mfr./sale/distribute window covering,*   Fax: 31-10-485-0621   Emp: 13,600
architectural products, metals trading,   www.hunterdouglas.com
precision machinery.

HUNTER DOUGLAS ARCHITECTURAL PRODUCTS

5015 Oakbrook Pkwy., Ste 100, Norcross, GA   30093-2265

CEO: Tom Ayres, VP   Tel: (770) 476-8803   %FO: 100

Bus: *Mfr./sales/distribution &*   Fax: (770) 623-3638
     warehousing of architectural
     products.

HUNTER DOUGLAS INC.

2 Parkway & Route 17 South, Saddle River, NJ   07458

CEO: Marvin Hopkins, Pres.   Tel: (201) 327-8200   %FO: 100

Bus: *Mfr./sale/distribute window*   Fax: (201) 327-5644   Emp: 3,355
     covering, architectural products.

● IFCO SYSTEMS NV

Rivierstaete, Amsteldijk 166, NL-1079 LH, Amsterdam, Netherlands

CEO: Karl Pohler, CEO   Tel: 31-20-504-1772   Rev: $375

Bus: *Holding company engaged in supply*   Fax: 31-20-646-0793   Emp: 5,000
     chain solutions, including round-trip   www.ifcosystems.de
     container management (RTC), pallet
     management services and industrial
     container services.

IFCO SYSTEMS NORTH AMERICA, INC.

4141 Singleton Blvd., Dallas, TX   75212

CEO: Brian Lewis   Tel: (214) 688-4108   %FO: 100

Bus: *Engaged in supply chain solutions,*   Fax: (214) 688-4043
     including round-trip container
     management (RTC), pallet
     management services and
     industrial container services.

IFCO SYSTEMS NORTH AMERICA, INC.

7507 Spur 331, Lubbock, TX   79404

CEO: Johnny Palmer, Plant Mgr.   Tel: (806) 762-6076   %FO: 100

Bus: *Engaged in supply chain solutions,*   Fax: (806) 762-6086
     including round-trip container
     management (RTC), pallet
     management services and
     industrial container services.

IFCO SYSTEMS NORTH AMERICA, INC.
1919 Trophy Road, McAllen, TX   78502
CEO: Genaro Elizando, Mgr.   Tel: (210) 631-3397   %FO: 100
Bus: *Engaged in supply chain solutions,* Fax: (210) 631-8329
including round-trip container
management (RTC), pallet
management services and
industrial container services.

IFCO SYSTEMS NORTH AMERICA, INC.
PO Box 97, New Boston, TX   75570
CEO: Jimmy Beard, Plant Mgr.   Tel: (903) 628-5695   %FO: 100
Bus: *Engaged in supply chain solutions,* Fax: (903) 628-5793
including round-trip container
management (RTC), pallet
management services and
industrial container services.

IFCO SYSTEMS NORTH AMERICA, INC.
PO Box 458, Plainview, TX   79073
CEO: Butch Palmer, Mgr.   Tel: (806) 293-3696   %FO: 100
Bus: *Engaged in supply chain solutions,* Fax: (806) 293-4655
including round-trip container
management (RTC), pallet
management services and
industrial container services.

IFCO SYSTEMS NORTH AMERICA, INC.
5250 Tacco Drive, San Antonio, TX   78244
CEO: J. R. Ramirez, Mgr.   Tel: (210) 662-7733   %FO: 100
Bus: *Engaged in supply chain solutions,* Fax: (210) 662-7735
including round-trip container
management (RTC), pallet
management services and
industrial container services.

IFCO SYSTEMS NORTH AMERICA, INC.
2810 W. Trade Street, Charlotte, NC   28208
CEO: Ned Rockecharlie, Mgr.   Tel: (704) 392-5386   %FO: 100
Bus: *Engaged in supply chain solutions,* Fax: (704) 392-5486
including round-trip container
management (RTC), pallet
management services and
industrial container services.

IFCO SYSTEMS NORTH AMERICA, INC.

1010 26th Street, Butner, NC   27509

CEO: Tony Fogleman, Mgr.   Tel: (919) 575-6491   %FO: 100

Bus: *Engaged in supply chain solutions,*   Fax: (919) 575-8467
including round-trip container
management (RTC), pallet
management services and
industrial container services.

IFCO SYSTEMS NORTH AMERICA, INC.

261 Rianda Circle, Salinas, CA   93901

CEO: J. Martinez, Plant Mgr.   Tel: (831) 422-4286   %FO: 100

Bus: *Engaged in supply chain solutions,*   Fax: (831) 422-4343
including round-trip container
management (RTC), pallet
management services and
industrial container services.

IFCO SYSTEMS NORTH AMERICA, INC.

PO Box 9001, Bartow, FL   33831

CEO: James Griffin, CEO   Tel: (863) 519-5688   %FO: 100

Bus: *Engaged in supply chain solutions,*   Fax: (863) 519-9259
including round-trip container
management (RTC), pallet
management services and
industrial container services.

IFCO SYSTEMS NORTH AMERICA, INC.

1587 NW 163rd Street, Miami, FL   33169

CEO: Mel Ball, Mgr.   Tel: (305) 592-3952   %FO: 100

Bus: *Engaged in supply chain solutions,*   Fax: (305) 592-3952
including round-trip container
management (RTC), pallet
management services and
industrial container services.

IFCO SYSTEMS NORTH AMERICA, INC.

6161 Jones Avenue, Zellwood, FL   32796

CEO: Jerry Butler, Mgr.   Tel: (407) 889-5000   %FO: 100

Bus: *Engaged in supply chain solutions,*   Fax: (407) 889-5587
including round-trip container
management (RTC), pallet
management services and
industrial container services.

IFCO SYSTEMS NORTH AMERICA, INC.
7152 First Avenue South, Seattle, WA 98108

CEO: Rick Cabuco, Mgr. Tel: (206) 763-2345 %FO: 100

Bus: *Engaged in supply chain solutions,* Fax: (206) 763-2345
including round-trip container
management (RTC), pallet
management services and
industrial container services.

IFCO SYSTEMS NORTH AMERICA, INC.
4808 North McCarty Drive, Houston, TX 77013

CEO: James Rice, Mgr. Tel: (713) 674-3491 %FO: 100

Bus: *Engaged in supply chain solutions,* Fax: (713) 674-3492
including round-trip container
management (RTC), pallet
management services and
industrial container services.

IFCO SYSTEMS NORTH AMERICA, INC.
6829 Flintlock Road, Houston, TX 77040

CEO: Edward Rhyne, EVP Tel: (713) 332-6145 %FO: 100

Bus: *Engaged in supply chain solutions,* Fax: (713) 332-6146
including round-trip container
management (RTC), pallet
management services and
industrial container services.

IFCO SYSTEMS NORTH AMERICA, INC.
727 W.W. White, San Antonio, TX 78219

CEO: Scott Gillum, Mgr. Tel: (210) 359-1425 %FO: 100

Bus: *Engaged in supply chain solutions,* Fax: (210) 359-1907
including round-trip container
management (RTC), pallet
management services and
industrial container services.

IFCO SYSTEMS NORTH AMERICA, INC.
PO Box 31943, Amarillo, TX 79111

CEO: Ed Renteria, Mgr. Tel: (806) 335-1746 %FO: 100

Bus: *Engaged in supply chain solutions,* Fax: (806) 335-3402
including round-trip container
management (RTC), pallet
management services and
industrial container services.

IFCO SYSTEMS NORTH AMERICA, INC.

2150 Peachtree, Balch Springs, TX   75180

CEO: Randy Foster, Mgr.   Tel: (972) 288-6220   %FO: 100

Bus: *Engaged in supply chain solutions,*   Fax: (972) 289-4727
including round-trip container
management (RTC), pallet
management services and
industrial container services.

IFCO SYSTEMS NORTH AMERICA, INC.

2401 Vinson Street, Dallas, TX   74222

CEO: Mark Foster, Mgr.   Tel: (214) 744-4840   %FO: 100

Bus: *Engaged in supply chain solutions,*   Fax: (214) 744-4840
including round-trip container
management (RTC), pallet
management services and
industrial container services.

IFCO SYSTEMS NORTH AMERICA, INC.

1300 East Berry Street, Ft. Worth, TX   76119

CEO: Steven East, Plant Mgr.   Tel: (817) 920-9711   %FO: 100

Bus: *Engaged in supply chain solutions,*   Fax: (817) 920-9722
including round-trip container
management (RTC), pallet
management services and
industrial container services.

IFCO SYSTEMS NORTH AMERICA, INC.

3117 Westminster Avenue, Dallas, TX   75212

CEO: Vance Maultsby, EVP   Tel: (713) 332-6145   %FO: 100

Bus: *Engaged in supply chain solutions,*   Fax: (713) 332-6146
including round-trip container
management (RTC), pallet
management services and
industrial container services.

IFCO SYSTEMS NORTH AMERICA, INC.

2903 Strickland Street, Jacksonville, FL   32254

CEO: Austin Cummings, Mgr.   Tel: (904) 387-6125   %FO: 100

Bus: *Engaged in supply chain solutions,*   Fax: (904) 387-6325
including round-trip container
management (RTC), pallet
management services and
industrial container services.

IFCO SYSTEMS NORTH AMERICA, INC.

165 Turkey Foot Road, Mocksville, NC   27028

CEO: Larry Draughn, Plant Mgr.   Tel: (336) 492-5565   %FO: 100

Bus: *Engaged in supply chain solutions,* Fax: (336) 492-5682
     including round-trip container
     management (RTC), pallet
     management services and
     industrial container services.

IFCO SYSTEMS NORTH AMERICA, INC.

1315 Main Street, Oakley, CA   95461

CEO: Vince Sheldon, Plant Mgr.   Tel: (925) 625-2020   %FO: 100

Bus: *Engaged in supply chain solutions,* Fax: (925) 625-5863
     including round-trip container
     management (RTC), pallet
     management services and
     industrial container services.

IFCO SYSTEMS NORTH AMERICA, INC.

8006 East Sligh Avenue, Tampa, FL   33610

CEO: Delbert L. Groene, Pres.   Tel: (813) 621-0063   %FO: 100

Bus: *Engaged in supply chain solutions,* Fax: (813) 623-3948
     including round-trip container
     management (RTC), pallet
     management services and
     industrial container services.

IFCO SYSTEMS NORTH AMERICA, INC.

1540 S. Greenwood Avenue, Montebello, CA   90640

CEO: Joe Cruz, Plant Mgr.   Tel: (323) 724-8507   %FO: 100

Bus: *Engaged in supply chain solutions,* Fax: (323) 887-6139
     including round-trip container
     management (RTC), pallet
     management services and
     industrial container services.

IFCO SYSTEMS NORTH AMERICA, INC.

PO Box 212, Staley, NC   27355

CEO: Gary Lawing, Plant Mgr.   Tel: (336) 622-5724   %FO: 100

Bus: *Engaged in supply chain solutions,* Fax: (336) 622-5728
     including round-trip container
     management (RTC), pallet
     management services and
     industrial container services.

- **INDIGO N.V.**

5 Limburglaan NL-6221 GA, Maastricht, Netherlands

CEO: Benzion Landa, Chmn.	Tel: 31-43-356-5656	Rev: $147
Bus: *Mfr. digital offset color printing presses.*	Fax: 31-43-356-5600	Emp: 760
	www.indigonet.com	

INDIGO AMERICA, INC.

400 Unicorn Park Drive, Woburn, MA   01801

CEO: Rob Secontine, Reg. Mgr.	Tel: (781) 937-8800	%FO: 100
Bus: *Mfr./sales digital offset color printing presses.*	Fax: (781) 937-8810	

- **ING GROUP N.V.**

Strawinskylaan 2631, PO Box 810, NL-1000 AV, Amsterdam, Netherlands

CEO: Ewald Kist, Chmn.	Tel: 31-20-541-5411	Rev: $72,597
Bus: *Commercial and investment banking and insurance services.*	Fax: 31-20-541-5444	Emp: 108,965
	www.inggroup.com	

BARING ASSET MANAGEMENT

353 Sacramento Street, Ste. 618, San Francisco, CA   94111

CEO: Donna Wills, Gen. Mgr.	Tel: (415) 834-1500	%FO: 100
Bus: *Asset management services.*	Fax: (415) 834-1722	

BARING ASSET MANAGEMENT

125 High Street, Ste. 2700, Boston, MA   02110-2713

CEO: Barclay Douglas, CEO	Tel: (617) 951-0052	%FO: 100
Bus: *Asset management services.*	Fax: (617) 330-7481	

BARING HOUSTON & SAUNDERS

667 Madison Avenue, 4th Fl., New York, NY   10021

CEO: Richard Saunders, Mgr.	Tel: (212) 527-7003	%FO: 100
Bus: *Securities broker/dealer & investment management services.*	Fax: (212) 350-7466	

EQUITABLE OF IOWA COMPANIES

909 Locust Street, Des Moines, IA   50306-1635

CEO: R. Glenn Hillard, Chmn.	Tel: (515) 698-7000	
Bus: *Insurance holding group.*	Fax: (515) 698-7615	

GOLDEN AMERICAN LIFE INSURANCE COMPANY

1475 Dunwood Drive, West Chester, PA   19380-1470

CEO: Barnett Chermow, CEO	Tel: (800) 366-0066	%FO: 100
Bus: *Engaged in life insurance.*	Fax:	

INDIANA INSURANCE COMPANY
350 East 96th Street, Indianapolis, IN   46240

CEO: R. L. Jean, CEO   Tel: (317) 581-6400   %FO: 100

Bus: *Engaged in life insurance.*   Fax: (317) 581-6405

ING (U.S.) SECURITIES FUTURES & OPTIONS
233 South Wacker Drive, Ste. 5200, Chicago, IL   60606

CEO: Margaret McGrath, COO   Tel: (312) 496-7000   %FO: 100

Bus: *Securities broker/dealer trading* Fax: (312) 496-7150
    services.

ING ADVISORS NETWORK
3424 Peachtree Road NE, Atlanta, GA   30326

CEO: Fred Hubbell, Pres.   Tel: (404) 841-6811   %FO: 100

Bus: *Investment banking.*   Fax: (404) 841-6965

ING BANK
1113 West St. Germain Street, St. Cloud, MN   56301

CEO: Brian Myers, Pres.   Tel: (320) 259-1413

Bus: *Corporate banking.*   Fax: (320) 259-1837

ING BARING FURMAN SELZ LLC
456 Montgomery Street, San Francisco, CA   94104

CEO: Val Huang, Gen. Mgr.   Tel: (415) 788-8870   %FO: 100

Bus: *Securities broker/dealer &*   Fax: (415) 788-8890
    investment management services.

ING BARING FURMAN SELZ LLC
230 Park Avenue, New York, NY   10169

CEO: Edmund A. Hajim, Chmn.   Tel: (212) 309-8200   %FO: 100

Bus: *Securities broker/dealer &*   Fax: (212) 309-8689
    investment management services.

ING BARINGS - Los Angeles
333 South Grand Ave., Ste. 4200, Los Angeles, CA   90071

CEO: Mark Vidergauz, Mng. Dir.   Tel: (213) 617-9100   %FO: 100

Bus: *Financial & investment banking* Fax: (213) 687-7324
    services

ING BARINGS
55 East 52nd Street, New York, NY   10055

CEO: David Duffy   Tel: (212) 409-1000   %FO: 100

Bus: *Investment banking and asset* Fax: (212) 409-1020
    management services.

ING BARINGS
200 Galeria Pkwy., Ste. 950, Atlanta, GA   30339
CEO: James W. Latimer, Mng. Dir.   Tel: (770) 956-9200   %FO: 100
Bus: *Insurance & financial services.*   Fax: (770) 951-1005

ING FURMAN SELZ ASSET MANAGEMENT
230 Park Avenue, New York, NY   10169
CEO: Edmund A. Hajim, Chmn.   Tel: (212) 309-8200   %FO: 100
Bus: *Investment banking and asset*   Fax: (212) 692-9608
management services.

ING FURMAN SELZ ASSET MANAGEMENT
150 North Wacker Drive, Ste. 2160, Chicago, IL   60606
CEO: R. Siegler, Mgr.   Tel: (312) 220-9620   %FO: 100
Bus: *Investment banking and asset*   Fax: (312) 220-0052
management services.

ING FURMAN SELZ ASSET MANAGEMENT
101 California Street, Ste. 4300, San Francisco, CA   94111
CEO: E. A. Hajim, CEO   Tel: (415) 659-3000   %FO: 100
Bus: *Investment banking and asset*   Fax: (415) 834-3694
management services.

ING INVESTMENT MANAGEMENT
300 Galleria Pkwy., NW, Ste. 1200, Atlanta, GA   30317-43909
CEO: Thomas J. Balachowski, Pres. &   Tel: (770) 690-4600   %FO: 100
CEO
Bus: *Asset management services.*   Fax: (770) 850-4801   Emp: 70

LIFE INSURANCE COMPANY OF GEORGIA
5780 Power Ferry Road, N.W., Atlanta, GA   30327
CEO: James D. Thompson, Pres.   Tel: (770) 980-3300   %FO: 100
Bus: *Insurance services.*   Fax: (770) 980-3301

MEDICAL RISK SOLUTIONS
5780 Powers Ferry Road, N.W., Atlanta, GA   30327
CEO: Valerie Brown, CEO   Tel: (770) 980-3300   %FO: 100
Bus: *Life insurance.*   Fax: (770) 980-3301

RELIASTAR LIFE INSURANCE COMPANY
20 Washington Avenue South, Minneapolis, MN   55401
CEO: John G. Turner, CEO   Tel: (612) 372-5432   %FO: 100
Bus: *Insurance services.*   Fax: (612) 342-3966

SECURITY LIFE OF DENVER INSURANCE COMPANY
1290 Broadway, Security Life Ctr., Denver, CO   80203
CEO: Jess Skrilletz, Pres.   Tel: (303) 860-1290   %FO: 100
Bus: *Life insurance.*   Fax: (303) 860-2260

SOUTHLAND LIFE INSURANCE COMPANY
5780 Powers Ferry Road, N.W., Atlanta, GA   30327
CEO: James D. Thompson, Pres.   Tel: (770) 980-5390   %FO: 100
Bus: *Life insurance.*   Fax: (770) 980-5800

SUCCESSFUL MONEY MANAGEMENT SEMINARS, INC.
12100 Tualatin Road, Tualatin, OR   97062
CEO: John H. P. Wheat, Pres.   Tel: (503) 691-6363   %FO: 100
Bus: *Presents seminars.*   Fax: (503) 691-5858

VESTAX SECURITIES CORPORATION
1931 Georgetown Road, Hudson, OH   44236
CEO: Jack Conley, Pres.   Tel: (330) 650-1660
Bus: *Investment banking and asset Fax: (330) 650-9941
    management services.*

• ISPAT INTERNATIONAL N.V.
Aert van Nesstraat 45, NL-3012 CA, Rotterdam, Netherlands
CEO: Lakshmi N. Mittal, Chmn.   Tel: 31-10-282-9465   Rev: $5,097
Bus: *Mfr. steel and iron.*   Fax: 31-10-282-9468   Emp: 15,000
                                    www.inland.com

ISPAT NORTH AMERICA, INC.
30 West Monroe Street, Chicago, IL   60603
CEO: Dr. Johannes Sittard, CEO   Tel: (312) 899-3412   %FO: 100
Bus: *Marketing/sales of steel products.* Fax: (312) 899-3562

ISPAT INLAND INC.
3210 Watling Street, East Chicago, IN   46312
CEO: Peter D. Southwick, Pres. & CEO Tel: (219) 399-1200   %FO: 100
Bus: *Mfr. flat-rolled steels and alloy Fax: (219) 399-5544
    bar products for industrial
    industries.*

• KLM ROYAL DUTCH AIRLINES (KLM NEDERLAND N.V.)
PO Box 7700, Schiphol Airport, NL-1117 ZL, Amstelveen, Netherlands
CEO: Leo Van Wijk, Pres. & CEO   Tel: 31-20-649-9123   Rev: $5,700
Bus: *International commercial air transport* Fax: 31-20-649-3001 Emp: 28,375
    services.   www.klm.nl

KLM-ROYAL DUTCH AIRLINES

3500 Interloop Road, North Cargo Bldg., Atlanta, GA   30320

CEO: William Blackwelder, Mgr.   Tel: (404) 762-3030   %FO: 100

Bus: *International commercial air*   Fax: (404) 767-5612
    transport services.

KLM-ROYAL DUTCH AIRLINES

565 Taxter Road, Elmsford, NY   10523

CEO: Jan Meurer, SVP   Tel: (914) 784-2000   %FO: 100

Bus: *International commercial air*   Fax: (914) 784-2413   Emp: 1,100
    transport services.

KLM-ROYAL DUTCH AIRLINES

9841 Airport Boulevard, Los Angeles, CA   90045

CEO: Paul T. Hanrath, Mgr.   Tel: (310) 646-4004   %FO: 100

Bus: *International commercial air*   Fax: (310) 649-0665
    transport services.

KLM-ROYAL DUTCH AIRLINES

Box 66357 AMF, O'Hare Intl Airport, Chicago, IL   60666

CEO: Michael Gerbino, Mgr.   Tel: (312) 686-6047   %FO: 100

Bus: *International commercial air*   Fax: (312) 601-8701
    transport services.

KLM-ROYAL DUTCH AIRLINES

5105 Northwest Drive, St. Paul, MN   55111-3034

CEO: Jan Willem Smeulers, VP   Tel: (612) 727-0688

Bus: *International commercial air*   Fax: (612) 727-8300
    transport services.

KLM-ROYAL DUTCH AIRLINES

PO Box 60277 AMF, Houston, TX   77205

CEO: Eric Jones, Mgr.   Tel: (713) 821-6642   %FO: 100

Bus: *International commercial air*   Fax: (713) 821-1251
    transport services.

• KPN ROYAL DUTCH TELECOM

Postbus 30000, NL-2500 GA, Den Haag, Netherlands

CEO: Paul Smits, Chmn.   Tel: 31-70-343-4343

Bus: *Engaged in telecommunications.*   Fax:
    www.kpn.com

KPN ROYAL DUTCH TELECOM

1270 Avenue of the Americas, Ste. 2212, New York, NY   10020

CEO: Dirk Jan Frijing, CEO   Tel: (212) 246-1818   %FO: 100

Bus: *Engaged in telecommunications.*   Fax: (212) 246-1905

- **LEASE PLAN HOLDING N.V.**

Postboks 6019, Etterstad, NL-0601, Oslo, Norway

CEO: Anton C. Goudsmit, Pres.

Tel: 47-2306-9800

Bus: *Corporate fleet leasing and management.*

Fax: 47-2306-9801

www.leaseplan.no

LEASE PLAN HOLDING

180 Interstate North Pkwy., Ste. 400, Atlanta, GA   30339

CEO: Dave Bush, SVP

Tel: (770) 933-9090

%FO: 100

Bus: *Engaged in vehicle leasing and fleet management solutions.*

Fax: (770) 933-9091

Emp: 65

- **MARTINAIR HOLLAND N.V.**

PO Box 7507, NL-1118 ZD, Schiphol Airport, Amsterdam, Netherlands

CEO: A. Van Bochove, Pres.

Tel: 31-20-601-1212

Rev: $811

Bus: *Passenger and cargo airline.*

Fax: 31-20-601-0123

Emp: 2,300

www.martinair.com

MARTINAIR SERVICES

11001 Aviation Blvd., Ste. 221, Los Angeles, CA   90045

CEO: Karen L. Olsen, Sales Mgr.

Tel: (310) 645-2570

%FO: 100

Bus: *International passenger/cargo air transportation.*

Fax: (310) 645-2852

MARTINAIR SERVICES N.A.

5550 Glades Road, Ste. 600, Boca Raton, FL   33431

CEO: Lucien Schroder, VP

Tel: (561) 391-6165

%FO: 100

Bus: *Airline sales/marketing and service.*

Fax: (561) 391-2188

Emp: 75

- **NAUTA DUTILH**

Prises Irenestraat 59, NL-1077 WV, Amsterdam, Netherlands

CEO: P. J. Verloop, Mng. Prtn.

Tel: 31-20-541-4646

Bus: *International law firm.*

Fax: 31-20-661-2827

Emp: 400

www.nautadutilh.com

NAUTA DUTILH

One Rockefeller Plaza, 23rd Fl., New York, NY   10178

CEO: Richard Norbruis, Mng. Ptnr.

Tel: (212) 218-2990

%FO: 100

Bus: *International law firm.*

Fax: (212) 218-2999

- **NEW SKIES SATELLITES NV**

Rooseveltplantsoen 4, NL-2517 KR, The Hague, Netherlands

CEO: Robert W. Ross, CEO

Tel: 31-70-306-4100

Rev: $200

Bus: *Engaged in satellite communications.*

Fax: 31-70-306-4240

Emp: 220

www.newskies.com

NEW SKIES SATELLITES, INC.
2001 L Street, Ste. 800, Washington, DC   20036
CEO: Robert Ross, CEO   Tel: (202) 478-7100   %FO: 100
Bus: *Engaged in satellite*   Fax: (202) 478-7101
    communications.

• **NUCLETRON B.V.**
Waardgelder 1, NL-3905 TH, Veenendaal, Netherlands.
CEO: Bert De Goort, CEO   Tel: 31-31-853-7133
Bus: *Mfr. medical, industrial and defense*   Fax: 31-31-855-0485
    imaging and optical instruments.   www.nucletron.com

   NUCLETRON INC.
   7080 Columbia Gateway Drive, Columbia, MD   21046
   CEO: Howard Motter, Pres. & CEO   Tel: (410) 312-4100   %FO: 100
   Bus: *Mfr./distributor medical,*   Fax: (410) 312-4199
       industrial and defense imaging
       and optical instruments.

• **OCÉ NEDERLAND N.V.**
St. Urbanusweg 43, NL-5914 CA, Venlo, Netherlands
CEO: R. L. van Iperen, CEO   Tel: 31-77-359-2222   Rev: $2,709
Bus: *Reprographics, copiers, printers, office*   Fax: 31-77-354-4700   Emp: 22,253
    automation.   www.oce.com

   ARKWRIGHT INC.
   538 Main Street, Fiskeville, RI   02823
   CEO: Joseph R. Marciano, CEO   Tel: (401) 821-1000   %FO: 100
   Bus: *Sales/service office automation*   Fax: (401) 826-3926
       equipment.

   OCÉ - USA HOLDING, INC.
   8600 West Bryn Mawr Avenue, 6th Fl., Chicago, IL   60631
   CEO: Giovanni Pelizzari, Pres.   Tel: (773) 714-3689   %FO: 100
   Bus: *Sales/service of reprographic*   Fax: (888) 308-8994
       equipment.

   OCÉ - USA INC.
   441 Lexington Avenue, 2nd Fl., New York, NY   10017
   CEO: Bob Thompson, Dir.   Tel: (212) 681-3700   %FO: 100
   Bus: *Sales/service of copier systems.*   Fax: (212) 986-9758

   OCÉ IMAGING SUPPLIES
   1800 Bruning Drive West, Itasca, IL   60153
   CEO: Giovanni Pelizzari, Pres.   Tel: (773) 714-8500   %FO: 100
   Bus: *Mfr. imaging supplies.*   Fax: (773) 714-4056

OCÉ PRINTING SYSTEMS INC.
5600 Broken Sound Blvd., PO Box 310710, Boca Raton, FL   33431-0710
CEO: Giovanni Pelizzari, Pres.   Tel: (561) 997-3100   %FO: 100
Bus: *Mfr. printing systems.*   Fax: (561) 997-3352

OCÉ USA INC.
5450 North Cumberland Avenue, Chicago, IL   60656
CEO: Giovanni Pelizzari, Pres.   Tel: (773) 714-8500   %FO: 100
Bus: *Mfr. mid/high volume copiers.*   Fax: (773) 714-0542

● **OLDELFT ULTRASOUND BV**
PO Box 5082, NL-2600 GB, Delft, Netherlands
CEO: Gerard Veld, CEO   Tel: 31-15-2698-900
Bus: *Mfr./distributes medical and industrial*   Fax: 31-15-2698-905
   products.   www.oldelft.nl

OLDELFT ULTRASOUND, INC.
9108 Guilford Road, Columbia, MD   21046
CEO: Don Phillips, CEO   Tel: (301) 498-4303   %FO: 100
Bus: *Mfr./distributes medical and*   Fax: (301) 498-9571
   industrial products.

● **PIE MEDICAL (LEISEGANG) N.V.**
Philipsweg 1, NL-6227 AJ, Maastricht, Netherlands
CEO: Bas Alberts, Pres.   Tel: 31-43-382-4600
Bus: *Mfr. diagnostic ultrasound systems.*   Fax: 31-43-382-4601   Emp: 200
          www.piemedical.com

CLASSIC MEDICAL SUPPLY, INC.
19900 Mona Road, Ste. 105, Tequesta, FL   33469
CEO: S. Dumond   Tel: (561) 746-9527   %FO: 100
Bus: *Mfr. diagnostic ultrasound systems.* Fax: (561) 746-4212

● **PURAC BIOCHEM**
PO Box 21, NL-4200 AA, Gorinchem, Netherlands
CEO: Gerry Bening, Pres.   Tel: 31-18-369-5695
Bus: *Produces natural lactic acid, lactates,*   Fax: 31-18-369-5600
   lactitol, lactides and polylactides.   www.purac.com

PURAC AMERICA INC.
111 Barclay Boulevard, Lincolnshire, IL   60069
CEO: Ellis Hogetoorn   Tel: (847) 634-6330   %FO: 100
Bus: *Mfr./sales lactic acid and*   Fax: (847) 634-1992
   derivatives.

● **QIAGEN N.V.**

Spoorstraat 50, NL-5911KJ, Venlo, Netherlands

CEO: Metin Colpan, CEO	Tel: 31-77-320-8400	Rev: $204
Bus: *Mfr. products for drug screening,*	Fax: 31-77-320-8409	Emp: 1,300
diagnostics and development of genetic	www.qiagen.com	
vaccinations. (JV of Quiagen Germany)		

QIAGEN INC.

28159 Avenue Stanford, Valencia, CA 91355

CEO: Mary Claire Bice	Tel: (661) 294-7940	%FO: 100
Bus: *Sales/distribution of products for*	Fax: (800) 718-8157	
drug screening, diagnostics and		
development of genetic		
vaccinations.		

● **RABOBANK NEDERLAND**

PO Box 17100, NL-3500 HG, Utrecht, Netherlands

CEO: Hans Smits, Chmn.	Tel: 31-30-216-9500	Rev: $15,630
Bus: *Banking and financial services.*	Fax: 31-30-216-3640	Emp: 45,000
	www.rabobank.nl	

RABOBANK INTERNATIONAL

300 South Wacker Dr., Ste. 3500, Chicago, IL 60606

CEO: William A. Padula, COO	Tel: (312) 786-0033	%FO: 100
Bus: *Banking and financial services.*	Fax: (312) 408-8240	

RABOBANK INTERNATIONAL

245 Park Avenue, 37th Fl., New York, NY 10167

CEO: Reinier Mesritz, Dir.	Tel: (212) 916-7800	%FO: 100
Bus: *Banking and financial services.*	Fax: (212) 818-0233	Emp: 330

RABOBANK INTERNATIONAL

245 Park Avenue, 37th Fl., New York, NY 10167

CEO: Sheldon Sussman, Mng. Dir.	Tel: (212) 916-7800	%FO: 100
Bus: *Engaged in investment banking.*	Fax: (212) 818-0233	

● **RANDSTAD HOLDING NV**

Diemermere 25, NL-1112 TC, Diemen, Netherlands

CEO: Hans Zwarts, Pres. & CEO	Tel: 31-20-569-5911	Rev: $5,604
Bus: *Engaged in office staffing, temporary*	Fax: 31-20-569-5520	Emp: 254,000
staffing, cleaning staffing and security	www.randstadholding.com	
personnel staffing.		

CREATIVE TALENT

55 West Monroe, Ste. 1010, Chicago, IL 60603

CEO: Alan Gershlak, Mng. Dir.   Tel: (312) 558-9199   %FO: 100

Bus: *Engaged in temporary office*   Fax: (312) 558-9176
staffing.

RANDSTAD

1400 Old Country Road, Ste. 211, Westbury, NY 11590

CEO: C. Doyle, Mgr.   Tel: (516) 333-2323   %FO: 100

Bus: *Engaged in temporary office*   Fax: (516) 333-6811
staffing.

RANDSTAT

55 West Monroe, Ste. 1010, Chicago, IL 60603

CEO: J. H. Reese, Pres.   Tel: (312) 558-9199   %FO: 100

Bus: *Engaged in temporary office*   Fax: (312) 558-9176
staffing.

RANDSTAD

486 Totten Pond Road, Waltham, MA 02451

CEO: Kristin Hilliard, VP   Tel: (781) 890-2727   %FO: 100

Bus: *Engaged in temporary office*   Fax: (781) 890-2727
staffing.

RANDSTAD STAFFING SERVICES

2015 South Park Place SE, Atlanta, GA 30339

CEO: Eric Vonk, Pres.   Tel: (770) 937-7000   %FO: 100

Bus: *Engaged in temporary office,*   Fax: (770) 937-7100
cleaning and security personnel
staffing.

TECH SPECIALISTS, DIV RANDSTAD

One Corporation Way, Peabody, MA 01960

CEO: Jason Bovey   Tel: (978) 538-9000   %FO: 100

Bus: *Engaged in temporary office*   Fax: (978) 538-9596
staffing.

● **REAL ABN AMRO BANK N.V.**

Foppingadreef 22, PO Box 283, NL-1102 BS, Amsterdam, Netherlands

CEO: Rijkman W. J. Groenink, Chmn.   Tel: 31-20-628-9898   Rev: $36,232

Bus: *Engaged in banking and financial*   Fax: 31-20-628-1229   Emp: 108,690
services.   www.abnamro.com

ABN AMRO BANK N.V.
One Post Office Square, 39th Fl., Boston, MA   02109
CEO: Carol A. Levine, Sr. VP
Bus: *International/domestic banking services.*
Tel: (617) 988-7900
Fax: (617) 988-7910
%FO: 100

ABN AMRO BANK N.V.
601 Second Avenue South, Minneapolis, MN   55401
CEO: James Pierpont, Mng. Dir.
Bus: *Banking and financial services.*
Tel: (612) 337-9868
Fax: (612) 338-8687
%FO: 100

ABN AMRO BANK N.V.
300 S. Grand Avenue, Ste. 1115, Los Angeles, CA   90017
CEO: Catheryn N. Fuller, SVP
Bus: *Banking and financial services.*
Tel: (213) 687-2050
Fax: (213) 687-2061
%FO: 100

ABN AMRO BANK N.V.
One PPG Place, Ste. 2950, Pittsburgh, PA   15222-5400
CEO: Andre Nel, SVP
Bus: *Banking and financial services.*
Tel: (412) 566-2250
Fax: (412) 566-2266
%FO: 100

ABN AMRO BANK N.V.
Three Riverway, Ste. 1700, Houston, TX   77056
CEO: Don Hanna, II, SVP
Bus: *Banking and financial services.*
Tel: (713) 629-6666
Fax: (713) 629-7533
%FO: 100

ABN AMRO BANK N.V.
200 S. Biscayne Blvd., 22nd Fl., Miami, FL   33131-1596
CEO: Paul Koch, SVP
Bus: *Banking and financial services.*
Tel: (305) 372-1596
Fax: (305) 372-2397
%FO: 100

ABN AMRO BANK N.V.
600 University Street, Ste. 2323, Seattle, WA   98101
CEO: Christian Sievers, SVP
Bus: *International/domestic banking services.*
Tel: (206) 587-2330
Fax: (206) 682-5641
%FO: 100

ABN AMRO BANK N.V.
101 California Street, Ste. 4550, San Francisco, CA   94111
CEO: Clayton Jackson, SVP
Bus: *International/domestic banking services.*
Tel: (415) 984-3700
Fax: (415) 362-3524
%FO: 100

ABN AMRO BANK N.V.
55 East 52nd Street, New York, NY   10055
CEO: Thomas Flemming, SVP   Tel: (212) 446-4271   %FO: 100
Bus: *International/domestic banking*   Fax: (212) 754-6114
    services.

ABN AMRO BANK N.V.
One Ravinia Drive, Ste. 1200, Atlanta, GA   30346
CEO: W. Patrick Fischer, SVP   Tel: (770) 396-0066   %FO: 100
Bus: *International/domestic banking*   Fax: (770) 395-9188
    services.

ALLEGHANY ASSET MANAGEMENT, INC.
135 South LaSalle Street, Chicago, IL   60603
CEO: Stuart Bilton, Pres.   Tel: (312) 904-2000   %FO: 100
Bus: *Banking and financial services.*   Fax: (312) 443-2819

EUROPEAN AMERICAN BANK
1345 Avenue of the Americas, New York, NY   10105
CEO: Edward Traicglianti, Chmn.   Tel: (212) 245-0247   %FO: 100
Bus: *Banking and financial services.*   Fax: (212) 704-0819

EUROPEAN AMERICAN BANK
One Rockefeller Plaza, New York, NY   10020
CEO: Harry Tempest, Pres.   Tel: (212) 765-3315   %FO: 100
Bus: *Banking and financial services.*   Fax: (212) 568-1613

EUROPEAN AMERICAN BANK
1107 Broadway, New York, NY   10005
CEO: Jim Paguaga, Mgr.   Tel: (212) 645-3200   %FO: 100
Bus: *Banking and financial services.*   Fax: (212) 645-8735

EUROPEAN AMERICAN BANK
E.A.B. Plaza, Uniondale, NY   11555
CEO: Edward Traicglianti, Chmn.   Tel: (516) 296-5000   %FO: 100
Bus: *Banking and financial services.*   Fax: (516) 296-6034

LASALLE NATIONAL BANK
135 South LaSalle Street, Chicago, IL   60603
CEO: S. K. Heitmann, Pres.   Tel: (312) 904-2000   %FO: 100
Bus: *Banking and financial services.*   Fax: (312) 443-2819

LASALLE TALMAN BANK, F.S.B.
30 West Monroe Street, 3rd Fl., Chicago, IL   60629
CEO: S. K. Heitmann, Pres.   Tel: (312) 726-8915   %FO: 100
Bus: *Banking and financial services.*   Fax: (312) 263-9042

STANDARD FEDERAL BANK

120 North LaSalle Street, Chicago, IL 60601

CEO: Scott K. Hietmann, Chmn.　　Tel: (312) 541-9696　　%FO: 100

Bus: *Banking and financial services.*　Fax: (312) 541-9797

STANDARD FEDERAL BANK

17430 West Thirteen Mile Road, Auburn Hills, MI 48326

CEO: Scott K. Hietmann, Chmn.　　Tel: (248) 647-0280　　%FO: 100

Bus: *Banking and financial services.*　Fax: (248) 647-0677

STANDARD FEDERAL BANK

2600 West Big Beaver Road, PO Box 3703, Troy, MI 48007-3703

CEO: Scott K. Hietmann, Chmn.　　Tel: (248) 643-9600　　%FO: 100

Bus: *Banking and financial services.*　Fax:

STANDARD FEDERAL BANK

17540 Grand River Avenue, Detroit, MI 48207

CEO: Scott Heidman, Pres.　　　　Tel: (313) 838-2950　　%FO: '

Bus: *Banking and financial services.*　Fax: (313) 838-0750

STANDARD FEDERAL BANK

18901 Kelly Road, Detroit, MI 48224

CEO: Scott Heidman, Pres.　　　　Tel: (313) 372-8877　　%FO: 100

Bus: *Banking and financial services.*　Fax: (313) 372-3150

STANDARD FEDERAL BANK

18620 Livernois, Detroit, MI 48223

CEO: Scott Heidman, Pres.　　　　Tel: (313) 345-6062　　%FO: 100

Bus: *Home lending services.*　　　Fax: (313) 372-3150

● **RODAMCO N.V.**

Coolsingel 120, Postbus 973, NL-3011 A6, Rotterdam, Netherlands

CEO: Gerald Egan, CEO　　　　　Tel: 31-10-224-1224　　Rev: $587

Bus: *Real estate development banking and*　Fax: 31-10-411-5288
　　investment services.　　　　　www.rodamco-na.com

RODAMCO NORTH AMERICA

950 East Paces Ferry Road, Ste. 2275, Atlanta, GA 30326

CEO: Peggy Liddel, VP　　　　　Tel: (404) 266-1002　　%FO: 100

Bus: *Real estate development banking*　Fax: (404) 239-6097
　　and investment services.

• ROYAL AHOLD N.V.

Albert Heijnweg 1, PO Box 33, NL-1500 EA, Zaandam, Netherlands

CEO: Cees H. van der Hoeven, CEO   Tel: 31-75-659-9111   Rev: $46,311

Bus: *Engaged in international food and*   Fax: 31-75-650-8350   Emp: 332,050
beverage retailing; interests include   www.ahold.com
food chains Stop & Shop, Tops, Giant
Food and Pathmark stores.

AHOLD USA, INC.

14101 Newbrook Drive, Chantilly, VA   20151

CEO: William Grize, Pres. & CEO   Tel: (703) 961-6000   %FO: 100

Bus: *U.S. headquarters holding*   Fax: (703) 961-6051   Emp: 140,000
company for food and beverage
retailing.

BI-LO INC.

PO Box 99, Maudlin, SC   29607

CEO: Jon Wilken Jr., CEO   Tel: (864) 234-1600   %FO: 100

Bus: *Retail food chain.*   Fax: (864) 297-1916

GIANT FOOD STORES INC.

1149 Harrisburg Pike, Carlisle, PA   17013

CEO: Tony Schiano, CEO   Tel: (717) 249-4000   %FO: 100

Bus: *Retail food chain.*   Fax: (717) 249-4970   Emp: 28,000

GIANT FOOD STORES INC.

6300 Sheriff Road, Landover, MD   20785

CEO: Richard Baird, CEO   Tel: (301) 341-4100   %FO: 100

Bus: *Retail food chain.*   Fax: (301) 618-4964

STOP & SHOP COMPANIES

1385 Hancock Street, Quincy, MA   02169

CEO: Marc Smith, Pres. & CEO   Tel: (781) 380-8000   %FO: 100

Bus: *Retail food chain*   Fax: (781) 770-8190

TOPS MARKETS

6363 Main Street, Williamsville, NY   14221

CEO: Frank Curci, Pres & CEO   Tel: (716) 635-5000   %FO: 100

Bus: *Retail food chain.*   Fax: (716) 635-5102

U.S. FOODSERVICE

9755 Patuxent Woods Drive, Columbia, MD   21046

CEO: James L. Miller, Pres. & CEO   Tel: (410) 312-7100   %FO: 100

Bus: *Engaged in restaurant, hotel and*   Fax: (410) 312-7598
school food distribution.

- **ROYAL CEBECO GROUP COOPERATIVE**

Blaak 31, Postbus 182, NL-3000 AD, Rotterdam, Netherlands

CEO: H. de Boon, Pres.

Bus: *Wholesale, agricultural products; mfr., agricultural machinery and food products.*

Tel: 31-10-454 4911
Fax: 31-10-411 3889
www.cebeco.com

  CEBECO INTERNATIONAL SEEDS, INC.

  820 West First Street, Halsey, OR   97348

  CEO: Rich Underwood, Pres.

  Bus: *Wholesale, agricultural products; mfr., agricultural machinery and food products.*

  Tel: (541) 369-2251
  Fax: (541) 369-2640

  %FO: 100

  CEBECO LILIES INC.

  14074 Arndt Road, NE, Aurora, OR   97002

  CEO: David Webber, Mgr.

  Bus: *Wholesale, agricultural products; mfr., agricultural machinery and food products.*

  Tel: (503) 678-1850
  Fax: (503) 678-1116

  %FO: 100

- **ROYAL DUTCH/SHELL GROUP**

30 Carel van Bylandtlaan, NL-2596 HR, The Hague, Netherlands

CEO: Maarten A. van den Bergh, Mng. Dir.

Bus: *Engaged in oil and natural gas exploration and production.*

Tel: 31-70-377-3395
Fax: 31-70-377-3115
www.shell.com

Rev: $149,146
Emp: 96,000

  CORAL ENERGY

  909 Fannin Street, Ste. 700, Houston, TX   77010

  CEO: Charles R. Crisp, Pres & CEO

  Bus: *Engaged in marketing of Shell's gas production.*

  Tel: (713) 767-5400
  Fax: (713) 230-3800

  %FO: 100

  MONTELL NORTH AMERICA INC.

  2801 Centerville Road, Wilmington, DE   19808

  CEO: Charles E. Platz, Pres.

  Bus: *Produces, market and sells polyolefins.*

  Tel: (302) 996-6000
  Fax: (302) 996-6051

  %FO: 100

  SHELL CHEMICALS

  PO Box 2463, Houston, TX   77252-2463

  CEO: Jerry L. Golden, EVP

  Bus: *Mfr. chemicals.*

  Tel: (713) 241-6161
  Fax: (713) 241-4044

  %FO: 100

SHELL EXPLORATION AND PRODUCTION COMPANY
PO Box 2463, Houston, TX   77252-2463

CEO: Walter van de Vijver, Pres.   Tel: (713) 241-6161   %FO: 100
Bus: *Produces oil and natural gas.*   Fax: (713) 241-4044

SHELL OIL COMPANY
One Shell Plaza, PO Box 2463, Houston, TX   77252

CEO: Steven L. Miller, CEO   Tel: (713) 241-6161   %FO: 100
Bus: *Global oil/gas company; JV with* Fax: (713) 241-4044   Emp: 19,000
UK.

SHELL SERVICE INTERNATIONAL INC.
PO Box 4855, Houston, TX   77252-4855

CEO: Guardie E. Banister, Pres.   Tel: (713) 241-1655   %FO: 100
Bus: *Provides business and IT services.* Fax: (713) 241-1376

● **ROYAL NEDLLOYD NV**

Postbus 487, NL-3000 AL, Rotterdam, Netherlands

CEO: Leo Berndsen, Chmn. & CEO   Tel: 31-10-400-7111   Rev: $1,906
Bus: *International shipping and transport* Fax: 31-10-404-6075   Emp: 13,500
services.   www.nedlloyd.com

DAMCO MARITIME CORPORATION
One Intercontinental Way, Peabody, MA   01960

CEO: David Powell, Pres.   Tel: (978) 535-1170   %FO: 100
Bus: *Sales/distribution of frozen* Fax: (978) 535-7028
pastries.

MAMMOET TRANSPORT USA INC.
20525 F.M. 521, Rosharon, TX   77583

CEO: Per Haugaard, Pres.   Tel: (281) 369-3900   %FO: 100
Bus: *Heavy transport operations.* Fax: (281) 369-3822

MAMMOET WESTERN INC.
1419 Potrero Avenue, South El Monte, CA   91733

CEO: Dennis Davenport, Pres.   Tel: (626) 442-5542   %FO: 100
Bus: *Heavy transport operations.* Fax: (626) 442-0841

P&0 NEDLLOYD LINES
Green Briar Point, Ste. 285, Chesapeake, VA   23320

CEO: Tom Dushatinski, Mgr.   Tel: (757) 420-4200   %FO: 100
Bus: *Steamship line.*   Fax: (757) 399-7887

NEDLLOYD LINES
3875 Faber Pl., Ste. 200, Charleston, SC   29405-8558

CEO: Chuck Csernica, AVP   Tel: (843) 566-7400   %FO: 100
Bus: *Ocean transportation services.* Fax: (843) 747-8238

P&O NEDLLOYD LINES
180 Howard Street, Ste. 300, San Francisco, CA   94105
CEO: Dick Hanft, Mgr.   Tel: (415) 817-3500   %FO: 100
Bus: *International shipping agency.*   Fax: (415) 817-3515

P&O NEDLLOYD LINES
2655 LeJeune Road, Ste. 703, Coral Gables, FL   33134
CEO: Michiel Messchaert, Mgr.   Tel: (305) 441-9140   %FO: 100
Bus: *International shipping agency.*   Fax: (305) 441-2984

P&O NEDLLOYD LINES U.S.A. CORPORATION
2100 River Edge Parkway, Ste. 300, Atlanta, GA   30328
CEO: Les Catrona, VP   Tel: (770) 951-3600   %FO: 100
Bus: *Ocean transportation services.*   Fax: (770) 980-4012   Emp: 65

• **ROYAL NUMICO N.V.**
PO Box 1, NL-2700 MA, Zoetermeer, The Netherlands
CEO: J. C. T. van der Wielen, CEO   Tel: 31-79-3539-000   Rev: $3,977
Bus: *Mfr. baby food products, dietary and*   Fax: 31-79-3539-620   Emp: 18,850
clinical nutritional products and   www.numico.com
supplements.

   GENERAL NUTRITION COMPANIES, INC.
   300 Sixth Avenue, Pittsburgh, PA   15222
   CEO: William E. Watts, Pres. & CEO   Tel: (412) 288-4600   %FO: 100
   Bus: *Mfr. nutritional supplements and*   Fax: (412) 338-8954
   self-care products.

   REXALL SUNDOWN, INC.
   6111 Broken Sound Parkway NW, Boca Raton, FL   33487
   CEO: Damon DeSantis, Pres. & CEO   Tel: (561) 241-9400   %FO: 100
   Bus: *Mfr. nutritional supplements and*   Fax: (561) 995-0197
   products.

• **ROYAL PHILIPS ELECTRONICS N.V.**
The Rembrandt Tower, Amstelplein NL-11096 HA, Amsterdam, Netherlands
CEO: Gerard J. Kleisterlee, CEO   Tel: 31-20-597-7777   Rev: $37,900
Bus: *Mfr. consumer electronics, lighting*   Fax: 31-20-597-7070   Emp: 219,400
components, appliances, professional   www.philips.com
system, communications and
information system, medical imaging
equipment.

ADAC LABORATORIES, INC.
540 Adler Drive, Milpitas, CA   95035

CEO: R. Andrew Eckert, CEO	Tel: (408) 321-9100	%FO: 100
Bus: *Mfr. nuclear medicine gamma cameras and work-stations, including computer cardiac software programs.*	Fax: (408) 321-9100	Emp: 900

ADVANCE TRANSFORMER COMPANY
10275 West Higgins Road, Rosemont, IL   60018-3816

CEO: Gary Lehman, Pres.	Tel: (847) 390-5000	%FO: 100
Bus: *Mfr./sales/distribution of professional light systems.*	Fax: (847) 390-5109	Emp: 300

ATL ULTRASOUND INC.
PO Box 3003, Bothell, WA   98041-3003

CEO: Timothy C. Mickelson, Pres.	Tel: (425) 487-7000	%FO: 100
Bus: *Mfr./sales of diagnostic medical ultrasound systems.*	Fax: (425) 485-6080	

MARANTZ AMERICA, INC.
440 Medinah Road, Roselle, IL   60172-2330

CEO: John McCrady, Pres.	Tel: (630) 307-3100	%FO: 100
Bus: *Mktg./sale high-performance audio and video components.*	Fax:	

NORELCO CONSUMER PRODUCTS COMPANY
1010 Washington Blvd., Stamford, CT   06901

CEO: Patrick J. Dinley, Pres.	Tel: (203) 973-0200	%FO: 100
Bus: *Mfr. razors, kitchen & travel appliances.*	Fax: (203) 975-1812	Emp: 120

PHILIPS ANALYTICAL
85 McKee Drive, Mahwah, NJ   07430

CEO: Ken Orsini, Pres.	Tel: (201) 529-3800	%FO: 100
Bus: *Mfr. x-ray and electron optics, analytical products.*	Fax: (201) 529-2252	

PHILIPS BROADBAND NETWORKS, INC.
64 Perimeter Center East, Atlanta, GA   30046-6400

CEO: Peter Gentsch, Chmn.	Tel: (770) 821-3269	%FO: 100
Bus: *Mfr. distribution equipment for cable TV & business information networks.*	Fax: (770) 682-9006	Emp: 150

PHILIPS BROADCAST INC.
2300 South Decker Lake Blvd., Salt Lake City, UT 84119
CEO: Joop Janssen, VP   Tel: (801) 972-8000   %FO: 100
Bus: *Mfr. professional television*   Fax: (801) 972-6304
systems for broadcast, production
and post-production and corporate
applications.

PHILIPS COMMUNICATIONS & SECURITY SYSTEMS INC.
1004 New Holland Avenue, Lancaster, PA 17601-5606
CEO: Jerry Gabberd, Pres.   Tel: (717) 295-6123   %FO: 100
Bus: *Mfr. closed-circuit television*   Fax: (717) 295-6097
equipment, access control
hardware and communication
products.

PHILIPS COMPONENTS INC.
1000 West Maude Avenue, Sunnyvale, CA 94086
CEO: M. T. Medeiros, CEO   Tel: (408) 617-7770   %FO: 100
Bus: *Mfr. components for auto,*   Fax: (408) 617-7705
telecommunications, computer,
and industrial electronics markets.

PHILIPS CONSUMER COMMUNICATIONS
66 Perimeter Center East, Ste. 700, Atlanta, GA 30346
CEO: Robert K. Faught, Pres.   Tel: (770) 821-2400   %FO: 100
Bus: *Mfr. and sales of digital and*   Fax:
analog cellular phones.

PHILIPS CONSUMER ELECTRONICS COMPANY
PO Box 14810, One Phillips Drive, Knoxville, TN 37914-1810
CEO: Robert Minkhorst, Pres.   Tel: (865) 521-4316   %FO: 100
Bus: *Mfr. home and portable audio and*   Fax: (865) 521-4308
video systems and components

PHILIPS CONSUMER ELECTRONICS NORTH AMERICA
PO Box 467300, Atlanta, GA 31146-7300
CEO: Robert Minkhorst, Pres.   Tel: (770) 821-2400   %FO: 100
Bus: *Mfr. digital convergence products*   Fax: (770) 821-2555
for Televisions, audio equipment,
PC monitors and peripherals.

PHILIPS DISPLAY COMPONENTS COMPANY
300 West Morgan Road, Ann Arbor, MI 48106
CEO: Cor Saris, Pres.   Tel: (734) 996-9400   %FO: 100
Bus: *Mfr./sales of color TV tubes and*   Fax: (734) 761-2886
data display tubes.

PHILIPS ELECTRONIC MANUFACTURING TECHNOLOGIES
5110 McGinnis Ferry Road, Alpharetta, GA   30005
CEO: Mike Buscher, Pres.   Tel: (770) 751-4420   %FO: 100
Bus: *Mfr. and sales color picture tubes*   Fax: (770) 751-4420
for TV and computer monitors.

PHILIPS ELECTRONICS NORTH AMERICA CORPORATION
1251 Avenue of the Americas, New York, NY   10020
CEO: William Curran, CEO   Tel: (212) 536-0500   %FO: 100
Bus: *Holding company.*   Fax: (212) 536-0500   Emp: 200

PHILIPS LIGHTING COMPANY
200 Franklin Square Drive, Somerset, NJ   08875-6800
CEO: Larry Wilton, Pres.   Tel: (732) 563-3000   %FO: 100
Bus: *Mfr./sales industrial, commercial*   Fax: (732) 563-3000
and consumer products.

PHILIPS MEDICAL SYSTEMS NA
710 Bridgeport Avenue, Shelton, CT   06484
CEO: Jack Price, Pres.   Tel: (203) 926-7674   %FO: 100
Bus: *Sales/service of medical*   Fax: (203) 929-6099
diagnostic imaging and
radiotherapy equipment.

PHILIPS RESEARCH
345 Scarborough Road, Briarcliff Manor, NY   10510
CEO: Barry Singer, Pres.   Tel: (914) 945-6000   %FO: 100
Bus: *Electronics R&D.*   Fax: (914) 945-6375

PHILIPS SEMICONDUCTORS
1240 McKay Drive, San Jose, CA   95131
CEO: Leon Husson, EVP   Tel: (408) 434-3000   %FO: 100
Bus: *Mfr. custom and semi-custom*   Fax: (408) 434-3100   Emp: 2,500
integrated circuits.

PHILIPS SEMICONDUCTORS
811 East Arques Avenue, Sunnyvale, CA   94088-3409
CEO: David Barringer   Tel: (408) 991-2000   %FO: 100
Bus: *Design/mfr./distribution integrated* Fax: (408) 991-2000
circuits

PHILIPS SPEECH PROCESSING
64 Perimeter Center East, 6th Fl., Atlanta, GA   30346
CEO: Ron van den Bos, Pres.   Tel: (770) 821-3678   %FO: 100
Bus: *Mfr. speech recognition products.* Fax: (770) 821-3678

- **ROYAL TEN CATE N.V.**
Egbert Gorterstraat 3, NL-7607 GB, Almelo, Netherlands

CEO: L. De Vries, Chmn.	Tel: 31-546-544911	Rev: $2,812
Bus: *Manufacture of industrial/agricultural/erosion control fabrics, fire hoses, geotextiles.*	Fax: 31-546-514145 www.tencate.com	Emp: 3,600

    BAYCOR CORPORATION
    PO Box 1979, Cornelia, GA   30531

CEO: Ron McKinney, VP Mfg.	Tel: (706) 778-9794	%FO: 100
Bus: *Geotextiles.*	Fax: (706) 778-2048	

    ROYAL TEN CATE (USA) INC.
    2170 Satellite Blvd., Ste. 350, Duluth, GA   30097-4074

CEO: Dave Clark, Pres.	Tel: (770) 689-2621	%FO: 100
Bus: *U.S. holding company.*	Fax: (770) 447-6272	

- **SHV HOLDINGS N.V.**
Rijinkade 1, Utrecht NL-3511 LC, Netherlands

CEO: P. C. Klaver, CEO	Tel: 31-30-233-8833	Rev: $10,265
Bus: *Engaged in energy and retail businesses.*	Fax: 31-30-233-8304 www.shv.nl	Emp: 33,400

    THE DAVID J. JOSEPH COMPANY
    PO Box 1078, 300 Pike Street, Cincinnati, OH   45201

CEO: Keith B. Grass, Pres. & CEO	Tel: (513) 345-4310	%FO: 100
Bus: *Metal recycling and marketing of scrap iron and steel.*	Fax: (513) 345-4396	Emp: 1,200

- **STIBBE SIMONT MONAHAN DUHOT**
PO Box 75640, NL-1070 AP, Amsterdam, Netherlands

CEO: Hans M. Van Veggel, Mng. Ptnr.	Tel: 31-20-546-0606	
Bus: *International law firm.*	Fax: 31-20-546-0123 www.stibbe.nl	Emp: 800

    SIBBE SIMONT MONAHAN DUHOT
    350 Park Avenue, 28th Fl., New York, NY   10022

CEO: T. H. Van Engelen, Mng. Ptnr.	Tel: (212) 972-4000	%FO: 100
Bus: *International law firm.*	Fax: (212) 972-4929	

● **STORK N.V.**

Amersfoortsestraatweg 7, NL-1412 KA, Naarden, Netherlands

CEO: Dr. Ir. A.W. Veenman, Chmn. Tel: 31-35-695-7411 Rev: $10,080

Bus: *Machinery and parts textile printing,* Fax: 31-35-694-1184 Emp: 20,000
complete systems for poultry processing www.storkgroup.com
and convenience foods.
• systems and services for aviation and
aerospace

H&E MACHINERY, INC.

334 Comfort Road, Ithaca, NY 14850

CEO: Elmer Locker, Pres. Tel: (607) 277-4968 %FO: 100

Bus: *Mfr. high-tech components for the* Fax: (607) 277-1193
transportation industry, including
steam turbine blades.

H&E TURBO COMPONENTS, INC.

4600 Technology Park, Auburn, NY 13021

CEO: Kevin Beck, Mgr. Tel: (607) 253-6461 %FO: 100

Bus: *Mfr. blading products.* Fax: (607) 277-1193

INSTROMET ULTRASONIC TECHNOLOGY, INC.

12650 Directors Dr., Ste. 100, Stafford, TX 77477

CEO: Richard E. Seif, VP Tel: (281) 491-5252 %FO: 100

Bus: *Mfr. gas measurement and control* Fax: (281) 491-8440
equipment.

STORK CELLRAMIC, INC.

8399 North 87th Street, Milwaukee, WI 53224

CEO: Frank van den Berge, Mgr. Tel: (414) 357-0260 %FO: 100

Bus: *Thermal spray coatings and anilox* Fax: (414) 357-0267
rolls.

STORK FOOD & DAIRY SYSTEMS

PO Box 1258, Gainesville, GA 30503

CEO: Brenda Morales Tel: (770) 535-1875 %FO: 100

Bus: *Sales/distribution/service of* Fax: (770) 536-0841
machinery for meat processing
industry

STORK ROTAFORM SCREENS AMERICA INC.

3201 North Interstate 85, Charlotte, NC 28213

CEO: John Costenoble Tel: (704) 598-7171 %FO: 100

Bus: *Sale of seamless rotary screens for* Fax: (704) 596-0858 Emp: 575
the textile printing industry.

STORK VECO INTERNATIONAL
3 Loomis Street, Bedford, MA   01730
CEO: David M. Haines, VP   Tel: (781) 275-3292   %FO: 100
Bus: *Sales/distribution of perforated*   Fax: (781) 275-4798
products

● **TELEPLAN INTERNATIONAL NV**
De Run 1120, NL-5503 LA, Veldhoven, Netherlands
CEO: Edmund Krix, CEO   Tel: 31-40-255-8670   Rev: $275
Bus: *Provides warranty services for*   Fax: 31-40-255-7311   Emp: 3,700
information technology products.   www.teleplan-int.com

   TELEPLAN (WHITE ELECTRONICS)
   8875 Washington Blvd., Roseville, CA   95678
   CEO: Jack Rockwood   Tel: (916) 677-4850   %FO: 100
   Bus: *Provides warranty services for*   Fax: (916) 677-4496
   information technology products.

   TELEPLAN (WHITE ELECTRONICS)
   6085 Sikorsky Street, Ventura, CA   93003
   CEO: Jim Wharmby   Tel: (805) 644-2944   %FO: 100
   Bus: *Provides warranty services for*   Fax: (805) 644-0593
   information technology products.

   TELEPLAN (WHITE ELECTRONICS)
   13581 Pond Springs Road, Ste. 315, Austin, TX   78729-4421
   CEO: Dene Jacobson   Tel: (512) 258-7590   %FO: 100
   Bus: *Provides warranty services for*   Fax: (512) 219-0021
   information technology products.

   TELEPLAN (WHITE ELECTRONICS)
   2305 Bering Drive, San Jose, CA   95131-1125
   CEO: Tom Ward   Tel: (408) 894-0800   %FO: 100
   Bus: *Provides warranty services for*   Fax: (408) 894-0880
   information technology products.

   TELEPLAN (WHITE ELECTRONICS)
   101 Coolidge Street, South Plainfield, NJ   07080
   CEO: Chris Walsh   Tel: (908) 561-3322   %FO: 100
   Bus: *Provides warranty services for*   Fax: (908) 561-3228
   information technology products.

● **TNT POST GROUP NV**
PO Box 13000, NL-1100 KG, Amsterdam, Netherlands
CEO: Ad J. Scheepbouwer, CEO   Tel: 31-20-500-6000   Rev: $9,358
Bus: *Engaged in international mail services.*   Fax: 31-20-500-7521   Emp: 129,675
www.tntpost-group.com

CTI LOGISTX, INC.
10407 Centurion Parkway North, Ste. 400, Jacksonville, FL   32256-0516
CEO: David G. Kulik, CEO   Tel: (904) 928-1400   %FO: 100
Bus: *Engaged in logistics services.*   Fax: (904) 928-1400

TNT LOGISTICS CORPORATION
1306 Concourse Drive, Ste. 401, Linthicum, MD   21090-1032
CEO: Jim Davidson, SVP   Tel: (410) 859-3313   %FO: 100
Bus: *International transport services.*   Fax: (410) 859-8844

● **TOOLEX INTERNATIONAL N.V.**
De Run 4315, NL-5503 AD, Veldhoven, Netherlands
CEO: Leon Giesen, CEO   Tel: 31-40-258-1581   Rev: $233
Bus: *Mfr. mastering equipment for music,*   Fax: 31-40-254-1985   Emp: 700
video and data compact discs.   www.toolex-alpha.com

TOOLEX USA INC.
6701 Carmel Road, Charlotte, NC   28226
CEO: Dave Johnson, EVP   Tel: (704) 752-8600   %FO: 100
Bus: *Sales/service of mastering*   Fax: (704) 752-1199
equipment for video, music and
data compact discs.

TOOLEX USA INC.
1601 Alton Parkway, Irvine, CA   92606-4878
CEO: Dave Johnson, EVP   Tel: (949) 794-8655   %FO: 100
Bus: *Sales/service of mastering*   Fax: (949) 794-8668
equipment for video, music and
data compact discs.

● **TRIPLE P N.V.**
Ir. D.S. Tuynmanweg 10, NL-4131 PN, Vianen, The Netherlands
CEO: Jan W. Baud, CEO   Tel: 31-34-735-3353   Rev: $121
Bus: *Computer software & services.*   Fax: 31-34-735-3354   Emp: 573
www.triple-p.com

TRIPLE P USA, INC.
11320 Random Hills Road, Suite 375, Fairfax, VA   22030
CEO: Goly Bouromand   Tel: (703) 385-1212   %FO: 100
Bus: *Computer software & services.*   Fax: (703) 385-2091

● **UNILEVER N.V.**

Weena 455, Postbus 760, NL-3000 DK, Rotterdam, Netherlands

CEO: Antony Burgmans, Chmn. & CEO   Tel: 31-10-217-4000   Rev: $44,813

Bus: *Soaps and detergents, foods, chemicals,*   Fax: 31-10-217-4798   Emp: 300,000
personal products (J/V of UNILVER   www.unilever.com
PLC, UK).

CALVIN KLEIN COSMETICS COMPANY

725 Fifth Avenue, New York, NY   10022

CEO: Paulanne Mancuso, Pres. & CEO   Tel: (212) 759-8888   %FO: 100

Bus: *Manufacturer of perfumes.*   Fax: (212) 755-8792

DIVERSEY LEVER

3630 East Kemper Road, Cincinnati, OH   45241-2046

CEO: V. Kasturirangan, SVP   Tel: (513) 554-4200   %FO: 100

Bus: *Mfr. specialty chemicals.*   Fax: (513) 554-4330

DIVERSEY LEVER

14496 Sheldon Road, Plymouth, MI   48170

CEO: Arwin Hughes, Pres.   Tel: (734) 414-1725   %FO: 100

Bus: *Mfr. specialty chemicals.*   Fax: (734) 414-3364

DIVERSEY LEVER INSTITUTIONAL

26935 Northwestern Hwy., Ste. 400, Southfield, MI   48034-8449

CEO: T. Gartland, Pres.   Tel: (248) 304-3400   %FO: 100

Bus: *Mfr. soaps, detergents and*   Fax: (248) 304-3567
chemical products.

ELIZABETH ARDEN

1345 Avenue of the Americas, New York, NY   10105

CEO: E. Scott Beattie, Pres.   Tel: (212) 261-1000   %FO: 100

Bus: *Mfr. cosmetics, perfumes.*   Fax: (212) 261-1350

HELENE CURTIS

325 North Wells Street, Chicago, IL   60610

CEO: Gene Zeffren, COO   Tel: (312) 661-0222   %FO: 100

Bus: *Mfr. cosmetics, perfumes.*   Fax: (312) 836-0125   Emp: 1,900

LIPTON

800 Sylvan Avenue, Englewood Cliffs, NJ   07632

CEO: Richard Goldstein, Pres.   Tel: (201) 567-8000   %FO: 100

Bus: *Manufacturer of tea products.*   Fax: (201) 871-8280

UNILEVER BESTFOODS, INC.

700 Sylvan Avenue, Englewood Cliffs, NJ   07632

CEO: C. R. Shoemate, Pres.   Tel: (201) 894-4000   %FO: 100

Bus: *Mfr. food products.*   Fax: (201) 894-2185

UNILEVER HPC USA
33 Benedict Place, Greenwich, CT   06830
CEO: Robert M. Phillips, Chmn.   Tel: (203) 661-2000   %FO: 100
Bus: *Mfr. home and personal care*   Fax: (203) 625-1602
  products. (Formerly
  Cheseborough-Pond's)

UNILEVER UNITED STATES INC.
390 Park Avenue, New York, NY   10022
CEO: Richard A. Goldstein, Pres.   Tel: (212) 688-6000   %FO: 100
Bus: *Mfr. soaps and detergents.*   Fax: (212) 318-3800   Emp: 38,000

• VAN LEEUWEN PIPE & TUBE B.V.
PO Box 50, NL-3330 AB, Zwijndrecht, Netherlands
CEO: B. van Dam, Pres. & CEO   Tel: 31-78-625-2525   Rev: $454
Bus: *Distribution of carbon steel, weld*   Fax: 31-78-625-2040   Emp: 1,000
  fittings, flanges and pipe.   www.vanleeuwen.com

VAN LEEUWEN PIPE AND TUBE CORPORATION
PO Box 40904, Houston, TX   77040
CEO: Charles Wolley, CEO   Tel: (713) 466-9966   %FO: 100
Bus: *Distribution of pipe, fittings,*   Fax: (713) 466-7423   Emp: 220
  flanges and valves.

• KONINKLIJKE VAN MELLE NV
Zoete Inval 20, NL-4800 DA, Breda, Netherlands
CEO: Izaak L .G. Van Melle, Pres.   Tel: 31-76-527-5000   Rev: $475
Bus: *Mfr. confectionery, biscuits, health*   Fax: 31-76-522-8560   Emp: 3,039
  foods.   www.van-melle.com

VAN MELLE USA INC.
One Van Melle Lane, PO Box 18190, Erlanger, KY   41018
CEO: Martin La Croix, Pres.   Tel: (859) 283-1234   %FO: 100
Bus: *Mfr./import candy.*   Fax: (859) 283-1316   Emp: 100

• VEDIOR NV
Tripolis Bldg. 100, Burgerweeshuispad 121, NL-1076 ET, Amsterdam, Netherlands
CEO: A. V. Martin, CEO   Tel: 31-20-573-5600   Rev: $6,200
Bus: *Engaged in temporary staffing solutions.* Fax: 31-20-573-5601   Emp: 22,450
                                     www.vedior.com

ACSYS INC.
75 14th Street, Ste. 2200, Atlanta, GA   30309
CEO: Jack Unroe, CEO   Tel: (404) 817-9440   %FO: 100
Bus: *Engaged in temporary staffing*   Fax: (404) 815-4703
  solutions.

● **VENDEX KBB N.V.**

PO Box 7997, NL-1008 AD, Amsterdam, Netherlands

CEO: Jan-Michiel Hessels, CEO   Tel: 31-20-549-0500   Rev: $2,837

Bus: *Mfr./sale of do-it-yourself fashion,*   Fax: 31-20-646-1954   Emp: 51,700
household and leisure items and toys..   www.venexbb.com

FAO SCHWARZ

767 Fifth Avenue, New York, NY   10153

CEO: Bud Johnson, CEO   Tel: (212) 644-9410   %FO: 100

Bus: *Toy store chain.*   Fax: (212) 644-2485   Emp: 150

● **VETUS DENOUDEN NV**

Fokkerstraat 571, NL-3125 BD, Schiedam, Netherlands

CEO: W.H.den Ouden, Pres.   Tel: 31-10-437-7700

Bus: *Mfr. marine equipment parts and*   Fax: 31-10-415-2623
accessories.   www.vetus.nl

VETUS DENOUDEN, INC.

7170 Standard Drive, Hanover, MD   21076

CEO: Leo J. van Hemert, Pres.   Tel: (410) 712-0740   %FO: 100

Bus: *Mfr. marine equipment parts and*   Fax: (410) 712-0985
accessories.

● **VITRONICS SOLTEC**

Karolusstraat 20, NL-4903 RJ, Oosterhout, Netherlands

CEO: Eelco Fokkens   Tel: 31-16-248-3000   Rev: $22

Bus: *Mfr. circuit board equipment.*   Fax: 31-16-248-3253   Emp: 130
www.vitronicscorp.com

VIRONICS SOLTEC INC.

2 Marin Way, Stratham, NH   03885

CEO: Jeroen Schmits   Tel: (603) 772-7778   %FO: 100

Bus: *Mfr./sales/service of circuit board*   Fax: (603) 772-7776
equipment.

● **VNU INTERNATIONAL BV**

Ceylonpoort 5-25, NL-2037 AA, Haarlem, Netherlands

CEO: R.F. van den Bergh, CEO   Tel: 31-23-546-3463   Rev: $3,187

Bus: *Publishes/distributes magazines,*   Fax: 31-23-546-3912   Emp: 18,720
newspapers, educational and business   www.vnu.com
information services.

AC NIELSEN CORPORATION
177 Broad Street, Stamford, CT   06901
CEO: Nicholas L. Trivisonno, CEO   Tel: (203) 961-3000   %FO: 100
Bus: *Engaged in research and media*   Fax: (203) 961-3190   Emp: 21,000
measurement including compiling
consumer data for businesses.

BILL COMMUNICATIONS
355 Park Avenue South, New York, NY   10010
CEO: John Wickersham, Pres. & CEO   Tel: (212) 592-6200   %FO: 100
Bus: *Provides communications services.*   Fax: (212) 592-6209

BILLBOARD MAGAZINE
1515 Broadway, 39th Fl., New York, NY   10036
CEO: John Babcock, Jr., Pres.   Tel: (212) 764-7300
Bus: *Entertainment trade magazine.*   Fax: (212) 536-5358

BPI COMMUNICATIONS, INC.
1515 Broadway, New York, NY   10036
CEO: John J. Babcock, Jr., Pres. & CEO   Tel: (212) 536-6520   %FO: 100
Bus: *Communications industry*   Fax: (212) 536-5243   Emp: 900
magazine publishers; Ad Week,
Media Week, et. al.

CLARITAS, INC.
1525 Wilson Blvd., Suite 1000, Arlington, VA   22209
CEO: Nancy Deck, Pres.   Tel: (703) 812-2700   %FO: 100
Bus: *Provides target marketing services.* Fax: (703) 812-2701   Emp: 150

COMPETITIVE MEDIA REPORTING
11 West 42nd Street, New York, NY   10036
CEO: Jeffrey Hale, Pres.   Tel: (212) 789-3680   %FO: 100
Bus: *Provides media & marketing*   Fax: (212) 789-3640   Emp: 75
consulting services.

INTERACTIVE MARKET SYSTEMS, INC.
5 Penn Plaza, 16th Fl., New York, NY   10001
CEO: Beverly Andal, Pres.   Tel: (212) 896-7100   %FO: 100
Bus: *Provides media & marketing*   Fax: (212) 896-7155   Emp: 55
consulting services.

LAKEWOOD PUBLICATIONS, INC.
50 South Ninth Street, Minneapolis, MN   55402
CEO: James P. Secord, Pres. & CEO   Tel: (612) 333-0471   %FO: 100
Bus: *Publishers of business book &*   Fax: (612) 340-4757
magazines.

MARKETING RESOURCES PLUS
555 Twin Dolphin Drive, Pacific Dolphin Pl., Redwood City, CA   94065

CEO: Beverly Andal, Pres.	Tel: (650) 595-1800	%FO: 100
Bus: *Develop/market software to advertising agencies.*	Fax: (650) 595-3410	Emp: 52

NATIONAL DECISION SYSTEMS INC.
5357 Mira Sorrento Place, Ste. 400, San Diego, CA   92121

CEO: Robert Nascenzi, Pres.	Tel: (619) 622-0800
Bus: *Engaged in site location information services.*	Fax: (619) 550-5800

NATIONAL RESEARCH GROUP INC.
5900 Wilshire Blvd., Los Angeles, CA   90036

CEO: Joseph Farrell, CEO	Tel: (213) 549-5000
Bus: *Provides marketing and information services.*	Fax: (213) 549-5111

NIELSEN MEDIA RESEARCH, INC.
299 Park Avenue, New York, NY   10171

CEO: John Dimling, Pres.	Tel: (212) 708-7500	%FO: 100
Bus: *Television audience measuring company.*	Fax: (212) 708-7795	

PERQ/HCI CORPORATION
3371 US Route One, Lawrenceville, NJ   08648

CEO: Marshall Paul, Pres.	Tel: (609) 452-0211
Bus: *Provides advertising and media buying services to the healthcare industry.*	Fax: (609) 734-8456

RTV/VIDEO MONITORING SERVICES OF AMERICA
330 West 42nd Street, New York, NY   10036

CEO: Robert Cohen, Pres.	Tel: (212) 736-2010
Bus: *Provides video monitoring services.*	Fax: (212) 629-0650

THE SACHS GROUP
1800 Sherman Avenue, Evanston, IL   60201

CEO: Michael Sachs, Chmn.	Tel: (847) 475-7526	%FO: 100
Bus: *Provides media & marketing consulting services.*	Fax: (847) 475-7830	Emp: 115

SCARBOROGH RESEARCH
11 West 42nd Street, New York, NY   10036

CEO: Robert Cohen, Pres.   Tel: (212) 789-3560   %FO: 100
Bus: *Provides media & marketing*   Fax: (212) 789-3577   Emp: 36
  consulting services.

SPECTRA MARKETING SYSTEMS
333 West Wacker Drive, Chicago, IL   60607

CEO: John Larkin, Pres.   Tel: (312) 263-0606   %FO: 100
Bus: *Provides media & marketing*   Fax: (312) 263-7022   Emp: 40
  consulting services.

STANDARD RATE AND DATA SERVICES (SRDS)
1700 West Higgins Road, Des Plaines, IL   60018

CEO: Christopher Lehman, Pres. & CEO Tel: (847) 375-5000   %FO: 100
Bus: *Provides media & marketing*   Fax: (847) 375-5005   Emp: 131
  consulting services.

TRADE DIMENSIONS/NRB
45 Danbury Road, Wilton, CT   06897

CEO: Harold Clark, Pres. & CEO   Tel: (203) 563-3000   %FO: 100
Bus: *Provides trade consulting services.* Fax: (203) 563-3131 Emp: 35

VNU USA INC.
770 Broadway, New York, NY   10003-9595

CEO: G. S. Hobbs, CEO   Tel: (646) 654-5500   %FO: 100
Bus: *Provides media and marketing* Fax: (646) 654-5001   Emp: 25
  consulting services.

● ROYAL VOPAK N.V. (FORMERLY ROYAL PAKHOED)
Blaak 333, NL-3011 GB, Rotterdam, Netherlands

CEO: A. H. Spoor, Chmn.   Tel: 31-10-44-2911   Rev: $3,900
Bus: *Engaged in logistics and distribution* Fax: 31-10-413-9829 Emp: 9,900
  services to the chemical and oil   www.vopak.nl
  industries and end-users of chemicals.

VOPAK USA INC.
PO Box 34325, Seattle, WA   98124

CEO: Paul H. Hough, Pres. & CEO   Tel: (425) 889-3400   %FO: 100
Bus: *Engaged in distribution of*   Fax: (425) 889-4138
  chemicals.

● WERELDHAVE N.V
23 Nassaulaan Postbus 85660, NL-2508 CJ, The Hague, Netherlands

CEO: Gijs Verweij, Chmn.   Tel: 31-70-346-9325   Rev: $120
Bus: *Real estate investment company.* Fax: 31-70-363-8990   Emp: 100
                                    www.wereldhave.nl

WEST WORLD HOLDING INC.
Four Manhattanville Road, 2nd Fl., Purchase, NY   10577
CEO: Charles O.W. Schouten, Pres.   Tel: (914) 694-5900   %FO: 100
Bus: *Real estate investment company.*   Fax: (914) 694-4642

● WESSANEN N.V.
Prof. E. M. Meijerslaan 2, Postbus 410, NL-1180 AK, Amsterdam, Netherlands
CEO: A. M. Zondervan, Chmn.   Tel: 31-20-574-9547   Rev: $3,037
Bus: *Global manufacturing and marketing of* Fax: 31-20-645-9160   Emp: 14,912
food and beverages.   www.bolswessanen.com

AMERICAN BEVERAGE CORPORATION
One Daily Way, Verona, PA   15147
CEO: David Bober, Pres.   Tel: (412) 828-9020   %FO: 100
Bus: *Production of fruit juices/drinks.*   Fax: (412) 828-5449

CROWLEY FOODS INC.
PO Box 549, Binghamton, NY   13902
CEO: Martin J. Margherio, Pres.   Tel: (607) 779-3289   %FO: 100
Bus: *Mfr./sales/distribution of dairy*   Fax: (607) 779-3439
     products.

CROWLEY FROZEN DESERTS, INC.
PO Box 7007, Lancaster, PA   17604
CEO: Bruce White, SVP   Tel: (717) 843-9891   %FO: 100
Bus: *Mfr./sales/distribution of dairy*   Fax: (717) 399-8584
     products.

HELUVA GOOD CHEESE, INC.
6551 Pratt Road, Sodus, NY   14551
CEO: Jay Snedeker, VP   Tel: (315) 483-6971   %FO: 100
Bus: *Distribution of cheese products.*   Fax: (315) 483-9927

MARIGOLD FOODS INC.
2929 University Avenue, SE, Minneapolis, MN   55414
CEO: James Green, Pres.   Tel: (612) 331-3775   %FO: 100
Bus: *Mfr./sales/distribution of milk and* Fax: (612) 378-8389
     dairy products.

TREE OF LIFE, INC.
1750 Tree Boulevard, St. Augustine, FL   32085
CEO: Henry Puente, Pres.   Tel: (904) 824-4699   %FO: 100
Bus: *Sales/distribution of natural and*   Fax: (904) 825-2013
     specialty foods to supermarkets
     and natural food stores.

WESSANEN USA
1750 Tree Boulevard, St. Augustine, FL   32086
CEO: Richard A. Thorne, Pres. & CEO   Tel: (904) 825-2002   %FO: 100
Bus: *U.S. headquarters.*   Fax: (904) 825-2230

● **WOLTERS KLUWER N.V.**
Apollolaan 153, P.O.Box 75248, NL-1070 AE, Amsterdam, Netherlands
CEO: Robert Pietersem, CEO   Tel: 31-20-607-0400   Rev: $3,215
Bus: *Legal, medical, science, educational,* Fax: 31-20-607-0490   Emp: 17,000
   professional and trade publishing.   www.wolterskluwer.com

   ASPEN PUBLISHERS INC.
   200 Orchard Ridge Road, Gaithersburg, MD   20878
   CEO: Edward T. Latta, Pres.   Tel: (301) 251-5000   %FO: 100
   Bus: *Publishing.*   Fax: (301) 251-5212

   BLESSING/WHITE INC.
   23 Orchard Road, Skillman, NJ   08558
   CEO: Christophe Rice, Pres.   Tel: (908) 904-1000
   Bus: *Provides training processes and* Fax: (908) 904-1774
      tools.

   CCH INC.
   2700 Lake Cook Road, Riverwoods, IL   60015
   CEO: Rebecca K. Hensley, Pres.   Tel: (847) 267-7000   %FO: 100
   Bus: *Provides tax and business law* Fax: (800) 224-8299
      information.

   CCH LEGAL INFORMATION SERVICES, INC.
   1111 Eighth Avenue, New York, NY   10011
   CEO: Christ Cartwright, CEO   Tel: (212) 894-8940
   Bus: *Legal information services.*   Fax: (212) 489-6101

   FACTS AND COMPARISONS
   111 West Port Plaza, Ste. 400, St. Louis, MO   63146
   CEO: Steve Hebel, CEO   Tel: (314) 878-2515   %FO: 100
   Bus: *Medical publications.*   Fax: (314) 878-5563

   LIPPINCOTT WILLIAM & WILKINS
   530 Walnut Street, Philadelphia, PA   19106
   CEO: J. K. Smith, CEO   Tel: (215) 521-8300   %FO: 100
   Bus: *Medical publisher.*   Fax: (215) 521-8902

OVID TECHNOLOGIES INC.
333 Seventh Avenue, 4th Fl., New York, NY   10001
CEO: Dean M. Vogel, CEO   Tel: (212) 563-3006
Bus: *Provides subscription based*   Fax: (212) 563-3784
     electronic services.

WOLTERS KLUWER U.S. CORPORATION
161 North Clark Street, 48th Fl., Chicago, IL   60601
CEO: Nancy McKinstry, CEO   Tel: (312) 425-7000   %FO: 100
Bus: *Publishing.*   Fax: (312) 425-0232

● **ZUREL & CO B.V.**
Lakenblekerstraat 49, NL-1431 BB, Aalsmeer, Netherlands
CEO: R. F. Zurel, Pres.   Tel: 31-29-733-3333   Rev: $2,500
Bus: *Import/export cut flowers.* Fax: 31-29-733-3318   Emp: 600
                                   www.zurel.nl

ZUREL USA, INC.
174 Touhy Court, Des Plaines, IL   60018
CEO: David J. Laird, Mgr.   Tel: (847) 296-8181   %FO: 100
Bus: *Import/export of cut flowers.* Fax: (847) 296-0312

Netherlands Antilles

• FUEL-TECH NV

Castorweg 22-24, Willemstad, Curacao, Netherlands Antilles

CEO: Ralph E. Bailey, CEO — Tel: 599-9-461-3754 — Rev: $22

Bus: *Mfr. products for the reduction of nitrogen oxide in industrial power generators.* — Fax: 599-9-461-6501 — Emp: 65

www.fuel-tech.com

CLEAN DIESEL TECHNOLOGIES, INC.

300 Atlantic Street, Stamford, CT 06901

CEO: James M. Valentine, COO — Tel: (203) 327-7050 — %FO: 100

Bus: *Mfr./sales of products for the reduction of nitrogen oxide in industrial power generators.* — Fax: (203) 323-0461

FUEL-TECH INC.

300 Atlantic Street, Stamford, CT 06901

CEO: Steven C. Argabright, CEO — Tel: (203) 425-9800 — %FO: 100

Bus: *Mfr./sales of products for the reduction of nitrogen oxide in industrial power generators.* — Fax: (203) 425-9823

FUEL-TECH INC.

512 Kingsland Drive, Batavia, IL 60510-2299

CEO: Dr. H. Sun, VP — Tel: (630) 845-4500 — %FO: 100

Bus: *Mfr./sales of products for the reduction of nitrogen oxide in industrial power generators.* — Fax: (630) 845-4501

• VELCRO INDUSTRIES B.V.

15 Pietermaai, Willemstad, Curacao, Netherlands Antilles

CEO: Robert W. Cripps, Chmn. — Tel: 603-669-4880 — Rev: $235

Bus: *Mfr. Velcro-brand fasteners for the apparel, auto, aerospace and consumer markets.* — Fax: 603-669-4860 — Emp: 1,200

www.velcro.com

VELCRO, AUTOMOTIVE DIV.

1210 Souter, Troy, MI 48083

CEO: K. Theodor Krantz, Pres. — Tel: (248) 583-6060 — %FO: 100

Bus: *Automotive division for manufacture of Velcro-brand fasteners.* — Fax: (248) 585-7861

VELCRO USA INC.
406 Brown Avenue, Manchester, NH   03108
CEO: K. Theodor Krantz, Pres.   Tel: (603) 669-4892   %FO: 100
Bus: *Industrial facility.*   Fax: (603) 669-9271

VELCRO USA INC.
800 DeMuro Drive, Douglas, AZ   85607
CEO: K. Theodor Krantz, Pres.   Tel: (520) 364-8478   %FO: 100
Bus: *Consumer products division for*   Fax: (800) 774-6166
    manufacture of Velcro-brand
    fasteners.

New Zealand

● **AHI ROOFING LTD. (SUB. TASMAN BUILDING PRODUCTS)**
PO Box 18071, Glen Innes, Auckland, New Zealand
CEO: Peter Stichbury, Gen. Mgr.   Tel: 64-9-978-9010
Bus: *Mfr. metal roofing systems.*   Fax: 64-9-978-9069
                                          www.ahiroofing.com

   TASMAN ROOFING, INC.
   1230 Railroad Street, Corona, CA   91720
   CEO: Natalie Tanner, Mgr.   Tel: (909) 272-8180   %FO: 100
   Bus: *Mfr. stone-coated steel roofing*   Fax: (909) 272-4476
        systems.

● **AIR NEW ZEALAND LTD.**
29 Customs Street West, Auckland, New Zealand
CEO: Selwyn Cushing, Chmn.   Tel: 64-9-336-2400   Rev: $926
Bus: *Commercial air transport services.*   Fax: 64-9-336-2764   Emp: 1,800
                                          www.airnz.co.nz

   AIR NEW ZEALAND
   1960 East Grand Avenue, Ste. 900, El Segundo, CA   90245
   CEO: Peter Walsh, VP   Tel: (310) 648-7000   %FO: 100
   Bus: *International commercial air*   Fax: (310) 648-7017
        transport services.

● **FLETCHER CHALLENGE FORSTS LTD.**
Fletcher Challenge House, 810 Great South Road, Penrose, New Zealand
CEO: Michael J. Andrews, CEO   Tel: 64-9-525-9000   Rev: $4,100
Bus: *Engaged in pulp and paper, building*   Fax: 64-9-525-9023   Emp: 20,000
     industries and energy.   www.fcl.co.nz

   FLETCHER CHALLENGE FORESTS USA INC.
   7458 New Ridge Road, Hanover, MD   21078
   CEO: Martin Plom, Pres.   Tel: (410) 850-5433   %FO: 100
   Bus: *Pulp and paper industry.*   Fax: (410) 850-5434

   FLETCHER CHALLENGE FORESTS USA INC.
   6505 226th Place SE, Ste. 120, Issaquah, WA   98027
   CEO: Ronald A. Johnson, Mgr.   Tel: (425) 837-9262   %FO: 100
   Bus: *Pulp and paper industry.*   Fax: (425) 837-0521

- **NEW ZEALAND LAMB CO (NA) LTD.**

5th Floor Seabridge House, 110 Featherstone Street, Wellington, New Zealand
CEO: Liew Pointon, Gen. Mgr.   Tel: 64-4-472-0236
Bus: *Produces/markets fresh meats.*   Fax: 64-4-499-9972
                                    www.nzlamb.com

  NEW ZEALAND LAMB COMPANY
  106 Corporate Park Drive, Ste. 113, White Plains, NY   10604
  CEO: Richard G. Lawrence, Pres.   Tel: (914) 253-6904   %FO: 100
  Bus: *Sales/distribution of fresh meats.*   Fax: (914) 253-8155

- **TELECOM NEW ZEALAND LIMITED**

Telecom Networks House,, 68-86 Jervois Quay, Wellington, New Zealand
CEO: Theresa Gattung, CEO   Tel: 64-4-801-9000   Rev: $1,826
Bus: *Provides telecommunications services*   Fax: 64-4-385-3469   Emp: 8,000
   and engaged in fiber optic cable   www.telecom.co.nz
   network.

  TELECOM NEW ZEALAND LIMITED
  251 South Lake Avenue, Ste. 540, Pasadena, CA   91101
  CEO: David Bedford, Pres.   Tel: (626) 432-4300   %FO: 100
  Bus: *Engaged in telecommunications.*   Fax: (626) 432-4303

Nigeria

● **UNITED BANK FOR AFRICA, PLC.**
UBA House 57, Marina, PMB 12002 Lagos, Nigeria
CEO: Mallam Abba Kyari, Dir.   Tel: 234-1-264-4722
Bus: *Commercial banking services.*   Fax: 234-1-264-465700
                                                                            www.absa.co.za

UNITED BANK FOR AFRICA, PLC
40 East 52nd Street, 20th Fl., New York, NY   10022
CEO: George H. Denniston Jr., Mgr.   Tel: (212) 308-7222   %FO: 100
Bus: *International commercial banking*   Fax: (212) 688-0870
      services.

Norway

● **AKER MARITIME ASA.**
Lileakervenien 8, PO Box 245 Lilleaker, N-0216 Oslo, Norway
CEO: Bjorn Rune Gjelsten, Chmn. Tel: 47-22-94-5000 Rev: $2,642
Bus: *Develops advanced solutions for* Fax: 47-22-94-6530 Emp: 14,925
 offshore exploration, development and www.akermaritime.no
 production of oil and gas fields.

 AKER GULF MARINE, INC.
 PO Box C-FM 1069 South, Ingleside, TX 78362-1302
 CEO: Myron Rodrigue, Pres. Tel: (361) 776-7551 %FO: 51
 Bus: *Engineering, procurement,* Fax: (361) 776-7245
  construction services &
  installation of offshore drilling &
  production systems.

 AKER MARITIME US, INC.
 11757 Katy Freeway, Ste. 500, Houston, TX 77079-1725
 CEO: Svein Eggen, Pres. Tel: (281) 588-7500 %FO: 100
 Bus: *Supplier of oil and gas related* Fax: (281) 588-7599
  technology and products.

 SPARS INTERNATIONAL, INC.
 11757 Katy Freeway, Ste. 500, Houston, TX 77079
 CEO: Robert M. Harrell, Pres. Tel: (281) 679-4900 %FO: JV
 Bus: *Markets and delivers deepwater* Fax: (281) 679-4910 Emp: 30
  platforms.

● **ANDERS WILHELMSEN & CO. AS**
PO Box 1583, Vika N-0118 Oslo, Norway
CEO: Arne Wilhelmsen, Pres. Tel: 47-22-01-4200
Bus: *Maritime enterprise engaged in* Fax: 47-22-01-4370
 shipping and investments. www.norwegian-shipping.com

 CELEBRITY CRUISES, INC.
 1050 Caribbean Way, Miami, FL 33132
 CEO: Richard E. Sasso, Pres. Tel: (305) 539-6000
 Bus: *Cruise shipping line.* Fax: (305) 374-7354

 ROYAL CARIBBEAN CRUISES LTD.
 1050 Caribbean Way, Miami, FL 33132
 CEO: Jack L. Williams, Pres. Tel: (305) 539-6000 %FO: 39
 Bus: *Cruise shipping line.* Fax: (305) 374-7354 Emp: 1,642

• **ASK PROXIMA ASA**
K. G. Meldahisvei 9, N-1602 Freedrikstad, Norway
CEO: Ole J. Fredriksen   Tel: 47-69-34-0155   Rev: $4,300
Bus: *Mfr. projectors and liquid crystal*   Fax: 47-69-34-0632   Emp: 887
display (LCD) screens used for   www.askproxima.no
presentations.

    ASK PROXIMA CORPORATION
    9440 Carroll Park Drive, San Diego, CA   92121
    CEO: William D. Yavorsky   Tel: (858) 457-5500   %FO: 100
    Bus: *Mfr. multimedia projectors.*   Fax: (858) 457-9647

    INFOCUS CORPORATION, DIV. ASK PROXIMA
    27700B SW Parkway Avenue, Wilsonville, OR   97070
    CEO: John V. Harker, Pres.   Tel: (503) 685-8888   %FO: 100
    Bus: *Mfr. multimedia projectors.*   Fax: (503) 685-8631

• **CHRISTIANIA BANK OG KREDITKASSE ASA**
Middelthunsgaten 17, PO Box 1166, N-0368 Oslo, Norway
CEO: Tom Ruud, Pres.   Tel: 47-22-48-5000   Rev: $2,162
Bus: *Banking services.*   Fax: 47-22-48-4749   Emp: 4,041
    www.kbank.no

    CHRISTIANIA BANK NEW YORK
    11 West 42nd Street, 7th Fl., New York, NY   10036
    CEO: Tore Nag, EVP   Tel: (212) 827-4800   %FO: 100
    Bus: *Commercial banking services.*   Fax: (212) 827-4888   Emp: 50

• **CORROCEAN, INC.**
Teglgarden, N-7485 Trondheim, Norway
CEO: Roe D. Strømmen, CEO   Tel: 47-73-82-5000   Rev: $20
Bus: *Mfr. corrosion monitoring equipment.*   Fax: 47-73-82-5050   Emp: 175
    www.corrocean.com

    CORROCEAN, INC.
    10333 Richmond Ave., Ste. 490, Houston, TX   77042
    CEO: Magne Ostby, Pres.   Tel: (713) 266-0941   %FO: 50
    Bus: *Corrosion monitoring equipment.*   Fax: (713) 266-0172   Emp: 7

• **DEN NORSKE BANK ASA**
Strandon 21, PO Box 1171, N-0150 Sentrum Oslo 2, Norway
CEO: Svein Aeser, Mng. Dir.   Tel: 47-22-48-1050   Rev: $2,544
Bus: *Banking services.*   Fax: 47-22-48-1870   Emp: 5,978
    www.dnb.no

DEN NORSKE BANK ASA

200 Park Avenue, 31st Fl., New York, NY   10166-0396

CEO: Berot Henriksen, Gen. Mgr.	Tel: (212) 681-3800	%FO: 100
Bus: *Commercial banking services.*	Fax: (212) 681-3900	Emp: 54

● DET NORSKE VERITAS A/S

Veritasveien 1, PO Box 300, N-1322 Høvik, Norway

CEO: Helge Midttun, CEO	Tel: 47-67-57-9900	Rev: $499
Bus: *Quality assurance services, ship classification & inspection.*	Fax: 47-67-57-9911 www.dnv.com	Emp: 5,500

AVITAS ENGINEERING, INC.

5040 Northwest 57th Street, Ste. 203, Miami, FL   33126

CEO: Lauren B. Nelson, Pres.	Tel: (305) 267-7332	%FO: 100
Bus: *Engineer/consultant, aircraft-FAA regulations.*	Fax: (305) 267-7356	Emp: 6

AVITAS INC.

14520 Avian Pkwy., Ste. 220, Chantilly, VA   20151

CEO: John W. Vitale, Pres.	Tel: (703) 476-2300	%FO: 100
Bus: *Quality assurance services, ship classification & inspection.*	Fax: (703) 860-5855	Emp: 13

DET NORSKE PROCESS

30700 Telegraph Road, Ste. 1530, Bingham Farms, MI   48025

CEO: John Glavey	Tel: (248) 540-5591	%FO: 100
Bus: *Engaged in consulting services to the oil, gas and process industries.*	Fax: (248) 540-5597	

DET NORSKE PROCESS

1001 Galaxy Way, Suite 101, Concord, CA   94520

CEO: Ronald T. Williams	Tel: (925) 521-0148	%FO: 100
Bus: *Engaged in consulting services to the oil, gas and process industries.*	Fax: (925) 521-0149	

DET NORSKE PROCESS

136 Ocean Ridge Drive, Fernandina Beach, FL   32034

CEO: Per Lea	Tel: (904) 277-1606	%FO: 100
Bus: *Engaged in consulting services to the oil, gas and process industries.*	Fax: (904) 277-2883	

DET NORSKE PROCESS

16340 Park Ten Place, Ste. 100, Houston, TX   77084

CEO: Davis Garnett	Tel: (281) 721-6600	%FO: 100
Bus: *Engaged in consulting services to the oil, gas and process industries.*	Fax: (281) 721-6906	

DET NORSKE PROCESS

110 Pine Avenue, Ste. 725, Long Beach, CA   90802

CEO: Sidney Vianna	Tel: (562) 435-1908	%FO: 100
Bus: *Engaged in consulting services to the oil, gas and process industries.*	Fax: (562) 432-3727	

DET NORSKE VERITAS AMERICAS

16340 Park Ten Place, Ste. 100, Houston, TX   77084-5143

CEO: Carl Arne Carlsen, Dir.	Tel: (281) 721-6600	%FO: 100
Bus: *Quality assurance services, ship classification & inspection.*	Fax: (281) 721-6900	

MARITIME NORTH AMERICA

70 Grand Avenue, Ste. 106, River Edge, NJ   07661

CEO: Blaine Collins, Mgr.	Tel: (201) 343-0800	%FO: 100
Bus: *Ship classification, certification & advisory services.*	Fax: (201) 488-1778	Emp: 500

SEATTLE MARITIME

14450 NE 29th Place, Suite 217, Bellevue, WA   98007

CEO: Philip Read	Tel: (425) 861-7977	%FO: 100
Bus: *Engaged in consulting services to the oil, gas and process industries.*	Fax: (425) 861-0423	

• DYNO NOBEL

Tollbugatan, PO Box 779 Sentrum, N-0106 Oslo, Norway

CEO: Dag Mejdell, Pres. & CEO	Tel: 47-22-31-7000	Rev: $1,338
Bus: *Mfr. chemicals and military explosives.*	Fax: 47-32-31-7000	Emp: 7,200
	www.dynonobel.com	

DYNO NOBEL INC.

50 South Main, Crossroad Towers, 11th Fl., Salt Lake City, UT   84144-0103

CEO: Douglas Jackson, Pres.	Tel: (801) 364-4800	%FO: 100
Bus: *Mfr. chemicals and military explosives.*	Fax: (801) 328-6452	

• ELKEM ASA

Hoffsveien 65B, PO Box 5211, N-0303 Majorstua Oslo, Norway

CEO: Ole Enger, Pres. & CEO	Tel: 47-22-45-0100	Rev: $1,337
Bus: *Produces products for steel industry, metallurgical technology, ceramics.*	Fax: 47-22-45-0155	Emp: 5,254
	www.elkem.com	

ELKEM METALS COMPANY

Airport Office Pk., Bldg.2, 400 Rouser Road, Moon Township, PA   15108

CEO: Anthony C. LaRusso, Pres.	Tel: (412) 299-7200	%FO: 100
Bus: *Sales, distribution steel products.*	Fax: (412) 299-7225	

ELKEM METALS COMPANY
2700 Lake Road East, PO Box 1040, Astabula, OH 44005-1040
CEO: Steve M. Dopuch, Pres. Tel: (440) 993-2300 %FO: 100
Bus: *Sales, distribution steel products.* Fax: (440) 993-2379

● **HELLY HANSEN ASA**
Solgaard Skog 139, N-1539 Moss, Norway
CEO: Jan Valdmaa, CEO Tel: 47-69-24-9000
Bus: *Outdoor wear wholesale manufacturer.* Fax: 47-69-24-9099
www.helly.com

HELLY HANSEN INC.
3326 160 N Avenue SE, Ste.200, Bellevue, WA 98008-5463
CEO: Jonathan Balley, VP Tel: (425) 378-8700 %FO: 100
Bus: *Wholesale manufacturer of* Fax: (425) 649-3740
outdoor wear.

● **HITEC GROUP**
Lagerveien 8, PO Box 8181, N-4069 Forus, Norway
CEO: Frederik Hvistendahl Tel: 47-51-81-8181 Rev: $180
Bus: *Technology group specializing in* Fax: 47-51-80-0507 Emp: 900
products and services to the petroleum www.hitec.no
industry.

HITEC DRILLING & MARINE SYSTEMS INC.
5225 Hollistter, Houston, TX 77040
CEO: Jon Gjedebo, Pres. & CEO Tel: (713) 462-7735 %FO: 100
Bus: *Provides systems for automation* Fax: (713) 462-7728
and remote control used on
drilling and production units.

NATIONAL OILWELL
10000 Richmond, 4th Fl., Houston, TX 77042
CEO: Gay Mather Tel: (713) 346-7500 %FO: 100
Bus: *Designs, manufactures, sells and* Fax: (713) 346-7775
services the major mechanical
components for both land and
offshore drilling rigs.

● **KONGSBERG MARITIME SHIP SYSTEMS (FORMERLY AUTRONICA)**
Bekkajordet 8A, PO Box 1009, N-3194 Horten, Norway
CEO: Per Branstad, Pres. Tel: 47-33-03-2000
Bus: *One-source, end-to-end supplier of* Fax: 47-33-04-2250
integrated ship systems. www.kmss.no

AUTRONICA MARINE USA INC.

234 Industrial Park, Northvale, NJ   07647

CEO: Ed Matthews, Mgr.   Tel: (201) 768-1886

Bus: *Provides fully integrated packages*   Fax: (201) 768-2570
     and stand-alone maritime
     instrumentation systems for the
     global maritime market.

● **KVAERNER ASA**

PO Box 169, Prof. Kohts Vei 15, N-1324 Lysaker, Norway

CEO: Kjell E Almskog, Pres. & CEO   Tel: 47-67-51-3400   Rev: $11,050

Bus: *Engaged in processing natural*   Fax: 47-67-51-3410   Emp: 61,955
     resources based on oil, gas and   www.kvaerner.com
     hydropower.

   HEAVYLIFT CARGO AIRLINES

   4600 Madison, Ste. 711, Kansas City, MO   64112

   CEO: Peter Clark, Mgr.   Tel: (816) 753-3337   %FO: 100

   Bus: *Air cargo charter company*   Fax: (816) 753-4664
        specializing in air transport of
        outsized loads.

   KVAERNER PROCESS

   PO Box 720421, Houston, TX   77272

   CEO: Thor Karlsen, Pres.   Tel: (713) 988-2002   %FO: 100

   Bus: *Engaged in processing natural*   Fax: (713) 772-4673
        resources based on oil, gas and
        hydropower.

   KVAERNER CONSTRUCTION INC.

   4950 West Kennedy Blvd., Ste. 600, Tampa, FL   33609

   CEO: Rich Rantala, Pres.   Tel: (813) 282-7100   %FO: 100

   Bus: *Construction services.*   Fax: (813) 289-0812

   KVAERNER CORPORATE DEVELOPMENT LTD.

   7909 Parkwood Circle Drive, Houston, TX   77036

   CEO: Thor Karlsen, Pres.   Tel: (713) 988-2002   %FO: 100

   Bus: *Charter air cargo services for*   Fax: (713) 772-4673
        outsized loads.

   KVAERNER MASA MARINE

   201 Defense Highway, Ste. 202, Annapolis, MD   21401

   CEO: John Avis, Pres.   Tel: (301) 970-2226   %FO: 100

   Bus: *Engaged in consulting services to*   Fax: (301) 970-2230
        ship design industry.

KVAERNER MASA MARINE INC.
201 Defense Highway, Ste. 202, Annapolis, MD   21401
CEO: John Avis, Pres.   Tel: (301) 970-2226   %FO: 100
Bus: *Consulting services to engineering*   Fax: (301) 970-2230
    and architecture industries.

KVAERNER PULPING INC.
8008 Corporate Center Drive, Charlotte, NC   28226
CEO: Roland Martin-Lof, Chmn.   Tel: (704) 541-1453   %FO: 100
Bus: *Engages in fiberline*   Fax: (704) 542-5969
    recausticizing, lime reburing,
    evaporation, and recovery boiler
    operations.

KVAERNER INC.
124 Roddy Avenue, South Attleboro, MA   02703
CEO: David Turton, Pres.   Tel: (508) 399-6400   %FO: 100
Bus: *Engaged in processing natural*   Fax: (508) 399-7883
    resources based on oil, gas and
    hydropower.

● **LAERDAL MEDICAL A/S**
PO Box 377, N-4002 Stavanger, Norway
CEO: Tore Laerdal, Pres.   Tel: 47-51-51-1700
Bus: *Emergency medical equipment and*   Fax: 47-51-52-3557   Emp: 700
    training.   www.laerdal.com

   LAERDAL MEDICAL CORPORATION
   PO Box 1840, Wappinger Falls, NY   12590-8840
   CEO: Terje Aasen, Pres.   Tel: (914) 297-7770   %FO: 100
   Bus: *Medical training equipment.*   Fax: (914) 297-1137   Emp: 200

● **O MUSTAD & SON A/S**
PO Box 40N, N-2801 Gjovik, Norway
CEO: Anders Liland, Mng. Dir.   Tel: 47-61-13-7700
Bus: *Mfr. fish hooks.*   Fax: 47-61-13-7951
                                              www.mustad.no

   O MUSTAD & SON (USA) INC
   241 Grant Avenue, Auburn, NY   13021
   CEO: John DeVries, EVP   Tel: (315) 253-2793   %FO: 100
   Bus: *Distributor fish hooks, fishing*   Fax: (315) 253-0157   Emp: 45
       tackle.

- **NCL HOLDING ASA**
PO Box 1861 Vika, N-0124 Oslo, Norway
CEO: Ole Lund, Chmn.   Tel: 47-23-11-8950   Rev: $770
Bus: *Holding company, passenger shipping,*   Fax: 47-22-83-1409   Emp: 6,028
     cruise line.   www.ncl.com

     NORWEGIAN CRUISE LINE
     7665 Corporate Center Drive, Miami, FL   33126
     CEO: Colin Veltch, CEO   Tel: (305) 436-4000   %FO: 100
     Bus: *Cruise line, travel industry.*   Fax: (305) 436-4120   Emp: 700

- **NERA ASA**
Kokstadveien 23, PO Box 7090, N-5020 Bergen, Norway
CEO: Bjorn Ove Skjeie, CEO   Tel: 47-55-22-5100   Rev: $288
Bus: *Mfr. microwave antennas, receivers and*   Fax: 47-55-22-5299   Emp: 1,500
     transmitters.   www.nera.no

     NERA NETWORKS INC.
     One SE 3rd Avenue, Ste. 1980, Miami, FL   33131
     CEO: Bjorn Ove Skjeie, Pres.   Tel: (305) 377-8370   %FO: 100
     Bus: *Mfr. microwave antennas,*   Fax: (305) 377-8371
        receivers and transmitters.

     NERA NETWORKS INC.
     660 N. Central Expwy., Ste. 250, Plano, TX   75074
     CEO: Bjorn Ove Skjeie, Pres.   Tel: (972) 422-6354   %FO: 100
     Bus: *Mfr. microwave antennas,*   Fax: (972) 422-4008
        receivers and transmitters.

     NERA NETWORKS INC.
     200 Research Drive, Wilmington, MA   01887
     CEO: Bjorn Ove Skjeie, Pres.   Tel: (978) 694-3000   %FO: 100
     Bus: *Mfr. microwave antennas,*   Fax: (978) 657-6097
        receivers and transmitters.

- **NORSK HYDRO A/S**
Bygdoy Alle 2, N-0240 Oslo, Norway
CEO: Egil Myklebust, Pres. & CEO   Tel: 47-22-43-2100   Rev: $13,088
Bus: *Mfr. mineral fertilizers, industrial gas,*   Fax: 47-22-43-2725   Emp: 40,000
     chemicals, aluminum, magnesium; oil   www.hydro.com
     and gas exploration, production,
     refining, mktg.

NORSK HYDRO USA INC

100 North Tampa Street, Ste. 3350, Tampa, FL   33601

CEO: Odd S. Gullberg, Pres. Tel: (813) 222-5714 %FO: 100

Bus: *Mfr./marketing fertilizers,* Fax: (813) 222-3880 Emp: 1,200
industrial chemicals, ammonia,
aluminum products, magnesium

● **ODFJELL ASA**

PO Box 25, N-5826 Bergen, Norway

CEO: Bjørn Sjaastad, Pres. & CEO Tel: 47-55-27-0000

Bus: *Engaged in shipping.* Fax: 47-55-28-4741

www.odfjell.no

ODFJELL TERMINALS INC.

12211 Port Road, Seabrook, TX   77586

CEO: Ake Gregertsen Tel: (713) 844-2300 %FO: 100

Bus: *Engaged in shipping.* Fax: (713) 844-2355

● **OFOTENS OG VESTERAALANS DAMPSKIBSSELSKAB AS**

Post Office Box 43, N-8501 Narvik, Norway

CEO: Jens Smkaar, Pres. Tel: 47-76-96-7600

Bus: *International passenger and cargo* Fax: 47-76-152469
shipping services. (JV of Troms Fylkes www.bergenline.com
Dampskibsselskap AS).

BERGEN LINE INC.

405 Park Avenue, New York, NY   10022

CEO: Rosalyn Gershell, Pres. Tel: (212) 319-1300 %FO: JV

Bus: *International passenger and cargo* Fax: (212) 319-1390
shipping services.

● **ORKLA, A.S.**

PO Box 218, N-1501 Moss, Norway

CEO: Jens P. Heyerdahl, CEO Tel: 47-69-24-99000 Rev: $4,138

Bus: *Mfr. chemicals and brand-name* Fax: 47-69-24-99290 Emp: 24,833
consumer products, including www.orkla.com
food/beverage, candy/biscuits,
outerwear and footwear, and cosmetics.

LIGNO TECH USA INC.

100 Grand Avenue, Rothschild, WI   54474-1198

CEO: Paul LaVanay, Pres. Tel: (715) 359-6544

Bus: *Mfr. chemicals.* Fax: (715) 355-3629

• PELTOR AB
Postboks 253, Solheimveien 56, N-1471 Skårer, Norway
CEO: Björn Anderssen — Tel: 46-370 -64200
Bus: *Mfr. personal hearing protectors and* — Fax: 46-370-15130 — Emp: 247
communications headsets for high noise — www.aearo.com
areas.

AEARO PELTOR COMPANY
90 Mechanic Street, Southbridge, MA   01550
CEO: Jack Curtin, Pres. — Tel: (508) 764-5500 — %FO: 85
Bus: *Mfr. personal hearing protectors* — Fax: (508) 764-5674 — Emp: 25
and communications headsets for
high noise areas.

EAR SPECIALTY COMPOSITES
650 Dawson Drive, Newark, DE   19713
CEO: Jack Curtin, Pres. — Tel: (302) 738-6800
Bus: *Mfr. of proprietary vinyls and* — Fax: (302) 738-6811
urethanes for noise and vibration
control, shock protection and
ergonomics.

EAR SPECIALTY COMPOSITES
7911 Zionsville Road, Indianapolis, IN   46268
CEO: Jack Curtin, Pres. — Tel: (317) 692-1111
Bus: *Mfr. personal hearing protectors* — Fax: (317) 692-3111
and communications headsets for
high noise areas.

• PETROLEUM GEO-SERVICES ASA
PGS House Strandveien 4, N-1366 Lysaker, Norway
CEO: Reidar Michaelsen, CEO — Tel: 47-67-52-6600 — Rev: $900
Bus: *Engaged in geophysical, gas and oil* — Fax: 47-67-53-6883 — Emp: 4,300
services. — www.pgs.com

PGS EXPLORATION SERVICES
16010 Barker's Point lane, Ste. 3200, Houston, TX   77079
CEO: Walter S. Lynn — Tel: (281) 589-8818 — %FO: 100
Bus: *Engaged in geophysical, gas and* — Fax: (281) 589-2826
oil services.

• ROLLS ROYCE MARINE SYSTEMS AS
PO Box 160 (Sjøgata 80), N-6067 Ulsteinuik, Norway
CEO: Jørn Heltne — Tel: 47-70-01-4000
Bus: *Mfr. diesel engines. (JV with Vickers* — Fax: 47-70-01-4013 — Emp: 350
PLC, England) — www.ulstein.no

BIRD-JOHNSON COMPANY
110 Norfolk Street, Walpole, MA   02081-1798
CEO: Peter J. Gwyn, Pres.

Tel: (508) 668-9610

Bus: *Produces marine propulsion and control systems.*

Fax: (508) 668-5638

ROLLS ROYCE MARINE INC.
100 UPM Drive, Mt. Holly, NC   28120
CEO: Owe Ring, Mgr.

Tel: (206) 281-7388

%FO: 100

Bus: *Mfr. diesel engines.*

Fax: (206) 284-1710

ROLLS ROYCE MARINE INC.
200 James Drive West, St. Rose, LA   70087
CEO: Nils Moerkeseth, Pres.

Tel: (504) 464-4561

%FO: 100

Bus: *Mfr. diesel engines.*

Fax: (504) 464-4565

Emp: 4

● ROXAR ASA
Lagerveien 12C Forus, PO Box 112, N-4065 Stavanger, Norway
CEO: Torkell Gjerstad, CEO

Tel: 47-51-81-0101

Rev: $50

Bus: *Provides integrated field development and reservoir management products and services for the upstream oil and gas industries.*

Fax: 47-51-802929

www.roxar.com

Emp: 300

ROXAR, INC.
2925 Briarpark Drive, Ste. 1000, Houston, TX   77042
CEO: Ab Abdalla, Pres.

Tel: (713) 974-4114

%FO: 100

Bus: *Mfr. multi-phase meters for gas and oil industries.*

Fax: (713) 339-2627

● STATOIL ASA (DEN NORSKE STATS OLJESELSKAP)
Forusbeen 50, N-4035 Stavanger, Norway
CEO: Olav Fjell, Pres. & CEO

Tel: 47-51-99-0000

Rev: $23,700

Bus: *Exploration, production, refining and marketing crude oil and natural gas.*

Fax: 47-51-99-0050

www.statoil.com

Emp: 18,000

STATOIL MARKETING & TRADING INC.
225 High Ridge Road, Stamford, CT   06905
CEO: David Jones

Tel: (203) 978-6900

%FO: 100

Bus: *Exploration, production, refining and marketing oil and gas, petrochemical products.*

Fax: (203) 978-6952

• **TELECOMPUTING, INC.**
Nesoyvelien 4, N-1377 Billingstad, Norway
CEO: Jason Donahue, CEO   Tel: 47-66-77-6570
Bus: *Computer software and services.*   Fax: 47-66-77-6572
                                           www.telecomputing.com

    TELECOMPUTING, INC.
    45999 Center Oak Plaza, Ste. 170, Sterling, VA   20166
    CEO: Marc Winkelstein, VP   Tel: (703) 948-2500   %FO: 100
    Bus: *Computer software and services.* Fax: (703) 948-2501

    TELECOMPUTING, INC.
    6700 N. Andrews Avenue, Ste. 200, Ft. Lauderdale, FL   33309
    CEO: Jason Donahue, CEO   Tel: (954) 229-2900   %FO: 100
    Bus: *Computer software and services.* Fax: (954) 229-2901

• **TFDS (TROMS FYLKES DAMPSKIBSSELSKAP AS)**
PO Box 548, N-9001 Tromso, Norway
CEO: Bjorn Bettum, Mng. Dir.   Tel: 47-77-64-8200
Bus: *Shipping, transportation, travel and* Fax: 47-77-64-8180   Emp: 5,087
tourism services.   www.bergenline.com

    BERGEN LINE SERVICES
    405 Park Avenue, New York, NY   10022
    CEO: Rosalyn Gershell, Pres.   Tel: (212) 319-1300   %FO: 100
    Bus: *Ticketing office for passenger*   Fax: (212) 319-1390   Emp: 10
    ferries, cruise ships and tour
    packages.

• **TOMRA SYSTEMS ASA**
Drengrudshaugen 2, PO Box 278, N-1372 Asker, Norway
CEO: Erik Thorsen, CEO   Tel: 47-66-79-9100   Rev: $309
Bus: *Mfr. reverse vending machines for*   Fax: 47-66-79-9111   Emp: 1,800
plastic bottle returns.   www.tomra.com

    TOMRA PACIFIC INC.
    150 Klug Circle, Crona, CA   92880-5424
    CEO: Erik Thorsen, CEO   Tel: (909) 520-1700   %FO: 100
    Bus: *Mfr. reverse vending machines for* Fax: (909) 520-1701
    plastic bottle returns.

    TOMRA PACIFIC INC.
    820 First Street, Ste. 200, West Des Moines, IA   50265
    CEO: Erik Thorsen, CEO   Tel: (515) 255-5103   %FO: 100
    Bus: *Mfr. reverse vending machines for* Fax: (515) 552-0746
    plastic bottle returns.

TOMRA PACIFIC INC.

1610 NW Couch Street, Portland, OR   97209

CEO: Erik Thorsen, CEO Tel: (503) 226-7015 %FO: 100

Bus: *Mfr. reverse vending machines for* Fax: (503) 226-7173
plastic bottle returns.

● **WALLENIUS WILHELMSEN LINES A/S**

PO Box 33, N-1324 Lysaker, Norway

CEO: Ingar Skaug, Pres. & CEO Tel: 47-67-58-4100

Bus: *Specialized shipping for motor vehicle* Fax: 47-67-58-4080 Emp: 2,800
and heavy cargo industries. www.2wglobal.com

WALLENIUS WILHELMSEN LINES

PO Box 1232, Woodcliff Lake, NJ   07677-1232

CEO: Raymond P. Ebeling, Pres. Tel: (201) 307-1300 %FO: 100

Bus: *Transportation automobiles,* Fax: (201) 307-9740
trucks and rolling cargo.

WALLENIUS WILHELMSEN LINES

5601 Edison Drive, Oxnard, CA   93033

CEO: Raymond P. Ebeling, Pres. Tel: (805) 488-4000 %FO: 100

Bus: *Transportation automobiles,* Fax: (805) 488-4009 Emp: 100
trucks and rolling cargo.

WALLENIUS WILHELMSEN LINES

PO Box 1560, Galveston, TX   77553

CEO: Raymond P. Ebeling, Pres. Tel: (723) 952-4390 %FO: 100

Bus: *Transportation automobiles,* Fax:
trucks and rolling cargo.

WALLENIUS WILHELMSEN LINES

200 Golden Oak Court, Ste. 480, Virginia Beach, VA   23452

CEO: Mary Tritch, Mgr. Tel: (757) 431-4760 %FO: 100

Bus: *Transportation automobiles,* Fax: (757) 431-4760
trucks and rolling cargo.

Pakistan

● **HABIB BANK LTD.**
Habib Bank Plaza, 11,Chundhrigh Road, Karachi 21, Pakistan
CEO: Zakir Mahmood, Pres.   Tel: 92-21-241-8000
Bus: *General banking services.* Fax: 92-21-241-4191
           www.habibbank.com

  HABIB BANK LTD.
  44 Wall Street, 10th Fl., New York, NY 10005
  CEO:Muhammad Hanif, Mgr. Tel: (212) 422-9720 %FO: 100
  Bus: *International banking services.* Fax: (212) 248-8506 Emp: 53

● **NATIONAL BANK OF PAKISTAN**
1-1 Chundrigar, Karachi, Pakistan
CEO: Mohammed Soomro, Pres. Tel: 92-21-241-1974
Bus: *Commercial banking services.* Fax: 92-21-241-6769
           www.nbp.com.pk

  NATIONAL BANK OF PAKISTAN
  100 Wall Street, 21st Fl., New York, NY 10005
  CEO:M. Rafiq Bengali, Gen. Mgr. Tel: (212) 344-8822 %FO: 100
  Bus: *International banking services.* Fax: (212) 344-8826 Emp: 40

  NATIONAL BANK OF PAKISTAN
  One United Nations Plaza, New York, NY 10017
  CEO:Raja Arshad Nazeer, Mgr. Tel: (212) 758-8900 %FO: 100
  Bus: *International banking services.* Fax: (212) 355-6211 Emp: 7

● **UNITED BANK LIMITED**
1-1 Chundrigar Road, Karachi, Pakistan
CEO: Zubyr Soomro, Pres.   Tel: 92-021-241-7100
Bus: *Commercial banking services.* Fax: 92-021-241-3492
           www.ubl.com.pk

  UNITED BANK LIMITED
  30 Wall Street, 10th Fl., New York, NY 10005
  CEO:Anwar Zaidl, Mgr.   Tel: (212) 294-3127 %FO: 100
  Bus: *International banking services.* Fax: (212) 968-0057

Panama

• BAC INTERNATIONAL BANK
Cl. Aquilino de la Guardia, Edificio Bac International Bank, Planta Baja, Panama

CEO: Carlos F. Pellas, Pres.

Bus: *International financial services, commercial & investment banking, securities and insurance services.*

Tel: 507-213-0822
Fax: 507-269-3879
www.bacbank.com

BAC INSURANCE CORPORATION
847 Brickell Avenue, Ste. 900, Miami, FL   33131

CEO: John Sordo, EVP

Bus: *International financial services, health and retirement insurance services.*

Tel: (305) 377-1046
Fax: (305) 375-0351

%FO: 100

• BANCO LATINOAMERICANO DE EXPORTACIONES SA (BLADEX)
Calle 50 y Aquillino de la Guardia, PO Box 6-1497, El Dorado, Panama City, Panama

CEO: Jose Castaneda, CEO

Bus: *International banking services.*

Tel: 507-263-6766
Fax: 507-269-6333
www.blx.com

Rev: $415
Emp: 160

BANCO LATINOAMERICANO DE EXPORTACIONES (BLADEX)
1185 Avenue of the Americas, 30th Fl., New York, NY   10036

CEO: Thomas Keresztes, Gen. Mgr.

Bus: *International banking services.*

Tel: (212) 754-2600
Fax: (212) 754-2606

%FO: 100
Emp: 8

• WILLBROS GROUP, INC.
Dresdner Bank Building at 50th Street, 8th Fl., PO Box 850048, Panama City 5, Panama

CEO: Larry J. Bump, CEO

Bus: *Engaged in independent contracting serving the oil and gas industries.*

Tel: 507-2-63-9282
Fax: 507-2-63-9294
www.willbros.com

Rev: $315
Emp: 2,200

WILLBROS GROUP, INC.
600 Willbros Place, 2431 East 61st Street, Tulsa, OK   74136-1267

CEO: Larry J. Bump, Chmn. & CEO

Bus: *Engaged in independent contracting serving the oil and gas industries.*

Tel: (918) 748-7000
Fax: (918) 748-7087

%FO: 100

Peru

● **BANCO DE CREDITO DEL PERU, SUB. CREDICORP LTD.**
Calle Centenario 156, Urbanizacion Laderas de Melgarejo, La Molina, Lima, Peru
CEO: Dionisio Romero, Chmn.   Tel: 51-1-437-3838   Rev: $1,009
Bus: *International banking services.*   Fax: 51-1-349-0638   Emp: 7,522
                                       www.viabcp.com

   BANCO DE CREDITO DEL PERU
   410 Park Avenue, 6th Fl., New York, NY   10022
   CEO: Alfredo Montero, Gen. Mgr.   Tel: (212) 644-6644   %FO: 100
   Bus: *International banking services.*   Fax: (212) 826-9852   Emp: 11

● **BANCO WIESE SUDAMERIS**
Dionisio Derteano, 102 Esquina con Miguel Seminario, Lima 27, Peru
CEO: Carlos Palacio, Pres.   Tel: 51-1-211-6243   Rev: $327
Bus: *Commercial banking services.*   Fax: 51-1-440-4832   Emp: 2,546
                                       www.bws.com.pe

   BANK WIESE SUDAMERIS
   One William Street, New York, NY   10004
   CEO: Claudio Marchiori, Rep.   Tel: (212) 509-7858   %FO: 100
   Bus: *International commercial banking*   Fax: (212) 943-0943
      services.

   BANK WIESE SUDAMERIS
   701 Brickell Avenue, 9th Fl., Miami, FL   33131
   CEO: Hubert de la Feld, SVP   Tel: (305) 372-2200   %FO: 100
   Bus: *International commercial banking*   Fax: (305) 374-1130
      services.

Philippines

- **BANK OF THE PHILIPPINE ISLANDS**
  BPI Building, Ayala Avenue, Makati Metro Manila, Philippines
  CEO: Xavier. P. Loinaz, Pres.   Tel: 63-2-816-9381   Rev: $800
  Bus: *Commercial banking services.*   Fax: 63-2-813-4066   Emp: 8,013
                                          www.bpi.com.ph

    BANK OF THE PHILIPPINE ISLANDS
    7 East 53rd Street, New York, NY   10022
    CEO: Marlene Alindogan, Gen. Mgr.   Tel: (212) 644-6700   %FO: 100
    Bus: *Commercial banking services.* Fax: (212) 752-5969

- **METROPOLITAN BANK & TRUST COMPANY**
  Senator Gil Puyat Avenue, Makati, Metro Manila, Philippines
  CEO: Antonio S. Abacan Jr., Pres.   Tel: 63-2-810-3311   Rev: $972
  Bus: *Commercial banking services.*   Fax: 63-2-813-4066   Emp: 7,223
                                          www.metrobank.com.ph

    ASIA MONEY LINK CORPORATION
    41-60 Main Street, 3rd Fl., Flushing, NY   11355
    CEO: Alfred V. Madrid, VP   Tel: (718) 463-2250   %FO: 100
    Bus: *International commercial banking* Fax: (718) 463-2259
        services.

    METROPOLITAN BANK & TRUST COMPANY
    10 East 53rd Street, New York, NY   10022
    CEO: Alfred V. Madrid, VP & Gen.   Tel: (212) 832-0855   %FO: 100
        Mgr.
    Bus: *International commercial banking* Fax: (212) 832-0993
        services.

- **PHILIPPINE AIRLINES (PAL)**
  Philippine Airlines Center 1/F, Legaspi Street, Legaspi Village, Makati City, Philippines
  CEO: Jose Garcia, Pres.   Tel: 63-2-815-6481
  Bus: *Commercial air transport carrier.* Fax: 63-2-818-0111   Emp: 14,000
                                          www.philippineair.com

    PHILIPPINE AIRLINES
    447 Sutter Street, San Francisco, CA   94018
    CEO: Alberto Lim, Deputy Mgr.   Tel: (415) 391-0270   %FO: 100
    Bus: *International airline carrier.* Fax: (415) 433-6733

PHILIPPINE AIRLINES
5959 W. Century Blvd., Ste. 600, Los Angeles, CA   90045
CEO: A. Ingles, District Sales Mgr.   Tel: (310) 338-9000   %FO: 100
Bus: *International airline carrier.*   Fax: (310) 338-7194

● **PHILIPPINE NATIONAL BANK**
PNB Financial Center, Roxas Blvd., Pasai City, Manila, Philippines
CEO: Benjamin P. Palma Gil, Pres.   Tel: 63-2-891-6040   Rev: $729
Bus: *Commercial banking services.*   Fax: 63-2-891-6267   Emp: 7,085
                                         www.philnabank.com

PHILIPPINE NATIONAL BANK
546 Fifth Avenue, 8th Fl., New York, NY   10036
CEO: Raul G. De Asis, SVP & Gen.Mgr. Tel: (212) 790-9600   %FO: 100
Bus: *International banking services.*   Fax: (212) 382-2238

Poland

- **BANK HANDLOWY W WARSZAWIE S.A.**
  Ul. Chalubinskiego 8, PO Box 129, PL-00-950 Warsaw, Poland
  CEO: Cezary Stypulkowski, Pres.   Tel: 48-22-6903-000   Rev: $733
  Bus: *Commercial banking services.*   Fax: Emp: 4,052
  www.bh.com

    BANK HANDLOWY W WARSZAWIE S.A.
    405 Park Avenue, Suite 1101, New York, NY   10022
    CEO: Eugeniusz Szewczyk, Chief Rep.   Tel: (212) 371-8390   %FO: 100
    Bus: *International banking services.*   Fax: (212) 371-8391

- **BANK POLSKA KASA OPIEKI S.A., GRUPA PEKAO**
  Ul. Grzybowska 53/57, P O Box 108, PL-00-950 Warsaw, Poland
  CEO: Maria Wisniewska, Pres.   Tel: 48-22-656-0000
  Bus: *Banking services.*   Fax: 48-22-656-0004
  www.pbg.pl

    BANK POLSKA KASA OPIEKI
    470 Park Avenue South, New York, NY   10016
    CEO: Alfred B. Biec, Gen. Mgr.   Tel: (212) 251-1200   %FO: 100
    Bus: *Commercial banking services.*   Fax: (212) 679-5910

- **MELEX VEHICLE PRODUCTION PLANT CO., LTD.**
  3 Wojska Polskiego Street, PL-39-300 Mielec, Poland
  CEO: Wieslaw Kosleradzki, Pres.   Tel: 48-196-88-7824
  Bus: *Mfr. golf cars and specialty vehicles.*   Fax: 48-196-88-7945
  www.melex.com

    MPI II, INC.
    3900 Business Hwy. 70 Business West, Clayton, NC   27520
    CEO: Scott Mallory, VP   Tel: (919) 938-3800   %FO: 100
    Bus: *Mfr./sale golf cars & specialty   Fax: (919) 938-3852
    vehicles.*

- **POLSKIE LINIE LOTNICZE LOT SA**
  39 Ul. 17 Stycznia, Warsaw PL-00697, Poland
  CEO: Jan Litwinski, Pres.   Tel: 48-26-66111   Rev: $2,700
  Bus: *International commercial air transport   Fax: 48-24-66409   Emp: 4,359
  services.*   www.lot.com

LOT POLISH AIRLINES
500 5th Avenue, New York, NY 10110
CEO: Genevieve Ziebinski, Mgr.   Tel: (212) 852-0244   %FO: 100
Bus: *International commercial air*   Fax: (212) 302-0191   Emp: 100
 transport services.

Portugal

- **BANCO COMMERCIAL PORTUGUES**
  Praça D. João I, 28, P-4000-295 Porto, Portugal
  CEO: Jorge M. Jardim Goncalves, Chmn.　　Tel: 351-21-321-1000　　　Rev: $4,707
  Bus: *General commercial banking.*　　　　Fax: 351-21-321-1079　　Emp: 12,600
  　　　　　　　　　　　　　　　　　　　www.bcp.pt

  ### BANCO COMMERCIAL PORTUGUES
  Two Wall Street, New York, NY　10005
  CEO:Pedro J. Bello, Gen. Mgr.　　　Tel: (212) 306-7800　　%FO: 100
  Bus: *International banking services.*　Fax: (212) 766-8047

- **BANCO FINANTIA**
  Rua General Firmino Miguel, 5, P-1600 Lisbon, Portugal
  CEO: António M. A. Guerreiro, Chmn. &　Tel: 351-1-720-2000
  　　CEO
  Bus: *Provides investment banking services.*　Fax: 351-1-726-8563
  　　　　　　　　　　　　　　　　　　　www.finantia.pt

  ### FINANTIA BROKERS LTD.
  437 Madison Avenue, New York, NY　10022
  CEO:Jennifer Howarth, Pres.　　　Tel: (212) 891-7300　　%FO: 100
  Bus: *Provides investment banking*　Fax: (212) 891-7310
  　　　services.

- **BANCO TOTTA & ACORES**
  Rua Do Ouro 88, P-1100 Lisbon, Portugal
  CEO: Antonio Horta Osorio, Chmn.　　Tel: 351-1-321-1500　　Rev: $2,315
  Bus: *Commercial banking services.*　　Fax: 351-1-321-2092　　Emp: 4,768
  　　　　　　　　　　　　　　　　　www.bta.pt

  ### BANCO TOTTA & ACORES
  590 Fifth Avenue, 8th Floor, New York, NY　10036
  CEO:Sergio Capela, Mgr.　　　　Tel: (212) 302-6870　　%FO: 100
  Bus: *International banking services.*　Fax: (212) 302-7369

Qatar

• DOHA BANK LIMITED
PO Box 3818, Doha, Qatar
CEO: Mohamad Atiq, Mgr.   Tel: 974-456600
Bus: *General banking services.*   Fax: 974-416631
                                          www.dohabank.com

DOHA BANK LTD.
100 Wall Street, 19th Fl., New York, NY   10005
CEO: Anjum Nisar, Mgr.   Tel: (212) 509-4030   %FO: 100
Bus: *General banking services.*   Fax: (212) 509-6433

Russia

● **AEROFLOT RUSSIAN INTERNATIONAL AIRLINES**
125167 Leningradsky Prospectus 37, Bldg. 9, Moscow, Russia
CEO: Sergi O. Frank, CEO   Tel: 7-95-156-8019   Rev: $1,166
Bus: *International air carrier.*   Fax: 7-95-155-6647   Emp: 14,995
                             www.aeroflot.org

     AEROFLOT (RUSSIAN) AIRLINES
     80 S.W. 8th Street, Miami, FL   33131
     CEO:N. A. Glushkov, Dir.   Tel: (305) 577-8500   %FO: 100
     Bus: *International air carrier.*   Fax: (305) 579-8666

     AEROFLOT (RUSSIAN) AIRLINES
     1411 4th Avenue, Ste. 420, Seattle, WA   98101
     CEO:N. A. Glushkov, Dir.   Tel: (206) 464-1005   %FO: 100
     Bus: *International air carrier.*   Fax: (206) 464-0452

     AEROFLOT (RUSSIAN) AIRLINES
     1620 "I" Street NW, Ste. 500, Washington, DC   20006
     CEO:N. A. Glushkov, Dir.   Tel: (202) 466-4080   %FO: 100
     Bus: *International air carrier.*   Fax: (202) 785-6618

     AEROFLOT (RUSSIAN) AIRLINES
     291 Geary Street, Ste. 200, San Francisco, CA   94102
     CEO:N. A. Glushkov, Dir.   Tel: (415) 434-2300   %FO: 100
     Bus: *International air carrier.*   Fax: (415) 403-4033

     AEROFLOT (RUSSIAN) AIRLINES
     225 North Michigan Avenue, Ste. 2304, Chicago, IL   60601
     CEO:N. A. Glushkov, Dir.   Tel: (312) 819-2350   %FO: 100
     Bus: *International air carrier.*   Fax: (312) 819-2352

     AEROFLOT (RUSSIAN) AIRLINES
     9100 Wilshire Blvd., Ste. 616, Beverly Hills, CA   90212
     CEO:N. A. Glushkov, Dir.   Tel: (310) 281-5300   %FO: 100
     Bus: *International air carrier.*   Fax: (310) 281-5304

     AEROFLOT (RUSSIAN) AIRLINES
     630 Fifth Avenue, New York, NY   10111
     CEO:N. A. Glushkov, Dir.   Tel: (212) 288-2125   %FO: 100
     Bus: *International air carrier.*   Fax: (212) 288-5973

- **BANK FOR FOREIGN ECONOMIC AFFAIRS OF USSR (VNESHECONOMBANK)**

3/5 Kopjevsky Lane, Moscow 103009, Russia

CEO: Andrei L. Kostin, Chmn.   Tel: 7-95-207-1037

Bus: *Provides centralized foreign economic*   Fax: 7-95-975-2134   Emp: 3,500
operations for Russian federation.   www.veb.ru

BANK FOR FOREIGN ECONOMIC AFFAIRS OF USSR (BFEA)

527 Madison Avenue, New York, NY   10022

CEO: Alexander Danilov, Pres.   Tel: (212) 421-8660   %FO: 100

Bus: *International banking services.*   Fax: (212) 421-8677   Emp: 2

- **ITAR-TASS (RUSSIAN NEWS AGENCY)**

10 Tverskoy Boulevard, Moscow 103009, Russia

CEO: Vitary Ignatenko, Director General   Tel: 7-95-229-64-03

Bus: *News and photo wires.*   Fax: 7-95-229-64-03   Emp: 3,500
     www.itar-tass.com

ITAR-TASS USA, INC.

50 Rockefeller Plaza, New York, NY   10020

CEO: Michael Koleshichenko, Pres.   Tel: (212) 664-0977   %FO: 100

Bus: *News wires, photos, advertising,*   Fax: (212) 245-4035   Emp: 15
public relations and consulting.

RUSSIAN NATIONAL TOURIST OFFICE

130 West 42nd Street, Ste. 504, New York, NY   10036

CEO: Michael Koleshichenko, Dir.   Tel: (212) 575-3431   %FO: 100

Bus: *Provides travel services.*   Fax: (212) 575-3434

- **UNIVERS BANK**

10 Bolshaya Morskaya Ulitsa, St. Petersburg 191186, Russia

CEO: Tate Ulsaker, Dir.   Tel: 7-812-164-8926

Bus: *Engaged in financial consulting and*   Fax: 7-812-278-9264
investment services.

PALMS & COMPANY OF RUSSIA INC.

Bldg. 103, 15 Lake Street South, Kirkland, WA   98033

CEO: Peter J. Palms, Pres.   Tel: (425) 828-6774

Bus: *Provides financial consulting and*   Fax: (425) 827-5528
investment services.

- **VAO INTOURIST**

Milyutinsky Lane 13/1, Moscow 101000, Russia

CEO: Alexander A. Uryupin, Pres.   Tel: 7-95-797-3065

Bus: *Engaged in international tourism and*   Fax: 7-95-797-3060   Emp: 3,750
investment operations.   www.intourist.ru

INTOURIST USA

12 South Dixie Hwy, Ste. 201, Lake Worth, FL   33460

CEO: Alexey N. Mesiatsev, Pres.　　Tel: (561) 585-5305　　%FO: JV

Bus: *International tourism and*　　Fax: (561) 582-1353　　Emp: 10
　　investment operations.

Saudi Arabia

- **ALIREZA GROUP**
  PO Box 90, Al-Khobar 31952, Saudi Arabia
  CEO: Ahmed Y. Z. Alireza, Pres. & CEO   Tel: 966-3-857-0234
  Bus: *Holding company engaged in*   Fax: 966-3-857-2846
        manufacturing and trading, energy,   www.alireza.com
        construction, transportation, healthcare
        and engineering.

  REZAYAT AMERICA INC.
  11000 Richmond Ave., Ste. 580, Houston, TX   77042
  CEO: Haroon Shadman, VP   Tel: (713) 782-0090   %FO: 100
  Bus: *Holding company engaged in*   Fax: (713) 782-7395
        diversified manufacturing and
        trading.

- **THE NATIONAL SHIPPING COMPANY OF SAUDI ARABIA**
  Al-Akariya Building, Sitteen Street, Malaz Area, PO Box 8931, Riyadh 11492, Saudi Arabia
  CEO: Abdulla Al-Shuraim, CEO   Tel: 966-1-478-5454
  Bus: *International shipping and cargo*   Fax: 966-1-477-7478
        services.   www.nscsaamerica.com

  NSCSA (America) INC.
  399 Hoes Lane, Ste. 100, Piscataway, NJ   08854
  CEO: Fahad Al-Megren, Pres.   Tel: (732) 562-8989   %FO: 100
  Bus: *International shipping/cargo*   Fax: (732) 562-0909
        services.

  NSCSA (America) INC.
  401 Pratt Street, 26th Fl., Baltimore, MD   21202
  CEO: Fahad Al-Megren, Pres.   Tel: (410) 625-7000   %FO: 100
  Bus: *International shipping/cargo*   Fax: (410) 625-7050
        services.

- **THE OLAYAN GROUP**
  PO Box 8772, Riyadh 11492, Saudi Arabia
  CEO: Khaled S. Olayan, Pres. & CEO   Tel: 966-1-477-8740
  Bus: *Holding company. (See Greece)*   Fax: 966-1-478-0988
                                          www.olayangroup.com

OLAYAN AMERICA CORPORATION

505 Park Avenue, 10th Fl., New York, NY   10022

CEO: John O. Wolcott, EVP   Tel: (212) 750-4800   %FO: 100

Bus: *Business development & advisory*   Fax: (212) 308-3654   Emp: 15
    services.

● RIYAD BANK

King Abdul Aziz Road, PO Box 22622, Riyadh 11416, Saudi Arabia

CEO: Mohammed Abalkhall, Chmn.   Tel: 966-1-4013030

Bus: *General banking services.*   Fax: 966-1-404 2707   Emp: 4,300
    www.riyadbank.com

RIYAD BANK

700 Louisiana, Ste. 4770, Houston, TX   77002

CEO: Samir A. Haddad, SVP   Tel: (713) 331-2001   %FO: 100

Bus: *International trade & project*   Fax: (713) 331-2043   Emp: 14
    financing services.

● SAUDI ARABIAN AIRLINES

Al Khaledyyah District, Jeddah 21231, Saudi Arabia

CEO: Dr. Khaled A. Ben-Bakr, Dir.   Tel: 966-2-686-2251   Rev: $2,500

Bus: *International commercial air transport*   Fax: 966-2-686-2251   Emp: 23,924
    services.   www.saudiairlines.com

SAUDI ARABIAN AIRLINES

725 Fifth Avenue, New York, NY   10022

CEO: Talal Mohsen, Gen.Mgr.   Tel: (212) 751-7000   %FO: 100

Bus: *International commercial air*   Fax: (212) 751-7270
    transport services.

● SAUDI ARABIAN OIL COMPANY

PO Box 5000, Central Mail Room T-51, Dhahran 31311, Saudi Arabia

CEO: Abdallah S. Jum'ah, CEO   Tel: 966-3-875-4915

Bus: *Oil exploration, transportation &*   Fax: 966-3-873-8490   Emp: 50,000
    refining.   www.aramco.com

ARAMCO SERVICES COMPANY

9009 West Loop South, Houston, TX   77096

CEO: Mustafa A. Jalali, Pres. & CEO   Tel: (713) 432-4000   %FO: 100

Bus: *Oil industry service and support.*   Fax: (713) 432-8566   Emp: 1,000

● SAUDI BASIC INDUSTRIES CORPORATION

PO Box 5101, Riyadh 11422, Saudi Arabia

CEO: Ibrahim A. Salamah, CEO   Tel: 966-1-401-2033

Bus: *Mfr./marketing chemicals, plastics,*   Fax: 966-1-401-2045   Emp: 600
    fertilizers & steels.   www.sabicusa.com

SABIC AMERICAS, INC.
2500 City West Blvd., Suite 650, Houston, TX   77042
CEO: Mohammad Al-Bat'hi   Tel: (713) 549-4999   %FO: 100
Bus: *Research/development,*   Fax: (713) 549-4994   Emp: 38
procurement & recruitment
petrochemical/fertilizer/steel
industries.

Scotland, U.K.

● **ABERDEEN ASSET MANAGEMENT PLC**
1 Albyn Place, Aberdeen Grampian AB10 1YG, UK
CEO: Martin J. Gilbert, Chmn. & CEO   Tel: 44-1224-631-999   Rev: $169
Bus: *Provides financial services.*   Fax: 44-1224-647-010   Emp: 465
    www.aberdeen-asset.com

    ABERDEEN ASSET MANAGEMENT, INC.
    45 Broadway, 31st Fl., New York, NY   10006
    CEO: Richard Strickler, Dir.   Tel: (212) 968-8800   %FO: 100
    Bus: *Provides financial services.*   Fax: (212) 363-5834

● **AGGREKO PLC**
121 West Regent Street, Glasgow G2 2SD, UK
CEO: Dr. Christopher Masters, Chmn.   Tel: 44-141-225-5900   Rev: $365
Bus: *Mfr./supplies temporary utility rental*   Fax: 44-141-225-5949   Emp: 1,485
    systems, compressors and accessories.   www.aggreko.com

    AGGREKO INC.
    124 North Langley Road, Glen Burnie, MD   21060
    CEO: Phil Harrower, CEO   Tel: (410) 760-6200   %FO: 100
    Bus: *Support services headquarters.*   Fax: (410) 760-6260

    AGGREKO INC.
    4607 W. Admiral Doyle Dr., New Iberia, LA   70560
    CEO: George Walker, Pres.   Tel: (337) 367-7884   %FO: 100
    Bus: *Provides temporary utility rental*   Fax: (337) 367-0870
    systems, compressors and
    accessories.

    AGGREKO INC.
    1803 Atlantic Boulevard, Jacksonville, FL   32207
    CEO: Phil Harrower, CEO   Tel: (904) 396-0040   %FO: 100
    Bus: *Latin American sales headquarters.*   Fax: (904) 396-1444

    AGGREKO INC.
    3732 Magnolia Street, Pearland, TX   77584
    CEO: Phil Harrower, CEO   Tel: (713) 512-6723   %FO: 100
    Bus: *National temperature repair.*   Fax: (713) 512-6796

AGGREKO INC.
PO Box 627, Chickasha, OK   73023
CEO: Phil Harrower, CEO   Tel: (405) 224-5301   %FO: 100
Bus: *Industrial cooling tower center.*   Fax: (405) 224-5352

AGGREKO INC.
1776 Woodstead Court, Ste. 206, The Woodlands, TX   77380
CEO: Phil Harrower, CEO   Tel: (888) 918-4874   %FO: 100
Bus: *Engaged in event services*   Fax: (281) 298-9152

AGGREKO INC.
One Chelsea Pkwy., Ste. 101, Boothwyn, PA   19061
CEO: Phil Harrower, CEO   Tel: (610) 364-4000   %FO: 100
Bus: *Engaged in business development.*   Fax: (610) 364-3900

AGGREKO INC.
655 Grigsby Way, Ste. B, Ceader Hill, TX   75104
CEO: Phil Harrower, CEO   Tel: (800) 269-5200   %FO: 100
Bus: *Engaged in critical air services.*   Fax: (972) 293-3667

● **BANK OF SCOTLAND**
PO Box 5, The Mound, Edinburgh EH1 1YZ, UK
CEO: Peter Burt, CEO   Tel: 44-131-442-7777   Rev: $7,861
Bus: *General banking services.*   Fax: 44-131-243-5437   Emp: 22,704
                                         www.bankofscotland.co.uk

BANK OF SCOTLAND
311 South Wacker Drive, Ste. 1625, Chicago, IL   60606
CEO: Jinn Halley, SVP   Tel: (312) 939-9710   %FO: 100
Bus: *International banking services.*   Fax: (312) 939-9710   Emp: 6

BANK OF SCOTLAND
The Haskell Bldg., 111 Riverside Drive, Jacksonville, FL   32202
CEO: Hugh Van Seaton, SVP   Tel: (904) 353-7766   %FO: 100
Bus: *International banking services.*   Fax: (904) 353-7833   Emp: 6

BANK OF SCOTLAND
1750 Two Allen Center, 1220 Smith Street, Houston, TX   77002
CEO: Rex McSwain, SVP   Tel: (713) 651-1870   %FO: 100
Bus: *International banking services.*   Fax: (713) 651-9714   Emp: 10

BANK OF SCOTLAND
660 Figueroa Street, Ste. 1760, Los Angeles, CA   90017
CEO: J. Craig Wilson   Tel: (213) 629-3057   %FO: 100
Bus: *International banking services.*   Fax: (213) 489-3594   Emp: 5

BANK OF SCOTLAND
565 Fifth Avenue, 5th Fl., New York, NY   10017
CEO: Jack Dykes, EVP   Tel: (212) 450-0800   %FO: 100
Bus: *International banking services.*   Fax: (212) 557-9460   Emp: 87

● **DEVRO PLC**
Gartferry Road, Moodiesburn, Chryston Glasgow G69 0JE, UK
CEO: Graeme Y. Alexander, CEO   Tel: 44-1236-879-191   Rev: $344
Bus: *Produces collagen casings and film for*   Fax: 44-1236-8111-005   Emp: 3,384
sausage products for the food industry.   www.devro.plc.uk

    DEVRO-TEEPAK INC.
    915 North Michigan, Danville, IL   51832
    CEO: Doug Cunningham, Mgr.   Tel: (217) 446-6460   %FO: 100
    Bus: *Produces collagen casings and*   Fax: (217) 442-2617
    film for sausage products.

    DEVRO-TEEPAK INC.
    133 West 10th Avenue, N. Kansas City, MO   64116
    CEO: Cliff Harper   Tel: (816) 421-0323   %FO: 100
    Bus: *Produces collagen casings and*   Fax: (816) 842-6909
    film for sausage products.

● **WILLIAM GRANT & SONS DISTILLERS LTD.**
Phoenix Crescent Stroth Clyde Business Park, Motherwell ML4 3AN, UK
CEO: Glen Gordon, Mng. Dir.   Tel: 44-169-884-3843
Bus: *Distillery/exporter liquor.*   Fax: 44-169-844-4788
     www.wmgrant.com

    WILLIAM GRANT & SON INC
    130 Fieldcrest Avenue, Edison, NJ   08837
    CEO: Derek Anderson, Pres.   Tel: (732) 225-9000   %FO: 100
    Bus: *Distillery/importer liquor.*   Fax: (732) 225-0950

● **INVERESK RESEARCH INTERNATIONAL LIMITED**
Tranent, Lothian EH33 2NE, UK
CEO: Walter Nimmo, CEO   Tel: 44-1875-614-545   Rev: $60
Bus: *Conducts clinical trials for*   Fax: 44-1875-614-555   Emp: 800
pharmaceutical companies.   www.inveresk.com

    CLIN TRIALS RESEARCH
    11000 Weston Pkwy., Ste. 100, Cary, NC   27513
    CEO: Tom Pilsworth   Tel: (800) 988-9845   %FO: 100
    Bus: *Conducts clinical trials for*   Fax: (919) 462-2520
    pharmaceutical companies.

INVERESK RESEARCH
5203 Leesburg Pike, Ste. 309, Falls Church, VA   22041
CEO: Walter Nimmo   Tel: (703) 824-7850   %FO: 100
Bus: *Conducts clinical trials for*   Fax: (703) 824-7851
       pharmaceutical companies.

INVERESK RESEARCH
3020 Kerner Blvd., Ste. D, San Rafael, CA   94901
CEO: Walter Nimmo   Tel: (415) 257-4243   %FO: 100
Bus: *Conducts clinical trials for*   Fax: (415) 257-4250
       pharmaceutical companies.

● **LOGITECH LTD., DIV. STRUERS**
Erskine Ferry Road, Old Kilpatrick, Glasgow G60 5EU, UK
CEO: David Humphries   Tel: 44-1389-875-444
Bus: *Engaged in precision materials*   Fax: 44-1389-890-956
       technology, including optics, lasers,   www.logitech.uk.com
       semiconductors.

   LOGITECH PRODUCT GROUP
   810 Sharon Drive, Westlake, OH   44145
   CEO: Charles Geyer   Tel: (440) 871-0071   %FO: 100
   Bus: *Mfr. precision sawing, lapping*   Fax: (440) 871-8188
          and polishing equipment.

● **MARTIN CURRIE LTD.**
20 Castle Terrace, Edinburgh EH1 2ES, UK
CEO: Willie Watt, CEO   Tel: 44-808-100-2125   Rev: $4,000
Bus: *Engaged in investment banking services.* Fax: 44-808-222-2532   Emp: 1,500
                                    www.martincurrie.com

   MARTIN CURRIE INC.
   53 Forest Avenue, Old Greenwich, CT   06870
   CEO: Steve Johnson, VP   Tel: (203) 698-9031   %FO: 100
   Bus: *Investment banking.*   Fax: (203) 698-9037

● **PPL THERAPEUTICS PLC**
Roslin, Edinburgh EH25 9PP, UK
CEO: Chris G. Greig   Tel: 44-131-440-4777   Rev: $3
Bus: *Engaged in biotechnology.*   Fax: 44-131-440-4888   Emp: 200
                                    www.ppl-therapeutics.com

   PPL THERAPEUTICS INC.
   1700 Kraft Drive, Ste. 2400, Blacksburg, VA   24060
   CEO: David Ayares, VP   Tel: (540) 961-5559   %FO: 100
   Bus: *Engaged in biotechnology.*   Fax: (540) 961-7958   Emp: 25

● **THE ROYAL BANK OF SCOTLAND GROUP PLC**

42 St. Andrew Square, Edinburgh EH2 2YE, UK

CEO: Fred A. Goodwin, CEO Tel: 44-131-556-8555 Rev: $17,713

Bus: *Financial services company; banking,* Fax: 44-131-557-6565 Emp: 19,620
insurance, investment advisory services. www.rbs.co.uk

CITIZENS BANK OF MASSACHUSETTS

28 State Street, Boston, MA 02109

CEO: Robert T. Gromley, Pres. Tel: (617) 742-6000 %FO: 100

Bus: *Financial services company;* Fax: (617) 523-0366
banking, insurance, investment
advisory services.

CITIZENS BANK OF RHODE ISLAND

One Citizens Plaza, Providence, RI 02903-4089

CEO: Mark J. Formica, Chmn. Tel: (401) 456-7000 %FO: 100

Bus: *Banking and savings.* Fax: (401) 455-5715

CITIZENS BANK OF RHODE ISLAND

One Citizens Plaza, Providence, RI 02903-4089

CEO: Robert T. Gormley, CEO Tel: (401) 456-7000 %FO: 100

Bus: *General banking services.* Fax: (401) 455-5715

CITIZENS FINANCIAL GROUP, INC.

One Citizens Plaza, Providence, RI 02903-4089

CEO: Lawrence K. Fish, Chmn. Tel: (401) 456-7000 %FO: 100

Bus: *Financial services company;* Fax: (401) 455-5715
banking, insurance, investment
advisory services. Holding
company.

CITIZENS LEASING CORPORATION, INC.

One Citizens Plaza, Providence, RI 02903-4089

CEO: John Chipman, Pres. Tel: (401) 456-7000 %FO: 100

Bus: *Lease financing subsidiary of the* Fax: (401) 455-5715
Royal Bank of Scotland PLC.

CITIZENS MORTGAGE CORPORATION, INC.

One Citizens Plaza, Providence, RI 02903-4089

CEO: Stephen E. Adamo, COO Tel: (401) 456-7000 %FO: 100

Bus: *Mortgage financing subsidiary of* Fax: (401) 455-5715
the Royal Bank of Scotland.

CITIZENS VENTURES, INC.
28 State Street, Boston, MA   02109

CEO: Robert E. Garrow, Pres.　　　Tel: (617) 742-6000　　　%FO: 100

Bus: *Financial services company;*　Fax: (617) 523-0366
banking, insurance, investment
advisory services.

COUTTS (USA) INTERNATIONAL
701 Brickell Avenue, Ste. 300, Miami, FL   33131

CEO: Camilo Patino, Pres.　　　　Tel: (305) 789-3714　　　%FO: 100

Bus: *International private banking*　Fax: (305) 789-3724
services.

GREENWICH CAPITAL MARKETS, INC.
600 Steamboat Road, Greenwich, CT   06830

CEO: Gary F. Holloway, Chmn.　　Tel: (203) 625-2700　　　%FO: 100

Bus: *Financial services company;*　Fax: (203) 629-4336
banking, insurance, investment
advisory services.

NATWEST GROUP N.A.
101 Park Avenue, 10th Fl., New York, NY   10178

CEO: Gareth Baker, COO　　　　Tel: (212) 401-3200　　　%FO: 100

Bus: *Financial services company;*　Fax: (212) 401-3623
banking, insurance, investment
advisory services.

ROYAL BANK OF SCOTLAND
101 Park Avenue, New York, NY   10178

CEO: Derek Weir, SVP　　　　　Tel: (212) 269-1700　　　%FO: 100

Bus: *Financial services company;*　Fax: (212) 269-8929
banking, insurance, investment
advisory services.

UNITED STATES TRUST COMPANY
40 Court Street, Boston, MA   02108

CEO: Domenic Colasacco, Pres.　　Tel: (617) 726-7250　　　%FO: 100

Bus: *Financial services company;*　Fax:
banking, insurance, investment
advisory services.

● SCOTTISH & NEWCASTLE, PLC.
50 East Fettes Avenue, Edinburgh EH4 1RR, UK

CEO: Brian Stewart, Chmn.　　　Tel: 44-131-528-2000　　Rev: $5,544

Bus: *Mfr./owner of breweries for distribution*　Fax: 44-131-528-2121　Emp: 57,750
of beers.　　　　　　　　　www.scottish-newcastle.com

SCOTTISH & NEWCASTLE IMPORTERS
990 A Street, Ste. 404, San Rafael, CA   94901
CEO: Kevin Moodie, Mgr.   Tel: (415) 257-2608   %FO: 100
  Bus: *Importer/distributor beer.*   Fax: (415) 257-2618

● **SCOTTISH POWER PLC**
One Atlantic Quay, Glasgow G2 8SP, UK
CEO: Charles Miller Smith, Chmn.   Tel: 44-141-248-8200   Rev: $9,000
  Bus: *Engaged in generation, transmission*   Fax: 44-141-248-8300   Emp: 24,115
    and distribution of electricity.   www.scottishpower.plc.uk

  PACIFICORP
  825 Northeast Multnomah Street, Portland, OR   97232
  CEO: Alan V. Richardson, CEO   Tel: (503) 813-5000   %FO: 100
    Bus: *Engaged in electric utility services.* Fax: (503) 813-7246

● **THE WEIR GROUP PLC.**
149 Newlands Road, Cathcart, Glasgow G44 4EX, UK
CEO: Mark Selway, CEO   Tel: 44-141-637-7111   Rev: $1,220
  Bus: *Mfr. valves, slurry pumps and process*   Fax: 44-141-637-2221   Emp: 9,646
    equipment.   www.weir.co.uk

  ATWOOD AND MORRILL CO. INC.
  285 Canal Street, Salem, MA   01970
  CEO: Paul Bowler, Pres.   Tel: (508) 744-5690   %FO: 100
    Bus: *Mfr./sales/distribution of valves.* Fax: (508) 741-3626

  C.S. LEWIS & COMPANY LTD.
  8625 Grant Road, St. Louis, MO   63123
  CEO: Bob Hanssen, Pres.   Tel: (314) 843-4437   %FO: 100
    Bus: *Mfr. centrifugal slurry pumps and* Fax: (314) 843-7964
      process equipment.

  ENVIRO TECH MOLDED PRODUCTS
  1075 West North Temple, Salt Lake City, UT   84116
  CEO: Scott Robinson, Pres.   Tel: (801) 323-2900   %FO: 100
    Bus: *Mfr./sales/distribution of molded* Fax: (801) 323-2913
      products.

  HAZELTON PUMPS, INC.
  225 North Cedar Street, Hazelton, PA   18201-0488
  CEO: Peter Haentjens, Mgr.   Tel: (570) 455-7711   %FO: 100
    Bus: *Mfr. centrifugal slurry pumps and* Fax: (570) 459-2586
      process equipment.

RUBBER ENGINEERING INC.
PO Box 96, Woodstock, GA 30118
CEO: Peter Krumm, Pres. & CEO   Tel: (770) 591-5858   %FO: 100
Bus: *Mfr. elastomer wear components.*   Fax: (770) 591-7057

RUBBER ENGINEERING INC.
PO Box 26188, Salt Lake City, UT 84126
CEO: Peter Krumm, Pres. & CEO   Tel: (801) 530-7887   %FO: 100
Bus: *Mfr. rubber wear products for the   Fax: (801) 261-5587*
mining, sand and gravel industries.

RUBBER ENGINEERING INC.
465 West Van Buren, Unit C, Colorado Springs, CO 80907
CEO: Peter Krumm, Pres. & CEO   Tel: (719) 389-0524   %FO: 100
Bus: *Mfr. elastomer wear components.*   Fax: (719) 389-0533

RUBBER ENGINEERING INC.
PO Box 653, Holicong, PA 18928
CEO: Peter Krumm, Pres. & CEO   Tel: (215) 794-7548   %FO: 100
Bus: *Mfr. elastomer wear components.*   Fax: (215) 794-7538

WEIR SLURRY GROUP, INC.
PO Box 7610, Madison, WI 53707-7610
CEO: John Parker, VP   Tel: (608) 221-5801   %FO: 100
Bus: *Mfr. centrifugal slurry pumps and   Fax: (608) 221-5807*
process equipment.

WEIR SPECIALTY PUMPS INC.
PO Box 209, Salt Lake City, UT 84110
CEO: Lee Bulson   Tel: (801) 359-8731   %FO: 100
Bus: *Mfr. centrifugal slurry pumps and   Fax: (801) 355-9303*
process equipment.

Singapore

● ASIA PULP & PAPER COMPANY LTD.
1 Maritime Square, #10-01 World Trade Centre, 099253 Singapore

CEO: Oei Tjie Goan, CEO

Tel: 65-272-9288

Rev: $3,135

Bus: *Engaged in the manufacture of paper and pulp for printing, including colored and uncoated papers.*

Fax: 65-374-9249

www.asiapulppaper.com

Emp: 79,000

ASIA PULP & PAPER TRADING, INC.
555 West Victoria Street, 2nd Fl., Compton, CA   90220

CEO: Ted Lin

Tel: (310) 638-4090

%FO: 100

Bus: *Engaged in the manufacture of paper and pulp for printing, including colored and uncoated papers*

Fax: (310) 631-9816

● BRIERLEY INVESTMENTS
16-02/03 Tung Centre, 20 Collyer Quay, 049319 Singapore

CEO: Sir Selwyn J. Cushing, Chmn.

Tel: 65-438-0002

Rev: $490

Bus: *Investment management services.*

Fax: 65-435-0040

www.bil.co.nz

Emp: 5,300

MOLOKAI RANCH LTD.
55 Merchant Street, Ste. 2000, Honolulu, HI   96813

CEO: James Mozley, Pres.

Tel: (808) 531-0158

%FO: 100

Bus: *Investment management services.*

Fax: (808) 521-2279

● CHARTERED SEMICONDUCTOR MANUFACTURING LTD.
60 Woodlands Industrial Park D, Street 2, 738406 Singapore

CEO: Ms. Ho Ching, Chair

Tel: 65-362-2838

Rev: $1,134

Bus: *Mfr. semiconductor chips.*

Fax: 65-362-2938

www.csminc.com

Emp: 4,340

CHARTERED SEMICONDUCTOR MANUFACTURING LTD.
1601 Trapelo Road, Waltham, MA   02154

CEO: Donald O'Rourke, Mng. Dir.

Tel: (781) 890-8711

%FO: 100

Bus: *Mfr. semiconductor chips.*

Fax: (781) 890-0617

CHARTERED SEMICONDUCTOR MANUFACTURING LTD.
1450 McCandless Drive, Milpitas, CA   95035

CEO: Michael J. Rekuc, Pres.

Tel: (408) 941-1100

%FO: 100

Bus: *Mfr. semiconductor chips.*

Fax: (408) 941-1101

● CREATIVE TECHNOLOGY LTD.
31 International Business Park, 609921 Singapore

CEO: Sim Wong Hoo, CEO   Tel: 65-895-4000   Rev: $1,344

Bus: *Mfr. digital entertainment products.*   Fax: 65-895-4999   Emp: 5,900

www.creative.com

CAMBRIDGE SOUNDWORKS, INC.
311 Needham Street, Newton Upper Falls, MA   02464

CEO: Mike Sullivan, Pres.   Tel: (617) 332-5936   %FO: 100

Bus: *Mfr. digital entertainment products.*   Fax: (617) 367-9229

CREATIVE LABS, INC.
1901 McCarthy Boulevard, Milpitas, CA   95035

CEO: Craig McHugh, Pres. & CEO   Tel: (408) 428-6600   %FO: 100

Bus: *Mfr. digital entertainment products.*   Fax: (408) 428-6611

● THE DEVELOPMENT BANK OF SINGAPORE
6 Shenton Way, Tower Two, 068809 Singapore

CEO: S. Dhanabalan, Pres.   Tel: 65-220-1111   Rev: $3,225

Bus: *Commercial banking services.*   Fax: 65-221-1306   Emp: 10,000

www.dbs.co.sg

THE DEVELOPMENT BANK OF SINGAPORE
445 South Figueroa Street, Ste. 3550, Los Angeles, CA   90017

CEO: Wil Kim Long, Gen. Mgr.   Tel: (213) 627-0222   %FO: 100

Bus: *Government banking institution.*   Fax: (213) 627-0228   Emp: 25

● FLEXTRONICS INTERNATIONAL LTD.
11 UBI Road 1, Meiban Industrial Bldg., Ste. 07-01/02, 408723 Singapore

CEO: Michael E. Marks, Chmn. & CEO   Tel: 65-844-3366   Rev: $12,110

Bus: *Provides contract electronics manufacturing services.*   Fax: 65-448-6040   Emp: 75,000

www.flextronics.com

FLEXTRONICS INTERNATIONAL
2090 Fortune Avenue, San Jose, CA   95131

CEO: Phil Koerper, Pres.   Tel: (408) 576-7000   %FO: 100

Bus: *Provides contract electronics manufacturing services.*   Fax: (408) 576-7454

• INTRACO LIMITED

430 Victoria Street, 1200 Bugis Junction Towers, 188024 Singapore

CEO: Au Eng Fong, CEO

Bus: *Diversified holding company; food, engineering, telecommunications and automotive dealerships.*

Tel: 65-337-0011
Fax: 65-337-7200
www.intraco.com.sg

Rev: $308
Emp: 660

INTRACO SYSTEMS, INC.

3998 Fau Boulevard, Ste. 210, Boca Raton, FL   33431

CEO: Bill Burbank, SVP

Bus: *Diversified holding company; food, engineering, telecommunications and automotive dealerships.*

Tel: (561) 367-0600
Fax: (561) 367-0600

%FO: 100

• NEPTUNE ORIENT LINES LIMITED

456 Alexandra Road, NOL Bldg., #06-00, 119962 Singapore

CEO: Flemming R. Jacobs

Bus: *Engaged in container shipping and logistics.*

Tel: 65-278-9000
Fax: 65-278-4900
www.nol.com.sg

Rev: $4,675
Emp: 8,550

AET SHIPPING

15 Exchange Place, Ste. 10, Jersey City, NJ   07302

CEO: G. McGrath

Bus: *Engaged in container shipping and logistics.*

Tel: (201) 985-0060
Fax: (201) 985-0527

%FO: 100

AET SHIPPING

1900 West Loop South, Ste. 920, Houston, TX   77027

CEO: Joseph Kwok, CEO

Bus: *Engaged in container shipping and logistics.*

Tel: (713) 622-1590
Fax: (713) 622-2256

%FO: 100

• OVERSEA-CHINESE BANKING CORP. LTD.

65 Chulia Street, OCBC Centre, 049513, Singapore

CEO: Seng Wee Lee, Chmn.

Bus: *Commercial banking services.*

Tel: 65-530-1515
Fax: 65-533-7955
www.ocbc.com.sg

Rev: $2,841

OVERSEA-CHINESE BANKING CORP LTD.

*Two World Financial Center, 36th Fl., New York, NY   10281

CEO: Eddie Lau, Mgr.

Bus: *International commercial banking services.*

Tel: (212) 587-0101
Fax: (212) 587-8235

%FO: 100
Emp: 18

● **OVERSEAS UNION BANK LTD.**
OUB Centre, 1 Raffles Place, 0104 Singapore
CEO: Peter Seah Lim Huat, Pres.   Tel: 65-533-8686   Rev: $1,762
Bus: *Commercial banking services.*   Fax: 65-533-2293
                                          www.1.oub.com

    OVERSEAS UNION BANK, LTD.
    *One World Trade Center, Ste. 3955, New York, NY   10048
    CEO: See-Inn Ong, VP   Tel: (212) 432-9482   %FO: 100
    Bus: *International banking services.*   Fax: (212) 432-9297   Emp: 17

    OVERSEAS UNION BANK, LTD.
    777 S. Figueroa Street, Ste. 3988, Los Angeles, CA   90017
    CEO: Chen Hoong, VP   Tel: (213) 624-3187   %FO: 100
    Bus: *International banking services.*   Fax: (213) 623-6407

● **RAFFLES HOLDINGS LTD.**
2 Stamford Road 06-01, Raffles City Convention Centre, 178882 Singapore
CEO: Richard Charles Helfer, CEO   Tel: 65-339-8377
Bus: *Worldwide hotel chain.*   Fax: 65-339-1713
                                          www.rafflesholdings.com

    THE DRAKE HOTEL
    440 Park Avenue, New York, NY   10022
    CEO: Guenther Richter, Mgr.   Tel: (212) 421-0900   %FO: 100
    Bus: *Hotel chain.*   Fax: (212) 371-4190

    RAFFLES L'ERMITAGE
    9291 Burton Way, Beverly Hills, CA   90210
    CEO: Jack Naderkhani, Mgr.   Tel: (310) 278-3344   %FO: 100
    Bus: *Luxury hotel accommodations.*   Fax: (310) 278-3344

    SWISSOTEL
    323 East Wacker Drive, Chicago, IL   60601
    CEO: Kevin Cuthbert, VP   Tel: (312) 565-0565   %FO: 100
    Bus: *Hotel chain.*   Fax: (312) 565-0540

    SWISSOTEL
    3391 Peachtree Road NE, Atlanta, GA   30326
    CEO: Kevin Cuthbert, VP   Tel: (404) 365-0065   %FO: 100
    Bus: *Hotel chain.*   Fax: (404) 365-8787

    SWISSOTEL
    One Avenue de Lafayette, Boston, MA   02111
    CEO: Kevin Cuthbert, VP   Tel: (617) 451-2600   %FO: 100
    Bus: *Hotel chain.*   Fax: (617) 451-0054

THE WATERGATE HOTEL
2650 Virginia Avenue NW, Washington, DC 20037
CEO: Julee Cooke   Tel: (202) 965-2300   %FO: 100
Bus: *Hotel chain.*   Fax: (202) 337-7915

● **SINGAPORE AIRLINES LTD.**
Airline House, 25 Airline Road, 819829 Singapore
CEO: Cheong Choong Kong, CEO   Tel: 65-542-3333   Rev: $5,510
Bus: *International air transport services.*   Fax: 65-542-1321   Emp: 28,300
                            www.singaporeair.com

SINGAPORE AIRLINES LTD.
899 West Cypress Creek Road, Ste. 104, Ft. Lauderdale, FL 33309
CEO: Teoh Tee Hooi, SVP   Tel: (954) 776-0166   %FO: 100
Bus: *International air transport*   Fax: (954) 776-1337
    services.

SINGAPORE AIRLINES LTD.
1050 17th Street, NW, Washington, DC 20036
CEO: Teoh Tee Hooi, SVP   Tel: (202) 466-3747   %FO: 100
Bus: *International air transport*   Fax: (202) 331-9318
    services.

SINGAPORE AIRLINES LTD.
8500 Stemmons Freeway, Ste. 1060, Dallas, TX 75247
CEO: Teoh Tee Hooi, SVP   Tel: (214) 631-6613   %FO: 100
Bus: *International air transport*   Fax: (214) 631-1412
    services.

SINGAPORE AIRLINES LTD.
3701 Kirby Drive, Ste. 1014, Houston, TX 77098
CEO: Teoh Tee Hooi, SVP   Tel: (713) 522-1631   %FO: 100
Bus: *International air transport*   Fax: (713) 522-0104
    services.

SINGAPORE AIRLINES LTD.
5670 Wilshire Blvd, Ste. 1800, Los Angeles, CA 90036-3709
CEO: Teoh Tee Hooi, SVP   Tel: (323) 934-8833   %FO: 100
Bus: *International air transport*   Fax: (323) 934-4482   Emp: 75
    services.

SINGAPORE AIRLINES LTD.
333 Bush Street, San Francisco, CA 94104
CEO: David Lau, VP   Tel: (415) 781-7304   %FO: 100
Bus: *International air transport*   Fax: (415) 296-8080   Emp: 50
    services.

SINGAPORE AIRLINES LTD.
55 East 59th Street, Ste. 20B, New York, NY   10022-1112
CEO: Koh Koh Chuan, VP   Tel: (212) 644-8801   %FO: 100
Bus: *International air transport*   Fax: (212) 319-6139   Emp: 50
    services.

SINGAPORE AIRLINES LTD.
3400 Peachtree Road NE, Ste. 1015, Atlanta, GA   30303
CEO: Teoh Tee Hooi, SVP   Tel: (404) 233-7300   %FO: 100
Bus: *International air transport*   Fax: (404) 233-1707
    services.

SINGAPORE AIRLINES LTD.
122 South Michigan Avenue, Ste. 1710, Chicago, IL   60603
CEO: Teoh Tee Hooi, SVP   Tel: (312) 419-6780   %FO: 100
Bus: *International air transport*   Fax: (312) 939-4079
    services.

● **SINGAPORE TECHNOLOGIES ENGINEERING LTD.**
51 Cuppage Road, Ste. 09-08, StarHub Centre, 229469 Singapore
CEO: Lim Neo Chian, CEO   Tel: 65-722-1818   Rev: $1,300
Bus: *Holding company engaged in*   Fax: 65-720-2293   Emp: 10,325
    engineering services for auto,   www.st.com.sg
    aerospace and marine.

   DAL FORT AEROSPACE LTD
   7701 Lemon Avenue, Dallas, TX   75209
   CEO: Alan Bragassam, EVP   Tel: (214) 358-6019
   Bus: *Engineering services.*   Fax: (214) 902-0938

   TERAFORCE TECHNOLOGY CORPORATION
   1240 East Campbell Road, Richardson, TX   75081
   CEO: Herman M. Frietsch   Tel: (469) 330-4960   %FO: JV
   Bus: *Provides custom engineering*   Fax: (469) 330-4972   Emp: 194
       design services.

● **SINGAPORE TELECOM LTD.**
31 Exeter Road, Comcentre 239732, Singapore
CEO: Lee Hsien Yang, Pres. & CEO   Tel: 65-838-3388   Rev: $3,060
Bus: *International telecommunications*   Fax: 65-738-3769   Emp: 12,000
    services & equipment.   www.singtel.com

SINGAPORE TELECOM USA

320 Post Road West, Ste. 100, Westport, CT   06880

CEO: Susan Napoli, Gen. Mgr.	Tel: (203) 454-6800	%FO: 100
Bus: *Representative office; service/sales telecommunications services/equipment.*	Fax: (203) 454-1923	Emp: 6

● ST ASSEMBLY TEST SERVICES LTD. (STATS)

5 Yhishun Street 23, 768442, Singapore

CEO: Tan Bock Seng, CEO	Tel: 65-755-5885	Rev: $332
Bus: *Mfr. leadframe and laminate packaging for semiconductors.*	Fax: 65-755-9006 www.stats.com.sg	Emp: 2,600

ST ASSEMBLY TEST SERVICES

9180 South Kyrene, Ste. 101, Tempe, AZ   85284

CEO: John McCarvel, SVP	Tel: (480) 961-7033	%FO: 100
Bus: *Mfr. lead frame and laminate packaging for semiconductors.*	Fax: (480) 961-9511	

ST ASSEMBLY TEST SERVICES

101 East Park Blvd., Ste. 1053, Plano, TX   75074

CEO: John McCarvel, SVP	Tel: (972) 422-2459	%FO: 100
Bus: *Mfr. lead frame and laminate packaging for semiconductors.*	Fax: (972) 881-0318	

ST ASSEMBLY TEST SERVICES

209 New Edition Court, Cary, NC   27511

CEO: John McCarvel, SVP	Tel: (919) 463-7648	%FO: 100
Bus: *Mfr. lead frame and laminate packaging for semiconductors.*	Fax: (919) 463-5484	

ST ASSEMBLY TEST SERVICES

144 Turnpike Road, Ste. 320, Southborough, MA   01772

CEO: John McCarvel, SVP	Tel: (508) 624-6800	%FO: 100
Bus: *Mfr. lead frame and laminate packaging for semiconductors.*	Fax: (508) 624-6850	

ST ASSEMBLY TEST SERVICES

1450 McCandless Drive, Milpitas, CA   95035

CEO: John McCarvel, SVP	Tel: (408) 941-1500	%FO: 100
Bus: *Mfr. lead frame and laminate packaging for semiconductors.*	Fax: (408) 941-1501	

● **TIMES PUBLISHING LIMITED**
Times Centre, One New Industrial Road, 536196 Singapore
CEO: Kua Hong Pak, Pres. & CEO   Tel: 65-284-8844   Rev: $275
Bus: *Engaged in publishing, distribution,*   Fax: 65-284-4733   Emp: 2,090
commercial printing, and online and   www.tpl.com.sg
retail bookstores.

    MARSHALL CAVENDISH CORPORATION
    99 White Plains Road, PO Box 2001, Tarrytown, NY   10591-9001
    CEO: Albert Lee, Pres.   Tel: (914) 332-8888   %FO: 100
    Bus: *Engaged in book publishing.*   Fax: (914) 332-8882

● **UNITED OVERSEAS BANK LTD.**
80 Raffles Place, UOB Plaza, 048624 Singapore
CEO: Wee Cho Yaw, Chmn.   Tel: 65-533-9898   Rev: $2,169
Bus: *Commercial banking and financial*   Fax: 65-534-2334   Emp: 6,500
services.   www.uob.com.sg

    UNITED OVERSEAS BANK LTD.
    592 Fifth Avenue, 10th Fl., New York, NY   10036
    CEO: Kwong Yew Wong, Pres.   Tel: (212) 382-0088   %FO: 100
    Bus: *Commercial banking and financial* Fax: (212) 382-1881   Emp: 25
    services.

    UNITED OVERSEAS BANK LTD.
    911 Wilshire Boulevard, Los Angeles, CA   90017-3478
    CEO: David Loh, Mgr.   Tel: (213) 623-8042   %FO: 100
    Bus: *Commercial banking and financial* Fax: (213) 623-3412
    services.

    UOB REALTY (USA) LTD PARTNERSHIP
    592 Fifth Avenue, UOB Bldg., New York, NY   10036
    CEO: Kwong Yew Wong, Gen. Mgr.   Tel: (212) 382-0088   %FO: 100
    Bus: *Develops/manages real estate*   Fax: (212) 382-1881
    investment partnerships.

● **VENTURE MANUFACTURING LTD.**
5006 Ang Mo Kio Avenue 5, #05-01/12 Techplace I, 569973 Singapore
CEO: Ngit Liong Wong, CEO   Tel: 65-482-1755
Bus: *Electronic services provider.*   Fax: 65-482-0122
          www.venture-mfg.com.sg

    VM SERVICES INC.
    6701 Mowry Avenue, Newark, CA   94560
    CEO: C. T. Wong, Pres.   Tel: (510) 744-3720   %FO: 100
    Bus: *Electronic services provider.*   Fax: (510) 744-3730

Slovenia

- **NOVA LJUBLJANSKA BANCA, D.D.**
  Trg Republike 2, 1520 Ljublijana, Slovenia
  CEO: Marko Voljc, Chmn.   Tel: 386-611-250-155
  Bus: *Banking services.*   Fax: 386-611-250-331
                                www.n-lb.si

  LBS BANK - NEW YORK
  12 East 52nd Street, New York, NY 10022
  CEO: Rudolf Gabrovec, Pres.   Tel: (212) 207-2200   %FO: 100
  Bus: *International banking services.*   Fax: (212) 593-1967   Emp: 40

South Africa

- **ANGLOGOLD LIMITED**
  11 Diagonal Street, Johannesburg 2001, South Africa
  CEO: Robert M. Godsell, CEO   Tel: 27-11-637-6000   Rev: $2,208
  Bus: *Engaged in gold production and mining.*   Fax: 27-11-637-6399   Emp: 84,000
      www.anglogold.com

      ANGLOGOLD LIMITED
      509 Madison Avenue, Ste. 1914, New York, NY   10022
      CEO: Charles Carter   Tel: (212) 750-5999   %FO: 100
      Bus: *Engaged in gold production and*   Fax: (212) 750-5626
         mining.

      ANGLOGOLD, c/o C. CARTER
      5251 DTC Parkway, Ste. 700, Englewood, CO   80111
      CEO: Charles Carter   Tel: (303) 694-4969   %FO: 100
      Bus: *Engaged in gold production.*   Fax: (303) 843-9255

- **INVESTEC GROUP**
  100 Grayston Drive, Sandown, Centon Johannesburg 2196, South Africa
  CEO: Stephen Koseff, CEO   Tel: 27-11-286-7000   Rev: $2,034
  Bus: *Engaged in investment banking.*   Fax: 27-11-286-7777   Emp: 2,706
      www.investec.co.za

      INVESTEC ERNST & COMPANY
      209 West Jackson Boulevard, Chicago, IL   60606
      CEO: Ray Hofer, Mgr.   Tel: (312) 554-2200   %FO: 100
      Bus: *Trades bonds and mutual funds.*   Fax: (312) 554-1009

      INVESTEC ERNST & COMPANY
      One Battery Park Plaza, 6th Fl., New York, NY   10004
      CEO: William Behrens, Pres.   Tel: (212) 898-6200   %FO: 100
      Bus: *Trades bonds and mutual funds.*   Fax: (212) 898-6455   Emp: 270

      PMG CAPITAL INC.
      Four Falls Corporate Center, West Conshohocken, PA   19428
      CEO: Peter Rawlings, Mng. Dir.   Tel: (610) 260-6400   %FO: 100
      Bus: *Engaged in investment banking.*   Fax: (610) 260-6404

- **MIH HOLDINGS LIMITED**

25 Oak Avenue, Randburg 2194, South Africa

CEO: Cobus Stofburg, CEO	Tel: 27-11-289-4800	Rev: $724
Bus: *Engaged in interactive and television services.*	Fax: 27-11-886-5785	Emp: 900
	www.mihholdings.co.za	

  OPEN TV CORP.

  45 Hayden Avenue, Lexington, MA   02421

CEO: Howard J. Hall	Tel: (781) 372-4600	%FO: 100
Bus: *Engaged in interactive television and media solutions.*	Fax: (781) 372-4650	

  OPEN TV CORP.

  1100 Marsh Road, Menlo Park, CA   94025

CEO: James Ackerman, CEO	Tel: (650) 330-7600	
Bus: *Engaged in interactive television and media solutions.*	Fax: (650) 330-7645	

  OPEN TV CORP.

  1240 East Diehl Road, Naperville, IL   60563

CEO: James Ackerman, CEO	Tel: (630) 505-1010	%FO: 100
Bus: *Engaged in interactive television and media solutions.*	Fax: (630) 505-4944	

  OPEN TV CORP.

  401 East Middlefield Road, Mountain View, CA   94043

CEO: James Ackerman, CEO	Tel: (650) 429-5500	%FO: 100
Bus: *Engaged in interactive television and media solutions.*	Fax: (650) 237-0808	

- **NEDCOR GROUP**

100 Main Street, PO Box 1144, Johannesburg 2001, South Africa

CEO: Dr. I.R. May	Tel: 27-11-630-7111	Rev: $3,342
Bus: *Commercial banking services.*	Fax: 27-11-630-7891	Emp: 18,722
	www.nedcor.co.za	

  NEDCOR BANK LIMITED

  230 Park Avenue, Ste. 1000, New York, NY   10169

CEO: Grant D. Tarr, Rep.	Tel: (212) 808-3011	%FO: 100
Bus: *International banking services.*	Fax: (212) 808-4987	Emp: 2

- **SAPPI LIMITED**

48 Ameshoff Street, Braamfontein, Gauteng 2001, South Africa

CEO: Eugene van As, CEO	Tel: 27-11-407-8111	Rev: $3,950
Bus: *Mfr. fine paper and paper products.*	Fax: 27-11-403-1493	Emp: 24,000
	www.sappi.com	

SAPPI FINE PAPER NORTH AMERICA
2700 Westchester Avenue, Ste. 300, Purchase, NY   10577
CEO: Tim Morgan   Tel: (914) 253-8660   %FO: 100
Bus: *Sales of fine paper products.*   Fax: (914) 253-8949

SAPPI FINE PAPER NORTH AMERICA
250 Baybridge Road, Mobile, AL   36610
CEO: Lynda Barr   Tel: (334) 330-2500   %FO: 100
Bus: *Sales of fine paper products.*   Fax: (334) 330-2934

SAPPI FINE PAPER NORTH AMERICA
225 Franklin Street, Boston, MA   02110
CEO: Les LaBov, Sales   Tel: (617) 423-7300   %FO: 100
Bus: *Sales of fine paper products.*   Fax: (617) 423-5491

SAPPI FINE PAPER NORTH AMERICA
11121 Carmel Commons Blvd., Ste. 430, Charlotte, NC   28226
CEO: Don Titherington   Tel: (800) 739-7704   %FO: 100
Bus: *Sales of fine paper products.*   Fax: (704) 542-8377

SAPPI FINE PAPER NORTH AMERICA
199 Wells Avenue, Newton, MA   02159
CEO: Brian Hilfrank   Tel: (617) 964-0020   %FO: 100
Bus: *Sales of fine paper products.*   Fax: (617) 332-1925

SAPPI FINE PAPER NORTH AMERICA
1818 Westlake Ave. North, Ste. 319, Seattle, WA   9109
CEO: Charles Painter   Tel: (206) 270-8991   %FO: 100
Bus: *Sales of fine paper products.*   Fax: (206) 270-8968

SAPPI MUSKEGON MILL
2400 Lakeshore Drive, Muskegon, MI   49443
CEO: Mark Gardner, VP   Tel: (231) 755-3761   %FO: 100
Bus: *Sales of fine paper products.*   Fax: (231) 759-5416

SAPPI PAPER SOMERSET MILL
RFD #3, Route 201, Skowhegan, ME   04092
CEO: Doug Daniels, VP   Tel: (207) 453-9301   %FO: 100
Bus: *Sales of fine paper products.*   Fax: (207) 453-4532

SAPPI PAPER/S.D. WARREN COMPANY
225 Franklin Street, Boston, MA   02110
CEO: Monte R. Haymon, Pres. & CEO Tel: (617) 423-7300   %FO: 100
Bus: *Sales of fine paper products.*   Fax: (617) 423-5491

● **SASOL LIMITED**
PO Box 5486, Johannesburg 2000, South Africa
CEO: Pieter V. Cox, Mng. Dir.   Tel: 27-11-441-3111
Bus: *Mfr. proprietary technologies for the*   Fax: 27-11-788-5092
production of synthetic fuels and   www.sasol.com
chemical products. (JV with Merisol UK)

    MERISOL USA LLC
    11821 East Freeway, Ste. 600, Houston, TX   77029
    CEO: Chris Lancaster, Pres.   Tel: (713) 428-5400   %FO: JV
    Bus: *Mfr. chemical products.*   Fax: (713) 455-8045

    SASOL NORTH AMERICA, INC.
    5177 Richmond Avenue, Ste. 1040, Houston, TX   77056
    CEO: Harry Hyatt, Pres.   Tel: (713) 871-8080   %FO: JV
    Bus: *Markets and distributes alpha*   Fax: (713) 871-1919
    olefins.

● **SOUTH AFRICAN AIRWAYS CORP.**
39 Wolmarans Street, Braamsontein PO Box 7778, Johannesburg 2000, South Africa
CEO: A. T. Moolman, Dir.   Tel: 27-11-356-2035
Bus: *Commercial air transport services.*   Fax: 27-11-356-2019   Emp: 11,100
                                                  www.saa.co.za

    SOUTH AFRICAN AIRWAYS CORPORATION
    515 East Las Olas Blvd., Suite 1600, Ft. Lauderdale, FL   33301
    CEO: Roberto Cuesta, VP   Tel: (954) 767-8722   %FO: 100
    Bus: *Commercial air transport services.* Fax: (954) 522-1287   Emp: 100

● **STANDARD BANK INVESTMENT CORP.**
PO Box 7725, 5 Simmonds Street, 9th Fl., Johannesburg 2001, South Africa
CEO: Dr. Conrad B. Strauss, Chmn.   Tel: 27-11-636-9111   Rev: $4,902
Bus: *Commercial banking services.*   Fax: 27-11-636-5117   Emp: 32,288
                                                 www.standatdbank.co.za

    THE STANDARD BANK OF SOUTH AFRICA LTD.
    153 East 53rd Street, 38th Fl., New York, NY   10022
    CEO: A. J. Strutt, SVP   Tel: (212) 407-5000   %FO: 100
    Bus: *International banking services.*   Fax: (212) 407-5025

    STANDARD NEW YORK INC.
    153 East 53rd Street, 38th Fl., New York, NY   10022
    CEO: Sean M.O' Connor, Mng. Dir.   Tel: (212) 407-5000   %FO: 100
    Bus: *International banking services.*   Fax: (212) 407-5025   Emp: 45

1156

South Korea

- **ANAM GROUP**

222-1, Dodang-dong, Wonmi-gu, Bucheon-si, Gyeonggi-do, 420-712, South Korea

CEO: Joojin Kim, CEO — Tel: 82-32-680-4800 — Rev: $1,120

Bus: *Assembly of semiconductor devices.* — Fax: 82-32-683-8105 — Emp: 8,180

www.anam.co.kr

AMKOR TECHNOLOGY

1345 Enterprise Drive, West Chester, PA   19380

CEO: John N. Boruch, CEO — Tel: (610) 431-9600 — %FO: 100

Bus: *Sale/distribution of semiconductor devices.* — Fax: (610) 431-5881 — Emp: 50

- **ASIANA AIRLINES**

10-1, 2-Ka, Hoehyun-Dong, Chung-Gu, Seoul, South Korea

CEO: Sam Koo Park, Pres. — Tel: 82-2-774-4000

Bus: *Air transport services.* — Fax: 82-2-758-8009 — Emp: 49

www.flyasiana.com

ASIANA AIRLINES

540 Madison Avenue, 14th Fl., New York, NY   10022

CEO: J. Lee, Mgr. — Tel: (212) 318-9200 — %FO: 100

Bus: *International air transport services.* — Fax: (212) 371-1212 — Emp: 100

ASIANA AIRLINES

1420 Fifth Avenue, Ste. 2950, Seattle, WA   98101

CEO: I. S. Park, CEO — Tel: (206) 340-0999 — %FO: 100

Bus: *International air transport services.* — Fax: (206) 343-1939

ASIANA AIRLINES

3530 Wilshire Blvd., Ste. 145, Los Angeles, CA   90010

CEO: K. S. Park, VP — Tel: (213) 365-4500 — %FO: 100

Bus: *International air transport services.* — Fax: (213) 365-9630

ASIANA AIRLINES

88 Kearny Street, Ste. 1450, San Francisco, CA   94108

CEO: I. S. Park, CEO — Tel: (415) 249-4200 — %FO: 100

Bus: *International air transport services.* — Fax: (415) 986-0653 — Emp: 18

● **AURORA TRADING CORPORATION**

Aurora Bldg., 385-10, Kil-Dong, Kangdong-Gu, Seoul, South Korea

CEO: Heui-Yul Noh, Pres.   Tel: 82-2-483-7731

Bus: *Develops and manufactures plush toys*   Fax: 82-2-484-9228
(stuffed animals).

    AURORA A&A PLUSH, INC.

    311 West Artesia Boulevard, Compton, CA   90220

    CEO: K. S. Hong, Pres.   Tel: (310) 631-0700   %FO: 100

    Bus: *Develops and manufactures plush*   Fax: (310) 631-0865   Emp: 53
    toys (stuffed animals).

● **CHEIL COMMUNICATIONS, INC., DIV. SAMSUNG**

736-1 Hannam-dong, Yongsan-gu, Seoul, South Korea

CEO: Myung-Kwan Hyun, CEO   Tel: 82-2-3780-2114   Rev: $134

Bus: *Worldwide advertising agency.*   Fax: 82-2-3780-2460   Emp: 4,740
                        www.cheil.co.kr

    CHEIL COMMUNICATIONS AMERICA, INC.

    105 Challenger Road, Ridgefield Park, NJ   07660

    CEO: Michael Kim, Pres.   Tel: (201) 229-6050   %FO: 100

    Bus: *Advertising and marketing*   Fax: (201) 229-6058   Emp: 25
    services.

● **CHOHUNG BANK, LTD.**

14, 1-Ga Namdaemoon-Ro, Chung-Gu, Seoul, South Korea

CEO: Sung Bok Wee, Pres. & CEO   Tel: 82-2-733-2000   Rev: $5,663

Bus: *Commercial banking services.*   Fax: 82-2-732-0835   Emp: 5,203
                        www.chohungbank.co.kr

    CHOHUNG BANK

    3000 Olympic Blvd., Los Angeles, CA   90006

    CEO: Dong Keon Sohn, Pres.   Tel: (213) 380-8300   %FO: 100

    Bus: *International commercial banking*   Fax: (213) 386-2170   Emp: 20
    services.

    CHOHUNG BANK LTD

    241 Fifth Avenue, New York, NY   10016

    CEO: Choon Kee Park, Pres.   Tel: (212) 679-7900   %FO: 100

    Bus: *International commercial banking*   Fax: (212) 447-7477
    services.

    CHOHUNG BANK LTD

    320 Park Avenue, New York, NY   10021

    CEO: Byung Soo Moon, Mgr.   Tel: (212) 935-3500   %FO: 100

    Bus: *International commercial banking*   Fax: (212) 355-2231   Emp: 40
    services.

CHOHUNG BANK LTD
136-68 Roosevelt Avenue, Flushing, NY   11354
CEO: Kyung Sik Kim, Mgr.   Tel: (718) 939-9595   %FO: 100
Bus: *International commercial banking*   Fax: (718) 939-3229
  services.

● **DADA TEXTILE MACHINERY CORP.**
Dada Bldg., 769-9 Yeoksam-Dong, Kangnam-Gu, Seoul, South Korea
CEO: B. Park, Pres.   Tel: 82-2-538-4271
Bus: *Mfr. stuffed toys and hats.*   Fax: 82-2-538-0113

    INKO HEADWEAR, INC.
    300 West Glen Oaks Boulevard, Glendale, CA   91202
    CEO: Ed Horowitz, VP   Tel: (818) 545-7002   %FO: 100
    Bus: *Hats and stuffed toys.*   Fax: (818) 545-7004

    INKO HEADWEAR, INC.
    12350 S. W. 132nd Court, Ste. 210, Miami, FL   33186
    CEO: Ed Horowitz, VP   Tel: (305) 234-9644   %FO: 100
    Bus: *Hats and stuffed toys.*   Fax: (305) 234-9258   Emp: 5

● **DAERIM CORPORATION**
482-2, Bangbae-Dong, Seocho-Gu, Seoul, South Korea
CEO: C. Oh, Pres.   Tel: 82-2-3470-6000
Bus: *Engaged in the processing and*   Fax: 82-2-523-8900
  distribution of the bottom fish fillet.   www.daerimi.com

    DAERIM AMERICA, INC.
    195-197 W. Spring Valley Avenue, Maywood, NJ   07607
    CEO: C. Oh, Pres.   Tel: (201) 587-8989   %FO: 100
    Bus: *Fresh and frozen seafood products.*   Fax: (201) 587-8959

● **DAEWOO ELECTRONICS**
925 Kongdan-dong, Kumi, Kyongsangbuk-do, South Korea
CEO: Chang Kiheyung, Pres.   Tel: 82-546-467-7114   Rev: $3,895
Bus: *Mfr. electronics including televisions,*   Fax: 82-546-461-8788   Emp: 7,800
  VCR's, refrigerators and washing   www.dwe.co.kr
  machines.

    DAEWOOD ELECTRONICS CORPORATION
    120 Chubb Avenue, Lyndhurst, NJ   07071
    CEO: Y. N. Cho, Pres.   Tel: (201) 460-2000   %FO: 100
    Bus: *Sales/distribution of electronics.*   Fax: (201) 935-5284

● **DAEWOO HEAVY INDUSTRIES, LTD.**
541 Namdaemunno 5-ga, Chung-gu, Seoul, South Korea
CEO: Choo Ho-Suk, Pres.   Tel: 82-2-726-3114   Rev: $4,625
Bus: *Mfr. machinery construction equipment.* Fax: 82-2-726-3307   Emp: 23,300
www.dhiltd.co.kr

    DAEWOO HEAVY INDUSTRIES INC.
    2905 Shawnee Industrial Way, Ste. 100, Suwanee, GA   30024
    CEO: Tim O'Malley, VP   Tel: (770) 831-2200   %FO: 100
    Bus: *Mfr. construction equipment.*   Fax: (770) 831-0480

    DAEWOO HEAVY INDUSTRIES INC.
    4350 Renaissance Parkway, Warrensville Heights, OH   44128
    CEO: I.S. Ki, Pres.   Tel: (216) 595-1212   %FO: 100
    Bus: *Mfr. forklift, truck and compact*   Fax: (216) 595-1214
        equipment.

● **DAEWOO INTERNATIONAL CORPORATION**
541 Namdaemun-ro 5-Ga, Chung-Gu, Seoul, South Korea
CEO: Tae-Yong Lee, CEO   Tel: 82-2-759-2114   Rev: $198
Bus: *Engaged in trading.*   Fax: 82-2-753-9489   Emp: 890
www.daewoo.com

    DAEWOO AMERICA
    1055 West Victoria Street, Compton, CA   90220
    CEO: D. J. Lee, Pres.   Tel: (310) 884-5800   %FO: 100
    Bus: *Mfr. auto parts, aerospace, textile.*   Fax: (310) 669-2020   Emp: 23

    DAEWOO INTERNATIONAL (AMERICA) CORPORATION
    85 Challenger Road, Ridgefield Park, NJ   07660
    CEO: H. K. Jhun, Pres.   Tel: (201) 229-4500   %FO: 100
    Bus: *Importing/exporting trading*   Fax: (201) 440-2244   Emp: 150
        services; sale of industrial &
        consumer products.

    DAEWOO INTERNATIONAL CORPORATION
    2855 Coolidge Highway, Troy, MI   48084
    CEO: Y. H. Park, Mgr.   Tel: (248) 649-0003   %FO: 100
    Bus: *Auto parts.*   Fax: (248) 649-0130   Emp: 6

    DAEWOO INTERNATIONAL CORPORATION
    3206 North Kennicott Road, Arlington Heights, IL   60004
    CEO: Y. H. Park, Pres.   Tel: (847) 590-9800   %FO: 100
    Bus: *Auto parts, electronics, textiles.*   Fax: (847) 590-9814   Emp: 5

• DAEWOO SECURITIES CO. LTD.

34-3 Youido-dong, Youngdungpo-ku, Seoul, South Korea

CEO: Jun Heo, Chmn.	Tel: 82-2-759-2114	Rev: $498
Bus: *Engaged in securities brokerage.*	Fax: 82-2-753-9489	Emp: 2,583
	www.securities.co.kr	

DAEWOO SECURITIES INC.

101 East 52nd Street, 28th Fl., New York, NY   10022

CEO: Andrew Kim, Pres.	Tel: (212) 407-1000	%FO: 100
Bus: *Engaged in securities brokerage.*	Fax: (212) 407-1010	

• DAI YANG METAL

730-1, Wonshi-Dong, Ansan-Shikyonggi, 425-090, South Korea
Korea

CEO: Sok Do Kang, Pres.	Tel: 82-345-494-0421	Rev: $79,040
Bus: *Manufacture of stainless steel panels.*	Fax: 82-345-494-6725	Emp: 240
	www.daiyangmetal.co.kr	

OCEAN METAL CORPORATION

227 North Sunset Avenue, City of Industry, CA   91744

CEO: H. B. Choi, Mgr.	Tel: (626) 333-0160	%FO: 100
Bus: *Sales of stainless steel tubes/coils.*	Fax: (626) 336-1702	Emp: 12

• DONGKUK STEEL MILL CO., LTD.

50 Suha-Dong, Chung-Gu, Seoul, 100-210, South Korea

CEO: Chan Kye, Pres.	Tel: 82-2-317-1114	Rev: $2,825
Bus: *Mfr. galvanized coil and sheet, steel*	Fax: 82-2-317-1391	Emp: 1,563
scrap, slab, plate, pipe and tubing.	www.dongkuk.co.kr]	

DONGKUK INTERNATIONAL

11211 Katy Pkwy., Ste 380, Houston, TX   77079

CEO: Hyoung Bin Hong, Pres.	Tel: (713) 467-4620
Bus: *Steel importing & exporting.*	Fax: (713) 467-5106

DONGKUK INTERNATIONAL

555 West Madison Street, Ste. 803, Tower 4, Chicago, IL   60666

CEO: Hyoung Bin Hong, Pres.	Tel: (312) 902-4435
Bus: *Steel importing & exporting.*	Fax: (312) 902-4609

DONGKUK INTERNATIONAL

460 Bergen Boulevard, Palisades Park, NJ   07650

CEO: Hyoung Bin Hong, Pres.	Tel: (201) 592-8600	%FO: 100
Bus: *Steel importing & exporting.*	Fax: (201) 592-8795	Emp: 35

DONGKUK INT'L INC.
19750 Magellan Drive, Torrance, CA   90502
CEO: Hyoung Bin Hong, Pres.   Tel: (310) 523-9595   %FO: 100
Bus: *Galvanized Coil and sheet/steel*   Fax: (310) 523-9599
    scrap, slab, plate, pipe, and tubing.

● **THE EXPORT-IMPORT BANK OF KOREA**
16-1 Yoido-dong, Youngdungpo-gu, Seoul, 150-010, South Korea
CEO: Man Ki Yang, Pres. & Chmn.   Tel: 82-2-784-1021
Bus: *Government owned financial institution.*   Fax: 82-2-784-1030
    www.koreaexim.go.kr

   THE EXPORT-IMPORT BANK OF KOREA
   460 Park Avenue, 8th Fl., New York, NY   10022
   CEO: Seung-Kon Kim, Rep.   Tel: (212) 355-7280   %FO: 100
   Bus: *Engaged in banking and finance.*   Fax: (212) 308-6106

● **HAITAI ELECTRONICS**
177, Chungchun-dong, Buk-gu, Inchon, South Korea
CEO: Heo Jin-Ho, Pres.   Tel: 82-32-510-4500
Bus: *Mfr. audio electronic products.*   Fax:
    www.hte.co.kr

   SHERWOOD AMERICA
   2346 East Walnut Avenue, Fullerton, CA   92831
   CEO: Terry Eastham, CEO   Tel: (714) 870-5100   %FO: 100
   Bus: *Sales/distribution of audio*   Fax: (714) 870-6300
      electronic products.

● **HAITAI INTERNATIONAL, INC.**
CPO Box 4488, Seoul, South Korea
CEO: Mr. C. W. Yoo, Pres.   Tel: 82-2-3270-1600
Bus: *Wholesaler/exporter of frozen*   Fax: 82-2-3701-7573   Emp: 85
    concentrated orange juice (Sunkist),   www.ht.co.kr
    wheat, beans, livestock.

   HAITAI GLOBAL, INC.
   7227 Telegraph Road, Montebello, CA   90640
   CEO: T. K. Min, Pres.   Tel: (323) 724-7337   %FO: 100
   Bus: *Food products, including dried*   Fax: (323) 724-7373
      laver (nori sheets).

● **HANJIN HEAVY INDUSTRIES & CONSTRUCTION CO., LTD.**

546-1 Kuui-Dong, Kwangjin-Gu, CPO Box 2034, Seoul, South Korea

CEO: Park Jae-Young, Pres. & CEO	Tel: 82-2-450-8114	Rev: $632
Bus: *General contracting, home building and developing; in-flight catering.*	Fax: 82-2-450-8101 www.hanjin.net	Emp: 3,000

HACOR, INC.

11220 Hindry Avenue, Los Angeles, CA   90045

CEO: Larry Cunningham	Tel: (310) 645-9011	%FO: 100
Bus: *Engaged in in-flight airline catering.*	Fax: (310) 645-9110	Emp: 140

● **HANJIN SHIPPING COMPANY, LTD.**

51 Sogong-Dong Chung-Ku, Seoul, South Korea

CEO: Chan-gil Kim, Pres.	Tel: 82-2-3782-1029	Rev: $4,454
Bus: *Containerized international shipping and cargo transport.*	Fax: 82-2-3770-6746 www.hanjin.com	Emp: 2,100

HANJIN SHIPPING COMPANY, LTD.

1500 NE Irving St., Ste. 300, Portland, OR   97232

CEO: Kimberly Boswell	Tel: (503) 234-4133	%FO: 100
Bus: *Cargo transport, containerized systems.*	Fax: (503) 234-4766	

HANJIN SHIPPING COMPANY, LTD.

444 W. Ocean Blvd. Suite 1200, Long Beach, CA   90802

CEO: Sam Berkowitz	Tel: (562) 449-4500	%FO: 100
Bus: *Cargo transport, containerized systems.*	Fax: (562) 441-0128	

HANJIN SHIPPING COMPANY, LTD.

1211 West 22nd Street, Ste. 1100, Oakbrook, IL   60523

CEO: Jack Budrick	Tel: (630) 891-7500	%FO: 100
Bus: *Cargo transport, containerized systems.*	Fax: (630) 891-7560	

HANJIN SHIPPING COMPANY, LTD.

401 Alaskan Way, Terminal 46, Seattle, WA   98104

CEO: Candy Moy	Tel: (206) 447-9422	%FO: 100
Bus: *Cargo transport, containerized systems.*	Fax: (206) 447-9428	

HANJIN SHIPPING COMPANY, LTD.

80 Route 4 East, Ste. 490, Paramus, NJ   07652

CEO: N. U. Park, Pres.	Tel: (201) 291-4600	%FO: 100
Bus: *Cargo transport, containerized systems.*	Fax: (201) 291-9393	Emp: 430

HANJIN SHIPPING COMPANY, LTD.
1415 Northloop West, Ste. 1200, Houston, TX   77008
CEO: Julie Villareal   Tel: (713) 802-7400   %FO: 100
Bus: *Cargo transport, containerized*   Fax: (713) 802-7410
    systems.

HANJIN SHIPPING COMPANY, LTD.
2000 Powers Ferry Road, Ste. 405, Marietta, GA   30067
CEO: Kue Ha Lee, Mgr.   Tel: (770) 952-0233   %FO: 100
Bus: *Marine transportation.*   Fax: (770) 952-0118   Emp: 45

HANJIN SHIPPING COMPANY, LTD.
80 East Route 4, Ste. 390, Paramus, NJ   07652-2655
CEO: Youngsook Kim   Tel: (201) 291-4500   %FO: 100
Bus: *Ocean shipping.*   Fax: (201) 291-9696

HANJIN SHIPPING COMPANY, LTD.
2128 Burnett Boulevard, Wilmington, NC   28401
CEO: Jennier Coulter   Tel: (910) 343-1464   %FO: 100
Bus: *Ocean shipping.*   Fax: (910) 251-2164

HANJIN SHIPPING COMPANY, LTD.
PO Box 248, Chesterfield, MO   63006-0248
CEO: Preston Smith   Tel: (636) 519-7739   %FO: 100
Bus: *Ocean shipping.*   Fax: (636) 519-7728

HANJIN SHIPPING COMPANY, LTD.
PO Box 7646, Garden City, GA   31418
CEO: Cindy Jun   Tel: (912) 447-7120   %FO: 100
Bus: *Ocean shipping.*   Fax: (912) 964-0945

HANJIN SHIPPING COMPANY, LTD.
One Market Spear Tower, Ste. 1700, San Francisco, CA   94105
CEO: Clara Quan   Tel: (415) 777-2600   %FO: 100
Bus: *Ocean shipping.*   Fax: (415) 777-9737

HANJIN SHIPPING COMPANY, LTD.
860 Greenbrier Circle, Ste. 200, Chesapeake, VA   23320
CEO: Debra Sommer   Tel: (757) 233-2202   %FO: 100
Bus: *Ocean shipping.*   Fax: (757) 233-2204

HANJIN SHIPPING COMPANY, LTD.
2277 W. Away 36, Ste. 312E, Roseville, MN   55113
CEO: Richard Szeliga   Tel: (651) 636-7726   %FO: 100
Bus: *Ocean shipping.*   Fax: (651) 636-7692

HANJIN SHIPPING COMPANY, LTD.
5255 Northwest 87th Avenue, Ste. 304, Miami, FL   33178
CEO: Maria Zacarias   Tel: (305) 594-0220   %FO: 100
Bus: *Ocean shipping.*   Fax: (305) 594-0207

HANJIN SHIPPING COMPANY, LTD.
5050 Popular Avenue, Ste. 627, Memphis, TN   38157
CEO: Samantha Swanner   Tel: (901) 259-4686   %FO: 100
Bus: *Ocean shipping.*   Fax: (901) 259-4692

HANJIN SHIPPING COMPANY, LTD.
17785 Center Court Drive, Ste. 750, Cerritos, CA   90703
CEO: Philip T. Wright   Tel: (562) 356-6600   %FO: 100
Bus: *Ocean shipping.*   Fax: (562) 356-6801

HANJIN SHIPPING COMPANY, LTD.
5727 Westpark Drive, Ste. 104, Charlotte, NC 28217
CEO: Missy Brown   Tel: (704) 679-3850   %FO: 100
Bus: *Ocean shipping.*   Fax: (704) 679-3853

HANJIN SHIPPING COMPANY, LTD.
Point Breeze Maritime Center 1, Ste. 201, Baltimore, MD   21224
CEO: Pat Frank   Tel: (410) 633-1902   %FO: 100
Bus: *Ocean shipping.*   Fax: (410) 633-1908

HANJIN SHIPPING COMPANY, LTD.
639 Granite Street, Ste. 315, Boston, MA   02184
CEO: Frank Goffredo   Tel: (781) 849-3130   %FO: 100
Bus: *Ocean shipping.*   Fax: (781) 849-1539   Emp: 5

HANJIN SHIPPING COMPANY, LTD.
175 South West Temple, Ste. 600, Salt Lake City, UT   84101
CEO: Stuart Johnson   Tel: (801) 258-2500   %FO: 100
Bus: *Ocean shipping.*   Fax: (801) 533-3232

● **HANVIT BANK**
130 Namdaemun ro, 2-ka, CPO Box 1033, Chung-gu, Seoul, 100-795, South Korea
CEO: Jin Man Kim, Pres. & CEO   Tel: 82-2-2002-3000   Rev: $5,466
Bus: *Commercial banking services.*   Fax: 82-2-2002-5690   Emp: 11,115
                                       www.hanvitbank.co.kr

HANVIT BANK
245 Park Avenue, New York, NY   10017
CEO: Jay Seung Yoo, Mgr.   Tel: (212) 949-1900   %FO: 100
Bus: *Provides wholesale banking*   Fax: (212) 973-1123
     services.

● HANWHA CORPORATION

1 Changkyo-dong, Chung-ku, Seoul, 100-797, South Korea

CEO: Kim Seung Youn, Pres.
Tel: 82-2-729-3791
Rev: $2,294

Bus: *Engaged in construction, trading of*
Fax: 82-2-729-3535
Emp: 4,799
petrochemicals and manufacture of
www.hanwha.co.kr
communication equipment and
machinery.

HANWHA INTERNATIONAL CORPORATION

2559 Golden Plaza, Rt. 130, Cranberry, NJ   08512

CEO: W. Yang
Tel: (609) 655-2500
%FO: 100

Bus: *Mfr. industrial furnaces, precision*
Fax: (609) 655-0711
equipment, aerospace and
machine tools.

UNION INCORPORATED HCC

14522 Myford Road, Irvine, CA   92606

CEO: Bob Hicks, Mgr.
Tel: (714) 734-2200
%FO: 100

Bus: *Mfr. industrial furnaces, precision*
Fax: (714) 734-2220
equipment, aerospace and
machine tools.

UNIVERSAL BEARINGS, INC.

431 North Birkey Drive, Bremen, IN   46506

CEO: Tom Kim, Pres.
Tel: (219) 546-2261
%FO: 100

Bus: *Mfr. loose rollers and related*
Fax: (219) 546-5085
Emp: 150
products.

● HUNG CHANG CO., LTD.

162-6 Dongkyo-Dong, Mapo-ku, Seoul, South Korea

CEO: Chung Soo Sohn, Pres.
Tel: 82-2-3140-0500
Rev: $86

Bus: *Mfr. electronic testing instruments,*
Fax: 82-2-3140-0505
Emp: 462
components, telecommunications
www.hungchang.co.kr
equipment.

HC ELECTRONICS AMERICA INC.

40 Boroline Road, Allendale, NJ   07401

CEO: Sin Gon Kim, Pres
Tel: (201) 818-9300
%FO: 100

Bus: *Distribution/sale, electronic*
Fax: (201) 818-0400
Emp: 13
testing instruments.

● HYNIX SEMICONDUCTOR INC.

San 136-1, Ami-Ri, Bubal-eub Ichon Si, Kyoungki-Do, 467-860, South Korea

CEO: Park Chong-Sup, Pres. & CEO
Tel: 82-336-741-0661
Rev: $5,260

Bus: *Mfr. electronic devices, including*
Fax: 82-336-741-0737
Emp: 13,930
memory chips and semiconductors..
www.heinix.com

HYNIX SEMICONDUCTOR AMERICA, INC.

3101 North First Street, San Jose, CA 95134

CEO: I. B. Jeon, Pres.   Tel: (408) 232-8200   %FO: 100

Bus: *Mfr./sales semi-conductors.*   Fax: (408) 232-8102

HYNIX SEMICONDUCTOR MANUFACTURING AMERICA, INC.

1830 Willow Creek Circle, Eugene, OR 97402

CEO: Seungil Kim, CEO   Tel: (541) 338-5000   %FO: 100

Bus: *Mfr. semiconductors.*   Fax: (541) 338-5200

MAXTOR CORPORATION

510 Cottonwood Drive, Milpitas, CA 95035

CEO: Michael R. Cannon, Pres.   Tel: (408) 432-1700   %FO: 100

Bus: *Mfr. hard disk drives for desktop*   Fax: (408) 432-4510
     computers.

MMC TECHNOLOGY, INC.

2001 Fortune Drive, San Jose, CA 95131

CEO: Ian L. Sanders, SVP   Tel: (408) 232-8600   %FO: 100

Bus: *Mfr. media disks.*   Fax: (408) 232-8139

● HYOSUNG GROUP LTD.

21-1, Seosomun-Dong, Chung-Gu, Seoul, South Korea

CEO: Jung-Rae, CEO   Tel: 82-2-771-1100   Rev: $2,082

Bus: *Mfr. tires, steel products, electronics,*   Fax: 82-2-754-9983   Emp: 7,098
     fabrics/yarns, and musical instruments.   www.hyosung.co.kr

HYOSUNG AMERICA, INC.

One Penn Plaza, Suite 2220, New York, NY 10119

CEO: Y. H. Suk, Pres.   Tel: (212) 736-7100   %FO: 100

Bus: *Agricultural products, chemicals,*   Fax: (212) 563-1323   Emp: 33
     electronics, textiles and garments.

HYOSUNG AMERICA, INC.

18000 Studebaker Road, Ste. 550, Cerritos, CA 90703

CEO: Y. H. Suk, Pres.   Tel: (562) 809-5050   %FO: 100

Bus: *Steel products, electronics,*   Fax: (562) 809-5251   Emp: 47
     fabrics/yarns, musical instruments.

● HYUNDAI CORPORATION

140-2 Kye-dong, Chongro-ku, Seoul, South Korea

CEO: Chung Chai-Kwan, Pres. & CEO   Tel: 82-2-746-1114   Rev: $32,870

Bus: *Engaged in construction, electronics,*   Fax: 82-2-741-2341   Emp: 1,025
     automobiles, financial services,   www.hyundai.net
     petrochemicals and shipbuilding.

HYUNDAI CORPORATION U.S.A

300 Sylvan Avenue, Englewood Cliffs, NJ   07632

CEO: Dong Soo Han, Pres.   Tel: (201) 816-4000   %FO: 100

Bus: *U.S. headquarters; administrative*   Fax: (201) 816-4036
      and trading operations.

• HYUNDAI ENGINEERING & CONSTRUCTION

140-2 Kye-Dong, Chongro-Gu, Seoul, South Korea

CEO: Chung Mong-hun, CEO   Tel: 82-2-746-1114   Rev: $4,840

Bus: *General contractor involved in overseas*   Fax: 82-2-743-8963   Emp: 28,300
      construction market.   www.hyundai.hdec.co.kr

HYUNDAI CORPORATION, ENGINEERING & CONSTRUCTION DIV.

300 Sylvan Avenue, Englewood Cliffs, NJ   07632

CEO: Dong Soo Han, Pres.   Tel: (201) 816-4000   %FO: 100

Bus: *U.S. headquarters; administrative*   Fax: (201) 816-4036
      and trading operations.

• HYUNDAI HEAVY INDUSTRIES CO., LTD.

1, Cheonha-dong, Dong-ku, Ulsan, 682-792, South Korea

CEO: Kil Seon Choi, CEO   Tel: 82-52-230-2114   Rev: $5,230

Bus: *Engaged in shipbuilding.*   Fax: 82-52-230-3850   Emp: 27,000
      www.hhi.co.kr

HYUNDAI HEAVY INDUSTRIES COMPANY

300 Sylvan Avenue, Englewood Cliffs, NJ   07632

CEO: J. S. Choi, Mgr.   Tel: (201) 816-4080   %FO: 100

Bus: *Engaged in shipbuilding, power*   Fax: (201) 816-4083
      plant and waste treatment plant
      construction.

HYUNDAI HEAVY INDUSTRIES COMPANY

Palladium 12124 Hi Tech Avenue, Orlando, FL   32817-1245

CEO: Yung Shin, Mgr.   Tel: (407) 249-7350   %FO: 100

Bus: *Production of construction*   Fax: (407) 275-4940
      equipment.

HYUNDAI HEAVY INDUSTRIES COMPANY

1400 Broadfield, Ste. 600 Park 10 Center, Houston, TX   77084

CEO: H. Kim, Pres.   Tel: (713) 578-7097   %FO: 100

Bus: *Production of construction*   Fax: (713) 578-7330
      equipment.

● **HYUNDAI MERCHANT MARINE CO., LTD.**
66, Chokson-dong, Jongro-ku Seoul, 110-052, South Korea
CEO: Choong Shik Kim, Pres. & CEO   Tel: 82-2-3706-5114   Rev: $4,000
Bus: *Marine transportation services.*   Fax: 82-2-3706-5876   Emp: 5,000
    www.hmm21.com

    HYUNDAI MERCHANT MARINE INC.
    300 Sylvan Avenue, Englewood Cliffs, NJ 07632
    CEO: J. L. Lee   Tel: (201) 816-4000   %FO: 100
    Bus: *Engaged in marine transportation.*   Fax: (201) 816-4036

● **HYUNDAI MOTOR CO. LTD., DIV. HYUNDAI GROUP**
231 Yangjae-Dong, Seocho-Gu, Seoul, 137-938, South Korea
CEO: Chung Mong-Ku, Chmn.   Tel: 82-2-3464-2545   Rev: $32,870
Bus: *Mfr., sales and service of automobiles.*   Fax: 82-2-3463-3484   Emp: 35,000
    www.hmc.co.kr

    HYUNDAI AUTO TECH CENTER INC.
    5075 Venture Drive, Ann Arbor, MI 48108
    CEO: Dupom Lee, Mgr.   Tel: (313) 747-6600   %FO: 100
    Bus: *Engaged in study of advanced*   Fax: (313) 747-6699
    technology and car performance.

    HYUNDAI MOTOR AMERICA
    10550 Talbert Avenue, Fountain Valley, CA 92728
    CEO: M. H. Juhn, Pres.   Tel: (714) 965-3000   %FO: 100
    Bus: *U.S. headquarters. Mfr./sales*   Fax: (714) 965-3816
    automobiles and parts.

    HYUNDAI MOTOR AMERICA FINANCE DIV.
    10550 Talbert Avenue, Fountain Valley, CA 92728
    CEO: William Thaxton, Pres.   Tel: (714) 965-3400   %FO: 100
    Bus: *Management of alternative*   Fax: (714) 965-7010
    financing for car purchase.

    KIA MOTORS AMERICA
    9801 Muirlands Boulevard, Irvine, CA 92618
    CEO: B. M. Ahn, Pres.   Tel: (949) 470-0700   %FO: 100
    Bus: *Engaged in sales and marketing.*   Fax: (949) 470-2803

● **HYUNDAI PRECISION INDUSTRY CO.**
140-2 Kye-Dong, Chongro-Gu, Seoul, 110-793, South Korea
CEO: Park Jung-In, Pres.   Tel: 82-2-746-1114   Rev: $2,279
Bus: *Shipping containers/trailers.*   Fax: 82-2-746-4244   Emp: 8,512
    www.hyundai.hdpic.co.jp

HYUNDAI PRECISION & INDUSTRY COMPANY
7314 19-Mile Road, Sterling Heights, MI   48314
CEO: J. Lee, Mgr. Tel: (810) 254-5600 %FO: 100
Bus: *Mfr. industrial materials.* Fax: (810) 254-5603 Emp: 6

HYUNDAI PRECISION AMERICA, INC.
8880 Rio San Diego, Ste. 600, San Diego, CA   92108
CEO: T. Y. Chung, Pres. Tel: (619) 574-1500 %FO: 100
Bus: *Manufactures shipping Fax: (619) 542-0301 Emp: 90
containers/trailers.*

HYUNDAI PRECISION INDUSTRY COMPANY
300 Sylvan Avenue, Englewood Cliffs, NJ   07632
CEO: J. M. Park, Mgr. Tel: (201) 816-4000 %FO: 100
Bus: *Container manufacturer.* Fax: (201) 816-4089 Emp: 2

● INDUSTRIAL BANK OF KOREA
50, Ulchiro 2-Ga, Chung-Gu, Seoul, 100-758, South Korea
CEO: Kyung Jun Lee, Gen. Mgr. Tel: 82-2-729-7004 Rev: $2,279
Bus: *Commercial banking services.* Fax: 82-2-729-7205 Emp: 7,590
www.kiup-bank.com

INDUSTRIAL BANK OF KOREA
16 West 32nd Street, 1st Fl., New York, NY   10001
CEO: Schoon Ko, Mgr. Tel: (212) 268-6363 %FO: 100
Bus: *Commercial banking services.* Fax: (212) 268-1090 Emp: 34

● JAMES VISION CO., LTD.
227-5 Nowon 3 Ga, Buk-Gu, Taegu, 702-083, South Korea
CEO: K. N. Kim, Pres. Tel: 82-53-351-9027
Bus: *Mfr. optical frames and sunglasses.* Fax: 82-53-351-2813
www.jamesvision.com

JAMES EYEWEAR CORPORATION
800 N.W. 31st Street, Miami, FL   33122
CEO: K. N. Kim, Pres. Tel: (305) 477-6336 %FO: 100
Bus: *Optical frames & sunglasses; Fax: (305) 477-9336 Emp: 5
mobile amusement products &
inflatable fun houses.*

● JINDO CO., LTD
371-62 Kansan-Dong, Kumchon-Gu, Seoul, 153-023, South Korea
CEO: Kim Young-Jim, Pres. Tel: 82-2-850-8200 Rev: $967
Bus: *Engaged in manufacture of shipping Fax: 82-2-864-7678 Emp: 1,304
containers and environment-related www.jindo.co.kr
products.*

JINDO AMERICA, INC.
580 Sylvan Avenue, Englewood Cliffs, NJ   07632
CEO: Y. W. Lee, Pres.   Tel: (201) 816-3434   %FO: 100
Bus: *Shipping containers; fur and*   Fax: (201) 816-1313
       leather goods.

• **KIA MOTORS CORPORATION**
992-28, Shihung-dong, Kumchun-gu, Seoul, South Korea
CEO: Soo Joong Kim, Pres.   Tel: 82-2-788-1114   Rev: $8,529
Bus: *Mfr. freight cars and commercial* Fax: 82-2-784-8347   Emp: 29,850
       vehicles.   www.kia.kr

   KIA MOTORS AMERICA, INC.
   Two Cromwell, PO Box 52410, Irvine, CA   92619-2410
   CEO: Hong-Rae Park, Pres.   Tel: (949) 470-7000   %FO: 100
   Bus: *Automotive company.*   Fax: (949) 470-2800   Emp: 170

• **KOLON INTERNATIONAL CORP.**
Kolon Bldg., 45 Mugyo Dong, Chung-Gu, Seoul, 100-170, South Korea
CEO: Lee Woong-Yeol, Chmn.   Tel: 82-2-311-7114   Rev: $1,912
Bus: *General international trading, including* Fax: 82-2-311-7988   Emp: 1,660
       film, video tapes, chemical and crude www.kolon.co.kr
       fibers.

   KOLON AMERICA INC
   One Madison Street East, Rutherford, NJ   07073
   CEO: S. Park, Pres.   Tel: (973) 470-9191   %FO: 100
   Bus: *Engaged in importing and*   Fax: (973) 470-9292
          exporting.

   KOLON AMERICA INC
   173 Kilgore Road, Carrollton, GA   30116
   CEO: S. Kim   Tel: (770) 832-7700   %FO: 100
   Bus: *Engaged in importing and*   Fax: (770) 832-1706
          exporting.

   KOLON AMERICA INC
   3 Sperry Road, Fairfield, NJ   07004
   CEO: Kim Jong   Tel: (973) 575-2550   %FO: 100
   Bus: *Video tape, polyester & nylon* Fax: (973) 575-1332   Emp: 15
          films.

   KOLON AMERICA INC
   350 Fifth Avenue, Ste. 5211, New York, NY   10118
   CEO: Jakwan Koo, Pres.   Tel: (212) 736-0120   %FO: 100
   Bus: *Engaged in importing and*   Fax: (212) 736-0933   Emp: 15
          exporting.

KOLON CALIFORNIA CORPORATION
17211 South Valley View Ave., Cerritos, CA 90703
CEO: M. H. Yoo, Pres.   Tel: (562) 802-9007   %FO: 100
Bus: *International trading.*   Fax: (562) 802-1425   Emp: 40

● **KOOKMIN BANK**
9-1, 2-Ga, Namdaemun-no, Chung-ku, Seoul, 100-703, South Korea
CEO: Kim Jung-Tae, CEO   Tel: 82-2-317-2460   Rev: $8,525
Bus: *Commercial and investment banking*   Fax: 82-2-317-2252   Emp: 11,643
    services.   www.kookmin-bank.com

　　KOOKMIN BANK
　　565 Fifth Avenue, 24th Fl., New York, NY   10017
　　CEO: Soo-Jong Choi, Mng. Dir.   Tel: (212) 697-6100   %FO: 100
　　Bus: *Wholesale & merchant banking*   Fax: (212) 697-1456
　　　services.

● **KOREA DATA SYSTEM CO., LTD. (KDS)**
170, Gongdan-Dong, Kumi-Si, Kyungbuk-Do, South Korea
CEO: J. Koh, Pres.   Tel: 82-546-461-3121
Bus: *Personal computer monitors.*   Fax: 82-546-461-8720
                          www.kdscomputers.com

　　KDS COMPUTERS INC.
　　12300 Edison Way, Garden Grove, CA   92841
　　CEO: Erin Rippee, VP Mktg.   Tel: (714) 379-5599   %FO: 100
　　Bus: *PC Monitors.*   Fax: (714) 379-5595   Emp: 50

● **THE KOREA DEVELOPMENT BANK**
10-2 Kwanchol-Dong, Chongno-gu, Seoul, 110-748, South Korea
CEO: Rak-Young Uhm, Gov.   Tel: 82-2-398-6114   Rev: $4,853
Bus: *Commercial banking services.*   Fax: 82-2-733-4768   Emp: 2,700
                          www.kdb.co.kr

　　THE KOREA DEVELOPMENT BANK
　　320 Park Avenue, 32nd Fl., New York, NY   10022
　　CEO: Woo-Yang Park, Pres.   Tel: (212) 688-7686   %FO: 100
　　Bus: *International commercial banking*   Fax: (212) 421-5028   Emp: 6
　　　services.

● **KOREA EXCHANGE BANK**
181 2-Ga Ulchiro Chung-Gu, Seoul, 100-192, South Korea
CEO: Gab Hyun Lee, Pres.   Tel: 82-2-729-8000   Rev: $5,387
Bus: *International commercial banking*   Fax: 82-2-775-9814   Emp: 5,732
    service.   www.koexbank.co.kr.

KOREA EXCHANGE BANK

460 Park Avenue, 15th Fl., New York, NY   10022

CEO: Tae Sung Park, Mgr.   Tel: (212) 838-4949   %FO: 100

Bus: *Commercial banking services.*   Fax: (212) 752-3964

PACIFIC UNION BANK

3530 Wilshire Blvd., Ste. 1800, Los Angeles, CA   90010

CEO: Kwang Soon Park, Pres.   Tel: (213) 385-0909   %FO: 100

Bus: *Commercial banking services.*   Fax: (213) 386-6869

• THE KOREA EXPRESS COMPANY LTD.

58-12 Seosomun-Dong, Chung-ku, Seoul, South Korea

CEO: Y. W. Kwak, Pres.   Tel: 82-2-3782-0114

Bus: *Engaged in cargo handling, storage and*   Fax: 82-2-3782-0098
transport.

KOREA EXPRESS USA INC.

901 Castle Road, Secaucus, NJ   07094

CEO: Myung Chung, Pres.   Tel: (201) 863-7505   %FO: 100

Bus: *Engaged in cargo handling,*   Fax: (201) 863-5036
storage and transport.

• KOREA FIRST BANK

100 Kong Pyong-Dong, Chongno-gu, Seoul, 110-1602, South Korea

CEO: Si Yul Ryu, Pres.   Tel: 82-2-3702-3114   Rev: $2,938

Bus: *Commercial banking services.*   Fax: 82-2-3702-3114   Emp: 4,853
www.kfb.co.kr

KOREA FIRST BANK

410 Park Avenue, 7th Fl., New York, NY   10022

CEO: Bang Yeung, Gen. Mgr.   Tel: (212) 593-2525   %FO: 100

Bus: *Commercial banking services.*   Fax: (212) 319-0255   Emp: 25

KOREA FIRST BANK

29 West 30th Street, New York, NY   10001

CEO: Seung Kim, Gen. Mgr.   Tel: (212) 279-2790   %FO: 100

Bus: *Commercial banking services.*   Fax: (212) 564-3278   Emp: 25

• KOREAN AIR CARGO

41-3, Seosomoon-dong, Joong-ku, Seoul, Korea

CEO: I.W. Nam   Tel: 82-2-751-7270

Bus: *Engaged in cargo transport*   Fax: 82-2-779-2578
www.cargo.koreanair.com

KOREAN AIR CARGO
Cargo Building 260, JFK Int'l Airport, Jamaica, NY   11430
CEO: J. H. Kim, Mgr.   Tel: (718) 632-5550   %FO: 100
Bus: *Engaged in cargo transport.*   Fax: (718) 632-5595

KOREAN AIR CARGO
6101 W. Imperial Highway, Los Angeles, CA   90045
CEO: Choong Nam Kim, Mgr.   Tel: (310) 417-5203   %FO: 100
Bus: *Engaged in cargo transport.*   Fax: (310) 337-0762

KOREAN AIR CARGO
2967 North Airfield Drive, Ste. 220, Dallas, TX   75281
CEO: Frank Choi, Sales Mgr.   Tel: (972) 574-1780   %FO: 100
Bus: *Engaged in cargo transport.*   Fax: (972) 574-1783

● KOREAN AIR LINES CO., LTD.
Kang Seo-gu, Gong Hang-dong, Seoul, 360-1, South Korea
CEO: Shim Yi Taek, Pres.   Tel: 82-2-656-7114   Rev: $2,810
Bus: *International passenger and cargo air*   Fax: 82-2-656-7788   Emp: 15,230
transport.   www.koreanair.com

KOREAN AIR LINES
1801 Broadway, Ste. 280, Denver, CO   80202
CEO: Diane Lee   Tel: (303) 292-3900   %FO: 100
Bus: *International air carrier.*   Fax: (303) 292-3999

KOREAN AIR LINES
2 Penn Center Plaza, Philadelphia, PA   19102
CEO: Young C. Chun   Tel: (215) 665-9080   %FO: 100
Bus: *International air carrier.*   Fax: (215) 665-8440

KOREAN AIR LINES
168 Federal Street, Boston, MA   02110
CEO: Ki Park   Tel: (617) 261-3883   %FO: 100
Bus: *International air carrier.*   Fax: (617) 261-3808

KOREAN AIR LINES
8700 N. Stemmons, Ste. 110, Dallas, TX   75247
CEO: Kwang Sung Kim   Tel: (214) 637-2444   %FO: 100
Bus: *International air carrier.*   Fax: (214) 905-6014   Emp: 20

KOREAN AIR LINES
1154 15th Street NW, Washington, DC   20005
CEO: Jay I. Bae   Tel: (202) 785-3644   %FO: 100
Bus: *International air carrier.*   Fax: (202) 785-3762   Emp: 20

KOREAN AIR LINES
609 Fifth Avenue, New York, NY   10017

CEO: B. S. Kim, Mgr.	Tel: (212) 326-5000	%FO: 100
Bus: *International air carrier.*	Fax: (212) 326-5090	Emp: 50

KOREAN AIR
6101 W. Imperial Highway, Los Angeles, CA   90045

CEO: Jung Heum Park	Tel: (310) 417-5200	%FO: 100
Bus: *Air transport services.*	Fax: (310) 417-3051	

KOREAN AIR LINES
PO Box 66259, Chicago, IL   60666-0259

CEO: Yun Cho, Mgr.	Tel: (773) 894-8030	%FO: 100
Bus: *International passenger & cargo air transport.*	Fax: (773) 601-5482	Emp: 45

● KUMHO INDUSTRIAL COMPANY LTD. (KUMHO TIRE)
Asiana Bldg. 10-1, 2-Ga, Hoehyun-Dong, Chung-Gu, Seoul, 100-052, South Korea

CEO: Shin Hyung-In, CEO	Tel: 82-2-758-1114	Rev: $1,238
Bus: *Mfr. passenger, truck and bus tires.*	Fax: 82-2-758-1515	Emp: 6,283
	www.kumhotire.co.kr	

KUMHO TIRE USA, INC.
14605 Miller Avenue, Fontana, CA   92336

CEO: Jong G. Kahng, Pres.	Tel: (909) 428-3300	%FO: 100
Bus: *Sales of passenger car, truck and bus tires.*	Fax: (909) 428-3989	Emp: 48

KUMHO TIRE USA, INC.
711 South Cleveland-Massillon Road, Akron, OH   44333

CEO: Ray Rowe	Tel: (330) 670-2600	%FO: 100
Bus: *Sales of passenger car, truck and bus tires.*	Fax: (330) 666-3972	

● KYUNG DONG INDUSTRIAL CO., LTD.
570-10 Gajwa-Dong, Seo-Gu, Inchon, 404-250, South Korea

CEO: Kyung Hwan Choy, Pres.	Tel: 82-32-577-0077	
Bus: *Manufacturer of stainless steel flatware/cookware, non-stick aluminum skillets.*	Fax: 82-32-577-0081	Emp: 2,500
	www.kyungdong.co.kr	

ESTIA CORP
350 Gotham Pkwy., Carlstadt, NJ   07072

CEO: Ye Sung Whang, EVP	Tel: (201) 939-7077	%FO: 100
Bus: *Distribution/sale of stainless steel flatware/cookware, non-stick aluminum skillets.*	Fax: (201) 939-4925	Emp: 10

• LG ELECTRONICS

20 Yoido-Dong, Youngdungpo-gu, Seoul, 150-721, South Korea

CEO: John Koo, Pres.	Tel: 82-2-3777-1114	Rev: $11,287
Bus: *Manufacture/sell home electronics, home appliances, computer office automation and magnetics.*	Fax: 82-2-3777-3400 www.lge.co.kr	Emp: 35,000

LG ELECTRONICS, INC.

201 James Record Road, PO Box 6126, Huntsville, AL 35824-0126

CEO: Y. W. Lee, Mgr.	Tel: (205) 772-6105	%FO: 100
Bus: *Engaged in home appliance, monitor, CD-ROM and multi-media sales.*	Fax: (205) 772-0628	

LG ELECTRONICS, INC.

355 West Second Street, Ste. 265, Callexico, CA 92231

CEO: J. B. Lee, Mgr.	Tel: (760) 768-7470	%FO: 100
Bus: *Engaged in home appliance, monitor, CD-ROM and multi-media sales.*	Fax: (760) 768-7575	

LG ELECTRONICS, INC.

40 Washington Road, Princeton, NJ 08550

CEO: Brian Lee, Mgr.	Tel: (609) 716-3502	%FO: 100
Bus: *Engaged in home appliance, monitor, CD-ROM and multi-media sales.*	Fax: (609) 716-3503	

LG ELECTRONICS, INC.

5255 N. W. 87th Avenue, Miami, FL 33178

CEO: Chang Sun Choi, Mgr.	Tel: (305) 477-1882	%FO: 100
Bus: *Sale of electronic products.*	Fax: (305) 471-0715	Emp: 5

LG ELECTRONICS, INC.

1000 Sylvan Avenue, Englewood Cliffs, NJ 07632

CEO: Bennett Norell	Tel: (201) 816-2000	%FO: 100
Bus: *Engaged in home appliance, monitor, CD-ROM and multi-media sales.*	Fax: (201) 816-2188	Emp: 105

LG ELECTRONICS, INC.

2021 South Archibald Avenue, Ontario, CA 91761

CEO: Chang Sun Choi, Mgr.	Tel: (909) 930-2300	%FO: 100
Bus: *Distributor/warehouse operation for electronic products.*	Fax: (909) 930-2366	Emp: 20

LG ELECTRONICS, INC.
6133 North River Road, Ste. 1100, Rosemont, IL   60018

CEO: N. K. Woo, Mgr.   Tel: (847) 692-4500   %FO: 100

Bus: *Electronic products.*   Fax: (847) 692-4501   Emp: 30

● LG GROUP INTERNATIONAL, LTD.
LG Twin Towers, 20 Yoido-Dong, Youngdungpo-Gu, Seoul, 150-721, South Korea

CEO: Koo Bon-Moo, Chmn.   Tel: 82-2-3773-1114   Rev: $72,615

Bus: *Chemicals and energy, electronics, machinery and metals, trade and services, finance and public services/sports and apparel manufacturing.*   Fax: 82-2-3773-2200   Emp: 100,000

www.lg.co.kr

LG CHEM LTD.
3252 Holiday Court, Ste. 101, La Jolla, CA   92037

CEO: M. Mok, Pres.   Tel: (619) 623-9068   %FO: 100

Bus: *Mfr. chemicals.*   Fax: (619) 623-8500

LG EPITAXY, INC.
PO Box 4778, 55 Aldo Avenue, Santa Clara, CA   95054

CEO: Rudi Morales, Mgr.   Tel: (408) 988-2161

Bus: *Engaged in manufacturing.*   Fax: (408) 988-1855

LG INSURANCE COMPANY LTD.
3700 Wilshire Blvd., Ste. 205, Los Angeles, CA   90010

CEO: T. Lim, Mgr.   Tel: (213) 382-7819

Bus: *Insurance services.*   Fax: (213) 382-8176

LG INTERNATIONAL AMERICA
1000 Sylvan Avenue, Englewood Cliffs, NJ   07632

CEO: Charles Koo, Pres. & CEO   Tel: (201) 816-2000   %FO: 100

Bus: *Chemicals and energy, electronics, machinery and metals, trade/services, finance, and public services/sports.*   Fax: (201) 816-0604   Emp: 1,200

LG INVESTMENT & SECURITIES AMERICA INC.
One World Trade Center, Ste. 8463, New York, NY   10048

CEO: M. Mok, Pres.   Tel: (212) 432-7660   %FO: 100

Bus: *Engaged in investments and securities.*   Fax: (212) 432-0442

LG PRECISION COMPANY
13013 East 166th Street, Cerritos, CA   90703

CEO: Lee Soo Ho, Pres.	Tel: (562) 483-8000	%FO: 100
Bus: *Mfr. test and measuring instruments.*	Fax: (562) 483-8080	Emp: 35

LG SILTRON INC.
150 East Brokaw Road, San Jose, CA   95112

CEO: Dae-Hong Kim	Tel: (408) 350-7770	%FO: 100
Bus: *Mfr. silicon wafers for the semiconductor industry.*	Fax: (408) 453-6148	

ZENITH ELECTRONICS CORPORATION
1000 Milwaukee Avenue, Glenview, IL   60025-2493

CEO: H. J. Lee, Chmn.	Tel: (847) 391-7000	%FO: 100
Bus: *Sales/distribution of video products.*	Fax: (847) 391-7523	

● LG INFORMATION & COMMUNICATIONS, LTD.
LG Twin Towers, 20 Youido-Dong, Youngdungpo-Gu, Seoul, 150-010, South Korea

CEO: B. H. Koo, Chmn.	Tel: 82-2-3777-2753	Rev: $2,027
Bus: *Mfr. wireless communication devices, machinery and metals.*	Fax: 82-2-3777-3400 www.lgic.co.kr	Emp: 5,704

LG INFOCOM, LTD.
1000 Sylvan Avenue, Englewood Cliffs, NJ   07632

CEO: J. Koo, Pres.	Tel: (201) 816-2072	%FO: 100
Bus: *Wireless communication devices.*	Fax: (201) 816-2073	Emp: 2

LG INFOCOM, LTD.
10225 Willowcreek Road, San Diego, CA   92131

CEO: Ick B. Kim, Pres.	Tel: (619) 635-5300	%FO: 100
Bus: *Wireless communication devices.*	Fax: (619) 623-9922	Emp: 40

● PACIFIC CORPORATION
181 Hangang-No, 2-Ga, Yongsan-Gu, Seoul, 140-77, South Korea

CEO: Soh Kyong-Bae, Pres.	Tel: 82-2-709-5114	Rev: $682
Bus: *Cosmetics, toiletries and hair care products*	Fax: 82-2-709-6029 www.pacific.co.kr	Emp: 3,398

PACIFIC CORPORATION OF AMERICA
270 Sylvan Avenue, Ste. 140, Englewood Cliffs, NJ   07632

CEO: J. Lee, Mgr.	Tel: (201) 503-0600	%FO: 100
Bus: *Cosmetics, toiletries and hair care products.*	Fax: (201) 503-0686	Emp: 15

PACIFIC COSMETICS, INC.
2610 West Olympic Blvd., Los Angeles, CA   90006

CEO: Woo K. Moon, Pres.	Tel: (323) 737-3333	%FO: 100
Bus: *Cosmetics, toiletries and hair care products.*	Fax: (323) 737-2022	Emp: 23

• POHANG IRON & STEEL CO., LTD
1 Koe-Dong, Nam-Gu, Kyongsangbuk-Do, Pohang City, 790-785, South Korea

CEO: Lee Ku-Taek, Pres.	Tel: 82-562-220-0114	Rev: $10,875
Bus: *Manufacturer of steel products.*	Fax: 82-562-220-4499	Emp: 26,250
	www.posco.co.kr	

POHANG IRON & STEEL COMPANY, LTD
1800 K Street, NW, Washington, DC   20006

CEO: Syon-Yong Shin, Chief Rep.	Tel: (202) 785-5643	%FO: 100
Bus: *Manufacturer of steel products (cold rolled, galvanized sheet, tin plate)*	Fax: (202) 785-5647	

POHANG IRON & STEEL COMPANY, LTD
2530 Arnold Drive, Martinez, CA   94553

CEO: Hoon-Kop Oh, Gen. Mgr.	Tel: (510) 228-9720	%FO: 100
Bus: *Manufacturer of steel products (cold rolled, galvanized sheet, tin plate)*	Fax: (510) 228-9729	

POHANG STEEL AMERICA COMPANY LTD.
300 Tice Blvd., Woodcliff Lake, NJ   07430

CEO: Byung Chang Yoo, Pres.	Tel: (201) 782-9200	%FO: 100
Bus: *Steel sales, investment development, holding company.*	Fax: (201) 782-9210	Emp: 17

USS-POSCO INDUSTRIES (UPI)
900 Loveridge Road, Pittsburgh, CA   94565

CEO: Robert Smith, Pres.	Tel: (925) 439-6300	%FO: 50
Bus: *Manufacturer of steel products (cold rolled, galvanized sheet, tin plate).*	Fax: (925) 782-9210	

• POONGSAN CORP.
60-1, 3-Ga, Chungmoo-Ro, Chung-Gu, Seoul, South Korea

CEO: Jin Roy Ryu, CEO	Tel: 82-2-3406-5114	Rev: $1,200
Bus: *Supplies fabricated copper and copper alloy products.*	Fax: 82-2-3406-5400	Emp: 4,261
	www.poongsan.co.kr	

PMX INDUSTRIES, INC.
5300 Willow Creek Drive, Cedar Rapids, IA   52404
CEO: M. Ahn, Pres.   Tel: (319) 368-7700   %FO: 100
Bus: *Copper and metal materials.*   Fax: (319) 368-7701   Emp: 260

● **PUSAN BANK**
830-38, Pomil-dong, Dong-gu, Pusan, 601-060, South Korea
CEO: Kim Kyung-Lim, Chmn.   Tel: 82-51-642-3300   Rev: $1,292
Bus: *Commercial banking services.*   Fax: 82-51-642-3151   Emp: 3,310
                                                www.pusanbank.co.jp

PUSAN BANK
29 West 30th Street, 10th Fl., New York, NY   10001
CEO: Yon Joo Jung, Rep.   Tel: (212) 244-2780   %FO: 100
Bus: *International banking services.*   Fax: (212) 244-2778

● **SAMJIN TRADING CO., LTD.**
1140-36, Jegi-Dong, Dongdaimoon-Gu, Seoul, South Korea
CEO: C. H. Kang, Pres.   Tel: 82-2-961-5501
Bus: *Oriental food, Ramen noodles, canned*   Fax: 82-2-961-5110
foods, gift and kitchenware   www.acorea.co.kr

SAMJIN AMERICA, INC.
3345 East Slauson Avenue, Vernon, CA   90058
CEO: S. K. Lee, Mgr.   Tel: (213) 622-5111   %FO: 100
Bus: *Oriental food, Ramen noodles,*   Fax: (213) 622-5285   Emp: 7
canned food, gift and kitchenware.

SAMJIN AMERICA, INC.
49-01 Maspeth Avenue, Maspeth, NY   11378
CEO: S. Jung, Mgr.   Tel: (718) 894-8383   %FO: 100
Bus: *Importer of Korean food and gift*   Fax: (718) 821-5858   Emp: 15
products.

● **SAMSUNG CORPORATION**
310 2 Ga, Taepyong-Ro, Chung-Gu, Seoul, 100-102, South Korea
CEO: Myung-Kwan Hyun, CEO   Tel: 82-2-3706-1114   Rev: $31,900
Bus: *Import/export, construction services, e-* Fax: 82-2-3706-1212   Emp: 4,740
business and housing development.   www.samsungcorp.com

AST RESEARCH, INC.
16215 Alton Parkway, Irvine, CA   92719
CEO: Soon-Taek Kim, Pres.   Tel: (949) 727-4141   %FO: 100
Bus: *Design/mfg./market desktop and*   Fax: (949) 727-9355
notebook computers.

SAMSUNG AMERICA INC.
105 Challenger Road, Ridgefield Park, NJ   07660-0511
CEO: Mansoo Lee, Pres.   Tel: (201) 229-5000   %FO: 100
Bus: *Imp/export general merchandise.*   Fax: (201) 229-5080

SAMSUNG AMERICA INC.
500-108th Avenue, N.E., Ste. 1095, Bellevue, WA   98004
CEO: Mansoo Lee, Pres.   Tel: (425) 646-6336   %FO: 100
Bus: *Import/export, textile*   Fax: (425) 646-9538
manufacturing, sportswear
apparel, heavy machinery,
communication technology and
construction services.

SAMSUNG AMERICA INC
1130 East Arapaho Road, Richardson, TX   75081-2328
CEO: D.J. Oh, Pres.   Tel: (972) 761-7000   %FO: 100
Bus: *Import/export, textile*   Fax: (972) 761-7001
manufacturing, sportswear
apparel, heavy machinery,
communication technology and
construction services.

SAMSUNG AMERICA INC.
14251 East Firestone Blvd., Ste. 201, La Mirada, CA   90638
CEO: J. Lee, Pres.   Tel: (562) 802-2211   %FO: 100
Bus: *Import/export, textile*   Fax: (562) 802-3011
manufacturing, sportswear
apparel, heavy machinery,
communication technology and
construction services.

SAMSUNG CARAVEL INC.
1359 Broadway, New York, NY   10018
CEO: J. Park, Mgr.   Tel: (212) 563-1022   %FO: 100
Bus: *Mfr. textiles.*   Fax: (212) 563-7663

SAMSUNG CARAVEL INC.
110 East Ninth Street, Ste. A-929, Los Angeles, CA   90079
CEO: J. Park, Mgr.   Tel: (213) 833-1735   %FO: 100
Bus: *Mfr. textiles.*   Fax: (213) 624-7388

SAMSUNG PACIFIC CONSTRUCTION INC.

14251 East Firestone Blvd., Ste. 101, La Mirada, CA   90638

CEO: D. L. Kim, Pres.   Tel: (562) 407-1862   %FO: 100

Bus: *Engineering and construction*   Fax: (562) 407-1864
      services, including plant
      construction and civil projects.

SAMSUNG PETRO CHEMICAL, INC.

5847 San Felipe, Ste. 2949, Houston, TX   77057

CEO: Jimmy Park, Mgr.   Tel: (713) 953-9700   %FO: 100

Bus: *Mfr. petro chemicals.*   Fax: (713) 953-9911

SAMSUNG SEMICONDUCTOR, INC.

3655 North First Street, San Jose, CA   95134

CEO: Han Joo Kim, Pres. & CEO   Tel: (408) 544-4000   %FO: 100

Bus: *Semi-conducting equipment,*   Fax: (408) 544-4980
      memory, TFT LCD, ASIC and
      MCU.

● **SAMSUNG DISPLAY DEVICES CO., LTD.**

575 Shin-dong, Paldal-gu, Suwon-shi, Kyonggi-do, South Korea

CEO: Son Wook, CEO   Tel: 82-331-210-1114   Rev: $3,590

Bus: *Mfr. color picture tube and computer*   Fax: Emp: 12,660
      monitors.   www.sdd.samsung.co.kr

SAMSUNG DISPLAY, INC.

18600 Broadwick Street, Rancho Dominguez, CA   90220

CEO: K. W. Park, Pres.   Tel: (310) 537-7000   %FO: 100

Bus: *Mfr. distributor computer monitors.*   Fax: (310) 537-1033   Emp: 9,000

● **SAMSUNG ELECTRONICS CO., LTD.**

250-2-Ga, Taepyung-Ro, Chung-Gu, Seoul, 100-742, South Korea

CEO: Yun Jong-Yong, Pres.   Tel: 82-2-727-7114   Rev: $22,861

Bus: *Computer memory discs, LCD panels,*   Fax: 82-2-727-7985   Emp: 55,000
      micro products.   www.sec.samsung.co.kr

SAMSUNG ELECTRONICS USA INC.

105 Challenger Road, Ridgefield Park, NJ   07660-0511

CEO: M. Oh, Pres. & CEO   Tel: (201) 229-4000   %FO: 100

Bus: *Mfr. consumer electronics,*   Fax: (201) 229-4000
      information systems, storage
      system products and office
      automation products.

SAMSUNG SEMICONDUCTOR, INC.
3655 North First Street, San Jose, CA   95234

CEO: B. S. Song, Pres.   Tel: (408) 954-7000   %FO: 100

Bus: *Computer memory discs, LCD*   Fax: (408) 954-7875   Emp: 480
    panels, micro products.

SAMSUNG TELECOMMUNICATIONS AMERICA (STA)
1130 East Arapaho Road, Richardson, TX   75081

CEO: Dr. Peter S. Rha, Pres.   Tel: (972) 761-7000   %FO: 100

Bus: *Telecommunications systems,*   Fax: (972) 761-7001
    consumer appliances, A/V
    equipment, computers, printers
    and semiconductors/

• SAMSUNG FIRE & MARINE INSURANCE CO., LTD.
Samsung Insurance Bldg., Euljiro 1-ka, Choong-ku, Seoul, 100-191, South Korea

CEO: Lee Chong-Ki, CEO   Tel: 82-2-758-7114   Rev: $2,491

Bus: *Sales non-life insurance.*   Fax: 82-2-758-7801   Emp: 4,000

                                       www.insurance.samsung.co.kr

SAMSUNG FIRE & MARINE INSURANCE CO., LTD.
105 Challenger Road, 5th Fl., Ridgefield Park, NJ   07660

CEO: Lee Chong-Ki, CEO   Tel: (201) 229-6011   %FO: 100

Bus: *Sales non-life insurance policies.* Fax: (201) 299-6015

• SAMSUNG LIFE INSURANCE CO., LTD.
Samsung Life Insurance Bldg., 150 Taepyongro 2-ga, Gunge-gu, Seoul, 100-716, South Korea

CEO: Lee Soo Bin, Chmn.   Tel: 82-2-751-8000   Rev: $18,610

Bus: *Individual and group life insurance* Fax: 82-2-751-8300   Emp: 8,280
    services.   www.sli.samsung.co.kr.

SAMSUNG LIFE INVESTMENT AMERICA LTD.
153 East 53rd Street, 36th Fl., New York, NY   10022

CEO: Min-Soo Ahn, Dir.   Tel: (212) 421-6751   %FO: 100

Bus: *Individual and group life*   Fax: (212) 421-6800
    insurance services.

• SEAH STEEL CORPORATION
40-153, Hangang-Ro, 3-Ga, Youngsan-Gu, Seoul, 140-013, South Korea

CEO: Jae Chul Cho, Chmn.   Tel: 82-2-709-8600   Rev: $874

Bus: *Iron and steel products.*   Fax: 82-2-797-2462   Emp: 956

                                       www.seahgroup.com

PUSAN PIPE AMERICA

9615 South Norwalk Blvd., Ste. B, Santa Fe Springs, CA   90670

CEO: B. J. Lee, Chmn.	Tel: (562) 692-0600	%FO: 100
Bus: *Iron and steel products.*	Fax: (562) 692-9295	Emp: 13

● **SEOUL BANK**

10-1 Namdaemun-no 2-ga Chung-gu, C.P.O. Box 276, Seoul, 100-746, South Korea

CEO: Chungwon Kang, Pres.	Tel: 82-2-3709-6114	Rev: $2,964
Bus: *Commercial banking services.*	Fax: 82-2-3709-6437	Emp: 7,511
	www.seoulbank.co.kr	

SEOUL BANK

280 Park Avenue, West Bldg., 24th Fl., New York, NY   10017

CEO: Deungno Lee, Mgr.	Tel: (212) 687-6160	%FO: 100
Bus: *International banking services.*	Fax: (212) 818-1721	Emp: 18

● **SHINHAN BANK**

120, 2-Ga, Taepyung-rNo, Chung-Gu, CPO Box 6999, Seoul, 100-102, South Korea

CEO: Heul-Keon Lee, Chmn.	Tel: 82-2-774-7674	Rev: $5,933
Bus: *Retail and international banking services.*	Fax: 82-2-774-7013	Emp: 4,450
	www.shinhanbank.co.kr	

SHINHAN BANK

800 Third Avenue, 32nd Fl., New York, NY   20033

CEO: Yong Sup Yoon, Gen. Mgr.	Tel: (212) 371-8000	%FO: 100
Bus: *International banking services.*	Fax: (212) 371-8875	

● **SK GLOBAL CO., LTD.**

36-1 Ulji-ro 2 ga Chung-gu, CPO Box 1780, Seoul, South Korea

CEO: Chang-Woo Nam, Pres. & CEO	Tel: 82-2-758-2114	Rev: $16,375
Bus: *Mfr. of petroleum and petrochemicals.*	Fax: 82-2-754-9414	Emp: 4,540
	www.skglobal.com	

SK CORPORATION BIO-PHARMACEUTICAL, INC.

140 A New Dutch Lane, Fairfield, NJ   07006

CEO: James Lee, Mgr.	Tel: (973) 227-3939	%FO: 100
Bus: *Bio-pharmaceutical research and development.*	Fax: (973) 227-4488	

SK CORPORATION

110 East 55th Street, 14th Fl., New York, NY   10022

CEO: Jae-Hong Lew, CEO	Tel: (212) 906-8140	%FO: 100
Bus: *Mfr. of petroleum and petrochemicals.*	Fax: (212) 906-8149	Emp: 4

SK CORPORATION
1300 Post Oak Blvd., Ste 780, Houston, TX   77056
CEO: Steve Lee, Mgr.   Tel: (713) 871-1088   %FO: 100
Bus: *Mfr. of petroleum and*   Fax: (713) 871-8050
     petrochemicals.

● SKC CO., LTD.
646-15, Yeoksam-dong, Kangnam-gu, Seoul, 135-080, Korea
CEO: Choi Dong Il   Tel: 82-2-3708-5151   Rev: $713
Bus: *Film and microfilm.*   Fax: 82-2-752-9088   Emp: 1,991
     www.skc.co.kr

SKC AMERICA INC.
One SKC Drive, Covington, GA   30014
CEO: Dal J. Yoo, Mgr.   Tel: (678) 342-1000   %FO: 100
Bus: *Film and microfilm.*   Fax: (378) 342-1800

SKC AMERICA INC.
850 Clark Drive, Mt. Olive, NJ   07828
CEO: Young S. Joo Yoon, VP   Tel: (973) 347-7000   %FO: 100
Bus: *Film and microfilm.*   Fax: (973) 347-7522

● SKM LTD.
216 1-Ga, Kwanghee-Dong, Chung-Gu, Seoul, South Korea
CEO: J. W. Chey, Pres.   Tel: 82-2-279-1611
Bus: *Professional and consumer audio tapes.*   Fax: 82-2-275-2144
     www.skm.co.kr

SKMA, INC.
4041 Via Oro Avenue, Long Beach, CA   90810
CEO: S. H. Cho, Pres.   Tel: (310) 830-6000   %FO: 100
Bus: *Professional & consumer audio*   Fax: (310) 830-0646   Emp: 20
     tapes.

● SSANGYONG CORPORATION
24-1, 2 Ga, Jeo-Dong, Chung Gu, CPO Box 409, Seoul, 100-748, South Korea
CEO: Ahn Jong-Won, Pres.   Tel: 82-2-270-8114   Rev: $7,152
Bus: *General trading company.*   Fax: 82-2-270-8775   Emp: 430
     www.ssy.co.kr

SSANGYONG (USA) INC.
115 West Century Road, Paramus, NJ   07652
CEO: C. W. Chung, Pres.   Tel: (201) 261-9400   %FO: 100
Bus: *import/export, general trading*   Fax: (201) 262-9120   Emp: 40
     company.

● **TONG IL INDUSTRIES, CO.**

62 B Sungsu Industrial Zone, Dalsu-Gu, Taegu, South Korea

CEO: Jong M. Kim, Pres.
Tel: 82-53-583-3690

Bus: *Manufacturer of polyethylene foam.*
Fax: 82-53-583-3698
www.toilon.com

    TOILON CORPORATION

    600 South Etiwanda Avenue, Ontario, CA 91761

    CEO: C. Kim, Mgr.
Tel: (909) 390-6644
%FO: 100

    Bus: *Manufacturer of polyethylene foam.*
Fax: (909) 390-6641
Emp: 20

● **TRIGEM COMPUTER, INC.**

1055 Shinkil-dong, Ansan, Kyonggi, South Korea

CEO: Hong Sun Lee, Pres.
Tel: 82-3-1489-3000
Rev: $4,328

Bus: *Manufacturing and trading of computers..*
Fax: 82-3-1489-3333
Emp: 1,770
www.trigem.com

    TRIGEM AMERICA CORPORATION

    14350 Myford Road, Bldg. 150, Irvine, CA 92606

    CEO: Chris Chung, Pres.
Tel: (714) 505-5051
%FO: 100

    Bus: *Manufacturing and trading of computers.*
Fax: (714) 505-5055
Emp: 80

● **UNION STEEL MFG. CO., LTD.**

Dabo Bldg., 140 Mapo-Dong, Kapo-Ku, Seoul, South Korea

CEO: Chulwoo W. Lee, Pres.
Tel: 82-2-3279-9114
Rev: $622

Bus: *Flat rolled galvanized steel sheets, steel pipes & tubes.*
Fax: 82-2-704-2450
Emp: 1,260
www.unionsteel.co.kr.

    UNION STEEL AMERICA, INC.

    460 Bergen Boulevard, Palisades Park, NJ 07650

    CEO: M. S. Lee, Pres.
Tel: (201) 947-7373
%FO: 100

    Bus: *Sale of flat rolled galvanized steel sheets, steel pipes & tubes.*
Fax: (201) 947-3999
Emp: 11

Spain

- **ACEITES BORGES PONT, SA**
  Avenida J. Trepat s/n, E-25300 Tàrrega, Spain
  CEO: Silvino Medina   Tel: 34-973-501-212
  Bus: *Production of olive oil, seeds, oil based*   Fax: 34-973-500-060   Emp: 240
        powders, nuts and agricultural products.   www.aceitesborges.es

    STAR FINE FOODS
    4652 E. Date Avenue, Fresno, CA   93725
    CEO: Stan Lewczyk, Pres.   Tel: (559) 498-2900   %FO: 100
    Bus: *Importers, processors, packers and*   Fax: (559) 498-2920
          distributors of specialty food
          products, including olives, olive
          oils, walnuts and seeds.

- **ACERINOX SA**
  Santiago de Compostela 100, E-28035 Madrid, Spain
  CEO: Victoriano Muñoz Cava, CEO   Tel: 34-91-398-5285   Rev: $1,500
  Bus: *Mfr. stainless steel.*   Fax: 34-91-398-5101   Emp: 3,500
                                        www.acerinox.es

    ACERINOX CORPORATION
    Two University Plaza, Hackensack, NJ   07601
    CEO: Francisco Nogus, Mgr.   Tel: (201) 489-6767   %FO: 100
    Bus: *Distributor stainless steel.*   Fax: (201) 489-7506   Emp: 14

    NORTH AMERICAN STAINLESS
    6870 Highway 42 East, Ghent, KY   41045
    CEO: Jose Lejeune, Pres.   Tel: (502) 347-6000   %FO: JV
    Bus: *Distributor stainless steel.*   Fax: (502) 347-6116

- **AGBAR (SOCIEDAD GENERAL DE AGUAS DE BARCELONA, SA)**
  39-43 paseo de San Juan, E-08009 Barcelona, Spain
  CEO: Ricardo Fornesa Ribo, Chmn.   Tel: 34-93-342-2000   Rev: $1,715
  Bus: *Provides water services.*   Fax: 34-93-342-2670   Emp: 1,150
                                        www.agbar.es

    WESTERN WATER COMPANY
    102 Washington Avenue, Point Richmond, CA   94801
    CEO: Michael Patrick George, CEO   Tel: (510) 234-7400   %FO: 100
    Bus: *Provides water services.*   Fax: (510) 307-7863

WESTERN WATER COMPANY
410 West Fallbrook Avenue, Ste. 102, Fresno, CA   93711

CEO: Michael Patrick George, CEO	Tel: (559) 437-1990	%FO: 100
Bus: *Provides water services.*	Fax: (559) 437-1992	

● **ALTADIS, S.A.**
10 Eloy Gonzalo, E-28010 Madrid, Spain

CEO: Pablo Isla, CEO	Tel: 34-91-360-9000	Rev: $2,639
Bus: *Mfr. premium cigars and cigarettes.*	Fax: 34-91-360-9100	Emp: 22,288
	www.altadis.com	

    ALTADIS USA, INC.
    5900 N. Andrews Avenue, Ft. Lauderdale, FL   33309-2369

CEO: Theo W. Folz, CEO	Tel: (954) 772-9000	%FO: 100
Bus: *Mfr. premium cigars.*	Fax: (954) 938-7811	

● **AMADEUS GLOBAL TRAVEL DISTRIBUTION, S.A.**
Salvador de Madariaga 1, E- 28027 Madrid, Spain
SpainMadrid, Spain

CEO: Jose A. Tazon, CEO	Tel: 34-915-820-100	Rev: $1,366
Bus: *Engaged in travel, ticketing, e-commerce and business to business services.*	Fax: 34-915-820-188	Emp: 3,200
	www.amadeuslink.com	

    AMADEUS GLOBAL TRAVEL DISTRIBUTION
    9250 North West 36th Street, Miami, FL   33178

CEO: Tony McKinnon, Pres. & CEO	Tel: (305) 499-6448	%FO: 100
Bus: *Engaged in travel, ticketing, e-commerce and business to business services.*	Fax: (305) 499-6866	

● **BANCO ATLANTICO, S.A.**
Avenita Diagonal 407, E-08008 Barcelona, Spain

CEO: Olimpio Fernandez, Dir.	Tel: 34-91-538-9084	Rev: $598
Bus: *Commercial banking services.*	Fax: 34-91-538-9568	Emp: 2,909
	www.batlantico.es	

    BANCO ATLANTICO, S.A.
    62 Williams Street, New York, NY   10005

CEO: Felipe Valbuena, Mgr.	Tel: (212) 422-3400	%FO: 100
Bus: *International banking services.*	Fax: (212) 742-9438	Emp: 45

- **BANCO BILBAO VIZCAYA ARGENTARIA, S.A.**
  Gran Via 1, E-48001 Bilbao, Viscaya, Spain

  CEO: Emilio de Ybara y Churruca, Chmn. &   Tel: 34-94-487-5555   Rev: $24,321
  CEO

  Bus: *International banking and financial*   Fax: 34-94-487-6161   Emp: 89,235
  services.   www.bbv.es

  ### BANCO DE BILBAO VIZCAYA, S.A.
  1345 Avenue of the Americas, 45th Fl., New York, NY   10105

  CEO: Raul Santoro, EVP   Tel: (212) 728-1500   %FO: 100

  Bus: *International banking and*   Fax: (212) 333-2906
  financial services.

  ### BBVA SECURITIES, INC.
  1345 Avenue of the Americas, 45th Fl., New York, NY   10105

  CEO: Ignacio Garijo, COO   Tel: (212) 728-1500   %FO: 100

  Bus: *Broker dealer securities.*   Fax: (212) 333-2906

- **BANCO ESPANOL DE CREDITO SA**
  Alcala 14, E-28014 Madrid, Spain

  CEO: Alfredo Sáenz, Pres.   Tel: 34-91-338-1000   Rev: $2,862

  Bus: *Commercial banking services.*   Fax: 34-91-262-8410   Emp: 13,190
                                                 www.banesto.es

  ### BANCO ESPAÑOL DE CRÉDITO
  730 Fifth Avenue, New York, NY   10019

  CEO: Luis Basagoiti, EVP   Tel: (212) 835-5300   %FO: 100

  Bus: *International commercial banking*   Fax: (212) 262-8410
  services.

- **BANCO SANTANDER CENTRAL HISPANO, S.A.**
  1 Plaza de Canalejas, E-28014 Madrid, Spain

  CEO: Ángel Corcóstegui Guraya, ceo   Tel: 34-91-558-1031   Rev: $24,332

  Bus: *Banking and investment products.*   Fax: 34-91-552-6670   Emp: 95,442
                                                 www.bancosantander.es

  ### BANCO SANTANDER CENTRAL HISPANO, S.A.
  45 East 53rd Street, New York, NY   10022

  CEO: Gonzalo De Las Heras, SVP   Tel: (212) 350-3699   %FO: 100

  Bus: *International banking services.*   Fax: (212) 350-3698

  ### BANCO SANTANDER INTERNATIONAL
  1401 Brickell Avenue, Ste. 1500, Miami, FL   33131

  CEO: Fernando Perez Hickman, Dir.   Tel: (305) 530-2930   %FO: 100

  Bus: *Private banking.*   Fax: (305) 530-2976   Emp: 130

● **BBVA INTERNATIONAL (BANCO BILBAO VIZCAYA ARGENTARIA)**
Pedro Rodríguez Tamayo, Pº Recoletos, 8, E-28001 Madrid, Spain
CEO: Francisco Gonzalez Rodriguez, CEO   Tel: 34-91-537-7000   Rev: $80,500
Bus: *Commercial banking services.*   Fax: 34-91-537-7805   Emp: 15,000
www.argentaria.es

    BANCO EXTERIOR DE ESPANA
    320 Park Avenue, 20th Fl., New York, NY   10022
    CEO: Jose Ignacio Leyun, Gen. Mgr.   Tel: (212) 605-7400   %FO: 100
    Bus: *Commercial banking; regional*   Fax: (212) 754-9306   Emp: 10
        office.

    BANCO EXTERIOR DE ESPANA
    701 Brickell Avenue, Ste. 1350, Miami, FL   33131
    CEO: Javier Barrutia, Gen. Mgr.   Tel: (305) 371-5008   %FO: 100
    Bus: *Commercial banking; regional*   Fax: (305) 371-5008
        office.

● **BERMARMOL SA**
Paraje Ledua 1, E-03660 Novelda, Spain
CEO: Manuel Fernandez-Cachorro   Tel: 34-96-560-0512   Rev: $4,200
Bus: *Distributes stone and marble.*   Fax: 34-96-560-5817   Emp: 215
www.bermarmol.es

    MB MARBLE & GRANITE COMPANY, INC.
    20005 South Rancho Way, Rancho Dominguez, CA   90220
    CEO: Javier Alfaro, VP & Gen.Mgr.   Tel: (310) 886-1844   %FO: 100
    Bus: *Natural stone distribution.*   Fax: (310) 886-0004   Emp: 6

● **CARRERA Y CARRERA, S.A.**
A.P. Correos 1 km 31.5 NI, E-28750 San Augustin de Guada, Spain
CEO: Manuel Carrera, CEO   Tel: 34-91-843-5193
Bus: *Manufacturer of gift items.*   Fax: 34-91-843-5825
www.carreraycarrera.com

    CARRERA Y CARRERA, INC.
    3 Bayberry Lane, Westport, CT   06880-4026
    CEO: R. Cristobal, Pres.   Tel: (203) 256-9461   %FO: 100
    Bus: *Sales of jewelry.*   Fax: (203) 227-8923   Emp: 5

● **CEMENTOS PORTLAND SA**
Calle Estella 6, E-31002 Pamplona, Navarra, Spain
CEO: Rafael Martinez, CEO   Tel: 34-948-42-6200   Rev: $426
Bus: *Engaged in the production and*   Fax: 34-948-10-6210   Emp: 1,715
    distribution of cement.   www.valderrivas.es

GIANT CEMENT HOLDING
320-D Midland Parkway, Summerville, SC   29485
CEO: Terry Kinder   Tel: (843) 851-9898   %FO: 100
Bus: *Engaged in the production and*   Fax: (843) 851-9881
    distribution of cement.

● **CHUPA CHUPS SA**
Avenida Diagonal 662, E-08034 Barcelona, Spain
CEO: Enric Bernat, Pres.   Tel: 34-3-495-2727
Bus: *Mfr. candy.*   Fax: 34-3-495-2707   Emp: 600
                                www.chupachups.com

   CHUPA CHUPS, USA
   1200 Abernathy Road NE, Ste. 1550, Atlanta, GA   30328
   CEO: Allan Slimming, VP   Tel: (770) 481-0440   %FO: 100
   Bus: *Candy distribution and product*   Fax: (770) 481-0340   Emp: 20
       development.

● **CODORNIU, S.A.**
Gran Via 644, E-08007 Barcelona, Spain
CEO: Jordi Raventos, CEO   Tel: 34-93-505-1551
Bus: *Mfr. wines.*   Fax: 34-93-317-9678
                                www.cordorniu.es

   CODORNIU NAPA INC.
   1345 Henry Road, Napa, CA   94558
   CEO: Michael Kenton, Pres.   Tel: (702) 224-1668   %FO: 100
   Bus: *Production/bottling wines.*   Fax: (702) 224-1672

● **ENDESA, S.A.**
Principe de Vergara 187, E-28002 Madrid, Spain
CEO: Rafael Miranda Robredo, CEO   Tel: 34-91-566-8800   Rev: $14,099
Bus: *Mines/produces coal; generates*   Fax: 34-91-563-8181   Emp: 29,000
    energy/electricity.   www.endesa.es

   ENDESA
   350 Park Avenue, 25th Fl., New York, NY   10022
   CEO: Jacinto Pariente, Dir.   Tel: (212) 750-7200   %FO: 100
   Bus: *Mines/produces coal; generates*   Fax: (212) 750-7433
       energy/electricity.

● **GARRIGUES & ANDERSEN**
José Abascal, 45, E-28003 Madrid, Spain
CEO: José María Alonso   Tel: 34-91-456-9800
Bus: *International law firm.*   Fax: 34-91-399-2408   Emp: 1,036
                                www.andersenlegal.com

GARRIGUES & ANDERSEN
115 East 57th Street, Ste.1230, New York, NY 10022
CEO: Miguel Gordillo   Tel: (212) 751-9233   %FO: 100
Bus: *International law firm.*   Fax: (212) 355-3594

● GRUPO DURO FELGUERA, SA
Calle Marques de Santa Cruz 14, E-33007 Oviedo, Asturias, Spain
CEO: Ramon Calao Caicoy, Pres.   Tel: 34-985-22-9700   Rev: $185
Bus: *Engaged in manufacturing and mining and material handling.*   Fax: 34-985-21-9339   Emp: 2,000
www.gdfsa.es

GRUPO DURO FELGUERA
205 Cadiz Court, Merritt Island, FL 32953
CEO: Florention Fernandez del Valle   Tel: (321) 452-6162   %FO: 100
Bus: *Engaged in mining and material handling.*   Fax: (321) 453-1170

● GRUPO PICKING PACK, SA
Calle Solsones 2, planta 3 Esc. B, Edi Muntades, E-08820 El Prat de Llobregat, Barcelona, Spain
CEO: Carlo U. Bonomi, CEO   Tel: 34-93-508-2424   Rev: $195
Bus: *Provides outsourcing services.*   Fax: 34-93-508-1212   Emp: 2,000
www.pickingpack.et

CHARRETTE INC.
31 Olympia Avenue, Woburn, MA 01801
CEO: Jack Ford   Tel: (781) 935-6000   %FO: 100
Bus: *Provides outsourcing services.*   Fax: (781) 938-1516

CHARRETTE PROGRAPHIC
285 Summer Street, Boston, MA 02210
CEO: Mike McFadyen   Tel: (617) 439-9981   %FO: 100
Bus: *Provides outsourcing services.*   Fax: (617) 428-3795

CHARRETTE PROGRAPHIC
629 Highland Avenue, Needham, MA 02494
CEO: David Gudejko   Tel: (781) 453-4013   %FO: 100
Bus: *Provides outsourcing services.*   Fax: (781) 536-6947

CHARRETTE PROGRAPHIC
545 Boylston Street, Boston, MA 02116
CEO: Heidi Houldcroft   Tel: (617) 859-0989   %FO: 100
Bus: *Provides outsourcing services.*   Fax: (617) 267-5236

CHARRETTE PROGRAPHIC
1000 Massachusetts Avenue, Cambridge, MA 02139
CEO: Vincent Kennedy   Tel: (617) 495-0235   %FO: 100
Bus: *Provides outsourcing services.*   Fax: (617) 492-7145

- **IBERIA AIRLINES (LINIAS AEREAS DE ESPANA)**
Calle Velasquez 130, E-28006 Madrid, Spain
CEO: Xabier de Irala Estevez, Pres.   Tel: 34-91-587-8787   Rev: $3,915
Bus: *International air transport.*   Fax: 34-91-587-7469   Emp: 29,080
                                        www.iberia.com

    IBERIA AIRLINES OF SPAIN
    6100 Blue Lagoon Dr, Ste. 200, Miami, FL 33126-2086
    CEO: Silvia Cairo, Mgr.   Tel: (305) 267-7747   %FO: 100
    Bus: *International air transport.*   Fax: (305) 267-9401   Emp: 20,000

- **INDITEX, S.A.**
Edificio Inditex, Avenida de la Diputación, E-15142 Arteixo, La Coruña, Spain
CEO: José María Castellano Ríos, CEO   Tel: 34-981-18-54-00   Rev: $2,422
Bus: *Clothing (men/women/children)*   Fax: 34-981-18-54-54   Emp: 24,000
manufacture and distribution to Inditex   www.inditex.com
600 worldwide stores.

    ZARA INTERNATIONAL, INC.
    750 Lexington Avenue, New York, NY 10022
    CEO: Moises Costas, Mng. Dir.   Tel: (212) 355-1415   %FO: 100
    Bus: *Zara chain of fashion stores.*   Fax: (212) 754-1128   Emp: 225

- **INDRA SISTEMAS, SA**
Velazquez 132, E-8006 Madrid, Spain
CEO: Humberto Figarola, VC   Tel: 34-91-396-3300   Rev: $652
Bus: *Engaged in information technology.*   Fax: 34-91-396-3131   Emp: 6,360
                                        www.indra.es

    INDRA SISTEMAS USA INC.
    3251 Progress Drive, Ste. A, Orlando, FL 32826
    CEO: Juan Carlos Baena, CEO   Tel: (407) 737-2688   %FO: 100
    Bus: *Engaged in information*   Fax: (407) 737-2689
    technology.

- **INSTRUMENTATION LABORATORY S.p.A.**
Aragon 90, Barcelona E-08015, Spain
CEO: Jose M. Ruberalta, Chmn.   Tel: 34-93-401-0101   Rev: $252
Bus: *Mfr. clinical diagnostic equipment.*   Fax: 34-93-451-3745   Emp: 1,200
                                        www.ilww.com

    INSTRUMENTATION LABORATORY COMPANY
    113 Hartwell Avenue, PO Box 9113, Lexington, MA 02173-3190
    CEO: Jose Manent, Gen. Mgr.   Tel: (781) 861-0710   %FO: 100
    Bus: *Sales/distribution of blood, urine*   Fax: (781) 861-1908
    and tissue diagnostic products.

● **IVEX - INSTITUTO VALENCIANO DE LA EXPORTACIÓN**

Iplaza de America, 2, E-46004 Valencia, Spain

CEO: Carmen de Miguel, Mgr.   Tel: 34-96-395-2001

Bus: *Government owned export services*   Fax: 34-96-395-4274
provider.   www.ivex.es

   IVEX - INSTITUTO VALENCIANO DE LA EXPORTACIÓN

   675 Third Avenue, New York, NY   10017

   CEO: Eva Blasco, Dir.   Tel: (212) 922-9000   %FO: 100

   Bus: *Government owned export services* Fax: (212) 922-9012
   provider.

● **LLADRO COMERCIAL SA**

Crta. de Alboraya, s/n. Tavernes Blanques, E-46016 Valencia, Spain

CEO: Francisco Varea, Exec. Dir.   Tel: 34-96-185 01 77

Bus: *Mfr./sales/marketing of high quality,*   Fax: 34-96-186-0420   Emp: 2,000
hand-crafted porcelain figurines, vases,   www.lladro.com
lamps and sculptures.

   LLADRÓ USA, INC.

   43 West 57th Street, New York, NY   10019

   CEO: Antonio F. Vargas, CEO   Tel: (212) 838-9356   %FO: 100

   Bus: *Sales/marketing of high quality,*   Fax: (212) 758-1928
   hand-crafted porcelain figurines,
   vases, lamps and sculptures.

   LLADRÓ USA, INC.

   One Lladró Drive, Moonachie, NJ   07074

   CEO: Antonio F. Vargas, CEO   Tel: (201) 807-1177   %FO: 100

   Bus: *Sales/marketing of high quality,*   Fax: (201) 807-1089   Emp: 165
   hand-crafted porcelain figurines,
   vases, lamps and sculptures.

● **MESTRE INFANTIL, S.A.**

Alberdo 42, E-28029 Madrid, Spain

CEO: Morris Hallak, Pres.   Tel: 34-91-315-9276

Bus: *Fine children's clothing and footwear.*   Fax: 34-91-315-2870
                        www.icex.es

   YES OUI SI, INC.

   131 West 33rd Street, Ste. 904, New York, NY   10001

   CEO: Morris Hallak, Pres.   Tel: (212) 564-2620   %FO: 100

   Bus: *Fine children's clothing and*   Fax: (212) 564-2450
   footwear.

- **NATRA CACAO S.A.**
Autovia A-3 salida 343 Cami de Torrent s/n, E-46930 Quart de Poblet Valencia, Spain
CEO: German San Juan, Pres.   Tel: 34-96-159-7300
Bus: *Mfr. of cocoa derivatives.*   Fax: 34-96-192-0453   Emp: 100
                                        www.natro-group.com

    NATRA US, INC.
    2801 Ponce DeLeon Blvd., Ste. 1070, Coral Gables, FL 33134
    CEO:Martin Brabenec, Mng. Dir.   Tel: (305) 447-8999   %FO: 100
    Bus: *Mfr./distribution of cocoa*   Fax: (305) 447-0885   Emp: 4
        derivatives.

- **RICHEL SA**
Carretera de Cornelia 125, E-08950 Espligas del Llobregat Barcelona, Spain
CEO: Michel Catris, CEO   Tel: 34-3-470-3333
Bus: *Mfr. neckties and women's scarves.*   Fax: 34-3-470-3345   Emp: 115
                                        www.richel.es

    RICHEL USA, INC.
    730 Fifth Avenue, New York, NY 10019
    CEO:Juan Catris, Mgr.   Tel: (212) 315-0777   %FO: 100
    Bus: *Sales/distribution neckties and*   Fax: (212) 315-0664
        scarves.

- **SOCIEDAD GENERAL DE AUTORES Y EDITORES (SGAE)**
Fernando VI 4, E-28004 Madrid, Spain
CEO: Eduardo Bautista-Garcia, Pres.   Tel: 34-91-349-9550
Bus: *Music licensing organization.*   Fax: 34-91-310-2120
                                        www.sgae.es

    SOCIEDAD GENERAL DE AUTORES Y EDITORES (SGAE)
    240 East 47th Street, Ste. 12B, New York, NY 10017
    CEO:Emilio Garcia, Pres.   Tel: (212) 752-7230   %FO: 100
    Bus: *Music licensing organization.*   Fax: (212) 754-4378

- **TELEFONICA, SA**
Gran Via 28, E-28013 Madrid, Spain
CEO: Julio Linares Lopez, CEO   Tel: 34-91-584-4700   Rev: $27,940
Bus: *Engaged in telecommunications.*   Fax: 34-91-531-9347   Emp: 118,500
                                        www.telefonica.es

    QUOTE.COM, INC.
    850 N. Shoreline Blvd., Mountain View, CA 94043
    CEO:Kaj Pedersen, Mgr.   Tel: (650) 428-5000   %FO: 100
    Bus: *Financial Website.*   Fax: (650) 428-5000

● **TORRAS SA**

Via de Ronda s/n, Caldes de Montour, E-08140 Barcelona, Spain
CEO: Juan Serra, Pres.
Bus: *Mfr. leather and knit jackets and sweaters.*

Tel: 34-93-865-3636
Fax: 34-93-865-4442
www.torras.com

Emp: 400

   BCN FASHIONS, INC.

   PO Box 951, Suffern, NY 10901
   CEO: Mel Singer, Dir.
   Bus: *Sales/distribution leather and knit jackets/sweaters.*

   Tel: (914) 368-1775
   Fax: (914) 357-6590

   %FO: 100

● **TUBACEX, S.A.**

Tres Cruces, 8, E-01400 Llodio Alava, Spain
CEO: Alvaro Videgain Muro, CEO
Bus: *Metals and mining, steel production.*

Tel: 34-94-671-9300
Fax: 34-94-672-5062
www.tubacex.com

Rev: $161
Emp: 1,145

   ALTX, INC.

   Spring Street Road, PO Box 91, Watervliet, NY 12189
   CEO: Ingacio Telleria
   Bus: *Metals & mining, steel production.*

   Tel: (518) 273-4110
   Fax: (518) 273-4128

   %FO: 100

   SALEM TUBE INC.

   951 Fourth Street, Greenville, PA 16125
   CEO: Charles Redzinak
   Bus: *Metals & mining, steel production.*

   Tel: (724) 646-4301
   Fax: (724) 646-4311

   %FO: 100

   TUBACEX INC.

   North Freeway, Suite 100, Houston, TX 77060
   CEO: Olga Elman
   Bus: *Metals & mining, steel production.*

   Tel: (281) 875-8660
   Fax: (281) 875-8665

   %FO: 100

● **URÍA & MENÉNDEZ**

Jorge Juan 6, E-28001 Madrid, Spain
CEO: Jesús Remón
Bus: *International law firm.*

Tel: 34-91-586-0400
Fax: 34-91-586-0403
www.uria.com

   URÍA & MENÉNDEZ

   320 Park Avenue, 28th Fl., New York, NY 10022
   CEO: Eduardo Geli
   Bus: *International law firm (Spain).*

   Tel: (212) 593-1300
   Fax: (212) 593-7144

   %FO: 100

- **VISCOFAN INDUSTRIA, SA**
Iturrama, 23 Entreplanta, E-31007 Pamplona, Navarra, Spain
CEO: Jimenez Muniain, CEO   Tel: 34-948-198-444
Bus: *Mfr. sausage casings.*   Fax: 34-948-198-430   Emp: 3,750
    www.viscofan.com

    VISCOFAN USA INC.
    50 County Court, Montgomery, AL   36105
    CEO: Roger Allen, VP Sales   Tel: (334) 396-0092   %FO: 100
    Bus: *Mfr. cellulosic food casings.*   Fax: (334) 396-0094   Emp: 200

- **ZARA (INDUSTRIA DE DISENO TEXTIL, SA)**
Edificio Inditex, Ave. de la Diputacion, E-15142 Arteixo La Coruna, Spain
CEO: Jose Maria Castellano Rios, CEO   Tel: 34-981-18-5400
Bus: *Women's clothing chain store.*   Fax: 34-981-18-5454   Emp: 24,000
    www.indetex.com

    ZARA USA INC.
    101 Fifth Avenue, New York, NY   10021
    CEO: Paula Spagnoli, Mgr.   Tel: (212) 355-1415   %FO: 100
    Bus: *Sales clothing.*   Fax: (212) 741-0555

    ZARA USA INC.
    1400 Willowbrook Blvd., Wayne, NJ   07470
    CEO: Jackie Lee   Tel: (973) 785-4845   %FO: 100
    Bus: *Sales clothing.*   Fax: (973) 785-4845

Sweden

● **ABA OF SWEDEN AB**
Scheelegatan 28, SE-112 28 Stockholm, Sweden
CEO: Lars Nordin, Pres. Tel: 46-8-654-1400
Bus: *Mfr. hose clamps.* Fax: 46-8-653-3410 Emp: 250
  www.abagroup.com

ABA OF AMERICA INC
4004 Auburn Street, Rockford, IL 61101
CEO: Arne Stegvik, Pres. Tel: (815) 965-5170 %FO: JV
Bus: *Mfr. hose clamps.* Fax: (815) 965-7559 Emp: 10

● **ABS PUMP AB, SUB. CARDO GROUP**
Kroksiätts Parkgata 4, Box 2053, SE-431 21 Moindal, Sweden
CEO: Thomas Widstrand, Pres. Tel: 46-31-706-1600 Rev: $320
Bus: *Mfr./import/distributor of pumps for* Fax: 46-31-272920 Emp: 2,000
  municipal, industrial and residential www.abspumps.com
  markets.

ABS PUMPS, INC.
970 Garcia Avenue, Pittsburgh, CA 94565
CEO: Tom Fogerty, Mgr. Tel: (925) 427-6400 %FO: 100
Bus: *Sales/distribution of pumps for* Fax: (925) 427-6404
  municipal, industrial and
  residential markets.

ABS PUMPS, INC.
140 Pond View Drive, Meriden, CT 06450
CEO: Gerald A. Assessor, Pres. Tel: (203) 238-2700 %FO: 100
Bus: *Sales/distribution of pumps and* Fax: (203) 238-0738
  pumping equipment.

ABS PUMPS, INC.
949 Shadick Avenue, Orange City, FL 32763
CEO: Paul Robinson, Mgr. Tel: (904) 775-6353 %FO: 100
Bus: *Sales/distribution of pumps for* Fax: (904) 775-3272
  municipal, industrial and
  residential markets.

- **AGA AB**
SE-181 81 Lidingö, Sweden
CEO: Lennart Selander, Pres. & CEO
Bus: *Mfr./sale industrial and medical gases and equipment.*

Tel: 46-8-731-1000
Fax: 46-8-767-6344
www.aga.se

Rev: $1,740
Emp: 10,500

   AGA GAS INC.
   PO Box 94737, Cleveland, OH   44101-4737
   CEO: Patrick F. Murphy, Mgr.
   Bus: *Industrial gas & gas equipment.*

   Tel: (216) 642-6600
   Fax: (216) 642-8516

   %FO: 100
   Emp: 1,177

- **AIMPOINT AB**
Jagershillgatan 15, SE-213 75 Malmo, Sweden
CEO: Per Sandberg, Pres.
Bus: *Electronic gun sights and mounting systems; red dot sights.*

Tel: 46-40-21-0390
Fax: 46-40-21-9238
www.aimpoint.com

   AIMPOINT INC.
   7702 Leesburg Pike, Falls Church, VA   22043
   CEO: Susan G. Smart, Mgr.
   Bus: *Import electronic gun sights, mounting systems; red dot sights for the military*

   Tel: (703) 749-2320
   Fax: (703) 749-2323

   %FO: 100
   Emp: 7

- **AKAB OF SWEDEN AB**
Bussgatan 4, Viared, SE-504 94 Borås, Sweden
CEO: Jan Karrman, Mng. Dir.
Bus: *Mfr. automatic sewing machines for home textile industry.*

Tel: 46-33-233600
Fax: 46-33-136867
www.akab.com

Emp: 80

   AKAB OF AMERICA INC.
   4209 Pleasant Road, Fort Mill, SC   29715
   CEO: Rolf Stridh, Pres.
   Bus: *Mfr. automatic sewing machines for home textile industry, spare parts and service.*

   Tel: (803) 548-6815
   Fax: (803) 548-6820

   %FO: 100
   Emp: 7

- **ÅKERLUND & RAUSING, AB**
P O Box 546, SE-201 25 Malmö, Sweden
CEO: Mats Pousette, Pres. & CEO
Bus: *Mfr. flexible, food packaging solution systems.*

Tel: 46-46-18-3000
Fax: 46-46-18-3127
www.akerlund-rausing.com

Rev: $347
Emp: 1,000

ÅKERLUND & RAUSING N.A., INC.

3450 Corporate Way, Ste. C, Duluth, GA   30136

CEO: Deborah Arnstein, Controller	Tel: (770) 623-8235	%FO: 100
Bus: *Food packaging systems.*	Fax: (770) 623-8236	Emp: 10

• ÅKERS INTERNATIONAL AB, DIV. INTER SCAN GROUP

SE-640 60 Åkers Styckebruk, Sweden

CEO: Ingvar Lundberg, Pres. & CEO	Tel: 46-159-32100	Rev: $257
Bus: *Mfr./marketing cast and forged steel rolls.*	Fax: 46-159-32101	Emp: 300
	www.akersrolls.com	

ÅKERS AMERICA INC

58 South Main Street, Ste. 4, Poland, OH   44514-1978

CEO: William D. Bigley, Pres.	Tel: (330) 757-4100	%FO: 100
Bus: *Mfr./sale cast and forged steel rolls.*	Fax: (330) 757-4235	

ÅKERS HYDE PARK FOUNDRY

326 First Avenue, Hyde Park, PA   15618

CEO: Andy Blaskovich, Pres.	Tel: (724) 842-1941	%FO: 100
Bus: *Mfr./sale cast and forged steel rolls.*	Fax: (724) 845-8865	

ÅKERS NATIONAL ROLL COMPANY

400 Railroad Avenue, Avonmore, PA   15641

CEO: Andy Blaskovich, Pres.	Tel: (724) 697-4533	%FO: 100
Bus: *Mfr./sale cast and forged steel rolls.*	Fax: (724) 697-4319	

ÅKERS VERTICAL SEAL COMPANY

RD 1, Box 147, Pleasantville, PA   16341

CEO: Andy Blaskovich, Pres.	Tel: (814) 589-7031	%FO: 100
Bus: *Mfr./sale cast and forged steel rolls and repair of mill components.*	Fax: (814) 589-7628	

• ALFA LAVAL AB

Borgen, Landerigrand, Ruben Rausings Gata, SE-221 86 Lund, Sweden

CEO: Sigge Haraldsson, CEO	Tel: 46-46-36-7000	Rev: $430
Bus: *Mfr., engineering and design services for diversified industrial systems.*	Fax: 46-46-36-4950	Emp: 11,000
	www.alfalaval.com	

ALFA LAVAL FLOW INC.

16516 Air Center Boulevard, Houston, TX   77032

CEO: Brian Tripoli, Pres.	Tel: (281) 443-0000	%FO: 100
Bus: *Sales/distribution valves.*	Fax: (281) 230-2121	

ALFA LAVAL FLOW, INC., INDUSTRIAL PUMP DIV.
PO Box 581909, Pleasant Prairie, WI 53158
CEO: Sammy Mulpiau, Pres.   Tel: (262) 947-8124   %FO: 100
Bus: *Marketing/distribution pumps.*   Fax: (262) 947-8126

ALFA LAVAL INC.
9201 Wilmot Road, PO Box 840, Kenosha, WI 53141-0840
CEO: Kirk Spitzer, Pres.   Tel: (262) 942-9315   %FO: 100
Bus: *U.S. headquarters. Engineering* Fax: (262) 942-3776
    and design services for diversified
    industrial systems.

ALFA LAVAL SEPARATION INC.
955 Mearns Road, Warminster, PA 18974-9998
CEO: Yannick Richomme, Pres.   Tel: (215) 443-4000   %FO: 100
Bus: *Mfr./marketing centrifuges.*   Fax: (215) 443-4205   Emp: 516

ALFA LAVAL THERMAL INC.
5400 International Trade Drive, Richmond, VA 23231
CEO: Sven Sjogren, Pres.   Tel: (804) 222-5300   %FO: 100
Bus: *Mfr./marketing plate heat* Fax: (804) 236-1333
    exchangers.

ALFA LAVAL THERMAL INC.
111 Parker Street, Newburyport, MA 01950
CEO: Dinko Mutak, Pres.   Tel: (978) 465-5777   %FO: 100
Bus: *Mfr./marketing plate heat* Fax: (978) 465-6006
    exchangers.

TRI-CLOVER INC.
PO Box 1413, Kenosha, WI 53141-1413
CEO: Keith Potts, Pres.   Tel: (262) 694-5511   %FO: 100
Bus: *Mfr. sanitary stainless steel* Fax: (262) 694-3173
    pumps, valves, fittings for food,
    pharmaceutical & biotech
    industries.

• ALIMAK AB
Box 720, SE-931 27 Skellefteå, Sweden
CEO: Krister Kempainen, Pres.   Tel: 46-910-87000
Bus: *Mfr. rack and pinion industrial and* Fax: 49-910-56690   Emp: 562
    passenger service elevators and mast www.alimak.com
    climbing work platforms.

ALIMAK ELEVATOR COMPANY

3040 Amwiler Road, Atlanta, GA   30360

CEO: Hans-Olof Lofstrand, Mgr.　　　Tel: (770) 441-9055　　　%FO: 100

Bus: *Distribution/service industrial and*　Fax: (770) 441-9095
passenger service elevators.

ALIMAK ELEVATOR COMPANY

1951-1 Johns Drive, PO Box 628, Glenview, IL   60025

CEO: John E. Dreyzehner, Mgr.　　　Tel: (847) 998-4646　　　%FO: 100

Bus: *Sales/distribution of industrial*　Fax: (847) 998-4660
rack and pinion elevators.

ALIMAK ELEVATOR COMPANY

16920 Texas Avenue, Ste. C-14, Webster, TX   77598

CEO: Tony Whaley, Mgr.　　　Tel: (281) 338-1114　　　%FO: 100

Bus: *Distribution/service industrial and*　Fax: (281) 338-0019
passenger service elevators.

ALIMAK ELEVATOR COMPANY

11912 Rivera Road, Unit E, Santa Fe Springs, CA   90670

CEO: Burt Zimmerling, Mgr.　　　Tel: (562) 698-2571　　　%FO: 100

Bus: *Distribution/service industrial and*　Fax: (562) 698-5513
passenger service elevators.

ALIMAK ELEVATOR COMPANY

1100 Boston Avenue, PO Box 1950, Bridgeport, CT   06601

CEO: Mike Repko, VP　　　Tel: (203) 367-7400　　　%FO: 100

Bus: *Distribution/service industrial and*　Fax: (203) 367-9251　　Emp: 80
passenger service elevators.

● **ALLGON AB**

Antennvägen 6, SE-187 80 Täby, Sweden

CEO: Lars Spongberg, CEO　　　Tel: 46-8-540-822-00

Bus: *Mfr. wireless equipment for*　Fax: 46-8-540-824-91　　Emp: 1,335
communications systems.　www.allgon.com

ALLGON TELECO LTD.

15051 FAA Boulevard, Ft. Worth, TX   76155

CEO: Stellan Ohrn, VP　　　Tel: (817) 684-4500　　　%FO: 100

Bus: *Mfr. wireless equipment for*　Fax: (817) 684-3500
communications systems.

● **AMERICAN SCANDINAVIAN STUDENT EXCHANGE (ASSE)**

Kindstugatan 1, Box 2017, SE-103 Stockholm, Sweden

CEO: Lena Bello, Mgr.　　　Tel: 46-8-230300

Bus: *Educational services.*　Fax: 46-8-240543　　Emp: 200

www.asse.com

ASPECT, INC.
350 Samsone Street, San Francisco, CA   94103
CEO: Tom Ericcson, Pres.   Tel: (415) 228-8000
Bus: *Worldwide educational*   Fax: (415) 228-8200   Emp: 100
     organization providing innovative,
     high-quality programs.

• APBIOTECH INC.
SE-751 84, Uppsala, Sweden
CEO: William M. Castell, Chmn.   Tel: 46-18-612-0000
Bus: *Mfr. equipment/supplies for*   Fax: 46-18-612-1200
     biotechnology and drug development. www.apbiotech.com
     (JV of Nycomed Amersham and
     Pharmacia).

APBIOTECH INC.
800 Centennial Ave., PO Box 1327, Piscataway, NJ   08855
CEO: Peter Coggins, CEO   Tel: (732) 457-8000   %FO: JV
Bus: *Mfr. Equipment/supplies for*   Fax: (732) 457-8000
     biotechnology and drug
     development. (JV of Nycomed
     Amersham and Pharmacia).

• ASKO CYLINDA AB
Jung, SE-534 82 Vara, Sweden
CEO: Hans Linnarson, Pres.   Tel: 46-512-32000   Rev: $20
Bus: *Household appliances, including steel* Fax: 46-512-22303   Emp: 100
     dishwashers, washers and dryers. www.asko.se

AM APPLIANCE GROUP
1161 Executive Drive West, PO Box 851805, Richardson, TX   75085
CEO: Joe Yoder   Tel: (972) 644-8595   %FO: 100
Bus: *Sales of dishwashers,*   Fax: (972) 644-8593   Emp: 20
     washers/dryers.

• ASSA ABLOY AB
Klarabergsviadukten 90, Box 70340, SE-107 23 Stockholm, Sweden
CEO: Carl-Henric Svanberg, Pres.   Tel: 46-8-698-8550   Rev: $1,178
Bus: *Mfr./sales door locks and hardware* Fax: 46-8-698-8585   Emp: 12,654
     products.   www.assaabloy.se

ARROW LOCK COMPANY, DIV. ASSA ABLOY
103-00 Foster Avenue, Brooklyn, NY   11236
CEO: Charles Armstrong, Pres.   Tel: (718) 257-4700   %FO: 100
Bus: *Sales/distribution of lock*   Fax: (718) 257-3299
     cylinders, deadlocks and door
     hardware products.

CURRIES GRAHAM COMPANY
1502 12th Street NW, Mason City, IA   50401
CEO: Jerry N. Currie, Pres. & CEO   Tel: (641) 423-1334   %FO: 100
Bus: *Mfr. residential security locks and*   Fax: (641) 424-8305
products.

SECURITRON MAGNALOCK CORP.
550 Vista Boulevard, Sparks, NV   89434
CEO: Bob Cook, Pres.   Tel: (775) 355-5625   %FO: 100
Bus: *Sales/distribution of lock*   Fax: (775) 355-5636
cylinders, deadlocks and door
hardware products.

YALE RESIDENTIAL SECURITY PRODUCTS, INC.
2725B Northwood Parkway, Norcross, GA   30017
CEO: Craig Dorsher, Pres.   Tel: (678) 728-7400   %FO: 100
Bus: *Mfr. residential security locks and*   Fax: (678) 728-7446
products.

YALE SECURITY CORP.
1902 Airport Road, Monroe, NC   28110
CEO: Claus Thelin, Pres.   Tel: (704) 283-2101   %FO: 100
Bus: *Mfr. architectural hardware and*   Fax: (704) 289-2875
security systems.

● ATLAS COPCO AB
SE-105 23 Stockholm, Sweden
CEO: Giulio Mazzalupi, Pres. & CEO   Tel: 46-8-743-8000   Rev: $4,226
Bus: *Mfr. power tools, mining and*   Fax: 46-8-644-9045   Emp: 23,393
construction equipment, pneumatic   www.atlascopco.com
tools, assembly systems.

ATLAS COPCO NORTH AMERICA, INC.
34 Maple Avenue, Pine Brook, NJ   07058
CEO: Mark Cohen, Pres.   Tel: (973) 439-3400   %FO: 100
Bus: *Mfr. compressors, mining*   Fax: (973) 439-9188   Emp: 2,000
construction equipment, pneumatic
tools, assembly systems.

ATLAS COPCO TOOLS, INC.
37735 Enterprise Court, Suite 300, Farmington Hills, MI   48331
CEO: Fredrik Moller, Pres.   Tel: (248) 489-1260   %FO: 100
Bus: *Mfr./distribution*   Fax: (248) 489-1260   Emp: 130
pneumatic/electric industrial
power tools.

ATLAS COPCO WAGNER, INC.
PO Box 20307, Portland, OR   97220-0307

CEO: John Noordwijk, Pres.	Tel: (503) 255-2863	%FO: 100
Bus: *Mfr./sale heavy mining/construction equipment.*	Fax: (503) 255-7075	

CHICAGO PNEUMATIC TOOL COMPANY
1800 Overview Drive, Rock Hill, SC   29730-7463

CEO: Charles Robison, Pres.	Tel: (803) 817-7000	%FO: 100
Bus: *Pneumatic & electric power tools, light construction equipment.*	Fax: (803) 817-7036	Emp: 1,700

MILWAUKEE ELECTRIC TOOL
13135 West Lisbon Road, Brookfield, WI   53005

CEO: Richard Grove, Pres.	Tel: (262) 781-3600	%FO: 100
Bus: *Mfr. heavy-duty tools.*	Fax: (262) 781-3611	

● ATLET AB
SE-435 82 Mölnlycke, Sweden

CEO: Marianne Nilson, Mng. Dir.	Tel: 46-31-984000	
Bus: *Mfr. lift trucks.*	Fax: 46-31-884686	Emp: 775
	www.atlet.se	

ATLET INC.
502 Pratt Avenue North, Schaumburg, IL   60173

CEO: Larry Couperthwaite, Pres.	Tel: (847) 352-7373	%FO: JV
Bus: *Sale/service lift trucks.*	Fax: (847) 352-8001	Emp: 15

● AUTOLIV INC.
World Trade Center, Klarabergsviadukten 70, PO Box 70381, SE-107 24 Stockholm, Sweden

CEO: Lars Westerberg, CEO	Tel: 46-8-587-20600	Rev: $4,116
Bus: *Mfr. car safety equipment, including airbags and seat belts.*	Fax: 46-8-411-7025	Emp: 30,000
	www.autoliv.com	

AUTOLIV ASP, INC.
3350 Airport Road, Ogden, UT   84405-1563

CEO: Tom Hartman, Pres.	Tel: (801) 625-9200	%FO: 100
Bus: *Sales/distribution car safety equipment, including airbags and seat belts.*	Fax: (801) 625-4911	

AUTOLIV NORTH AMERICA
1000 West 3300 South, Ogde, UT   84401

CEO: Jonathan Sommer	Tel: (801) 629-9800	%FO: 100
Bus: *Airbag module facility.*	Fax: (801) 629-9619	

AUTOLIV NORTH AMERICA
3250 Pennsylvania Avenue, Ogden, UT   84401
CEO: Tom Hartman, Pres.   Tel: (801) 625-9800   %FO: 100
Bus: *Sales/distribution car safety*   Fax: (801) 629-9619
     equipment, including airbags and
     seat belts.

AUTOLIV NORTH AMERICA
281 Enterprise Court, Ste. 100, Bloomfield Hills, MI   48302
CEO: Lars Westerberg   Tel: (248) 338-4959   %FO: 100
Bus: *Sales/distribution car safety*   Fax: (248) 338-3208
     equipment, including airbags and
     seat belts.

AUTOLIV NORTH AMERICA
2910 Waterview Drive, Rochester Hills, MI   48309
CEO: Ray Pekar, Mgr.   Tel: (248) 853-8600   %FO: 100
Bus: *Sales/distribution car safety*   Fax: (248) 853-8620
     equipment, including airbags and
     seat belts.

AUTOLIV NORTH AMERICA
1320 Pacific Drive, Auburn Hills, MI   48326-1569
CEO: Barry Murphy   Tel: (248) 475-9000   %FO: 100
Bus: *Technical center.*   Fax: (248) 475-9044

AUTOLIV NORTH AMERICA
PO Box 100488, Denver, CO   80250
CEO: Troy Hanks   Tel: (303) 693-1248   %FO: 100
Bus: *Mfr. inflators.*   Fax: (303) 699-6991

AUTOLIV NORTH AMERICA, SEAT BELT DIV.
5851 West 80th Street, Indianapolis, IN   46278-1321
CEO: Peter Tomsing, Mgr.   Tel: (317) 875-7579
Bus: *Mfr./distribution seat belts.*   Fax: (317) 875-8171

AUTOLIV, INC.
410 Autoliv Belt Way, Madisonville, KY   42431
CEO: Mike Ward   Tel: (270) 825-9809   %FO: 100
Bus: *Mfr. seat belts.*   Fax: (270) 825-9809

QAUTOLIV NORTH AMERICA, STEERING WHEEL DIV.
4868 East Park 30 Drive, Columbia City, IN   46725
CEO: Erv Glass, Mgr.   Tel: (219) 244-4941
Bus: *Mfr./distribution steering wheels.*   Fax: (219) 244-4951

- **AXEL JOHNSON AB**

Villagatan 6, Box 26008, SE-100 41 Stockholm, Sweden

CEO: Göran Ennerfelt, Pres.   Tel: 46-8-701-6100   Rev: $763

Bus: *Mfr. industrial machinery.*   Fax: 46-8-701-6159   Emp: 3,358

www.axel-johnson.se

    AXEL JOHNSON INC

    300 Atlantic Street, Stamford, CT   06901

    CEO: Lawrence D. Milligan, CEO   Tel: (203) 326-5200   %FO: 100

    Bus: *Mfr./sales/service industrial*   Fax: (203) 326-5280
          machinery.

    HEKIMIAN LABORATORIES, INC.

    15200 Omega Drive, Rockville, MD   20850-3240

    CEO: Desmond P. Wilson III, Pres.   Tel: (301) 590-3600   %FO: 100

    Bus: *Mfr./sales/service industrial*   Fax: (310) 590-3599
          electronic machinery.

    LARSCOM INC.

    1845 McCandless Drive, Milpitas, CA   95035

    CEO: Robert Coackley, CEO   Tel: (408) 941-4000   %FO: 100

    Bus: *Mfr./sales/service*   Fax: (408) 956-0118
          telecommunications equipment.

    PARKSON CORPORATION

    2727 Northwest 62nd St., Ft. Lauderdale, FL   33309-1171

    CEO: William C. Acton, Pres.   Tel: (954) 974-6610   %FO: 100

    Bus: *Mfr./sales/service liquids and*   Fax: (954) 974-6182
          solids separation devices and
          aeration systems for the treatment
          of water.

    SPRAGUE ENERGY CORPORATION

    Two International Drive, Ste. 200, Portsmouth, NH   03801-6809

    CEO: James M. Kantells, Pres.   Tel: (603) 431-1000   %FO: 100

    Bus: *Mkt. Heavy fuel oil, coal, jet fuel,*   Fax: (603) 431-5324
          gasoline and provides bulk
          material handling services.

- **AXIS COMMUNICATIONS AB**

Scheelevägen 34, Ideon, SE-223 63 Lund, Sweden

CEO: Peter Ragnarsson, Pres. & CEO   Tel: 46-46-2721800

Bus: *Mfr. computer and office equipment.*   Fax: 46-46-136130   Emp: 100

www.axis.se

AXIS COMMUNICATIONS INC.
100 Apollo Drive, Chelmsford, MA   01824

CEO: Peter Ragnarsson, Pres.   Tel: (978) 614-2000   %FO: 100
Bus: *Computer and office equipment.*   Fax: (978) 614-2100

AXIS COMMUNICATIONS INC.
2655 South Bayshore Drive, Ste. 302, Miami, MI   33133

CEO: Peter Ragnarsson, Pres.   Tel: (305) 860-8226   %FO: 100
Bus: *Computer and office equipment.*   Fax: (305) 860-9266

AXIS COMMUNICATIONS INC.
800 El Camino Real, Ste. 180, Mountain View, CA   94040

CEO: Bengt Christensson, VP   Tel: (650) 903-2221   %FO: 100
Bus: *Computer and office equipment.*   Fax: (650) 903-2224   Emp: 100

● BESAM AB
Lodjursgatan 10, Box 131, SE-261 22 Landskrona, Sweden

CEO: Bertil Samuelsson, Pres.   Tel: 46-418-51000   Rev: $1,951
Bus: *Mfr. automatic swing, slide, folding and*   Fax: 46-418-23800   Emp: 11,000
revolving doors.   www.besam.com

BESAM AUTOMATED ENTRANCE SYSTEMS, INC.
84 Twin Rivers Drive, Hightstown, NJ   08520

CEO: Joseph Loria, Pres.   Tel: (609) 443-5800   %FO: 100
Bus: *Sales/distribution of automatic*   Fax: (609) 443-3440
door systems.

● BINDOMATIC AB
Vretenborgsvägen 9, Box 42101, SE-126 12 Stockholm, Sweden

CEO: Sture Wiholm, Mng. Dir.   Tel: 46-8-709-5800
Bus: *Mfr. binding systems.*   Fax: 46-8-188-652
                                     www.bindomatic.se

COVERBIND CORP
3200 Corporate Drive, Wilmington, NC   28405

CEO: Howard Wilkes, Mgr.   Tel: (910) 799-4116   %FO: 100
Bus: *Mfr. binding systems.*   Fax: (910) 799-3935

● BIORA AB
Medeon Science Park, SE-205 12 Malmo, Sweden

CEO: Rickard Söderberg, CEO   Tel: 46-40-32-1340   Rev: $10
Bus: *Mfr. products for treatment of*   Fax: 46-40-32-1335   Emp: 75
periodontal disease and products used   www.biora.se
during oral surgery.

BIORA, INC.
415 North LaSalle Street, Ste. 615, Chicago, IL   60610
CEO: Maria Nyholm   Tel: (312) 832-1414   %FO: 100
Bus: *Mfr. products for use during oral*   Fax: (312) 832-1429
surgery and for treatment of
periodontal disease.

• BRIO AB
Västra Järnvägsgatan 9, Box 3, SE-283 00 Osby, Sweden
CEO: Tomas Persson, CEO   Tel: 46-479-19000   Rev: $200
Bus: *Mfr./marketing specialty toys.*   Fax: 46-479-14124   Emp: 1,075
www.brio.se

BRIO CORP
North 120 W.18485 Freistadt Road, Germantown, WI   53022
CEO: Peter F. Reynolds, Pres.   Tel: (262) 250-3240   %FO: 100
Bus: *Importer marketing/distribution*   Fax: (262) 250-3255   Emp: 30
toys.

• BROMMA CONQUIP AB
Krossgatan 31-33, SE-162 50 Vallingby, Sweden
CEO: Terry E. Howell, Mng. Dir.   Tel: 46-8-620-0900
Bus: *Mfr. spreaders and container handling*   Fax: 46-8-739-3786   Emp: 146
equipment.   www.bromma.com

BROMMA, INC.
2285 Durham Road, PO Box 451, Roxboro, NC   27573
CEO: Terry E. Howell, Pres.   Tel: (336) 599-3141   %FO: 100
Bus: *Mfr. container-handling*   Fax: (336) 599-4499
equipment & related attachments.

• BT INDUSTRIES AB, DIV. TOYOTA
Syarvargatan 8, SE-595 81 Mjolby, Sweden
CEO: Carl-Erik Ridderstråle, Pres. & CEO   Tel: 46-1-428-6000   Rev: $1,206
Bus: *Mfr. material handling trucks.*   Fax: 46-1-428-6080   Emp: 7,900
www.bt-industries.com

BP PRIME-MOVER INC.
3305 North Highway 38, Muscatine, IA   52761
CEO: Dick Lowendahl   Tel: (319) 262-7700   %FO: 100
Bus: *Mfr. electric lift trucks.*   Fax: (319) 262-7600

BT RAYMOND INC.
PO Box 130, South Canal Street, Greene, NY   12778
CEO: James J. Malvaso, Pres. & CEO   Tel: (607) 656-2311   %FO: 100
Bus: *Mfr. electric lift trucks.*   Fax: (607) 656-9005

CAROLINA HANDLING INC.

Airport Industrial Park, 3101 Piper Lane, Charlotte, NC   28241

CEO: Tim Hilton, Pres.
Tel: (704) 357-6273
%FO: 100

Bus: *Mfr. handling equipment.*
Fax: (704) 329-3858

DOCKSTOCKER CORPORATION

3305 North Highway 38, Muscatine, IA   52761-8800

CEO: Dick Lowendahl
Tel: (319) 262-7700
%FO: 100

Bus: *Mfr. material-handling equipment.*
Fax: (319) 262-7600
Emp: 300

RAYMOND LEASING CORPORATION

20 South Canal Street, Greene, NY   13778

CEO: Patrick McManus, Pres.
Tel: (607) 656-2458
%FO: 100

Bus: *Mfr. electric lift trucks.*
Fax: (607) 656-9005

● CARDO AB

Roskildevagen 1, Box 486, SE-201 24 Malmo, Sweden

CEO: Kjell Svensson, Pres. & CEO
Tel: 46-40-35-0400
Rev: $1,040

Bus: *Mfr. centrifugal pumps, doors, brake systems and garage doors.*
Fax: 46-40-97-6440
www.cardo.se
Emp: 8,135

ABS PUMPS, INC.

140 Pond View Drive, Meriden, CT   06450

CEO: Gerald Assesson, Pres.
Tel: (203) 238-2700
%FO: 100

Bus: *Mfr. centrifugal pumps.*
Fax: (203) 238-0738

PUMPEX, INC.

49 Molasses Hill Road, Lebanon, NJ   08833

CEO: Rob Montenagro, Pres.
Tel: (908) 730-7004
%FO: 100

Bus: *Mfr. submersible pumps.*
Fax: (908) 730-7580

● CARNEGIE HOLDING AB

Vastra Tradgardsgatan 15, SE-103 38 Stockholm, Sweden

CEO: Lars Bertmar, CEO
Tel: 46-8-676-8800

Bus: *Stockbroker, asset management services.*
Fax: 46-8-205783
www.carnegieholding.com
Emp: 908

CARNEGIE INC.

20 West 55th Street, New York, NY   10019

CEO: Tore Bjark, Pres.
Tel: (212) 262-5800
%FO: 100

Bus: *Stockbroker, investment management services.*
Fax: (212) 265-3946
Emp: 10

● **CAR-O-LINER AB**

Granlidsvigen 4, Box 7, SE-736 00 Kungsör, Sweden

CEO: Björn Ramberg, Pres.   Tel: 46-227-41200

Bus: *Mfr. collision repair equipment.*   Fax: 46-227-31900   Emp: 200

www.car-o-liner.com

CAR-O-LINER COMPANY

29900 Anthony Drive, Wixom, MI   48393-3609

CEO: Larry J. Carter, Pres.   Tel: (248) 624-5900   %FO: 100

Bus: *Distribution collision repair*   Fax: (248) 624-9529   Emp: 15
equipment.

● **CELLMARK GROUP**

Ö Hamngatan 17, PO Box 11927, SE-404 39 Gothenburg, Sweden

CEO: Hans Kling   Tel: 46-31-100300   Rev: $1,200

Bus: *Produces printing papers.*   Fax: 46-31-136421   Emp: 500

www.perkinsgoodwin.com

AMERISOUTH HOLDINGS INC.

3799 Brownsmill Road, Atlanta, GA   30354

CEO: Edward A. Collier   Tel: (404) 209-0002   %FO: 100

Bus: *Paper pulp sales and marketing.*   Fax: (404) 209-0005

CELLMARK PULP INC.

2112 Whalen Drive, Point Roberts, WA   98281

CEO: Peter Fraser   Tel: (360) 945-0345   %FO: 100

Bus: *Paper pulp sales and marketing.*   Fax: (360) 945-1399

CELLMARK PULP INC.

4321 W. College Avenue, Ste. 320, Appleton, WI   54914

CEO: Don Lang   Tel: (920) 739-8980   %FO: 100

Bus: *Paper pulp sales and marketing.*   Fax: (920) 739-4298

GFI FLORIDA

109 St. Eustacius Lane, Bonita Springs, FL   33923

CEO: Gus Flier   Tel: (941) 495-2665   %FO: 100

Bus: *Paper pulp sales and marketing.*   Fax: (941) 495-2213

LEXINGTON RECYCLING SERVICES INC.

845 Angliana Avenue, Lexington, KY   40508

CEO: George Sherrill   Tel: (606) 231-7770   %FO: 100

Bus: *Engaged in paper recycling.*   Fax: (606) 255-6220

PACFOR PACKAGING

50 Carolinas Way, Fayetteville, GA   30215

CEO: James B. Casavan   Tel: (770) 716-7302   %FO: 100

Bus: *Paper pulp sales and marketing.*   Fax: (770) 716-7127

PACFOR RECYCLING
3525 Colby Avenue, Ste. 211, Everett, WA   98201
CEO: Robes Nelson   Tel: (425) 259-1999   %FO: 100
Bus: *Engaged in paper recycling.*   Fax: (425) 252-4365

PACFOR RECYCLING
4240 Ancroft Circle, Norcross, GA   30092
CEO: Ben C. Smith   Tel: (770) 662-8002   %FO: 100
Bus: *Engaged in paper recycling.*   Fax: (770) 290-9050

PERKINS-GOODWIN COMPANY, INC.
300 Atlantic Street, 5th Fl., Stamford, CT   06901
CEO: Joe Hoffman, Pres.   Tel: (203) 363-7800   %FO: 100
Bus: *Distributes forest products.*   Fax: (203) 363-7809

PITTSBURGH RECYCLING SERVICES LLC
50 Vespucius Street, Pittsburgh, PA   15201
CEO: Bart Rigg   Tel: (412) 420-6000   %FO: 100
Bus: *Engaged in paper recycling.*   Fax: (412) 420-6009

TRIBORO FIBERS INC.
770 Barry Street, Bronx, NY   10474
CEO: Fred Sears   Tel: (718) 378-4600   %FO: 100
Bus: *Paper pulp sales and marketing.*   Fax: (718) 378-2385

● **CHRIS-MARINE AB**
Box 9025, SE-200 39 Malmö, Sweden
CEO: Matts Persson   Tel: 46-40-671-2600
Bus: *Sales grinding equipment for diesel*   Fax: 46-40-671-2699
engines.   www.chris-marine.com

CHRIS-MARINE USA, INC.
732 Parker Street, Jacksonville, FL   32202
CEO: Kent Ekenberg, VP   Tel: (904) 354-8784   %FO: 100
Bus: *Diesel engine & turbocharger*   Fax: (904) 358-7862
repairs.

● **CYCORE AB**
Dragarbrunnsgatan 35, SE-753 20, Uppsala, Sweden
CEO: Bengt Starke, CEO   Tel: 46-18-656-560
Bus: *Mfr. interactive, 3-D software for the*   Fax: 46-18-656-566
internet.   www.cycore.com

CYCORE INC.
3130 La Selva Drive, Ste. 100, San Mateo, CA   94403
CEO: Jim Madden, Pres. & CEO   Tel: (650) 627-5000   %FO: 100
Bus: *Mfr. interactive, 3-D software for*   Fax: (650) 358-8419
the internet.

● **DUNI AB**
Box 95, SE-101 21 Stockholm, Sweden
CEO: Hans von Uthmann, CEO   Tel: 46-8-402-1300   Rev: $591
Bus: *Food service and table products for*   Fax: 46-8-206-6609   Emp: 4,700
airlines, trains and ferries.   www.duni.com

DUNI DE STER CORP.
W 165 N5830 Ridgewood Drive, Menomonee Falls, WI   53051-5655
CEO: Aad Dorleijn, Pres.   Tel: (262) 252-7700   %FO: 100
Bus: *Mfr. disposable food service and*   Fax: (262) 252-7710   Emp: 200
table products.

DUNI DE STER CORP.
225 Peachtree Street, Ste. 400, Atlanta, GA   30303
CEO: Aad Dorleijn, Pres.   Tel: (404) 659-9100   %FO: 100
Bus: *Mfr. disposable food service and*   Fax: (404) 659-5226
table products.

DUNI DE STER CORP.
2260 Delray Road, Thomaston, GA   30286
CEO: Aad Dorleijn, Pres.   Tel: (706) 647-2205   %FO: 100
Bus: *Mfr. disposable food service and*   Fax: (706) 647-1360
table products.

● **DUX INDUSTRIER AB**
Strandridargatan 8, SE-231 61 Trelleborg, Sweden
CEO: Claes Ljung, Pres.   Tel: 46-410-16500
Bus: *Mfr. furniture & mattresses.*   Fax: 46-410-17615
www.dux.se

DUX INTERIORS, INC.
235 East 58th Street, New York, NY   10022-1201
CEO: Bo Gustafsson, Pres.   Tel: (212) 752-3897   %FO: 100
Bus: *Wholesale furniture and*   Fax: (212) 319-9638
mattresses.

● **DYNARC AB**
Norgegatan 2, SE-164 32 Kista, Sweden
CEO: Olov Schagerlund, Pres. & CEO   Tel: 46-8-566-12100
Bus: *Computer integrated system design.*   Fax: 46-8-566-12121   Emp: 25
                                              www.dynarc.com

    DYNARC
    2815 Zanker Road, San Jose, CA   95134
    CEO: Lars Romfelt, VP   Tel: (408) 571-8000   %FO: 100
    Bus: *Develops products for high-*   Fax: (408) 571-8001
       performance network solutions.

● **EGE WESTIN AB**
Lertagsgatan 7, Box 20, SE-694 21 Hallsberg, Sweden
CEO: Jan-Erik Westin, Pres.   Tel: 46-582-613950
Bus: *Mfr. blinds, awnings and sunscreens.*   Fax: 46-582-611922   Emp: 25
                                              www.ege.se

    EGE SYSTEM SUN CONTROL INC.
    15203 Northeast 95th Street, Redmond, WA   98052
    CEO: Wayne Sneva, Pres. & CEO   Tel: (425) 869-6575   %FO: JV
    Bus: *Mfr./retail sale awnings & sun*   Fax: (425) 869-6581   Emp: 22
       screens.

● **EISER TRIKÅ AB**
Planteringsgatan 36, Box 3, SE-275 21, Sjöbo, Sweden
CEO: Per Höiby, Pres.   Tel: 46-416-188 15
Bus: *Children's clothing manufacturer.*   Fax: 46-416-128 96   Emp: 10
                                              www.eisertrika.se

    EISER INC.
    235 NW Park Street, Portland, OR   97209
    CEO: Per Höiby, Pres.   Tel: (503) 224-6218   %FO: 100
    Bus: *Children's clothing manufacturer.*   Fax: (503) 224-8656   Emp: 10

● **EKA NOBEL AB, DIV. AKZO NOBEL**
Bohus, SE-445 80 Bohus, Sweden
CEO: Jan Svärd, Pres.   Tel: 46-31-587000   Rev: $7,000
Bus: *Mfr. chemicals and allied products for*   Fax: 46-31-587400   Emp: 2,800
  the pulp and paper industries..   www.ekachemicals.se.com

    EKA CHEMICALS, INC.
    8401 B Quartz Avenue, South Gate, CA   90280
    CEO: Mark Suder   Tel: (213) 562-5266   %FO: 100
    Bus: *Mfr. chemicals and allied products.*   Fax: (213) 562-5268

EKA CHEMICALS, INC.
PO Box 2167, Columbus, MS 39704
CEO: Andy Gressett   Tel: (601) 327-0400   %FO: 100
Bus: *Mfr. chemicals and allied products.* Fax: (601) 329-3004

EKA CHEMICALS, INC.
PO Box 6286, Augusta, GA 30916
CEO: Billy Johnson   Tel: (706) 790-9364   %FO: 100
Bus: *Mfr. chemicals and allied products.* Fax: (706) 790-0534

EKA CHEMICALS, INC.
12 Beeches Lane, Woodstock, CT 06281
CEO: Charles Sweet   Tel: (860) 963-2061   %FO: 100
Bus: *Mfr. chemicals and allied products.* Fax: (860) 963-2164

EKA CHEMICALS, INC.
6653 Kimball Drive, Bldg. E, Gig Harbour, WA 98335
CEO: Al Hazelquist   Tel: (253) 858-7113   %FO: 100
Bus: *Mfr. chemicals and allied products.* Fax: (253) 858-5064

EKA CHEMICALS, INC.
PO Box 1079, Moses Lake, WA 98837
CEO: Scott Isherwood   Tel: (509) 765-6400   %FO: 100
Bus: *Mfr. chemicals and allied products.* Fax: (509) 765-5557

EKA CHEMICALS, INC.
1775 West Oak Commons Court, Marietta, GA 30062
CEO: Börje Andersson, Pres.   Tel: (770) 578-0858   %FO: 100
Bus: *Mfr. chemicals and allied products.* Fax: (770) 578-1359   Emp: 100

EKA CHEMICALS, INC.
2432 Doug Barnard Parkway, Augusta, GA 30906
CEO: Glenn Mankin   Tel: (706) 790-6520   %FO: 100
Bus: *Mfr. chemicals and allied products.* Fax: (706) 790-7286

● **ELECTROLUX AB**
St. Göransgatan 143, Stockholm, Sweden
CEO: Michael Treschow, Pres. & CEO   Tel: 46-8-738-6000   Rev: $13,209
Bus: *Mfr. household and commercial   Fax: 46-8-656-4478   Emp: 87,125
     appliances and outdoor lawn and leaf   www.electrolux.com
     products.*

AMERICOLD
2340 Second Avenue NW, Cullman, AL 35058-9816
CEO: Bill Colson, EVP   Tel: (256) 734-9160   %FO: 100
Bus: *Mfr. refrigeration compressors.*   Fax: (256) 739-0217

BARING INDUSTRIES
17901 Northwest Miami Court, Miami, FL   33169
CEO: Chuck Sperry, Pres.   Tel: (305) 653-1600   %FO: 100
Bus: *Mfr. household appliances.*   Fax: (305) 654-1217

BEAM INDUSTRIES
PO Box 788, Webster City, IA   50595
CEO: John Coghlan, Pres.   Tel: (515) 832-4620   %FO: 100
Bus: *Mfr. central vacuum systems.*   Fax: (515) 832-6659

DOMETIC CORPORATION
2320 Industry Parkway, Box 490, Elkhart, IN   46515-0490
CEO: John Waters, Pres.   Tel: (219) 294-2511   %FO: 100
Bus: *Mfr. products for recreational Fax: (219) 293-9686
    vehicles.*

ELECTROLUX LLC
5956 Sherry Lane, Dallas, TX   75225
CEO: Gary Griffin, Pres.   Tel: (214) 378-4000   %FO: 100
Bus: *Sales of vacuums and accessories.* Fax: (214) 378-7561

ELX GROUP
5000 Central Freeway, Wichita Falls, TX   76306
CEO: Chuck Schott, VP   Tel: (940) 855-3990   %FO: 100
Bus: *Mfr. professional laundry   Fax: (940) 855-9349
    equipment.*

THE EUREKA COMPANY
1201 East Bell Street, Bloomington, IL   61701
CEO: Leo Cadelo, Pres.   Tel: (309) 828-2367   %FO: 100
Bus: *Mfr. floorcare products.*   Fax: (309) 823-5203

FRIGIDAIRE COMMERCIAL PRODUCTS COMPANY
707 Robins Street, PO Box 4000, Conway, AR   72032-6565
CEO: John Waters, Pres.   Tel: (501) 327-8945   %FO: 100
Bus: *Mfr./sale commercial refrigeration Fax: (501) 450-3782
    equipment.*

FRIGIDAIRE HOME PRODUCTS
104 Warren Road, Augusta, GA   30907
CEO: Norman E. Topping, Pres.   Tel: (706) 860-2290   %FO: 100
Bus: *Corporate headquarters for   Fax: (706) 860-2274
    household appliances & lawn &
    garden equipment.*

FRIGIDAIRE HOME PRODUCTS
250 Bobby Jones Expressway, Martinez, GA   30907
CEO: Robert Cook, Pres.   Tel: (706) 651-1751   %FO: 100
Bus: *Mfr./sales household appliances*   Fax: (706) 651-1751
and outdoor lawn & garden
products.

HUSQVARNA FOREST & GARDEN COMPANY
9006 Perimeter Woods Drive, Charlotte, NC   28216
CEO: David Zerfoss, Pres.   Tel: (704) 597-5000   %FO: 100
Bus: *Distributor/service chain saws,*   Fax: (704) 597-8802
lawn & garden equipment.

WCI INTERNATIONAL COMPANY
3 Parkway Center, Pittsburgh, PA   15220
CEO: Giovan Borsetti, Pres.   Tel: (412) 928-3321   %FO: 100
Bus: *Exporter/marketer household*   Fax: (412) 928-9407
appliances.

WHITE CONSOLIDATED INDUSTRIES INC.
PO Box 35920, Cleveland, OH   44135-0920
CEO: George Weigand, SVP   Tel: (216) 898-1800   %FO: 100
Bus: *Headquarters office for US*   Fax: (216) 898-2393   Emp: 22,316
operations.

● **ELECTROLUX ORIGO**
Box 9052, SE-300 09 Halmstad, Sweden
CEO: Anders Magnusson, Pres.   Tel: 46-35-218860
Bus: *Mfr. stoves/heaters for mobile homes* Fax: 46-35-130238   Emp: 20
and boats.   www.origo-sweden.com

ORIGO USA INC.
1121 Lewis Avenue, Sarasota, FL   34237
CEO: Anders Ebbeson, Pres.   Tel: (941) 365-3660   %FO: 100
Bus: *Sale/service heaters, ventilation* Fax: (941) 955-2596   Emp: 4
systems for boats, mobile homes.

● **ELEKTA AB**
Birger Jarlsgatan 53, Box 7593, SE-103 93 Stockholm, Sweden
CEO: Laurent Laksell, Pres.   Tel: 46-8-587-25400   Rev: $232
Bus: *Mfr./sales technical instrument and* Fax: 46-8-587-25500   Emp: 1,135
supplies for medical and dental surgery. www.elekta.se

ELEKTA INC.
3155 Northwoods Parkway NW, Norcross, GA   30071
CEO: Gerald Woodard, Pres.   Tel: (770) 315-1225   %FO: 100
Bus: *Sales/distribution of surgical and*   Fax: (770) 315-7850
    medical instruments.

● **ELMO CALF AB**
SE-512 81, Svenljunga, Sweden
CEO: Jan Ohlsson, Chmn.   Tel: 46-325-66-1400
Bus: *Design/mfr. high quality furniture and*   Fax: 46-325-61-1004   Emp: 369
    automotive leathers.   www.elmocalf.se

    ELMO LEATHER OF AMERICA
    24 Kilmer Road, Edison, NJ   08817
    CEO: Evert Emauelsson, EVP   Tel: (732) 777-7800   %FO: 100
    Bus: *Design/mfr./marketing high*   Fax: (732) 777-7373   Emp: 50
        quality furniture & automotive
        leathers.

    ELMO LEATHER OF AMERICA
    312 South Hamilton Street, Ste. 201, High Point, NC   27260
    CEO: Jim Hollomon, VP   Tel: (336) 885-3566   %FO: 100
    Bus: *Design/mfr./marketing high*   Fax: (336) 885-3565   Emp: 123
        quality furniture & automotive
        leathers.

● **ELOF HANSSON BYGG-GROSS AB**
Exportgatan 73, Box 446, SE-401 26 Göteborg, Sweden
CEO: Thomas Pettersson, Pres.   Tel: 46-31-589-885   Rev: $1,700
Bus: *Mfr. pulp, paper & wood products.*   Fax: 46-31-528-601   Emp: 400
                      www.elof-hansson.se

    ELOF HANSSON INC
    565 Taxter Road, Elmsford, NY   10523
    CEO: Ulf Hammarstold, Pres.   Tel: (914) 345-8380   %FO: 100
    Bus: *Importer; pulp, paper products.*   Fax: (914) 345-8114

● **ELTEX OF SWEDEN AB**
Box 608, SE-343 24 Almhult, Sweden
CEO: Steffan Ferm, Dir.   Tel: 46-476-48800
Bus: *Mfr. electronic yarn monitoring*   Fax: 46-476-13400   Emp: 180
    equipment; battery chargers; catalogers. www.eltex.se

ELTEX US INC.
PO Box 868, Greer, SC 29651
CEO: Jonathan Bell, Pres.   Tel: (864) 879-2131
Bus: *Sales/service electronic yarn*   Fax: (864) 879-3734   Emp: 6
monitoring equipment; battery
chargers; dataloggers.

● **TELEFONAKIEBOLAGET AB ERICSSON**
Telefonvägen 30, SE-126 25 Stockholm, Sweden
CEO: Kurt Hellström, Pres. & CEO   Tel: 46-8-719-0000   Rev: $29,026
Bus: *Mfr. telecommunications systems, radio* Fax: 46-8-719-1976   Emp: 103,300
communications and electronic defense   www.ericsson.com
systems.

   ERICSSON USA INC.
   740 East Campbell Road, Richardson, TX 75081
   CEO: Per-Arne Sandstrom   Tel: (972) 583-8800   %FO: 100
   Bus: *Mfr./distribution/service*   Fax: (972) 437-6627   Emp: 1,700
   telecommunications, switching &
   cellular radio systems.

   ERICSSON USA INC. PUBLIC AFFAIRS
   1634 I Street NW, Ste. 600, Washington, DC 20006-4083
   CEO: John P. Giere, VP   Tel: (202) 783-2200
   Bus: *Public affairs office.*   Fax: (202) 783-2206

● **ETON SYSTEMS AB**
Djupdal, S-507 71 Gånghester, Sweden
CEO: Mikael Davidson   Tel: 46-33-23-1200
Bus: *Unit production systems for apparel and* Fax: 46-33-24-9167   Emp: 10
home fashion.   www.eton.se

   ETON SYSTEMS, INC.
   4000 McGinnis Ferry Road, Alpharetta, GA 30005
   CEO: Toivo Anttila, Pres.   Tel: (770) 475-8022   %FO: 100
   Bus: *Unit production systems for*   Fax: (770) 442-0216
   apparel and home fashion.

● **FLEXLINK SYSTEMS AB**
Kullagergatan 50, CFL/SFS-4, SE-415 50 Göteborg, Sweden
CEO: Fredrik Jönsson, CEO   Tel: 46-31-337-3100   Rev: $84
Bus: *Mfr. industrial machinery.*   Fax: 46-31-337-2233   Emp: 330
                                             www.flexlink.com

FLEXLINK SYSTEMS INC.
1530 Valley Center Pkwy., Ste. 200, Bethlehem, PA   18017
CEO: Dave Clark, Pres.   Tel: (610) 954-7000   %FO: 100
Bus: *Mfr. plastic chain conveyors and*   Fax: (610) 954-7045   Emp: 75
     automation components.

● **FOLKSAM INTL**
Bohusgatan 14, SE-106 60 Stockholm, Sweden
CEO: Anders Henricksson, Mng. Dir.   Tel: 46-8-772-6000   Rev: $5,733
Bus: *Insurance services.*   Fax: 46-8-7641-6304   Emp: 3,900
     www.folksam.se

     FOLKSAMERICA REINSURANCE CO
     *900 South Avenue, Staten Island, NY   10314-3403
     CEO: Steven E. Fass, Pres.   Tel: (718) 568-2264   %FO: 100
     Bus: *Reinsurance services.*   Fax: (718) 568-2265   Emp: 70

● **FORSHEDA AB**
Storgatan, SE-330 12 Forsheda, Sweden
CEO: Sonny Lindquist, Pres.   Tel: 46-370-89000
Bus: *Mfr. pipe and shaft seals, industrial*   Fax: 46-370-81872   Emp: 1,200
     polymers, automotive components.   www.varnamo.se

     FORSHEDA PIPE SEAL CORPORATION
     2200 South McDuffie Street, Anderson, SC   29624
     CEO: Larry Fatt, Mgr.   Tel: (864) 261-3445   %FO: 100
     Bus: *Mfr. pipe seals, custom rubber*   Fax: (864) 226-9834   Emp: 60
     extrusions, automotive components.

● **FRANGO AB**
Göta Ark 111, Medborgarplasten 25, SE-118 72 Stockholm, Sweden
CEO: Tom Löfstedt, Pres.   Tel: 46-8-555 775 00   Rev: $12
Bus: *Mfr. computer software applications.*   Fax: 46-8-555-775-01   Emp: 90
     www.frango.com

     FRANGO INC.
     500 Park Boulevard, Ste. 1245, Itasca, IL   60143
     CEO: Rick Smith, Pres.   Tel: (630) 773-4700   %FO: 100
     Bus: *Provides software systems.*   Fax: (630) 773-9796

● **GAMBRO AG**

PO Box 7373, SE 103 91, Stockholm, Sweden

CEO: Sören Mellstig, Pres. & CEO Tel: 46-8-613-6500 Rev: $2,316

Bus: *Engaged in medical technology and* Fax: 46-8-611-2830 Emp: 17,000
healthcare, including renal care www.gambro.com
services, blood component technology
and cardiopulmonary care. (Gambro
was created from the mixed industrial
conglomerate, Incentive AB.)

GAMBRO BCT USA, INC.

10810 West Collins Avenue, Lakewood, CO   80215-4498

CEO: Kevin Simpson, VP Tel: (303) 232-6800 %FO: 100

Bus: *Engaged in medical technology* Fax: (303) 231-4923
and healthcare.

GAMBRO HEALTHCARE, INC.

225 Union Blvd, Ste. 600, Lakewood, CO   80228

CEO: Brad Nutter, CEO Tel: (303) 232-6800 %FO: 100

Bus: *Operate renal care healthcare* Fax: (303) 231-4915
clinics.

GAMBRO, INC.

225 Union Blvd, Ste. 600, Lakewood, CO   80228

CEO: David Perez, Pres. Tel: (303) 232-6800 %FO: 100

Bus: *Engaged in medical technology* Fax: (303) 231-4915
and healthcare.

● **GATESPACE AB**

Stora Badhusgatan 18-20, SE-411 21 Göteborg, Sweden

CEO: Staffan Truvé, Pres. & CEO Tel: 46-31-743-9800

Bus: *Software products and professional* Fax: 46-31-711-6416
consulting services for Internet. www.gatespace.com

GATESPACE INC.

720 San Antonio Road, Palo Alto, CA   94303

CEO: Ulf Corné, Pres. Tel: (650) 846-6580 %FO: 100

Bus: *Software products and* Fax: (650) 846-9345
professional consulting services
for Internet.

● **GETINGE AB**

PO Box 69, SE-310 44 Getinge, Sweden

CEO: Johan Malmquist, Pres. & CEO Tel: 46-35-155500

Bus: *Mfr. sterilization, disinfection and* Fax: 46-35-54952 Emp: 3,812
surgical products. www.getinge.com

ARJO INC.
50 North Gary Avenue, Roselle, IL   60172
CEO: Hans Lingegård   Tel: (630) 307-2756
Bus: *Provides ergonomically adapted*   Fax: (888) 594-2756
lifting systems for therapy and
transport, as well as personal
hygiene products.

GETINGE-CASTLE INC.
1777 East Henrietta Road, Rochester, NY   14623-3133
CEO: Creighton A. White, CEO   Tel: (716) 475-1400   %FO: 100
Bus: *Mfr. sterilization, disinfection and*   Fax: (716) 272-5033
surgical products.

GETINGE-CASTLE INC.
371 B Spartan Blvd. East, N. Charleston, SC   29418
CEO: Pete Koste, Dir.   Tel: (843) 552-8652   %FO: 100
Bus: *Mfr. sterilization, disinfection and*   Fax: (843) 552-8652   Emp: 65
surgical products.

PEGASUS AIRWAVE INC.
791 Park of Commerce Blvd., Boca Raton, FL   33487
CEO: Ross Scavuzzo, Pres.   Tel: (561) 989-9898
Bus: *Produces pressure area care*   Fax: (561) 989-9898
products and medical equipment.

● **GRÄNSFORS BRUKS AB**
Gränsfors Yxsmedja, SE-820 70 Bergsjo, Sweden
CEO: Gabriel Bränby, Pres.   Tel: 46-652-71090
Bus: *Mfr. axes, wrecking bars & protective*   Fax: 46-652-14002   Emp: 75
material.   www.gransfors-bruks.com

GRÄNSFORS BRUKS INC.
821 West 5th North Street, PO Box 818, Summerville, SC   29484
CEO: Yvonne Caruso, Pres.   Tel: (843) 875-0240   %FO: 100
Bus: *Mfr./marketing safety apparel for* Fax: (843) 821-2285   Emp: 20
forest industry.

● **GRINDEX AB**
Hantverkarvägen 24, Box 538, SE-136 25 Haninge, Sweden
CEO: Goran Holmen, Mng. Dir.   Tel: 46-8-606-6600
Bus: *Mfr. electronic submersible heavy duty*   Fax: 46-8-745-1606   Emp: 80
drainage and sludge pumps.   www.pitandquarry.com

GRINDEX PUMPS
18524 South 81st Avenue, Tinley Park, IL   60477

CEO: Magnus Lundberg, Gen. Mgr.   Tel: (708) 532-9988   %FO: 100

Bus: *Sale/service drainage & sludge*   Fax: (708) 532-8767   Emp: 8
   pumps.

● H&M HENNES & MAURITZ AB
Norrlandsgatan 15, Box 1421, SE-111 84 Stockholm, Sweden

CEO: Rolf Eriksen, CEO   Tel: 46-8-796-5500   Rev: $3,000

Bus: *Mfr. of reasonably priced, trendy*   Fax: 46-8-796-9919   Emp: 20,700
   clothing.   www.hm.com

H&M STORES
Brass Mill Center, 495 Union Street, Waterbury, CT   06706

CEO: Christian Bagnoud   Tel: (203) 753-4000   %FO: 100

Bus: *Mfr. of clothing.*   Fax: (203) 753-4000

H&M STORES
1328 Broadway at Herald Square, New York, NY   10001

CEO: Christian Bagnoud   Tel: (212) 472-1165   %FO: 100

Bus: *Mfr. of clothing.*   Fax: (212) 472-1165

● HÄGGLUNDS DRIVES AB
SE-890 42 Mellansel, Sweden

CEO: Anders Lindblad, Pres.   Tel: 46-660-87-000

Bus: *Armored and all-terrain vehicles,*   Fax: 46-660-87-160
   marine transport equipment, hydraulic   www.hagglunds.com
   drives.

HÄGGLUND DRIVES INC.
2275 International Street, Columbus, OH   43228

CEO: Christer Sahlberg, Pres.   Tel: (614) 527-7400   %FO: 100

Bus: *Mfr. hydraulic drives and motors.*   Fax: (614) 527-7401

HÄGGLUND DRIVES INC.
719 Sawdust Road, Ste. 330, Spring, TX   77380

CEO: Gary Sauder, Reg. Mgr.   Tel: (281) 292-6700   %FO: 100

Bus: *Sales of hydraulic drives and*   Fax: (281) 292-6768
   motors.

● HALDEX AB
Biblioteksgatan 11, Box 7200, SE-103 88 Stockholm, Sweden

CEO: Claes Waranders, Pres.   Tel: 46-8-678-7270   Rev: $3,374

Bus: *Mfr. automatic brake adjusters, air*   Fax: 46-8-418-57700   Emp: 3,741
   dryers, drain valves and air oil   www.haldex.com
   separators for commercial vehicle
   market.

HALDEX BARNES CORPORATION
2222 15th Street, PO Box 6166, Rockford, IL 61125-1166
CEO: John Pepe, Pres. Tel: (815) 398-4400 %FO: 100
Bus: *Mfr. hydraulic pumps, electro-* Fax: (815) 398-5977 Emp: 325
hydraulic powerpacks.

HALDEX BRAKE PRODUCTS CORPORATION
10930 North Pomona Avenue, Kansas City, MO 64153-4918
CEO: Charles Kleinhagen, Pres. Tel: (816) 891-2470 %FO: 100
Bus: *Mfr. wire.* Fax: (816) 891-9447

HALDEX GARPHYTTAN CORPORATION
4404 Nimitz Parkway, South Bend, IN 46628
CEO: Leif Ericksson, Pres. Tel: (219) 232-8800 %FO: 100
Bus: *Mfr. wire.* Fax: (219) 232-2565

● **HALLDE MASKINER AB**
Box 1165, SE-164 22 Kista, Spanga, Sweden
CEO: Christer Lithander, Pres. Tel: 46-8-752-0400
Bus: *Mfr. food process equipment.* Fax: 46-8-750-4887 Emp: 75
www.hallde.com

PAXTON CORPORATION
897 Bridgeport Avenue, Shelton, CT 06484
CEO: Leif Jensen, Pres. Tel: (203) 925-8720 %FO: 100
Bus: *Distribution food process* Fax: (203) 925-8722 Emp: 5
equipment.

● **HOLMEN AB (FORMERLY MODO)**
PO Box 5407, SE-114 84 Stockholm, Sweden
CEO: Per Ericson, Pres. & CEO Tel: 46-8-666-2100 Rev: $1,610
Bus: *Engaged in paper business, newsprint* Fax: 46-8-666-2130 Emp: 5,275
and magazine paper, paperboard and www.holmen.com
packaging paper.

IGGESUNG PAPERBOARD, INC.
107 John Street, Southport, CT 06490
CEO: Uno Lausen, Pres. Tel: (203) 256-9064 %FO: 100
Bus: *Mfr./distributor forestry products;* Fax: (203) 256-9097
wood, pulp, and paper.

IGGESUNG PAPERBOARD, INC.
1050 Wall Street West, Ste. 640, Lyndhurst, NJ 07071
CEO: Uno Lausen, Pres. Tel: (201) 804-9977 %FO: 100
Bus: *Mfr./distributor forestry products;* Fax: (201) 804-9890
wood, pulp, and paper.

● **HÖRNELL ELEKTROOPTIK AB**
Ernst Hedlundsvågen 35, SE-780 41 Gagnef, Sweden
CEO: Mats Erkers   Tel: 46-241-62400
Bus: *Mfr. of auto darkening welding lenses*   Fax: 46-241-62107   Emp: 100
and air purifying systems.   www.hornell.se

    HORNELL SPEEDGLAS, INC.
    2374 Edison Boulevard, Twinsburg, OH   44087
    CEO: James Miklandek, Pres.   Tel: (330) 425-8880   %FO: 100
    Bus: *Auto darkening welding lenses and* Fax: (330) 425-4576
    personal air purifying systems.

● **HUSQVARNA AB**
SE-56182, Husqvarna, Sweden
CEO: Bengt Andersson, Pres.   Tel: 46-36-146600   Rev: $676
Bus: *Mfr. sewing machines, chainsaws and*   Fax: 46-36-144179
household products.   www.husqvarna.se

    HUSQVARNA FOREST AND GARDEN COMPANY
    9006 Perimeter Woods Drive, Charlotte, NC   28216
    CEO: David Zerfoss, Pres.   Tel: (704) 597-5000   %FO: JV
    Bus: *Sales/distribution of sewing*   Fax: (704) 597-8802
    machines, chainsaws & household
    products.

● **ICON MEDIALAB INTERNATIONAL AB**
Sa Hamnvagen 22, Box 27214, SE-101 37 Stockholm, Sweden
CEO: Pier Carlo Falotti, CEO   Tel: 46-8-588-99000   Rev: $15
Bus: *Media service provider including web*   Fax: 46-8-588-99097   Emp: 300
publishing, technology and Website   www.iconmedialab.com
production.

    ICON MEDIALAB SAN FRANCISCO
    22 Fourth Street, 9th Fl., San Francisco, CA   94103-3139
    CEO: Torben Bolvig   Tel: (415) 932-5500   %FO: 100
    Bus: *Media service provider of websites.* Fax: (415) 932-5560

    ICON MEDIALAB
    7600 Leesburg Pike, Ste. 410, Falls Church, VA   22043
    CEO: Greg Moore   Tel: (703) 714-0096   %FO: 100
    Bus: *Engaged in Internet development.* Fax: (703) 714-0096   Emp: 20

    ICON MEDIALAB
    700 Goddard Avenue, Chesterfield, MO   63005
    CEO: Patrick Cherniawski   Tel: (636) 530-7776   %FO: 100
    Bus: *Engaged in Internet development.* Fax: (636) 530-4644   Emp: 70

ICON NICHOLSON
295 Lafayette Street, 8th Fl., New York, NY   10012
CEO: Debra Boulanger   Tel: (212) 274-0470   %FO: 100
Bus: *Engaged in Internet development.*   Fax: (212) 274-0380

● INDIGO AVIATION AB
Sodra Forstadsgatan 4, SE-21143 Marimo, Sweden
CEO: Mat Andersson   Tel: 46-40-660-3001   Rev: $63
Bus: *Owns and leases aircraft to major*   Fax: 46-40-302-350   Emp: 25
    airlines.   www.flyindigo.com

INDIGO AIRLEASE CORPORATION
100 NE Third Avenue, Ste. 800, Ft. Lauderdale, FL   33301
CEO: John Evans, Pres. & CEO   Tel: (954) 760-7777   %FO: 100
Bus: *Owns and leases aircraft to major*   Fax: (954) 760-7716
    airlines.

● INDUSTRI-MATEMATIK INTERNATIONAL AB
Stadsgården 10, Box 15044, SE-104 65 Stockholm, Sweden
CEO: Stig G. Durlow, Pres. & CEO   Tel: 46-8-676-5000   Rev: $75
Bus: *Provides high-performance supply*   Fax: 46-8-676-5010   Emp: 620
    chain and customer service software.   www.im.se

INDUSTRI-MATEMATIK AMERICAN OPERATIONS, INC.
1315 50th Street, West Des Moines, IA   50266
CEO: J. P. Joei, VP   Tel: (515) 224-2307   %FO: 100
Bus: *Provides high-performance supply*   Fax: (515) 224-2036
    chain and customer service
    software.

INDUSTRI-MATEMATIK AMERICAN OPERATIONS, INC.
8410 West Bryn Mawr Ave., Ste. 400, Chicago, IL   60631
CEO: Stephen J. D'Angelo, Pres.   Tel: (773) 380-1231   %FO: 100
Bus: *Provides high-performance supply*   Fax: (773) 380-1262
    chain and customer service
    software.

INDUSTRI-MATEMATIK AMERICAN OPERATIONS, INC.
305 Fellowship Road, Ste. 200, Mt. Laurel, NJ   08054
CEO: David J. Simbari, Pres.   Tel: (856) 793-4400   %FO: 100
Bus: *Provides high-performance supply*   Fax: (856) 793-4401
    chain and customer service
    software.

● **INTENTIA INTERNATIONAL AB**

Vendevägen 89, Box 59, SE-182 15 Danderyd, Sweden

CEO: Björn Algkvist, Pres. & CEO　　Tel: 46-8-555-25-000　　　Rev: $361

Bus: *Mfr. software for the paper, food and*　Fax: 46-8-555-25-999　　　Emp: 3,380
beverage industries.　　　　　　　www.intentia.com

　　INTENTIA INTERNATIONAL AMERICA GROUP

　　Two Century Centre, 1700 East Golf Road, 9th Fl., Schaumburg, IL　60173

　　CEO: Mike Nutter, Pres. & CEO　　Tel: (847) 762-0900　　　%FO: 100

　　Bus: *Mfr. software for the paper, food*　Fax: (847) 762-0901
　　and beverage industries.

● **INTERSPIRO AB**

Box 10060, SE-181 10 Lidingo, Sweden

CEO: Bengt Egerkrantz, CEO　　　Tel: 46-8-636-5110

Bus: *Mfr. breathing apparatus.*　　Fax: 46-8-765-4853　　　Emp: 170
　　　　　　　　　　　　www.interspiro.se

　　INTERSPIRO INC.

　　31 Business Park Drive, Branford, CT　06405

　　CEO: Mike Brookman, Pres.　　　Tel: (203) 481-3899　　　%FO: 100

　　Bus: *Mfr./sales breathing apparatus.*　Fax: (203) 483-1879　　　Emp: 30

● **INVESTOR AB**

Arsenalsgatan 8C, SE-103 32, Stockholm, Sweden

CEO: Marcus Wallenberg, CEO　　Tel: 46-8-614-2000　　　Rev: $8,860

Bus: *Industrial holding company.*　Fax: 46-8-614-2150　　　Emp: 663
　　　　　　　　　　　　www.investorab.com

　　INVESTOR GROWTH CAPITAL, INC.

　　12 East 49th Street, New York, NY　10017-1028

　　CEO: Henry E. Gooss, Dir.　　　Tel: (212) 515-9000　　　%FO: 100

　　Bus: *Holding company.*　　　　Fax: (212) 515-9029

● **ITT FLYGT AB**

Svetsarvagen 12, Box 1309, SE-171 25 Solna, Sweden

CEO: Lief E. Carlsson, Pres.　　Tel: 46-8-475-6700　　　Rev: $593

Bus: *Mfr. pumps.*　　　　　　Fax: 46-8-475-6970
　　　　　　　　　　　　www.flygt.com

　　ITT FLYGT CORPORATION

　　N27 W23291 Roundy Dr., Pewaukee, WI　53072

　　CEO: Jim Randall, Reg. Mgr.　　Tel: (414) 544-1922　　　%FO: JV

　　Bus: *Mfr./sales electric pumps,*　Fax: (414) 544-1399
　　hydroturbines, mixers.

ITT FLYGT CORPORATION
790-A Chadborne Road, Fairfield, CA 94533
CEO: Darryl Smith, Reg. Mgr.   Tel: (707) 422-9894   %FO: JV
Bus: *Mfr./sales electric pumps,*   Fax: (707) 422-9808
hydroturbines, mixers.

ITT FLYGT CORPORATION
PO Box 1004, Trumbull, CT 06611-0943
CEO: K.I. Ericsson, Pres.   Tel: (203) 380-4700   %FO: JV
Bus: *Mfr./sales electric pumps,*   Fax: (203) 380-4705   Emp: 205
hydroturbines, mixers.

ITT INDUSTRIES (FLYGT CORPORATION)
2400 Tarpley Road, Carrollton, TX 75006-2407
CEO: Ed Bailey, Reg. Mgr.   Tel: (972) 418-2400   %FO: JV
Bus: *Regional sales office.*   Fax: (972) 416-9570

● **JOHNSON PUMP AB**
Nastagatan 19, Box 1436, SE-701 14 Orebro, Sweden
CEO: Lena Ottosson   Tel: 46-19-21-8300
Bus: *Mfr. pumps and pumping equipment.*   Fax: 46-19-27-2330   Emp: 600
www.johnson-pump.com

JOHNSON PUMPS OF AMERICA, INC.
10509 United Parkway, Schiller Park, IL 60176
CEO: Hans Kragh   Tel: (847) 671-7867   %FO: 100
Bus: *Mfr./sales of pumps and pumping*   Fax: (847) 671-7909
equipment.

● **KANTHAL AB, DIV. SANDVIK GROUP**
Box 502, SE-734 27 Hallstahammar, Sweden
CEO: Harry Furuberg, Pres.   Tel: 46-220-21000
Bus: *Mfr. resistance alloys, heating elements,*   Fax: 46-220-21154
bimetals.   www.kanthal.se

THE KANTHAL CORP
119 Wooster Street, Bethel, CT 06801-0281
CEO: Jack Beagley, Pres.   Tel: (203) 744-1440   %FO: 100
Bus: *Mfr. resistance alloys, heating*   Fax: (203) 748-2229   Emp: 107
elements, hi-temp tubing.

● **KAROLIN MACHINE TOOL AB**
Box 2001, SE-931 31 Skellefteå, Sweden
CEO: Björn Kumlin, Pres. & CEO   Tel: 46-910-71-1030   Rev: $95
Bus: *Mfr. fabrication machinery and systems,*   Fax: 46-910-71-1039   Emp: 450
punching & beveling machinery, laser   www.kmt.se
systems.

PULLMAX, INC.
1201 Lunt Avenue, Elk Grove Village, IL   60007

CEO: Johann Arnberg, Pres.

Bus: *Mfr. fabrication machinery and systems, punching and beveling machinery, laser systems.*

Tel: (847) 228-5600
Fax: (847) 228-5650

%FO: 100
Emp: 12

● KOCKUM SONICS AB
Industrigatan 39, Box 1035, SE-212 10 Malmö, Sweden

CEO: Claes Paulsson, Dir.

Bus: *Mfr. marine signal and lighting, industrial sonic cleaning, and civil alarm equipment.*

Tel: 46-40-671-8800
Fax: 46-40-216513
www.kockumsonics.com

Emp: 100

KOCKUM SONICS INC.
903 Industry Road, Ste. 105, Kenner, LA   70062

CEO: William C. Edwards, Gen. Mgr.

Bus: *Sales/service marine signal light equipment, industrial sonic cleaning and civil alarm equipment.*

Tcl: (504) 466-9740
Fax: (504) 466-9792

%FO: 100
Emp: 7

RADIO HOLLAND USA
8943 Gulf Freeway, Houston, TX   77017

CEO: Rich Beattie, Mgr.

Bus: *Sales/service marine signal light equipment, industrial sonic cleaning and civil alarm equipment.*

Tel: (713) 943-3325
Fax: (713) 943-3802

%FO: 100

● LAGERLÖF & LEMAN
Strandvägen 7A, PO Box 5402, SE-114 84 Stockholm, Sweden

CEO: I. Zander, Mng. Ptnr.

Bus: *International law firm.*

Tel: 46-8-665-6600
Fax: 46-8-667-6883
www.icclaw.com

Emp: 43

LAGERLÖF & LEMAN
712 Fifth Avenue, 30th Fl., New York, NY   10019

CEO: Magnus Andren, Mng. Ptnr.

Bus: *International law firm.*

Tel: (212) 424-9150
Fax: (212) 424-9155

%FO: 100

● MANNHEIMER SWARTLING ADVOKATBYRÅ
Norrmalmstorg 4, Box 1711, SE-111 87 Stockholm, Sweden

CEO: Magnus Wallander, Mng. Ptnr.

Bus: *International law firm.*

Tel: 46-8-613-5500
Fax: 46-8-613-5501
www.msa.se

Emp: 200

MANNHEIMER SWARTLING ADVOKATBYRÅ LLP
101 Park Avenue, 26th Fl., New York, NY 10178
CEO: Maria Tufvesson Shuck   Tel: (212) 682-0580   %FO: 100
Bus: *International law firm.*   Fax: (212) 682-0982   Emp: 5

● MODERN TIMES GROUP MTG AB
Skeppsbron 18, Box 2094, SE-103 13 Stockholm, Sweden
CEO: Hans-Holger Albrecht, CEO   Tel: 46-8-5620-0050   Rev: $575
Bus: *Media holding company.*   Fax: 46-8-2050-74   Emp: 1,475
www.mtg.se

METRO PHILADELPHIA
100 South Broad Street, Ste. 1210, Philadelphia, PA 19110
CEO: Jens Torpe, VP   Tel: (215) 717-2600   %FO: 100
Bus: *Develops smart card electronic*   Fax: (215) 717-2626
payment systems.

● MORGARDSHAMMAR AB
SE-777 82 Smedjebacken, Sweden
CEO: Lars Almhed, Pres.   Tel: 46-240-668500   Rev: $53
Bus: *Mfr. equipment for steel mills & mines.*   Fax: 46-240-668501   Emp: 300
www.morgardshammar.com

MORGARDSHAMMAR INC.
9800-L Southern Pine Blvd., PO Box 240582, Charlotte, NC 28273
CEO: Grant Philip, Pres.   Tel: (704) 522-8024   %FO: 100
Bus: *Sales/service equipment for steel*   Fax: (704) 522-0264   Emp: 6
mills & mines.

● MUNKSJÖ PAPER AB
Box 624, SE-551 18 Jönköping, Sweden
CEO: Sture Bjarholt, Mng. Dir.   Tel: 46-36-30-3300
Bus: *Mfr. paper and paper products.*   Fax: 46-36-30-3383
www.munksjo.se

MUNKSJÖ PAPER DÉCOR, INC.
642 River Street, Fitchburg, MA 01420
CEO: Dennis Bunnell, Pres.   Tel: (978) 342-1080   %FO: 100
Bus: *Mfr. paper products for interior*   Fax: (978) 345-4268
design.

● NEDERMAN & CO, AB
Sydhamnsgatan 2, SE-252 28, Helsingborg, Sweden
CEO: Per Yngve Larsson, Pres.   Tel: 46-42-18-8700
Bus: *Environmental pollution control for dust*   Fax: 46-42-14-7971   Emp: 10
and fume.   www.nederman.com

NEDERMAN INC.
39115 Warren Road, Westland, MI   48185
CEO: B. V. Converse, Pres. & CEO   Tel: (734) 729-3344   %FO: 100
Bus: *Environmental pollution control*   Fax: (734) 729-3358   Emp: 10
for dust and fume.

● **NEFAB AB**
Box 2184, SE-550 02 Jönköping, Sweden
CEO: Lars-Åke Rydh, Pres. & CEO   Tel: 46-36-345050   Rev: $1,128
Bus: *Mfr. of plywood and steel customized*   Fax: 46-36-150444   Emp: 714
packaging solutions.   www.nefab.se

   NEFAB, INC.
   736 West Estes Avenue, Schaumburg, IL   60193-4405
   CEO: Tor Helenius, Pres.   Tel: (847) 985-1600
   Bus: *Mfr. plywood packaging systems.*   Fax: (847) 985-3200   Emp: 33

● **NOBEL BIOCARE AB**
Bohusgatan 15, Box 5190, SE-402 26, Göteborg, Sweden
CEO: Jack Forsgren, Pres.   Tel: 46-31-818800   Rev: $164
Bus: *Surgical, medical and dental supplies.*   Fax: 46-31-163152   Emp: 1,200
        www.nobelbiocare.se

   NOBEL BIOCARE USA INC.
   22715 Savi Ranch Parkway, Yorba Linda, CA   92887
   CEO: Martin J. Dymek, Pres. & CEO   Tel: (714) 282-4800   %FO: 100
   Bus: *Distributor of*   Fax: (714) 998-9236   Emp: 500
   surgical/medical/dental equipment.

● **NOLATO AB**
Box 66, SE-260 93 Torekov, Sweden
CEO: Tomas Sjolin, CEO   Tel: 46-431-442290   Rev: $208
Bus: *Mfr. molded rubber and plastic*   Fax: 46-431-442291   Emp: 1,870
products.   www.nolato.se

   NALATO SHIELDMATE INC.
   761 District Drive, Itasca, Il   60143
   CEO: Torsten Nilson, Pres.   Tel: (630) 773-8801   %FO: 100
   Bus: *Designs polymer components and*   Fax: (630) 773-8807
   assembly systems.

   NOLATO TEXAS
   1500-L Peterson Court, Ft. Worth, TX   7617
   CEO: Per Ahlund, Pres.   Tel: (817) 430-4744   %FO: 100
   Bus: *Mfr. plastic components.*   Fax: (817) 430-2889

SUNNEX INC.
3 Huron Drive, Natick, MA   01760
CEO: Lars A. Lundholm, Pres.   Tel: (508) 651-0009   %FO: 100
Bus: *Mfr./sales machine mounts and*   Fax: (508) 651-0099   Emp: 24
       industrial work lights.

● **NORDEA AB (FORMERLY MERITANORDBANKEN PLC)**
Hamngatan 10, SE-10571 Stockholm, Sweden
CEO: Vesa Vainio, Pres. & CEO   Tel: 46-8-614-7000   Rev: $6,003
Bus: *International commercial banking*   Fax: 46-8-105-069   Emp: 18,896
       services.   www.meritanordbanken.com

    NORDEA AB
    437 Madison Avenue, New York, NY   10022
    CEO: Jukka Niemi, Gen. Mgr.   Tel: (212) 318-9300   %FO: 100
    Bus: *International banking services.*   Fax: (212) 421-4420

● **NORDEN PAC INTERNATIONAL AB**
Södra Vägen 30, Box 845, SE-391 28 Kalmar, Sweden
CEO: Henrik Cornell   Tel: 46-480-44-7700
Bus: *Provides advanced packaging systems.*   Fax: 46-480-44-7764
                                       www.norden-pac.se

    NORDEN ANDBRO INC.
    430 Andbro Drive, Pittman, NJ   08070
    CEO: Brian Anderson   Tel: (609) 589-1250   %FO: 100
    Bus: *Sales/distribution of rubber and*   Fax: (609) 589-2052
           plastic products.

    NORDEN INC.
    230 Industrial Parkway, Branchburg, NJ   08876
    CEO: Göran Adolfsson, Pres.   Tel: (908) 534-1222   %FO: 100
    Bus: *Provides advanced packaging*   Fax: (908) 534-9555
           systems.

● **ORIGOVERKEN AB**
Box 9052, SE-30009 Halmstad, Sweden
CEO: Anders Ebbeson   Tel: 46-35-218-860
Bus: *Mfr. stoves/heaters for mobile homes*   Fax: 46-35-130-238
       and boats.

    ORIGO AB SWEDEN
    1540 Northgate Boulevard, Sarasota, FL   34234
    CEO: Rick Butler, Mgr.   Tel: (941) 355-4488
    Bus: *Sales/distribution of stoves and*   Fax: (941) 355-1558
           heaters for mobile homes and
           boats.

● **ORREFORS AB (DIV. OF INCENTIVE AB)**
Box 8, SE-380 40 Orrefors, Sweden
CEO: Olle Markoo, Pres.   Tel: 46-481-34000
Bus: *Mfr. crystal products.*   Fax: 46-481-30400   Emp: 200
                                           www.orrefors.com

    GALLERI ORREFORS KOSTA BODA
    58 East 57th Street, New York, NY   10022
    CEO: Amy, Gallery Dir.   Tel: (212) 752-1095   %FO: 100
    Bus: *Sale/distribution crystal products.*   Fax: (212) 752-3705   Emp: 50

    GALLERI ORREFORS KOSTA BODA
    Crystal Court, 3333 Bear Street, Costa Mesa, CA   92626
    CEO: Scott Smith, Gallery Dir.   Tel: (714) 549-1959   %FO: 100
    Bus: *Sale/distribution crystal products.*   Fax: (714) 549-8247   Emp: 8

    GALLERI ORREFORS KOSTA BODA
    140 Bradford Drive West, Berlin, NJ   08091
    CEO: Oyvind Saetre, Pres.   Tel: (609) 768-5400   %FO: 100
    Bus: *Sale/distribution crystal products.*   Fax: (609) 768-9726   Emp: 100
        Sub of INCENTIVE AB.

● **PERBIO SCIENCE AB**
Knutpunkten 34, SE-252 78 Sweden
CEO: Mats Fischier, CEO   Tel: 46-42-26-9090
Bus: *Engaged in biotechnology.*   Fax: 46-42-26-9098
                                           www.perbio.com

    ENDOGEN, INC.
    30 Commerce Way, Woburn, MA   01801-1059
    CEO: Owen A. Dempsey, Pres.   Tel: (781) 937-0890   %FO: 100
    Bus: *Provides immunoassay test kits.* Fax: (781) 937-3096

● **PERSTORP AB**
Box 500, SE-284 80 Perstorp, Sweden
CEO: Ake Fredriksson, Pres. & CEO   Tel: 46-435-38000   Rev: $1,345
Bus: *Mfr. specialty chemicals, analytic* Fax: 46-435-38100   Emp: 6,512
    instruments, decorative laminates,   www.perstorp.com
    flooring and wood products.

    PERGO FLOORING INC.
    524 New Hope Road, Raleigh, NC   27610
    CEO: Lars von Kantzow, Pres.   Tel: (919) 773-6000   %FO: 100
    Bus: *Mfr. laminate flooring.*   Fax: (919) 773-6004

PERSTORP COMPOUNDS INC.
238 Nonotuck Street, Florence, MA 01060

CEO: Per Dahlen, Pres.	Tel: (413) 584-2472	%FO: 100
Bus: *Mfr. melamine & urea molding compounds.*	Fax: (413) 586-4089	Emp: 55

PERSTORP INC.
PO Box 60010, Florence, MA 01062

CEO: David Tracy, Pres.	Tel: (413) 584-9522	%FO: 100
Bus: *Holding company.*	Fax: (413) 587-3040	Emp: 4

PERSTORP POLYOLS INC.
600 Matzinger Road, Toledo, OH 43612-2695

CEO: David Wolf, Pres.	Tel: (419) 729-5448	%FO: 100
Bus: *Mfr. pentaerythritol, sodium formate, trimethylolpropane, specialty polyols, other chemicals.*	Fax: (419) 729-3291	Emp: 86

PERSTORP UNIDUR INC.
7343-L W. Friendly Avenue, Greensboro, NC 27410

CEO: Jan Bergstrom, Pres.	Tel: (910) 316-0166	%FO: 100
Bus: *Sale decorative laminate.*	Fax: (910) 316-0139	

YLA, INC.
2970 C Bay Vista Court, Benicia, CA 94510

CEO: Gary Patz, Pres.	Tel: (707) 747-2750	%FO: 61
Bus: *Mfr. components in composite materials.*	Fax: (707) 747-2754	

● **PUMPEX**
PO Box 5207, SE-121 16 Johanneshov, Sweden

CEO: Robert Montenegro, Pres.	Tel: 46-8-725-4930
Bus: *Mfr. of submersible pumps.*	Fax: 46-8-659-3314
	www.pumpex.com

PUMPEX, INC.
49 Molasses Hill Road, Lebanon, NJ 08833

CEO: Rob Montenagro, Pres.	Tel: (908) 730-7004	%FO: 100
Bus: *Mfr. submersible pumps.*	Fax: (908) 730-7580	

● **RAPID GRANULATOR AB**
Industrivagen 4, Box 9, SE-330 10 Bredaryd, Sweden

CEO: Karl-Valter Fornell, Pres.	Tel: 46-370-865-00
Bus: *Mfr. granulators.*	Fax: 46-370-802-51
	www.rapidgranulator.com

RAPID GRANULATOR INC.
PO Box 5887, Rockford, IL   61125
CEO:Carl Caldeira, Pres.　　　　Tel: (815) 399-4605　　%FO: 100
Bus: *Mfr. granulators.*　　　　Fax: (815) 399-0419

RAPID GRANULATOR, INC.
PO Box 5887, Rockford, IL   61125
CEO:Carl Caldeira, Pres.　　　　Tel: (815) 399-4605　　%FO: 100
Bus: *Mfr./distribute granulators.*　　Fax: (815) 399-0419　　Emp: 20

RAPID GRANULATOR, INC.
Crowfield Industrial Parkway, Goose Creek, SC   29445
CEO:Carl Caldeira, Pres.　　　　Tel: (843) 572-8226　　%FO: 100
Bus: *Mfr./distribute granulators.*　　Fax: (843) 572-8226

● **RESULT VENTURE KNOWLEDGE INTERNATIONAL**
Peter Myndes Backe 12, SE-118 46 Stockholm, Sweden
CEO: Ola Ahlvarsson, CEO　　　　Tel: 46-8-556-09-200
Bus: *Engaged in venture capital; develops*　Fax: 46-8-556-09-201
international business and　　www.result.com
communications strategies.

　　RESULT VENTURE KNOWLEDGE INTERNATIONAL
　　160 Mercer Street, New York, NY   10012
　　CEO:Urban Pettersson　　　　Tel: (212) 979-1700　　%FO: 100
　　Bus: *Develops international business*　Fax: (212) 979-1773
　　and communications strategies.

● **ROTTNE INDUSTRI AB**
Fabriksvägen 12, SE-360 40 Rottne, Sweden
CEO: Jarl Petersson, Pres.　　　　Tel: 46-470-91170　　Rev: $33
Bus: *Mfr. forestry equipment.*　　Fax: 46-470-92268　　Emp: 230
　　　　　　　　　　　　www.rottne.com

　　BLONDIN INC.
　　85 Cool Spring Road, PO Box 1287, Indiana, PA   15701
　　CEO:Rikard Olofsson, Pres.　　Tel: (724) 349-9240　　%FO: JV
　　Bus: *Sales/distribution forestry*　Fax: (724) 349-9242　　Emp: 7
　　equipment.

● **SAAB AIRCRAFT AB**
SE-581 88, Linköping, Sweden
CEO: Hans Krüger, Pres.　　　　Tel: 46-13-18-2616　　Rev: $1,033
Bus: *Design/mfr. aircraft and parts.*　Fax: 46-13-18-4495　　Emp: 7,890
　　　　　　　　　　　　www.saabaircraft.se

SAAB AIRCRAFT LEASING INC.

21300 Ridgetop Circle, Sterling, VA 20166

CEO: Marlin Schultz, Pres. Tel: (703) 406-7200 %FO: 100

Bus: *Design/mfr. aircraft & parts.* Fax: (703) 406-7309

● SAAB AUTOMOBILE AB

SE-461 80 Trollhättan, Sweden

CEO: Peter Augustsson, CEO Tel: 46-520-85000 Rev: $3,500

Bus: *Mfr. automobiles.*   Fax: 46-520-35016 Emp: 9,100

         www.saab.com

SAAB CARS USA INC.

4405-A International Blvd., Norcross, GA 30093

CEO: Daniel Chasins, Pres. & COO Tel: (770) 279-0100 %FO: 100

Bus: *Import/distribution/service* Fax: (770) 279-6499 Emp: 182
  automobiles.

● SAAB ERICSSON SPACE AB

Delsjömotet, SE-405 15 Göteborg, Sweden

CEO: Bengt Halse, Pres. & CEO Tel: 46-31-735-0000

Bus: *Design/mfr. components for satellites* Fax: 46-31-735-9520 Emp: 600
  and launch vehicles.   www.space.se

SAAB ERICSSON SPACE, INC.

1634 I Street, N.W., Ste. 600, Washington, DC 20006-4083

CEO: Andreas Derntl   Tel: (202) 783-1700 %FO: 100

Bus: *Marketing of Saab Ericsson space* Fax: (202) 783-2625
  products.

SAAB ERICSSON SPACE, INC.

222 N. Sepulveda Blvd., Ste. 2000, El Segundo, CA 90245

CEO: Marino Poppe, Office Mgr. Tel: (310) 662-4760 %FO: 100

Bus: *Marketing of Saab Ericsson space* Fax: (310) 662-4762
  products.

● SAAB ROSEMONT AB

Box 13045, SE-402 51 Goteborg, Sweden

CEO: Malcolm Burke, Pres   Tel: 46-31-337-000

Bus: *Research, design and manufacture of* Fax: 46-31-253-022
  telecommunications software tools for www.saabradar.com
  tank gauging solutions.

SAAB ROSEMONT TANK CONTROL USA

10700 Hammerly Blvd., Ste.115, Houston, TX 77043

CEO: Malcolm Burke, Pres.   Tel: (713) 722-9199 %FO: 100

Bus: *Sales/technical support*   Fax: (713) 722-9115 Emp: 10
  telecommunications software tools.

- **SANDVIK AB**

Storgatan 2, SE-811 81 Sandviken, Sweden
CEO: Claes Åke Hedström, Pres. & CEO   Tel: 46-26-26-0000   Rev: $4,646
Bus: *Mfr. cemented carbide and steel*   Fax: 46-26-26-1022   Emp: 34,300
products, tools, specialty steels and   www.sandvik.com
alloys, conveyors and industrial systems.

DORMER TOLS, INC.

135 Sweeten Creek Road, Asheville, NC   28803
CEO: Richard Tunstill, Dir.   Tel: (828) 274-6078
Bus: *Mfr./distribution tools and tooling* Fax: (828) 274-6076
systems for metalworking and rock
drilling.

DRILTECH MISSION LLC

PO Box 338, Alachua, FL   32615
CEO: Olaf Lundblad, Pres.   Tel: (904) 462-4100   %FO: 100
Bus: *Mfr. tools and rock drilling*   Fax: (904) 423-3247
systems.

EIMCO LLC

PO Box 1100, Bluefield, NV   27401
CEO: Bill Reid, Pres.   Tel: (304) 327-0260   %FO: 100
Bus: *Mfr. tools and rock drilling*   Fax: (304) 324-3658
systems.

KANTHAL GLOBAR

PO Box 339, Niagara Falls, NY   14302
CEO: Jack Beagley, Pres.   Tel: (716) 286-7600   %FO: 100
Bus: *Mfr. tools and rock drilling*   Fax: (716) 286-7602
systems.

KANTHAL PALM COAST

One Commerce Blvd., Palm Coast, FL   32164
CEO: Jack Beagley, Pres.   Tel: (904) 445-2000   %FO: 100
Bus: *Mfr. tools and rock drilling*   Fax: (904) 445-2244
systems.

PENNSYLVANIA EXTRUDED TUBE COMPANY

PO Box 1820, Scranton, PA   18501
CEO: Orjan Blom, Pres.   Tel: (717) 586-5555
Bus: *Mfr./distribution high-speed steel*   Fax: (717) 586-3333
tools.

PRECISION TWIST DRILL COMPANY

One Precision Plaza, Crystal Lake, IL   60039-9000

CEO: Tony Elfstrom, Pres.   Tel: (815) 459-2040

Bus: *Mfr./distribution tools and tooling*   Fax: (815) 459-2804
systems for metalworking and rock
drilling.

PROK INTERNATIONAL INC.

1225 East Crosby, Ste. 17, Carrollton, TX   75006

CEO: Charles Sturgell, Mgr.   Tel: (972) 466-0334   %FO: 100

Bus: *Sales/distribution of machinery,*   Fax: (972) 466-0431
equipment and tools for mining
and construction industries.

SANDVIK COROMANT COMPANY

1702 Nevins Road, PO Box 428, Fair Lawn, NJ   07410

CEO: James T. Baker, Pres.   Tel: (201) 794-5000   %FO: 100

Bus: *Mfr./distribution/service cemented*   Fax: (201) 794-5032   Emp: 500
carbide metalworking tools &
systems.

SANDVIK HARD MATERIALS COMPANY

1050 Wilshire Drive, Ste. 110, Troy, MI   48084

CEO: Per Erik Hansson, Pres.   Tel: (248) 458-4100   %FO: 100

Bus: *Mfr. metal products; cemented*   Fax: (248) 458-1168   Emp: 20
carbide.

SANDVIK MILFORD CORPORATION

PO Box 817, Branford, CT   06405

CEO: William Lavelle Jr., Pres.   Tel: (203) 481-4281   %FO: 100

Bus: *Mfr. cemented carbide & steel*   Fax: (203) 483-1384
products, tools, specialty steels &
alloys, conveyors & industrial
systems.

SANDVIK PROCESS SYSTEMS INC

21 Campus Road, Totowa, NJ   07512

CEO: Walter Miller, Pres.   Tel: (973) 790-1600   %FO: 100

Bus: *Mfr./sale/service conveyors,*   Fax: (973) 790-9247   Emp: 100
handling & automatic sorting
systems.

SANDVIK SORTING SYSTEMS, INC.

500 East Burnett Avenue, Louisville, KY   40217

CEO: Thomas Barry, Pres.   Tel: (502) 636-1414   %FO: 100

Bus: *Design/mfr./service industrial*   Fax: (502) 636-1491   Emp: 100
handling systems.

SANDVIK SPECIAL METALS CORPORATION
PO Box 6027, Kennewick, WA   99336
CEO: Wayne Banko, Pres. & CEO   Tel: (509) 586-4131   %FO: 100
Bus: *Mfr./distribution tube products in*   Fax: (509) 582-3552   Emp: 50
titanium & zirconium alloys.

SANDVIK STEEL COMPANY
PO Box 1220, Scranton, PA   18501
CEO: Edward R. Nuzzaci, Pres.   Tel: (717) 587-5191   %FO: 100
Bus: *Mfr./distribution stainless, high*   Fax: (717) 586-1722   Emp: 500
alloy steel & specialty metal tubes,
strip & wire, welding consumables

TAMROCK INC.
345 Patton Drive, Atlanta, GA   30336
CEO: Jean-Guy Coulombe, Pres.   Tel: (404) 505-0005   %FO: 100
Bus: *Mfr./distribution tools and tooling*   Fax: (404) 505-0029
systems for metalworking and rock
drilling.

UNION BUTTERFIELD CORPORATION
268 Beltline Road, Gaffney, SC   29341
CEO: Jan Lindahl, Gen. Mgr.   Tel: (864) 848-9023   %FO: 100
Bus: *Mfr. loom parts.*   Fax: (864) 848-9031   Emp: 8

● **SCAN COIN AB**
Jägershillgatan 26, SE-213 75 Malmö, Sweden
CEO: Rickard Ovin, Mng. Dir.   Tel: 46-40-600-0600   Rev: $243
Bus: *Mfr. coin counting sorting machinery,*   Fax: 46-40-600-0700   Emp: 400
currency counters, coin wrappers.   www.scancoin.se

SCAN COIN INC
21580 Beaumeade Circle, Suite 150, Ashburn, VA   20147
CEO: Per Lundin, Pres.   Tel: (703) 729-8600   %FO: 100
Bus: *Currency handling equipment.*   Fax: (703) 729-8606   Emp: 5

● **SCANCEM AB**
Anetorpsbagen 100, Box 60066, SE-21610 Malmö, Sweden
CEO: Sven Ohlsson, CEO   Tel: 46-40-16-5000   Rev: $2,200
Bus: *Mfr. construction materials, cement,*   Fax: 46-40-16-5143   Emp: 10,965
concrete, aggregates, brick and   www.scamcem.com
paperboard products.

LEHIGH PORTLAND CEMENT COMPANY

7660 Imperial Way, Allentown, PA   18195

CEO: Helmut S. Erhard, Pres.   Tel: (610) 366-4600   %FO: 100
Bus: *Mfr. cement, aggregates, ready-*   Fax: (610) 366-4684   Emp: 6,000
mix cement.

SCANCEM INC.

PO Box 619, Blandon, PA   19510-0619

CEO: Richard Kline   Tel: (610) 926-1024
Bus: *Mfr. construction materials,*   Fax: (610) 926-1906   Emp: 600
cement, concrete, aggregates,
brick and paperboard products.

VINELAND GORUP

158 Route 73 North, Voorhees, NJ   08043

CEO: William Steele, Pres.   Tel: (609) 768-6800
Bus: *Mfr. construction materials,*   Fax: (609) 768-6592
cement, concrete, aggregates,
brick and paperboard products.

VINELAND GROUP

PO Box 1247, Marlton, NJ   08053-6247

CEO: William Steele, Pres.   Tel: (609) 767-0609   %FO: 100
Bus: *Mfr. construction materials,*   Fax: (609) 767-7458
cement, concrete, aggregates,
brick and paperboard products.

● SCANDECOR MARKETING AB

Box 656, SE-751 27 Uppsala, Sweden

CEO: Goran W. Huldtgren, CEO   Tel: 46-18-54-9190
Bus: *Mfr. posters, greeting cards, art prints,*   Fax: 46-18-52-5290
etc.   www.scandecor-marketing.se

SCANDECOR INC.

430 Pike Road, Southampton, PA   18966

CEO: R. Gary Beatty, Pres.   Tel: (215) 355-2410   %FO: 100
Bus: *Distribution of posters, greeting*   Fax: (215) 364-8737   Emp: 25
cards and art prints.

● SCANDINAVIAN AIRLINES SYSTEM

Frösundaviks allé 1, SE-161 87 Stockholm, Sweden

CEO: Jan Stenberg, Pres. & CEO   Tel: 46-8-797-0000   Rev: $4,900
Bus: *International air transport services.*   Fax: 46-8-797-1290   Emp: 25,060
www.sas.se

SCANDINAVIAN AIRLINES OF NORTH AMERICA, INC.
9 Polito Avenue, Lyndhurst, NJ   07071

CEO: Jorgen Hoe-Knudsen, Gen.Mgr.	Tel: (201) 896-3600	%FO: 100
Bus: *Commercial airline services.*	Fax: (201) 896-3725	Emp: 200

SCANDINAVIAN AIRLINES SYSTEM
1301 Fifth Avenue, Ste. 2727, Seattle, WA   98101-2669

CEO: Klavs Pedersen, Reg. Mgr.	Tel: (206) 682-5250	%FO: 100
Bus: *Commercial airline (Western regional sales office).*	Fax: (206) 625-9057	

SCANDINAVIAN AIRLINES SYSTEM
150 North Michigan Avenue, Ste. 2110, Chicago, IL   60601

CEO: Palle Christensen, Mgr.	Tel: (312) 855-3900	%FO: 100
Bus: *Commercial airline services.*	Fax: (312) 855-3925	

• SCANIA AB, DIV. VOLVO AB
SE-151 87 Sodertalje, Sweden

CEO: Leif Ostling, Pres. & CEO	Tel: 46-8-55-38-1000	Rev: $5,853
Bus: *Mfr. heavy-trucks, buses, industrial and marine engines.*	Fax: 46-8-55-38-1037 www.scania.com	Emp: 23,540

SCANIA USA INC.
121 Interpark, Ste. 601, San Antonio, TX   78216

CEO: Claus Sundberg, Pres.	Tel: (210) 403-0007	%FO: 100
Bus: *Sales/distribution of heavy-trucks, buses and industrial and marine engines.*	Fax: (210) 403-0211	

• SECURITAS AB
Lindhagensplan 70, Box 12307, SE-102 28 Stockholm, Sweden

CEO: Thomas Berglund, Pres. & CEO	Tel: 46-8-657-7400	Rev: $5,300
Bus: *Provides security guards and cash transport services and provides and maintains alarm systems.*	Fax: 48-6-657-7072 www.securitasgroup.com	Emp: 210,000

PINKERTON'S INC.
4330 Park Terrace Drive, Westlake Village, CA   91361

CEO: Don W. Walker, Pres. & CEO	Tel: (818) 706-6800	%FO: 100
Bus: *Provides security systems integration including private guards and high-tech electronic access control monitoring.*	Fax: (818) 706-5515	Emp: 40,000

● **SELDEN MAST AB**

Redegatan 11, SE-426 77 Västra Frölunda, Sweden

CEO: Per Lindburg, CEO

Bus: *Mfr. of spar, masts and rigging systems for yachts.*

Tel: 46-31-69-6900
Fax: 46-31-29-7137
www.seldenmast.com

> **SELDEN MAST INC.**
>
> 4668 Franchise Street, N. Charleston, SC 29418
>
> CEO: Per Lindburg, Pres.
>
> Bus: *Mfr. of masts and rigging systems for yachts.*
>
> Tel: (843) 760-6278   %FO: 100
> Fax: (843) 760-1220

● **SIEMENS ELEMA AB**

Rontgenvagen 2, SE-171 94 Solna, Sweden

CEO: Carl Goran Myrin, Pres.

Bus: *Hospital/medical equipment; mammography, imaging, mobile x-ray.*

Tel: 46-8-730-7000   Rev: $339
Fax: 46-8-986-017   Emp: 1,100
www.siemens.se

> **ELEMA-SCHONANDER INC.**
>
> 2501 North Barrington Road, Hoffman Estates, IL 60195
>
> CEO: Russell Hall, Gen. Mgr.
>
> Bus: *Service medical imaging equipment; mfr./sales/service film viewing equipment.*
>
> Tel: (847) 842-2150   %FO: 100
> Fax: (847) 842-2195   Emp: 23

● **SKANDIA INSURANCE COMPANY LTD.**

Sveavägen 44, SE-103 50 Stockholm, Sweden

CEO: Lars-Eric Peterson, Pres. & CEO

Bus: *Insurance; property and casualty.*

Tel: 46-8-788-1000   Rev: $15,995
Fax: 46-8-788-3080   Emp: 7,161
www.skandia.se

> **AMERICAN SKANDIA LIFE ASSURANCE CORPORATION**
>
> One Corporate Drive, Shelton, CT 06484
>
> CEO: Wade A. Dokken, CEO
>
> Bus: *Property and casualty insurance services.*
>
> Tel: (203) 926-1888   %FO: 100
> Fax: (203) 929-8071

> **SKANDIA U.S. INSURANCE COMPANY**
>
> 55 Alahambra Plaza, Coral Gables, FL 33134
>
> CEO: Maria Rodriguez-Scott, Pres.
>
> Bus: *Property and casualty insurance services.*
>
> Tel: (305) 461-7400   %FO: 100
> Fax: (305) 461-4399   Emp: 10

- **SKANDINAVISKA ENSKILDA BANKEN**

Kungstradgardsgatan 8, SE-106 40 Stockholm, Sweden

CEO: Jacob Wallenburg, Chmn.	Tel: 46-8-763-8000	Rev: $3,504
Bus: *International banking services.*	Fax: 46-8-763-7163	Emp: 20,368
	www.sebank.se	

SKANDINAVISKA ENSKILDA BANKEN - NY BRANCH

245 Park Avenue, New York, NY 10167

CEO: Milton Brady, Pres.	Tel: (212) 907-4700	%FO: 100
Bus: *International banking & financial services.*	Fax: (212) 370-1642	Emp: 50

- **SKANSKA AB**

Klarabergsuiadukten 90, SE-11191 Stockholm, Sweden

CEO: Claus Bjork, Pres. & CEO	Tel: 46-8-753-8800	Rev: $11,475
Bus: *Engaged in engineering, construction, development and rental of real estate properties.*	Fax: 46-8-755-1256	Emp: 63,370
	www.skanska.com	

BARCLAY WHITE SKANSKA

518 Township Line Road, Suite 100, Bluebell, PA 19422

CEO: Edward Jorden, Pres. & CEO	Tel: (267) 470-1000	%FO: 100
Bus: *Engaged in engineering and construction.*	Fax: (267) 470-1010	

BEERS CONSTRUCTION COMPANY

70 Ellis Street, Atlanta, GA 30303

CEO: Ted Hudginn, Pres.	Tel: (404) 659-1970	%FO: 100
Bus: *General contractor/construction services.*	Fax: (404) 656-1665	Emp: 500

KOCH SKANSKA, INC.

400 Roosevelt Avenue, Carteret, NJ 07008

CEO: Robert W. Koch Jr., Pres.	Tel: (732) 969-1700	%FO: 100
Bus: *General contractor; heavy construction, steel.*	Fax: (732) 969-0197	Emp: 50

PATTEN-BEERS CONSTRUCTORS

1901 21st Avenue South, Nashville, TN 37212

CEO: Martha Kitchens, Pres.	Tel: (615) 329-3353
Bus: *Heavy construction, construction management & development, rental of real estate.*	Fax: (615) 329-7015

SKANSKA (USA) INC.

16-16 Whitestone Expressway, Whitestone, NY 11357

CEO: Stuart E. Graham, Pres. Tel: (718) 767-2600 %FO: 100

Bus: *Heavy construction, construction* Fax: (718) 767-2663
  management & development,
  rental of real estate.

SLATTERY SKANSKA, INC.

16-16 Whitestone Expressway, Whitestone, NY 11357

CEO: Salvatore Mancini, Pres. Tel: (718) 767-2600 %FO: 100

Bus: *Provides design-build operations* Fax: (718) 767-2663
  and maintenance contracting.

SORDONI SKANSKA CONSTRUCTION COMPANY

400 Interpace Pkwy., Bldg. C, Parsippany, NJ 07054

CEO: Michael J. Healy, Pres. Tel: (973) 334-5300 %FO: 100

Bus: *Heavy construction, construction* Fax: (973) 334-5376
  management & development,
  rental of real estate.

SPECTRUM SKANSKA INC.

115 Stevens Avenue, Valhalla, NY 10595

CEO: Mitchell Hochberg, Pres. Tel: (914) 773-1200 %FO: 100

Bus: *Provides construction* Fax: (914) 773-0301
  management and contracting
  services.

TIDEWATER SKANSKA GROUP, INC.

809 South Military Highway, Virginia Beach, VA 23464

CEO: David J. Eastwood, Pres. Tel: (757) 420-4140 %FO: 100

Bus: *Provides construction services.* Fax: (757) 420-3551

UNDERPINNING & FOUNDATION CONSTRUCTORS, INC.

46-36 54th Road, Maspeth, NY 11378

CEO: Peter MacKenna, Pres. Tel: (718) 786-6557 %FO: 100

Bus: *Provides heavy foundation* Fax: (718) 786-6987
  construction, pile driving and
  marine construction services.

● SKF GROUP AB

Aktiebolaget SKF, Hornsgatan 1, SE-415 50 Göteborg, Sweden

CEO: Sune Carlsson, Pres. Tel: 46-31-337-1000 Rev: $6,000

Bus: *Mfr. roller bearings, seals and special* Fax: 46-31-337-2832 Emp: 41,000
  steels, and control measurement and www.skf.com
  testing equipment.

CHICAGO RAWHIDE AMERICAS
900 North State Street, Elgin, IL   60123
CEO: William Diggory, VP   Tel: (847) 742-7840   %FO: 100
Bus: *Mfr. heat testing, surface finishing*   Fax: (847) 742-7845
    and assembly machinery.

MRC BEARINGS
PO Box 280, Jamestown, NY   14702-0280
CEO: Steve J. Koehler   Tel: (716) 661-2600   %FO: 100
Bus: *Mfr. roller bearings.*   Fax: (716) 661-2740

ROLLER BEARING INDUSTRIES
PO Box 9, Elizabethtown, KY   42702
CEO: Mary Currlin, VP   Tel: (270) 737-5120   %FO: 100
Bus: *Mfr. heat testing, surface finishing*   Fax: (270) 769-1633
    and assembly machinery.

RUSSELL T. GILMAN INC.
1230 Cheyenne Avenue, Grafton, WI   53023
CEO: Andrew Fletcher, Pres.   Tel: (262) 377-2434   %FO: 100
Bus: *Mfr. heat testing, surface finishing*   Fax: (262) 377-9438
    and assembly machinery.

SKF AERO BEARING SERVICE CENTER
PO Box 41908, North Charleston, SC   19143-1907
CEO: John Bennett, VP   Tel: (843) 207-3377   %FO: 100
Bus: *Mfr. heat testing, surface finishing*   Fax: (843) 207-3399
    and assembly machinery.

SKF AUTOMOTIVE DIVISION
1084 International Place, Graniteville, SC   29829
CEO: Dan Iacconi, Gen. Mgr.   Tel: (803) 663-8600   %FO: 100
Bus: *Mfr. heat testing, surface finishing*   Fax: (803) 663-8610
    and assembly machinery.

SKF AUTOMOTIVE DIV.
46815 Port Street, Plymouth, MI   48170
CEO: Josie Boar   Tel: (734) 414-6800   %FO: 100
Bus: *Mfr. roller bearings.*   Fax: (734) 414-6850

SKF CONDITION MONITORING, INC.
4141 Ruffin Road, San Diego, CA   92123-1841
CEO: Dan Bradley, Pres.   Tel: (858) 496-3400   %FO: 100
Bus: *Mfr. and markets sensors,*   Fax: (858) 496-3531
    instruments, software, turn-key
    systems, and services for condition
    monitoring of plant machinery.

SKF MOTION TECHNOLOGIES

1530 Valley Center Parkway, Ste. 180, Bethlehem, PA   18017

CEO: Poul Jeppesen   Tel: (800) 541-3624   %FO: 100

Bus: *Engaged in motion technologies.*   Fax: (610) 861-4811

SKF USA INC.

4392 Run Way, York, PA   17406

CEO: Jeffrey Brickner, VP   Tel: (717) 751-2900   %FO: 100

Bus: *Mfr. heat testing, surface finishing*   Fax: (717) 751-2901
and assembly machinery.

SKF USA INC.

1510 Gehman Road, Kultsville, PA   19443

CEO: Jane Richmond, Gen. Mgr.   Tel: (215) 513-4400   %FO: 100

Bus: *Mfr. heat testing, surface finishing*   Fax: (215) 513-4401
and assembly machinery.

SKF USA INC.

1111 Adams Avenue, Norristown, PA   19403

CEO: Jane Richmond, Gen. Mgr.   Tel: (610) 630-2800   %FO: 100

Bus: *Mfr./import ball and roller*   Fax: (610) 630-2801   Emp: 25
*bearings; actuation systems. (U.S.
headquarters).*

SKF USA INC.

5385 McEver Road, Box 545, Flowery Branch, GA   30542

CEO: Steve Stuart, Gen. Mgr.   Tel: (770) 967-3311   %FO: 100

Bus: *Mfr. heat testing, surface finishing*   Fax: (770) 967-4258   Emp: 100
and assembly machinery.

SKF USA INC.

7310 Tilghman Street, Ste. 650, Allentown, PA   18106

CEO: Linda Leuters   Tel: (610) 391-8054   %FO: 100

Bus: *Corporate purchasing.*   Fax: (610) 481-9070

● SMEDBO AB

Grustagsgatan 1, Box 13063, SE-250 13 Helsingborg, Sweden

CEO: Svante Andrae, Pres.   Tel: 46-42-151500

Bus: *Mfr. brass, decorative hardware and*   Fax: 46-42-155135
bathroom accessories.   www.smedbo.com

SMEDBO INC.

1001 Sherwood Drive, Lake Bluff, IL   60044

CEO: John W. Dixon, Mgr.   Tel: (847) 615-0000   %FO: 100

Bus: *Import/distribution decorative*   Fax: (847) 615-1001   Emp: 12
hardware, bathroom accessories.

• SMT MACHINE AB
PO Box 800, SE-72 122 Vasteräs Sweden

CEO: C.G. Johansson, CEO   Tel: 46-21-80-5100   Rev: $15

Bus: *Mfr. lathe equipment.*   Fax: 46-21-80-5111   Emp: 115

www.smt-machine.se

AMERICAN SMT INC.
613 Lunt Avenue, Schaumburg, IL 60193

CEO: Stig Schedin, CEO   Tel: (847) 352-0013

Bus: *Sales lathe equipment.*   Fax: (847) 352-0388   Emp: 3

• SMZ INDUSTRIER AB
Mossvagen 8, SE-641 49 Katrineholm, Sweden

CEO: Lennart Bobman, Pres.   Tel: 46-150-16220

Bus: *Mfr. hydraulic liftgates.*   Fax: 46-150-10428   Emp: 300

www.waltco.com

WALTCO TRUCK EQUIPMENT CO
227 East Compton Boulevard, Gardena, CA 90248

CEO: Marshall Walker, Gen. Mgr.   Tel: (310) 243-6800   %FO: 100

Bus: *Mfr./distribution/sale hydraulic*   Fax: (310) 538-1136
liftgates & cylinders.

WALTCO TRUCK EQUIPMENT CO
285 Northeast Avenue, Tallmadge, OH 44278

CEO: Rod Robinson, Pres.   Tel: (330) 633-9191   %FO: 100

Bus: *U.S. headquarters location;*   Fax: (330) 633-1418   Emp: 300
mfr./distribution/sale hydraulic
liftgates & cylinders.

• SSAB SWEDISH STEEL AB (FORMERLY SVENSKT STÅL AKTIEBOLAG)
Birger Jarlsgätan 58, PO Box 26208, SE-100 40 Stockholm, Sweden

CEO: Anders Ullberg, CEO   Tel: 46-8-45-45-700   Rev: $1,933

Bus: *Mfr. steel.*   Fax: 46-8-45-45-725

www.ssab.se

SSAB HARDOX, INC.
4700 Grand Avenue, Pittsburgh, PA 15225

CEO: Ralf Norden, Pres.   Tel: (412) 269-3231

Bus: *Mfr. and sale of steel and steel*   Fax: (412) 269-3251
products.

SSAB HARDTECH

200 Kipp Road, Mason, MI   48854

CEO: Sten Sjoberg, Pres.   Tel: (517) 244-8800

Bus: *Mfr. and sale of steel and steel*   Fax: (517) 244-8899
      products.

SSAB SWEDISH STEEL, INC.

4700 Grand Avenue, Pittsburgh, PA   15225

CEO: Ralf Norden, Pres.   Tel: (412) 269-2120   %FO: 100

Bus: *Mfr. and sale of steel and steel*   Fax: (412) 269-2124
      products.

● **SVEDALA INDUSTRI AB**

Kaptensgatan 1, Box 4004, SE-203 11 Malmö, Sweden

CEO: Alf Goransson, CEO   Tel: 46-40-245800   Rev: $1,820

Bus: *Design/mfr./sales systems and*   Fax: 46-40-245876   Emp: 11,000
      equipment for mineral processing,   www.svedala.com
      material handling, road construction,
      and waste processing.

SVEDALA DYNAPAC INC.

16435 IH-35 North, Selma, TX   78154

CEO: Art Kaplan, Pres.   Tel: (210) 651-9700   %FO: 100

Bus: *Construction/mining/materials*   Fax: (210) 651-6784
      handling equipment.

SVEDALA INDUSTRIES

PO Box 500, Danville, PA   17821

CEO: Don Gaughenbaugh, Mgr.   Tel: (717) 275-3050   %FO: 100

Bus: *Construction/mining/materials*   Fax: (717) 275-6789
      handling equipment.

SVEDALA INDUSTRIES INC.

800 First Avenue NW, Cedar Rapids, IA   52405

CEO: Dan Ferguson, Gen. Mgr.   Tel: (319) 365-0441   %FO: 100

Bus: *Mfr. construction/mining heavy*   Fax: (319) 369-5440   Emp: 100
      materials handling equipment.

SVEDALA INDUSTRIES, INC.

PO Box 2219, Appleton, WI   54913-2219

CEO: Patrick Quinn, Gen. Mgr.   Tel: (920) 734-9831   %FO: 100

Bus: *Mfr. construction/mining &*   Fax: (920) 734-9756   Emp: 1,000
      materials handling equipment.

SVEDALA INDUSTRIES, INC.

20965 Crossroads Circle, PO Box 1655, Waukesha, WI   53187-1655

CEO: Nina Hemberger, Pres.   Tel: (414) 798-6200   %FO: 100

Bus: *Design/mfr./sales systems and*   Fax: (414) 798-6211
equipment for mineral processing,
material handling, road
construction, and waste processing.

SVEDALA INDUSTRIES, INC., NORTHWEST DESIGN & EQUIPMENT

North 2020 Dollar Road, Spokane, WA   99212

CEO: Tom Gilligan, Gen. Mgr.   Tel: (509) 535-1044   %FO: 100

Bus: *Mfr./sales construction/mining*   Fax: (509) 535-7164   Emp: 15
handling equipment.

SVEDALA INDUSTRIES, INC., BULK MATERIALS HANDLING

4800 Grand Avenue, Neville Island, Pittsburgh, PA   15225-1599

CEO: Ray M. Koper, Pres.   Tel: (412) 269-5000   %FO: 100

Bus: *Mfr./sales bulk handling*   Fax: (412) 269-5050   Emp: 100
equipment.

SVEDALA INDUSTRIES, INC., INSTRUMENTATION DIV.

200 Rio Grande Blvd., Denver, CO   80223

CEO: James D. Shotton, Gen. Mgr.   Tel: (303) 893-0022   %FO: 100

Bus: *Mfr. construction handling*   Fax: (303) 623-3807   Emp: 10
equipment.

SVEDALA INDUSTRIES, INC., SVEDALA TRELLEX

3588 Main Street, Keokuk, IA   52632

CEO: Pat Boyd, Plant Mgr.   Tel: (319) 524-8430   %FO: 100

Bus: *Mfr./sales rubber and plastic*   Fax: (319) 524-7290   Emp: 100
products.

SVEDALA INDUSTRIES, PUMPS & PROCESS

621 South Sierra Madre, Box 340, Colorado Springs, CO   80901

CEO: Ron Robinson, Pres.   Tel: (719) 471-3443   %FO: JV

Bus: *Design/mfr./sale of equipment;*   Fax: (719) 471-4469   Emp: 100
mineral & food processing;
environmental controls.

SVEDALA MC NALLY MFG.

1308 North Walnut, Drawer D, Pittsburg, KS   66762

CEO: Timothy F. McNally, VP & Gen.   Tel: (316) 231-3000   %FO: 100
Mgr.

Bus: *Mfr. industrial process equipment.*   Fax: (316) 231-0343   Emp: 100

SVEDALA PACIFIC
12760 Earhart Avenue, Auburn, CA 95602
CEO: Brad Critchfield, Gen. Mgr.   Tel: (530) 885-0204   %FO: 100
Bus: *Import/distribution crusher &*   Fax: (530) 885-1715   Emp: 25
     screening equipment.

● **SVENSKA CELLULOSA AKTIEBOLSGET (SCA)**
Box 7827, SE-103 97 Stockholm, Sweden
CEO: Sverker Martin-Löf, CEO   Tel: 46-8-788-5100   Rev: $7,674
Bus: *Mfr. forestry and paper products.*   Fax: 46-8-660-7430   Emp: 32,100
     www.sca.se

     SCA HYGIENE PAPER INC.
     500 Baldwin Tower, Eddystone, PA 19022
     CEO: Scott Jungles   Tel: (610) 499-3700   %FO: 100
     Bus: *Mfr./sales forestry and paper*   Fax: (610) 499-3410
         products.

     SCA HYGIENE PAPER INC.
     650 Distribution Drive, Atlanta, GA 30336
     CEO: Jon Peterson, Mgr.   Tel: (404) 696-5270   %FO: 100
     Bus: *Paper plant manufacturing facility.*   Fax: (404) 696-4470

     SCA NORTH AMERICA, INC.
     500 Baldwin Tower, Eddystone, PA 19022
     CEO: Colin J. Williams, Pres.   Tel: (610) 499-3700   %FO: 100
     Bus: *Mfr./sales forestry and paper*   Fax: (610) 499-3410
         products.

     SCA PROTECTIVE PACKAGING
     800 Fifth Avenue, New Brighton, PA 15066
     CEO: John P. O'Leary Jr., Pres.   Tel: (724) 843-8200   %FO: 100
     Bus: *Mfr. packaging and protective*   Fax: (724) 843-0326
         products.

     SCA TISSUE INC.
     PO Box 719, San Ramon, CA 94583
     CEO: Dan Filipinni, Mgr.   Tel: (925) 327-8300   %FO: 100
     Bus: *Mfr./sales forestry and paper*   Fax: (925) 830-0628
         products.

     SCA TISSUE NORTH AMERICA
     210 Riverside Drive, Brattleboro, VT 05301
     CEO: Colin J. Williams, Pres.   Tel: (802) 257-0511   %FO: 100
     Bus: *Mfr. packaging and protective*   Fax: (802) 254-8411
         products.

SCA TISSUE NORTH AMERICA
984 Winchester Road, Dock 53, Neenah, WI   54956
CEO: Jeff R. Walch, VP   Tel: (920) 720-4545   %FO: 100
Bus: *Mfr. packaging and protective*   Fax: (920) 720-4535
   products.

SCA TISSUE NORTH AMERICA
500 Baldwin Tower, Eddystone, PA   19022
CEO: Jan Waldauer   Tel: (610) 499-3700   %FO: 100
Bus: *Mfr. tissue products.*   Fax: (610) 499-3391

SCA TISSUE, INC.
2527 Camino Ramon, Ste. 325, San Ramon, CA   94583
CEO: Stefan Angwald, Pres.   Tel: (925) 830-2970   %FO: 100
Bus: *Sale of industrial wipes and other*   Fax: (925) 830-0628   Emp: 95
   paper products.

● SVENSKA HANDELSBANKEN
Kungsträdgårdsgatan 2, SE-106 70 Stockholm, Sweden
CEO: Arne Mårtensson, Pres. & CEO   Tel: 46-8-701-1000   Rev: $8,122
Bus: *Commercial banking services.*   Fax: 46-8-611-5071   Emp: 8,575
                                        www.handelsbanken.se

SVENSKA HANDELSBANKEN
153 East 53rd Street, New York, NY   10022
CEO: Anders Bouvin, Mgr.   Tel: (212) 326-5100   %FO: 100
Bus: *Commercial banking services.*   Fax: (212) 326-5196

● SVERIGES TELEVISION AB
SE-105 10 Stockholm, Sweden
CEO: Allan Larsson, Chmn.   Tel: 46-8-784-8484
Bus: *Broadcasting, telecommunications.*   Fax: 46-8-784-1515
                                        www.svt.se

SWEDISH BROADCASTING COMPANY
747 Third Avenue, New York, NY   10017
CEO: Elizabeth Johansson   Tel: (212) 644-1224   %FO: 100
Bus: *Broadcasting representative.*   Fax: (212) 644-1227

● SWEDBANK (SPARBANKEN SVERIGE AB)
Brunkebergstorg 8, SE-105 34 Stockholm, Sweden
CEO: Goran Collert, Chmn.   Tel: 46-8-5859-0000
Bus: *Commercial banking services.*   Fax:
                                        www.swedbank.se

SWEDBANK NEW YORK
12 East 49th Street, 20th Fl., New York, NY   10017
CEO: John Matthews, Mgr.   Tel: (212) 486-8400   %FO: 100
Bus: *Commercial banking services.*   Fax: (212) 486-3220   Emp: 30

● **SWEDISH MATCH AB**
Rosenlundsgatan 36, SE-118 85 Stockholm, Sweden
CEO: Lennart Sundén, Pres. & CEO   Tel: 46-8-658-0200   Rev: $1,224
Bus: *Mfr./sales of smokeless tobacco, pipe*   Fax: 46-8-658-3263   Emp: 13,675
tobacco and lighters.   www.swedishmatch.ch

   GENERAL CIGAR/SWEDISH MATCH
   700 Columbia Highway, Dolthan, AL   36301
   CEO: Jim Fowler, Reg. Mgr.   Tel: (334) 793-7289   %FO: 100
   Bus: *Mfr./factory facility for cigars.*   Fax: (334) 615-8288

   SWEDISH MATCH CORPORATION
   Lookout Corporate Ctr., 1717 Dixie Highway, 5th Fl., Ft. Wright, KY   41011
   CEO: John Burrus, Reg. Mgr.   Tel: (606) 344-6511   %FO: 100
   Bus: *Sales/distribution of tobacco*   Fax: (606) 344-6551
      products.

   SWEDISH MATCH CORPORATION, CHEWING TOBACCO DIV.
   PO Box 11588, Richmond, VA   23230-1588
   CEO: Alain Tremblais, Reg. Mgr.   Tel: (804) 287-3220   %FO: 100
   Bus: *Sales/distribution of chewing*   Fax: (804) 287-3282
      tobacco products.

   SWEDISH MATCH CORPORATION, LEAF TOBACCO DIV.
   PO Box 1872, Owensboro, KY   40302-1872
   CEO: Doug Pajak, Reg. Mgr.   Tel: (502) 685-7200   %FO: 100
   Bus: *Sales of smokeless tobacco, pipe*   Fax: (502) 685-7353
      tobacco and lighters.

   SWEDISH MATCH CORPORATION, SOUTHERN SALES DIV.
   2951 Flowers Road South, Ste. 200, Atlanta, GA   30341
   CEO: Jim Fowler, Reg. Mgr.   Tel: (770) 454-6204   %FO: 100
   Bus: *Sales of smokeless tobacco, pipe*   Fax: (770) 454-6919
      tobacco and lighters.

● **SWEDTEL AB, SUB. TELIA AB**
Sankt Eriksgatan 117, Box 6296, SE-102 35 Stockholm, Sweden
CEO: Lennart Mikaelsson, Pres.   Tel: 46-8-690-2200
Bus: *Telecommunication products and*   Fax: 46-8-318319
services.   www.swedtel.com

SWEDTEL INC.
10520 NW 26th Street, Ste. C-101, Miami, FL   33172
CEO: Jan Karlsson, Pres.   Tel: (305) 593-9559   %FO: 100
Bus: *Telecommunications products and*   Fax: (305) 593-8482   Emp: 10
    services.

● **TELIA AB**
Marbackagatan 11, SE-123 86 Farsta, Sweden
CEO: Marianne Nivert, Pres. & CEO   Tel: 46-8-713-10-00   Rev: $5,742
Bus: *Telecommunications services.*   Fax: 46-8-713-33-33   Emp: 29,868
                                      www.telia.se

    TELIA INTERNATIONAL CARRIER, INC.
    Switch Location, 111 8th Avenue, Suite 818, New York, NY   10011
    CEO: Erik Heilborn, Dir.   Tel: (212) 989-5931   %FO: 100
    Bus: *Telecommunications.*   Fax:

    TELIA INTERNATIONAL CARRIER, INC.
    800 El Camino Real, Suite 210, Menlo Park, CA   94025
    CEO: Erik Heilborn, Dir.   Tel: (650) 470-0841   %FO: 100
    Bus: *Telecommunications.*   Fax:

    TELIA INTERNATIONAL CARRIER, INC.
    10780 Parkridge Blvd., Suite 300, Reston, VA   20191
    CEO: Erik Heilborn, Dir.   Tel: (703) 546-4000   %FO: 100
    Bus: *Telecommunications.*   Fax: (703) 546-4130

● **TRELLEBORG INDUSTRI AB**
Nygatan 102, PO Box 153, SE-231-22 Trelleborg, Sweden
CEO: Fredrik Arp, Pres. & CEO   Tel: 46-410-67000   Rev: $3,136
Bus: *Mfr. molded rubber products, wear* Fax: 49-410-42763   Emp: 13,890
    resistant rubber, industrial hoses, www.trelleborg.com
    protective clothing, v-belt, motor
    vehicle parts/equipment.

    GOODALL RUBBER COMPANY
    790 Birney Highway, Aston, PA   19014
    CEO: Joseph Mika, Pres.   Tel: (610) 361-0800
    Bus: *Mfr. rubber goods for all* Fax: (610) 361-0810
        appliances.

    METECH INTERNATIONAL INC.
    120 Mapleville Main Street, Mapleville, RI   02839
    CEO: John D. Koskinas, Pres.   Tel: (401) 568-0711   %FO: 100
    Bus: *Metals recycling systems.* Fax: (401) 568-6003

TRELLEBORG INC.
3000 Northwoods Parkway, Suite 350, Norcross, GA 30071
CEO: Sven Olsson, Pres.   Tel: (770) 729-8030   %FO: 100
Bus: *Mfr./sale motor vehicle equipment.*   Fax: (770) 729-1820

TRELLEBORG MONARCH INC.
61 State Route 43 North, Box 430, Hartville, OH 44632-0430
CEO: Timothy Ryan, Pres.   Tel: (330) 877-1211   %FO: 100
Bus: *Mfr./sale rubber motor vehicle products.*   Fax: (330) 877-2346

TRELLEBORG VIKING INC.
170 West Road, Ste. 1, Portsmouth, NH 03801
CEO: Richard Bauer, Mgr.   Tel: (603) 436-1236   %FO: 100
Bus: *Mfr./sale protective textile products.*   Fax: (603) 436-1392

TRELLEBORG WHEEL SYSTEMS INC.
61 State Route 43 North, Hartville, OH 44632
CEO: Tim Ryan, Pres.   Tel: (330) 877-1211   %FO: 100
Bus: *Mfr. resilient, solid and pneumatic industrial tires, and forest, farm and special application tires.*   Fax: (330) 877-2346

● **AB VOLVO**
Torslandaverken, SE-405 08 Göteborg, Sweden
CEO: Leif Johansson, Pres. & CEO   Tel: 46-31-590000   Rev: $26,670
Bus: *Mfr. trucks, marine, industrial/aircraft engines, aerospace components, hydraulic systems, construction equipment.*   Fax: 46-31-532602   www.volvo.com   Emp: 79,800

VOLVO CAR FINANCE INC.
25 Philips Pkwy, Montvale, NJ 07645
CEO: Tony Nicolosi, Pres.   Tel: (201) 358-6600   %FO: 20
Bus: *Financial services.*   Fax: (201) 307-6749

VOLVO CONSTRUCTION EQUIPMENT NORTH AMERICA
One Volvo Drive, Asheville, NC 28801
CEO: Jay Roszell, Pres.   Tel: (828) 650-2000   %FO: 50
Bus: *Mfr. construction and mining equipment.*   Fax: (828) 650-2501

VOLVO TRUCKS NORTH AMERICA INC.
7900 National Service Road, Greensboro, NC 27402-6115
CEO: Michel Gigou   Tel: (336) 393-2000   %FO: 87
Bus: *Mfr./sale trucks.*   Fax: (336) 393-2277

VOLVO MONITORING & CONCEPT CENTER

700 Via Alondra, Camarillo, CA   93012

CEO: Doug Frasier

Tel: (805) 388-0399

%FO: 100

Bus: *Research/development motor vehicles.*

Fax: (805) 388-1403

Emp: 20

VOLVO NORTH AMERICA CORP

570 Lexington Avenue, New York, NY   10022

CEO: Tomas Ericson, Pres.

Tel: (212) 754-3300

%FO: 100

Bus: *Administers subsidiaries and investments.*

Fax: (212) 418-7437

VOLVO PENTA OF THE AMERICAS

1300 Volvo Penta Drive, Chesapeake, VA   23320-9860

CEO: Clint Moore, Pres.

Tel: (757) 436-2800

%FO: 100

Bus: *Designer and manufacturer of specialist engines and drive systems for marine and industrial use.*

Fax: (757) 436-5150

Emp: 100

Switzerland

• ABB LTD.

Affolternstrasse 44, PO Box 8131, CH-8050 Zürich Oerlikon, Switzerland

CEO: Jörgen Centerman, Pres. & CEO   Tel: 41-1-317-7111   Rev: $24,680

Bus: *Engineering services for power,*   Fax: 41-1-317-7321   Emp: 165,000
process, industrial automation, mass   www.abb.com
transit, environment control.

ABB ANALYTICAL DIVISION

843 North Jefferson Street, Lewisburg, WV   24901

CEO: Lawrence J. Mueller, Pres.   Tel: (304) 647-4358   %FO: 100

Bus: *On-line process analyzers for*   Fax: (304) 645-4236
detection, analysis and monitoring
of chemical compounds.

ABB AUTOMATION

29801 Euclid Avenue, Wickliffe, OH   44092

CEO: Mike Zaharna, CEO   Tel: (440) 585-8500   %FO: 100

Bus: *Mfr. robotic cells and systems and*   Fax: (440) 585-8756
process automation systems.

ABB AUTOMATION

560 Kirts Boulevard, Ste. 119, Troy, MI   48084

CEO: Patrick Kirby, Pres.   Tel: (248) 740-8496   %FO: 100

Bus: *Paint surface finishing systems,*   Fax: (248) 740-8496
spray application equipment,
abatement systems, spray booths
and drying ovens.

ABB AUTOMATION ETSI

2 Acee Drive, Natrona Heights, PA   15065

CEO: Ronald Walko, Pres.   Tel: (724) 295-6000   %FO: 100

Bus: *Products/services for power,*   Fax: (724) 295-6560
process, industrial automation,
mass transit, environmental
control markets.

ABB AUTOMATION INC. / ETSI

2 Acee Drive, Natrona, PA   15065

CEO: William Fluhrer   Tel: (724) 295-6000

Bus: *Mfr. process automation*   Fax: (724) 295-6560
equipment and related services.

ABB C-E BOILER SYSTEMS
2000 Day Hill Road, Windsor, CT   06095
CEO: Fritz Gautschi, Pres.   Tel: (860) 688-1911   %FO: 100
Bus: *Engineers and designs utility,*   Fax: (860) 285-5877
marine and industrial boiler
systems.

ABB ENERGY VENTURES
202 Carnegie Center, Ste. 100, Princeton, NJ   08540
CEO: Chris Antonopoulou, Pres.   Tel: (609) 243-7575   %FO: 100
Bus: *Development and ownership of*   Fax: (609) 243-9175
independent power plants
worldwide.

ABB FAN GROUP NORTH AMERICA
1701 Terminal Road, PO Box 760, Niles, MI   49120
CEO: Daniel Hartlein, Pres.   Tel: (616) 683-1150   %FO: 100
Bus: *Heavy duty and high temperature*   Fax: (616) 683-2622
fans for power generation and
process systems.

ABB FINANCIAL SERVICES
One Stamford Plaza, 263 Tresser Blvd., Stamford, CT   06901
CEO: E. Nayar, Pres.   Tel: (203) 961-7800   %FO: 100
Bus: *Engaged in ABB financial services.* Fax: (203) 961-7943

ABB FLEXIBLE AUTOMATION, INC.
2487 South Commerce Drive, New Berlin, WI   53151
CEO: Silas Nichols, Pres.   Tel: (262) 785-3400   %FO: 100
Bus: *Industrial automation systems.*   Fax: (262) 785-3466

ABB INC., CE SERVICES
1000 Day Hill Road, Windsor, CT   06095
CEO: William A. Kitchen, Pres.   Tel: (860) 688-1911   %FO: 100
Bus: *Boilers for the utility industry and* Fax: (860) 285-5877
cogeneration applications.

ABB INDUSTRIAL SYSTEMS
1460 Livingston Avenue, North Brunswick, NJ   08902
CEO: J. Randall Baker, Mgr.   Tel: (732) 932-6399   %FO: 100
Bus: *Industrial automation.*   Fax: (732) 932-6456

ABB INSTRUMENTATION
125 East County Line Road, Warminster, PA   18974
CEO: Dane Maisel, Pres.   Tel: (215) 674-6000   %FO: 100
Bus: *Field and control room*   Fax: (215) 674-7183
instrumentation.

ABB LUMMUS GLOBAL, INC.
1515 Broad Street, Bloomfield, NJ   07003
CEO: Stephen Solomon, Pres.   Tel: (973) 893-1515   %FO: 100
Bus: *Construction services, engineering*   Fax: (973) 893-2000
    and power-generation equipment.

ABB POWER AUTOMATION
208 South Rogers Lane, Raleigh, NC   27610
CEO: John Reckleff, Pres.   Tel: (919) 212-4700   %FO: 100
Bus: *Power engineering services.*   Fax: (919) 212-4821

ABB POWER T & D COMPANY
1021 Main Campus Drive, Raleigh, NC   27606
CEO: David Slump, Pres.   Tel: (919) 856-3806   %FO: 100
Bus: *Provides electrical power*   Fax: (919) 856-3810
    transmission and distribution
    solutions.

ABB POWER T & D COMPANY
201 Hickman Drive, Sanford, FL   32771
CEO: Norb Hagenhoff, VP   Tel: (407) 323-8220   %FO: 100
Bus: *Provides electrical power*   Fax: (407) 322-4434
    transmission and distribution
    solutions.

ABB POWER T & D COMPANY
333 Turnpike Road, Southboro, MA   01772
CEO: Scott Kennedy, Mgr.   Tel: (508) 485-1331   %FO: 100
Bus: *Provides electrical power*   Fax: (508) 485-1712
    transmission and distribution
    solutions.

ABB POWER T & D COMPANY
2 Waterside Crossing, Windsor, CT   06095
CEO: D. Howard Pierce, CEO   Tel: (860) 683-8781   %FO: 100
Bus: *Provides electrical power*   Fax: (860) 285-2565
    transmission and distribution
    solutions.

ABB PROCESS ANALYTICS
2516 Highway 35, Manasquan, NJ   08736
CEO: Pete Gilbert, Mgr.   Tel: (732) 223-0443   %FO: 100
Bus: *On-line process analyzers for* Fax: (732) 223-4444
    detection, analysis and monitoring
    of chemical compounds.

ABB VETRO GRAY, INC.
PO Box 2291, Houston, TX   77252

CEO: Donald Grierson, Pres.   Tel: (713) 681-4685   %FO: 100

Bus: *Provides piping and pressure*   Fax: (713) 878-5155
vessel connections for power
generation.

ABB, INC.
501 Merritt Seven, PO Box 5308, Norwalk, CT   06556-5308

CEO: D. Howard Pierce, Pres. & CEO   Tel: (203) 750-2200   %FO: 100

Bus: *Products/services for power,*   Fax: (203) 750-2263   Emp: 22,000
process, industrial automation,
mass transit, environmental
control markets.

• **ACUTRONIC SCHWEIZ AG, SUB. JUNG TECHNOLOGIES AG**
Techcenter Schwarz, CH-8608 Bubikon, Switzerland

CEO: Thomas W. Jung, Chmn. & CEO   Tel: 41-55-253-2323

Bus: *Develop motion simulation and inertial*   Fax: 41-55-253-2333
navigation test systems.   www.acutronic.com

    ACUTRONIC USA INC.
    139 Delta Drive, Pittsburgh, PA   15238

    CEO: Dr. Louis A. DeMore, Pres.   Tel: (412) 963-9400   %FO: 100

    Bus: *Production, sales and service of*   Fax: (412) 963-0816   Emp: 25
    motion simulators.

• **ADECCO SA**
Rue de Langallerie 11, Case Postal 2, CH-1000 Lausanne 4, Switzerland

CEO: John Bowmer, CEO   Tel: 41-21-321-6666   Rev: $11,130

Bus: *International recruitment, temporary*   Fax: 41-21-321-6628   Emp: 350,000
employment, outplacement and career   www.adecco.com
and human resources service.

    ACCOUNTANTS ON CALL
    Park 80 West, Plaza II, GSP I-80, 9th Fl., Saddle Brook, NJ   07663

    CEO: Diane O'Meally, Pres.   Tel: (201) 843-0006   %FO: JV

    Bus: *Recruitment, temporary*   Fax: (201) 843-4936
    employment, outplacement and
    career and human resources
    business.

ADECCO, INC.
100 Redwood Shores Parkway, Redwood City, CA   94065
CEO: Debbie Pond-Heide, Pres.   Tel: (650) 610-1000   %FO: 100
Bus: *Recruitment, temporary*   Fax: (650) 610-1076
employment, outplacement and
career and human resources
business.

AJILON SERVICES, INC.
210 West Pennsylvania Avenue, Ste. 650, Towson, MD   21204-5348
CEO: Roy F. Haggerty, Pres.   Tel: (410) 821-0435   %FO: 100
Bus: *Recruitment, temporary*   Fax: (410) 828-0106
employment, outplacement and
career and human resources
business.

BCI INCORPORATED
4440 Brookfield Corporate Drive, Chantilly, VA   20151-1641
CEO: Robert Kipp, Pres.   Tel: (703) 222-8300   %FO: 100
Bus: *Recruitment, temporary*   Fax: (703) 222-8324
employment, outplacement and
career and human resources
business.

LEE HECHT HARRISON
11400 West Olympic Blvd., Ste. 1544, Los Angeles, CA   90064
CEO: Ruby Huizar, Mgr.   Tel: (310) 445-8685   %FO: 100
Bus: *Recruitment, temporary*   Fax: (310) 444-1419
employment, outplacement and
career and human resources
business.

LEE HECHT HARRISON
235 Pine Street, San Francisco, CA   94104
CEO: Andrea Huff, Mgr.   Tel: (415) 434-0125   %FO: 100
Bus: *Recruitment, temporary*   Fax: (415) 362-3585
employment, outplacement and
career and human resources
business.

LEE HECHT HARRISON
100 South Wacker Drive, Ste. 1900, Chicago, IL   60606
CEO: Chuck Ziale, Mgr.   Tel: (312) 726-1880   %FO: 100
Bus: *Recruitment, temporary*   Fax: (312) 726-1574
employment, outplacement and
career and human resources
business.

LEE HECHT HARRISON
15303 Dallas Parkway, Dallas, TX   75248
CEO: Patricia Rutherford, Mgr.   Tel: (972) 383-7400   %FO: 100
Bus: *Recruitment, temporary*   Fax: (972) 383-7420
employment, outplacement and
career and human resources
business.

LEE HECHT HARRISON
50 Tice Boulevard, Woodcliff Lake, NJ   07675
CEO: Stephen G. Harrison, Pres.   Tel: (201) 930-9333   %FO: 100
Bus: *Recruitment, temporary*   Fax: (201) 307-0864
employment, outplacement and
career and human resources
business.

OLSTEN STAFFING SERVICES
111 Speen Street, Framingham, MA   01701
CEO: Susan Acorn   Tel: (508) 875-1970   %FO: 100
Bus: *Temporary staffing services.* Fax: (508) 875-7779

● AGIE CHARMILLES GROUP, DIV. GEORG FISCHER
Case postale 373, 8-10 rue du Pré-de-la-Fontaine, CH-1217 Meyrin Geneva 1, Switzerland
CEO: Dr. Kurt E. Stirnermann, CEO   Tel: 41-22-783-3469   Rev: $650
Bus: *Mfr. of electric discharge machines*   Fax: 41-22-783-3268   Emp: 3,000
(EDM) and high-speed machining   www.agie-charmilles.com
(HSM) centers and leading system
suppliers to the tool and mold making
industry.

AGIE LTD. & ELOX CORP.
565 Griffith Street, PO Box 220, Davidson, NC   28036
CEO: Gabriele G. Carinci, Pres. & CEO   Tel: (704) 892-8011   %FO: 100
Bus: *Industrial machinery &*   Fax: (704) 896-7512   Emp: 5
equipment, machine tool
accessories.

CHARMILLES TECHNOLOIES CORP.
560 Bond Street, Lincolnshire, IL   60069
CEO: Harry Moser, Pres.   Tel: (847) 913-5300   %FO: 100
Bus: *U.S. headquarters operation for*   Fax: (847) 913-5340
manufacture and distribution of
electric discharge machines.

CHARMILLES TECHNOLOGIES MANUFACTURING CORP.
1555 Industrial Drive, Owosso, MI   48867
CEO: Mark Lorencz   Tel: (989) 725-2129   %FO: 100
Bus: *Mfr. of electric discharge   Fax: (989) 723-7266
    machines.*

INTECH EDM
2001 West Parkes Drive, Broadview, IL   60155
CEO: Linda Radtke   Tel: (708) 661-6110   %FO: 100
Bus: *Distribution of EDM wire,   Fax: (708) 681-0447
    graphite, supplies and accessories.*

MECATOOL LTD.
575 Bond Street, Lincolnshire, IL   60069
CEO: David Lynch, Pres.   Tel: (847) 478-5771   %FO: 100
Bus: *Mfr. ICS and GPS work-holding Fax: (847) 478-5784
    systems for EDM and chip making
    applications.*

MIKRON BOSTOMATIC CORP.
125 Fortune Boulevard, Milford, MA   01757
CEO: Mary Pascal, Pres.   Tel: (508) 473-4561   %FO: 100
Bus: *Mfr. of precision machining   Fax: (508) 478-7224
    systems for milling, profiling,
    contouring, and engraving.*

SYSTEM 3R USA INC.
40-D Commerce Way, Totowa, NJ   07512
CEO: Nick Giannotte, Pres. & CEO   Tel: (973) 785-8200   %FO: 100
Bus: *Sales/service of machine tools.* Fax: (973) 785-9612

● **AGRO AG**
Korbackerweg 7, CH-5502 Hunzenschwil, Switzerland
CEO: Christoph Lehmann, Mng. Dir. Tel: 41-62-889-4747
Bus: *Mfr. of cable connectors.*   Fax: 41-62-889-4750
                                   www.agro.ch

AGRO USA SALES, INC.
115 North Union Avenue, Ste. 202, Cranford, NJ   07016-2120
CEO: Mark P. Birchmeier, Mgr.   Tel: (908) 497-1300   %FO: 100
Bus: *Sales/distribution of cable   Fax: (908) 497-0915
    connectors.*

CSC COMMUNICATIONS
33162 Sterling Ponds Blvd., Sterling Heights, MI   48312
CEO: J. Bush   Tel: (810) 276-4888   %FO: 100
Bus: *Sales/distribution of cable*   Fax: (810) 276-2144
   connectors.

● AKRIS AG
Felsenstrasse 40, PO Box 31, CH-9001 St. Gallen, Switzerland
CEO: Peter Kriemler, Pres.   Tel: 41-71-22-77722
Bus: *Mfr. ladies wear.*   Fax: 41-71-22-77700
                                      www.akris.ch

AKRIS
16 Newbury Street, Boston, MA   02116
CEO: Ellen Gradwohl, Mgr.   Tel: (617) 536-6225   %FO: 100
Bus: *Sales of ladies wear.*   Fax: (617) 424-0227   Emp: 7

● ALOS HOLDING AG
Raffelstrasse 12, CH-8045 Zürich, Switzerland
CEO: Stephan Kopp, Chmn.   Tel: 41-1-468-7111   Rev: $933
Bus: *Mfr./sales of document management and* Fax: 41-1-468-7100 Emp: 1,031
   imaging systems.   www.alosmc.com

ALOS MICROGRAPHICS CORPORATION
118 Bracken Road, Montgomery, NY   12549
CEO: Gregory Schloemer   Tel: (845) 457-4400   %FO: 100
Bus: *Sales/distribution of document* Fax: (845) 457-9083   Emp: 40
   management and imaging systems

● ALU MENZIKEN HOLDING AG
CH-5737, Menziken, Switzerland
CEO: Martin Bahnmüller   Tel: 41-62-765-2121
Bus: *Mfr. of aluminum products and modular* Fax: 41-62-765-2145
   assembly systems and components. www.alu-menziken.com

UNIVERSAL ALLOY CORPORATION
2871 La Mesa Avenue, PO Box 6316, Anaheim, CA   92816-6316
CEO: John C. Ball, Pres. & CEO   Tel: (714) 630-7200
Bus: *Mfr./sales of aluminum extrusions.* Fax: (714) 630-7207   Emp: 600

● ALGROUP (ALUSUISSE-LONZA GROUP), DIV. ALCAN
Feldeggstrasse 4, Postfach 495, CH-8034 Zürich, Switzerland
CEO: Sergio Machionne, CEO   Tel: 41-1-386-2222   Rev: $4,786
Bus: *Mining and engineering; produces* Fax: 41-1-386-2585   Emp: 23,115
   aluminum and packaging.   www.algroup.ch

ALUSUISSE COMPOSITES INC.
208 West 5th St., PO Box 507, Benton, KY 42025

CEO: Jim Burr, Pres.	Tel: (502) 527-4200	%FO: 100
Bus: *Mfr./distribution of composite materials.*	Fax: (502) 527-1552	Emp: 140

ALUSUISSE COMPOSITES INC.
55 West Port Plaza, Ste. 625, St. Louis, MO 63146

CEO: Jim McCormick, Mgr.	Tel: (314) 878-2303	%FO: 100
Bus: *Mfr./distributor composite materials.*	Fax: (314) 878-7596	Emp: 140

LAWSON MARDON FLEXIBLE INC.
5303 St. Charles Road, Bellwood, IL 60104

CEO: Tim Nicholson, Mgr.	Tel: (708) 544-1600	%FO: 100
Bus: *Mfr. flexible packaging, aluminum foil.*	Fax: (708) 649-3888	Emp: 6,000

LAWSON MARDON WHEATON INC.
1101 Wheaton Avenue, Millville, NJ 08332

CEO: Hank Carter, EVP	Tel: (609) 825-1400	%FO: 100
Bus: *Glass/plastic containers, caps, closures for the pharmaceutical, cosmetic and scientific lab markets.*	Fax: (609) 825-7785	Emp: 400

● AMEDA AG
Bosch 106, CH-6331 Hunenberg, Switzerland

CEO: Robert Riedweg, Chrm. & Pres.	Tel: 41-4178-55138	
Bus: *Mfr. neonatal products, breast pumps & breastfeeding accessories, medical suction pumps, bloodflow monitors.*	Fax: 41-4178-55150 www.ameda.ch	Emp: 120

HOLLISTER INCORPORATED
2000 Hollister Drive, Libertyville, IL 60048

CEO: Allen Herbert, Pres.	Tel: (847) 680-1000	%FO: 100
Bus: *Sales, leasing and service of medical equipment.*	Fax: (847) 918-3453	Emp: 20

HOLLISTER MEDICAL SERVICES
755 Industrial Drive, Cary, IL 60013

CEO: Roland Müller, VP	Tel: (847) 639-2900	%FO: 100
Bus: *Neonatal products, breast pumps, breastfeeding accessories, medical suction pumps, bloodflow monitors.*	Fax: (847) 639-7895	Emp: 45

● **THE ARES-SERONO GROUP SA**

15 bis, Chemin des Mines, Case Postale 54, CH-1211 Geneva 20, Switzerland

CEO: Ernesto Bertarelli, CEO	Tel: 41-22-739-3000	Rev: $1,147
Bus: *Development/marketing pharmaceutical* *& diagnostics products.*	Fax: 41-22-739-3000 www.serono.com	Emp: 4,300

    ARES ADVANCED TECHNOLOGY, INC.

    280 Pond Street, Randolph, MA 02368

CEO: Scott Chappel, EVP	Tel: (781) 963-0890	%FO: 100
Bus: *Research/development life* *sciences.*	Fax: (781) 963-6058	Emp: 140

    SERONO LABORATORIES, INC.

    100 Longwater Circle, Norwell, MA 02061-1616

CEO: Hisham Samra, Pres.	Tel: (781) 982-9000	%FO: 100
Bus: *Mfr./research/marketing/distributio n pharmaceutical products.*	Fax: (781) 871-6754	Emp: 200

● **ASCOM HOLDING AG**

Belpstrasse 37, PO Box 3000, Bern 14, Switzerland

CEO: Urs T. Fischer, CEO	Tel: 41-31-999-1111	Rev: $2,000
Bus: *Development/sales of public telephone/data switching systems, security systems, paging equipment, ticket vending machines and parking systems.*	Fax: 41-31-999-2700 www.ascom.ch	Emp: 12,000

    ASCOM AUTOMATION INC.

    444 North Third Street, Philadelphia, PA 19123

CEO: Steven S. Keller, Pres. & CEO	Tel: (215) 629-1540	%FO: 100
Bus: *Sales/distribution of automatic signaling and fee collection systems for garages.*	Fax: (215) 592-7490	

    ASCOM ENERGY SYSTEMS, INC.

    One Pine Lakes Parkway North, Palm Coast, FL 32137

CEO: Robert Rhonehouse, Pres.	Tel: (904) 445-0311	%FO: 100
Bus: *Mfr. of custom AC-to-DC and DC- to-DC power supplies for use in mainframe computers and supercomputers.*	Fax: (904) 445-0322	

    ASCOM HASIER MAILING SYSTEMS, INC.

    19 Forest Parkway, Shelton, CT 06484

CEO: John Vavra, Pres.	Tel: (203) 925-2368	%FO: 100
Bus: *Mfr./sales of postage meters and mailing machines.*	Fax: (203) 929-6084	

ASCOM HOLDING INC.
19 Forest Parkway, Shelton, CT   06484
CEO: Michael A. Allocca, Pres.	Tel: (203) 925-2373	%FO: 100
Bus: *U.S. headquarters.*	Fax: (203) 627-5355	Emp: 1,100

ASCOM TRANSPORT SYSTEMS, INC.
3100 Medlock Bridge Road, Ste. 370, Norcross, GA   30071-1439
CEO: Peter E. Sands, Pres.	Tel: (770) 368-2003	%FO: 100
Bus: *Installs/maintains computerized parking control and toll road systems.*	Fax: (770) 368-2093	Emp: 50

● AVL MEDICAL INSTRUMENTS AG
Stettemerstrasse 28, CH-8207 Schafhausen, Switzerland
CEO: Helmut List, CEO	Tel: 41-848-800-885
Bus: *Mfr. biomedical devices.*	Fax: 41-848-800-875
	www.avlmed.com

ROCHE DIAGNOSTICS, INC.
235 Hembree Park Drive, Roswell, GA   30076
CEO: Steve Lundy, VP	Tel: (770) 576-5000	%FO: 100
Bus: *Mfr./sales of medical analyzers.*	Fax: (770) 576-5010	

● BACHEM AG
Hauptstrasse 144, CH-4416 Bubendorf, Switzerland
CEO: Rolf Nyfeler, COO	Tel: 41-61-931-2333	Rev: $70
Bus: *Mfr. of bulk peptide pharmaceuticals and amino acid derivatives.*	Fax: 41-61-931-2549	Emp: 330
	www.bachem.com	

BACHEM BIOSCIENCE, INC.
3700 Horizon Drive, King of Prussia, PA   19406
CEO: Jose de Chastonay, COO	Tel: (610) 239-0300	%FO: 100
Bus: *Mfr. organic chemicals.*	Fax: (610) 239-0800	Emp: 20

BACHEM CALIFORNIA, INC.
6868 Nancy Ridge Drive, San Diego, CA   92121
CEO: Dr. Josè de Chastonay, Pres	Tel: (619) 455-7051	%FO: 100
Bus: *Mfr. peptides and organic chemicals.*	Fax: (619) 455-5741	Emp: 85

PENINSULA LABORATORIES INC.
601 Taylor Way, San Carlos, CA   94070
CEO: Jim Hampton, VP	Tel: (650) 592-5392	%FO: 100
Bus: *Mfr. peptides and organic chemicals.*	Fax: (650) 595-4071	

● **BALLY MANAGEMENT LTD.**
Via Industria 1, CH-6987 Caslano, Switzerland
CEO: Gérald Mazzalovo, Pres. Tel: 41-91-612-9111 Rev: $624
Bus: *Mfr./design leather shoes and* Fax: 41-91-612-9112 Emp: 3,000
  accessories. www.bally.ch

  BALLY, INC.
  628 Madison Avenue, New York, NY 10153
  CEO: Susan K. Sussman, Pres. & CEO Tel: (212) 751-9082 %FO: 100
  Bus: *Markets shoes, accessories,* Fax: (212) 751-9126
   leather goods and apparel.

  BALLY, INC.
  One Bally Place, New Rochelle, NY 10801
  CEO: Susan K. Sussman, Pres. & CEO Tel: (914) 632-4444 %FO: 100
  Bus: *Markets shoes, accessories,* Fax: (914) 632-8264 Emp: 507
   leather goods and apparel.

● **BAUMANN FEDERN AG**
CH-8630, Rüti, Switzerland
CEO: Hans R. Rüegg, CEO Tel: 41-55-286-8111
Bus: *Mfr. of springs.* Fax: 41-55-286-8516
   www.baumann-springs.com

  BAUMANN SPRINGS USA INC.
  10710 Southern Loop Blvd., PO Box 410167, Charlotte, NC 28241
  CEO: Urs Schaffützel, VP Tel: (704) 588-2700 %FO: 100
  Bus: *Mfr. of springs/wire products.* Fax: (704) 588-8354 Emp: 70

  BAUMANN SPRINGS USA INC.
  3075 N. Great Southwest Pkwy., Ste. 100, Grand Prairie, TX 75051
  CEO: Frank Mauro, Gen, Mgr. Tel: (972) 641-7272 %FO: 100
  Bus: *Mfr. of springs/wire products.* Fax: (972) 641-0180 Emp: 60

● **BELIMO AUTOMATION AG**
Guyer-Zeller-Strasse 6, CH-8620 Wetzikon, Switzerland
CEO: Prof. Hans-Peter Wehrli, Chmn. Tel: 41-1-933-1111 Rev: $111
Bus: *Mfr./sales/marketing of air damper* Fax: 41-1-933-1221 Emp: 446
  actuators for the HVAC industries. www.belimo.com

  BELIMO AIRCONTROLS USA INC.
  43 Old Ridgebury Road, PO Box 2928, Danbury, CT 06813
  CEO: Werner A. Buck, Pres. Tel: (203) 791-9915 %FO: 100
  Bus: *Mfr./sales/marketing of air* Fax: (203) 791-9919 Emp: 65
   damper actuators for the HVAC
   industries.

BELIMO AIRCONTROLS USA INC.
1675 East Prater Way, Suite 101, Sparks, NV 89434

CEO: Werner A. Buck, Pres.	Tel: (800) 987-9042	%FO: 100
Bus: *Mfr./sales/marketing of air damper actuators for the HVAC industries.*	Fax: (702) 857-4255	

• THE BENNINGER GROUP AG
Fabnik Strasse, Postfach 68 CH-9240 Uzwil, Switzerland

CEO: Hans Balmer	Tel: 41-71-955-8585	
Bus: *Mfr. textile machinery.*	Fax: 41-71-955-8747	Emp: 830
	www.benninger.ch.com	

BENNINGER/SYMTECH INC.
885 Simuel Road, PO Box 2548, Spartanburg, SC 29301

CEO: Adolf Peter, Pres.	Tel: (864) 574-6968	%FO: 100
Bus: *Sales/service of textile machinery.*	Fax: (864) 574-7033	Emp: 15

• BERNA BIOTECH LTD.
Rehhagstrasse 79, PO Box 8234, CH-3018 Berne, Switzerland

CEO: Peter Giger, Chmn.	Tel: 41-31-980-6111	
Bus: *Mfr. pharmaceuticals.*	Fax: 41-31-980-6775	
	www.berna.org.	

BERNA PRODUCTS, INC.
4216 Ponce de Leon Boulevard, Coral Gables, FL 33146

CEO: Andres Murai, Pres.	Tel: (305) 443-2900	%FO: 100
Bus: *Sales of pharmaceuticals.*	Fax: (305) 567-0143	Emp: 8

• BERNEX, DIV. BERNA GROUP
Industriestrasse 211, CH-4601 Olten, Switzerland

CEO: Thomas Weilenmann, Chmn.	Tel: 41-62-287-8787	
Bus: *Produce PVD and CVD thin film coatings.*	Fax: 41-62-287-8788	
	www.berna.ch	

MULTI-ARC INC.
200 Roundhill Drive, Rockaway, NJ 07866-1215

CEO: Peter D. Flood, Pres.	Tel: (973) 625-3400	%FO: 100
Bus: *Sales of CVD (chemical vapor deposition) and PVD (physical vapor deposition) thin film coatings.*	Fax: (973) 625-2244	Emp: 380

XALOY, INC.

102 Xaloy Way, Pulaski, VA   24301
CEO: Bill Talbot
Bus: *Mfr. high-performance screws.*
Tel: (540) 980-7560
Fax: (540) 980-5670
%FO: 100

● BIRCHER, AG

Bircher Reglomat, Wiesengasse 20, CH-8222 Beringen, Switzerland
CEO: Rémy Höhener, Mgr.
Bus: *Mfr. industrial safety equipment and automation and controls.*
Tel: 41-52-687-1111
Fax: 41-52-687-1210
www.bircher.com

BIRCHER AMERICA, INC.

909 East Oakton Street, Elk Grove Village, IL   60007
CEO: Roland Schibli, Mgr.
Bus: *Sales/distribution of industrial safety equipment and automation and controls.*
Tel: (847) 952-3730
Fax: (847) 952-2005
%FO: 100
Emp: 7

● BISCHOFF TEXTIL AG

Bogenstrasse 9, PO Box 362, CH-9001 St. Gallen, Switzerland
CEO: Rudi Sieber
Bus: *Mfr. of lace, embroidery, couturier fabrics and luxury bedding.*
Tel: 41-71-72-0111
Fax:
www.bischoff-august.com

BISCHOFF ROYAL EMBROIDERED LACE

1329 East Thousand Oaks Blvd., Thousand Oaks, CA   91362
CEO: Georges Ulmer, CEO
Bus: *Sales/distribution of lace, embroidery, couturier fabrics and luxury bedding.*
Tel: (805) 379-1099
Fax: (805) 379-3548
%FO: 100
Emp: 5

BISCHOFF-AUGUST INTERNATIONAL

37 Industrial Avenue, Fairview, NJ   07022
CEO: Ralph August, CEO
Bus: *Sales/distribution of embroidered goods.*
Tel: (201) 295-3400
Fax: (201) 861-1030
%FO: 100
Emp: 10

● BLASER SWISSLUBE AG

Winterseistrasse, CH-3415 Hasle-Rüegsau, Switzerland
CEO: Peter Blaser, Pres.
Bus: *Mfr./distribution of metalworking fluids and lubricants.*
Tel: 41-34-460-0101
Fax: 41-34-460-0100
www.blaser-swisslube.com

BLASER SWISSLUBE INC.

31 Hatfield Lane, Goshen, NY   10924

CEO: Uli Krahenbuhl, Pres.

Tel: (914) 294-3200   %FO: 100

Bus: *Sales/distribution of metalworking*   Fax: (914) 294-3102   Emp: 25
fluids and lubricants.

● BOBST S.A.

PO Box 1001, CH-1001 Lausanne, Switzerland

CEO: Andreas Koopmann, CEO

Tel: 41-21-621-2111   Rev: $930

Bus: *Mfr. equipment and services for the*   Fax: 41-21-626-1270   Emp: 5,050
folding carton, corrugated, and flexible   www.bobstgroup.com
packaging industries.

BOBST GROUP

1995 North Place, NW, Atlanta, GA   30339

CEO: Jonathan Abbis

Tel: (770) 952-2310   %FO: 100

Bus: *Mfr., distribution, & servicing*   Fax: (770) 984-8830
printing & converting machines
for paper and cardboard.

BOBST GROUP

4825 North Scott Street, Chiller Park, IL   60176

CEO: Philippe Michel, Pres.

Tel: (847) 678-9390   %FO: 100

Bus: *Mfr., distribution, & servicing*   Fax: (847) 678-6809
printing & converting machines
for paper and cardboard.

BOBST GROUP

140 Harrison Avenue, PO Box 2800, Roseland, NJ   07068

CEO: Philippe Michel, Pres.

Tel: (973) 226-8000   %FO: 100

Bus: *Mfr., distribution, & servicing*   Fax: (973) 226-8625   Emp: 464
printing & converting machines
for paper and cardboard.

CORRUGATING ROLL CORPORATION

607 Market Street, Ste. 801, Knoxville, TN   37902

CEO: Bob Sukenik, Pres.

Tel: (865) 522-6874   %FO: 100

Bus: *Mfr., distribution, & servicing*   Fax: (865) 521-9576   Emp: 35
printing & converting machines
for paper and cardboard.

● BOSSARD HOLDING AG

Steinhauserstrasse 70, CH-6301 Zug, Switzerland

CEO: Heinrich Bossard, CEO

Tel: 41-41-749-6611   Rev: $207

Bus: *Develop and manufacture systems,*   Fax: 41-41-749-6622   Emp: 1,200
methods and elements for industry   www.bossard.com
assembly.

BOSSARD IIP INC.
11305 Meredith Drive, Des Moines, IA 50322
CEO: Janneth I. Marcelo   Tel: (515) 278-7030   %FO: 100
Bus: *Mfr. metric fasteners.*   Fax: (515) 278-8620

BOSSARD LARSON, INC.
3801 West Green Tree Road, Milwaukee, WI 53212
CEO: Peter Vogel   Tel: (414) 247-1100   %FO: 100
Bus: *Develop and manufacture systems,*   Fax: (414) 247-8713
methods and elements for industry
assembly.

BOSSARD METRICS INC.
PO Box 9556, Greenville, SC 29615-9556
CEO: Bill Unferth, VP   Tel: (864) 297-3881   %FO: 100
Bus: *Mfr. metric fasteners.*   Fax: (864) 297-9042   Emp: 14

BOSSARD METRICS INC.
235 Heritage Avenue, Portsmouth, NH 03801
CEO: R. Doane, Mgr.   Tel: (603) 433-5900   %FO: 100
Bus: *Provides metric fastening*   Fax: (603) 433-4695   Emp: 100
solutions and technical support.

MATERIAL MANAGING GROUP, DIV. BOSSARD
2319 East Pensar Drive, Appleton, WI 54911
CEO: J. Fitzpatrick   Tel: (920) 749-1212   %FO: 100
Bus: *Mfr. fasteners.*   Fax: (920) 749-9370

● BOURDON-HAENNI HOLDING AG
Bernstrasse 59, CH-3303 Jegenstorf, Switzerland
CEO: Peter Gloor, Pres. & CEO   Tel: 41-31-764-9911
Bus: *Design and manufacture of scales and*   Fax: 41-31-764-9922
measuring equipment.   www.haenni-str.com

HAENNI INSTRUMENTS, INC.
1107 Wright Avenue, Gretna, LA 70056
CEO: David Morgan, Gen. Mgr.   Tel: (504) 392-3344   %FO: 100
Bus: *Sales of pressure gauges, scales*   Fax: (504) 392-6500   Emp: 5
and measuring equipment.

LOADOMETER CORPORATION
3G Nashua Court, Baltimore, MD 21221
CEO: Ernst Werthmueller   Tel: (410) 574-0102   %FO: 100
Bus: *Sales of measuring equipment.*   Fax: (410) 574-2865

- **BRUDERER AG**

CH-9320, Frasnacht, Switzerland

CEO: Markus E. Bruderer, Pres.   Tel: 41-71-447-7500

Bus: *Mfr./sales high speed punching presses.*   Fax: 41-71-447-7780   Emp: 750

www.bruderer-presses.com

> **BRUDERER INC.**
>
> 1619 Highway 72, East, PO Box 208, Huntsville, AL 35804-0208
>
> CEO: Werner Vieh, VP   Tel: (256) 859-4050   %FO: 100
>
> Bus: *Mfr. high speed presses.*   Fax: (256) 859-0944   Emp: 100
>
> **BRUDERER MACHINERY INC.**
>
> 1200 Hendricks Causeway, Ridgefield, NJ 07657
>
> CEO: Alois Rupp, Pres.   Tel: (201) 941-2121   %FO: 100
>
> Bus: *Sales high speed presses.*   Fax: (201) 886-2010   Emp: 40

- **BSI - BANCA DELLA SVIZZERA ITALIANA (SUB.ASSICURAZIONA GENERALI, S.p.A.**

Via Magatti 2, PO Box 2833, CH-6901 Lugano, Switzerland

CEO: Hugo von der Crone, Chmn.   Tel: 41-91-809-3111

Bus: *International commercial and private*   Fax: 41-91-809-3678   Emp: 300
banking services.   www.bsi.ch

> **BSI - BANCA DELLA SVIZZERA ITALIANA**
>
> 65 East 55th Street, New York, NY 10022
>
> CEO: Yves G. Gaden, SVP   Tel: (212) 326-3100   %FO: 100
>
> Bus: *International commercial and*   Fax: (212) 326-3105   Emp: 20
> *private banking services.*

- **BUHLER LTD.**

CH-9240, Uzwil, Switzerland

CEO: Urs Bühler, Chmn.   Tel: 41-71-955-1111

Bus: *Mfr./sales of food processing and*   Fax: 41-71-955-3379   Emp: 3,000
industrial machinery.   www.buhler.ch

> **BUHLER LTD.**
>
> 1100 Xenium Lane North, PO Box 9497, Minneapolis, MN 55441-4499
>
> CEO: Dr. Eric von Euw, Pres.   Tel: (763) 847-9900   %FO: 100
>
> Bus: *Mfr./sales food processing;*   Fax: (763) 847-9911   Emp: 280
> *industrial machinery.*
>
> **SORTEX, INC.**
>
> 2385 Arch-Airport Road, Ste. 300, Stockton, CA 95206
>
> CEO: Mike Clay, Pres.   Tel: (209) 983-8400   %FO: 100
>
> Bus: *Provides sorting solution*   Fax: (209) 983-4800
> *machinery.*

- **BYSTRONIC MASCHINEN AG, DIV. BYSTRONIC GROUP**

Industriestrasse 5, CH-4922 Bützberg, Switzerland

CEO: Heinz Wäiti

Bus: *Mfr. of machinery for cutting, breaking, grinding, drilling and handling of flat glass.*

Tel: 41-62-958-7777
Fax: 41-62-958-7676
www.bystronic.com

BYSTRONIC INC.

30 Commerce Drive, Hauppauge, NY   11788

CEO: Ulrich Trösch, VP

Bus: *Sales/service of machinery for the glass industry, laser cutting machines and waterjet cutting machines.*

Tel: (631) 231-1212
Fax: (631) 231-1040

%FO: 100

- **CU CHEMIE UETIKON AG**

CH-8707, Uetikon am Zee, Switzerland

CEO: Dr. Moritz Braun, CEO

Bus: *Mfr. fertilizers, organic and inorganic fine chemicals, bulk pharmaceuticals and molecular sieves.*

Tel: 41-1-922-9111
Fax: 41-1-920-2093
www.uetikon.com

ZEOCHEM

562 Prince Edward Road, Glen Ellyn, IL   60137

CEO: M. Schneider

Bus: *Producer of molecular sieve adsorbents used in natural gas processing, petroleum refining, and petrochemicals.*

Tel: (630) 545-0109
Fax: (630) 545-0109

Emp: 100

ZEOCHEM

3303 FM 1960 West, Ste. 300, Houston, TX   77068

CEO: M. Schneider

Bus: *Producer of molecular sieve adsorbents used in natural gas processing, petroleum refining, and petrochemicals.*

Tel: (281) 444-3731
Fax: (281) 444-3731

Emp: 100

ZEOCHEM

PO Box 35940, Louisville, KY   40232

CEO: Kenneth J. Gustafson, Gen. Mgr.

Bus: *Producer of molecular sieve adsorbents used in natural gas processing, petroleum refining, and petrochemicals.*

Tel: (502) 634-7600
Fax: (502) 634-8133

%FO: 50
Emp: 100

● **CIBA SPECIALTY CHEMICALS HOLDING**
Klybeckstrasse 141, CH-4002 Basel, Switzerland
CEO: Armin Meyer, CEO   Tel: 41-61-636-1111   Rev: $4,896
Bus: *Mfr. specialty chemicals.*   Fax: 41-61-636-3019   Emp: 24,500
                                 www.cibasc.com

    CIBA SPECIALTY CHEMICALS CORPORATION
    PO Box 820, Suffolk, VA   23439-0820
    CEO: Judy Orey   Tel: (757) 538-3700   %FO: 100
    Bus: *Sales/distribution of water*   Fax: (757) 538-3989
      treatment products.

    CIBA SPECIALTY CHEMICALS CORPORATION
    4050 Premier Drive, High Point, NC   27265
    CEO: Brenda Speth   Tel: (888) 873-2422   %FO: 100
    Bus: *Mfr. pigments, textile dyes and*   Fax: (336) 801-2808
      paper chemicals.

    CIBA SPECIALTY CHEMICALS CORPORATION
    540 White Plains Road, Tarrytown, NY   10591
    CEO: Fred Vigeant, Mgr.   Tel: (914) 785-2000   %FO: 100
    Bus: *Mfr. specialty chemicals including*   Fax: (914) 785-2183   Emp: 500
      water treatment products.

● **CLARIANT INTERNATIONAL LTD.**
Rothausstrasse 61, CH-4132 Muttenz, Switzerland
CEO: Reinhard Handte, CEO   Tel: 41-61-469-5111   Rev: $6,566
Bus: *Mfr./sales of dyes and specialty*   Fax: 41-61-469-5999   Emp: 31,550
  chemicals   www.clariant.com

    CLARIANT CORPORATION
    4000 Monroe Road, Charlotte, NC   28205
    CEO: Ken Golder, Pres.   Tel: (704) 331-7000   %FO: 100
    Bus: *Mfr./sales of dyes and specialty*   Fax: (704) 377-1063   Emp: 1,200
      chemicals

    CLARIANT LIFE SCIENCES
    2114 Larry Jeffers Road, Elgin, SC   29045
    CEO: Ken Golder, Pres.   Tel: (803) 438-3471   %FO: 100
    Bus: *Mfr./sales of dyes and specialty*   Fax: (803) 438-4497
      chemicals

● **COM TELCO INTERNATIONAL INC.**

Hechtackerstrasse 41, CH-9014 St. Gallen, Switzerland

CEO: Ulrich Berkmann, CEO   Tel: 41-71-276-8633   Rev: $11

Bus: *Mfr. computer software systems for the*   Fax: 41-71-278-8640   Emp: 250
hospitality industry.   www.comtelco.com

    COM TELCO INC.

    One Market Street, 2nd Fl., Lynn, MA   01901

    CEO: Don Armstrong, VP   Tel: (781) 595-2002   %FO: 100

    Bus: *Mfr. computer software systems*   Fax: (781) 595-3003
    for the hospitality industry.

● **COMPAGNIE FINANCIÈRE RICHEMONT AG**

Rigistrasse 2, CH-6300 Zug, Switzerland

CEO: Johann Rupert, Chmn. & CEO   Tel: 41-41-710-3322   Rev: $7,700

Bus: *Holding company for Dunhill and*   Fax: 41-41-711-7102   Emp: 29,000
Winfield tobacco products, high value   www.richemont.com
jewelry and watches and luxury goods
subsidiary, Vendome Group.

    ALFRED DUNHILL OF LONDON INC.

    450 Park Avenue, New York, NY   10022

    CEO: Vincent Robin, Pres.   Tel: (212) 888-4000   %FO: 100

    Bus: *Sales/distribution of tobacco and*   Fax: (212) 750-8841
    tobacco products, clothing,
    leathergoods, and jewelry.

    MONTBLANC USA

    75-100 North Street, Bloomsbury, NJ   08804

    CEO: Fred Reffsin, Pres.   Tel: (908) 479-1600   %FO: 100

    Bus: *Sales/distribution of high-quality*   Fax: (908) 479-4566
    writing instruments and pen
    products.

● **COMPAGNIE FINANCIÈRE TRADITION**

11, rue de Langallerie, P.O.Box 2400, CH-1002 Lausanne, Switzerland

CEO: Patrick Combes, Chmn.   Tel: 41-21-343-5252   Rev: $584

Bus: *International securities broker.*   Fax: 41-21-343-5500
    www.traditiongroup.com

    CAPSTONE GLOBAL ENERGY

    1330 Lake Robbins Drive, Ste. 350, The Woodlands, TX   77380

    CEO: Riaz Siddiqi   Tel: (281) 296-7080   %FO: 100

    Bus: *International securities broker.*   Fax: (281) 296-7034

THE RECRUITEMENT COMPANY
17 State Street, 41st Fl., New York, NY 10004
CEO: Doug King, Mgr.   Tel: (212) 943-6916   %FO: 1
Bus: *International securities broker.*   Fax: (212) 943-8504

TFS DERIVATIVES CORPORATION
17 State Street, 41st Fl., New York, NY 10004
CEO: Raymond C. Baccala, Mng. Dir.   Tel: (212) 943-6916   %FO: 100
Bus: *International securities broker.*   Fax: (212) 943-8504   Emp: 60

TRADITION DERIVATIVES CORPORATION
180 Maiden Lane, 20th Fl., New York, NY 10038
CEO: Jeff Mehan, Pres.   Tel: (212) 943-6916   %FO: 100
Bus: *International securities broker.*   Fax: (212) 943-8504   Emp: 5

TRADITION FINANCIAL SERVICES INC.
680 Washington Blvd., 5th Fl., Stamford, CT 06901
CEO: Julian Harding, Mng. Dir.   Tel: (203) 351-9555   %FO: 100
Bus: *International securities broker.*   Fax: (203) 351-9566   Emp: 35

TRADITION FINANCIAL SERVICES INC.
180 Maiden Lane, 20th Fl., New York, NY 10038
CEO: David Pinchin, Pres.   Tel: (212) 943-2787   %FO: 100
Bus: *International securities broker.*   Fax: (212) 943-0720   Emp: 35

TRADITION GLOBAL CLEARING INC.
61 Broadway, 4th Fl., New York, NY 10006
CEO: Emil Assentato, Mng. Dir.   Tel: (212) 797-5300   %FO: 100
Bus: *International securities broker.*   Fax: (212) 797-7207   Emp: 200

TRADITION INC.
865 S. Figueroa Street, Ste. 1320, Los Angeles, CA 90017
CEO: William G. Whyte, SVP   Tel: (213) 622-4127   %FO: 100
Bus: *International securities broker.*   Fax: (213) 622-9561   Emp: 9

● CORIM AG
Dufourstrasse 65, CH-8702 Zolikon, Switzerland
CEO: Ben H. Willilngham, Jr., CEO   Tel: 41-1-391-7123
Bus: *Investment financing.*   Fax: 41-1-391-2726
     www.corim.com

INTREPID, INC., DIV. CORIM
100 Laura Street, PO Box 359, Jacksonville, FL 32201
CEO: Bill Wellingham, Pres.   Tel: (904) 355-3500   %FO: 100
Bus: *U.S. headquarters; real estate investment/property management.*   Fax: (904) 355-2099   Emp: 25

INTREPID, INC., DIV. CORIM
7 Drayton Street, Savannah, GA   31401
CEO: Sylvia King, Mgr.   Tel: (912) 233-5520   %FO: 100
Bus: *Real estate investment/property*   Fax: (912) 233-9163   Emp: 5
  management.

INTREPID, INC., DIV. CORIM
3951 Pleasantdale Road, Atlanta, GA   30340
CEO: Deshion Weatherly, VP   Tel: (770) 953-3434   %FO: 100
Bus: *Real estate investment/property*   Fax: (770) 953-3737   Emp: 8
  management.

● **COTECNA INSPECTION SA**
58, rue de la Terrassiere, PO Box 6155, CH-1211 Geneva 6, Switzerland
CEO: Robert M. Massey, CEO   Tel: 41-22-849-6900
Bus: *Customs values inspection services for*   Fax: 41-22-849-6989   Emp: 4,000
  international traded goods.   www.cotecna.com

   COTECNA INSPECTION INC.
   14505 Commerce Way, Ste. 501, Miami Lakes, FL   33016
   CEO: Peter Schnyder, Mgr.   Tel: (305) 828-8141   %FO: 100
   Bus: *Engaged in quality control*   Fax: (305) 827-0616   Emp: 40
     services.

   COTECNA INSPECTION INC.
   10102 Sands Trail Court, Houston, TX   77064
   CEO: H. Olaya, Mgr.   Tel: (281) 477-8662   %FO: 100
   Bus: *Engaged in quality control*   Fax: (281) 477-0891
     services.

● **CREDIT SUISSE GROUP**
Paradeplatz 8, PO Box 1, CH-8070 Zürich, Switzerland
CEO: Lukas Mühlemann, CEO   Tel: 41-1-333-1111   Rev: $7,000
Bus: *Engaged in financial advisory services*   Fax: 41-1-333-2587   Emp: 62,300
  and sales/trading financial products   www.csg.ch
  worldwide.

   BLUE RIDGE INSURANCE COMPANIES
   86 Hopmeadow Street, PO Box 519, Simsbury, CT   06070
   CEO: Peter Christen, Pres. & CEO   Tel: (860) 651-1065   %FO: 100
   Bus: *Engaged in insurance services.*   Fax: (860) 408-3267

CREDIT SUISSE ASSET MANAGEMENT

277 Park Avenue, New York, NY   10172

CEO: Charles Stonehill   Tel: (212) 892-3000   %FO: 100

Bus: *Engaged in financial advisory*   Fax:
     services and sales/trading
     financial products.

CREDIT SUISSE ASSET MANAGEMENT

445 South Figueroa Street, 27th Fl., Los Angeles, CA   90017

CEO: John Mack   Tel: (213) 489-6807   %FO: 100

Bus: *Engaged in financial advisory*   Fax: (213) 489-6811
     services and sales/trading
     financial products.

CREDIT SUISSE ASSET MANAGEMENT

466 Lexington Avenue, New York, NY   10017

CEO: John Mack   Tel: (212) 875-3500   %FO: 100

Bus: *Engaged in financial advisory*   Fax: (646) 658-0728
     services and sales/trading
     financial products.

CREDIT SUISSE ASSET MANAGEMENT

Two Mid America Plaza, Oakbrook Terrace, Ste. 800, Chicago, IL   60181

CEO: William McKenzie, Mgr.   Tel: (630) 954-2220   %FO: 100

Bus: *Engaged in financial advisory*   Fax: (630) 954-2219
     services and sales/trading
     financial products.

CREDIT SUISSE FIRST BOSTON

11 Penn Center Plaza, 26th Fl., Philadelphia, PA   19103-2929

CEO: Charles Stauffer, Mng. Dir.   Tel: (215) 851-1000   %FO: 100

Bus: *Engaged in financial advisory*   Fax: (215) 851-0352   Emp: 15
     services and sales/trading
     financial products.

CREDIT SUISSE FIRST BOSTON

227 West Monroe, Chicago, IL   60606-5016

CEO: Mark Berny   Tel: (312) 750-3000   %FO: 100

Bus: *Engaged in financial advisory*   Fax: (312) 750-1823   Emp: 135
     services and sales/trading
     financial products.

CREDIT SUISSE FIRST BOSTON

633 West Fifth Street, 64th Fl., Los Angeles, CA   90017

CEO: Kenneth Moelis	Tel: (213) 955-8200	%FO: 100
Bus: *Engaged in financial advisory services and sales/trading financial products.*	Fax: (213) 955-8245	Emp: 45

CREDIT SUISSE FIRST BOSTON

201 Spear Street, PO Box 115802, San Francisco, CA   94105-1637

CEO: John Mack	Tel: (415) 836-7600	%FO: 100
Bus: *Engaged in financial advisory services and sales/trading financial products.*	Fax: (415) 836-7751	

CREDIT SUISSE FIRST BOSTON

2400 Hanover Street, Palo Alto, CA   94304-1135

CEO: John Mack	Tel: (650) 614-5000	%FO: 100
Bus: *Engaged in financial advisory services and sales/trading financial products.*	Fax: (650) 614-5030	

CREDIT SUISSE FIRST BOSTON

11 Madison Avenue, New York, NY   10010-3629

CEO: John Mack	Tel: (212) 325-2000	%FO: 100
Bus: *Engaged in financial advisory services and sales/trading financial products.*	Fax: (212) 318-1188	Emp: 4,000

CREDIT SUISSE FIRST BOSTON

100 Federal Street, 30th Fl., Boston, MA   02110-1802

CEO: Joe L. Roby, Pres.	Tel: (617) 556-5500	%FO: 100
Bus: *Engaged in financial advisory services and sales/trading financial products.*	Fax: (617) 542-1814	Emp: 45

CREDIT SUISSE FIRST BOSTON

133 Peachtree Street N.E., Atlanta, GA   30303-1841

CEO: Scott Hinchman	Tel: (404) 897-2800	%FO: 100
Bus: *Engaged in financial advisory services and sales/trading financial products.*	Fax: (404) 522-3043	

CREDIT SUISSE FIRST BOSTON
600 Travis Street, Ste. 3030, Houston, TX   77002-3003

CEO: Gordon Hall, Mng. Dir.	Tel: (713) 220-6700	%FO: 100
Bus: *Engaged in financial advisory services and sales/trading financial products.*	Fax: (713) 236-9222	Emp: 35

GENERAL CASUALTY INSURANCE COMPANIES
One General Drive, Sun Prairie, WI   53596

CEO: Lukas Muhlemann, CEO	Tel: (608) 837-4440	%FO: 100
Bus: *Engaged in insurance services.*	Fax: (608) 837-0583	

REPUBLIC UNDERWRITERS INSURANCE
2727 Turtle Creek Boulevard, Dallas, TX   75219

CEO: John Mack	Tel: (214) 559-1222	%FO: 100
Bus: *Engaged in financial advisory services and sales/trading financial products.*	Fax: (214) 748-9590	

SOUTHERN GUARANTY INSURANCE
2545 Taylor Road, Montgomery, AL   36123

CEO: John Mack	Tel: (334) 270-6000	%FO: 100
Bus: *Engaged in financial advisory services and sales/trading financial products.*	Fax: (334) 270-6226	

SWISS AMERICAN SECURITIES INC.
12 East 49th Street, New York, NY   10017

CEO: Peter Bretscher, Chmn.	Tel: (212) 612-8700	%FO: 100
Bus: *Engaged in financial advisory services and sales/trading financial products.*	Fax: (212) 813-0625	

UNIGARD INSURANCE GROUP
15805 N. E. 24th Street, Bellevue, WA   98008

CEO: John Mack	Tel: (425) 641-4321	%FO: 100
Bus: *Engaged in financial advisory services and sales/trading financial products.*	Fax: (425) 562-5256	

WINTERTHUR INTERNATIONAL AMERICA
40 Wall Street, New York, NY   10005

CEO: John Mack	Tel: (212) 530-4545	%FO: 100
Bus: *Engaged in financial advisory services and sales/trading financial products.*	Fax: (212) 530-4544	

● **DANZAS GROUP AG**

Peter Merian Strasse, CH-4051 Basel, Switzerland

CEO: Peter Wagner, CEO   Tel: 41-61-274-7474   Rev: $7,800

Bus: *International air and land*   Fax: 41-61-274-7475   Emp: 43,250
transportation.   www.danzas.com

       DANZAS CORPORATION

       3650 131st Avenue, SE, Ste. 700, Bellevue, WA   98006

       CEO: Hans Toggweiler, CEO   Tel: (425) 649-9339   %FO: 100

       Bus: *U.S. headquarters office for*   Fax: (425) 649-4940
       air/land transport and custom
       house brokerage.

● **EBEL SA, DIV. LVMH GROUP**

113, rue de la Paix, CH-2300 La Chaux-de-Fonds, Switzerland

CEO: Pierre-Alain Blum, CEO   Tel: 41-32-9123-123

Bus: *Mfr. watches.*   Fax: 41-32-9123-124
                    www.ebel.ch

       EBEL, INC., DIV. LVMH GROUP

       750 Lexington Avenue, New York, NY   10022

       CEO: Ronald L. Wolfgang, Pres. & CEO Tel: (212) 888-3235   %FO: 100

       Bus: *Sales/distribution of watches.* Fax: (212) 888-6719   Emp: 55

● **EMS-CHEMIE HOLDING AG**

Kugelgasse 22, CH-8708 Mannedorf, Switzerland

CEO: Christoph Blocher, Chmn. & CEO   Tel: 41-1-921-0000   Rev: $720

Bus: *Mfr. chemicals, including airbag*   Fax: 41-1-921-0001   Emp: 2,750
igniters, coating and sealing products www.emschemie.com
and generators.

       EMS-CHEMIE INC.

       2060 Corporate Way, PO Box 1717, Sumter, SC   29151-1717

       CEO: Guido J. Hobi   Tel: (803) 481-9173   %FO: 100

       Bus: *Mfr. chemicals, including airbag* Fax: (803) 481-3820
       igniters, coating and sealing
       products and generators.

● **ENDRESS + HAUSER FLOWTEC AG**

Kägenstrasse 7, CH-4153 Reinach, Switzerland

CEO: Klaus Endress, CEO   Tel: 41-61-715-6111   Rev: $702

Bus: *Mfr./distribution level, pressure, flow* Fax: 41-61-711-0989   Emp: 3,000
and moisture instrumentation and   www.endress.com
process recorders.

A. D. INSTRUMENTS, DIV. ENDRESS + HAUSER INC.
4711-A Nations Crossing Road, Charlotte, NC   28217
CEO: Aloaire Cramer, Mgr.   Tel: (704) 522-8415   %FO: 100
Bus: *Mfr./sales of level, pressure, flow*   Fax: (704) 527-5005
and moisture instrumentation
process recorders.

ENDRESS + HAUSER FLOWTEC INC.
2350 Endress Place, PO Box 246, Greenwood, IN   46143
CEO: Hans Peter Blaser, Mng. Dir.   Tel: (317) 535-7138   %FO: 100
Bus: *Mfr./sales of electronic process*   Fax: (317) 535-8498   Emp: 25
control instrumentation.

ENDRESS + HAUSER INSTRUMENTS INC.
942 Town Center, New Britain, PA   18901
CEO: Joe Shaffer   Tel: (267) 880-1750   %FO: 100
Bus: *Mfr./sales of level, pressure, flow*   Fax: (267) 880-1759
and moisture instrumentation
process recorders.

ENDRESS + HAUSER INSTRUMENTS INC.
2350 Endress Place, PO Box 246, Greenwood, IN   46143
CEO: Joseph W. Schaffer, VP   Tel: (317) 535-7138   %FO: 100
Bus: *Mfr./sales of level, pressure, flow*   Fax: (317) 535-8498   Emp: 180
and moisture instrumentation
process recorders.

● GEORG FISCHER LTD.
Amsler-Laffon-Strasse 9, PO Box 671, CH-8201 Schaffhausen, Switzerland
CEO: Martin Huber, Pres. & CEO   Tel: 41-52-631-1111   Rev: $2,210
Bus: *Mfr. automotive castings and products;*   Fax: 41-52-631-2847   Emp: 12,200
piping systems; machine tools, plant   www.georgfischer.com
engineering and construction.

AGIE CORPORATION
565 Griffith Street, PO Box 220, Davidson, NC   2803
CEO: Gabriele Carinci, Pres.   Tel: (704) 892-8011
Bus: *Mfr. electrical discharge machines.*   Fax: (704) 896-7512   Emp: 60

BUSS AMERICA INC.
230 Covington Drive, Bloomingdale, IL   60108
CEO: Dan Nierste, Pres.   Tel: (630) 307-9900   %FO: 100
Bus: *Sales/service of compounding*   Fax: (630) 307-9905
equipment.

CHARMILLES TECHNOLOGIES CORPORATION
560 Bond Street, Lincolnshire, IL 60069-4224

CEO: Harry C. Moser, Pres.	Tel: (847) 913-5300	%FO: 100
Bus: *Distributor/service electrical discharge machines*	Fax: (847) 913-5340	Emp: 120

CHARMILLES TECHNOLOGIES MANUFACTURING CORP
1555 Industrial Drive, Owosso, MI 48867

CEO: Mark Lorencz, Pres.	Tel: (517) 725-2129	%FO: 100
Bus: *Machining & assembly facility for electrical discharge machines.*	Fax: (517) 723-7266	Emp: 140

FISCHER ELECTRONIC CONNECTORS
115 Perimeter Center Place, Ste. 1060, Atlanta, GA 30346

CEO: Steve DeFeo, Pres.	Tel: (770) 352-0606	%FO: 100
Bus: *Sales of electrical connectors.*	Fax: (770) 352-0992	

GEORGE FISCHER AUTOMOTIVE PRODUCTS INC.
2655 Woodward Avenue, Ste. 300, Bloomfield Hills, MI 48304

CEO: Thomas Bischoff, Pres.	Tel: (248) 745-5952	%FO: 100
Bus: *Sales/distribution of automotive products.*	Fax: (248) 745-5957	

GEORGE FISCHER CORP
230 Covington Drive, Bloomingdale, IL 60108-3106

CEO: Michael Reynolds, Pres.	Tel: (630) 351-5593	%FO: 100
Bus: *Holding company.*	Fax: (630) 307-9905	Emp: 46

GEORGE FISCHER INC
2882 Dow Avenue, Tustin, CA 92680-7285

CEO: Christof Blumer, CEO	Tel: (714) 731-8800	%FO: 100
Bus: *Distribution plastic piping systems, plastic values, fluid sensor products.*	Fax: (714) 731-6201	Emp: 52

GEORGE FISCHER SLOANE INC.
7777 Sloane Drive, Little Rock, AR 72206

CEO: Mario Bettini, Pres.	Tel: (501) 490-7777	%FO: 100
Bus: *Mfr./sales industrial machinery.*	Fax: (501) 490-7100	

MECATOOL USA
575 Bond Street, Lincolnshire, IL 60069

CEO: David Lynch, Pres.	Tel: (847) 478-5771	%FO: 100
Bus: *Mfr./sales machine tools.*	Fax: (847) 478-5784	

SIGNET SCIENTIFIC CO
3401 Aerojet Ave., PO Box 5770, El Monte, CA 91734-1770
CEO: Michael Gioseffi, Pres.   Tel: (626) 571-2770   %FO: 100
Bus: *Mfr. fluid sensor products.*   Fax: (626) 573-2057   Emp: 110

WAESCHLE INC.
230 Covington Drive, Bloomingdale, IL 60108
CEO: Heinz W. Schneider, Pres.   Tel: (630) 539-9100   %FO: 100
Bus: *Design/construction components, operating units & plans.*   Fax: (630) 539-9196   Emp: 30

● **FORBO INTERNATIONAL SA**
Bauelenzelgstrasse 20, CH-8193 Eglisau Zürich, Switzerland
CEO: Werner Kummer, CEO   Tel: 41-1-868-2525   Rev: $1,251
Bus: *Decorative building products and construction materials holding company.*   Fax: 41-1-868-2526   Emp: 6,781
www.forbo.com

    FORBO AMERICA, INC.
    1105 North Market Street, Ste. 1300, Wilmington, DE 19899
    CEO: Eugene Chace, Pres. & CEO   Tel: (302) 427-2139   %FO: 100
    Bus: *Mfr. /sales building materials & home products.*   Fax: (302) 427-2139

    FORBO INDUSTRIES INC
    PO Box 667, Hazelton, PA 18201
    CEO: Denis P. Darragh, Pres.   Tel: (570) 459-0771   %FO: 100
    Bus: *Sales/distribution of floor coverings.*   Fax: (570) 450-0258   Emp: 63

    SIEGLING AMERICA, INC.
    12201 Vanstory Road, Huntersville, NC 28078
    CEO: Wayne E. Hoffman, Pres.   Tel: (704) 948-0800   %FO: 100
    Bus: *Systems technology.*   Fax: (704) 948-0995   Emp: 250

● **FRANKE HOLDING AG**
CH-4663 Aarburg, Switzerland
CEO: Michael Pieper, Chmn.   Tel: 41-62-787-3131   Rev: $762
Bus: *Sales/distribution of kitchen sinks and accessories, food service equipment, industrial and medical equipment.*   Fax: 41-62-791-6761   Emp: 4,042
www.franke.com

    FRANKE COMMERICAL SYSTEMS
    680 Overmeyer Road, Sparks, NV 89431
    CEO: William M. Cherkitz, Pres.   Tel: (702) 359-6663   %FO: 100
    Bus: *Mfr. food service equipment, kitchen sinks & accessories.*   Fax: (702) 359-0407   Emp: 40

FRANKE CONSUMER PRODUCTS INC., KITCHEN DIV.

3050 Campus Drive, Ste. 500, Hatfield, PA   19440

CEO: Tom Smith, Pres.   Tel: (215) 822-6590   %FO: 100

Bus: *Mfr./distribution of kitchen sinks,*   Fax: (215) 822-5873   Emp: 15
     faucets and accessories.

FRANKE CONTRACT GROUP

One Franke Boulevard, Fayetteville, TN   37334

CEO: L. Affolter   Tel: (931) 433-7455

Bus: *Mfr. of food service equipment.*   Fax: (931) 433-3309

FRANKE GROUP

310 Tech Park Drive, La Verge, TN   37086

CEO: L. Affolter   Tel: (615) 793-5990   %FO: 100

Bus: *Sales/distribution spare parts.*   Fax: (615) 793-5940   Emp: 75

FRANKE INC.

685 Glendale Avenue, Sparks, NV   89431-5812

CEO: L. Affolter   Tel: (775) 358-8484

Bus: *Mfr. of food service equipment.*   Fax: (775) 359-1005

O'BRIEN BUDD INC.

PO Box 1307, St. Charles, IL   60174-7307

CEO: Mike McCabe, VP   Tel: (630) 513-4255

Bus: *Mfr./distribution of kitchen sinks,*   Fax: (630) 513-1069
     faucets and accessories.

● GIVAUDAN, S.A.

5 Chemin de la Parfumerie, CH-1214 Vernier, Switzerland

CEO: Jüerg Witmer, CEO   Tel: 41-22-780-9111   Rev: $1,223

Bus: *Mfr. flavors and fragrances.*   Fax: 41-22-780-9150   Emp: 4,800
                                          www.givaudan.com

GIVAUDAN CORPORATION

225 Avenue I, Ste. 202, Redondo Beach, CA   90277

CEO: Rebecca Delapiedru, Mgr.   Tel: (310) 792-0200   %FO: 100

Bus: *Mfr. and sales of flavors and*   Fax: (310) 792-0211
     fragrances.

GIVAUDAN CORPORATION

300 Waterloo Valley Road, Mount Olive, NJ   07828

CEO: Dave Johnson, Pres.   Tel: (973) 448-6500   %FO: 100

Bus: *Mfr. and sales of flavors and*   Fax: (973) 448-6517
     fragrances.

GIVAUDAN CORPORATION
6250 River Road, Ste. 4010, Rosemont, IL   60018
CEO: Chris Johnson, Mgr.   Tel: (847) 735-0221   %FO: 100
Bus: *Mfr. and sales of flavors and*   Fax: (847) 735-0221
    fragrances.

GIVAUDAN CORPORATION
7 West 57th Street, New York, NY   10019
CEO: Art Alvardo, Mgr.   Tel: (212) 593-1601   %FO: 100
Bus: *Mfr. and sales of flavors and*   Fax: (212) 829-8495
    fragrances.

GIVAUDAN FLAVORS CORP.
1199 Edison Drive, Cincinnati, OH   45201
CEO: Mike Davis, Pres.   Tel: (513) 948-8000   %FO: 100
Bus: *Mfr. and sales of flavors.*   Fax: (513) 948-5637

GIVAUDAN FRAGRANCES CORP.
1775 Windsor Road, Teaneck, NJ   07666
CEO: Errol Stafford, Pres.   Tel: (201) 833-7500   %FO: 100
Bus: *Mfr. and sales of fragrances.*   Fax: (201) 833-8165

● HABASIT AG
Römerstrasse 1, CH-4153 Reinach, Switzerland
CEO: Giovanni Volpi, Pres.   Tel: 41-61-715-1515   Rev: $228
Bus: *Mfr./distribution of power transmission*   Fax: 41-61-715-1555   Emp: 1,850
and conveyor belts.   www.habasit.com

HABASIT ABT INC.
150 Industrial Park Road, Middletown, CT   06457
CEO: Dennis Goodwin, Pres. & CEO   Tel: (860) 632-2211   %FO: 100
Bus: *Mfr./sales of power transmission*   Fax: (860) 632-1710
    and conveyor belts.

HABASIT BELTING INCORPORATED
305 Satellite Blvd., PO Box 80507, Suwanee, GA   30024
CEO: John G. Wallace, Pres.   Tel: (678) 288-3600   %FO: 100
Bus: *Sales/distribution of power*   Fax: (678) 288-3651   Emp: 350
    transmission and conveyor belts.

HABASIT GLOBE, INC.
1400 Clinton Street, PO Box 1062, Buffalo, NY   14206-2919
CEO: Harry Cardillo, Pres. & CEO   Tel: (716) 824-8484   %FO: 100
Bus: *Mfr./distribution of power*   Fax: (716) 827-0375
    transmission and conveyor belts.

● **HANRO LTD.**
PO Box 4410, CH-4410 Liestal, Switzerland
CEO: Lothar Peters, Dir.   Tel: 41-61-921-0294
Bus: *Manufacturer of sleepwear and*   Fax: 41-61-921-0294   Emp: 500
underwear.   www.hanro.com

    HANRO USA, INC.
    40 East 34th Street, Ste. 205, New York, NY   10016
    CEO: Niki Kalish-Sachs, Pres.   Tel: (212) 532-3320   %FO: JV
    Bus: *Distributor underwear, sleepwear.* Fax: (212) 685-4823   Emp: 20

● **HERMANN BUHLER AG**
Spinnerei Spinning Mill, CH-8482 Sennhof (Winterthur), Switzerland
CEO: Martin Kägi, CEO   Tel: 41-52-234-0404
Bus: *Spinning mill for high quality yarns.* Fax: 41-52-234-0494   Emp: 265
www.buhleryarn.com

    BUHLER QUALITY YARNS CORP.
    1881 Athens Hwy., PO Box 50, Jefferson, GA   30549
    CEO: Jean Claude Allemann, COO   Tel: (706) 367-9834   %FO: 100
    Bus: *Spinning mill for high quality*   Fax: (706) 367-9837   Emp: 120
    yarns.

● **HOLDERBANK FINANCIÈRE GLARIS LTD.**
Zurchenstrasse 156, CH-8745 Jona, Switzerland
CEO: Thomas Schmidheiny, Chmn.   Tel: 41-55-222-8700   Rev: $8,190
Bus: *Mfr. cement and building materials.* Fax: 41-55-222-8629   Emp: 40,500
www.holderbank.com

    HOLNAM INC.
    6211 North Ann Arbor Road, Dundee, MI   48131
    CEO: Paul A. Yhouse, Pres.   Tel: (734) 529-2411   %FO: 100
    Bus: *Mfr./supplier cement, aggregates* Fax: (734) 529-5512   Emp: 2,500
    & concrete.

    ST. LAWRENCE CEMENT COMPANY
    3 Columbia Circle, Albany, NY   12203
    CEO: Dennis Skidmore, SVP   Tel: (518) 452-3563   %FO: 100
    Bus: *Mfr./supplier cement. (JV with*   Fax: (518) 452-3045   Emp: 350
    Holderbank & St. Lawrence
    Cement, Canada)

● **HUBER & SUHNER AG**

Tumbelenstrasse 20, CH-8330 Pfäffikon, Switzerland

CEO: Marc C. Cappis, Chmn. & CEO	Tel: 41-1-952-2211	Rev: $450
Bus: *Provides components and subsystems for cellular communication, and automotive, railway, building and civil engineering systems.*	Fax: 41-1-952-2424 www.hubersuhner.com	Emp: 3,474

CHAMPLAIN CABLE CORPORATION

12 Hercules Drive, Colchester, VT   05446

CEO: Bob Job, Pres.	Tel: (802) 655-2121	%FO: 100
Bus: *Mfr. datacom, industrial, and automotive cables.*	Fax: (802) 654-4224	

EM&C ENGINEERING ASSOCIATES

3535 Hyland Avenue, Ste. 202, Costa Mesa, CA   92626

CEO: Mohamed El Gafi	Tel: (714) 957-6429	%FO: 100
Bus: *Engaged in waste water treatment solutions.*	Fax: (714) 957-6414	

HUBER & SUHNER INC.

19 Thomas Drive, Essex, VT   05452

CEO: George Pouch, Chmn.	Tel: (802) 878-0555	%FO: 100
Bus: *Sales/distribution of microwave products and specialty insulated cables.*	Fax: (802) 878-9880	

HUBER & SUHNER INC.

31291 Via Mari Posta Court, Bonsall, CA   92003

CEO: John E. Jacob	Tel: (760) 630-0093	%FO: 100
Bus: *Distributes antenna systems solutions.*	Fax: (760) 630-3903	

JOOS EQUIPMENT COMPANY

Station Square Two, Ste. 114 North Valley Road, Paoli, PA   19301

CEO: Eric R. Joos	Tel: (610) 644-5875	%FO: 100
Bus: *Engaged in waste water treatment solutions.*	Fax: (610) 889-0819	

SYSTEM COMPONENTS CORP.

6750 West Hwy. 40, Ocala, FL   34482

CEO: Charlie McAllister	Tel: (352) 237-8848	%FO: 100
Bus: *Engaged in waste water treatment solutions.*	Fax: (352) 237-8558	

TC&M SYSTEMS INC.
745-Y Cinema Court, Kernersville, NC   27284

CEO: Edward L. Wentz	Tel: (336) 993-6110	%FO: 100
Bus: *Engaged in waste water treatment solutions.*	Fax: (336) 993-6110	

● **INFICON**
Maienfelderstrasse 2, 7310 Bad Ragaz, Switzerland

CEO: James L. Brissenden, CEO	Tel: 41-81-302-4646	Rev: $170
Bus: *Mfr. instrumentation for monitoring, analysis, control, leak detection and plasma cleaning in the semiconductor, vacuum coatings, air conditioning/refrigeration and industrial markets.*	Fax: www.inficon.com	Emp: 700

INFICON
Two Technology Place, East Syracuse, NY   13057

CEO: James L. Brissenden, CEO	Tel: (315) 434-1100	%FO: 100
Bus: *Mfr. instrumentation for monitoring, analysis, control, leak detection and plasma cleaning in the semiconductor, vacuum coatings, air conditioning/refrigeration and industrial markets.*	Fax: (315) 437-3803	Emp: 700

● **INFRANOR INTER AG**
Scharenmoosstrasse 117, CH-8052 Zürich, Switzerland

CEO: Nicholas Eichenberger, CEO	Tel: 41-1-302-2727	Rev: $53
Bus: *Mfr./service systems, motors and industrial equipment.*	Fax: 41-1-302-7189 www.infranor.com	Emp: 280

INFRANOR INC
45 Great Hill Road, PO Box 1307, Naugatuck, CT   06770

CEO: J. C. Carbone, Pres.	Tel: (203) 729-8258	%FO: 100
Bus: *Mfr./service systems, motors and industrial equipment.*	Fax: (203) 729-6969	Emp: 20

● **INTERNATIONAL BIOMEDICINE MANAGEMENT PARTNERS AG**
Aeschenplatz 7, PO Box 136, CH-4010 Basel, Switzerland

CEO: Stefan Ryser, CEO	Tel: 41-61-206-9030
Bus: *Engaged in financial services.*	Fax: 41-61-206-9031
	www.biomedicine.ch

INTERNATIONAL BIOMEDICINE, INC.
2121 N. California Blvd., Ste. 250, Walnut Creek, CA   94596

CEO: Andrienne Burgess	Tel: (925) 952-3870	%FO: 100
Bus: *Engaged in financial services.*	Fax: (925) 952-3871	

● JET AVIATION INTERNATIONAL, INC.
Zollikerstrasse 228, PO Box 586, CH-8034 Zürich, Switzerland

CEO: Thomas M. Hirschmann, CEO	Tel: 41-1-382-2202	Rev: $520
Bus: *Engaged in leasing chartered jets worldwide.*	Fax: 41-1-382-1060	Emp: 3,800
	www.jetaviation.com	

JET AVIATION BUSINESS JETS, INC.
1515 Perimeter Road, West Palm Beach, FL   33406

CEO: Thomas W. Mitchell, SVP	Tel: (561) 233-7242	%FO: 100
Bus: *Engaged in aircraft charter, management and flight support.*	Fax: (561) 233-7240	

JET AVIATION BUSINESS JETS, INC.
4511 Empire Avenue, Hangar 5, Burbank, CA   91505

CEO: Lisa Schiebelhut, Sales Mgr.	Tel: (818) 843-8400	%FO: 100
Bus: *Engaged in aircraft charter, management and flight support.*	Fax: (818) 843-6606	

JET AVIATION BUSINESS JETS, INC.
5200 West 63rd Street, Bldg. A, Chicago, IL   60638

CEO: James Short, Sales Mgr.	Tel: (773) 581-6575	%FO: 100
Bus: *Engaged in aircraft charter, management and flight support.*	Fax: (773) 581-2635	

JET AVIATION BUSINESS JETS, INC.
111 Charles Lindbergh Drive, Teterboro, NJ   07608

CEO: Patricia Pattermann, Mgr.	Tel: (201) 462-4000	%FO: 100
Bus: *Engaged in aircraft charter, management and flight support.*	Fax: (201) 462-4005	

JET AVIATION BUSINESS JETS, INC.
Westchester County Airport, White Plains, NY   10604

CEO: Bruce McNeely, SVP	Tel: (914) 761-0711	%FO: 100
Bus: *Engaged in aircraft charter, management and flight support.*	Fax: (800) 221-0197	

JET AVIATION BUSINESS JETS, INC.
Washington National Airport, General Aviation Terminal, Washington, DC   20001

CEO: Bruce McNeely, SVP	Tel: (800) 736-8538	%FO: 100
Bus: *Engaged in aircraft charter, management and flight support.*	Fax: (800) 221-0197	

JET AVIATION, INC.
380 Hanscom Drive, Bedford, MA   01730

CEO: Michael Gregory, SVP	Tel: (781) 274-0030	%FO: 100
Bus: *Engaged in leasing corporate and private jets and helicopters.*	Fax: (781) 274-6573	

• JULIUS BAER HOLDING LTD.
Bahnhofstrasse 36, Postfach, CH-8010 Zürich, Switzerland

CEO: Walter Knabenhans, CEO	Tel: 41-1-228-5111	Rev: $1,491
Bus: *Engaged in securities and investment banking.*	Fax: 41-1-211-2026 www.juliusbaer.com	Emp: 2,285

BANK JULIUS BAER
1900 Avenue of the Stars, Ste. 2701, Los Angeles, CA   90067

CEO: Roger Wacker, Gen. Mgr.	Tel: (310) 286-0201	%FO: 100
Bus: *Engaged in securities and investment banking.*	Fax: (310) 286-0306	

BANK JULIUS BAER
251 Royal Palm Way, Ste. 601, Palm Beach, FL   33480

CEO: Michael A. Blank, Rep.	Tel: (561) 659-4440	%FO: 100
Bus: *Engaged in securities and investment banking.*	Fax: (561) 659-4744	

BANK JULIUS BAER
330 Madison Avenue, New York, NY   10017

CEO: Bernard Spiiko, Mgr.	Tel: (212) 297-3600	%FO: 100
Bus: *Engaged in private banking.*	Fax: (212) 557-7839	

BANK JULIUS BAER
101 California Street, Ste. 4525, San Francisco, CA   94111

CEO: Pius Kämpfen, Gen. Mgr.	Tel: (415) 986-1622	%FO: 100
Bus: *Engaged in securities and investment banking.*	Fax: (415) 398-7159	

BANK JULIUS BAER ASSET MANAGEMENT
330 Madison Avenue, New York, NY   10017

CEO: Michael Byl, Mgr.	Tel: (212) 297-3800	%FO: 100
Bus: *Engaged in securities and investment banking.*	Fax: (212) 557-7839	

• KABA HOLDING AG
Hofwisenstrasse 24, CH-8153 Rumlang, Switzerland

CEO: Ulrich Graf, Pres. & CEO	Tel: 41-1-818-9061	Rev: $275
Bus: *Leading technology developers and providers in the field of access management.*	Fax: 41-1-818-9052 www.kaba.com	Emp: 2,000

KABA HIGH SECURITY LOCKS CORPORATION
PO Box 490, Southington, CT   06489

CEO: Tom DiVito, Pres. & CEO	Tel: (860) 621-3605	%FO: 100
Bus: *Mfr. keys, key mach, locks, locksmith supplies.*	Fax: (860) 621-5972	

● KUDELSKI SA
Route de Geneve 22, CH-1033 Cheseaux-sur-Lausanne, Switzerland

CEO: Andre Kudelski, CEO	Tel: 41-21-732-0101	Rev: $223
Bus: *Mfr. digital TV access systems.*	Fax: 41-21-732-0100	Emp: 425
	www.kudelski.com	

NAGRA USA, INC.
240 Great Circle Road, Ste. 326, Nashville, TN   37228

CEO: Glen Trew	Tel: (615) 726-5191	%FO: 100
Bus: *Mfr./sales digital TV access systems.*	Fax: (615) 726-5189	

NAGRASTAR LLC
90 Inverness Circle East, Englewood, CO   80112

CEO: Charles Egli, COO	Tel: (303) 706-5700	%FO: 100
Bus: *Mfr./sales digital TV access systems.*	Fax: (303) 706-5719	

NAGRAVISION
2041 Rosecrans Avenue, Ste. 350, El Segundo, CA   90245

CEO: Charles Egli, COO	Tel: (310) 335-5225	%FO: 100
Bus: *Mfr./sales digital TV access systems.*	Fax: (310) 335-5227	

● KUONI TRAVEL HOLDING LTD.
Neue Hard 7, CH-8010 Zürich, Switzerland

CEO: Hans Lerch, Chmn.	Tel: 41-1-277-4444	Rev: $2,552
Bus: *Leisure travel firm.*	Fax: 41-1-271-5282	Emp: 7,700
	www.kuoni.com	

INTRAV
7711 Bonhomme Avenue, St. Louis, MO   63105

CEO: David Dreier, COO	Tel: (314) 727-0500	%FO: 100
Bus: *Engaged in leisure travel.*	Fax: (314) 727-0908	

● LAMPRECHT TRANSPORT AG
Peter-Merian Strasse 48, Postfach, CH-4002 Basel, Switzerland

CEO: Thomas A. Lamprecht, Dir.	Tel: 41-61-284-7474	
Bus: *Freight forwarding and logistics services.*	Fax: 41-61-284-7444	Emp: 300
	www.lamprecht.ch	

AMERICAN LAMPRECHT TRANSPORT INC.
2801 NW 74 Avenue, Ste. 220, Miami, FL 33122
CEO: Jean Dill   Tel: (305) 597-5979   %FO: 100
Bus: *Air/ocean, import/export*   Fax: (305) 597-5975
     forwarding and customhouse
     brokers.

AMERICAN LAMPRECHT TRANSPORT INC.
Ridgeview Centre Drive, Ste. 197-B, Duncan, SC 29334
CEO: Oscar Christen   Tel: (864) 433-8585   %FO: 100
Bus: *Air/ocean, import/export*   Fax: (864) 433-8555   Emp: 7
     forwarding and customhouse
     brokers.

AMERICAN LAMPRECHT TRANSPORT INC.
2218 Landmeier Road, Elk Grove Village, IL 60007
CEO: Hans-Peter Widmer, Pres.   Tel: (847) 364-0555   %FO: 100
Bus: *Air/ocean, import/export*   Fax: (847) 364-9350   Emp: 5
     forwarding and customhouse
     brokers.

AMERICAN LAMPRECHT TRANSPORT INC.
5757 West Century Blvd., Ste. 480, Los Angeles, CA 90045
CEO: John M. Bruckner, Pres.   Tel: (310) 645-4736   %FO: 100
Bus: *Air/ocean, import/export*   Fax: (310) 645-5985
     forwarding and customhouse
     brokers.

AMERICAN LAMPRECHT TRANSPORT INC.
700 Rockaway Turnpike, Lawrence, NY 11559
CEO: Alain Tiercy, EVP   Tel: (516) 239-6200   %FO: 100
Bus: *Air/ocean, import/export*   Fax: (516) 239-0844   Emp: 7
     forwarding and custom house
     brokerage services.

● **LEICA GEOSYSTEMS AG**
CH-9435 Heerbrugg, Switzerland
CEO: Hans Hess, Pres. & CEO   Tel: 41-71-727-3131
Bus: *Develop, manufacture and sales of*   Fax: 41-71-727-4678
     microscopes and optoelectronic sensors, www.leica-geosystems.com
     surveying instrument and
     photogrammetic equipment.

LEICA GEOSYSTEMS INC.
4855 Peachtree Industrial Blvd., Ste. 235, Norcross, GA   30092
CEO: Lisa Corbett   Tel: (770) 447-6361   %FO: 100
Bus: *Sales of microscopes and*   Fax: (770) 447-0710
     optoelectronic sensors, surveying
     instrument and photogrammetic
     equipment.

LEICA GEOSYSTEMS INC.
23868 Hawthorne Blvd., Torrance, CA   90505
CEO: Neil VanCans, Pres.   Tel: (310) 791-5300   %FO: 100
Bus: *Development/mfr./sales of Global*   Fax: (310) 378-6627   Emp: 85
     Positioning Systems for navigation
     and surveying.

LEICA MICROSYSTEMS INC.
111 Deerlake Road, Deerfield, IL   60015
CEO: Hank Smith, Pres.   Tel: (847) 405-0123   %FO: 100
Bus: *Mfr. of hand held refractometers,*   Fax: (847) 405-0147   Emp: 300
     diagnostic equipment and
     microscopes.

LEICA MICROSYSTEMS INC.
3362 Walden Avenue, Depew, NY   14043
CEO: Art Alix, Pres.   Tel: (716) 686-3000   %FO: 100
Bus: *Mfr. of hand held refractometers,*   Fax: (716) 686-3085   Emp: 200
     diagnostic equipment and
     microscopes.

● **LIEBHERR-INTERNATIONAL AG**
Rue de l'Industrie 19, PO Box 272, CH-1630 Bulle, Switzerland
CEO: Paul Wagishauser, Mng. Dir.   Tel: 41-26-913-3111   Rev: $3,090
Bus: *Mfr. industrial machinery, cranes,*   Fax: 41-26-912-1240   Emp: 19,400
     machine tools, assembly lines,   www.liebherr.com
     automation, and aviation machinery.

LIEBHERR CONSTRUCTION EQUIPMENT COMPANY
4100 Chestnut Avenue, Newport News, VA   23605
CEO: Eduard Sprow, Pres.   Tel: (757) 245-5251   %FO: 100
Bus: *Mfr. construction machinery and*   Fax: (757) 928-8701
     concrete mixes.

LIEBHERR MINING EQUIPMENT CO.
4100 Chestnut Avenue, Newport News, VA   23607
CEO: Dr. Andreas Pielczyk, Pres.   Tel: (757) 245-5251   %FO: 100
Bus: *Mfr. industrial machinery.*   Fax: (757) 928-8755   Emp: 60

LIEBHERR AEROSPACE SALINE COMPANY
1465 Woodland Drive, Saline, MI   48176
CEO: Peter Kozma, VP   Tel: (734) 429-7225   %FO: 100
Bus: *Mfr. industrial machinery.*   Fax: (734) 429-2294

LIEBHERR-AMERICA, INC.
4100 Chestnut Avenue, Newport News, VA   23605
CEO: Ronald Jacobson, Pres.   Tel: (757) 245-5251   %FO: 100
Bus: *Mfr. industrial machinery.*   Fax: (757) 928-8701   Emp: 60

• LINDT & SPRÜNGLI INTERNATIONAL
Seestrasse 204, CH-8802 Kitchberg, Switzerland
CEO: Ernst Tanner, CEO   Tel: 41-1-716-2233   Rev: $971
Bus: *Mfr./trading of chocolate products.*   Fax: 41-1-716-2662   Emp: 5,820
                                 www.lindt.com

GHIRARDELLI CHOCOLATE COMPANY
1111 139th Avenue, San Leandro, CA   94578-2631
CEO: John Anton, CEO   Tel: (510) 483-6970   %FO: 100
Bus: *Mfr./sales of chocolate, cocoa and*   Fax: (510) 297-2649
    candy bars.

LINDT & SPRUENGLI INC.
One Fine Chocolate Place, Stratham, NH   03885
CEO: Lee Mizusawa, Pres.   Tel: (603) 778-8100   %FO: 100
Bus: *Mfr./sales of Swiss chocolates.*   Fax: (603) 778-3102

• LOGITECH INTERNATIONAL SA
Moulin du Choc D, CH-1122 Romanel-sur-Morges, Switzerland
CEO: Daniel V. Borel, Chmn.   Tel: 41-21-863-5111   Rev: $761
Bus: *Mfr. digital video cameras, keyboards,*   Fax: 41-21-863-5311   Emp: 4,795
    trackballs, 3-D game controllers and   www.logitech.com
    joysticks.

LOGITECH INC.
6505 Kaiser Drive, Fremont, CA   94555
CEO: Guerrino DeLuca, Pres. & CEO   Tel: (510) 795-8500   %FO: 100
Bus: *Sales/distribution of digital video*   Fax: (510) 792-8901
    cameras, keyboards, trackballs, 3-
    D game controllers and joysticks.

• LONZA GROUP LTD.
Munchensteinerstrasse 38, CH-4002 Basel, Switzerland
CEO: Sergio Marchionne, CEO   Tel: 41-41-61-316-8111   Rev: $1,526
Bus: *Engaged in biotechnology and fine*   Fax: 41-41-61-316-9111   Emp: 6,000
    chemicals.   www.lonzagroup.com

LONZA BIOLOGICS INC.
101 International Drive, Portsmouth, NH 01801
CEO: David Jackson, VP   Tel: (603) 334-6100   %FO: 100
Bus: *Pharmaceuticals.*   Fax: (603) 334-6262

LONZA INC.
17-17 Route 208, Fair Lawn, NJ 07410
CEO: Fred F. Schauder, CEO   Tel: (201) 791-5200   %FO: 100
Bus: *Mfr./distributor chemicals,*   Fax: (201) 794-2597   Emp: 900
    packaging, & aluminum.

LONZA INC.
2031 East 65th Street, Los Angeles, CA 90001
CEO: Louis Bollag, Mgr.   Tel: (323) 584-5600   %FO: 100
Bus: *Pharmaceuticals.*   Fax: (323) 584-5650

LONZA INC.
3500 Trenton Avenue, Williamsport, PA 17701
CEO: Dennis Shaffer   Tel: (570) 321-3900   %FO: 100
Bus: *Mfr. chemicals and acids.*   Fax: (570) 321-3925

● **LUWA, DIV. ZELLWEGER LUWA AG**
Wilstrasse 11, CH-8610 Ulster, Switzerland
CEO: Konrad Peter   Tel: 41-1-943-5151
Bus: *Engaged in textile air engineering and*   Fax: 41-1-943-5152   Emp: 2,525
    environmental and energy engineering.   www.luwa.com

LUWA LEPCO, INC.
1750 Stebbins Drive, Houston, TX 77043
CEO: Timothy J. Whitener, Pres.   Tel: (713) 461-1131   %FO: 100
Bus: *Engaged in textile and industrial*   Fax: (713) 461-6319
    air engineering and building
    management services.

LUWA LEPCO, INC.
3901 West Point Boulevard, PO Box 10458, Winston Salem, NC 27103
CEO: Timothy J. Whitener, Pres.   Tel: (336) 760-3434   %FO: 100
Bus: *Engaged in textile and industrial*   Fax: (336) 760-0283   Emp: 700
    air engineering and building
    management services.

● **MARCEL BOSCHUNG AG**
Maschinenfabrik. Ried bei Berg 4, CH-3185 Schmitten, Switzerland
CEO: Paul Boschung, Mng. Dir.   Tel: 41-26-497-8585
Bus: *Development, production and sales of*   Fax: 41-26-497-8590
    machines and devices for cleaning   www.boschung.ch
    airports, highways and cities.

BOSCHUNG COMPANY INC.

4115 Castle Butte Drive, Castle Rock, CO   80104

CEO: Gerry Waldman   Tel: (303) 681-8942   %FO: 100

Bus: *Sales of mechanical and electronic*   Fax: (303) 681-8944
      equipment to clean and clear
      airports from ice, snow and dirt.

● **MEDITERRANEAN SHIPPING COMPANY SA**

40, Avenue Eugene Pittard, CH-1206 Geneva, Switzerland

CEO: Gianluigi Aponte, Pres.   Tel: 41-22-703-8888   Rev: $1,000

Bus: *Steamship company.*   Fax: 41-22-703-8787   Emp: 6,000

     MEDITERRANEAN SHIPPING COMPANY (USA) INC.

     420 Fifth Avenue, New York, NY   10018

     CEO: Nicola Arena, Pres.   Tel: (212) 764-4800   %FO: 90

     Bus: *Steamship agents.*   Fax: (212) 764-8592   Emp: 250

● **METRO HOLDING AG**

Neuhofstrasse 4, PO Box 400, CH-6340 Baar, Zug, Switzerland

CEO: Dr. Hans-Joachim Koerber, Chmn.   Tel: 41-41-768-7171   Rev: $39,800

Bus: *Holding company for department and*   Fax: 41-41-761-2523   Emp: 153,800
     electronic stores and home improvement   www.metro.de
     centers and wholesale hypermarkets.

     JETRO CASH & CARRY ENTERPRISES, INC.

     15-24 132nd Street, Flushing, NY   11356

     CEO: Andrea Rosen, Mgr.   Tel: (718) 762-8700   %FO: JV

     Bus: *Distribution center for*   Fax: (718) 463-8058
        manufacturers.

● **METTLER-TOLEDO INTERNATIONAL INC.**

PO Box MT-100, CH-8606 Greifensee, Switzerland

CEO: Robert F. Spoerry, Pres. & CEO   Tel: 41-1-944-2211   Rev: $936

Bus: *Mfr. precision weighing instruments*   Fax: 41-1-944-3060   Emp: 8,250
     used in industrial, laboratory and retail   www.mt.com
     food markets.

     ASI APPLIED SYSTEMS, INC.

     8223 Cloverleaf Drive, Ste. 120, Millersville, MD   21108

     CEO: M. Pavlosky   Tel: (410) 987-3241   %FO: 100

     Bus: *Sales/distribution of precision*   Fax: (410) 987-2626
        weighing instruments used in
        industrial, laboratory and retail
        food markets.

GARVINS USA INC.
PO Box 2033, Pine Brook, NJ 07058

CEO: L. Hugill

Tel: (973) 276-1093

%FO: 100

Bus: *Sales/distribution of precision weighing instruments used in industrial, laboratory and retail food markets.*

Fax: (973) 276-1094

METTLER-TOLEDO INC.
1900 Polaris Parkway, Columbus, OH 43240

CEO: Mary Finnegan

Tel: (614) 438-4511

%FO: 100

Bus: *Sales/distribution of precision weighing instruments used in industrial, laboratory and retail food markets.*

Fax: (614) 438-4900

● **MICRONAS SEMICONDUCTOR HOLDING AG**
Technopark, Technoparkstrasse 1, CH-8005 Zürich, Switzerland

CEO: Wolfgang Kalsbach, CEO

Tel: 41-1-445-3960

Bus: *Develops microchips, integrated circuits (ICs) and sensors.*

Fax: 41-1-445-3961
www.micronas.com

Emp: 500

MICRONAS SEMICONDUCTORS INC.
2635 North First Street, Ste. 101, San Jose, CA 95134-2031

CEO: Rainer Hoffman, Pres.

Tel: (408) 526-2080

%FO: 100

Bus: *Mfr. semiconductors.*

Fax: (408) 324-1379

● **MONTRES ROLEX SA**
Rue Francois-Dussaud 3, CH-1211 Geneva 24, Switzerland

CEO: Patrick Heiniger, CEO

Tel: 41-22-308-2200

Rev: $300

Bus: *Manufacturer of watches.*

Fax: 41-22-300-2255
www.rolex.com

ROLEX WATCH, INC.
665 Fifth Avenue, New York, NY 10022

CEO: Walter Fisher, Pres. & CEO

Tel: (212) 758-7700

%FO: 100

Bus: *Import/sales/service of watches.*

Fax: (212) 223-7443

Emp: 330

● **MOTURIS LTD.**
Flughstrasse 55, CH-8152 Glattbrugg, Switzerland

CEO: Ernst Dähler, Pres.

Tel: 41-1-808-7000

Bus: *Rental of motor homes and motorcycles.*

Fax: 41-1-808-7001
www.moturis.com

MOTURIS INC.
3901 NW 16th Street, Lauderhill, FL   33311
CEO: Mike Castro, Mgr.   Tel: (954) 587-6450   %FO: 100
Bus: *Rental of motor homes and*   Fax: (954) 587-6452
       motorcycles.

MOTURIS INC.
420 San Leandro Boulevard, San Leandro, CA   94577
CEO: Roger Löhrer, Mgr.   Tel: (510) 562-7566   %FO: 100
Bus: *Rental of motor homes and*   Fax: (510) 562-7567
       motorcycles.

MOTURIS INC.
4175 West Dewey Drive, Las Vegas, NV   89118
CEO: Dominique Zbinden, Mgr.   Tel: (702) 597-5978   %FO: 100
Bus: *Rental of motor homes and*   Fax: (702) 597-5980
       motorcycles.

MOTURIS INC.
5300 Colorado Boulevard, Commerce City, CO   80022
CEO: Martin Steinemann, Mgr.   Tel: (303) 295-6837   %FO: 100
Bus: *Rental of motor homes and*   Fax: (303) 295-6849
       motorcycles.

MOTURIS INC.
42, Highway 36, Middletown, NJ   07748
CEO: Daniele Sarasino, Mgr.   Tel: (732) 495-0959   %FO: 100
Bus: *Rental of motor homes and*   Fax: (732) 583-8932
       motorcycles.

MOTURIS INC.
425 North Industrial Drive, Naperville, IL   60563
CEO: Lorenz Neukom, Mgr.   Tel: (630) 369-8472   %FO: 100
Bus: *Rental of motor homes and*   Fax: (630) 369-8717
       motorcycles.

● **NESTLÉ SA**
Avenue Nestle 55, CH-1800 Vevey, Switzerland
CEO: Peter Brabeck-Letmathe, CEO   Tel: 41-21-924-2111   Rev: $50,522
Bus: *Develop/mfr. foods, beverages,*   Fax: 41-21-924-2813   Emp: 224,550
       pharmaceuticals and petfoods.   www.nestle.com

ALCON LABORATORIES INC
6201 South Freeway, Ft. Worth, TX   76134
CEO: Tim R. Sear, Pres.   Tel: (817) 293-0450   %FO: 100
Bus: *Mfr./sale pharmaceuticals*   Fax: (817) 551-4705   Emp: 9,500
       products; ophthalmic products.

FALCON PHARMACEUTICALS, LTD.

6201 South Freeway, Ft. Worth, TX   76134

CEO: George Neal, VP   Tel: (800) 343-2133   %FO: 100

Bus: *Mfr. pharmaceuticals.*   Fax: (817) 551-8893

FRISKIES PETCARE

1200 Market Street, NE, PO Box 548, Decatur, AL   35602

CEO: Dave Gamet, Mgr.   Tel: (256) 552-7411   %FO: 100

Bus: *Mfr./distribute pet food.*   Fax: (256) 552-7435

GALDERMA LABORATORIES, INC.

3000 Alta Mesa Blvd., Ste. 300, Ft. Worth, TX   76133

CEO: Stephen Clark, Pres.   Tel: (817) 263-2600   %FO: 100

Bus: *Mfr./sales skin care products.* Fax: (817) 263-2609   Emp: 150

NESTLÉ COFFEE SPECIALTIES INC.

214 East 52nd Street, New York, NY   10022

CEO: Sebastiano Pagano, Pres.   Tel: (212) 755-0585   %FO: 100

Bus: *Mfr./sales specialty   Fax: (212) 755-0043   Emp: 100
coffees/beverages.*

NESTLÉ FROZEN FOOD INC., ICE CREAM DIV.

30000 B. Bainbridge Road, Solon, OH   44139

CEO: James Dintaman, Pres.   Tel: (440) 349-5757   %FO: 100

Bus: *Mfr./sales frozen consumer foods.* Fax: (440) 498-0830   Emp: 4,500

NESTLÉ HOLDINGS INC.

Five High Ridge Road, Stamford, CT   06905

CEO: Michael Davis, VP   Tel: (203) 322-4567   %FO: 100

Bus: *Commodities international trading.* Fax: (203) 322-7756   Emp: 28

NESTLÉ USA

637 South Pine Street, Burlington, WI   53105

CEO: Peter Ferris, Plant Mgr.   Tel: (414) 763-9111   %FO: 100

Bus: *Mfr. foods, candies, and   Fax: (414) 763-5037   Emp: 550
confections.*

NESTLÉ USA INC.

800 North Brand Boulevard, Glendale, CA   91203

CEO: Joseph M. Weller, Chmn. & CEO Tel: (818) 549-6000   %FO: 100

Bus: *U.S. holding company: food,   Fax: (818) 549-6952   Emp: 38,500
beverages, pet food and
pharmaceuticals.*

NESTLÉ USA INC.
1133 Connecticut Avenue, NW, Suite 310, Washington, DC   20036
CEO: Maxine C. Champion, VP   Tel: (202) 296-4100   %FO: 100
Bus: *Government relations*   Fax: (202) 296-8555
    representative.

● **NEXTROM HOLDING SA**
Route Du Bois 37, CH-1024 Ecublens-Lausanne, Switzerland
CEO: Jouni Heinonen, Pres.   Tel: 41-21-694-4111
Bus: *Engaged in telecommunication, energy*   Fax: 41-21-694-4714
    and plastic production.   www.nextrom.com

    NEXTROM, INC.
    1650 Satellite Boulevard, Center 2, Duluth, GA   30097
    CEO: Y. Kohpala, Sales Mgr.   Tel: (678) 957-3500   %FO: 100
    Bus: *Supplier of manufacturing systems*   Fax: (678) 957-3512   Emp: 21
        to the wire and cable industry.

● **NOVARTIS INTERNATIONAL AG**
Lichstrasse 35, CH-4002 Basel, Switzerland
CEO: Dr. Daniel Vasella, CEO   Tel: 41-61-324-1111   Rev: $40,790
Bus: *Pharmaceutical company;*   Fax: 41-61-324-8001   Emp: 68,000
    research/mfr./marketing of healthcare   www.novartis.com
    and nutritional products.

    CHIRON/BIOCINE COMPANY
    4560 Horton Street, Emeryville, CA   94608
    CEO: Sean Lance, Pres.   Tel: (510) 655-8730   %FO: 100
    Bus: *Biotechnology research.*   Fax: (510) 655-9910   Emp: 2,000

    CIBA SPECIALITY CHEMICALS CORPORATION
    540 White Plains Road, PO Box 2005, Tarrytown, NY   10561-9005
    CEO: Stanley Sherman, Pres. & CEO   Tel: (914) 785-2000   %FO: 100
    Bus: *Mfr./sale specialty chemicals.*   Fax: (914) 785-2227   Emp: 15,000

    CIBA SPECIALTY CHEMICALS CORPORATION, PLASTICS DIV.
    281 Fields Lane, Brewster, NY   10509
    CEO: Edward Bozzi, Pres.   Tel: (914) 785-3000   %FO: 100
    Bus: *Mfr. epoxy resins and formulated*   Fax: (914) 785-3476   Emp: 400
        industrial systems.

    CIBA VISION CORP
    11460 Johns Creek Parkway, Duluth, GA   30155
    CEO: Dr. C. Glen Bradley, Pres.   Tel: (770) 448-1200   %FO: 100
    Bus: *Mfr./distribution soft contact*   Fax: (770) 418-4261
        lenses & lens care products.

GENETIC THERAPY INC., DIV. OF SYSTEMIX
938 Clopper Road, Gaithersburg, MD   20878-1301

CEO: Mike Perry, Pres.   Tel: (301) 590-2626
Bus: *Biotechnical research.*   Fax: (301) 948-3774

GENEVA PHARMACEUTICALS INC.
2655 West Midway Blvd., Broomfield, CO   80038-0469

CEO: David Hurley, Pres.   Tel: (303) 466-2400   %FO: 100
Bus: *Mfr./distribution generic*   Fax: (303) 466-3717   Emp: 1,000
    pharmaceuticals.

GERBER LIFE INSURANCE COMPANY
66 Church Street, White Plains, NY   10601

CEO: Ron Masiero, Pres.   Tel: (914) 761-4404   %FO: 100
Bus: *Life insurance services. Sub. of*   Fax: (914) 761-4772 Emp: 230
    Gerber products company.

GERBER PRODUCTS COMPANY
445 State Street, Fremont, MI   49413

CEO: Al Piergallini, Pres. & CEO   Tel: (616) 928-2000   %FO: 100
Bus: *Mfr./markets baby/children's*   Fax: (616) 928-2723   Emp: 1,200
    nutritional products.

NOVARTIS
2001 Pennsylvania Avenue, NW, Suite 925, Washington, DC   20006

CEO: Michael Ailsworth, VP   Tel: (202) 293-3019   %FO: 100
Bus: *Industry government relations and*   Fax: (202) 659-0249 Emp: 11
    public affairs office.

NOVARTIS CONSUMER HEALTH CORPORATION
556 Morris Avenue, Summit, NJ   07901

CEO: Fred Huser, Pres.   Tel: (908) 598-7600   %FO: 100
Bus: *Mfr./markets consumer over-the-*   Fax: (908) 273-2869
    counter healthcare products.

NOVARTIS CORPORATION
5550 Morris Avenue, Summit, NJ   07901

CEO: Wayne Wetter, CEO   Tel: (908) 277-5000   %FO: 100
Bus: *Research/mfr./marketing of*   Fax: (908) 277-5752
    healthcare, agribusiness and
    nutritional products.

NOVARTIS CROP PROTECTION, INC.
410 Swing Road, PO Box 18300, Greensboro, NC   27419-8300
CEO: Emilio J. Bontempo, Pres.   Tel: (332) 632-6000   %FO: 100
Bus: *Develops/mfr. agricultural*   Fax: (332) 632-7353
      products & services for crop
      protection.

NOVARTIS FINANCE CORPORATION
608 Fifth Avenue, New York, NY   10022
CEO: Kamran Tavangar   Tel: (212) 307-1122   %FO: 100
Bus: *Corporate administrative &*   Fax: (212) 246-0185
      financial services.

NOVARTIS NUTRITION CORPORATION
5100 Gamble Drive, PO Box 370, Minneapolis, MN   55440
CEO: David Hurley, Pres. & CEO   Tel: (612) 925-2100   %FO: 100
Bus: *Clinical enteral nutrition*   Fax: (612) 593-2087   Emp: 700
      products, and food services.

NOVARTIS PHARMACEUTICALS CORPORATION
59 Route 10, East Hanover, NJ   07936
CEO: Douglas G. Watson, Pres.   Tel: (908) 522-6700   %FO: 100
Bus: *Develop/mfr./market*   Fax: (908) 522-6818   Emp: 7,000
      pharmaceuticals.

NOVARTIS SEEDS, INC.
PO Box 4188, Boise, ID   83711-0727
CEO: John Sorenson, Pres. & CEO   Tel: (208) 322-7272   %FO: 100
Bus: *Research/mfr. vegetable seeds.*   Fax: (208) 322-1436   Emp: 700

NOVARTIS SEEDS, INC.
5300 Katrina Avenue, Downers Grove, IL   60515
CEO: Fred Fuller, Pres.   Tel: (630) 969-6300   %FO: 100
Bus: *Mfr./distribution flower seeds,*   Fax: (630) 696-6373   Emp: 600
      plugs, plants & other horticultural
      products.

NOVARTIS SEEDS, INC.
7500 Olson Memorial Highway, Golden Valley, MN   55427
CEO: Ed Shonsey, Pres.   Tel: (612) 593-7333   %FO: 100
Bus: *Research/mfr./market agricultural*   Fax: (612) 542-0194   Emp: 2,000
      products & seeds: corn, wheat,
      soybean, alfalfa, sorghum &
      sunflower.

RED LINE HEALTHCARE CORPORATION
8121 10th Avenue North, Golden Valley, MN   55427
CEO: Robert Carr, Pres.   Tel: (612) 595-6000   %FO: 100
Bus: *Distribution of medical supplies.*   Fax: (612) 595-6677   Emp: 700

SYSTEMIX, DIV. OF NOVARTIS
3155 Porter Drive, Palo Alto, CA   94304
CEO: Mike Perry, Pres.   Tel: (650) 856-4901
Bus: *Biotechnical research.*   Fax: (650) 856-4919

● **PANALPINA WORLD TRANSPORT LTD.**
Viaduktstrasse 42, CH-4002 Basel, Switzerland
CEO: Gerhard Fischer, Pres.   Tel: 41-61-226-1111   Rev: $2,643
Bus: *International forwarding agents.*   Fax: 41-61-226-1101   Emp: 11,000
                                   www.panalpina.com

PANALPINA INC.
67 Park Place, Morristown, NJ   07960
CEO: Christian Ryser, Pres.   Tel: (973) 683-9000   %FO: 100
Bus: *International freight*   Fax: (973) 254-5799   Emp: 1,000
    forwarder/custom house broker.

● **PUBLIGROUPE LTD.**
Avenue des Toises 12, CH-1002 Lausanne, Switzerland
CEO: Jean-Jacques Zaugg, CEO   Tel: 41-21-317-7111   Rev: $1,682
Bus: *Engaged in advertising magazine sales.*   Fax: 41-21-317-7555   Emp: 4,300
                                   www.publigroupe.com

REAL MEDIA, INC.
260 Fifth Avenue, New York, NY   10001
CEO: Walter Annasohn, CEO   Tel: (212) 725-4537   %FO: 1
Bus: *Engaged in advertising magazine*   Fax: (212) 725-4573
    sales.

● **RATHOR AG, DIV. FLM HOLDING**
Rütistrasse, CH-9050 Appenzell, Switzerland
CEO: Stefan Miczka, Pres.   Tel: 41-71-788-3660
Bus: *Mfr. polyurethane foam.*   Fax: 41-71-788-3600
                                   www.polypag.ch

FOMO PRODUCTS INC.
2775 Barber Road, PO Box 1078, Norton, OH   44203
CEO: Stefan Gantenbein, Gen. Mgr. Tel: (330) 753-4585   %FO: 100
Bus: *Sales/distribution of polyurethane*   Fax: (330) 753-7213
    foam.

• WALTER REIST HOLDING AG (WRH)

Industriestrasse 1, CH-8340 Hinwil, Switzerland

CEO: Walter Reist, Pres.	Tel: 41-1-938-7000
Bus: *Mfr. conveying and processing system for printing industry.*	Fax: 41-1-938-7070 Emp: 1,700
	www.walter-reist-holding.ch

FERAG INC.

190 Rittenhouse Circle, PO Box 137, Bristol, PA   19007-0137

CEO: Michael Paschall	Tel: (215) 788-0892	%FO: 100
Bus: *Mfr. conveying and processing system for printing industry*	Fax: (215) 788-7597	Emp: 150

• RICOLA AG

PO Box 130, CH-4242 Laufen, Switzerland

CEO: Felix Richterich, Pres.	Tel: 41-61-765-4121
Bus: *Manufacturer of confections.*	Fax: 41-61-765-4122
	www.ricola.ch

RICOLA USA, INC.

51 Gibraltar Drive, Morris Plains, NJ   07950

CEO: Dan Thomas, Pres.	Tel: (201) 984-6811	%FO: 100
Bus: *Distribution and marketing of Ricola confectionery products.*	Fax: (201) 984-6814	Emp: 10

• RIETER HOLDING AG

Schlosstalstrasse 43, CH-8406 Winterthur Zürich, Switzerland

CEO: Kurt E. Feller, CEO	Tel: 41-52-208-7171	Rev: $1,818
Bus: *Mfr. spinning systems and noise control systems for motor vehicles.*	Fax: 41-52-208-7060	Emp: 11,162
	www.rieter.com	

RIETER AUTOMOTIVE N.A.

38555 Hills Tech Drive, Farmington Hills, MI   48331

CEO: Lars O. Larsson, Pres.	Tel: (248) 848-0100	%FO: 100
Bus: *Sales/distribution of noise control systems for motor vehicles.*	Fax: (248) 848-4279	Emp: 1,700

RIETER CORPORATION

PO Box 4383, Spartanburg, SC   29305

CEO: Ueli Schmid, CEO	Tel: (864) 582-5468	%FO: 100
Bus: *Mfr./distribution/service spinning systems.*	Fax: (864) 585-1643	Emp: 160

● **RIRI SA**

Via Catenazzi 23, PO Box 277, CH-6850 Mendrisio, Switzerland
CEO: Benedetto Bonaglia, Dir.   Tel: 41-91-64-65-822
Bus: *Mfr. zippers.*   Fax: 41-91-64-06-161
                                                 www.riri.com

> **RIRI USA INC.**
> 14 East 60th Street, New York, NY   10022
> CEO: Giovanna Cugnasca, Mgr.   Tel: (212) 583-9180   %FO: 100
> Bus: *Sales of zippers.*   Fax: (212) 583-9185

● **RMB ROULEMENTS MINIATURES SA**

Eckweg 8, Box 6121, CH-2500 Biel-Bienne, Switzerland
CEO: Alparsoan Kutukcuoglu, Dir.   Tel: 41-32-3444-300
Bus: *Mfr. miniature ball/rollerbearings.*   Fax: 41-32-414721   Emp: 1,600
                                                 www.rmb-group.com

> **RMB MINIATURE BEARINGS INC.**
> 29 Executive Pkwy., Ringwood, NJ   07456
> CEO: Jeffrey H. Perkins, Pres.   Tel: (973) 962-1111   %FO: 100
> Bus: *Mfr. bearing & ballscrews.*   Fax: (973) 962-1101   Emp: 12

● **ROCHE HOLDING AS**

Grenzacherstrasse 124, CH-4070 Basel, Switzerland
CEO: Dr. Franz B. Humer, CEO   Tel: 41-61-688-1111   Rev: $17,900
Bus: *Research/mfr./marketing*   Fax: 41-61-691-9391   Emp: 67,000
pharmaceuticals, medicinals,   www.roche.com
botanicals, biological products and
drugs. (20% owned by Novartis AG)

> **HOFFMANN-LA ROCHE INC.**
> 1301 I Street, NW, Suite 520 West, Washington, DC   20005-3314
> CEO: William M. Burns, Pres.   Tel: (202) 408-0090   %FO: 100
> Bus: *Corporate government relations.* Fax: (202) 408-1750

> **HOFFMANN-LA ROCHE INC.**
> 340 Kingsland Street, Nutley, NJ   07110-1199
> CEO: George Abercrombie, Pres.   Tel: (973) 235-5000   %FO: 100
> Bus: *Mfr./distribution/research*   Fax: (973) 235-4264   Emp: 17,327
> *pharmaceuticals, chemicals,*
> *diagnostics & lab services.*

> **LABCORP**
> 358 South Main Street, Burlington, NC   27215
> CEO: Thomas McMann, Pres.   Tel: (336) 584-5171   %FO: JV
> Bus: *Clinical laboratory.*   Fax: (336) 584-5171   Emp: 18,000

ROCHE BIOSCIENCE
3401 Hillview Avenue, Palo Alto, CA   94304-1320
CEO: Dr. James N. Woody, Pres.   Tel: (650) 855-5050   %FO: 100
Bus: *Mfr./distribution pharmaceuticals*   Fax: (650) 354-7646   Emp: 1,100

ROCHE DIAGNOSTICS CORP.
9115 Hague Road, Indianapolis, IN   46250
CEO: Martin Madaus, Pres. & CEO   Tel: (317) 845-2000   %FO: 100
Bus: *Mfr./distribution health diagnostic*   Fax: (317) 845-2221
     equipment, pharmaceuticals and
     health related products.

ROCHE DIAGNOSTICS CORPORATION
9115 Hague Road, PO Box 50457, Indianapolis, IN   46250-0457
CEO: Martin Madaeus, CEO   Tel: (317) 845-2000
Bus: *Mfr./distribution health diagnostic*   Fax: (317) 845-2090
     equipment, pharmaceuticals and
     health related products.

ROCHE DIAGNOSTICS, INC.
235 Hembree Park Drive, Roswell, GA   30076
CEO: Heino von Prondzynski   Tel: (770) 576-5000   %FO: 100
Bus: *Mfr./sales of medical analyzers.*   Fax: (770) 576-5010

ROCHE MOLECULAR SYSTEMS, INC.
4300 Hacienda Drive, Pleasanton, CA   94588
CEO: Heiner Dreismann, CEO   Tel: (925) 730-8200   %FO: 100
Bus: *Mfr./distribution health diagnostic*   Fax: (925) 225-0758
     equipment, pharmaceuticals and
     health related products.

ROCHE VITAMINS
45 Waterview Boulevard, Parsippany, NJ   07054
CEO: Chris Goppelsroeder, Pres.   Tel: (973) 257-1063   %FO: 100
Bus: *Mfr./distribution vitamins.*   Fax: (973) 257-8616

● SAIR GROUP (FORMERLY SWISSAIR)
Batz Zimmermannstrasse, POBox 8058 Zürich-Airport, CH-8058 Zürich, Switzerland
CEO: Wolfgang Werle, Pres. & CEO   Tel: 41-1-812-1212   Rev: $10,070
Bus: *International air transport, duty free*   Fax: 41-1-810-8046   Emp: 72,000
     and retail travel services.   www.sairgroup.com

SWISSAIR
3391 Peachtree Road, Ste. 210, Atlanta, GA   30326
CEO: E. Suhr, Gen. Mgr.   Tel: (404) 814-6300   %FO: 100
Bus: *International air transport*   Fax: (404) 814-6319   Emp: 20
     services.

SWISSAIR

150 N. Michigan Ave., Ste. 2900, Chicago, IL   60601

CEO: J. Patrick O'Brien, Gen. Mgr.	Tel: (312) 630-5820	%FO: 100
Bus: *International air transport services.*	Fax: (312) 630-5825	Emp: 100

SWISSAIR

608 Fifth Avenue, New York, NY   10022

CEO: R. Annette	Tel: (212) 969-5760	%FO: 100
Bus: *International air transport services.*	Fax: (212) 969-5746	Emp: 15

SWISSAIR

41 Pinelawn Road, Melville, NY   11747

CEO: R. Wilhel, VP	Tel: (516) 844-4550	%FO: 100
Bus: *U.S. headquarters location; international air transport services.*	Fax: (516) 844-4559	Emp: 174

● **SANTEX AG**

Fliegeneggstrasse 9, CH-9555 Tobel, Switzerland

CEO: Christian Strahm, Pres.	Tel: 41-71-918-6666	Rev: $50
Bus: *Mfr. textile finishing machines and systems.*	Fax: 41-71-918-6600	Emp: 145
	www.santex-group.com	

AMERICAN SANTEX INC.

485 Simuel Road, PO Box 8648, Spartanburg, SC   29305-8648

CEO: Richard Horton, Pres.	Tel: (864) 574-7222	%FO: 100
Bus: *Mfr., sales, service textile machines.*	Fax: (864) 574-0804	Emp: 12

● **SARNAFIL AG**

Industriestrasse, CH-6060 Sarnen, Switzerland

CEO: Karl Brandenburg, Pres.	Tel: 41-41-666-9966	Rev: $504
Bus: *Processing and application of roofing and polumeric materials.*	Fax: 41-41-666-9817	Emp: 3,780
	www.sarnafilus.com	

SARNAFIL INC.

100 Dan Road, Canton, MA   02021

CEO: Richard K. Foley, Pres. & CEO	Tel: (781) 828-5400	%FO: 100
Bus: *Sales/distribution of roofing.*	Fax: (781) 828-5365	

● **SAURER LTD.**

Stelzenstrasse 6, CH-9320 Arbon, Switzerland

CEO: Dr. Manfred Timmermann	Tel: 41-71-447-5274	
Bus: *Mfr. textile machinery and textile system components.*	Fax: 41-71-447-5288	Emp: 11,350
	www.saurer.com	

NEUMAG CORPORATION
13504 South Point Boulevard, Charlotte, NC 28273
CEO: Manfred Timmermann   Tel: (704) 587-9307   %FO: 100
Bus: *Sales synthetic fiber machinery.*   Fax: (704) 587-9311

SCHLAFHORST INC
8801 South Boulevard, Charlotte, NC 28273
CEO: Dan W. Loftis, CEO   Tel: (704) 554-0800   %FO: 100
Bus: *Sale/service textile equipment,*   Fax: (704) 554-7350   Emp: 188
machinery and parts.

● **SCHINDLER HOLDING AG**
Seestrasse 55, CH-6052 Hergiswil, Switzerland
CEO: Alfred N. Schindler, Vice Chmn.   Tel: 41-41-958550   Rev: $4,800
Bus: *Elevators and escalators.*   Fax: 41-41-393134   Emp: 39,000
www.schindler.com

SCHINDLER ELEVATOR CORPORATION
1900 Center Park Drive, Suite J, Charlotte, NC 28217
CEO: Ray Falduti, District Mgr.   Tel: (704) 329-1471   %FO: 100
Bus: *Install and service/modernize*   Fax: (704) 329-1478
elevators and escalators

SCHINDLER ELEVATOR CORPORATION
20 Whippany Road, PO Box 1935, Morristown, NJ 07962-1935
CEO: Roland Hess, Pres.   Tel: (973) 397-6264   %FO: 100
Bus: *Manufacture/sales/service of*   Fax: (973) 397-6142   Emp: 5,900
elevators and escalators

● **SCHOLL SWITZERLAND AG**
Striegelstrasse 8, PO Box 224, CH-5745 Safenwil, Switzerland
CEO: Thomas Gerhard, Pres. & CEO   Tel: 41-62-789-8383
Bus: *Mfr./sales of dyeing units and stainless*   Fax: 41-62-789-8384   Emp: 200
units for chemical industries.   www.scholl-global.com

SCHOLL AMERICA INC.
PO Box 286, Gibsonville, NC 27249
CEO: Charlie Ward, Pres.   Tel: (336) 449-2000   %FO: 100
Bus: *Sales/service of dyeing units for*   Fax: (336) 449-0329   Emp: 80
textile industry and stainless steel
process equipment.

• SCINTILLA AG
PO Box 632, CH-4501 Solothurn, Switzerland

CEO: Urs Rinderknecht	Tel: 41-32-686-3111	Rev: $1,357
Bus: *Mfr. Bosch electrical and battery tools for industrial and domestic applications.*	Fax: 41-32-686-3703 www.scintilla.ch	Emp: 1,850

ROBER BOSCH POWER TOOL CORPORATION
2800 South 25th Avenue, Broadview, IL 60153

CEO: Frederick W. Hohage, Pres.	Tel: (708) 865-5200	%FO: JV
Bus: *Holding company. (JV with Bosch GmbH).*	Fax: (708) 450-8561	

S-B POWER TOOL COMPANY.
4300 West Peterson Avenue, Chicago, IL 60646-5999

CEO: Paddy Maguire, Pres.	Tel: (773) 794-6617	%FO: JV
Bus: *Develop/mfr./distribution power tools.*	Fax: (773) 794-6618	Emp: 3,000

• SERONO SA
Chemin des Mines 15bis, PO Box 54, CH-1211 Geneva 20, Switzerland

CEO: Ernesto Bertarelli, CEO	Tel: 41-22-739-3000	Rev: $1,054
Bus: *Engaged in biotechnology.*	Fax: 41-22-731-2179 www.serono.com	Emp: 3,966

SERONO INC.
100 Longwater Circle, Norwell, MA 02061

CEO: Carolyn Castel	Tel: (781) 982-9000	%FO: 100
Bus: *Engaged in biotechnology.*	Fax: (781) 871-6754	

• SGS SOCIETE GENERALE DE SURVEILLANCE HOLDING S.A.
97 rue de Lyon, PO Box 2152, CH-1211 Geneva, Switzerland

CEO: Antony M. Czura, CEO	Tel: 41-22-739-9111	Rev: $1,939
Bus: *Provides inspection and monitoring services for traded agricultural products, minerals, petroleum, petrochemicals and consumer goods.*	Fax: 41-22-739-9886 www.sgsgroup.com	Emp: 37,500

COMMERCIAL TESTING & ENGINEERING COMPANY
1919 South Highland Avenue, Ste. 210B, Lombard, IL 60148

CEO: Scott Morrison, Mgr.	Tel: (630) 953-9300	%FO: 100
Bus: *Engaged in inspection services for minerals.*	Fax: (630) 953-9306	

INTERMODAL TRANSPORTATION SERVICES, INC.
9 Campus Drive, Ste. 7, PO Box 316, Parsippany, NJ 07054-0316

CEO: John McHale, Pres.	Tel: (973) 993-3400	%FO: 100
Bus: *Engaged in inspection services.*	Fax: (973) 993-9579	

SGS CONTROL SERVICES INC.

333 Thornall Street, Edison, NJ   08818

CEO: Norman Powell, Pres. Tel: (732) 906-1700 %FO: 100

Bus: *Engaged in inspection services for* Fax: (732) 494-1832
redwood, petroleum and
petrochemicals.

SGS INTERNATIONAL CERTIFICATION SERVICES INC.

201 Route 17 North, Rutherford, NJ   07070

CEO: Ernani Pires, Pres. Tel: (201) 935-1500 %FO: 100

Bus: *Engaged in international* Fax: (201) 935-4555
certification services.

SGS NORTH AMERICA INC.

42 Broadway, New York, NY   10004

CEO: Bernard Yip, Pres. Tel: (212) 482-8700 %FO: 100

Bus: *U.S. headquarters; services to the* Fax: (212) 968-8343
government and international
institutions.

SGS U.S. TESTING COMPANY INC.

291 Fairfield Avenue, Fairfield, NJ   07004

CEO: Jeffrey Horner, Pres. Tel: (973) 575-5252 %FO: 100

Bus: *Consumer products services and* Fax: (973) 575-8271
pre-certification services for the
Russian market.

TESTCOM, INC.

25 Walker Way, Albany, NY   12205-4946

CEO: Dan Stone, Pres. Tel: (518) 452-0300 %FO: 100

Bus: *Provides inspection and* Fax: (518) 452-1019
monitoring services.

• SIEGFRIED LTD.

Untere Brühlstrasse 4, CH-4800 Zofingen, Switzerland

CEO: Dr. B. Siegfried, Chmn. Tel: 41-62-746-1111

Bus: *Mfr. pharmaceuticals and bulk medical* Fax: 41-62-746-1212
chemicals. www.siegfried-cms.ch

GANES CHEMICALS INC.

33 Industrial Park Road, Pennsville, NJ   08070

CEO: Douglas Gunthardt, Pres. Tel: (856) 678-3601 %FO: 100

Bus: *Mfr. bulk medical chemicals.* Fax: (856) 678-4008 Emp: 250

● **SIEMENS BUILDING TECHNOLOGIES LTD.**
Bellerivestrasse 36, CH-8034 Zürich, Switzerland
CEO: Oskar K. Ronner, CEO   Tel: 41-1-385-2211
Bus: *Engaged in building control, fire*   Fax: 41-1-385-2555
   detection, engineering and contracting.   www.2.sibt.com

   SIEMENS BUILDING TECHNOLGIES, INC.
   8 Fernwood Road, Florham Park, NJ   07932
   CEO: Ronald Matson, Pres.   Tel: (973) 593-2600   %FO: 100
   Bus: *Provides fire protection services.*   Fax: (973) 593-6670

   SIEMENS BUILDING TECHNOLGIES, INC.
   1000 Deerfield Parkway, Buffalo Grove, IL   60089
   CEO: John J. Grad, CEO   Tel: (847) 215-1000   %FO: 100
   Bus: *Provides building control*   Fax: (847) 215-1093
     solutions for commercial facilities.

● **SIG CAMBIBLOC INTERNATIONAL AG, DIV. SIG HOLDING AG**
Rolf-Dieter Rademacher Industrieplatz, CH-8212 Neuhausen Rhine Falls, Switzerland
CEO: Dr. Kormer, CEO   Tel: 41-52-674-7500
Bus: *Mfr. aseptic packages and filling*   Fax: 41-52-674-7200   Emp: 2,250
   systems.   www.sig-group.com

   SIG COMBIBLOC INC.
   4800 Roberts Road, Columbus, OH   43228
   CEO: Terry Derrico, CEO   Tel: (614) 876-0661   %FO: 100
   Bus: *Mfr./sales packaging systems for*   Fax: (614) 876-8678   Emp: 230
     fresh and long-life liquid food.

● **SIG HOLDING AG (SIG)**
Industrieplatz, CH-8212 Neuhausen am Rheinfall, Switzerland
CEO: Dr. Roman Boutellier, CEO   Tel: 41-52-674-6111   Rev: $1,424
Bus: *Mfr. packaging machines and systems.*   Fax: 41-52-674-6556   Emp: 7,307
                                          www.sig-group.com

   BYESVILLE ASEPTICS, INC.
   100 Hope Road, Byesville, OH   43723
   CEO: Tom Szymanick   Tel: (740) 685-2548   %FO: 100
   Bus: *Mfr./sales packaging machines*   Fax: (749) 685-6550
     and systems.

SIG HOLDING USA INC.
869 South Knowles Avenue, New Richmond, WI 54017-1797

CEO: John F. DeBoer	Tel: (715) 246-6511	%FO: 100
Bus: *Holding company; sales/distribution of packaging systems and machines.*	Fax: (715) 246-6539	

SIG PACK DOBOY, INC.
869 South Knowles Avenue, New Richmond, WI 54017-1797

CEO: William Heilhecker, Pres.	Tel: (715) 246-6511	%FO: 100
Bus: *Mfr./sales of packaging lines and machines.*	Fax: (715) 246-6539	

SIG PACK EAGLE CORP.
2107 Livingston Street, Oakland, CA 94606

CEO: John Staruch	Tel: (510) 533-3000	%FO: 100
Bus: *Mfr./sales packaging machines and systems.*	Fax: (510) 534-3000	

SIG PACK SERVICES INC.
2401 Brentwood Road, Raleigh, NC 27604

CEO: Harold Carr	Tel: (919) 877-0886	%FO: 100
Bus: *Mfr./sales packaging machines and systems.*	Fax: (919) 877-0887	

SIG PLASTICS TECHNOLOGY USA, INC.
PO Box 5329, North Branch, NJ 08876

CEO: Wolfgang Meyer	Tel: (908) 252-9350	%FO: 100
Bus: *Mfr./sales packaging machines and systems.*	Fax: (908) 252-9807	

• SOCIÉTÉ INTERNATIONALE PIRELLI SA
St. Jakobs-Strasse, CH-4052 Basle, Switzerland

CEO: Alfred E. Sarasin, Chmn.	Tel: 41-61-316-4111	Rev: $49
Bus: *Mfr. tires and cables. (Owns 40% of Pirelli SpA, Italy).*	Fax: 41-61-316-4355 www.pirelli.com	

PIRELLI CABLE CORPORATION
246 Stoneridge Drive, Columbia, SC 29210

CEO: Kevin E. Riddett, Pres.	Tel: (803) 951-4800	%FO: 100
Bus: *Mfr./sales cables.*	Fax: (803) 951-1069	

PIRELLI TIRE NORTH AMERICA
300 George Street, New Haven, CT 06511

CEO: Carlo Bianconi, CEO	Tel: (203) 784-2200	%FO: 100
Bus: *Mfr./sales/distribution of tires.*	Fax: (203) 784-2408	

● **STAEUBLI AG**

Seestrasse 240, Postfach 492, CH-8810 Horgen, Switzerland

CEO: Anthony O. Stäeubli, Pres. & CEO   Tel: 41-1-728 6111

Bus: *Mfr. textile machinery, robot systems,*   Fax: 41-1-728 6122   Emp: 2,000
weaving preparation systems and quick   www.staeubli.com
connect couplings.

     STAEUBLI CORPORATION

     201 Parkway West, PO Box 189, Duncan, SC   29334

     CEO: Harald Behrend, VP   Tel: (864) 433-1980   %FO: 100

     Bus: *Sales/service for textile machines,*   Fax: (864) 433-1988   Emp: 115
     robot systems, weaving
     preparation systems and quick
     safety couplings.

● **STMICROELECTRONICS NV**

20 Route de Pre-Bois, ICC Bldg., CH-1215 Geneva 15, Switzerland

CEO: Pasquale Pistorio, CEO   Tel: 41-22-929-2929   Rev: $7,814

Bus: *Mfr. semiconductors.*   Fax: 41-22-929-2900   Emp: 43,650
   www.st.com

     STMICROELECTRONICS

     17197 N. Lauren Park Drive, Ste. 253, Livonia, MI   48152

     CEO: Richard Pieranunzi, VP   Tel: (734) 953-1700   %FO: 100

     Bus: *Mfr./sales semiconductors.*   Fax: (734) 462-4071

     STMICROELECTRONICS

     16350 West Bernardo Drive, San Diego, CA   92127

     CEO: Richard Pieranunzi, VP   Tel: (858) 485-8900   %FO: 100

     Bus: *Mfr./sales semiconductors.*   Fax: (858) 485-9110

     STMICROELECTRONICS

     1060 East Brokaw Road, San Jose, CA   95131

     CEO: Richard Pieranunzi, VP   Tel: (408) 452-8585   %FO: 100

     Bus: *Mfr./sales semiconductors.*   Fax: (408) 452-1549

     STMICROELECTRONICS

     1000 East Bell Road, Phoenix, AZ   85022

     CEO: Richard Pieranunzi, VP   Tel: (602) 485-6100   %FO: 100

     Bus: *Mfr./sales semiconductors.*   Fax: (602) 485-6102

     STMICROELECTRONICS

     1310 Electronics Drive, Carrollton, TX   75006

     CEO: Richard Pieranunzi, VP   Tel: (972) 466-6000   %FO: 100

     Bus: *Mfr./sales semiconductors.*   Fax: (972) 466-6001

• SULZER GROUP AG

8401 Winterthur, PO Box 414, CH-8401 Winterthur, Switzerland

CEO: Leonardo E. Vannotti, CEO	Tel: 41-52-262-1122	Rev: $3,559
Bus: *Engineering systems: textile, energy,*	Fax: 41-52-262-0101	Emp: 21,170
oil, gas and chemicals, mining, water	www.sulzer.com	
technology, wood and food products		
industries.		

HICKHAM INDUSTRIES, INC.

11518 Old La Porte Road, La Porte, TX   77571

CEO: Brian McKenzie, Pres.	Tel: (713) 471-6540	%FO: 100
Bus: *Service of thermal turbomachinery.*	Fax: (713) 471-4821	Emp: 250

SULZER METCO (US) INC.

1101 Prospect Avenue, PO Box 1006, Westbury, NY   11590

CEO: Jerry L. Mariar, Pres.	Tel: (516) 334-1300	%FO: 100
Bus: *Design/mfr. industrial spraying*	Fax: (516) 338-2488	Emp: 360
materials & systems.		

SULZER PUMPS INC.

2800 Northwest Front Avenue, Portland, OR   97210

CEO: Antonio Moscon, Pres.	Tel: (503) 226-5200	%FO: 100
Bus: *Design/sales/service pumps;*	Fax: (503) 226-5286	Emp: 850
energy industry .		

SULZER TEXTILE INC.

745 Landers Road, Spartanburg, SC   29303

CEO: Peter Egloff, Pres.	Tel: (864) 585-5255	%FO: 100
Bus: *Sales/service textile machinery.*	Fax: (864) 585-5064	Emp: 75

SULZER TURBOSYSTEMS INTERNATIONAL

2901 Wilcrest, Ste. 345, Houston, TX   77042

CEO: Dan Jones, Pres.	Tel: (713) 780-4200	%FO: 100
Bus: *Water technology.*	Fax: (713) 780-2848	Emp: 25

SULZER USA INDUSTRIES HOLDING INC.

555 Fifth Avenue, New York, NY   10017

CEO: Philip T. Hauser, Pres.	Tel: (212) 949-0999	%FO: 100
Bus: *Import/sales/service of machinery*	Fax: (212) 661-0533	Emp: 35
and systems for process		
technology.		

● **SULZER MEDICA LTD., DIV. SULZER CORP.**
Zurcherstrasse 12, CH-8401 Winterthur, Switzerland
CEO: André P. Buchel, Pres.	Tel: 41-52-262-7250	Rev: $1,120
Bus: *Develop/mfr. orthopedic, oral rehabilitation, implantable medical devices and biomedicals for cardiovascular and orthopedics markets.*	Fax: 41-52-262-0059 www.sulzermedica.com	Emp: 5,100

   SULZER CARBOMEDICS, INC.
   1300 East Anderson Lane, Austin, TX 78752
CEO: Terry L. Marlatt, Pres.	Tel: (512) 873-3200	%FO: 100
Bus: *Design/mfr. medical devices.*	Fax: (512) 873-3350	

   SULZER DENTALS INC.
   2320 Faraday Avenue, Carlsbad, CA 92008
CEO: Steven Hanson, Pres.	Tel: (760) 431-9515	%FO: 100
Bus: *Design/mfr. dental implants.*	Fax: (760) 431-9753	

   SULZER MEDICA USA INC.
   3 East Greenway Plaza, Houston, TX 77046
CEO: Andre P. Buchel, Pres.	Tel: (713) 561-6300	%FO: 100
Bus: *U.S. holding company; develop/mfr. Implantable medical devices and biomaterials for cardiovascular and orthopedic markets.*	Fax: (713) 561-6380	

   SULZER ORTHOPEDICS, INC.
   9900 Spectrum Drive, Austin, TX 78717
CEO: Gary Sabins, Pres.	Tel: (512) 432-9900	%FO: 100
Bus: *Design/mfr. orthopedic medical devices.*	Fax: (512) 432-9014	

   SULZER SPINE-TECH INC.
   7375 Bush Lake Road, Minneapolis, MN 55439
CEO: Rich Lunsford, Pres.	Tel: (952) 832-5600	%FO: 100
Bus: *Mfr. medical devices.*	Fax: (952) 832-5620	

● **SWAROVSKI INTERNATIONAL HOLDING AG**
General-Wille-Strasse 88, PO Box 163, CH-8706 Feldmeilen, Switzerland
CEO: Manuela Sieberer	Tel: 41-19-257-111
Bus: *Mfr./sales/service fashion jewelry, crystal objects and gifts.*	Fax: 41-19-257-210 www.swarovski.com

SWAROVSKI CONSUMER GOODS LTD
2 Slater Road, Cranston, RI   02920-4468

CEO: Daniel Cohen, Pres.	Tel: (401) 463-6400	%FO: 100
Bus: *Mfr. fashion jewelry, gifts and collectors objects.*	Fax: (401) 463-3261	Emp: 700

● **THE SWATCH GROUP AG**
Seevorstadt 6, CH-2502 Biel Bern, Switzerland

CEO: Nicholas G. Hayek, Chmn.	Tel: 41-32-343-6811	Rev: $2,645
Bus: *Mfr./marketing of microelectronics and major brand watches including Blancpain, Omega, Longines, Hamilton, Balmain, Swatch.*	Fax: 41-32-343-6911 www.swatchgroup.com	Emp: 17,750

SWATCH GROUP
1200 Harbor Boulevard, Weehawken, NJ   07087

CEO: Yann Y. Gamard, Pres.	Tel: (201) 271-4680	%FO: 100
Bus: *Sale/distribution and repair of watches, clocks and movements, including brands Swatch, Longines, Omega and Hamilton.*	Fax: (201) 271-4709	Emp: 400

● **SWISS REINSURANCE COMPANY**
Mythenquai 50/60, CH-8022 Zürich, Switzerland

CEO: Walter Kielholz, CEO	Tel: 41-1-285-2121	Rev: $20,393
Bus: *Insurance and reinsurance services.*	Fax: 41-1-285-2999 www.swissre.com	Emp: 8,770

LINCOLN RE, DIV. LINCOLN NATIONAL
1500 Market Street, Ste. 3900, Philadelphia, PA   19102-2112

CEO: Jon A. Boscia, CEO	Tel: (215) 448-1400	%FO: 100
Bus: *Provides universal life, term life and variable universal life insurance.*	Fax: (215) 448-3956	

NORTH AMERICAN SPECIALTY INSURANCE COMPANY
650 Elm Street, Manchester, NH   03101

CEO: Robert M. Solitro, Pres. & CEO	Tel: (603) 644-6600	%FO: 100
Bus: *Specialty insurance services.*	Fax: (603) 644-6696	

SWISS RE LIFE & HEALTH AMERICA, INC.
969 High Ridge Road, Stamford, CT   06905

CEO: Jacques Dubois, CEO	Tel: (203) 321-3000	%FO: 100
Bus: *Life insurance.*	Fax: (203) 321-3232	

SWISS REINSURANCE AMERICA CORPORATION
175 King Street, Armonk, NY   10504
CEO: James P. Slattery, CEO   Tel: (914) 828-8000   %FO: 100
Bus: *Property and casualty reinsurance*   Fax: (914) 828-7000

UNDERWRITERS REINSURANCE COMPANY
26050 Mureau Road, Calabasas, CA   91302
CEO: Steven H. Newman, CEO   Tel: (818) 878-9500   %FO: 100
Bus: *Reinsurance products and services.*   Fax: (818) 878-9335

● **SWISSCOM AG**
Alte Tiefenaustrasse 6, CH-3050 Bern, Switzerland
CEO: Jens Alder, CEO   Tel: 41-31-342-1111   Rev: $8,750
Bus: *Engaged in telecommunications;*   Fax: 41-31-342-2549   Emp: 17,450
provides local, long distance and   www.swisscom.ch
international services.

   SWISSCOM, INC.
   2001 L Street NW, Ste. 750, Washington, DC   20036
   CEO: Markus Lickert, EVP   Tel: (202) 785-1145   %FO: 100
   Bus: *Engaged in telecommunications*   Fax: (202) 457-8915
   services.

● **SWISSLOG HOLDING AG**
PO Box 4003, CH-5001 Aarau, Switzerland
CEO: Juhani Antilla, CEO   Tel: 41-62-837-9537   Rev: $402
Bus: *Mfr. automated material handling*   Fax: 41-62-837-9510   Emp: 2,063
systems.   www.swisslog.com

   MUNCK AUTOMATION TECHNOLOGY, INC.
   161 Enterprise Drive, Newport News, VA   23603-3135
   CEO: Bradley Moore, SVP   Tel: (757) 887-8080   %FO: 100
   Bus: *Sales/distribution of automated*   Fax: (757) 887-5588
   material handling systems.

● **SYNGENTA AG**
Schwarzwaldalle 215, CH-4058 Basel, Switzerland
CEO: Michael Pragnell   Tel: 41-61-697-1111   Rev: $4,876
Bus: *Mfr. agrochemicals and seeds.*   Fax: 41-61-697-1111   Emp: 25,000
     www.syngenta.com

   SYNGENTA CROP PROTECTION, INC.
   PO Box 18300, Greensboro, NC   27409
   CEO: Heiri Gugger, Pres.   Tel: (336) 632-6000   %FO: 100
   Bus: *Mfr./sales agrochemicals.*   Fax: (336) 632-6000

SYNGENTA SEEDS INC.
PO Box 4188, Boise, ID   83804-4188
CEO: Zhangliang Chen   Tel: (208) 322-7272   %FO: 100
Bus: *Mfr./sales seeds.*   Fax: (208) 322-7272

● **TEUSCHER CONFISERIE**
Storchengasse 9, CH-8001 Zürich, Switzerland
CEO: R. Teuscher, Pres. & CEO   Tel: 41-1-211-5151
Bus: *Handmade Swiss chocolates.*   Fax: 41-1-212-2958
                                        www.truffesdor.com

  TEUSCHER CHOCOLATES OF SWITZERLAND
  410 University Street, Seattle, WA   98101
  CEO: Alex Hernandez, Mgr.   Tel: (206) 340-1747   %FO: 100
  Bus: *Sales of handmade Swiss*   Fax: (206) 340-0887
       chocolates.

  TEUSCHER CHOCOLATES OF SWITZERLAND
  620 Fifth Avenue, New York, NY   10020
  CEO: Brad Bloom, Mgr.   Tel: (212) 246-4416   %FO: 100
  Bus: *Sales of handmade Swiss*   Fax: (212) 765-8134   Emp: 18
       chocolates.

  TEUSCHER CHOCOLATES OF SWITZERLAND
  230 Newbury Street, Boston, MA   02116
  CEO: Per Wyrsch, Mgr.   Tel: (617) 536-1922   %FO: 100
  Bus: *Sales of handmade Swiss*   Fax: (617) 536-1787
       chocolates.

● **UBS AG (UNION BANK OF SWITZERLAND)**
Bahnhofstrasse 45, CH-8098 Zürich, Switzerland
CEO: Marcel Ospel, Chmn.   Tel: 41-1-234-4100   Rev: $49,498
Bus: *Banking, securities trading and* Fax: 41-1-234-3414   Emp: 49,050
     underwriting, asset management and www.ubs.com
     corporate finance services.

  BRINSON PATNERS, INC.
  209 South LaSalle St., Ste. 114, Chicago, IL   60604-1295
  CEO: B. Lenhardt, CEO   Tel: (312) 220-7100   %FO: 100
  Bus: *Engaged in asset management*   Fax: (312) 220-7110
       services.

  MITCHELL HUTCHINS INSTITUTIONAL INVESTORS
  1285 Avenue of the Americas, New York, NY   10019
  CEO: Brian M. Storms, CEO   Tel: (212) 713-4800   %FO: 100
  Bus: *Institutional investors.*   Fax: (212) 713-4800

TIMBER INVESTMENTS, DIV. UBS ASSET MANAGEMENT
24 Airport Road, 4th Fl., West Lebanon, NH 03784
CEO: Joan Moschello   Tel: (603) 298-4940   %FO: 100
Bus: *Engaged in asset management.*   Fax: (603) 298-7620

UBS - LOS ANGELES
633 West Fifth Street, 69th Fl., Los Angeles, CA 90017
CEO: Richard Schaefer, Mng. Dir.   Tel: (213) 253-1900   %FO: 100
Bus: *Banking, securities trading and   Fax: (213) 680-1944
     underwriting, asset management
     and corporate finance services.*

UBS - SAN FRANCISCO
101 California Street, Ste. 2500, San Francisco, CA 94111
CEO: Caesar Ruegg, Exec. Dir.   Tel: (415) 774-3318   %FO: 100
Bus: *Banking, securities trading and   Fax: (415) 788-2067
     underwriting, asset management
     and corporate finance services.*

UBS AG
1100 Louisiana Street, Ste. 4500, Houston, TX 77002
CEO: W. Rovere, SVP   Tel: (713) 655-6500   %FO: 100
Bus: *Banking, securities trading &   Fax: (713) 655-6553
     underwriting, asset management
     and corporate finance services.*

UBS AGRIVEST LLC
242 Trumbull Street, Hartford, CT 06103-1212
CEO: Joan Moschello   Tel: (860) 275-3600   %FO: 100
Bus: *Engaged in realty investment.* Fax: (860) 275-3012

UBS ASSET MANAGEMENT, INC.
10 East 50th Street, New York, NY 10022
CEO: Joan Moschello   Tel: (212) 335-1000   %FO: 100
Bus: *Engaged in investment banking   Fax: (212) 335-1626
     and asset management.*

UBS PAINEWEBBER
1285 Ave. of the Americas, 17th Fl., New York, NY 10019
CEO: John H. Decker, Mgr.   Tel: (212) 713-7800   %FO: 100
Bus: *Engaged in investment banking   Fax: (212) 713-3938
     and asset management.*

UBS PAINEWEBBER

500 Grant Street, 46th Fl., Pittsburgh, PA   15219

CEO: Paul R. Meese, Mgr.   Tel: (412) 562-6711   %FO: 100

Bus: *Engaged in investment banking*   Fax: (412) 562-6740
and asset management.

UBS PAINEWEBBER

100 South Main Street, Greensburg, PA   15601

CEO: Andrew J. Newman, Mgr.   Tel: (724) 837-2300   %FO: 100

Bus: *Engaged in investment banking*   Fax: (724) 830-6559
and asset management.

UBS PAINEWEBBER

1725 North Main Street, High Point, NC   27262

CEO: Charles William Kern III, Mgr.   Tel: (336) 885-4001   %FO: 100

Bus: *Engaged in investment banking*   Fax: (336) 885-5520
and asset management.

UBS PAINEWEBBER

200 Concord Plaza Drive, Ste. 300, San Antonio, TX   78216

CEO: Jeffrey Roger Weissman, Mgr.   Tel: (210) 824-0014   %FO: 100

Bus: *Engaged in investment banking*   Fax: (210) 824-0014
and asset management.

UBS PAINEWEBBER

One Blue Hill Plaza, 1st Fl., Pearl River, NY   10965

CEO: Thomas Reichert, Mgr.   Tel: (845) 735-8200   %FO: 100

Bus: *Engaged in investment banking*   Fax: (845) 735-7386
and asset management.

UBS PAINEWEBBER

140 Broadway, 24th Fl., New York, NY   10005

CEO: Peter A. Ambrose, Mgr.   Tel: (212) 607-3200   %FO: 100

Bus: *Engaged in investment banking*   Fax: (212) 607-3343
and asset management.

UBS PAINEWEBBER

433 Hackensack Avenue, Hackensack, NJ   07601

CEO: Ricardo Capozzi, Mgr.   Tel: (201) 487-1050   %FO: 100

Bus: *Engaged in investment banking*   Fax: (201) 441-4903
and asset management.

UBS PAINEWEBBER

33 South 6th Street, 37th Fl., Minneapolis, MN   55402

CEO: Mark E. Kenyon, Mgr.   Tel: (612) 371-4000   %FO: 100

Bus: *Engaged in investment banking*   Fax:
and asset management.

UBS REALTY INVESTORS LLC
12001 North Central Expwy., Ste. 650, Dallas, TX   75243-3735
CEO: Joan Moschello   Tel: (972) 458-3300   %FO: 100
Bus: *Engaged in realty investment.*   Fax: (972) 490-9440

UBS REALTY INVESTORS LLC
242 Trumbull Street, Hartford, CT   06103-1212
CEO: Jayne Brundage   Tel: (860) 275-3080   %FO: 100
Bus: *Engaged in realty investment.*   Fax: (860) 275-4225

UBS REALTY INVESTORS LLC
455 Market Street, Ste. 1540, San Francisco, CA   94105-2443
CEO: Joan Moschello   Tel: (415) 538-4800   %FO: 100
Bus: *Engaged in realty investment.*   Fax: (415) 538-8141

USB CAPITAL LLC
299 Park Avenue, New York, NY   10171-0026
CEO: C. Delaney, Pres.   Tel: (212) 821-3000   %FO: 100
Bus: *Banking, securities trading and*   Fax: (212) 821-3073   Emp: 2,200
     underwriting, asset management
     and corporate finance services.

USB PAINEWEBBER
777 South Figueroa Street, 50th Fl., Los Angeles, CA   90017
CEO: David Andrew Jones, Mgr.   Tel: (213) 830-2100   %FO: 100
Bus: *Engaged in investment banking*   Fax: (213) 972-1440
     and asset management.

USB PAINEWEBBER
400 Water Street, Ste. 100, Rochester, MI   48307
CEO: Stephen D. Arkwright, Mgr.   Tel: (248) 652-3200   %FO: 100
Bus: *Engaged in investment banking*   Fax: (248) 650-1629
     and asset management.

USB PAINEWEBBER
9 Old Kings Highway South, 3rd Fl., Darien, CT   06830
CEO: Ralph V. Balzano, Mgr.   Tel: (203) 655-0200   %FO: 100
Bus: *Engaged in investment banking*   Fax: (203) 655-9586
     and asset management.

USB PAINEWEBBER
2525 E. Camelback Road, Ste. 600, Phoenix, AZ   85016
CEO: James Van Steenhuyse, Mgr.   Tel: (602) 957-5100   %FO: 100
Bus: *Engaged in investment banking*   Fax: (602) 957-5150
     and asset management.

USB PAINEWEBBER
10 Park Street, Concord, NH 03301
CEO: Richard F. P. Crews, Mgr.　　Tel: (603) 225-6601　　%FO: 100
Bus: *Engaged in investment banking*　Fax: (603) 226-2953
and asset management.

USB PAINEWEBBER
700 Fifth Avenue, Seattle, WA 98104
CEO: Gilbert C. Powers, Mgr.　　Tel: (206) 628-8511　　%FO: 100
Bus: *Engaged in investment banking*　Fax: (206) 628-8550
and asset management.

USB PAINEWEBBER
703 Trancas Street, Napa, CA 94558
CEO: George Shick, Mgr.　　Tel: (707) 257-1880　　%FO: 100
Bus: *Engaged in investment banking*　Fax: (707) 254-1550
and asset management.

USB PAINEWEBBER
2029 Century Park East, Ste. 3000, Century City, CA 90067
CEO: David B. Harberson, Mgr.　　Tel: (310) 772-7000　　%FO: 100
Bus: *Engaged in investment banking*　Fax: (310) 772-8030
and asset management.

USB PAINEWEBBER
200 Clock Tower Place, Ste. C-100, Carmel, CA 93923
CEO: David R. Stewart, Mgr.　　Tel: (831) 624-1222　　%FO: 100
Bus: *Engaged in investment banking*　Fax: (831) 626-2300
and asset management.

USB PAINEWEBBER
One Broad Street Plaza, 2nd Fl., Glens Falls, NY 12801
CEO: Glenn L. Pearsall, Mgr.　　Tel: (518) 745-5500　　%FO: 100
Bus: *Engaged in investment banking*　Fax: (518) 745-0924
and asset management.

USB PAINEWEBBER
200 Concord Plaza Drive, Ste. 300, San Antonio, TX 78216
CEO: Jeffrey R. Weissman, Mgr.　　Tel: (210) 824-0014　　%FO: 100
Bus: *Engaged in investment banking*　Fax:
and asset management.

USB PAINEWEBBER
5285 East Williams Circle, Tucson, AZ 85711
CEO: Jonathan G. Heller, Mgr.　　Tel: (520) 750-7500　　%FO: 100
Bus: *Engaged in investment banking*　Fax:
and asset management.

USB PAINEWEBBER
One Pointe Drive, Ste. 140, Brea, CA   92821
CEO: William R. Spruston, Mgr.   Tel: (714) 256-5400   %FO: 100
Bus: *Engaged in investment banking*   Fax: (714) 256-5498
      and asset management.

USB PAINEWEBBER
5200 North Palm, Ste. 101, Fresno, CA   93704
CEO: John T. Marino Jr., Mgr.   Tel: (559) 226-2800   %FO: 100
Bus: *Engaged in investment banking*   Fax: (559) 248-4078
      and asset management.

USB PAINEWEBBER
8 Essex Center Drive, 2nd Fl., Peabody, MA   01960
CEO: Judson S. Potter, Mgr.   Tel: (978) 538-1900   %FO: 100
Bus: *Engaged in investment banking*   Fax: (978) 538-1490
      and asset management.

USB PAINEWEBBER
1100 Town & Country Rd., Ste. 1000, Orange, CA   92868
CEO: Steven V. Arrigo, Mgr.   Tel: (714) 973-6000   %FO: 100
Bus: *Engaged in investment banking*   Fax: (714) 973-6086
      and asset management.

USB PAINEWEBBER
318 Canyon Avenue, Ft. Collins, CO   80521
CEO: Gary E. Birdsell, Mgr.   Tel: (970) 498-4000   %FO: 100
Bus: *Engaged in investment banking*   Fax: (970) 498-4002
      and asset management.

USB PAINEWEBBER
733 Bishop Street, Ste. 1600, Honolulu, HI   96813
CEO: Elliot L. Luke, Mgr.   Tel: (808) 536-4511   %FO: 100
Bus: *Engaged in investment banking*   Fax: (808) 521-2798
      and asset management.

USB WARBURG
141 West Jackson Blvd., Chicago, IL   60604
CEO: Roger Peterson, Pres.   Tel: (312) 554-5000   %FO: 100
Bus: *Securities trading and*   Fax: (312) 554-5835
      underwriting services.

USB WARBURG

677 Washington Boulevard, Stamford, CT   06901

CEO: John Costas, COO   Tel: (203) 719-3000   %FO: 100

Bus: *Banking, securities trading and*   Fax: (203) 719-5499
     underwriting, asset management
     and corporate finance services.

USB WARBURG

555 California Street, Suite 4650, San Francisco, CA   94104

CEO: Max Straubb, Dir.   Tel: (415) 352-5555   %FO: 100

Bus: *Investment banking.*   Fax: (415) 698-6521

● **UNAXIS HOLDING (FORMERLY OERLIKON-BÜHRLE HOLDING AG)**

Hofwiesenstrasse 135, PO Box 2409, CH-8021 Zürich, Switzerland

CEO: Dr. Will Kissling, Chmn. & CEO   Tel: 41-1-363-4060   Rev: $1,817

Bus: *Engaged in information technology,*   Fax: 41-1-363-7260   Emp: 8,366
     surface technology and components.   www.unaxis.com

    LEYBOLD VACUUM USA INC.

    5700 Mellon Road, Export, PA   15632

    CEO: Dr. Monika Mattern-Klosson   Tel: (724) 327-5700   %FO: 100

    Bus: *Provides vacuum solutions for the*   Fax: (724) 325-4353
       semiconductor industry,
       chemical/pharmaceutical
       applications and industrial
       research.

    LEYBOLD VACUUM USA INC.

    8 Sagamore Park Road, Hudson, NH   03051

    CEO: Dr. Monika Mattern-Klosson   Tel: (603) 595-3270   %FO: 100

    Bus: *Provides vacuum solutions for the*   Fax: (603) 595-3280
       semiconductor industry,
       chemical/pharmaceutical
       applications and industrial
       research.

    UNAXIS MATERIALS

    16035 Vineyard Boulevard, Morgan Hill, CA   95037

    CEO: Soheil Hosseini   Tel: (408) 779-0636   %FO: 100

    Bus: *Mfr. thin film.*   Fax: (408) 779-0291

    UNAXIS OPTICS USA INC.

    16080 Table Mountain Pkwy., Ste. 100, Golden, CO   80403

    CEO: Ed Yousse   Tel: (303) 273-9700   %FO: 100

    Bus: *Mfr. thin film.*   Fax: (303) 273-2995

UNAXIS OPTICS USA INC.
10050 16th Street North, St. Petersburg, FL   33716
CEO: Notker Kling Tel: (727) 577-4999 %FO: 100
Bus: *Mfr. thin film.* Fax: (727) 577-7035 Emp: 1,000

UNAXIS OPTICS USA INC.
191 Harvard Circle, Newton, MA   02460
CEO: Roger Kirschner Tel: (617) 572-1960 %FO: 100
Bus: *Mfr. thin film.* Fax: (617) 558-3245

UNASIX USA INC.
25 Sagamore Park Road, Hudson, NH   03051
CEO: Hans Quaderer, Mgr. Tel: (603) 594-1514 %FO: 100
Bus: *Engaged in optics and information* Fax: (603) 594-1515
   technology.

● **UNION BANCAIRE PRIVEE**
96-98 rue du Rhone, CH-1211 Geneva, Switzerland
CEO: Maurice de Picciotto, Rep. Tel: 41-22-819-2111
Bus: *International private investment* Fax: 41-22-819-2432
   banking services.

  UNION BANCAIRE PRIVEE
  630 Fifth Avenue, Suite 1525, New York, NY   10111
  CEO: Maurice de Picciotto, Rep. Tel: (212) 265-3320 %FO: 100
  Bus: *International private investment* Fax: (212) 247-4310
     baking services.

● **VIBRO-METER SA**
PO Box 1071, CH-1701 Fribourg, Switzerland
CEO: Dr. Richard W. Greaves, Pres. Tel: 41-26-407-1111 Rev: $60
Bus: *Design/mfr. transducers and electronic* Fax: 41-26-407-1731 Emp: 500
   measuring instruments. www.vibro-meter.com

  VIBRO-METER CORP
  3995 Via Oro Avenue, Long Beach, CA   90810
  CEO: Ronald Vadas, Pres. Tel: (310) 830-7778 %FO: 100
  Bus: *Design/mfr. transducers and* Fax: (310) 830-2300 Emp: 40
     electronic measuring instruments.

● **VITRA INTERNATIONAL AG**
Klünenfeldstrasse 22, CH-4127 Birsfelden, Switzerland
CEO: Rolf Fehlbaum, CEO Tel: 41-61-377-0000
Bus: *Mfr. of ergonomic office chairs, sofas* Fax: 41-61-377-1510
   and desks. www.vitra.com

VITRA INC.
6560 Stonegate Drive, Allentown, PA   18106

CEO: Al Severance, VP — Tel: (610) 391-9780 — %FO: 100

Bus: *Production facility for manufacture of office furniture.* — Fax: (610) 391-9816 — Emp: 30

VITRA INC.
149 Fifth Avenue, New York, NY   10010

CEO: Stefan Golinski, Pres. — Tel: (212) 539-1900 — %FO: 100

Bus: *Mfr./distribution of ergonomic office chairs, sofas and desks.* — Fax: (212) 539-1977 — Emp: 15

• VOLKART BROTHERS HOLDING LTD.
PO Box 343, CH-8401 Winterthur, Switzerland

CEO: Andreas Reinhart, Pres. — Tel: 41-52-268-6868

Bus: *Holding company.* — Fax: 41-52-268-6889

www.volkart.ch

VOLKART AMERICA, INC.
6840 North First Avenue, Phoenix, AZ   85013

CEO: Walter Locher — Tel: (602) 222-9213 — %FO: 100

Bus: *Cotton trading.* — Fax: (602) 222-9214 — Emp: 15

• VON ROLL MANAGEMENT AG
Edenstrasse 20, CH-8045 Zürich, Switzerland

CEO: Martin A. messner, CEO — Tel: 41-1-204-3111 — Rev: $1,056

Bus: *Environmental engineering and services, electrical insulation, casting, pressure pipes and valves.* — Fax: 41-1-204-3112 — Emp: 5,802

www.vonroll.ch

VON ROLL INC.
302 Research Drive, Ste. 130, Norcross, GA   30092

CEO: Mitch Gorski, VP — Tel: (770) 613-9788 — %FO: 100

Bus: *Waste management, sewage treatment, multiple hearth plants, recovery systems.* — Fax: (770) 613-9860 — Emp: 10

VON ROLL INC.
1250 St. George Street, East Liverpool, OH   43920-5919

CEO: Fred Sigg, VP — Tel: (330) 385-7337 — %FO: 100

Bus: *Waste incineration, waste management, remedial consulting.* — Fax: (330) 385-7813 — Emp: 170

VON ROLL ISOLA INC.
One Campbell Road, Schenectady, NY   12306

CEO: Jurg Brunner, VP — Tel: (518) 344-7200 — %FO: 100

Bus: *Mfr./sale insulation materials.* — Fax: (518) 344-7287 — Emp: 230

● **VONTOBEL HOLDING LTD.**

Tödistrasse 27, CH-8022 Zürich, Switzerland

CEO: Robert Zingg, CEO Tel: 41-1-283-5900 Rev: $6,418

Bus: *Banking and financial services.* Fax: 41-1-283-7500 Emp: 890

www.vontobel.ch

VONTOBEL USA INC.

450 Park Avenue, New York, NY 10022

CEO: Henry Schlegel, Pres. & CEO Tel: (212) 415-7000 %FO: 100

Bus: *Investment advisory.* Fax: (212) 750-7853 Emp: 20

● **WAGNER INTERNATIONAL AG**

Industriestrasse 22, CH-9450 Altstaetten, Switzerland

CEO: Gunter Cott, CEO Tel: 41-71-757-2268

Bus: *Mfr. paint spray equipment.* Fax: 41-71-757-2268

www.wagner-group.com

WAGNER SPRAY TECH CORPORATION

1770 Fernbrook Lane, PO Box 279, Minneapolis, MN 55440

CEO: Sean C. James, Pres. Tel: (763) 553-7000 %FO: 100

Bus: *Mfr. paint spray equipment.* Fax: (763) 553-7288 Emp: 300

WAGNER SYSTEMS, INC.

700 High Grove Boulevard, Glendale Heights, IL 60139

CEO: Sean C. James, Pres. Tel: (630) 924-2400

Bus: *Mfr. paint spray equipment.* Fax: (630) 924-2419

● **WEITNAUER HOLDING LTD.**

Petersgasse 36-38, CH-4001 Basel, Switzerland

CEO: Max Oriet, CEO Tel: 41-61-266-4488

Bus: *Watchmakers.* Fax: 41-61-261-4981

www.weitnauer.ch

DUTREPEX

Expressport Plaza, 1160 McLester Street, Unit 5, Elizabeth, NJ 07201

CEO: Richard McCormick, Gen. Mgr. Tel: (908) 355-0178 %FO: 100

Bus: *Operation of airport duty free* Fax: (908) 355-0930 Emp: 25
    shops.

WEITNAUER AMERICA TRADING SERVICES INC.

2335 N.W. 107th Avenue, Ste. B-38, Miami, FL   33172

CEO: Manuel Sosa, Gen. Mgr.	Tel: (305) 591-1763	%FO: 100
Bus: *Supplier of duty free merchandise to cruise/cargo ships, duty free retailers, airliners, military/diplomatic corps.*	Fax: (305) 593-9893	Emp: 30

WEITNAUER GROUP OF COMPANIES

11420 Kendall Drive, Ste. 202, Miami, FL   33178

CEO: Jose Gonzales, Reg. Dir.	Tel: (305) 595-7907	%FO: 100
Bus: *Regional headquarters.*	Fax: (305) 595-1388	Emp: 2

WEITNAUER HOUSTON, INC.

PO Box 279, Humble, TX   77347

CEO: Leo Dotolo, Gen. Mgr.	Tel: (281) 233-7380	%FO: 100
Bus: *Operation of airport duty free shops.*	Fax: (281) 233-7385	Emp: 65

WEITNAUER INC.

200 East Robinson Street, Ste. 500, Orlando, FL   32801

CEO: Robert Hendry	Tel: (407) 843-5880	%FO: 100
Bus: *Operation of airport duty free shops.*	Fax: (407) 843-5880	

WEITNAUER NEW YORK INC.

JFK Airport Bldg. 142, Bergen Road, Jamaica, NY   11430

CEO: David Bachenheimer, Gen. Mgr.	Tel: (718) 553-6325	%FO: 100
Bus: *Operation of airport duty free shops.*	Fax: (718) 553-6328	Emp: 45

WEITNAUER PHILADELPHIA INC.

Philadelphia Intl. Airport Terminal A, Duty Free, Philadelphia, PA   19153

CEO: Michael Elia, Gen. Mgr.	Tel: (215) 365-1300	%FO: 100
Bus: *Operation of airport duty free shops.*	Fax: (215) 365-8116	Emp: 25

● **WINTERTHUR SWISS INSURANCE CO., DIV. CREDIT SUISSE GROUP**

General Guisanstrasse 40, CH-8401 Zürich, Switzerland

CEO: Peter Späiti, Chmn.	Tel: 41-52-261-1111	Rev: $23,184
Bus: *General insurance services.*	Fax: 41-52-261-6620	Emp: 28,722
	www.winterthur.com	

BLUE RIDGE INSURANCE COMPANIES
86 Hopmeadow Street, Simsbury, CT   06070
CEO: Larry E. Lawrence, CEO   Tel: (860) 651-1065   %FO: 100
Bus: *General insurance services.*   Fax: (860) 408-3266   Emp: 200

GENERAL CASUALTY INSURANCE
One General Drive, Sun Prairie, WI   53596
CEO: John R. Pollock, Pres. & CEO   Tel: (608) 837-4440   %FO: 100
Bus: *General insurance services.*   Fax: (608) 837-0583   Emp: 1,200

REPUBLIC DIVERSIFIED SERVICES, INC.
PO Box 600302, Dallas, TX   75266-0302
CEO: Bruce R. Milligan, VP   Tel: (214) 559-1134   %FO: 100
Bus: *International insurance services.* Fax: (214) 559-0883   Emp: 60

REPUBLIC UNDERWRITERS INSURANCE COMPANY
2727 Turtle Creek Boulevard, Dallas, TX   75219
CEO: Bruce R. Milligan, Pres. & CEO   Tel: (214) 559-1222   %FO: 100
Bus: *Holding company: finance,*   Fax: (214) 748-9590   Emp: 430
    general insurance services.

SOUTHERN GUARANTY INSURANCE COMPANIES
8445 Taylor Road, Montgomery, AL   36123
CEO: James L. Riding, Pres. & CEO   Tel: (334) 270-6000   %FO: 100
Bus: *General insurance services.*   Fax: (334) 270-6115   Emp: 280

UNIGARD INSURANCE GROUP
15805 Northeast 24th Street, Bellevue, WA   98008
CEO: Peter K. Christen, CEO   Tel: (425) 641-4321   %FO: 100
Bus: *General insurance services.*   Fax: (425) 562-5256   Emp: 630

● **DR. EGON ZEHNDER & PARTNER AG**
Toblerstrasse 80, PO Box 231, CH-8044 Zürich, Switzerland
CEO: Dr. Mark R. Hoenig, CEO   Tel: 41-1-267-6969
Bus: *Engaged in executive and board search;* Fax: 41-1-267-6967   Emp: 2,000
    management consulting.   www.zehnder.com

EGON ZEHNDER INTERNATIONAL, INC.
100 Spear Street, Suite 920, San Francisco, CA   94105
CEO: Jennifer C. McElrath   Tel: (415) 228-5200   %FO: 100
Bus: *Executive and board search,*   Fax: (415) 904-7801   Emp: 7
    management consulting services.

EGON ZEHNDER INTERNATIONAL, INC.

3475 Piedmont Road NE, Ste.1900, Atlanta, GA   30305

CEO: Graham W. Galloway	Tel: (404) 836-2800	%FO: 100
Bus: *Executive and board search, management consulting services.*	Fax: (404) 876-4578	Emp: 15

EGON ZEHNDER INTERNATIONAL, INC.

30 South Wacker Drive, Ste. 3400, Chicago, IL   60606-7487

CEO: Keith B. Meyer	Tel: (312) 260-8800	%FO: 100
Bus: *Executive and board search, management consulting services.*	Fax: (312) 782-2846	Emp: 26

EGON ZEHNDER INTERNATIONAL, INC.

350 Park Avenue, 8th Fl., New York, NY   10022-6022

CEO: Marc P. Schappell	Tel: (212) 519-6000	%FO: 100
Bus: *Executive and board search, management consulting services.*	Fax: (212) 519-6060	Emp: 40

EGON ZEHNDER INTERNATIONAL, INC.

300 S. Grand Avenue, Ste. 3580, Los Angeles, CA   90017

CEO: George C. Fifield	Tel: (213) 621-8900	%FO: 100
Bus: *Executive and board search, management consulting services.*	Fax: (213) 621-8900	Emp: 25

EGON ZEHNDER INTERNATIONAL, INC.

1290 Page Mill Road, Palo Alto, CA   94304

CEO: Jon F. Carter	Tel: (650) 847-3000	%FO: 100
Bus: *Executive and board search, management consulting services.*	Fax: (650) 847-3050	Emp: 20

EGON ZEHNDER INTERNATIONAL, INC.

75 Park Plaza, 4th Fl., Boston, MA   02116

CEO: George L. Davis, Jr.	Tel: (617) 535-3500	%FO: 100
Bus: *Executive and board search, management consulting services.*	Fax: (617) 457-4949	Emp: 20

● ZEHNDER HOLDING LTD.

Moortalstrasse 1, CH-5722 Gränichen, Switzerland

CEO: Paul Aeschimann, Pres.	Tel: 41-62-855-1500	Rev: $305
Bus: *Industrial group, specializing in aluminum radiators and space heaters.*	Fax: 41-62-855-1515 www.zehnderholding.com	Emp: 2,014

RUNTAL NORTH AMERICA, INC.

187 Neck Road, PO Box 8278, Ward Hill, MA   01835

CEO: Wesley Owens, EVP	Tel: (508) 373-1666	%FO: 100
Bus: *Mfr./sales of radiators and space heaters..*	Fax: (508) 372-7140	Emp: 40

- **ZELLWEGER LUWA LTD.**

Wilstrasse 11, CH-8610 Uster, Switzerland

CEO: Konrad Peter, CEO

Bus: *Engaged in textile electronics, environmental monitoring and ventilation and air conditioning engineering.*

Tel: 41-1-943-2211
Fax: 41-1-943-3838
www.zeluwa.com

Rev: $976
Emp: 4,695

LUWA BAHNSON INC.

3901 West Point Boulevard, PO Box 10458, Winston Salem, NC 27108

CEO: Timothy J. Whitener, Pres.

Bus: *Engaged in textile and industrial air engineering and building management services.*

Tel: (336) 760-3111
Fax: (336) 760-8548

%FO: 100
Emp: 700

LUWA BAHNSON INC.

78068 Ordnance Road, Hermiston, OR 97838

CEO: Robin Summers

Bus: *Engaged in plumbing, heating and air conditioning.*

Tel: (541) 564-7371
Fax: (541) 564-7371

%FO: 100

ZELLWEGER ANALYTICS, INC.

4331 Thurmond Tanner Road, Flowery Branch, GA 30542-2100

CEO: Kevin York, Pres.

Bus: *Sales/services of portable detection systems for air monitoring.*

Tel: (770) 967-2196
Fax: (770) 967-1854

%FO: 100
Emp: 40

ZELLWEGER ANALYTICS, INC.

405 Barclay Boulevard, Lincolnshire, IL 60069

CEO: Kevin York, Pres.

Bus: *Sales/services of portable detection systems for air monitoring.*

Tel: (847) 955-8200
Fax: (847) 955-8208

%FO: 100

ZELLWEGER USTER, INC.

456 Troy Circle, PO Box 51270, Knoxville, TN 37950-1270

CEO: Eddie Bradley, CEO

Bus: *Suppliers of quality control machinery for the textile industry.*

Tel: (865) 588-9716
Fax: (865) 558-0914

%FO: 100
Emp: 175

ZELLWEGER USTER, INC.

2200 Executive Street, Charlotte, NC 28202

CEO: Eddie Bradley, CEO

Bus: *Suppliers of quality control machinery for the textile industry.*

Tel: (704) 392-7421
Fax: (704) 393-1706

%FO: 100

- **ZUEST & BACHMEIER AG**

Palazzo Zuest & Bachmeier, CH-6830 Chiasso, Switzerland
CEO: E Scherer, Chmn.   Tel: 91-44-6942-4344
Bus: *Engaged in freight forwarding and* Fax: 91-44-6942-4377
 logistics.   www.zust.com

ZUST BACHMEIER OF SWITZERLAND, INC.

601-A Hammonds Ferry Road, Baltimore, MD   21090
CEO: Thomas Graefe, Pres. Tel: (410) 789-5340 %FO: 100
Bus: *International freight forwarding.* Fax: (410) 789-0792

ZUST BACHMEIER OF SWITZERLAND, INC.

6201 Rankin Road, Humble, TX   77396
CEO: Thomas Graefe, Pres. Tel: (281) 446-0852 %FO: 100
Bus: *International freight forwarding.* Fax: (281) 446-3475

ZUST BACHMEIER OF SWITZERLAND, INC.

14 East 4th Street, Ste. 607, New York, NY   10012
CEO: Thomas Graefe, Pres. Tel: (212) 388-1815 %FO: 100
Bus: *International freight forwarding.* Fax: (212) 388-1908 Emp: 35

- **ZURICH FINANCIAL SERVICES GROUP**

Mythenquai 2, CH-8022 Zürich, Switzerland
CEO: Rolf F. Hüppi, Chmn. Tel: 41-1-205-2121 Rev: $39,100
Bus: *Insurance, risk management products,* Fax: 41-1-205-3618 Emp: 68,900
 investment advisory services. www.zurich.com

AMERICAN FEDERATION INSURANCE CO.

5600 Beech Tree Lane, Caledonia, MI   49316
CEO: Richard L. Antonini, CEO Tel: (616) 942-3000 %FO: 100
Bus: *Provides insurance for* Fax: (616) 956-3990
 manufactured homes and
 recreational vehicles.

THE EMPIRE COMPANIES

13810 FNB Parkway, Omaha, NE   68154-5202
CEO: John J. McCartney, CEO Tel: (402) 963-5000 %FO: 100
Bus: *Provides financial services.* Fax: (402) 963-5109

FARMERS GROUP, INC.

4680 Wilshire Boulevard, Los Angeles, CA   90010
CEO: Martin D. Feinstein, CEO Tel: (323) 932-3200 %FO: 100
Bus: *Provides financial services.* Fax: (323) 932-3200

FARMERS GROUP INC.
4680 Wilshire Boulevard, Los Angeles, CA   90010

CEO: Martin D. Feinstein, Chmn.   Tel: (323) 932-3200   %FO: 100

Bus: *Insurance, risk management*   Fax: (323) 634-1881
     products and services.

FARMERS NEW WORLD LIFE INSURANCE COMPANY
3003 77th Avenue, SE, Mercer Island, WA   98040

CEO: C. Paul Patsis, Pres.   Tel: (206) 232-8400   %FO: 100

Bus: *Financial services; property and*   Fax: (206) 236-6547
     casualty insurance.

FEDERAL KEMPER LIFE ASSURANCE CO.
One Kemper Drive, Long Grove, IL   60049

CEO: Gale K. Caruso, CEO   Tel: (847) 320-4500   %FO: 100

Bus: *Insurance services.*   Fax: (847) 550-5530

FIDELITY AND DEPOSIT COMPANIES
300 St. Paul Place, Baltimore, MD   21202

CEO: Richard F. Williams, CEO   Tel: (410) 539-0800   %FO: 100

Bus: *Small business insurance services.*   Fax: (410) 539-7002

FIDELITY AND DEPOSIT COMPANIES
300 Saint Paul Place, PO Box 1227, Baltimore, MD   21203

CEO: Richard F. Williams, Chmn.   Tel: (410) 539-0800   %FO: 100

Bus: *Surety bonding services.*   Fax: (410) 539-7002

FOREMOST COUNTY MUTUAL INSURANCE CO.
5600 Beech Tree Lane, Caledonia, MI   49316

CEO: F. Robert Woudstra, COO   Tel: (616) 942-3000   %FO: 100

Bus: *Provides financial services.*   Fax: (616) 956-3990

KEMPER CORPORATION
1400 American Lane, Schaumburg, IL   60196-1056

CEO: Loren J. Alter, CEO   Tel: (847) 605-6000   %FO: 100

Bus: *Insurance, risk management*   Fax: (847) 605-6011   Emp: 9,800
     products and services.

SCUDDER KEMPER INVESTMENTS INC.
345 Park Avenue, New York, NY   10154

CEO: Edmond D. Villani, Pres.   Tel: (212) 326-6200   %FO: 100

Bus: *Insurance, risk management*   Fax: (212) 751-3451
     products and services.

UNIVERSAL UNDERWRITERS GROUP
6363 College Boulevard, Overland Park, KS   66211
CEO: Stephen Smith, CEO   Tel: (913) 339-1000   %FO: 100
Bus: *Provides financial services.*   Fax: (913) 339-1026

ZURICH RE NORTH AMERICA INC.
One Chase Manhattan Plaza, New York, NY   10005
CEO: Richard E. Smith, Pres. & CEO   Tel: (212) 898-5000   %FO: 100
Bus: *Reinsurance and insurance*   Fax: (212) 898-5052
   services.

ZURICH U.S.
1400 American Lane, Schaumburg, IL   60196
CEO: Constantine Iordanou, CEO   Tel: (847) 605-6000   %FO: 100
Bus: *Provides financial services.*   Fax: (847) 605-6011

Taiwan (ROC)

● **ACER INC.**

21/F, 88 Hsin Tai Wu Road, Sec. 1 Hsichih, Taipei Hsien 221, Taiwan ROC

CEO: Stan Shih, Chmn.   Tel: 886-2-2696-1234   Rev: $5,300

Bus: *Mfr. computers and peripheries.*   Fax: 886-2-8696-1777   Emp: 23,000

www.acer.com

    ACER AMERICA CORPORATION

    2641 Orchard Parkway, San Jose, CA   95134

    CEO: Patrick Lin, CEO   Tel: (408) 432-6200   %FO: 100

    Bus: *Mfr./sales computers &*   Fax: (408) 922-2933
       peripherals.

● **ADI CORP.**

14/F No. 1, Section 4, Nanking East Road, Taipei 10569, Taiwan, ROC

CEO: James C. C. Liao, Pres. & CEO   Tel: 886-22-2713-3337   Rev: $1,200

Bus: *Computer peripherals and color*   Fax: 886-22-2713-6555
monitors.   www.adi.com.tw

    ADI SYSTEMS INC.

    2115 Ringwood Avenue, San Jose, CA   95131

    CEO: Alan Chai, Pres.   Tel: (408) 944-0100   %FO: 100

    Bus: *Mfr./sales display monitors.*   Fax: (408) 944-0300   Emp: 60

● **ASUSTEK COMPUTER, INC.**

150 Li-Te Road, Peitou District, Taipei 112, Taiwan ROC

CEO: Jonney Shih, Pres.   Tel: 886-2-2894-3447   Rev: $1,520

Bus: *Mfr. computer hardware.*   Fax: 886-2-2894-3449

www.asus.com.tw

    ASUS COMPUTER INTERNATIONAL, INC.

    6737 Mowry Avenue, Bldg. 2, Newark, CA   94560

    CEO: Ivan Ho, Pres.   Tel: (510) 739-3777   %FO: 100

    Bus: *Distributes computer hardware.*   Fax: (510) 608-4555

● **BANK OF TAIWAN**

120 Chungking South Road Section I, PO Box 305, Taipei 1100, Taiwan ROC

CEO: Mu Tsai Chen, Chmn.   Tel: 886-22-349-3456

Bus: *Commercial banking services.*   Fax: 886-22-314-6699

www.bot.com.tw

BANK OF TAIWAN

*The Crown Building Center, 730 Fifth Avenue Suite 907, New York, NY   10019

CEO: Maw Yan Lin, SVP	Tel: (212) 333-8613	%FO: 100
Bus: *International banking services.*	Fax: (212) 333-8670	

BANK OF TAIWAN

601 South Figueroa Street, Ste. 4525, Los Angeles, CA   90017

CEO: H. H. Lin, Mgr.	Tel: (213) 629-6600	%FO: 100
Bus: *International banking services.*	Fax: (213) 629-6610	

● **CHANG HWA COMMERCIAL BANK, LTD.**

38 Tsu Yu Road, Sec.2, Taichung, Taiwan ROC

CEO: Chiung-Shin Wu, Pres.	Tel: 886-4-222-2001	Rev: $2,048
Bus: *Commercial, savings, trust &*	Fax: 886-4-223-1297	Emp: 6,234
international banking services.	www.chb.com.tw	

CHANG HWA COMMERCIAL BANK - L. A. Branch

Wells Fargo Ctr. 1, 6th Fl.
333 S. Grand Ave., Los Angeles, CA   90071

CEO: James Lin, Gen. Mgr.	Tel: (213) 620-7200	%FO: 100
Bus: *Bank branch operations, lending*	Fax: (213) 620-7227	Emp: 26
and treasury services.		

CHANG HWA COMMERCIAL BANK - N. Y. Branch

*c/o The Chase Manhattan Bank, 4 Chase Metro Tech Ctr. 20th Fl/Rm B, Brooklyn, NY 11245

CEO: Wan Tu Yeh, VP & Gen. Mgr.	Tel: (718) 242-6880	%FO: 100
Bus: *Bank branch operations, lending*	Fax: (718) 242-7159	Emp: 21
and treasury services.		

● **CHINA AIRLINES**

131 Nanking Road East, Section 3, Taipei, Taiwan, ROC

CEO: Christine Tsai-yi Tsung, Pres.	Tel: 886-22-715-2626	Rev: $1,940
Bus: *Commercial air transport services.*	Fax: 886-22-514-6005	Emp: 8,980
	www.china-airlines.com	

CHINA AIRLINES

633 Third Avenue, Ste. 800, New York, NY   10017

CEO: David Yao, Mgr.	Tel: (917) 368-2000	%FO: 100
Bus: *Commercial airline services.*	Fax: (917) 368-2078	Emp: 32

CHINA AIRLINES

6053 West Century Blvd, Ste. 800, Los Angeles, CA   90045

CEO: T. S.Chang, CEO	Tel: (310) 641-8888	%FO: 100
Bus: *Commercial airline services.*	Fax: (310) 641-0864	Emp: 30

- **CHINA GENERAL PLASTICS (CGPC)**

No. 3, 2/F, Tun Hwa South Road, Sec. 1, Taipei City, Taiwan ROC

CEO: Chang Chihchieh, Chmn.	Tel: 886-2-577-3661	
Bus: *Mfr. plastics, PVC powder and related products.*	Fax: 886-2-578-8248 www.cgpc.com.tw	Emp: 1,400

    CGPC (CHINA GENERAL PLASTICS CORPORATION)

    14104 Arbor Place, Cerritos, CA   90703

CEO: Rob Kahn, Pres.	Tel: (562) 926-8399	%FO: 100
Bus: *Sales/distribution of plastics, PVC powder and related products.*	Fax: (562) 926-9286	

- **CHINESE PETROLEUM CORPORATION**

83 Chung Hwa Road, Section 1, Taipei 10031, Taiwan ROC

CEO: Wen-Yen Pan, Pres.	Tel: 886-22-361-0221	Rev: $11,600
Bus: *Petroleum exploration, refining and sales.*	Fax: 886-22-331-9645 www.cpc.com.tw	Emp: 19,900

    OPICOIL AMERICA, INC.

    3040 Post Oak Boulevard, Ste. 800, Houston, TX   77056

CEO: K. Y. Ysai, Pres.	Tel: (713) 840-7171	%FO: 100
Bus: *Petroleum marketing services.*	Fax: (713) 297-8108	

- **D-LINK CORPORATION**

2/F, 233-2 Pao-Chiao Road, Hsin-Tien, Taipei, Twain ROC

CEO: Ken Kao, CEO	Tel: 886-2-2916-1600	Rev: $422
Bus: *Mfr. data communications hardware.*	Fax: 886-2-2914-6299 www.dlink.com.tw	Emp: 1,900

    D-LINK SYSTEMS, INC.

    53 Discover, Irvine, CA   92618

CEO: Roger Kao	Tel: (800) 326-1688	%FO: 100
Bus: *Mfr. data communications hardware.*	Fax: (949) 753-7033	

- **EVERGREEN MARINE CORPORATION (TAIWAN) LTD.**

166 Minsheng East Road, Sec 2, Taipei 10444, Taiwan ROC

CEO: Captain S. Y. Kuo, Chmn.	Tel: 886-22-505-7766	Rev: $1,421
Bus: *International container shipping and cargo services.*	Fax: 886-22-505-5255 www.evergreen-america.com.tw	Emp: 1,440

EVERGREEN AMERICA CORPORATION (EVA)
60 Patriots Plaza, Bldg. B, Morristown, NJ 07960
CEO: Owen Wu, Pres.   Tel: (973) 349-3214   %FO: 100
Bus: *International commercial shipping*   Fax: (973) 349-3011
    & air cargo and transport - US,
    Canada & Caribbean operations..

● **FIRST COMMERCIAL BANK**
30 Chungking Road, Section #1, Taipei, Taiwan ROC
CEO: An-Chyr Chen, Pres.   Tel: 886-22-311-1111
Bus: *General banking services.*   Fax: 886-22-331-6962
    www.firstbank.com.tw

    FIRST COMMERCIAL BANK
    200 East Main Street, Alhambra, CA 91801
    CEO: Tzuooyau Lin, Mgr.   Tel: (626) 300-6000   %FO: 100
    Bus: *General banking services.*   Fax: (626) 300-6030   Emp: 20

    FIRST COMMERCIAL BANK
    18725 East Gale Avenue Suite 150, City of Industry, CA 91748
    CEO: An-Chyr Chen, Pres.   Tel: (626) 964-1888   %FO: 100
    Bus: *General banking services.*   Fax: (662) 696-4006

    FIRST COMMERCIAL BANK
    1141 South De Anza Boulevard, San Jose, CA 95129
    CEO: An-Chyr Chen, Pres.   Tel: (408) 253-4666   %FO: 100
    Bus: *General banking services.*   Fax: (408) 343-0666

● **FORMOSA PLASTICS, DIV. FORMOSAN RUBBER GROUP**
201 Tun Hwa North Road, Taipei, Taiwan ROC
CEO: C. T. Lee, Pres.   Tel: 886-22-712-2211   Rev: $1,566
Bus: *Mfr. rubber, PU and PVC-coated*   Fax: 886-22-712-9211   Emp: 3,000
    fabrics and a wide range of logistical   www.fpc.com.tw
    support equipment, plastic resins and
    petrochemicals.

    FORMOSA PLASTICS CORPORATION
    9 Peach Tree Hill Road, Livingston, NJ 07039
    CEO: C. L. Tseng, EVP   Tel: (973) 992-2090   %FO: 100
    Bus: *Mfr. plastic resins and*   Fax: (973) 992-9627   Emp: 700
    petrochemicals.

    FORMOSA PLASTICS CORPORATION
    201 Formosa Drive, PO Box 700, Point Comfort, TX 77978
    CEO: Paul Huang, VP   Tel: (361) 987-7000   %FO: 100
    Bus: *Mfr. plastic resins and*   Fax: (361) 987-2721
    petrochemicals.

● **HUA NAN COMMERCIAL BANK LTD.**
No. 38 Section One, Chung King South Road, Taipei, Taiwan ROC
CEO: Edward H. T. Chien, Chmn.   Tel: 886-22-371-3111   Rev: $2,153
Bus: *Commercial banking services.*   Fax: 886-22-382-1060   Emp: 6,046
www.hncb.com.tw

   HUA NAN COMMERCIAL BANK LTD.
   *Two World Trade Center, Ste. 2846, New York, NY   10048
   CEO: Derek Chang, SVP   Tel: (212) 488-2330   %FO: 100
   Bus: *Commercial banking services.*   Fax: (212) 912-1050   Emp: 14

● **THE INTERNATIONAL COMMERCIAL BANK OF CHINA**
100 Chi Lin Road, Taipei 104, Taiwan ROC
CEO: Yung-San Lee, Chmn.   Tel: 886-22-563-3156   Rev: $1,471
Bus: *Commercial banking services.*   Fax: 886-22-563-2614   Emp: 3,000

   THE INTERNATIONAL COMMERCIAL BANK OF CHINA
   65 Liberty Street, New York, NY   10005
   CEO: Owen S. Y Hu, SVP   Tel: (212) 608-4222   %FO: 100
   Bus: *Commercial banking services.*   Fax: (212) 608-4943   Emp: 60

   THE INTERNATIONAL COMMERCIAL BANK OF CHINA
   445 S. Figueroa Street, Ste. 1900, Los Angeles, CA   90071
   CEO: Ruey Jen Liu, SVP   Tel: (213) 489-3000   %FO: 100
   Bus: *Commercial banking services.*   Fax: (213) 489-1183   Emp: 25

   THE INTERNATIONAL COMMERCIAL BANK OF CHINA
   2 North Lasalle Street, Ste 1803, Chicago, IL   60602
   CEO: Chia-Jang Liu, VP   Tel: (312) 782-8035   %FO: 100
   Bus: *Commercial banking services.*   Fax: (312) 782-2402   Emp: 25

● **MACRONIX INTERNATIONAL CO., LTD.**
No. 16 Li-Hsin Road, Science-Based Industria Park, Hsinchu, Taiwan ROC
CEO: Miin Wu, CEO   Tel: 886-3-578-6688   Rev: $974
Bus: *Mfr. memory chips.*   Fax: 886-3-563-2999   Emp: 3,700
www.macronix.com

   MACRONIX AMERICA, INC.
   800 NW Highway, Ste. 820, Palatine, IL   60067
   CEO: Roland Tseng   Tel: (847) 963-1900   %FO: 100
   Bus: *Mfr. memory chips.*   Fax: (847) 963-1909

   MACRONIX AMERICA, INC.
   491 Fairview Way, Milpitas, CA   95035-0302
   CEO: Roland Tseng   Tel: (408) 453-8088   %FO: 100
   Bus: *Mfr. memory chips.*   Fax: (408) 453-8488

● MICROTEK INTERNATIONAL INC.

6 Industry East Road, III Science-Based Industrial Park, Hsinchu, Taiwan ROC

CEO: Benny Hsu, Chmn. & Pres.	Tel: 886-3-577-2155	Rev: $91
Bus: *Mfr. of microcomputer simulators and desktop video image processors.*	Fax: 886-3-577-2598 www.microtek.com.tw	Emp: 76

MICROTEK

3715 Doolittle Drive, Redondo Beach, CA   90278

CEO: Mary Dell, Mgr.	Tel: (310) 297-5000	%FO: 100
Bus: *Sales/distribution of scanners, microcomputer simulators and desktop video image processors.*	Fax: (310) 297-5050	

● MOSEL VITELIC INC.

No. 19, Li Hsin Road, Science Based Industrial Park, Hsinchu, Taiwan ROC

CEO: H. C. Hu, CEO	Tel: 886-3-579-5888	Rev: $825
Bus: *Mfr. memory integrated circuits.*	Fax: 886-3-566-5888 www.moselvitelic.com	Emp: 1,075

MOSEL VITELIC INC.

3910 North First Street, San Jose, CA   95134

CEO: Hsing Tuan, Pres.	Tel: (408) 433-6000	%FO: 100
Bus: *Mfr. memory integrated circuits.*	Fax: (408) 433-0952	

● NAN YA PLASTICS CORPORATION

201 Tun Hwa North Road, Taipei, Taiwan ROC

CEO: Y.C. Wang, Chmn. & CEO	Tel: 886-22-712-2211	Rev: $3,010
Bus: *Mfr. plastics, PVC leather, sheeting, pipe; polyester fibers, laminates, plate and engineering plastics. (Sub of Formosa Plastics Corp.)*	Fax: 886-22-717-8533 www.npc.com.tw	Emp: 18,817

NAY YA PLASTICS CORPORATION, AMERICA

PO Box 700, Point Comfort, TX   77978

CEO: George Chang	Tel: (361) 987-7000	%FO: 100
Bus: *Mfr. plastics; PVC sheeting, polyester fibers.*	Fax: (361) 987-7481	

NAY YA PLASTICS CORPORATION, AMERICA

9 Peachtree Hill Road, Livingston, NJ   07039

CEO: George Chang	Tel: (973) 716-7488	%FO: 100
Bus: *Mfr. plastics; PVC sheeting, polyester fibers.*	Fax: (973) 716-7470	

NAY YA PLASTICS CORPORATION, AMERICA
5561 Normandy Road, Batchelor, LA   70715

CEO: George Chang	Tel: (225) 492-2435	%FO: 100
Bus: *Mfr. plastics; PVC sheeting, polyester fibers.*	Fax: (225) 492-2134	

NAY YA PLASTICS CORPORATION, AMERICA
700 Highway 59 Loop RR, Wharton, TX   77488

CEO: George Chang	Tel: (979) 532-5494
Bus: *Mfr. plastics; PVC sheeting, polyester fibers.*	Fax: (979) 532-4836

NAY YA PLASTICS CORPORATION, AMERICA
140 East Beulah Road, Lake City, SC   29560

CEO: George Chang	Tel: (843) 389-7800	%FO: 100
Bus: *Mfr. plastics; PVC sheeting, polyester fibers.*	Fax: (843) 389-3559	

• SILICONWARE PRECISION INDUSTRIES CO., LTD.
No. 123 Sec. 3, Da-Fong Road, Tantzu, Taichung, Taiwan ROC

CEO: Bough Lin, CEO	Tel: 886-3-579-5678	Rev: $570
Bus: *Mfr. electronics.*	Fax: 886-3-577-0173	
	www.spil.com.tw	

SPIL BUSINESS DEVELOPMENT
1735 Technology Drive, Ste. 300, San Jose, CA   95110

CEO: Bough Lin, Pres.	Tel: (408) 573-5530	%FO: 100
Bus: *Mfr. electronics.*	Fax: (408) 573-5530	

• TAIWAN SEMICONDUCTOR MFG. CO.
Science Based Industrial Park, 121 Park Avenue 3, Hsin-Chu, Taiwan ROC

CEO: Morris Chang, Chmn. & Pres.	Tel: 886-3-5780-221	Rev: $1,566
Bus: *Provides manufacturing services for advanced integrated circuits.*	Fax: 886-3-5781-546	Emp: 6,000
	www.tsmc.com.tw	

TSMC, INC.
1740 Technology Drive, Ste. 660, San Jose, CA   95110

CEO: Ed Ross, Pres.	Tel: (408) 437-8762	%FO: 100
Bus: *Provides manufacturing services for advanced integrated circuits.*	Fax: (408) 441-7713	

• TATUNG CO.
22 Chungshan North Road, Sec. 3, Taipei, Taiwan ROC

CEO: Lin Weishan, Pres. & CEO	Tel: 886-22-592-5252	Rev: $4,133
Bus: *Engaged in telecommunications.*	Fax: 886-22-598-4509	Emp: 60,675
	www.tatung.com.tw	

TATUNG USA CORPORATION
2850 El Presidio Street, Long Beach, CA   90810
CEO: Mike Lee, VP Sales   Tel: (800) 827-2850   %FO: 100
Bus: *Engaged in telecommunications.*   Fax: (310) 637-2105

• TECO WESTINGHOUSE MOTOR COMPANY
No. 156-2, Sung Chiang Road, Taipei City, Taiwan ROC
CEO: Huang Machsiung, Chmn.   Tel: 886-22-562-1111   Rev: $634
Bus: *Mfr. electric motors.*   Fax: 886-22-536-6862   Emp: 3,400
                                       www.tecowestinghouse.com

TECO WESTINGHOUSE MOTORS INC.
1600 Eldridge Parkway, Ste. 3708, Houston, TX   77077
CEO: C. Yiho, Pres.   Tel: (281) 596-9611   %FO: 100
Bus: *Sales/distribution of motors.*   Fax: (281) 596-9304

• ULEAD SYSTEMS, INC.
2F, 358 Neihu Road, Section 1, Taipei, Taiwan ROC
CEO: Danielle H.L. Liao, Pres.   Tel: 886-2-2659-7588
Bus: *Computer software & services.*   Fax: 886-2-2659-8388
                                       www.ulead.com

ULEAD SYSTEMS, INC.
20000 Mariner Ave., Suite #200, Torrance, CA   90503
CEO: Lewis Liaw, SVP   Tel: (310) 896-6388   %FO: 100
Bus: *Computer software & services.*   Fax: (310) 896-6389

• UMAX DATA SYSTEMS, INC.
No. 1-1, R&D Road, Science-Based Industrial Park, Hsinchu, Taiwan ROC
CEO: Frank C. Huang, Chmn. & CEO   Tel: 886-3-577-4955
Bus: *Mfg.. computer hardware &*   Fax: 886-3-577-0140
peripherals, scanners, monitors,   www.umax.com.tw
speakers, & digital cameras.

UMAX TECHNOLOGIES INC.
3561 Gateway Blvd., Fremont, CA   94538
CEO: Vincent Tai, CEO   Tel: (510) 651-4000   %FO: 100
Bus: *Mfr. computer hardware &*   Fax: (510) 651-8834
peripherals, scanners, monitors,
speakers, & digital cameras.

• UNITED MICROELECTRONICS CORPORATION
3 Li-Hsin 2nd Road, Science Based Industrial Park, Hsinchu, Taiwan ROC
CEO: Peter Change, CEO   Tel: 886-3-578-2258   Rev: $3,492
Bus: *Mfr. of semiconductors.*   Fax: 886-3-577-9392   Emp: 9,500
                                       www.umc.com

UMC USA INC.
488 De Guigne Drive, Sunnyale, CA   94086
CEO: Jim Kupec, Pres.   Tel: (408) 523-7800   %FO: 100
Bus: *Sales/distribution of*   Fax: (408) 733-8090
     semiconductors.

● **UNITED WORLD CHINESE COMMERCIAL BANK**
65 Kuan-Chien Road, Taipei, Taiwan ROC
CEO: Gregory Khwang, Pres.   Tel: 886-22-312-5555   Rev: $1,206
Bus: *Commercial banking services.*   Fax: 886-22-213-78

UNITED WORLD CHINESE COMMERCIAL BANK
555 West Fifth Street, Suite 3850, Los Angeles, CA   90013
CEO: Shihchen Joseph Jao, Gen. Mgr.   Tel: (213) 243-1234   %FO: 100
Bus: *International banking services.*   Fax: (213) 627-6817   Emp: 18

● **VIA TECHNOLOGIES, INC.**
533 Chung Cheng Road, 8/F, Hsin-Tien, Taipei 231, Taiwan ROC
CEO: Wen Chi Chen, CEO   Tel: 886-2-2218-5452   Rev: $934
Bus: *Engaged in electronics.*   Fax: 886-2-2218-5453   Emp: 1,000
                                 www.viatech.com

CENTAUR TECHNOLOGY, INC.
9111 Jollyville Road, Ste. 206, Austin, TX   78759
CEO: Glenn Henry, Pres.   Tel: (512) 418-5700   %FO: 100
Bus: *Mfr. small PC's.*   Fax: (512) 794-0717

● **WINBOND ELECTRONICS CORPORATION**
No. 4, 3 Creation Road, Science Based Industrial Park, Hsinchu, Taiwan ROC
CEO: Ching-Chu Chang, Pres. & CEO   Tel: 886-3-577-0066   Rev: $1,487
Bus: *Mfr. semiconductors.*   Fax: 886-3-579-2668   Emp: 4,477
                                 www.winbond.com.tw

WINBOND
2727 North First Street, San Jose, CA   95134
CEO: Tom Sullivan, VP   Tel: (408) 943-6666   %FO: 100
Bus: *Mfr. semiconductors.*   Fax: (408) 544-1798

Thailand

- **BANGKOK BANK PUBLIC COMPANY**
  333 Silom Road, Bangkok 10500, Thailand
  CEO: Chatri Sophonpanich, Chmn. Tel: 66-2-231-4333 Rev: $3,711
  Bus: *Banking services.* Fax: 66-2-231-4742 Emp: 21,652
  www.bbl.co.th

  BANGKOK BANK PUBLIC COMPANY LTD.
  29 Broadway, 20th Fl., New York, NY   10006
  CEO: Chalit Phaphan, VP Tel: (212) 422-8200 %FO: 100
  Bus: *General banking services.* Fax: (212) 422-0728 Emp: 40

- **BANK OF THAILAND**
  273 Samsen Road, Bankhunprom, PO Box 154, Bangkok 10200, Thailand
  CEO: Rerngchai Marakanond, Gov. Tel: 66-2-283-5353
  Bus: *Government, Central Bank of Thailand.* Fax: 66-2-280-0449
  www.bot.or.th

  BANK OF THAILAND
  40 East 52nd Street, New York, NY   10017
  CEO: Aroonsri Tivakul, CEO Tel: (212) 750-0310 %FO: 100
  Bus: *Central Bank of Thailand.* Fax: (212) 223-7454 Emp: 10

- **HANA MICROELECTRONICS CO., LTD.**
  10/4 Moo 7, Vibhavadi-Rangsit Rd., Don Muang, Bangkok 10210, Thailand
  CEO: Richard D. Han, CEO Tel: 66-2-551-1297
  Bus: *Engaged in electronics and* Fax: 66-2-552-1299
  semiconductors. www.hanagroup.com

  ADVANCED INTERCONNECT TECHNOLOGIES (AIT), INC.
  7011 Koll Center Pkwy., Ste. 150, Pleasanton, CA   94588
  CEO: Tom Reynolds, Pres. Tel: (925) 426-3100 %FO: 100
  Bus: *Engaged in electronics.* Fax: (925) 426-2323

- **KRUNG THAI BANK LTD.**
  35 Sukhumvit Road, Bangkok 10110, Thailand
  CEO: Singh Tangtatswas, Pres. Tel: 66-2-255-2222 Rev: $2,497
  Bus: *Commercial banking services.* Fax: 66-2-255-9391 Emp: 18,422
  www.ktb.co.th

KRUNG THAI BANK - New York Branch
415 Madison Avenue, 8th Fl., New York, NY 10017
CEO: Pannipa Apichatabutra, SVP   Tel: (212) 832-5600   %FO: 100
Bus: *International commercial banking*   Fax: (212) 832-5993   Emp: 10
    services.

KRUNG THAI BANK - Los Angeles Branch
707 Wilshire Boulevard, Ste. 3150, Los Angeles, CA 90017
CEO: Chai Hongvisitkul, Mgr.   Tel: (212) 488-9897   %FO: 100
Bus: *International commercial banking*   Fax: (213) 891-0734   Emp: 15
    services.

● **SAHA-UNION PUBLIC COMPANY LTD.**
1828 Sukhumvit Road, Bangchak, Phrakanong Bangkok 10250, Thailand
CEO: Damri Darakananda, Exec.Chrm.   Tel: 66-2-311-5111-9   Rev: $458
Bus: *Distributor of textile products,*   Fax: 66-2-332-5616   Emp: 2,100
    exploration fabrics, garment   www.sahaunion.co.th
    accessories, footwear, plastics, etc.

    SAHA-UNION INTL (USA) INC
    419 Allan Street, Daly City, CA 94014
    CEO: Ong-Arj Kriengkripetch, Pres.   Tel: (415) 467-5330   %FO: 100
    Bus: *Mfr. textiles, sewing threads.*   Fax: (415) 239-2625

● **SIAM COMMERCIAL BANK PLC**
9 Rutchadatick Road, Latyao, Chatuchak, Bangkok 10900, Thailand
CEO: Jada Wattanasiritham, CEO   Tel: 66-2-544-1111   Rev: $2,334
Bus: *Commercial banking services.*   Fax: 66-2-937-7763   Emp: 12,220
    www.scb.co.th

    SIAM COMMERCIAL BANK PLC - NEW YORK AGENCY
    One Exchange Place, 8th Fl., New York, NY 10006
    CEO: Chulatip Nitibhon, Mgr.   Tel: (212) 344-4101   %FO: 100
    Bus: *International banking services.*   Fax: (212) 747-0106   Emp: 25

    SIAM COMMERCIAL BANK PLC
    601 S. Figueroa Street, Ste. 3575, Los Angeles, CA 90017
    CEO: Joe Crestejo, Mgr.   Tel: (213) 614-1805   %FO: 100
    Bus: *International banking services.*   Fax: (213) 622-0049   Emp: 20

● **THAI AIRWAYS INTERNATIONAL**
89 Vibhavadi Rangsit Road, Bangkok 10900, Thailand
CEO: Chai-anan Samudavanija, Chmn.   Tel: 66-2-513-0120   Rev: $2,936
Bus: *Commercial air transport services.*   Fax: 66-2-513-3398   Emp: 24,222
    www.thaiairways.com

THAI AIRWAYS INTERNATIONAL
222 N. Sepulveda Boulevard, Ste. 1950, El Segundo, CA   90245
CEO: M. Somchainuek, Pres.   Tel: (310) 640-0097   %FO: 100
Bus: *International commercial air*   Fax: (310) 640-8202
      transport services.

THAI AIRWAYS INTERNATIONAL
630 Fifth Avenue, Suite 351, New York, NY   10111
CEO: Prin Yooprasert, Mgr.   Tel: (212) 265-6021   %FO: 100
Bus: *International commercial air*   Fax: (212) 644-9351   Emp: 150
      transport services.

● **THAI FARMERS BANK LTD.**
1 Thai Farmers Lane, Ratburana Road, Bangkok 10140, Thailand
CEO: Banyong Lamsam, Chmn.   Tel: 66-2-470-1122   Rev: $2,414
Bus: *Commercial banking services.*   Fax: 66-2-470-1144
                                         www.tfb.co.th

THAI FARMERS BANK LTD.
333 South Grand Avenue
Suite 3570, Los Angeles, CA   90070
CEO: S. Kueworakulchai, Gen. Mgr.   Tel: (213) 680-9331   %FO: 100
Bus: *International banking services.*   Fax: (213) 620-9362   Emp: 17

THAI FARMERS BANK LTD.
*27 Sapphire Drive, West Windsor, NJ   08550
CEO: Pipat Visuttiporn, Gen. Mgr.   Tel: (609) 213-2387   %FO: 100
Bus: *International banking services.*   Fax: (606) 275-6510   Emp: 17

Turkey

- **GLOBAL SECURITIES**

100-102 Buyukdere Caddesi, Maya Akar Centre, 80280 Esentepe Istanbul, Turkey

CEO: Mehmet Kutman, Chmn.

Tel: 90-212-3179797

Bus: *Provides investment banking and asset management services.*

Fax: 90-212-317-9727

Emp: 300

GLOBAL SECURITIES

101 East 52nd Street, New York, NY 10012

CEO: Patrick Desan, Mgr.

Tel: (212) 317-9797

%FO: 100

Bus: *Investment banking and asset management services.*

Fax: (212) 317-9727

- **HACI ÖMER SABANCI HOLDING A.S.**

Sabanci Center, 4 Levent, 80745 Istanbul, Turkey

CEO: Sakip Sabanci, Chmn.

Tel: 90-212-281-6600

Rev: $5,399

Bus: *Financial services; banking, insurance.*

Fax: 90-212-281-0272

www.sabanci.com.tr

Emp: 30,150

HOLSA INC.

650 Fifth Avenue, 16th Fl., New York, NY 10019

CEO: Halit Ozbelli, Gen. Mgr.

Tel: (212) 307-6522

%FO: 100

Bus: *Financial services; banking, insurance.*

Fax: (212) 307-6710

Emp: 4

- **KOÇ HOLDING A.S.**

Nakkastepe Azizbey Sokak No.1, 81207 Istanbul, Turkey

CEO: Temel Atay, CEO

Tel: 90-216-531-0000

Rev: $3,240

Bus: *Holding company; automotive, consumer goods, financial, tourism and energy industry services.*

Fax: 90-216-343-1944

www.koc.com.tr

Emp: 45,625

RAMERICA INTERNATIONAL, INC.

One Rockefeller Plaza, Ste. 204, New York, NY 10020

CEO: Feyzi Celik, Pres. & CEO

Tel: (212) 218-6990

%FO: 100

Bus: *U.S. representative: automotive & consumer goods, financial, tourism and energy industry services.*

Fax: (212) 218-6999

Emp: 6

● **T.C. ZIRAAT BANKASI**
Bankalar Cad, No. 42, Ankara, Turkey
CEO: Osman Tunaboylu, Chmn.　　　　Tel: 90-312-310-2480
Bus: *General banking services.*　　　　Fax: 90-312-490-8076　　　　Emp: 40,000

　　T.C. ZIRAAT BANKASI
　　330 Madison Avenue, 32nd Fl., New York, NY　10017
　　CEO: Mehmet Akkoc　　　　Tel: (212) 557-5612　　　%FO: 100
　　Bus: *International banking services.*　　Fax: (212) 490-8076　　Emp: 40

● **TURKISH AIRLINES (TURK HAVA YOLLARI AO)**
Ataturk International Airport, Yesilkoy, 34834 Istanbul, Turkey
CEO: Yusuf Bolayirli, Pres.　　　　Tel: 90-212-663-6300
Bus: *International commercial air transport*　　Fax: 90-212-663-4744　　Emp: 9,000
　　services.　　　　　　　　　　www.turkishairlines.com

　　TURKISH AIRLINES
　　437 Madison Avenue, Ste. 17B, New York, NY　10022
　　CEO: Raha Pakkan, Dir.　　　　Tel: (212) 339-9650　　　%FO: 100
　　Bus: *International commercial air*　　Fax: (212) 339-9683　　Emp: 43
　　　transport services.

　　TURKISH AIRLINES
　　625 North Michigan Avenue, Ste. 1400, Chicago, IL　60611
　　CEO: Semira Kirgiz, Dir.　　　　Tel: (312) 943-7858　　　%FO: 100
　　Bus: *International commercial air*　　Fax: (312) 943-7843
　　　transport services.

　　TURKISH AIRLINES
　　1001 Brickell Bay Dr.. Ste. 2414, Los Angeles, CA　90045
　　CEO: Phil Westernoff, Dir.　　　　Tel: (310) 258-0530　　　%FO: 100
　　Bus: *International commercial air*　　Fax: (310) 258-0535
　　　transport services.

● **TURKIYE CUMHURIYET MERKEZ BANKASI**
Istiklal Caddeis, No.10, 06100 Ankara, Turkey
CEO: Gazi Ercel, Gov.　　　　Tel: 90-312-310-3646
Bus: *Central banking institution of Turkey;*　Fax: 90-312-310-7434
　　issues currency, sets monetary policy.　www.tcmb.gov.tr

　　CENTRAL BANK OF TURKEY
　　821 United Nations Plaza, 7th Fl., New York, NY　10017
　　CEO: Nurhayat Bezgin, Rep.　　　　Tel: (212) 682-8717　　　%FO: 100
　　Bus: *Central banking institution of*　　Fax: (212) 867-1958　　Emp: 4
　　　Turkey.

United Arab Emirates

● **EMIRATES AIR**

Dubai International Airport, Dubai, United Arab Emirates

CEO: H.H. Sheikh Ahmed Bin Saeed Al Maktoum, CEO   Tel: 971-421-5544   Rev: $600

Bus: *Commercial air transport services.*   Fax: 971-423-9817   Emp: 3,400

www.emirates.com

    EMIRATES AIR

    405 Park Avenue, Suite 403, New York, NY 10022

    CEO: James Baxter, VP North America   Tel: (212) 758-4252   %FO: 100

    Bus: *International commercial air transport services.*   Fax: (212) 758-4434   Emp: 26

● **EMIRATES SKY CARGO (DNATA)**

Airline Centre A", 3rd Fl., PO Box 686, Dubai, United Arab Emirates

CEO: Fay Thompson   Tel: 971-4-22-71-04

Bus: *Travel management services, handling agency and cargo and freight forwarding.*   Fax: 971-4-28-20-49

www.sky-cargo.com

    SKY CARGO / EC INTERNATIONAL (GSA)

    147-29 182nd Street, Springfield Gardens, NY 11413

    CEO: Ed Chism, Pres.   Tel: (718) 340-7500

    Bus: *International freight forwarding.*   Fax: (718) 244-6881

● **MASHREQ BANK PSC**

PO Box 1250, Deira, Dubai, United Arab Emirates

CEO: Abdulla Ahmed Al Ghurair, Chmn.   Tel: 971-422-9131

Bus: *Commercial banking services.*   Fax:

    MASHREQ BANK PSC.

    255 Fifth Avenue, 1st Fl., New York, NY 10016

    CEO: Muhammad A. Ghafoor, Mgr.   Tel: (212) 545-8200   %FO: 100

    Bus: *Commercial banking services.*   Fax: (212) 545-0919   Emp: 32

● **NATIONAL BANK OF ABU DHABI**

Khalidiya Office Bldg., PO Box 4, Abu Dhabi, United Arab Emirates

CEO: John Symonds, CEO   Tel: 971-2-666-6800

Bus: *Commercial banking services.*   Fax: 971-2-667-2081

www.nbad.co.ae

ABU DHABI INTERNATIONAL BANK INC.
1020 19th Street NW, Suite 500, Washington, DC   20036

CEO: Nagy S. Kolta, Dir.	Tel: (202) 842-7900	%FO: 100
Bus: *International commercial banking services.*	Fax: (202) 842-7955	Emp: 22

Uruguay

- **BANCO DE LA REPUBLICA ORIENTAL DEL URUGUAY**
Edificio 19 de Junio, Cerrito y Zabala, Montevideo, Uruguay
CEO: Antonio G. Correa, CEO   Tel: 598-2-915-0157
Bus: *General banking services.*   Fax: 598-2-916-2064
                                        www.brounet.com.uy

BANCO DE LA REPUBLICA ORIENTAL DEL URUGUAY
1270 Avenue of the Americas, Suite 3001, New York, NY   10020
CEO: Walter Calcagno, SVP   Tel: (212) 307-9600   %FO: 100
Bus: *International commercial banking*   Fax: (212) 307-6786   Emp: 25
    services.

Venezuela

- **AEROVIAS VENEZOLANAS SA**
  Torré Humbolt, Av. Rio Cavro, 25th Fl., Caracas, Venezuela
  CEO: Henry Lord Boulton, Pres   Tel: 58-2-907-8000
  Bus: *Commercial air transport carrier.*   Fax: 58-2-907-8027   Emp: 2,700
       www.avensa.com.ve

  - **AVENSA AIRLINES**
    JFK International Airport, West Wing, Bldg. 52, Jamaica, NY   11430
    CEO: Irene Sanchez, Mgr.   Tel: (718) 244-6857   %FO: 100
    Bus: *International commercial air*   Fax: (718) 244-7500
         transport carrier.

  - **AVENSA AIRLINES**
    800 Brickell Avenue, Ste. 1109, Miami, FL   33131
    CEO: Tony Lutz, Mgr.   Tel: (305) 381-8706   %FO: 100
    Bus: *International commercial air*   Fax: (305) 381-6079
         transport carrier.

- **BANCO INDUSTRIAL DE VENEZUELA**
  Tercera Ave. Cruce con Francisco Solano, Torre Financiera, Caracas, Venezuela
  CEO: Maria D. Parada, VP   Tel: 58-2-545-9222
  Bus: *Commercial banking services.*   Fax: 58-2-952-4139
       www.biv.com.ve

  - **BANCO INDUSTRIAL DE VENEZUELA**
    900 Third Avenue, Suite 1400, New York, NY   10022
    CEO: Mario C. Caires, EVP   Tel: (212) 688-2200   %FO: 100
    Bus: *International banking services.*   Fax: (212) 888-4921   Emp: 23

- **BANCO MERCANTIL, C.A. VENEZUELA**
  PO Box 789, Avenida Andres Bello 1, Edificio Mercantil, Caracas 1050, Venezuela
  CEO: Gustavo A. Marturet, Chrm.   Tel: 58-12-503-1111   Rev: $505
  Bus: *Commercial banking services.*   Fax: 58-12-503-1391   Emp: 7,303
       www.bancomercantil.com

  - **BANCO MERCANTIL**
    11 East 51st Street, New York, NY   10022
    CEO: Diego Arnal, Mgr.   Tel: (212) 891-7400   %FO: 100
    Bus: *Bank agency.*   Fax: (212) 891-7411   Emp: 19

BANCO MERCANTIL
2199 Ponce de Leon Boulevard, Coral Gables, FL   33134
CEO: Alberto Gonzalez, Gen. Mgr.   Tel: (305) 460-8500   %FO: 100
Bus: *Banking agency.*   Fax: (305) 460-8595

COMMERCE BANK NATIONAL ASSOCIATION
220 La Hambre Circle, Coral Gables, FL   33134
CEO: Juan Carlos Martinez, Mgr.   Tel: (305) 460-4000   %FO: 100
Bus: *Banking agency.*   Fax: (305) 448-9027

● **THE CISNEROS GROUP OF COMPANIES**
Edificio Venevisión, Quinto Piso, Final Avenida La Salle, Colina de los Caobos, Caracas 1050,
Venezuela
CEO: William T. Keon III, CEO   Tel: 58-2-781-8286   Rev: $3,500
Bus: *Owns media conglomerates, including*   Fax: 58-2-781-5957   Emp: 35,000
Spanish-language broadcasting and   www.cisneros.com
engaged in gold mining.

   CISNEROS TELEVISION GROUP
   420-426 Jefferson Avenue, Miami Beach, FL   33139
   CEO: Carlos E. Cisneros, Pres. & CEO   Tel: (305) 535-5733   %FO: 100
   Bus: *Spanish-language broadcasting.*   Fax: (305) 531-9446

   HIGHGATE PROPERTIES, DIV. CISNEROS
   36 East 61 Street, New York, NY   10021
   CEO: Alejandro Rivera, EVP   Tel: (212) 355-0620   %FO: 100
   Bus: *Engaged in media.*   Fax: (212) 838-1836

   UNIVISION
   1999 Avenue of the Stars, Los Angeles, CA   90067
   CEO: Henry Cisneros, Pres & CEO   Tel: (310) 556-7676
   Bus: *Engaged in media.*   Fax: (310) 556-7615

   VENEVISION INTERNATIONAL
   550 Biltmore Way, 9th Fl., Coral Gables, FL   33134
   CEO: Luis Villanueva, Pres. & CEO   Tel: (305) 442-3487   %FO: 100
   Bus: *Spanish-language broadcasting.* Fax: (305) 448-4762

● **CORP BANCA, C.A.**
Torre Corp Banca, Avenida Principal, Plaza La Castellana, Caracas 1060, Venezuela
CEO: Lautaro Aguilar, Pres.   Tel: 58-2-206-3299
Bus: *International banking services.* Fax: 58-2-206-3130   Emp: 3,500
                                       www.Corpbanca.com.ve

CORP BANCA CA

845 Third Avenue, 5th Fl., New York, NY   10022

CEO: Felipe M. Lesser, Mgr.   Tel: (212) 980-1770   %FO: 100

Bus: *International commercial banking*   Fax: (212) 753-1206   Emp: 30
services.

● **PETRÓLEOS DE VENEZUELA SA (PDVSA)**

Avda Libertador Apdo. 169, La Campina, Caracas 1010-A, Venezuela

CEO: Gualcalpuro Lameda Montero, Pres.   Tel: 58-2-708-4111   Rev: $32,648

Bus: *Engaged in exploration, production,*   Fax: 58-2-708-4662   Emp: 56,600
distribution of petrochemicals, oil and   www.pdv.com
coal.

   BITOR AMERICA, INC.

   5200 Town Center Circle, Ste. 301, Boca Raton, FL   33486

   CEO: Eduardo Hernandez-Carstens, VP   Tel: (561) 392-0026   %FO: 100

   Bus: *U.S. sub. of Petroleos de*   Fax: (561) 392-0490   Emp: 8
   Venezuela SA

   CITGO PETROLEUM CORP

   PO Box 3758, Tulsa, OK   74102

   CEO: Oswaldo Contreras Maza, Pres.   Tel: (918) 495-4000   %FO: 100

   Bus: *Oil refining & marketing.*   Fax: (918) 495-4511   Emp: 4,500

   PDV AMERICA, INC.

   750 Lexington Avenue, 10th Fl., New York, NY   10022

   CEO: Jose I. Moreno, Mgr.   Tel: (212) 339-7770   %FO: 100

   Bus: *U.S. headquarters. Petroleum*   Fax: (212) 339-7727   Emp: 8
   information systems & services.

   PDVSA SERVICES, INC.

   11490 Westheimer, Ste. 1000, Houston, TX   77077

   CEO: Manuel Vila, Mgr.   Tel: (281) 531-0004   %FO: 100

   Bus: *Petroleum information systems &*   Fax: (281) 588-6290
   services.

Wales, U.K.

● **GYRUS GROUP PLC**
Fortran Road, St. Mellons, Cardiff CF3 0LT, UK

CEO: N. Mark Goble	Tel: 44-29-20-776300	Rev: $40
Bus: *Engaged in the development, manufacturing, and marketing of bipolar electrosurgical instrumentation for the minimally invasive surgery market.*	Fax: 44-29-20-776301 www.gyrus.co.uk	Emp: 300

GYRUS MEDICAL, INC.
6655 Wedgwood Road, Ste. 105, Maple Grove, MN 55311-3602

CEO: Keith Poppe, VP	Tel: (763) 416-3000	%FO: 100
Bus: *Engaged in the development, manufacturing, and marketing of bipolar electrosurgical instrumentation for the minimally invasive surgery market.*	Fax: (763) 416-3001	

● **IQE (INTERNATIONAL QUANTUM EPITAXY) PLC**
Pascal Close, Cypress Drive, St. Mellons Cardiff CF3 OEG, UK

CEO: Drew Nelson, CEO	Tel: 44-2920-839-400	Rev: $45
Bus: *Mfr. compound semiconductors.*	Fax: 44-2920-839-401 www.iqeplc.com	Emp: 200

IQE INCORPORATED
119 Technology Drive, Bethlehem, PA 18015

CEO: Lorraine Ball, HR	Tel: (610) 861-6930	%FO: 100
Bus: *Mfr. compound semiconductors.*	Fax: (610) 861-5273	

ALPHABETICAL
LISTING
OF FOREIGN FIRMS

Part Two is an alphabetical listing of all the foreign firms in Part One, giving the name, an abbreviation in parenthesis identifying the country, and the number of the page where the complete listing can be found in Part One.

B

BANCO BOZANO, SIMONSEN S.A. (Brazil)	70
BANCO BRADESCO SA (Brazil)	70
BANCO COLPATRIA SA (Colombia)	205
BANCO COMMERCIAL PORTUGUES (Portugal)	1127
BANCO DE BOGOTA (Colombia)	205
BANCO DE CHILE (Chile)	195
BANCO DE CREDITO DEL PERU, SUB. CREDICORP LTD. (Peru)	1122
BANCO DE GALICIA Y BUENOS AIRES (Argentina)	4
BANCO DE LA NACION ARGENTINA (Argentina)	4
BANCO DE LA PROVINCIA DE BUENOS AIRES (Argentina)	4
BANCO DE LA REPUBLICA ORIENTAL DEL URUGUAY (Uruguay)	1351
BANCO DI NAPOLI SPA (Italy)	775
BANCO DI SICILIA S.p.A (Italy)	775
BANCO DO BRASIL (Brazil)	71
BANCO DO ESTADO DE SÃO PAULO SA (Brazil)	71
BANCO DO ESTADO DO PARANÁ SA (Brazil)	72
BANCO DO ESTADO DO RIO GRANDE DO SUL SA (Brazil)	72
BANCO ESPANOL DE CREDITO SA (Spain)	1188
BANCO FIBRA SA (Brazil)	72
BANCO FINANTIA (Portugal)	1127
BANCO INDUSTRIAL DE VENEZUELA (Venezuela)	1352
BANCO INDUSVAL S.A (Brazil)	72
BANCO INTERNACIONAL DE COSTA RICA, S.A. (Costa Rica)	207
BANCO INTERNACIONAL, S.A. (Mexico)	1017
BANCO ITAÚ S.A. (Brazil)	73
BANCO LATINOAMERICANO DE EXPORTACIONES SA (BLADEX) (Panama)	1121
BANCO MERCANTIL DE SÃO PAULO S.A (Brazil)	73
BANCO MERCANTIL, C.A. VENEZUELA (Venezuela)	1352
BANCO NACIONAL DE MEXICO S.A. (BANAMEX) (Mexico)	1017
BANCO PACTUAL S.A. (Brazil)	73
BANCO REAL SA (Brazil)	73
BANCO SANTANDER CENTRAL HISPANO, S.A. (Spain)	1188
BANCO SANTIAGO (Chile)	195
BANCO TOTTA & ACORES (Portugal)	1127
BANCO WIESE SUDAMERIS (Peru)	1122
BANG & OLUFSEN HOLDING A/S (Denmark)	212
BANGKOK BANK PUBLIC COMPANY (Thailand)	1344
BANK AUDI, SAL (Lebanon)	1010
BANK AUSTRIA CREDITANSTALT, DIV. HVB GROUP (Austria)	24
BANK BNI (BANK NEGARA INDONESIA) (Indonesia)	724
BANK CENTRAL ASIA (Indonesia)	724
BANK FOR FOREIGN ECONOMIC AFFAIRS OF USSR (VNESHECONOMBANK) (Russia)	1130
BANK HANDLOWY W WARSZAWIE S.A. (Poland)	1125
BANK HAPOALIM BM (Israel)	742
BANK INDONESIA (Indonesia)	724
BANK LEUMI LE ISRAEL B.M. (Israel)	742
BANK MELLI IRAN (Iran)	726
BANK MUAMALAT MALAYSIA BERHAD (Malaysia)	1014
BANK NEGARA MALAYSIA (Malaysia)	1014
BANK OF BARODA (India)	716
THE BANK OF BERMUDA LTD. (Bermuda)	61
BANK OF CHINA (China (PRC))	198
BANK OF COMMUNICATIONS (China (PRC))	199
THE BANK OF EAST ASIA, LIMITED (Hong Kong)	697
BANK OF INDIA (India)	716
BANK OF IRELAND (Ireland)	729
BANK OF JAPAN (Japan)	817
BANK OF MONTREAL (Canada)	92
BANK OF SCOTLAND (Scotland, U.K.)	1136
BANK OF TAIWAN (Taiwan (ROC))	1335
BANK OF THAILAND (Thailand)	1344
BANK OF THE PHILIPPINE ISLANDS (Philippines)	1123
BANK OF TOKYO MITSUBISHI, LTD. (Japan)	817
THE BANK OF YOKOHAMA, LTD. (Japan)	818
BANK POLSKA KASA OPIEKI S.A., GRUPA PEKAO (Poland)	1125
BANK SADERAT IRAN (Iran)	726
BANK SEPAH-IRAN (Iran)	726
BANQUE BRUXELLES LAMBERT (Belgium)	38
BANQUE FRANÇAISE DU COMMERCE EXTERIEUR (France)	466
BANQUE SUDAMERIS (Brazil)	74
BARALAN INTL SPA (Italy)	775
BARBEQUES GALORE LIMITED (Australia)	8
BARCLAYS BANK PLC (England, U.K.)	259
BARCO N.V. (Belgium)	38
BARCONET NV (Belgium)	39
BARILLA G & R RATELLI SPA (Italy)	776
BARLOW INTERNATIONAL PLC (England, U.K.)	260
BARMAG AG, DIV. SAURER GROUP (Germany)	556
BARRATT DEVELOPMENTS PLC (England, U.K.)	261
BARRICK GOLD CORP. (Canada)	92
BASF AG (Germany)	556
BATA LIMITED (Canada)	93

C

D

DAI NIPPON PRINTING CO LTD. (Japan)	827	DECOMA INTERNATIONAL INC. (Canada)	110
DAI YANG METAL (South Korea)	1160	DEGUSSA AG (Germany)	579
DAIDO STEEL CO INC (Japan)	827	DELANO TECHNOLOGY CORPORATION (Canada)	110
DAIDO TSUSHO CO LTD. (Japan)	828	DELCAM PLC (England, U.K.)	289
DAIDOH, LTD. (Japan)	828	DELFT INSTRUMENTS N.V. (Netherlands)	1050
THE DAIEI, INC. (Japan)	828	DELHAIZE LE LION GROUP SA (Belgium)	42
DAIHATSU MOTOR CO., LTD. (Japan)	829	DELI UNIVERSAL (Netherlands)	1051
DAIICHI CHUO KK (Japan)	829	DELLE VEDOVE LEVIGATRICI S.p.A. (Italy)	780
THE DAI-ICHI KANGYO BANK LIMITED, DIV. MIZUHO FINANCIAL GROU (Japan)	829	DELTA PLC (England, U.K.)	289
DAIICHI PHARMACEUTIAL CO. LTD. (Japan)	830	DELTA-GALIL INDUSTRIES LTD. (Israel)	746
DAIKIN INDUSTRIES, LTD. (Japan)	830	DEMAREST E ALMEIDA (Brazil)	75
DAILY MAIL AND GENERAL TRUST (DMGT) PLC (England, U.K.)	286	DEN NORSKE BANK ASA (Norway)	1108
DAIMLER-CHRYSLER AG (Germany)	576	DENISON INTERNATIONAL PLC (England, U.K.)	290
DAINICHISEIKA COLOUR & CHEMICALS MFR. CO., LTD. (Japan)	831	DENKI KAGAKU KOGYO KK (Japan)	833
DAINIPPON INK & CHEMICALS INC. (Japan)	831	DENSO CORPORATION (Japan)	834
DAIO PAPER CORPORATION (Japan)	832	DENTECH PRODUCTS LTD. (Canada)	111
DAISHOWA INTL CO LTD. (Japan)	832	DENTSU INC. (Japan)	835
DAIWA HOUSE INDUSTRY CO. LTD. (Japan)	832	DEPFA DEUTSCHE PFANDBRIEF BANK AG (Germany)	580
DAIWA SB INVESTMENTS LTD. (Japan)	833	DERLAN INDUSTRIES LTD. (Canada)	112
DAIWA SECURITIES GROUP INC. (Japan)	833	DEROMA SPA (Italy)	781
DANFOSS A/S (Denmark)	213	THE DESCARTES SYSTEMS GROUP INC. (Canada)	112
DANFOSS SOCLA SA (France)	482	DESCENTE LTD. (Japan)	835
DANISCO A/S (Denmark)	215	DET NORSKE VERITAS A/S (Norway)	1109
DANKA BUSINESS SYSTEMS PLC (England, U.K.)	286	DETA BATTERIES US LTD. (England, U.K.)	290
GROUPE DANONE SA (France)	483	DEUTSCHE BABCOCK AG (Germany)	580
DANSKE BANK A/S (FORMERLY DEN DANSKE BANK) (Denmark)	216	DEUTSCHE BANK AG (Germany)	580
DANZAS GROUP AG (Switzerland)	1280	DEUTSCHE BUNDESBANK (Germany)	581
DASSAULT AVIATION (France)	483	DEUTSCHE GELATINE FABRIKEN STOESS AG (Germany)	581
DATAMIRROR CORPORATION (Canada)	109	DEUTSCHE LUFTHANSA AG (Germany)	582
DATAMONITOR PLC (England, U.K.)	287	DEUTSCHE MESSE AG (Germany)	582
DATAWAVE SYSTEMS, INC. (Canada)	109	DEUTSCHE TELEKOM AG (Germany)	582
DAVIES, WARD, PHILLIPS & VINEBERG LLP (Canada)	110	DEUTZ AG (Germany)	583
DAVNET LIMITED (Australia)	12	DEVELOPMENT BANK OF JAPAN (Japan)	836
DAWSON HOLDINGS PLC (England, U.K.)	287	THE DEVELOPMENT BANK OF SINGAPORE (Singapore)	1144
DAYTON MINING CORPORATION (Canada)	110	DEVRO PLC (Scotland, U.K.)	1137
DBT DEUTSCHE BERGBAU-TECHNIK GMBH (Germany)	578	DEXIA BANQUE INTERNATIONALE A LUXEMBOURG (Belgium)	42
DCM LTD. (India)	717	DFDS A/S (Denmark)	216
DCS GROUP PLC (England, U.K.)	287	DG BANK (Germany)	583
DE BANDT, VAN HECKE & LAGAE (Belgium)	41	DG BANK (DEUTSCHE GENOSSENSCHAFTSBANK) (Germany)	583
DE BRAUW BLACKSTONE WESTBROEK, LINKLATERS ALLIANCE (Netherlands)	1050	DIAGEO PLC (England, U.K.)	290
DE DIETRICH & CIE, DIV. ABN AMRO (France)	484	DIALOG SEMICONDUCTOR PLC (Germany)	584
WALTER DE GRUYTER & CO (Germany)	578	DIA-NIELSEN GMBH (Germany)	584
DE LA RUE PLC (England, U.K.)	288	FRIEDR. DICK GMBH (Germany)	584
DE LONGHI SPA (Italy)	780	DIE NORDDEUTSCHE LANDESBANK (Germany)	585
DECLEOR PARIS (France)	485	DIENES-WERKE (Germany)	585

DIESEL S.p.A. (Italy) — 781

DIGICA LTD., SUB DCS GROUP (England, U.K.) — 291

PT DJAKARTA LLOYD (Indonesia) — 724

D-LINK CORPORATION (Taiwan (ROC)) — 1337

DOCDATA N.V. (Netherlands) — 1052

DOFASCO, INC. (Canada) — 113

DOHA BANK LIMITED (Qatar) — 1128

DOLCE & GABBANA (Italy) — 781

DOLLFUS MIEG & CIE (DMC) (France) — 485

DONCASTERS PLC, SUB. ROYAL BANK PRIVATE EQUITY (England, U.K.) — 291

DONGKUK STEEL MILL CO., LTD. (South Korea) — 1160

DOREL INDUSTRIES INC. (Canada) — 113

ALOYS F. DORNBRACHT GMBH & CO. KG (Germany) — 585

DOSATRON INTL SA (France) — 485

DOUGHTY HANSON & CO. (England, U.K.) — 292

DOUGLAS HOLDING AG (Germany) — 585

DRÄGERWERK AG (Germany) — 586

DRAKA HOLDING B.V. (Netherlands) — 1052

DRESDNER BANK AG, DIV. ALLIANZ GROUP (Germany) — 586

DRESDNER KLEINWORT WASSERSTEIN PLC, DIV. DRESDNER BANK GROUP (England, U.K.) — 292

DREW SCIENTIFIC GROUP PLC (England, U.K.) — 292

DRUCK LTD (England, U.K.) — 293

DSG INTERNATIONAL LIMITED (Hong Kong) — 699

DSM N.V. (Netherlands) — 1053

DTZ HOLDINGS PLC (England, U.K.) — 293

DUCATI MOTOR HOLDING SPA (Italy) — 781

DUERKOPP ADLER AG (Germany) — 587

DUNI AB (Sweden) — 1212

DUNLOP SLAZENGER INTERNATIONAL LTD. (England, U.K.) — 295

DUOPLAN OYJ (Finland) — 439

DURATEX SA (Brazil) — 75

DÜRKOPP ADLER AG, DIV. FAG KUGELFISCHER GROUP (Germany) — 587

DURR AG (Germany) — 587

DUTCH SPACE INDUSTRY, FORMERLY FOKKER SPACE BV (Netherlands) — 1054

DUX INDUSTRIER AB (Sweden) — 1212

DYCKERHOFF AG (Germany) — 587

DYNACARE INC. (Canada) — 114

DYNARC AB (Sweden) — 1213

DYNEGY CANADA INC. (Canada) — 115

DYNO NOBEL (Norway) — 1110

E

E.ON AG (Germany) — 588

EAST JAPAN RAILWAY COMPANY (Japan) — 836

EASYSCREEN PLC (England, U.K.) — 295

EBARA CORPORATION (Japan) — 836

EBEL SA, DIV. LVMH GROUP (Switzerland) — 1280

ECI TELECOM LTD. (Israel) — 746

THE ECONOMIST GROUP (England, U.K.) — 295

ED&F MAN GROUP PLC (England, U.K.) — 296

EDEL MUSIC AG (Germany) — 589

EDITIONS QUO VADIS (France) — 485

EDUARD LOEHLE SEN GMBH (Germany) — 589

EDUSOFT LTD. (Israel) — 746

EGE WESTIN AB (Sweden) — 1213

EGYPTAIR (Egypt) — 234

EIDOS PLC (England, U.K.) — 297

EIKI INDUSTRIAL COMPANY, LTD. (Japan) — 838

EIRCOM PLC (Ireland) — 730

EISAI CO., LTD. (Japan) — 838

EISELE GMBH & CO (Germany) — 589

EISER TRIKÅ AB (Sweden) — 1213

EKA NOBEL AB, DIV. AKZO NOBEL (Sweden) — 1213

EL AL ISRAEL AIRLINES LTD. (Israel) — 747

ELA MEDICAL SA, DIV. SANOFI-SYNTHELABO (France) — 486

ELAMEX, S.A. DE C.V. (Mexico) — 1019

ELAN CORPORATION PLC (Ireland) — 731

ELATERAL LIMITED (England, U.K.) — 297

ELECTROCOMPONENTS PLC (England, U.K.) — 297

ELECTROLUX AB (Sweden) — 1214

ELECTROLUX ORIGO (Sweden) — 1216

ELECTRONICS LINE LTD. (Israel) — 747

ELEKTA AB (Sweden) — 1216

ELEKTRO-PHYSIK KOLN GMBH & CO. KG (Germany) — 590

ELEMENTIS PLC (England, U.K.) — 298

ELIN EBG ELEKTROTECHNIK GMBH (Austria) — 26

ELKEM ASA (Norway) — 1110

ELMO CALF AB (Sweden) — 1217

ELMO COMPANY, LTD. (Japan) — 838

ELOF HANSSON BYGG-GROSS AB (Sweden) — 1217

ELRON ELECTRONIC INDUSTRIES LTD. (Israel) — 747

ELSEVIER NV (Netherlands) — 1054

ELTEX OF SWEDEN AB (Sweden) — 1217

EM.TV & MERCHANDISING AG (Germany) — 590

EMBLAZE SYSTEMS LTD. (Israel) — 748

EMBRAER, EMPRESA BRASILEIRA DE AERONAUTICA S.A. (Brazil) — 76

EMCO LTD. (Canada) — 115

EMCO MAIER GMBH (Austria) — 26

F

G

GEORG VON HOLTZBRINCK GMBH (Germany)	601
GERDAU SA (Brazil)	77
GERLING-KONZERN VERSICHERUNGS-BETEILIGUNGS AG (Germany)	601
GETINGE AB (Sweden)	1220
GETRONICS NV (Netherlands)	1060
GIANFRANCO FERRE SPA, DIV. IT HOLDING (Italy)	787
GILAT SATELLITE NETWORKS LTD. (Israel)	750
GILDEMEISTER AG (Germany)	602
GIRMES AG (Germany)	602
GIULIANI, IGMI S.p.A. (Italy)	787
GIVAUDAN, S.A. (Switzerland)	1284
GIVEN IMAGING LTD. (Israel)	750
GKN, PLC. (GUEST, KEEN, NETTLETOLDS) (England, U.K.)	312
GLANBIA PLC (Ireland)	732
GLAXO SMITHKLINE PLC (England, U.K.)	315
GLOBAL CROSSING LTD. (Bermuda)	62
GLOBAL LIGHT TELECOMMUNICATIONS INC. (Canada)	125
GLOBAL SECURITIES (Turkey)	1347
GLOBAL SOURCES LTD. (Hong Kong)	700
GLOBALSTAR TELECOMMUNICATIONS LIMITED (Bermuda)	62
GLOBO CABO SA (Brazil)	77
GLOCK GMBH (Austria)	26
GN RESOUND AS, SUB. GN GREAT NORDIC A/S (Denmark)	218
GOLIATH INTERNATIONAL TOOLS LTD. (England, U.K.)	315
GORAN CAPITAL INC. (Canada)	125
GORANN LTD. (Ireland)	733
GOTTEX MODELS LTD. (Israel)	751
GPC BIOTECH AG (Germany)	603
GRANADA PLC (England, U.K.)	315
GRANARIA HOLDINGS B.V (Netherlands)	1060
GRÄNSFORS BRUKS AB (Sweden)	1221
WILLIAM GRANT & SONS DISTILLERS LTD. (Scotland, U.K.)	1137
GRAPHISOFT NV (Hungary)	711
GRAPHTEC CORPORATION (Japan)	846
GRASS HOLDING AG (Austria)	27
GRASSO PRODUCTS N.V. (Netherlands)	1061
GREAT NORDIC A/S (Denmark)	218
GREAT PACIFIC ENTERPRISES (Canada)	126
THE GREAT UNIVERSAL STORES PLC (England, U.K.)	316
THE GREAT-WEST LIFE ASSURANCE COMPANY (Canada)	126
R. GRIGGS GROUP LIMITED (England, U.K.)	316
GRINDEX AB (Sweden)	1221
GROB WERKE GMBH & CO KG (Germany)	603

GROSFILLEX SARL (France)	493
GROUP 4 FALCK A/S (Denmark)	219
GROUPE AB S.A. (France)	493
GROUPE BULL (France)	493
GROUPE CASINO (France)	494
GROUPE DES ASSURANCES NATIONALES SA (France)	495
GROUPE INGENICO (France)	495
GROUPE LACTALIS (France)	495
GROUPE LIMAGRAIN HOLDING (France)	496
GROUPE SCHNEIDER SA (France)	496
GROUPE STERIA SCA (France)	497
GROUPE TRANSCONTINENTAL GTC LTEE (Canada)	127
GROVE DRESSER ITALIA S.p.A. (Italy)	787
GROZ-BECKERT K.G. (Germany)	603
GRUMA, S.A. DE C.V. (Mexico)	1019
GRUNER + JAHR AG & CO. (Germany)	604
GRUPO BIMBO, SA (Mexico)	1020
GRUPO CARSO, S.A. DE C.V. (Mexico)	1020
GRUPO CEMENTOS DE CHIHUAHUA, SA DE CV (Mexico)	1020
GRUPO DURO FELGUERA, SA (Spain)	1191
GRUPO FINANCIERO BBVA BANCOMER, SA (Mexico)	1021
GRUPO FINANCIERO SERFIN S.A. (Mexico)	1022
GRUPO IMSA, S.A. DE C.V. (Mexico)	1022
GRUPO INDUSTRIAL DURANGO, SA DE CV (Mexico)	1023
GRUPO INDUSTRIAL MASECA (Mexico)	1023
GRUPO MEXICO SA DE CV (Mexico)	1024
GRUPO MINSA, SA DE CV (Mexico)	1025
GRUPO NACIONAL PROVINCIAL, S.A. (Mexico)	1025
GRUPO PICKING PACK, SA (Spain)	1191
GRUPO TACA (El Salvador)	235
GRUPPO CERAMICHE RICCHETTI SPA (Italy)	787
GRUPPO GFT (Italy)	788
GRUPPO RCS EDITORI SPA (Italy)	788
GSI LUMONICS INC. (Canada)	127
GUCCI GROUP N.V. (Netherlands)	1061
GUERLAIN SA (France)	497
GUINNESS LTD., DIV. DIAGEO (England, U.K.)	317
GUIRAUDIE-AUFFEVE SA (France)	497
GULF AIR COMPANY GSC (Bahrain)	35
GULF INTERNATIONAL BANK (GIB) (Bahrain)	35
THE GUNMA BANK, LTD. (Japan)	847
GUNOLD + STICKMA GMBH (Germany)	605
GYRUS GROUP PLC (Wales, U.K.)	1355

H

I

INDUSTRIA MACCHINE AUTOMATICHE SPA
(Italy) 790

INDUSTRIAL AND COMMERCIAL BANK OF
CHINA (China (PRC)) 204

INDUSTRIAL BANK OF JAPAN LTD. (SUB.
MIZUHO HOLDINGS) (Japan) 859

INDUSTRIAL BANK OF KOREA (South Korea) 1169

INDUSTRIAL-ALLIANCE LIFE INSURANCE
CO. (Canada) 131

INDUSTRIAS METALURGICAS
PESCARMONA SAIC (Argentina) 5

INDUSTRIE NATUZZI S.p.A. (Italy) 791

INDUSTRI-MATEMATIK INTERNATIONAL
AB (Sweden) 1225

INFICON (Switzerland) 1288

INFINEON TECHNOLOGIES AG (Germany) 622

INFOGRAMES ENTERTAINMENT, SA (France) 501

INFORMA GROUP PLC (England, U.K.) 327

INFOSYS TECHNOLOGIES LIMITED (India) 717

INFOVISTA SA (France) 502

INFOWAVE SOFTWARE INC. (Canada) 131

INFRANOR INTER AG (Switzerland) 1288

ING GROUP N.V. (Netherlands) 1069

INGENTA PLC (England, U.K.) 328

INMARSAT VENTURES PLC (England, U.K.) 329

INMET MINING CORPORATION (Canada) 131

THE INNOVATION GROUP PLC (England,
U.K.) 329

INSIGNIA SOLUTIONS PLC (England, U.K.) 329

INSTITUT DR. FÖRSTER (Germany) 623

INSTRUMENTATION LABORATORY S.p.A.
(Spain) 1192

INTENTIA INTERNATIONAL AB (Sweden) 1226

INTERBREW S.A (Belgium) 46

INTERMATRIX LTD. (England, U.K.) 330

INTERNATIONAL ABSORBENTS INC.
(Canada) 132

INTERNATIONAL BIOMEDICINE
MANAGEMENT PARTNERS AG
(Switzerland) 1288

THE INTERNATIONAL COMMERCIAL BANK
OF CHINA (Taiwan (ROC)) 1339

INTERNATIONAL GREETINGS PLC (England,
U.K.) 330

INTERNATIONAL POWER PLC (England, U.K.) 330

INTERPUMP GROUP SPA (Italy) 791

INTERSPIRO AB (Sweden) 1226

INTERTAINMENT AG (Germany) 623

INTERTAPE POLYMER GROUP (Canada) 132

INTERTEK TESTING SERVICES (England,
U.K.) 330

INTERWAVE COMMUNICATIONS
INTERNATIONAL, LTD. (Bermuda) 62

INTESABCI SPA (FORMERLY BANCA
COMMERCIALE ITALIANA) (Italy) 791

INTRACO LIMITED (Singapore) 1145

INTRAWEST CORPORATION (Canada) 132

INVENSYS PLC (England, U.K.) 332

INVERESK RESEARCH INTERNATIONAL
LIMITED (Scotland, U.K.) 1137

INVESTCORP BANK E.C. (Bahrain) 36

INVESTEC GROUP (South Africa) 1152

INVESTOR AB (Sweden) 1226

IOCHPE-MAXION S.A. (Brazil) 77

IONA TECHNOLOGIES PLC (Ireland) 733

IPSCO, INC. (Canada) 133

IPSOS SA (France) 502

IQE (INTERNATIONAL QUANTUM EPITAXY)
PLC (Wales, U.K.) 1355

IRISH LIFE & PERMANENT PLC (Ireland) 734

ISETAN COMPANY, LTD. (Japan) 860

ISHIKAWAJIMA-HARIMA HEAVY
INDUSTRIES COMPANY, LTD. (Japan) 860

ISPAT INTERNATIONAL N.V. (Netherlands) 1072

ISRAEL AIRCRAFT INDUSTRIES LTD. (Israel) 752

ISRAEL DISCOUNT BANK LTD. (Israel) 752

ISUZU MOTORS LTD. (Japan) 861

ITALDESIGN S.p.A. (Italy) 791

ITAR-TASS (RUSSIAN NEWS AGENCY)
(Russia) 1130

ITOCHU CORPORATION (Japan) 861

ITO-YOKADA COMPANY, LTD. (Japan) 863

ITT FLYGT AB (Sweden) 1226

IVACO INC. (Canada) 133

IVANHOE ENERGY INC. (Canada) 134

IVECO SPA (Italy) 792

IVEX - INSTITUTO VALENCIANO DE LA
EXPORTACIÓN (Spain) 1193

IWATANI INTERNATIONAL CORPORATION
(Japan) 863

IXOS SOFTWARE AG (Germany) 623

THE IYO BANK LTD. (Japan) 864

J

JAAKKO PÖYRY GROUP OYJ (FINVEST)
(Finland) 444

JAFCO CO., LTD. (Japan) 864

JAGENBERG AG (Germany) 623

JAMES VISION CO., LTD. (South Korea) 1169

JAPAN AIRLINES COMPANY, LTD. (Japan) 864

JAPAN AVIATION ELECTRONICS INDUSTRY
LTD. (Japan) 865

JAPAN BANK FOR INTERNATIONAL CORP.
(Japan) 865

JAPAN ENERGY CORPORATION (Japan) 866

JAPAN RADIO COMPANY, LTD. (Japan) 866

THE JAPAN STEEL WORKS, LTD. (Japan) 867

K

N

O

P

S

SANYO SPECIAL STEEL COMPANY, LTD. (Japan) 954

SANYO TRADING COMPANY, LTD. (Japan) 954

SÃO PAULO ALPARGATAS S.A. (Brazil) 79

SAP AG (Germany) 658

SAPIENS INTERNATIONAL CORPORATION NV (Israel) 763

SAPPI LIMITED (South Africa) 1153

SAPPORO BREWERIES, LIMITED (Japan) 954

SAPUTO GROUP INC. (Canada) 168

SARNAFIL AG (Switzerland) 1307

SASIB SPA (Italy) 802

SASOL LIMITED (South Africa) 1155

SATYAM COMPUTER SERVICES LTD. (India) 719

SAUDI ARABIAN AIRLINES (Saudi Arabia) 1133

SAUDI ARABIAN OIL COMPANY (Saudi Arabia) 1133

SAUDI BASIC INDUSTRIES CORPORATION (Saudi Arabia) 1133

SAURER LTD. (Switzerland) 1307

SAVIA, SA DE CV, DIV. GRUPO PULSAR (Mexico) 1026

SCAN COIN AB (Sweden) 1238

SCAN SHIPPING SERVICES LIMITED (England, U.K.) 391

SCANCEM AB (Sweden) 1238

SCANDECOR MARKETING AB (Sweden) 1239

SCANDINAVIAN AIRLINES SYSTEM (Sweden) 1239

SCANIA AB, DIV. VOLVO AB (Sweden) 1240

SCAPA GROUP PLC (England, U.K.) 392

CARL SCHENCK AG, DIV. DURR GROUP (Germany) 659

SCHENKER AG, DIV. STINNES (Germany) 660

SCHERING AG (Germany) 661

SCHINDLER HOLDING AG (Switzerland) 1308

SCHLEICHER & SCHUELL KG & COMPANY (Germany) 662

SCHMALBACH-LUBECA AG (Germany) 663

SCHNEIDER ELECTRIC SA (France) 525

ADOLF SCHNORR GMBH & CO KG (Germany) 663

FELIX SCHOELLER JR. PAPIERFABRIKEN GMBH (Germany) 663

SCHOLL SWITZERLAND AG (Switzerland) 1308

SCHOTT GLAS (Germany) 664

SCHRODERS PLC (England, U.K.) 392

SCHUMAG AG (Germany) 665

SCHUNK GROUP GMBH (Germany) 665

SCHWARZ PHARMA AG (Germany) 666

SCIENCE SYSTEMS PLC (England, U.K.) 393

SCINTILLA AG (Switzerland) 1309

SCITEX CORPORATION LTD. (Israel) 763

SCOR SA (France) 525

SCOTIABANK (THE BANK OF NOVA SCOTIA) (Canada) 169

SCOTTISH & NEWCASTLE, PLC. (Scotland, U.K.) 1140

SCOTTISH POWER PLC (Scotland, U.K.) 1141

SCRIPTA, SA (France) 526

SDL PLC (England, U.K.) 393

SEA CONTAINERS LTD. (England, U.K.) 394

SEA HORSE INTERNATIONAL (Monaco) 1029

THE SEAGRAM COMPANY LTD. (Canada) 170

SEAH STEEL CORPORATION (South Korea) 1182

SEAT PAGINE GIALLE SPA (Italy) 802

SEB S.A. (France) 527

SECOM CO., LTD. (Japan) 955

SECURICOR PLC (England, U.K.) 395

SECURITAS AB (Sweden) 1240

SEDIVER SA (France) 527

SEFAC EQUIPMENT (France) 528

SEGA CORPORATION, DIV. CSK (Japan) 955

SEIKO CORPORATION (Japan) 956

SEIKO EPSON CORPORATION (Japan) 956

SEINO TRANSPORTATION COMPANY, LTD. (Japan) 957

SEKISUI CHEMICAL COMPANY, LTD. (Japan) 957

SELDEN MAST AB (Sweden) 1241

SELECT APPOINTMENTS HOLDINGS LIMITED (England, U.K.) 396

SEMANTIX, INC. (Canada) 172

SEMIKRON INTL GMBH & CO (Germany) 667

SENIOR PLC (England, U.K.) 396

SENSE TECHNOLOGIES INC. (Canada) 172

SEOUL BANK (South Korea) 1183

SER SYSTEMS AG (Germany) 668

SERCO GROUP PLC (England, U.K.) 398

SERONO SA (Switzerland) 1309

SERVICE POWER TECHNOLOGIES PLC (England, U.K.) 398

SEVEN WORLDWIDE, INC. (England, U.K.) 398

SEVERN TRENT, PLC. (England, U.K.) 399

SEZ AG (Austria) 29

SGL CARBON AG (Germany) 668

SGS SOCIETE GENERALE DE SURVEILLANCE HOLDING S.A. (Switzerland) 1309

SHANGHAI COMMERCIAL BANK LTD. (Hong Kong) 706

SHARP CORPORATION (Japan) 957

SHAWCOR LTD. (Canada) 173

SHERWOOD INTERNATIONAL PLC (England, U.K.) 399

SHIBA SOKU COMPANY, LTD. (Japan) 957

SHIMIZU CORPORATION (Japan) 958

SHIN-ETSU CHEMICAL COMPANY, LTD. (Japan) 958

SHINHAN BANK (South Korea) 1183

SHINKAWA LTD. (Japan) 960

SOLVAY SA (Belgium)	50
SOMMER ALLIBERT, SA (France)	531
SONERA CORPORATION (Finland)	450
SONY CORPORATION (Japan)	964
SOPHEON PLC (England, U.K.)	406
SOPHUS BERENDSEN A/S (Denmark)	229
SOPREMA SA (France)	532
SOTHYS (France)	532
SOUTH AFRICAN AIRWAYS CORP. (South Africa)	1155
SPC ELECTRONICS CORPORATION (Japan)	965
SPECTRAL DIAGNOSTICS INC. (Canada)	178
SPECTRIS GROUP (FORMERLY FAIREY GROUP PLC) (England, U.K.)	407
SPECTRUM SIGNAL PROCESSING INC. (Canada)	178
SPHERETEX GMBH (Germany)	674
SPIRAX SARCO ENGINEERING PLC (England, U.K.)	408
SPIRENT PLC (FORMERLY BOWTHORPE HOLDINGS PLC) (England, U.K.)	409
SPODE LIMITED (England, U.K.)	410
SPORTSWORLD MEDIA GROUP PLC (England, U.K.)	410
SPOT IMAGE SA (France)	533
SRS WORLDHOTELS - STEIGENBERGER RESERVATION SERVICE (Germany)	674
SSAB SWEDISH STEEL AB (FORMERLY SVENSKT STÅL AKTIEBOLAG) (Sweden)	1246
SSANGYONG CORPORATION (South Korea)	1184
SSL INTERNATIONAL PLC (England, U.K.)	410
ST ASSEMBLY TEST SERVICES LTD. (STATS) (Singapore)	1149
ST MICROELECTRONICS N.V. (France)	533
ST. IVES PLC (England, U.K.)	411
ST. LAWRENCE CEMENT, INC. (Canada)	178
STAEDTLER MARS GMBH & CO. (Germany)	675
STAEUBLI AG (Switzerland)	1313
STAGECOACH HOLDINGS PLC (England, U.K.)	411
R. STAHL GMBH, DIV. HEIDELBERG GROUP (Germany)	675
STAKE TECHNOLOGY LTD. (Canada)	179
STANDARD BANK INVESTMENT CORP. (South Africa)	1155
STANDARD CHARTERED, PLC (England, U.K.)	411
STAR MICRONICS COMPANY, LTD. (Japan)	966
STARHOTELS SPA (Italy)	803
STATE BANK OF INDIA (India)	721
STATE TRADING CORP. OF INDIA LTD. (India)	722
STATOIL ASA (DEN NORSKE STATS OLJESELSKAP) (Norway)	1117
STEAG HAMA TECH AG (Germany)	675
STEINER LEISURE LIMITED (Bahamas)	34
STELCO, INC. (Canada)	179
W. P. STEWART & CO. LTD. (Bermuda)	65
STIBBE SIMONT MONAHAN DUHOT (Netherlands)	1089
ANDREAS STIHL (Germany)	675
STINNES AG, SUB. E.ON (Germany)	676
STMICROELECTRONICS NV (Switzerland)	1313
STOCKCUBE PLC (England, U.K.)	412
STOLT-NIELSEN SA (England, U.K.)	412
STORA ENSO OYJ FINLAND (Finland)	450
STORK N.V. (Netherlands)	1090
STRATUS HOLDINGS PLC (England, U.K.)	413
STRAT-X SA (France)	533
STRUERS A/S (Denmark)	229
STS SYSTEMS, INC. (Canada)	179
STUDIO LEGALE BISCONTI (Italy)	803
SÜD-CHEMIE AG (Germany)	677
SUEZ (FORMERLY SUEZ LYONNAISE DES EAUX) (France)	534
SUGINO MACHINE, LTD. (Japan)	966
SULZER GROUP AG (Switzerland)	1314
SULZER MEDICA LTD., DIV. SULZER CORP. (Switzerland)	1315
SUMIKIN BUSSAN CORPORATION (DIV. SUMITOMO GROUP) (Japan)	966
SUMITOMO BAKELITE COMPANY, LTD. (Japan)	967
SUMITOMO CHEMICAL COMPANY, LTD. (Japan)	967
SUMITOMO CORPORATION (Japan)	967
SUMITOMO ELECTRIC INDUSTRIES, INC. (Japan)	968
SUMITOMO FORESTRY CO., LTD. (Japan)	970
SUMITOMO HEAVY INDUSTRIES, LTD. (Japan)	970
SUMITOMO MARINE & FIRE INSURANCE COMPANY, LTD. (Japan)	971
SUMITOMO METAL INDUSTRIES, LTD. (Japan)	971
SUMITOMO METAL MINING COMPANY, LTD. (Japan)	971
SUMITOMO MITSUI BANKING CORPORATION (SMBC) (Japan)	971
SUMITOMO REALTY & DEVELOPMENT CO., LTD. (Japan)	972
SUMITOMO RUBBER INDUSTRIES LTD. (Japan)	972
THE SUMITOMO TRUST & BANKING CO., LTD. (Japan)	973
SUN INTERNATIONAL HOTELS LIMITED (Bahamas)	34
SUN LIFE FINANCIAL SERVICES OF CANADA (Canada)	180
SUNBASE ASIA, INC. (Hong Kong)	707
SUNHAM & COMPANY, LTD. (Hong Kong)	707
SUNTORY, LTD. (Japan)	973

TERROT STRICKMASCHINEN GMBH (Germany)	679
TERUMO CORPORATION (Japan)	981
TESCO CORPORATION (Canada)	182
TEUSCHER CONFISERIE (Switzerland)	1318
TEVA PHARMACEUTICALS IND LTD. (Israel)	765
TFDS (TROMS FYLKES DAMPSKIBSSELSKAP AS) (Norway)	1118
THAI AIRWAYS INTERNATIONAL (Thailand)	1345
THAI FARMERS BANK LTD. (Thailand)	1346
THALES (FORMERLY THOMSON-CSF SA) (France)	536
THALES ANTENNAS LIMITED (England, U.K.)	417
THAMES WATER PLC (England, U.K.)	417
THIEFFRY ET ASSOCIÉS (France)	537
THIES GMBH & CO. (Germany)	679
THINKPATH.COM INC. (Canada)	183
THOLSTRUP CHEESE A/S (Denmark)	230
THE THOMAS COOK GROUP LTD. (England, U.K.)	418
THE THOMSON CORP. (Canada)	184
THOMSON MULTIMEDIA SA (France)	537
THYSSEN KRUPP AG (Germany)	680
TIBBETT & BRITTEN GROUP PLC (England, U.K.)	418
TIMES PUBLISHING LIMITED (Singapore)	1150
TIMMINCO LIMITED (Canada)	185
TIOGA TECHNOLOGIES LTD. (Israel)	766
TLC LASER EYE CENTERS INC. (Canada)	185
TNT POST GROUP NV (Netherlands)	1091
TOAGOSEI CO. LTD. (Japan)	982
TODA CORPORATION (Japan)	983
TOHOKU ELECTRIC POWER CO., INC. (Japan)	983
THE TOKAI BANK, LTD., DIV. UNITED FINANCIAL OF JAPAN (UFJ) (Japan)	983
TOKAI CARBON CO., LTD. (Japan)	984
TOKINA OPTICAL COMPANY, LTD. (Japan)	984
THE TOKIO MARINE & FIRE INSURANCE CO., LTD (Japan)	984
TOKYO AIRCRAFT INSTRUMENT COMPANY, LTD. (Japan)	985
THE TOKYO ELECTRIC POWER COMPANY, INC. (Japan)	985
TOKYO ELECTRON LIMITED (Japan)	985
TOKYO ROPE MANUFACTURING CO., LTD. (Japan)	986
TOKYO SEIMITSU COMPANY, LTD. (Japan)	986
TOKYU CORPORATION (Japan)	987
TOMEN CORPORATION (Japan)	987
TOMKINS PLC (England, U.K.)	418
TOMRA SYSTEMS ASA (Norway)	1118
TONG IL INDUSTRIES, CO. (South Korea)	1185
TOOLEX INTERNATIONAL N.V. (Netherlands)	1092
TOPCALL INTERNATIONAL AG (Austria)	29
TOPPAN PRINTING COMPANY, LTD. (Japan)	987
TOPY INDUSTRIES LIMITED (Japan)	988
TORAY INDUSTRIES INC. (Japan)	988
TOROMONT INDUSTRIES LTD. (Canada)	186
TORONTO-DOMINION BANK (Canada)	186
TORRAS SA (Spain)	1195
TORSTAR CORPORATION (Canada)	186
TOSHIBA CORPORATION (Japan)	989
TOSHIBA MACHINE COMPANY, LTD. (Japan)	990
TOSOH CORPORATION (Japan)	990
TOTAL FINA ELF S.A. (France)	538
TOTO LTD. (Japan)	991
TOWER SEMICONDUCTOR LTD. (Israel)	766
TOYO SUISAN KAISHA, LTD. (Japan)	991
TOYO TIRE & RUBBER CO., LTD. (Japan)	991
TOYOBO CO., LTD. (Japan)	992
TOYODA AUTOMATIC LOOM WORKS, LTD. (Japan)	992
TOYODA MACHINE WORKS (Japan)	992
TOYOSHIMA SPECIAL STEEL COMPANY, LTD. (Japan)	993
TOYOTA MOTOR CORPORATION (Japan)	993
TOYOTA TSUSHO CORPORATION (Japan)	994
TRACTEBEL S.A. (FORMERLY POWERFIN SA) (Belgium)	52
TRACTEL LTD. SWINGSTAGE GROUP (Canada)	187
TRANS ALTA CORPORATION (Canada)	187
TRANSBRASIL LINHAS AEREAS (Brazil)	79
TRANSCANADA PIPELINES LTD. (Canada)	188
TRANSGENE S.A. (France)	539
TRANSMISIONES Y EQUIPOS - MECANICOS SA DE CV (Mexico)	1027
TREATT PLC (England, U.K.)	421
TRELLEBORG INDUSTRI AB (Sweden)	1252
TREND MICRO INC. (Japan)	995
TREVI-FINANZIARIA INDUSTRIALE SpA (Italy)	804
TRIANON INDUSTRIES CORP. (France)	539
TRICOM, S.A. (Dominican Republic)	233
TRIGEM COMPUTER, INC. (South Korea)	1185
TRIKON TECHNOLOGIES, INC. (England, U.K.)	421
TRINITY BIOTECH PLC (Ireland)	738
TRINTECH GROUP PLC (Ireland)	738
TRIPLE P N.V. (Netherlands)	1092
TRIVERSITY INC. (Canada)	188
TRIZEC HAHN CORP. (Canada)	188
TROJAN TECHNOLOGIES INC. (Canada)	189
ALFRED TRONSER GMBH (Germany)	681
TRUMPF GMBH & CO (Germany)	681
TSUBAKIMOTO CHAIN COMPANY (Japan)	995
TSUKAMOTO SOGYO COMPANY, LTD. (Japan)	995

U

V

W

ALPHABETICAL LISTING OF AMERICAN AFFILIATES

Part Three is an alphabetical listing of all the American affiliates in Part One, giving the name, and in parenthesis the country in which its foreign parent or investor is located, and the number of the page where the complete listing can be found in Part One.

AP TECHNOGLASS (Japan)	815	ASAHI BEER USA INC. (Japan)	814
AP TECHNOGLASS COMPANY (Japan)	815	ASAHI GLASS AMERICA, INC. (Japan)	815
APBIOTECH INC. (Sweden)	1202	ASAHI KASEI AMERICA, INC. (Japan)	815
APEM WORLDWIDE (France)	459	ASAP SOFTWARE EXPRESS (Netherlands)	1044
APPLETON FABRICS (Germany)	686	ASARCO INCORPORATED (Mexico)	1024
APPLETON PAPERS, INC. (England, U.K.)	250	ASATSU AMERICA (Japan)	816
APV AMERICAS (England, U.K.)	249	ASCOM AUTOMATION INC. (Switzerland)	1264
APV BAKER INC. (England, U.K.)	249	ASCOM ENERGY SYSTEMS, INC. (Switzerland)	1264
AQUA-LUNG AMERICA (France)	454	ASCOM HASIER MAILING SYSTEMS, INC.	
AQUARION COMPANY (England, U.K.)	336	(Switzerland)	1264
AQUASOURCE LLC (France)	534	ASCOM HOLDING INC. (Switzerland)	1265
AQUIONICS INC. (England, U.K.)	317	ASCOM TRANSPORT SYSTEMS, INC.	
ARAB BANK PLC (Jordan)	1006	(Switzerland)	1265
ARAB BANKING CORPORATION (Bahrain)	35	ASHTEAD TECHNOLOGY, INC. (England,	
ARACRUZ CORPORATION (Brazil)	69	U.K.)	251
ARAKAWA CHEMICAL USA, INC. (Japan)	813	ASI APPLIED SYSTEMS, INC. (Switzerland)	1296
ARAMCO SERVICES COMPANY (Saudi Arabia)	1133	ASI ENTERTAINMENT (Australia)	7
ARAMEX INTERNATIONAL (Jordan)	1006	ASIA MONEY LINK CORPORATION	
ARAMEX INTERNATIONAL, C/O AIRBORNE		(Philippines)	1123
EXPRESS (Jordan)	1006	ASIA PULP & PAPER TRADING, INC.	
ARBI TRANSNATIONAL, INC. (Brazil)	70	(Singapore)	1143
ARC INTERNATIONAL/DURAND GLASS		ASIANA AIRLINES (South Korea)	1156
(France)	460	ASICS TIGER CORPORATION (Japan)	817
ARCADIS G&M (Netherlands)	1037	ASK PROXIMA CORPORATION (Norway)	1108
ARCADIS GIFFELS (Netherlands)	1039	ASM AMERICA INC. (Netherlands)	1040
ARCADIS JSA (Netherlands)	1039	ASM PACIFIC ASSEMBLY PRODUCTS INC.	
ARCO PERMIAN (England, U.K.)	269	(Netherlands)	1040
AREMISSOFT CORPORATION (England, U.K.)	250	ASO CORPORATION (Japan)	817
ARES ADVANCED TECHNOLOGY, INC.		ASPECT, INC. (Sweden)	1202
(Switzerland)	1264	ASPEN PUBLISHERS INC. (Netherlands)	1100
ARIANESPACE, INC. (France)	461	ASPREY & GARRARD HOLDINGS INC.	
ARISTA RECORDS INC. (Germany)	562	(England, U.K.)	252
ARISTOCRAT TECHNOLOGIES INC.		ASSET BACKED MANAGEMENT CORP.	
(Australia)	7	(France)	511
ARJO INC. (Sweden)	1221	ASSOCIATED FUEL PUMP SYSTEMS	
ARKOPHARMA INC. (France)	461	CORPORATION (Germany)	568
ARKWRIGHT INC. (Netherlands)	1075	ASSOCIATED HYGIENIC PRODUCTS LLC	
ARM, INC. (England, U.K.)	250	(Hong Kong)	699
ARMSTRONG PUMPS INC. (Canada)	90	ASSOCIATED NEWSPAPERS N.A., INC.	
AROMAT CORPORATION (Japan)	892	(England, U.K.)	253
ARQUATI USA INC. (Italy)	772	ASSURANT GROUP (Belgium)	44
ARROW LOCK COMPANY, DIV. ASSA		AST RESEARCH, INC. (South Korea)	1179
ABLOY (Sweden)	1202	ASTENJOHNSON, INC. (Germany)	610
ARROW MAP INC. (Germany)	632	ASTRA ZENECA PHARMACEUTICALS	
ARROWPAK INC. (Italy)	776	(England, U.K.)	253
ARTHUR COX (Ireland)	730	ASTRO ARC POLYSOUDE, INC. (France)	462
ARTS & ENTERTAINMENT (A&E) NETWORK		ASTRO BUSINESS SOLUTIONS, INC. (Japan)	821
(France)	493	ASUS COMPUTER INTERNATIONAL, INC.	
ASACA/SHIBA SOKU CORP. (Japan)	813	(Taiwan (ROC))	1335
ASACA-SHIBASOKU CORPORATION OF		AT PLASTICS CORPORATION (Canada)	90
AMERICA (Japan)	958	ATC CORPORATION (Japan)	996
ASAHI AMERICA INC. (Japan)	815	THE ATHLETE'S FOOT GROUP INC. (France)	519
THE ASAHI BANK, LTD. (Japan)	813	ATI TECHNOLOGIES SYSTEMS CORP.	
		(Canada)	91
		ATKINS BENHAM (England, U.K.)	255

B

BACOU DALLOZ USA INC. (France) 466
BADGER FIRE PROTECTION (England, U.K.) 429
BAE ADVANCED SYSTEMS (England, U.K.) 257
BAE AEROSPACE SECTOR (England, U.K.) 257
BAE SYSTEMS NA (England, U.K.) 257
BAER SUPPLY COMPANY, INC. (Germany) 691
BAHLSEN GMBH & CO. (Germany) 556
BAI GLOBAL INC. (England, U.K.) 238
BALFOUR BEATTY INC. (England, U.K.) 258
BALLANTINE DELL PUBLISHING GROUP
    (Germany) 562
BALLARD POWER SYSTEMS CORPORATION
    (Canada) 92
BALLAST NEDAM CONSTRUCTION, INC.
    (Netherlands) 1042
BALL-FOSTER GLASS CONTAINER
    COMPANY (France) 521
BALLY, INC. (Switzerland) 1266
BALTIMORE TECHNOLOGIES INC. (England,
    U.K.) 259
BALZERS, INC. (Liechtenstein) 1011
BANC WEST CORPORATION (France) 468
BANCA CRT SPA (Italy) 804
BANCA DI ROMA (Italy) 773
BANCA MONTE DEI PASCHI DI SIENA SPA.
    (Italy) 774
BANCA NAZIONALE DEL LAVORO (Italy) 774
BANCA NAZONALE DELL' AGRICOLTURA
    (Italy) 774
BANCA POPOLARE DI MILANO (Italy) 775
BANCA POPOLARE DI NOVARA (Italy) 775
BANCA SERFIN SA (Mexico) 1022
BANCAFE INTERNATIONAL MIAMI
    (Colombia) 205
BANCO ATLANTICO, S.A. (Spain) 1187
BANCO BANDEIRANTES S.A. (Brazil) 70
BANCO BRADESCO SA (Brazil) 70
BANCO COLPATRIA S.A. (Colombia) 205
BANCO COMMERCIAL PORTUGUES
    (Portugal) 1127
BANCO DE BILBAO VIZCAYA, S.A. (Spain) 1188
BANCO DE BOGOTA (Colombia) 205
BANCO DE BOGOTA INTERNATIONAL
    CORPORATION (Colombia) 205
BANCO DE CHILE - New York Branch (Chile) 195
BANCO DE CHILE - Miami Agency (Chile) 195
BANCO DE CREDITO DEL PERU (Peru) 1122
BANCO DE GALICIA Y BUENOS AIRES
    (Argentina) 4
BANCO DE LA NACION ARGENTINA
    (Argentina) 4
BANCO DE LA PROVINCIA DE BUENOS
    AIRES (Argentina) 4
BANCO DE LA REPUBLICA ORIENTAL DEL
    URUGUAY (Uruguay) 1351

BANCO DI NAPOLI (Italy) 775
BANCO DI SICILIA (Italy) 775
BANCO DO BRASIL S.A. (Brazil) 71
BANCO DO ESTADO DE SÃO PAULO SA
    (Brazil) 71
BANCO DO ESTADO DO PARANA SA (Brazil) 72
BANCO ESPAÑOL DE CRÉDITO (Spain) 1188
BANCO ESPIRITO SANTO (Luxembourg) 1013
BANCO EXTERIOR DE ESPANA (Spain) 1189
BANCO INDUSTRIAL DE VENEZUELA
    (Venezuela) 1352
BANCO INTERNACIONAL DE COSTA RICA,
    S.A. (Costa Rica) 207
BANCO INTERNACIONAL, S.A. (Mexico) 1017
BANCO ITAÚ S.A. (Brazil) 73
BANCO LATINOAMERICANO DE
    EXPORTACIONES (BLADEX) (Panama) 1121
BANCO MERCANTIL (Venezuela) 1352
BANCO MERCANTIL DE SÃO PAULO S.A
    (Brazil) 73
BANCO NACIONAL DE MEXICO (Mexico) 1018
BANCO REAL INTL INC (Brazil) 73
BANCO REAL SA (Brazil) 74
BANCO SANTANDER CENTRAL HISPANO,
    S.A. (Spain) 1188
BANCO SANTANDER INTERNATIONAL
    (Spain) 1188
BANCO SANTIAGO (Chile) 195
BANCO TOTTA & ACORES (Portugal) 1127
BANG & OLUFSEN (Denmark) 212
BANGKOK BANK PUBLIC COMPANY LTD.
    (Thailand) 1344
BANGOR HYDRO ELECTRIC COMPANY
    (Canada) 115
BANK AUDI (Lebanon) 1010
BANK AUSTRIA CREDITANSTALT (Austria) 24
BANK BNI (Indonesia) 724
BANK BRUSSELS LAMBERT (Belgium) 38
BANK CENTRAL ASIA (Indonesia) 724
BANK FOR FOREIGN ECONOMIC AFFAIRS
    OF USSR (BFEA) (Russia) 1130
BANK HANDLOWY W WARSZAWIE S.A.
    (Poland) 1125
BANK HAPOALIM (Israel) 742
BANK INDONESIA (Indonesia) 724
BANK JULIUS BAER (Switzerland) 1290
BANK JULIUS BAER ASSET MANAGEMENT
    (Switzerland) 1290
BANK LEUMI LE ISRAEL (Israel) 742
BANK LEUMI LE ISRAEL - Chicago Branch
    (Israel) 742
BANK LEUMI LE ISRAEL - Beverly Hills Branch
    (Israel) 742
BANK LEUMI LEASING CORPORATION
    (Israel) 742

BCI INCORPORATED (Switzerland)	1259	BERLICHEM INC. (Germany)	662
BCN FASHIONS, INC. (Spain)	1195	BERMANS (England, U.K.)	264
BCOM3 GROUP (Japan)	835	BERMUDA DEPARTMENT OF TOURISM (Bermuda)	62
BEAM INDUSTRIES (Sweden)	1215	BERNA PRODUCTS, INC. (Switzerland)	1267
BEAR CREEK CORPORATION (Japan)	1001	BERNARD C. CHOCOLATERIE (Canada)	94
BEERS CONSTRUCTION COMPANY (Sweden)	1242	BERNDORF BELT SYSTEMS, INC. (Austria)	25
BEHR AMERICA INC. (Germany)	560	BERNDORF ICB (Austria)	25
BEHR AMERICA, INC. (Germany)	560	SANFORD C. BERNSTEIN & CO. INC. (France)	464
BEHR CLIMATE SYSTEMS, INC. (Germany)	560	BERTELSMANN INDUSTRY SERVICES (Germany)	563
BEHR HEAT TRANSFER SYSTEMS, INC. (Germany)	561	BESAM AUTOMATED ENTRANCE SYSTEMS, INC. (Sweden)	1207
BEI PECAL (Canada)	179	BESPAK INC. (England, U.K.)	265
BEIERSDORF JOBST, INC. (Germany)	561	BEST SOFTWARE, INC. (England, U.K.)	390
BEIERSDORF, INC. (Germany)	561	BETA LASERMIKE, INC. (England, U.K.)	407
BEITEN BURKHARDT MITTL & WEGENER (Germany)	561	BETHNOVA TUBE, LLC (Canada)	152
BEKAERT CORPORATION (Belgium)	39	BEVAN FUNNELL, LTD. (England, U.K.)	265
BEKAERT CORP. (Belgium)	39	BFC FRONTIER, INC. (Canada)	90
BEL KAUKAUNA CHEESE USA, INC. (France)	492	BGF INDUSTRIES, INC. (France)	516
BELFOR USA (Germany)	595	BHARAT ELECTRONICS LTD. (India)	717
BELFORD INC. (Hong Kong)	706	BHD CORP. (Dominican Republic)	233
BELGACOM NORTH AMERICA (Belgium)	41	BHF SECURITIES CORPORATION (Germany)	565
BELIMO AIRCONTROLS USA INC. (Switzerland)	1266	BHK OF AMERICA INC. (Germany)	565
BELL SYSTEMS, DIV. DIGIQUANT (Denmark)	213	BHP BUILDING PRODUCTS, INC. (Australia)	8
BELLTECH (Japan)	815	BHP COPPER (Australia)	9
BELMONT OF AMERICA, DIV. BGF INDUSTRIES (France)	516	BHP PETROLEUM (AMERICA) INC. (Australia)	9
BELWITH INTERNATIONAL, LTD. (England, U.K.)	308	BIC CORPORATION (France)	467
		BID.COM INTERNATIONAL INC. (Canada)	94
BEN VENUE LABORATORIES, INC. (Germany)	567	BIESSE GROUP AMERICA INC. (Italy)	777
MATTHEW BENDER (Netherlands)	1054	BILL COMMUNICATIONS (Netherlands)	1096
BENETEAU MANUFACTURERS (France)	476	BILLABONG USA, INC. (Australia)	9
BENETEAU USA INC. (France)	476	BILLBOARD MAGAZINE (Netherlands)	1096
BÉNÉTEAU USA INC. (France)	467	BI-LO INC. (Netherlands)	1082
BENETTON USA CORPORATION (Italy)	776	BIMBO BAKERIES USA, INC. (Mexico)	1020
BENFIELD BLANCH INC. (England, U.K.)	264	BIO MERIEUX, INC. (France)	515
BENIER USA INC., DIV. KAAK (Netherlands)	1043	BIO-CHEM VALVE INC. (England, U.K.)	317
BENNINGER/SYMTECH INC. (Switzerland)	1267	BIOGLAN PHARMA INC. (Canada)	173
BENSONS INTERNATIONAL SYSTEMS INC. (England, U.K.)	300	BIOKYOWA, INC. (Japan)	887
BENTALL US PARTNERS (Canada)	93	BIONOVA HOLDING (Mexico)	1026
BENTALL US, INC. (Canada)	97	BIORA, INC. (Sweden)	1208
BENTELER AUTOMOTIVE CORPORATION (Germany)	562	BIOSOUND ESAOTE INC. (Italy)	783
BERENDSEN FLUID POWER INC. (Denmark)	229	BIOTRACE, INC. (England, U.K.)	266
BERETTA USA CORPORATION (Italy)	777	BIRCHER AMERICA, INC. (Switzerland)	1268
BERGEN LINE INC. (Norway)	1115	BIRD-JOHNSON COMPANY (Norway)	1117
BERGEN LINE SERVICES (Norway)	1118	BIRD-JOHNSON, DIV. ROLLS-ROYCE (England, U.K.)	385
BERKELEY INTERNATIONAL CAPITAL (Channel Islands, U.K.)	194	BISCHOFF ROYAL EMBROIDERED LACE (Switzerland)	1268
BERK-TEL, DIV. ALCATEL (France)	456	BISCHOFF-AUGUST INTERNATIONAL (Switzerland)	1268
BERLEX LABORATORIES, INC. (Germany)	662	BITOR AMERICA, INC. (Venezuela)	1354
BERLEX LABORATORIES, INC. (Germany)	662	BIW CABLE SYSTEMS, INC. (Netherlands)	1052

BRITISH GAS U.S. HOLDINGS, INC. (England, U.K.) 265

BRITISH TRAVEL INTERNATIONAL (England, U.K.) 353

BROKAT INFOSYSTEMS INC. (Germany) 571

BROMMA, INC. (Sweden) 1208

BROOKFIELD HOMES (Canada) 95

BROOKS BROTHERS (England, U.K.) 347

BROSSE USA, INC. (France) 544

BROTHER INTERNATIONAL CORPORATION (Japan) 820

BROWN & WILLIAMSON TOBACCO CORPORATION (England, U.K.) 273

BROWNING (Belgium) 41

BRUDERER INC. (Switzerland) 1271

BRUDERER MACHINERY INC. (Switzerland) 1271

BRYAN, GONZALEZ VARGAS Y GONZALEZ BAZ, S.C. (Mexico) 1018

BSI - BANCA DELLA SVIZZERA ITALIANA (Switzerland) 1271

BSN MEDICAL INC. (Germany) 572

BT NORTH AMERICA, INC. (England, U.K.) 274

BT OFFICE PRODUCTS INTERNATIONAL, INC. (Netherlands) 1044

BT RAYMOND INC. (Sweden) 1208

BTM CAPITAL CORPORATION (Japan) 817

BTM INFORMATION SERVICES INC. (Japan) 818

BTM LEASING AND FINANCE, INC. (Japan) 818

THE BUDD COMPANY (Germany) 680

BUEHLER MOTOR INC. (Germany) 572

BUENA VISTA WINERY, INC./RACKE USA (Germany) 652

BUHLER LTD. (Switzerland) 1271

BUHLER QUALITY YARNS CORP. (Switzerland) 1286

BUHRMANN US INC. (Netherlands) 1047

BULGARI (Italy) 778

BULL & BEAR SECURITIES, INC. (Canada) 166

BULL HN INFORMATION SYSTEMS INC. (France) 469

BULL HN INFORMATION SYSTEMS, INC. (France) 493

BULL HN INFORMATION SYSTEMS INC. (France) 494

BULL INFORMATION SYSTEMS INC. (France) 494

BUNZL USA INC. (England, U.K.) 276

BURBERRY'S LIMITED (England, U.K.) 316

BURGER KING CORPORATION (England, U.K.) 290

BURMAH CASTROL HOLDINGS INC (England, U.K.) 270

BURNTSAND INC. (Canada) 96

BURRELL COMMUNICATIONS GROUP (France) 518

BUSINESS MEN'S ASSURANCE CO. OF AMERICA (Italy) 772

BUSINESS OBJECTS AMERICAS (France) 470

BUSS AMERICA INC. (Switzerland) 1281

BUTTERWORTH HEINEMANN INC. (England, U.K.) 373

BYESVILLE ASEPTICS, INC. (Switzerland) 1311

BYRLANE INC. (France) 515

BYSTRONIC INC. (Switzerland) 1272

C

C&C BOAT MANUFACTURING INC. (Japan) 999

C.S. LEWIS & COMPANY LTD. (Scotland, U.K.) 1141

CA IB SECURITIES INC. (Austria) 24

CABLE & WIRELESS COMMUNICATIONS, INC. (England, U.K.) 276

CAD CAM INC. (Canada) 183

CADENCE CAPITAL MANAGEMENT CORP. (Germany) 551

CAE RANSOHOFF INC. (Canada) 97

CAE USA, INC. (Canada) 97

CAHNERS BUSINESS INFORMATION (England, U.K.) 373

CAHNERS ELECTRONIC MEDIA GROUP (England, U.K.) 373

CAHNERS TRAVEL GROUP INC. (England, U.K.) 374

CAHNERS TRAVEL GROUP INC. (Netherlands) 1054

CAISSE DES DEPOTS SECURITIES INC. (France) 470

CALEB BRETT USA (England, U.K.) 331

CALGAZ, DIV. AIR LIQUIDE (France) 455

CALIFORNIA CLOSETS COMPANY, INC. (Canada) 121

CALIFORNIA COMMERCE BANK (Mexico) 1018

CALIFORNIA MEC, INC. (Japan) 898

CALIFORNIA WOODFIBER CORPORATION (Japan) 832

CALMAR INC. (France) 521

CALTY DESIGN RESEARCH, INC. (Japan) 993

CALVIN KLEIN COSMETICS COMPANY (England, U.K.) 423

CALVIN KLEIN COSMETICS COMPANY (Netherlands) 1093

CAMBIOR USA INC. (Canada) 97

CAMBRIDGE SOUNDWORKS, INC. (Singapore) 1144

THE CANADA LIFE ASSURANCE COMPANY OF AMERICA (Canada) 98

CANADIAN IMPERIAL BANK OF COMMERCE. (Canada) 98

CANADIAN NATIONAL ILLINOIS CENTRAL (Canada) 99

CIBA SPECIALITY CHEMICALS
   CORPORATION (Switzerland) 1300

CIBA SPECIALTY CHEMICALS
   CORPORATION, PLASTICS DIV.
   (Switzerland) 1300

CIBA SPECIALTY CHEMICALS
   CORPORATION (Switzerland) 1273

CIBA VISION CORP (Switzerland) 1300

CINCINNATI ELECTRONICS CORP. (England,
   U.K.) 258

CIRQUE DU SOLEIL INC. (Canada) 102

CISNEROS TELEVISION GROUP (Venezuela) 1353

CIS-US INC. (France) 477

CITEL AMERICA INC. (France) 477

CITGO PETROLEUM CORP (Venezuela) 1354

CITIC KA WAH BANK LTD. (Hong Kong) 698

CITIFOR INC. (China (PRC)) 200

CITIGATE ALBERT FRANK (England, U.K.) 325

CITIGATE BROADCAST (England, U.K.) 325

CITIGATE BROADSTREET (England, U.K.) 326

CITIGATE CORPORATE BRANDING (England,
   U.K.) 326

CITIGATE CORPORATE BRANDING INC.
   (England, U.K.) 326

CITIGATE CUNNINGHAM (England, U.K.) 326

CITIGATE CUNNINGHAM INC. (England, U.K.) 326

CITIGATE DEWE ROGERSON (England, U.K.) 326

CITIGATE HUDSON (England, U.K.) 327

CITIZEN AMERICA CORPORATION (Japan) 825

CITIZEN SERVICE HDQRTS. (Japan) 825

CITIZEN WATCH COMPANY OF AMERICA
   (Japan) 825

CITIZENS BANK OF MASSACHUSETTS
   (Scotland, U.K.) 1139

CITIZENS BANK OF RHODE ISLAND
   (Scotland, U.K.) 1139

CITIZENS FINANCIAL GROUP, INC. (Scotland,
   U.K.) 1139

CITIZENS LEASING CORPORATION, INC.
   (Scotland, U.K.) 1139

CITIZENS MORTGAGE CORPORATION, INC.
   (Scotland, U.K.) 1139

CITIZENS VENTURES, INC. (Scotland, U.K.) 1140

CLAAS OF AMERICA INC. (Germany) 574

CLARENDON INSURANCE AGENCY, INC.
   (Canada) 180

CLARENDON NSURANCE GROUP (Germany) 607

CLARIANT CORPORATION (Switzerland) 1273

CLARIANT LIFE SCIENCES (Switzerland) 1273

CLARICA LIFE INSURANCE COMPANY
   (Canada) 103

CLARIFOIL, DIV. ACORDIS ACETATE
   CHEMICALS LTD. (Netherlands) 1031

CLARINS USA INC (France) 477

CLARION CORPORATION OF AMERICA
   (Japan) 826

CLARITAS, INC. (Netherlands) 1096

THE CLARK COMPANIES (England, U.K.) 282

CLARKE AMERICAN INC. (England, U.K.) 356

CLASSIC MEDICAL SUPPLY, INC.
   (Netherlands) 1076

CLAUSING INDUSTRIAL INC. (England, U.K.) 236

CLEAN DIESEL TECHNOLOGIES, INC.
   (Netherlands Antilles) 1102

CLEXTRAL, INC. (France) 490

CLICKSOFTWARE, INC. (Israel) 743

CLIENTLOGIC CORPORATION (Canada) 153

CLIFFORD CHANCE ROGERS & WELLS
   (England, U.K.) 282

CLIN TRIALS RESEARCH (Scotland, U.K.) 1137

CLINICAL ONE (England, U.K.) 396

CLOCKWORK SOLUTIONS, INC. (Israel) 744

CLUB MED INC. (France) 477

CLUB MED SANDPIPER (France) 477

CMG WIRELESS DATA SOLUTIONS, INC.
   (England, U.K.) 282

CMR INC. (England, U.K.) 415

CN BIOSCIENCES, INC. (Germany) 640

COACH USA, INC. (England, U.K.) 411

COATS & CLARK, INC. (England, U.K.) 282

COATS VIYELLA NORTH AMERICA, INC.
   (England, U.K.) 282

CODELCO USA INC. (Chile) 196

CODORNIU NAPA INC. (Spain) 1190

COFACE NORTH AMERICA (France) 478

COFAP OF AMERICA, INC. (Italy) 784

COFLEXIP STENA OFFSHORE INC. (France) 478

COGEMA INC. (France) 479

COGNICASE INC. (Canada) 103

COGNOS CORPORATION (Canada) 104

COLBOND INC., DIV. ACORDIS (Netherlands) 1031

COLDWATER SEAFOOD CORPORATION
   (Iceland) 713

COLGATE DEWE ROGERSON (England, U.K.) 327

COLGATE SARD VERBINNEN (England, U.K.) 327

COLLEGE PRO PAINTERS LTD. (Canada) 121

THE COLONNADE HOTEL (France) 530

COLUMBUS LINE USA INC. (Germany) 606

COM TELCO INC. (Switzerland) 1274

COMERCIAL AMERICAN INS. CO., DIV.
   SEGCOAM (Mexico) 1026

COMINCO AMERICAN INC. (Canada) 105

COMMERCE BANK NATIONAL
   ASSOCIATION (Venezuela) 1353

COMMERCIAL BANK OF KUWAIT (Kuwait) 1008

COMMERCIAL TESTING & ENGINEERING
   COMPANY (Switzerland) 1309

COMMERICAL RISK SERVICES INC. (France) 526

COMMERZ FUTURES (Germany) 574

COMMERZBANK - New York Branch (Germany) 575

COMMONWEALTH BANK OF AUSTRALIA (Australia)	10
COMPASS GROUP FOOD SERVICE CORP. (England, U.K.)	283
COMPETITIVE MEDIA REPORTING (Netherlands)	1096
COMPUGEN, INC. (Israel)	744
COMPUTALOG INC. (Canada)	106
COMPUTALOG USA INC. (Canada)	162
CONAX FLORIDA CORPORATION (England, U.K.)	283
CONCERT COMMUNICATIONS COMPANY (England, U.K.)	274
CONDEA VISTA COMPANY (Germany)	658
CONGRESSIONAL INFORMATION SERVICE (England, U.K.)	374
CONNECT ONE SEMICONDUCTORS, INC. (Israel)	745
CONSOL ENERGY INC. (Germany)	658
CONSOLIDATED PAPERS, INC. (Finland)	450
CONTACT ELECTRONICS INC. (Germany)	575
CONTINENTAL GENERAL TIRE INC. (Germany)	575
CONTINENTAL SUPERBAG COMPANY (Canada)	126
CONTOURS, LTD. (Belgium)	41
CONTROL DEVICES, INC. (England, U.K.)	307
COOK COMPOSITES AND POLYMERS (France)	538
COOKSON AMERICA INC. (England, U.K.)	284
COOLBRANDS INTERNATIONAL INC. (Canada)	106
CORAL ENERGY (Netherlands)	1083
CORE INC. (Belgium)	44
CORE LABORATORIES, INC. (Netherlands)	1049
CORE TECH CONSULTING GROUP, INC. (Israel)	754
CORESTAFF SERVICES (England, U.K.)	284
CORGI CLASSIC LTD. (Hong Kong)	710
CORONA USA CORPORATION (Japan)	826
CORP BANCA CA (Venezuela)	1354
CORPORATE EXPRESS, INC. (Netherlands)	1047
CORROCEAN, INC. (Norway)	1108
CORRUGATING ROLL CORPORATION (Switzerland)	1269
CORUS STEEL INC. (England, U.K.)	285
COSCAN WASHINGTON INC. (Canada)	96
COSCAN WATERWAYS, INC. (Canada)	96
COSCO (China (PRC))	202
COSCO INC. (Canada)	113
COSMO OIL OF USA INC. (Japan)	826
COSTA CRUISE LINES NV (Italy)	780
COSTCO COMPANIES (Mexico)	1019
CO-STEEL (Canada)	106
CO-STEEL RARITAN INC. (Canada)	107
CO-STEEL SAYREVILLE (Canada)	107
COSWORTH TECHNOLOGY INC. (Germany)	686
COTECNA INSPECTION INC. (Switzerland)	1276
COTT BEVERAGES (Canada)	107
COURTAULDS FIBERS INC. (Netherlands)	1034
COURTAULDS PACKAGING LAMINATE TUBES N.A. (Netherlands)	1034
COUTTS (USA) INTERNATIONAL (England, U.K.)	285
COUTTS (USA) INTERNATIONAL (Scotland, U.K.)	1140
COVERBIND CORP (Sweden)	1207
COVISINT, INC. (France)	517
CRATE & BARREL (Germany)	648
CREANOVA INC. (Germany)	579
CREATIVE LABS, INC. (Singapore)	1144
CREATIVE SALES CORPORATION (Germany)	632
CREATIVE TALENT (Netherlands)	1078
CRÉDIT AGRICOLE INDOSUEZ (France)	480
CRÉDIT AGRICOLE INDOSUEZ SECURITIES, INC. (France)	481
CREDIT INDUSTRIEL ET COMMERCIAL DE PARIS (France)	481
CRÉDIT LYONNAIS - New York (France)	482
CRÉDIT LYONNAIS - Los Angeles (France)	482
CRÉDIT LYONNAIS - Chicago (France)	482
CRÉDIT LYONNAIS - Dallas (France)	482
CRÉDIT LYONNAIS SECURITIES (France)	482
CREDIT SUISSE ASSET MANAGEMENT (Switzerland)	1277
CREDIT SUISSE FIRST BOSTON (Switzerland)	1277
CREDITO ITALIANO (Italy)	805
CREDITO ITALIANO - Los Angeles Agency (Italy)	805
CREDITO ITALIANO - Chicago Agency (Italy)	804
CREE CORPORATION (Japan)	948
CREO SCITEX AMERICA, INC. (Israel)	763
CREST FOAM INDUSTRIES INC. (England, U.K.)	275
CRISPLANT, INC. (Denmark)	213
CRODA INC. (England, U.K.)	286
CRONOS CONTAINERS INC. (Luxembourg)	1012
CROWLEY FOODS INC. (Netherlands)	1099
CROWLEY FROZEN DESERTS, INC. (Netherlands)	1099
CROWN CHEMICAL (Germany)	570
CROWN CHEMICAL CORPORATION (Germany)	676
CROWN PUBLISHING (Germany)	563
CRUM & FORSTER HOLDINGS, INC. (Canada)	118
CRYSTAL AMERICA INC. (Israel)	745
CRYSTAL CRUISES, INC. (Japan)	928
CRYSTAL SYSTEMS AMERICA, INC. (Israel)	749
CRYSTAL TECHNOLOGY, INC. (Germany)	669

D

DUNLOP SLAZENGER GROUP AMERICAS (England, U.K.) 295
DUNLOP TIRE CORPORATION (Japan) 972
DURANGO INC. (Mexico) 1023
DURATEX NORTH AMERICA, INC. (Brazil) 76
DURA-VENT (England, U.K.) 404
DUERKOPP ADLER AMERICA INC. (Germany) 587
DURHAM TRANSPORTATION (England, U.K.) 353
DÜRKOPP ADLER AMERICA INC. (Germany) 587
DURR INDUSTRIES INC. (Germany) 587
DUTREPEX (Switzerland) 1327
DUX INTERIORS, INC. (Sweden) 1212
THE DYLAN HOTEL (France) 530
DYNACARE INC. (Canada) 114
DYNAGEL INC. (Germany) 581
DYNAMIC DIAGRAMS INC. (England, U.K.) 328
DYNARC (Sweden) 1213
DYNARIC INC. (Japan) 831
DYNEGY INC. (Canada) 115
DYNEGY, INC. (England, U.K.) 265
DYNO NOBEL INC. (Norway) 1110

E

E.ON NORTH AMERICA, INC. (Germany) 588
EADS AEROFRAME SERVICES (France) 488
EADS, INC. (France) 488
EAGLE BEND MANUFACTURING INC. (Canada) 140
EAGLE MANUFACTURING LLC (Canada) 138
EAGLE-PICHER INDUSTRIES, INC. (Netherlands) 1061
EAR SPECIALTY COMPOSITES (Norway) 1116
EARTH TECH (Bermuda) 66
EARTHRISE FARMS (Japan) 831
EAST JAPAN RAILWAY COMPANY (Japan) 836
EAST SMITHFIELD FARMS INC. (France) 469
EASTECH CHEMICAL INC. (Germany) 676
EASYSCREEN INC. (England, U.K.) 295
EBARA AMERICA CORPORATION (Japan) 837
EBARA INTERNATIONAL CORPORATION (Japan) 837
EBARA SOLAR, INC. (Japan) 837
EBARA TECHNOLOGIES INC. (Japan) 837
EBEL, INC., DIV. LVMH GROUP (France) 508
EBEL, INC., DIV. LVMH GROUP (Switzerland) 1280
ECI TELECOM, INC. (Israel) 746
ECO SNOW SYSTEMS, INC. (Canada) 91
THE ECONOMIST (England, U.K.) 296
THE ECONOMIST/SHENANDOAH VALLEY PRESS (England, U.K.) 296

THE ECONOMIST ADVERTISING DIV. (England, U.K.) 296
THE ECONOMIST EDITORIAL DIV. (England, U.K.) 296
EDCO TOOL AND SUPPLY, INC. (Canada) 116
EDGEWING, DIV. PLAUT (Austria) 27
EDUSOFT INC. (Israel) 747
EF&F MAN ALCOHOLS INC. (England, U.K.) 296
EF&F MAN COCOA INC. (England, U.K.) 296
EF&F MAN SUGAR INC. (England, U.K.) 297
EFFRON ENTERPRISES INC. (England, U.K.) 327
EFI ELECTRONICS CORP. (France) 525
EFKA OF AMERICA INC. (Germany) 595
EGE SYSTEM SUN CONTROL INC. (Sweden) 1213
EGON ZEHNDER INTERNATIONAL, INC. (Switzerland) 1329
EGYPTAIR (Egypt) 234
EIDOS INTERACTIVE USA, INC (England, U.K.) 297
EIKI INTERNATIONAL INC. (Japan) 838
EIMCO LLC (Sweden) 1236
EIMSKIP USA INC. (Iceland) 713
EIRCOM U.S. LTD. (Ireland) 730
EISAI CORPORATION OF NORTH AMERICA (Japan) 838
EISAN RESEARCH INSTITUTE OF BOSTON, INC. (Japan) 838
EISAI USA INC. (Japan) 838
EISELE CORPORATION (Germany) 589
EISER INC. (Sweden) 1213
EKA CHEMICALS, INC. (Sweden) 1213
EKONO INC. (Finland) 439
EL AL ISRAEL AIRLINES (Israel) 747
ELA MEDICAL INC. (France) 486
ELAMEX USA INC. (Mexico) 1019
ELAN CORPORATION (Ireland) 731
ELAN DIAGNOSTICS (Ireland) 731
ELAN PHARMA INC. (Ireland) 731
ELAN PHARMACEUTICAL RESEARCH CORPORATION (Ireland) 731
ELAN PHARMACEUTICAL RESEARCH CORPORATION & ELAN HOLDINGS, IN (Ireland) 731
ELAN PHARMACEUTICALS (Ireland) 732
ELAN TRANSDERMAL TECHNOLOGIES (Ireland) 732
ELATERAL INC. (England, U.K.) 297
ELECROCHEMICALS INC. (England, U.K.) 339
ÉLECTRICITÉ DE FRANCE INTERNATIONAL NORTH AMERICA, INC. (France) 486
ELECTROLUX LLC (Sweden) 1215
ELECTRONIC MICRO SYSTEMS INC. (England, U.K.) 318
ELECTRONICS LINE USA INC. (Israel) 747

ELECTRO-PHYSIK USA INC. (Germany)	590
ELEKTA INC. (Sweden)	1217
ELEMA-SCHONANDER INC. (Sweden)	1241
ELEMENTIS AMERICA INC. (England, U.K.)	298
ELEMENTIS CHROMIUM LP (England, U.K.)	298
ELEMENTIS INC. (England, U.K.)	298
ELEMENTIS LTP (England, U.K.)	298
ELEMENTIS PIGMENTS INC. (England, U.K.)	298
ELF LUBRICANTS NORTH AMERICA (France)	538
ELG METALS, INC. (Germany)	595
ELISRA GROUP (Israel)	753
ELITE COLOR GROUP (Ireland)	737
ELIZABETH ARDEN (Netherlands)	1093
ELIZABETH ARDEN (England, U.K.)	423
ELKEM METALS COMPANY (Norway)	1110
ELMO LEATHER OF AMERICA (Sweden)	1217
ELMO MANUFACTURING CORPORATION (Japan)	838
ELOF HANSSON INC (Sweden)	1217
ELRON TELESOFT INC. (Israel)	747
ELSEVIER SCIENCE INC. (England, U.K.)	374
ELSEVIER SCIENCE INC. (Netherlands)	1054
ELTEX US INC. (Sweden)	1218
ELX GROUP (Sweden)	1215
EM INDUSTRIES, INC. (Germany)	641
EM INDUSTRIES, INC. (Germany)	641
EM SCIENCE (Germany)	641
EM&C ENGINEERING ASSOCIATES (Switzerland)	1287
EMBRAER AIRCRAFT CORPORATION (Brazil)	76
EMCO MAIER CORPORATION (Austria)	26
EMD PHARMACEUTICALS, INC. (Germany)	641
EMI GROUP, INC. (England, U.K.)	299
EMI MUSIC PUBLISHING (England, U.K.)	299
EMIRATES AIR (United Arab Emirates)	1349
EMITEC INC. (England, U.K.)	313
THE EMPIRE COMPANIES (Switzerland)	1332
EMS-CHEMIE INC. (Switzerland)	1280
ENDEAVORS TECHNOLOGY (England, U.K.)	414
ENDESA (Spain)	1190
ENDEVCO CORPORATION (England, U.K.)	349
ENDOGEN, INC. (Sweden)	1232
ENDRESS + HAUSER FLOWTEC INC. (Switzerland)	1281
ENDRESS + HAUSER INSTRUMENTS INC. (Switzerland)	1281
ENI REPRESENTATIVE FOR THE AMERICAS (Italy)	782
ENKOTEC CO INC (Denmark)	216
ENOVIA CORPORATION (France)	484
ENRAF INC. (Netherlands)	1051
ENTERPRISE OIL SERVICES INC (England, U.K.)	300
ENTRELEC INC. (France)	486
ENVIRO TECH MOLDED PRODUCTS (Scotland, U.K.)	1141
ENVIROVAC, INC. (Finland)	445
EPM CORPORATION (Italy)	792
EPOKE INC. (Denmark)	217
EPSON AMERICA, INC. (Japan)	956
EPSON PORTLAND INC. (Japan)	956
EPSON RESEARCH & DEVELOPMENT (Japan)	956
EQUANT NETWORK SERVICES DIVISION (Netherlands)	1055
EQUITABLE OF IOWA COMPANIES (Netherlands)	1069
ERAMET NORTH AMERICA, INC. (France)	487
ERICSSON USA INC. (Sweden)	1218
ERICSSON USA INC. PUBLIC AFFAIRS (Sweden)	1218
ERIDANIA BEGHIN-SAY AMERICA (Italy)	795
ERIKS AIRSPACE (Netherlands)	1057
ERIKS CORPORATION (Netherlands)	1058
ERIKS MIDWEST (Netherlands)	1058
ERIKS, INC. (Netherlands)	1058
ERMENEGILDO ZEGNA (Italy)	783
ERSTE BANK (Austria)	26
ESAB WELDING & CUTTING GROUP (England, U.K.)	281
ESC MEDICAL SYSTEMS (Israel)	748
ESCADA BOUTIQUE (Germany)	591
E-SIM INC. (Israel)	749
ESKIMO PIE CORPORATION (Canada)	106
ESPIRITO SANTO BANK (Luxembourg)	1013
ESPIRITO SANTO FINANCIAL SERIVCES, INC. (Luxembourg)	1013
ESSELTE AMERICA CORPORATION (England, U.K.)	301
ESSELTE OFFICE PRODUCTS (England, U.K.)	301
ESSROC CORPORATION (France)	476
ESTIA CORP (South Korea)	1174
ETERNIT, INC., DIV. ETEX (Belgium)	43
ETL SEMKO (England, U.K.)	331
ETON SYSTEMS, INC. (Sweden)	1218
ETS SCHAEFER CORPORATION (Canada)	192
EULER ACI (France)	487
EULER ACI (France)	487
THE EUREKA COMPANY (Sweden)	1215
EURO LLOYD TRAVEL INC. (Germany)	592
EURO LLOYD TRAVEL INC. (Germany)	592
EURO RSCG TATHAM (France)	498
EURO RSCG WORLDWIDE (France)	499
EUROCLEAN USA INC. (Denmark)	225
EUROP ASSISTANCE WORLDWIDE SERVICES (France)	488
EUROPEAN AMERICAN BANK (Netherlands)	1080

FORTIS BENEFITS INSURANCE COMPANY (Belgium) 44
FORTIS FAMILY INS. (Netherlands) 1059
FORTIS FAMILY INSURANCE (Belgium) 44
FORTIS FINANCIAL GROUP (Belgium) 44
FORTIS FINANCIAL SERVICES (Belgium) 44
FORTIS HEALTH, DIV. FORTIS INC. (Belgium) 45
FORTIS INC. (Belgium) 45
FORTIS INSURANCE (Belgium) 45
FORTIS PRIVATE CAPITAL, INC. (Netherlands) 1060
FOSBEL INC. (England, U.K.) 271
FOSECO INC. (England, U.K.) 271
FOSS NIRSYSTEMS (Denmark) 218
FOSS NORTH AMERICA (Denmark) 218
FOSTER'S USA LLC (Australia) 13
FOUR SEASONS & REGENT HOTELS (Canada) 122
FOUR SEASONS HOTELS (Canada) 123
FOUR SEASONS REGENT HOTELS & RESORTS (Canada) 123
FOUR SEASONS RESORTS & HOTELS (Canada) 123
FOX BROADCASTING COMPANY (Australia) 17
FOX ENTERTAINMENT GROUP, INC. (Australia) 17
FOX KIDS WORLDWIDE (Australia) 17
FOX NEWS (Australia) 18
FOXBORO COMPANY (England, U.K.) 332
FRAMATOME CONNECTORS USA, INC. (France) 491
FRAMATOME TECHNOLOGIES, INC. (France) 491
FRAMATOME USA, INC. (France) 491
FRANCE TELECOM NORTH AMERICA INC. (France) 491
FRANCOTYP-POSTALIA INC. (Germany) 595
FRANGO INC. (Sweden) 1219
FRANKE COMMERICAL SYSTEMS (Switzerland) 1283
FRANKE CONSUMER PRODUCTS INC., KITCHEN DIV. (Switzerland) 1284
FRANKE CONTRACT GROUP (Switzerland) 1284
FRANKE GROUP (Switzerland) 1284
FRANKE INC. (Switzerland) 1284
FRASER PAPER, LTD. (Canada) 147
FREEDOM INVESTMENTS, INC. (Canada) 118
W. H. FREEMAN & COMPANY (Germany) 601
FREIBERG PUBLISHING COMPANY (England, U.K.) 327
FREIGHTLINER CORPORATION (Germany) 577
FRENCH CONNECTION (England, U.K.) 309
FRESENIUS MEDICAL CARE N.A. (Germany) 596
FRESHFIELDS BRUCKHAUS DERINGER LLP (England, U.K.) 310
FREUDENBERG NONWOVENS (Germany) 596

FREUDENBERG NONWOVENS VITECH LTD. (Germany) 597
FREUDENBERG NORTH AMERICA, LTD. (Germany) 597
FREUDENBERG SPUNWEB COMPANY (Germany) 597
FREUDENBERG-NOK GENERAL PARTNERSHIP (Germany) 597
FRIEDR. DICK CORPORATION (Germany) 584
FRIENDS IVORY & SIME NORTH AMERICA, INC. (England, U.K.) 310
FRIGIDAIRE COMMERCIAL PRODUCTS COMPANY (Sweden) 1215
FRIGIDAIRE HOME PRODUCTS (Sweden) 1215
FRISCO BAY INDUSTRIES INC. (Canada) 123
FRISKIES PETCARE (Switzerland) 1299
FRU-CON CONSTRUCTION CORPORATION (Germany) 566
FRU-CON DEVELOPMENT CORP (Germany) 566
FRU-CON ENGINEERING INC. (Germany) 566
FRU-CON HOLDING CORPORATION (Germany) 566
FRU-CON TECHNICAL SERVICES INC (Germany) 566
FRUIT OF THE LOOM, INC. (Cayman Islands) 193
F-SECURE, INC. (Finland) 442
FST CONSULTING (Italy) 800
FUCHS LUBRICANTS CO. (Germany) 598
FUCHS SYSTEMS, INC. (Germany) 600
FUDICIARY MANAGEMENT ASSOCIATES (England, U.K.) 359
FUEL-TECH INC. (Netherlands Antilles) 1102
THE FUJI BANK & TRUST COMPANY - NY Agency (Japan) 839
THE FUJI BANK LTD. (Japan) 839
THE FUJI BANK LTD. - Chicago Agency (Japan) 839
THE FUJI BANK LTD. - LA Agency (Japan) 839
FUJI CAPITAL MARKETS CORPORATION (Japan) 840
FUJI ELECTRIC CORPORATION OF AMERICA, INC. (Japan) 840
FUJI HEAVY INDUSTRIES INC. (Japan) 841
FUJI HI-TECH, INC. (Japan) 840
FUJI HUNT PHOTO. CHEMICALS, INC. (Japan) 841
FUJI MARINE CORPORATION (Japan) 840
FUJI MEDICAL SYSTEMS USA, INC. (Japan) 841
FUJI PHOTO FILM HAWAII, INC. (Japan) 842
FUJI PHOTO FILM, INC. (Japan) 842
FUJI PHOTO FILM USA, INC. (Japan) 842
FUJIKURA AMERICA INC. (Japan) 842
FUJISAWA HEALTHCARE, INC. (Japan) 843
FUJITA CORPORATION USA, INC. (Japan) 843
FUJITEC AMERICA, INC. (Japan) 843
FUJITSU AMERICA, INC. (Japan) 844

G

GEORGE FISCHER CORP (Switzerland) 1282
GEORGE FISCHER INC (Switzerland) 1282
GEORGE FISCHER SLOANE INC. (Switzerland) 1282
GEORGE FUNARO & ASSOCIATES (Italy) 786
GEORGIA-PACIFIC GROUP (Chile) 197
GERBER LEDENDARY BLADES (Finland) 441
GERBER LIFE INSURANCE COMPANY
(Switzerland) 1301
GERBER PRODUCTS COMPANY (Switzerland) 1301
GERLING GLOBAL REINSURANCE
CORPORATION (Germany) 602
GET MUSIC LLC (Germany) 563
GETINGE-CASTLE INC. (Sweden) 1221
GETRONICS INC. (Netherlands) 1060
GETTER CORPORATION OF AMERICA (Italy) 800
GFI FLORIDA (Sweden) 1210
GFT USA INC. (Italy) 788
GHIRARDELLI CHOCOLATE COMPANY
(Switzerland) 1294
GIANT CEMENT HOLDING (Spain) 1190
GIANT FOOD STORES INC. (Netherlands) 1082
GIDDINGS & LEWIS INC. (Germany) 680
THE GIFT WRAP COMPANY (England, U.K.) 330
GIORGIO ARMANI (Italy) 772
GIULIANA, DIV. IGMI USA INC. (Italy) 787
GIVAUDAN CORPORATION (Switzerland) 1284
GIVAUDAN FLAVORS CORP. (Switzerland) 1285
GIVAUDAN FRAGRANCES CORP.
(Switzerland) 1285
GIVEN IMAGING, INC. (Israel) 750
GKN AEROSPACE CHEM-TRONICS, INC.
(England, U.K.) 313
GKN AEROSPACE INC. (England, U.K.) 313
GKN ARMSTRONG WHEELS (England, U.K.) 313
GKN AUTOMOTIVE INC. (England, U.K.) 313
GKN DRIVETECH INC. (England, U.K.) 313
GKN SINTER METALS DIV. (England, U.K.) 314
GKN TECHNOLOGY US (England, U.K.) 314
GKN WALTERSCHEID, INC. (England, U.K.) 314
GKN WESTLAND INC. (England, U.K.) 314
GLANBIA FOODS, INC. (Ireland) 733
GLASTEEL USA INC. (Mexico) 1022
GLAXOSMITHKLINE (England, U.K.) 315
GLEN-GERY CORPORATION (England, U.K.) 323
GLENS FALLS LEHIGH CEMENT CO.
(Germany) 588
GLOBAL CROSSING INC. (Bermuda) 62
GLOBAL SECURITIES (Turkey) 1347
GLOBAL SOURCES USA, INC. (Hong Kong) 700
GLOBALSTAR (Bermuda) 62
GLOBECAST NORTH AMERICA (France) 491
GLOBO INTERNATIONAL TV NETWORK
(Brazil) 77

GLOCK INC. (Austria) 27
GN RESOUND NORTH AMERICA (Denmark) 218
GN RESOUND, INC. (Denmark) 218
GOLDEN AMERICAN LIFE INSURANCE
COMPANY (Netherlands) 1069
GOLDWELL COSMETICS INC. (Japan) 872
GOLIATH THREADING TOOLS INC. (England,
U.K.) 315
GOODALL RUBBER COMPANY (Sweden) 1252
GORANN INC. (Ireland) 733
GOTTEX INDUSTRIES, INC. (Israel) 751
GOULD ELECTRONICS INC. (Japan) 866
GPC BIOTECH INC. (Germany) 603
GRANADA ENTERTAINMENT USA (England,
U.K.) 316
GRANITE STATE ELECTRIC COMPANY
(England, U.K.) 354
GRANITE STATE ENERGY, INC. (England,
U.K.) 354
GRÄNSFORS BRUKS INC. (Sweden) 1221
WILLIAM GRANT & SON INC (Scotland, U.K.) 1137
GRAPHISOFT US INC. (Hungary) 711
GRAPHTEC CORPORATION (Japan) 847
GRASS AMERICA INC. (Austria) 27
GRASSO INC. (Netherlands) 1061
GREAT ATLANTIC & PACIFIC TEA
COMPANY INC. (A&P) (Germany) 679
GREAT BRANDS/DANONE INTERNATIONAL
(France) 483
GREAT LAKES GAS TRANSMISSION
COMPANY (Canada) 188
GREAT-WEST LIFE & ANNUITY INSURANCE
COMPANY (Canada) 126
THE GREAT-WEST LIFE ASSURANCE
COMPANY (Canada) 162
GREEN LIND & McNULTY, INC. (Israel) 741
GREENWICH CAPITAL MARKETS, INC.
(Scotland, U.K.) 1140
GREENWOOD PUBLISHING GROUP INC.
(England, U.K.) 374
GREYHOUND LINES, INC. (Canada) 135
GRINDEX PUMPS (Sweden) 1222
GROB SYSTEMS,INC. (Germany) 603
GROSFILLEX, INC. (France) 493
GROSVENOR MARKETING LTD. (England,
U.K.) 253
GROUP 4 INC. (Denmark) 219
GROUP 4 SECURITIES TECHNOLOGY CORP.
(Denmark) 219
GROUPE SCHNEIDER (France) 497
GROVES DICTIONARIES, INC. (England, U.K.) 344
GROZ-BECKERT USA INC. (Germany) 603
GRUMA CORPORATION/AZTECA MILLING
(Mexico) 1019

H

HARPER COLLINS PUBLISHERS INC. (Australia) 18

HARRIS BANKCORP INC. (Canada) 92

HARRIS INVESTMENT MANAGEMENT CORP (Canada) 92

HARRIS INVESTORS DIRECT, INC. (Canada) 92

HARRIS MORAN (France) 545

HARRIS MORAN SEED COMPANY (France) 496

HARRIS-TARKETT INC. (Germany) 679

HART & COOLEY, INC. (England, U.K.) 419

HART-LATIMER ASSOCIATES, INC. (England, U.K.) 365

HASEKO CORPORATION (Japan) 849

HASEKO HAWAII INC. (Japan) 849

HAVAS ADVERTISING (France) 499

HAVER FILLING SYSTEMS INC. (Germany) 608

HAYS HOME DELIVERY SERVICES (England, U.K.) 321

HAYS INFORMATION MANAGEMENT, INC. (England, U.K.) 321

HAZAMA CORPORATION (Japan) 850

HAZELTON PUMPS, INC. (Scotland, U.K.) 1141

HC ELECTRONICS AMERICA INC. (South Korea) 1165

HEADLAND DIGITAL MEDIA (England, U.K.) 363

HEATHWAY INC. (England, U.K.) 321

HEAVYLIFT CARGO AIRLINES (Norway) 1112

HECKLER & KOCH, INC. (England, U.K.) 258

HECNY TRANSPORTATION INC. (Hong Kong) 701

HEDWIN CORP (Belgium) 50

HEIDELBERG INC. (Germany) 608

HEIDENHAIN CORPORATION (Germany) 609

HEINEKEN U.S.A., INC. (Netherlands) 1062

HEISEI MINERALS CORPORATION (Japan) 900

HEITMAN FINANCIAL LLC (England, U.K.) 359

HEKIMIAN LABORATORIES, INC. (Sweden) 1206

HEKIMIAN LABORATORIES, INC. (England, U.K.) 409

HELENE CURTIS (England, U.K.) 423

HELENE CURTIS (Netherlands) 1093

HELIX / HITEMP CABLES, INC. (Netherlands) 1053

HELLA NORTH AMERICA, INC. (Germany) 611

HELLA NORTH AMERICA INC. (Germany) 611

HELLER FINANCIAL, INC. (Japan) 840

HELLER FIRST CAPITAL CORPORATION (Japan) 840

HELLER REAL ESTATE FINANCIAL SERVICES (Japan) 840

HELLERMANN TYTON (England, U.K.) 409

HELLMANN WORLDWIDE LOGISTICS, INC. (Germany) 611

HELLY HANSEN INC. (Norway) 1111

HELM NEW YORK INC. (Germany) 612

HELMITIN INC. (Japan) 861

THE HELMSLEY PARK LANE HOTEL (France) 530

HELUVA GOOD CHEESE, INC. (Netherlands) 1099

HEMOSOL USA INC. (Canada) 128

HENGELER MUELLER WEITZEL WIRTZ (Germany) 612

HENKEL CORPORATION (Germany) 612

HENKEL CORPORATION CHEMICALS GROUP (Germany) 613

HENKEL CORPORATION SURFACE TECHNOLOGIES (Germany) 613

HENKEL SURFACE TECHNOLOGIES (Germany) 613

HENRY & HENRY INC. (Netherlands) 1050

HENRY HOLT & COMPANY (Germany) 601

HENRY HOLT AND COMPANY, INC. (Germany) 685

HERAEUS AMERSIL (Germany) 614

HERAEUS ELECTRO-NITE COMPANY (Germany) 614

HERAEUS INC. CERMALLOY DIV. (Germany) 614

HERAEUS PRECIOUS METALS MANAGEMENT INC. (Germany) 614

HERAEUS KULZER, INC. (Germany) 614

HERAEUS PRECIOUS METALS MANAGEMENT, INC. (Germany) 615

HERAEUS SHIN-ETSU AMERICA, INC. (Japan) 959

HERAEUS SYSTEMS, INC. (Germany) 615

HERION USA INC. (Germany) 622

HERMES PARIS (France) 499

HERMLE BLACK FOREST CLOCKS (Germany) 596

HETTICH AMERICA LP (Germany) 615

HFNM (HACHETTE FILIPACCHI) (France) 498

HI SPECIALTY AMERICA, INC. (Japan) 853

HICKHAM INDUSTRIES, INC. (Switzerland) 1314

HIDDEN CREEK INDUSTRIES (Canada) 153

HIGH POINT TEXTILE AUXILARIES (Japan) 872

HIGHGATE PROPERTIES, DIV. CISNEROS (Venezuela) 1353

TOMMY HILFIGER CORPORATION (Hong Kong) 701

HILTON INTERNATIONAL CO. (England, U.K.) 321

HILTON INTERNATIONAL COMPANY (England, U.K.) 321

HINO DIESEL TRUCKS USA, INC. (Japan) 850

HIRANO DESIGN INTL INC. (Japan) 850

THE HIROSHIMA BANK LTD. (Japan) 851

HIRSCHMANN ELECTRONICS (Germany) 616

HITACHI AMERICA, LTD. (Japan) 851

HITACHI COMPUER PRODUCTS AMERICA, INC. (Japan) 852

HITACHI DATA SYSTEMS CORPORATION (Japan) 852

HITACHI INSTRUMENTS (Japan) 852

HITACHI KOKI IMAGING SOLUTIONS, INC. (Japan) 851

IRISH LIFE FINANCIAL SERVICES (Ireland) 734

IRISH LIFE OF NORTH AMERICA INC. (Ireland) 734

IROQUOIS GAS TRANSMISSION SYSTEM (Canada) 188

IRVINE SCIENTIFIC SALES COMPANY INC. (Japan) 866

ISETAN COMPANY, LTD. (Japan) 860

ISOLA USA INC. (Germany) 657

ISPAT INLAND INC. (Netherlands) 1072

ISPAT NORTH AMERICA, INC. (Netherlands) 1072

ISRAEL AIRCRAFT INDUSTRIES INTERNATIONAL INC. (Israel) 751

ISRAEL DISCOUN BANK LTD. (Israel) 752

ISRAEL DISCOUNT BANK OF NY (Israel) 753

ISUZU AUTOMOTIVE, INC. (Japan) 861

ISUZU MOTORS AMERICA (Japan) 861

ISUZU MOTORS AMERICA, INC. (Japan) 861

ITALCARDANO NA INC. (England, U.K.) 314

ITAR-TASS USA, INC. (Russia) 1130

ITOCHU COTTON INC. (Japan) 862

ITOCHU INTERNATIONAL INC. (Japan) 862

ITS INC. (England, U.K.) 263

ITT FLYGT CORPORATION (Sweden) 1226

ITT FLYGT CORPORATION (Sweden) 1227

ITT INDUSTRIES (FLYGT CORPORATION) (Sweden) 1227

IVACO STEEL MILLS LTD. (Canada) 133

IVACO STEEL PROCESSING, INC. (Canada) 133

IVANHOE ENERGY USA INC. (Canada) 134

IVECO TRUCKS OF NORTH AMERICA, INC. (Italy) 785

IVECO TRUCKS OF NORTH AMERICA (Italy) 792

IVEX - INSTITUTO VALENCIANO DE LA EXPORTACIÓN (Spain) 1193

IVI CHECKMATE CORP. (France) 495

IWATANI INTERNATIONAL CORPORATION OF AMERICA (Japan) 863

IXOS SOFTWARE, INC. (Germany) 623

THE IYO BANK LTD. (Japan) 864

J

J&L SPECIALTY STEEL INC. (France) 540

J&L SPECIALTY STEEL, INC. (France) 540

J. A. JONES CONSTRUCTION COMPANY (Germany) 618

J. F. JELELENKO & COMPANY (Germany) 615

J. L. FRENCH AUTOMOTIVE CASTINGS (Canada) 153

J. P. LEVESQUE & SONS LTD. (Canada) 148

J. WALTER THOMPSON COMPANY (England, U.K.) 433

JAAKKO PÖYRY CONSULTING (NORTH AMERICA), INC. (Finland) 444

JACKSON NATIONAL LIFE INSURANCE COMPANY (England, U.K.) 370

JAE ELECTRONICS INC. (Japan) 865

JAFCO AMERICA VENTURES, INC. (Japan) 864

JAGENBERG INC. (Germany) 624

JAMES EYEWEAR CORPORATION (South Korea) 1169

JAMES HARDIE EXPORT (Australia) 14

JAMES HARDIE INC. (Australia) 14

JANUS ELEVATOR PRODUCTS INC. (England, U.K.) 318

JAPAN AIR LINES (USA) Ltd. (Japan) 865

JAPAN BANK FOR INTERNATIONAL CORP. (JBIC) (Japan) 865

JAPAN RADIO COMPANY, LTD. (Japan) 866

JAPAN STEEL WORKS AMERICA INC. (Japan) 867

JAPAN TOBACCO INC. (Japan) 868

JARDINE MOTORS BEVERLY HILLS LTD. (Hong Kong) 703

JCB INC. (England, U.K.) 335

JCI USA INC. (Japan) 920

JEANTET & ASSOCIES (France) 503

JEOL USA, INC. (Japan) 868

JET AVIATION BUSINESS JETS, INC. (Switzerland) 1289

JET AVIATION BUSINESS JETS, INC. (Switzerland) 1289

JET AVIATION, INC. (Switzerland) 1290

JETRO CASH & CARRY ENTERPRISES, INC. (Switzerland) 1296

JFC INTERNATIONAL, INC. (Japan) 878

JI INTERNATIONAL (France) 478

JIJI PRESS AMERICA, LTD. (Japan) 869

THE JIM HENSON COMPANY, INC. (Germany) 590

JINDO AMERICA, INC. (South Korea) 1170

JLT SERVICES CORPORATION (England, U.K.) 335

JOHN ALDEN FINANCIAL CORPORATION (Belgium) 45

JOHN CRANE NORTH AMERICA (England, U.K.) 405

H & R JOHNSON, INC. (England, U.K.) 336

JOHNSON MATTHEY INC. (England, U.K.) 335

JOHNSON PUMPS OF AMERICA, INC. (Sweden) 1227

HOTEL JOLLY (Italy) 780

J. A. JONES INC. (Germany) 618

J. A. JONES CONSTRUCTION CO (Germany) 618

J. A. JONES ENVIRONMENTAL SERVICES (Germany) 619

JOOS EQUIPMENT COMPANY (Switzerland) 1287

JOUAN, INC. (France) 503

THE JOYO BANK LTD. (Japan) 869

JT INTL, INC. (Japan) 868

K

L

LERNOUT & HAUSPIE DIRECT INC. (Belgium) 47
LERNOUT & HAUSPIE SPEECH PRODUCTS INC. (Belgium) 47
LEVEL 8 INC. (Israel) 753
LEVER BROTHERS COMPANY (England, U.K.) 423
LEXIGEN PHARMACEUTICAL (Germany) 641
LEXINGTON RECYCLING SERVICES INC. (Sweden) 1210
LEXIS-NEXIS (England, U.K.) 374
LEXIS NEXIS (Netherlands) 1054
LEYBOLD VACUUM USA INC. (Switzerland) 1324
LFA INDUSTRIES INC. (France) 459
LG CHEM LTD. (South Korea) 1176
LG ELECTRONICS, INC. (South Korea) 1175
LG EPITAXY, INC. (South Korea) 1176
LG INFOCOM, LTD. (South Korea) 1177
LG INSURANCE COMPANY LTD. (South Korea) 1176
LG INTERNATIONAL AMERICA (South Korea) 1176
LG INVESTMENT & SECURITIES AMERICA INC. (South Korea) 1176
LG PRECISION COMPANY (South Korea) 1177
LG SILTRON INC. (South Korea) 1177
LOUISVILLE GAS AND ELECTRIC (England, U.K.) 367
LIBERTY INTERNATIONAL UNDERWRITERS (Netherlands) 1032
LIEBHERR CONSTRUCTION EQUIPMENT COMPANY (Switzerland) 1293
LIEBHERR MINING EQUIPMENT CO. (Switzerland) 1293
LIEBHERR AEROSPACE SALINE COMPANY (Switzerland) 1294
LIEBHERR-AMERICA, INC. (Switzerland) 1294
LIEBIG INTERNATIONAL INC. (Germany) 610
LIFE INSURANCE COMPANY OF GEORGIA (Netherlands) 1071
LIFESERV CORPORATION (Canada) 100
LIGNO TECH USA INC. (Norway) 1115
LILOGIX RD AUTOMATION (Netherlands) 1043
LIMAGRAIN GENETICS CORP. (France) 496
LIMCO AIREPAIR INC. (Israel) 764
LINAMAR USA INC. (Canada) 138
LINATEX CORPORATION OF AMERICA (England, U.K.) 299
LINCOLN PRODUCTS (England, U.K.) 433
LINCOLN RE, DIV. LINCOLN NATIONAL (Switzerland) 1316
LINDBERG CORPORATION (England, U.K.) 268
LINDE HYDRAULICS CORPORATION (Germany) 634
LINDE LIFT TRUCK CORP. (Germany) 634
LINDT & SPRUENGLI INC. (Switzerland) 1294
LINKLATERS & ALLIANCE (England, U.K.) 340
LION BIOSCIENCE INC. (Germany) 635

LIPHA PHARMACEUTICALS, INC. (Germany) 641
LIPHA TECH INC. (Germany) 641
LIPPINCOTT WILLIAM & WILKINS (Netherlands) 1100
LIPPO BANK (Indonesia) 725
LIPTON (England, U.K.) 423
LIPTON (Netherlands) 1093
LISEGA USA INC. (Germany) 635
LISTER-PETTER INC. (England, U.K.) 341
LIU CHONG HING BANK LTD. (Hong Kong) 704
LLADRÓ USA, INC. (Spain) 1193
LLOYD'S AMERICA LIMITED (England, U.K.) 341
LLOYDS BANK PLC (England, U.K.) 341
LMI TECHNOLOGIES, INC. (Canada) 138
LML PAYMENT SYSTEMS CORP. (Canada) 138
LMT - FETTE INC. (Germany) 593
LOADOMETER CORPORATION (Switzerland) 1270
LOBLAW COMPANIES LIMITED (Canada) 139
LOCKWOOD GREENE (Germany) 619
LOCKWOOD GREENE ENGINEERS, INC. (Germany) 619
LOCTITE CORPORATION (Germany) 613
LOEWEN GROUP (Canada) 139
LOGIC INNOVATIONS, INC. (England, U.K.) 434
LOGICA, INC. (England, U.K.) 342
LOGITECH INC. (Switzerland) 1294
LOGITECH PRODUCT GROUP (Scotland, U.K.) 1138
LOHER DRIVE SYSTEMS (Germany) 555
LOHER DRIVE SYSTEMS, INC. (Germany) 554
LOHMANN THERAPY SYSTEMS, INC. (Germany) 636
LOMBARDINI USA INC. (Italy) 792
LONDON BRIDGE GROUP (England, U.K.) 342
LONDON BRIDGE PHOENIX SOFTWARE, INC. (England, U.K.) 342
LONDON PACIFIC GROUP LTD. (Channel Islands, U.K.) 194
LONESTAR INDUSTRIES, INC. (Germany) 588
LONZA BIOLOGICS INC. (Switzerland) 1295
LONZA INC. (Switzerland) 1295
THE LORD GROUP (Japan) 835
L'OREAL (France) 506
LORIEN, INC. (England, U.K.) 343
LOS ANGELES DODGERS INC. (Australia) 18
LOT POLISH AIRLINES (Poland) 1126
LOTEPRO CORPORATION (Germany) 634
LOUIS VUITTON USA INC. (France) 508
LOUISVILLE LADDERS INC. (Mexico) 1022
LOVELL WHITE DURRANT (England, U.K.) 343
L-SQUARED INC. (Cayman Islands) 193
LTM CORP OF AMERICA (France) 507
LTU CARGO c/o DITCO PACIFIC (Germany) 636

M

MARUBENI INTERNATIONAL ELECTRONICS
   CORPORATION (Japan) 888

MARUBENI METAL BLANKING INC. (Japan) 889

MARUBENI PROJECT INVESTMENT
   COMPANY (Japan) 889

MARUBENI STEEL PROCESSING, INC. (Japan) 889

MARUBENI TUBULARS, INC. (Japan) 889

MARUICHI AMERICAN CORPORATION
   (Malaysia) 1015

MARUKAI CORPORATION (Japan) 890

MARZOTTA USA CORPORATION (Italy) 787

MASHREQ BANK PSC. (United Arab Emirates) 1349

MASSACHUSETTS ELECTRIC COMPANY
   (England, U.K.) 354

MATERIAL MANAGING GROUP, DIV.
   BOSSARD (Switzerland) 1270

MATSUBO COMPANY, INC. (Japan) 837

MATSUSHITA AVIONICS SYSTEMS
   CORPORATION (Japan) 891

MATSUSHITA ELECTRIC CORPORATION OF
   AMERICA (Japan) 891

MATSUSHITA ELECTRIC WORKS, R&D
   LABORATORY INC (Japan) 892

MATSUZAKAYA AMERICA, INC. (Japan) 892

MAUELL CORPORATION (Germany) 612

MAUNA LANI RESORT INC. (Japan) 987

MAXI/BROOKS PHARMACY INC. (Canada) 134

MAXTOR CORPORATION (South Korea) 1166

MAYBELLINE INC. (France) 506

MAYER TEXTILE MACHINE CORPORATION
   (Germany) 639

MAYFRAN INTERNATIONAL, INC. (England,
   U.K.) 420

MAZDA MOTOR MFG USA, CORPORATION
   (Japan) 893

MB MARBLE & GRANITE COMPANY, INC.
   (Spain) 1189

MBL (USA) CORPORATION (Japan) 903

MC CAIN FOODS USA, INC. (Canada) 142

MC KECHNIE PLASTIC COMPONENTS, N.A.
   (England, U.K.) 348

MC QUAY, C/O SCHWAB, VOLLHABER,
   LUBRATT, INC. (Malaysia) 1016

MCA NASHVILLE (Canada) 170

MCA RECORDS (Canada) 170

MCKESSON WATER PRODUCTS COMPANY
   (France) 483

MCM, INC. (England, U.K.) 328

MCS BUSINESS SOLUTIONS, INC. (Japan) 822

MCS LTD. (Japan) 907

MDL INFORMATION SYSTEMS, INC.
   (England, U.K.) 375

MDS PANLABS (Canada) 142

MEAT AND LIVESTOCK AUSTRALIA LTD.
   (Australia) 16

MEC FINANCE USA INC. (Japan) 898

MECATOOL LTD. (Switzerland) 1261

MECATOOL USA (Switzerland) 1282

MEDAL LP (France) 455

MEDASYS USA INC. (France) 509

MEDEVA PHARMACEUTICALS (England,
   U.K.) 279

MEDIA ADVISORS INTERNATIONAL
   (Australia) 7

MEDIAGATE INC. (Israel) 748

MEDIC COMPUTER SYSTEMS, INC. (England,
   U.K.) 352

MEDICAL RISK SOLUTIONS (Netherlands) 1071

MEDIPHARM INC. (Denmark) 212

MEDITERRANEAN SHIPPING COMPANY
   (USA) INC. (Switzerland) 1296

MEDRAD INC. (Germany) 662

MEGA INTERNATIONAL, INC. (Canada) 187

MEGGITT AVOINICS INC. (England, U.K.) 349

MEGGITT DEFENSE SYSTEMS (England, U.K.) 349

MEGGITT SAFETY SYSTEMS, INC. (England,
   U.K.) 349

MEGGITT SILICONE PRODUCTS (England,
   U.K.) 350

MEGTEC SYSTEMS COMPANY INC. (France) 509

MEIJI SEIKA (USA), INC. (Japan) 893

MEIKO AMERICA, INC. (Japan) 893

MEINEKE DISCOUNT MUFFLER SHOPS, INC.
   (England, U.K.) 314

MELITTA NORTH AMERICA INC. (Germany) 640

MELITTA USA INC. (Germany) 640

MEMC INC. (Germany) 588

MENTERGY (Israel) 755

THE MENTHOLATUM COMPANY (Japan) 950

MEPLA-ALFIT INC. (Germany) 691

MEPLA-ALFIT, INC. (Germany) 691

MERANT INC. (England, U.K.) 350

MERCEDES-BENZ ADVANCED DESIGN OF
   N.A., INC. (Germany) 577

MERCEDES-BENZ LATINA, INC. (Germany) 577

MERCEDES-BENZ OF NORTH AMERICA,
   INC. (Germany) 577

MERCEDES-BENZ US INTERNATIONAL INC.
   (Germany) 577

MERIDIAN PRINTING, INC. (Ireland) 737

MERISOL USA LLC (South Africa) 1155

MERO STRUCTURES INC. (Germany) 642

MESSE DÜSSELDORF NORTH AMERICA
   (Germany) 642

MESSER ADVANCED GAS SYSTEMS (France) 463

MESSNER VETERE BERGER McNAMEE
   SCHMETTERER/EURO RCG (France) 499

METAL BULLETIN, INC. (England, U.K.) 350

METAL COATINGS INTERNATIONAL INC.
   (Japan) 935

METCRAFT INC (Canada) 115

N

NATIONAL BANK OF CANADA - Agency (Canada) 147

NATIONAL BANK OF CANADA - Chicago Branch (Canada) 147

NATIONAL BANK OF GREECE (Greece) 694

THE NATIONAL BANK OF KUWAIT S.A.K. (Kuwait) 1009

NATIONAL BANK OF PAKISTAN (Pakistan) 1120

NATIONAL DECISION SYSTEMS INC. (Netherlands) 1097

NATIONAL ELECTRICAL CARBON PRODUCTS, INC. (England, U.K.) 353

NATIONAL EXPRESS CORPORATION (England, U.K.) 353

NATIONAL FOAM, INC. (England, U.K.) 430

NATIONAL GRID USA (England, U.K.) 354

NATIONAL OILWELL (Norway) 1111

NATIONAL RESEARCH GROUP INC. (Netherlands) 1097

NATIONAL STARCH & CHEMICAL COMPANY (England, U.K.) 324

NATIONAL STEEL CORPORATION (Japan) 935

NATRA US, INC. (Spain) 1194

NATURE AMERICA INC (England, U.K.) 344

NATUZZI AMERICAS (Italy) 791

NATWEST GROUP N.A. (Scotland, U.K.) 1140

NAUTA DUTILH (Netherlands) 1074

NAVINVEST MARINE SERVICES, DIV. B+H OCEAN (Bermuda) 61

NAVISION US, INC. (Denmark) 225

NAY YA PLASTICS CORPORATION, AMERICA (Taiwan (ROC)) 1340

NCIPHER INC. (England, U.K.) 355

NCS PEARSON (England, U.K.) 363

NDC INFRARED ENGINEERING LTD. (England, U.K.) 408

NDS AMERICAS INC. (England, U.K.) 355

NEC AMERICA, INC. (Japan) 912

NEC COMPUTER SYSTEMS INC (Japan) 912

NEC COMPUTERS (Japan) 912

NEC ELECTRONICS, INC. (Japan) 912

NEC ELUMINANT TECHNOLOGIES, INC. (Japan) 912

NEC INDUSTRIES, INC. (Japan) 912

NEC INDUSTRIES, INC. (Japan) 912

NEC RESEARCH INSTITUTE, INC. (Japan) 913

NEC SYSTEMS, INC. (Japan) 913

NEC TECHNOLOGIES, INC. (Japan) 913

NEC USA, INC. (Japan) 913

NEDCOR BANK LIMITED (South Africa) 1153

NEDERMAN INC. (Sweden) 1230

NEFAB, INC. (Sweden) 1230

NERA NETWORKS INC. (Norway) 1114

NESS TECHNOLOGIES INC. (Israel) 756

NESTE CORPORATE HOLDING INC. (Finland) 442

NESTLÉ COFFEE SPECIALTIES INC. (Switzerland) 1299

NESTLÉ FROZEN FOOD INC., ICE CREAM DIV. (Switzerland) 1299

NESTLÉ HOLDINGS INC. (Switzerland) 1299

NESTLÉ USA (Switzerland) 1299

NESTLÉ USA INC. (Switzerland) 1299

NET CREATIONS, INC. (Italy) 802

NETAFIM USA INC. (Israel) 757

NETSTAL MACHINERY, INC. (Germany) 638

NETVALUE USA INC. (France) 511

NETZSCH INC. (Germany) 645

NETZSCH INCORPORATED (Germany) 590

NETZSCH THERMAL ANALYSIS, DIV. NETZSCH INC. (Germany) 647

NEUMAG CORPORATION (Switzerland) 1308

THE NEUMAYER COMPANY (Finland) 447

NEW ENGLAND ELECTRIC SYSTEM INC. (NEES) (England, U.K.) 354

NEW ENGLAND HYDRO FINANCE COMPANY, INC. (England, U.K.) 355

NEW ENGLAND INSTRUMENTS (England, U.K.) 334

NEW ENGLAND POWER COMPANY (England, U.K.) 355

NEW FRONTIERS INC. (France) 511

NEW HAMPSHIRE BALL BEARINGS INC. (Japan) 895

NEW HERBOLD INC. (Germany) 647

NEW HOLLAND CONSTRUCTION INC. , DIV. CNH GLOBAL (Netherlands) 1049

NEW JAPAN SECURITIES INTL, INC. (Japan) 914

THE NEW OTANI HOTEL & GARDEN (Japan) 914

NEW SKIES SATELLITES, INC. (Netherlands) 1075

NEW UNITED MOTOR MFG., INC. (Japan) 993

NEW WORLD NETWORK USA INC. (Canada) 125

THE NEW YORK HELMSLEY (France) 530

NEW YORK POST (Australia) 18

NEW ZEALAND LAMB COMPANY (New Zealand) 1105

NEWARK ELECTRONICS (England, U.K.) 367

NEWARK ELECTRNICS (England, U.K.) 368

NEWPORT PRECISION (Japan) 854

NEWS AMERICA MARKETING (Australia) 18

NEWS AMERICA PUBLISHING GROUP (Australia) 18

NEWS CORP ONE (Australia) 18

NEWS CORPORATION (Australia) 18

THE NEWS GROUP (Canada) 156

NEWTOWN CPC (Canada) 124

NEXTEXIS BANQUES POPULAIRES (France) 511

NEXTROM, INC. (Switzerland) 1300

O

OFFSET PAPERBACK MANUFACURERS INC. (Germany) 564

OGILVY & MATHER WORLDWIDE (England, U.K.) 433

OHIO STAR FORGE COMPANY (Japan) 827

OJI PAPER COMPANY, LTD. (Japan) 940

OKAMOTO CORPORATION (Japan) 941

OKAMOTO USA, INC (Japan) 940

OKAYA ELECTRIC AMERICA, INC. (Japan) 941

OKI NETWORK TECHNOLOGIES, INC. (Japan) 941

OKI TELECOM, INC. (Japan) 942

OKIDATA, INC. (Japan) 942

OKLAHOMA SAFETY EQUIPMENT CO. INC. (England, U.K.) 319

OKUMA CORPORATION (Japan) 942

OLAYAN AMERICA CORPORATION (Saudi Arabia) 1133

OLDCASTLE, INC. (Ireland) 730

OLDELFT ULTRASOUND INC. (Netherlands) 1051

OLDELFT ULTRASOUND, INC. (Netherlands) 1076

OLICOM USA INC. (Denmark) 228

OLIVETTI USA, INC. (Italy) 795

OLSTEN STAFFING SERVICES (Switzerland) 1260

OLYMPIC AIRWAYS (Greece) 694

OLYMPUS AMERICA, INC. (Japan) 942

OMRON ELECTRONICS, INC. (Japan) 943

OMRON HEALTHCARE, INC. (Japan) 943

OMRON MANUFACTURING OF AMERICA, INC. (Japan) 943

OMRON OFFICE AUTOMATION PRODUCTS, INC. (Japan) 943

OMSCO (Canada) 173

ONDEO DEGREMONT INC. (France) 512

ONDEO DEGRÉMONT INC. (France) 512

ONDEO NALCO COMPANY (France) 512

ONESOURCE, DIV. CARLISLE GROUP US (Belize) 55

ONEX FOOD SERVICES, INC. (Canada) 153

ONEX INVESTMENT CORP. (Canada) 153

ONO PHARMA, INC. (Japan) 943

ONTARIO DIE COMPANY OF AMERICA (Canada) 154

ONTARIO DIE OF TENNESSEE (Canada) 154

ONTARIO DIE OF TEXAS (Canada) 154

OOCL (USA), INC. (Hong Kong) 704

OOZX USA INC. (Japan) 827

OPC DRIZO, INC. (France) 491

OPEN TEXT (Canada) 154

OPEN TV CORP. (South Africa) 1153

OPHIR OPTRONICS INC. (Israel) 759

OPICOIL AMERICA, INC. (Taiwan (ROC)) 1337

OPTIBASE INC. (Israel) 759

OPTIMA MACHINERY CORPORATION (Germany) 648

OPTIONS TAI PING CARPETS INC. (Hong Kong) 708

OPTO INTERNATIONAL INC. (England, U.K.) 360

OPTOBAHN CORPORATION (Israel) 757

ORBITAL ENGINE COMPANY INC. (Australia) 19

ORBOTECH INC. (Israel) 759

ORCHESTREAM HOLDINGS (England, U.K.) 360

ORCKIT COMMUNICATIONS (Israel) 760

ORCKIT COMMUNICATIONS, INC. (Israel) 760

ORICA USA INC. (Australia) 20

ORIENTAL MOTOR USA CORPORATION (Japan) 944

ORIGO AB SWEDEN (Sweden) 1231

ORIGO USA INC. (Sweden) 1216

ORION PHARMA INC. (Finland) 447

ORIX REAL ESTATE CAPITAL MARKETS, LLC (Japan) 944

ORIX REAL ESTATE EQUITIES, INC. (Japan) 944

ORIX USA CORPORATION (Japan) 944

ORMAT SYSTEMS INC. (Israel) 760

GALLERI ORREFORS KOSTA BODA (Sweden) 1232

ORTOFON INC. (Denmark) 228

OSAKA GAS COMPANY, LTD. (Japan) 944

OSHAWA GROUP PRODUCE, INC. (Canada) 177

OSLER, HOSKIN & HARCOURT (Canada) 155

OSMETECH INC. (England, U.K.) 360

OSRAM SYLVANIA INC. (Germany) 670

OST INC. (France) 513

OTIM USA INC. (Italy) 795

OTSUKA AMERICA PHARMACEUTICALS, INC. (Japan) 945

OTSUKA AMERICA, INC. (Japan) 945

OTSUKA CHEMICAL COMPANY (Japan) 945

OUTOKUMPU COPPER AMERICAS, INC. (Finland) 448

OUTOKUMPU COPPER FRANKLIN INC. (Finland) 448

OUTOKUMPU COPPER USA, INC. (Finland) 448

OUTOKUMPU MINTEC USA INC. (Finland) 448

OUTOKUMPU TECHNOLOGY, INC. (Finland) 448

OUTOKUMPU TECHNOLOGY, INC., CARPCO DIV. (Finland) 448

OVERHEAD DOOR CORPORATION (Japan) 952

OVERSEA-CHINESE BANKING CORP LTD. (Singapore) 1145

OVERSEAS UNION BANK, LTD. (Singapore) 1146

OVERSEAS UNION BANK, LTD. (Singapore) 1146

OVID TECHNOLOGIES INC. (Netherlands) 1101

OXFORD INSTRUMENTS MEDICAL SYSTEMS DIV. (England, U.K.) 361

OXFORD ORGANICS INC. (England, U.K.) 435

OYO CORPORATION (Japan) 946

OZ.COM (Iceland) 715

OZONIA NORTH AMERICA (France) 534

P

Q

ROLLS-ROYCE GEAR SYSTEMS INC.
(England, U.K.) 386

ROLLS-ROYCE MOTOR CARS, INC. -
NORTHERN REGION (Germany) 686

ROLLS-ROYCE MOTOR CARS, INC. (Germany) 686

ROLLS-ROYCE MOTOR CARS, INC. 687
CENTRAL REGION (Germany)

ROLLS-ROYCE MOTOR CARS, INC. -
SOUTHERN REGION (Germany) 687

ROLLS-ROYCE, INC. (England, U.K.) 386

ROSENBAUER AMERICA (Austria) 29

ROSENLEW INC. (Finland) 451

ROSENTHAL USA LTD. (Germany) 656

ROSIE MAGAZINE (Germany) 604

ROSSIGNOL SKI CO NC. (France) 529

ROTHSCHILD NORTH AMERICA, INC.
(England, U.K.) 387

ROTORK COMPANY (England, U.K.) 387

ROTORK CONTROLS INC. (England, U.K.) 387

ROVEMA PACKAGING MACHINES, INC.
(Germany) 656

ROWENTA INC. (France) 527

ROWLAND WORLDWIDE INC. (France) 518

ROXANE LABORATORIES, INC. (Germany) 567

ROXAR, INC. (Norway) 1117

ROYAL & SUN ALLIANCE FINANCIAL
SERVICES (England, U.K.) 388

ROYAL & SUN ALLIANCE INC. (England,
U.K.) 388

ROYAL AIR MAROC (Morocco) 1030

ROYAL BANK OF SCOTLAND (Scotland, U.K.) 1140

ROYAL CARIBBEAN CRUISES LTD. (Norway) 1107

ROYAL CHINA & PORCELAIN COMPANIES
(England, U.K.) 410

ROYAL DOULTON USA INC. (England, U.K.) 389

ROYAL JORDANIAN AIRLINES (Jordan) 1007

ROYAL OLYMPIC CRUISES, INC. (ROC USA)
(Greece) 695

ROYAL ORDINANCE NA (England, U.K.) 258

ROYAL TEN CATE (USA) INC. (Netherlands) 1089

ROYALBLUE GROUP, INC. (England, U.K.) 389

RTS WRIGHT INDUSTRIES (England, U.K.) 385

RTSE USA INC. (England, U.K.) 389

RTV/VIDEO MONITORING SERVICES OF
AMERICA (Netherlands) 1097

RUBBER ENGINEERING INC. (Scotland, U.K.) 1142

RUETGERS ORGANICS CORPORATION
(Germany) 656

RUNTAL NORTH AMERICA, INC. (Switzerland) 1330

RUSKIN COMPANY (England, U.K.) 420

RUSSELL T. GILMAN INC. (Sweden) 1244

RUSSIAN NATIONAL TOURIST OFFICE
(Russia) 1130

RÜTGERS ORGANICS CORPORATION
(Germany) 657

RYOBI DIE CASTING INC. (Japan) 950

S

S&B INTERNATIONAL CORPORATION
(Japan) 950

S&S BIOPATH INC. (Germany) 663

S. A. HEALY COMPANY (Italy) 790

SAAB AIRCRAFT LEASING INC. (Sweden) 1235

SAAB CARS USA INC. (Sweden) 1235

SAAB ERICSSON SPACE, INC. (Sweden) 1235

SAAB ROSEMONT TANK CONTROL USA
(Sweden) 1235

SAATCHI & SAATCHI WORLDWIDE INC.
(England, U.K.) 390

SABENA BELGIAN WORLD AIRLINES
(Belgium) 48

SABIC AMERICAS, INC. (Saudi Arabia) 1134

THE SACHS GROUP (Netherlands) 1097

SACHS NORTH AMERICA (Germany) 639

SACM TEXTILE INC. (France) 524

SAES GETTERS USA INC. (Italy) 800

SAES PURE GAS, INC (Italy) 800

SAFEGUARD INSURANCE COMPANY
(England, U.K.) 388

SAFELITE AUTO GLASS (England, U.K.) 263

SAFETY FIRST (Canada) 114

SAFETY-KLEEN CORPORATION (Canada) 135

SAFILO USA INC. (Italy) 800

SAGE LABORATORIES, INC., DIV.
FILTRONIC (England, U.K.) 306

SAGE SOFTWARE, INC. (England, U.K.) 391

SAGEM CORPORATION (France) 521

SAHA-UNION INTL (USA) INC (Thailand) 1345

SAI AUTOMOTIVE, INC. (France) 532

SAINT GOBAIN WINTER INC. (Germany) 690

SAINT-GOBAIN CORPORATION (France) 522

SAINT-GOBAIN PERFORMANCE PLASTICS
(France) 522

SAIPEM USA INC. (Italy) 801

SAIPEM, INC. (Italy) 782

SAKI MAGNETICS, INC. (Japan) 979

SALANS HERTZFELD HEILBRONN CHRISTY
& VIENER (France) 524

SALEM TUBE INC. (Spain) 1195

SAMJIN AMERICA, INC. (South Korea) 1179

SAMSUNG AMERICA INC. (South Korea) 1180

SAMSUNG AMERICA INC (South Korea) 1180

SAMSUNG CARAVEL INC. (South Korea) 1180

SAMSUNG DISPLAY, INC. (South Korea) 1181

SAMSUNG ELECTRONICS USA INC. (South
Korea) 1181

SCHOLL AMERICA INC. (Switzerland)	1308
SCHOTT CORPORATION (Germany)	664
SCHOTT DONNELLY LLC (Germany)	664
SCHOTT ELECTRONIC PACKAGING (Germany)	664
SCHOTT FIBER OPTICS INC. (Germany)	664
SCHOTT GLASS TECHNOLOGIES INC. (Germany)	664
SCHOTT PHARMACEUTICAL PACKAGING, INC. (Germany)	665
SCHOTT SCIENTIFIC GLASS, INC. (Germany)	665
SCHOTT-FOSTEC LLC (Germany)	665
THE SCHRADER GROUP (England, U.K.)	420
SCHRODERS & COMPANY INC. (England, U.K.)	392
SCHUMAG-KIESERLING MACHINERY, INC. (Germany)	555
SCHUNK GRAPHITE TECHNOLOGY, INC. (Germany)	666
SCHUNK INEX, INC. (Germany)	666
SCHUNK QUARTZ, INC. (Germany)	666
SCHWARZ PHARMA INC. (Germany)	666
SCHWARZKOPF & DEP INC. (Germany)	614
SCIENTIFIC AMERICAN (Germany)	601
SCIENTIFIC DESIGN COMPANY, INC. (Germany)	635
SCOR REINSURANCE (France)	526
SCOR REINSURANCE COMMERICIAL RISK RE-INSURANCE (France)	526
SCOR REINSURANCE COMPANY (France)	526
SCOR U.S. CORPORATION (France)	526
SCOTIABANK (Canada)	169
SCOTSMAN INDUSTRIES INC. (England, U.K.)	300
SCOTTISH & NEWCASTLE IMPORTERS (Scotland, U.K.)	1141
SCRIPTA MACHINE TOOL CORPORATION (France)	527
SCUDDER KEMPER INVESTMENTS INC. (Switzerland)	1333
SDL USA INC. (England, U.K.)	393
SEA HORSE INTERNATIONAL (Monaco)	1029
JOSEPH E. SEAGRAM & SONS INC. (Canada)	170
SEAGRAM AMERICAS (Canada)	170
SEAGRAM CHATEAU & ESTATE WINES COMPANY (Canada)	171
THE SEAGRAM SPIRITS & WINE GROUP (Canada)	171
SEALRIGHT, DIV. HUHTAMAKI (Finland)	444
SEATTLE MARITIME (Norway)	1110
SECURICOR NEW CENTURY, INC. (England, U.K.)	395
SECURICOR WIRELESS INC. (England, U.K.)	395
SECURITRON MAGNALOCK CORP. (Sweden)	1203
SECURITY FIRST NETWORK BANK (Canada)	166

SECURITY LIFE OF DENVER INSURANCE COMPANY (Netherlands)	1072
SEDIVER INC. (France)	527
SEFAC LIFT & EQUIPMENT CORPORATION (France)	528
SEGA CORPORATION, INC. (Japan)	955
SEGA GAMEWORKS LLC (Japan)	955
SEGA OF AMERICA DREAMCAST, INC. (Japan)	955
SEGASOFT NETWORKS INC. (Japan)	955
SEI BRAKES INC. (Japan)	968
SEIKO CORPORATION OF AMERICA, INC. (Japan)	956
SEIKO OPTICAL PRODUCTS, INC. (Japan)	956
SEINO AMERICA, INC. (Japan)	957
SEKISUI AMERICA CORPORATION (Japan)	957
SELDEN MAST INC. (Sweden)	1241
SELES FLUID PROCESSING CORPORATION (Germany)	635
SEMANTIX, INC. (Canada)	172
SEMIA, INC. (Japan)	968
SEMIKRON INTL INC. (Germany)	667
SEMINIS, INC. (Mexico)	1026
SENIOR AEROSPACE DIV. (England, U.K.)	396
SENIOR AEROSPACE, INC. (England, U.K.)	397
SENIOR FLEXONICS INC. (England, U.K.)	397
SENIOR FLEXONICS, INC. (England, U.K.)	397
SENIOR HOLDINGS INC. (England, U.K.)	398
SENOV LIMITED (Czech Republic)	210
SENSE TECHNOLOGIES INC. (Canada)	172
SENSTAR-STELLAR CORP. (Israel)	754
SEOUL BANK (South Korea)	1183
SER SOLUTIONS, INC. (Germany)	668
SERCEL INC. (France)	480
SERCO GROUP INC. (England, U.K.)	398
SERICOL INC. (England, U.K.)	271
SERONO INC. (Switzerland)	1309
SERONO LABORATORIES, INC. (Switzerland)	1264
SERVICE BUILDING PRODUCTS, INC. (Germany)	658
SERVICE MANAGEMENT SYSTEMS (England, U.K.)	393
SERVICE POWER TECHNOLOGIES (England, U.K.)	398
SETFAIR USA INC. (England, U.K.)	329
SETRA/KASSBOHRER OF NORTH AMERICA, INC. (Germany)	578
SEVEN WORLDWIDE, INC. (England, U.K.)	398
SEVERN TRENT ENVIRONMENTAL SERVICES (England, U.K.)	399
SEVERN TRENT SYSTEMS, INC. (England, U.K.)	399
SEVERN TRENT US, INC. (England, U.K.)	399
SEZ AMERICA, INC. (Austria)	29

ST. LAWRENCE CEMENT COMPANY
(Switzerland) 1286

ST. MARTIN'S PRESS, INC. (England, U.K.) 344

ST. MARTIN'S PRESS, INC. (Germany) 601

STABILUS (Germany) 639

STAEDTLER, INC. (Germany) 675

STAEUBLI CORPORATION (Switzerland) 1313

R. STAHL INC. (Germany) 675

STAINED GLASS OVERLAY, INC. (Canada) 121

THE STANDARD BANK OF SOUTH AFRICA
LTD. (South Africa) 1155

STANDARD CHARTERED, PLC. (England,
U.K.) 412

STANDARD FEDERAL BANK (Netherlands) 1081

STANDARD NEW YORK INC. (South Africa) 1155

THE STANT GROUP (England, U.K.) 420

STAPLA ULTRASONICS CORPORATION
(Germany) 666

STAR FINE FOODS (Spain) 1186

STAR MICRONICS AMERICA INC (Japan) 966

H.C. STARK INC. (Germany) 559

STATE BANK OF INDIA (India) 722

STATE TRADING CORP OF INDIA (India) 722

STATOIL MARKETING & TRADING INC.
(Norway) 1117

THE STAUBACH COMPANY (England, U.K.) 294

STEAG HAMA TECH, INC. (Germany) 675

STEINER USA INC. (Bahamas) 34

STELCO INC. (Canada) 179

STERIA USA INC. (France) 497

W. P. STEWART & CO. (Bermuda) 65

STEWART SMITH GROUP INC. (England, U.K.) 431

STIHL INC. (Germany) 676

STINNES CORPORATION (Germany) 677

STMICROELECTRONICS (Switzerland) 1313

STOLT OFFSHORE INC. (England, U.K.) 412

STOLTHAVEN TERMINALS (HOUSTON) INC.
(England, U.K.) 412

STOLT-NIELSEN TRANSPORTATION GROUP
LTD. (England, U.K.) 413

STOP & SHOP COMPANIES (Netherlands) 1082

STORA ENSO NORTH AMERICA
CORPORATION (Finland) 451

STORK CELLRAMIC, INC. (Netherlands) 1090

STORK FOOD & DAIRY SYSTEMS
(Netherlands) 1090

STORK ROTAFORM SCREENS AMERICA INC.
(Netherlands) 1090

STORK VECO INTERNATIONAL (Netherlands) 1091

STRATEGY RESEARCH CORPORATION
(England, U.K.) 241

STRAT-X INTERNATIONAL (France) 533

STRECK LABORATORIES INC. (Japan) 974

STROUT PLASTICS, DIV. JIM PATTISON
GROUP (Canada) 156

STRUERS INC. (Denmark) 229

STS SYSTEMS, INC. (Canada) 179

STUDIO LEGALE BISCONTI (Italy) 803

STYRENICS TECHNOLOGY (Canada) 150

SUBARU OF AMERICA (Japan) 841

SUBARU RESEARCH & DESIGN (Japan) 841

SUCCESSFUL MONEY MANAGEMENT
SEMINARS, INC. (Netherlands) 1072

SUD-CHEMIE PERFORMANCE PACKAGING,
INC. (Germany) 677

SUD-CHEMIE PROTOTECH, INC. (Germany) 678

SUD-CHEMIE RHEOLOGICALS (Germany) 678

SUGINO CORPORATION (Japan) 966

SULZER CARBOMEDICS, INC. (Switzerland) 1315

SULZER DENTALS INC. (Switzerland) 1315

SULZER MEDICA USA INC. (Switzerland) 1315

SULZER METCO (US) INC. (Switzerland) 1314

SULZER ORTHOPEDICS, INC. (Switzerland) 1315

SULZER PUMPS INC. (Switzerland) 1314

SULZER SPINE-TECH INC. (Switzerland) 1315

SULZER TEXTILE INC. (Switzerland) 1314

SULZER TURBOSYSTEMS INTERNATIONAL
(Switzerland) 1314

SULZER USA INDUSTRIES HOLDING INC.
(Switzerland) 1314

SUMIDEN WIRE PRODUCTS CORP (Japan) 968

SUMIKIN BUSSAN INTERNATIONAL
CORPORATION (Japan) 966

SUMITOMO CHEMICAL AMERICA INC
(Japan) 967

SUMITOMO CORPORATION OF AMERICA
(Japan) 968

SUMITOMO CRYOGENICS OF AMERICA INC.
(Japan) 970

SUMITOMO ELECTRIC CARBINE INC. (Japan) 968

SUMITOMO ELECTRIC FIBER OPTICS
CORPORATION (Japan) 968

SUMITOMO ELECTRIC FINANCE INC. (Japan) 969

SUMITOMO ELECTRIC INTERCONNECT
PRODUCTS INC. (Japan) 969

SUMITOMO ELECTRIC LIGHTWAVE
CORPORATION (Japan) 969

SUMITOMO ELECTRIC MAGNET WIRE
COMPANY (Japan) 969

SUMITOMO ELECTRIC USA, INC. (Japan) 969

SUMITOMO ELECTRIC WIRING SYSTEMS
INC. (Japan) 969

SUMITOMO ELECTRIC WIRING SYSTEMS,
INC. (Japan) 969

SUMITOMO FORESTRY INC. (Japan) 970

SUMITOMO HEAVY INDUSTRIES (USA) INC.
(Japan) 970

SUMITOMO MACHINERY CORPORATION OF
AMERICA (Japan) 970

T

TABUCHI ELECTRIC COMPANY OF AMERICA (Japan) 974

TADPOLE-CARTESIA (England, U.K.) 414

TAI FOOK SECURITIES (U.S.) INC. (Hong Kong) 708

TAIHEIYO CEMENT INC. (Japan) 974

TAISEI CONSTRUCTION CO., LTD. (Japan) 974

TIASHO PHARMACEUTICALS CALIFORNIA INC. (Japan) 975

TAIYO YUDEN USA INC. (Japan) 975

TAKARA SAKE USA, INC. (Japan) 976

TAKASHIMAYA CALIFORNIA, INC. (Japan) 976

TAKASHIMAYA ENTERPRISES, INC. (Japan) 976

TAKASHIMAYA NEW YORK, INC. (Japan) 976

TAKATA FABRICATION CORPORATION (Japan) 977

TAKEDA AMERICA, INC. (Japan) 977

TAKEDA VITAMIN & FOOD INC. (Japan) 977

TAKENAKA (USA) CORPORATION (Japan) 978

TAKEUCHI MFG (USA), LTD. (Japan) 978

TAKISAWA USA, INC. (Japan) 978

TALBOTS, INC. (Japan) 870

TAMFELT, INC. (Finland) 451

TAMROCK INC. (Sweden) 1238

TAMRON INDUSTRIES, INC. (Japan) 979

TANDEM RESEARCH ASSOCIATES, INC (England, U.K.) 241

TAP HOLDINGS INC. (Japan) 977

TARGETTI-TIVOLI, INC. (Italy) 804

TARO PHARMACEUTICALS USA INC. (Canada) 181

TASMAN ROOFING, INC. (New Zealand) 1104

TATA INC. (India) 723

TATE & LYLE, INC. (England, U.K.) 414

TATE & LYLE SUGARS INC. (England, U.K.) 415

TATE ACCESS FLOORS INC. (Ireland) 737

TATUNG USA CORPORATION (Taiwan (ROC)) 1342

TAYLOR & FRANCIS GROUP (England, U.K.) 415

TAYLOR NELSON SOFRES INTERSEARCH (England, U.K.) 416

TAYLOR WOODROW COMMUNITIES, INC. (England, U.K.) 416

TAYLOR WOODROW FLORIDA (England, U.K.) 416

TAYLOR WOODROW HOMES CALIFORNIA LTD. (England, U.K.) 416

TC&M SYSTEMS INC. (Switzerland) 1288

TD SECURITIES INC. (Canada) 186

TD WATERHOUSE SECURITIES (Canada) 181

TD WATERHOUSE INVESTOR SERVICES, INC. (Canada) 186

TDK COMPONENTS USA, INC. (Japan) 979

TDK CORPORATION OF AMERICA (Japan) 979

TDK ELECTRONICS CORPORATION (Japan) 979

TDK FERRITES CORPORATION (Japan) 980

TDK SEMICONDUCTOR CORPORATION (Japan) 980

TDK SYSTEMS, INC. (Japan) 980

TDK TEXAS CORPORATION (Japan) 980

TDK USA CORPORATION (Japan) 980

TEAC AMERICA, INC. (Japan) 980

TECH SPECIALISTS, DIV RANDSTAD (Netherlands) 1078

TECHALLOY COMPANY INC. (France) 541

TECHNICOLOR ENTERTAINMENT SERVICES (France) 537

TECHNICOLOR FILM SERVICES (England, U.K.) 278

TECHNICOLOR PACKAGED MEDIA GROUP (France) 538

TECHNIP USA INC (France) 535

TECK COMINCO INC. (Canada) 181

TECNIMONT, INC. (Italy) 795

TECNOMATIX-UNICAM, INC. (Israel) 765

TECO WESTINGHOUSE MOTORS INC. (Taiwan (ROC)) 1342

TECSYN INC., DIV. EXCO (Canada) 116

TEIJIN AMERICA, INC. (Japan) 981

TEIJIN SEIKI AMERICA INC. (Japan) 981

TEIJIN SHOJI USA, INC. (Japan) 981

TEKNION CORPORATION (Canada) 181

TEKSID ALUMINUM FOUNDRY, INC. (Italy) 785

TEKSID, INC. (Italy) 785

TELCO SYSTEMS, INC. (Israel) 743

TELE DENMARK USA INC. (Denmark) 230

TELECOM ITALIA (Italy) 804

TELECOM NEW ZEALAND LIMITED (New Zealand) 1105

TELECOMET INC. (Japan) 877

TELECOMPUTING, INC. (Norway) 1118

TELEGLOBE COMMUNICATIONS CORP. (Canada) 182

TELEPLAN (WHITE ELECTRONICS) (Netherlands) 1091

TELEVISION FRANCAISE 1 (France) 535

TELIA INTERNATIONAL CARRIER, INC. (Sweden) 1252

TELRAD NETWORKS INC. (Israel) 765

TELSTRA INC. (Australia) 22

TENCEL, DIV. ACORDIS (Netherlands) 1031

TENGU COMPANY INC. (Japan) 917

TENNESSEE WATER CRAFTS, INC. (Japan) 1000

TERAFORCE TECHNOLOGY CORPORATION (Singapore) 1148

TERROT KNITTING MACHINES INC. (Germany) 679

TERUMO CARDIOVASCULAR SYSTEMS (TCVS) (Japan) 981

TERUMO MEDICAL CORPORATION (Japan) 982

TORAY COMPOSITE (AMERICA), INC. (Japan) 988
TORAY INDUSTRIES (AMERICA), INC. (Japan) 989
TORAY MARKETING & SALES (AMERICA), INC. (Japan) 989
TORAY PLASTICS (AMERICA), INC. (Japan) 989
TORAY RESIN COMPANY (Japan) 989
TORAY ULTRASUEDE INC. (Japan) 989
TORONTO-DOMINION HOLDINGS (USA) INC. (Canada) 186
TOSHIBA AMERICA CONSUMER PRODUCTS, INC. (Japan) 989
TOSHIBA AMERICA ELECTRONIC COMPONENTS, INC. (Japan) 989
TOSHIBA AMERICA, INC. (Japan) 990
TOSHIBA AMERICA INFORMATION SYSTEMS, INC. (Japan) 990
TOSHIBA AMERICA MEDICAL SYSTEMS, INC. (Japan) 990
TOSHIBA INTERNATIONAL CORPORATION (Japan) 990
TOSHIBA MACHINE COMPANY OF AMERICA (Japan) 990
TOSOH USA, INC. (Japan) 990
TOTAL FINA ELF SERVICES, INC. (France) 539
TOTO INDUSTRIES, INC. (Japan) 991
TOTO USA INC. (Japan) 991
TOWER SEMICONDUCTOR USA, INC. (Israel) 766
THE TOWNSEND & SCHUPP COMPANY (England, U.K.) 328
TOYO SEIKAN (Japan) 991
TOYO TIRE USA CORPORATION (Japan) 991
TOYOBO AMERICA, INC. (Japan) 992
TOYODA MACHINERY USA, INC. (Japan) 992
TOYOSHIMA INDIANA, INC. (Japan) 993
TOYOTA INDUSTRIAL EQUIPMENT MFG INC. (Japan) 992
TOYOTA MOTOR NA INC. (Japan) 993
TOYOTA MOTOR CREDIT CORPORATION (Japan) 994
TOYOTA MOTOR MFG. INDIANA, INC. (Japan) 994
TOYOTA MOTOR MFG, INC. (Japan) 994
TOYOTA MOTOR MFG. WEST VIRGINIA INC. (Japan) 994
TOYOTA MOTOR SALES USA, INC. (Japan) 994
TOYOTA TECHNICAL CENTER USA INC. (Japan) 994
TOYOTA TSUSHO AMERICA, INC (Japan) 994
TPC WIRE & CABLE (England, U.K.) 368
TR METRO CHEMICALS INC. (Germany) 651
TRACE ANALYTICAL (Italy) 800
TRACFONE WIRELESS, INC. (Mexico) 1017
TRACTEBEL ENERGY MARKETING INC. (Belgium) 52
TRACTEBEL POWER INC. (Belgium) 52

TRACTEL LTD., SWINGSTAGE DIV. (Canada) 187
TRADE ARBED INC. (Luxembourg) 1012
TRADE DIMENSIONS/NRB (Netherlands) 1098
TRADE SOURCES, INC. (Hong Kong) 700
TRADITION DERIVATIVES CORPORATION (Switzerland) 1275
TRADITION FINANCIAL SERVICES INC. (Switzerland) 1275
TRADITION GLOBAL CLEARING INC. (Switzerland) 1275
TRADITION INC. (Switzerland) 1275
TRAKKER MAP INC. NATIONWIDE DISTRIBUTORS INC. (Germany) 632
TRANS ALTA CORPORATION (Canada) 188
TRANS ALTA ENERGY MARKETING (Canada) 188
TRANSAMERICA BUSINESS CREDIT CORP. (Netherlands) 1032
TRANSAMERICA CORPORATION (Netherlands) 1032
TRANSAMERICA DISTRIBUTION FINANCE CORP. (Netherlands) 1033
TRANSAMERICA OCCIDENTAL LIFE INSURANCE (Netherlands) 1033
TRANSAMERICA REAL ESTATE TAX SERVICE (Netherlands) 1033
TRANSBRASIL AIRLINES INC. (Brazil) 79
TRANSCO AGENCIES INC. (Chile) 196
TRANSCON PRINTING INC. (Canada) 124
TRANSCONTINENTAL PRINTING, INC. (Canada) 127
TRANSETTLEMENT, DIV. DESCARTES (Canada) 113
TRANSGENE, INC. (France) 539
TRANSMISSIONS TECHNOLOGY INC. (Mexico) 1027
TRANSTECTOR SYSTEMS, INC. (England, U.K.) 406
TRAVEL SERVICES INTERNATIONAL, INC. (England, U.K.) 243
TREE OF LIFE, INC. (Netherlands) 1099
TREFILARBED ARKANSAS INC. (Luxembourg) 1012
TRELLEBORG INC. (Sweden) 1253
TRELLEBORG MONARCH INC. (Sweden) 1253
TRELLEBORG VIKING INC. (Sweden) 1253
TRELLEBORG WHEEL SYSTEMS INC. (Sweden) 1253
TREND MICRO INC. (Japan) 995
TREVI - ICOS CORPORATION (Italy) 804
TRIBORO FIBERS INC. (Sweden) 1211
TRI-CLOVER INC. (Sweden) 1200
TRICO (England, U.K.) 421
TRICOM U.S.A. (Dominican Republic) 233
TRIGEM AMERICA CORPORATION (South Korea) 1185
TRIGEN BIO POWER INC. (France) 534

U

V

X

Y

Z

PART FOUR

PUBLISHER'S NOTES

RELATED PUBLICATIONS

The 16th Edition
DIRECTORY OF AMERICAN FIRMS OPERATING IN FOREIGN COUNTRIES

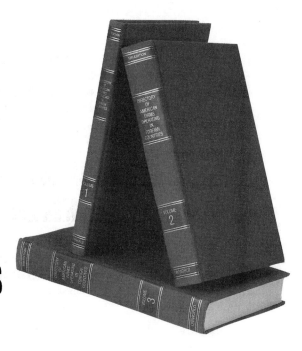

EDITED & PUBLISHED BY UNIWORLD BUSINESS PUBLICATIONS, INC.
Published January 2001

THREE VOLUMES   PRICE: $325.00
4200 PAGES   ISBN: 0-8360-0045-5

CD ROM one year subscription $ 975.00
CD ROM two year subscription $1500.00
(see insert for details)

COMPREHENSIVE LISTINGS

- **2,600** American Firms
- Over **34,500** Foreign subsidiaries, affiliates, or branches
- **190** Countries

EASY AND FLEXIBLE ACCESS

The firm(s) you are looking for are found:

- **by name**-----US companies listed alphabetically (Part 1)
- **by country**--US companies and their affiliates and branches by foreign country (Part 2)

Principal Product or service

Names and address of subsidiary, affiliate or branch

Where available, telephone, fax and local contacts for foreign subsidiaries

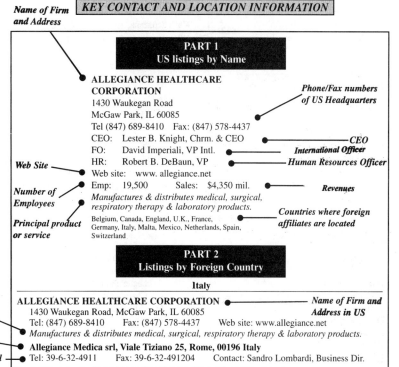

Name of Firm and Address

KEY CONTACT AND LOCATION INFORMATION

PART 1
US listings by Name

ALLEGIANCE HEALTHCARE CORPORATION
1430 Waukegan Road
McGaw Park, IL 60085
Tel (847) 689-8410   Fax: (847) 578-4437
CEO: Lester B. Knight, Chrm. & CEO
FO: David Imperiali, VP Intl.
HR: Robert B. DeBaun, VP
Web site: www. allegiance.net
Emp: 19,500   Sales: $4,350 mil.
Manufactures & distributes medical, surgical, respiratory therapy & laboratory products.
Belgium, Canada, England, U.K., France, Germany, Italy, Malta, Mexico, Netherlands, Spain, Switzerland

Phone/Fax numbers of US Headquarters
CEO
International Officer
Human Resources Officer
Revenues
Countries where foreign affiliates are located
Web Site
Number of Employees
Principal product or service

PART 2
Listings by Foreign Country

Italy

ALLEGIANCE HEALTHCARE CORPORATION
1430 Waukegan Road, McGaw Park, IL 60085
Tel: (847) 689-8410   Fax: (847) 578-4437   Web site: www.allegiance.net
Manufactures & distributes medical, surgical, respiratory therapy & laboratory products.
Allegiance Medica srl, Viale Tiziano 25, Rome, 00196 Italy
Tel: 39-6-32-4911   Fax: 39-6-32-491204   Contact: Sandro Lombardi, Business Dir.

Name of Firm and Address in US

NEW 11th Edition

DIRECTORY OF FOREIGN FIRMS OPERATING IN THE UNITED STATES

EDITED & PUBLISHED BY
UNIWORLD BUSINESS PUBLICATIONS, INC.
Published January 2002

ONE VOLUME • 1480 PAGES • PRICE: $250.00 • ISBN: 0-8360-0046-3

ONE VOLUME   PRICE: $225.00
1480 PAGES   ISBN: 0-8360-46-3

CD ROM one year subscription $ 675.00
CD ROM two year subscription $1000.00
(see insert for details)

COMPREHENSIVE LISTINGS

- **2,800** Foreign Firms
- **7,200** U.S. Affiliates
- **79** Countries

EASY AND FLEXIBLE ACCESS

The firm(s) you are looking for can be found:
- _by country_ --(Part I)
- _by name_------the name of the parent company (Part II)
- _by affiliate_---the name of the American based affiliate (Part III)

KEY CONTACT AND LOCATION INFORMATION

Name of Parent Foreign Firm and Address — _Revenue_

Italy

• LUXOTTICA GROUP, S.p.A.
Via Vacozzena, 10, I-32021 Agordo Belluno, Italy
CEO — ●CEO: Leonardo Del Vecchio, Pres.   _Telephone/Fax Number_   Tel: 39-0437-63746   Rev: $2,275
Bus: _Mfr. eyeglass frames, retail eyecare and_   Fax: 39-0437-63840   Emp: 19,400
clothing stores.   www.luxottica.it ●— _Web_

Number of Employees

AVANT GARDE OPTICS INC.
44 Harbor Park Drive, Port Washington, NY 11050
CEO — ●CEO: Claudio Del Vecchio, Pres.   Tel: (516) 484-3800   %FO: 100
Bus: _Distribution, eyeglass frames._   Fax: (516) 484-4481   Emp: 326

LENSCRAFTERS INC.
8650 Governor's Hill Drive, Cincinnati, OH 43068   _Telephone/Fax Number_
CEO: Cliff Bartow, COO   Tel: (513) 583-6000   %FO: 100
Bus: _Eyeglass frames, eyecare retail_   Fax: (513) 583-6388   Emp: 12,800
stores.

Principal Product or Service   _Principal Product or Service_   _% Foreign Owned_   _Number of Employees_

PARTIAL BUYERS LIST

Country, Regional, State Editions & Mailing Lists

11th Edition of the *Directory of Foreign Firms Operating in The United States and the*
16th Edition of *Directory of American Firms Operating in Foreign Countries*
in **Country**, **Regional** or **State** editions with all the same information that is in the library set.

- **Country and Regional Editions** ~ list the companies alphabetically within each country.

- **State Editions** ~ *Directory of Foreign Firms Operating in The United States,*
  lists by State the Foreign Firms (alphabetically), at each American
  Affiliate headquarters location within the state..

  ~ *Directory of American Firms Operating in Foreign Countries,*
  lists by State the American firms (alphabetically), at the headquarters
  location within the state

- **Mail Lists-Labels** ~ available for all directories, **Country**, **Regional** or the complete
  World List: *Name and American Address of the Parent Company*
  with a corporate officer: *CEO, International Operations Officer or
  Human Resources Director* (where available), with telemarketing
  list.

- **Custom Order** ~ Create your own regions or country groupings to suit your project needs.

  To place an order, please call (212)-496-2448 or send the attached **Order
  Form** by FAX (212) 769-0413. Orders for Country, Regional, State
  editions and Mailing lists require pre-payment by credit card, check or
  money order in U.S. dollars, drawn on a U.S. Bank. **All sales are final.**

  Please see reverse side for title and pricing information.

Print/CD Rom

AFRICA — $ 79.00/$199.00
Algeria, Angola, Benin, Botswana, Burkina Faso, Burundi, Cameroon, Cent. African Rep., Chad Congo, Dem. Rep. Of Congo, Djibouti, Egypt, Ethiopia, Gabon, Ghana, Guinea, Ivory Coast, Kenya, Lesotho, Liberia, Libya, Madagascar, Malawi, Mali, Mauritius, Morocco, Mozambique, Namibia, Niger, Nigeria, Reunion, Senegal, Seychelles, Sierra Leone, South Africa, Sudan, Swaziland, Tanzania, Tunisia, Uganda, Zambia & Zimbabwe

ASIA — $189.00/$420.00
Bangladesh, Brunei, Cambodia, China, Hong Kong, India, Indonesia, Japan, Kazakhstan, Kirgnizia, Laos, Macau, Malaysia, Mongolia, Myanmar, Nepal, Pakistan, Philippines, Singapore, South Korea, Sri Lanka, Taiwan, Tajikistan, Thailand, Uzbekistan & Vietnam

South Asia — $ 49.00/$125.00
Bangladesh, India, Myanmar, Pakistan & Sri Lanka

South East Asia — $ 99.00/$249.00
Brunei, Cambodia, Indonesia, India, Laos, Malaysia, Philippines, Singapore, Thailand & Vietnam

Japan & South Korea — $ 79.00/$199.00

China Group — $109.00/$275.00
China, Hong Kong, Macau, Singapore & Taiwan

NEAR & MIDDLE EAST — $ 69.00/$175.00
Bahrain, Cyprus, Iran, Israel, Jordan, Kuwait, Lebanon, Oman, Palestine, Qatar, Saudi Arabia, Syria, Turkey, United Arab Emirates & Yemen

The Arabic Countries — $ 69.00/$175.00
Algeria, Bahrain, Egypt, Iran, Jordan, Kuwait, Lebanon, Libya, Morocco, Oman, Palestine, Qatar, Saudi Arabia, Sudan, Syria, Tunisia, United Arab Emirates & Yemen

Near & Middle East & Arabic Countries Combined — $ 79.00/$199.00

AUSTRALIA GROUP — $ 79.00/ $199.00
Australia, New Zealand, Fiji, French Polynesia, Guam, New Caledonia, No. Mariana Isl., Palau, Papua New Guinea, Polynesia, Solomon Isl. & Vanuatu

EUROPE WESTERN — $189.00/$475.00
Austria, Belgium, Channel Isl., Denmark, England, Finland, France, Germany, Gibraltar, Greece, Iceland, Ireland, Isle of Man, Italy, Liechtenstein, Luxembourg, Madeira, Malta, Monaco, Netherlands, No. Ireland, Norway, Portugal, San Marino, Scotland, Spain, Sweden, Switzerland & Wales

British Isles — $109.00/$275.00
Channel Is., England, Gibraltar, Ireland, Isle of Man, No. Ireland, Scotland & Wales

Europe West. Excl. British Isles — $169.00/$375.00
Belgium	$ 49.00/$125.00
France	$ 69.00/$175.00
Germany	$ 79.00/$199.00
Italy	$ 59.00/$149.00
Netherlands	$ 59.00/$149.00
Spain	$ 49.00/$125.00
Sweden	$ 49.00/$125.00
Switzerland	$ 39.00/$ 99.00
Scandinavia (Denmark, Finalnd, Iceland, Norway & Sweden)	$ 79.00/$199.00

Europe Eastern — $ 89.00/$225.00
Albania, Armenia, Azerbaijan, Belarus, Bosnia-Herzegovina, Bulgaria, Croatia, Czech Rep., Estonia, Georgia, Hungary, Kazabhstan, Kirgnizia, Latvia, Lithuania, Macedonia, Poland, Romania, Russia, Slovakia, Slovenia, Tajikistan, Turkmenistan, Ukraine, Uzbekistan & Yugoslavia

NORTH AMERICA — $109.00/$275.00
Canada, Greenalnd & Mexico
Canada
Mexico

Central America — $ 49.00/$125.00
Belize, Costa Rica, El Salvador, Guatemala, Honduras, Nicaragua & Panama

Caribbean Islands — $ 49.00/$125.00
Anguilla, Antigua, Aruba, Bahamas, Barbados, Bermuda, British Virgin Is., Cayman Isl., Dominican Rep., French Antilles, Grenada, Haiti, Jamaica, Neth. Antilles, Trinidad/Tobago & Turks/Caicos

South America — $109.00/$275.00
Argentina, Bolivia, Brazil, Chile, Colombia, Ecuador, French Guiana, Guyana, Paraguay, Peru, Surinam, Uruguay, Venezuela
Argentina	$ 39.00/$ 99.00
Argentina, Brazil & Chile	$ 79.00/$199.00
Brazil	$ 59.00/$125.00
Venezuela	$ 39.00/$ 99.00

AFRICA — $ 29.00/$ 79.00
Burkina Faso, Egypt, Ivory Coast, Nigeria, & South Africa

ASIA — $ 89.00/$225.00
China, Hong Kong, India, Indonesia, Japan, Malaysia, Pakistan, Philippines, Singapore, South Korea, Taiwan & Thailand

Japan & South Korea — $ 79.00/$199.00

China Group — $ 39.00/$ 99.00
China, Hong Kong, Singapore & Taiwan

NEAR & MIDDLE EAST — $ 39.00/$ 99.00
Bahrain, Cyprus, Egypt, Iran, Israel, Jordan, Kuwait, Lebanon, Saudi Arabia, Turkey & United Arab Emirates

AUSTRALIA GROUP — $ 29.00/$ 79.00
Australia & New Zealand

NORTH AMERICA — $49.00/$125.00
Canada Mexico

LATIN AMERICA — $ 39.00/$ 99.00
Argentina, Bahamas, Barbados, Bermuda, Bolivia, Brazil, British Virgin Is., Cayman Isl., Chile, Colombia, Costa Rica, Dominican Rep., El Salvador, Guatemala, Guyana, Mexico, Panama, Peru, Uruguay & Venezuela

EUROPE — $149.00/$375.00
Austria, Belgium, Czech Rep., Denmark, England, Finland, France, Germany, Greece, Hungary, Iceland, Ireland, Italy, Liechtenstein, Luxembourg, Monaco, Netherlands, Norway, Poland, Portugal, Romania, Russia, Scotland, Slovenia, Spain, Sweden, Switzerland & Wales

British Isles — $ 69.00/$175.00
Channel Is., England, Ireland Scotland & Wales

Europe West. Excl. British Isles — $119.00/$299.00
France	$ 49.00/$125.00
Germany	$ 59.00/$149.00
Italy	$ 39.00/$ 99.00
Netherlands	$ 39.00/$ 99.00
Scandinavia	$ 59.00/$175.00
Sweden	$ 39.00/$ 99.00
Switzerland	$ 49.00/$125.00

Europe Eastern — $ 29.00/$ 79.00
Czech Rep., Hungary, Poland, Russia & Slovenia

Uniworld Business Publications, Inc.
257 Central Park West, Suite 10A
New York, New York 10024
Tel: (212) 496-2448
Fax: (212) 769-0413
E-mail: uniworldbp@aol.com
Website: http://uniworldbp.com

Prices subject to change without notice

ORDER FORM

UNIWORLD BUSINESS PUBLICATIONS, INC.

257 Central Park West, Suite 10A New York, New York 10024-4110
Tel: 212-496-2448 Fax: 212-769-0413
E-mail: uniworldbp@aol.com   WEBsite: http://www.uniworldbp.com

Order by Title	Standing Order*	Quantity	Price	Subtotal
Directory of Foreign Firms Operating in The United States			$ 250.00	
CD ROM Directory of Foreign Firms Operating in the United States **1 year subscription**			$ 675.00	
CDROM Directory of Foreign Firms Operating in the United States **2 year subscription**			$ 1000.00	
Directory of American Firms Operating in Foreign Countries			$ 325.00	
CD Rom Directory of American Firms Operating in Foreign Countries **1 year subscription**			$ 975.00	
CD Rom Directory of American Firms Operating in Foreign Countries **2 year subscription**			$ 1500.00	

PAYMENT INFORMATION

☐ Check or money order enclosed for $_____ payable to:

  Uniworld Business Publications, Inc. (in U.S. dollars drawn on a U.S. bank)

☐ Charge to
  └ American Express ☐ MasterCard ☐ VISA

  Credit card holder:_____

  Card number:_____

  Expiration Date:__/__/___Signature:_____

Subtotal	_____
Shipping & Handling	_____
NY & CT buyers and sales tax	_____
Total	_____

☐ Bill me (Public Libraries and Educational Institutions only)

P.O.#:_____Name:_____

Signature:_____

MAILING ADDRESS

Name:_____

Title/Dept.:_____

Firm/Org.:_____

Address:_____

City:_____State:____Zip:_____

Tel. #:_____Fax #:_____

E-mail:_____

Website:_____

BUILLING ADDRESS (if different than mailing address)

Name:_____

Title/Dept.:_____

Firm/Org.:_____

Address:_____

City:_____State:____Zip:_____

Tel. #:_____Fax #:_____

E-mail:_____

Website:_____

SHIPPING AND HANDLING

Via UPS: Directory of American Firms Operating in Foreign Countries **$13.50**
Directory of Foreign Firms Operating in the United States **$8.50**.
Via US Mail: CD Rom one year $7.50, two year $15.00
Shipping outside the United States or next day delivery rates
please call **212-496-2448**.

TAX EXEMPTION STATUS

Purchasers whose organizations are tax-exempt must include the tax-exemption
number below or enclose a copy of the tax-exemption certificate.

#_____

FEDERAL TAX ID NUMBER

Uniworld Business Publications, Inc. **Federal Tax ID# is 13-2897346**

*STANDING ORDERS

All publications in this brochure are available on a continuation basis
ensuring immediate receipt upon publication of the new editions.
Mark "Y" in Standing Order column above.

SATISFACTION GUARANTEED

Hardbound directories may be returned in salable condition within 10 days
for a refund of the purchase price, excluding shipping and handling.
CDRoms and soft bound Regional and Country Editions are "Final Sale."

Office Use Only
Received_____Amount $_____
Check #_____Order #_____